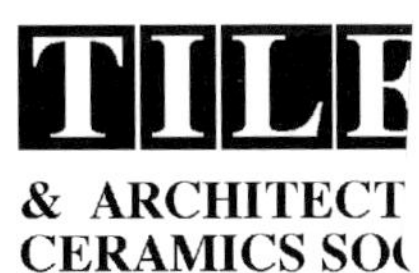

TILE GAZETTEER

A Guide to British Tile and Architectural Ceramics Locations

Lynn Pearson

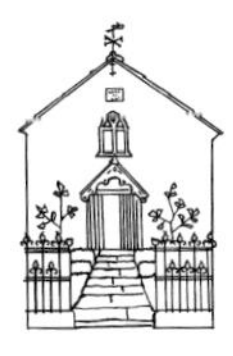

RICHARD DENNIS
2005

Preface and Acknowledgements

The Tiles and Architectural Ceramics Society (TACS), the national society responsible for the study and protection of tiles and architectural ceramics, was founded in 1981. From the start, details were collected on *in situ* ceramic locations and notes were published for the Society's site visits. By the mid-1990s a considerable amount of information had been amassed, and the Society decided to compile a computerised location database, which is currently being made available on the TACS website at www.tilesoc.org.uk, and to produce the *Gazetteer*, a guide to *in situ* British locations.

The *Gazetteer* project took almost ten years to complete and involved hundreds of people and organisations. Initial funding was provided from the Society's own resources, followed in 1997 by a grant from the Manifold Trust. As *Gazetteer* Editor I was awarded the 1999 Cumming Ceramic Research Foundation Scholarship, which enabled the project to focus on Staffordshire churches and their Minton tile pavements. Work on the *Gazetteer* continued with my 1999-2003 Research Fellowship at the School of Art & Design, University of Wolverhampton, where Ed Bird, Keith Cummings and Antonia Payne were all hugely supportive. Essential extra funding came in the form of grants from the Scouloudi Foundation (in association with the Institute of Historical Research), the Manifold Trust and the Pilgrim Trust. The project had almost reached fruition when an unforeseen crisis necessitated an appeal for funds in summer 2003. An excellent response from the TACS membership followed by a further generous donation from the Manifold Trust enabled the project to be completed, and I am deeply grateful to all the individuals and organisations who have contributed financially to the production of the *Gazetteer*.

Aside from financial considerations, the *Gazetteer* project was based on the hard work of numerous individuals who gave their time to research specific areas and sites, and took responsibility in other ways. Its progress was overseen by an Editorial Board comprising Judy Rudoe, Alan Swale, Hans van Lemmen, Biddy Macfarlane and Sue Hudson, and chaired with enthusiasm and expertise by Tony Herbert. It was a constant source of support, as was the TACS Committee and its chair (throughout most of the project) Alan Swale, whose personal drive and energy were crucial to the project's successful outcome.

Many archives, libraries and other organisations were consulted, and many locations throughout Britain, from the Orkney Islands to the Isles of Scilly, were visited, often by public transport, sometimes by bicycle, and on one occasion by rowing boat. I am particularly grateful to all those who let me have access to their homes and places of work or worship. Dennis Hadley very kindly allowed us to see (and publish on the TACS website) his invaluable listing of the Powell's of Whitefriars opus sectile works. Angella Streluk gave us free access to her research on Gibbs & Canning, and also provided many site photographs. Malcolm Shifrin's website www.victorianturkishbath.org was splendidly helpful, as was its webmaster. Chris Blanchett dealt patiently and constructively with a seemingly endless series of queries concerning tile identification. Sue Beckett, Collections Officer, Poole Museum Service, provided much useful advice during my repeated visits to Poole in relation to the Carter Archive. I am grateful to Ian Betts and the Museum of London Specialist Services for allowing us generous access to a draft of his forthcoming book *London Delftware Tiles*.

My thanks also go to all the contributors of the introductory sections of the *Gazetteer*, and to the staff of the many organisations encountered during the life of the project including the Brewery History Society, British Library, British Museum, English Heritage, Gladstone Working Pottery Museum (Angela Lee), Hampshire Museums and Archive Service, Heritage Tile Conservation Ltd (Jeremy Southorn), Huddersfield Gem (Chris Marsden, Adrian Evans), Ironbridge Gorge Museum Trust Library, Isle of Man Victorian Society (Peter and Ruth Kelly), Jackfield Conservation Studio (Lesley Durbin), Jackfield Tile Museum (Michael Vanns), Manchester Victoria Baths Trust (Gill Wright), NADFAS (Angela Goedicke, Wendy Woods), Newcastle City Library, Pilkington's Ceramic Tiles, Pilkington's Lancastrian Pottery Society, Potteries Museum and Art Gallery, Potteries Pub Preservation Group (Mervyn Edwards), Public Monument and Sculpture Association, Robinson Library at the University of Newcastle upon Tyne,

Shaws of Darwen (Jon Wilson), Shropshire Archives, Tile Heritage Foundation (Sheila Menzies, Joe Taylor), Twentieth Century Society, Victoria and Albert Museum (National Art Library, Prints and Drawings Study Room), Victorian Society (Geoff Brandwood, Charles Smith) and the William Morris Gallery (Amy Clarke).

For help with the project in many and various ways my grateful thanks go to Josie Adams, Kath Adams, Mary Alexander, Charles Allen, Mike Allen, Phil Almond, David Andrews, Katie Arber, Frank and Sue Ashworth, Penny Beckett, Douglas Bedwell, Mary and John Bentley, Maggie Angus Berkowitz, James Bettley, Myra Brown, Philip and Dorothy Brown, Anne and John Bundock, Lawrence Burton, Richard Camp, Ann M. Carter, Christina Casement, Cynthia Church, Kenneth Clark, Peter and Diana Clegg, Rosemary Cochrane, Jo Connell, Alison Copeland, Zena Corrigan, Chris Cox, Peter Creffield, Helene Curtis, Simon Curtis, Susan and Douglas Dalgleish, Felicity Davies, Tony Davies, Anne Diver, Ian Dobson, Mick Downs, Don Ekless, Gwyn and Marie Evans, Robert Evans, Harry and Margaret Fancy, Ray Farleigh, Rachel Faulding, Robert Field, Anna Flowers, Jean Foster, John Fox, Lance Fuller, Ellie Gabbay, Denis Gahagan, Laura Gardner, Steve Gendall, Margaret A. V. Gill, Simon Gispert, Joan Godfrey, Elaine Godina, Mike Godwin, Rosemary Grazebrook, Betty Greene and the late John Greene, Eleanor Greeves, Diana Hall, Rosemary Hall, Philip Hampel, Pam and Robert Hardy, Steve Hartgroves, Lisa Hawker, Charmain Hawkins, Leslie Hayward, Roger and Doreen Hensman, Ned Heywood, Violet Hobbs, Peter Hodson, Geoff Hollis, Jenny Holzer, Jean Howard, Kathryn Huggins, Rod Humby, Maggie Humphry, Douglas Hunter, Laurence Hurst, Dave Hutchins, Willem Irik, Neil Irons, Louise Irvine, Ray Jenkins, Catherine Johns, Joan Jones, Martin Jones, Ivor Kamlish, Geoffrey Kay, Christopher Ketchell, Elspeth King, the late Bryan Lacey, John Leroux, Ian Lewis, Ted Lightbown, M. R. Lippiatt, Sara Lunt, Helen Major, Judith Martin, Serena Mills, Neil Moat, Peggy Moir, Martin Mosebury-Smith, Celia Mycock, Richard and Hilary Myers, Beverley Nenk, Barry and Julia Norman, Helen Norman, Clare from Oddbins, Jan O'Highway, Linette O'Sullivan, David Parker, Judith Patrick, Ian Peaty, Irene Pellett, Jim and Margaret Perry, Richard and Caroline Pizey, Andrew Plummer, Jean Powell, William Prescott, Trish Radford, Anthony Ray, Keith Reedman, Graham Roberts, Douglas Rose, Peter Rose, Helen Ross, John Rotheroe, Paul Rothery, Paul Rowbottom, John Scott, Paul Scott, Joseph Sharples, Thelma and Stewart Shepley, Deborah Skinner, Joan Skinner, Don Slade, Gordon Smith, Margaret Newlands Smith, Di Stiff, Jennie Stopford, the late Michael Stratton, June Stubbs, R. E. Tapping, Philippa Threlfall, Laura Trelford, Robert Thorne, Marilyn Tweddle, Peter Tyler, John Vigar, Jane Wainwright, Sue Ward, Mark Watson, Tony Watts, Jane Webb, Leslie Weber, Rob Whatley, Hilary White, Mark Whyman, Anne Wilkins, Bronwyn Williams-Ellis, Julie Gillam Wood, A. J. Wootton, Caroline Worthington, Carolyn Wraight, Sheelagh Wurr and Kathleen Young.

Many of the colour plates in the *Gazetteer* have kindly been supplied by Richard Dennis Publications, to whom go our grateful thanks; the majority of the black and white illustrations have been provided by Hans van Lemmen and Lynn Pearson. We should like to thank the following contributors for providing illustrations of specific sites: Penny Beckett (butcher's shop, Broseley, Shropshire); Mary and John Bentley (Berkshire: St Mary's Church, Beech Hill; St Luke's Church, Maidenhead; St Mary's Church, Winkfield); Geoff Brandwood (Coachmakers PH, Wednesbury, Staffordshire); Jean Foster (Ashbourne, Monyash and Tideswell Churches, Derbyshire); Roger Hensman (Sainsbury's, Wilmslow, Cheshire); Willem Irik (Rhinefield House and Itchen Stoke Church, Hampshire; Abbey Dore Church and Hereford All Saints Church, Herefordshire); Martin Jones (Eve Memorial, Kidderminster, and Little Comberton Church, Worcestershire); Linette O'Sullivan (Methodist Chapel, Batford, Harpenden, Hertfordshire); Helen Ross (Bishop Wilton Church, East Yorkshire; Foxholes Church, North Yorkshire; Jubilee Fountain, Torpichen, West Lothian); Thelma Shepley (St Peter and St Paul Old Church, Albury, Surrey); Malcolm Shifrin (Haywain PH, Epsom, Surrey); Joan Skinner (Lloyds Bank, Loughborough, Leicestershire); Don Slade (Meppershall Church, Bedfordshire); and Sheelagh Wurr (Christ Church, Epsom Common, Surrey).

Complementary to seeing tiles and architectural ceramics *in situ* are the museum collections. It is impossible to list here all the museums which have good collections of tiles, but the following three institutions are of national importance with collections including many items specifically related to buildings. The British Museum, Great Russell Street, London WC1B 3DG (020 7323 8000) has an extensive tile collection including medieval pavements; the collection can be searched online using the 'Compass' function at www.thebritishmuseum.ac.uk. Gladstone Working Pottery Museum, Uttoxeter Road, Longton, Stoke-on-Trent ST3 1PQ (01782 311378, www.stoke.gov.uk) includes the Tile Gallery displaying the history of the decorative tile. Jackfield Tile Museum, Telford, Shropshire (one of the Ironbridge Gorge Museums, 01952 882030, www.ironbridge.org.uk), is housed in the former Craven Dunnill tileworks with a wide-ranging display including reconstructed architectural settings; the associated website www.tessellations.org.uk gives access to a national database of historic tile designs.

The *Gazetteer* is arranged geographically, in the case of England by county, although these have been defined so as not to split up any administrative areas, for instance the *Gazetteer* entry for Cheshire covers the administrative areas of Cheshire County Council, Halton Borough Council, Stockport Metropolitan Borough Council, Warrington Borough Council and Wirral Metropolitan Borough Council. The area covered by each English county is given at the end of its introduction. London is treated by borough, Scotland and Wales by unitary authority, and the Isle of Man is taken separately. Within these counties and authorities, entries are arranged alphabetically by town, often with a suggested walking route around major sites; London sites are listed alphabetically by street. It must be stressed that mention of a building in the *Gazetteer* does not in any sense imply that it is open to the public. The reader should always assume that there is no access, and should check before visiting. Every effort has been made to provide accurate location descriptions, but readers should be aware that buildings are subject to change; tile pavements, for instance, may be hidden beneath carpets at short notice. The Editor and the Tiles and Architectural Ceramics Society accept no liability of any kind whatsoever, however arising, which may result from the use of the *Gazetteer*. However, many locations may be inspected from the public highway, and the TACS programme of site visits often allows access to normally private locations, as do the events held annually in September and known as Heritage Open Days (England), London Open House, Scotland's Doors Open Days and European Heritage Days (Wales).

It is now three decades since Alec Clifton-Taylor, in *English Parish Churches as Works of Art* (Batsford, London, 1974, p158), fulminated against Victorian tile pavements, suggesting that 'The removal of these 'lavatory-tiles' would not be a very costly matter, and it should be done all over the country'. The status of Victorian and later tilemakers and their products is now rather higher, but encouraging conservation and appreciation of architectural ceramics of all types remains a constant challenge. As Editor, I count myself lucky to have already seen and enjoyed many of Britain's most amazing ceramic sites, which I hope the *Gazetteer* will reveal to a wider public.

Lynn Pearson, Newcastle upon Tyne,
26th March 2005

Foreword

The abundant locations of tiles and architectural ceramics recorded in this *Gazetteer* are a fitting tribute to the hard work put in by members of the Tiles and Architectural Ceramics Society over many years. From the very beginning, the Society has always encouraged visiting tiles and architectural ceramics in their original sites and made this an important part of their annual programme of events. The Society's first event was a tour of Birmingham in June 1981 led by the late Michael Stratton. Since then scores of visits have been made every year to tile locations throughout Britain, the information from which has been preserved in TACS Tour Notes. Society members were also encouraged to record tile sites they came across on Index Location Cards and many have responded to this call over the years. These two elements were the initial foundation of the *Gazetteer*.

By the mid 1990s it had become clear that this project could only be advanced and expanded if a more systematic approach was adopted and this eventually crystallised into the idea of compiling a *Gazetteer* of important tile locations in Britain arranged county by county (including Scotland and Wales) with Lynn Pearson as the editor in charge. This major project has now been successfully completed and has been published by Richard Dennis as *The Tiles and Architectural Ceramics Society Gazetteer of British Tile and Architectural Ceramics Locations*, better known as the 'Tile *Gazetteer* ' for short. The completion of this publication is a great achievement and has involved Lynn Pearson in thousands of miles of travel to many towns and cities and to places in some of the remotest parts of Britain to assess, record, and photograph tile sites worth entering in the *Gazetteer*. Although she has been assisted and helped by many people, it must be said that without her continuous drive and sustained efforts this publication would not have seen the light of day.

The tile *Gazetteer* with its thousands of entries and choice selection of illustrations is the first of its kind to record significant tile and architectural ceramics locations nationwide in a comprehensive and systematic way. No matter where you are in the British Isles, there will be something worth seeing in your area. This book is therefore bound to become a standard reference work and should be a constant guide and companion for those interested in tiles and architectural ceramics.

Hans van Lemmen
Chairman of the Tiles and Architectural Ceramics Society

Front Cover : Glasgow's Doulton Fountain (1887-8) was restored in 2002-3 and moved to its present location on Glasgow Green; in the background is the former Templeton's Carpet Factory.

Edited by Lynn Pearson
Book production by Flaydemouse, Yeovil, Somerset, England
Published by Richard Dennis, The Old Chapel, Shepton Beauchamp, Somerset, TA19 0LE

ISBN 0 903685 97 3

British Library Cataloguing-in-Production Data.
A catalogue record for this book is available from the British Library
Colour Photography by Magnus Dennis
Black and White Photography by Lynn Pearson, Hans van Lemmen and TACS members and friends.

Contents

Introduction: Decorative Ceramics in Architecture

The Gazetteer

Introduction

Decorative Ceramics in Architecture

FIRED CLAY TILES IN ROMAN BRITAIN

by Catherine Johns

When Britain became a province of the Roman Empire in AD 43, extensive changes took place in all aspects of life, from language, law and administration to countless material details of everyday living. Amongst the latter was the introduction of sophisticated and carefully planned buildings designed and constructed according to Mediterranean traditions, most of them incorporating manufactured materials, principally concrete and fired clay.

Ceramic bricks and tiles were ubiquitous in Roman architecture, but they were employed almost entirely for structural, rather than decorative, purposes. Decorative surface treatments of exterior elevations and of interior walls, ceilings and floors, were nearly always carried out in stone or painted plaster; except on the roof, the bricks or tiles were generally covered up.

There is, therefore, no direct line of descent from Roman tiles to those used in the medieval and later periods, but it is important to remember that fired-clay tiles, though used almost exclusively for structural rather than decorative functions, were commonplace in Britain for the first four hundred years of the Christian era.

Walls

Roman bricks intended for wall construction are thin, flat squares, and are therefore often referred to as tiles. Standard sizes were used, based on the Roman foot of c28 cm, and ranging from about 20 cm up to about 58 cm square, with a thickness of only around 5-7 cm. In areas where plenty of stone was available for building, horizontal tile-courses were still very often included in walls. When used alone, brick-built walls were normally faced or rendered.

Roofs

Tiles were visible on roofs, however. Roof-tiles were made in two standard forms that were used together, the *tegula* and the *imbrex*. The *tegula* was a large, almost square tile only about 2 cm thick, with upturned narrow flanges on the longer sides. The *imbrex* was of half-cylindrical form. When *imbrices* were laid over the adjacent flanges of the *tegulae*, they formed the characteristic ridged tiled roof of shallow pitch (about 30 degrees) that is still often to be seen in parts of Italy and France today. There were further details of the shaping of both tile types, such as the slight tapering of the *imbrices,* that enabled them to interlock for stability.

Ridge-tiles were generally plain, but many roofs also had decorative finials of stone or fired clay at the apex of the gable, and some roofs featured antefixes, vertical decorative tiles placed along the lower edges where the roof met the wall. Antefixes were of roughly triangular form, and bore mould-made decoration. This might be purely ornamental or of an official and informative nature. For example, the antefix tiles made in tileries controlled by the Roman army would bear the name and emblem of the relevant legion.

Heating Systems

The other major use of standardised fired-clay building materials was in the construction of the Roman hypocaust, the under-floor heating system that was considered desirable in at least some of the principal rooms of a private house of any pretension. This form of heating was not merely desirable but essential in a Roman bath-house, and proper facilities for bathing were, in turn, essential to the Roman way of life.

The cavity beneath the floor of the space to be heated was supported by *pilae,* small, very stable columns composed of a series of small square tiles firmly mortared together. The heat from the adjacent furnace would then circulate freely in the space, and would warm the room above. In the case of a bath-house, where it was necessary to heat the walls as well as the floor, heat was conducted further, up through the interior of the walls, in flues made of interlocking fired-clay box-tiles. These tiles are open-ended boxes of square or rectangular cross-section.

Floors

Complete tiles were not used as flooring in Roman buildings, though the characteristic orange-red of tile fabric does sometimes appear in other guises, either as a constituent of *opus signinum*, which was concrete mixed with crushed fired clay, or as some of the tiny individual 'tiles' (*tesserae*) in mosaic flooring. The *tesserae* varied in size from about 2-3 cm square for plain borders down to as little as 1 cm when they formed part of an elaborate polychrome pattern. *Tesserae* were cut as required, mainly from stone of varying types and colours, but also when made of tile, pottery vessels or glass; they were not purpose-made from fired ceramic materials.

Names And Decoration On Roman Tiles

The manufacture of tiles, like that of many types of Roman pottery, was a highly organised industry capable of producing very large quantities of standardised products. Official and military name-stamps in very abbreviated form are found on the tiles used at certain sites, and indicate that manufacturers fulfilled government contracts, and marked the products intended for those consignments accordingly. Some ordinary building tiles have other simple marks on them that may have been intended as production control marks within the factory. Decorative antefixes with mould-made designs have already been mentioned; these are the only Roman tiles whose decoration was intended to be seen after they were incorporated into a building.

It is all the more surprising, therefore, that the box- or flue-tiles used in heating systems are often quite elaborately decorated in low relief with geometric, floral and even figural ornament. The designs were applied to the tiles before firing using roller-stamps, presumably of carved hardwood. Obviously these patterns served as identification of the products of particular manufacturers, and they would also have been of use in providing a key for the mortar and plaster applied to the flue-tiles once they were in place, but the zig-zag lines, rosettes, and even a hunting-scene of a stag pursued by a hound, were not intended to been seen once the building was finished.

MEDIEVAL TILES

by Beverley Nenk

The majority of tiles produced during the medieval period were roof tiles and decorated and plain floor tiles. They were used on many medieval buildings, from royal palaces and castles, to abbeys and churches, manor houses and town houses. Limited production of ceramic roof tiles, and what are thought to be wall tiles, occurred during the later Anglo-Saxon period. However widespread production of roof tiles did not become established until the twelfth century, and of decorated tile pavements until the mid thirteenth century. Initially these were specially commissioned for the monarchy or for religious houses, but subsequently, commercial tileries were established.

Roof Tiles

During the medieval period ceramic tiles, as well as thatch, wooden shingles and stone slate were all commonly used as roofing materials. Glazed roof tiles may have been introduced into England by Continental tilers working on Norman castles and abbeys. In London, the earliest forms were being made by the mid twelfth century, and include flanged and curved tiles (used in the same way as Roman roof tiles), shouldered peg tiles and decorated ridge tiles. At Guildford Castle, roof tiles were being made c1175. Elsewhere, by the late thirteenth century the range of forms had increased to include peg tiles, hip tiles, valley tiles, and half-tiles. During the fourteenth century, commercial tileries were established, such as that at Penn, Buckinghamshire. Although production of roof tiles occurred at places such as Exeter, York and North Wales, the widespread use of ceramic roof tile occurred mainly in the south-east during the medieval period.

The roofs of medieval houses might be decorated with elaborate ornamental louvers to provide ventilation, or with decorative finials at the end of the ridge, often in the form of human or animal figures. Ridge tiles, or crests, often decorated with knife-cut shapes or steps, provided a decorative roof-line to medieval houses. Ceramic chimney pots occur in southern and south-eastern England from the thirteenth century onwards.

Floor Tiles

The other major use of ceramic tiles during the medieval period was in the manufacture of paved floors. These were formed usually of either square or mosaic tiles. Floor tiles were decorated with a range of techniques, including inlaid, slip-decorated, line-impressed, relief, counter-relief, or more rarely, sgraffito. The earliest pavements were probably special commissions for ecclesiastical institutions and for the monarchy. The earliest post-Conquest floor tiles may be relief-decorated monochrome-glazed tiles from the Chapter House, St Albans Abbey, dated to the 1150s or 1160s. The technique may have been introduced by continental tilers.

Mosaic tiled pavements were made at a number of sites, mainly Cistercian abbeys in northern England and southern Scotland, principally during the second and third quarters of the thirteenth century. The mosaic tiles were arranged in square, rectangular or circular panels, surrounded by borders also formed of mosaic tiles. The overall polychrome effect of the floor was created by the use of tiles of different shapes each glazed a single, different colour. The technique was probably introduced by craftsmen from the Continent working under monastic patronage.

Two-colour, inlaid floor tiles were probably introduced into England in the second quarter of the thirteenth century, probably by tilers from the Continent working under royal patronage. The first pavements were specially commissioned for the building works of Henry III. The earliest surviving inlaid Wessex tiles were made in the 1240s for the pavements laid at Winchester Castle (1241-2) and in the King's Chapel at Clarendon Palace, Wiltshire (1240-4). Itinerant Wessex tilers subsequently influenced production over a wide area of western England and South Wales from the mid thirteenth to early fourteenth century. In London, the earliest decorated pavements were being laid in the Palace of Westminster in the late 1230s and 1240s, while the pavement which survives in the Chapter House of Westminster Abbey dates to the 1250s. Royal patronage is also reflected in the high-quality series of tiles from Chertsey Abbey, the most beautifully decorated of all medieval tiles, which may have been commissioned originally for Westminster Palace. Their production spans the period c1250-1300. They are decorated with several series of designs, notable among which are the scenes of combat, including tiles depicting Richard I and Saladin, and a series illustrating episodes from the medieval romance of Tristram and Isolde.

Commercial floor tile production became widespread during the second half of the thirteenth and fourteenth centuries, with the establishment of such tileries as the 'Westminster' industry in London, the South Midlands industry (the 'stabbed Wessex' series), Tyler Hill, near Canterbury, and Penn, Buckinghamshire. Large-scale production at this time sometimes led to a decline in quality. Many industries produced slip-decorated tiles; others made relief-decorated tiles, such as the industry at Bawsey, Norfolk, and line-impressed tiles, such as those produced in the Midlands and the North, notably at Chester. During the fourteenth and fifteenth centuries floor tiles were increasingly used in parish churches, manor houses and town houses.

Monastic patronage was the impetus for the late medieval revival of decorated floor tile production, notably at Great Malvern Priory during the mid fifteenth century. Commercial production continued during the later fifteenth and sixteenth centuries, such as the industry at Bristol. The latest slip-decorated tiles, made in the mid-sixteenth century, incorporate Renaissance motifs into their designs. During the late sixteenth and seventeenth centuries, the production of medieval earthenware tiles was superseded by the fashion for polychrome tin-glazed floor tiles. The latest industry to produce decorated earthenware floor tiles in the medieval tradition was at Barnstaple, Devon, where glazed relief-decorated tiles were made from the later sixteenth to the early eighteenth century.

Wall Tiles

With a few notable exceptions, tiles intended to decorate walls during the medieval period have rarely been identified. Anglo-Saxon polychrome relief tiles, known from major Anglo-Saxon ecclesiastical sites such as St Albans, Winchester, Bury St Edmunds and York, are thought to have been used either as a facing to the altar, as part of a retable, or on the walls or steps surrounding the altar. They may have been the earliest ceramic tiles produced after the Roman period, and were probably produced from the mid tenth to late eleventh century. Monastic patronage may have been significant in their production.

The so-called Tring tiles, a series of rectangular tiles decorated with figural scenes from the Apocryphal Gospels of the Childhood of Christ, may have been intended as wall tiles. The decoration on these unusual tiles is carried out in the sgraffito technique, which would not have survived had the tiles been used as floor tiles. A further series of wall tiles was made in the 1450s during the revival of tile making which occurred at Great Malvern. Wall and floor tiles were made for the rebuilt Priory church, including panels of wall tiles decorated with architectural and heraldic designs, inscriptions and dates.

FROM 1500 TO 1830

by Hans van Lemmen

Tiles

The history of tiles and architectural ceramics was at a pivotal moment at the beginning of the sixteenth century. On the one hand the era of medieval tiles was drawing to an end and came to a final halt with the Dissolution of the Monasteries, while on the other hand new forms of tile making and architectural terracotta were being introduced into Britain.

The production of tin-glazed tiles was introduced from Flanders by potters skilled in the manufacture of colourful Italian maiolica. An early sixteenth century example of this type of tile can still be seen on the floor of the chapel at the Vyne (Sherborne St John, Hampshire). The technique involves covering tiles with an opaque white tin glaze which can be painted in polychrome or blue-and-white. The first potteries to make tin-glazed tiles were set up in London during the sixteenth century, often by craftsmen who had come from Flanders or Holland like Jasper Andries and Jacob Jansen who petitioned Queen Elizabeth to be allowed to make tin-glazed ware in 1570. In the seventeenth century, potteries in London made tin-glazed tiles as a small sideline to their main output of tin-glazed pottery. It is likely that these early maiolica tiles were used on the floor rather then the wall and could only be afforded by a privileged clientele.

Tin-glazed tiles were also imported from the Netherlands where the tile industry had grown enormously in the seventeenth century and the Dutch-produced tiles were better made and more skilfully painted than English tiles. When King William III needed high quality tiles for the walls of the dairy at Hampton Court in the 1680s he placed the order with a factory in Delft. The term 'delftware' which entered the English language at the end of the seventeenth century is therefore derived from the Dutch town of Delft which had become famous for its high quality blue-and-white ware.

The production of delftware tiles in Britain did not come into its own until the eighteenth century. Greater demand led to the already existing potteries in London making more tiles and new potteries were set up in Liverpool, Bristol and Glasgow. The range of pictorial motifs on delftware tiles is extensive and it is not difficult to see why these tiles with hand painted images are now represented in so many public and private collections. Landscapes, scenes from daily life, animals, ships, fables and biblical scenes are some of the topics found on delftware tiles. If tiles made in London often closely followed Dutch examples, tiles made in Liverpool and Bristol took on a more uniquely English character. Tiles with *bianca-sopra-bianca* borders and finely painted polychrome tiles with birds and chinoiserie scenes became a speciality not seen in Dutch tiles.

Delftware tiles were used in fireplaces and dairies and as splashbacks for hand basins and sometimes in baths and toilet areas. Few examples from this period have withstood the ravages of time, but some notable surviving tile installations include the eighteenth century fireplace in Aston Hall, Birmingham, with polychrome Liverpool tiles depicting chinese scenes. Basin wall recesses rescued from eighteenth century houses are now on show in the Victoria & Albert Museum in London and the Ashmolean Museum in Oxford. Visitors to Chatham Dockyard in Kent can see the 'Blue Loo' covered with landscape tiles made in London, and delftware tiles are to be found in the bath in the Water Tower at Carshalton, in the London Borough of Sutton. They were also used as inn signs and one tile panel probably made for the Cock & Bottle Inn in London is now in the Museum of London.

It was in the production of delftware tiles that the first steps towards mechanical decorating methods were made. In 1756 John Sadler of Liverpool hit on the idea of decorating plain white delftware tiles with printed images taken from woodcuts and engraved copperplates. Better clay bodies were developed by Josiah Wedgwood and Josiah Spode who were important entrepreneurs in the early industrialisation of the British ceramics industry. During the 1760s and 1770s Wedgwood produced a 'cream-ware' body which was much harder and stronger than the earthenware used in delftware. Cream-ware tiles were also produced and therefore only needed a transparent glaze to finish them instead of the white opaque glaze used in traditional delftware tiles. They could be left plain or decorated with on-glaze printed and painted designs. The Wedgwood tiles in the dairy at Endsleigh, Devon, installed around 1815 are a fine example of creamware tiles.

Josiah Spode was instrumental in introducing underglaze transfer printed decorations on various types of ceramic ware. Transfer printed designs on the glaze of tiles are very vulnerable to wear but if they were covered by a transparent glaze they would last as long as the piece of ceramics they decorated. Cobalt blue in particular proved very successful as an underglaze colour and although this was not immediately used on a large scale for tile production at the beginning of the nineteenth century, underglaze transfer printing was to become one of the main methods of decorating tiles from about 1830 onwards.

Architectural Ceramics

An early instance of the use of architectural ceramics in Britain can be found at the beginning of the sixteenth century when there was a short-lived fashion for the use of terracotta in the reign of Henry VIII. He employed foreign craftsmen including the Italian Giovanni da Maiano from Florence where there was a well-established tradition of architectural terracotta and faience. Da Maiano made some fine terracotta roundels showing Roman emperors, which still decorate the exterior of Hampton Court Palace. It is possible that local rather than foreign craftsmen were responsible for the remarkable terracotta interior of the Bedingfield Chapel in Oxborough Church, Norfolk, where the terracotta tombs date from around 1525. The terracotta screens in the chapel are still in remarkably good condition and feature ornate Renaissance decorations. The vogue for Renaissance-style terracotta work spread to other great Tudor houses such as Sutton Place in Surrey, Layer Marney in Essex and East Barsham Hall, Norfolk.

Another interesting feature of sixteenth century architectural ceramics is the decorative brick chimneys on the roofs of Tudor manor houses. The ornate chimneys on the roof of Hampton Court with their chevron, honeycombed and diamond patterns were amongst the first examples in the country. Brick chimneys became a status symbol for the nobility as they indicated the size of the house. The more chimneys there were on the roof, the more rooms there were in the house. East Barsham Hall in Norfolk and Plaish Hall in Shropshire are good examples of this tendency.

A renewed interest in architectural ceramics occurred during the second half of the eighteenth century, when Eleanor Coade (1733-1821) established a terracotta factory at Lambeth, London in 1769. Like Wedgwood and other ceramic entrepreneurs, she was responding to the period's rising consumer demands. The prevailing neo-classical style in architecture meant a demand for all manner of classical decoration like ornamental capitals for columns, balusters, keystones, chimneys, friezes, medallions and plaques, and also garden sculpture, sundials, urns and vases. Replicating these in stone was expensive, so a grey-coloured terracotta closely resembling stone was the answer. In fact Mrs Coade's products were marketed as 'artificial stone'; in her factory all kinds of architectural ornaments and sculptures were made with the aid of plaster moulds and then fired in large kilns. Well known architects of the day like Robert Adam, Samuel Wyatt and John Nash made use of Coade stone products. Since terracotta products were closely associated with brick making, a possible reason for marketing terracotta as 'artificial stone' was to avoid the brick tax that was levied between 1784 and 1850. Many examples of Coade stone remain throughout the country, like the keystones with classical heads and rusticated blocks framing doorways in Bedford Square, London and the decorative plaques on Radcliffe Observatory, Oxford. There are also fine examples in Scotland like the swans and lions at Gosford House, East Lothian, and the elaborate roofware on Dalmeny House, Edinburgh.

An important ecclesiastical example is St Pancras Church, London, consecrated in 1822 and built in the Greek Revival style. The church has two porticos with terracotta decorations projecting from the north and south sides. They are embellished with striking female Greek figures known as caryatids. These load-bearing columns in the shape of Greek women were manufactured from grey-coloured terracotta by John Rossi who until 1814 had worked for Coade.

After Mrs Coade's death in 1821, the manufacture of Coade stone continued under the direction of William Croggon. However, production ceased around 1840 and the moulds and equipment were sold off. Mark Henry Blanchard, who probably bought some of the moulds, became an important Victorian architectural terracotta manufacturer.

THE VICTORIAN PERIOD TO THE FIRST WORLD WAR: AN OVERVIEW

by Tony Herbert

The years from 1840 until the First World War were in many respects a golden period for the use of ceramics in architecture. They coincided with a great variety of architectural styles and fashions for which decorative tiles and terracotta were eminently suited by virtue of their readily adapted forms and colours.

Beginning in the 1840s with a surge in the gothic revival, the boom in new and restored churches, driven by Tractarianism and the Oxford Movement, opened up a big market for inlaid (or as they became known encaustic) tiles largely based on medieval originals. The two largest companies of the period – Minton in Stoke-on-Trent and Maw in the Ironbridge Gorge - were founded on this market. Both subsequently diversified and were joined by a host of other large-scale manufacturers.

The choice of geometric and encaustic floor tiles by Queen Victoria and Prince Albert for Osborne House in the mid 1840s gave the royal seal of approval to a rapidly burgeoning domestic market, which was soon amplified by wall and fireplace tiles. Soon the arbiters of domestic taste such as Charles Eastlake were writing enthusiastically about the virtues of tiles in the home. Victorian tile designs served as a barometer of taste and fashion and rapidly changed to meet new stylistic demands such as the post 1860s interest in Japan and the Orient. In a world where travel and exploration were informing new trends in architecture and design, colourful glazed ceramics had a big part to play. Whether you wanted a Moroccan billiard room, a Moorish smoking room, or a Chinese dairy it was the ceramic elements of the style which contributed most to a sense of the exotic.

Whilst the response to fashion and style may have been paramount in the Victorian revival of architectural ceramics there was an underlying practical element too. Because of the widespread use of coal as a fuel, both for domestic fires and as a source of steam power for industry, Victorian cities were sooty and grimy. Many natural building stones soon became disfigured, but this went hand in hand with a growing realisation that ceramic building materials were much more resistant. Indeed glazed architectural faience and the unglazed red and buff terracotta blocks with their characteristic fireskin were somewhat optimistically described as 'self cleaning' in the rain.

The size and scale of the major tile and terracotta factories was immense and the buoyant home market was amplified by demands from other corners of the British Empire, which this volume makes no attempt to cover. The offices and headquarters buildings of these manufacturers were frequently developed architecturally as outdoor pattern books of their products, shown in an architectural context for all to admire. The designs themselves were extremely varied and it is perhaps difficult now to perceive just how much choice was available to the Victorian builder or architect. Mass production meant that tiles were relatively cheap and so even a modest terrace house might be brightened by a panel of tiles in its porch, affording the occupants of the house colour and a degree of individuality formerly the preserve of the wealthy. Most large companies not only made use of in-house design staff but also commissioned designs from leading architects so that the ceramic decoration was frequently integrated into architecture in a way that rarely happens today.

During the Edwardian period, new philosophies of architecture and design began to emerge, especially in Europe. The eclectic style revivals of the High Victorian period were replaced by art nouveau and the beginnings of modernism. Ceramics (and glass) were natural mediums for art nouveau and although full-blown schemes using the style in Britain are few and far between, those that survive, such as the Everard Building in Bristol, completed in 1901, still have the power to stop passers-by in the street. Modernism brought a new agenda to architecture and design in which, contrary to common belief, architectural ceramics had a significant role to play. The four years of World War One, with all their social and economic upheavals, represent a very clear full stop to the kaleidoscopic output of architectural ceramics which marked the previous seventy years.

ECCLESIASTICAL TILES

by Hans van Lemmen

The history of nineteenth century ecclesiastical tiles is inextricably linked with the building of new churches in the Gothic Revival style and the accompanying restoration of old churches and cathedrals. Church architects like A. W. N. Pugin, William Butterfield and Sir George Gilbert Scott recommended the use of encaustic floor tiles reminiscent of medieval inlaid floor tiles, particularly those made from red clay with an impression stamp filled with white clay and covered with a transparent lead glaze. Victorian tile manufacturers were therefore actively encouraged to produce replicas.

Samuel Wright of Shelton had revived the technique of making encaustic tiles for which he had taken out a patent in 1830. He had problems developing it commercially, and disposed of it to Herbert Minton in Stoke-on-Trent and Walter Chamberlain in Worcester in 1835 on a royalty basis. Encaustic tiles were made by using plaster moulds with raised designs at the bottom into which red plastic clay was pressed with aid of a small screw press. When the tiles came out of the mould, they had indented designs on their surface. The tiles were then covered with white or buff coloured clay the consistency of butter or with liquid slip and left to settle. When leather hard, the surface of the tiles was scraped level revealing the inlaid designs clearly against the darker body of the tiles. Chamberlain's tiles were covered with a transparent lead glaze, which made the white inlaid design look honey-coloured yellow and the red body a deep red brown, just like medieval tiles. Good examples of Chamberlain tiles dating from the early 1840s can still be found on the back wall of the sanctuary of Great Malvern Priory, Worcestershire.

Minton tiles were not glazed in this way, but a special yellow enamel glaze was painted over the inlaid sections of the tiles creating a vivid colour contrast with the unglazed background. By 1845 Minton had begun using blue and white clays for the inlaid parts of the designs making more colourful patterns possible. A prestigious early commission for Minton was the paving of the Temple Church in the City of London in 1841-2 with many of the designs based on the medieval tiles at Westminster Abbey Chapter House which had recently been discovered by antiquarians. The result of this commission was the publication of the first commercial catalogue of encaustic tiles entitled *Examples of Old English Tiles.* It was also in 1842 that Minton paid for the building of Holy Trinity Church in Hartshill, Stoke-on-Trent to which he donated a series of his early encaustic tiles. However it was Minton's cooperation with the architect A. W. N. Pugin that made him the leading manufacturer of church tiles. Pugin was a prolific designer of new Catholic churches and paved them with Minton tiles using his own designs. The most magnificent example of Pugin's and Minton's collective efforts is St Giles R. C. Church in Cheadle, Staffordshire, built for Lord Shrewsbury and opened in 1846, where there is a splendid array of colourful Minton tiles designed by Pugin.

By the early 1850s other manufactures of encaustic church tiles had come on to the scene. The Maw family had acquired the Chamberlain factory in 1850 and moved production from Worcester to Benthall in Shropshire in 1852. Maw & Co became one of the largest tile producers in the second half of the nineteenth century and their output included many encaustic tiles for church use. They employed architects like George Goldie and J. P. Seddon to design encaustic tiles for them. Good examples of Maw's encaustic tiles can be found in Battlefield Church (1861), Shropshire, in the sanctuary of St Asaph Cathedral (1867-75), Denbighshire, and the Lady Chapel of Chester Cathedral (1860s).

William Godwin and his brother Henry set up a company in Lugwardine, Hereford in 1852. Godwin became a major producer of church tiles, and Hereford Cathedral (1857-63) has good examples of their early production. They took advantage of the invention by William Boulton and Joseph Worthington in 1863 of dust-pressed encaustic tiles and their dust-pressed tiles can be found in churches throughout Britain. Holy Trinity Church (1870) in Hull, East Yorkshire, and St Peter's Church (1876) in Leeds, West Yorkshire, are cases in point. Godwin had a special relationship with George Gilbert Scott who often used their tiles in his church restoration work.

Although Craven Dunnill in Jackfield were relative late comers on to the encaustic scene, only starting to make tiles in the early 1870s, they produced a range of encaustic tiles, many of which were used in the restoration of cathedrals like Chester Cathedral and St Magnus Cathedral, Kirkwall, Orkney. They also made glazed relief floor tiles in red, yellow and green, which were used in the restoration of Bangor Cathedral (1875), Gwynedd.

All church tiles depict an array of Gothic decorative motifs of which the fleur-de-lys is the most common, but they would also sometimes incorporate pictorial designs. Minton made many encaustic tiles showing the four Evangelists and also the Holy Lamb and in one instance produced special sets of encaustic tiles with scenes from the Bible for the sanctuary floor of Lichfield Cathedral (c1860), Staffordshire. The Campbell Brick & Tile Co in Stoke-on-Trent made a series of tiles depicting the Instruments of the Passion (c1880). These pictorial tiles were always placed in a prime spot in the church, usually in front of the altar. Manufacturers like Minton also made encaustic commemorative tiles which were placed diagonally either on the floor or on the walls of churches to remember the lives of particular people such as the plaques on the walls of St Peter ad Vincula in Stoke-on-Trent which were installed from 1859 onward.

Hand painted wall panels for ecclesiastical interiors were also produced. Pictorial tile panels designed by the architect William Butterfield from 1873 can be found in All Saints Church, Margaret Street, Westminster, while Morris & Company produced wall tiles with minstrel angels for Findon Church in West Sussex in the late 1860s. Not far from Findon is Clapham Church (West Sussex) with a tiled reredos of Morris & Co tiles showing archangels installed in 1873-4. The same church has W.B. Simpson tile panels with apostles flanking the windows.

The strong fashion for ecclesiastical tiles tailed off towards the end of the nineteenth century and by the beginning of the twentieth century their application was far less common. An interesting late example can be found in St John the Evangelist, Rhosymedre, Ruabon (Wrexham), where there is reredos consisting of a mixture of encaustic and majolica tiles made by the workers of the local terracotta firm J. C. Edwards in 1906 in remembrance of their employer J. C. Edwards.

CIVIC AND PUBLIC BUILDINGS
by Alan Swale

Borne of the increasing prosperity of the mid-Victorian period, a surge of civic and public buildings appeared throughout the land, many providing architects with an opportunity to lavish these with architectural ceramic ornamentation. New purpose-built government buildings, museums, libraries, town and other public halls, schools and law courts received this treatment. Later in the period, new public baths, post offices, telephone exchanges and police and railway stations became recipients of tiles, terracotta, faience or all three at once, often in great profusion.

Not surprisingly, the most prominent of these structures appeared in the capital. Surely, the most important new building of the era was the gothic New Palace of Westminster, resplendent in Pugin's glowing encaustic pavements. St Stephen's Hall, the Royal Gallery and Central Lobby provide some of the finest examples of what can be achieved with the use of rich polychromatic patterning; the huge spaces ideally suiting Pugin's grand schemes. Here, Minton's recently-introduced new tile product was given a great boost leading to its mass use in churches, town halls and domestic dwellings. The new Foreign Offices, designed by G. G. Scott in 1861, and former India Office interiors of 1866 designed by Matthew Digby Wyatt both feature tiles used in quite a different manner to the Palace of Westminster, reflecting the classical style of architecture employed. Scott's generally more restrained scheme has pavements of geometric tiles while majolica tiles and roundels appear on the brackets supporting the ceilings. Wyatt's more exuberant scheme utilised majolica tiles made by Maw & Co in the coved ceiling to the loggia of the Durbar Court and on the balcony.

Also prominent were London's new museums featuring terracotta. The new Quadrangle extensions at the Victoria & Albert Museum (formerly South Kensington Museum), commenced in 1860, featuring buff and red terracotta ornament combined with red brick were indeed intended to promote this material. In line with this aim, the Central Refreshment Rooms and Ceramic (or West) Staircase are both vehicles for a superabundance of ceramics in the form of majolica (faience) clad columns, high relief figurative dados, mosaic work, coved ceilings using Campbell's vitrified enamel painting process and relief majolica friezes of alphabet letters. Godfrey Sykes designed and modelled much of the finest decorative work on the quadrangle. His figuratively decorated terracotta columns supporting the Lecture Theatre facade's first floor arcade are among the more spectacular examples of his artistry. Identical columns support the arcade of the former Science Schools (now the museum's Henry Cole Wing) along Exhibition Road.

On an even more prominent site was Alfred Waterhouse's Natural History Museum (1873-81) where terracotta demonstrated its viability as a structural walling material on a massive scale, as well as providing copious amounts of figurative sculpture and ornament. Supplied by Gibbs & Canning of Tamworth, Staffordshire, the terracotta also forms the majestic interior. Of particular note are the pale blue bands that intersperse the mainly buff terracotta used throughout the building. The abundant sculpture, all meticulously designed by Waterhouse himself and modelled by M. Dujardin, features huge extinct and existing species of animals alongside quite small details such as monkeys playfully climbing the ribs of the interior arches. Also supplied by Gibbs & Canning, the multi-use Royal Albert Hall (Westminster) was the final public building at South Kensington to feature abundant amounts of terracotta dressings as well as a prominent mosaic tiled figurative frieze beneath its dome.

In a similar manner to the V&A Museum Quadrangle complex, the Wedgwood Memorial Institute, Burslem, Stoke-on-Trent was intended to promote the use of architectural ceramics and stimulate local pottery manufacturers to diversify into this branch of the craft. Opened in 1869, the institute was designed as a multi-purpose building, serving as an art school, reference library and museum. A remarkable testament to the decorative potential of terracotta to provide colour, sculptural and ornamental detail at a moderate cost compared to stone, the institute bears an impressive array of terracotta in the form of illustrative 'Process' panels above the highly ornamented ground floor windows, while 'Month' panels adorn the windowless upper storey. Sadly, local manufacturers were unable to rise to the challenge and the terracotta was supplied by Blanchard's of London and Blashfield's of Stamford. At least, locally supplied encaustic tiles grace some of the interior rooms.

Newly built town halls and other public structures soon proliferated in London and elsewhere, frequently providing great opportunities for fictile products. One of the great attractions these offered in terms of their suitability for public spaces was their durability and easy maintenance. In the provinces, one of the earliest public buildings to feature ceramics conspicuously was Liverpool's St George's Hall (1854) where Minton's encaustic tiles provided a spectacular and immense display. Cuthbert Brodrick's Leeds Town Hall (1858) is a further example of the genre, again provided by Minton's.

In terms of external architectural ceramic, terracotta was increasingly incorporated into many red brick town halls where it provided decorative and sculptural details. An illustration of a town hall bearing an entirely terracotta facade can be seen at Hereford where the pseudo Jacobean Renaissance mansion is one of the most flamboyant examples to be seen. Designed by Harry Cheers and completed in 1904, this buff terracotta structure has intricate corner towers and a huge mullioned windowed central gable over a massive carapace covering the porch. Faience provides a creamy and light interior with a fine curved stairway leading to the upper floors, as well as a relief-tiled dado and floor mosaic. Among the many other town halls (there are some thirty-five on the TACS Location Database), that at East Ham, Newham, London, a late example completed in 1903, is also massively impressive with its red brick and buff terracotta supplied by Doulton's. Of particular note here are the entrances with Romanesque detailing and prominent clock tower. The Free Style employed on the Bishopgate Institute (City of London, completed 1894) encouraged a lavish use of block terracotta ornamentation where a huge arts and crafts movement-inspired *Tree of Life* dominates the facade.

So much cheaper than carved stone and offering far greater resistance to corrosive atmospheres, terracotta detailing became commonplace on technical schools, college buildings and elementary schools throughout the country, frequently purchased as ready made stock designs from the manufacturers' catalogues. However, an outstanding example of a school designed with terracotta created specially for the purpose, an early and pioneering example too, is Charles Barry Junior's Dulwich College, Southwark, opened in 1870. This colourful and highly decorative Italianate structure features mainly buff terracotta manufactured by Blashfield, combined with light red brick. Widely distributed throughout this large structure, the ornamentation is most prominent along the roofline as pierced parapeting, in the huge window of the great hall and the ornate pedimented main door. During the erection of this building, Blashfield conducted widely publicised scientific tests on his material providing strong arguments for its use in preference to stone.

Birmingham (Warwickshire), well served by many terracotta edifices, sports the impressive, richly red Victoria Law Courts designed by Aston Webb and Ingress Bell and completed in 1891. Here, high gothic architecture and terracotta combine to produce an imposing symbol of the might of the law. J. C. Edwards provided the block terracotta for the exterior while Gibbs & Canning produced the muted stone coloured terracotta of the interior. Terracotta is also to be seen adding ornamentation to a number of elementary schools in the city designed by the Martin & Chamberlain office. By the same office, the School of Art (now part of the University of Central England) of 1883-5 is a triumph of arts and crafts terracotta detailing. Birmingham libraries also come in for this treatment, Bloomsbury Public Library, Nechells (1891-3) being a conspicuously fine example with excellent sculpture and ornament. A number of highly distinctive public baths complete the panoply of terracotta to be seen on Birmingham's public buildings. In particular, the entrance facades of Moseley Road Baths (Balsall Heath, 1907) and Nechells Park Road Baths, Nechells, opened 1910, are especially impressive. Among other regional libraries is that at Wolverhampton, Staffordshire, which is a further and fine example of Free Style architecture featuring Doulton's buff terracotta combined with bright red brick. It was designed by Henry T. Ware and completed in 1902.

Post offices and telephone buildings frequently feature terracotta ornament combined with brick. The former post office at Wolverhampton (1898, now a University of Wolverhampton building) with its frothy array of Dennis's buff terracotta set against red brick, and Birmingham's entirely red terracotta and brick Bell Edison former telephone exchange (1896) provide two of the more exuberant examples.

Architectural faience first appeared in the 1880s when, frequently coupled with encaustic tiled floors and relief glazed tiles, it became increasingly popular as a material for the interiors, if not the exteriors, of public buildings in the later Victorian and Edwardian periods. Once again, Alfred Waterhouse led the charge, employing a glittering array of Burmantofts faience in the hall of his Victoria Building of Liverpool University, completed in 1892. Here can be seen entire faience chequerwork and striped wall surfaces with a magnificent fireplace and framed clock, a balustraded staircase and shining array of triangular-tiled columns. Terracotta detailing appears on the exterior of the building too. Waterhouse used the same material in the entrance hall to his Yorkshire College (1892-5, now part of Leeds University). Public libraries also came in for this treatment. The impressive Old Library, Cardiff (1880-2) originally had copious quantities of faience, rich dados of Maw's tiles including Walter Crane's *Times of Day* and *Seasons*, mosaic-floored corridors and two fine faience drinking fountains. Stoke Library (1878), Stoke-on-Trent, and its once spectacular external tiles panels at first floor level, would have merited a more detailed mention here except that a faulty cleaning scheme all but eradicated these. As it is, there is a remarkable array of Moyr Smith tiles hidden behind wallpaper in the basement waiting to be fully revealed.

Faience became a feature of a large number of London Underground stations. Here, the rich victoria plum coloured faience provided by Burmantofts for the forty or so stations built in 1906-7 makes them immediately identifiable. Leslie Green's design featured a large central archway flanked by pilastered side arches and its use on all of these stations provides an excellent early example of corporate style. This concept extended below street level, where the platform areas bear decorated tiles assembled in bold geometric arrangements incorporating the station name, the tile and faience clad entrances being equally noteworthy. Indeed, one and a half million tiles went into the ninety-four platforms and passageways of these deep-level tube stations, making this one of the largest tiling projects of the period.

In the provinces, the most notable examples of faience associated with the railways were to be seen in their hotels. Probably the most impressive remaining instance is the former First Class Refreshment Room of the Station Hotel, Newcastle upon Tyne, Northumberland (currently the Centurion Bar) in the centre of the present station complex. Clad in Burmantofts faience and dating from 1892-3, it provides a lofty array of glittering ceramic surfaces extending from walls to ceiling where it culminates in a top-lit lantern. At York, although detached from the station itself, the dining room of the former Royal Station Hotel, now Royal York Hotel, is equally impressive with faience walls and ceiling including an elaborate faience fireplace. Even more detached is the Midland Hotel (1898-1903) of the former Midland Railway at Manchester, but here Leeds Fireclay's gingery brown faience with sculpture by Spruce forms the entire massive exterior. Of incidental interest are the tiled or sometimes glazed brick railway network maps to be seen at some stations including Manchester Victoria, York and Tynemouth (Northumberland).

HOSPITALS

by Biddy Macfarlane

In 1987, the Tiles and Architectural Ceramics Society (TACS) published a book called *Brightening the Long Days*, a tour de force by one of the Society's founding members, John Greene, which was an abundantly illustrated record of hospital tile pictures. Some of the information as to the location of the pictures had been provided by children who had answered two Blue Peter television appeals and much had been based on the author's own finds in his experience of working in hospitals and on hospital management committees. Since 1987, lots of things have changed in the hospital world. In-patient stays are much shorter. Wards may have needed to be adapted, to produce smaller or larger units. Many of the older institutions have been extensively modernised, or destroyed and replaced, and although in many cases the authorities have realised the importance of their tiles and have managed to preserve these treasures for the future delight of patients and staff, some have been lost.

Sadly, some panels have been stolen, always a risk when work is being carried out in a hospital. Others have been covered up or destroyed. (There is some cheerful news: some of the important tile panels stolen from a London hospital were recovered because of a tip-off from a TACS member, who recognised their provenance.)

The three great surges in the use of tiles in hospitals came in the Victorian, Edwardian and interwar periods. The last forty years of the nineteenth century saw a huge output of encaustic and patterned tiles, as well as plain tiling and plain faience. Two factors had led to a large increase in urban populations: agricultural depression and sharp population growth. As a result, there was a boom in the planning of hospitals (as well as churches), coming to fruition in the thirty years following 1880.

In 1860, Joseph Lister had pioneered the the use of an antiseptic system which had revolutionised British surgery. Glazed tiling provided a surface entirely suitable for promoting antiseptic conditions on wards; they could be quickly and easily washed down and disinfected. The various potteries must have had an easy task in persuading the builders of the new urban hospitals to incorporate their products into the buildings and no doubt the salesmen would have been able to point to the desirability of including more decorative panels in the tiling scheme.

Public health was a topic which became of great importance in the late nineteenth century, Florence Nightingale, on her return from the Crimean War, threw herself into a campaign to open and regulate hospitals and her influence was wide-reaching. Funding was, of course, in private hands and in many cases appeals for donations or endowments were successfully launched. Queen Victoria's Golden and Diamond Jubilees, in 1887 and 1897, each provided occasions for raising money for hospitals, and a number of tiled wards carry memorials showing that one of the jubilees had been the reason for loosening private or municipal purse-strings.

The prosperity of the Edwardian age, up to the Great War, also led to benevolence (particularly private charitable giving) on an impressive scale. Hospitals planned earlier were now built. For example, the red brick and terracotta Royal Waterloo Hospital for Children and Women in Lambeth, London (1903-5, now Schiller International University) has splendid green Doulton faience and bold lettering proclaiming its title and making it known that it was supported by voluntary contributions and that its patrons were Edward VII, Queen Alexandra and their Royal Highnesses the Prince and Princess of Wales.

Donors sometimes had family members who had spent time in hospital, while others acted altruistically, as a thank-offering for their own good health. Although the popularity of tiles for home use was beginning to wane a little, their efficacy as an attractive and hygienic decoration for hospitals had been proved in the previous century, and they remained extremely popular for that purpose.

In the years between the two world wars, hospitals which had been built in the nineteenth century began to need updating and in many cases new wards were added. For children's wards, in particular, bright, cheerful decoration was favoured and a number of tile-makers and decorators (including Carter's, Doulton's and W. B. Simpson & Sons) produced lively pictures of nursery rhyme and fairy tale characters, or animals in human clothes, in clear colours and glazes and simple designs, making an immediate appeal and literally, for young patients, brightening the long days.

Since the end of the Second World War, another problem has arisen. Whereas among the virtues of tiles in the older hospitals were their permanency and their resistance to damage, more recently the emphasis has moved to flexibility. Many of the old tiling schemes have had to be covered up, drilled through or abandoned as bedside machinery has become essential. This has told against the introduction of more tiles into wards and instead prints or photographs are displayed. However, several hospitals have installed tiling or mosaic murals outside or in entrance halls, waiting rooms or corridors. Excellent examples by modern tile-makers are to be found in many parts of the country, but even they are under threat as whole hospitals move and the old buildings are demolished. In Greenwich, for example, a new district hospital was built in the 1970s, with a large panoramic mural on an exterior wall designed by Philippa Threlfall in 1972, depicting Greenwich's royal and maritime history. That 'new' hospital has, in its turn, been moved to a different site, leaving the 1972 mural behind and at risk. In Carlisle, the Carlisle Royal Infirmary had three tiled panels designed by Christine Constant as recently as

1991; but when the hospital building was demolished in 2000-1, the panels were destroyed as well.

What is more, benefaction for private purposes in public buildings has gone a little out of fashion. Tight budgets in the NHS mean there is often no money available for expensive rescue work for tiles in disused hospitals; but we must all fight if we can to preserve these little gems of our architectural heritage, which may be just as valuable to patients on the new site as they have been on the old. The restructured Jackfield Tile Museum, one of the Ironbridge Gorge Museums, includes among its exhibits part of a tiled hospital ward as an example of the happy marriage of function and ornament which was once such an alleviation of a tedious and painful episode in people's lives.

FACTORIES
by Joan Skinner

The factory system of production has its origins largely in the mechanization of processes in the textile industry. The earliest factories were in rural areas, water operated, stone-built and assumed a Palladian appearance to appease the sensitivities of the aristocracy, as at Arkwright's Masson Mill, Cromford, Derbyshire (1783). Technical advances in materials, methods and energy sources (firstly steam) brought factories into towns. Increasing in size and number to accommodate even larger machines and demand for their products, their appearance was distinguished only by their scale and the unremitting monotony of their design, blackened by smoke from chimneys that identified their sites. A few of these giants remain at Ancoats, Manchester. Seaport warehouses, housing bulk quantities of sugar, cotton, tobacco and the like, were of similar pattern, sometimes enhanced by a little neo-classicism. But the mid-nineteenth century town warehouses could be mistaken in scale and grandeur for palaces, still stone built and stone decorated at, for instance, Whitworth Street and Portland Street in Manchester, the Lace Market, Nottingham and Little Germany, Bradford, West Yorkshire.

By the 1850s, many other products were being made in factories, built in a range of architectural styles. Importantly, too, by this time, the middle classes were establishing their power and taste and were prepared to display their wealth, confidence and civic pride. Their houses saluted the gothic revival but their factories were in elegant Italianate style, for instance Saltaire, Bradford (1851-3), Dean Clough, Halifax (1854-85) and Whitmore, Leicester (1848). And often factories were being built in brick - Accrington red, Staffordshire blue, Leicester peach, Ruabon plum - but generally stone-dressed to preserve the tradition.

And then came High Victorian eclectic opulence. Ceramic decoration came into its own as cleaner, more durable, more colourful, with advertising potential and superb modelling possibilities to echo the splendour of the Manchester warehouses. Smaller factories were fairly reserved, even domestic in appearance, but a decorated entrance for the owner and important visitors, a fancy first-floor hanging-bay to the owner's office, and perhaps a frieze of coloured tiles below the eaves were not unusual. Decorative bricks were also frequent - moulded, carved, rubbed or in dentillated polychromatic patterns. The Staffordshire potteries were almost always reticent in their factory design, but when the tile manufacturers Minton Hollins & Co built their large factory at Stoke-on-Trent around 1870, the architect Charles Lynam boldly exhibited the company's products on its roadside elevation, in lintels, spandrels and cornice, with the company name in blue and white mosaic above the vehicular entrance. Lynam repeated this succesful means of decoration in his design for tilemakers Craven Dunnill & Co (1871-4), Jackfield, Shropshire.

In informing the public of its wares, however, Doulton's factory at High Street, Lambeth, London (1876-8, Tarring, Son & Wilkinson) showed no restraint. Resplendent in Venetian gothic dress, Staffordshire blue brick and Fareham red were enhanced by red and buff terracotta. *The Builder* of 2nd August 1879 noted that the use of terracotta 'is steadily on the increase'. Fashion was following attitude. Less flamboyant but elegantly attractive is St Paul's House, Park Square, Leeds (1878, Thomas Ambler), brick-built with fine Doulton buff terracotta dressing in an exotic Moorish gothic. The skyline decoration deteriorated at a time when makers were unwilling to take on small batch work; replacements are in fibreglass. Much more ornate, however, is Templeton's carpet factory, Glasgow (1888, William Leiper) with patterned red, light green and cream brick and blue glass mosaic. Flamboyance had become respectable, particularly when used with grace. The Faire Brothers warehouse, Alexandra House, Leicester (1895-8, Edward Burgess) lost its dome in warfare but fortunately its Burmantofts buff faience external skin is undamaged. The flatware is probably catalogue, but is highly decorated with specially-designed, three-dimensional references to the trade, export regions and locality.

Into the twentieth century, the Michelin Tyre Company interpreted 'free design' to mean exotic in their multi-coloured tiled headquarters and stockrooms in Fulham Road, South Kensington, London (1910, architect François Espinasse), but for the Sanderson wallpaper factory at Turnham Green (1902-3) C. F. A. Voysey preferred a sophisticated version of English domestic revival cum arts and crafts. White glazed brick over-all with wavy string-courses and the skyline in black, such modernity may have been considered more appropriate to their product. Northern factories were also modernizing, with steel frame construction and large windows, as at Coppull Mills, south-west of Chorley, Lancashire (1906, Joseph Stott & Sons) but the walls are of Accrington red brick, yellow glazed brick and buff terracotta. Of similar ilk is Broadstone Mill, Reddish (around 1910) also banded in Accrington red and yellow glazed brick. Both factories have marvellously decorated Byzantine towers. Manchester's twentieth century warehouse owners also began to appreciate the values and attractiveness of ceramic decoration. India House, Whitworth Street (1905-9, Henry Fairhurst) is red brick with glazed sienna tiles above a rusticated base; Lancaster House, Princess Street (1907-10, also Fairhurst) has bright sienna terracotta which, it was claimed, was self-washing and shone like gold after rain; and Orient House, Granby Row (c1914, George H. Goldsmith) has a white glazed brick facade.

There were, too, other uses for ceramics in factories. Coloured floor tiles and tiled dados frequently grace the vestibules and entrance halls of factories and warehouses, and tiled fireplaces were often found in directors' offices. Canteen walls and floors were tiled, the kitchens for fire-resistance and cleanliness, the dining and rest rooms, with tiles in colours and patterns, to differentiate between workplace and leisure. By the 1870s white glazed brick was meeting the Right of Light in preference to whitewashing common stone or brick. White glazed brick spelled out a company's name high on the chimney or along the fascia or skyline, and high dados of golden brown glazed brick still protect the pavement-side walls of many town factories.

SHOPS AND COMMERCIAL BUILDINGS
by Chris Blanchett

The Victorian era saw a whole new emphasis on cleanliness and hygiene, with an awareness of the advantages of proper sanitation and a desire for more healthy food supplies and surroundings. Ceramics had a very important part to play in this social revolution. The person in the street wanted to be able to purchase fresh, healthy food from shops that had clean, hygienic surfaces which could be hosed down or scrubbed clean. Shopkeepers turned first to marble, but because this was so expensive they rapidly considered the use of ceramic tiles which offered a cheaper and more decorative finish.

One of the earliest companies to explore the use of ceramics in their shop interiors was J. Sainsbury whose second shop at 159 Queens Crescent, London, which opened in 1875, was completely decorated with tiles. A dado of low relief moulded tiles ran around the whole shop, and above this were hand-painted tile panels depicting exotic birds. All the tiles were selected from the current catalogue of Minton Hollins & Co who were to supply Sainsbury's with tiles right up to the late 1930s. Relief moulded tiles were also used for the front of the counters and the floor was set with ceramic mosaic, also supplied by Minton Hollins. Counter tops were of marble, easy to clean and a natural 'refrigerated' surface.

Soon, most butcher's shops, fishmongers and dairies had at least some tile decoration, often plain, but on occasion featuring large hand-painted tile panels depicting idyllic country scenes, fishing trawlers or even in one instance, musical instruments. Not only were tiles easy to clean, but they were very durable, showed what the shop sold (in times when literacy was not particularly high), and gave a 'high-class' air to the premises. Architectural ceramics were used on exteriors too: faience columns, tiled stall-risers, porch tile panels and tiled name signs soon started to change the look of Britain's High Streets. Not only were they durable, but a shower of rain and they looked like new!

The prestige factor also brought about the use of architectural ceramics in financial establishments, banks, insurance companies and gentlemen's clubs. Their main aim here was to impress, to show how strong and permanent the company was, and to provide opulent surroundings where the wealthy could feel at home. The adoption of steel frame construction meant that large, open spaces, essential to such buildings could be created easily and cheaply, and ceramics were the ideal materials with which to clad the frame. Ornate terracotta created the right impression outside achieving the effect of sandstone at a fraction of the cost and with patterns that could be moulded ad infinitum. Faience, its glazed equivalent, ran rampant inside: dados, panels, staircases and columns, even ceilings, were all clad in beige and brown faience; tiled fireplaces, counters and interior fittings proliferated. Heavy mouldings and ornate cornices became the order of the day, sometimes enlivened with mosaics or painted tile panels. J. C. Edwards, Burmantofts and Doulton's were the main companies involved, they too being seen as prestigious organisations in a world of smaller manufacturers.

Occasionally, restaurants and tea-rooms too adopted ceramics as a decorative material, the Turkey Café (1900-1) in Leicester being a classic example with its wonderful polychrome Doulton exterior. For sheer exuberance of a kind seldom seen in Britain the Doulton ceramic ornamentation of the Everard Building (1901), Edward Everard's printing works in Bristol, Gloucestershire, is hard to beat. However the austerity dictated by the onset of war in 1914 meant that such schemes never proliferated.

ENTERTAINMENT ARCHITECTURE
by Lynn Pearson

The architecture of the Victorian and Edwardian entertainment industry was very varied, encompassing everything one might encounter during a day at the races or a night at the opera. Theatres, and related buildings such as music halls, opera houses and circuses, were particularly important in numerical terms, with some 800 theatres being built between the 1860s and 1920, although the real boom in their construction occurred in the period between the 1880s and 1914. The substantial amount of terracotta (made by Gibbs & Canning) used very visibly at the Royal Albert Hall, an all-purpose cultural venue which was begun in 1867, paved the way for its specification by theatre architects, although only at major sites was its use especially lavish, for instance at two theatres designed by Frank Matcham, the Hackney Empire (1901) and the rather less decorative London Coliseum (1902-4), Westminster, where Hathern terracotta formed the entire facade. Creamy-white Doulton Carraraware in Edwardian baroque style clad the whole facade of Torquay's Pavilion (1911-12), a seafront music hall.

As well as making striking facades, ceramics were used decoratively inside theatres, an early example being the Criterion, Piccadilly Circus (Westminster), where the W. B. Simpson & Sons pictorial tiling dates from 1884. Although the currently derelict Chatham Theatre Royal (1897-9), Kent, had a good interior decorative scheme including several pictorial panels, its quality was nowhere near the equal of the Burmantofts work inside the Blackpool Tower buildings (1891-4), Lancashire, where the high relief blue-glazed panels of birds by E. C. Spruce come alive as the visitor walks the tile-lined corridors. Blackpool Winter Gardens, a huge leisure centre always in competition with its rival the Tower, included twenty-eight hand-painted Doulton tile panels designed by W. J. Neatby in its extension of 1896. Although dado tiling, normally in relatively plain designs, was fairly common in theatres, pictorial panels were rare, and external pictorial panels most unusual, but in Plymouth, Devon, pictorial tile panels by Doulton featured on the exterior of the New Palace Theatre (1898-9).

Terracotta was also popular with early cinema architects; two good examples are Great Yarmouth's Gem (1908) and Empire (1911), Norfolk, in rather different styles, their cream faience and grey terracotta respectively providing a good contrast with the same town's circus, the Hippodrome (1903), faced in bright pinky-red art nouveau terracotta. Entertainment venues other than theatres and the like included sports grounds, where the architecture was generally purely functional, although there were exceptions: the pavilion (1889-90) at Lord's Cricket Ground, St John's Wood (Westminster), sports bright salmon-pink terracotta dressings; the ornate ceramics include corbel heads of cricketers.

In general, although there were some spectacular instances of the use of tiles and architectural ceramics in the buildings of the Victorian and Edwardian entertainment industry, it is not entertainment buildings which come to mind as being the most decorative of this era. Entertainment is bound up with the requirement for novelty, especially at the seaside - then such an important element of the leisure industry - and buildings with fun as their purpose often tend towards the ephemeral, eyecatching and cheap, rather than being expensively and permanently decorated. It was only in the interwar years that the use of faience on an almost heroic scale for cinema facades became popular, the smooth, clean material then presenting precisely the modern image required by the film industry.

THE BREWING INDUSTRY

by Lynn Pearson

The relationship between the brewing and ceramics industries was always close, even before 1850, when tile pictures were first used to decorate a pub interior (at Gurton's tavern, in London's Old Bond Street). Sanitaryware, stoneware barrels, flasks and jugs were all required by sellers of beer, but it was only towards the end of the nineteenth century, when brewing became increasingly competitive, that the use of tiles, architectural ceramics and glazed bricks in pubs and breweries became widespread.

Tiles and colourful glazed bricks were used as exterior decoration on breweries from the early 1870s, with the emphasis usually being on the brewhouse tower or chimney, to attract attention to the brewery. Inside, glazed bricks were preferred by brewers' architects from the early 1880s as the most hygienic finish for brewhouse and fermenting room walls. Initially these were plain white, but coloured glazed bricks were introduced by the late 1880s, often forming attractive decorative features. Terracotta dressings were most often used to emphasise brewery entrances or names, but the material was occasionally used on a larger scale, as in the rebuilding of Cain's Mersey Brewery, Liverpool, completed in 1902. The rich, red Ruabon terracotta makes an emphatic architectural statement complete with the brewery's trademark unicorn, a superb example of the art of terracotta manufacturing. Brewery offices were often given a more ornate architectural treatment, with interiors fitted out to a high standard, although few could compete with the Newcastle Breweries Offices (1896-1901), Newcastle upon Tyne, Northumberland; its interior is faced with glazed faience, almost certainly by Burmantofts, in shades of brown, green and buff, even including the Breweries name and logo.

The brewery wars of the late nineteenth and early twentieth centuries had a dramatic effect on pub construction, although the results of competition were far from identical throughout the country. Attractive, colourful, easily cleaned, hygienic tiles and faience could be used on the pub facade to catch the eye of the passer-by, to present the symbol or brand image of pub or brewery, to brighten up long corridors, to add colour and intricate form to the bar area, and to provide a modern appearance for toilets. Ceramics were widely used in the public house from the early 1880s, but their finest hour came in the late 1890s and especially the early 1900s. The exact nature of the relationship between brewer, architect, builder, tiler and ceramic manufacturer determined the ultimate look of the public house, and designs show considerable local peculiarities.

Carter's started to produce historical tile murals for public houses around 1883. They could be found in the entrance halls of several leading London taverns by 1886, and although other ceramic manufacturers rapidly developed their own tile murals, Carter's remained successful in this field until well into the next century as they tended to be cheaper than their competitors. Picture panels were eventually combined with wall tiling and even ceramic bar fronts, a Craven Dunnill speciality, to give a complete ceramic interior. An outstanding example of this type of design, which peaked in popularity in the early years of the twentieth century, is the Mountain Daisy, Sunderland (1900-2), County Durham. Here Craven Dunnill supplied seven hand-painted tile panels showing local scenes as well as decorative wall tiling and a quarter-circle bar front.

Coloured ceramic facades, branding the pub as part of a particular brewer's estate, began to be seen around the turn of the century. There are clear regional differences, including the Birmingham 'tile and terracotta' style - a terracotta facade with an ornate interior including tilework - which was popular during 1896-1904. In the Edwardian period, use of the pub facade as an advertisement developed to the extent that products - beer, India Pale Ale, lager and so forth - the brewery name (sometimes as a logo) and the pub name (often in pictorial form) were all portrayed in ceramics.

These complex tile and terracotta facades and interiors were not always profitable for the ceramics manufacturers; indeed, they were often seen as loss leaders, sold in the hope of obtaining the more lucrative contracts for bricks and sanitaryware. Long-term relationships between brewers, architects and ceramics manufacturers were not uncommon, with Carter's, Doulton's and (later) Shaws being the most important manufacturers, although Maw, Minton Hollins and Craven Dunnill become more significant the further north the location of the pub or brewery. Doulton's produced all types of ware for brewers and publicans, including everything from barrels, bottles and jugs to internal and external decorative faience for public houses; this important element of their overall production began in the mid-nineteenth century and continued until the 1930s.

Local relationships between brewers and ceramics manufacturers produced local styles for the 'local', but the innovatory capacity of the ceramics industry was crucial in creating the timeless image of the British public house. Eventually the turn-of-the-century pub became the apotheosis of integral colour in architecture, although perhaps this was not exactly what the Arts and Crafts architect (and partner in William De Morgan's tileworks) Halsey Ricardo, an enthusiastic proponent of more colour in the environment, had in mind when he wrote in 1902 'We have tried mass and form, and light and shade, might we not now have an attempt at colour?'

BATHS, WASHHOUSES AND TOILETS

by Tony Herbert

During the nineteenth century the growth of the urban population of towns and cities led to overcrowding, with all its associated problems and unsanitary conditions and disease. The rising concern for public health and hygiene took a variety of architectural forms many of which relied on the hard, smooth glazed surfaces of ceramic materials. At its most basic level this started with the building of a proper piped water supply and the removal of subsequent waste through a network of sewers. Miles of salt glazed ceramic pipes were made and used in London in the 1850s, buried unglamorously underground, but with some still in use today. The fortunes of Henry Doulton were built on this industry and the great Doulton ceramic empire, which grew to include tiles, faience and terracotta, was a profound legacy.

An Act of Parliament in 1864 heralded the desirability 'for the Health, Comfort and Welfare of the Inhabitants of Towns and populous Districts to encourage the Establishment therein of public Baths and Wash-Houses'. Some cities, like Birmingham, were driven by a philanthropic municipal vision and the provision of public baths brought architectural opportunities where huge quantities of glazed ceramics, including brick, could serve as clean and hardwearing materials in the cause of human hygiene.

The provision of public baths accelerated considerably towards the end of the nineteenth century and the Duke of Westminster captured the mood of civic concern for cleanliness in the collect written for the opening of Woolwich Public Baths, London in 1894 which began 'O God, who has taught us by thy servant John Wesley that cleanliness is next to Godliness, we thank thee for the public spirit which has caused these Baths to be erected in our midst'. Fortunately, the survival (and impending restoration) of the Victoria Baths complex in Manchester enables us to sense the unique Victorian blend of elaborate architectural detail and functional design which characterised these buildings.

As the concept of leisure grew, the emphasis gradually moved from bath cubicles catering for people without baths at home to public swimming baths, which provided opportunities for long runs of decorative tiled dados and more ornate work, for instance at Newcastle upon Tyne's Gibson Street Baths (1907) with its series of Carter's aquatic pictorial panels. But the full flowering of tiled decoration came with the development of Russian or Vapour baths and Turkish baths. Anyone who has seen the surviving schemes at Carlisle, Cumbria, or Harrogate, North Yorkshire, cannot fail to be impressed by the sense of the exotic which coloured, glazed tiles were able to create.

Although not usually so exotic, the public lavatory was a building type that relied very heavily on glazed materials. The ubiquitous use of white or cream glazed tiles in these circumstances may well be responsible for the term 'lavatorial' with which many Victorian tiling schemes were labelled at the height of their unfashionability in the 1960s. Some fine examples feature in the Gazetteer, notably the Market Place toilets in Hull, East Yorkshire, and the beautifully restored gents on the pier head at Rothesay on the Isle of Bute (Argyll & Bute). Other examples survive as part of public houses and arguably the best is the gents at the Philharmonic Hotel in Liverpool, where the landlord is quite accustomed to requests for unisex access to view the tiles!

MONUMENTS

by Alan Swale and Lynn Pearson

Monuments incorporating or constructed entirely of ceramics come in all shapes and sizes, from huge fountains and mausoleums to the lozenge-shaped memorial tiles seen in some churches. One of the largest is the towering column of the Martyrs' Memorial (1878-9) in the grounds of St John's Church, Stratford Broadway, Newham, London. Constructed from buff terracotta supplied by a Sussex manufacturer, its crisp gothic detailing has barely weathered. Unusually, it was put up at a time when terracotta had hardly come into fashion as a building material. Most ceramic memorials date from the period between the late 1880s and the early 1900s, when terracotta was far more generally popular, and it is no coincidence that many monuments were executed by Doulton & Co, who employed a number of talented sculptors and artists in their London studio, thus placing them in a highly favourable position to receive such commissions.

Three of the largest ceramic monuments of the period, all made by Doulton's, were erected in Glasgow. The most spectacular of these is the 43' high salmon-pink terracotta Victoria Fountain on Glasgow Green. Made as an exhibit for the 1888 Glasgow International Exhibition, but serving as a monument to Queen Victoria and the empire she ruled, it includes sculptural groups symbolising Australia, Canada, India and South Africa, all surmounted by the Queen herself. After years of neglect, the Victoria Fountain was restored to its former glory in 2002-4 and resited in front of the People's Palace. The second monument was the matt white glazed Carraraware Hamilton Fountain (1907) in Maxwell Park, Pollokshields. This commemorated a local merchant, Thomas Hamilton, whose figure could be seen standing on top of the central shaft. Although restored in 1953, the Hamilton Fountain was mostly dismantled in the late 1980s. Glasgow's third and rather smaller Doulton terracotta monument is the Cameron Memorial Fountain (1895-6) on Sauchiehall Street, which survives although tilting badly.

Among a number of Doulton monuments to Queen Victoria, at home and abroad, is that in Victoria Park, Newbury, Berkshire of around 1901. Modelled by John Broad in Doulton red terracotta, the Queen is seen accompanied by reclining lions. Also by Broad is the 1893 Doulton terracotta statue of General Gordon to be found in Gravesend, Kent, the General's birthplace. This has survived the years relatively undamaged, but the drinking fountain memorial to Richard Eve in Brinton Park, Kidderminster, Worcestershire of 1902 has not been so lucky. In highly colourful salt-glazed Doultonware, the striking tower-like structure features a relief portrait of Eve and superb art nouveau panels.

Turning to funerary monuments, it is no surprise that Henry Doulton's own mausoleum is constructed of Doulton terracotta combined with red brick, featuring panels of low relief terracotta sculpture. Dating from around 1888 and built for his wife Sarah, this is in West Norwood Cemetery, Lambeth. In Burslem Cemetery, Stoke-on-Trent stands the impressive dark green glazed Doultonware tomb of Thomas Hulm of 1905. Although damaged, it is still complete with its main elements, a tall pyramid, once capped with an urn and at the base, an angel with a piped instrument reflecting Hulm's long service as an organist. There are also relief panels of local views connected with his life, the whole again being modelled by Broad. Very few of these coloured glazed ceramic monuments were made, the Hulm tomb and the Richard Eve memorial being the best surviving examples.

Finally, to tiles. The most common form of memorial tile was the 12" square glazed tile, set on the diagonal on the interior walls of churches; often manufactured by Minton Hollins, these were especially popular from the 1870s to the 1890s. In contrast, the unusual array of memorials in Postman's Park, City of London, is dedicated to those who died heroically in the act of saving others. These hand-painted glazed ceramic panels, installed during 1900-31, were initially executed by William De Morgan and then by Doulton & Co; they feature decorative inscriptions, some bearing symbols representing the event. Sheltered by a lean-to roof, these memorial tiles are in good condition.

TILES IN THE DOMESTIC CONTEXT

by Peter Rose

Tiles were used in domestic settings, at all social levels, for centuries before the Victorian period, both for practical and decorative purposes. Indeed, by the eighteenth century Horace Walpole at Strawberry Hill (Richmond upon Thames) was using not only the genuine article but also wallpaper in 'imitation of Dutch tiles'. By the mid-nineteenth century his successor Lady Waldegrave was refurbishing and enlarging the house with Minton tiles in fire surrounds and domestic offices, while the newly fashionable encaustic tiles were used for the floors. The wider use of tiles was much facilitated by inventions such as Richard Prosser's process of making ceramic articles from pressed, powdered clay, patented in 1840 and immediately exploited by Minton & Co. Tiles soon spread from floors and walls to furniture: they were set into objects such as sideboards, washstands, jardinieres, tabletops, hall stands and chairs, as well as a range of smaller portable items such as teapot stands, plant holders and trays.

Designs were commissioned from leading artists for clients who wished to integrate tile panels into an overall scheme of decoration. For instance Morris, Marshall, Faulkner & Co created panels of pictorial tiles designed by Edward Burne-Jones, soon after the start of the firm in 1861, for the artist Myles Birket Foster's newly built home 'The Hill', Witley, Surrey. Initially Morris himself also designed tiles, which had a marked influence on his friend and associate, William De Morgan, the most famous tile designer of the nineteenth century. De Morgan was responsible for creating many hundreds of designs, which were hugely popular with the expanding taste for 'aesthetic' interiors. The most complete surviving scheme is the Debenham House (1904-7), Holland Park (Kensington & Chelsea), designed by the architect and De Morgan's one-time partner, Halsey Ricardo.

Minton & Co were from the beginning the leading manufacturers of tiles, although as the century progressed other firms such as Maw & Co, Craven Dunnill, and Wedgwood increasingly challenged that position. In the Great Exhibition of 1851 Minton showed a spectacular example of the use of the newly developed majolicaware tiles in high relief designed by A. W. N. Pugin; the celebrated Great Stove was vividly colourful and caused a sensation. But these were exceptional; most domestic wall tiles were smooth or in low relief. At a time when grime in the form of smoke and grease was becoming a greater problem in the home, the easily washed and impervious surface of glazed tiles offered an irresistible attraction to architects and clients seeking permanent freshness of effect.

By great good fortune the boom time in demand for domestic tiles coincided with a renaissance in design standards encouraged by the newly established Schools of Design. From the middle of the century onwards major artists like Burne-Jones, Edward Poynter, Albert Moore and William Coleman turned their hand to designing tiles in the spirit of the newly emerging arts and crafts movement. Architects included A. W. N. Pugin, William Burges and E. W. Godwin. Some of the new breed of trained designers, but not the majority, devoted themselves almost exclusively to this form of decoration. These designers included Christopher Dresser, John Moyr Smith, Henry Stacy Marks and William Wise.

The ubiquitous cast iron fire-grate set in a marble or wood surround created an irresistible opening for designers. The established pattern was to provide space for flanking columns of four or five tiles surmounted by a frieze, frequently accommodating the standard set of twelve tiles, together with extra spacers if necessary. Sometimes the column tiles were designed to show a continuous design such as a flowering plant in a pot. More commonly they would comprise a series of designs based on a theme such as months of the year, scenes from Shakespeare, the novels of Walter Scott, Aesop's fables, classical figures or animals or birds. The emphasis on the hearth in Victorian family life meant that storytelling subjects were especially popular. More progressive designers like Dresser or Charles Bevan, by contrast, favoured geometric designs.

The use of terracotta as a decorative material in the domestic interior was unusual, but external terracotta ornament was common, with much being supplied straight from the manufacturers' catalogues. Two-foot square red terracotta Queen Victoria jubilee plaques may be found on houses throughout the country, with the greatest concentration in central and southern England. The plaques show a relief bust of the Queen and were produced by Stanley Brothers of Nuneaton. Initially they were made to mark the Queen's fiftieth jubilee in 1887, but the design was later adapted for the 1897 Diamond Jubilee, the later version being much more common.

From the beginning of the twentieth century the use of tiles in the home was on the decline. Voysey, however, remained committed to the arts and crafts ethos and designed tiles which he used in the traditional manner. In the more typical Edwardian terraces, ornament was still in favour and the firegrates continued to sport decorative tile surrounds but usually in the then current taste for art nouveau. After the First World War the fashion for highly wrought interiors was replaced by the minimal decoration of the modern movement.

BETWEEN THE WARS

by Chris Blanchett

The era immediately following World War One was a comparatively quiet period for British architectural ceramic manufacturers. The war had claimed many of Britain's young men who died in the fighting, and for a number of years, industry found it hard to recruit staff to rebuild their businesses. Inspiration in design was at a low ebb too - in fact most of the British tiles made during the early 1920s were either plain glazed or simplified versions of basic art nouveau designs from a decade or more earlier. The Depression did not help and a number of long-established tile manufacturers went under at this time. Those that survived sought technological solutions to their problems, such as the development of the tunnel kiln invented by Conrad Dressler in 1914 and first installed by J. H. Barratt & Co in Stoke-on-Trent. The new kilns dramatically reduced costs and firing times and enabled manufacturers to keep up continuous production. Stocks of tiles were thus reduced and standard designs could be quickly glazed in colour as and when required to meet specific orders. Many of the complex older designs were deleted from catalogues and a new rationalized approach to design is apparent from many contemporary catalogues.

The companies that did succeed were the companies that innovated, in the field of design as well as technology, and chief among these was Carter & Co at Poole in Dorset. Their links with Poole Pottery meant they had access to some of the leading designers of their day and they were quick to take advantage of the fact. A steady stream of fresh, bright designs appeared, mainly hand-painted which meant that the tiles were expensive, but they could be used sparingly in a fireplace or surrounded by plain tiles to keep the cost down. Carter's products also featured in the home magazines of the day which, together with the high profile of Poole Pottery, established a market for the tiles amongst a younger clientele. Carter's revived the Victorian idea of producing tile designs in sets and got their designers to come up with complete sets of Nursery Rhymes, Farmyard Scenes, Flowers etc that could be used en masse in a fireplace or scattered at random in a field of plain tiles.

Seeing the success of Carter's Tiles and Poole Pottery, a number of other, smaller companies sprang up, often the brainchild of students from the new Art Colleges established by the government to foster British design. One such company was Dunsmore Tiles established in about 1927 by Miss Brace and Miss Pilsbury. Like Carter's, they started with hand-painted tiles, but soon turned to stencilled designs in order to fulfil demand and keep costs down. They too designed sets of tiles, notably series of Exotic Birds, Rural Scenes and an especially fine set of characters from *Alice in Wonderland* based on C. F. A. Voysey's illustrations for the book.

Packard & Ord were another company to be established in the late twenties although their business didn't really flourish until the mid 1930s. Started by Sylvia Packard and Rosalind Ord, two art teachers from the Royal School for the Daughters of Officers at Bath, the company produced hand-painted designs, and, like Dunsmore, worked on commercial tiles bought in from Carter's and others. Initially they bought Carter tiles, decorated them and returned them to Poole for glazing and firing, not having their own kilns until 1936, when demand for Coronation tiles necessitated the purchase of their own small electric kiln and the employment of a young lady, Thea Bridges, to help in the decorating. The fact that companies such as Dunsmore and Packard & Ord were established and run by women was a direct result of the emancipation women experienced in the 1920s and 1930s.

The larger commercial tile manufacturers such as Henry Richards, H. & R. Johnson, T. & R. Boote and Wades continued to produce art nouveau designs well on into the 1930s, but their catalogues gradually began to feature 'room settings' incorporating the latest design trend, art deco. Characterized by strongly geometric forms, art deco is not a style that works well on single tiles, so the featured interiors (and a few exteriors too), show the use of large areas of plain tiling in bright, bold colours, put together in strongly geometric shapes, often with the use of narrow borders of contrasting plain or vividly-decorated border tiles. The use of highly glossy glazes went out of fashion, and eggshell glazes dominated the market as manufacturers experimented with new reactive glaze techniques that achieved rich, mottled surfaces. New materials were used to create the glazes, including the recently-discovered uranium and cadmium compounds that produced vibrant, bold colours not achievable before.

In the mid 1930s, tube-lining made a come-back as a major decorating technique. The process lent itself to the production of small runs, and also worked very effectively with the new boldly coloured, matt glazes. Pilkington's were one of the major exponents of the technique, utilising it to advantage in scenes of galleons and sailing ships, as well as series of Nursery Rhymes, Animals and Landscapes. It is possible that both Pilkington's and Carter's locations, well away from the Potteries, led them to create tiles that were different from those of the major Staffordshire tile companies.

Tiles did not feature heavily on commercial buildings of this period although a few tiled butchers and fishmongers have survived, often with a neo-classical swag design set at the top of the walls above fields of plain tiling. Faience, however, experienced something of a revival as a material for facing department stores and especially cinemas. The buildings themselves were often starkly art deco in design and the bold colours and shapes achievable with faience led to its widespread use on such buildings. Although the influence was art deco, there were often neo-classical overtones with the use of pilasters and columns and architectural swags and drapes. In Britain, this decoration was often meant to resemble marble and the use of names such as Carraraware (Doulton) and Marmo (Burmantofts) reinforces this allusion.

Substantial parts of the London Underground system underwent expansion and refurbishment in the 1930s and Carter's were commissioned to create a series of tiles, moulded in relief with 'Symbols of London'. Designed by Harold Stabler, the tiles were made in off-white and pale buff eggshell glazes and feature stylized images of famous London landmarks in early modernist form. The patterned tiles were used quite sparingly, set amongst the ubiquitous plain tiling that dominated architectural schemes of the time. On the whole, the impression is one of a brighter, more airy feel than that of earlier Underground tiling schemes and this was to set the trend for post-war underground rebuilding too.

POST-WAR TO THE PRESENT
by Chris Blanchett

World War Two left much of Britain's industry in ruins, many factories having been commandeered for the war effort. Machinery was in a bad state of repair if not completely useless, buildings often neglected or bombed out. The housing stock was seriously depleted too, due to bomb damage. The Government's short term answer was to build pre-fabricated homes (prefabs) which had little architectural ceramic embellishment, apart perhaps from a few plain white tiles in the kitchen or bathroom. To stimulate manufacturers to produce utilitarian plain tiles, the Government slapped a very high rate of Purchase Tax on decorated tiles. Larger companies could cope with the production of plain white and cream tiles, but smaller companies such as Packard & Ord relied on making hand-decorated tiles. The novel means by which they survived was to make the tiles into tea-trays which were seen as utilitarian items!

Slowly the economy began to boom and by the early 1950s, there was a return to the use of decorated tiles, but in an endeavour to keep costs down, manufacturers turned to new ways of putting pattern on to tiles. One of the leading companies was again Carter's of Poole who first developed the production of silk screen printed tiles. This technique had been employed before, but as a method of hand decoration; Carter's mechanized the process so that tiles could be mass produced. Soon, new designs were being commissioned, and again, Carter's innovated by involving commercial designers such as Peggy Angus. Her designs were fresh and original, relying on the use of simple geometric forms that could be used in repeat as 'pattern-making tiles' to cover whole areas of wall. The designs were popular with schools and local authorities and were used to good advantage in many public buildings in the mid to late 1950s, when large-scale pictorial and abstract ceramic murals also began to be commissioned, often by corporate clients. In addition, the large number of Catholic churches built throughout Britain between around 1953 and the mid-1960s provided a continuing opportunity for ceramic decoration, notably by the Polish-born artist Adam Kossowski.

In the 1960s, Shaw-Hathernware's mass production of plain 9″ by 3″ 'Twintiles' was an initial success with progressive architectural practices, leading to huge areas of Twintile cladding appearing on the redeveloped buildings of the period. However, the material came to be associated with on-site failures of tile-clad architecture, and demand (like some of the tiles) fell away. In the domestic context, 'Do It Yourself' became the country's leading spare time occupation, fuelled by popular DIY television programmes, and British tile manufacturers began to make much thinner tiles that could be cut and fixed by the man (or woman) in the street. The designs for these were fairly basic, consisting mainly of mottled or marbled patterns that created an all-over pattern requiring little design skill. With the advent of package holidays abroad however,

British consumers came in contact with the much more vibrant designs of tiles produced in Spain and Italy, and rapidly became disillusioned with British tile design. Some retailers were quick to see the opportunity and began to import tiles from these countries and to sell them through retail outlets rather than through the builder's merchant, the traditional tile suppliers in the UK. Foreign producers dominated the tile market by the end of the 1960s and many of the old names in British tiles were swallowed up by the two giants, H. & R. Johnson and Pilkington's Tiles, who accounted for 90% of UK production in the 1970s.

After the relatively fallow decade of the 1970s, when it sometimes seemed that only tiled underpasses kept architectural ceramic decoration alive, the 1980s saw a rise of interest in tiles as a decorative medium and a resurgence of interest in hand made and decorated tiles, often with a 'rustic' appearance. A large number of smaller companies were born that specialised in just one or two forms of decoration; relief moulding and majolica glazes becoming most popular. The larger companies such as H. & R. Johnson and Pilkington's retaliated with mass-produced tiles that mimicked the rustic qualities of the hand-made tiles by having wavy edges! Imports from abroad continued to supply a wider part of the market with new producers such as Greece and Brazil flooding the UK with cheap imports. Few of these were used in commercial buildings; they were more at home in a domestic setting.

From the 1980s, historically-themed hand made ceramic murals were often provided as public artworks by bodies such as local councils and supermarkets. However, the late 1980s and early 1990s also heralded a return to nostalgia with companies making copies of Victorian tiles, often for use in reproduction cast-iron fireplaces designed to replace those ripped out in the modernisation of the 1960s DIY era. Bathrooms were fitted out with reproduction Victorian suites and Victorian-style tiles were needed to complete the picture. As this move gained momentum, so architects began to design shops and pubs in 'nostalgic' mood, often, sadly, something of a pastiche of the original. Reproductions were not limited to wall tiles, demand for reproductions of historic encaustic tiles for refurbishment work led to a whole new market, which included shopping malls and clubs as well as pubs and shops.

The end of the twentieth century and expectations for the twenty-first have seen a new vigour introduced to tile design. Designers are no longer confined to clay materials for tiles: metals, glass and even plastics have offered a whole new design sphere within which it is possible to create entirely fresh pattern and image. These materials have yet to prove their value as architectural embellishments, but the fact that they are being used bodes well for the British tile industry of the twenty-first century.

England
Bedfordshire

Bedfordshire is generally a county of clay, but the Lower Greensand ridge, running south-west to north-east below Bedford and the Great Ouse valley, provides rolling country with expansive views and a plethora of fascinating churches of great ceramic interest. Often built from the iron-brown version of the Greensand known as carstone, many of these churches were restored by the Victorians, leaving a legacy of medievally-inspired ceramic decoration. Indeed Willington Church, just east of Bedford, offers a tantalising vision of the true colours of medieval tile pavements in a setting both romantic and historic. In contrast, the towns - apart from the hospital tile panels - are a ceramic disappointment, the local clay providing ample supplies of brick but little else. Suggested reading: Jill Somerscales, 'Bedford Hospital Tile Pictures', *Glazed Expressions* 34, 1997, pp4-6; J. M. Bailey, 'Decorated 14th-century tiles at Northill Church, Bedfordshire', *Medieval Archaeology*, vol 19, 1975, pp209-13. The *Gazetteer* entry for Bedfordshire covers the administrative areas of Bedfordshire County Council and Luton Borough Council.

BEDFORD

The **Shire Hall**, set beside the Great Ouse and fronting ST PAUL'S SQUARE, is instantly recognisable because of its abundant red brick and deep red, almost scarlet, terracotta dressings provided by J. C. Edwards of Ruabon.[1] The building, which now houses law courts, was erected in 1879-81, its architect being Alfred Waterhouse. Across the square is the former **Corn Exchange** (built 1871-4), with a cornice of knobbly terracotta dressings. The architects, J. Ladds & W. H. Powell, won the commission in a competition; perhaps the assessors were swayed by the emphatic quartet of chimneys and the unusual decorative features. East along the pleasant riverside promenade is Bedford Museum, where superb medieval tile pavements found at Warden Abbey (which stood about six miles south-east of Bedford) are on display.

South of the river on AMPTHILL ROAD is the south wing of **Bedford General Hospital**, built in 1897-8 (architect H. Percy Adams, a specialist in hospital design) with a separate ward designed specifically for children, the Victoria Ward.[2] Here a remarkable set of twenty Simpson's nursery rhyme panels has survived, along with a tiled panel listing the names of the sixteen generous lady benefactors who provided them in commemoration of Queen Victoria's sixtieth jubilee.[3] Eighteen of the panels measure 6′ by 3′, while two are larger at 6′ by 6′; the tiles were made by Maws, and the pictures were designed and hand-painted by Philip H. Newman for W. B. Simpson & Sons, who carried out the final firing. Apart from the happily named *Woman and Pig*, all portray well-known nursery rhymes. The drawing and painting is of exceptional quality, although the predominantly green colouring results in a rather anaemic appearance. Manufactured in the 1890s, these tiles form one of only three sets of early Simpson's nursery rhyme panels still in existence.

HAYNES

St Mary's is a most unusual church, medieval in origin but much rebuilt by Henry Woodyer in 1850; it stands, hidden by hedgerows, just south of Hawnes, a largely eighteenth-century mansion. Reconstruction of the church was the responsibility of the Reverend Lord John Thynne, an indirect descendant of the Carterets for whom Hawnes was built. Woodyer, an architect known for his inventiveness, was an adherent of Ecclesiological principles, thus St Mary's interior focuses on the colourful chancel, with its Minton pavement and reredos. The designs of the chancel tiles increase in complexity through the choir, where buff and red fleur-de-lys tiles form patterns defined by black diagonals, while the first step towards the altar has fleur-de-lys tiling in buff and blue. The next - narrow - step sports lozenge-shaped geometrics in red, green and yellow, while the sanctuary pavement is still more ornate. Two designs, a cross and the monogram IHS (for Jesus) are combined in the east wall tiling, which is topped by a reredos with lettering reading, rather oddly, 'Lo I am with you alway'. *The Builder* reported that the reredos was given to St Mary's by Minton & Co, but Haynes does not appear in the published list of churches to which Herbert Minton donated tiles between 1844 and his death in 1858.[4] This unrecorded donation is the first such case to be identified, and at present appears to be a unique occurrence, although the reredos (apart from its spelling) is not an especially unusual design.

A surprise is in store behind the elegant iron screen which bars entrance to the north or Thynne Chapel: inside this multicoloured but gloomy cavity is the recumbent white figure of Lady Thynne (1868), angels at her head, set above a patterned marble floor with a central pictorial roundel in black on buff marble; there are also a few encaustic border tiles. The floor, the canopy over the statue and probably the whole decorative scheme were designed by Sir George Gilbert Scott, while screen and floor were manufactured by Poole & Sons. At the head of the south aisle, railed off by fine ironwork, is the Carteret Chapel, its pavement composed of geometric tiles in a pattern made up of six-pointed green stars within red hexagons.

NORTHILL

On a sunny spring morning, the interior of **St Mary's Church** is dominated by golden light emanating from the pair of heraldic windows suspended above the south aisle. This remarkable painted glass - originally a single window at the east end - was commissioned from John Oliver in 1664 by the Worshipful Company of Grocers, patrons of the church, to commemorate the 1663-4 restoration of St Mary's. The church was restored again in 1862-3, by the architect Henry Woodyer, when the chancel pavement was added; it is mostly single-coloured Minton encaustic tiling with repeats of one early design, and there are also three pairs of white on blue letter tiles, with different combinations of letters (JM, CB and JT), perhaps referring to those involved with the restoration.[5] It is interesting to note that although Northill retains a large number of early fourteenth century line-impressed tiles (not normally on view), with motifs including well-drawn figures, apparently no attempt was made to replicate these designs during the 1862-3 restoration.[6]

TURVEY

All Saints Church is isolated from the parkland of Turvey House and the village by an intimidating wall of yew, undulating its way around the churchyard, in which a mausoleum's giant lettering proclaims 'What man is he that liveth and shall not see death?' Beyond its iron-clad door, the church does not disappoint, with an excellent double-decker monument - the second Lord Mordaunt reclining above his two wives - and a chancel built by Sir George Gilbert Scott in 1852-4. Here there is much colour, created by the use of two Minton designs, a cross and the agnus dei, in the sanctuary pavement; there is Biblical letter tiling across the altar step riser, and fleur-de-lys tiling in the choir and around the font.

WILLINGTON

The village of Willington lies in the broad Great Ouse plain a few miles east of Bedford. Sir John Gostwick (d1545), Master of the Horse to Cardinal Wolsey, and later in the service of King Henry VIII, owned the manor from 1529 and rebuilt the church of St Lawrence during 1539-41. Sir John's manor house is long gone, but close to the church, in quiet parkland well away from the Bedford road, are his stables and a most unusual dovecote, a tall, louvred structure with nesting boxes for 1,500 pigeons.

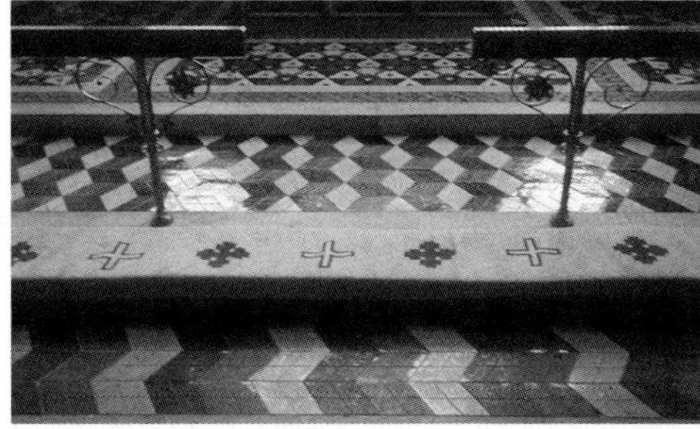

Fig 1.

Inside the church, the medieval atmosphere remains intense. The magnificent tomb of Sir William Gostwick (d1615) almost fills the little north chapel, where there are a few medieval tiles at the base of Sir John's rather smaller tomb. The chancel's Victorian pavement, however, is a complete visual shock: in the choir are line-impressed and relief tiles, square and rectangular, in red, green and black, while the sanctuary is floored with highly glazed yellow, green and black geometric tiles along with a few line-impressed tiles, the latter buff, with a flower motif. The geometric tiles, many of them rhomboidal in shape, are arranged so as to create an illusion of three-dimensionality, provoked by the optically-reversing rhomboids (Fig 1).

The pavement was installed as part of the 1876-7 restoration by that highly original architect Henry Clutton (1819-93), convert to Catholicism (in 1856), expert on French medieval architecture and friend of William Burges. The source of its inspiration lies in the north chapel, with its lozenge-shaped medieval tiles; the new chancel tiling was apparently intended to be a copy of the original medieval pavement. It is unclear whether the pavement survived from the original church (the church guidebook suggests it dated from the fourteenth century), or was added in the 1539-41 rebuilding; if the latter, it would be a very late example of the genre. It is interesting to note that soon after 1537, the Gostwicks built a house four miles to the south of Willington at Warden Abbey, part of their Bedfordshire estate. The abbey itself was a Cistercian foundation dating from 1135, and the Gostwicks incorporated some of its buildings into their new house, a fragment of which is still extant.[7] Excavations during late twentieth-century repairs to this curious remnant uncovered superb fourteenth-century tile pavements; these were part of the original abbey and were probably made and fired on site. The pavements are now displayed at Bedford Museum. Their designs show remarkable similarities to the Victorian chancel pavement at Willington, and it seems likely that the St Lawrence pavement is a copy of its fourteenth-century predecessor, which may have been installed by the same hand responsible for the Warden Abbey pavement.

The Victorian tiling certainly gives a real insight into the appearance of medieval pavements at the time they were laid. The brightness and intensity of the colours is unexpected, as is the stark geometry of the pattern and the optical illusion generated by the rhomboidal groups. Apart from its intrinsic attraction, the Willington scheme is therefore highly significant in that it effectively replicates the contemporary visual experience of a medieval pavement, in a way that excavated pavements, with their muted colours and lack of glaze, cannot. As to its manufacturer, the Willington tiles with a floret motif are based on a medieval design which also occurs at Bolton Abbey, West Yorkshire.[8] Godwin's made replacement tiles for Bolton Abbey, and Willington also has some green-glazed buff tiles, typical of Godwin's, thus it would appear that this firm is the most likely manufacturer.

One remaining question concerns the reason for installation of this spectacular pavement. The 1876-7 restoration appears to have been largely funded by the Duke of Bedford, whose family took over the Willington estate in 1779. He was an active landlord who took an interest in the church, and was assisted in the rebuilding by the Reverend Augustus Orlebar. Both men may have been concerned about the effect on the congregation of the opening of a methodist church in the village in 1868; the lavish restoration was perhaps an attempt to combat the forces of non-conformism. Although Willington was by no means the only church where medieval tiling was replicated by Victorian restorers, it appears unique in the scale and accuracy of its reproduction.

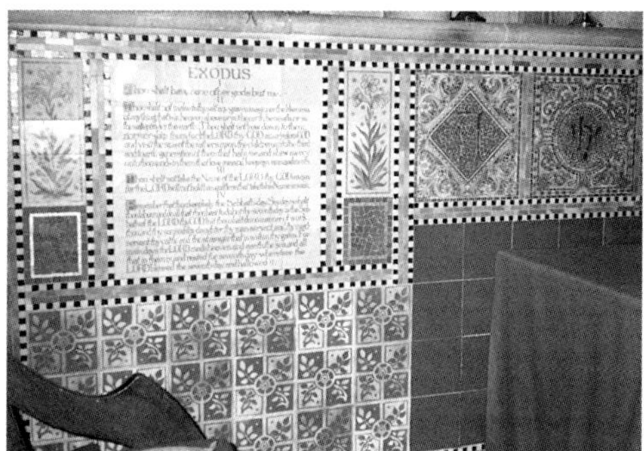

Fig 2.

Bedfordshire Roundup

All Saints Church, **Clifton** has a chancel pavement of decorative Minton tiles, installed in 1863.[9] At St Peter and St Paul, **Flitwick**, there are a few Minton tiles on the altar step risers, and Powell's opus sectile panels either side of the altar on the east wall, showing Christ as the *Good Shepherd* and *Light of the World*; they were installed in 1907 in memory of Major Brooks of Flitwick Manor. In **Luton**, the little-changed Painters Arms, 79 Hightown Road (1913) has a green glazed brick exterior with floor and dado tiling inside; in Holy Trinity Church, Trinity Road there is an encaustic tiled chancel pavement and tiled east wall. The Church of the Virgin Mary, **Meppershall**, has a large Powell's opus sectile and red glass tile reredos, installed in 1880; it includes extracts from *Exodus* (Fig 2). All Saints

Church, **Renhold** was restored in 1863, when the attractive Minton encaustic tiled chancel pavement was laid. At St Peter's Church, **Sharnbrook**, the Powell's opus sectile reredos of the Last Supper was installed in 1901; its bright, robed figures are set upon a background of gold mosaic, with red glass tile panels to the sides.

References

1. J. C. Edwards, *Bricks, Tiles & Terracotta - Catalogue of Patterns* (Ruabon, 1903), p6.
2. Jill Somerscales, 'Bedford Hospital Tile Pictures', *Glazed Expressions*, (1997) 34, pp4-6.
3. John Greene, *Brightening the Long Days* (Tiles and Architectural Ceramics Society, 1987), p2.
4. *The Builder*, vol 9, 9th August 1851, p502; *Glazed Expressions* 32, 1996, pp3-6.
5. *The Builder*, vol 21, 28th February 1863.
6. J. M. Bailey, 'Decorated 14th-century tiles at Northill Church, Bedfordshire', *Medieval Archaeology*, 19 (1975), pp209-213.
7. *Landmark Trust Handbook*, 19th ed (Landmark Trust, Shottesbrooke, 2001).
8. Elizabeth S. Eames, *Catalogue of Medieval Lead-Glazed Earthenware Tiles in the Department of Medieval and Later Antiquities, British Museum*, (British Museum Publications, London, 1980), vol 1 pp91-2, vol 2 design 122.
9. *The Builder*, vol 21, 9th May 1863.

Berkshire

Berkshire might be described as the home of polychromy, with the strength of anglo-catholicism in the county reflected in its brilliantly colourful churches by G. E. Street (Boyn Hill, Maidenhead), William Butterfield (Beech Hill) and Henry Woodyer (Clewer Convent), as well as (in secular terms) Reading's mix of local terracotta and coloured brickwork. An undoubted highlight is the eighteenth-century Coade stone screen at St Mary's Church, Langley Marish, Slough, while the delightful Royal Dairy at Frogmore (Windsor) is a building of international importance to ceramic history, although access is highly restricted. In addition, Reading's Civic Centre houses John Piper's ceramic frieze of the town's coat-of-arms. Suggested reading: Charles Handley-Read 'Prince Albert's Model Dairy', *Country Life*, vol 129, 29th June 1961, pp1524-6; John Elliott and John Pritchard (eds), *George Edmund Street: A Victorian architect in Berkshire* (University of Reading, 1998); John Elliott and John Pritchard (eds), *Henry Woodyer: Gentleman Architect* (University of Reading, 2002); TACS Tour Notes *Reading* (1992), *Windsor* (1991). The *Gazetteer* entry for Berkshire covers the administrative areas of Bracknell Forest Borough Council, Reading Borough Council, Slough Borough Council, West Berkshire Council, Windsor and Maidenhead Borough Council, and Wokingham District Council.

BEECH HILL

At the hamlet of Beech Hill, a few miles south of Reading, is **St Mary's Church** (1866-7), its bright interior violently colourful even by William Butterfield's standards (Fig 3). In the chancel, and especially the sanctuary, Butterfield carried polychromy to an extreme. The base of the east wall is faced with diagonal bands of Godwin tiles in black, red and buff on red, the latter with fleur-de-lys and bird motifs. Above this dado is a horizontal strip of bright red brickwork with black and white stone inserts, and piled still higher is the uppermost layer, comprising red, white and black headers laid chequerboard-style. More tiles, some forming a cross, decorate the tall white stone reredos, while the sanctuary pavement and tiling in the sedilia continue the theme; recently-embroidered kneelers, taking tile designs as their motifs, provide a modern echo.

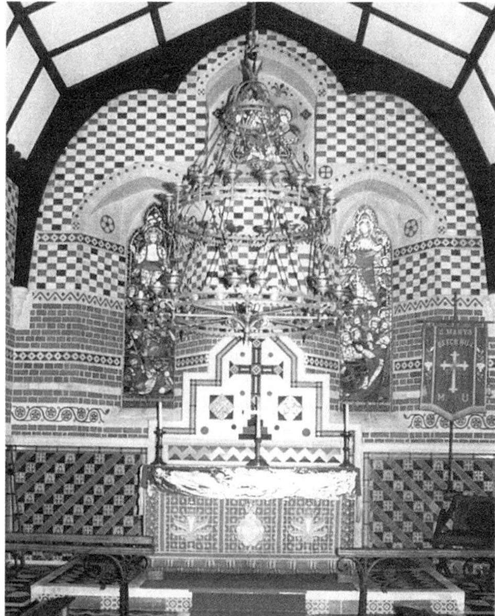

Fig 3.

BRACKNELL

Tower blocks in Bracknell's apparently tree-lined centre are portrayed on attractive 1960s industrial tiling in the High Street walkway leading to the shopping precinct; just south on Station Road is the **Railway Station**, where another modern panel - showing steam engine 488 - welcomes passengers. On a rather grander scale, and about a mile further south, is the **Church of St Michael and St Mary Magdalene**, Easthampstead. It was reconstructed in 1866-7, the architect being J. W. Hugall, who worked on several local churches. Aside from exceptional stained glass, the real delight here is a pair of colourful reredoses in tiles, mosaic, opus sectile, marble and mother-of-pearl made by Powell's of Whitefriars. The main east end reredos (1873), which shows the crucifixion, was designed by H. J. Burrow; its side panels, showing the evangelists, were designed by Henry Holiday and installed in 1877. The north aisle reredos (1905) portrays the *Walk to Emmaus* and was designed by John W. Brown.[1]

ETON

Construction of the College Hall at **Eton College** began in the mid fifteenth century, although it was given a classical makeover in 1720-1; the medieval look was restored by the architect Henry Woodyer in 1856-8. Visitors (guided tours only) will see a fine tile pavement whose layout was possibly designed by Woodyer himself.[2] It includes many standard Minton patterns as well as specials with armorial and other symbolic motifs.

In the centre of Eton at 110 HIGH STREET is the **Christopher Hotel**; its pleasing 1902 facade of lime and lemon faience includes good lettering.

MAIDENHEAD

In the centre of Maidenhead on MARLOW ROAD is the former Technical School (1895-6), now **Social Services Department**, designed by local architect E. J. Shrewsbury. There is much good red terracotta detailing on its porch and on the unusual, oversized Dutch gable-like pediment; the manufacturer was the Measham Terra Cotta Company.[3] West of the centre on ST MARK'S ROAD is the Shrewsbury-designed Maidenhead Union Workhouse, now part of **St Mark's Hospital**. It was built in 1896 and again shows ornate terracotta detailing, but in pink rather than the red of the Technical School.

Slightly north of Maidenhead's centre, amidst the Victorian villas of NORFOLK ROAD, is one of the town's pair of exotic churches, **St Luke**, built in 1866 and designed by the little-known architect George Row Clarke. Running above and across the whole of its chancel arch is a striking tile painting entitled *Jacob's Ladder* and featuring many colourful angels (Fig 4). The painting, which was obscured by dirt for many years and only revealed by cleaning in 1991, dates from 1885 and was produced by W. B. Simpson & Sons; the firm's name, written in dark script, is beneath the foot of the angel furthest to the right. The tiles were presented to the church by Thomas J. Nunns in memory of his mother.

Even more surprising is **All Saints Church**, BOYN HILL ROAD in Boyn Hill, a mile or so west of the town centre; it was described in Betjeman & Piper's *Murray's Berkshire Architectural Guide* as the 'Tractarian Cathedral of an Upper-class Suburb'.[4] Its architect, George Edmund Street, was appointed by Samuel Wilberforce, Bishop of Oxford, as architect to the Diocese of Oxford in 1850. Wilberforce, who was reasonably sympathetic to the ideas of the Oxford or Tractarian Movement, had also instigated a Church Building Society in order to provide accommodation in new or restored churches for the rapidly expanding population. In architectural terms, the Oxford Movement expected churches once again to symbolise Catholic principles, with the emphasis laid upon the altar and chancel rather than the pulpit. The crusade to restore continuity with the Catholic past was led by *The Ecclesiologist*, the journal founded in 1841 by the Cambridge Camden Society, which had considerable influence over church design.

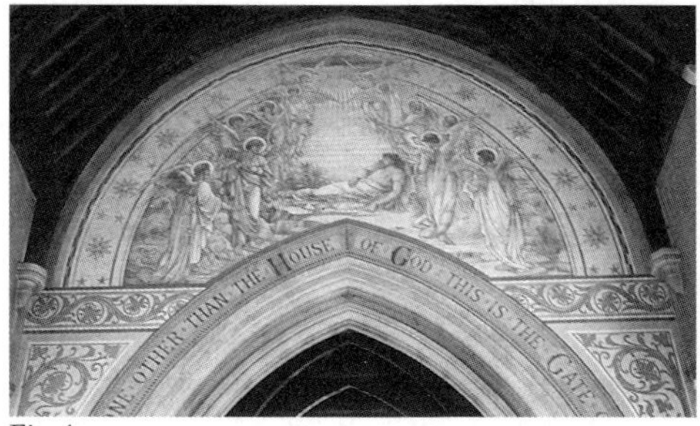

Fig 4.

Generous local benefactors donated land and funds for a church at Boyn Hill, and also enabled Street to produce a collegiate-style quadrangle of buildings comprising vicarage, stables, school, schoolmaster's house and clergy house. These harked back to the medieval idea of communal living, to which Street was attracted. The church, one of Street's first major commissions, was erected in 1854-7, while the final part of the associated complex was completed in 1859; he added the campanile tower in 1864-5. Street visited Italy just before beginning work on Boyn Hill, and his design, which reflected the colour and warmth of Venetian buildings, was a personal and very English version of what *The Ecclesiologist* described as 'Geometrical Middle Pointed'. The exterior of the church is banded in red brick, yellow Bath stone and black brick, while the remainder of the complex is made almost equally polychromatic in appearance with varying designs of diaper work in black brick. Inside the church, the unique chancel is a tour-de-force of the art of polychromy, its walls banded horizontally in green, yellow, red and buff tiles alternating with alabaster slabs. The tile pavement is by Minton, with floral and geometric designs in green, black, red and cream. And then there is colourful stencilling, stained glass, wrought ironwork, sculptures and ornate woodwork, all carried out to Street's designs.[5] Not surprisingly, *The Ecclesiologist* approved.

NEWBURY

Inside the **West Berkshire Museum**, situated right in the centre of Newbury at THE WHARF, are over 150 Dutch tiles, probably dating from the seventeenth and eighteenth centuries, which were installed in the museum as skirting in 1902-3 and remain in place; the building housing the museum is a seventeenth century house. To the north, hidden away in an obscure corner of **Victoria Park**, PARK WAY is a salmon-pink terracotta statue of Queen Victoria protected by four reclining lions; the memorial was modelled for Doulton by the sculptor and designer John Broad (1873-1919) around 1901. Broad was a prolific artist whose output included several monumental statues. This Queen Victoria statue was given to Newbury by Lord George Sanger and originally stood in the Market Place, but was removed in 1933 to allow the traffic to flow more freely. The statue (and lions) were re-erected at nearby Greenham Park, but the construction of a by-pass caused them all to be moved again, this time ending up at the council depot; two of the lions then escaped to Beale Park, a wildlife park in Lower Basildon (see Pangbourne). Queen Victoria and her two remaining lions were finally re-sited in Victoria Park in 1966 and, with the assistance of the Child-Beale Trust, the missing lions were returned to Newbury as part of the Queen's Jubilee celebrations in 2002. A happy ending indeed.

PANGBOURNE

A couple of miles north-west of Pangbourne is **Beale Park**, Lower Basildon, a wildlife and fun park beside the Thames which is run by the Child-Beale Trust; the park was created by Gilbert Beale (1868-1967), a benefactor renowned for his eccentricity and love of the countryside. In the park is a large sculpture collection, including the unglazed white Doultonware groups of *Commerce* and *Britannia*, sculpted by John Broad, which flanked the entrance of the Birkbeck Bank (1895-6), a thoroughgoing ceramic extravaganza which stood near the north end of London's Chancery Lane until its demolition in summer 1965.[6]

READING

The most memorable tiles in Reading are hidden away in the Council Chamber of the **Civic Centre** (1975), which is dominated by a large and dramatic tile frieze centred on a ceramic version of the town's coat-of-arms. This was designed by the artist John Piper (1903-92) and made by the artist-potter Geoffrey Eastop (b1921), then lecturer in ceramics at Reading College of Technology. In 1969 Eastop helped to establish a pottery at Piper's home in Fawley Bottom, about ten miles north of Reading, and the two collaborated on the production of ceramics until the early 1980s.[7] There are few other tiles in Reading, but much colourful local brick and terracotta, the latter largely produced by Collier's (1848-1929), the only firm to use Reading clays for making terracotta on a large scale. John Piper approved of the town's abundance of terracotta facades, saying that 'The washable, weather resisting surface that will hardly change with centuries of wear changes its look constantly with the different lights of different days and has plenty of delights to satisfy an unprejudiced eye'.

The most notable manifestation of Collier's products is the **Town Hall** (which also houses the Museum of Reading), just south-east of the station in BLAGRAVE STREET. The central towered section was designed by Alfred Waterhouse and built in 1872-5 of local red and grey brick, with some terracotta supplied by Gunton's of Norwich. The adjoining concert hall (1879-82, architect Thomas Lainson) uses deep red and blue bricks with terracotta dressings by J. C. Edwards, but the most striking part of the municipal ensemble is the museum and art gallery (1894, architect W. R. Howell) curving round the corner into Valpy Street, with several buff carved terracotta reliefs showing local historical scenes.[8] Another highlight is the orangey-red terracotta canyon of nearby QUEEN VICTORIA STREET, which has an extensive display of lofty facades dating from the early 1900s; in adjoining BROAD STREET, the terracotta front of **W. H. Smith's** was restored by Hathernware in 1989. Turning into WEST STREET, the **Palmer Memorial Building** and the **West Street Hall** display beautiful terracotta frontages, the latter by Collier's. There is a reset panel of medieval floor tiles (from the Penn tilery) in **Greyfriars Church**, which began life as a thirteenth-century Franciscan foundation. West of the centre in DOWNSHIRE SQUARE is **All Saints Church** (1865-74); its ornate interior was completed in 1891-6 by the addition of several substantial panels of Powell's opus sectile work.[9]

Tilehurst

St Michael's Church was almost completely rebuilt in 1854-5 by G. E. Street, who specified the decorative and colourful Minton tiles which form the chancel pavement; the nave tiling was relaid in 1975, using tiles similar in design to those of the original pavement.[10]

SLOUGH

In the town centre is **St Mary's Church** on CHURCH STREET, its chancel dating from 1876-8. The sanctuary walls are faced with bright blue and white floral-pattern glass tiles by Powell's; gold mosaic with red and unusual green glass tiles enhance the overall effect. The east wall tiling is topped by a row of opus sectile cherubic heads encased in angel wings on a background of more gold mosaic, making a rather odd reredos. The sanctuary's encaustic tiled pavement, which includes some mosaic work, is by Minton Hollins. Also in the centre is the **Robert Taylor Library**, HIGH STREET, where the stairs are hung with three tile panels designed in 1988 by the artist Geoffrey Carr, working with local schoolchildren. The scratched designs on unglazed, 40-tile orange panels show local buildings and activities, with motifs ranging from Concorde to a multistorey car park by way of the railway station and the Mars factory.

To the east in Langley Marish is **St Mary's Church**, ST MARY'S ROAD, where the presence of mid nineteenth-century east wall tiling by Minton & Co (the evangelists, albeit set in unusual circular borders) and fourteenth-century tiles in the sanctuary pavement is completely overshadowed by the glorious additions to the church made by Sir John Kedermister in the early seventeenth century. Sir John was granted the manor in 1626, but had already begun to build the Kedermister chapel in the south transept. This is now entered through an airy, vaulted Gothic Coade stone screen, added by the Harvey family (to whom the manor eventually passed) in 1792; it was probably designed by Henry Emlyn (c1729-1815), an architect and builder from Windsor.[11] On the south side of the chapel is the Kedermister pew, an entrancing family pew whose latticework openings ensured privacy. Its interior is painted to resemble marble, with several all-seeing eyes implying God's presence. More amazing still is the tiny library, just behind the pew, where the Kedermister book collection, generously donated to the parish, is kept; over 200 books and medieval manuscripts are stored behind the elaborately painted panelled doors of its book cupboards.

WINDSOR

The stunning fan-vaulted Coade stone screen in St George's Chapel, **Windsor Castle**, was designed by the architect Henry Emlyn in about 1788 as a replacement for the original stone screen, which was removed during alterations. This remarkable work features vaults springing from unbelievably thin columns rather than from the wall. As Alison Kelly put it, Mrs Coade's camouflage was perfect and few visitors to the Chapel guess they are looking at 'a vast piece of pottery'.[12] Adjacent to the Chapel are the collegiate buildings of the College of St George, founded by Edward III in 1348. Its main entrance, built in 1353-4, is the Porch of Honour or Aerary Porch, which took its name from the treasury (or errarium) housed on its upper floor. The Aerary itself is now used as an archive room (no public access) and has a complete but badly worn and much-repaired floor of two-colour decorated Penn tiles dating from 1355. The building accounts of Windsor Castle provide a wealth of detail on the purchase, transport and laying of these tiles.[13]

For a view of Windsor as it was, seek out the narrow passageway running west from THAMES STREET, for here is a blue and white tiled picture entitled *Prospect of Windsor Castle based upon the engraving by Wenceslaus Hollar AD1663*. This attractive panel, which is dated 1918 and measures about 6' by 12', is by the artist Leslie MacDonald Gill, known as Max, who was the oldest of Eric Gill's six brothers. MacDonald Gill specialised in decorative graphics, and was the designer of the *Wunderground* map for London Underground. Apart from the detailed drawing of town and castle, the panel also indicates the future position of 'Boots Cash Chemists'; it appears that the panel was commissioned to mark the opening of a branch of Boots in the adjacent building, which is dated 1917.

Clewer

Clewer Convent, HATCH LANE, was set up in 1849 by Mrs Tennant, a clergyman's widow, as a House of Mercy - a home for 'fallen' girls. It soon became clear to the local vicar that a larger organisation was necessary to undertake the task of caring for the girls, and a sisterhood was then founded. Its convent was designed by the architect Henry Woodyer, who began working on the complex of buildings in 1853 and continued, without ever charging a fee, until his death in

1896.[14] The original plan for a quadrangle of red brick buildings (including a chapel which still has a colourful geometric Minton pavement) was completed in 1858, then extra wings were added during the 1870s and a grand new chapel was erected in 1881. The chapel's interior features spectacular stained glass and ironwork, as well as polychromatic red and black brick, with monogrammed terracotta panels in the choir and a Minton pavement; the latter is mainly of plain tiles in red, yellow and black but includes a few patterned tiles in early Minton designs. There are also two ceramic plaques on the chapel's exterior, one commemorating Woodyer. This ornate 1881 chapel is now listed II*, although its future is uncertain, as Clewer Convent was undergoing a change of use in 2002.

Nearly a mile north-east of Clewer Convent is **St Stephen's Church**, VANSITTART ROAD, built in 1870-4 to cater for Clewer's rapidly expanding population. The architect was Henry Woodyer, who also designed most of the fittings, which were added when funds allowed. The east wall decoration (1881) includes two pairs of mosaic figures of saints, while the chancel pavement - probably of around the same date - is elaborate patterned Minton tiling.[15]

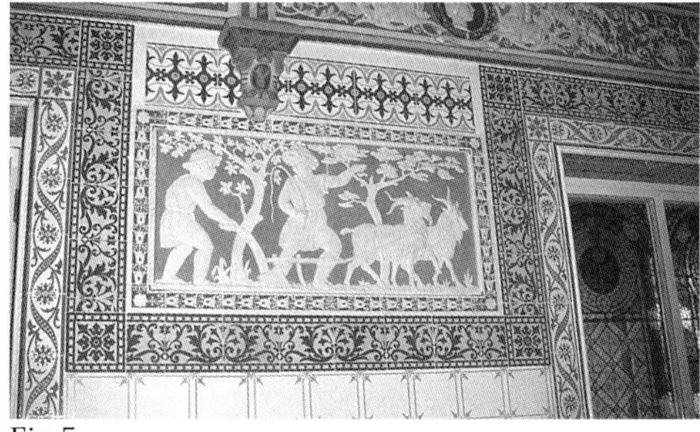

Fig 5.

Frogmore

Stretching south of Windsor Castle is the Home Park, where the **Royal Dairy** (no public access) stands about half a mile south-east of Frogmore House, at the Prince Consort's HOME FARM. The picturesque Dairy, which includes a two-storey house and offices as well as the tiled creamery, was built in 1858, though its internal decoration was not completed until 1861 (Fig 5).[16] The Dairy was built under the Prince's personal direction, with John Thomas (1813-62), a sculptor and occasional architect who was a protégé of Prince Albert's, acting as executive architect; the buildings were erected by the Board of Works. Behind the anticlimactic facade, all is light and bright, as the pristine Minton tiles emanate cleanliness and coolness. The generous use of colour is surprising, as earlier tiled dairies were generally plain-tiled, but here Minton's used new majolica glazes to enrich the overall effect.

The creamery's painted timber roof shelters a series of long marble tables which carry the separating basins. A ceramic frieze of sea horses with relief portraits of the Royal children runs above the windows, which are framed by block printed border tiles in five different patterns, while relief panels in orange and white portray cherubic, idyllic versions of rural activities. Pierced tiles assist with ventilation and the decorative non-slip floor tiling has white glaze recessed into the buff body of the tiles.[17] Most striking of all are the two exotic majolica fountains, with deep, rich green glazes, and motifs of herons supporting a shell, surmounted by figures of a mermaid and merman. Both *The Builder* and the *Illustrated London News* reported on the completion of the Royal Dairy in 1861, and versions of its design were emulated elsewhere; it remains an early example of a polychromatic ceramic secular interior, with an atmosphere completely different from the many churches which incorporated tiled decoration from the 1840s.

WINKFIELD

The unusual wooden nave roof (1592) of **St Mary's Church** is supported by a central row of piers, dividing the nave into two, but the chancel, rebuilt in 1858 to a design by G. E. Street, is tripartite.[18] This apparent east-west dislocation may have been ameliorated by the architect Henry Woodyer's alterations of 1888, which included lowering the floor of the choir, and the lavish chancel decoration which was added shortly afterwards (Fig 6).

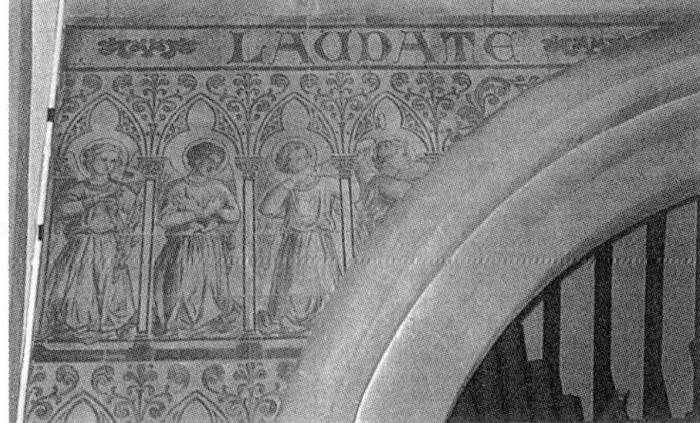

Fig 6.

Above a geometric pavement, all three walls of the chancel were decorated from dado level upward with painted tiling depicting gothicised biblical figures, some angelic, in colour reddish-brown on an off-white ground. This unexpected scheme, signed E. I. and bearing the dates 1889, 1890 and August 1891, was carried out at the behest of the vicar's wife, Mrs Daubeny, who bought tiles and pigment from Powell's of Whitefriar's; after decoration, the tiles were then fired by Powell's.[19] *Pevsner* suggests the tiles were designed by Henry Woodyer and painted by Mrs Daubeny, although it seems just as likely that Mrs Daubeny could have been the designer.[20]

WRAYSBURY

An extremely high-relief terracotta panel designed by George Tinworth for Doulton & Co can be found on the outside wall of the tower (1880) of the polychromatic brick **Baptist Church** (1862) in the HIGH STREET. This unusually-sited panel depicts *The City of Refuge* and is signed with Tinworth's 'GT' monogram.[21]

Berkshire Roundup

The sanctuary pavement at St Bartholomew's Church (1863), Church Lane, **Arborfield** is by Minton; the church was designed by the architect and antiquary James (later Sir James) Allanson Picton of Liverpool (1805-89). The encaustic tile pavement in the chancel of St Peter's Church (rebuilt 1869-72), **Brimpton** was manufactured by Maw & Co and laid by Simpson's.[22] Out of sight in the disused late Victorian chapel at **Datchet** Cemetery on Ditton Road (near the Queen Mother Reservoir) is a blue, white and yellow-tiled memorial panel, probably Iberian and dating from 1924, as well as several terracotta panels. At St James the Greater (1851-3, architect G. E. Street), **Eastbury**, there is a decorative encaustic tile pavement in the chancel and sanctuary. There are good sixteenth century floor tiles in the chancel of the now-redundant St Thomas Church, **East Shefford**. St Mary's Church (1864-6, Street), **Fawley**, looks northward over the downs; the encaustic tile pavement in the chancel is by Godwin's. St Mary's Church, **Purley** (rebuilt 1869-70, design by G. E. Street) has an elaborate chancel pavement of Godwin tiles with motifs based on patterns used at the medieval Penn tilery.[23] St Nicholas Church, **Remenham** has mid fourteenth-century Penn tiles around the pulpit and an encaustic tiled chancel pavement, probably from one of the Minton works, added during restoration in 1870. There are unusual fourteenth century tiles at the church of St Denys, **Stanford Dingley**; the tiles are thicker than normal, with inlaid designs on two sides. St Paul's Church, Reading Road, **Wokingham** (1862-4, architect Henry Woodyer) has rich Minton tiling in the chancel.

References

1. Dennis W. Hadley, *James Powell & Sons: A listing of opus sectile, 1847-1973*, (2001).
2. Nikolaus Pevsner and Elizabeth Williamson, *Buckinghamshire* 2nd ed. Buildings of England (Penguin, London, 1994), p311.
3. Details of the building and the terracotta manufacturer were given in contemporary editions of the *Maidenhead Advertiser*.
4. Bridgeen Fox, *The Church of All Saints, Boyne Hill, Maidenhead*, in *George Edmund Street: A Victorian architect in Berkshire*, John Elliott and John Pritchard, Editors, (Centre for Continuing Education, University of Reading, Reading, 1998) pp47-60.
5. John Elliott and John Pritchard, eds. *George Edmund Street: a Victorian architect in Berkshire* (Centre for Continuing Education, University of Reading, Reading, 1998), pp100-2. G. E. Street's first wife is buried in the churchyard to the north of the church; the gravestone was designed by Street.
6. Nicholas Taylor, 'Ceramic Extravagance', *Architectural Review*, 138 (1965) November, pp338-41.
7. Margot Coatts and Geoffrey Eastop, *Geoffrey Eastop: a potter in practice* (Ecchinswell Studio, 1999).
8. *J. C. Edwards: Catalogue of Patterns*, 1890.
9. Hadley, *Powell's opus sectile* (2001).
10. Elliott and Pritchard (eds), *George Edmund Street* (University of Reading, 1998), p115-6.
11. Howard Colvin, *A Biographical Dictionary of British Architects, 1600-1840* 3rd ed (Yale University Press, New Haven and London, 1995), pp345-6.
12. Alison Kelly, *Mrs Coade's Stone* (Self Publishing Association, Upton-upon-Severn, 1990), pp17, 216-7, 335.
13. Laurence Keen, *Windsor Castle and the Penn tile industry*, in *Windsor: Medieval Archaeology, Art and Architecture of the Thames Valley*, Laurence Keen and Eileen Scarff, Editors, (British Archaeological Association, Leeds, 2002) pp219-37.
14. John Pritchard, 'Clewer Convent under threat', *Ecclesiology Today*, (2000) 22, pp39-40.
15. John Elliott and John Pritchard, eds. *Henry Woodyer: Gentleman Architect* (Department of Continuing Education, University of Reading, Reading, 2002), p145-6.

16. Charles Handley-Read, 'Prince Albert's Model Dairy', *Country Life*, 129 (1961) 29th June, pp1524-6.
17. Tony Herbert and Kathryn Huggins, *The Decorative Tile in Architecture and Interiors* (Phaidon Press, London, 1995), pp94-6; see also 'Prince Albert's Dairy', *Architectural Review*, vol 146, December 1969, pp414-6.
18. Elliott and Pritchard (eds), *George Edmund Street* (University of Reading, 1998), p128-9.
19. Hadley, *Powell's opus sectile* (2001).
20. Pevsner, *Berkshire* (1966), p306.
21. Desmond Eyles and Louise Irvine, *The Doulton Lambeth Wares* (Richard Dennis, Shepton Beauchamp, 2002), p49.
22. *The Builder*, 27th Nov 1869, vol 27, p953.
23. Elliott and Pritchard (eds), *George Edmund Street* (University of Reading, 1998), p108.

Buckinghamshire

The tilery which functioned during the 1330s to the 1380s at Tylers Green, Penn, near High Wycombe, was the best known and most successful of all the medieval commercial tileries, while there was also a tilery in the north of the county at Little Brickhill, on Watling Street, which worked in the late fifteenth and early sixteenth centuries. Ironically, much more evidence remains in situ of the work of these medieval tileries, especially Penn, than of the Medmenham Pottery, established at Marlow Common by the soap manufacturer Robert Hudson around 1897. Victorian church restoration provided the opportunity for the installation of numerous tiles pavements, and the most frequently used manufacturer turned out to be Godwin's, although examples of Maw and Minton pavements also survive. There is, however, little significant use of terracotta, in secular or ecclesiastical contexts. The county's ceramic highlights include a Little Brickhill medieval pavement at Great Linford church (Milton Keynes); good Victorian church tiles at Edlesborough, Hughenden and Westcott; modern ceramic church furnishings at Coffee Hall (Milton Keynes); and a 1979 tile mural at Stantonbury (Milton Keynes). Suggested reading: Elizabeth Eames, *English Tilers* (British Museum Press, London, 1992); Miles Green, *Medieval Penn Floor Tiles* (Penn, 2003); Robert Prescott Walker, 'Conrad Dressler and the Medmenham Pottery', *Journal of the Decorative Arts Society*, 18, 1994, pp50-60. The *Gazetteer* entry for Buckinghamshire covers the administrative areas of Buckinghamshire County Council and Milton Keynes Council.

CALVERTON

All Saints Church stands at Lower Weald, just outside Milton Keynes, although the remainder of Calverton lies within the city. The church was initially rebuilt in 1817-18, but much more reconstruction work was carried out later, probably in the 1850s, when much emphasis was laid on the interior, which is full of carved naturalistic decoration. A Minton tile pavement was laid in the chancel, whose walls have *sgraffito* patterns, while the mosaic reredos was probably added during further alterations made by E. Swinfen Harris in 1871-2. Harris, from Stony Stratford (now Milton Keynes), was a good and prolific architect who worked on numerous houses, churches and schools in the north of the county.

CHEDDINGTON

The little church of **St Giles** was restored by G. E. Street in 1855-6; the Minton tiles probably date from this period, while the east wall decoration (1870) is by Powell's of Whitefriars.[1] The opus sectile reredos, portraying the Last Supper, was exhibited at the South Kensington Museum before installation at St Giles; it was the first large figurative opus sectile panel made by Powell's.[2] The reredos is flanked by panels of patterned glass tiles in very subdued tones, characteristic of Powell's early experiments in this field.

DRAYTON BEAUCHAMP

St Mary's Church, delightfully sited outside the village, was restored in 1866-7 by the appropriately-named pair of London architects Slater & Carpenter. The abundant Minton tiles in the chancel were added during the restoration, their designs being copied from those of medieval tiles found during construction work.[3] Part of the tile pavement is set in an uncommon chevron pattern, while some tile designs, in particular the combination of a fleur-de-lys with a pair of stylised birds, are most unusual; these Minton designs have not not been recorded elsewhere.

DROPMORE

St Anne's Church, Boveney Wood Lane, was built in 1865-6 and although small is Butterfield through and through, from its flint and brick banded exterior to the frieze of glazed red and black bricks inside. William Butterfield also designed the timber screen separating chancel from nave, and much of the other furnishings. The polychrome interior scheme includes a small number of Minton tiles in the reredos; they have a buff pattern on red ground, the design being made to appear more emphatic by the use of a majolica glaze over the inlay. Minton tiles with glaze over the inlay are not unusual in themselves, but the Dropmore tiles appear to be very late examples of this technique.

EDLESBOROUGH

The tower of **St Mary's Church** stands proud on its hill above the A4146, aloof from the straggling village of Edlesborough away to the north. Clamber up the hill to find a rewarding interior with a sprinkling of fourteenth-century tiles, although the Victorian work dominates, especially in the chancel, restored in 1875. The Godwin encaustic chancel pavement incorporates single tiles bearing a decorative 'B' for Lord Brownlow, but more unusual is the dado tiling, with pink and red tiles in a zigzag pattern topped by biblical quotations. Best of all is the reredos of 1895 by W. B. Simpson & Sons, comprising seven sections of mosaic and painted tiles within a stone surround. The large central panel shows a figure of Christ, while to either side are three panels with strong imagery of the Four Evangelists, ears of wheat and a bunch of grapes, the latter pair a reference to the bread and wine of the Eucharist. The church is in the care of the Churches Conservation Trust.

GREAT MISSENDEN

The church of **St Peter and St Paul** is one of those interesting cases where the Victorian tiles in the choir - made by Godwin's and possibly introduced during the 1899-1901 restoration by John Oldrid Scott, or perhaps earlier - mimic some designs (notably a shield bearing three crescents) of the remaining medieval tiles, located north and south of the altar; these originated at the nearby Penn tilery via Missenden Abbey.

HORSENDEN

St Michael's Church is an odd structure which combines the chancel of the ancient church, restored in 1855, with a mini-chancel, all of six feet long, built on to its east end in 1869. The architect of this addition, the polychromatic brick enthusiast William White, also decorated the reredos and east wall with colourful Godwin tiles, complementing the many medieval tiles which survived the destruction of the original nave. The reredos includes two portrayals of a six-winged lion.

HUGHENDEN

St Michael's Church lies halfway up the broad slope leading to Disraeli's home, Hughenden Manor; his grave is in the churchyard. The church is medieval in origin but was restored and partly rebuilt by Sir Arthur Blomfield in 1874-5, when the chancel pavement of Godwin tiles was probably installed, a brilliantly colourful contrast to the pervading gloom of the remainder of the church. At **Hughenden Manor** (NT) itself, there is a Maw geometric encaustic pavement in the loggia (1874) and odd grey-green hexagonal wall tiling - possibly by Minton Hollins - in the stables.

LITTLE KIMBLE

The nave walls of little **All Saints Church** are almost completely covered by early fourteenth century wall paintings, showing a large collection of saints as well as the devil at the mouth of hell. Continuing the pictorial theme in the chancel are several thirteenth century floor tiles made in the kilns of Chertsey Abbey, Surrey; here the images - on four-tile roundels - include a pair of fighting knights and a king with his dog.

MARLOW COMMON

The pretty woodland of Marlow Common became something of an artists' colony during the late nineteenth century. Conrad Dressler, sculptor and art potter, moved into the White Cottage (now **Monks Corner**) around 1897, to work as director of the Marlow Common-based Medmenham Pottery, founded and funded by the soap manufacturer Robert Hudson of nearby Medmenham. Dressler used the cottage, which is near the west end of the hamlet, to display trial runs of items commissioned from the pottery. On its exterior is the 25' polychrome ceramic frieze *Industry* (showing women working), later to be seen on Sunlight Chambers in Dublin, as well as portrait roundels and other panels, while a few of Dressler's tiles remain inside. The service wing (now **Jerome Cottage**) displays another fine Medmenham piece, a plain frieze of laundrywomen.

MEDMENHAM

During 1895-6, the wealthy soap magnate Robert Hudson bought Medmenham Abbey, the remains of a Thames-side Cistercian foundation once used by Sir Francis Dashwood for meetings of his

Medmenham Club (popularly known as the Hell-Fire Club). Hudson brought in the architect W. H. Romaine-Walker (later mainly a designer of town houses) to restore and enlarge the abbey in 1898. Romaine-Walker went on to create a series of estate buildings, and in 1899-1901 built Danesfield House, a new and vast home for his client. Hudson was an admirer of the Arts & Crafts theories of William Morris, and around 1897, in true *News from Nowhere* style, put up pottery workshops and kilns by the clay pits of Marlow Common (two miles north-east of Medmenham) in order to foster rural crafts and encourage local talent. This concern became known as the Medmenham Pottery, and the sculptor Conrad Dressler, who had previously been employed at the Della Robbia Pottery in Birkenhead, was brought in as its director.[4] The individuality and handmade look of Medmenham tiles soon attracted the attention of architects, and they were used in prestigious locations such as the Law Society's Hall in London and Sunlight Chambers in Dublin. Presumably Hudson must have been quietly satisfied when the Medmenham Pottery obtained the latter commission, as the building was the Irish headquarters of his rivals, Lever Brothers.

Despite these successes, Dressler became disillusioned with the entire project and by 1905 production at Medmenham had ceased, although a few architectural remnants still survive in the village (and at Marlow Common) to remind the observer of the unusual and high-quality output of this little pottery. As originally built, all the many bathrooms of **Danesfield House** were decorated with Dressler's early handmade tiles, exotic and richly colourful cuenca-style designs including an especially striking fish, all scales and attitude; however, conversion of the house to an hotel, along with a series of fires, has resulted in the loss of all but a single tiled bathroom. A happier fate befell **Westfield Cottages**, a little west of the village off the main Marlow-Henley road; these six pairs of picturesque estate cottages were built around 1900 and probably designed by Romaine-Walker (Fig 7). Over each front doorway is a semicircular tympanum of low relief Medmenham ware, showing the labours of the months, from gathering firewood (January) through the corn harvest (June) to ploughing (November) and digging (December).

MILTON KEYNES

The new city of Milton Keynes was designated in 1967, taking in an area stretching from Bletchley in the south to Stony Stratford and Wolverton in the north. The uninspiringly-named centre is known as Central Milton Keynes, and the city was laid out around it on a rough grid square system incorporating the existing towns and villages.

Coffee Hall

The residential grid square Coffee Hall, south of the centre, was developed at speed during the 1970s and early 1980s. **Our Lady of Lourdes R.C. Church** was built in 1974-6; as with many of the city's early buildings, it was designed by Milton Keynes Development Corporation's own architects, in this case Derek Walker (Chief Architect and Planning Officer) and Peter Barker. The circular exterior of the church hides a square interior, in which the furnishings - altar, font, pulpit and Stations of the Cross - are of sculpted glazed stoneware by Norman and Anna Adams. The font, with its pastel imagery of flowers and birds, is relatively restrained but the altar frontal is altogether more hectic, with pale blue angels descending from above through a jagged network of white crosses.

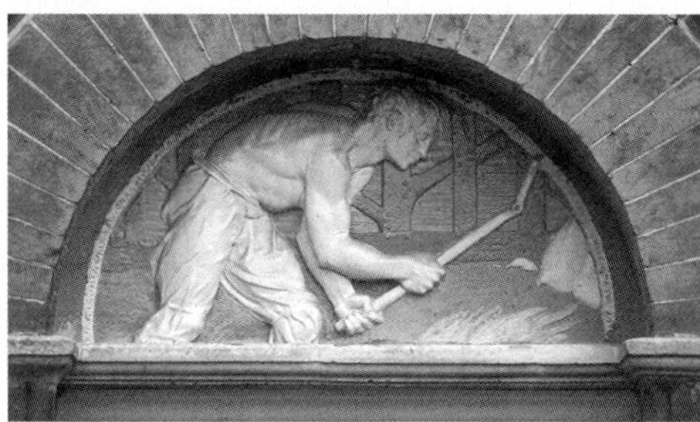

Fig 7.

Galley Hill

Galley Hill was developed from 1971, and was the first major housing scheme in Milton Keynes. Covering the gable end of one of the buildings at **Watling Way County Middle School** is the tile mural *Climbing Frame* which was designed and made by the painter John Watson and installed in 1978. Its flowing brushwork depicts children, many holding animal masks, weaving their way around a prominent white frame; it includes the names of individual children.

Great Linford

St Andrew's Church stands on the northern fringe of Great Linford and thus of Milton Keynes itself, not far from the Grand Union Canal. It is a medieval church, and at the east end of the nave is a pavement of Little Brickhill tiles, made at the tilery (its site now just south-east of the city limits) which was in production during the late fifteenth and early sixteenth centuries. Its products were two-colour tiles of relatively primitive design, but the addition of small amounts of copper or brass to the glaze made for bright and attractive pavements.[5] A memorial brass records that the St Andrews pavement, which is normally kept covered, was bequeathed to the church by Roger Hunt (d1473).

Stantonbury

The Stantonbury grid square was developed from 1972; over a third of it is devoted to the **Stantonbury Campus** which includes a shopping centre where the *Bicycle Wall* tile mural was installed in 1979. The artist John Watson created the mural with the help of children from one of the local comprehensive schools; many pupils (as well as bicycles) are depicted on the mural, which is intended to portray 'childhood happiness and enthusiasm'. The 60′ by 24′ mural comprises around 1,200 tiles, which were made and fired in the school's art department, decorated and glazed in the artist's studio, then refired at the school before being fixed directly to the brick wall.[6]

Wolverton

Wolverton was a railway town, involved first in building locomotives (from 1845) and then carriages (from around 1865); the works dominated the town until the early 1960s. The church of **St George Martyr**, CHURCH STREET, was built in 1843-4 to cater for the railway workforce; transepts were added in 1895-6 and the chancel was extended in 1903. The opus sectile reredos, showing four angels on a gold ground, was bought from Powell's of Whitefriars in 1887, so presumably was resited when the chancel was altered.

PENN

Penn, and the adjacent settlement of Tylers Green, formed a major centre of tile production during the fourteenth century. As part of the millennium restoration of **Holy Trinity Church**, Penn tiles which had been found in the churchyard and the neighbouring area were built into the altar platform of the Lady Chapel. Tiles with twenty-five different designs were used to make a mosaic in combination with an area of reproduction Penn tiles made by Diana Hall.[7]

SHALSTONE

St Edward's Church was rebuilt in 1861-2 by George Gilbert Scott for Mrs Fitz-Gerald of Shalstone House. He spared the chancel much improvement, although its tile pavement and the tile and mosaic reredos of the Evangelists both probably date from the time of the reconstruction.

WESTCOTT

St Mary's Church was built by G. E. Street in 1866-7. Its stark interior is given some warmth by the use of pale pink brick throughout, while there is a surprise in the chancel in the form of an east wall decorated by pretty tiling bearing the Lord's Prayer and Creed on a cream ground.

Buckinghamshire Roundup

At the church of St James, **Bierton**, are many fourteenth and fifteenth century floor tiles. Urns and balustrades on the garden front of **Cliveden** were restored in 1985-8 using terracotta by Ibstock Hathernware.[8] The church of St James, **Great Horwood**, has an opus sectile reredos of the Crucifixion designed by Bladen for Powell's and installed in 1886; there is also a Godwin encaustic tile pavement. The Powell's opus sectile reredos at St Mary's Church, **Hardwick** dates from 1901; its design, by H. J. Strutt, includes six angels with shields. The polygonal chancel added to St John Evangelist, **Lacey Green**, in 1871 by the architect and tile designer J. P. Seddon has brightly coloured floor tiling in red and yellow - complementing the polychromatic brickwork - and green and blue. William Butterfield installed a Minton tile pavement in the chancel of St Michael's Church, **Lavendon**, during restoration in 1858-9. The Powell's opus sectile reredos of the Nativity was installed at **Leckhampstead** church - the Assumption of the Virgin - in 1899; it cost £145. In the sanctuary of St Nicholas Church, **Lillingstone Dayrell**, are several groups of four medieval tiles with relief designs. St Mary's Church, **Mursley** was restored in 1865-7 when the colourful Godwin tile pavement was added. There are colourful Minton tiles in the sanctuary of Holy Trinity Church (1849), **Penn Street**. The chancel of St Mary's Church, Church End, **Pitstone** (now in the care of the Churches Conservation Trust) is floored largely with fourteenth and fifteenth century tiles. St Mary's Church, Church Lane, **Princes Risborough** (restored 1867-8) has a sanctuary pavement by Maw & Co, probably dating from the 1880s; rather more unusual is the mosaic floor beneath the altar, probably also by Maw's. The colourful tiles in the side panels of the reredos (1871) at St Mary's Church, Church Lane, **Wendover** are by Frederick Garrard, while the sanctuary encaustic pavement is by Godwin's. St Laurence's Church, **Winslow**, was restored by John Oldrid Scott in 1883-4, when the richly patterned Godwin chancel pavement was laid.[9]

References

1. Dennis W. Hadley, *James Powell & Sons: A listing of opus sectile, 1847-1973*, (2001).
2. Philip Brown and Dorothy Brown, 'Glass tiles', *Glazed Expressions*, (1994) 28, pp2-3; D. W. Hadley, 'From Rees mosaic to opus sectile: the development of opaque stained glass', *Glass Technology*, (2004) 45, October, pp192-6.
3. *The Builder*, vol 25, 2nd March 1867.
4. Robert Prescott Walker, 'Conrad Dressler and the Medmenham Pottery', *Journal of the Decorative Arts Society*, (1994) 18, pp50-60.
5. Elizabeth Eames, *English Tilers* (British Museum Press, London, 1992), p58.
6. *Ceramic Industries Journal*, vol 88, February 1979, p10.
7. Miles Green, *Medieval Penn Floor Tiles* (Miles Green, Penn, 2003).
8. Michael Stratton, *The Terracotta Revival* (Victor Gollancz, London, 1993), p222.
9. *The Builder*, vol 48, 10th January 1885, p85.

Cambridgeshire

Although there are interesting church tiles, from medieval examples to a Victorian maze, throughout Cambridgeshire, most of the county's ceramic highlights are in Cambridge. The splendid Morris & Co overmantel at Queens' College must rank first among the city's sites, but the octagonal banking hall at Lloyds Bank comes a close second. The most unusual sites in Cambridgeshire, however, are Waterbeach Church with its Ten Commandments tile panel, and the delightful Adam and Eve medieval tiled pavement at Ely, a location of national importance. In Peterborough, the Law Courts (1978) and the Mosque (2002-3) both provide modern brickwork of significant interest. Suggested reading: TACS Tour Notes *Cambridge* (1996); Jane Cochrane, 'Medieval Tiled Floor Patterns', *TACS Journal* 5, 1994, pp11-19. The *Gazetteer* entry for Cambridgeshire covers the administrative areas of Cambridgeshire County Council and Peterborough City Council.

BOTTISHAM

Just east of Cambridge, right on the edge of the Fens, stands the fine medieval church of **Holy Trinity**. Several changes were made to its chancel in the 1860s and 1870s. The step up to the altar was initially laid with Maw & Co encaustic tiles (designed by J. P. Seddon) around 1860, but its central panel was replaced in 1877 with Pugin-designed Minton tiles including a Lamb of God roundel, while the altar dais was also paved with Minton tiles; the border tiles have an unusual red and green design. The walls to either side of the altar were faced with polychrome Spanish majolica tiles at some point during this period, perhaps when the east window was replaced in 1875. The main four-tile repeating motif copies the early Dutch *Pompadour* pattern, and there is a *bead and bud* border in blue and white.

BOURN

Beneath the west tower of the church of **St Helen and St Mary** is a rectangular maze in the form of a pavement of red and black tiles, measuring 15′ by 12′ and constructed in 1875; its design was based on the Hampton Court hedge maze of 1690, a plan much repeated elsewhere. Since ancient times, the maze or labyrinth had been seen as a symbol of pilgrimage to the Holy Land. George Gilbert Scott included a black and white stone maze pavement in his 1870 restoration of Ely Cathedral; its path length is the same as the height of the west tower, beneath which it situated. It would appear likely that the Ely maze was the inspiration behind the Bourn maze, installed when the entire church floor was being relaid.[1]

CAMBRIDGE

In the very centre of Cambridge is the towered and extravagantly striped form of **Lloyds TSB Bank** on SIDNEY STREET, built as Fosters' Bank in 1891-4 and designed by Alfred Waterhouse (Fig 8). The interior is completely unexpected: a domed octagonal banking hall whose walls are totally clad in cream, green and buff Burmantofts faience in a variety of relief patterns.[2] This wonderful arcaded space is entered through faience-clad arches leading from the street, and although slightly cluttered with modern banking equipment, retains its Victorian grandeur. Restoration of the faience was carried out during the early 1990s by Shaws of Darwen, with assistance from specialist tilemaker John Burgess for the smaller dust-pressed tiles. Shaws matched the colour of the original raw lead glaze (now not permitted under Health & Safety regulations) by using a low solubility lead glaze with specially prepared metal-based colour pigments.

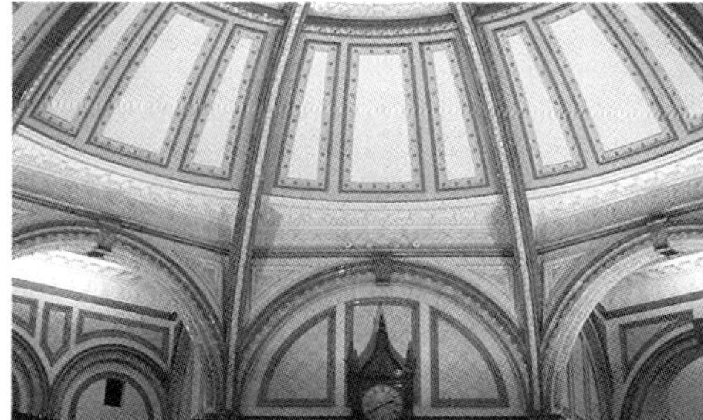

Fig 8.

Just north on JESUS LANE is **All Saints Church**, now in the care of the Churches Conservation Trust. The church was designed by George Frederick Bodley and built during 1860-4, the landmark spire being added in 1869-71. The lofty interior, a Tractarian gem, is remarkable for the patterned, painted decoration which covers the walls throughout the church. This was carried out by F. R. Leach, a local artist, under the direction first of William Morris, later C. E. Kempe, and finally Bodley himself, who directed the bulk of the wall decoration in 1878-9; its restoration was completed in 2003. The Godwin encaustic tiles in the chancel, however, play only a minor role in this fine decorative scheme. Across the road is **Jesus College**, where the chapel restoration of 1846-9 by A. W. N. Pugin included the installation of a Minton chancel pavement.

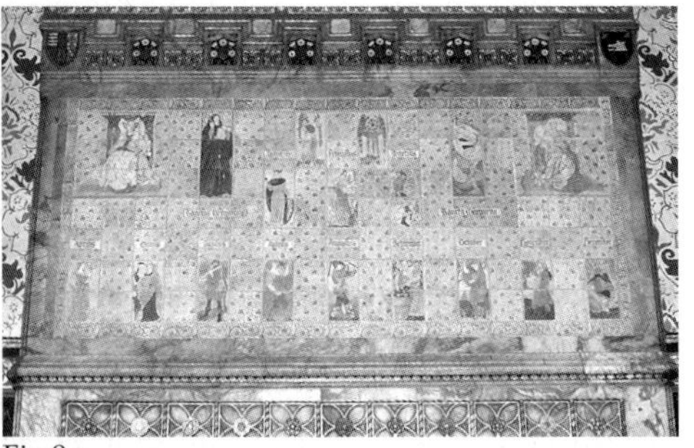

Fig 9.

Return to the centre via TRINITY STREET, where the former **St Michael's Church** (now a café) retains its late Victorian encaustic tiled pavement, and continue south to **Queens' College**, QUEENS' LANE, whose Old Hall - in the range opposite the gatehouse - was restored over a period of about thirty years from the 1840s. The architect G. F. Bodley supervised work from 1861, opening up the original fireplace and adding an alabaster panel above it; a new floor was also laid, using tiles by Godwin. In 1862-3 Bodley brought in the firm Morris, Marshall, Faulkner & Co to provide tiles for the overmantel, in an ambitious scheme which included eighteen separate panels of between two and nine tiles, set in a surround of the *Swan* pattern within a border of oblong tiles (Fig 9).[3] The panels, which used overglaze polychrome decoration on 6" tin-glazed tiles, show the twelve *Labours of the Months*, the *Angels of Night and Day*, the College's two patron saints (St Margaret and St Bernard), and the founding queens of the college, Margaret of Anjou (Henry VI) and Elizabeth Woodville (Edward IV). All but the pair of queen panels were installed during 1862-3 and variously designed by William Morris, Edward Burne-Jones, Dante Gabriel Rossetti and Ford Madox Brown; an important source for the designs were notes taken by William Morris from fifteenth century Books of Hours.[4] During this period, Godwin's encaustic tiles were introduced to flank the fireplace itself, and in 1864 the shields on the alabaster frieze below the tile panels were painted by Philip Webb to his own designs; the nine-tile queen panels were designed by Ford Madox Brown and added in 1873. This ornate overmantel forms just a small part of the lavish decorative scheme in this surprisingly small and intimate space. In 2003 the 1862-3 tiled floor was removed and replaced with a reproduction made by Craven Dunnill of Jackfield.

Just south of Queens' on TRUMPINGTON STREET is **Peterhouse**, where the thirteeth century Hall was restored, almost rebuilt, in 1868-70 by George Gilbert Scott junior, who also restored the adjoining fifteenth century Combination Room. The William Morris tiles in the Hall fireplace date from 1870, while in the Combination room are two fireplaces with tiles said to have been painted by Lucy Faulkner, sister of Charles Faulkner.[5] The larger fireplace has allegorical figures of the seasons designed by Burne-Jones and incorporating verses by William Morris. The earliest building at **Girton College** on the HUNTINGDON ROAD was erected in 1873 by Alfred Waterhouse, who chose the Norfolk firm Gunton's to supply red terracotta for his neo-Tudor design; the clock near the original front door has a mosaic face by Powell's of Whitefriars.[6] Finally, out west to **Robinson College**, GRANGE ROAD, a brick tour-de-force built in 1977-80, where the superb chapel has tiling (1979) by the artist-potter Geoffrey Eastop. His unusual deep khaki-coloured ceramic slabs form part of the wall and floor of the ante-chapel, and are complemented by stained glass designed by John Piper; Piper, with whom Eastop collaborated on ceramic works from 1969 until the early 1980s, also designed the ceramic of the Deposition in the main chapel.[7]

ELY

Difficult as it is to divert one's attention from the preposterous octagon which dominates **Ely Cathedral**, there are tiles worth seeking out, firstly in the choir, where the pavement is a mix of marble and Minton's tile tesserae, installed in 1851 during restoration by George Gilbert Scott.[8] Bishop West's Chantry, a small chapel at the east end of the cathedral, has an encaustic tile pavement dating from 1868.[9] It includes depictions of a cockerel, part of the rebus (in its entirety a cockerel above a globe) of one of those who endowed the chapel (Fig 10). Most of the yellow enamel which originally covered the buff inlay of these Minton tiles has worn away.[10]

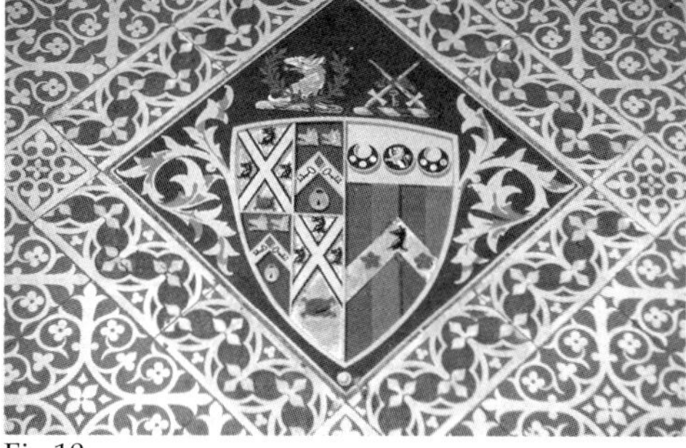

Fig 10.

There are also relaid fourteenth-century line-impressed tiles (normally covered) in the south transept, whose door leads out into the cloister and thence **Prior Crauden's Chapel**; its key may be obtained from the Cathedral. The chapel, built by Prior John de Craudene for his private prayers and directly connected to his study (now demolished), was probably completed around 1324; it may even have been designed before the octagon. Entry into this perfect little medieval world is via a small doorway and stairs in a tiny turret, which deposit the visitor into a wonderfully elegant, light space, originally full of colour from frescoes and gilding, painted glass and glazed tiles. Little of the frescos and glass remain, but the tile pavement is one of the most important and complex *in situ* survivals in the country.[11] Initially the loss of glaze makes it difficult to read the opus sectile shapes by the altar, but soon the main image emerges: Adam and a rather apprehensive Eve grappling with the serpent (which has a female head) and the forbidden fruit of the Tree of Knowledge (Fig 11). The picture was glazed in yellow, green and brown, while the background was black; although all is now almost reduced to monochrome, the dulled colours do not diminish its impact. Either side of Adam and Eve are tiles depicting lions, while the nave is paved with plain mosaic tiles, some with line-impressed decoration, in a pattern based on interlocking circles arranged in three long strips defined by borders.[12]

The chapel has had a difficult history, at one time being used as a laundry, and was in a ruinous condition by 1846. The tiles have suffered, although rather less than its other decorative features, but the nave pavement is very worn and sixteen tiles were stolen from around the altar in the late 1980s. Manufacture of replacements was undertaken in 1990 by Diana Hall, who used a mixture of clays to obtain the colours and textures required to match the patination (rather than the original appearance) of the remaining tiles.[13]

PETERBOROUGH

The entrance hall of the ancient **Bishop's Palace** was rebuilt in 1864-5, when the handsome Minton encaustic tile pavement was installed.[14] In the foyer of the **Law Courts**, RIVERGATE, is a brick wall with an incised pattern created by the letter-cutter David Kindersley in 1978. North of the centre, the **Mosque** (2002-3, by Archi-Structure of Bradford) has large panels of glazed brickwork as well as its glistening, deep green dome.

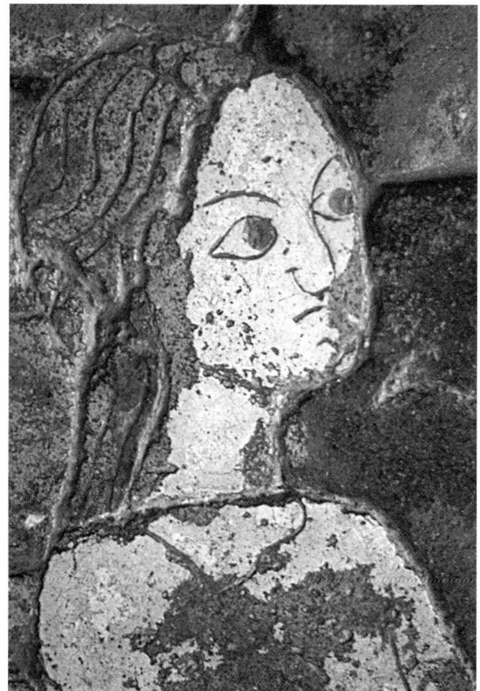

Fig 11.

WATERBEACH

St John's Church originated around 1200 but was successively extended and rebuilt in the early thirteenth century, the fifteenth century, 1616, 1821, 1849 and finally 1878 when the chancel was enlarged to accommodate the organ and choir (and to compete with the thriving local nonconformist church). This much-altered church is full of ceramic surprises, beginning in the porch, where a five-tile square encaustic floor panel bears the eagle symbol of St John the Evangelist above the wording 'St Johannes'; unusually, the eagle's head is depicted on a single small tile. The manufacturer of these tiles is unknown, but could be Godwin's, who produced a similar St Johannes group.

Following its enlargement, the chancel was redecorated in 1879-80 to designs by the diocesan architect, J. Ladds. This scheme featured a large opus sectile reredos by Powell's of Whitefriars, which was ordered in 1878; the central three-figure section (including the Virgin Mary and John the Baptist) is flanked by side pieces each with a further three figures. This substantial work, with much gold mosaic, cost £155. Two more colourful Powell's opus sectile panels adorn the marble pulpit of 1883. They were designed by Charles Hardgrave, then Powell's top designer, and show the sermon on the mount and Paul at Athens.[15] But the major tile interest of this fascinating church is the series of large and attractive panels running across the east ends of north and south aisles, complemented by a continuous tiled strip around the whole nave. The tile panels, in mainly black lettering on cream ground, and with multicoloured ornament in the style of medieval manuscript illumination, carry the text of various prayers and the Ten Commandments; the dado has a single line of lettering in the same manner. The Ten Commandments panel is signed 'W. H. Constable, Cambridge 1879'. It seems probable that Constable's was a local stained glass firm specialising in church decoration.

Cambridgeshire Roundup

The Old Butcher's Shop at **Barnack** has two stall risers with pictorial tile panels. Buckden Towers (1872, now a religious community), in the centre of the village of **Buckden**, has several fireplaces with pictorial tiles signed by the Gower Street stained glass maker G. E. Cook and his designer F. Hart.[16] As well as excellent mural painting, the chancel of Holy Trinity Church, **Hildersham** contains a fine Maw tile pavement, probably dating from the 1878-90 restoration. The R. C. Church of Our Lady and St Philip, Newmarket Road, **Kirtling**, stands next to Kirtling Tower, which is dominated by the twin-towered gatehouse of 1530 remaining from the mansion demolished in 1801; the church (1877, architect C. A. Buckler) has interesting patterned floor tiling. There are Minton floor tiles at the Church of St James, **Newton**, near Wisbech. Pig, sheep and bull interwar pictorial tile panels feature on the shop which was formerly Harry Anderson's the butcher at 12 The Waits, **St Ives**. St Peter's Church, **Snailwell**, has a good geometric pavement, letter tile risers to the sanctuary and a memorial floor tile. There is tilework by the architect William Butterfield at St Giles Church, **Tadlow**, which he restored in 1860; the sanctuary wall shows his typical plain and encaustic tile patterning. The church of St James the Great, **Waresley**, was designed by William Butterfield and built in 1855-7; in the chancel is an excellent polychromatic display including geometrical stencilling in pink, buff and green, and tiling in red, green and yellow. The entrance hall of **Wimpole Hall** (NT), near Arrington, has a spectacular pavement of Maw & Co encaustic tiles made at their Benthall works, Broseley, around 1880; in addition, there are Wedgwood tiles in the dairy.

References

1. Randoll Coate, Adrian Fisher and Graham Burgess, *A Celebration of Mazes* (Minotaur Designs, St Alban's, 1986), pp21-2.
2. Colin Cunningham and Prudence Waterhouse, *Alfred Waterhouse, 1830-1905: Biography of a Practice* (Clarendon Press, Oxford, 1992), pp134-5, 265.
3. Richard Myers and Hilary Myers, *William Morris Tiles - The tile designs of Morris and his Fellow-Workers* (Richard Dennis, Shepton Beauchamp, 1996), pp62-3, 81.
4. Michaela Braesel, 'The tile decoration by Morris & Co. for Queens' College, Cambridge', *Apollo*, 149 (1999) January, pp25-33.
5. Myers, *William Morris Tiles* (1996), p80
6. Michael Stratton Archive; Nikolaus Pevsner, *Cambridgeshire*, (Penguin, London, 1970), p190.
7. June Osborne, *John Piper and Stained Glass* (Sutton Publishing, Stroud, 1997).
8. *The Builder*, vol 9, 19th July 1851, p450.
9. Nikolaus Pevsner, *Cambridgeshire* 2nd ed. Buildings of England (Penguin, Harmondsworth, 1970), p367.
10. Kenneth Beaulah and Hans van Lemmen, *Church Tiles of the Nineteenth Century* 2nd ed (Shire Publications, Princes Risborough, 2001), p17.
11. Elizabeth Eames, *English Tilers* (British Museum Press, London, 1992), pp33-5.
12. Jane Cochrane, 'Medieval Tiled Floor Patterns', *TACS Journal*, 5 (1994), pp11-19.
13. Diana Hall, 'Prior Crauden's Chapel, Ely Cathedral', *Glazed Expressions*, (1991) 22, pp10.
14. Jeremy Musson, 'Bishop's Palace, Peterborough', *Country Life*, 195 (2001) 11th January, pp52-7.
15. Dennis W. Hadley, *James Powell & Sons: A listing of opus sectile, 1847-1973*, (2001).
16. David Thomas, *Arthur W. Marshall: Owner of Buckden Towers*, (1999).

Cheshire

Most of Cheshire's ceramic interest lies in the north of the county, where tightly packed urban terraces yield numerous tiled pubs and terracotta shop facades. But there is much more: Birkenhead, on the Wirral, was the home of the Della Robbia Pottery, founded by Harold Rathbone in 1894. He aspired to produce ornamental architectural pieces in the manner of the fifteenth-century Florentine sculptor Luca Della Robbia, which he hoped to sell to the rising business classes. The domestic flat and hollow wares were succcessful, but his decorative, arts and crafts-inspired wares were not, and the pottery closed in 1906; *in situ* examples of Della Robbia architectural ware are therefore rare. Cheshire's highlights include the Della Robbia panels at Wallasey's Memorial Church, tiling possibly from Liverpool's Swan Tile Works at the Stork Hotel in Birkenhead, the porch tiles of Crewe, and - out in the countryside - Alfred Waterhouse's golden terracotta Parrot House at Eaton Hall. Suggested reading: Williamson Art Gallery & Museum, *Della Robbia Pottery, Birkenhead, 1894-1906: An Interim Report* (Metropolitan Borough of Wirral, Birkenhead, 1980); the facsimile *1896 Catalogue of the Della Robbia Pottery* (Williamson Art Gallery & Museum, 1994); TACS Tour Notes *Birkenhead* (1999). The *Gazetteer* entry for Cheshire covers the administrative areas of Cheshire County Council, Halton Borough Council, Stockport Metropolitan Borough Council, Warrington Borough Council and Wirral Metropolitan Borough Council. Note that Trafford, including Hale and Sale, is covered in the Lancashire section.

BIRKENHEAD

The most rewarding approach to Birkenhead is via the Mersey ferry; on alighting, passengers may ascend HAMILTON STREET in search of the town's landmark Town Hall clock tower. On the right is the **Pier Hotel**, its unusual grey-green stoneware facade bearing fine lettering and a superb high relief coat of arms, both signifying the pub's original owners as the Birkenhead Brewery Company, which brewed in Oxton Road (west of the centre) until 1962 (Fig 12). The maker of the facade is unknown; unlike many brewing companies, the Birkenhead Brewery apparently had no clear long-term relationship with any single ceramics manufacturer. Even the date of this spectacular facade, offering us *Peerless Ales & Stout*, remains a mystery, but is probably just pre-1914.

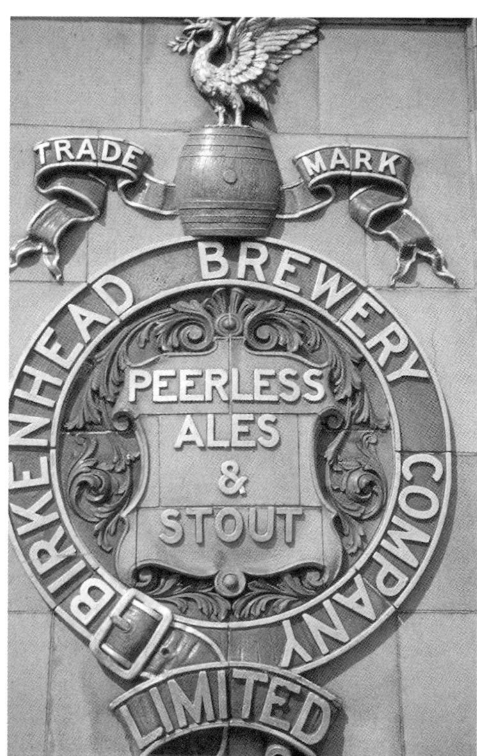

Fig 12.

Into HAMILTON SQUARE, the largest early nineteenth-century grade I listed square outside London, where the impressive Town Hall - redundant since the 1974 local government reorganisation - has now been transformed into **Wirral Museum**. The classical pile was built in 1883-7 and restored, following a fire, in 1901. Behind the grey stone facade are several unexpected pleasures, beginning with the grand entrance hall and stairs, where there is an unusual combination of blue and green tiles in a pavement probably made by Minton Hollins and dating from the original building. Also on the ground

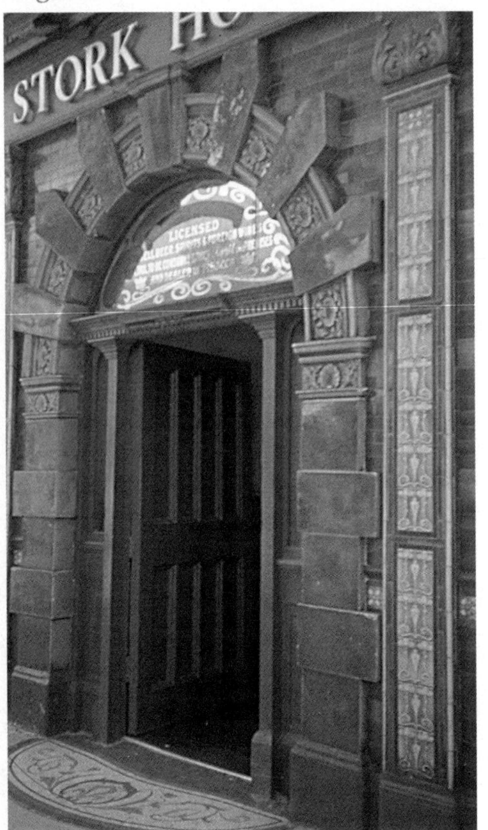

Fig 13.

floor, in the room immediately north of the entrance, is a fireplace grate decorated with Wedgwood's Marsden's patent tiles; the floral designs combine stencilling and a clear transparent glaze to achieve their unique effect.[1] Upstairs, the tile pavement continues, reinforced by mainly red wall tiling, leading the visitor into the lavish council chamber. In a side room is an ornate fireplace with colourful mottled tiling and the borough coat of arms; this was apparently painted on the central tile four-tile group then glazed. It is probably mid-1880s Minton Hollins work, as are the hexagonal Pugin-designed tiles, depicting a red clover leaf on cream ground, to be found lurking in an upstairs toilet. To the rear, in a room which may have been converted into a kitchen during the 1920s, is slip trailed art deco wall tiling, possibly by the Henry Richards Tile Company.

Leave Hamilton Square at its south-west corner, passing in short order the home of Conrad Dressler, sculptor and co-director of the Della Robbia Pottery (34a Hamilton Square), and the central Della Robbia studio (2a Price Street). Head along Price Street as far as the junction with ADELPHI ROAD to find the **Stork Hotel**, a most unusual public house built in 1840 but thoroughly refurbished inside and out, probably by the Birkenhead Brewery, around 1903 (Fig 13). Its turquoise tile and brown glazed brick facade looks distinctly odd, an Edwardian interpretation of classical decoration, with heavily ornamented tiled pilasters and doorcases set upon the shiny brick ground. Inside, as well as the perfectly preserved glass and woodwork of the curved bar counter, is rather more elegant art nouveau dado tiling featuring tulip-pattern designs in yellow and green, and a fine mosaic floor, revealed in 2000 after some years in hiding beneath lino. This gem of a pub, which has managed to remain intact despite many threats of modernisation, is now listed grade II. Its singular appearance results not only from the brewery's need for a flagship pub near both its brewery and the town centre, but the employment of a local tile fixer and maker to carry out the ceramics contract, rather than one of the nationally-known manufacturers. The tiles were fixed by George Swift and may also have been made at his Swan Tile Works, Liverpool, once a substantial concern; if so, the Stork Hotel would be the only remaining *in situ* location of Swan Tile Works products in the Liverpool area.[2]

Adelphi Street ends at CONWAY STREET; just west is another pub, the **Crown**, with a mostly plain turn-of-the-century purple faience exterior with a sprinkling of well-moulded, high relief crowns. It illustrates the local propensity for visual renditions of the pub name to be included in the facade. Turn east along Conway Street to the **Conway Centre**, a hulking red brick and buff terracotta pile built as the Higher Elementary School in 1903 (Fig 14). It is an unexpected tour-de-force. The modelling of terracotta figures and lettering is excellent; a bending caryatid holds aloft a balcony inscribed with 'Elementary', while other figures pose in niches beneath terracotta domes, and the borough arms plus supporters stand proud above it all. The Dennis Ruabon catalogue of 1903 lists the company's terracotta as being used in the nearby (now demolished) Board of Guardian Offices on Conway Street, whose architect was Edmund Kirby. It is possible that the same firm's terracotta may have been used for the Conway Centre.

East along Conway Street to Argyle Street; just south, on the corner of GRANGE ROAD, is the

George & Dragon, whose white-tiled 1930s facade sports a colourful St George and dragon relief plaque; note the green dragon's tail sliding off into space. Shaws of Darwen, who supplied the Liverpool (and Salford) brewers Threlfalls with ceramic materials for their tied estate during the 1930s, made a plaque in similar style for the St George Hotel in Liverpool, which suggests the George & Dragon is also by Shaws.[3] Turning north up Argyle Street, then right into Market Street, pass the **Market Inn**, with its Threlfall's lettering and cream and blue tiling - doubtless by Shaws - then return along Hamilton Street to the Town Hall.

Well south of the Town Hall area in BOROUGH ROAD, three Della Robbia panels may be seen at **Birkenhead Central Library**, in the ground floor lending library beyond the foyer. They were presented by the Pottery's founder Harold Rathbone (1858-1929) in memory of Charles Gatehouse, chairman of the Libraries Committee. The two smaller panels are a pair, *The Sower* and *The Reaper*, designed by Conrad Dressler; the most attractive of the three is *The Sower*, a highly three-dimensional representation. Finally, there is more Della Robbia ware in Birkenhead's main shopping area at CHARING CROSS, in the form of two male figures by Carlo Manzoni above the entrance to a wine bar (formerly the **Midland Bank**, originally the North and South Wales Bank).

Bidston

The **R. C. Church of the Holy Cross** (1959), HOYLAKE ROAD was designed by the architect Francis Xavier Velarde (d1960), known for his (mainly Roman Catholic) churches built in north-west England from 1930 onward.[4] Although it was not the last of Velarde's church designs, it was the last he was able to complete himself; surprisingly, the building is not listed. Externally it is the intriguing geometric fenestration which catches the eye, but inside is a wonderfully atmospheric mosaic scheme by the Art Pavements & Decorations Co, whose parent company was Carter's of Poole.

CHEADLE

In 1849 the wholesale draper (later Mayor of Manchester) James Watts bought the villa **Abney Hall**, on MANCHESTER ROAD, and in the following two or three years turned it into a Tudorised red brick country house. The architects of this transformation were Travis & Mangnall of Manchester, but the real importance of the house lies in its interior, created around 1852 by J. G. Crace. Following the success of their Medieval Court at the Great Exhibition, the combination of Crace, Pugin, Minton and Hardman obtained commissions to carry out several interior furnishing schemes, of which Abney Hall was one; in this case, Pugin's designs were executed after his death by Crace.[5] The house was one of the first to be equipped with gas (the gasoliers were by Hardman), while the extensive areas of encaustic floor tiles were by Minton's; the hall tiling is particularly impressive.[6] Cheadle Town Hall occupied Abney Hall until 1974, but the house now functions as private office accommodation, standing in the lee of the M63.

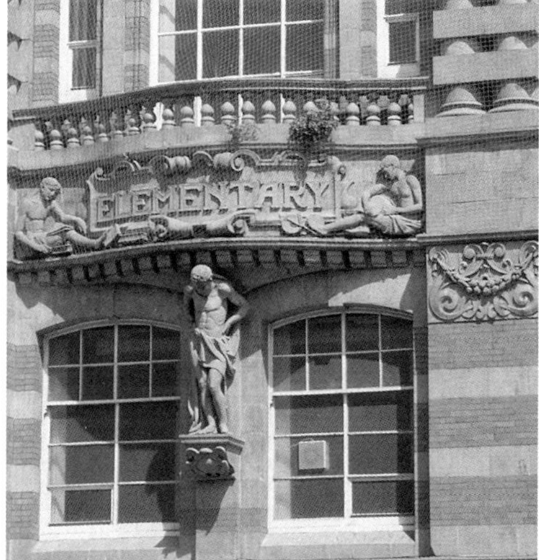

Fig 14.

CHESTER

Chester Cathedral, off ABBEY STREET, not only provides a quiet contrast to the famous double-decker black-and-white Rows, but offers displays of both Victorian and medieval tilework, the latter being Chertsey border tiles with a fleur-de-lys and castle design. Much more extensive is the encaustic tile pavement in the choir, installed as part of George Gilbert Scott's restoration around 1880. The tiles were manufactured by Craven Dunnill, and were a relatively unusual venture into cathedral work for this firm. Their designs, based on medieval tile motifs, have a Celtic feel and incorporate several gargoyle-like faces. In addition there is an attractive Maw & Co pavement, dating from 1863-4, beyond the choir in the Lady Chapel; its rich brown and white tiles were designed for Maw's by the architect George

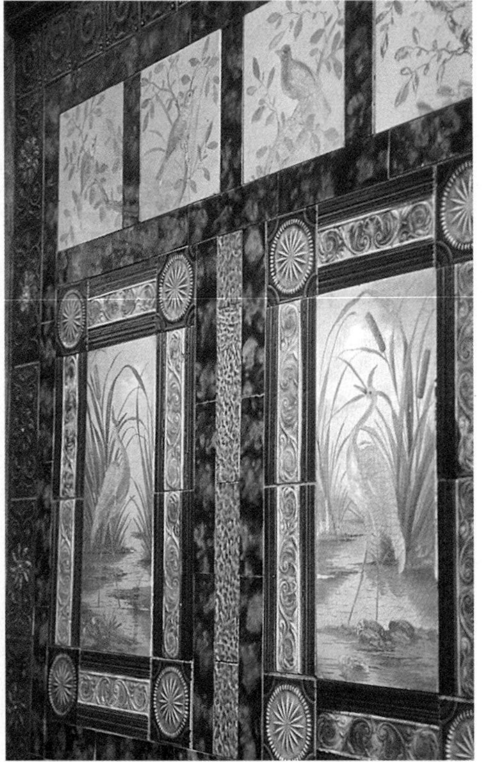

Fig 15.

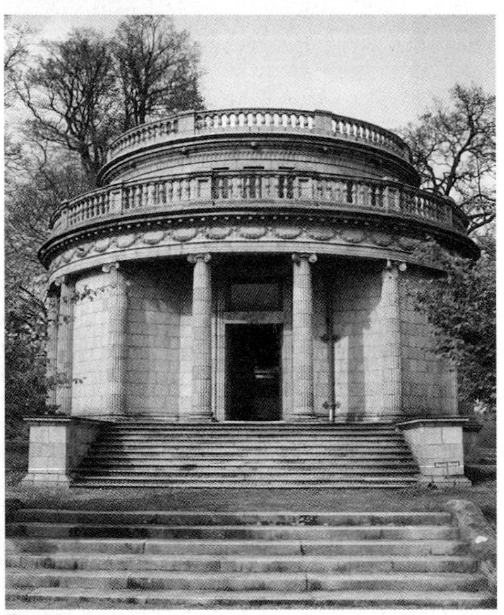

Fig 16.

Goldie, one of their regular designers. The tiles were supplied by W. B. Simpson & Sons, who were responsible for the overall layout.[7] There are smaller tile pavements in several other chapels, and the north wall of the nave has a splendid series of four full-height mosaic panels dating from 1883-6. They show Old Testament characters and were designed by the stained glass artist J. R. Clayton of the church decorators Clayton & Bell, here working in conjunction with the Venetian mosaicist Salviati.[8]

Across NORTHGATE STREET from the Cathedral is **Chester Library**, built in 1914 as the Westminster Coach and Motor Car Works for J. A. Lawton & Co to the designs of the architect Philip H. Lockwood; its shiny pinkish-buff terracotta was designed and made by Dennis Ruabon, a picture of the building appearing in the firm's catalogue.[9] The two-storey structure is dominated by a row of three semicircular windows at first floor level; above is a richly ornamented relief frieze topped by a massive balustrade, broken only by a curved pediment bearing the name of the works. The building was converted to a library and arts centre during its restoration in 1983-4, when the balusters - which had been replaced by brickwork - were reinstated; at that time, the new balusters were the largest ever made by Shaws of Darwen. Next to the Library is the Town Hall, with the **Forum Shopping Centre** to its rear. Its HAMILTON PLACE facade is ornamented with several terracotta plaques showing shopping-related motifs; they were made by Timothy Clapcott in 1995.

South towards the River Dee lies BRIDGE STREET; on its east side is the towering black-and-white form of **St Michael's Buildings**, built in 1910 for the Grosvenor estate. Its five storeys were originally faced in white faience, but this was replaced immediately by half-timbering on the orders of the second Duke of Westminster. Some faience remains, however, on the ground floor exterior, and more importantly inside the two-storey St Michael's Arcade, entered at Rows level. Here the renaissance-style decoration combines grey and green faience, including an elaborate frieze, with cream and pink tiling. This is probably a Doulton scheme; there are heads - perhaps of Magog - near the entrance, modelled in a style resembling that of Doulton's designer W. J. Neatby.[10]

CREWE

In the streets off NANTWICH ROAD, just west of Crewe's fabled railway station, is one of the country's finest collections of porch tiles, dating from around 1890 up to the First World War. The open porches of these simple terraced houses are adorned with a dazzling variety of colourful wall tiles, the basic pattern being a dado, with border tiles top and bottom, enclosing a five tile by four tile area with a pictorial centrepiece; there is often an encaustic geometric pavement (Fig 15). However, some porches are completely tiled and there appears to be almost infinite variation of tiling even within the confines of a few streets. The centre tile panels are especially striking, and include elegant female figures on tiles made by the Photo Decorated Tile Co (Catherine Street), as well as rural scenes signed E. J. B. Evans (Bedford Street). Many manufacturers and many tilemaking techniques are represented in this magic miscellany, for instance a single house in Furnival Street displays turn of the century dust-pressed transfer printed and relief moulded tiles by T. G. & F. Booth and T. & R. Boote.

The best of the porch tiles can be seen by heading west from the station along Nantwich Road, then following this route: Gresty Road, Catherine Street, Bedford Street, Ernest Street, Furnival Street, returning along Nantwich Road past the **Earl of Crewe** pub, which retains its Queen Victoria Jubilee terracotta plaque made by Stanley Brothers of Nuneaton. The two-foot square terracotta plaque shows a relief bust of Queen Victoria, with an inscription including named parts of the British Empire and the date in a cartouche at the top. Stanley's made the plaques to mark the Queen's fiftieth jubilee in 1887, and the mould was later adapted for use on the occasion of the Diamond Jubilee; roughly equal numbers of each design survive.[11]

A deviation from Furnival Street into RUSKIN ROAD will allow a view of **Ruskin County High School**, opened in 1909 as the County Grammar School. Its lofty (and lengthy, at twenty-three bays) classical facade and masses of salmon-pink terracotta are totally out of scale with the surrounding houses. The school, more imposing than attractive, was designed by the county architect H. Beswick, and was mentioned in the 1908 Dennis Ruabon catalogue.

EATON HALL

Although the first Duke of Westminster's astonishingly palatial Eaton Hall (1870-83, architect Alfred Waterhouse) was demolished in 1961, many of its estate buildings remain, including the exquisite classical **Parrot House** (Fig 16). This circular garden temple was also designed by Waterhouse and built in 1881-3; it was constructed from golden yellow terracotta manufactured by J. C. Edwards of Ruabon.[12] The walls are block terracotta through and through; inside, caryatids support the ceiling. The temple, now surrounded by greenery, has been restored using terracotta supplied by by Shaws of Darwen. Near the stable block is Waterhouse's gothic **Chapel**, which retains its Godwin tile pavement, and the large **Summer House** with an unusual Minton-tiled fireplace.

HOYLAKE

In CABLE ROAD, Hoylake are a few houses with groups of five colourful handmade Della Robbia tiles - showing flower fairies and gardening scenes - set into their porches; it is very unusual to find Della Robbia ware used on house exteriors (Fig 17).

Fig 17.

NEW BRIGHTON

Facing the PROMENADE is the **Floral Gardens Theatre**; a few remnants of the original late Edwardian theatre are intact, including the tiled shelter just west of the theatre. Decorative ironwork suggests that the shelter was once glass-roofed, while the tiled dado along its rear wall is mainly yellow with some relief-patterned tiles. Its front is open to what would originally been a fine view across the Mersey, but now looks on to the crazy golf course. Uphill into the town's shopping centre, where **Rowson's Building**, on the corner of VICTORIA ROAD and Rowson Street, features a good red terracotta plaque by Dennis Ruabon depicting the insignia of the Prince of Wales.[13] The building probably began life around 1900 as a branch of the North & South Wales Bank.

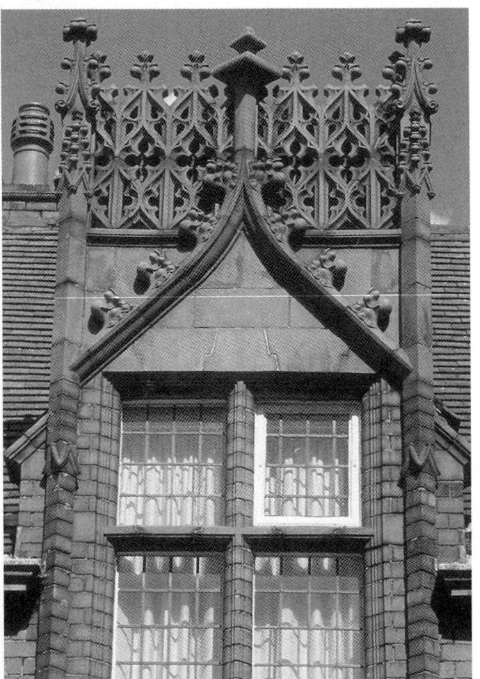

Fig 18.

SANDIWAY

St John's Church, NORLEY ROAD, is unusual for several reasons: not only was it designed by the architect John Douglas, who became lord of the manor, donated the site for the church and contributed towards its cost, but it contains a Della Robbia wall panel. The body of the church was built in 1902-3, but the tower was erected later as a memorial to Douglas.

STOCKPORT

The monumental stripped classical white faience facade of the **Plaza Cinema** (1932) still dominates MERSEY SQUARE in the middle of Stockport; it was listed grade II in 1997 and began to show films again in 2000, having been dark since 1966. About two miles south of the centre, just off the A6 on POPLAR GROVE, is the **Stepping Hill Hospital**, where two ceramic panels by Gerald Buchanan - one showing a tree house, the other entitled *Waterside* - were installed at the Treehouse Children's Centre during the mid 1990s.

WALLASEY

The **Memorial Church**, MANOR ROAD (1898-9) is a testament to the creative potential of nonconformism combined with arts and crafts ideals. The Unitarian church was built in memory of William Elam (1821-96) by his wife Martha, the architects being Frederick Waring and Edmund Rathbone, brother of Harold Rathbone, founder of the Della Robbia Pottery; the Rathbones were also a Unitarian family.[15] The intention behind the decoration of the church was to portray the new religious and social ideas, thus the interior includes work by Benjamin Creswick, Bernard Sleigh and members of the influential Bromsgrove Guild. This rare arts and crafts interior is completed by a Della Robbia reredos, a triptych signed by Harold Rathbone and dated 1899. It shows beautifully sculpted figures set amongst verdant scenery, with a biblical inscription winding its way through the trees. The church is now in the care of the Historic Chapels Trust.

Weatherhead High School, a specialist media arts college, moved to its new site on BRECK ROAD in 2003; in the entrance is a large mural by ceramicist Jean Powell showing the original school building, where she was a pupil.

WARRINGTON

Warrington offers some substantial terracotta and faience facades, firstly at the **King's Head** on WINWICK STREET, almost opposite the railway station. There is a Burmantofts look about its olive

PORT SUNLIGHT

There is much of external ceramic interest in the Lever Brothers' model village Port Sunlight (founded 1888), including lacy, bright red terracotta decoration above the dormers of a row of houses (1896) in CROSS STREET (Fig 18). The village's first public building was the **Gladstone Hall** (1891), which bears a pretty ceramic plaque commemorating its opening (Fig 19).

ROSTHERNE

St Mary's Church, which has a beautiful setting above Rostherne Mere, was restored in 1888 at the expense of Wibraham, second baron Egerton of Tatton; the work included encaustic tiling around the font and a reredos with two Powell's opus sectile panels of angels by Frank Mann.[14] The east wall of the church was further embellished in 1910 with the addition of two large and elaborate tile panels (around 6 feet in height) showing St John the Baptist and the Virgin Mary; these were erected by the Countess of Albemarle and were also designed by Powell's.

green faience, the moulding involving a jumble of faces and flowers. Winwick Street leads south towards the town centre and BRIDGE STREET, which displays a good range of partly terracotta facades, the best being that of **Howard Buildings** (now Boots); this late Victorian work includes two picture panels and four lion finials. **St Mary's R. C. Church**, BUTTERMARKET STREET, has an ornate sanctuary pavement, while east of town in GORSEY LANE is the grade II listed **Orford Hotel**, built around 1908 with a terracotta pseudo-Tudor facade; inside is a tiled frieze in the corridor. Finally, well south in Stockton Heath is **St Thomas Church**, with unusual Victorian tilework in the chancel.

WEST KIRBY

West Kirby Residential School (1886-8), MEOLS DRIVE was originally a children's convalescent home which moved to West Kirby from Hoylake in 1888. The facade has good, bright red terracotta decoration by J. C. Edwards of Ruabon; the building was mentioned in the firm's 1890 and 1903 catalogues. Over the years the children's home built up a collection of Doulton pictorial tile panels commemorating the endowment of individual cots, ranging in date from 1889 to 1953. Donors were mainly local families, the plaques being individual memorials, but also included the Freemasons of Cheshire. The panels had some unusual designs featuring children and animals.[16] By the 1990s only nine panels remained; all were moved from their original positions and some required restoration, but they were once again on display in the school in 1997. The surviving panels date from between 1909, when the open-air ward was added, and 1951.[17]

WILMSLOW

A scary, bearded wizard, storm-driven trees and all manner of animals greet shoppers arriving at **Sainsbury's** supermarket in the centre of Wilmslow on ALDERLEY ROAD. They are players in *The Legend of the Iron Gates*, a lengthy (around 80 feet) terracotta mural depicting a local story; it was designed in 1989 by Judith Bluck and fired by Ibstock Brick Nostell Ltd. The installation is around nine feet in height, and uses terracotta in the form of tile-like squares; the moulding of figures is excellent, the animals having an especially weirder-than-life quality (Fig 20).

About a mile north-west of the centre near Pownall Park is **Pownall Hall** (now a school, no public access), CARRWOOD ROAD, furnished for the brewer Henry Boddington by the Century Guild in 1886-8; the glass was an important commission for Shrigley & Hunt, who were also tile painters. There are De Morgan tiles on four fire surrounds, the best being in the former drawing room where no fewer than twenty-four different fabulous green beasts cavort. More De Morgan tilework may be found in a bathroom, and the products of other manufacturers including Minton Hollins decorate still more fire surrounds.

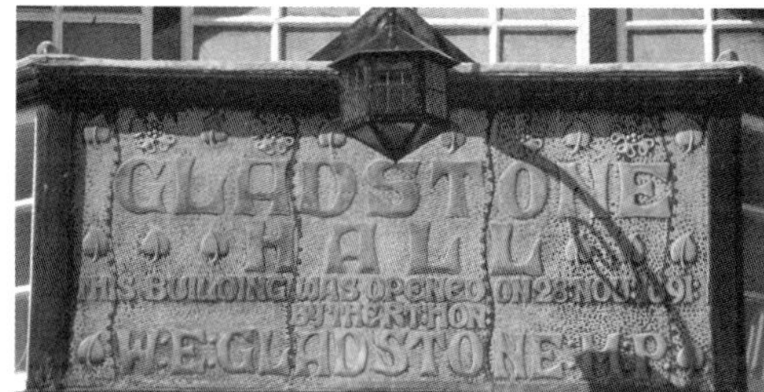

Fig 19.

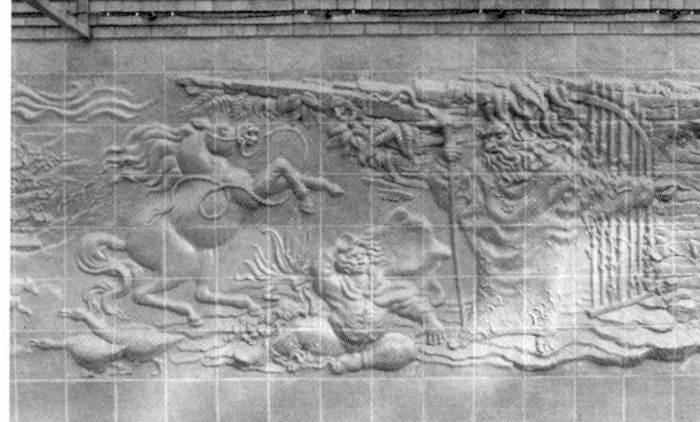
Fig 20.

Cheshire Roundup

The pair of cemetery chapels (1860-80) sited off Cheshire Street in **Audlem** have external tile decoration as well as rich encaustic tile pavements. St James Church, **Christleton** (1875-7) was William Butterfield's only church in Cheshire; its polychromatic interior includes a chequered red-and-white stone chancel, tiled floors, and Minton mosaics in the 1893 reredos. Inside Antrobus Street United Reformed Church, **Congleton**, is a Second World War memorial to the Netherlands Forces comprising twelve delft tiles. St Michael's Church (1856-8), **Crewe Green** (the Crewe Hall estate church), was designed by George Gilbert Scott in polychromatic brick, the interior being of red and yellow brick with tile bands above. St Cross Church, Mobberley Road,

England

Knutsford (1880-1, architects Paley & Austin) was built using brick and red terracotta both supplied by the Knutsford Brick & Tile Company; inside is a Craven Dunnill line-impressed tile pavement, typical of Paley & Austin's work after the late 1870s.[18] Cheshire School of Art and Design (1897), London Road, **Northwich** bears a large figurative terracotta plaque depicting the Arts.

References

1. Hans van Lemmen, *Victorian Tiles* 2nd ed (Shire Publications, Princes Risborough, 2000), p22.
2. Penny Beckett, 'George Swift and Liverpool's Swan Tile Works', *TACS Journal*, 10 (2004), pp24-31.
3. Lynn Pearson, 'Decorative ceramics in the buildings of the British brewing industry', *TACS Journal*, 8 (2000), pp26-36.
4. Fiona Ward, *Merseyside Churches in a Modern Idiom: Francis Xavier Verlade & Bernard Miller*, in *The Twentieth Century Church*, (Twentieth Century Society, London, 1998) pp93-102.
5. Paul Atterbury and Clive Wainwright, *Pugin: A Gothic Passion* (Yale University Press, New Haven and London, 1994), p58.
6. Mark Girouard, *The Victorian Country House* (Yale University Press, New Haven and London, 1979), pp24, 393.
7. 'The Lady Chapel, Chester Cathedral', *The Builder*, 24 (1866) 15th December, pp922-3.
8. Peter Larkworthy, *Clayton and Bell, Stained Glass Artists and Decorators* (Ecclesiological Society, London, 1984).
9. Andrew Connolly, *Life in the Victorian brickyards of Flintshire and Denbighshire* (Gwasg Carreg Gwalch, Llanrwst, 2003), p237; however, Ifor Edwards, 'Claymasters and Clayworkers in the old parish of Ruabon', *Transactions of the Denbighshire Historical Society*, vol 35 (1986), pp83-98, states that the terracotta for the coachworks was provided by J. C. Edwards, and that the building appeared in one of the firm's catalogues. As the 1914 building replaced an earlier coachworks destroyed by fire, perhaps this may be a reference to the older structure.
10. Michael Stratton Archive.
11. Arthur Sadler, 'Victorian Commemorative Plaques', *Leicestershire Historian*, (1999) 35, pp1-2.
12. Colin Cunningham and Prudence Waterhouse, *Alfred Waterhouse, 1830-1905: Biography of a Practice* (Clarendon Press, Oxford, 1992), p236.
13. *Dennis Ruabon Catalogue*, (1903).
14. Dennis W. Hadley, *James Powell & Sons: A listing of opus sectile, 1847-1973*, (2001).
15. Williamson Art Gallery and Museum, *Della Robbia Pottery, Birkenhead, 1894-1906: An interim report* (Metropolitan Borough of Wirral, Department of Leisure Services, Birkenhead, 1980).
16. John Greene, *Brightening the Long Days* (Tiles and Architectural Ceramics Society, 1987).
17. Lesley Durbin, 'Hospital Tiles - The Continuing Story', *TACS Newsletter*, (1997) 40, pp3.
18. *The Builder*, vol 41, 1st October 1881, p437; Philip and Dorothy Brown, 'Lancaster architects - church terracotta and tiles', *Glazed Expressions*, 21, (1990), pp8-10.

Cornwall

There are no grand ceramic gestures in this part of the world, well away as it is from the major tilemaking areas, although there is a good example of post-medieval Barnstaple tiles at Launcells church. Victorian tile pavements and wall tiles, including Butterfield tiling at Mawgan-in-Pydar, may be found throughout the county, while other highlights are Coade stone decoration at the Egyptian House in Penzance, and Bernard Leach tiles on the tomb of Alfred Wallis at St Ives. Such is the paucity of research on tiles and architectural ceramics in Cornwall that it is hard to suggest anything useful to read which is specific to this neglected county. The *Gazetteer* entry for Cornwall (Kernow) covers the administrative areas of Cornwall County Council and Isles of Scilly Council.

BODMIN

A brilliant blue glazed brick wall bearing the name **Bodmin Hospital** in large, coloured ceramic letters greets visitors to the hospital, which stands in WESTHEATH AVENUE and opened in 2002. The ceramic wall, a product of the Percent for Art scheme, is the work of Camelford-based potter Roger Michell, the hospital's artist in residence.

HAYLE

Near the harbour is an old butcher's shop (1894, architect Samson Hill of Redruth) which is now the **Carnsew Gallery**. Its unusual facade includes a series of high-relief gold and green ceramic panels bearing three-dimensional sheep heads, and full-height Staffordshire-made porch tiling showing a handsome horned cow in a floral cartouche. Another cow's head is the central image of the well-preserved doorway mosaic, while a broad row of geometric encaustic tiles (perhaps by Minton Hollins) separates the shopfront from the pavement. The derelict former **Palace Cinema**, COPPERHOUSE TERRACE, was built around 1900 as a drill hall (St George's Hall) and later converted into one of Cornwall's earliest cinemas. The cinema closed in 1983, but its richly decorative salmon-pink terracotta facade, which features a set of unusual conical finials, is to be incorporated into a new arts centre development.

ISLES OF SCILLY

The **Abbey Garden**, on the island of TRESCO, was created by Augustus Smith, who leased the Isles of Scilly from the Duchy of Cornwall in 1834. Although the islands reverted to the Duchy in 1920, Smith's heirs, the Dorrien-Smith family, still lease Tresco and continue to improve the gardens. The Shell House (1994), a pretty shell grotto designed and made by Lucy Dorrien-Smith, has a shell-themed tile floor, and individual tiles commemorating members of the family can be seen amongst the shells on its internal walls.

KINGSAND

On the edge of Kingsand is a **bus shelter** with a spectacular ceramic interior. Along with highly glazed, colourful tiles by Sarah McCormack are tiles made by schoolchildren, all showing locally-related scenes.

Cawsand

Not far from Kingsand, the **ferry shelter** (1999) in the nearby hamlet of Cawsand is also tiled. Here tiles by Zoe Coles are combined with more work from local schoolchildren.

LAUNCELLS

Rare sixteenth-century Barnstaple relief tiles form the sanctuary pavement of **St Swithin's Church**; the designs include a fleur-de-lys, Tudor rose, pelican and lion. The post-medieval Barnstaple tilers were the last to use relief decoration, producing tiles long after they had become unfashionable elsewhere. The fabric was coarse thus motifs were necessarily bold, and only a clear lead glaze was used; the resulting tiles (many with a reduced grey body) appear olive-green or - if the glaze has oxidised - brown.[1] The designs were created with a wooden stamp, which was placed on the dried tile and struck. Relief tiles were produced at Barnstaple from the late sixteenth century until the early eighteenth century.

PENZANCE

The town's architectural star turn is undoubtedly the **Egyptian House** in CHAPEL STREET, its colourful facade a delicious example of the style popular following Napoleon's 1798 campaign in Egypt (Fig 21). It was built around 1835 and its elevation is a copy of the Egyptian Hall in Piccadilly (1812, architect P. F. Robinson); either Robinson or John Foulston, Plymouth's leading architect of the time, may have been responsible for its design. The original purpose of the building, whose facade is heavily enriched with Coade stone, was to act as a museum and geological repository; the Coade ornamentation includes Egyptian figures and winged serpents. To the west of Chapel Street is MORRAB ROAD and the late nineteenth-century **Public Library** (architect Henry White), with a facade displaying much terracotta decoration, including swags, roundels and tiles with foliate motifs; the tiles may have been made at nearby Marazion Marsh, where brickmaking was carried out.

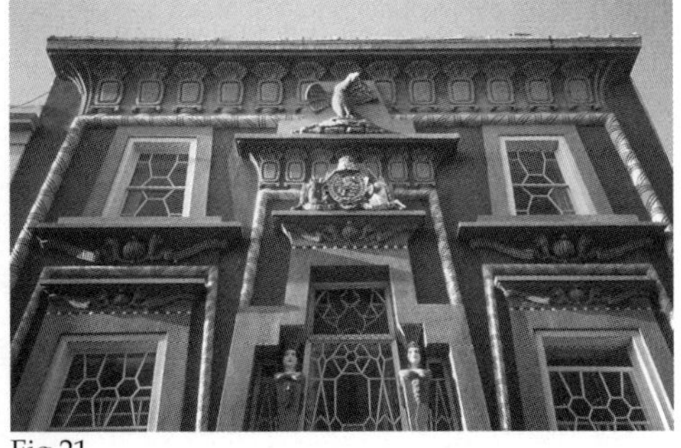

Fig 21.

The **Railway Station** lies just east of the town centre, at the north end of WHARF ROAD. A tile mural designed by Cornish ceramicist Genevieve Val Baker - a huge map of Cornwall featuring lighthouses, tin mines and much more - was installed inside the trainshed in 1999; the tiles were made, painted and glazed by local children. Outside the station, a group of artworks (2003) marking the **Penzance Passenger Transport Interchange** includes a pair of oval bench seats with ceramic tops by Teena Gould, the Carmarthenshire ceramicist. These comprise 140 hand-moulded blocks in white clay, with low reliefs of shells, leaves and Celtic patterns decorated with a variety of black and white glazes; similar ceramic inserts can be found on the adjacent planters. The muted colours and mysterious shapes complement the constantly changing seaside light. These benches, together with a pavement map of Cornwall in granite and marble, and twin steel sculptures-cum-signposts, have transformed the previously messy station forecourt into an unexpectedly attractive public space.

QUETHIOCK

The Reverend William Willimott was rector of the **Church of St Hugh of Lincoln** during 1878-88, and was responsible for the appearance of many of its furnishings. He initiated the tiling of the east wall of the chancel, which includes the ten commandments amongst its decorative motifs, and was also in office when the chancel floor was relaid with Minton encaustic tiles in 1878-9; tiles from Webb's Worcester Tileries were laid throughout the remainder of the church at the same time.

ST IVES

Above Porthmeor Beach and not far from the Tate St Ives is the town's **Old Cemetery**, where the primitive artist Alfred Wallis (1855-1942), inspiration of many of the St Ives School, is buried beneath a grave cover of painted stoneware tiles made by Bernard Leach around 1942. The seven-by-three tile grave cover (which tops a low brick tomb) shows a lighthouse and seascape, and describes Wallis as an *Artist & Mariner*.[2]

Cornwall Roundup

The late fifteenth-century chapel at **Cotehele** (NT), the seat of the Edgcumbe family, has an original green and white tile pavement. There are tiles by Maw & Co at St Peter's Church, **Dobwalls**. At 31 Church Street, **Falmouth** is a shop with an art nouveau relief-tiled stall riser showing fish in grey, blue and green glazes. The floor of **Germoe** church was paved with Bridgwater tiles during its restoration by the priest-architect Ernest Geldart of Essex in 1889-91. The aesthetic movement architect E. W. Godwin designed the fairly plain encaustic pavement in the Church of St Grada (1862), **Grade**; he also designed some of its furnishings.[3] Just south-west of **Lostwithiel** church is a butcher's shop whose tiled stall riser proclaims it as Liddicoat's; the name and art deco tulips on its central panel were apparently hand-painted by a local artist, but the flanking panels of floral relief tiles are by Maw & Co. There is a nineteenth-century encaustic tile pavement in the sanctuary of All Saints Church, **Marazion** (1861). St Mawgan's Church, **Mawgan-**

in-Pydar, which originated in the thirteenth century, was restored and partly rebuilt in 1860-1 by William Butterfield; his work included typically colourful tiling on the north and east walls of the chancel. Pretty blue and white six-tile panels of boats on Stevenson's buildings in **Newlyn** identify the company's fishing fleet; the tilemaker is Peter Ellery. The Church of St Probus and St Grace, **Probus** has the tallest tower in Cornwall; in its cell-like chancel is a substantial Powell's opus sectile reredos, dating from 1886 and showing the Crucifixion.[4] St Anthony's Church, **St Anthony-in-Roseland**, was rebuilt around 1850 by Samuel Spry, to whose family home - the Place - it is connected; restoration included the installation of Minton floor tiles. Unusual features of St Michael's Church, **St Michael Caerhays**, are the attractive commandment tables of nineteenth-century tiles. St Pynnochus Church, **St Pinnock** has Maw & Co floor tiling while St Tudius Church, **St Tudy** has a Powell's tiled altar surround dating from 1874. There is a Powell's tile and mosaic reredos, probably installed in 1873, at St Wenna Church, **St Wenn**. The Godwin encaustic tile pavement at St Sancredus Church, **Sancreed** includes many of the firm's common motifs - fish, fleur-de-lys, Tudor rose - as well as a four-tile group showing a jaunty lion. At St Sidinius Church, **Sithney**, the encaustic tile sanctuary pavement is mainly buff and brown designs, but there is also a black tile initialled *JL* in memory of the vicar John Lidman. There is an excellent terracotta panel by George Tinworth of *Via Crucis* in the north choir aisle of **Truro** Cathedral; there are also a few gothic revival tiles in St Mary's aisle.

References

1. Elizabeth Eames, *English Medieval Tiles* (British Museum Publications, London, 1985).
2. Michael Tooby, *Tate St Ives* (Tate Gallery Publications, London, 1993), pp34-5.
3. Catherine Arbuthnott, *E. W. Godwin and Ceramics*, in *E. W. Godwin: Aesthetic Movement Architect and Designer*, Susan Weber Soros, Editor, (Yale University Press, New Haven and London, 1999) pp297-311.
4. Dennis W. Hadley, *James Powell & Sons: A listing of opus sectile, 1847-1973*, (2001).

Cumbria

Apart from ecclesiastical tiling and the work of local ceramic artists Paul Scott and Maggie Angus Berkowitz, the vast majority of Cumbria's ceramic sites are located in Carlisle, with the staggering Burmantofts excesses of the County Hotel to the fore. Other Cumbrian highlights are the unusual encaustic tiling at Greystoke Church and a complete Edwardian turkish bath scheme in Carlisle, while the 1960s abstract mural by Pilkington's in Carlisle's intriguing Civic Centre is also worthy of note. Finally, hidden away in Milnthorpe is a fine ceramic mural of the Stations of the Cross (1971) by Adam Kossowski. Suggested reading: TACS Tour Notes *Carlisle* (1997). The *Gazetteer* entry for Cumbria covers the administrative area of Cumbria County Council.

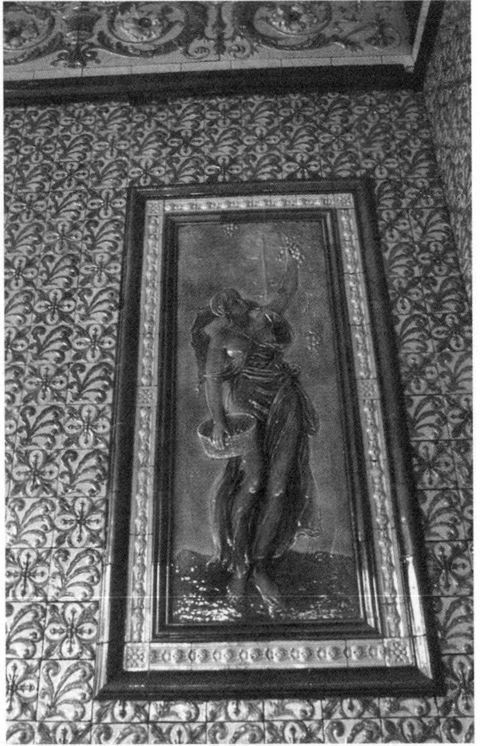

Fig 22.

BARROW-IN-FURNESS

The former **Technical School** (1900-3), ABBEY ROAD has lavish buff terracotta detailing (probably by Burmantofts) including a domed tower and two figurative panels depicting technology and the arts. The terracotta continues as an ornate frieze inside the entrance hall, while the stairwell has a glazed brick dado.

BOWNESS-ON-WINDERMERE

The arts and crafts house **Blackwell** (1900) stands about a mile and a half south of Bowness on the B5360, well above Windermere. It was the holiday home of Manchester brewer Sir Edward Holt, for whom it was designed by the architect M. H. Baillie Scott. The interior was intended by Scott to be a work of art in itself, and to this end great care was taken with the detailing, down to door furniture, light fittings and of course fireplaces, whose tiling was an integral part of the colour scheme. One of the three delft tiled fireplaces is in the dining room; its extraordinarily massive surround is of slate and sandstone sections (all the delft tiles are probably by Ravesteijn of Utrecht). In addition there are seven fireplaces with a few decorated but mostly plain tiles from William De Morgan's Sands End Pottery. The house was restored for use as an art centre during 1999-2001, since when it has been open to the public.

CARLISLE

Henry VIII would not be disappointed with the current appearance of his Citadel, the twin-towered guardian of the south-east gateway to Carlisle. The king modernised the castle (half a mile north-west on the bank of the Eden) and built the Citadel in 1541-3; Sir Robert Smirke completed modifications to the Citadel in 1812, creating circular assize court rooms in the castellated towers. Their monumentality still humbles mere passengers arriving at the railway station in COURT SQUARE, whose east side is occupied by the **Lakes Court Hotel** (originally the County Hotel), which owes its origins to the railway. The railway came to Carlisle in 1836, but the station - which became the terminus for seven railway companies - was built in 1847-8 by Sir

William Tite. The gently italianate hotel appears to have been started in 1852 and is usually credited to Anthony Salvin; further building work was done in 1866-8. The major tile features of the building are the broad frieze of geometrics high on the tower and the tiled window reveals using enamelled encaustic tiles. The latter use of tiling is rare in Britain, although much commoner in southern Europe; the encaustic tiles, which feature much bright yellow in their design, are probably by Minton.

Just across BOTCHERGATE is the **County Hotel**, formerly the Red Lion, a complex building erected during 1885-1900. An elegant, electric blue tile-lined lightwell in the inner foyer (perhaps by Burmantofts) does not prepare one for the stunning former dining room (1893-6), where a Burmantofts ceramic coffered ceiling hovers above two identical ceramic fireplaces, both complete with bevelled mirrors, and a ceramic doorcase with a red lion motif. The corner of the building facing the Citadel, known as **1 Botchergate**, is dated externally 1885; this originally formed a sumptuous entrance to the hotel (Fig 22). Indeed it is a room fit for a queen, and was intended for the use of Queen Victoria when breaking her journey to Balmoral. Its exquisite Burmantofts interior, complete with ceramic ceiling and pale blue dragon frieze, was revealed again in its full glory after a conservation project which began in 1995 and was carried out by the Jackfield Conservation Studio and the Decorative Tile Works.

Overpainting and damage necessitated the manufacture of at least seven different types of replacement wall tiles, while the ceiling (held in a mahogany framework) also required reconstruction. The large ceiling tiles, with a compex yellow and green rose and thistle design unique to Botchergate, were originally made in five pieces. It seems likely that Burmantofts produced the dining room ceiling after learning from the experience of constructing and installing the ceiling in the hotel entrance; the dining room ceiling is completely ceramic and uses smaller tiles, thus avoiding the difficulties inherent in fitting large, heavy tiles into a wooden framework. The Café Solo now occupies 1 Botchergate, and the glistening pale blue and cream wall tiles along with numerous figurative relief panels (including the *Seasons*) and the magnificent ceiling make for an atmospheric and surprisingly delicate interior.

Head west towards English Street and the market place, then left over the railway tracks on the Victoria Viaduct, built in 1877 by the council and the railway companies in order to connect the city centre and the western suburbs. This leads into JAMES STREET and **The Pools**, a swimming pool complex with that rarity, a completely tiled turkish bath (now known as the Victorian Health Suite). The five rooms of varying temperature, which include a plunge pool, were added to the main baths complex of 1883-4 in 1909.[1] The ceramic facing is in shades of green and white, the most striking elements of this beguiling interior being the striped, moorish-style keyhole arch and curious capitals; this is a remarkable survivor (Fig 23). The ceramics manufacturers may have been Craven Dunnill, who were the leading suppliers of ceramics for turkish baths, or possibly Pilkington's. Potential visitors to The Pools should note that Sunday is normally the sole day for mixed bathing, the remainder of the week being divided into gents days and ladies days.

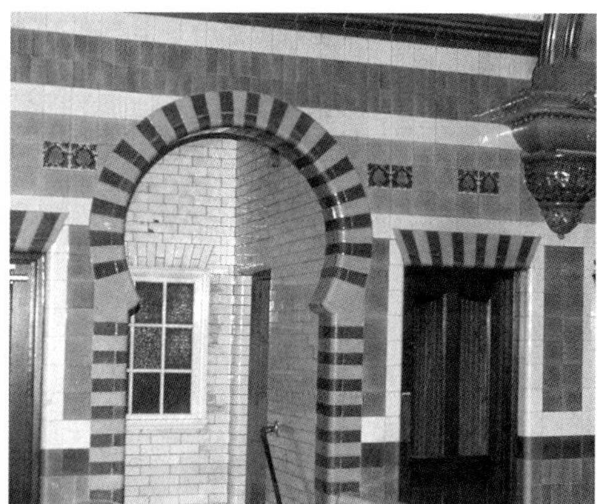

Fig 23.

Return to the city centre then turn left into CASTLE STREET to reach **Tullie House Museum and Art Gallery**, a combination of Old Tullie House (1689), which was bought for the city around 1890, and its extension of 1892-3, designed by the architect C. J. Ferguson. The building opened as a museum in 1893. A Craven Dunnill tiled staircase dado, in olive green relief moulded tiles with a colourful decorative frieze, runs throughout most of the museum; this dates from the 1892-3 works. In addition, a robust tile and faience fireplace can be found in the room adjacent to the tearoom. A more modern extension to the museum is commemorated in the new entrance: a ceramic wall plaque designed and made by Paul Scott, showing delicate black and white images relating to the museum, records the opening of the new building by the Queen on the 3rd May 1991.

Now to the **Civic Centre** in RICKERGATE for an architectural treat. At first glance this is simply an anonymous 1960s office block, but the unusual octagonal protrusion on its southern flank gives a clue as to its purpose. The search for a unified administrative building had begun in 1914, but war and land shortages delayed progress until an architectural competition was held in 1956-7. It was won by Charles B. Pearson & Partners, and the Civic Centre finally opened in 1964.[2] Entering the building is what might be termed an Alice in Cumberland experience: much of the internal wall surfaces are faced with small panels of rustic abstract mock brown stone, while unsupported stairways criss-cross upward and the airy, double-height rates hall has white mushroom columns reminiscent of the Johnson Wax Building. The first floor is stranger still, with a reception room where an unbelievable pendant ceiling shelters behind a moorish-style latticework screen, while the council chamber (in the isolated octagon, of course) has a back-lit fibrous plasterwork panel by T. F. Copplestone showing local scenes. The street entrance to the council chamber is via a stairwell lined with a dramatic abstract tile mural by Pilkington's. It stretches vertically over two floors and uses mainly bright purple and green tiles, with a pattern of white circles exploding away from an off-centre group of coloured squares, the whole perhaps symbolising the growth of the city. This excellent building with its fine sixties decorative art deserves wider appreciation.

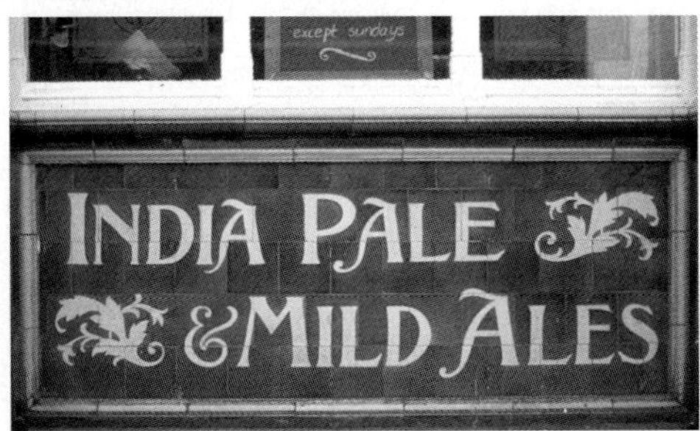

Fig 24.

Return to the city centre along LOWTHER STREET, passing the yellow and green Doulton faience and tile facade of the **Howard Arms**, which advertises 'India Pale and Mild Ales', 'Lager Beer & Stout' and 'Wines Spirits & Liqueurs' (Fig 24). The Doulton signature is at the bottom right, close to 'Liqueurs'. Off to the left (via Victoria Place) is CHATSWORTH SQUARE, where **Red Gables** - on the south corner with Currie Street - displays bright red external terracotta by Burmantofts, including massed panels of sunflowers and high-relief fruit. There is more terracotta further east at 161-3 WARWICK ROAD, where two terrace houses have red terracotta plaques, showing sunflowers in a vase, between ground and first floor windows. Almost back in the centre, the **White House**, Warwick Road is a Spanish-style pub (originally the Crescent) built in 1932 and designed by Harry Redfern; it sports Medmenham tiles in a foyer frieze and two fire surrounds on the first floor.

GREYSTOKE

Behind the drab curtains which hide the east wall inside **St Andrew's Church**, all is tiles, and very strange they are. A frieze of deep relief tiles, bearing a biblical quotation, runs along the top; its colours are mostly yellow and a bright pink. Below is mainly darker geometric tiling, but stretching across the width of the altar is an area of small tiles with a floral motif. In the middle of these floral tiles is a colourful mosaic panel surrounding a circular gold-coloured metal boss with a jewel-like hemisphere of coloured glass at its centre. This unusual and attractive piece was probably installed during the 1848 restoration of the chancel by Henry Howard of Greystoke Castle, where the architect Anthony Salvin had just completed work.

KENDAL

In the ELEPHANT YARD shopping centre is a large Ruabon tile panel by the ceramicist Maggie Angus Berkowitz showing images of Kendal and its twin town, Rinteln, which is in north-west Germany. Berkowitz was also responsible for the extensive tiled floors in the **Brewery Arts Centre** on nearby HIGHGATE. East of the town centre, at the coffee shop of the **Abbot Hall Art Gallery** (in the ladies' toilet), is an attractive tile panel entitled *Venice* (1963) by Diana Braithwaite. Additionally, several good examples of ornate Victorian chimney pots may be found in Kendal.

KESWICK

The **Theatre by the Lake**, LAKESIDE, opened in 1999, replacing the 'blue box' Century Theatre which had served the town since 1975; inside are six high-fired porcelain panels by Paul Scott. The theme of the distinctive blue-framed panels celebrates the theatre's history and setting, with imagery in painted and printed under-glaze colour. The transparent glaze was fired to 1,200°C.

MARYPORT

In the centre of Maryport is the excellent tiled facade of **Gearing's** butcher's shop (currently vacant). The stall riser sports twin bull's heads and chequerwork borders, while the porch tiles include a larger bull's head within an ornate golden wreath, set above a pretty blue and white 16-tile panel of grazing sheep; the latter is signed 'W. Lambert, 1904'. Unusually, assorted fowl are portrayed on another panel; most of the decoration is underglaze. The artist was probably William Lambert, who was taken on by the Lancaster stained glass firm Shrigley & Hunt in the mid-1870s to oversee their tile department, but left in 1891 to establish a rival stained glass firm and went bankrupt in 1895.[3] W. Lambert is known to have painted two large tile panels in 1896 on Wooliscroft tiles, so it is possible that the butcher's shop panels were also manufactured by George Wooliscroft and Sons.[4]

MILNTHORPE

The polygonal stone box of the **R. C. Church of Christ the King**, HAVERFLATTS LANE, holds all manner of wonders executed by the Polish-born artist Adam Kossowski (1905-86). The most dramatic is his irregularly-shaped ceramic mural of the *Way of the Cross* (1971), linking the twelve Stations of the Cross in one long, complex figurative composition. There is also a ceramic plaque of Our Lady (1970) and another representing *Christ the King* (1970), the latter a welcoming figure on the outer wall near the broad doorway (Fig 25). Kossowski's *Way of the Cross* is one of his most powerful expressions of the Stations of the Cross, which he produced in various forms for several other churches.[5]

ROSLEY

Rosley Church of England Primary School stands in a delightful rural setting opposite Holy Trinity Church (1841); the school was built in 1960-61. A tile panel showing a female figure is to the left of the entrance, its date and artist unknown. In the school hall is a map-like, irregular porcelain mural made by pupils, staff, parents and other members of the local community in autumn 1996, designed and supervised by Paul Scott. Individual elements of the panel show local scenes and activities.

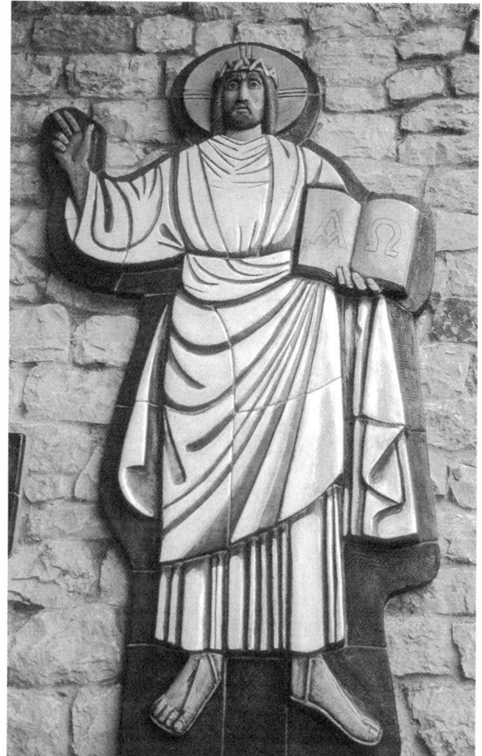

Fig 25.

ST BEES

The present **Priory Church of St Mary and St Bega** dates from its refoundation in the twelfth century, although its chancel is almost wholly Butterfield, with a superb decorative scheme which suits the strengths of church, its colours strong but spare. William Butterfield carried out the bulk of the restoration work around 1855-71, although his majestic and brightly coloured ironwork screen dates from 1886. There are some delightful Minton encaustic tiles in the chancel: a series of 36-tile red and yellow panels in the choir, then black and yellow zigzag risers, with more patterned tiles in the sanctuary and two thin bands of wall tiles running around the east end. The patterned tiles, including a fleur-de-lys with serrated border, have a majolica glaze over their white inlay, suggesting a date of 1845-55. This would be possible if the tiles had been installed during the early part of the restoration work, or reserved until the chancel restoration, which appears to date from 1867-9. Their overall effect is one of delicacy and elegance in the context of a powerful polychromatic scheme.

Cumbria Roundup

St Mary's Church, **Ambleside**, was built in 1850-4 by Sir George Gilbert Scott; Herbert Minton donated tiles for its chancel pavement in 1853. Appleby War Memorial Swimming Pool, Chapel Street, **Appleby**, has a large pictorial tile panel (1995) by Maggie Angus Berkowitz. In the Parish Room (formerly village school) at **Blencogo** is an early community mural by Paul Scott. Eighteenth century English tin-glazed tiles line the sides of a fireplace at the Wordsworth House (NT), Main Street, **Cockermouth**; the house was William Wordsworth's birthplace. St Andrew's Church, **Coniston** dates from the sixteenth century, although its chancel was added in 1891, when the Maw & Co tiling was also installed. The medieval church of St Lawrence, **Crosby Ravensworth** has a complex building history; its south chapel, separated from the body of the church by a wooden screen, dates from the nineteenth century and includes Minton tiling. Remote St Paul's Church, **Irton** (NY 091005) has an expansive view of Wasdale Head; the church, which has interesting stained glass, was built in 1857 but the Maw & Co nave tile pavement (which includes a single memorial tile) dates from the 1887 works undertaken in celebration of the Queen's golden jubilee. The entrance of Burlington Slate Limited's head office Cavendish House, **Kirkby-in-Furness**, has a 1982 tile panel by Maggie Angus Berkowitz entitled *Riving Slate, Elterwater Quarry*; its rich appearance was achieved by outlining the figures in black then building up the colours with layers of multi-fired glazes. At **Seascale** School is a ceramic mural created in 1996 by pupils under the guidance of Paul Scott; it shows the history of Seascale. Clayton's the butcher's in Crescent Road, **Windermere** has a complete tiled interior (probably interwar) although no picture panels; its tiled stall riser bears the shop name.

References

1. Marcus Binney, Hana Laing and Alastair Laing, *Taking the Plunge: The architecture of bathing* (Save Britain's Heritage, London, 1981), p22
2. 'Civic Centre', *Architects' Journal*, 141 (1965) 15, pp883-898
3. William Waters, *Stained Glass from Shrigley & Hunt of Lancaster and London* (Centre for North-West Regional Studies, University of Lancaster, Lancaster, 2003), pp25-7
4. *TACS Tour Notes: South-East London Adventure*, (1998)
5. *Adam Kossowski: Murals and Paintings*, (Armelle Press, London, 1990)

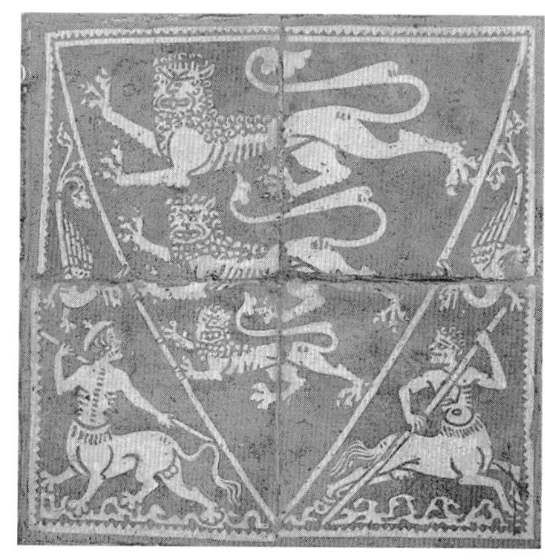

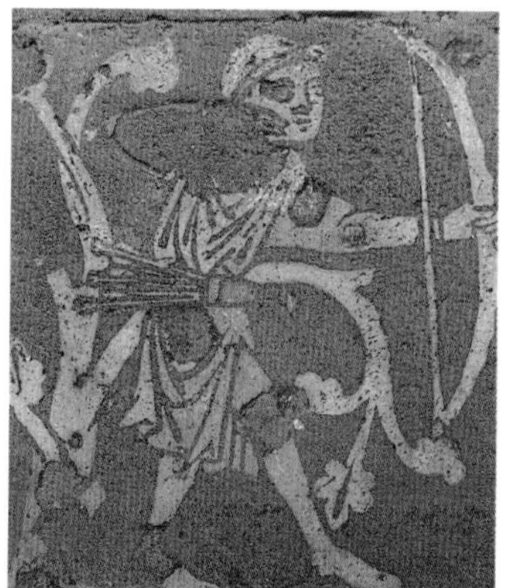

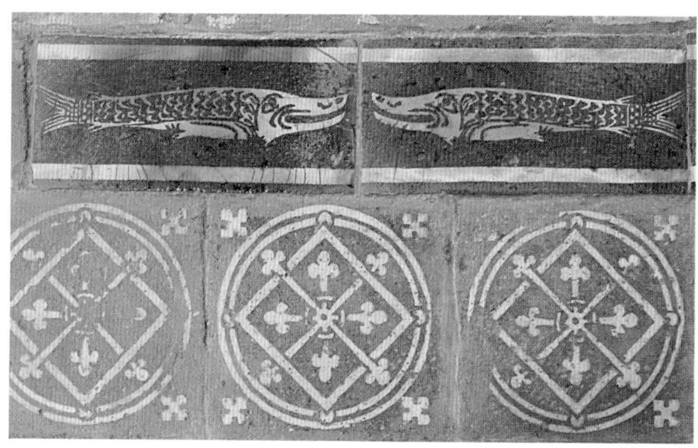

Thirteenth century tile pavement, Chapter House, Westminster Abbey, London.

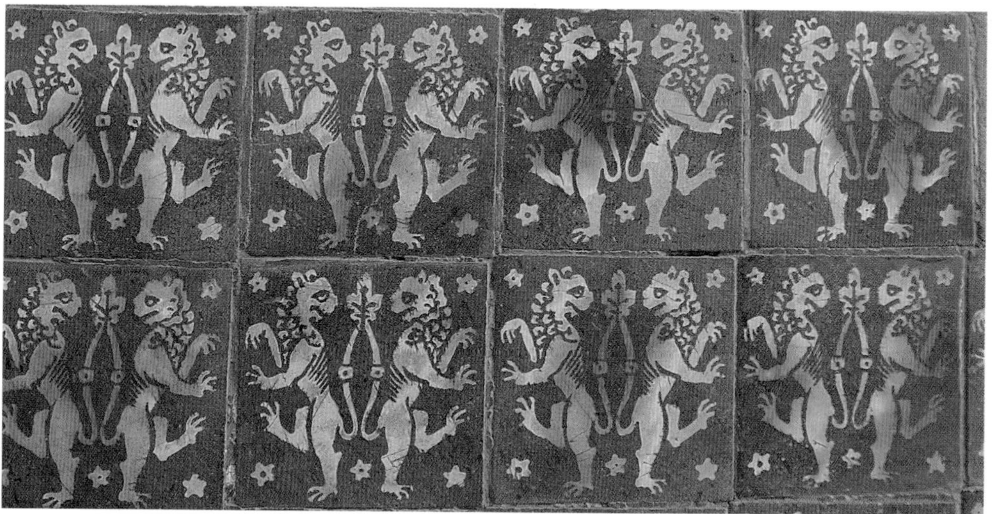

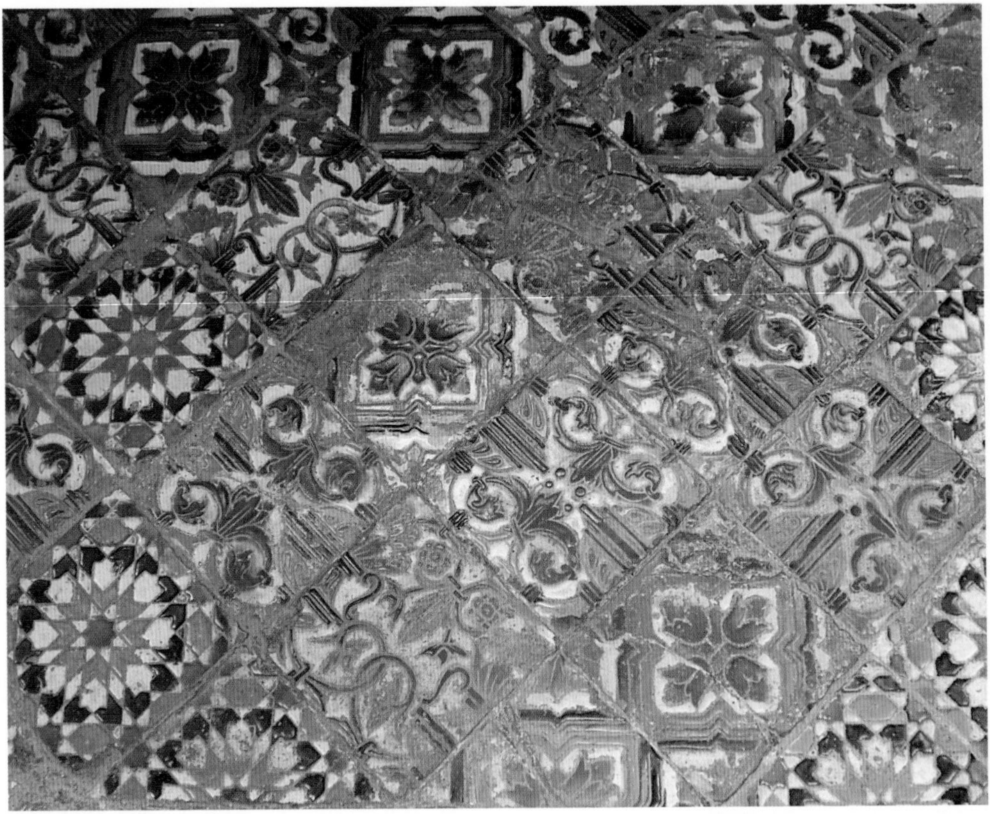

Sixteenth century pavement, Lord Mayor's Chapel, Bristol, Gloucestershire.

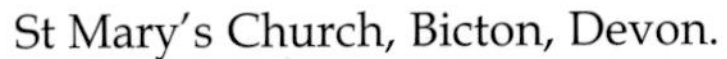

St Mary's Church, Bicton, Devon.

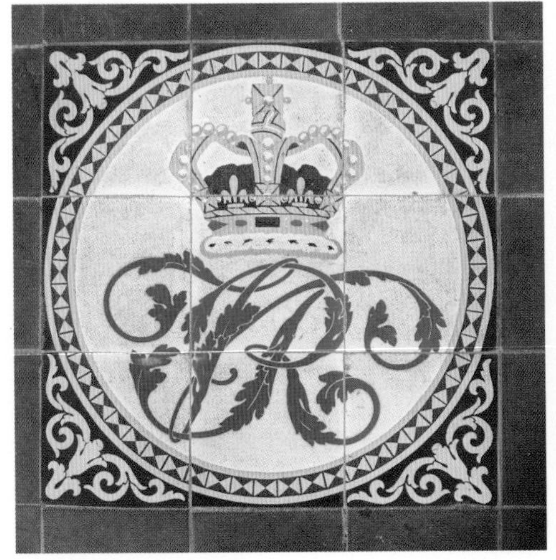

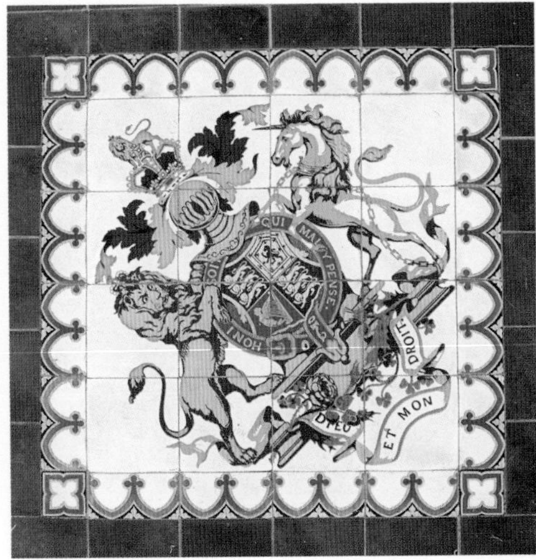

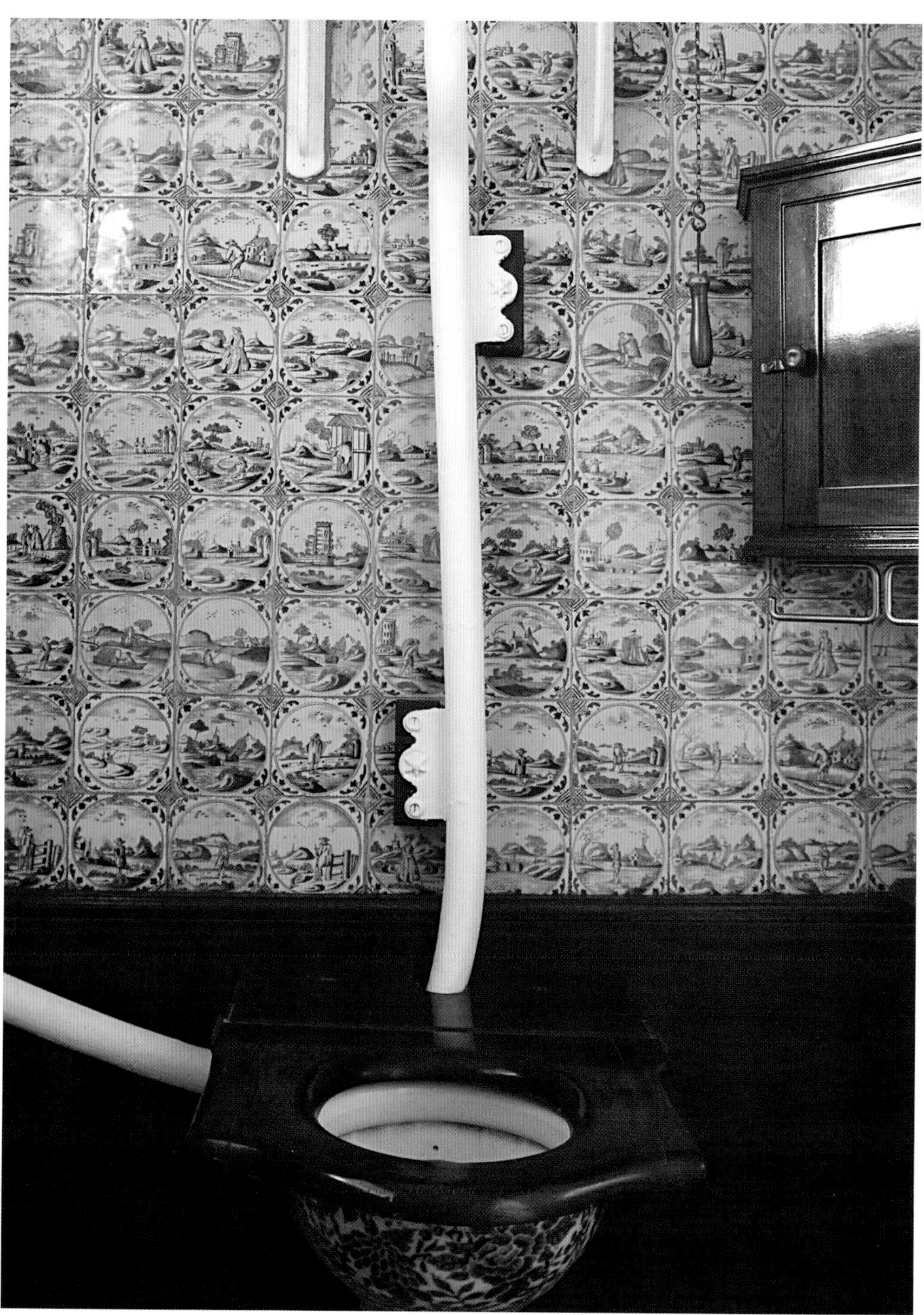
Commissioner's House, Chatham, Kent.

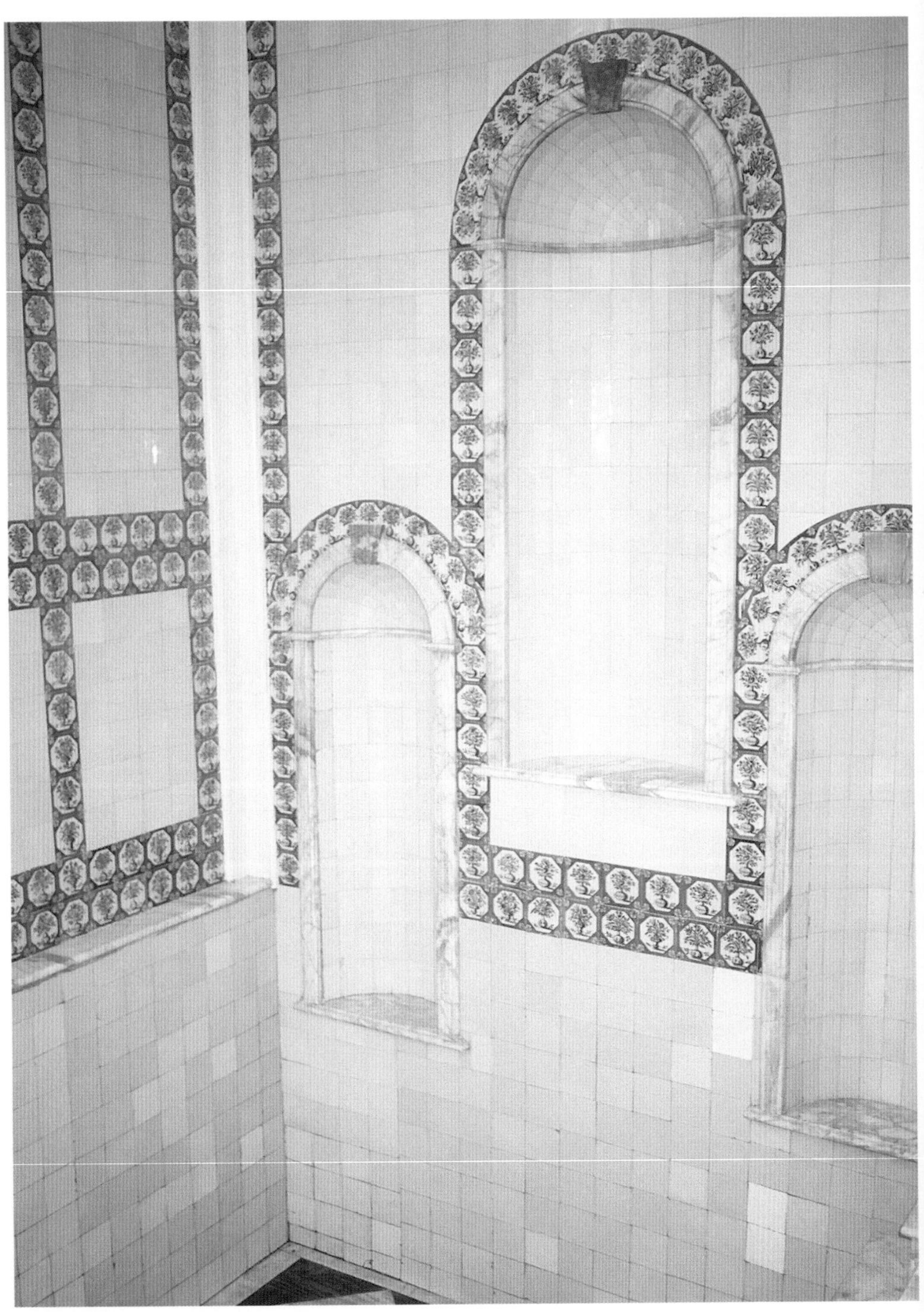

Water Tower, Carshalton, Sutton, London.

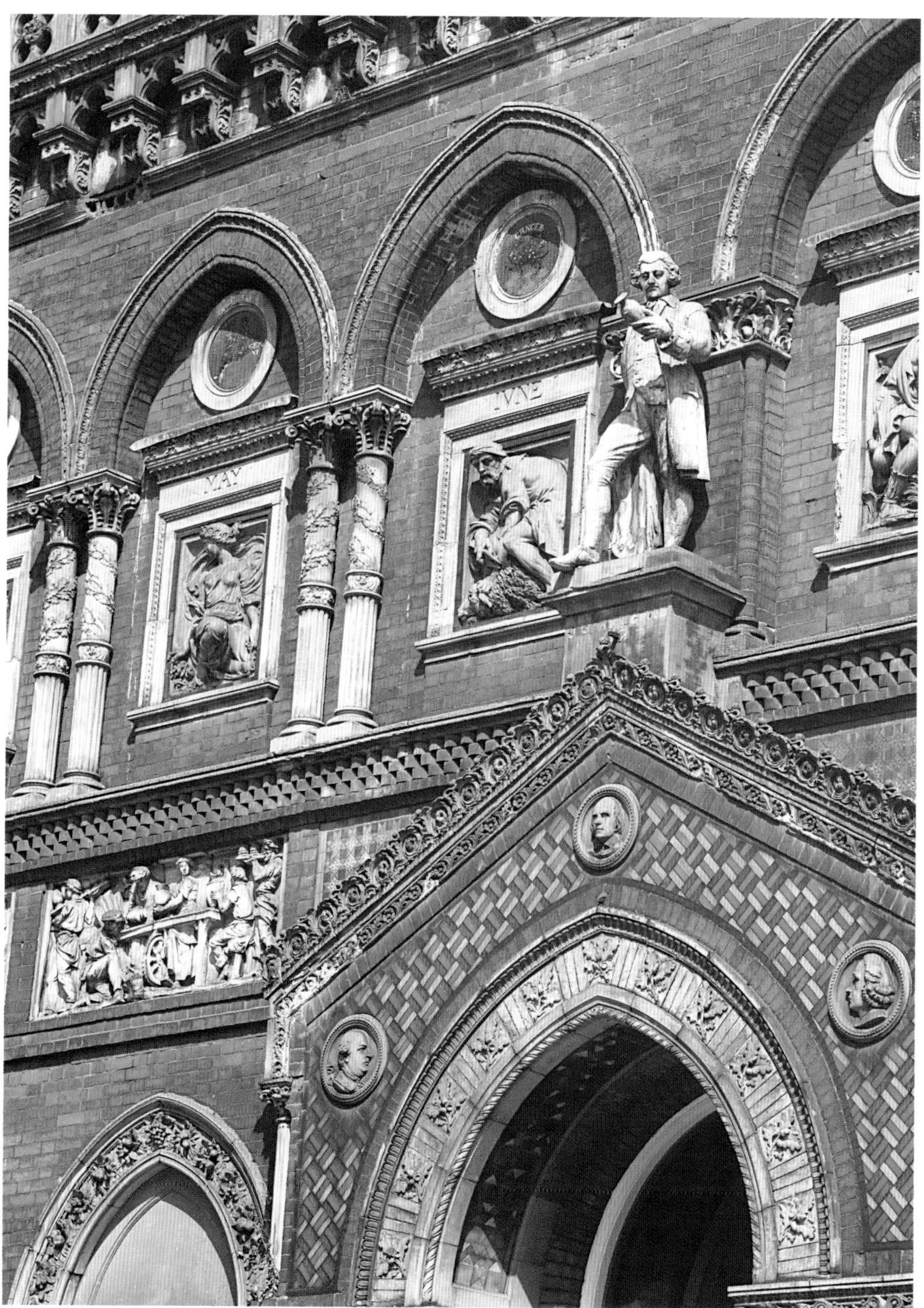

Wedgwood Memorial Institute, Burslem, Stoke-on-Trent, Staffordshire.

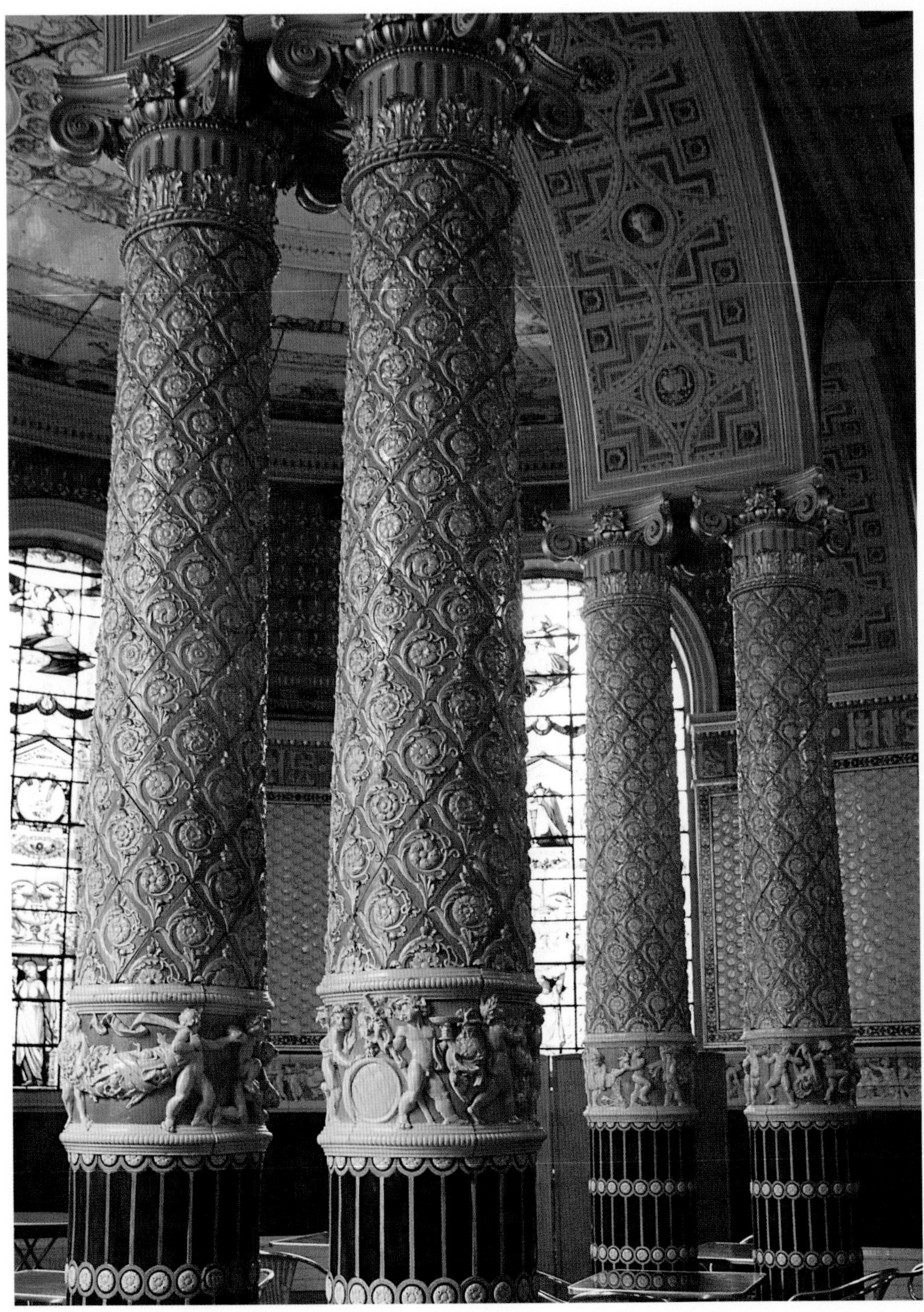

Centre Refreshment Room, V&A Museum, Kensington & Chelsea, London.

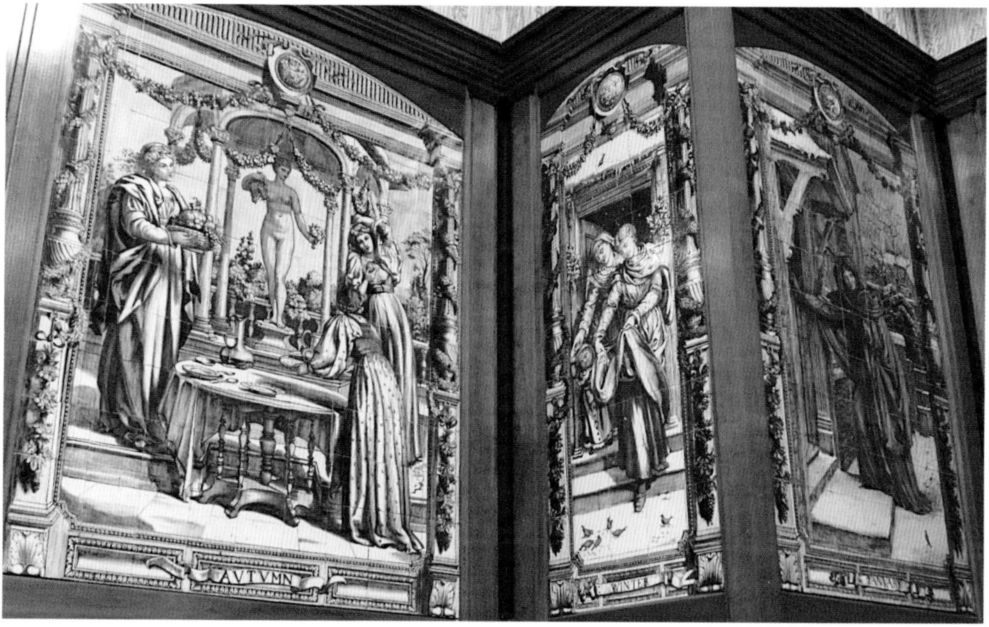

Grill Room, V&A Museum, Kensington & Chelsea, London.

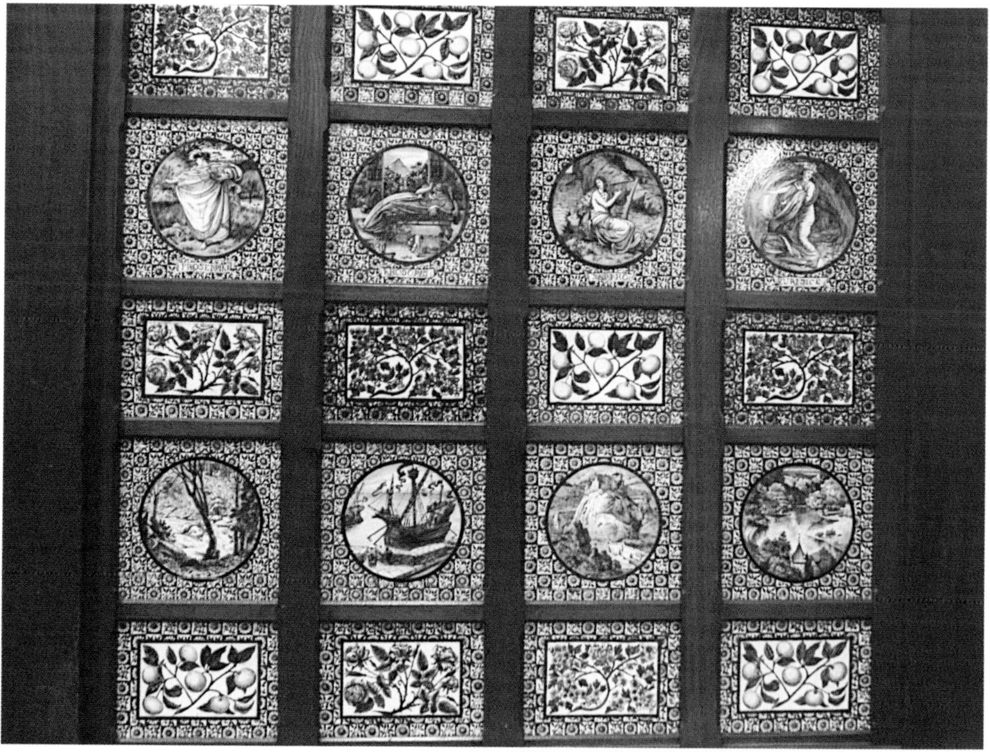

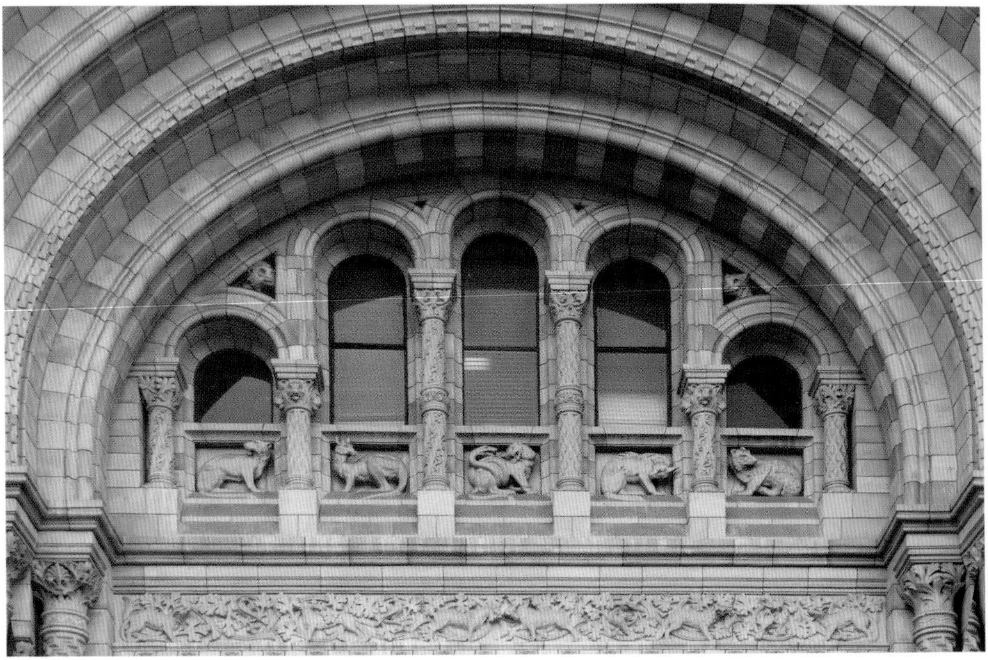

Natural History Museum, Kensington & Chelsea, London.

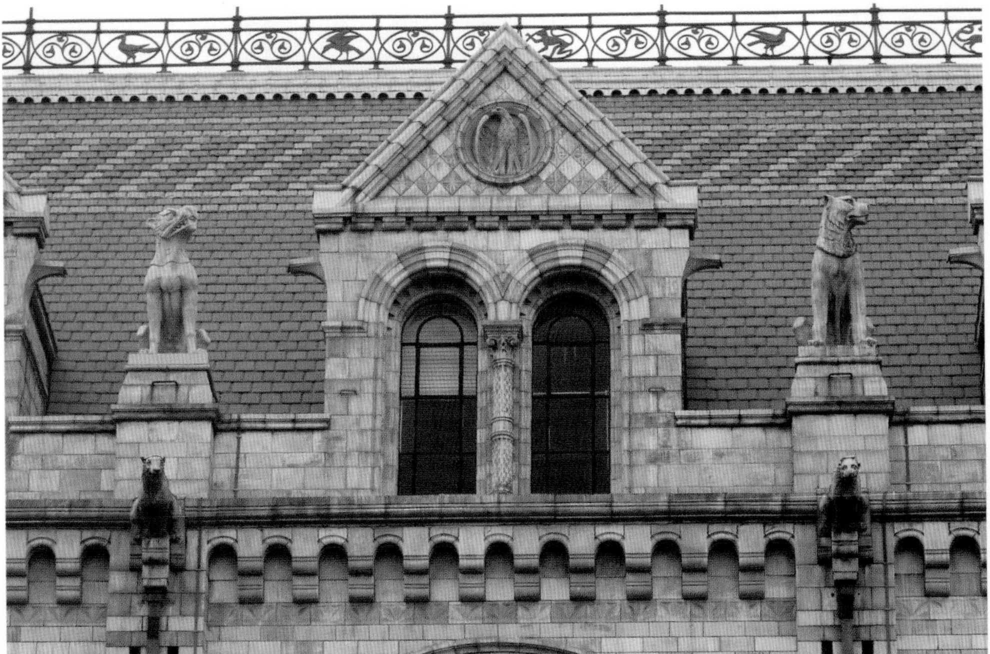

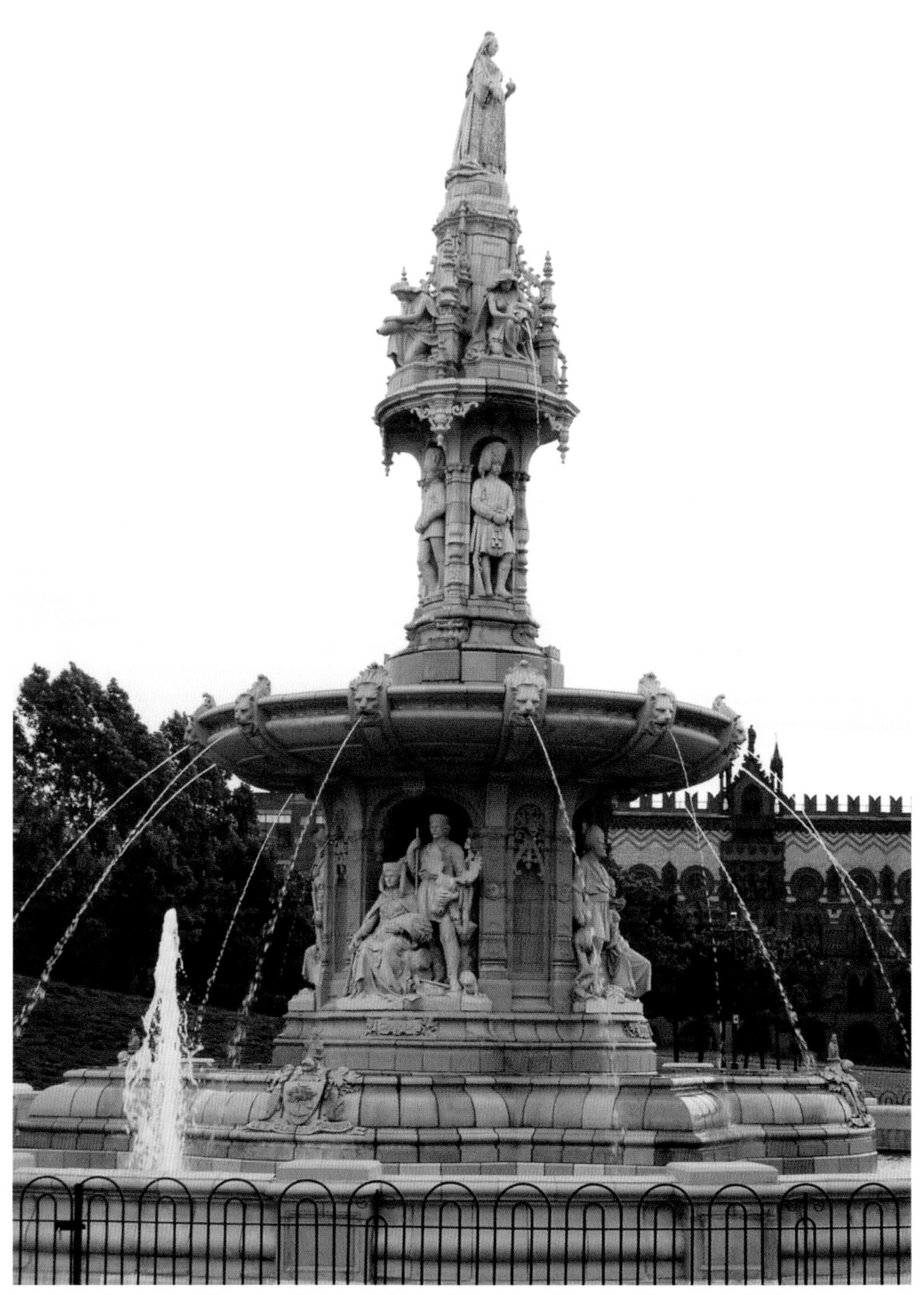

Doulton Fountain, Glasgow Green, with the Templeton Business Centre in the background.

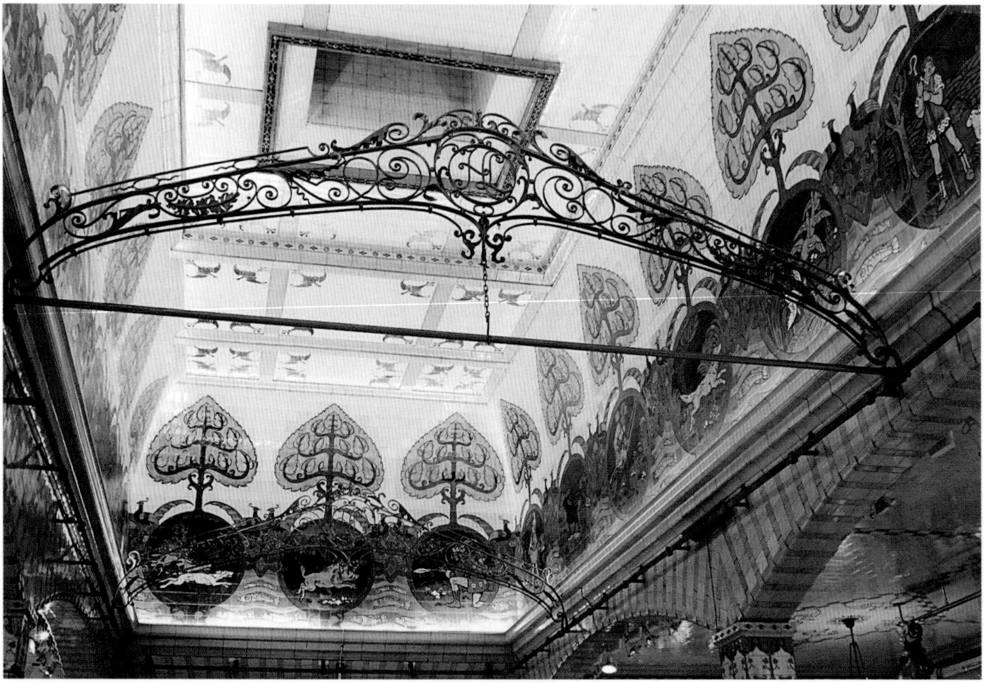

Meat Hall, Harrods, Kensington & Chelsea, London.

Arab Hall, Leighton House, Kensington & Chelsea, London.

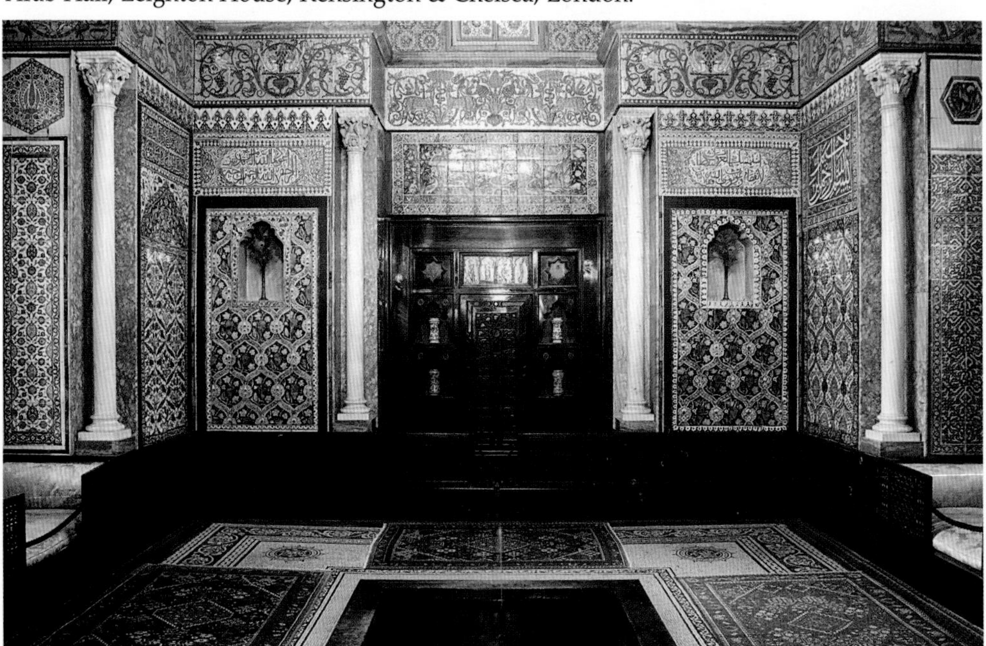

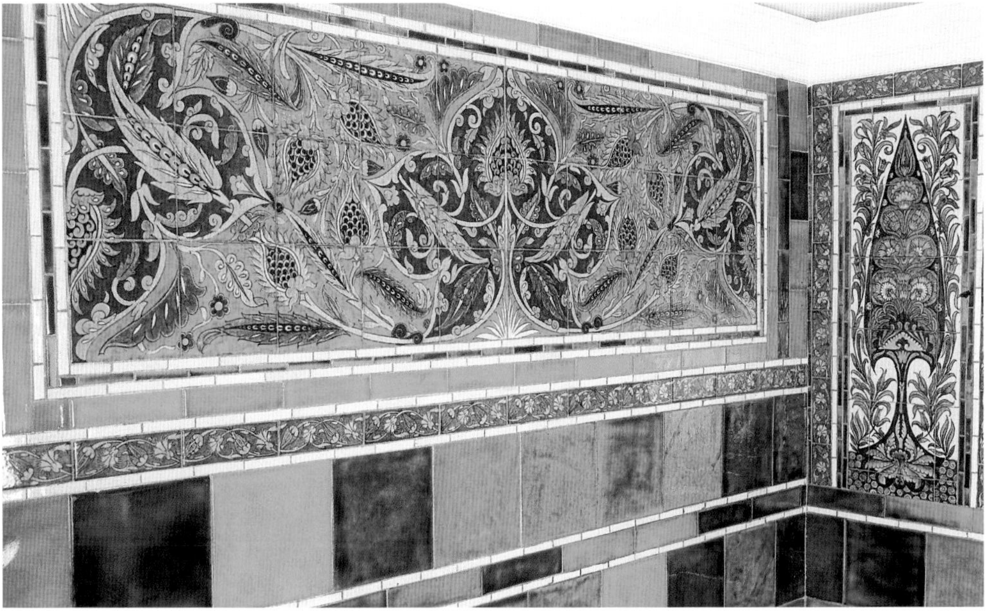

Debenham House, Kensington & Chelsea, London.

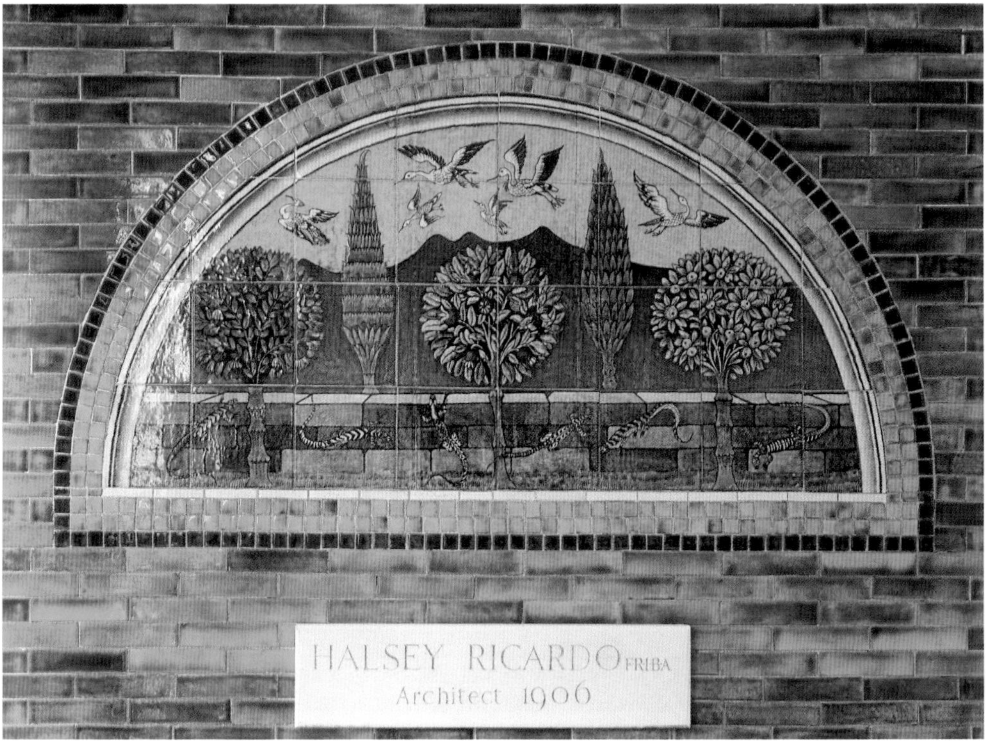

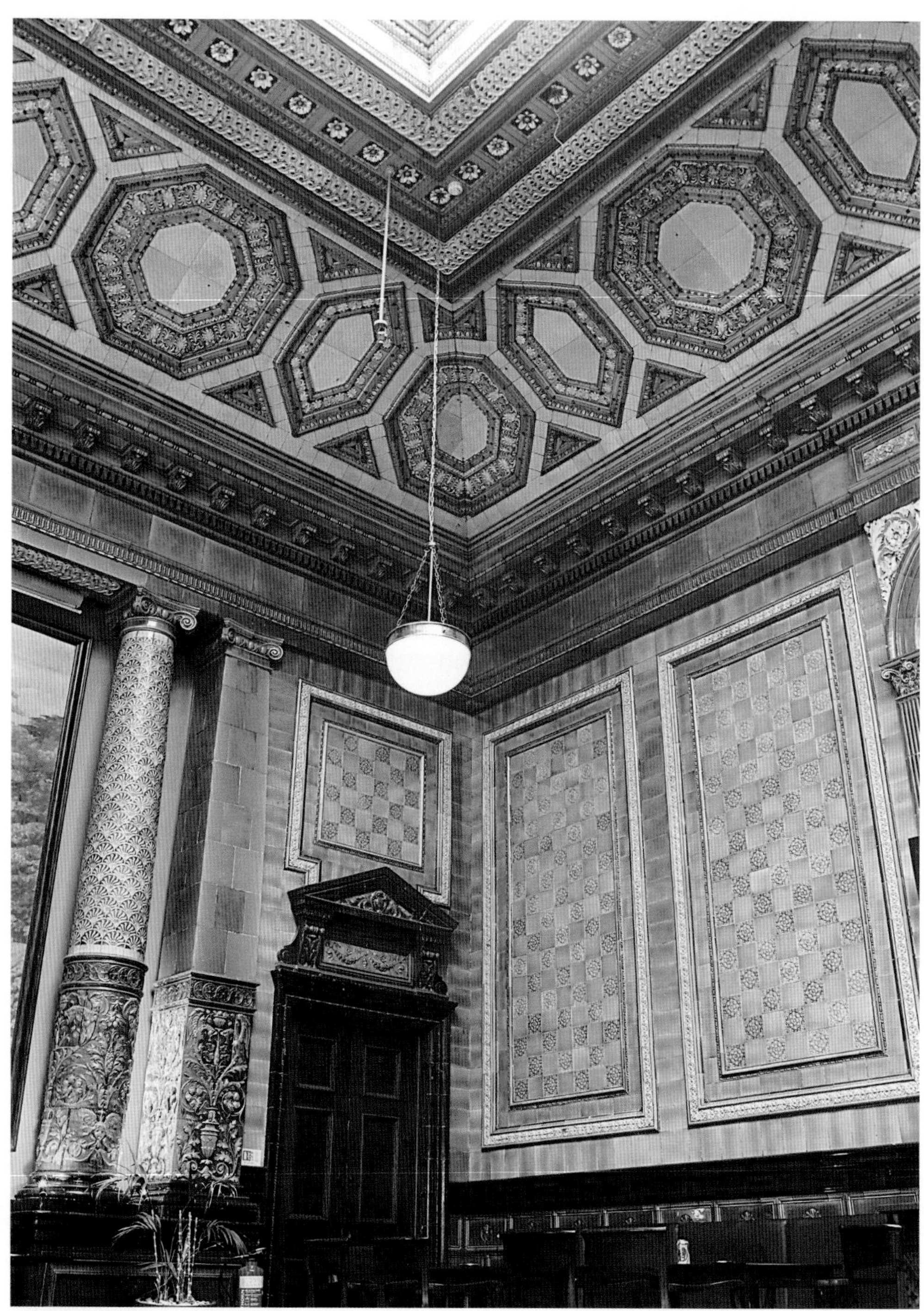

Centurion Bar, Central Station, Newcastle upon Tyne, Northumberland.

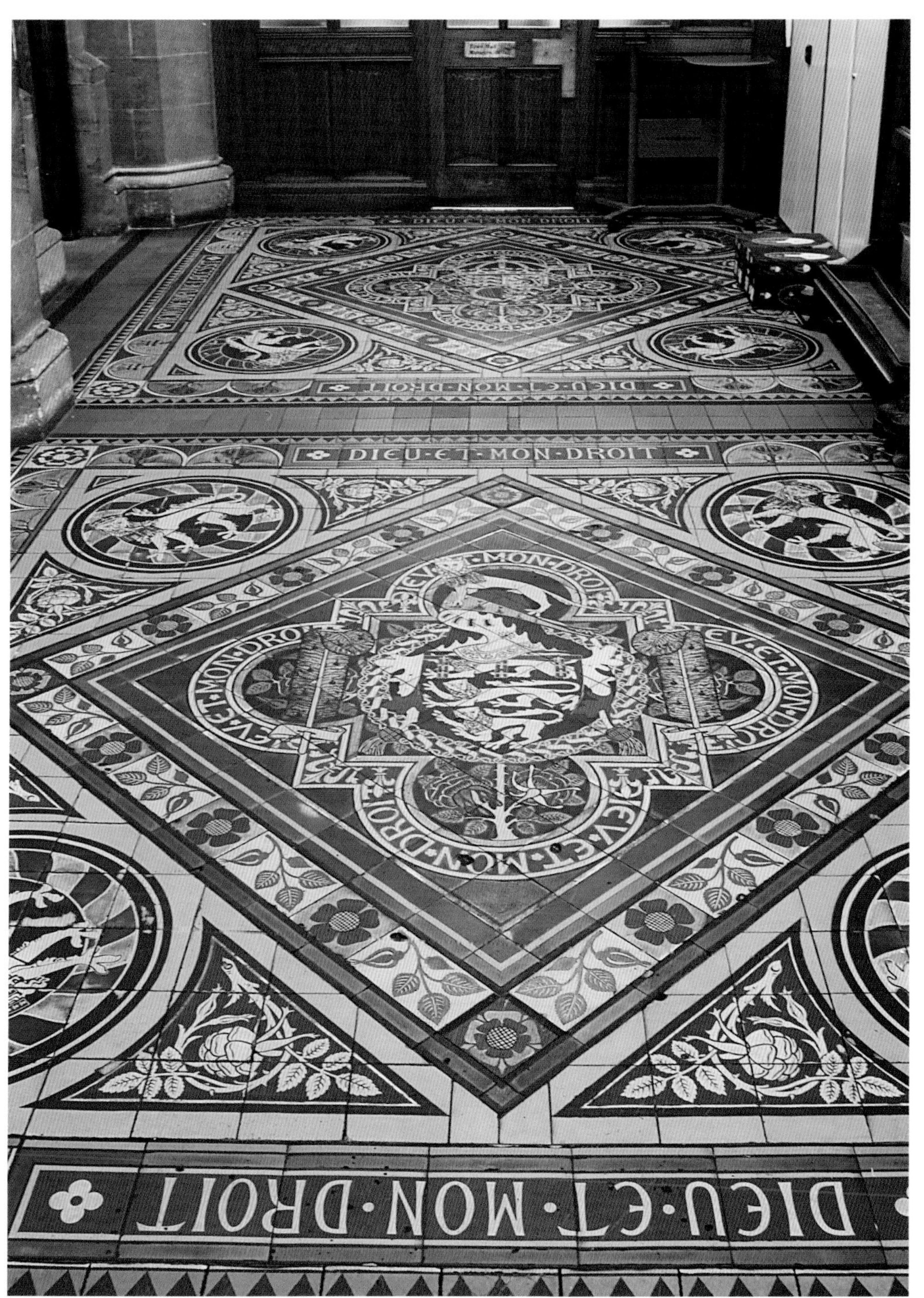

Town Hall, Rochdale, Lancashire.

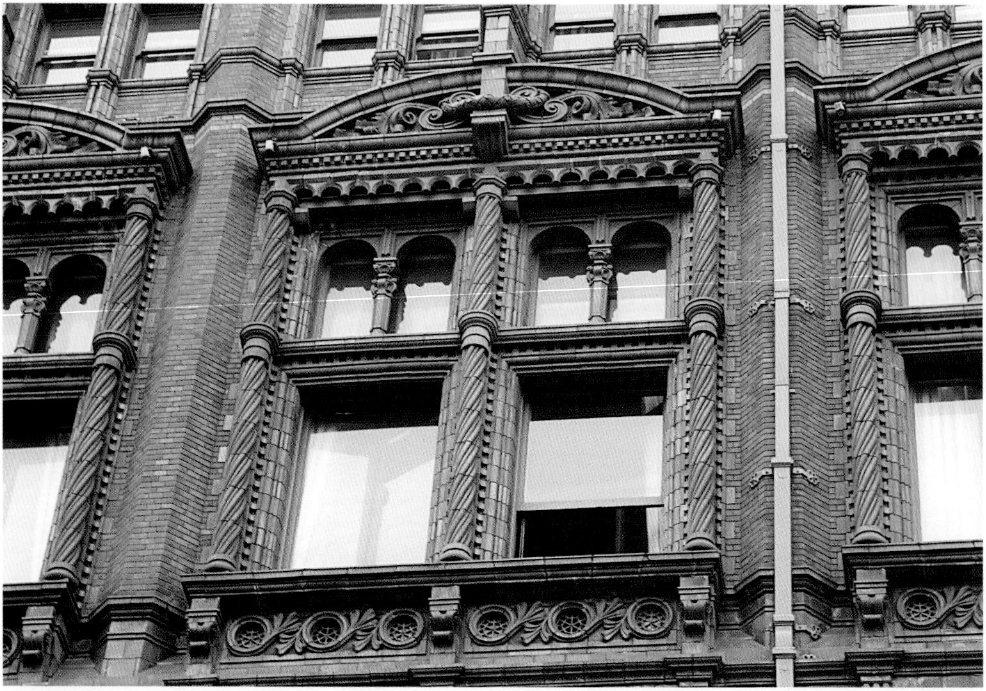

Palace Hotel (Refuge Assurance Building), Manchester, Lancashire.

Central Arcade, Newcastle upon Tyne, Northumberland.

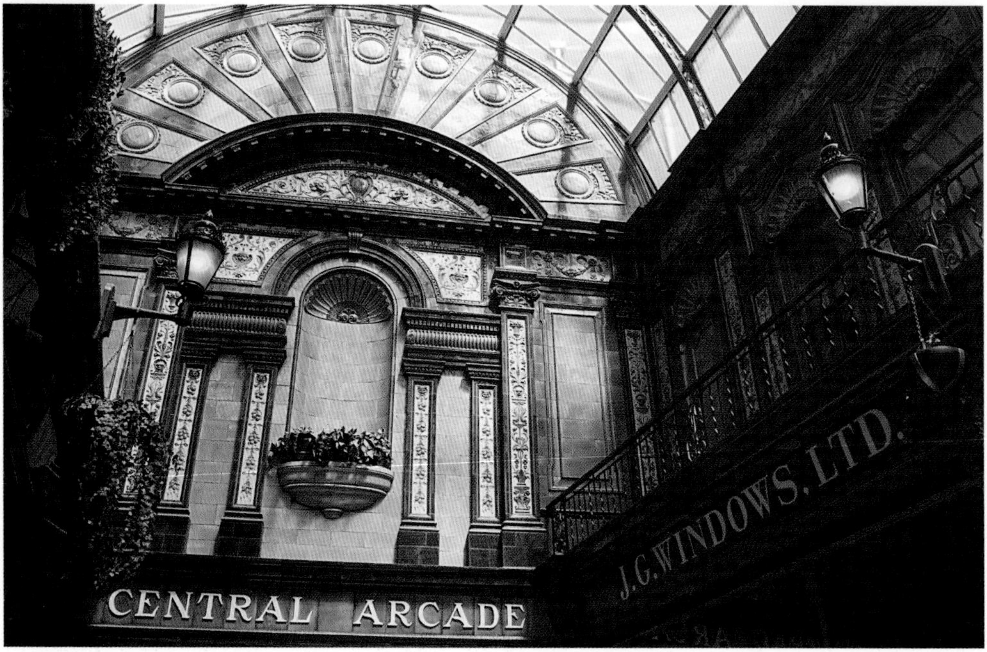

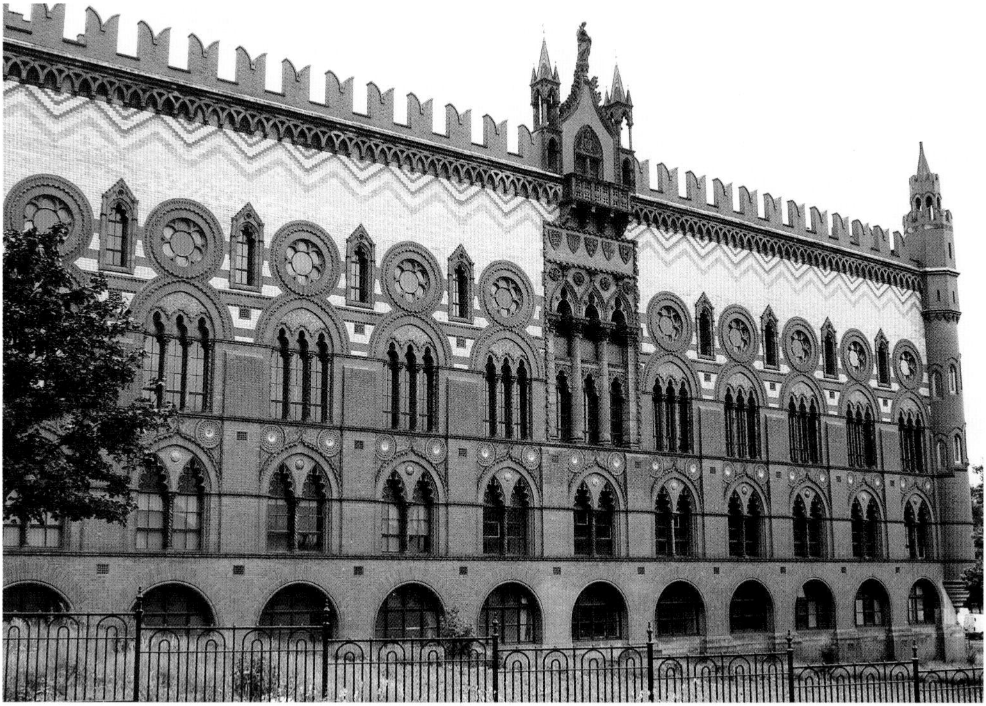

Templeton Business Centre, Glasgow Green.

Mountain Daisy Public House, Sunderland, County Durham.

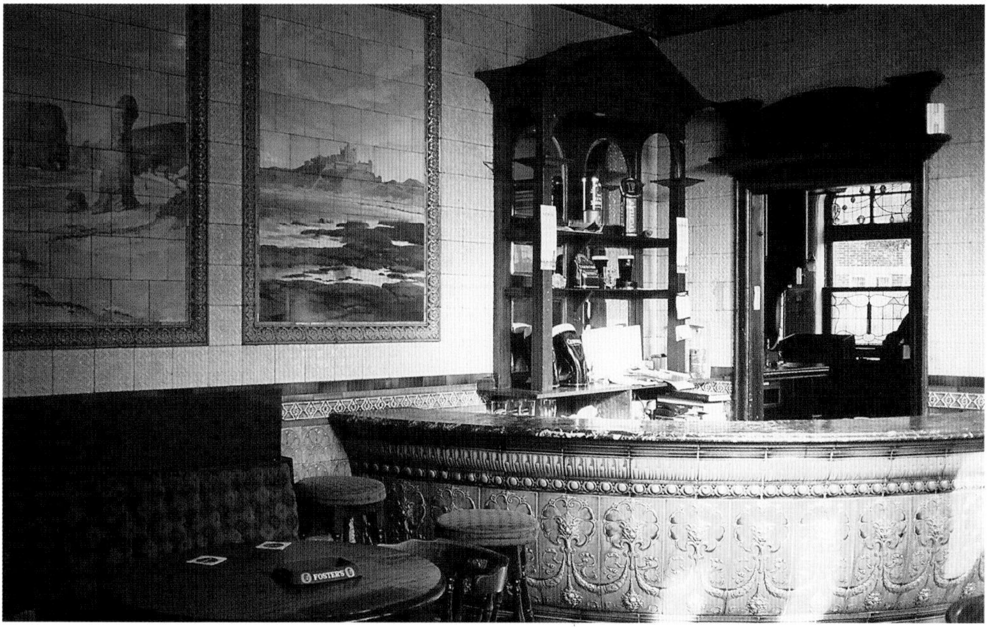

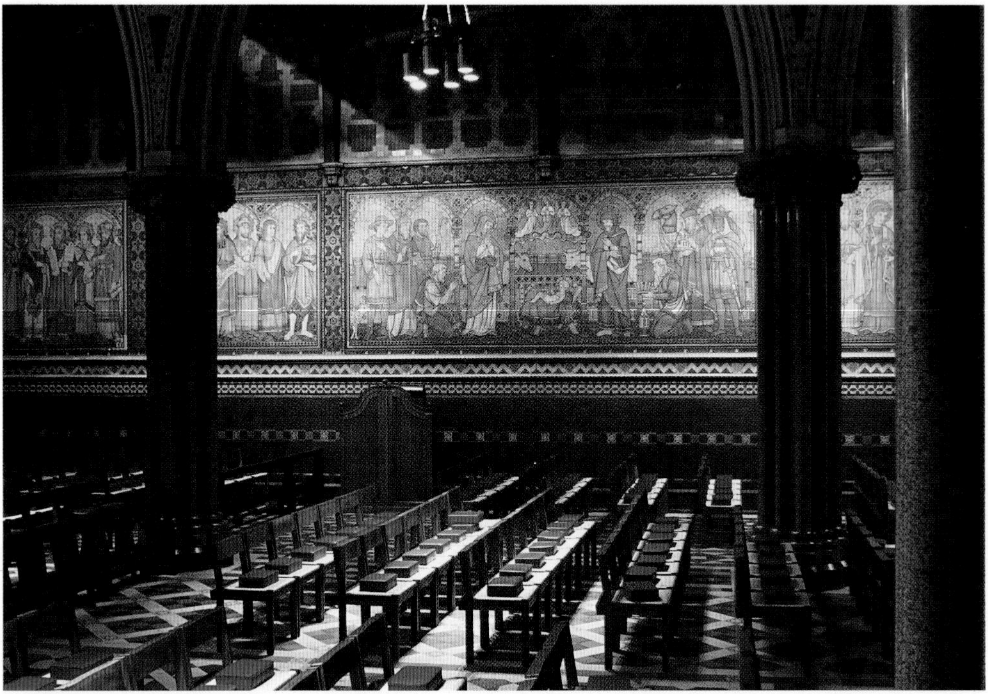

All Saints Church, Margaret Street, Westminster, London.

Doulton House, Lambeth, London.

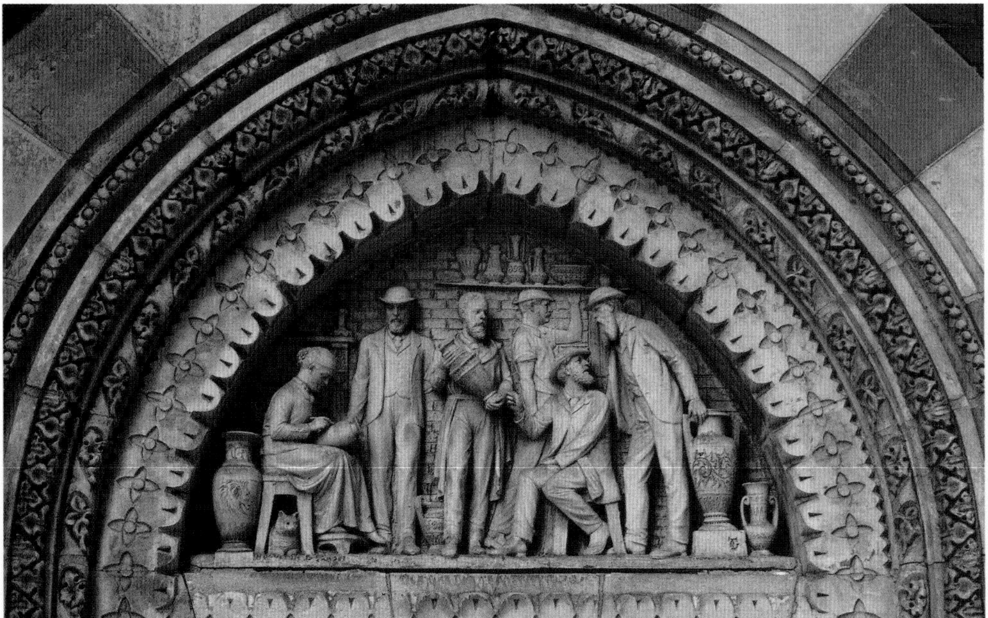

Derbyshire

Tiles from Derbyshire's medieval tilery at Dale Abbey have survived in situ at a few locations, notably Morley church, and have provided exemplars for tile pavements installed during late nineteenth-century restoration of several churches, for instance Ashbourne. Churches provide the bulk of the county's locations; little, however, remains of the tiling at the half dozen churches to which Herbert Minton donated tiles during the 1840s and 1850s. Major items of interest include the 1920s art deco tile scheme at Buxton's Natural Baths, a completely intact former Lipton's shop in Chesterfield, 'Green Man' tiles by Godwin's at Monyash Church, a Compton Potters' Arts Guild plaque at Tideswell church and a seventeenth-century Flemish tile pavement at Church Wilne church. The *Gazetteer* entry for Derbyshire covers the administrative areas of Derby City Council and Derbyshire County Council.

ASHBOURNE

The tall spire of **St Oswald's Church** dominates the view westward along CHURCH STREET. There has been a church in Ashbourne from Saxon times, but the oldest part of the present structure - best known for its monuments and stained glass - dates from the thirteenth century; its medieval tiles (a few still on display) provided the inspiration for the line-impressed and encaustic tiles installed during George Gilbert Scott's 1876-81 restoration.[1] The sparkling encaustics of the chancel pavement, their yellow glaze protected by being let into the surface of the tiles, have unusual designs including a four-winged butterfly and a pair of long-tailed birds; they were made by the Campbell Brick & Tile Co (Fig 26). Back towards the centre of town (still on Church Street) is the **Methodist Church** (1880), bespattered with buff terracotta roundels, while round the corner in DIG STREET is a shop with a stall riser of brown glazed brick with two four-tile panels in a flower and grape design.

ATLOW

The little church of **St Philip and St James**, built in 1874, has an unexpectedly colourful interior, the highlight of which is a largely blue and white majolica reredos including a fine black-framed plaque of the Holy Lamb by the Campbell Brick & Tile Co. The reredos is topped by biblical quotations, some in plain brown-on-cream letter tiles, others within lavish floral decoration. Decorative tiling also features on the walls, where single tiles are dotted about on contrasting brick and stone bands; there is also a nine-tile group centred on a pelican in its piety. The geometric tile pavement complements the wall tiling but is less ornate.

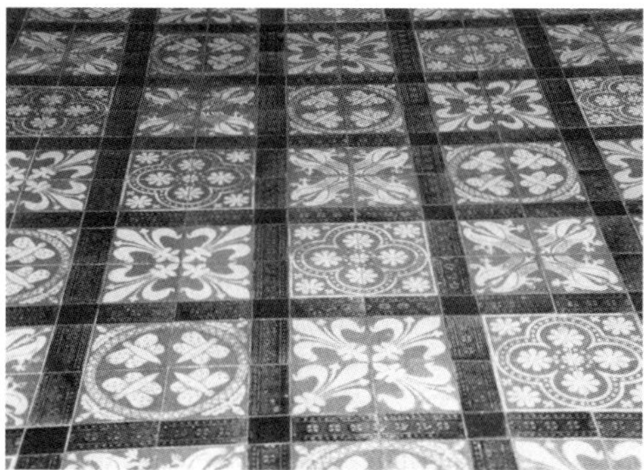

Fig 26.

AULT HUCKNALL

The tiling at **St John's Church**, Ault Hucknall (near Glapwell) was installed during restoration of the church by William Butterfield in 1885-8; the manufacturer was very probably Minton. The sanctuary pavement combines a grey fossil marble with plain tiles in blue (almost turquoise), red, yellow and black as well as buff on red decorative encaustics. Typical Butterfield chevrons in the nave pavement echo the sanctuary wall tiling, in which strings of yellow on red chevron tiles make zig-zag bands; these form the borders to panels displaying the letters alpha and omega.[2]

BUXTON

The **Natural Baths** (1853), just west of THE CRESCENT, lie close to the site of a Roman baths and were designed by the Duke of Devonshire's architect Henry Currey. The gentlemen's baths and the plunge baths were included in the original plan, but all was rebuilt in 1924 when a ladies baths was added. The interior is completely tiled, mainly in white but with coloured friezes carrying classical motifs; the manufacturer was Craven Dunnill. This is an important survival of a major art deco interior tiling scheme, comparable to only a few others remaining in the south-east of England. The Natural Baths have been largely derelict since the 1970s, but are currently the subject of a development proposal intended to transform the structure into a mineral water spa. The nearby **Cavendish Arcade**, at the east end of The Crescent, was created in the mid 1980s from the Hot Baths. Most of its heavily moulded faience decoration, which probably dates from the late nineteenth century, was preserved in the conversion, although some replication was involved.

CHATSWORTH

The Oak Room, created around 1840 at **Chatsworth House**, has German woodwork, a tiled fireplace and a most unusual tiled floor. The tin-glazed fireplace tiles are grey with a relief pattern and were probably taken from a late eighteenth century German tiled stove before their installation in the Oak Room. The unexpectedly colourful mosaic-style majolica floor tiles in yellow, blue and white are probably Italian in origin and date from the early to mid-nineteenth century, the period when the room was being put together.

CHESTERFIELD

The bulky and inelegant **Market Hall** (1857) occupies most of the MARKET PLACE. Upstairs is the Assembly Rooms Main Hall, a huge high-ceilinged space with dado tiling all around, mainly in shades of dark brown but topped by a single row of colourful majolica tiles. Then there is a delightful survivor just to the east: **Jackson's the Bakers**, 7 CENTRAL PAVEMENT is a brilliant, near-perfectly preserved 1920s Lipton's; only the exterior stall risers have suffered damage. Inside, the shop is completely tiled in white with colourful floral swags, and four large stall riser tile panels offer 'Cooked Meats' and suchlike in green on white. Finally, a high-level frieze of pale blue and white tiles announces that Lipton's is 'The business on which the sun never sets'. The tiles were probably made at Wade's Flaxman Tile Works in Burslem.

Old Whittington

In the encaustic pavement at **St Bartholomew's Church** in the suburb of Old Whittington, on the northern edge of Chesterfield, are several patterned designs shown in Maw & Co catalogues, along with unusual green border tiles and a four-tile buff and red memorial tablet. Its slightly clumsy lettering is very similar to drawings for tablets in Maw's design books, which show experiments with the lay-out of lettering for tablets dating from the 1870s into the 1890s.[3]

CHURCH WILNE

The Willoughby Chapel (1622) at **St Chad's Church** is floored with tiles of an unusual design in which groups of four tiles centre on a yellow, white, blue and green flower. These tiles were initially made in the Netherlands during 1580-1600, then copied in England in the first quarter of the seventeenth century, mainly in the London area, for instance at Pickleherring Quay, Southwark. The St Chad's tiles appear to have a pinkish body, which identifies them as the Flemish version, as opposed to the London tiles which have a hard, grey body. To confuse the issue still further, faithful reproductions of this design were made in the late nineteenth century by Frederick Garrard of London; these latter tiles have a deep red body. The church was gutted by fire in 1917 and restored during 1917-23, so it is possible that Garrard tiles were introduced at that point, although the chapel's original stained glass survived the flames. It may even be that the chapel floor is a mixture of Flemish and Garrard tiles.

CRICH

In the Tramway Village at the NATIONAL TRAMWAY MUSEUM is the **Red Lion** public house, erected in Stoke-on-Trent around 1830 and rebuilt at the Museum during 1991-2002. The pub was about to be demolished in 1973, to make way for a new road, but was rescued by volunteers from the Museum (notably Jim Soper) who had the pub taken down brick by brick and moved to Crich. The ornate pub exterior features tiling by the Campbell Tile Co of Stoke, dating from about 1890, and a magnificent balustrade topped by a fibreglass replica of the original terracotta lion. The pub was part of the estate of Showell's

Brewery of Oldbury, and the tiled lettering refers to their 'Amber Bitter' and 'Nut Brown Ales' as well as 'Showell's Stingo'.

DERBY

As a result of modern road building, A. W. N. Pugin's **St Marie's R. C. Church** (1838-41), off St Alkmund's Way, now stands perilously close to roaring traffic. The Lady Chapel, added in 1854-5 by E. W. Pugin, has a Minton tile pavement leading to its high altar. The tiling is mainly in buff, brown and sky blue, with fleur-de-lys designs in white on a stronger blue ground. **Derbyshire Children's Hospital** (now closed) originally had a fine selection of tiles dating from its construction in 1882-3 and extension during the 1930s. The earlier tiles were probably made by J. C. Edwards of Ruabon, while the 1930s tiles (mainly animal designs) came from two manufacturers: Pilkington's and Dunsmore, the latter printing on to Minton blanks. The tiles were moved by the Jackfield Conservation Studio to a new children's hospital in 1997.

MONYASH

St Leonard's Church was restored by William Butterfield in 1884-7. His tile pavement includes many plain red, yellow and blue tiles as well as a most unusual and striking 'Green Man' tile, found four times over within a nine-tile group (Fig 27). There are also tiles with a paired bird design, and an area of Butterfield's trademark chevron patterning, here carried out in red, yellow and black. The 'Green Man' tile, its motif an ancient and enigmatic fertility symbol, was manufactured by Godwin's; the design was taken directly from that of a fourteenth century Wessex tile. Examples of this medieval design have been found at churches in Berkshire (Great Shefford) and Hampshire (Stoke Charity); they are now in the British Museum collection. [4]

TIDESWELL

The fourteenth century **Church of St John the Baptist**, Commercial Road, known as the cathedral of the Peak, is packed with high-quality wood carving. Above the altar in its Lady Chapel (in the north transept), restored in 1924, is a coloured, moulded ceramic plaque measuring about 3′ by 1′ 6″ and depicting the Nativity; this apppears to be the work of the Compton Potters' Arts Guild (Fig 28).

WIRKSWORTH

St Mary's Church was restored by George Gilbert Scott in 1870-6. He added a Campbell Brick & Tile Co encaustic tile pavement in the choir with designs, derived from local medieval examples, similar to those he used a few years later at Ashbourne but without any plain tile bands. The resulting effect is much brighter than the restrained tiling of the sanctuary.

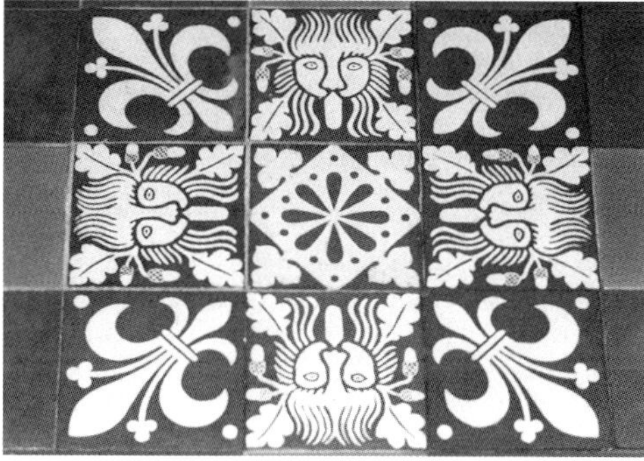

Fig 27.

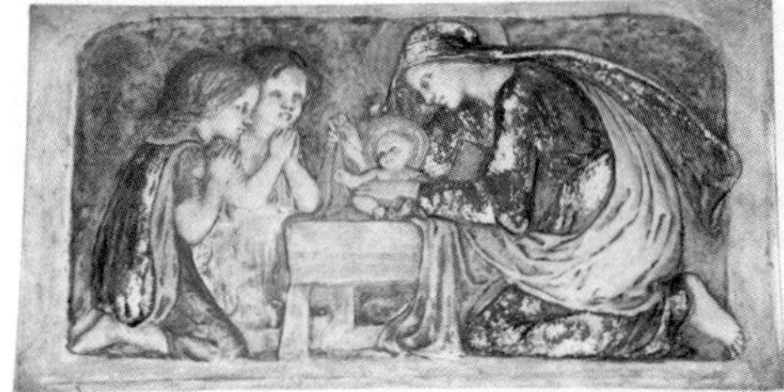

Fig 28.

Derbyshire Roundup

The Godwin chancel pavement at St Michael's Church, **Church Broughton** was laid in 1886 during restoration of the church by the architect J. R. Naylor of Derby; it comprises mainly four-tile groups of common designs, divided by black-tiled diagonal bands.[5] St Peter's Church (1867), built by George Gilbert Scott for the 7th Duke of Devonshire in the gloriously sited Chatsworth estate village of **Edensor**, has a chancel pavement of Godwin dust-pressed encaustic tiles, the designs a mixture of fleur-de-lys, roses, birds and lions. The Ritz Cinema (1938), South Street, **Ilkeston** is one of the best surviving works of the architect Reginald Cooper of Nottingham, a specialist in cinema design; for the facade, he used Doulton Carraraware around the main entrance and on the fin-shaped tower. There are cream, green and blue art nouveau floral tiles in the tympanum of York Chambers (1903, formerly the Midland Counties Bank, architects Gorman & Ross, now a café), 40 Market Place, **Long Eaton**; the town also has many examples of art nouveau porch tilies. All Saints Church, **Lullington** has a Minton chancel dado (a geometric pattern in brown, buff and blue) dating from restoration in 1861-2; in addition, there are four roundels of the Evangelists in the dais pavement.

The richly decorative 1851 restoration of All Saints Church, **Mackworth** included its Minton encaustic tiled sanctuary pavement.[6] Medieval tiles survive in the north chancel chapel (c1370) of St Matthew's Church, **Morley**; the tiles, which include butterfly and paired-bird designs (like those copied by Scott at Ashbourne) were probably made in the kilns of Dale Abbey, four miles to the south-east.[7] As well as a Minton encaustic tile pavement (1863) in the chancel of St Michael's Church, **Sutton on the Hill**, there are elegant encaustic roundels and squares set into the font surround.[8] St Mary's Church (1840-3), **Wensley** was designed by the architect Joseph Mitchell of Sheffield, his son J. B. Mitchell-Withers extending the tiny chancel in 1885-6 when the Minton Hollins tiling was installed. All Saints Church, **Youlgreave** was restored by Norman Shaw in 1869-70; he designed the mosaic reredos and the tile pavements in sanctuary and chancel.

References

1. Philip and Dorothy Brown, 'Victorian Varieties - Church tiles at Lichfield and Ashbourne', *Glazed Expressions*, (1989) 18, pp2.
2. Philip and Dorothy Brown, 'Obliterating Butterfield', *Glazed Expressions*, (1989) 19, pp8-9.
3. Maw & Co Collection, D/MAW/9/2 Modern Encaustic Tile Design vol 4, design numbers 611-613, Ironbridge Gorge Museum Trust Library.
4. Elizabeth S. Eames, *Catalogue of Medieval Lead-Glazed Earthenware Tiles in the Department of Medieval and Later Antiquities, British Museum*, (British Museum Publications, London, 1980), vol 2, design 1822.
5. *The Builder*, 3rd July 1886, vol 51.
6. *The Builder*, 29th November 1851, vol 9, p752.
7. Eames, *Catalogue of Medieval Lead-Glazed Earthenware Tiles*, vol 1, p231.
8. *The Builder*, 9th January 1864, vol 22, p33.

Devon

Devon is a county brim-full of colourful ceramics. This is partly due to its profusion of churches, whose interiors often combine medieval tile pavements with Victorian ceramic decoration. Tile production in the county began with the late medieval tileries of the Barnstaple and Bideford area, which specialised in relief decoration and were active from the late sixteenth to the early eighteenth century. Their tiles are found in many of the county's churches; the more notable examples are listed in the main text, with other locations included in the Devon Roundup. Torquay's terracotta industry and the North Devon art potters flourished during the late nineteenth and early twentieth century, while Candy & Co of Newton Abbot continued in production until the 1990s; however, in situ examples of these local wares are uncommon.

Victorian restoration was responsible for tile pavements being installed at many churches, particularly those rebuilt by the Barnstaple Borough Surveyor Richard Davie Gould (1817-1900) during the mid-nineteenth century. Other than church tiles, the prosperity of the smaller Devon resorts, for instance Ilfracombe and Exmouth, encouraged shops to use tile decoration to attract custom; fortunately for today's tile-seekers, many of these towns did not become overdeveloped and thus retained their tiles. Indeed, one of the great highlights of the county's tile locations is Ilfracombe's High Street, with its four excellent tiled butcher's shops. Where development was more intense, for instance at Torquay, much tiling has been lost.

Other important sites include the former Brannam's Pottery in Barnstaple, a superb Minton encaustic tile pavement at Bicton Church, the wide variety of tiling at Exeter Cathedral and Haccombe Church, and the unusual external pictorial tile panels at Plymouth's New Palace Theatre. A full list of locations of the ceramic plaques installed in 1994 as part of the Alphabet of Parishes Project, which celebrated local identity, may be found in the Devon Roundup. Suggested reading: Audrey Edgeler and John Edgeler, *North Devon Art Pottery* (North Devon Museums Service, Barnstaple, 1995); TACS Tour Notes *English Riviera* (1997). The *Gazetteer* entry for Devon covers the administrative areas of Devon County Council, Plymouth City Council and Torbay Council.

ARLINGTON

St James Church (mainly rebuilt 1846 by R. D. Gould), in the grounds of the National Trust property Arlington Court, has an unusual chancel pavement of black tiles bearing a white scrollwork design; they were apparently made by Powell's of Whitefriars.

ASHFORD

St Peter's Church was rebuilt by R. D. Gould in 1854, although it was 1863 before the chancel was complete. Maw & Co tiles were used for the chancel pavement, and a decorative tiled reredos was also installed.[1]

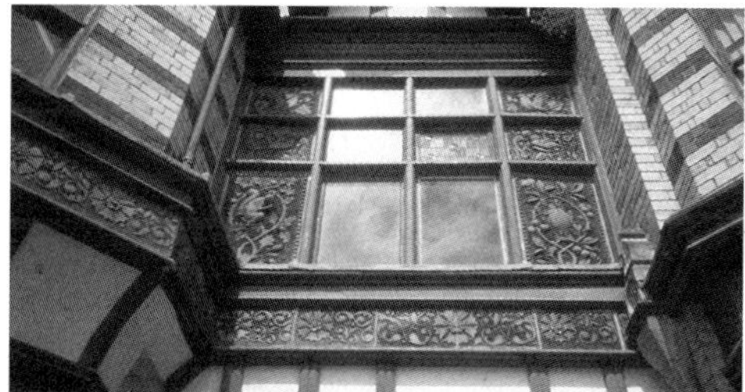

Fig 29.

BARNSTAPLE

Barnstaple was the home of North Devon's art pottery industry during the late nineteenth and early twentieth centuries. Several substantial firms were involved, and **Brannam's Pottery**, the largest works, can still be seen in LITCHDON STREET, just south of the town centre (Fig 29). It was owned by C. H. Brannam, maker of Barum Ware, and built in two stages during 1886-7; the architect was W. C. Oliver.[2] The jolly facade combines terracotta pictorial plaques (mainly of animals and birds) at first floor level above a carriage entrance below, with colourful bands of specially-made tiles on the showroom and office to the east. The showroom has a chamfered doorway supported by twin yellow floral ceramic columns, with a distinctive knobbly surface. The whole is very attractive, as it needed to be to encourage tourists, and the pottery only ceased production in 1989. The buildings were then converted to offices and shops, while Brannam's moved to Roundswell Industrial Estate, on the southern edge of Barnstaple (just off the A39). The shed-like home of **Brannam's** new works is enlivened on its exterior by three large, circular shaped-brick panels designed by the artist Jeffrey Salter (Fig 30). Before carving the unfired 'green' brick Salter documented the works using drawing and photography.[3] The finished panels, made from red bricks up to four times the normal cut brick size, show scenes from the old works and a royal coat-of-arms.

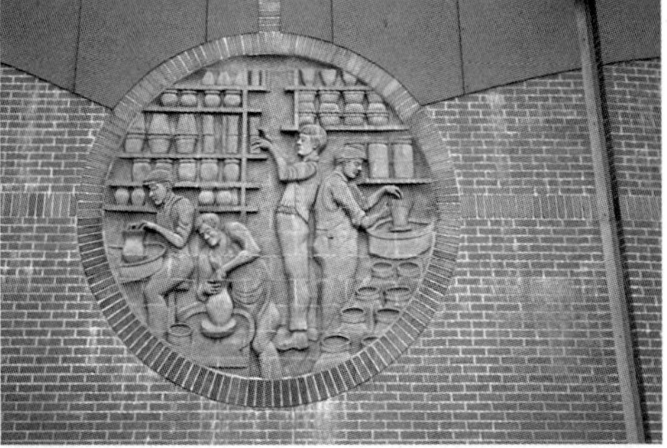

Fig 30.

Back in the centre of Barnstaple, terracotta panels by Alexander Lauder, a rival of Brannam's, may be seen on the facade of the **Squire & Sons** building (1903) in Tuly Street. Lauder was the architect of the building, which included ornamental brickwork from his Pottington works. As befits an agricultural supply merchants, it has a pair of terracotta reliefs of agricultural subjects high on its gables. Lauder also designed and built **Ravelin Manor**, well east of the town centre off Constitution Hill, in 1889; its lavish external terracotta decoration (including full-size figures) was the product of his own works, as was the artistic tile and terracotta ornament of the interior. Although it was designed for a client, Lauder eventually lived at Ravelin Manor himself.[4]

Several of Barnstaple's streets still retain their Craven Dunnill blue and white encaustic tiled names, which date from the end of the nineteenth century. There is also some external tiling on houses in residential streets just north of Brannam's works, but given the strength of the art pottery industry here (not to mention the presence of Barnstaple's late medieval tilery on North Walk), the ceramic showing in the town is rather disappointing. However, tube-lined work (perhaps 1920s) is visible at **Ayre's** butchers in Bear Street; its fairly plain exterior tiling is complemented by an interior panel of a pig's head within an iridescent wreath, probably made at Wade's Flaxman Tile Works, Burslem. Finally, the entrance hall of the **Museum of Barnstaple and North Devon**, The Square, has a sparkling encaustic tiled floor.

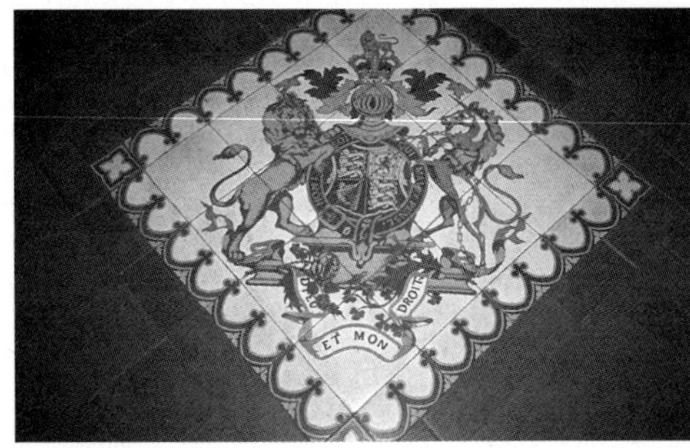

Fig 31.

BICTON

Three Coade stone busts - Sir Walter Raleigh, Lord Nelson and (perhaps) the Duke of Wellington - look down over the lush perfection of the Italian gardens from the orangery at **Bicton Park**. The busts, by Coade & Sealy, date from 1806.[5] Orangery and garden are but a small part of the extensive landscaped park largely created by John, Lord Rolle (1750-1842) and his second wife Louisa. Although their mansion (now an agricultural college) is managed independently of the park, the logic of their planning is still easily appreciated. At the southern tip of the grounds, in woodland beside the road, are **St Mary's Church** and the Rolle mausoleum, both commissioned by Lady Rolle to commemorate the death of her husband. John Hayward of Exeter, an enthusiastic Ecclesiologist, was chosen as architect for St Mary's, which was erected during 1848-50 next to the remains of a medieval church. Hayward's gothic design is notable for its surprising display of fifty sculpted heads of kings and queens of England, from Edward I to Victoria, on the dripstones; the heads of Lord and Lady Rolle also feature on the north porch. Inside, the gloom is dissipated by a stunning Minton encaustic tile pavement running throughout the church, with a unique display of armorial and monogrammed tiles in the chancel and sanctuary (Fig 31). The sixteen-tile group showing the Royal Arms on a white background is the most eye-catching, but other, mostly nine-tile groups depict the arms of Lord and Lady Rolle (with a pale blue ground),

Louisa Rolle's monogram and - in the sanctuary - unusually ornate symbols of the evangelists. The risers of the two steps leading into the sanctuary are decorated with letter tiles in red on pale blue.

Just west of the church is the **Rolle mausoleum**, built by A. W. N. Pugin for Lady Rolle in 1850. The little mortuary chapel (as Pugin preferred to call it) with its steeply-pitched roof is attached to the ruins of the old church, which Pugin partially demolished to create the required background for the mausoleum. Inside, beneath the painted roof are monuments to John, Lord Rolle (by Pugin) and the baroque tomb of Denys Rolle (d1638), standing above a fine Minton encaustic tile pavement in mainly blue on cream, with white and maroon as secondary colours. The tiles were designed especially for the mausoleum; those bearing Rolle monograms and heraldic emblems alternate with plainer tiles in geometric patterns. Unfortunately there is normally no public access to the interior of this significant and thoroughly Puginian structure, but the church (generally open) may be entered through the grounds of Bicton Park.

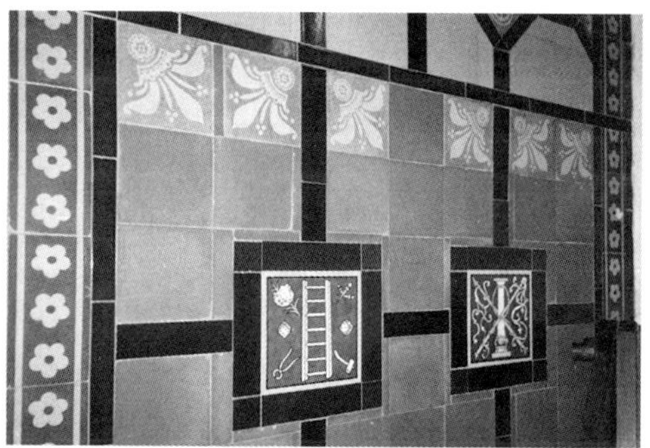

Fig 32.

BRIDESTOWE

The most unusual ceramic feature of **St Bridget's Church** is the 28-tile plaque to be found on the north interior wall. It bears a list of previous rectors (latest date 1889), has a brown glazed ceramic frame and is signed Doulton of Lambeth; the church was restored around 1890. This type of list was intended to emphasise the continuity of the church, the incumbent during the Commonwealth being marked here as an 'Intruder'. There is also interesting tiling by Maw & Co on the north and south walls of the sanctuary, including a series of oversize bright red tiles showing the instruments of the passion (Fig 32).

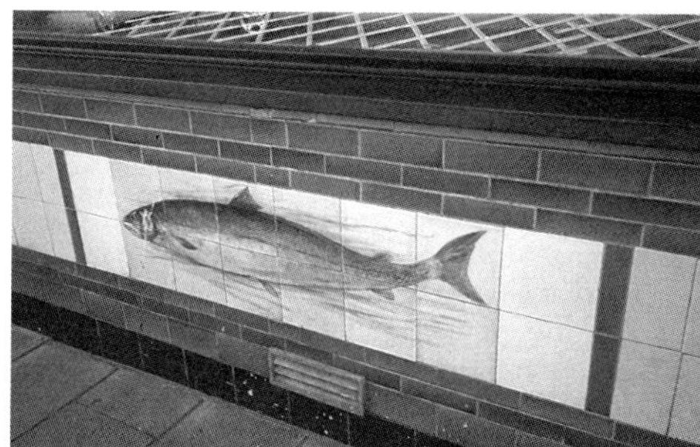

Fig 33.

BUDLEIGH SALTERTON

Several shops in the town's HIGH STREET sport green glazed brick stall risers, and the baker's has a good geometric pavement running from the porch right through into the shop, but **G. & K. Sanders** the fishmongers have the finest shop of all: its pale green, blue and yellow tiled facade has a central 12-tile panel below the window showing a nicely drawn fish, and a 16-tile porch panel of a sailing boat (Fig 33). The latter is signed Carter's of Poole with a blurred date which could read 1957 or 1932. Unfortunately Carter's records do not mention this site, but judging from the style of the panels 1932 would appear the more likely.

DARTMOUTH

The excellent green and yellow faience facade of the **Dolphin**, MARKET SQUARE includes a column supporting the porch over a chamfered corner doorway (Fig 34). There is a ceramic advertisement for Star Ales (with a distinctive white star on red circle logo) produced by Plymouth Breweries Limited; the company was registered in 1889, thus the facade probably dates from the end of the nineteenth century.

DAWLISH

St Gregory's Church (Dawlish parish church) has a remarkable collection of opus sectile panels by Powell's of Whitefriars. The chancel was rebuilt in 1874 but the reredos - an opus sectile depiction of the Last Supper designed by William Burton - was installed about 1879. Burton, who was born in London around 1831, spent some time in Florence during the early 1870s; the Last Supper reredos (after the Last Supper by Raphael in Florence) was his only recorded work for Powell's. It shows Christ and the apostles at a table set upon a red and white chequerboard floor, with glinting gold mosaic arcading above. According to Powell's records, the reredos was extended several times, and the fine evangelist panels at either side, including opus sectile symbols, much gold mosaic and floral tiles, would seem to constitute these extensions.[6]

Opus sectile panels of Isiah, Daniel, Ezekiel and Jeremiah were installed on the north wall of the chancel in 1899, while above the altar in the Lady Chapel is another large opus sectile reredos, in this case depicting the Adoration of the Magi; alongside are blue glass tiles of a floriate design often used by Powell's. This reredos dates from 1914-15 and was designed by Guy Miller, a Powell's studio employee who was a prolific cartoonist; the colours are considerably cooler than the main reredos. The total cost of opus sectile work ordered from Powell's for St Gregory's was well over £400; perhaps the benefactor was a visitor to the little resort.

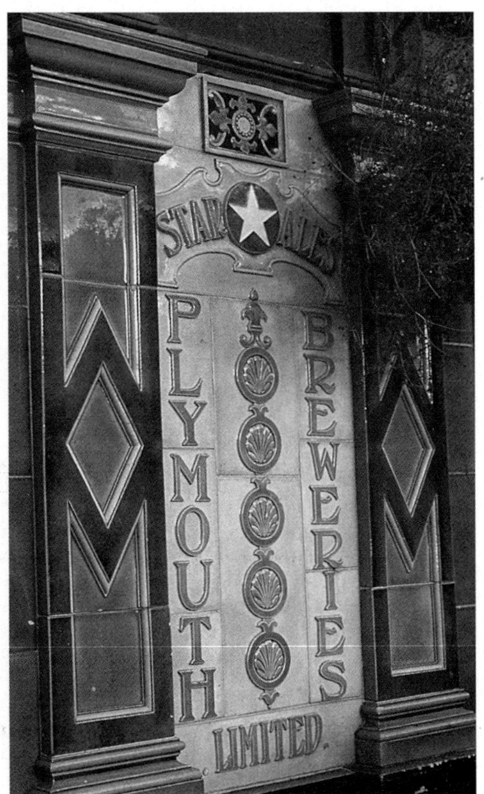

Fig 34.

ENDSLEIGH

The mansion known as Endsleigh Cottage was designed in 1810 by Sir Jeffry Wyatville for the 6th Duke of Bedford. The delightful site for this combination of family holiday home and evocation of English Picturesque taste was chosen by the Duchess, while Humphrey Repton designed the grounds (over 300 acres) in 1814; estate buildings included the Swiss Cottage and a Shell Grotto. In Repton's Dairy Dell, north-west of the house, Wyatville designed Pond Cottage, which stands next to a dark pool, and the nearby octagonal **Dairy** (c1815). Its marble and tile-clad chamber ensured coolness; the marble was local while the tiling, by Wedgwood, was mainly plain white but with a delicate border bearing a trailing ivy design. Transfer printing, then a new technique, was used to produce the outline, which was hand-coloured.[7] The doorway to the dairy, with inset tiled archways, is particularly attractive. The dairy, which is now in the care of the Landmark Trust, was an early example of the picturesque tiled dairies which became popular in the early to mid-nineteenth century, the most exotic being the Royal Dairy at Windsor.

EXETER

A tile tour of Exeter must begin at the wonderfully colourful **Cathedral**, whose impressive array of vaults and chapels is paved by tiles ranging from medieval (a chapel on the north side) to Victorian encaustic, mainly installed during restoration by Sir George Gilbert Scott during 1870-7. There are good displays by Godwin's in several side chapels (especially the Lady Chapel) and notably in the choir, where the tiles - some with uncommon designs - are combined with local marble work.[8] In the Oldham Chantry, at the east end of the south aisle, is a small Minton encaustic pavement, while a Powell's opus sectile panel depicting the Good Shepherd may be found in the choir aisle.

Head west from the Cathedral precincts into Broadgate, swiftly bearing right into the HIGH STREET to find the **St Petrock Centre**, formerly St Petrock's Church. Inside, the walls of this strangely configured space house a series of ceramic memorial plaques, each lozenge-shaped but all set within tiled borders thus making a band of tiling midway along the wall. Dates on the tablets cover 1857 to 1925; the time of their installation is unknown, but such commemorative tablets appear to have been fashionable during the last quarter of the nineteenth century, particularly in the midlands. A little way north along the High

Street is the **Guildhall**, where a substantial chimneypiece installed during its 1887-8 restoration, in celebration of Queen Victoria's golden jubilee, is tiled in white with symbols of Queen and city (crown and castle) in yellow and black; the imagery is repeated in the stained glass of the main hall (Fig 35). To the rear of the Guildhall is the **Guildhall shopping precinct**; in its centre is the 22′ by 9′ Exeter Millennium Mosaic (2000), designed by Garry Plastow and Sam Watts and entitled *A Moment in Time*. It was made from identical tiles which were given to local people and groups who created their own designs; the completed tiles were then assembled as a wall installation.

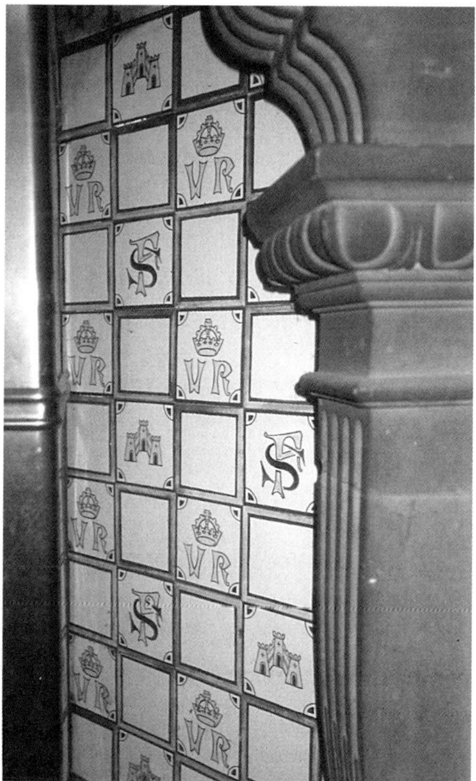

Fig 35.

South-east of the city centre, on the pediment of the red brick **Wyvern Barracks** (1804), BARRACK ROAD, is a large (about 12 ft by 10 ft) and brightly-painted Coade stone Royal Arms, marked Coade and Sealy, 1806; this is one of a series of Royal Arms made by the firm for various barracks and similar locations. Also in Barrack Road is the **Royal Devon and Exeter Hospital**, where Exeter Health Care Arts has developed a programme of artworks including several ceramic installations. The fish-strewn Swim Fountain (1997) by ceramic artist Kate Malone stands in the Bramble Courtyard; its pools have semi-submerged rainbow-coloured fish dotted around deep blue-tiled walls. Yet more fish line the walls of the Hydrotherapy Pool (Reptile Ceramics, 1997), while the Brick Sofa (1999) by Rodney Harris is patterned with imprints of hearts and lungs.

In Newtown, the polychromatic interior of **St Matthew's Church** (1881-90) includes colourful tiling and a partly terracotta pulpit of 1891.

Alphington

The medieval **Church of St Michael and All Angels**, DAWLISH ROAD was restored in 1876-8. The work, carried out by the local architectural practice Hayward & Son, included rebuilding and extending the east end of the church; this new section was floored with Godwin tiles.[9] The window recesses along the south aisle have memorial tiles made by Doulton, their dates ranging from 1898 to 1919.

EXMOUTH

In the middle of Exmouth, **Spindals** in ROLLE STREET has a most unusual facade, with hefty faience pilasters in dark olive green, plus an open porch tile panel depicting a large and unsmiling sun, symbol of the Sun Fire Office (Fig 36). The shop appears originally to have been the base of a firm of builders and contractors, who were also agents for the insurance company. **Julie's Restaurant** in EXETER ROAD sports a good, complete faience facade in grey, green and yellow; two large lettered panels at first floor height advertise fish and vegetables respectively.

HACCOMBE

The **Church of St Blaise**, in the grounds of Haccombe House, has an excellent range of floor tiling, including twenty-nine different designs of medieval inlaid tiles in and around the chancel; the designs appear to have developed from those produced in Exeter around 1280. Some bear the arms of the Archdeacon family, who inherited the manor in 1330, thus the tiles probably date from the mid-fourteenth century, perhaps soon after 1335 when a college was established at St Blaise. There are also green glazed white tiles, likely to have been imported from France or Spain in the early fifteenth century, and 1860s patterned encaustic tiles in the north aisle.

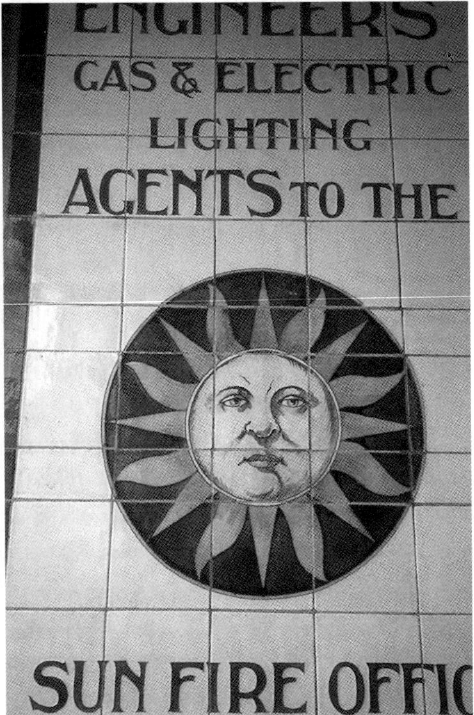

Fig 36.

HATHERLEIGH

The quiet market town of Hatherleigh has much of ceramic interest, including an attractive ceramic mural on a gable end above the central square (opposite the George Hotel) erected to mark town's millennium in 1981. There is also a collection of public artworks resulting from the Hatherleigh Project, which began in 1994 when West Devon Borough Council and the townspeople combined forces in an effort to attract more visitors to their then-declining town and to raise the profile of the region's artists. Locations given 'the Hatherleigh treatment' included various seats and bridges, and there is a ceramic map with a difference on the side of the supermarket in the main street; this was created by local children and the artist Roger Dean in 1996. The **Church of St John the Baptist** has Barnstaple tiles around the font at the rear, and a lozenge-shaped unglazed memorial tile dated 1877 on a north window sill at the east end of the church. The east wall of the chancel is decorated with an odd arrangement of encaustic tiles dating from around 1840, and there is a large area of mosaic floor; it is altogether a rather strange church.

ILFRACOMBE

This little town, tightly squeezed into crevices of the rocky coastline, became an important seaside resort after the arrival of the railway in 1874. To its attractions was added in 1997 the two-and-a-half white brick 'cooling towers' of the **Landmark Theatre** on the PROMENADE, replacing the Victoria Pavilion Theatre (1925) which had been damaged in a storm (Fig 37). The striking design was by Tim Ronalds Architects, and the bricks - over 30,000 of them - were made from German clay fired in Belgium.[10] Close to, the brickwork is rather banal, with some discolouration, but viewed from Capstone Hill the grouping is delightfully picturesque. The contrast between inside and outside is instructive: the bland exterior turns out to house wonderful curving, airy spaces defined by strong colours and forms. This homage to nautical style might have been enhanced by the use of black brick, even glazed black brick, rather than mimsy white. But perhaps a black cooling tower on the seafront would have held less appeal.

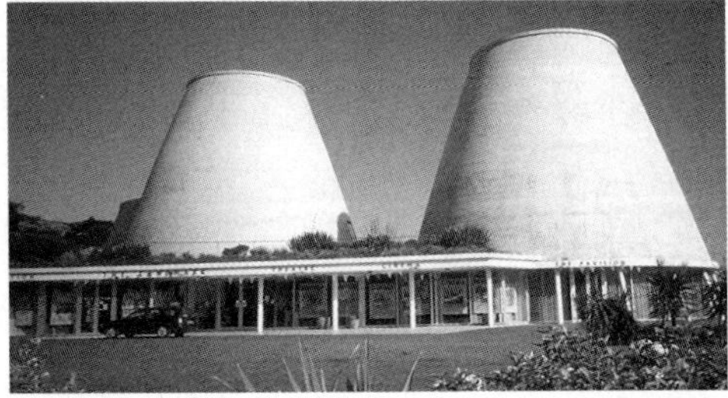

Fig 37.

Opposite the Landmark is the first of Ilfracombe's unexpectedly large collection of ceramic shops, most built at the time of the main resort expansion in the 1890s but these, on the PROMENADE, date from the 1880s. This terrace of small shops has a single course of Minton Hollins picture tiles in brown on white (some from the signs of the zodiac series) along its stepped facade, surprisingly effective given that the individual images are far too high, at well above first floor level, to be seen clearly. Then east to the QUAY and the harbour, whose 1952 entrance, all flyaway white fins, is marked by a colourful 1994 ceramic roundel showing several boats. It was made by Devon potter Harry Juniper and installed as part of the Alphabet of Parishes project which commemorated local distictiveness, in this case using Q for the Quay.[11] Back in BROAD STREET, the former **Crang's Pharmacy** has many original fittings and an excellent geometric tiled floor, with a brown encaustic pavement in the doorway bearing the pharmacy name.

Round and uphill to the HIGH STREET, and the multiplicity (a shambles?) of ceramic butcher's shops: first, on the left, is **Turton's**, which probably dates from the 1890s. It has a Craven Dunnill interior tile panel showing a large brown animal which, according to the butcher, has the front end of a cow and the rear end of a bull. Outside is a broad vertical band of white tiling with lettering on a pale blue ribbon, and a bull's head below. The lettering reads: 'W. H. Andrew Purveyor & Family Butcher Estd. 1855'.

Oddments of encaustic pavements and wall tiles pop up here and there throughout Ilfracombe; even the street names are tiled, in white on blue ground. Many of these are relatively modern replacements, especially the nicely crafted ones showing the acorn sign of the South West Coast Path, but look for the large gloved pointing hand on the Minton Hollins originals. A newer hand is in the alleyway leading from High Street (opposite a large shop with the remains of lime green tiled pilasters) down to the seafront. A series of pretty tiles and small plaques bearing colourful seaside images can be found in the alley running parallel to the High Street and just to its north; these were installed by Ilfracombe Civic Trust in 1993.

Towards the west end of High Street is Ilfracombe's most spectacular ceramic shop, **Scarrett's** the butcher's (formerly Mogridge & Sons). Its tiling dates from 1896 and was carried out by a Barnstaple firm, probably either Brannam's or Lauder's, who were the largest tile producers in the town (Fig 38). The interior is totally tiled, in white above a blue and white art nouveau dado; even the wooden cash booth has a tiled dado. There are two mostly blue picture panels, one of sheep and one of cows. Outside, a new name board has been fixed over the fascia, although fortunately this does not obscure a pair of bulls heads. Although some of the internal tiling is obscured by shop fittings, little has been changed permanently; this is an excellent shop interior, and a fine illustration of the profitability of the town's late Victorian tourist trade.

Just a few doors west is a complementary interior: a **Dewhursts**, with at least ten examples of the Carter's four-tile Farmyard series of

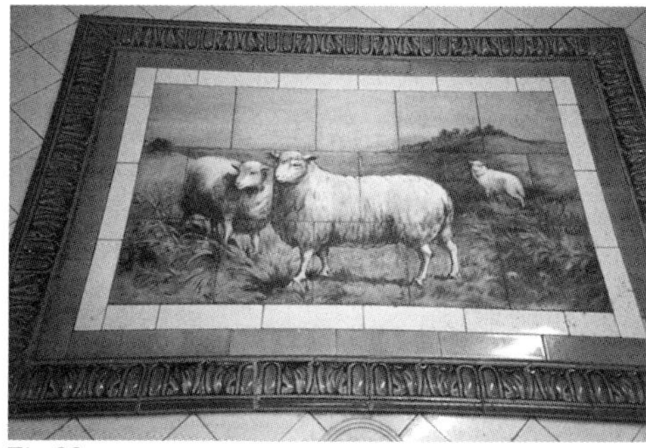

Fig 38.

animals and birds designed by E. E. Stickland around 1922 and used for many years in this chain of butcher's. This, too, is well preserved. High Street eventually becomes CHURCH STREET where the **Angel Restaurant** occupies the fourth ceramic butcher's. Here, the interior is tiled floor to ceiling: a blue and white patterned dado is topped by a maroon and white anthemium frieze, while set in the white tiling above are two superb lozenge picture panels showing bull's heads in ornate borders. This pretty scheme is set off by geometric paving in the adjacent hallway.

KINGSWEAR

Coleton Fishacre (NT) was built in 1923-6 for Rupert D'Oyly Carte, the second generation of the family which managed production of the Gilbert and Sullivan operettas; the architect was Oswald Milne (1881-1968), once assistant to Sir Edwin Lutyens. The calm, stone-built exterior hides a more modern interior, with details including jazzy bathroom tiles designed by the young Edward Bawden for Carter's of Poole.

MARY TAVY

In the south porch of **St Mary's Church** is an unsigned 3 foot high by 2 foot wide turquoise-framed ceramic plaque, bearing a list of previous rectors ('intruders' during the 1649-60 interregnum are in red lettering) within an ornate border (Fig 39). The latest date on the plaque is 1892, so it was probably added in 1893 when the south transept was built. As to the maker, it could well have been one of the many late nineteenth-century firms specialising in church decoration.

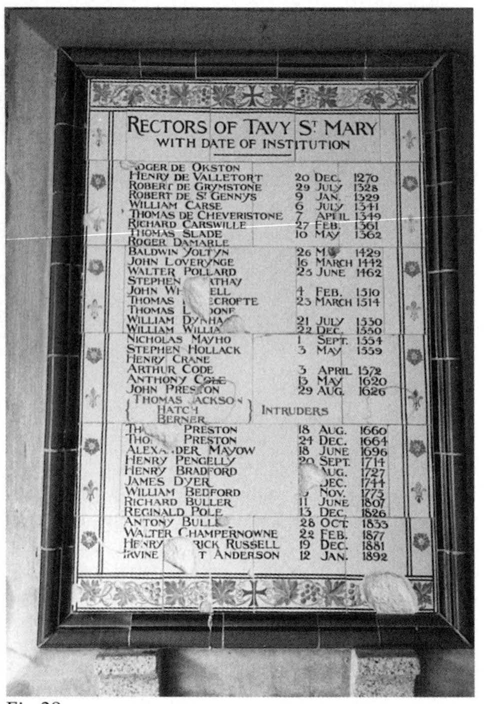

Fig 39.

MORTEHOE

The most immediately impressive feature of the interior of **St Mary's Church** is the large figurative mosaic work above its chancel arch. It was designed by Selwyn Image in 1903 and made by Powell's of Whitefriars who also installed it; the mosaic, which was given to the church by Dr G. B. Longstaffe (churchwarden 1878-1916) in memory of his wife, was unveiled in 1905. There is an encaustic tile pavement in the chancel, the most decorative section being in the choir where there are two royal coats of arms; the plainer sanctuary pavement appears to be of a different date.

NEWTON ABBOT

Begin toward the eastern end of QUEEN STREET, the main shopping street, and head west, soon passing **St Joseph's R. C. Church** (1915) with its colourful opus sectile and mosaic tympanum showing Mary, Joseph and their donkey; the panel is showing few signs of wear despite its unusual exterior situation. At the corner of COURTENAY STREET and Queen Street is **Drum Sports**, whose gable carries a large ceramic plaque in green and yellow with the name 'Invertére Buildings'. Turn right then left to find the groovy Pompidou-style multistorey **Car Park** opposite the Market Hall in SHERBORNE ROAD; it sports a ceramic wall mural (1995) by Taja entitled *Dartmoor Landscape*, with rugged images of sheep and cows, and the names of assorted sponsors.

Continuing westward and round into BANK STREET, a surprise awaits in the form of the **Passmore Edwards Public Library, Science, Art and Technical School**. The huge structure, restored in 2004 and now Newton Abbot Library, uses bright ochre terracotta on the grand scale; masses of grey local limestone contrast with the eyecatching terracotta dressings to make a memorable exterior. It was designed by the Truro-based architect, politician and businessman Silvanus Trevail (1851-1903), who was responsible for several libraries (in similar robust style) funded by the philanthropist John Passmore Edwards, and was built in 1901-4 using terracotta supplied by Dennis Ruabon.[12] The library was one of the last works carried out by the unfortunate Trevail, who committed suicide in 1903, soon after his fifty-second birthday, in a Great Western Railway train passing near Par in Cornwall. Trevail's assistant, Alfred Cornelius, completed the library largely to the original design.

OTTERY ST MARY

The collegiate **Church of St Mary** was rebuilt from 1342 by Bishop Grandison of Exeter, the design being modelled on Exeter Cathedral. The original furnishings were lavish, and included encaustic tiles, some of which remain in the ambulatory, behind the altar (although they may have been moved from the chancel). Dissolution and Victorian restoration changed the appearance of the interior, although the 1977 repainting attempted to revive its medieval colouring. The Surrey architect Henry Woodyer restored the Lady Chapel in 1848, paving the floor with tiles; its tiled reredos, which depicts the Annunciation, was installed in 1881.[13] A moderately decorative tile pavement runs throughout the chancel and into the minstrel's gallery beyond, but more unusual are the wall mosaics in the south transept, which was restored by William Butterfield in 1878 for the Coleridge family. Butterfield designed the mosaic tiling, which is mainly in grey and red with dark patterns; the work was executed by W. B. Simpson & Sons of London.[14]

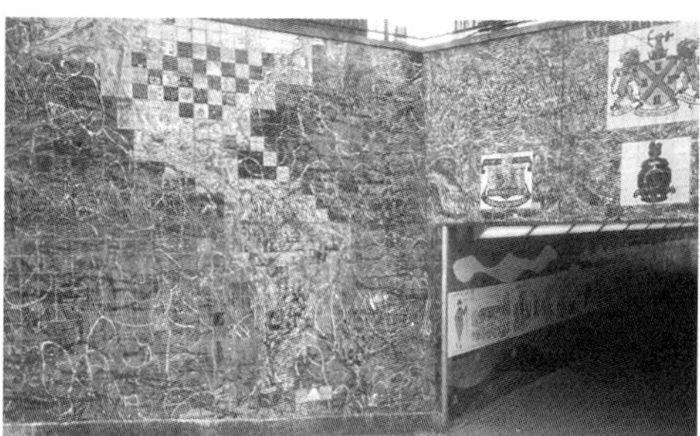

Fig 40.

PLYMOUTH

'Note: this text was written before the Armada Way underpass was filled in during late 2004.

The grand scale of the **Armada Underpass Mural**, dating from 1987-90 and designed by Edward Pond, is appropriate for a city so dramatically reconstructed following the Second World War (Fig 40). Technical aspects of the ARMADA WAY mural, which depicts the naval history of Plymouth and the ships which took part in the battle with the Spanish Armada, were handled by Kenneth Clark Ceramics, whose team included Joanna Espiner.[15] The words beautiful and underpass do not generally coexist happily but here they most certainly do; the quality of the glazes, the exciting colours and the complexity of the design all make this a wonderful mural. Black vitrified tiles were used for the outer wings with standard commercial earthenware tiles in the 300 foot long underpass. For the subterranean section, the designs were outlined in trailed black glaze, then coloured glazes added by brushing and tube-lining. The density of colour in the outer wings was achieved by tube-lining on top of light-toned glazes, followed by the addition of yet more coloured glazes.[16] The signature of Edward Pond can be found at the north end of the mural on its west side. Here, all the original tiling is still intact, and dramatic, swirling lines and deep blues and greens cover the flanking walls. Alas, at the southern end of the underpass, both flanks of the mural have been replaced by insipid pale blue industrial tiling. The remaining upper section, with its three coats of arms, gives only a small clue as to the lost design. The partial loss of this groundbreaking mural is nothing short of a ceramic tragedy.

Heading west of Armada Way, at the west end of NEW GEORGE STREET is a row of 1960s shops with striking blue, yellow and black geometric tiling (probably by Carter's) on their first floor facades. Further west still is the city's most spectacular ceramic building: the former **New Palace Theatre** and adjoining Great Western Hotel in UNION STREET. The theatre was built in 1898 then reopened in 1899 after a fire; the architects were Wimperis & Arber. The facade, by W. J. Neatby for Doulton, is of brown faience and buff terracotta with much maritime symbolism. The finishing touch is a pair of semicircular tiled panels showing scenes from the Armada after paintings by Sir Oswald Brierly: *Spanish Armada leaving Ferrol* and *Defeat of Spanish Armada*. Like most other examples of nineteenth century exterior tile paintings in Britain, these vitreous enamel panels have lost much of their original colour.[17] Across the street is a tiled pub, now the **Theatre** but originally the Grand, named for the Grand Theatre, built in 1889 and demolished in 1963.

Just south-east of Union Street is MILLBAY ROAD and the **Duke of Cornwall Hotel** (1863-7), a showy gothic grand hotel built for passengers arriving on the Great Western Railway; it was designed by the London architect Charles Forster Hayward. The hotel was one of a series of early 1860s buildings in which the use of terracotta, in this case by Blashfield, was increasingly evident.[18]

Devonport

In Devonport, west of the modern city centre, are two good late Victorian ceramic pubs, the **Kings Arms** on PEMBROKE STREET, with heraldic faience panels and good lettering, and the **Royal Naval Arms** on SALTASH ROAD, with an ornate, columned facade of deep green and brown faience.

SOWTON

Medieval **St Michael's Church** was largely rebuilt for the high church Garratt family in 1844-5 by the Exeter architect and Ecclesiologist John Hayward, who went on to design Bicton Church shortly afterwards. It remains an untouched example of early Tractarian village church design; the decorative scheme includes a tile pavement throughout (incorporating symbols of the evangelists in the sanctuary), tiled stair risers and a tiled east wall.

TIVERTON

St Peter's Church is notable for the romantic nautical stone carving of the Greenway Chapel and an astounding brass candelabra dating from

1709. At first glance the tiling - an encaustic choir pavement - is unmemorable, but behind the drab grey cobwebbed curtain covering the east wall is a colourful encaustic tile dado stretching the width of the sanctuary. The tiles, probably by Minton, include roundels of the four evangelists and a lamb of god, along with various monograms; they were installed when the chancel was rebuilt by the Exeter architect Edward Ashworth in 1853-6. The awful fawn carpet covering the sanctuary floor also hides a tile pavement which dates from 1895 (when the floor was raised). If revealed, the richness of the chancel tiling would enliven the interior and certainly complement the stone carving; it is sad that the church authorities still appear so ashamed of their Victorian tilework.

TOPSHAM

Several shops in FORE STREET have tiled stall risers. At number 74, there are white and cream tiles with a blue floral border and good lettering reading 'Established 1835'. The cheese shop stall riser is obscured in the centre, but still visible are a cow's head at one end and a sheep's head at the other, both in pale blue on white tiles. Finally, the butcher's has a complete blue glazed brick exterior.

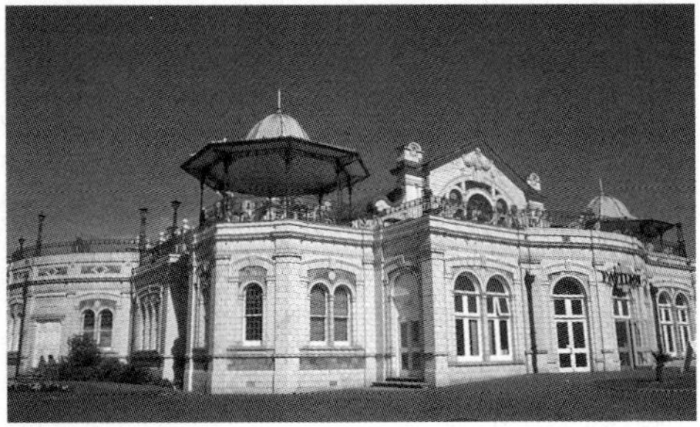

Fig 41.

TORQUAY

At the centre of Torquay's sea front on PRINCESS PARADE is the splendid **Pavilion**, opened in 1912 and saved from the threat of demolition in the early 1970s (Fig 41). The initial plan for the Pavilion appeared in 1906, but this was redesigned in 1908-11 by Major Henry Augustus Garrett, Torbay's Borough Engineer and Surveyor during 1890-1932; the Pavilion was finally built in 1911-12 by local contractor R. E. Narracott. The intention behind its rather late appearance at the resort was to attract more visitors by providing the cultural attractions of music and theatre combined with an enjoyable meeting place in the tea garden and café. The Pavilion's style is an Edwardian Baroque version of Art Nouveau, and the steel-framed building is clad in white Doulton Carraraware with some pale green banded decoration. There are numerous swags, urns and assorted flowery faience decorative elements. The long, elaborately plastered barrel-vaulted theatre has an especially attractive facade facing the bay, with twin domed corner canopies at first floor level. Pretty ironwork, and a central dome topped by a figure of Britannia, completes the picture. The original interior contained a theatre, with a music hall-style balcony around three sides of the auditorium.

The building was a success, and became home to the municipal orchestra; the 1920s and 1930s were the Pavilion's heyday, and it was extended to the east in 1939. In the 1950s the orchestra was disbanded and the Pavilion eventually fell into disrepair, although the 1960s saw it used for roller skating and bingo, amongst other disparate entertainments. The Friends of the Pavilion saved it from demolition in the 1970s, and it was listed grade II in 1973. The Pavilion was remodelled in 1986-7 as a shopping centre and restaurant; the 1939 extension was removed, and the eastern facade - with a new entrance - was reconstructed in faience blocks specially manufactured by Hathern. The new use is a great success; while entertainment buildings at other resorts continue to disappear, the Pavilion shows what can be done. And the glistening white Carraraware is still very attractive.

Standing high above the harbour, and visible from most of Torquay, is the church of **St John the Evangelist** in MONTPELLIER ROAD. It was designed by G. E. Street and erected - over four building campaigns - during 1862-85, the tower being completed by Street's son A. E. Street after his father's death in 1881. The major building material was limestone, quarried on the site. The church was one of the leading centres of late nineteenth-century Anglo-Catholicism, thus there are rich furnishings including north aisle mosaics by Salviati showing scenes from the life of St John, stained glass by Morris & Co, and an extensive (although not terribly decorative) Minton tile pavement. There is also a fine display of colourful South Devon marbles, which are tough and highly polished limestones. They are very varied, and have been used in a decorative context throughout Devon, although their most lavish use was in local churches.

Not far from the town centre, at the west end of Babbacombe Road, is **Torquay Museum**, built for Torbay Natural History Society in 1874-6 by William Harvey, one of a family of local architects and builders responsible for much of Torquay's early development. Its facade displays an attractive pair of allegorical scenes - the arts and nature - in local buff terracotta, above the first floor windows. Inside, hanging above the tiled floor of the entrance hall, are a dozen or so interesting tiles and ceramic plaques, one early Persian and very unusual, another dating from the 16th century.

Throughout Torquay, although mainly east of the centre amongst the villa-laden hills, are ceramic street names in blue with white lettering. Each letter has its individual tile, and some display the pointing finger, for instance the sign for Lincombe Drive, which leads off HIGHER WOODFIELD ROAD opposite a villa which was the retirement home of Herbert Minton. The villa, built on Lincombe Hill in 1835 and originally known as Belmont (now **Mintons**, no public access), was acquired by Minton in 1856; following his death in 1858, it remained in the Minton family until around 1890. The verandah is paved with Minton's geometric and encaustic tiles, and the hall has an attractive black and white pseudo-mosaic, with a glazed maroon and green dado. In the former kitchen are Pugin-designed block-printed blue and white wall tiles, while the bathroom has red and green block-printed tiling, also ascribed to Pugin. On the fire surround in what is now known as the butler's pantry are Mintons China Works tiles dating from the mid to late 1880s.

Outside in the garden, looking towards the sea, is a pretty hexagonal gazebo with pierced, blue-glazed ceramic seats, some now replaced by poor concrete copies (Fig 42). Round its exterior, just below roof height, runs a series of colourful majolica plaques, while the inside has a mosaic floor and three large wall panels of *cuenca* tiles; in the centre of the ceiling is a single hexagonal majolica tile. The gazebo probably dates from the mid-1870s, and the house has undergone many alterations, including the installation, in the late 1980s, of around sixty medieval inlaid tiles in the floor of the conservatory. The tiles, which mostly retain their glaze and have clearly recognisable motifs, originated in Shropshire.

Herbert Minton made over 150 donations of his firm's tiles to churches during the 1840s and 1850s. One recipient, amongst several similarly fortunate Devon churches, was St Mark's Church, ST MARK'S ROAD, only half a mile from Minton's home. The church was built by Anthony Salvin in 1856-7 on a site given by the Palk family; the

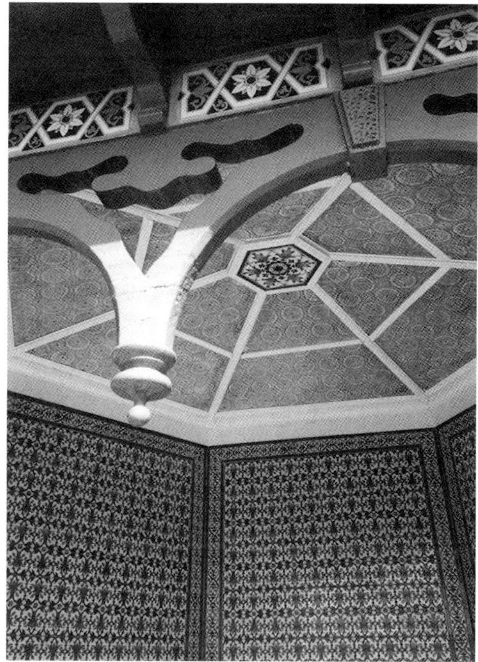
Fig 42.

central tower collapsed in 1856 and was rebuilt lower than its architect originally intended. Minton, a parishioner, gave the tiles for the nave pavement in 1856. St Mark's Church was converted in 1986-7 to the **Little Theatre**, which was built within the nave; its raked floor thus conceals the original floor. It is especially sad that Minton's gift to his very own and final church is no longer visible, if indeed it is extant beneath the seating. Also unknown is the fate of the Powell's art nouveau tiled dado in the sanctuary, dating from its 1890-1 restoration. Minton also presented tiles to St Mary's Church in Marychurch, three miles to the north, but this was rebuilt in the 1950s after war damage and again the tiles have been lost.

Finally in the west of central Torquay there is an excellent tiled butcher's shop: **Terry Prentice** at 78 BELGRAVE ROAD (at its north end, almost opposite Church Street). The interior is fully tiled with plain white tiles and a gold and maroon border, but both porches display picture panels of a bull's head; the scheme is probably interwar.

Babbacombe

All Saints Church, Cary Avenue was built for £10,000 in 1865-7 (the east end and tower 1872-4) by William Butterfield, and the typically polychromatic interior includes chancel mosaics by Salviati and unusual wall tiles high up in the nave; there are patterned encaustic tiles around the font. It is one of Butterfield's most important churches, built for the booming resort, but the gloomy interior is unencouraging. The diaper motif is everywhere, along with fifty varieties of the local marbles; although one can eventually discern a feast of colour, the ceramic contribution is relatively insignificant.

Just south of All Saints Church in **Reddenhill Road** is a taste of how shop fronts in Babbacombe used to be. There are several examples in green glazed brick, especially fine being 'Traces Dairy and Creamery', proclaimed in white lettering on the green brick below the windows. There is also a tiled butcher's shop, W. A. Eastley at number 118; no picture panels, but (probably interwar) cream, yellow and brown tiling inside and out.

Ilsham

The **Church of St Mattias**, on Babbacombe Road and ST MATTIAS CHURCH ROAD at Ilsham, is one of the rare Torquay churches which is usually open to the public, often through the adjacent church centre. Salvin's church of 1858 was much extended by J. L. Pearson in 1882-5; there is an extremely lavish and attractive sanctuary of 1882, with much marble and mosaic, and encaustic tiles paving the chancel steps.

Shiphay

Torbay Hospital, a couple of miles to the north of the centre, off NEWTON ROAD in Shiphay, was built in 1926-8; its children's ward originally contained 21 tile picture nursery rhyme panels by Simpson's, each measuring 2 ft 6 in by 4 ft 6 in. There were extensive alterations to these wards in 1977, resulting in several panels being obscured or painted over, but eight are still visible. A large new addition to the hospital was made around 1968, and in the Outpatients Entrance is a colourful ceramic mural by Arthur Goodwin, called *Tree of Life*; the design is based on a simple tree form and includes references to Torbay.[19]

WASHFORD PYNE

St Peter's Church was almost completely rebuilt by the inventive architect Robert Medley Fulford in 1882-4; Fulford, the son of a vicar, gave up the profession when he was ordained in 1891. The Craven Dunnill dado and floor tiling forms part of its wholly intact decorative scheme, making the little church a fine example of Victorian design.

WEMBWORTHY

St Michael's Church has an unusual collection of tiles. Encaustic memorial tablets to the Reverend Peter Johnson (d1869) and his wife Gratiana (d1845) are set in the tiled floor of the porch; it is unclear when they were installed. The nave floor includes some seventeenth century green-glazed relief tiles, moved from elsewhere, while the chancel floor is paved with Victorian patterned encaustic tiles.

Devon Roundup

St Stephen's Church (1882), **Ashill** has a tiled sanctuary pavement and dado. The 1848 rebuilding of the chancel of St Mary's Church, **Bickleigh**, near Tiverton included the installation of Minton tiling in the sanctuary. St Bridget's Church, **Bridgerule** has a Godwin encaustic tile pavement in the chancel. At St Andrew's Church, **Buckland Monachorum** is a Maw encaustic tile pavement and a Powell's opus sectile reredos (1891, cartoon by Drake). The 1888 renovation of St Michael's Church, **Chagford** included the installation of colourful east wall relief tiling depicting a peacock. The architect James Crocker (1850-1922) of Exeter restored St Matthew's Church, **Cheriton Fitzpaine** during 1883-5, installing a chancel pavement of encaustic tiles by Maw & Co. St Mary's Church, **Chulmleigh** has a few late medieval tiles and a decorative sanctuary pavement dating from around 1880. On the Tarka Trail in the **East Yarde** area are four ceramic sculptures in the form of large seats, whose forms reflect characters from Henry Williamson's *Tarka the Otter*; they were made around 2000 by the artist Katy Hallett in collaboration with pupils from local schools. St Michael's Church, **Gittisham** has a colourful chancel tile pavement dating from the 1860s. There is a complex sanctuary tile pavement dating from 1887 at St Andrew's Church, **Halberton**. St Thomas Church, **Kentisbury** has an elaborate tile pavement running through the chancel and sanctuary; it dates from the 1873-5 rebuilding of the chancel. St Peter's Church, **Lamerton** has an opus sectile reredos designed by Charles Hardgrave of Powell's and depicting the Last Supper; it was installed around 1879, during rebuilding of the church following a fire. The construction of St Peter's Church (1882), **Noss Mayo** was financed by the banker Edward Baring; it has a richly decorative interior (completed by the early 1890s) including a partly-tiled reredos designed by the Plymouth stained glass firm Fouracre & Watson. St Mary's Church, **Morchard Bishop** (whose tower is visible for miles around) has dado and floor tiling dating from its restoration in 1887-91. Lloyd's Bank, **Paignton**, (Palace Avenue/Torquay Road), has terracotta urns on its balustrade and a marble and mosaic porch pavement with the word 'Bank' and (in the corner) 'Diespeker's Patent'. Christ Church (1878), **Parracombe** has encaustic tile pavements by Maw & Co in nave and chancel.[20] The Courtenay Memorial Chapel in the south aisle of St Clement's Church, **Powderham** has interesting tiling by Godwin of Hereford. There are particularly good Barnstaple floor tiles at St Andrew's Church, **Sutcombe**. Apart from its fine fifteenth century stone screen, St Mary's Church, High Street, **Totnes** has a Godwin encaustic tiled chancel pavement, probably dating from the 1867-74 restoration; outside is a ceramic church name board erected in 1966. The Minton tiled reredos installed around 1875 at St Mary's Church, **Upton Hellions** includes the signs of the zodiac in blue. The floor tiles for the sanctuary and chancel of Holy Trinity Church, **Weare Giffard** were supplied by Maw & Co in 1863, when the church was restored by the architect Edward Ashworth.[21] The polychromatic interior of St Peter's Church, **West Buckland** mostly rebuilt by R. D. Gould in 1860-3, unusually includes tiling on the chancel arch and tile banding in the nave as well as a patterned tiled reredos. There are medieval Barnstaple tiles with uncommon designs at St Peter's Church, **Westleigh**. The elaborate chancel tiling at St John Baptist Church, **Witheridge** dates from restoration carried out in 1882-3. The interior of St Bartholomew's Church, **Yealmpton**, rebuilt by William Butterfield in 1850, displays his typical constructional polychromy as well as colourful chancel tiling.

Apart from those mentioned above, the following churches have Barnstaple or other medieval tiles *in situ*: Abbots Bickington, Alverdiscott, Alwington, Ashreigney, Black Torrington, Bradford, Bradworthy, Broadwood Kelly, Cadeleigh, Clawton, Coldridge, Cookbury, Frithelstock, Horwood, Huntshaw, Instow, Monkleigh, Newton St Petrock, West Putford.

Twenty-six *Alphabet of Parishes* commemorative ceramic plaques, made by Harry Juniper from designs provided by local communities, were installed in 1994 at locations in the following towns and villages: Atherington; Beaford; Berrynarbor; Bishopsnympton; Brendon; Burrington; Cheldon; Chittlehamholt, Warkleigh & Satterleigh; Chulmleigh; Combe Martin; Fremington; Frithelstock; Great Torrington; Holsworthy Hamlets; Ilfracombe; Landkey; Molland; North Molton; West and East Putford; Rose Ash; Shebbear; Sheepwash; South Molton; Taddiport & Little Torrington; Winkleigh; Yarnscombe.

References

1. *The Builder*, 4th July 1863, vol 21.
2. Audrey Edgeler and John Edgeler, *North Devon Art Pottery* (North Devon Museums Service, Barnstaple, 1995).
3. Gwen Heeney, *Brickworks* (A & C Black, London, 2003), pp116-8.
4. Audrey Edgeler, *The Art Potters of Barnstaple* (Nimrod Press, Alton, 1990).
5. Alison Kelly, *Mrs Coade's Stone* (Self Publishing Association, Upton-upon-Severn, 1990).
6. Dennis W. Hadley, *James Powell & Sons: A listing of opus sectile, 1847-1973*, (2001).
7. Tony Herbert and Kathryn Huggins, *The Decorative Tile in Architecture and Interiors* (Phaidon Press, London, 1995), pp38-9.
8. Victoria & Albert Museum, *Victorian Church Art* (HMSO, London, 1971), p174.
9. *The Builder*, 3rd August 1878, vol 36.
10. Tim Ronalds, *Swimming against the tide: The Landmark, Ilfracombe*, in *Shaping Earth*, (University of Wolverhampton, 2000), pp82-87.
11. *Alphabet of Parishes*, (Beaford Arts Centre, Winkleigh, 1995).
12. *Dennis Ruabon Catalogue*, (1903).
13. John Elliott and John Pritchard, eds. *Henry Woodyer: Gentleman Architect* (Department of Continuing Education, University of Reading, Reading, 2002), p161.
14. *The Builder*, 5th October 1878, vol 36.
15. Lynda Relph-Knight, 'Art Under the Arches', *Building (Supplement)*, 253 (1988), pp34-35.
16. Kenneth Clark, *The Tile: Making, Designing and Using* (Crowood Press, Marlborough, 2002).
17. Paul Atterbury and Louise Irvine, *The Doulton Story* (Royal Doulton Tableware, Stoke on Trent, 1979), p80.
18. Bridget Cherry and Nikolaus Pevsner, *Devon*, Buildings of England (Penguin Books, London, 1989), p665.
19. John Greene, *Brightening the Long Days* (Tiles and Architectural Ceramics Society, 1987).
20. *The Builder*, 9th November 1878, vol 36.
21. *The Builder*, 31st October 1863, vol 21.

Dorset

Poole in Dorset has been the home of Carter & Co, later Poole Pottery, since 1873. Although the original Poole Pottery factory was demolished in 2001, production continues elsewhere and many examples of the Pottery's architectural output remain in situ throughout the county. In addition, the 2004 auction sale of the contents of the Poole Pottery Museum and Archive resulted in many items being acquired for Poole Museum Service. Other Dorset highlights include its wealth of medieval tiles, for instance at Milton Abbas and Shaftesbury, while Eleanor Coade's house in Lyme Regis provided an excellent advertisement for her manufactory's wares. From the Victorian period there are numerous instances of encaustic church pavements, including tiles designed by J. D. Sedding at St Clement's Boscombe (Bournemouth), but Dorset also offers the best surviving example of an Owen Jones decorative scheme at Sutton Waldron Church, the architectural oddities of Purbeck House in Swanage, and unusual local terracotta at Child Okeford and Iwerne Minster. Carter's provided lavish terracotta for one of the most unusual churches in the country, the early twentieth century St Osmund's, Parkstone (Poole), and colourful faience beside the interwar seaside at San Remo Towers, Boscombe (Bournemouth). Interesting contemporary installations include the Waitrose mural at Dorchester. Suggested reading: Leslie Hayward, *Poole Pottery* (Richard Dennis, Shepton Beauchamp, 2002); Jennifer Hawkins, *Poole Potteries* (Barrie & Jenkins, London, 1980); A. B. Emden, *Medieval Decorated Tiles in Dorset* (Phillimore, Chichester, 1977); TACS Tour Notes *Poole and Bournemouth* (1985). The *Gazetteer* entry for Dorset covers the administrative areas of Bournemouth Borough Council, Dorset County Council and Poole Borough Council.

BERE REGIS

Part of a fourteenth century tile pavement was found in the south aisle of the church of **St John the Baptist** during its restoration by G. E. Street in 1874-5. Only one medieval patterned tile survives, but Street installed a superb Godwin encaustic pavement including four-tile groups whose motifs were copies of the armorial designs present in the medieval pavement. The 1875 tiles also feature copies of the large medieval tile showing three lions (the arms of England) found a few miles to the south at Bindon Abbey, although this design was apparently not originally present at Bere Regis.[1]

BOURNEMOUTH

Bournemouth's centre is THE SQUARE, where the town's delightfully spacious gardens swoop down to meet its imposing shops, most noticeably the unusual curved facade of **Debenham's** on the west side. The appearance of the store, which results from piecemeal development during 1900-20, is marred by a dreadful canopy which makes a mockery of the stylish Edwardian Baroque facade, its grey Carter's ceramic marble set into red terracotta. OLD CHRISTCHURCH ROAD runs east of The Square, passing **Dingles** store, with an impressive interwar art deco Carter's Ceramic Marble facade including coloured, vaguely Egyptianate motifs.

Just east of Dingles is **St Peter's Church**, ST PETER'S ROAD. This is a visual feast, with a wonderfully colourful interior where it seems almost every surface is painted. This complex church was designed by G. E. Street and built during 1854-79, using the south aisle of the earlier church on the site as its basis. Pass through the crossing arch, covered by a Clayton and Bell fresco of 1873, and then the adjacent openwork stone arch (shades of Wells Cathedral), to reach the sanctuary and a reredos with mosaic panels dating from 1899; these replaced an earlier decorative scheme including tiles by William Morris. The original tiles were the first of only three church commissions for tilework obtained by Morris. Two east wall panels, showing processing angels, were designed by Morris himself, while four panels on the north and south walls were New Testament scenes by Burne-Jones. However, soon after their installation around 1866 the panels began to disintegrate, and they were removed in 1899.[2] The present mosaics, whose subjects - angelic wings to the fore - match the originals were designed by Arthur Blomfield and made by Powell & Sons; below the mosaics are red and white glass tiles, also by Powell's.

These tiles were made by crushing fragments of flint glass, contaminated by clay, and then fusing the resulting powder to create opaque glass; this material could then be shaped and used just as a normal ceramic tile, but one having only the tiniest clay content.[3] They were often used in the context of decorative schemes including glass mosaic and opus sectile work. There is, indeed, a multicoloured opus sectile panel at the east end of the north aisle wall. It shows Christ preaching and bears the inscription 'In memory of Walter Scott Evans for more than 30 years churchwarden of this parish Jan 10th 1908'. The addition of gold mosaic makes this a lively panel, but there is no sign of its designer.

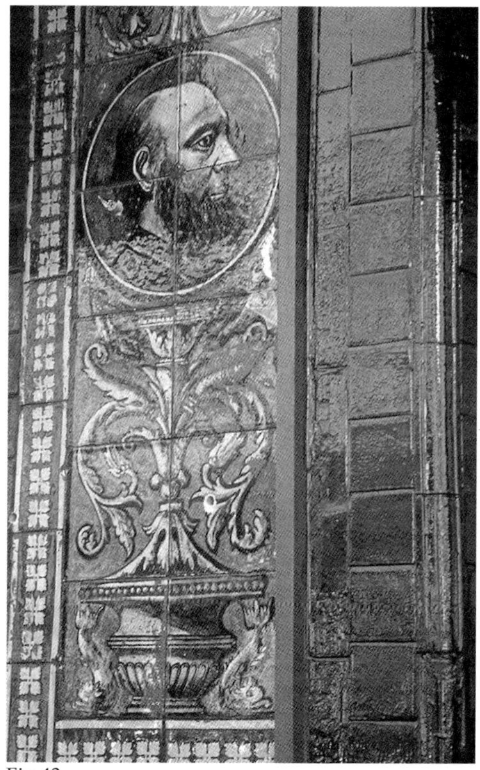

Fig 43.

Leaving the churchyard, wherein lies the heart of Percy Shelley, further east is **Joseph's Terrace**, 216-36 OLD CHRISTCHURCH ROAD, developed by Joseph Cutler around 1880, and still bearing (at 222-6) one and a half portraits of the bearded developer in painted circular panels on green glazed tile pilasters with floral ornament (Fig 43). These primitive but endearing images were probably produced by the Patent Architectural Pottery. Across the roundabout at the end of Old Christchurch Road rises the unlikely tower of **The College** (Lansdowne College), CHRISTCHURCH ROAD. A floor mosaic outside its entrance carries the date 1910, while inside are extensive floor mosaics including a coat of arms. South-east of The College on GERVIS ROAD is **St Swithun's Church**, designed by Richard Norman Shaw and built in 1876-8 (chancel) and 1891 (nave). The east wall has a dado of Hispano-Moorish style *cuenca* tiles, one of Shaw's favourite finishes because of their handmade look; they were probably made by Frederick Garrard.

West of St Swithun's on the clifftop is the unlikely Scottish Baronial pile of the **Russell-Cotes Art Gallery and Museum**, EAST CLIFF, built in 1897-1907 (as East Cliff Hall) for Sir Merton and Lady Russell-Cotes as a house-cum-museum. The design was by the Irish engineer and architect John Frederick Fogerty, who practised in Bournemouth from 1893. Sir Merton, who became mayor of Bournemouth, owned the town's Royal Bath Hotel; the interior decoration of East Cliff Hall was carried out by John Thomas and his son Oliver, who were responsible for decorating the hotel. A Japanese theme ran through both house and hotel, although the house also had a Moorish alcove (inspired by the Alhambra) and much decoration related to the family's Scottish background. The ceramics include Maw & Co tiles in the porch (which dates from 1907), Persian tiles in several toilets and terracotta busts on the picture gallery (1918-19). The fireplace tiles in the study, decorated by Carter's of Poole, allude to Sir Merton's position in society, showing his monogram, a cockerel and the motto from his coat of arms. Out in the garden are edging tiles, urns and an eagle made by the South Western Pottery of Poole and illustrated in their 1878 catalogue. Modern commissions complement the historic ceramics: in the family gallery is a panel of fish tiles (1990) by Dorset designer-makers John Hinchcliffe and Wendy Barber, and in the adjacent café is a bold, abstract tile mural (1999) by Hinchcliffe on the theme of the sea.

Back in central Bournemouth and west of The Square, the superb **Branksome Arms** on POOLE HILL, built around 1905, displays a brightly coloured tiled advertisement for Eldridge Pope's Dorchester Ales in its porte cochere; the brewer's arms lie within a green oval on a yellow ground, surrounded by ornate scrollwork (Fig 44). The pub's main facade is an exuberant combination of green glazed brick with pale grey Carter's ceramic

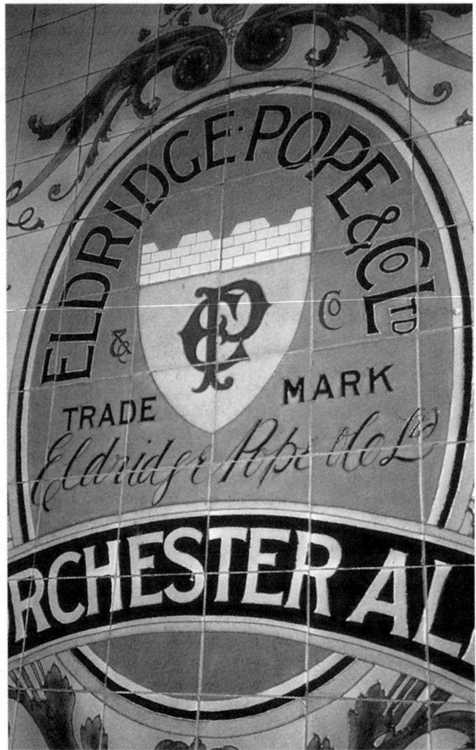

Fig 44.

marble dressings. Just south in West Hill Road is the **Pembroke Arms**, now the Goat and Tricycle, which was built about 1900 and designed by the Bournemouth architect C. T. Miles. Its pleasingly fishy green faience facade was produced by Carter's for Marston's Dolphin Brewery of Poole; note the beady-eyed fish on either pilaster.[4]

On the northern edge of town in Castle Lane East is the **Royal Bournemouth Hospital**, where sixteen W. B. Simpson tile panels - originally installed at the Royal Victoria Hospital in Boscombe - may be found, mounted on the stairs. The panels, which date from 1910 and show nursey rhymes and fairy tales, were moved from the now-demolished hospital in 1993.

Boscombe

In Michelgrove Road, on the cliffs above Boscombe Pier and overlooking Boscombe Chine, is **San Remo Towers** (1935-8), a massive block of 164 flats designed by the American architect Hector O. Hamilton for Armstrong Estates of Guildford (Fig 45). The flats were intended to attract a superior type of clientele, their modern conveniences including central heating, an 'auto vac' cleaning system, a residents' club and a restaurant. Hamilton created an aspirational exterior to match, the six entrances being emphasised by surrounds of candy-striped Carter's faience in barley-sugar engaged columns. The five blocks were identified by faience lettering (A to E and the main entrance) and were partly faience tiled. This superlative piece of seaside architecture bears more relation to Miami's colourful art deco hotels than to the white modernist houses which colonised the English coast during the 1930s. The flats were restored during 2000-2 using coloured faience mullions replicated by the terracotta and brick manufacturers Lamb's of Billingshurst, West Sussex.

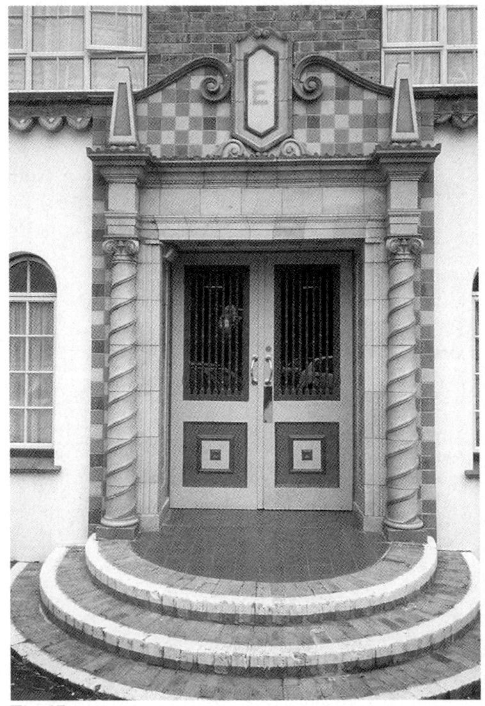

Fig 45.

To the north is **St Clement's Church**, St Clement's Road, the first major church to be designed by the architect J. D. Sedding; it was largely built in 1871-3, the tower being added in 1890-3. Sedding's decorative treatment included encaustic floor tiles showing an anchor motif within a large square pavement of patterned tiles; elaborate encaustic tiling runs throughout the nave, chancel and lady chapel. J. D. Sedding married the sister of the first vicar of St Clement's, and designed three gravestones for the churchyard.

Southbourne

In the side aisles of **St Katherine's Church**, CHURCH ROAD is a series of nine-tile encaustic groups bearing an unusual catherine wheel motif in buff on red ground with yellow glaze; the tiles may have been manufactured by Carter's. To the west at 128-44 SEABOURNE ROAD (just south of Pokesdown Station) is **Julian Terrace**, built around 1920 with much Carter's buff terracotta and red faience ornament including two enormous rectangular cartouches bearing the terrace name. A little further south at 1-17 FISHERMANS AVENUE is a row of two-storey houses dating from about 1900. The porches have elaborate glazed tile dadoes in the form of green or blue-grey panels with embossed art nouveau plants, all within a yellow and dark green border.

Westbourne

The former **Grand Cinema** (now Grand Bingo), POOLE ROAD opened in 1922 and was designed by J. E. Hawker; the building also included four shops. Its grey Carter's ceramic marble facade is topped by reclining figures each side of a central pediment. The cinema had a sliding roof which could be opened during intervals; it showed its final film in 1977. Close by, the house 5 PINE TREE GLEN, dating from about 1880, is faced entirely with red floor tiles and bands of buff and black encaustic tiles. A buff panel on the east chimney stack bears a motif in green glazed tiles.

BROWNSEA ISLAND

St Mary the Virgin Church was built in 1853-4 by Colonel William Petrie Waugh of Branksea Castle, who bought the island in 1852 hoping to exploit its resources of china clay. In the chancel are a few strips of single tiles, but in the room beneath the tower - a private family pew - is a superb fireplace, with Minton tiles also dating from the 1850s (Fig 46). It stands beneath a timber ceiling taken from Sir John Crosby's house in the City of London, which was built in 1466; the ceiling was removed in the early nineteenth century and the house demolished around 1906. Adjoining the private pew is another private room containing a chest tomb supporting the recumbent effigy of a later owner of the island, Charles van Raalte. Altogether, this is a most unusual church in a most unusual situation.

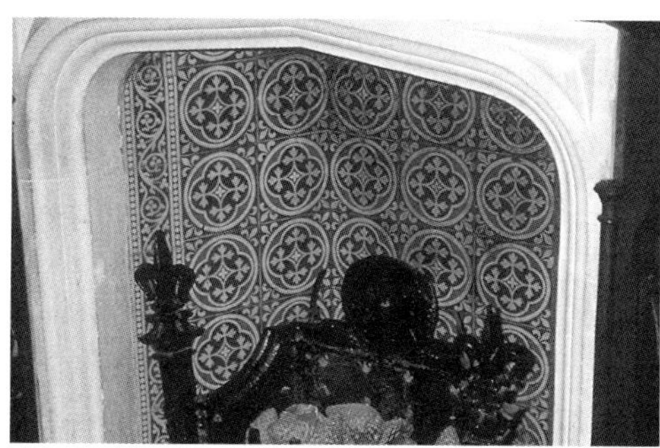

Fig 46.

CHARMINSTER

The **Herrison Hospital**, just north of Charminster, was erected in 1859-63 as the Dorset County Asylum; its exterior was notable for strongly polychromatic brickwork. Several wards were added during 1870-80, and were kitted out with fifteen fireplaces decorated with series of Minton Hollins picture tiles. The extension known as Herrison House, dating from around 1904-14, has much decorative buff terracotta used in combination with red brickwork; the central part of this building was undergoing conversion to flats in 2002.

CHRISTCHURCH

At **Christchurch Priory**, medieval encaustic tiles may be found in the north transept (beneath a wooden trap door against the north wall), and under the monumental Salisbury Chantry in the chancel, where one design is of a church with a central tower. Godwin's supplied tiles for the Priory during nineteenth century restoration works. In the centre of town at SAXON SQUARE, on the wall of the shopping development overlooking the roundabout, is the beautifully executed Saxon Warrior (1982) tile mural by the artist and potter David Ballantyne, made soon after his retirement from teaching at Bournemouth College of Art. His first architectural commission had been a tile mural at Oxford Railway Station (1974, demolished).[5]

DORCHESTER

Dorchester South Station, opened in 1986, was sponsored and built for British Rail by the local brewers Eldridge Pope & Co, whose ornate brewery may be seen from the train. On platform

1 is a hand-painted 'Welcome to Dorchester' tile panel, showing a town scene combined with the words 'Home of Eldridge Pope & Co plc'; the panel, which has a semicircular top, is about four feet high by two feet wide and was made by Florian Tiles of Sturminster Newton. On the station's exterior is a circular terracotta commemorative plaque, dated 1986. Nearby, at Eldridge Pope's Dorchester Brewery (the **Thomas Hardy Brewery** since 1997), WEYMOUTH AVENUE, there is much attractive polychromatic brickwork, a green tiled plaque bearing the EP logo at the base of the chimney stack, some terracotta ornamentation and tiles in the segmental blanks above two windows. The Dorchester Brewery was largely built in 1880, although some of the associated buildings date from the mid-1880s and the brewhouse was rebuilt after a fire in 1922. The highly decorative nature of the brewery arose from Eldridge Pope's decision to employ brewers' architects Scamell & Colyer, known for their ornate structures, in combination with the Weymouth architect G. R. Crickmay, best known for his work on local churches.

In the centre of Dorchester there is a good late Victorian tile and faience butcher's shop with an original interior at 14 HIGH EAST STREET, while the nearby **Borough Arms** has a tiled stall riser showing the words 'J. Goldie Ltd' (probably the pub's owner rather than the brewer) in brown art nouveau style lettering on yellow ground. In the foyer of **Dorchester Central Library**, HIGH WEST STREET is an attractive ceramic mural of Old Dorchester, made by the pupils of St Mary's School, Puddletown. Also in High West Street is **St Peter's Church**, whose east wall bears a two-section opus sectile scene of the *Nativity* (1922). Still in the town centre, outside **Waitrose** is an unglazed ceramic mural depicting the history of the town; it was designed by John Hodgson and installed in 1986. It comprises five rectangular panels, each 46" by 64", connected by a horizontal band of tiles just over eight yards in length; the colours are mainly cream and brown.

HAMWORTHY

St Michael's Church, BLANDFORD ROAD was built in 1958-9 by Morley & Bolden of Poole. Inside this brick-built church is a colourful reredos in the form of a semicircular Carter's panel showing a virile St Michael triumphing over a spectacular green dragon. It was probably designed by Harold and Phoebe Stabler, who were then much influenced by the Della Robbia style, expressed most strongly in the cherubs around the panel's border. The Carter archives also suggest the presence of a panel in a niche above a doorway, showing 'The Good Shepherd'.[6] Further along Blandford Road, near Poole Bridge, is **Old Rope Walk**, a 1905 almshouse-style development by Carter's for their workers. Here the end cottage has a small triangular ceramic inset in its gable, showing a decorative cream 'C' with green scrollwork on a cream ground.

IWERNE COURTNEY

The nineteenth century terracotta reredos of **St Mary's Church** was designed by Lady Baker and made in her own local pottery; its motifs include grapes, angels and a bust of Christ.

KINGSTON

St James Church at Kingston on the Isle of Purbeck was designed by G. E. Street in 1873-4 and built during 1874-80 for John Scott, 3rd Earl of Eldon. It was part of a building programme devised by the Earl to keep his Encombe estate labourers in employment, and all materials were obtained from the Encombe quarries. Street called it his jolliest church, although its interior feels cool and monumental; there is an encaustic tile pavement.

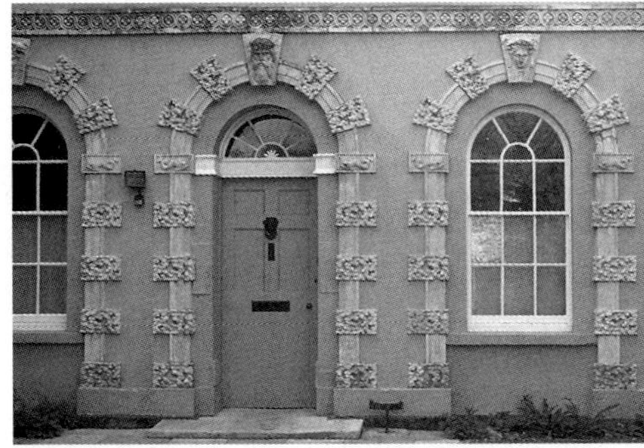

Fig 47.

LYME REGIS

Eleanor Coade took over the lease of **Belmont** (then Bunter's Castle), POUND STREET, from her uncle Samuel Coade in 1784, and used the house to put on a fine display of wares from her Artificial Stone Manufactory in Lambeth (Fig 47).[7] Both house and garden are ornamented with Coade stone, some pieces having designs not seen elsewhere, including dolphins and a crowned king (a keystone); the family crest, a coot, features on gate piers. The urns dotted along the parapet and the rest of the profuse decoration were all executed in Coade stone.

In the 1990s the stone-carver Philip Thomason of the Somerset firm Thomason Cudworth revived the manufacture of a Coade-type stone, using (amongst twelve ingredients) ball clay which may be the same as that used by Eleanor Coade. An ammonite public footpath in neo-Coade stone made by Thomason Cudworth was laid at the **Lyme Regis Philpot Museum**, BRIDGE STREET around 2000.[8]

MILTON ABBAS

Sir George Gilbert Scott restored the church at **Milton Abbey** (founded around 935) in 1865. On removing the Portland stone paving (laid in 1789) from the chancel he found the remains of a medieval tile pavement, whose designs included birds, animals, and heraldic and geometrical devices in red and buff. Godwin's were asked to reproduce the tile designs, and the substitute pavement was laid so as to resemble the medieval arrangement as far as possible, with new elements being added where necessary, although it is now impossible to tell new and old apart.[9] On a hill just to the east of the church is **St Catherine's Chapel**, a Norman pilgrim chapel. Some of the medieval tiles displaced from the Abbey church in 1789 were laid in the chapel's chancel, although they were relaid in 1901, with the addition of others found by Scott and initially relaid in the rood-screen gallery of the Abbey church. The chapel's floor now comprises over 670 rather worn Wessex medieval patterned tiles, along with border tiles by Godwin's. The medieval tiles date from the thirteenth to the fifteenth centuries and have a greta variety of designs.

POOLE

Until its demolition in 2001, the obvious place to begin a tour of Poole would have been Poole Pottery itself, sited on THE QUAY, beside the huge and dramatic expanse of the harbour. The site has now been occupied by the towering Dolphin Quays development comprising shops and flats, into which it is intended to incorporate some of the large-scale tile panels which originally decorated the Pottery. Of course, examples of Poole Pottery's output remain on buildings throughout the town. To find them, head west along the quayside past the first of many local pubs with ceramic facades, the buff, brown and black glazed brick **Jolly Sailor**. The pub also has a good door canopy, in dark brown - almost lustrous - faience; two further ceramic panels may be hidden by later signage. Next is the entrancing **Poole Arms** whose facade, a massive emerald green faience gable end, shimmers in reflected light from the water opposite. Dark green dressings, a classical doorcase, a central panel with the pub's name in gold lettering, and the town's coat of arms - also a trademark of the local brewers, Marston's - on yellow ground in a circular panel at the top of the gable make this a most memorable pub front. It is the work of Carter's (later Poole Pottery), who showed the pub's mosaic doorway panel in a catalogue dating from about 1908.[10]

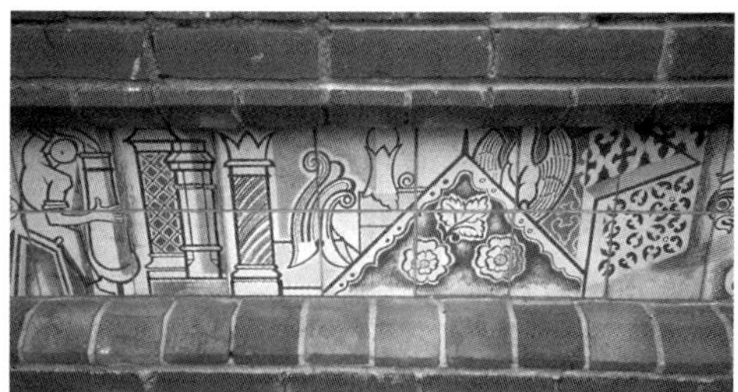

Fig 48.

A slight deviation away from the quayside is required to reach the Tourist Information Centre and **Waterfront Museum**, 4 HIGH STREET, where a Carter's plaque of the town arms is topped by a voluptuous figure of mermaid, supposedly based on a shapely local lass who was a one-time 'Miss World' winner. Back on the Quay is the 1990 residential development **Barber's Wharf**, with a charming series of pictorial tile panels strung out at low level along its frontage (Fig 48). Depicting local industries and activities, these well-produced panels deserve better than to be mounted only a few inches above the pavement. They were one of the last works of the artist and potter David Ballantyne (1913-90), who taught at Bournemouth College of Art between 1950 and his retirement in 1978, after which he undertook several commissions concerned with architecture and restoration.[11] At the Quay's end is **Poole Bridge** (opened 1927), with large, high relief Della Robbia ware panels proudly showing the town's coat of arms on the outside of each of its four piers; all are signed 'Carter, Stabler & Adams Ltd 1926' (Fig 49).

To explore the town itself, return to the Poole Pottery site and head inland along OLD ORCHARD, passing the former **Swan Inn** (now a shop), rebuilt by the architect C. T. Miles of Bournemouth in 1906. The glazed brick facade is in lime and emerald green, with rich brown

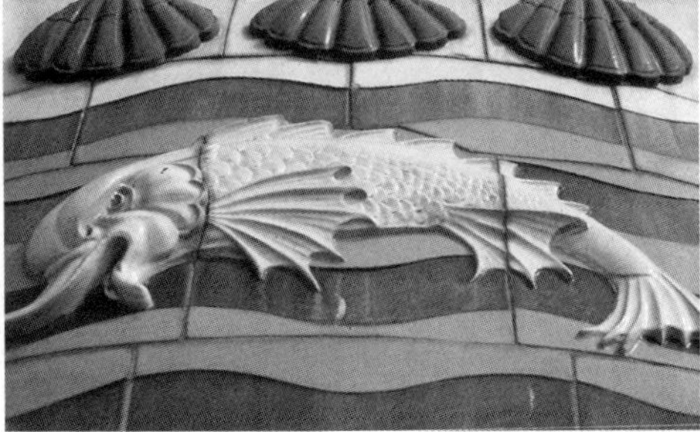

Fig 49.

faience dressings and a green faience keystone - a rather startled dolphin - above the door. On the fascia two elegant tube-lined swans bear decorative swags in their beaks, and a panel reads 'Marston's Poole Ales'. The dolphin refers to Marston's Dolphin Brewery, which stood nearby on Market Street. On the corner of Old Orchard and HIGH STREET is **Peri Ice Cream** shop, once Yeatman's the florists, as suggested by two pretty tube-lined Carter's panels of flowers in natural colours on black ground (Fig 50). The design of these six-inch tiles was by Reginald Till, and they were fixed on the Old Orchard facade in December 1949.[12]

Round the corner in LOWER HIGH STREET is the **Old Orchard** office building (no public access); inside is a 1976 Carter's tile panel showing the Old Orchard area around 1600; it was designed by the Jones Design Co-partnership. Continue northward through the pedestrianised area, soon reaching a well-preserved **Dewhurst's** at 135 High Street, with at least eleven Carter's pictorial four-tile panels from the pretty *Farmyard* series designed by E. E. Stickland around 1922; they were used in many Dewhurst shops until the 1960s. Just off the High Street in LAGLAND STREET the former **Norton Free Library** (now Wetherspoon's) has red terracotta decoration and a discreet tile plaque in buff and brown worded 'These buildings were erected and presented to the Borough of Poole as a Free Library by John J. Norton Esq. Novr 19th 1887'. Inside, the pub's decorative theme is Poole Pottery, with large photographic copies of the well-known Poole map tile panel of around 1930 (designed by Edward Bawden and painted by Margaret Holder) and several of the firm's interwar advertisements displayed on the walls.

This endorsement of the value of local history is rather a contrast to the fate of an actual Carter's tile panel at Poole Library, which can be found on the northern edge of the town centre in a typically sprawling Arndale Centre; this was designed in 1963-9 by architects W. Leslie Jones & Partners, and is now known as the **Dolphin Shopping Centre**. At first floor level inside the Centre is the Library, where - until refurbishment took place around 2002 - readers were greeted by a jolly full-height Carter's tube-lined panel in black and white on pale blue depicting the architectural wonders of Poole (Fig 51). At the far end of the same floor is still a brightly coloured mosaic of similar size showing a breezy yachting scene; this is unsigned. The new-style Library is certainly more open and welcoming, but there seems no apparent reason why this little piece of the town's history could not have been left on display rather than boarded over.

Fig 50.

Heading out of town on PARKSTONE ROAD we find **Parkstone Court**, a small block of flats built in 1999 with a pleasingly detailed decorative terracotta roundel in its gable showing the date and a galleon. Well outside the town at the end of Parkstone Road stands the Municipal Buildings, now **Civic Centre**, designed by L. Magnus Austin

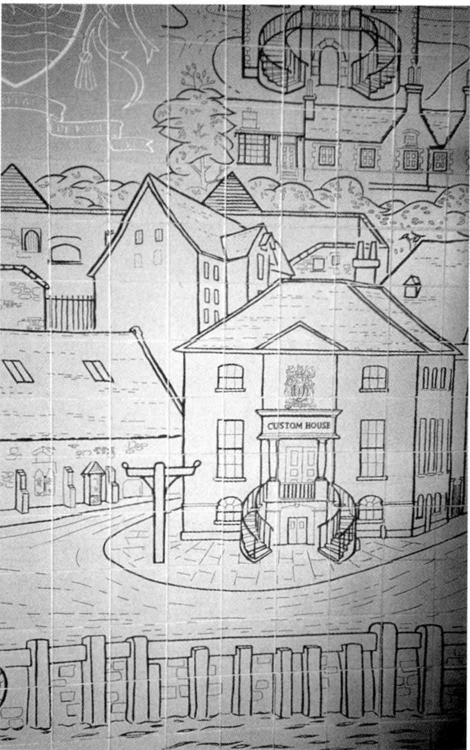

Fig 51.

working under the Borough Surveyor E. J. Goodacre in 1931-2. It has decorative Moderne stonework reliefs of local scenes, and a coat of arms in Carter's faience above the main entrance. Just inside is a mosaic floor depicting the arms and an assortment of Poole landmarks.

Broadstone

Yaffle House in WATER TOWER ROAD was designed by the architect Edward Maufe in Spanish Mission style and built in 1930 for Charles Carter, managing director of Carter & Co until his retirement in 1928. Ceramic decoration on the semi-butterfly plan house include reliefs of a yaffle (a green woodpecker) on the balcony; the doorway has a black faience architrave which is dated and bears the initials of client and architect. The still-complete contemporary interior includes mosaics.

Parkstone

Just north of Parkstone station, across the main Bournemouth road, is **St Peter's Church**, PARR STREET. The chancel of this large, spire-less stone church was built by Frederick Rogers of London in 1876-7; John Loughborough Pearson consolidated the chancel in 1881, then added the nave and transepts in 1891-2; his son F. L. Pearson completed the church in 1900-1. Carter's supplied and laid the tiled floors in 1877.[13]

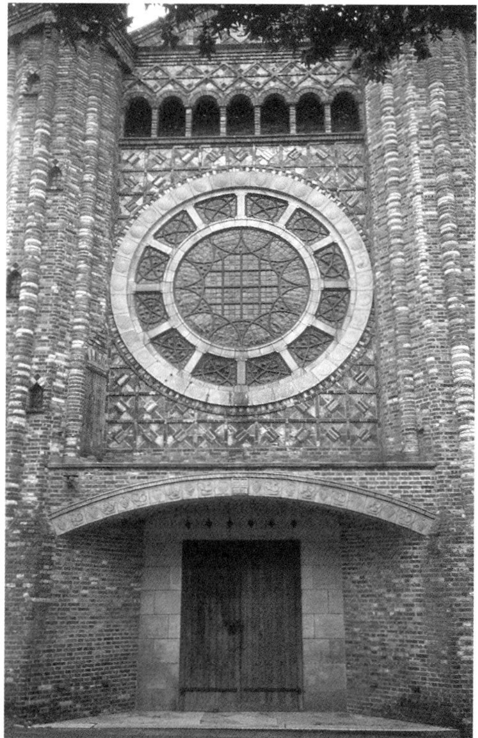
Fig 52.

Half a mile east along BOURNEMOUTH ROAD, at its junction with St Osmund's Road, is the **Church of St Osmund** (Fig 52). The foundation stone of the church was laid in 1904, but it was 1916 before this most unusual structure was complete. Its Byzantine-style design originated with a Parkstone architect, George Bligh Livesay, who had erected a temporary nave and aisles - based on the church of San Zeno, Verona - by July 1905. St Osmund's was one of the last large churches to be built in this area, at a time when terracotta and faience were popular as facing materials, and Livesay's design used Carter's cream terracotta blocks with capitals and cornices in red.[14] A hiatus of several years followed this initial activity, and further building did not take place until 1913, by which time Livesay was unable to continue as architect. He may have already joined the army by then; he died at sea on the 29th May 1916. It fell to the architect E. S. Prior, in partnership with Arthur Grove, to complete the church, and it turned out to be Prior's final work. He altered the external detailing, specifying thin, specially-textured wire-cut bricks (hand-made at Newtown Vale Brickworks in Poole) and only a limited amount of buff terracotta work.[15]

The interior features fluted Ionic columns of red terracotta in the apse, with a low wall in cream terracotta, its coping wide enough to form a seat for the clergy. Behind the high altar is the bishop's throne, made entirely of terracotta and supported by feet decorated with lion's heads; an amazing white faience baldachino, partly gilded, soars above while twelve winged angel heads look on. The copper-roofed dome is of cast concrete within an octagonal brick shell; it was found to be unsafe in 1922 and its crown was rebuilt by Sidney Tugwell (1869-1938) of Bournemouth, a leading arts and crafts architect in the area. There is much more red and cream terracotta in the nave, with many specials (one-off pieces) and hardly any standard mouldings; St Osmund's was a major undertaking for Carter's, who provided all the terracotta. This unforgettable and original church is also rich with mosaics and has excellent hand-made abstract stained glass by Prior. Sadly, the experimental nature of its construction, involving an unusually early use of reinforced concrete, resulted in structural problems leading to the closure of the church in 2001; it was declared redundant in the same year.

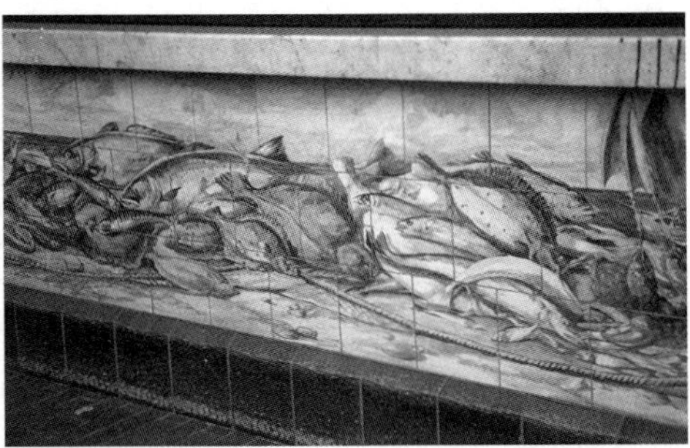

Fig 53.

Turn south along St Osmund's Road and left into PENN HILL AVENUE to find (at its far end) 7-8 **Bank Chambers**, where the twin fishmonger's and butcher's shops behind the dark green and brown faience arcade are now one under the name Bankes Bistro; the unique tiled fish mural (signed Carter & Co Ltd, Poole) and lettering survive in good condition (Fig 53). The shop, originally Jenkins & Sons, was built in 1923 and designed by architects Lawson & Reynolds, while the delicately drawn fish panel, with its inevitable yachts, was designed and painted by James Radley Young. Even the lettering, advertising cooked meats and family butchers, on the butchery half of this double feature is unusual; the 'A' has what might be called a flying serif.

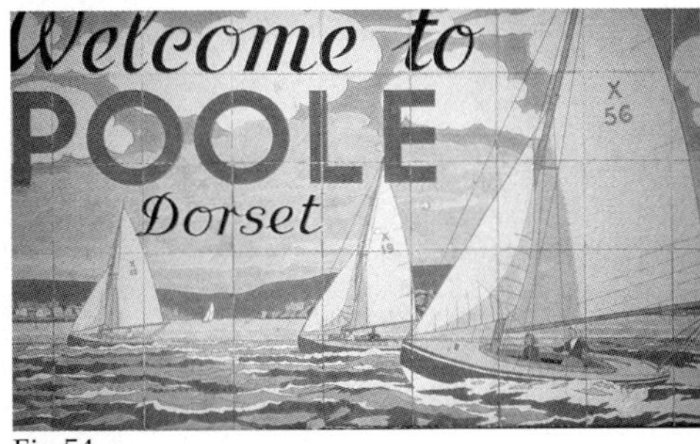

Fig 54.

Sandbanks

From Sandbanks a chain ferry runs across to South Haven Point (thence Swanage), while a smaller ferry crosses to Brownsea Island. Near the ferry terminal, at the junction with PANORAMA ROAD, a Carter's 'Welcome to Poole' tube-lined tile panel survives *in situ*; it shows yachts in Poole harbour and a distant Brownsea Castle (Fig 54). These town panels, designed by Arthur Nickols in the 1950s, could originally be found on a number of Poole's local approach roads, and were also made for Swanage and Wareham. Another is still to be found about three miles north-east along the coast, on ALUM PROMENADE at the Poole-Bournemouth border.

SHERBORNE

Relaid medieval floor tiles remain in the Lady Chapel and the Chapel of St Mary le Bow at **Sherborne Abbey**. All surviving medieval tiles were removed from the choir during restoration by Carpenter & Slater in 1849-58, and exact replicas were made by Minton's; the designs included a four-tile group showing herons fishing. Although some Minton tiling is extant, notably in the aisles where scattered tiles feature the Digby arms and initials, the choir pavement was replaced by Purbeck stone in 1963. The redundant tiles were destroyed or sold as tea pot stands.[16]

SUTTON WALDRON

The interior of **St Bartholomew's Church** (built in flint in 1847) was decorated by Owen Jones in pure Ecclesiological style; the surfaces were painted with abstract patterns (partly derived from Jones's study of the Alhambra) in red, blues and gold. The scheme is probably the most important by Jones to survive. The chancel pavement is of Pugin-designed Minton encaustic tiles, and there are also Minton tiles around the font.

SWANAGE

The Weymouth architect George R. Crickmay rebuilt **Purbeck House** (1875, now an hotel) in what might be called Dorset Baronial style for George Burt (1816-94), nephew and successor of the London contractor John Mowlem. Its position on the HIGH STREET brings the visitor into direct contact with its walls, which are partly faced with granite left over from Burt's then-current construction project, the Albert Memorial. Also incorporated into this architectural emporium of a house are several terracotta plaques which originated at the Great Exhibition. The terrace has a pavement of Minton's patterned encaustic tiles, deemed surplus to requirements at the Houses of Parliament, and the billiard room was built partly of terracotta tiles. In the garden, amongst an odd variety of structures salvaged from Mowlem's London demolitions, is a temple erected after 1878; this has terracotta dragon finials and a floor of encaustic tiles removed from the House of Commons around 1880. Burt also built Swanage's market hall (1892, now the **Heritage Centre**), which has a mosaic floor of broken tiles salvaged from from various London building works.

TRENT

St Andrew's is a medieval church full of interest, with a superb collection of carved sixteenth - century bench ends as well as a fine rood screen and a seventeenth century Dutch pulpit. There are tile pavements in the north chapel, where hexagonal plain tiles form an interesting pattern, and in the chancel, where polychrome Minton encaustics were laid during restoration by the Rev. William Henry Turner around 1840. To the Rev. Turner the chancel also owes its north and south wall dado of what appears to be a diaper of moulded terracotta. The pattern is formed by repetition of a six-petalled flower within a concave-sided hexagon, surrounded by smaller convex-sided triangles enclosing round-lobed trefoils. The diaper appears to have been painted in green, blue, red and gold.

A possible attribution for this terracotta is suggested by similar work at St Stephen's Church, Westminster. The British Archaeological Association held its first annual meeting at Canterbury in 1844, and the cathedral was examined by the architectural section, presided over by Robert Willis and with Benjamin Ferrey as an honorary secretary.[17] In 1845, Willis published his architectural account of the cathedral, drawing attention to the diaper stonework of what was considered to be the remains of St Dunstan's shrine. He even used the diaper design as an illustration on the title page of the book.[18] Shortly after its publication, Ferrey designed St Stephen's, Westminster and the *Ecclesiologist* reported that 'the reredos is the reproduction of that beautiful diapering of the fragment of S. Dunstan's shrine at Canterbury, executed in terra cotta by Mr. Minton' and 'richly picked out with gold and colours'.[19] The painted stone diaper is still to be seen at Canterbury and is closely similar to the terracotta at Trent. The terracotta on the east wall at St. Stephen's has been painted white, but the design and measurements are the same. There seems to be no evidence to connect any of the Trent work with Ferrey, but he was the local diocesan architect from 1841.

WEYMOUTH

Weymouth's intricate network of back lanes has many reminders of the wealth of ceramics which once cheered the urban scene. Next to the railway station, on the corner of RANELAGH ROAD and Queen Street, is a former pub with rich red faience slabs to dado level, and two cornucopia panels plus another decorative floral panel, all in pale olive-green. The **South West Tools** shop in KING STREET, opposite the station, has a facade of green patterned tiles; turn into PARK STREET to see the remains of several small-scale glazed brick facades including that of the **Duke of Albany**, whose complete green glazed brick facade has survived intact. Divert east to the splendidly curving ESPLANADE for a glimpse of the Coade stone statue of **George III**, a regular visitor to Weymouth around the end of the eighteenth century. The monarch and accompanying lion and unicorn are all life-size, and the ensemble has been brightly painted since 1949. The original purpose of the statue, which was ordered in 1803 and made the following year, was to express the gratitude of the town for the king's continued patronage. However, he ceased to visit the town in 1805, and the statue was eventually erected in 1809 to mark the fiftieth year of his reign.[7]

South into the maze of tiny alleys to find the green faience facade of the **Wellington Arms**, ST ALBAN STREET, its fascia covered over; at 22 St Alban Street there are yellow abstract floral pattern tiles below a shop window. Nearby at 10-12 MARKET STREET are tile panels of yellow fleur-de-lys design on a green background, set below windows in first and second floor oriels; this attractive arrangement seems to be something of a local custom. Cross the Town Bridge, to the far side of the harbour, to see a repeat of this treatment at 12 TRINITY ROW, where there is a row of floral tiles beneath an oriel window. At **Holy Trinity Church**, TRINITY ROAD, is a large Powell's opus sectile reredos dating from 1920.[20] Then to **Brewers Quay**, HOPE SQUARE, originally the Hope Brewery of John Groves & Sons. Its imposing, well-fenestrated red brick Queen Anne facade dates from 1903-4 and was designed by Arthur Kinder & Son, a leading London firm of brewers'architects. The brewery was taken over by its near-neighbours, Devenish & Co, in 1960, but ceased brewing in 1985; the structure now functions as a shopping centre with associated heritage elements. To the right of the brewhouse, on a building which probably dates from the early 1960s (soon after the Devenish takeover), is a handsome full length framed tiled sign reading 'Devenish's Brewery' in red sans serif lettering with a black shadow on yellow ground; this could well be the work of Carter's.

West of the town centre on the ABBOTSBURY ROAD is **St Paul's Church**; the encaustic tile pavement in the chancel dates from the construction of the church in 1893-6. Cross back to the north of the harbour to find DORCHESTER ROAD leading out of town from the far end of the Esplanade; the **Royal Oak**, on the east side, dates from around 1900 and has a green faience facade with good lettering. This Devenish pub was probably designed by George R. Crickmay & Son, who worked on several of the brewery's houses as well as on Eldridge Pope's Dorchester Brewery. **St John's Church** (1850-4), on the same side of the road, has a Minton tiled sanctuary pavement.

Preston

St Andrew's Church, CHURCH ROAD was restored in 1855; there is an encaustic tiled chancel pavement.

Upwey

The **Church of St Laurence**, CHURCH STREET has a Minton tiled chancel pavement.

WIMBORNE MINSTER

The **Minster**, which was restored in 1855-7 by T. H. Wyatt, has an extensive Minton encaustic tile pavement in the choir and sanctuary. It features several unusual designs, including (at either side of the altar) circular tiles showing a fish beneath a feathered coronet, and a portcullis with single feather. The arrangement is articulated by bands of plain red and black tiles, and the sanctuary step riser carries a tiled biblical quotation. In addition, the sanctuary has a richly coloured tile and mosaic dado.

Dorset Roundup

St Nicholas Church, **Abbotsbury** has a patterned Victorian encaustic tiled pavement. There is a tiled inn sign for the former Five Bells in South Street, **Bridport**. In **Castletown**, Isle of Portland, the Portland Roads Hotel has a massive, partly striped gold and brown faience facade with high relief ornament, art nouveau touches and good Devenish lettering; the manufacturer was probably Burmantofts. Apart from its sixteenth century tower, St Mary's Church, **Chettle** (which stands in the grounds of Chettle House) dates from 1849-50; there is an encaustic tile pavement in the chancel. A cottage in Hayward's Lane, half a mile south-west of **Child Okeford**, is constructed entirely of terracotta made in a local pottery owned by Lady Baker. At **East Lulworth**, the exterior decoration of St Mary's R. C. Church, built in the grounds of Lulworth Castle in 1786-7, includes nine Coade stone vases. The Minton tile pavement at St Andrew's Church, **Fontmell Magna** was installed when the church was rebuilt in 1862-3.[21] The Britannia Inn at **Fortuneswell** on the Isle of Portland has a good (although overpainted) Eldridge Pope faience facade including lettering and brewer's motifs. There is much encaustic tiling at St Thomas Church (1851-2), **Melbury Abbas**. The encaustic tile pavement at St Nicholas Church, **Moreton** includes symbols of the passion (a theme continued by the 1958 engraved glass). There are patches of rather worn late thirteenth century and fourteenth century floor tiles in **Shaftesbury** Abbey Church, and more in the site museum. The east wall on either side of the altar at Holy Trinity Church, **Stourpaine** is faced with late Victorian tiling. St John's Church, **Tolpuddle**, has good 1850s Minton tiling. There is a Victorian encaustic tile pavement at St Mary's Church, **Turnworth**. Down on the quayside at **Wareham** is a Carter's map of the town by A. Lee; on the Railway Tavern, North Port (next to the railway station) is an interwar tile panel of a railway engine. There are Roman tiles in the external walls of the north transept and chancel (north side) at St Wite's Church, **Whitchurch Canonicorum**.

References

1. B. Emden, *Medieval decorated tiles in Dorset* (Phillimore, London & Chichester, 1977), p34.
2. Richard Myers and Hilary Myers, *William Morris Tiles - The tile designs of Morris and his Fellow-Workers* (Richard Dennis, Shepton Beauchamp, 1996), pp71-3.
3. Philip and Dorothy Brown, 'Glass tiles', *Glazed Expressions*, (1994) 28, pp2-3.
4. Carter Archive, Poole Museum Service, 2D 16.
5. Mike Allen, ed. *David Ballantyne: Creative Genius*, (Highcliffe Castle, 2003).
6. Carter Archive, Poole Museum Service, 2D 27.
7. Alison Kelly, *Mrs Coade's Stone* (Self Publishing Association, Upton-upon-Severn, 1990), pp230-2.
8. Amicia De Moubray, 'The Secret Coade Unlocked', *Country Life*, 197 (2003), pp106-8.
9. Emden, *Medieval decorated tiles in Dorset*, pp24-7.
10. Leslie Hayward, *Poole Pottery: Carter & Company and their successors, 1873-1995* 1st ed, ed. Paul Atterbury (Richard Dennis Publications, Shepton Beauchamp, 1995), p20.
11. Peter Stoodley, 'David Ballantyne - Renaissance Man of Clay', *Ceramic Review*, (1991) 128, pp20-23.
12. Carter Archive, Poole Museum Service, 2C 14.
13. *The Builder*, 5th January 1878, vol 36.
14. Martin Hammond, 'Worth a Detour 6: St Osmund's Church, Parkstone, Poole, Dorset', *Glazed Expressions*, (1985) 11, pp10-11.
15. Martin Hammond, 'The Bricks and Brickmakers of St Osmund's Church, Parkstone, Poole, Dorset', *British Brick Society Information*, (2003) 92, pp21-4.
16. Emden, *Medieval decorated tiles in Dorset*, p31.
17. *Archaeological Journal*, 1846, 1, pp267-83.
18. Robert Willis, *The Architectural History of Canterbury Cathedral* (Longman, London, 1845).
19. *Ecclesiologist*, June 1850, 11 (ns 8), p115.
20. Dennis W. Hadley, *James Powell & Sons: A listing of opus sectile, 1847-1973*, (2001).
21. *The Builder*, 26th December 1863, vol 21.

Durham

Like neighbouring Northumberland, County Durham is not known for its ceramic manufacturing, other than sanitary ware. The Gateshead Art Pottery produced hand-decorated tiles and earthenware around 1884-1900, but none of its tiles has yet been found in or on the county's buildings. However, unlike its northern neighbour, Durham does possess some impressive examples of decorative terracotta, for instance the facades of the Miners' Memorial Hall in Esh Winning and Sunderland's Elephant Tea Rooms. Tile and faience highlights include Pugin's work at Ushaw, Hartlepool's rare Doultonware fountain, the magnificent Burmantofts interior of Durham City's Old Shire Hall, and the Mountain Daisy in Sunderland, arguably the best ceramic pub interior in the country, let alone the county. Although listed grade II, it occupies a vulnerable site and needs greater statutory protection, which might already have been forthcoming if the Mountain Daisy had been located in Southwark rather than Sunderland. Finally, from the 1960s come the set of abstract tile panels at Sunderland Museum and Winter Gardens, which provide a heartening story of successful conservation work. Suggested reading: TACS Tour Notes *County Durham* (1998). The *Gazetteer* entry for Durham covers the administrative areas of Darlington Borough Council, Durham County Council, Gateshead Metropolitan Borough Council, Hartlepool Borough Council, South Tyneside Metropolitan Borough Council, Stockton-on-Tees Borough Council and Sunderland City Council.

DARLINGTON

On the southern edge of the town centre at 22 GRANGE ROAD, behind a mildly art nouveau stone facade, is a ceramic interior of national importance: **Sloan's Billiard Room**, built in 1907 and now the Drum art furniture showroom, is completely fitted out with Craven Dunnill wall tiling and pictorial panels. The tiles begin the moment one enters the small foyer, with a basic green and white tile scheme above a green-tiled dado; a tile-lined stair takes the visitor up to the billiard room itself on the first floor. What makes this building remarkable is the profusion of colourful pictorial wall panels, each measuring approximately 2 foot by 3 foot, showing landscapes and townscapes from home and abroad (in fact from nearby Brancepeth Castle to Venice). All the panels, which number at least twenty, are signed Craven Dunnill, and the scheme also includes faience frames for mirrors and windows. The room, original floorboards and all, is totally intact; it is easy to imagine it busy with Edwardian billiard players. The survival of the room in such good condition (some panels may have been overpainted in the past) is a tribute to its current owners.

Just north of the town centre on NORTHGATE is the old **Technical College**, now council offices, an imposing pile designed in 1893-6 by G. Gordon Hoskins, once clerk to Alfred Waterhouse. This handsome building displays an abundance of buff Burmantofts terracotta in vaguely perpendicular style, culminating in a pair of inspiring apotropaic figures on its pediment; it was shown in the firm's 1902 catalogue. Inside is more terracotta, used as arcading and balusters in combination with brown glazed brick on the stairwell. Opposite the college is a real curiosity, a heavily overpainted faience facade, part of a terrace, displaying a plaque commemorating Edward Pease, backer of the Stockton & Darlington Railway; this facade, however, is in poor condition. Across the rather soulless town centre in PARKGATE is **Darlington Civic Theatre**, built as the Hippodrome (or Palace) in 1907 and also designed by Hoskins. Again there are lashings of buff terracotta, in just the same shade as that of the Technical College, thus the manufacturer is very probably Burmantofts; the theatre was renovated in 1990. Just east on the corner of HARGREAVE TERRACE is the **Black Swan**. This fine pub has a dark green glazed brick facade incorporating five superb (although somewhat battered) tube-lined panels, each bearing a black swan in one of three different designs (Fig 55). The maker is unknown, but given the northerly location, could well be Duncan's of Glasgow. East again beneath the railway bridge to NEASHAM ROAD, where **St John's Church** - the railwayman's church - stands at the junction with Yarm Road (close to Darlington railway station). St John the Evangelist, whose imposing square tower was never crowned with the spire it clearly deserves, was built in 1847-9 by local architect John

Middleton. The chancel pavement, donated by Herbert Minton in 1849, includes vine leaves and symbols of St John on blue ground, in an arrangement unlike those seen in the Staffordshire churches to which Minton also gave tiles.

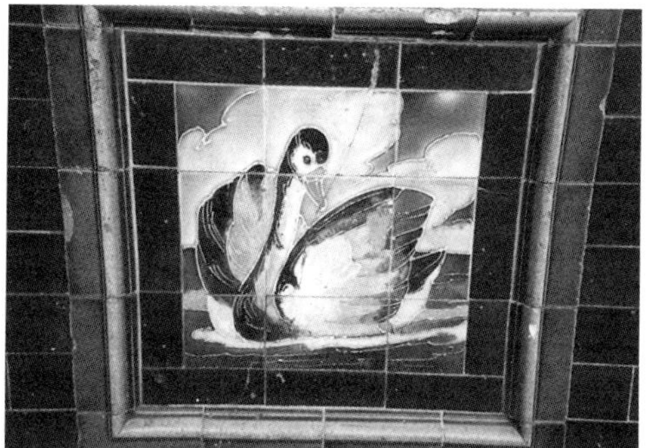

Fig 55.

On the eastern outskirts of Darlington, at the Morrison's Shopping Complex, MORTON PALMS (near the junction of the A66 and A67) is the landmark sculpture **Train**, designed by the artist David Mach and built from around 185,000 bricks in 1997 (Fig 56). The brick train, which appears to be steaming out from a hillside, stands near the route of the original Stockton & Darlington Railway; at over 150 feet in length, it was the largest single sculpture in Britain. Its apparent solidity conceals a hollow interior, which bats may enter via specially-made bat bricks.

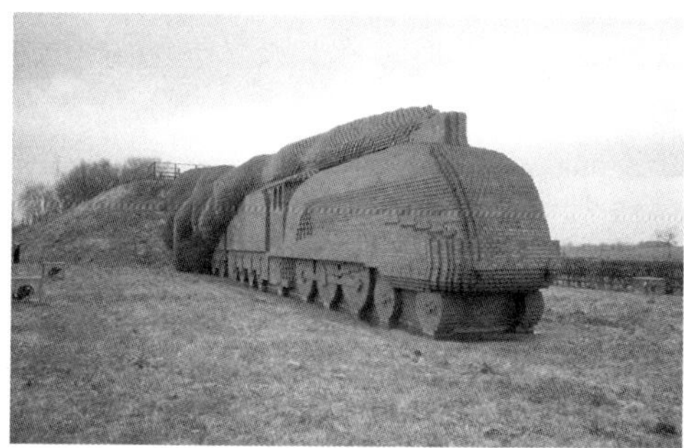

Fig 56.

DURHAM

Durham's major ceramic attraction, a monumental red-domed edifice, stands on OLD ELVET, to the east of the Cathedral peninsula: it is the **Old Shire Hall**, part of the University of Durham since 1963 and currently the University Office (Fig 57). The red brick and terracotta pile was built in 1896-8, the architects being Barnes & Coates of Sunderland; a blander (but still polychromatic) east wing was added in 1905. The sturdy, bright red terracotta balustrade and brick-lined stairway give an inkling of the stunning Burmantofts scheme within, where faience is all around, on walls and even ceilings. The staircase hall and most ground floor rooms are completely faced in hugely ornate faience, its colours ranging from cream through yellows and blue-greens to brown, the latter with superb colour variations. Even the staircase balusters are faience, with a brown faience 'handrail' almost a foot wide. This amazing scheme shows Burmantofts' unique ability to manufacture faience panels up to two feet in length but little more than an inch thick.[1] The lavish interior also includes wrought ironwork and colourful stained glass, while wall tiling in the 1905 extension is pinky-brown with a linenfold-style pattern; there is some doubt about the manufacturer.

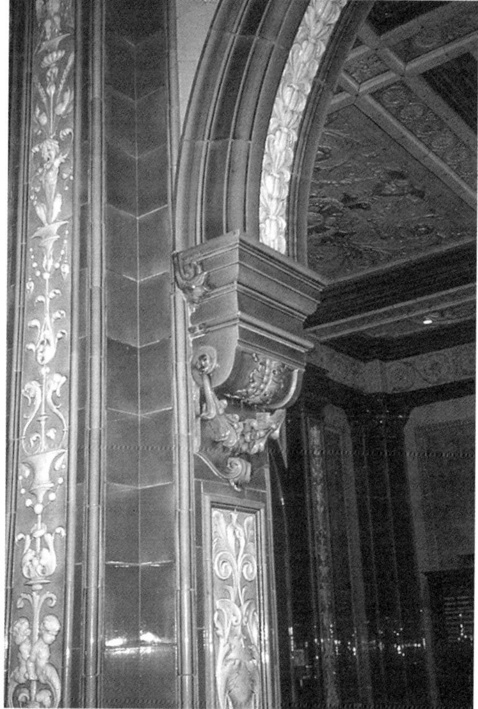

Fig 57.

Old Elvet leads westward to the junction with NEW ELVET and the **Half Moon** public house, whose facade displays five tiled pilasters.

The tiles, showing almost three-dimensional flowers on a strong pinky-red ground, are probably by Sherwin & Cotton, and date from an 1894 rebuilding by the Newcastle upon Tyne architects Oswald & Son.

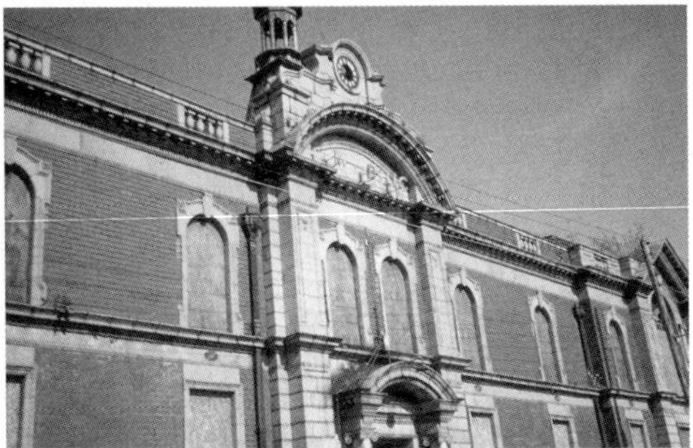

Fig 58.

ESH WINNING

The derelict **Esh Winning Miners' Memorial Hall**, a miniature French chateâu in red brick and yellow terracotta, stands forlorn and apparently unloved in BRANDON ROAD (Fig 58). Built in 1923 and designed by John Arthur Robson of nearby Langley Moor, it was one of several such halls put up in coalfield communities after the First World War. Inside, miners could enjoy a fine range of facilities, including cinema, concert hall, swimming bath, billiard room, games room and library. The £10,024 cost, including copious Edwardian baroque terracotta of unknown attribution, was met by contributions from local miners and the colliery company Pease & Partners, 543 of whose employees had died in the war.[2]

GATESHEAD

Central Gateshead is something of a ceramic desert, especially when compared with the riches available across the Tyne, but down on the quayside larger-than-life black glazed ceramic lettering on the exterior of the **Baltic** Centre for Contemporary Art, SOUTH SHORE ROAD, reveals its origins as a 1950s flour mill. Then to an unexpected gem: just west of central Gateshead in Bensham is Bensham Grove, now **Bensham Grove Community Centre**, BENSHAM ROAD. The house was the home of Robert Spence Watson (1837-1911), a political, social and educational reformer who was one of the founders of Newcastle University, a member of the Alpine Club and president of the National Liberal Federation 1890-1902. At Bensham Grove, which he extended between the mid-1850s and the 1870s, he entertained Rossetti and William Morris. Indeed, the library has stained glass, tiles and fittings designed by Morris & Co, and there are similar stained glass and fireplace tiles elsewhere in the house; the tiles date from the early 1870s. The library tiles are the *Seasons* pattern on five-inch tiles interspersed with the *Longden* pattern attributed to Philip Webb.[3] The house has been rather institutionalised, but surviving portraits of Spence Watson and his wife remind the observer of its original use. In the entrance is a colourful tile panel, its design based around a tree, produced at Bensham Grove by local ceramics course members soon after 1990; many of the images refer to local events, such as the 1990 Gateshead Garden Festival.

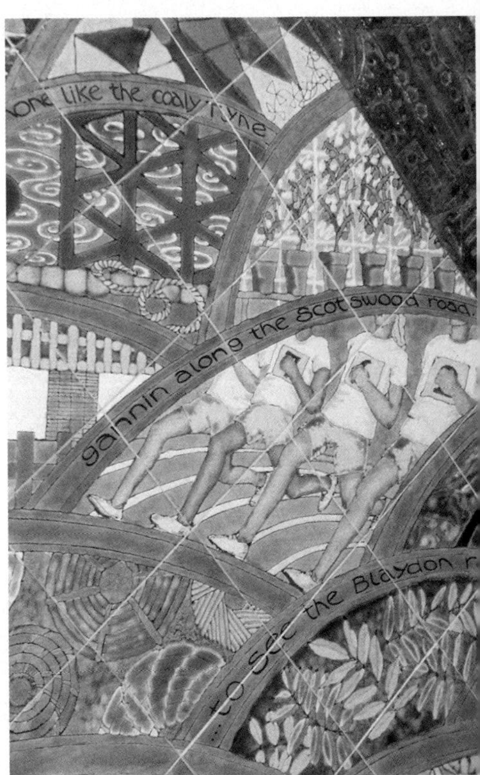

Fig 59.

An unusual and highly successful collaboration during 1994-6 between ceramicists in the north-east and Japan resulted in two spectacularly colourful installations at **Gateshead Leisure Centre** and **Gateshead Central Library**, PRINCE CONSORT ROAD. The town's artistic connections with Japan stretch back to the early 1990s; Komatsu is twinned with Gateshead and an artists exchange had long been discussed.[4] The potters Christine Constant and Jane Hufton of Gateshead visited Komatsu in 1994, with Junko Tokuda and Shuhei Koshita making the return trip the following year. Design ideas for the collaborative ceramic mural were collected from local people, who also helped with making and glazing the tiles. The design was drawn on to white biscuit tiles using a blend of wax resist and white oxide, giving a black line; coloured earthenware glazes were then painted between the lines and fired to 1040°C. The mural *Bridges of Friendship* was sited in the Leisure Centre in November 1996, and the smaller *Across Two Cultures* was later installed in the Central Library.[5] Both show wonderful use of highly coloured glazes; the Leisure Centre panel, around 3′ high by 25′ long, depicts images from the two countries and cultures, including the Tyne Bridge, athletes, origami designs and the tea ceremony (Fig 59). The English ceramicists were particularly inspired by the Japanese custom of wrapping and presenting everything in an ordered manner.

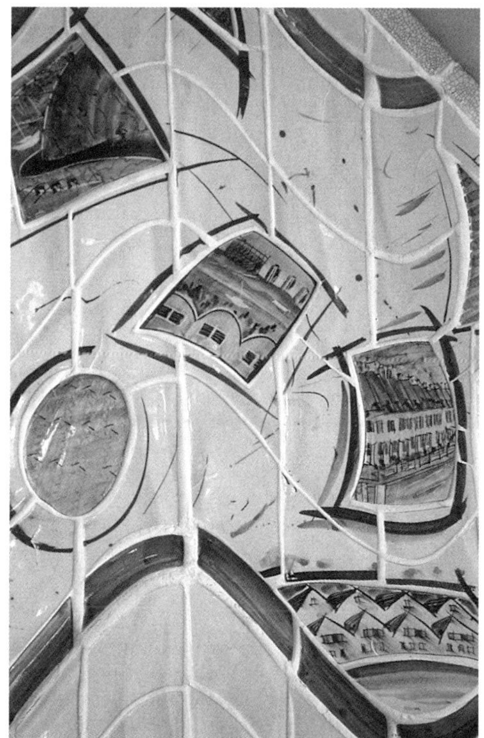

Fig 60.

Further south, in the main entrance to the **Queen Elizabeth Hospital**, on its hilly site in QUEEN ELIZABETH AVENUE, is a ceramic mural created in 1994 by Paul Scott and funded by Northern Arts (Fig 60). The basically abstract design begins outside the foyer and continues for about 15′ inside, its white ground laden with tiny but colourful depictions of local sites, all beautifully detailed.[6] In shape, the mural is a large-scale wave form, and the hand-made glazed porcelain tiles are anything but square. North of the hospital in Felling, the **Victorian Baker's Shop**, CARLISLE STREET, was created by Neil Talbot in 1986. It is a complete shopfront in ochre tiling, and includes a window display of carefully sculpted cakes and pies. Its shock effect has diminished of late as it has become rather grubby.

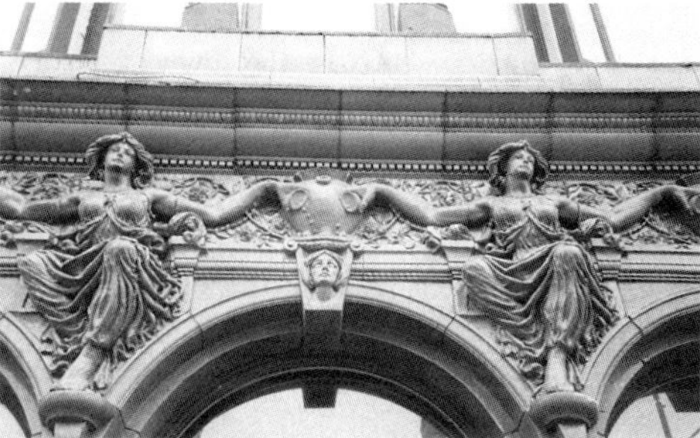

Fig 61.

HARTLEPOOL

Ceramic interest in Hartlepool centres on the new town of West Hartlepool, begun with the construction of new docks in 1847, rather than old Hartlepool itself, away on the distant headland. The **Railway Station** - whose sole remaining platform houses a Craven Dunnill North Eastern Railway map, dating from the early 1900s - stands just off CHURCH STREET, where a truly bizarre faience facade is to be found at the **Shades Hotel** (Fig 61). Barley-sugar style columns define the fenestration, while above runs a frieze of womanly (and rather bored) bacchantes, their arms outstretched and holding fast to urns, themselves supported by keystones in the shape of female heads. The facade was put up around 1900 and is made all the stranger by the almost non-ceramic appearance of the faience, perhaps a result of overpainting. The Shades is on the corner of LYNN STREET, wherein stands another ceramic pub, the **Market Hotel** (now a restaurant). Here the facade, which dates from the same period, is a more restrained but still decorative composition in green, buff and brown, with a nicely rounded bay window.

At the west end of Church Street, one of the town's earliest streets, is CHURCH SQUARE and the striking pinky-red brick and terracotta of the old **Municipal Buildings**, which dates mostly from 1886-9. The architect in this period of building was Richard Knill Freeman of Manchester, who won the commission in competition. There is much ceramic decoration, and perhaps this abundance of ornamentation is only to be expected from an architect who became something of a specialist in the design of pleasure pier pavilions. Just north of the square, in the grounds of the Gray Art Gallery and Museum, CLARENCE ROAD, is the **Henry Withy Memorial Fountain**, a tall, triangular faience structure in olive green, grey-blue and chestnut brown, topped by a royal blue ball finial; it dates from 1902 and was presented to the town by Withy, a local Justice of the Peace. It is one of the few remaining such faience memorials, most of which date from the Edwardian period and have often been damaged by weather and vandals; it has survived in remarkably good condition, possibly because of its present slightly out-of-the-way site. The Richard Eve fountain (Kidderminster, 1900) and the Hulm tomb (Burslem, 1905) are better-known and rather more ornate examples of these colourful but now rare objects. The Withy fountain is almost certainly Doultonware, and was probably one of the series - including the Eve fountain, with which it shares the same colour palette - designed in conjunction with Doulton's by the architects Meredith & Pritchard of Kidderminster.[7]

West of the central area at 125-7 PARK ROAD is a splendidly preserved butcher's shop interior dating from 1898. **Leighton's** was originally just one in a row of similarly tiled shops, but is now the sole working survivor. It was designed by the local architect James Garry, and its interior features meat rails and massive metal hooks as well as decorative (but not pictorial) wall tiling, mainly in blue and white and possibly by Minton Hollins.

HEBBURN

The heavily baroque brown and gold faience facade (very probably Burmantofts) of the **Albert**, ALBERT STREET, Hebburn was designed by South Shields architect Joseph W. Wardle for Gateshead brewer John Rowell & Son in 1908 (Fig 62). The pub would have catered for customers from the tightly packed terraced housing near the shipyards; much of this environment, including the music hall across the road, has now gone. Half a mile east along WAGONWAY ROAD is **Hebburn Business Park**, its location signalled by a large roadside ceramic panel designed by Christine Constant around 1996 (Fig 63). Bright colours and large images appeal to viewers in passing cars, but when examined closely there is also a wealth of detail and a variety of beautiful glaze effects.

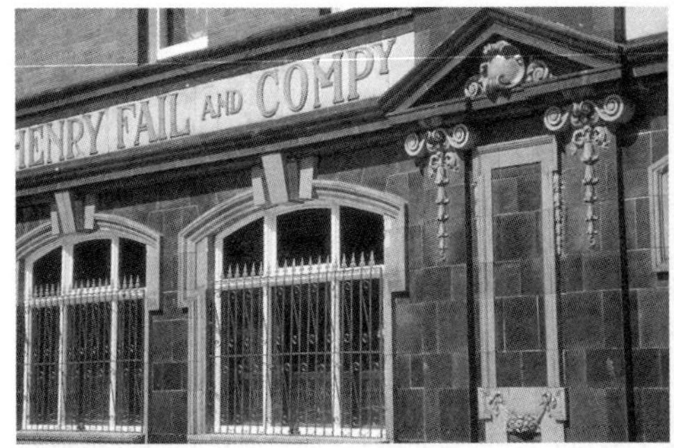

Fig 62.

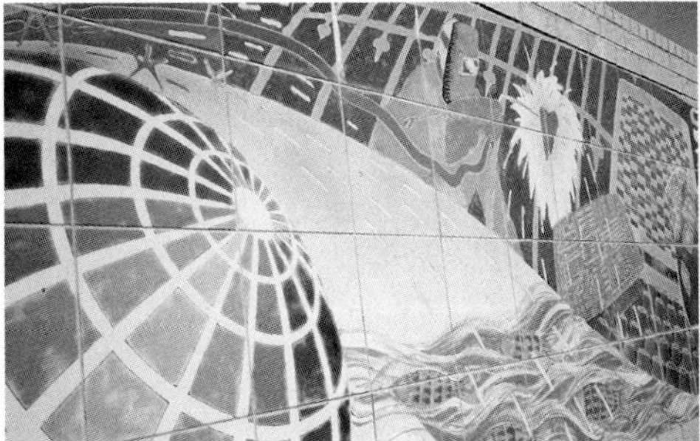
Fig 63.

JARROW

In the middle of what remains of Jarrow's town centre is the tall spire of **Christ Church** (1868) on CLAYTON STREET. The chancel's east wall and parts of its north and south walls were clad around 1891 with moulded terracotta in a pattern formed by repeats of a six-petalled flower within a concave-sided hexagon, surrounded by smaller convex-sided triangles. Similar terracotta, although dating from the late 1840s to 1851, may be found at Trent Church, Somerset and Church Leigh, Staffordshire; the manufacturer was Minton's and its design was inspired by St Dunstan's shrine at Canterbury Cathedral. As the Christ Church terracotta is of a later date, it is impossible to confirm its maker. The church suffered a fire during 2003, following which the intention was to restore the terracotta, which had been overpainted, to its original appearance.

Just east of Christ Church is the **Town Hall**, on GRANGE ROAD. It was built in 1902 and designed by South Shields architect Fred Rennoldson. The initial impression is red and spectacular, but it is clear that repetition of a number of basic decorative terracotta elements is responsible for this effect. Although there are numerous florid cartouches and a heavily overhanging porch there is little flair, no 'specials'; the most attractive part is the little octagonal openwork terracotta tower. The building was mentioned in the 1903 catalogue issued by terracotta manufacturers J. C. Edwards of Ruabon. The town hall's interior is much more memorable, however, with lavish mosaic, marble and stained glass, and a large Powell's opus sectile panel dating from 1904 in the council chamber. The design, a copy of a 1922 picture of a local shipbuilding yard, is carried out in vibrant colours, particularly the blues and greens of the rippling water.[8]

Opposite the Town Hall is the the VIKING CENTRE, a 1960s shopping experience, which is linked to the bus and metro stations by a **pedestrian underpass**; a second subway is nearby. The entrances of both are much enhanced by recent tile installations; the vivid images, including the Venerable Bede and the Jarrow Crusade, were based on the drawings of local schoolchildren and painted by Christine Constant. Beyond the Town Hall to the north on ORMONDE STREET and the (alas no longer) Market Square is a good **ex-Burton's**, complete with name, its inter-war white white faience facade stretching around the corner site. Off TYNE STREET, in Jarrow Riverside Park, is the southern entrance to the **Tyne Pedestrian and Cycle Tunnels**; for description, see Howdon, Northumberland.

SUNDERLAND

Elephants and other peculiar beasts peer down from the facade of the wonderfully wacky indo-gothic **Elephant Tea Rooms** (now Royal Bank of Scotland), which stands at the important High Street and FAWCETT STREET corner (Fig 64). Since 1879, when the elegant Wear Bridge opened to provide a direct rail connection with Newcastle, this has been the crossing point of the two main axes of this new city. Behind Fawcett Street is the railway station, while High Street West provides a link with Sunderland's original centre near the dockside. The Tea Rooms was designed by the idiosyncratic and imaginative local architect Frank Caws in 1873-7; the elephants and the rest of the eccentric, almost white terracotta dressings are by Doulton (whose name is high up on the corner turret). The replacement ground floor facade is dreadful, but above it the elephants and other beasties are well preserved.

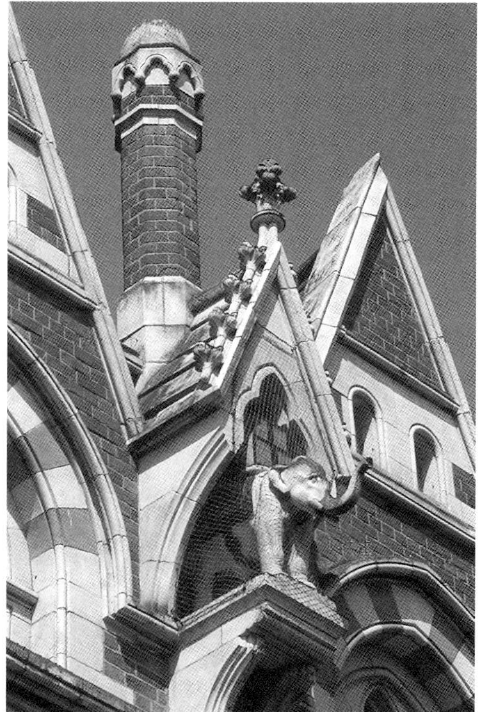

Fig 64.

Opposite is **Walkers Buildings** (1926), a decent enough off-white faience facade with much classical ornamentation, but rather overwhelmed in comparison with the elephants. Just west, hiding round the corner in narrow Pann Lane, are the forlorn remains of the Three Crowns pub: part of its good faience facade, now incorporated into later rebuilding. At **21-22 Fawcett Street** is another Caws extravaganza, this time in bright red brick and pinky-red terracotta from J. C. Edwards of Ruabon.[9] Above the dross of the modern facade are three layers of bow windows with oodles of frilly terracotta dressings, the whole topped by elongated shaped gables and finished off with a turret. This Moorish-inspired pair, built for Corder's the drapers, date from

1889-90. Caws loved colour and decoration, and planned to build a Tea Rooms-style bazaar down the east side of Fawcett Street; it would have been a great improvement on its current appearance.[10]

At the southern end of Fawcett Street is BOROUGH ROAD and the **Sunderland Museum and Winter Gardens**, refurbished and much expanded during 2000-1. On the rear elevation, near the exotic new circular winter garden and overlooking Mowbray Park, is a striking group of three abstract tile panels designed in 1963 by Walter Hudspith, Senior Lecturer at Sunderland College of Art (Fig 65). These unusual and attractive panels, each comprising 400 tiles, were the first examples of public art to be commissioned in Sunderland, and were made for the 1962-4 extension to the building (which then included a library). The designs, which relate to the functions of the building, represent Music, Art and Literature, and all feature a brightly coloured abstract formation on a black background. The panels were restored by Lesley Durbin at the Jackfield Conservation Studio in 2000-1, and replaced close to their previous position; they are now completely demountable. Looking southward into the park, a series of terracotta lions - manufactured by Shaws of Darwen to match the originals - lie upon a balustrade demarcating terrace and gardens.

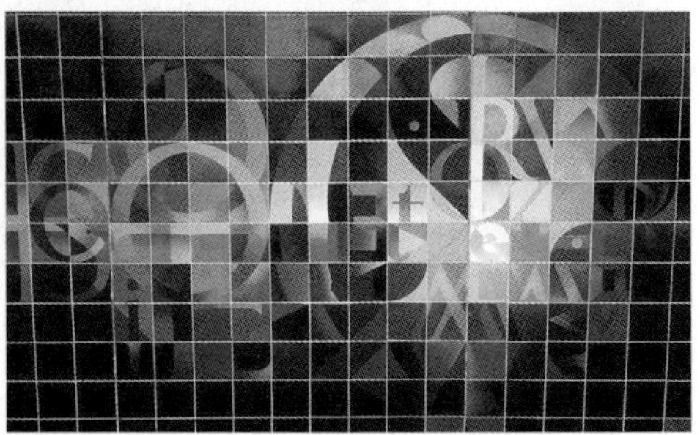

Fig 65.

Just west of the centre in GREEN TERRACE is the old **Technical College** (1900-1), whose Hathernware dressings include two fine figurative panels, while north of the Wear in Southwick the **Tram Car Inn** on THE GREEN has a decorative yellow and green faience facade dating from 1906 (Fig 66).[11]

Finally, and well west of the city centre, one of the best pub interiors in the country hides behind a stern red-brick facade in HYLTON ROAD (close to Millfield Metro station). The **Mountain Daisy** was rebuilt by local architects William & T. R. Milburn - best known for their theatres - in 1900-2 (Fig 67). Even before its reconstruction the pub had been large, but the new version was even bulkier, its main bar, two sitting rooms and news room all needed to cope with demand in still-booming Sunderland, where recession was not to arrive for another five years. Much of the pub has been altered but the west sitting room remains completely as built, a miniature Edwardian drinking palace lined with Craven Dunnill ceramics. The floor-to-ceiling wall tiling features seven different hand-painted 3′ by 4′ 6″ panels showing Northumbrian scenes including Cragside, Bamburgh Castle and Durham Cathedral.[12] A ceramic-fronted quarter-circle bar counter fits snugly across the corner of the room, while contemporary stained glass completes the picture. The toilets and upper rooms of the pub also retain the original decorative scheme, with ornate fittings and much colourful pictorial stained glass.

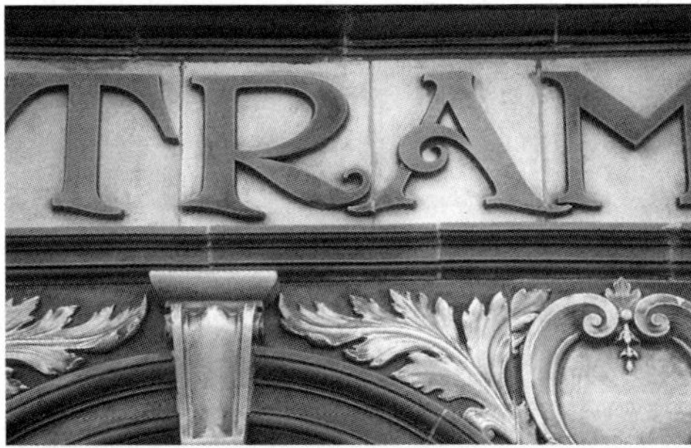

Fig 66.

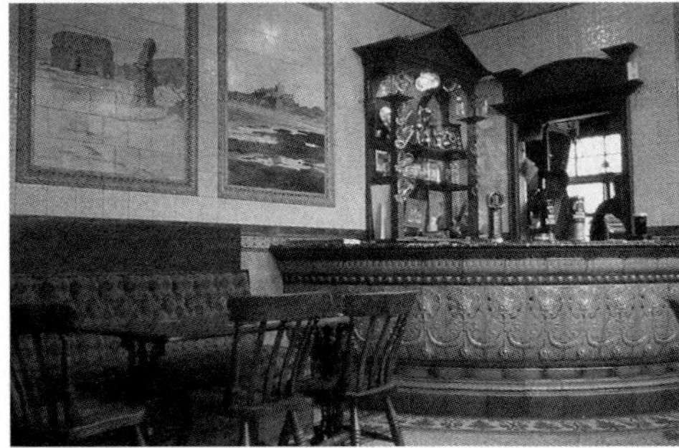

Fig 67.

USHAW

St Cuthbert's College, a Roman Catholic seminary in a beautiful moorland setting, began life as the Northern District College; its first buildings were erected in 1804-8. The original plan was a Gothic quadrangle, but the college grew to three times its initial size between 1837 and 1934 (Fig 68). A. W. N. Pugin produced an initial design for a chapel in 1840 (the drawings survive), but this was found to be too small; his second and larger attempt was built in 1844-8. This in turn was replaced by the present chapel, built in 1882-4 by Dunn & Hansom. In fact the College interior is an overwhelmingly Puginian experience, almost a small-scale Palace of Westminster, including an astonishing hammerbeam roof above a small concert hall and rooms equipped with original Pugin furniture.

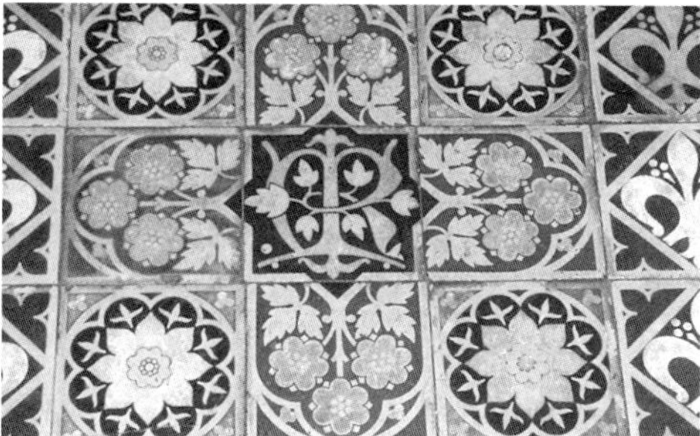
Fig 68.

The main college chapel, which has a Minton nave pavement, retained many of Pugin's decorative features. An antechapel lies at its west end, and off its south-east side is the Lady Chapel, redecorated in 1899 by Bentley. Here are the altar, stained glass and fleur-de-lys floor tiles from Pugin's original chapel. The altar has been raised on a partly-tiled dias; there is a small area of yellow and brown tiles with a strong geometric design, and a few larger tiles on a second step. Although these dias tiles are said to date from Pugin's 1848 chapel, it may be that they were additions from the 1884 rebuilding; the Pugin fleur-de-lys tiles cover the centre part of the Lady Chapel. Floor tiles can also be found in St Michael's Chapel, a memorial chapel built in 1858-9 by E. W. Pugin.

Durham Round-Up

The butcher's shop almost opposite the castle in **Barnard Castle** has a delightful but small exterior tiled panel showing the castle (Fig 69). The Railway Hotel, Durham Road, **Birtley** sports an excellent brown faience facade in classical style with ionic columns; a steam train puffs its way around the curving window. There is a Minton encaustic tile pavement, probably dating from the 1864 restoration, at St Mary's Church, Low Green,

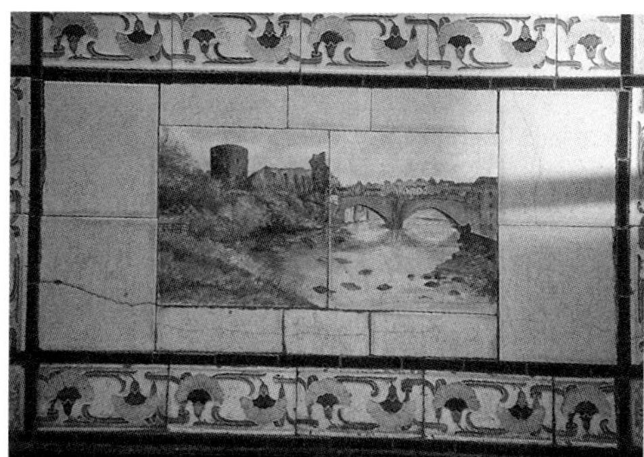
Fig 69.

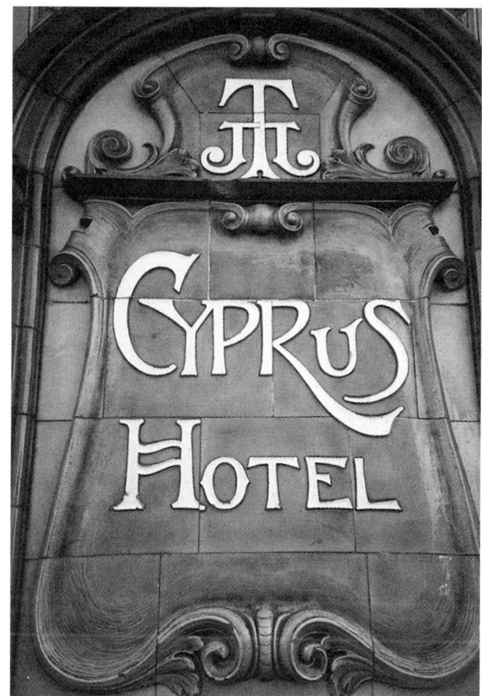

Fig 70.

Gainford; the church is beautifully sited above the Tees. St James, **Hamsterley**, in Weardale, has an unusual neo-Gothic pulpit probably dating from the church's restoration in 1884; it has panels of Minton Hollins tiles, signed by John Moyr Smith, showing biblical scenes and the Pilgrim's Progress. A pair of tile panels, probably inter-war, depicting healthy pink porkers is set in green glazed brick below the windows of an old butcher's shop in Church Street, **Seaham**. Stranded on the northern fringe of **Sedgefield** at the old Winterton Hospital site - once the Durham County Lunatic Asylum, now housing - is **St Luke's Church** (built 1884), designed by the architect William Crozier junior, son and chief assistant to the Engineer and Architect of County Durham; this impressive brick church has Doulton of Lambeth terracotta in the nave arcade, while the encaustic tile chancel pavement is by Maw's.[13] The Cyprus pub (built 1901) in Chichester Road, **South Shields**, has an excellent faience facade, probably Burmantofts, incorporating good large-scale lettering (Fig 70). Debenhams (also 1901), High Street, **Stockton-on-Tees**, is remarkable for its very early steel-framing; the steel columns were protected by polygonal red terracotta blocks, later overpainted.[14]

References

1. Michael Stratton, *The Terracotta Revival* (Victor Gollancz, London, 1993), pp102-3.
2. Norman Emery, 'The Esh Winning Miners Memorial Hall', *Durham Archaeological Journal*, 8 (1992), pp87-94.
3. Richard Myers and Hilary Myers, *William Morris Tiles - The tile designs of Morris and his Fellow-Workers* (Richard Dennis, Shepton Beauchamp, 1996), p60.
4. *Across Two Cultures: The Gateshead and Komatsu Ceramic Artists Exchange*, (Gateshead MBC Libraries and Arts Service, Gateshead, 1998).
5. Christine Constant, 'Across Two Cultures', *Studio Pottery*, (1998) 31, pp8-14.
6. Paul Scott, 'Queen Elizabeth Hospital, Gateshead', *TACS Newsletter*, (1994) 27, pp2.
7. Paul Atterbury and Louise Irvine, *The Doulton Story* (Royal Doulton Tableware, Stoke on Trent, 1979).
8. Dennis W. Hadley, *James Powell & Sons: A listing of opus sectile, 1847-1973*, (2001).
9. *J. C. Edwards: Catalogue of Patterns*, (1890).
10. Graham R. Potts, *Buildings and Architects 1780-1914*, in *Sunderland: River, Town and People*, eds Geoffrey E. Milburn and Stuart T. Miller, (Sunderland Borough Council, Sunderland, 1988), pp155-168.
11. *Brick and Pottery Trades Journal*, vol 4, December 1901, p61.
12. Lynn F. Pearson, *The Northumbrian Pub - An Architectural History* (Sandhill Press, Warkworth, 1989), pp81-2, 123-7.
13. *The Builder*, vol 47, 1st November 1884, pp607-8.
14. Michael Stratton, 'New Materials for a New Age: Steel and Concrete Construction in the North of England, 1860-1939', *Industrial Archaeology Review*, 21 (1999) 1, pp5-24.

Essex

Although far from the heartlands of tile or terracotta production, Essex has several interesting ceramic locations, notably a handful of rare fifteenth century Spanish tiles in Billericay, early sixteenth century terracotta at Layer Marney Tower, the unique maritime memorial tiles at Brightlingsea Church, and tile panels marking the various works carried out by the architect-priest Ernest Geldart (1848-1929) of Little Braxted. Geldart worked on a total of fifty-seven projects in Essex, and his tile panels, often bearing biblical texts, can be found in several of his church restorations along with his distinctive paving designs. Finally, in the postwar period, there is the curious story of the Basildon Bus Station tile murals. Suggested reading: James Bettley, ''The Master of Little Braxted in his prime': Ernest Geldart and Essex, 1873-1900', *Essex Archaeology and History*, 31 (2000), pp169-194; Lynn Pearson, 'Memorial and Commemorative Tiles in Nineteenth and Early Twentieth Century Churches', *TACS Journal*, 9 (2003), pp13-23; Alfred L. Wakeling and Peter Moon, *Tiles of Tragedy: Brightlingsea's Unique Maritime Memorial*, (Ellar Publications, Stockton-on-Tees, 2003). The *Gazetteer* entry for Essex covers the administrative areas of Essex County Council, Southend-on-Sea Borough Council and Thurrock Borough Council.

ARDLEIGH

The peaceful churchyard and unexceptional, though pleasant, exterior view of **St Mary the Virgin** does not prepare the visitor for the spectacular colour of its ravishing chancel decoration, which was largely carried out in 1894-5, following restoration work begun by William Butterfield in 1882. St Mary's vicar during 1872-91 was T. W. Perry, a high churchman who had previously been a curate at All Saints, Margaret Street. Perry raised funds for the restoration and brought in Butterfield as his architect, although the dramatic chancel decorative scheme was only completed after Perry's death in 1891.[1] The chancel's encaustic tile pavement, which features examples of the *Green Man* design, is by Godwin's and was part of the 1882-3 works. Perry's successor as vicar called on the Essex architect-priest Ernest Geldart to produce a decorative scheme for the remainder of the chancel, and this was executed by Percy Bacon & Brothers during 1894-5. It includes a highly glazed seven-tile plaque on the wall below the south chancel window; the black lettering on cream ground largely commemorates Perry.

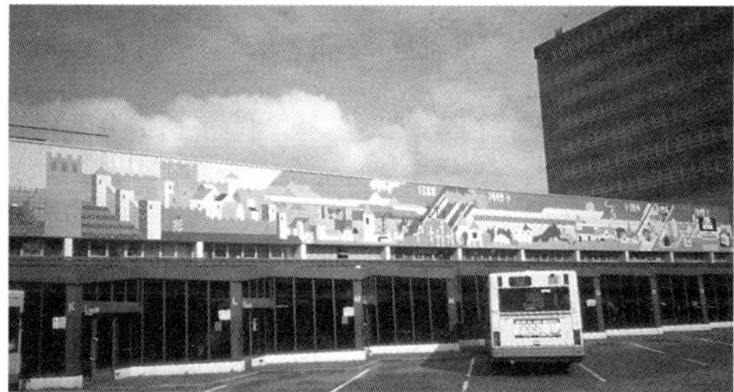

Fig 71.

BASILDON

Basildon's **Bus Station** on SOUTHERNHAY, on the southern edge of the new town's shopping precinct, is distinguished by a brightly coloured tile panel at first floor height stretching along its entire length and portraying scenes from the town's history (Fig 71). This impressive installation, about 60 yards long by 10 feet high, probably dates from the early 1980s as it shows the railway station, which was opened in the late 1970s. Its mixture of square and oblong tiles can easily be seen by passers-by on road and train, although not by passengers waiting at the bus station, whose shelter is directly beneath. The shelter was added in front of a row of shops during the 1966 rebuilding of the bus station. Curiously, the original 1958 layout of the bus station also featured a large tile mural, in exactly the same place as the present installation. This mural, designed by William Gordon for Carter's of Poole, was made up from hand-painted tiles in an abstract pattern using mainly geometric motifs.[2] Photographs show it to be an impressive piece, but it was fairly short-lived; the alterations to the bus station do not appear to have necessitated its removal, and indeed the present tiling may simply have been installed on top of the older mural (which perhaps may have been weathering badly). Or was the vivid 1958 abstract scheme so unpalatable to Basildon that it had to be replaced with the blander, more figurative design?

BILLERICAY

The **Church of St Mary Magdalene**, HIGH STREET, with its oddly battlemented brick tower, has some intriguing but easily overlooked objects of ceramic interest: six scruffy dark blue and white tiles are set in the spandrels above the outside of the west doorway, through which one enters from the High Street. These tiles, four showing flowers and two bearing coats of arms, are from Manises, near Valencia, and date from the early part of the fifteenth century. This type of metallic lustre tile is very rare in Britain, and their appearance - built into the wall of a fifteenth century church tower - seems to replicate heraldic building decoration of the time, albeit in an otherwise unknown fashion. The tiles, luxury items, were probably installed during the construction of the tower, although they could have been added when the church was remodelled during the eighteenth century.

BRAINTREE

The inn sign at the **White Hart Hotel**, COGGESHALL ROAD (in the middle of the town centre) is an attractive pentagonal pictorial tile panel high up on the pub main facade. It probably dates from the interwar period and shows a white hart (a male deer bearing antlers) and a colourful rural scene within a cream frame. The panel measures about three feet by four feet and is signed Doulton of Lambeth in the bottom right hand corner.

BRIGHTLINGSEA

All Saints Church stands a good mile out of Brightlingsea, on a breezy hilltop at the north end of CHURCH ROAD. It has a unique collection of 213 six-inch square ceramic memorial tiles dated between 1872 and 1988; they form a dado on the walls of the nave and south aisle (Fig 72). The memorial scheme originated in 1883 with the loss of nineteen Brightlingsea fishermen in a storm at sea. Brightlingsea's incumbent, the Reverend Arthur Pertwee, was so shocked by the disaster that he decided to make a commemorative record of all parishioners lost at sea since his arrival in 1872. Many of the casualties were fishermen, but as the tradition was maintained into the twentieth century, wartime losses became more frequent. Each tile gives on successive lines the name, age, brief summary of the loss, and the date it occurred; many of them use gothic lettering on a pale ground, and there is little additional decoration. The tiles are hand-painted overglaze on white ground and were initially supplied by the church decorating firm Cox, Sons, Buckley & Co.[3]

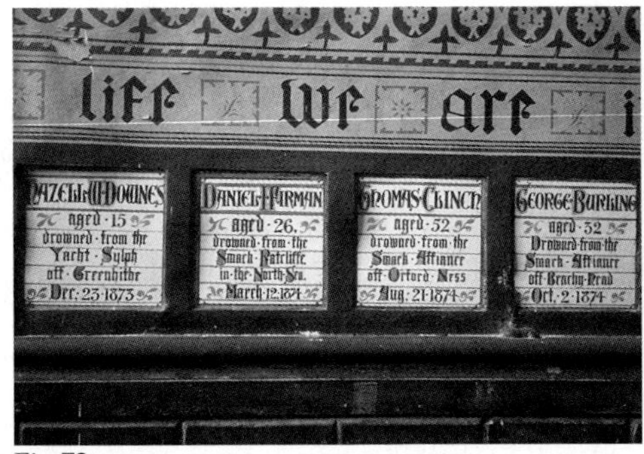

Fig 72.

The Brightlingsea memorial tiles are unusual not only because of their number, which could be approached by a handful of Staffordshire churches, but in their design; the norm for these memorials is a lozenge shape, and few from other areas date from after the First World War.[4] In fact there is also a ceramic memorial of the more common type and design at All Saints, on an inner wall of the tower; it comprises a four-tile group set diagonally, is dated 1886 and commemorates the tower's restoration. It seems certain that the influence of the priest-architect Ernest Geldart, rector of Little Braxted, played a strong part in the decision to begin the extraordinary memorial tile frieze at All Saints. Geldart, who first used commemorative tiles in 1882, occasionally preached at Brightlingsea, having met its vicar for the first time in late 1884; the first of the memorial tiles was not installed until the following year.[5] Geldart also worked on St Mary's Church at Southery in Norfolk, where there is a tile frieze comparable to Brightlingsea's although lacking the maritime connection.

Down in the town itself, beside Brightlingsea Creek on WATER SIDE, is a substantial building, formerly a pub, rather out of scale with its neighbours and topped by four fine red terracotta dragon finials.

CHELMSFORD

The **Shire Hall** (1790-2), DUKE STREET, has Coade stone capitals and three high relief panels of

Justice, Wisdom and Mercy, all modelled by the artist John Bacon. The architect of the Shire Hall was John Johnson, County Surveyor for Essex, who also used Coade stone in his partial rebuilding in 1801-3 of the nearby parish church of St Mary following its collapse in 1800; the church became the **Cathedral** in 1914. The south aisle piers, and the clerestory tracery and figures are all of Coade stone.[6]

Galleywood Common

St Michael's Church has a tile and mosaic reredos dating from 1874; this was probably designed by Harry Burrow for Powell's of Whitefriars.

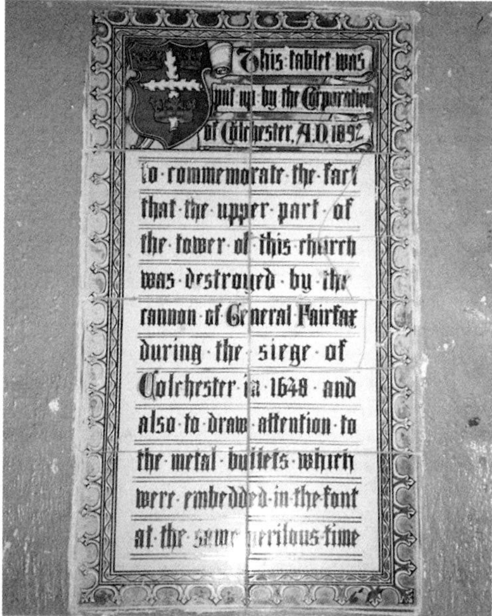

Fig 73.

COLCHESTER

Just north of Colchester's imposing Town Hall is **St Martin's Church**, WEST STOCKWELL STREET (Fig 73). The now-redundant church was restored by Ernest Geldart in 1890-1 and a small glazed tile wall plaque in the south aisle records this fact, along with the names of the churchwardens, in strong gothic lettering; these tile plaques were a feature of Geldart's restorations. Another Geldart trademark is striking geometric design of the paving, here carried out in red, black and yellow. There is also an ornate eight-tile wall plaque, installed at the west end of the north wall in 1892, which records the partial destruction of the tower in 1648.

West of the main shopping area on CHURCH STREET (in the shadow of the Jumbo water tower) is **Colchester Arts Centre**, formerly the church of St Mary-at-the-Walls, which was rebuilt (apart from its tower) in 1871-2 by Sir Arthur Blomfield. There is a decent encaustic tile pavement in the sanctuary, hidden away backstage, but the real surprise is in the nave (now auditorium), where the shiny buff columns with their elaborate capitals turn out to be faced in terracotta. The cladding was added to the original cast iron columns in 1911, when the topmost part of the tower was also built.

Well north of the centre at **Colchester General Hospital**, TURNER ROAD, two large mosaic panels by Cleo Mussi, made from a mix of broken and recycled hand-made and mass-produced tiles, form part of the 65 art and craft commissions carried out during the late 1990s; all the work was funded through the Colchester and Tendring Hospital Arts Project, which aimed to de-institutionalise the hospital atmosphere. Mussi's colourful panels are mounted on the staircase wall of the Constable wing, where the overall theme for art commissions was air, water and earth.[7]

FRINTON-ON-SEA

Frinton's first pub, on the quiet little town's main street CONNAUGHT AVENUE, is a conversion of a shop with an unusual green faience facade incorporating curved glasswork and a singular green faience column as well as tiled pilasters; it probably dates from around 1900. Almost opposite is **Maynard's** the fishmongers, with a porch whose blue art nouveau tiling continues inside the shop; one interior wall has white tiling with two lozenge-shaped blue pictorial panels, both probably of sheep but partly obscured by shop furnishings.

GOOD EASTER

The chancel of **St Andrew's Church** was restored in 1879-81 by Ernest Geldart, who designed the IHS tile which can be seen in the piscina, as well as the painted decoration. There is also a tile pavement by Maw & Co.

HARLOW

Harlow New Town began life in 1947, with Frederick Gibberd responsible for its overall planning. The first part of the centre to be completed was the MARKET SQUARE, overlooked by **Adams House** with its clock on a blue and white tiled background. The square retains much of the integrity of the original design, as does the main shopping street, Broad Walk, and WEST SQUARE. Here, beyond the bridge, is **Gate House** with a large abstract tile mural in lustrous blue and dark blue relief tiles, the latter with an attractive rippling motif; it was made by Pilkington's in 1955.[8]

There was a clear emphasis on architectural decoration throughout Harlow's centre, with several external mosaics and marble-slab murals, along with sculpture from the Harlow Arts Trust collection. Although much of the artwork is still present, it is generally ignored and not well-presented; even the listed Gibberd-designed water gardens have been demolished (although they are to be rebuilt) to make way for a modern shopping experience. Unlike the Hertfordshire new towns of Stevenage and Hemel Hempstead, where alterations have respected the initial conception, Harlow's 1950s layout has not been valued, while much of the new building is wildly out of scale; the bus station, however, using terracotta slabs and green-faced bricks, is a welcome exception.

As a decorative finish, mosaic was more popular than tiling in late fifties Harlow - the broad slabs of the listed Frank Lloyd Wright-style Harlow Town railway station are mostly faced with it - and a mosaic by the artist John Piper is the town's great (but normally hidden) glory. Just south of the centre in PLAYHOUSE SQUARE is **St Paul's Church** (1959-61, architects Humphrys & Hurst) where the east wall is completely covered by Piper's mosaic representation of the Madonna and child, in bright colours on a looming black ground (Fig 74). But this dark presence does not overwhelm the wonderfully light interior, where glazing bars cast a rectangular grid of shadows.

HARWICH

The major landmark of this odd town - a bracing mixture of high-tech port and old-fashioned buildings - is **St Nicholas Church**, CHURCH STREET, built in 1820-2 and designed by the Essex architect M. G. Thompson; it took the place of an earlier chapel which had become dilapidated and was pulled down. The materials are London brick combined with iron columns and window frames, all topped by a series of eyecatching Coade stone pinnacles. One of the three fonts is made from terracotta (its origin is unclear); it was used until 1873 when it was replaced by a stone and marble

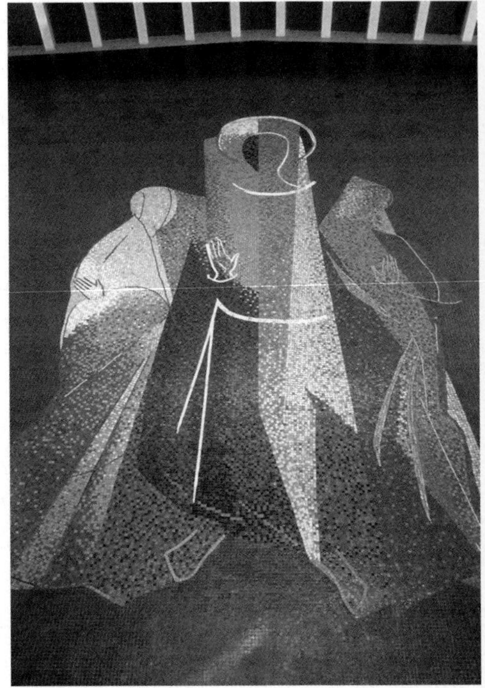

Fig 74.

model. At the rear of the church is a collection of Dutch seventeenth century tin glazed tiles, removed from a house in West Street where they had been reused to line a pantry. The tiles portray biblical scenes as well as familiar images of landscapes and windmills. Just north of the church at 21 MARKET STREET is a former fruit and vegetable shop with a mainly green and blue tiled facade probably dating from around 1900; it includes a signed Carter's porch panel showing a boy and girl picking apples (Fig 75).

HATFIELD BROAD OAK

St Mary's Church, CHURCH YARD has an encaustic tile pavement; its broadly terracotta colouring inspired the design of the 1988-9 set of kneelers. There is also a patterned chancel tile pavement at the **Church of St John the Evangelist** (1856), BUSH END.

LAYER MARNEY

Sir Henry Marney (Baron Marney from 1522), whose family had held Layer Marney since the twelfth century, was born in the mid-fifteenth century and rose to become Sheriff of Essex and Captain of the King's Bodyguard under Henry VIII

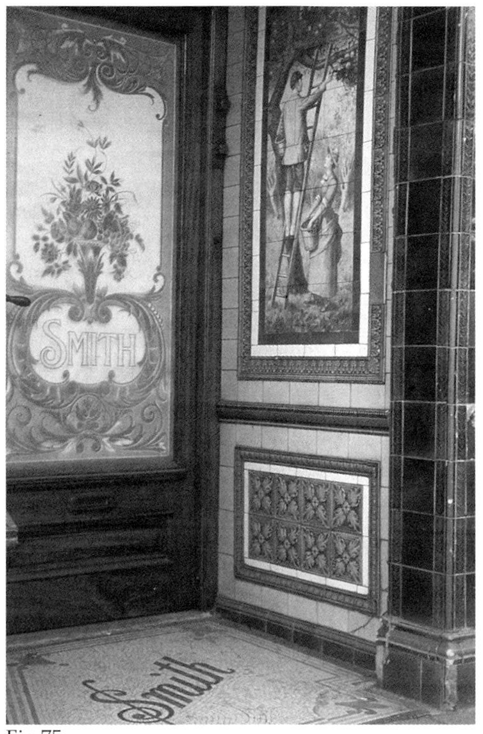

Fig 75.

He was eventually made Keeper of the Privy Seal, but died shortly afterwards, his position as the King's chief adviser having already been taken over by Thomas Wolsey, European diplomat and builder of Hampton Court (from 1514), which passed to the King in 1528. Wolsey's architectural ambitions knew few bounds. Foreign travel ensured that his extensive patronage was not restricted to home-grown artists and sculptors; he floored the (lost) Manor of the More, Rickmansworth, with fine tiles from Flanders, and commissioned terracotta roundel busts by the Italian sculptor Giovanni da Maiano for Hampton Court. Dating from 1521, these roundels were some of the earliest examples of a brief, passing fashion for terracotta - then seen as a foreign material - lasting from the early 1520s until its abandonment about a quarter-century later, as the country became more insular following the dissolution of the monasteries.

Sir Henry Marney, who also had contacts with Italian craftsmen, began to build a palace on his country estate at Layer Marney around 1520, having rebuilt the church a few years before. **Layer Marney Tower** was intended to rival Wolsey's Hampton Court in size and grandeur, with a gatehouse taller, at about eighty feet, than any other domestic building in England. Ostentation was all, as fortified gatehouses were no longer any real proof against attack; indeed, the style is transitional between medieval and renaissance, with rather more terracotta decoration (possibly provided by English craftsmen) than at Hampton Court itself. Ornament on the red brick tower includes bands of terracotta trefoils, stylised dolphins and shell-like battlements, giving good views of the Essex countryside.[9]

Lord Marney died in 1523, after the gatehouse had been completed but before very much of his palace had been built. His tomb, in **St Mary's Church**, has an elaborate canopy above a black marble effigy which rests on a terracotta tomb chest. The monument to Lord Marney's son John, who died in 1525, just two years after his father, also has a terracotta tomb chest. The design of these tombs appears to have been the inspiration behind the extravagant terracotta tombs of Lord Marney's sister Margaret and her husband Sir Edmund Bedingfield at Oxborough, Norfolk, which in turn brought the material into fashion in that county.

LITTLE BRAXTED

Little Braxted was the only parish of the architect-priest Ernest Geldart (1848-1929), whose architectural career encompassed 163 projects, of which 57 were in Essex.[10] He worked for the firm of church decorators and furnishers Cox & Sons (later Cox, Sons, Buckley & Co), from at least 1881, when he also became rector of remote little **St Nicholas Church**. He soon made changes to the arrangement and decoration of St Nicholas, so that it would accord with his ritualist view of worship; it seems as if every inch of the church's interior is covered with meaningful pattern, lettering or figurative decoration. His five chronongrams, in which the letters used for Roman numerals within an unrelated text are added together to form a date, are particularly strange. Major alterations followed in 1883-6; the 'before' and 'after' plans are recorded on a single six-inch tile in the vestry. Within this amazingly colourful decorative scheme are a few tiles, including a vicars list inscribed on glazed tiles, in Geldart's own handwriting, on the west wall of the north aisle; this type of small ceramic panel was a trademark of Geldart's church restorations, along with his striking designs for paving. Another tile panel, bearing the commandments, is on a north aisle column of St Nicholas, although this dates from after Geldart resigned the living (on grounds of ill-health) in 1900.

LOUGHTON

There are three relatively minor items of ceramic interest here, two right in the town centre on LOUGHTON HIGH ROAD, where the **Royal Standard** pub has a good external ceramic panel of the eponymous flag on its canted corner. Across the road from the pub stands the **Lopping Hall**, a public hall built in 1883-4 partly as compensation for the loss of lopping rights; lopping was the ancient commoners' practice of cutting branches of trees in nearby Epping Forest for firewood. Above the hall's entrance in STATION ROAD is a high-relief red terracotta tympanum showing lopping taking place. Further north in RECTORY LANE is **St Nicholas Church** (1877), which has a dado of *cuenca* tiles made by Frederick Garrard of Millwall.

RAYLEIGH

The **Dutch Cottage**, 33 CROWN HILL, is a pretty little timber-framed and thatched octagonal cottage dating from 1621. It is believed to have been built by Dutch refugees, and includes a broad selection of Delft tiles dating from 1630 to the late nineteenth century, which were probably introduced into the building in the nineteenth century.

STANFORD-LE-HOPE

The tower of **St Margaret of Antioch Church** was rebuilt in 1882-4 by Ernest Geldart; the work is recorded inside the tower on a small tile panel. A large ceramic mural, designed and made by the Essex ceramicist Lisa Hawker in collaboration with staff and pupils, was installed in 2001 at Stanford-le-Hope **Infant School**. The *Super Square of Stanford* is a colourful relief map of the school's catchment area.[11]

STAPLEFORD ABBOTTS

The medieval parish church of **St Mary the Virgin**, CHURCH LANE was largely rebuilt during the nineteenth century; the architect of its chancel, which dates from 1862, was Thomas Jeckell of Norwich. The unusual ceramic feature of the chancel is the Minton encaustic tiled dado on the east wall. The designs, which are all familiar, include roundels of the four evangelists, the Lamb of God and an ornate cross, but these tiles are normally found in pavements rather than being used as wall tiles. As a result of their position, the tiles remain in perfect condition.

THUNDERSLEY

Tyrells Arch, a ceramic entrance archway at the **Tyrells Centre** (for the care of the elderly), 39 SEAMORE AVENUE, was created by the artist Lisa Hawker and members of the local community in a project which culminated in the unveiling of the dramatic artwork in June 2004.

TIPTREE

On an outside wall of **Tesco's**, CHURCH ROAD, is a large tile mural, about 12 feet high by 10 feet wide, showing an Edwardian-style picnic with the local preserves to the fore. The mural, in mostly pale blue on white ground within a dark blue frame, was installed in 2002 (when the store opened) and was designed by Ned Heywood and Julia Land of Chepstow.

TWINSTEAD

Henry Woodyer's rebuilding of the **Church of St John Evangelist** in 1859-60 included the installation of its attractive pavement of red, black and yellow tiles from Poole and Minton's.[12] In the churchyard is a memorial cross whose base is decorated with encaustic tiles.

WALTHAM ABBEY

On the ground floor of Waltham Abbey's art nouveau **Town Hall** in HIGHBRIDGE STREET is a corridor with an elegant dado of green art nouveau floral relief tiles, dating from around 1905 and probably manufactured by one of the Burslem firms T. & R. Boote or J. & W. Wade.

Essex Roundup

In the main shopping street of **Dovercourt** is a Dewhurst's with at least six of the usual Carter's *Farmyard* series of four-tile panels; the one nearest the window shows an attractive piggy scene. Restoration of Holy Cross Church, **Felsted**, by the architect Henry Woodyer in 1874-8 included the installation of a Minton tiled floor in the chancel. The State Cinema, George Street, **Grays**, a huge 'super cinema' built in 1938 for Frederick's Electric Theatres, has a cream and black moderne faience facade. Nine medieval tiles (dating from around 1300) which formerly lay close to the altar of the Church of St Mary the Virgin, **Great Bentley** are now on display at the rear of the church; although worn, their designs can still be made out, including a stag and a complex knot.

There is an encaustic-tiled reredos (probably 1857-8) at the Church of St James the Great, **Great Saling**. The patterned tiled pavements at St Giles Church, **Langford** probably date from the extensive restoration carried out around 1880; the church has a unique western apse. **Rawreth** Church was rebuilt by Ernest Geldart in 1880-2; he used glazed tiles here for the first time, to record the donors of the reredos in 1882. The chapel at St Osyth's Priory, The Bury, **St Osyth** has encaustic and impressed medieval floor tiles, as well as a nineteenth century tile pavement installed during the building's conversion to a chapel. St Peter's Church (1888), Church Lane, **Shelley** has a gently polychromatic interior including a patterned tile pavement. A thirteen square metre mural with much ceramic content was installed on the platform wall of **Southminster** Railway Station in autumn 2004; the design was by Lisa Hawker and local community groups. The fourteenth century south porch of the Church of St Mary Magdalene, off Clacton Road, **Thorrington** is partly constructed of Roman bricks and tiles; inside is a floor combining herringbone-style wooden blocks and fairly plain nineteenth century tiling. There is a Godwin encaustic tile pavement in the sanctuary of St Nicholas Church, **Witham**, probably dating from its 1877 restoration.

References

1. James Bettley, *Ritualism rampant in the diocese of St Albans: Victorian Society visit to Essex, 24th August 2002* (Victorian Society, 2002).
2. Carter Archive, Poole Museum Service; Carter Photograph Catalogue and photographs 3c/37/5a,b.
3. Alfred L. Wakeling and Peter Moon, *Tiles of Tragedy: Brightlingsea's Unique Maritime Memorial* 2nd ed (Ellar Publications, Stockton-on-Tees, 2003).
4. Lynn Pearson, 'Memorial and Commemorative Tiles in Nineteenth and Early Twentieth Century Churches', *TACS Journal*, 9 (2003), pp13-23.
5. Personal communications, James Bettley, 25th August, 17th September and 7th October 2002.
6. Alison Kelly, *Mrs Coade's Stone* (Self Publishing Association, Upton-upon-Severn, 1990), pp81-2, 109.
7. Pamela Buxton, 'Colchester General Hospital', *Crafts*, (2000) 163, pp20-23.
8. 'The Artist in Tilemaking', *Hot Pot: A Newsletter from Pilkington's Tiles Ltd*, (1955) Spring, p4.
9. Jane A. Wight, *Brick Building in England from the Middle Ages to 1550* (John Baker, London, 1972), p181.
10. James Bettley, ''The Master of Little Braxted in his prime': Ernest Geldart and Essex, 1873-1900', *Essex Archaeology and History*, 31 (2000), pp169-194.
11. *Ceramic Review*, Sept/Oct 2001, no 191, p64.
12. John Elliott and John Pritchard, eds. *Henry Woodyer: Gentleman Architect* (Department of Continuing Education, University of Reading, Reading, 2002), pp166-7.

Gloucestershire

Gloucestershire is a county packed with ceramic locations from the medieval to the Victorian, but sadly lacking in examples of twentieth century work. Two outstanding medieval sites are Hailes Abbey, where the thirteenth century pavement is on site (in the Abbey Museum) if not exactly *in situ*, and the fifteenth century Seabroke pavement in Gloucester Cathedral, the latter well complemented by George Gilbert Scott's late Victorian pavement. Bristol was a centre for tile manufacture in the late medieval period, although the location of the tilery is unknown. Its most famous product, the Canynges House pavement, discovered in 1820 beneath the wooden floor of a merchant's house in Redcliffe Street, Bristol, is now on display at the British Museum. These tiles date from around 1480-1515, just predating the cuenca tiles of the pavement in the Lord Mayor's Chapel, Bristol, which were probably imported from Spain in 1527. This is a location of European importance in ceramic history; the dramatic sight of these sparkling, colourful new tiles doubtless hastened the end of local encaustic tile manufacture.[1]

Production of delftware tiles in Bristol began around 1720.[2] The Limekiln Lane and Redcliffe Back potteries made Dutch-influenced tiles with biblical and landscape designs, and later went on to produce high-quality polychrome chinoiserie tiles, but none of these exist *in situ* in Gloucestershire. The eighteenth century is represented by the unique encaustic pavement at Goldney Grotto, Bristol (1762-5); here the source of the tiles was not Spain but Shropshire. Coade stone was used for the delicate tracery of St Mary's Church, Tetbury around 1780, and also for the caryatids of Montpellier Walk, Cheltenham in the mid 1830s.

From that point onward the ceramic story of Gloucestershire is really that of the building and restoration of its many churches. About 120 new Anglican churches were built during the nineteenth century in the county, and a huge amount of restoration took place.[3] The firm of tile manufacturers founded in 1852 by William Godwin in neighbouring Herefordshire provided encaustic pavements for many of these new and rebuilt churches. Research by the indefatigable Betty Greene has provided detailed information on the firm's Gloucestershire church pavements, and many Godwin sites - for instance the fine pavement at Tewkesbury Abbey - have their own *Gazetteer* entries while others have been appended to the Roundup section.

Apart from the Godwin installations, there are remarkable Minton pavements at the Church of Our Lady of the Annunciation, Woodchester (1846-9) and, of course, Holy Innocents Church, Highnam (1849-51), the latter designed by the Surrey architect Henry Woodyer, many of whose sixteen Gloucestershire commissions included tilework. Two local architects also produced churches with notable ceramic content: John Middleton of Cheltenham, who designed some fine polychromatic schemes, and the Tractarian Francis Niblett, whose work is almost always of interest.

The end of ceramic history in Gloucestershire arrived in 1901 with the completion of the Everard Building in Bristol, its polychrome Doulton Carraraware facade designed by W. J. Neatby. It is a building of international significance in terms of both architectural and ceramic history, but had little impact upon the local use of architectural ceramics, which withered away almost completely after the early 1900s. One exception was St Paul's Church, Clifton, Bristol, which contains one of the best collections of Powell's opus sectile work in the country, dating from 1903-27.

Unfortunately one site which cannot be recommended is Hartcliffe School, on the southern edge of Bristol, as the mural designed in 1961 by Ivor Kamlish for Carter's of Poole, and sited above the school's entrance, has been removed. It seems that the ceramic heritage of the late twentieth century is still unrecognised and unprotected. Suggested reading: Betty Greene, 'The Godwins of Hereford', *TACS Journal*, 1 (1982), pp8-16. The *Gazetteer* entry for Gloucestershire covers the administrative areas of Bristol City Council, Gloucestershire County Council and South Gloucestershire Council.

ABENHALL

The **Church of St Michael and All Angels**, a medieval red sandstone structure standing on the edge of the Forest of Dean, was restored in 1873-4. On the altar dais are some unusual six-inch encaustic tiles: a complete set of the signs of the zodiac, in cream on black ground, with six tiles at each side of the altar. Behind this extraordinary (in an ecclesiastical setting) display is a mosaic and moulded terracotta reredos by Powell's; it bears the words *Holy Holy Holy* and dates from 1884.

Fig 76

BRISTOL

Before exploring central Bristol, there is one worthwhile (but rarely accessible) ceramic location to be found on the eastern fringe of the centre, behind Temple Meads Station and beyond the floating harbour. **St Vincent's Works**, SILVERTHORNE LANE (at the junction with Gas Lane), was based on a galvanising plant taken over by John Lysaght in 1857, but it grew swiftly, encompassing a foundry, and in 1891-3 was completed by the addition of offices, whose initial plan was by Lysaght's brother, the architect Thomas Lysaght. However, it seems he either died or left Bristol before much of the building work was completed, and the final design is due to the local architect R. Milverton Drake. He produced an L-shaped castellated block with fairytale-castle aspirations in which the various departments lead off from a domed octagonal lobby (Fig 76). This was an entrance hall intended to impress both workers and customers: it is faced in gleaming cream Doulton faience with panels of yellow and white relief patterned tiles, and green relief tiles on the staircase dado.[4] There are assorted faience grotesques and, at gallery height, a majolica-glazed faience arcade with more grotesques in the spandrels. Above this, just below the lantern, is a painted frieze, a golden armada in full sail; looking down, the observer sees a mosaic floor with an ornate border and the city's coat-of-arms in the centre. It is an imposing space from all angles. The company, which exported prefabricated buildings, clearly saw its headquarters as part of the Bristol tradition of palatial mercantile premises. St Vincent's Works was acquired by the wind energy engineering consultancy Garrad Hassan & Partners in 2000; their restoration of the office building in 2001 removed many unsightly 1960s and 1970s alterations.

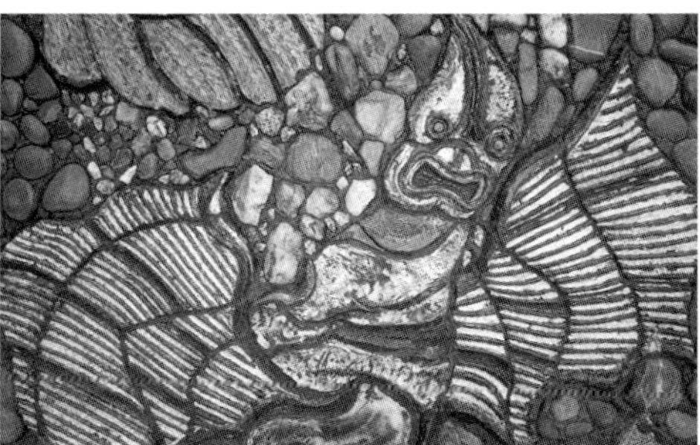

Fig 77.

From Temple Meads, the bulk of the city lies west along Victoria Street, but just before crossing the bridge over the Floating Harbour, turn left along the quayside pathway to find REDCLIFF QUAY and **Exploration** (1991), a sculpture celebrating Bristol's seafaring heritage, particularly the exploits of fifteenth-century mariners who sailed from the city to cross uncharted waters (Fig 77). The shiny ceramic obelisk - *The Unknown Deep* by Philippa Threlfall and Kennedy Collings - is topped with a steel armillary sphere designed and made by James

Blunt, which functions as a sundial; the whole work was commissioned by the Standard Life Assurance Company. The design of the obelisk features sea monsters and serpents based on drawings from medieval bestiaries. Return to Bristol Bridge and cross the Floating Harbour; immediately to the right is CASTLE PARK, in whose north-east corner is **Only Dead Fish go with the Flow** (1993), a sculpture in white-glazed *ceramica do Douro* by Victor Moreton.[5] Close to the waterside near the park's centre is **Fish** (1993), a bronze water fountain, its bowl formed by erupting fishes, which stands on a brick and terracotta-tiled plinth. The ceramic original of the fountain, by Kate Malone (b1959), who was brought up in Bristol, may be seen in the foyer of Bristol City Museum and Art Gallery, Park Row. Bronze was chosen as a medium for the fountain because of the vulnerability of three-dimensional ceramics to vandalism. After it was cast, Malone glazed the pot with complex layers of colour evoking deep sea images.

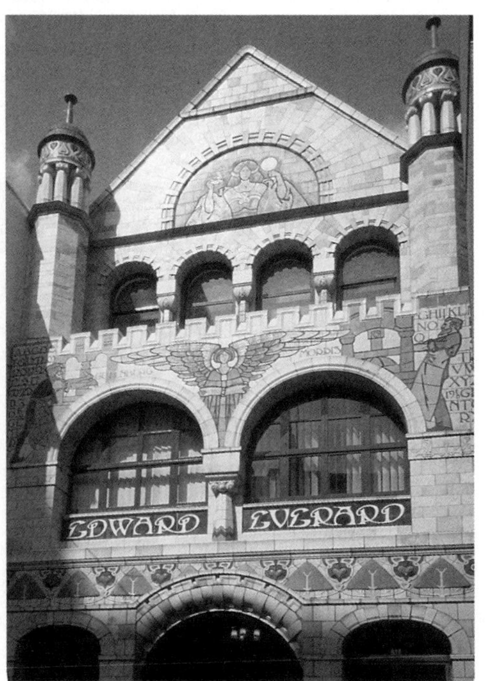

Fig 78.

Back at the bridge, continue along the High Street into the narrow thoroughfare known as BROAD STREET, to reach the iconic - and in its time iconoclastic - facade of the **Everard Building**, now NatWest Insurance Services (Fig 78). The Everard Printing Works, designed by the architect Henry Williams with the ceramic facade by W. J. Neatby for Doulton's, was completed in 1901. The first public sight of the building caused such a stir that the crowds had to be controlled by police for two days before the shock of the polychrome Carraraware facade wore off. The owner of the new Works, Edward Everard, intended his building to honour the masters of the art of printing, and initially favoured a Celtic theme. Neatby, however, put forward the design as executed, with Gutenberg and William Morris appearing on the first floor of the facade, both at work on their presses.[6] An angel hovers between the two printers and their alphabets, while in the gable above is an allegorical female figure representing light and truth. The whole is set back from the general building line of the street, and therefore all the more unexpected. The tile fixing was carried out by Walter Yoxall, a local craftsman; a plaque in the foyer (where there is another tile panel) commemorates his part in the enterprise. The Works was demolished in 1971, leaving the facade with new offices to the rear; round the corner at 1 JOHN STREET, however, there is a remnant of the old building: a red terracotta dragon (probably supplied by Barham Bros of Bridgwater) can still be seen peering into a downpipe. Today, the Everard Building is a monument to the lost cause of colour in the townscape. Around the time of its construction, the use of external colour was being discussed as part of the general concern about suitable architectural styles for the new century. The architect Halsey Ricardo (partner of William De Morgan during 1888-98) wrote in 1902: 'We have tried mass and form, and light and shade, might we not now have an attempt at colour?'[7] The answer, despite the success of the Everard Building, was in the negative, although it has certainly come to be accepted, as its owner hoped, by 'futurity'.

Wend your way down to the Centre Promenade, perhaps via CORN STREET; on the north side amongst many impressive structures is the **Commercial Rooms** (now a bar), built in 1809-11 as a club for the city's merchants; later remodelling included the addition of a green faience ceiling to its entrance lobby. The single-storey former **Stock Exchange**, on the left in ST NICHOLAS STREET, was built in 1903 and designed by Henry Williams; its fine interior, which featured in Pilkington's trade literature, includes art nouveau tiling running up the oval stairwell from the basement.[8] Nearby in CLARE STREET is a typical **Prudential Assurance** building by Alfred Waterhouse, put up in 1899-1901. Its relatively unspectacular facade combines red terracotta, manufactured by J. C. Edwards of Ruabon, and pink granite. Rather more interesting is the former **warehouse** (1878) at 13 ST STEPHEN'S STREET, where red terracotta busts of Shakespeare, Milton and Tennyson gaze forth from a bright yellow glazed brick facade.

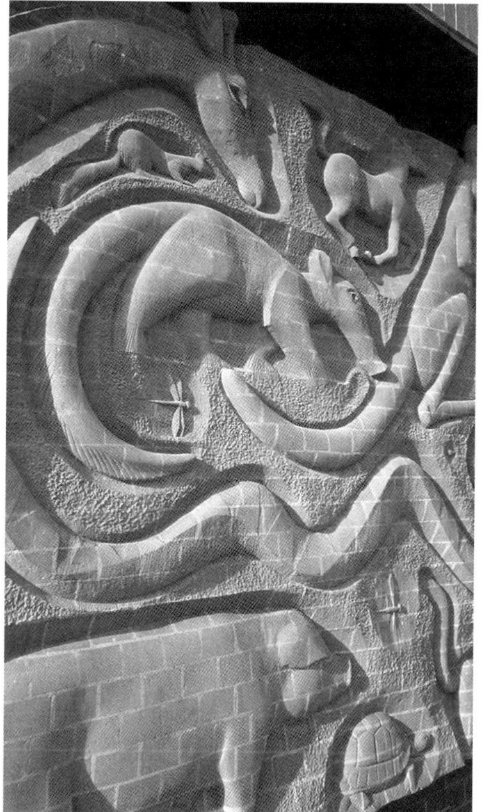

Fig 79.

At the bottom of the hill is the broad expanse of the Centre Promenade; the main route leads south, but a deviation north at this point, into the main shopping area, will bring you to the **Bristol Eye Hospital**, opened on LOWER MAUDLIN STREET in 1986 (Fig 79). Decorating the front of the building are five massive carved-brick reliefs designed and sculpted by Walter Ritchie (1919-97), who was a pupil of Eric Gill during 1938-9. The panels, each measuring 5′ 7″ by 12′, depict *The Creation* and were executed in 1983-6; the material was Ibstock Red Marl brick. The relief of *Animal Life* is especially attractive, with a giraffe, kangaroo and a multitude of other creatures cunningly interwoven. When installed, these panels were the largest non-reinforced brick reliefs ever carved.[9] From Centre Promenade, head south to BROAD QUAY and **Broad Quay House** (1981), looking out over Bordeaux Quay. On the eastern facade of this anonymous office block is a series of fifteen complex ceramic panels, each measuring about three foot by four foot, designed and made by Philippa Threlfall and Kennedy Collings. They were commissioned by Standard Life Assurance and depict elements of local maritime history.

West of the quayside is the triangular space of COLLEGE GREEN, bounded by the Council House on the west and the cathedral to the south. On the north side is St Mark's Chapel, which was built in the early thirteenth century and became the official place of worship for the Mayor and Corporation of Bristol in 1721; it is now owned by the City Council and known as the **Lord Mayor's Chapel**, and - as well as a wealth of fabulous tombs - has a good Godwin pavement in its chancel. The splendidly perpendicular Poyntz Chapel, a chantry chapel to the south of the chancel, was added by Sir Robert Poyntz between 1510 and 1520; he was interred in the (unfinished) chapel in 1520. Sir Robert's home, Acton Court near Bristol, was partly floored with late fifteenth century tiles made in or near Bristol; their design is ornate but their buff and brown colouring dull in comparison with the chapel's colourful cuenca pavement. These latter tiles were probably brought back from Spain by Francis, third son of Sir Robert, in 1527.[10] The cuenca tiles, which have a wide variety of glazes, are likely to have been manufactured in Seville and have two main types of design, geometric patterns and Renaissance motifs including animals and heraldic symbols (Fig 80). It seems that Seville tiles were undergoing a brief

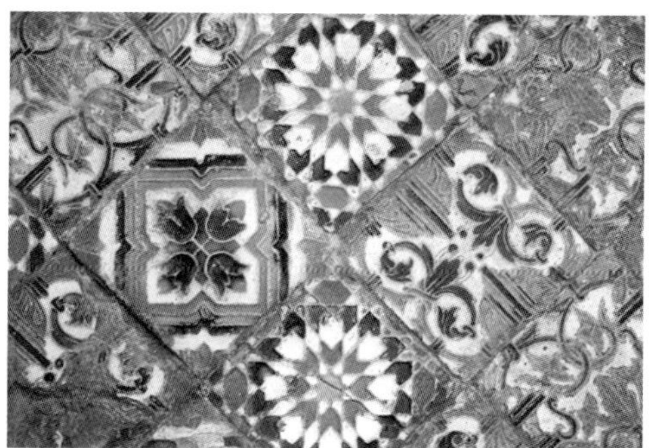

Fig 80.

period of popularity in Britain during the early sixteenth century, as a floor including tiles of the same origin and period, and with similar colouration, exists at The Vyne in Hampshire.[11] The floor of the Poyntz Chapel was successfully restored during 1992-3, and the tiles on the dais are normally visible, although the main floor area is now covered by a carpet.

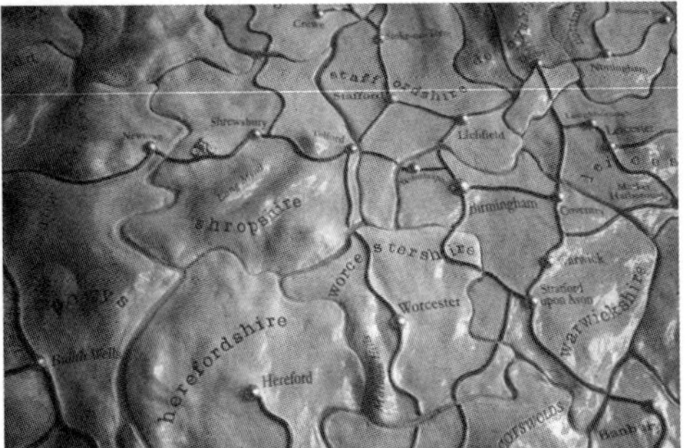

Fig 81.

Cross College Green and make for the steps at the east end of the Cathedral, which lead down towards the quayside. At the bottom, across Anchor Road, is the **Tourist Information Centre** in ANCHOR SQUARE; on its west side is a full height ceramic map (2003) of the National Cycle Network by Marian Tucker, Sue Ford (a Bristol-based ceramicist) and Carol Arnold (Fig 81). Its 110 individual pieces were made from white stoneware paper clay, a combination of clay and paper pulp which has the same strength as normal clay but is less likely to shrink or warp; the clay was pressed into county-shaped moulds then fired three times. Several months of experimentation were required to produce a material which could withstand the elements. Similar ceramic maps featuring the Sustrans routes can be found on other cycle paths in Britain and Northern Ireland; one stands on Belfast's quayside while the first was unveiled in Birmingham's Centenary Square in 2000.[12] From Anchor Square, return to Temple Meads via Pero's Bridge and Redcliffe Bridge.

Clifton

Heading out of the city centre towards Clifton, in JACOB'S WELLS ROAD is the opulent buff terracotta of the former **Hotwells Public Baths** (1881-7), converted into a gymnasium around 1980; its architect was Josiah Thomas, Bristol's City Surveyor. Immediately above the single-storey baths is a row of terraced houses which continue the buff terracotta theme almost to excess, using the material for assorted relief decoration as well as in vertical strips of patterned hollow bricks apparently acting as vents.

Half a mile west of Jacob's Wells Road on CLIFTON HILL is Goldney House, now owned by the University of Bristol and known as Goldney Hall. The house was built around 1720 for the Quaker merchant Thomas Goldney, whose family created the garden to the south of the house, in which stands the **Goldney Grotto**. The grotto, dated 1739 (in shells) but constructed during the period 1737-65, is a substantial subterranean fantasy whose pillared interior - a miniature dance hall in scale - is decorated with a mixture of shells, quartz and rock crystal; there is also a cascade, a rock pool and a lion's den. Once the walls of the enchanting grotto were complete it seems that the Goldneys turned their attention to the floor, which is a unique encaustic pavement formed from two types of red and buff marbled tile interspersed with plain buff tiles. Marbled tiles are made by wedging together clays of two colours; after slicing and rearranging the clay, the colours remain separate, forming streaks and random shapes running right through the tile. Thomas Goldney's account book records that he bought quarry tiles from the Dale brick and tile works in Coalbrookdale, then paid Thomas Paty for 'grinding, gageing and laying them' during 1762-5.[13] The swirling colours of the floor enhance the weird atmosphere of the grotto.

Continuing into Clifton proper, the late nineteenth century butcher's shop at 12 THE MALL has a partly green-tiled facade and good interior tiling. Half a mile east in ST PAUL'S ROAD is **St Paul's Church**, rebuilt in 1867 by the architect C. F. Hansom. The church has a good collection of Powell's opus sectile work: the reredos, which cost £347 and was one of the firm's largest commissions, was completed in 1903; two more panels followed in the same year, then two more in 1905 and another in 1906, by which time the church had become something of a Powell's showcase (Fig 82). The firm supplied a further panel in 1910, then two war memorial panels in 1919 and the final three panels in 1923 and 1927 (two), taking the display of opus sectile work almost up to the point at which Powell's ceased production. Together with the chancel tile pavement and the excellent set of Hardman stained glass windows, the opus sectile panels form part of an elaborate (and expensive) decorative scheme.[14]

Fishponds

At the **Avon Orthopaedic Centre**, Southmead Hospital, is a modern tile mural by Alan Lloyd showing a map and images of Avonmouth. The former site of Fishponds railway station in STATION ROAD is now marked by a huge brick sculpture of a fish diving into a pond: *Fish on its Nose* by Doug Cocker.

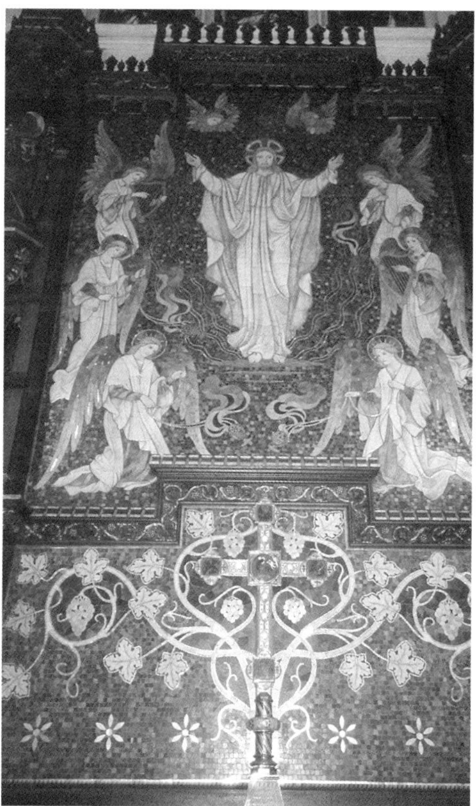

Fig 82.

CHELTENHAM

Cheltenham is something of a disappointment in ceramic terms. Many of its churches have hidden their encaustic tile pavements beneath carpeting, while its tiled shop interiors have disappeared completely, so it is only possible to recommend two secular sites and a trio of churches, the latter all by the town's leading ecclesiastical architect John Middleton (1820-85), a designer of strongly polychromatic interiors. The best of his churches is **All Saints Church**, ALL SAINTS ROAD, on the northern edge of the town centre. It was built in 1866-8 (with alterations in 1877) and the vibrant interior, intended for Tractarian worship, includes nave and aisle pavements by Godwin and an elaborate Minton chancel pavement. The Lizard Serpentine Company supplied the Minton tiles. There is also a fine ironwork chancel screen and mural paintings at the west end.

West of All Saints in WINCHCOMBE STREET is a shop with delightful late nineteenth century tiled pilasters showing an assortment of well-detailed fish and fowl; it was the premises of Messrs Morris, fishmonger and poulterer. Right in the middle of Cheltenham, on the busy junction between HIGH STREET and St James's Street, is the pub originally known as the **Coopers Arms**. Its lime green faience facade and red fascia (good lettering) make it easy to identify even allowing for the changes of name which so often afflict licensed premises. The pub was built in 1909 by the Cheltenham Original Brewery Company, its predecessor on the site having been destroyed by fire. Half a mile south-west of the High Street, the shopfronts of MONTPELLIER WALK are supported by a series of tall caryatids, two of which are painted terracotta figures sculpted by John Rossi; the remainder are stone. The Walk was designed by the local architect William Hill Knight (1814-95) and put up between 1843 and around 1860. Rossi, who modelled the well-known caryatids on St Pancras Church, London during 1818-22, died in 1839, so it appears that he gained the contract for the Cheltenham caryatids in the mid 1830s but was only able to complete a few of the figures. Rossi's terracotta caryatids (which were used as models for the stone figures) represented an unusual and unfashionable choice of material on the part of the young architect. A further half-mile south is the **Church of St Philip and St James** (1879-82), GRAFTON ROAD, another polychromatic feast designed by John Middleton. Here the encaustic pavement, which runs throughout, is by Maw & Co.

Charlton Kings

The patron of the **Church of the Holy Apostles**, LONDON ROAD, was Charles Cook-Higgs; he lived nearby and donated the site and much of the construction costs. It was put up in 1865-71 to John Middleton's design, but Cook-Higgs wanted to control the appointment of the incumbent and the church was not consecrated until after its patron's death in 1884. The main feature of the interior is the scheme of stone carving, but there is also a good Godwin encaustic pavement in chancel and sanctuary, its tile designs including a stag's head motif.

CIRENCESTER

In the MARKET PLACE, the centre of Cirencester, is the **Church of St John the Baptist**, the largest parish church in Gloucestershire; its excellent Godwin encaustic pavement, installed by George Gilbert Scott during his restoration of 1865-7, is currently under threat of replacement by marble flooring. The tiles seem never to have been a popular addition to the church, whose guidebook describes the nave tiling as Scott's 'only real mistake'; even before the altar was raised by a step in 1970, the brightly coloured sanctuary pavement had been 'discreetly covered with carpet'.[15] At the far end of West Market Place is BLACK JACK STREET and the superb Edwardian butcher's shop of **Jesse Smith & Co**. The facade has much art nouveau lettering, including a stall riser reading 'Pork Butchers', and a four-tile pig's head panel in the doorway. A little south of the centre in WATERMOOR ROAD is **Holy Trinity Church**, built in 1847-51 by George Gilbert Scott; there is a good Minton pavement in the chancel.

CLEARWELL

St Peter's Church, an estate church erected in 1863-4 and designed by John Middleton, has one of his typically polychromatic interiors: horizontal stripes are formed from layers of white Bath stone and local blue and red Forest stone, and there is a Godwin encaustic tile pavement in the chancel, as well as a lavish reredos. The church remains very much as it was built.

COLESBOURNE

The **Church of St James** is set in the grounds of Colesbourne Park. On its exterior east wall is a single embossed tile, about a foot square and bearing a crucifix; it may be fourteenth century. The encaustic pavement in the chancel is probably by Godwin's while the tiled dado, most of which was covered by panelling in 1921, was by Minton's. A small patch of this glazed encaustic wall tiling is still visible, however, hiding behind a radiator.

COWLEY

St Mary's Church (which stands in the grounds of Cowley Manor) was restored in 1871-2; the encaustic tile pavement is by Minton Hollins while the opus sectile reredos of 1875 was designed by Charles Hardgrave of James Powell & Sons. It cost £85 and shows the Last Supper, with accompanying text in small blue tiles.[16]

DAYLESFORD

The medieval home of the Hastings family was at Daylesford; the estate was sold off in 1715 but Warren Hastings, formerly Governor-General of Bengal, bought it back in 1788 and built the present house. He also rebuilt medieval **St Peter's Church**, purchasing two angel head corbels from the Coade factory in 1817, but died the following year. His grave, in the churchyard immediately east of the chancel, is marked by a fine Greek revival Coade stone monument.[17] The church itself was seen as unsuitable for modern worship by the 1850s and an almost completely new church was built in 1859-63; its architect was John Loughborough Pearson. There is an elaborate geometric pavement by Maw & Co inside, part of a largely untouched polychromatic decorative scheme.

FRAMPTON-ON-SEVERN

St Mary's Church was consecrated in 1315, restored in 1850-2 and then again in 1869-70, the latter work being carried out by the gentleman architect Henry Woodyer; his main contribution was to enlarge the chancel. The east wall of the new chancel was faced with Powell's eight-inch glass tiles, and there is an attractive sanctuary encaustic pavement by Godwin's. An opus sectile reredos of the Last Supper, also by Powell's and designed by Harry Burrow, completed the decorative scheme in 1878.

FRETHERNE

St Mary's Church was rebuilt in 1846-7. The new church was commissioned by the Rev. Sir William Lionel Darell, who appears to have wanted a church suited to Tractarian worship, as his chosen architect was Francis Niblett (1814-83), the architect member of the Niblett family of nearby Haresfield Court and a member of the Cambridge Camden Society from 1845. Niblett eventually had a busy general architectural practice in Gloucestershire, but this early opportunity to build a complete church in accord with his own and the incumbent's principles was the chance of an architectural lifetime. No expense was spared, and the result was a perfect, if small, vision of the Victorian version of medieval worship, with much colour and decoration; even the roof has fishscale patterned tiles. The nave has a brilliant geometric pavement in red, black, green, yellow, blue and white tiles, while the chancel and sanctuary have bright Minton encaustic pavements. Later additions to the church by the architect John West

Hugall include the Tierney chapel (1857-9), which also has an encaustic pavement, and the ornate Darell chapel (1866-7).

GLOUCESTER

Gloucester Cathedral originated as the Benedictine monastery of St Peter, and its best-known medieval encaustic tiles - the Seabroke pavement - were laid during the abbacy of Thomas Seabroke (1450-7).[18] But this pavement is only one of the Cathedral's many tile installations, which range from early medieval to late Victorian and include an unusual Minton memorial (Fig 83). A good view of the heart of this complex building may be obtained from the tribune gallery, which looks down on to the choir and presbytery, restored by George Gilbert Scott during 1867-73. At the east end is the Seabroke pavement, in front of the high altar; it was carefully restored in the early nineteenth century, and around 1873 the medieval tiles originally on the altar dais were removed to the south-east chapel of the tribune gallery. The Seabroke tiles are from Great Malvern and most of their twenty-nine different designs - apart from those bearing the arms of Abbot Seabroke - have also been found at Malvern Priory, although no original pavement is now extant at Malvern. Also in the Cathedral sanctuary are some Droitwich tiles of around 1370 which predate the Seabroke pavement.

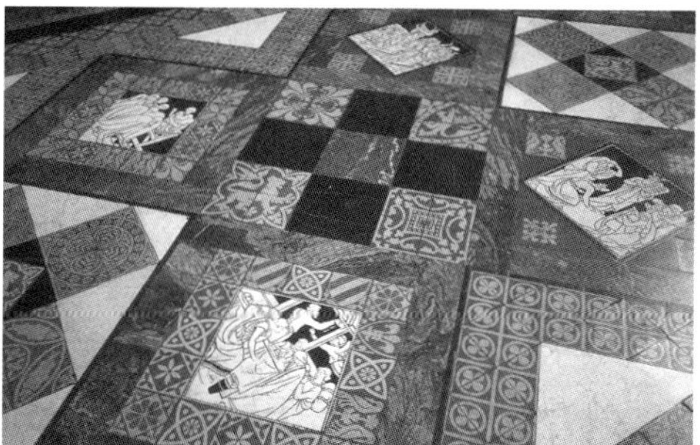

Fig 83.

George Gilbert Scott, who had been consulted about restoration proposals for the Cathedral in 1855, set out his proposed programme of restoration in 1867; it included preservation of the Seabroke pavement and paving the presbytery and choir with a mixture of marble and encaustic tiles. His proposals were accepted, and Scott commissioned Godwin's of Lugwardine to produce copies of medieval tiles found around the high altar and elsewhere in the Cathedral. In the choir these were combined with black and white marble, while for the presbytery Scott designed eighteen white-on-black sgraffito marble squares depicting incidents from the Old Testament, which are used with the tiles and various coloured marbles to form an intricate decorative scheme. In the presbytery pavement, laid in 1871, is a plain-tiled area marking the presumed burial site of Duke Robert, eldest son of William the Conquerer, who died at Cardiff Castle in 1134. Seen from above, this is a dramatic pavement, full of life and colour, but opinion following its installation was not all in its favour. An observer writing in 1899 gave this verdict:

'New tiles, ostensibly copied from the old ones, but of a different size, with an excessive glaze, and very stiff design and execution have been put down. It is hard to judge what the effect of the tiles would have been, as it has been quite killed by the white marble which has been mixed with them. The glaring white marble in the floor of the presbytery has been inlaid with biblical scenes filled in with black cement. It is possible from the triforium to get a general idea of the crudity and tastelessness of the pavement, which is so composed and arranged that time - the softener of all things - can never make it look appreciably better.'

East of the high altar is the Lady Chapel, where the sanctuary tile pavement dates from around 1475. The pavement is thought originally to have covered the entire floor area, but burials in the seventeenth and eighteenth centuries resulted in the floor being relaid, with the surviving tiles being moved. Elewhere in the Cathedral are many more medieval tiles, notably in the chapel of St Edmund and St Edward (north-east), around the tomb of Edward II and in Abbot Parker's chantry chapel (north ambulatory). The chapter house, whose medieval tiled floor had been boarded over in the seventeenth century, was restored in 1856-8 and a new tile pavement laid. This was made by Minton's and kept as far as possible to the design of the original floor. The much brighter encaustic pavement in the Chapel of St Andrew, in the south transept, probably dates from 1866-8 when its excellent wall paintings were executed by Thomas Gambier Parry, making it a Highnam in miniature (see below). Finally, out in the east walk of the cloister is the unusual floor memorial of Lieutenant General Sir Giles Nightingall (d1829), a stone rectangle framed in polychrome Minton tiles. The tiles were added to the original memorial by the architect John West Hugall in 1865 in memory of the Rev. Sir W. L. Darell of Fretherne.[19] Hugall had built a chapel at Fretherne Church in memory of Darell's father-in-law in 1857-9, and added the Darell chapel in 1866-7.

After the Cathedral, the rest of Gloucester is something of a ceramic anticlimax. However, turn southward to find WESTGATE STREET and the redundant **St Nicholas Church**; its elaborate sanctuary wall tiling, in a slightly shocking red, dates from restoration in 1865. Just south in UPPER QUAY STREET, on the facade of the extension to the **Shire Hall**, is a fine six-part ceramic mural by Peter Saysell, a potter from Bream in the Forest of Dean, depicting local scenes, including the new building itself, in bright colours and high relief; it was installed when the building was completed in 1966. Just north of the main crossroad, in NORTHGATE STREET is the **Imperial Inn**, with an attractive (though small) tile and faience facade dating from 1904 when the pub was owned by the brewers Mitchells & Butlers, who were attempting to expand their tied estate beyond Birmingham; the architects were the Cheltenham practice Knight & Chatters. A rather more spectacular pub facade of about the same date is that of the **Vauxhall Inn** in BARTON STREET, the continuation of Eastgate Street; it displays many similar elements to the Imperial, although on a larger scale suitable for its corner site with good lettering and emphatic doorcases. In SOUTHGATE STREET is the **Church of St Mary de Crypt**, restored in 1844-5 (not normally open); the complex Chamberlain encaustic pavement in the sanctuary includes a trade tile at the corner of the altar dais. Turn left into GREYFRIARS to find a tree-shaped ceramic mural above the entrance to **Eastgate Market Hall** (1968), through which one can return to EASTGATE STREET and Lloyds Bank (1898, now **Lloyds TSB**) with buff terracotta dressings including lion finials.

Kingsholm

St Mark's Church, WORCESTER STREET was built in 1845-7 and designed by the local architect Francis Niblett, whose Fretherne Church was being put up almost simultaneously. Unlike Fretherne, which was fully funded by its incumbent, construction of St Marks, which stood in a poor area of town, was funded by the Diocesan Church Building Association and various grants and voluntary contributions. It was therefore impossible for Niblett to produce as lavish an interior as at Fretherne, and indeed St Mark's was enlarged in 1888-90, the alterations to the chancel being carried out by Richard William Drew, once a pupil of Henry Woodyer. The sanctuary encaustic pavement is by Godwin's. In addition, St Mark's has a First World War memorial, dedicated in 1920, in the form of an oblong, coloured tile plaque edged with mosaic; it was made by G. J. Hunt.

Wotton

About half a mile north-east of Gloucester railway station on the LONDON ROAD is **St Catherine's Church**, the third St Catherine's to be built in Wotton. The first was a medieval church, the second was put up in 1868, then both were demolished and the present church built on a new site in 1912-15 for the Gloucester Church Extension Society; it was designed by the Gloucester architect Walter B. Wood (1852-1926). The nave of the stone-built church is not divided from the chancel, but there is a small sanctuary and - most surprisingly - a decorative encaustic tile pavement running throughout the church. The tiles, which were manufactured by Godwin's, must have been brought from the Victorian church along with the font. There is also a carved and painted reredos (1937) and a wooden screen (1948); the mixture of Victorian and twentieth century furnishings is intriguing.

Just south of St Catherine's, the new **Gloucestershire Royal Hospital** opened in 2004 on a large triangular site bordered by the London Road and the GREAT WESTERN ROAD, close to the railway station. Artist Marion Brandis was commissioned to produce a tile and mosaic *Welcome Wall* for the Children's Centre, basing the images - which include a funky blue cat - on designs created by local children.

HAILES

Hailes Abbey, a Cistercian house, was founded in 1246 by Richard, Earl of Cornwall, younger brother of Henry III. In 1270 Richard's son, Edmund of Cornwall, presented an important relic to the Abbey; it was kept in a shrine at the east end of the presbytery, which was rebuilt during 1271-7. This new section of the Abbey was paved with specially designed tiles which were probably made on site, although no kiln has yet been located. The tile designs were mainly heraldic, with oxidised and reduced tiles laid alternately to introduce colour variation. Shortly before its dissolution in 1539, the chapter house and other areas of the Abbey were repaved using tiles of heraldic design which were decorated with poured slip.[20] Part of this early sixteenth century pavement was relaid at Southam Delabere, six miles south-west of Hailes, following the dissolution. This house was once the home of Sir

John Huddleston, whose arms featured on one of the bosses in the thirteenth century chapter house. The pavement was eventually returned to Hailes and may now be seen in the Abbey Museum, along with sundry thirteenth century floor tiles. In **Hailes Church**, which predates the foundation of the Abbey, is a substantial collection of mostly late thirteenth century tiles, probably brought from the Abbey.

HIGHNAM

Holy Innocents Church is a monument to the taste of Thomas Gambier Parry of Highnam Court, to his wife Isabella, who died three years before its consecration, and to the ideals of the High Church revival. Gambier Parry, who was educated at Eton and Cambridge, joined the Camden Society in 1840 and began to plan a new church for Highnam in 1848, the year of his wife's death at the age of thirty-two. His chosen architect was Henry Woodyer, a school friend from Eton who shared Gambier Parry's High Church views, and the foundation stone was laid in 1849. Construction and the provision of ornate fittings (including the Minton pavement) took just twenty-one months, and the church was consecrated on the 29th April 1851.[21] The elaborate Minton tiling - including unusual multicoloured encaustics with a roughly circular brass inlay - becomes increasingly rich towards the east end, where red glass roundels are set into the pattern; tiling in the side chapel was removed in 1968. The tiles are only one element in the overall decorative scheme, which was finished around 1880 when Gambier Parry completed his remarkable series of 'spirit fresco' wall paintings, whose colour and vitality make the church so memorable.

KEMPSFORD

The architect G. E. Street worked at **St Mary's Church** in 1856-8, restoring the chancel and adding a chapel. The Godwin sanctuary pavement dates from this period but the glass tile and mosaic installation on the east wall is later; it was ordered from Powell's of Whitefriars in 1891. The design includes tiles bearing heraldic symbols and the sacred monogram, as well as a foliate motif identical to those of the glass tiles at St Mary, Frampton-on-Severn.[22]

LITTLETON-UPON-SEVERN

Around the font of the **Church of St Mary of Malmesbury** are some early sixteenth century heraldic tiles showing the arms of the Duke of Buckingham and probably made in Bristol. They were brought from **Thornbury Castle**, a few miles to the east, which was begun by Edward Stafford, third Duke of Buckingham, around 1511; he was executed in 1521, before the building was complete. The castle was restored in 1854 and a few of the original tiles remain on the ground floor.

MINCHINHAMPTON

The alterations made to the chancel of **Holy Trinity Church** by William Burges in 1869-71 included the installation of a Godwin encaustic tile pavement and the unusual 'double plane tracery' of the east window.[23] This double set of tracery caused the light to fall in a grid pattern on the shining tiles, an effect Burges also used at the memorial church of Christ the Consoler, Skelton, North Yorkshire, begun in 1871.

OWLPEN

The interior of the **Church of the Holy Cross** is one of the richest in the Cotswolds. Its encaustic pavement (by Godwin) probably dates from the alterations carried out in 1874-5, but it is the work of Powell's of Whitefriars which really catches the eye, in the chancel and most impressively the baptistery. The decoration of the east end (1887), in mosaic and opus sectile, includes lettering and figures of the Virgin Mary, the four Evangelists and St Helena, all designed by Charles Hardgrave. The church tower was rebuilt in 1911-12, then in 1913 its interior (which serves as the baptistery) was treated with a superb opus sectile scheme of angels which cost £400.[24]

OXENTON

St John the Baptist is a thirteenth century church with a puzzle - optical, ceramic and chronological - on its chancel floor. The chancel paving comprises plain red, yellow and black diamond-shaped tiles, with sides 115mm in length; their arrangement produces a three-dimensional effect akin to that achieved in some medieval pavements.[25] The Oxenton tiles are identical to tiles found a few miles south-west at **Tredington Court**, and just over the border at Bredon Church in Worcestershire. Analysis suggests that the Tredington tiles (which are in a part of the house added in the seventeenth century) probably date from the mid seventeenth to early eighteenth centuries and originate in the Midlands, although similar clays were also in use in the late sixteenth and early seventeenth centuries. Thus a probable date of the seventeenth century also seems appropriate for the Oxenton tiles.

REDMARLEY D'ABITOT

Apart from its tower (rebuilt 1738), **St Bartholomew's Church** was rebuilt by the Gloucestershire architect Francis Niblett in 1855-6. The vivid geometric tile pavements in the chancel and especially the sanctuary doubtless date from this period, as does the similarly colourful (but overpainted) sanctuary wall tiling. The manufacturer may have been Maw & Co.

TETBURY

St Mary's Church, CHURCH STREET was designed by the architect Francis Hiorne of Warwick and built in 1776-81 to replace the ruined medieval church. Hiorne often worked in the decorative Gothic style, and here he specified Coade rather than Tetbury stone as a "proper and suitable stone" for the delicate cream tracery of the soaring windows.[26] In NEW CHURCH STREET is **St Saviour's Church** (redundant since 1976), built in 1846-8 in thoroughgoing Ecclesiological style by the Gloucester architect Samuel Whitfield Daukes, a member of the Camden Society from 1844. The array of fine furnishings provided by Hardman & Co of Birmingham includes an unusually good encaustic tile pavement by Chamberlain & Co, one of the last such pavements to be produced at their Worcester works.

TEWKESBURY

Tewkesbury Abbey was restored by Sir George Gilbert Scott and his sons during 1875-9. The work included the excavation of most of the Abbey's medieval tiles, and the laying of a pavement in the choir made up of careful copies of the designs of those found in the eastern part of the Abbey. The new encaustic pavement, which steps up to the sanctuary, was manufactured by Godwin's in 1879 and includes many images typical of the medieval Malvern tilers. There are groups of four, twelve and sixteen tiles divided by black bands, and the designs, in buff and brown, suggest that most of the original pavements were laid in the first half of the fifteenth century, although some were earlier. This exemplary (and extraordinarily highly polished) Victorian pavement may be compared with the remaining medieval tiles in the Abbey which are scattered around various sites, some having been relaid; the best are in the north chantry chapel, the Beauchamp Chapel, which was erected around 1430.[27] Tewkesbury Abbey's over-restoration, as William Morris saw it, was one of the crucial events leading to the formation of the Society for the Protection of Ancient Buildings in 1877. Lastly, in the town itself, at the main **Post Office**, HIGH STREET, is a large 1970s tube-lined pictorial tile panel.

TWYNING

The Cheltenham architect John Middleton rebuilt the **Church of St Mary Magdalene** in 1867-70, although the Godwin encaustic tile pavement in the chancel dates from 1885-6, as do most of the other chancel furnishings. Outside in the churchyard are two unusual memorials dating from 1916: a pair of pale buff glazed ceramic hearts, for the wife and daughter of Owen Thomas of Rose Villa, Twyning. The heart-shaped plaques are mounted on rustic vernacular stems of rough brown ceramic, resembling trees, with the top branch holding the heart and the two side branches hollowed out to hold flowers. These ingenious memorials have recently been described as being 'of unbelievable hideousness and unsuitability'; in addition 'they have failed to weather or attract lichens and can only be left as an example of inappropriate materials'.[28] Large ceramic memorials are rarely found in churchyards, partly because they may have been thought to be vulnerable to the effects of the weather; the Hulm memorial (Doulton) in Burslem Cemetery, Stoke-on-Trent dates from the same period as the Twyning hearts and has suffered considerable damage. It seems that despite their weather-beating qualities, the design of the ceramic hearts did not generally appeal to those searching for suitable memorials; perhaps they would have fared better in the Potteries.

UPPER SLAUGHTER

The mortuary chapel on the north side of the chancel of **St Peter's Church** was designed by Francis Niblett, built in 1854 and paid for by public subscription; it houses the tomb of Francis Edward Witts (1783-1854), rector and lord of the manor, who was best known for publishing *The diaries of a Cotswold parson*. The elaborate decoration of the chapel includes encaustic floor tiling, a painted frieze and modern abstract stained glass; the chancel pavement is by Godwin. Near the church is the **Lords of the Manor Hotel**, the home of the Witts family from 1855; its tile pavement probably dates from enlargements made in that year.

WOODCHESTER

Deep in a secluded valley south of Stroud is the astonishing and incomplete house originally known as Woodchester Park; it now goes by the name of Woodchester Mansion, to avoid confusion with the surrounding landscape park which is now in the care of the National Trust. In 1845 the Woodchester Park estate was bought by the Staffordshire landowner and recent Catholic convert William Leigh, who commissioned A. W. N. Pugin to draw up plans for a new house. Pugin withdrew in 1846 because of pressure of work, and Leigh then concentrated on the construction work required to house a new Passionist religious community on a site at the east end of his estate. Work on Leigh's mansion did not begin until 1854, but much of its unique Gothic stone-built structure was complete by 1862; work continued through the 1860s but the mansion was abandoned around 1870 and Leigh died in 1873. The mansion, now conserved but never to be complete, is now in the care of the Woodchester Mansion Trust.

Leigh also asked Pugin to provide plans for the Passionist community buildings, but the architect gave up the commission after Leigh asked for the size of the church to be reduced, and C. F. Hansom took it on. His **Church of Our Lady of the Annunciation**, ST MARY'S HILL was built in 1846-9 and taken over by the Dominicans in 1850; Hansom's priory, to the north of the church, was built in 1850-3 but demolished in 1971. The church, which stands high above the Bath Road, now serves as a Roman Catholic parish church. The richly patterned encaustic chancel pavement, which includes distinctive six-inch tiles in a mixture of brown, red, blue and cream, is only a small part of the superlative original interior decorative scheme, most of which has been lost. The tiles, some of which were designed by Hansom, were manufactured by Minton's.

Woodchester's parish church, **St Mary's Church**, is in the settlement of North Woodchester, well to the north of the mansion; it was built in 1862-4 (architect S. S. Teulon). The original tile pavement is now hidden following alterations to the floor levels, but there is a tiled reredos of the Last Supper designed by Frederick Preedy (1820-98), the stained glass artist and architect, who also designed three windows at St Mary's. The reredos, which was reset in the thirties, was probably part of the first decorative scheme. The remains of the Old Church of St Mary, abandoned in 1863, stand less than half a mile to the north. Beneath the churchyard is a Roman palace excavated in 1793-6; in one of its rooms (still buried) is the Orpheus mosaic pavement, the largest north of the Alps.

WYCK RISSINGTON

The architect J. E. K. Cutts restored the **Church of St Laurence** in 1879, contributing one of his typically well designed (mainly geometric) tile pavements, which often featured eight triangular tiles of alternating colours set within a square. The tiles were made by Godwin's. Beneath a monument to Canon Harry Cheales (d1984) is a 3′ by 2′ wall mosaic representing the design of the hedge maze he created in the rectory garden. In 1947 Cheales had a vision instructing him to create the Maze of the Mysteries of the Gospels, which was complete by 1950 (but has been lost). The mosaic version, by Adrian Fisher Maze Design, dates from 1988.

Gloucestershire Roundup

Terracotta by Gibbs & Canning was used in the works carried out at Holy Trinity Church (1855-6), **Apperley** in 1896-7 by its original architect, Francis Cranmer Penrose. Forty-eight tube-lined tiles designed by Kit Williams and made at Jackfield decorate the central pavilion of the Dragonfly Maze, Rissington Road, **Bourton-on-the-Water**; the maze was begun in 1995. There is an attractive Godwin tile pavement in the chancel and sanctuary of St Michael's Church, **Brimpsfield**, dating from its restoration in 1883-4. There is an unusual encaustic pavement (possibly Godwin, 1892) in the sanctuary of St Swithin's Church, **Brookthorpe**. Relaid in the south aisle of St Michael's Church, **Buckland** is a group of fifteenth century tiles, while the Godwin encaustic pavement in nave, chancel and sanctuary dates from the 1885 restoration and includes copies of medieval tile designs particular to this church. The tile and mosaic reredos (1876) at St Matthew's Church, **Coates** is by James Powell & Sons. On the west wall of St John the Baptist, **Coln St Aldwyns**, is a highly glazed panel of plain and encaustic tiles, perhaps dating from the late 1890s. The Butterfield-influenced 1863 restoration of St Mary's Church, **Driffield**, included a sanctuary pavement and colourful dado tiling, possibly using tiles from several manufacturers. There are medieval tiles in St Peter's Church, **Dyrham** (at the east end of the south aisle) and the walls of the dairy at Dyrham Park are faced with seventeenth century Delft tiles. St Mary's Church, **Flaxley** was rebuilt in 1856 by George Gilbert Scott; the rich decoration includes a fine Godwin encaustic tile pavement. St John the Baptist (1856-7), **France Lynch** was only the second complete church to be built by G. F. Bodley; its polychromatic interior includes a superb encaustic tile pavement, probably attributable to Minton's. Christ Church (1867-8) **Gretton** has some unusual Godwin designs in its chancel encaustic pavement and an embossed majolica tile memorial (dated 1865) on a transept wall. The Godwin chancel encaustic pavement at St Michael's Church, **Guiting Power** dates from the 1902-3 restoration and includes symbols of the evangelists. St George's Church, **Hampnett** was restored by G. E. Street in 1868; the Godwin pavement includes some uncommon tile designs. The Godwin pavement at St John the Baptist, **Harescombe** dates from the restoration of the church by Francis Niblett in 1870-1. William Butterfield's 1863-7 restoration of St Mary Magdalene, **Hewelsfield** included the addition of plain Minton tiling (nave) and a Godwin encaustic pavement (sanctuary). The interior of a garden building at Hidcote Manor, **Hidcote Bartrim** is faced with Dutch tiles, mostly dating from the eighteenth and nineteenth centuries and largely of Friesian manufacture. St John the Baptist, **Huntley** was built (apart from its earlier tower) in 1862-3 by the architect S. S. Teulon; the very rich interior has a Minton Hollins pavement throughout. The brightly coloured Godwin encaustic pavement running throughout St Mary's Church, **Icomb** dates from its 1870-1 restoration. All Saints Church, **Kemble** has a tiled reredos by Maw & Co and a Godwin pavement, both dating from the late 1870s. St Mary's Church, **Painswick** has an unspectacular Godwin pavement and an opus sectile reredos (1893-4) by Powell's in the north chapel. William Butterfield's uncommonly colourless interior at St Michael's Church (1873-4), **Poulton** includes an encaustic pavement by Maw & Co. The chancel of St Lawrence Church, **Sandhurst** (rebuilt 1857-8) has an excellent Godwin encaustic pavement including eight-inch tiles of the evangelists. There is an elaborate encaustic tile pavement (probably Minton) in the chancel of St Andrew's Church, **Sevenhampton**, dating from the 1892-3 restoration. William Butterfield's restoration of little All Saints Church, **Shorncote** (now redundant) in 1882-3 included the installation of chancel floor tiling. The elaborate encaustic chancel pavement at St Peter's Church, **Siddington** formed part of Henry Woodyer's 1864-5 restoration, as did the blue glazed tiled dado, which has been overpainted. The mostly plain Godwin tile pavement (1872) at St Mary's Church, **Upper Swell** includes four six-inch memorial tiles on the altar step. Henry Woodyer's 1849 restoration of St Leonard's Church, **Upton St Leonards** included the installation of a sanctuary tile pavement and a gold mosaic reredos, both from Minton's.[29] The unusual sanctuary pavement by Maw & Co at St Lawrence, **Weston Sub Edge** dates from around 1853. The colourful Minton pavement (in mostly buff, brown, blue and white) at St Peter's Church, **Willersey** dates from its 1866-72 restoration. The extensions and alterations (1873-5) to St Peter's Church, **Windrush** carried out by Henry Woodyer included the installation of a geometric nave pavement (Minton Hollins) and an encaustic pavement in the chancel.

Apart from those mentioned above, the following churches have Godwin tile pavements: St Bartholomew, Aldsworth; St Margaret, Alstone; Holy Rood, Ampney Crucis; St Peter, Ampney St Peter; St Margaret, Bagendon; St Mary Magdalene, Baunton; All Saints, Bisley; St Michael, Blaisdon; Holy Trinity, Brimscombe; St Michael, Bulley; St Andrew, Churcham; St Bartholomew, Churchdown; St Bartholomew, Coaley; St Andrew, Cold Aston; St Mary, Down Hatherley; St Peter, Framilode; St Edward, Hawling; St Andrew, Hazleton[30]; St Swithun, Hempsted; St Martin, Horsley; St Lawrence, Lechlade (also Minton wall plaque); St Mary, Lower Slaughter; St Stephen, Moreton Valence; St Andrew, Naunton; St Mary, Norton; St Bartholomew, Notgrove; All Saints, Somerford Keynes; Holy Trinity, Stroud; St Laurence, Stroud; St Thomas À Becket, Todenham; St Luke, Tutshill; St Margaret, Whaddon; St Peter, Winchcombe; St Bartholomew, Winstone.

There are tile pavements by other manufacturers at St Mary, Barnsley; St Martin, Charlton Abbots (Minton); St Edward, Evenlode (Maw); St Peter, Frampton Cotterell (Minton); St Peter, Hasfield (Minton); St Nicholas, Hatherop; St Mary the Virgin, Lower Swell (part Wedgwood); St Mary, Meysey Hampton (Maw); Holy Ascension, Oddington (Minton); St John the Baptist, Old Sodbury (Maw); St Cyr, Stinchcombe (Minton); St John the Baptist, Shipton Moyne (supplied by Simpson's, so probably by Maw's); St Edward, Stow-on-the-Wold; St Matthew, Twigworth (Minton).

References

1. David Gaimster and Beverley Nenk, *English Households in Transition c1450-1550: the ceramic evidence*, in *The Age of Transition: the archaeology of English culture 1400-1600*, David Gaimster and Paul Stamper, Editors, (Oxbow Books, Oxford, 1997), pp171-195.

2. Hans van Lemmen, *Delftware Tiles* (Laurence King, London, 1997), pp123-5.

3. David Verey and Alan Brooks, *Gloucestershire 1: The Cotswolds* 3rd ed. Buildings of England (Penguin, London, 1999), p100.

4. Paul Atterbury and Louise Irvine, *The Doulton Story* (Royal Doulton Tableware, Stoke on Trent, 1979).

5. Andrew Foyle, *Bristol* Pevsner Architectural Guides (Yale University Press, New Haven and London, 2004), p171.

6. J. Barnard, 'A monument to the printers' craft', *Country Life*, 149 (1971), pp412-3.

7. H. Ricardo, 'The architect's use of enamelled tiles', *British Clayworker*, 10 (1902) March, pp431-7.

8. Pilkington's Tile & Pottery Co. Ltd., Clifton Junction in British Library, Trade Literature, OM06y. This brochure, comprising twelve photographs of interiors with Pilkington's faience and tilework, was probably produced shortly after the opening in 1903 of two buildings featured: Corporation Baths, Lister Drive, Liverpool and the Stock Exchange, Bristol. It includes two photographs of Lister Drive Baths, one showing the entrance hall and staircase which is captioned 'Faience Balustrade & Wall Tiling'; the other shows the main baths. Seven out of the twelve photograph captions mention faience, suggesting that Pilkington's was a major producer of coloured slab faience during the early 1900s.

9. Douglas Merritt, *Sculpture in Bristol* (Redcliffe Press, Bristol, 2002).

10. Carol E. Brown and Jeremy Hutchings, *The Conservation of the Spanish Tile Floor in the Lord Mayor's Chapel, Bristol*, in *Architectural Ceramics: their history, manufacture and conservation*, Jeanne Marie Teutonico, ed, (James & James (Science Publishers) Ltd, London, 1996), pp113-118.

11. Chris Blanchett, 'The floor tiles at The Vyne, Hampshire, England', *Glazed Expressions*, (2000) 41, pp2-31.

12. David Wickers, *Millennium Miles: The Story of the National Cycle Network* (Good Books (GB Publications Lmited), Whitley, 2000), p93.

13. Tony Herbert, 'Early Encaustics in Bristol', *Glazed Expressions*, (1985) 10, pp5.

14. Martin Laker, 'A new look at St Paul's mosaics', *St Paul's Church, Clifton, Parish Magazine*, (2003).

15. Canon Rowland E. Hill, *Cirencester Parish Church: An account of its History and Architecture* 4th ed (The Friends of Cirencester Parish Church, Cirencester, 2000).

16. Dennis W. Hadley, *James Powell & Sons: A listing of opus sectile, 1847-1973*, (2001).

17. Alison Kelly, *Mrs Coade's Stone* (Self Publishing Association, Upton-upon-Severn, 1990), p349.

18. David Welander, *The History, Art and Architecture of Gloucester Cathedral* (Alan Sutton Publishing, Stroud, 1991).

19. David Verey and Alan Brooks, *Gloucestershire 2: The Vale and the Forest of Dean* 3rd ed. Buildings of England (Yale University Press, New Haven and London, 2002), p428.

20. Elizabeth Eames, *English Tilers* (British Museum Press, London, 1992).

21. Tom Fenton, *To raise a perfect monument to taste* (Smith & Associates, Much Wenlock, 2001).

22. Philip and Dorothy Brown, 'Glass tiles', *Glazed Expressions*, (1994) 28, pp2-3.

23. J. Mordaunt Crook, *William Burges and the High Victorian Dream* (John Murray, London, 1981), p232.

24. Hadley, *James Powell & Sons* (2001).

25. Betty Greene, 'Some unusual tiles at Bredon, Oxenton and Tredington', *Glazed Expressions*, (1992) 24, p8.

26. Kelly, *Mrs Coade's Stone* (1990), pp115, 350.

27. Jane A. Wight, *Mediaeval Floor Tiles* (John Baker, London, 1975).

28. Hilary Lees, *Exploring English Churchyard Memorials* (Tempus Publishing, Stroud, 2000).

29. John Elliott and John Pritchard, eds, *Henry Woodyer: Gentleman Architect* (Department of Continuing Education, University of Reading, Reading, 2002).

30. *The Builder*, vol 25, 2nd February 1867.

Hampshire

The influence of Carter's in nearby Poole is seen largely in the design of the pubs and shops of Hampshire's large ports. Away from the shore, although the county is by no means a paradise for the tile-hunter, there are several sites of national importance, including the thirteenth century pavement at Winchester Cathedral and the sixteenth century maiolica pavement at The Vyne. Other highlights are the Moorish smoking room in Rhinefield House, Brockenhurst and the huge area of Carter's mosaic on the twin towers of Gosport's 1960s flat blocks. The Isle of Wight, whose sites are listed at the end of the main Hampshire section, is perhaps a more fruitful area for exploration than the county's hinterland, with the seminal Minton's encaustic tile pavements of Osborne House, the unique brickwork of Quarr Abbey and the products of the island's own terracotta works frequently on view. Suggested reading: 'The Floor Tiles at The Vyne', *Glazed Expressions* 41 (2000). The *Gazetteer* entry for Hampshire covers the administrative areas of Hampshire County Council, Isle of Wight County Council, Portsmouth City Council and Southampton City Council.

BORDON WHITEHILL

The seven classrooms at **Woodlea Primary School** (1992) each have a tiled wet floor area, their wide variety of colourful designs being provided by guest artists. The encaustic tiles were supplied by the Life Enhancing Tile Company, whose founder, Robert Manners, contributed one of the designs.

BROCKENHURST

The honeymoon of Mabel Walker, a Nottinghamshire coal heiress, and Captain Lionel Munro was a grand tour which allowed them to take their pick of the world's interior designs for use in their new home, **Rhinefield House** (1888-90). Their architect, W. H. Romaine-Walker, combined the couple's ideas and produced a tudorbethan pile including Hampton Court-style chimneys and Lionel Munro's Moorish smoking room, which was a replica of a room in the Alhambra Palace (Fig 84). It has a mosaic floor in a bold floral pattern outlined in black and white, while the walls are tiled to dado level with cuenca tiles (in orange, green, black and white) manufactured in Triana, Seville; above, the walls are faced with beaten copper. The Walker-Munro family retained the house until the 1950s, and it was eventually converted to an hotel in 1985; the smoking room or Alhambra is now a private dining room.

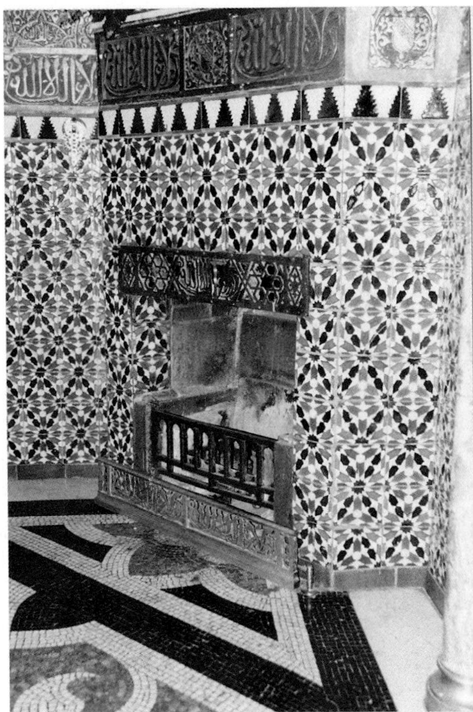

Fig 84.

FARLEIGH WALLOP

The Coade stone mermaids on the gatepiers of **Farleigh House** were made around 1785 (for Lord Portsmouth at Hurstbourne Priors) and later removed to Farleigh Wallop. Around 2000 they were joined by another mermaid, part of the Whale Fountain which was executed in neo-Coade stone by Thomason Cudworth for the Earl and Countess of Portsmouth. The whale itself weighs one and a half tons and took two weeks to fire.[1]

FARNBOROUGH

The mansion **Farnborough Hill** (now a school) was built in 1863 by the architect Henry E. Kendall (1805-85) for the publisher T. G. Longman, and bought in 1881 by the Empress Eugénie (d1920), widow of Napoleon III, last Emperor of France. The facade of this unusual house, where English half-timbering meets Germanic gothic, includes a frieze of small plasterwork relief panels showing angels, galleons and swans; this runs around most of the house generally between ground and first floor levels. Inside, the entrance hall has an encaustic pavement, probably by Minton's, in which groups of four decorated tiles are divided by strings of plain red and black tiles. In the library and lower gallery are pretty window boxes faced with Minton's tiles, and other rooms have tiled fireplaces. There are ornate fittings throughout the house, particularly the sunflower-themed ironwork on the staircase.

FARRINGDON

Apart from the many medieval tiles that have been relaid in the chancel of **All Saints Church**, the great ceramic attraction of Farringdon is the **Village Hall**, an idiosyncratic bright red brick and terracotta monster designed and mostly built by the Reverend Thomas Hackett Massey, who came to the village as rector in 1857, having been ordained four years earlier. He rebuilt the chancel of All Saints and put up a new rectory before turning to Stone House, a former school. He bought the property and around the late 1880s began to build, with the assistance of bricklayer Henry Andrews (1838-1924), carpenter George Gilbert (1867-1930) and young labourer Frank Bone (1871-1936). The strange construction, made from red brick and decorative terracotta from Rowlands Castle brickworks, quickly became known as Massey's Folly. The reverend would demolish parts of the building and add other sections as the whim took him; not surprisingly, it was still unfinished when he died in 1919, and lay boarded up for many years afterwards .

GOSPORT

The ferry journey across Portsmouth Harbour provides a dramatic view of **Seaward Tower** and **Harbour Tower**, a pair of sixteen-storey tower blocks built in 1963 on the ESPLANADE; the brick campanile (1889) of Holy Trinity Church rises incongruously beside them. Both blocks of flats have pairs of 135′ murals of Carter's unglazed mosaic in red, white, blue and black running the whole height of the buildings (Fig 85). These staggering murals were designed by Kenneth Barden, although the initials JET are also to be found on two of them. Between the blocks is **Timespace**, a public timepiece (a sundial with 50′ high gnomon) and arena installed around 2001 as part of the Millennium Promenade development; its theme is Einstein's theory of relativity. Running round the edge of the circular space is a mosaic by Mosaic Works of London showing events and characters from the town's maritime history. Now that Gosport has recognised the value of its 'initially controversial' (according to the Millennium Promenade Trail Guide) tower block mosaics, the town seems to have gone mosaic mad, with further recent installations in the bus station and near the ferry landing.

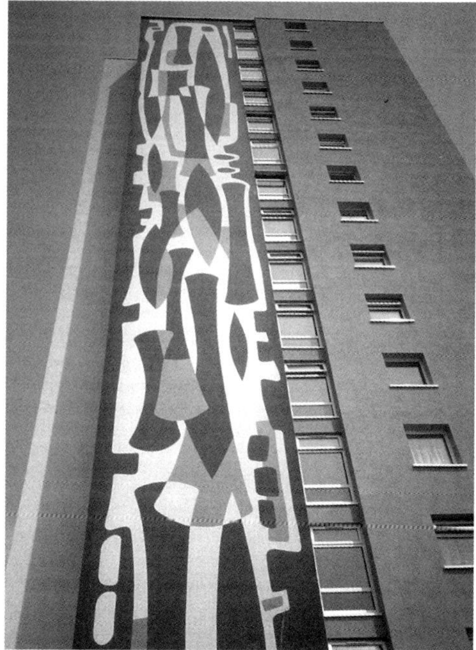

Fig 85.

One of the glories of Gosport is its collection of small but very ornate public houses, built to serve the 7,000 or more people who lived within the bounds of the town's ramparts in the late nineteenth century.[2] Perhaps the prettiest is the **Fox Tavern** in NORTH STREET (north of the High Street), with a glazed brick facade in green, yellow, red, blue and black which includes a tiny pair of faience fox heads; the fascia lettering reminds us that the pub was part of the estate of Long's Southsea Brewery. Gosport's own breweries, notably Blake's, also attempted to entice customers into their pubs with colourful ceramics. Of their thirty Gosport pubs, the **King's Head** in BROCKHURST ROAD and the former **Royal Oak** in AVERY LANE (both west of the centre), and the **Royal Arms** in STOKE ROAD (west of the High Street) have fancy displays of tiling in green and yellow featuring the Blake's name. The brewers Brickwoods, from over the waters in Portsmouth, made their contribution with the green tiles and glazed brick of the **Gipsy Queen**, WHITWORTH ROAD (west of Stoke Road).

There are many more examples of brewer's ceramics throughout the town, but once the pub crawl is complete, head for BEMISTER'S LANE, which links the High Street with South Street, to relax on an unusual, cone-shaped commemorative seat (1999) with ceramics designed by Jan O'Highway.

HURSLEY

All Saints Church was rebuilt in 1847-8 for its incumbent during 1836-66, John Keble, pioneer of the Oxford Movement; the architect was J. P. Harrison of Oxford. Its extensive encaustic tiling includes large red, buff and blue roundels depicting the four evangelists; these were made by Minton's to designs by Pugin. Following bad rain damage, All Saints was extensively restored in 1910, the rotten wooden side aisle flooring being replaced with floral encaustics and a border of swirling grapes and vine leaves. There is a memorial brass to Keble, designed by William Butterfield.

ITCHEN STOKE

The floor of the apsidal chancel of **St Mary's Church** (1866) takes the form of a maze around 15′ in diameter made from plain glazed reddish-brown and green tiles of various shapes, the design being based on that of the labyrinth laid in 1202 at Chartres Cathedral, perhaps the best known of the medieval Christian labyrinth designs and certainly one of the most frequently copied (Fig 86). The design of the church itself was by the architect Henry Conybeare, brother of the incumbent (who paid for its construction), and was inspired by the then recently restored Sainte Chapelle in Paris. The church, which is in the care of the Churches Conservation Trust, also has many unusual furnishings including a pulpit with cast iron tracery.

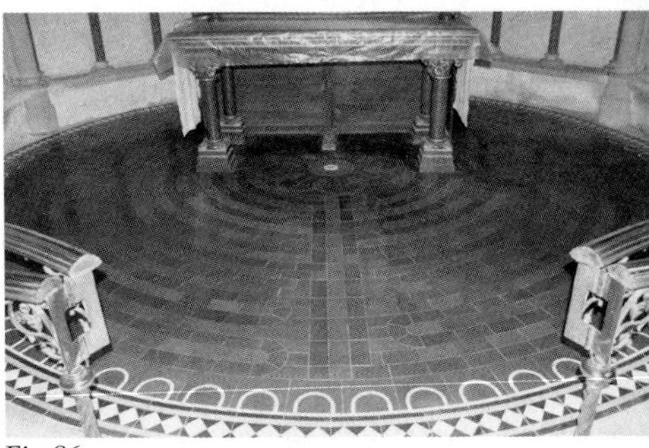

Fig 86.

LISS

At the **Newman Collard Recreation Ground** is the Liss Millennium Mosaic, a colourful 35′ by 8′ tile and mosaic mural incorporating about 100 contributions from local groups, organisations and individuals which was completed in 2000. A river flows along the mural's base while the various scenes are divided by trees; the project was overseen by the artist Sally Maltby.

PETERSFIELD

The reredos of **St Peter's Church**, on THE SQUARE, was made by Powell's of Whitefriars in 1902 to a design by Charles Hardgrave. Most of the remaining decoration in the chancel, which includes tiling and terracotta to shoulder height, was added by Sir Arthur Blomfield in 1873-4, although the terracotta, which may have been made in Newick, East Sussex, is possibly slightly earlier.

PORTSMOUTH

Portsmouth's main contribution to ceramic history results from competition between two of its brewers, Brickwoods and Portsmouth United Breweries (whose apposite acronym is PUB), from the 1900s into the interwar years. Their tied estates included many pubs with memorable ceramic facades designed to attract customers. Brickwoods were first to use glazed bricks and faience, normally in dark red or brown with white lettering, while United preferred green; most of the ceramics used on the pub facades, along with the doorway mosaics, came from Carter's of Poole. Many pubs with relatively plain ceramic facades still survive, but three of the more ornate deserve mention.[3]

The former **Mediterranean**, just north of Portsmouth's centre in STAMSHAW ROAD, was built in 1904 by the local architect Arthur E

Cogswell (1858-1934), who was something of a pub specialist. It has been converted into flats but retains its Carter's tiled mural of Gibraltar at first floor level. Also by Cogswell is the **Tangier**, TANGIER ROAD, Baffins (well east of the centre), built for United. This was licensed in 1911 and has a green glazed brick and faience facade; it was the first to be designed in what became the typical United style. There is also much faience lettering as well as two tile murals, both by Carter's, depicting a market in Tangiers and an Arab horseman. The pub (and the road) took their names from the nearby Tangier Farm, and it is said that the design of the pub tiles resulted from a holiday taken in Morocco by the chairman of Portsmouth United Breweries, Sir William Dupree.[4]

Southsea

On the northern edge of Southsea, just south of Portsmouth's main railway station, is the former Yorkshire Grey public house (1897, architect A. H. Bone, now **Grey's**) at 25 GUILDHALL WALK. Inside are two large Carter's pictorial tile panels, a third having been destroyed. Head south to find another good ceramic pub, the **India Arms**, GREAT SOUTHSEA STREET, the north part of which was designed by A. E. Cogswell and built in 1902; next door is a former butcher's and fishmonger's shop (1900) which became part of the pub around 1980. The original section of the pub has a tiled ground floor with a tile mural bearing the pub's name and the date 1902, while the old shop has two tiled panels by Carter's showing a shooting party and fishing boats. Continuing seaward, the **Queen's Hotel** (1903), CLARENCE PARADE displays some excellent salmon-pink terracotta dressings including a pair of domes and elaborate figurative corbels. Finally, just east along Osborne Road is NETLEY ROAD and a smaller pub, the **Auckland Arms**, with a colourful facade of glazed brick and faience. It was once part of the estate of Long's Southsea Brewery, and is very similar to the same brewer's Fox Tavern in Gosport.

SELBORNE

Resited around the altar of **St Mary's Church**, Selborne is a collection of thirteenth and fourteenth century inlaid tiles, some found at nearby Selborne Priory during excavations begun in 1953 and others from beneath the floor of the church itself, in the south aisle. The motifs include eagles, birds, fish and a pair of castles with a fault caused by a damaged stamp, the latter design being identical to tiles found in Winchester and made at the Otterbourne tilery.[5]

SHERBORNE ST JOHN

The Vyne (NT) stands about a mile north of Sherborne St John. It is a large red brick house built in 1526-8 by William Lord Sandys, a member of the court of Henry VIII; additions were made in the seventeenth, eighteenth and nineteenth centuries. Over the fireplace in the Stone Gallery is a large early renaissance terracotta roundel. The sumptuous private chapel, built by Lord Sandys and as lavish as any in the country at the time, has three areas paved with early sixteenth century maiolica tiles made in Antwerp, several panels of early sixteenth century Spanish cuenca tiles and two fourteenth century medieval inlaid tiles set amongst the maiolica tiles (Fig 87). The maiolica tiles are brightly coloured and have a wide range of renaissance motifs including portraits and a surprisingly cheery skull and crossbones. Similar maiolica pavements, dating from the 1520s to the 1540s, a period when new renaissance-style interiors were fashionable, are known to have existed at a number of high-status sites in England.[6]

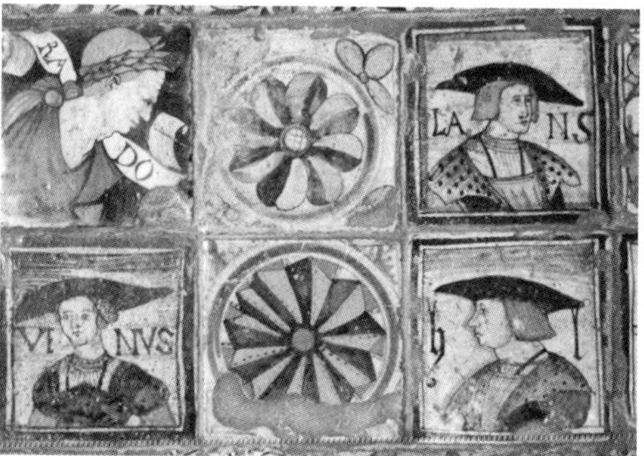

Fig 87.

The Vyne's maiolica tiles were thought for many years to have come from Italy, but in 1926 Bernard Rackham suggested that they were in fact Flemish in origin, made at the workshops of Guido Andries, an Italian immigrant who established a workshop in Antwerp in the early sixteenth century.[7] None of the tiles at The Vyne are in their original position, the tradition being that they were laid in a part of the house which was demolished around 1654 and were subsequently rediscovered in the gardens towards the end of the nineteenth century before being relaid in the chapel. However, the *Journals* of

Wiggett Chute, owner of the house during much of the nineteenth century, state that he repositioned the tiles during the 1840s; he thought that Lord Sandys brought some of the tiles from France in the sixteenth century. An alternative theory is that they were collected during the second half of the eighteenth century by John Chute, then owner of The Vyne, and his friend Horace Walpole during their frequent trips to the continent; Chute and Walpole's 'gothicising' of the house can be seen as a forerunner of the nineteenth century gothic revival.

The maiolica tiles fall into four distinct groups: rectangular border tiles, hexagonal tiles which surround small square tiles, and large square tiles. There are three different combinations of hexagonal and small square tiles, each of slightly differing size, suggesting that the tiles came from different workshops and/or were made at different times. There are only small areas of each type, not enough to make up a whole room floor, and this, together with the inclusion of the Spanish tiles, indicates that the tiles are more likely to have been acquired piecemeal by Lord Sandys or by Chute and Walpole. It is almost certain that some, if not all the maiolica tiles at The Vyne were made at the Antwerp workshops of Guido Andries, probably at different periods, but until further research on early Flemish tile production has been undertaken, no firm attribution can be made.[8]

SOUTHAMPTON

From the main **Railway Station**, where a tile and mosaic frieze of a liner may be found on the footbridge, the heart of Southampton lies to the east, just beyond the major public buildings which overlook Guildhall Square. The square is bordered by ABOVE BAR STREET, where there is a former **Prudential Assurance** building designed by Waterhouse & Son and built in 1901-4, with much red terracotta and a dramatic double porch and window surrounds. The building is something of a curiosity as it was the last Prudential to be erected in the lifetime of Alfred Waterhouse (1830-1905), although it was almost certainly designed by Paul Waterhouse as his father had a stroke in 1901 and passed control of the firm to his son. The Prudential has been restored after being damaged by fire.[9]

Southward to BARGATE STREET, where a statue of George III (in Roman dress) may be seen in a niche high on the south face of the gateway, **The Bargate**. It is signed Coade and Sealy and dates from 1809, the design being a copy of a statue of Emperor Hadrian originally in the British Museum. The statue was given to the Mayor of Southampton by the 2nd Marquess of Lansdowne in 1809, and took the place of a statue of Queene Anne which had previously occupied the niche.[10] Continue southward into the HIGH STREET to find the former **Post Office** (now housing) at number 57-58, with a decorative red terracotta facade including scrolls and shields. At 56 are the former premises of the fruit merchants **Oakley and Watling**, built in 1890 and faced in Doulton's white Carraraware, a material introduced by the firm in 1888. The facade displays lively decorative touches including roundels of fruit and a Southampton Hulk (a sailing vessel). Almost opposite at 123-4 High Street is **Market Chambers**, a former fishmonger's (now restaurant), whose interior has very fine Carter's painted tile panels showing subjects linked to the sea: boats, fish, goddesses and whales amongst them. The surrounds of the panels are moulded shells and fish in shades of ochre.

In contrast, just east of the High Street on BACK OF THE WALLS is a modern office building, **The Friary**, on the side of which is a series of fifteen tile panels by John Hodgson, installed in 1987 and showing the activities of medieval friars. Further east along Bernard Street is OXFORD STREET; at its junction with John Street is a former shipping office with good red terracotta dressings. At the corner of Oxford Street and TERMINUS TERRACE is the **London Hotel**, with spectacular, heavily rusticated green Carter's tiling.

Freemantle

Christ Church, PAYNE'S ROAD, Freemantle was built in 1865-6 and designed by the architect William White, but the chancel tiling - a Godwin encaustic pavement in red, cream, black and glazed green with some uncommon designs - was laid in 1897. Just over half a mile north west in ENGLISH ROAD is the **Englishman**, a pub with an unusual art deco tiled frieze in red and white on its fascia. The tiles probably date from the early 1920s, when the pub was owned by the Winchester Brewery; the design is made up from elongated repeats of the letters 'WB'.

Portswood

St Denys Church, ST DENYS ROAD, was designed by George Gilbert Scott and built in 1868 on a site close to that of the Augustinian Priory of St Denys, which was founded in the twelfth century. Some medieval encaustic tiles from the Priory are mounted as a wall panel inside the church, which also has a Godwin tile pavement and a reredos (1871) comprising three opus sectile and mosaic panels by Powell and Son.

Powell's also supplied the superb opus sectile and mosaic reredos to be found at **Christ Church**, HIGHFIELD LANE, Highfield. The church was built in 1846-7, with additions in 1855, 1878, 1915 and later. The 1878 work included the construction of a new chancel, which was paved with Minton tiles; if these are still extant, they are now hidden by carpet. The reredos, which was probably given by the family of the Reverend Thomas McCalmont after his death, shows the Last Supper and was purchased from Powell's in 1885 for £160. Its design was carried out for the firm by Harry Burrow, who died in 1882; designs were often used by Powell's on more than one occasion. This colourful reredos is flanked by panels of red glass tiles with grain and grape motifs (symbols of the Eucharist), making a very striking composition.[11]

TITCHFIELD

The remains of thirteeenth century **Titchfield Abbey** (EH) stand half a mile north of Titchfield, and are overlooked by the massive Tudor gatehouse of Place House, the (otherwise mostly demolished) mansion formed by the conversion of part of the Abbey buildings following the Dissolution. There are several areas of late thirteenth or early fourteenth century encaustic tiles in the former Abbey cloister, which was retained as the mansion's courtyard. The tiles may have been manufactured locally or at the Otterbourne tilery, although some of their designs are common to other Premonstratensian foundations; they show birds, beasts and a variety of heraldic motifs, as well as two contemporary portraits: a man with a round cap and a woman with a chin-strap and thrust-back hair-net.

WINCHESTER

The thirteenth century tiling in the three-aisled retrochoir of **Winchester Cathedral** is one of the most important surviving indoor medieval pavements in the country. There are over 5,000 five-and-a-half inch square Wessex tiles, most of which are in their original positions, laid around 1260-80 in carpet patterns using over sixty different designs.[12] The pavement was recorded and successfully conserved during 1990-6; the work included the introduction of some replica tiles made by Diana Hall (Fig 88).[13] Another medieval tiled floor is still in situ beneath boarding in the Cathedral Verger's office, and in the Muniments Tower of **Winchester College** are two medieval tile pavements, one in excellent condition.

In SOUTHGATE STREET, running south of the Cathedral, is the former **Church of St Thomas and St Clement** (1845-6) which has been converted to office use with the sanctuary partitioned off as a storeroom. Hidden away in the store is a very fine Powell's of Whitefriars opus sectile, tile and mosaic reredos, ordered from the firm in 1893. The design, Christ in Majesty flanked by a band of angels, was by George Parlby. Also in Southgate Street is **Fiennes House**, with heavily ornamented terracotta cladding. Half a mile further along the street, which continues as ST CROSS ROAD, is the **Hospital of St Cross**, founded in 1132, although the church is rather later, being completed in the thirteenth century. There are medieval inlaid tiles in its porch, west end and side aisles; these are mainly thirteenth century but some, dating from the late fourteenth century, are thought to have come from the Otterbourne tilery. The Minton encaustic pavements in nave and chancel date from alterations made by William Butterfield in 1864-5; he was architect to the hospital (which Pugin chose as his symbol of medieval charity in *Contrasts*) from 1853 until the end of his career. Butterfield's work also included the application of colourful wall decoration, following what survived of the original Norman fresco designs; however, this outraged local antiquarians and was later removed.

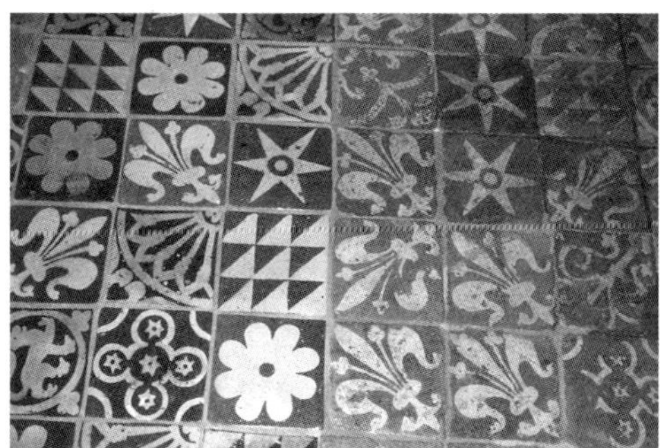

Fig 88.

ISLE OF WIGHT

Apart from the locations listed below, terracotta produced by Pritchett & Co is widespread. The firm made bricks, tiles, pottery and terracotta around the early 1900s, with works near Cowes and Carisbrooke. Harry Pritchett was their architectural modeller, and his lively, often hand-crafted figures (including many dragon finials) may be seen throughout the island.

COWES

In the main shopping area, the **butchers** at 62 HIGH STREET has unusual starburst-style ventilators and a mostly hexagonal, white-tiled interior with strips of coloured relief tiles. **Holy Trinity Church**, CHURCH ROAD has an excellent encaustic tile pavement by Maw & Co.

EAST COWES

The grandly Italianate pile **Osborne House** (EH), just east of East Cowes, was built for Queen Victoria and Prince Albert following their purchase of a smaller house on the site overlooking the Solent in 1845. Construction began in 1845, with the Pavilion Wing being completed in 1846 and the Household Wing in 1851; the Durbar Wing was added in 1890-1. Prince Albert, who was responsible for the design of the house, attended an exhibition of tile pressing by Herbert Minton in 1843, and was so interested in the process that Minton prepared a description of it for him. Soon afterwards Minton's made a geometric and encaustic tile pavement for Osborne, and tiles were used widely in the the house and grounds, leading to a growth in their popularity in the domestic market (Fig 89). Blue, green and white geometric tiles decorated the ornamental fountains on the terraces (1847-53) of Osborne House, while the kitchen of the Swiss Cottage (1853), built for the royal children and standing half a mile to the east of the house, has wall tiling in white with a pattern of dark blue spots.[14]

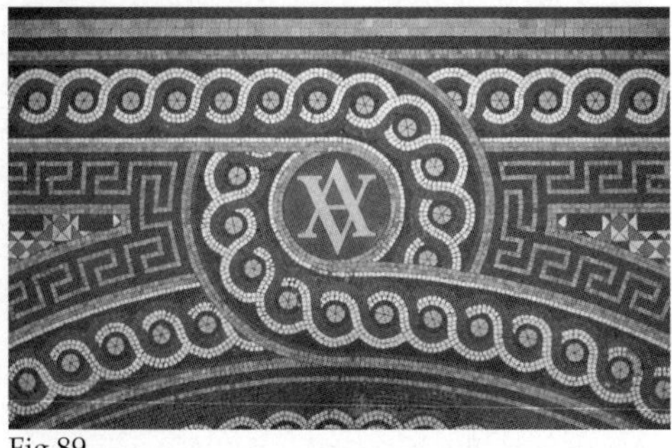
Fig 89.

Inside the house, there are many tiled fire surrounds, including one with royal monograms by Minton's, and the Marble Corridor has ornate Minton's encaustic floor tiles. The lavish Minton tile pavement in the Grand Corridor of the Household Wing includes many heraldic and other symbols, but is covered along the whole of its central length by a beige carpet. This fantastic pavement, along with those of St George's Hall, Liverpool (on view occasionally) and the Palace of Westminster is one of the three grandest and most complex encaustic tile pavements in the country. Surely the conservation difficulties associated with allowing full access to these pavements have contributed to their being undervalued in terms of the decorative arts; the appearance of the Grand Corridor would certainly be transformed by substituting the bold colours and patterns of the tiles for the grim carpet.

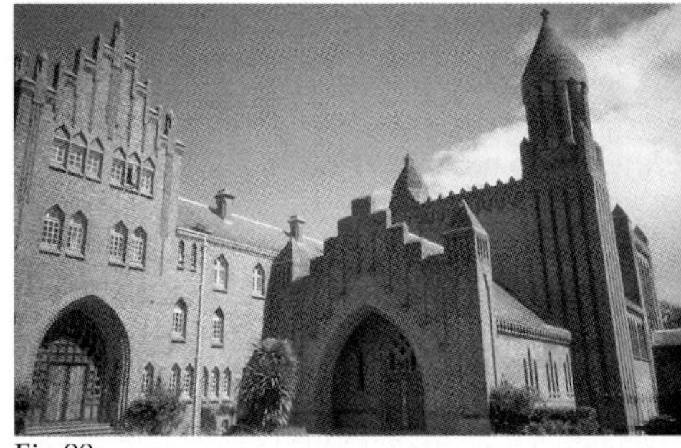
Fig 90.

QUARR ABBEY

Quarr Abbey, a mile and a half west of Ryde, was built for French Benedictine monks in 1907-14 and designed by the architect-turned-monk Dom Paul Bellot (1876-1944). His church (1911-12) was built from rough Belgian bricks, left bare inside and out, with decoration in the form of cut-brick friezes and stepped patterns (Fig 90). With its almost-Byzantine campanile and raw brick, it is an entirely unexpected architectural event, adrift in the lush countryside of the northern part of the island. Bellot studied architecture at the École des Beaux-Arts in Paris during 1894-1901, but in 1902 joined a Benedictine community from Solesmes which had settled at Appuldurcombe House on the Isle of Wight. He designed monastic buildings in the Netherlands in 1906, then was recalled to Appuldurcombe where he designed Quarr Abbey, the community moving there in 1908. He went on to build in France, Belgium and the Netherlands in his distinctive style, experimenting with polychromatic brickwork, parabolic arches and dramatic lighting.[15] Quarr Abbey is his only British building, and though rather restrained in comparison with his later output, is a stunning essay in the use of brick to create soaring spaces and spiritual feeling.

RYDE

St Michael's Church, WRAY STREET, Swanmore was built by the Reverend William Grey, supervised by the Ryde architect Richard J. Jones, in 1861-3; the chancel was completed in 1874. A large and ritualistic church, the polychromatic interior features red, yellow and black brick as well as stone, and the tiling by Maw & Co dates from around 1865.

SANDOWN

Southern Water's **Pumping Station** sports a mosaic (2001) by Rebecca Newnham featuring images of primitive fish.

WHIPPINGHAM

St Mildred's Church, the Osborne House estate church, was built in 1854-5 (chancel only) and 1861-2; the design was by the architect A. J. Humbert with strong input from Prince Albert, who died in 1861. There is a good encaustic tile pavement.

Hampshire Roundup

The interior decorative scheme of St Joseph's R. C. Church (1912-13), QUEEN'S ROAD, **Aldershot** includes terracotta and multicoloured brick and tiles. St Mary's Church, Eastrop Lane, **Basingstoke** has glazed tiling with prayers, commandments and biblical creeds on the east wall; this probably dates from the 1886 alterations. There are many thirteenth and fourteenth century inlaid floor tiles in the chancel of St Andrew's Church, **Chilcomb**. Christ Church (1870), **Colbury** has a glittering mosaic reredos, either side of which are vertical panels of red and buff stencilled tiles produced by Maw's. The elaborate pinnacles and chancel screen of All Saints Church (1818), **Deane**, are of Coade stone, as are the windows. There are elaborate Minton encaustic tiles in the sanctuary of St Mary's Church, **Monxton**, installed during its 1852-3 rebuilding by the architect Henry Woodyer. A large tile mural showing yachts, windsurfers and swimmers features on the Public Baths at **New Milton**; it was made in 1990 from plain coloured 6" tiles manufactured by H. & R. Johnson, cut where necessary to form the required shapes. In the chancel of **Old Burghclere** parish church (in the grounds of the manor house) is a tiled wall memorial to members of the Herbert family of nearby Highclere Castle; the memorial predates the estate church at Highclere, which was built in 1870. The Church of St Peter and St Paul (1853-5), Market Place, **Ringwood** has ornate chancel tiling bearing inscriptions. There is a good early Minton tile pavement in the sanctuary of the Church of St Peter and St Paul, **Thruxton**. The facade of the Rising Sun pub, by the quay at **Warsash**, sports an unusual pictorial tile panel possibly dating from the 1950s.

References

1. Amicia De Moubray, 'The Secret Coade Unlocked', *Country Life*, 197 (2003), pp106-8.
2. *A Toast to Gosport* (Gosport Borough Council and CAMRA, Gosport, 1996).
3. Lynn Pearson, 'Decorative ceramics in the buildings of the British brewing industry', *TACS Journal*, 8 (2000), pp26-36.
4. Philip Eley and R. C. Riley, *The demise of demon drink? Portsmouth Pubs, 1900-1950*, Portsmouth Papers vol 58 (Portsmouth City Council, Portsmouth, 1991).
5. Elizabeth S. Eames, *Catalogue of Medieval Lead-Glazed Earthenware Tiles in the Department of Medieval and Later Antiquities, British Museum*, (British Museum Publications, London, 1980), vol 1, pp215-6.
6. David Gaimster and Michael Hughes, *South Netherlands maiolica floor tiles from Broad Arrow Tower, Tower of London*, in *Maiolica in the North: the archaeology of tin-glazed earthenware in north-west Europe c1500-1600*, ed David Gaimster, (British Museum, London, 1999).
7. Bernard Rackham, *Early Netherlands Maiolica with special reference to the tiles at The Vyne in Hampshire* (Geoffrey Bles, London, 1926).
8. Chris Blanchett, 'The floor tiles at The Vyne, Hampshire, England', *Glazed Expressions*, (2000) 41, pp2-31.
9. Colin Cunningham and Prudence Waterhouse, *Alfred Waterhouse, 1830-1905: Biography of a Practice* (Clarendon Press, Oxford, 1992).
10. Alison Kelly, *Mrs Coade's Stone* (Self Publishing Association, Upton-upon-Severn, 1990).
11. Dennis W. Hadley, *James Powell & Sons: A listing of opus sectile, 1847-1973*, (2001).
12. Christopher Norton, *The Medieval Tile Pavements of Winchester Cathedral*, in *Winchester Cathedral: Nine Hundred Years, 1093-1993*, ed John Crook, (Phillimore, Chichester, 1993) pp167-176.
13. Peter Bird, *Winchester Cathedral: Conserving the retrochoir pavement*, in *Historic Floors: Their history and conservation*, ed Jane Fawcett, (Butterworth-Heinemann, Oxford, 1998) pp113-119.
14. Tony Herbert and Kathryn Huggins, *The Decorative Tile in Architecture and Interiors* (Phaidon Press, London, 1995).
15. Peter Willis, *Dom Paul Bellot: Architect and Monk* (Elysium Press, Newcastle upon Tyne, 1996).

Herefordshire

The tile manufacturing firm of Godwin's, in its several manifestations, dominates the later ceramic history of Herefordshire, with Godwin encaustic tile pavements in churches throughout the county. Aside from Victorian encaustics, there are several significant medieval tile locations, while the unusual Sadler & Green transfer printed tile fire surround survives at Croft Castle, as do Minton block-printed tiles at Eastnor Castle in another fire surround, along with spectacular moulded terracotta panels on a seat in Eastnor churchyard. Suggested reading: Betty Greene, 'The Godwins of Hereford', *TACS Journal*, vol 1 (1982), pp8-16. The *Gazetteer* entry for Herefordshire covers the administrative area of Herefordshire Council.

ABBEY DORE

Dore Abbey was a twelfth century Cistercian foundation, its church (minus the original nave) now being known as **St Mary's Church**. Thirteenth century inlaid and impressed tiles found during the 1902 restoration of the church were relaid in the chancel and around the font; the inlaid tiles have heraldic motifs, while the impressed tiles appear to have designs unique to Dore Abbey (Fig 91).

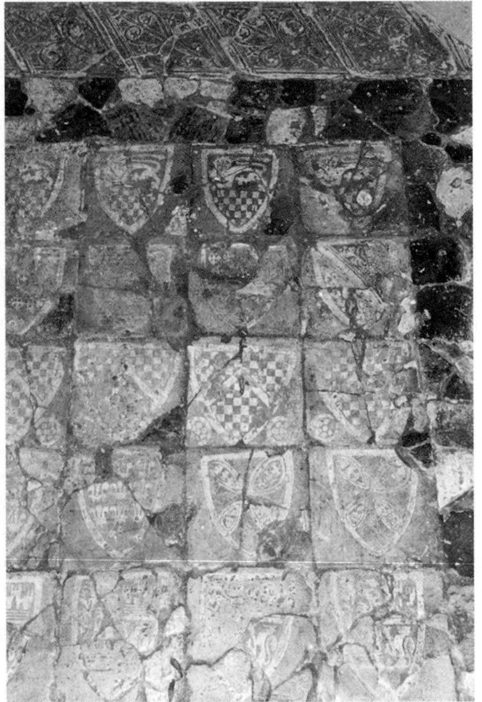

Fig 91.

CROFT

Croft Castle (NT) dates from the late fourteenth or early fifteenth century, but a Gothick facade was added in the mid-eighteenth century after the castle passed to Richard Knight, uncle of Richard Payne Knight of Downton Castle, which lies six miles north through rolling countryside. The fashionable interior decoration introduced by Knight includes one great rarity, a fire surround of Sadler & Green's transfer printed tin-glazed tiles dating from around 1765-75. The tiles used images taken from engraved copper plates and were printed in one colour, resulting in intensely detailed pictures, tiny scenes from everyday life which ranged from romantic ruins and high society to contemporary actors and actresses.[1] The thirty-two tiles of the Croft fireplace include rural scenes and society figures, and is one of very few such fire surrounds to have survived in its original location.

The parish church, **St Michael**, stands below the castle in Croft Park, and has an extensive collection of medieval floor tiles along the centre of the chancel and on the step risers. They date mainly from the latter part of the fifteenth century and may originate from a local tilery, a previously unrecognised late production centre.

DOWNTON ON THE ROCK

Almost completely cut off, down in the valley of the Teme, Richard Payne Knight's magic kingdom of Downton even has its own road signs, as well as the castle put up around 1772-8 to Knight's own designs, a mixture of picturesque exterior, all battlements and towers, and classical interior. Downton Castle and its park formed a Picturesque landscape, wild and rugged in contrast to the tame parklands Knight felt were produced by Capability Brown. The ruins of Downton's medieval church stand in the village, and new **St Giles Church** was built in the park, about half a mile south-west of the castle, to complete a vista, although the castle is now hidden from view by greenery. This perfectly preserved estate church was built for Andrew Rouse Boughton Knight in 1861-2 and designed by the architect Samuel Pountney Smith of Shrewsbury. Pountney Smith built and restored many churches, and also had his own contracting business, whose high standards of craftsmanship may be seen at Downton. The church has a delightful conservatory-like porch with stained glass, and is tiled throughout with the products of Godwin's of Lugwardine. Plain red and black tiling in the nave changes to a decorative encaustic pavement in the chancel, and - unusually - a colourful, mostly geometric tiled dais. A little gem, miles from nowhere.

EASTNOR

Eastnor Castle, dramatically sited at the southern end of the Malvern Hills, was built in 1811-20 by Sir Robert Smirke for the 2nd Baron Somers. Behind the battlements is a lavish interior mostly created for Earl Somers by A. W. N. Pugin and J. G. Crace in 1846 and 1849-50, with some redecoration by G. E. Fox in the 1860s. In particular, the hugely ornate drawing room fireplace (1849), with a painted genealogical tree above it, is lined with Minton tiles bearing Somers heraldic emblems. These strongly coloured tiles were produced by the block-printing process patented by Collins & Reynolds in 1848; Herbert Minton bought an interest in the patent and was able to manufacture this type of tile by the following year, their earliest use appearing to be in the smoking rooms of the Palace of Westminster.[2]

Down on the village green is a **Well** erected by Lady Henry Somerset (Lady Isabella Caroline Somerset, daughter of the last Earl Somers, who married Lord Henry Somerset in 1872); she devoted her life to temperance work, and was president of the British Women's Temperance Association during 1890-1903. The late nineteenth or early twentieth century well has a brick rear wall with two good terracotta reliefs in Italian Renaissance style, now overpainted. In the north-west corner of the nearby churchyard of **St John the Baptist** is a spectacular seat, probably dating from the same period as the well, with five moulded terracotta relief panels, each measuring about 3′ wide by 4′ high. These impressive works show the sower, Ceres, an angel, Christ the King, and another angel holding a Christ child, and are said to have been modelled by hand by Lady Henry Somerset (1851-1921). The church itself, which was mostly rebuilt in 1852 by George Gilbert Scott, has two-colour Minton enamelled encaustic tiles in the sanctuary.

HEREFORD

In 1852 William Godwin (1813-83) began making encaustic tiles at Lugwardine, just north-east of Hereford; production was in full flow by 1853, and in 1863 the firm began tile manufacture on an extensive new site at Withington, a few miles east of Lugwardine. Although the fortunes of the firm declined after Godwin's death in 1883, there was production on the Withington site until 1988; the firm (and its successors) had a complex history, with splits and changes of hands. Almost inevitably local tiles feature strongly in the churches of Hereford and notably in **Hereford Cathedral**, BROAD STREET, for which Godwin of Lugwardine supplied tiles as part of George Gilbert Scott's 1857-63 restoration.[3] The floors throughout were laid with Godwin encaustic and enamelled tiles, the chancel pavement being designed by Scott himself. As well as patterned encaustics there are large areas of plain tiling made up from red, green and black tiles; many of the green tiles have lost their glazing, rendering them buff, which does little for the visual quality of the cathedral. Scott's brilliantly colourful metalwork chancel screen, removed in the late 1960s (and now, after conservation, on display at the V&A Museum) would have enlivened the scene considerably.

Just beyond the north end of Broad Street is the HIGH STREET and **All Saints Church**, where the pick of the town's Godwin pavements may be inspected in an unusual setting, as the medieval church was partly rebuilt during 1992-7 to include a café, south gallery and various related offices (in free-standing 'pods') while still retaining all normal parish functions (Fig 92). The new installations, by the Hereford architectural practice Rod Robinson Associates, are brilliantly designed and allow the Godwin chancel pavement to be seen at its best. The encaustic tiles were made and donated by Godwin & Hewitt in 1892-3, and are laid mainly in groups of four (some of sixteen) divided by bands of plain black tiles; there is also a section where the tile groups form chevron shapes. The overall effect is densely patterned, due to the preponderance of buff in the various designs. A few medieval floor tiles survive, found during the 1890s restoration and now mounted in the north chapel.

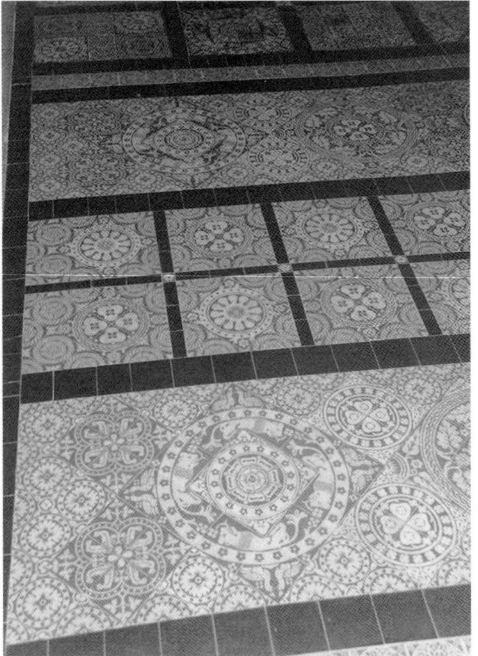

Fig 92.

East of All Saints on ST PETER'S SQUARE is **St Peter's Church** with yet more Godwin tiling, this time donated to the church by William Henry Godwin of Lugwardine in 1885.[4] The design of the nave and chancel pavements was by Thomas Nicholson (1823-95), the Hereford Diocesan Architect, who was in charge of the 1884-5 restoration of the medieval church. The smaller Godwin pavement in the Lady Chapel dates from 1905. Just south of the church is the **Town Hall** in ST OWEN STREET, designed by the architect Henry Cheers, a specialist in municipal buildings, and erected in 1902-4. The exterior is bursting with baroque yellow terracotta; there are two openwork towers and a hefty canopy over the main entrance. Inside is a superb cream faience staircase and a dark brown relief tiled dado, with vine leaf and grape patterns, which runs through the porch and ground floor; the porch also has a good floor mosaic showing Hereford's arms. Continue south into GREEN STREET to find **St James Church**, built in 1868-9 and again designed by Thomas Nicholson, but burnt out on the 23rd December 1901. The original church had tiling by Godwin of Lugwardine, including both a chancel pavement and a reredos, the latter 'peculiarly rich in colour and harmonious in design'.[5] After the fire, the church was rebuilt during 1901-3, with colourful tile pavements in chancel and sanctuary (now partly covered by carpet); William Henry Godwin of Lugwardine supplied the tiles at half-price.

Following the death of William Godwin in 1883, the firm was taken on by his son, William Henry Godwin, and was in competition with the firm set up by Godwin's brother Henry Godwin in 1876, which eventually became Godwin & Hewitt. Both strands of the old Godwin company donated tiles to local churches, William Henry Godwin to St Peter's in 1885 and Godwin & Hewitt to All Saints in 1892-3, probably for a combination of commercial and family reasons. Although Henry Godwin sold out to Hewitt in 1894, it appears William Henry Godwin (a Baptist) still felt moved to generosity in the case of St James in 1901-3, when his business was in decline; he may have felt that charity would be followed by further orders, as was the case with Herbert Minton's donations of tiles to many churches.

HOARWITHY

Coming upon the Italian Romanesque vision of **St Catherine's Church**, set above the Wye valley, is astonishing; the building was a bare brick chapel before being brought to life by J. P. Seddon in its conversion (which took place around 1874 to 1903) for wealthy local vicar William Poole. The Byzantine interior, inspired by Poole's knowledge of European churches, is rich in marble and mosaics, including mosaic pavements. G. E. Fox had overall responsibility for the interior decoration during the 1880s, but the powerful mosaic of the head of Christ in the semi-domed apse was designed by Ada Currey (1852-1913) for Powell's of Whitefriars in 1893. It took Currey 193 hours to produce the cartoon for this mosaic, which cost £350.[6]

LEDBURY

In Ledbury's HIGH STREET, opposite the Market House, is a handsome **war memorial** commemorating the dead of First and Second World Wars. The stone column was built by King & Co of Hereford and dedicated in 1920; at its base a pedestal, with three mosaics of a soldier, sailor and angel, forms the earlier memorial, while the upper and later section has a hand-painted four-tile panel showing a Biggles-like World War Two flying ace, complete with leather flying jacket, helmet and goggles, and two aircraft in the background. This unusual tile panel may date from the late 1980s. Nearby, on the west side of the High Street, is **St Katherine's Hospital**, whose medieval chapel floor has an impressive range of fourteenth and fifteenth century Malvern tiles mainly arranged in circles surrounded by lettering; some tiles show heraldic motifs or Christian symbols. The hospital, most of which was put up in the early to mid-nineteenth century, also has good Victorian encaustic floor tiling.

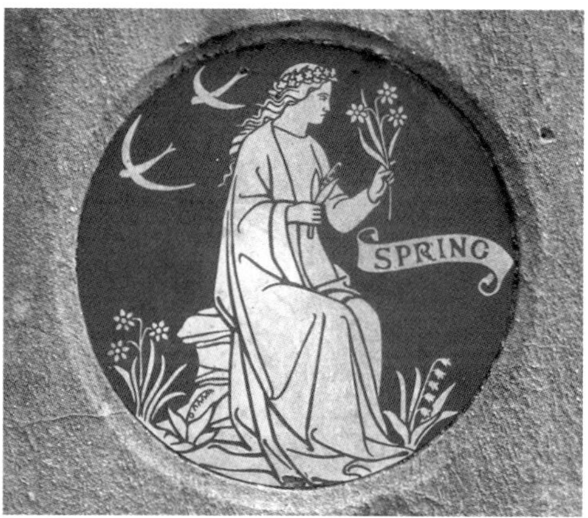

Fig 93.

LUGWARDINE

It is no surprise to find the products of William Godwin's Lugwardine tile works, founded in 1852 on a site just north of the church, used in and around the village. **St Peter's Church** itself was supplied with a Godwin pavement, probably in the course of its 1871-2 restoration, and in the churchyard is a tomb (dated 1872) with a colourful Godwin glazed encaustic tile set into its headstone. William Godwin lived in Porch House, opposite the church, while his son William Henry Godwin, who probably joined the firm during the 1860s, built two houses on the main road (A4103) midway between Lugwardine and the new works at Withington, two miles to the north-east.[7] The interior of **The Ferns**, put up in 1870 using polychrome brick with stone dressings and bands of decorative tiling, was embellished with a wild variety of decorative and letter tiles, the latter in all sorts of colourways: white on black, buff on red, white on blue and its reverse; there are also masses of different four-tile groups jammed together higgledy-piggeldy. **Penkelly** (1875) is rather less ornate, although its gateposts bear Godwin glazed encaustic roundels of the Four Seasons (Fig 93). Finally, a sampler floor in the main chapel of **Lugwardine Chapel**, LUMBER ROAD contains around 5,000 Godwin tiles in a huge variety of different designs.

WIGMORE

In the sanctuary of **St James Church** is an important encaustic tile pavement by Chamberlain & Co of Worcester, including several of the designs featured in the firm's first catalogue, which was issued in 1844, along with four-tile panels of the evangelists and another panel dated 1845.

WITHINGTON

Henry Godwin (1828-1910) worked at Maw's in Worcester before joining his brother William Godwin in their tilemaking venture at Lugwardine in the early 1850s. The firm opened a factory at Withington in 1863, and Henry built his villa **'Mayfield'** (no public access) adjoining the site in 1863 or shortly afterwards. The house retains copious amounts of Godwin tiling, including panels on the facade, a complex pavement running throughout most of the ground floor and friezes with many different tile designs. The house seems to have acted as a showroom for the firm's wares.

YAZOR

Part of the exotic and colourful decorative scheme of **St Mary the Virgin Church** (1843-55) is a richly patterned tile pavement in the chancel. The church, which is now in the care of the Churches Conservation Trust, was built for the Price family of the nearby Foxley estate, a few years after the death of Sir Uvedale Price (1747-1829), theorist of the Picturesque.

Herefordshire Roundup

St Lawrence Church, **Canon Pyon** has a Godwin enaustic pavement including an uncommon design in the sanctuary, a four-tile group centred on four hearts within a circlular border. A thirteenth century tile depicting a man digging, a 'labour of the month', is one of several medieval tiles relaid on the north wall of St James Church, **Colwall**. The walls of the dairy (c1783) at Berrington Hall (NT), a mile east of **Eye**, are faced with plain tin-glazed tiles bordered by Liverpool printed tiles bearing a Greek key pattern. Restoration of St Mary's Church, **Fownhope** in 1881 involved the laying of an extensive Godwin encaustic pavement including many decorative four-tile groups, mostly in common designs; there is also a memorial tile dated 1881. At Hergest

England

Croft Gardens, **Kington** there is a De Morgan tiled fire surround in the old dining room (now tea rooms) of the house, which was built from 1895 onward. Unusual terracotta tiles form the chancel pavement of St James Church, **Kinnersley**, restored in 1868; the rich chancel decoration was designed by G. F. Bodley and executed by the incumbent. The Priory Church of St Peter and St Paul, **Leominster** has a small but important collection of medieval floor tiles in a recess at its west end, in the south nave; some tiles bear a lion motif (a pun on the town's name) while other designs are unique to this site. A Powell's opus sectile reredos of the Virgin and child, with flanking panels of glass tiles, was installed in 1912 at St John the Baptist Church, **Whitbourne**.

References

1. Hans van Lemmen, *Delftware Tiles* (Laurence King, London, 1997).
2. Paul Atterbury and Clive Wainwright, *Pugin: A Gothic Passion* (Yale University Press, New Haven and London, 1994).
3. *The Builder*, vol 21, 11th July 1863.
4. Margaret A. V. Gill, 'A Munificent Benefaction: Godwin tiles in St Peter's Church, Hereford', *TACS Journal*, 9 (2003), pp24-34.
5. Margaret A. V. Gill, 'Godwin tiles in St James' Church, Hereford', *Glazed Expressions*, (2001) 43, pp5-7.
6. Dennis Hadley, 'Ada Currey (1852-1913): a forgotten artist', *The Journal of Stained Glass*, 24 (2000), pp29-37.
7. Betty Greene, 'The Godwins of Hereford', *TACS Journal*, 1 (1982), pp8-16.

Hertfordshire

The best of the county's *in situ* medieval tile locations is the brightly coloured circular mosaic at Meesden Church, but the churches of the Victorian era, aside from Ayot St Peter with its unique Martin Brothers stoneware chancel arch, are rather a ceramic disappointment. Much more intriguing are the postwar New Town tile murals, or at least what remains of them, for one large-scale Carter's mural in Hemel Hempstead has already disappeared. However, another remains there, on a car park, along with two murals in Stevenage's Town Square, one being part of its listed Clock Tower. Hertfordshire is also significant in that it retains several locations where the pattern-making tiles of Peggy Angus may still be seen. Suggested reading: Katie Arber, *Patterns for Post-War Britain: the tile designs of Peggy Angus*, Middlesex University Press, 2002. The *Gazetteer* entry for Hertfordshire covers the administrative area of Hertfordshire County Council.

AYOT ST PETER

For a taste of the exotic and experimental in the context of the Victorian church, visit **St Peter's Church**, Ayot St Peter, in the middle of nowhere west of Welwyn. The church, which was designed by J. P. Seddon and built during 1874-5, has a red brick exterior with buff and black brick banding, and a clock with a blue mosaic face; inside the church, all is colour. As well as green and brown tiles in the chancel, there is a complete Arts and Crafts furnishing scheme which dates from around 1880 and includes a circular font with colourful mosaics of landscape and sea on the bowl, and painted panels on the chancel roof. But the outstanding feature is the unique stoneware chancel arch made by the Martin Brothers at Pomona House, Fulham, to Seddon's design, which was a contemporary adaptation of medieval work with birds, flowers and foliage.[1] Robert Wallace Martin, the eldest of the brothers, had already established a working relationship with J. P. Seddon before their pottery moved to Pomona House, and the Martins produced a variety of smaller architectural elements, such as fireplace surrounds, for Seddon and other architects. The chancel arch, however, was far and away the biggest item of architectural ware the brothers ever produced. It was never to be repeated, by the Martin Brothers or any other makers, and it would be interesting to know if there were problems with its manufacture or construction, or if the cost of such a large ceramic piece proved prohibitive.

GREAT AMWELL

Sir Hugh Myddelton (1560?-1631), banker and Member of Parliament, brought fresh water to London by building the New River, a thirty-eight mile long canal which was fed by springs in and around Great Amwell. The canal was ten feet wide and four feet deep, and was built in 1609-13. When it was decided to commemorate Myddelton's feat in 1800, Robert Mylne, architect to the New River Company, designed a water garden (off AMWELL LANE) at the source of the springs, comprising several grassy islands amidst streams. On the main island is an urn to Myddelton, and on another island a pedestal and globe, all in Coade stone.[2] While working on the water garden Mylne erected his family's mausoleum in the churchyard of **St John the Baptist** above. The white brick structure is topped by a Coade stone urn and also has a Coade roundel of a mourning woman.

HARPENDEN

Ernest Heasman (1874-1927) was a stained glass artist who also designed and painted tiles at his studio in Harpenden. The tiles were used in domestic and church settings, for instance at the **Methodist Chapel**, LOWER LUTON ROAD, Batford (on the northern edge of Harpenden) where there is an eight-tile First World War memorial plaque including two finely drawn angels (Fig 94).

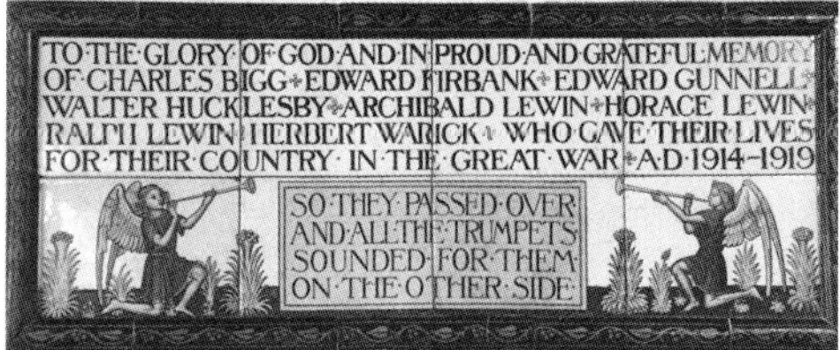

Fig 94.

HEMEL HEMPSTEAD

Hemel Hempstead was designated a New Town in 1947 and building began, south of the old town centre, in the early 1950s. The master plan was devised by Geoffrey Jellicoe, whose water gardens adjoin the new town centre; the mid-fifties shopping area, Marlowes, bounded by offices and car parks, lies south of the main civic buildings. Hemel Hempstead stood out from the other six post-war London satellite towns as several of its public buildings sported large-scale ceramic murals in striking geometric designs, for instance the bowling alley (built 1962-3, demolished) just east of the shopping centre with its Carter's tiling. Although other new towns commissioned the occasional ceramic mural, as at Basildon bus station (1958), the use of tiling was most widespread at Hemel Hempstead. Unfortunately only one such installation survives, the *Tile Mosaic Map* (1960) by Rowland Emett (1906-90). This can be found on the south side of the **Hillfield Road NCP Car Park** which fronts on to Marlowes, opposite the market. Emett was best-known for his eccentric mechanical sculptures, but began his career as a cartoonist and developed a drawing style depicting a quaint, rather old fashioned world. The Hemel Hempstead images, hand-painted by Phyllis Butler at Carter's on white tile panels against a background of grey mosaic, show historic and modern local attractions connected by roads, although assorted methods of transport - from trams to space ships - also play a part. It is a delightful and unexpected work, which only encourages the observer to wonder about the vanished murals.[3]

There is another surprising and important survivor in Hemel Hempstead, however, at **South Hill Primary School**, HEATH LANE, just west of the central area. Here the entrance hall still displays wall tiling designed by Peggy Angus around 1950, its dense pattern incorporating the Hertfordshire stag, oak leaves and acorns. The tiles were commissioned by Hertfordshire County Council and the school's architects, Harrison & Steel, and made by Carter's, with whom Angus worked from about 1949. Angus's distinctive screen-printed pattern-making tiles were popular with school architects throughout the 1950s.[4]

HERTFORD

Right in the centre of Hertford is **St Andrew's Church**, ST ANDREW STREET, restored in 1869-70. There is an encaustic tile pavement in the chancel and an impressively large opus sectile and mosaic reredos designed by E. Penwarden for Powell's of Whitefriars and installed in 1914. Just east in PARLIAMENT SQUARE is the former **Green Dragon Hotel** (1903), converted to offices in 1975 but still displaying fine terracotta lettering inviting prospective customers to enjoy its 'good stabling & motor pit' as well as the products of local brewers McMullen's.

HIGH WYCH

Opinions vary about **St James Church** (Pevsner called it 'High Victorian design at its most revolting' and 'perversely ugly'), but it certainly has some items of ceramic interest. It was designed by the architect George Edward Pritchett (1824-1912) of Bishop's Stortford and built during 1860-1, most of the funds being provided by the Reverend H. F. Johnson. The exterior is of knapped flints with red brick and stone dressings, but brick is the dominant material inside, with bands of red brick set into walls of buff brick, and brick vaulting in the chancel, which has a colourful encaustic tile pavement. There are also glazed ceramic plaques, bearing alpha and omega symbols, set into the exterior of the west doorway.

MEESDEN

The important tile pavement in the sanctuary of **St Mary's Church** dates from around 1315 and is a wheel-plan mosaic, measuring about nine feet by seven feet, although with some impressed and inlaid tiles. The tiles radiate from the round central tile like spokes on a wheel, each segment being made up from six different tile shapes in alternating colours. Those colours - bright yellow and deep green - its circular lay-out and good condition make this a most memorable pavement, and, now, a great rarity.[5]

OLD HALL GREEN

A mile south-west of Standon village is Old Hall Green and **St Edmund's College**, a Roman Catholic foundation whose extensive school buildings mostly date from the late 1790s. The chapel is an addition of 1845-53 by A. W. N. Pugin, with some later alterations including floor tiles of 1897 in the choir and ante-chapel; Pugin's decorative scheme included a pavement of red, blue and yellow tiles.[6]

ST ALBANS

Sir Edmund Beckett (1816-1905), later Lord Grimthorpe, was a member of the notable Leeds banking family; he was a lawyer (and something of a bully) who enjoyed theological discussion and took a great interest in ecclesiastical architecture. His opinion of architects was low. He lectured members of the architectural profession on their incompetence and went so far as to design several churches in Yorkshire himself.[7] Without his generosity, however, the restoration of **St Albans Cathedral**, almost ruinous in the early nineteenth century, could not have been completed. Restoration had been planned from the 1850s, but nothing was done until the 1870s when Sir George Gilbert Scott began work; his death in 1878, combined with lack of funds, brought the process to a halt. At that point Lord Grimthorpe took a hand and is said to have spent £130,000 on the Cathedral, the most obvious of his often controversial interventions being the almost complete rebuilding of the west front. The Cathedral's encaustic tile pavements were made for Lord Grimthorpe by Minton & Co around 1885. Many of the new tiles were copies of medieval designs found during the building work; a few of the medieval tiles were relaid in the north transept.

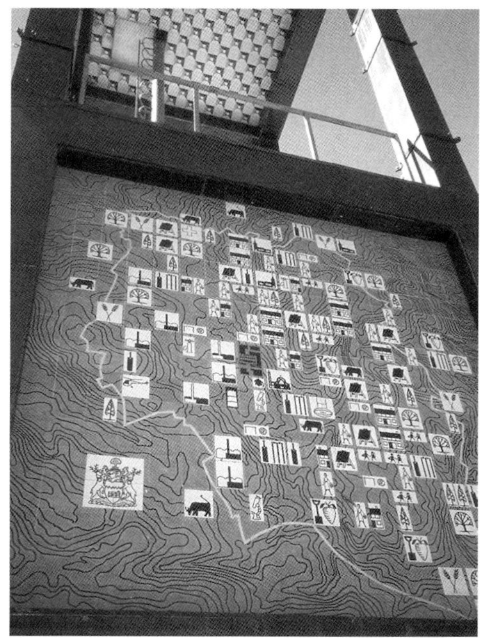

Fig 95.

STEVENAGE

Stevenage was the first New Town to be designated as such, in 1946, and housebuilding began in 1949; its new town centre (1957-9) included the first pedestrian-only shopping area in England. An openwork concrete **Clock Tower** designed by Leonard Vincent, one of the planners of the town centre, forms the focal point of the TOWN SQUARE. Its frame, which rises from a rectangular pool lined with tiles in primary colours, is clad in black granite and encloses two cubes; the upper cube bears clock faces and a bell compartment, which is illuminated at night (Fig 95). The lower cube carries inscriptions and reliefs, one with a backing of Carter's cream textured tiles, and on its east face a Carter's painted tile panel, about five feet square; this shows a contour map of the area (in black lines on grey ground) on which information logos are dotted about. These are mostly black on white but a few, for instance the bus station, are in red. There are also Carter's pattern-making tiles in black, grey, yellow and white, in three different designs, on the undersides of both cubes and the roof of the tower.[8] The Town Square is small, with a good sense of enclosure; the clock tower and its recently installed fountain make a strong and unusual centrepiece.

Unlike Hemel Hempstead, where the integrity of the centre has been lost, modern developments in Stevenage have generally been on the fringes of the original new town centre. It retains not only its fifties feel (although still functioning as a successful shopping centre) but much of its late fifties decorative work, including a large pictorial tile mural on the **Primark** store on the south side of the Town Square, overlooking the pool (Fig 96). The shop was built for the Letchworth, Hitchin & District Co-op in 1958-9 and the mural, which is about 15' high by 10' wide, was designed by G. Bajo of the CWS Architects' Department. Its jolly, slightly idealised old-fashioned imagery - is there some rustic Spanish influence here? - was intended to depict 'the spirit and activities of the Co-operative Movement as a whole and in relation to Stevenage', and includes elements representing 'the architectural atmosphere of the town' and transport, industry, commerce, science, technology and agriculture.[9] The tiles may also have been made by Carter's, or could have originated abroad.

The bright colours of the Primark mural are a contrast to another panel just north in QUEENSWAY; here an area of similar size is filled with black textured and plain tiles making a striking abstract pattern. There are other areas of

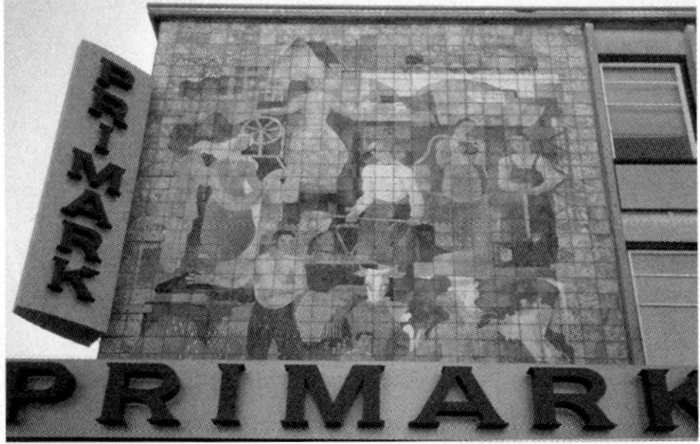

Fig 96.

similar tiling around Queensway. This is one of the few remaining shopping centres where it is possible to see how tiles were used externally in the late 1950s; they were almost ubiquitous, but due to the ever-changing nature of shopping, most examples have disappeared.

Just east of the old town centre, which lies a mile to the north of the new town centre, is **Barclay School**, WALKERN ROAD, built by Yorke, Rosenberg & Mardall (YRM) in 1950-1; it was the first significant secondary school to be built after the war, and its broad foyer still retains wall tiling by Peggy Angus. The architect F. R. S. Yorke commissioned Angus to design her first tiles in 1948, and thereafter YRM used Angus's tiles in their school projects until about 1958.[10]

TRING

The **Church of St Peter and St Paul** stands just north of the High Street in CHURCH YARD. The restoration of 1861-2 included the installation of encaustic tiles by Maw & Co in the nave, while those in the chancel were made by Maw's from patterns of old tiles dug up during excavations. The chancel pavement comprises mainly nine-tile groups of buff and brown tiles divided from each other by diagonal black-tiled bands.[11]

WARE

South-east of Ware, across the River Ash, is the site of Easneye Park (now a school) designed by Alfred Waterhouse and built in 1866. The mansion, in red brick and much red terracotta, is significant because it was the first time Waterhouse had specified a substantial amount of terracotta in a design. The estate outbuildings, which included **Easneye Dairy**, a quarter-mile north-east of the house on Hollycross Road, were probably designed by a local architect working in the Waterhouse style.[12] The octagonal Dairy, which is attached to the farmhouse, was built around 1868. Its interior tiling is exceptionally decorative, with a flowery frieze, blue tiles impressed with a geometric pattern and an ornate encaustic tile floor.

On the north-east edge of Ware is Fanhams Hall, now an hotel, which has six bathrooms lined with reused seventeenth and eighteenth century delft tiles; these were probably installed during alterations to the house carried out during 1898-1901.

WATERFORD

St Michael's Church lies a mile or so north of Hertford, on the main Stevenage road, at the entrance to the grounds of Goldings, a mansion built in 1871-7 for the banker Robert Abel Smith. The little church (1871-2), designed by gentleman architect Henry Woodyer, was also built for Smith, who financed a lavish decorative scheme including fourteen stained glass windows by William Morris and Philip Webb, amongst others.[13] The brilliant mosaic angels which hover around the chancel were made by Powell's of Whitefriars in 1909-12; their designer may have been Gerald Hutchinson, who is known to have visited the church but was on Powell's salaried staff, rather than working as a designer, by that time. The stone reredos, also by Powell's, includes six angelic figures in opus sectile.[14] The tile pavements, mostly geometrics, are by Minton.

WATFORD

Holy Rood R. C. Church, MARKET STREET, was one of only four churches to be built by John Francis Bentley (1839-1902), the architect of Westminster Cathedral. He was offered the commission in 1889 by S. Taprell Holland, a member of the building firm to which Bentley had been apprenticed, and the church was complete by 1899.[15] Holland funded the church, Bentley's masterpiece, and its sumptuous furnishings; the chancel is ablaze with colour. The sanctuary has opus sectile panels designed by George Daniels, and a partly encaustic tiled floor incorporating tiles bearing one of Bentley's favourite motifs, a lion with its tongue protruding. In addition, there are lettered tiles on the risers to the altar.

Hertfordshire Roundup

The Powell's of Whitefriars opus sectile reredos (1874) at St Peter's Church, **Berkhamsted**, was designed by Harry Burrow. **Flaunden** parish church, St Mary Magdalene, was built in 1838 by George Gilbert Scott; it was his first church, and has medieval tiles from the old parish church (a mile or so to the south) on the porch floor. An unusual, mostly green-tiled, pavement occupies the chancel of St Peter's Church, **Lilley** (1870-1). At St Mary's Church, **Puttenham** there is a Godwin encaustic pavement (comprising four-and-a-half inch tiles) of 1887 in the chancel, as well as a few fifteenth century tiles. St Bartholomew's Church, Hemp Lane, on the northern edge of **Wigginton**, was restored in 1881; it has an encaustic tile pavement and a reredos which includes two mosaic and opus sectile panels of angels (*The Annunciation*) designed by Ada Currey for Powell's in 1899.[16]

In addition, the following churches have encaustic or geometric tile pavements which were installed during late Victorian restoration or rebuilding: St John the Baptist, **Aldbury** (also medieval tiles); St Mary's, **Aspenden**; St Margaret of Antioch, **Barley** (also wall tiling); St Mary's, **Bayford**; St Andrew's, **Buckland**; St James, **Bushey**; St John the Baptist, **Cottered**; St Botolph, **Eastwick**; St Mary, **Graveley**; St Nicholas, **Great Hormead** (and tiled east wall); St Peter & St Paul, **Little Gaddesden** (by Maw's and Minton Hollins); St Cecilia, **Little Hadham** (also medieval tiles); St Mary's, **Standon** (also reredos); St Mary the Virgin, **Walkern**; and Holy Trinity, **Weston**.

References

1. *The Builder*, vol 33, 27th November 1875, p1068.
2. Alison Kelly, *Mrs Coade's Stone* (Self Publishing Association, Upton-upon-Severn, 1990).
3. Carter Archive, Poole Museum Service; 3A-28 and 3D-6. See Kenneth Clark, The Tile, Crowood Press, Marlborough, 2002, p19 for an early 1960s sketch by Ivor Kamlish showing a mural designed for Hemel Hempstead town centre.
4. Katie Arber, 'Peggy Angus, designer of modern tiles for a modern Britain', *Decorative Arts Society Journal*, 26 (2002), pp120-134.
5. Jane A. Wight, *Mediaeval Floor Tiles* (John Baker, London, 1975).
6. David J. S. Kay, *The Buildings of St Edmund's College* (St Edmund's College, 2000), p39.
7. Derek Linstrum, *West Yorkshire: Architects and Architecture* (Lund Humphries, London, 1978), pp36-7.
8. Carter Archive, Poole Museum Service, 3C-73.
9. Kathryn A. Morrison, *English Shops and Shopping: An Architectural History* (Yale University Press, New Haven and London, 2003), p156.
10. Arber, 'Peggy Angus' (2002).
11. *The Builder*, vol 21, 17th January 1863.
12. Colin Cunningham and Prudence Waterhouse, *Alfred Waterhouse, 1830-1905: Biography of a Practice* (Clarendon Press, Oxford, 1992), pp100, 160.
13. John Elliott and John Pritchard, eds. *Henry Woodyer: Gentleman Architect* (Department of Continuing Education, University of Reading, Reading, 2002).
14. Dennis W. Hadley, *James Powell & Sons: A listing of opus sectile, 1847-1973*, (2001).
15. Peter Howell, 'John Francis Bentley: Homage for his Centenary', *The Victorian*, (2002) 9, pp12-15.
16. Dennis Hadley, 'Ada Currey (1852-1913): a forgotten artist', *The Journal of Stained Glass*, 24 (2000), pp29-37.

Kent

Many East Kent churches still retain the distinctive tiles made between around 1275 and 1350 on Tyler Hill, just north of Canterbury; its four tile kilns produced tiles with purplish-brown and cream glazes. The 'blue loo' at Chatham Historic Dockyard is one of the few locations where eighteenth century English delftware tiles have been preserved in situ, but Kent's two most dramatic ceramic locations - The Grange, Ramsgate and The Friars, Aylesford - both centre on the creation of Catholic communities. The Grange was the home of A. W. N. Pugin, who also designed its associated church, St Augustine, according to his 'True Principles', while the 1950s-70s ceramic installations at The Friars were the masterwork of the Polish-born artist Adam Kossowski. More generally, Kent has a series of high quality turn-of-the-century ceramic pub facades at its ports and seaside towns. Suggested reading: Libby Horner and Gill Hunter, *A Flint Seaside Church* (Pugin Society, Ramsgate, 2000); James H. Sephton, *The Friars, Aylesford* (Sephton, Aylesford, 1999); *Adam Kossowski: Murals and Paintings* (Armelle Press, London, 1990); and TACS Tour Notes *North Kent* (2002). The *Gazetteer* entry for Kent covers the administrative areas of Kent County Council and Medway Council.

AYLESFORD

Aylesford Priory, normally known as **The Friars**, stands on the north bank of the Medway just west of Aylesford. Founded in 1242, it was one of the first two Carmelite houses in England, both of which were established in that year. Following the Dissolution the church was pulled down and part of the cloisters eventually became a mansion. In 1949 The Friars was put up for sale and the Carmelites were able to buy the house and return to their former home. The first Prior, Fr Malachy Lynch, began restoration of the buildings and in time The Friars became a pilgrimage centre. The architect Adrian Gilbert Scott, younger brother of Giles Gilbert Scott, was brought in to design the new church, comprising the Main Shrine and four radiating chapels, which was built in 1958-65 by a combination of Italian masons, local craftsmen and volunteers. Activities at The Friars, including furniture and pottery manufacture, printing and publishing (the *Aylesford Review*, a literary magazine, was published from 1955 to 1969) expressed the Catholic arts and crafts ideal. The pottery was set up in 1955 and run by David Leach, who lived at Aylesford for five years, with Br Michael as his assistant.[1]

The unique and moving ceramics which decorate the shrine and chapels are by the artist Adam Kossowski, who was born in Poland in 1905 (Fig 97). He studied architecture in Warsaw and painting in Cracow before working at Warsaw Academy of Fine Arts from 1929, where he became tutor in mural techniques. He was arrested by Soviet troops in 1939 and interned in labour camps until his release in 1942, eventually arriving in London in 1943. He initially worked for the Polish Ministry of Information, then with three other artists established a Decorative Arts Studio at Old Brompton Road in 1946. They exhibited at Heal's in 1948, and the following year he showed ceramic figures in the Catholic Art Exhibition at the RIBA. In 1950 the sculptor Philip Lindsay-Clark, who had previously invited Kossowski to join the Guild of the Catholic Artists, introduced Adam Kossowski to Fr Malachy Lynch, who commissioned the artist to produce seven tempera paintings showing the history of the Aylesford Carmelites, for the Chapter Room; this was the start of an association which was to last until 1971.[2]

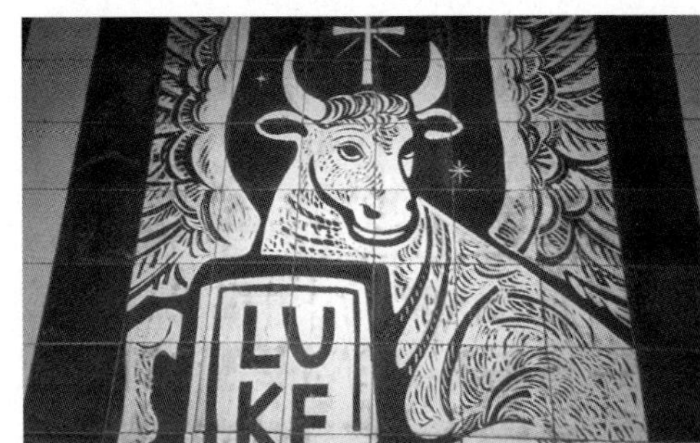

Fig 97.

While work on the tempera paintings was still under way, Fr Malachy Lynch asked Kossowski to make a Rosary Way - a series of shrines illustrating the fifteen mysteries of the Rosary - in ceramics. Kossowski was hesitant as his only previous experience with the medium had been on a much smaller scale, but he produced the fifteen glazed high reliefs during 1950-1. Framed in oak and set on stone pedestals, these colourful images mark the stages along the Rosary Way, a pathway to the east of the Main Shrine; they are also a reminder of traditional Polish roadside shrines. In 1951 the relic of St Simon Stock, the English Carmelite, was brought back to Aylesford, and Kossowski began his next project, the massive Scapular Vision Shrine, which stands at the north-east corner of the Rosary Way and represents the Virgin Mary appearing to St Simon Stock. It was the largest ceramic composition he had undertaken, and was fired in the old kiln at the Fulham Pottery; a limited range of majolica glazes was used on unfired white clay. The shrine also included the first tiles (sculpted and irregular) Kossowski had ever produced.[3]

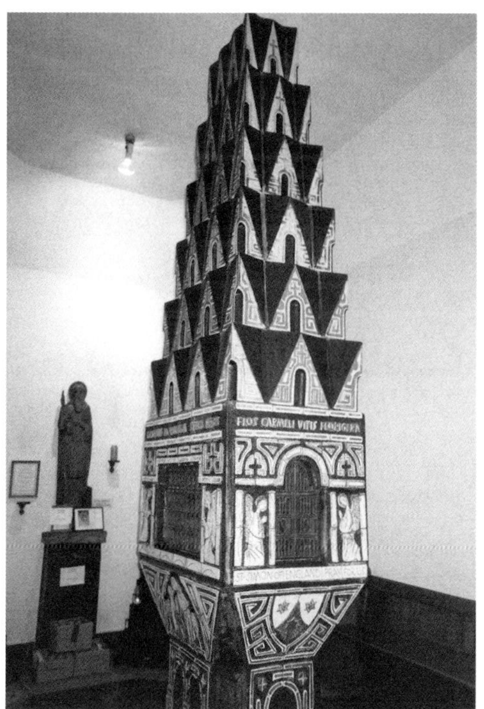

Fig 98.

Between 1951 and the completion of construction of the Main Shrine, Kossowski worked at Aylesford only occasionally, but from the early 1960s until 1971 much of his time was devoted to The Friars (Fig 98). Eventually he produced more than one hundred individual works for Aylesford, carried out in mainly in ceramics but also in tempera, oil, mosaic, wrought iron and stained glass (Fig 99).[4] In the Main Shrine, which overlooks the piazza, a statue of the Glorious Virgin of the Assumption (by Michael Clark, son of Philip Lindsay-Clark, 1960) stands in a tall, arched niche lined with blue ceramic tiles designed by Kossowski and fired in The Friars pottery with the help of the Brothers and pottery workers. The angels on the side walls, including the Angel of Aylesford holding the shrine while standing above the village, were created using black slip and amber-orange translucent glaze; their strongly figurative composition and bold colour is characteristic of Kossowski's work. The altar ceramics and candlesticks were also by Kossowski.

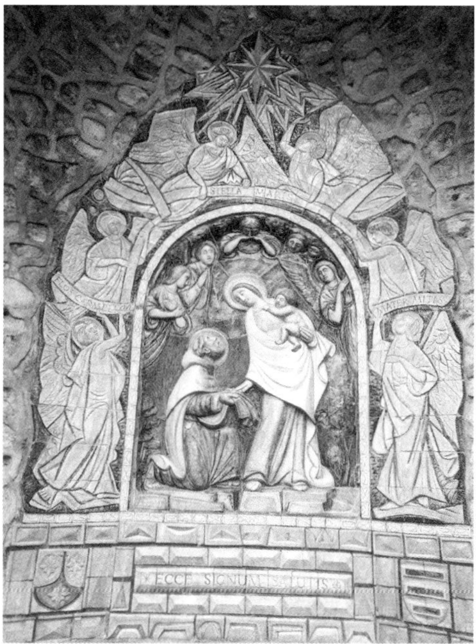
Fig 99.

The decoration of St Anne's Chapel, just to the right of the Main Shrine, was completed during 1961-3. Green sgraffito murals with ceramic reliefs including high-flying angels are complemented by a floor of 2,000 green, grey and black glazed tiles, fired at The Friars. A corridor leads north from the Main Shrine towards the Relic Chapel, which is dominated by one of Kossowski's favourite Aylesford works, the Reliquary of St Simon Stock (1963-4), an astonishing black and white ceramic tower twelve feet in height. The body of the tower is concrete, its tiled exterior representing the hermits' cells of Mount Carmel. There is also a ceramic relief altar frontal in red glaze on black, the fourteen Stations of the Cross (1963-6) and an additional 'fifteenth station', the Empty Tomb (1966). Leading east from the Relic Chapel is the Chapel of the Carmelite Saints, decorated during 1964-5, while to the west is the Chapel of the English Martyrs (1965-7), the most atmospheric of these magical spaces, its intensity deriving from ceramic reliefs in red glaze on dark blue ground along with highly coloured glass.

Kossowski's final contribution to The Friars was in St Joseph's Chapel, west of the Main Shrine, where the decoration was carried out in 1966-71. Figurative panels march across the walls whilst the focus is the altar, backed by a ceramic relief representing the universal church and standing on a superb tile pavement showing the four symbols of the evangelists, in ceramic sgraffito on green tiles. Here the eagle and the winged ox, lion and man are not just mere symbols but powerful images in their own right, outstanding in the totality of Kossowski's work at The Friars, which is one of the most compelling twentieth-century ceramic visions in Britain. Kossowski's work as a ceramicist ceased when he had to abandon his massive studio in 1971; he died in 1986 and was interred at Aylesford.

CHATHAM

Towards the west end of the HIGH STREET is the site of the former **Theatre Royal**, designed by the Rochester architect George Edward Bond and built in 1897-9. Its interior had tiling as good as any theatre in Britain, with a series of hand-painted pictorial panels of Shakespearean characters and the Greek Muses set into cream dado tiling along the corridors and stairs leading to the stalls and royal circle (Fig 100). The pictorial panels were interspersed with panels bearing a floral motif, which appear in a catalogue produced by George Wooliscroft and Sons, and there was other, less decorative tilework throughout the building, including chequerwork wall tiles in the balcony bar. One pictorial panel was signed 'W. Lambert 1899', and as Lambert is known to have painted two large tile panels in 1896 on Wooliscroft tiles, it is very probable that the Theatre Royal's pictorial panels were also manufactured by George Wooliscroft and Sons. Tiles from Pilkington's and the Marsden Tile Co have also been identified from the theatre, so the architect and builders appear to have used the products of a wide range of manufacturers.

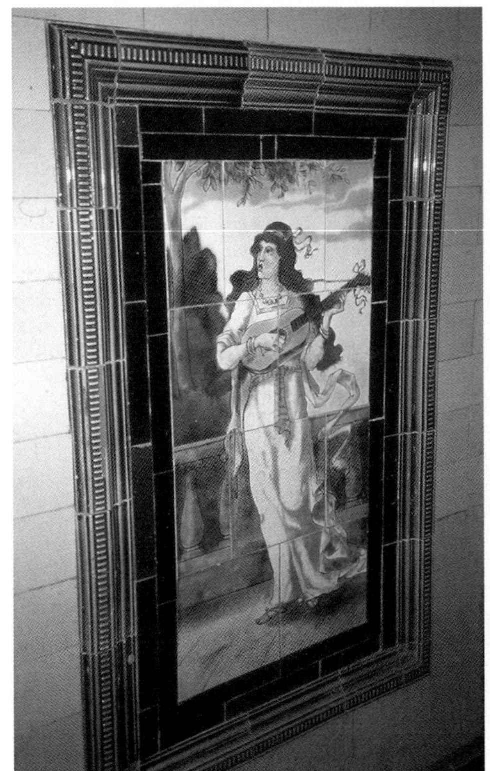

Fig 100.

The theatre closed in 1955 and was sold in 1956. Under constant threat of demolition, the fabric deteriorated and the proscenium opening was bricked up. The Theatre Royal Chatham Trust Ltd was formed in 1992 to work towards reopening the building as a live theatre, and initially made good progress. A large area of tilework survived the years of neglect, including several pictorial panels, although three were removed and are on display at the Guildhall Museum, Rochester. However, in 2003 the Trust had to sell the building and by mid 2004 the interior had deteriorated considerably; at the time of writing it seems likely that the structure will be demolished.

At the east end of the High Street is the former **Fountain Inn**, now the bookmakers William Hill; it was probably built in the 1890s and ceased to be a pub around 1980 (Fig 101). Inside its lofty porch is full-height wall tiling, with panels of colourful relief tiles and a very delicately painted blue and white fountain, flanked by a pair of urns, on white ground; it could well have been made by Mintons China Works. Similar tiling exists in the former entrance on the other side of the building, although this is now concealed behind boarding. The porch tiles are all that remain of a fine ceramic interior, which included a mosaic floor and two tiled bars. In RICHARD STREET, which runs slightly south of and parallel to the High Street, is the **Shipwright's Arms**. This small pub has a good, probably early Edwardian, faience facade in mostly green and gold advertising the 'Burton Ales' and 'London Porter and Stout' of brewers Truman Hanbury Buxton & Co.

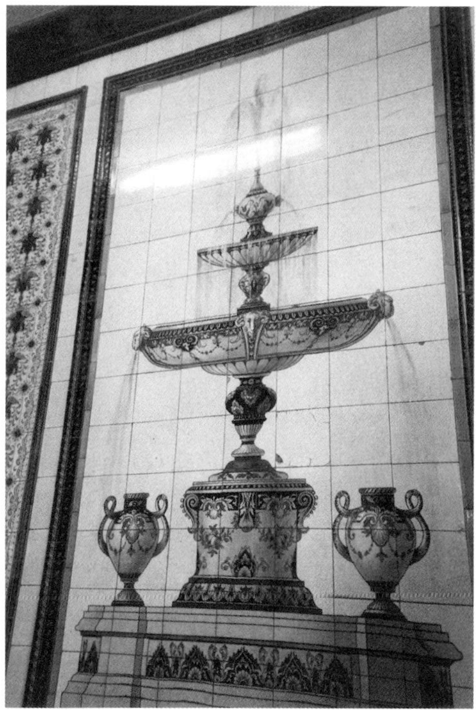

Fig 101.

From the centre of Chatham, DOCK ROAD runs north to the Dockyard, whose **Main Gate** (1720) bears an impressively large and colourful relief of the Royal Arms. This well-preserved example of a Coade stone Royal Arms dates from 1812 and is signed Coade & Sealy. Beyond is Chatham Historic Dockyard and one of the few locations where eighteenth century English delftware tiles have been preserved in situ: the 'blue loo' in the **Commissioner's House**. This little room provides an intensely blue experience as the walls are completely tiled, floor to ceiling, with delftware tiles; the loo itself is also blue on white. The tiles were made in London around 1760-90 and show a variety of landscape scenes. The room was conserved by Heritage Tile Conservation Ltd in 1990, who removed a complete wall of tiles which was in danger of falling off due to a combination of dry rot and rising damp. The tiles were then restored before being refixed after remedial work to the wall.

DEAL

In and around RANELAGH ROAD, towards the south end of Deal, is a unique set of extravagantly tiled tall terrace houses in an area which used to be naval docks, but was infilled and the houses built from the 1880s onward. They display all manner of tiles, in lancet-shaped panels below the eaves, horizontal panels between ground and first floor windows and vertical installations beside the sash windows. There are large plaques which almost seem to take the place of windows, as well as tiles on gateposts and in encaustic pavements. There are several examples from the Minton Hollins hand-coloured transfer printed *Birds* series, and art nouveau style lettered tiles reading 'Southampton Terrace', and the variety of tiles - from heavily relief-moulded fruit to transfer printed to majolica to encaustic, mostly by Maw's and Minton Hollins - is enormous. These houses were built at a time of prosperity, while Deal was still the naval equivalent of a garrison town, but nowhere else in the town is there showy external tiling, clearly a part of the original architectural conception, on this scale.

DOVER

In the centre of Dover is the MARKET SQUARE and an excellent turn-of-the-century public house, the **Sir John Falstaff**. Its mainly buff and brown faience facade, striped in the lower part, is topped by heavily moulded consoles bearing grotesques. There is also lavish decorative tiling inside the pub. North to CASTLE STREET, which is connected to the waterfront by means of a **pedestrian underpass** beneath the dual carriageway. This unpromising location was transformed in 1993 by Tessera, whose expansive tile mural covers the entire wall area. The theme is shipping through the ages, the colours a maritime red, white and blue, and the effect appropriate.

The church of **St Mary in the Castle** stands above and to the north-east of the town on Castle

Hill, just south of Dover Castle. The late Saxon church was restored by George Gilbert Scott in 1860-2, then in 1888-9 William Butterfield carried out the chancel decoration, with its flowing scrolls of mosaic on the upper part of the walls and elaborate tilework elsewhere. The tiling includes Butterfield's typical bright yellow zigzag motif.

FOLKESTONE

In TONTINE STREET, right in the centre of Folkestone, is the splendid **Brewery Tap**, its late Victorian faience and tile facade proclaiming the merits of Mackeson's Hythe Ales. The pub was originally the brewery tap of Langton's Brewery, also situated in Tontine Street, but this firm was taken over by Mackeson's of Hythe in 1886; the pub doubtless acquired its new facade shortly after this date. To the west of the town centre, THE LEAS runs along the cliffs past **Leas Cliff Hall**, a neo-classical theatre designed by J. L. Seaton Dahl in 1913 and built in 1925-7 from reinforced concrete partly clad in faience. Little can be seen at clifftop level but the entrance (added in 1980); however, to the rear, and with superb sea views, a series of broad, glazed terraces runs down the cliffside.

GRAVESEND

Gravesend was the first port of note downriver from London, and was a popular destination for day-trippers from the capital. Not surprisingly the town is well endowed with pubs, several of which have tile and faience facades; the best remaining example is the **Trocadero** in WINDMILL STREET, in the town centre. Here a deep central bow window is flanked by wall tiling at each side entrance bearing the pub's name and signed Millington & Co, 139 Shaftesbury Avenue, London. Millington's was a firm of shopfitters who also produced stained glass and probably decorated the Trocadero tiles themselves. The route down to the riverside passes along THE TERRACE, where the lustrous green and white faience facade of the **Terrace Tavern** advertises the gloriously-named 'Shrimp Brand Beers' produced by local brewery Russell's (Fig 102). Unusually, the lettering also includes what appears to be the name of the licensee, T. A. Hooper.

On GORDON PROMENADE, beside the Thames, is the delightful **Promenade Café** and its petite ice cream kiosk, both probably erected in the 1930s and completely faced in large creamy-yellow and black ceramic tiles. Behind the café is GORDON PARK, where the larger-than-life Doulton terracotta figure of **General Gordon** can be found mounted upon a tall pedestal; General Charles George 'Chinese' Gordon (1833-85) was born in Gravesend (Fig 103). The statue, commissioned by George M. Arnold, Mayor of Gravesend in 1897, was unveiled in 1893 and bears the marks Broad - the sculptor was John Broad - and Doulton. Arnold also donated the Doulton statue of **Queen Victoria** (1897-8, John Broad) which can be found west of the railway station in DARNLEY ROAD. Doulton's originally sent a faulty statue of Queen Victoria, and this can still be seen in the **Borough Market House**, PRINCES STREET.

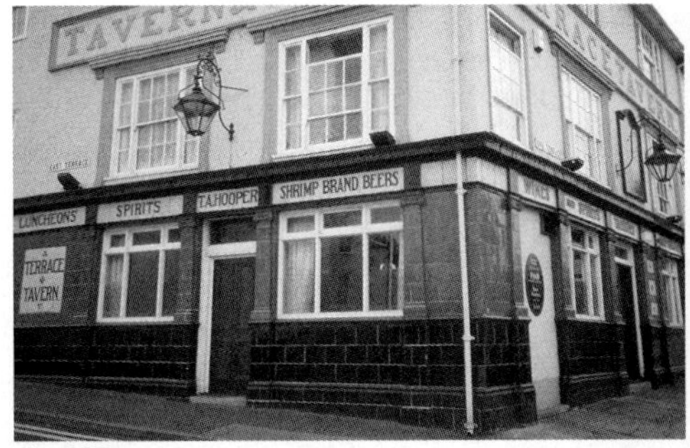

Fig 102.

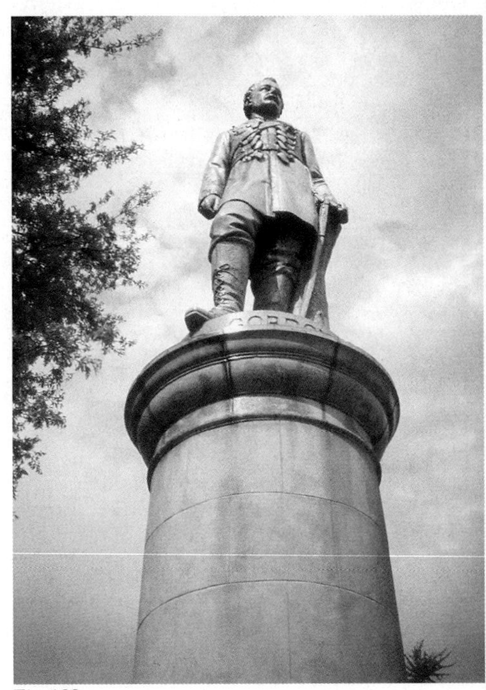

Fig 103.

KEMSING

The topographical artist Donald Maxwell (1877-1936) wanted to make a permanent record of every town and village in his adopted county, Kent. He experimented with hand-painting scenes on tiles at the Pembury Glazed Tile Company, but eventually his 'clay etchings' were produced during 1933-6 by Doulton's of Lambeth as the Domesday (or Maxwell) Tile series. Maxwell worked with Doulton's Art Director, Joseph Mott, to perfect the reproduction process in which Maxwell's etched copper plate sketches were transferred to the earthenware tile surface, the colours then being painted in by Annie Lyons and Doris Johnson.[5] The full ceramic 'modern Domesday Book of Kent' was never completed, but there were fifty-four different tile designs, including two showing Kemsing. Two of the Domesday Tiles, as well as other tiles relating to the village, may be seen inside **Kemsing Church**.[6]

MARGATE

East of Margate's centre the promenade rises to NEWGATE and eventually crosses Newgate Gap, a mini-gorge which leads to some of the town's famous caves. The promenader's route lies across **Newgate Bridge**, erected by the Borough of Margate to commemorate its fiftieth jubilee and opened in 1907; this jolly little seaside structure was built from steel with faience facing. Cream Doulton Carraraware is combined with blue and green faience insets in an attractive design which includes octagonal corner turrets; the bridge is a listed building, although that did not stop its closure in 2000 due to its dangerous condition, a sad state for an unusual example of integral colour in a building.

Back in the town centre, the view across the harbour takes in that icon of the seaside, the **Dreamland Cinema** on MARINE TERRACE. The cinema which gave us the phrase 'Meet me tonight in Dreamland' is a steel-framed, mostly brick, structure built in 1935; its fantastic fin tower is an effective landmark, but the faience panels of its facade are barely visible now. It was designed by the specialist cinema architects Julian Leathart and W. F. Granger, and its audacious tower went on to become the model for many Odeons, which often featured much more faience. In STATION ROAD, just inland from the cinema, is the **Railway Station**, a substantial neo-classical pile built in 1926 to cater for the vast numbers of trippers heading towards Dreamland and the beach; the architect was probably Edwin Maxwell Fry of the Southern Railway. The exterior is executed in a stone-like, almost matt grey faience, and includes a frieze of pictorial roundel reliefs depicting locomotives and other railway scenes. To the west of the centre on the CANTERBURY ROAD stands the former **Royal Sea Bathing Hospital**, whose polychrome brick chapel (architect James Knowles) was added in 1883; an encaustic tiled pavement runs through the sanctuary, choir and central nave aisle.

NORTHFLEET

St Botolph's Church was restored by the architect and designer E. W. Godwin in 1862. His work included the design of an elaborate encaustic tile chancel pavement which incorporates several green-glazed tiles in nine-tile and sixteen-tile groups; there is also an uncommon 'running hare' motif. He also produced tile designs for the lower part of the chancel walls, depicting St Botolph kneeling before a canopied throne and holding a crown.[7]

Perry Street

All Saints Church was designed by James Brooks and built in 1869-70; its chancel and sanctuary have an encaustic tiled pavement by Maw & Co.

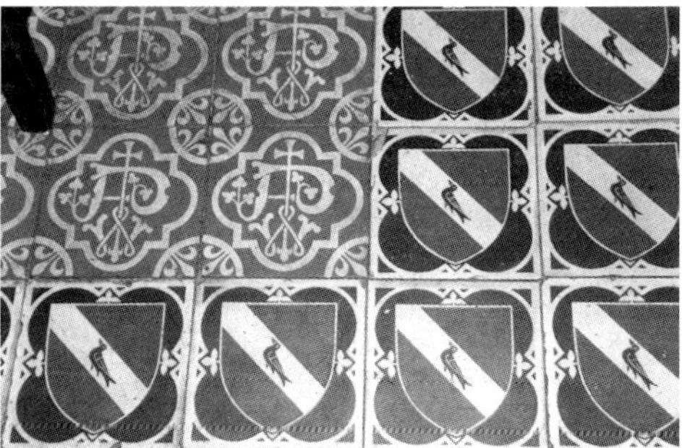

Fig 104.

RAMSGATE

The first port of call in Ramsgate must be **The Grange**, the home of A. W. N. Pugin from 1844 until his death in 1852; it stands in ST AUGUSTINE'S ROAD, at the west end of the town (Fig 104). Pugin was drawn to Ramsgate, then a respectable, middle class seaside resort, for several reasons: he stayed there with his aunt after his mother died in 1833, he loved sailing and the sea, and there was a strong connection with his patron saint, St Augustine of Canterbury. He bought the plot of land in 1843 then designed and built The Grange, which he saw as the basis of a

Catholic community, during 1843-4. Its severe, buff brick exterior is enlivened only by the lookout tower from which Pugin could watch the goings-on at sea, while the interior is a highly functional family home. Pugin's second wife died in 1844, but by 1851 he had remarried and the household comprised Pugin, his wife Jane, five children and four servants.[8]

Although the house appears rather gloomy from the north, all the main reception rooms on the south (and garden) side have a sea view; Pugin did his work in the library and there was a small chapel at the east end of the garden range. Decoration inside the house included Minton encaustic floor tiles in the entrance staircase hall, some of which still remain. Here criss-cross rows of plain black tiles surround groups of four tiles, two bearing Pugin's monogram and two with his crest, which included a martlet. The martlet is an heraldic representation of a martin or swallow without feet, thus a bird which never rests.

As soon as The Grange was complete Pugin began work on St Augustine's Church, which stands immediately east of the house. Despite being funded wholly by Pugin, he always intended that it should benefit the local religious community, and in it he was able, for once, to incorporate his own 'True Principles' of architecture, being his own 'paymaster and architect'. It was built between 1845 and 1852, and was not quite complete even at his death. Pugin also bought land on the opposite side of St Augustine's Road in 1849, although the community was not extended to the north until 1860-1 when St Augustine's Abbey was built by E. W. Pugin for local Benedictine monks; it is connected to the church by a tunnel beneath the road.

The main entrance to the church, now known as **St Augustine's Abbey Church**, is at the north-west corner of the cloister; around the cloister are brightly painted terracotta Stations of the Cross, erected in 1893 and made by the De Beule brothers of Ghent. Before the Altar of the Sacred Heart are encaustic tiles depicting dice (which the centurions threw for the robe of Jesus) and the story of the raven carrying away poisoned bread which was fed to St Augustine. The interior of the church is faced with Whitby sandstone, its tones varying from grey to yellow. Puginian brilliance of colour arises from the fittings, including many Minton's patterned encaustic tiles, for instance in the chancel and Lady Chapel. The tomb of A. W. N. Pugin lies in the Pugin Chantry (above the family vault), which is entered through a screen. The floor tiles around the base of the tomb, which was made in 1852-3, were specially produced by Minton and - apart from the martlet and other personal symbols - bear the legend 'Pray for the soul of Augustus Welby Pugin the founder of this church'.

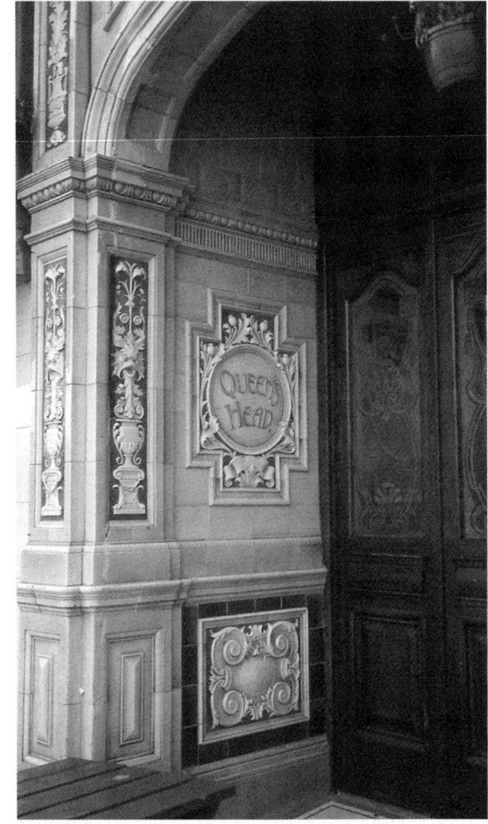

Fig 105.

The Pugin family remained at The Grange until the death of Cuthbert Pugin, last surviving son of A. W. N. Pugin, in 1928. The church continued as a working church, and is now both an abbey and a parish church. Although The Grange was purchased by the monastery in 1931, it suffered many years of neglect, remaining empty and unrepaired until taken on by the Landmark Trust in 2002 for restoration and future use as a holiday home.

Beside the harbour, in the centre of Ramsgate, the **Queen's Head**, all ornate green and yellow faience, looks out across the water from HARBOUR PARADE. In its spectacular frontage a carriage entrance is set beside a broad archway, topped by a faience-floored balcony and enclosing a deep bay though which one may enter the pub, although there are also doorways at either side (Fig 105). The excellent faience detailing includes circular lamp-holders in the side porch ceilings. The interior is tiled to dado level with brown relief tiling which runs around and a brown faience fireplace. The pub's faience has been restored by Shaws of Darwen, who also worked on the neighbouring domed red terracotta **Custom House** (1893-4). Overlooking the harbour from the rear is the **Royal Sailors Rest**, built as a sailors' hostel in 1904 by the Royal British and Foreign Sailors' Society; its impressive buff terracotta pilasters stretch the full height of the building.

RIVERHEAD

The decoration of the sanctuary of **St Mary's Church** (1831), LONDON ROAD was carried out in opus sectile by Powell's of Whitefriars, apart from a central mosaic figure in the reredos which was executed by Salviati; this dates from 1894. In 1909 Powells supplied opus sectile figures of angels for the reredos (from a sketch by A. F. Coakes, one of the firm's leading designers, and cartoons by Charles Hardgrave) at a cost of £130, then in 1911 provided four evangelists (by W. C. Hodges), also for the reredos. The south sanctuary wall was decorated in 1912, and finally the north wall in 1916, both with opus sectile figures of old testament characters.[9]

ROCHESTER

The present buildings of **Rochester Cathedral**, which lies just off the HIGH STREET, date largely from the twelfth century. Medieval tiles, some with patterns still visible, remain in the north transept and the south choir transept, but far more dramatic is the Godwin encaustic tile pavement in the presbytery, installed by Sir George Gilbert Scott during his restoration work which took place around 1870 (Fig 106). Many of the tile designs were copied from those of the Cathedral's medieval tiles, but towards the altar step the tiling grows increasingly elaborate, climaxing with a stunning circular arrangement (normally covered by carpet) including the Signs of the Zodiac. In front of the altar a series of tile roundels represent the Seven Virtues, and either side of the altar are two roundels of jaunty angels each bearing a banner inscribed 'Alleluia'. Also in the Cathedral is the monument to Lady Anne Henniker (d1793) with Coade stone figures of *Truth* and *Father Time*, the latter apparently designed by the sculptor Thomas Banks (1735-1805); it is his only known work for the Coade firm.[10]

Head up Boley Hill, which runs south of the Cathedral, and continue into ST MARGARET'S STREET to find the **Church of St Margaret of Antioch**. Its chancel, added in 1839-40, has complete floor tiling dating from the 1870s. Further out of town in MAIDSTONE ROAD is **St John Fisher R. C. Church**, designed by the architect H. S. Goodhart-Rendel and opened in 1955 (although not consecrated until 1979). Because of its durability, at that time Goodhart-Rendel favoured tile decoration, and commissioned Carter & Co to produce a ceramic reredos for the church. The design work was undertaken by Joseph Ledger (b1926), who carried out this type of commission for Carter's from the early 1950s until his departure to become Design Director of Royal Doulton in 1955. He also designed the reredos for Goodhart-Rendel's Church of St Mary the Virgin, Hounslow, completed in 1955, and (in 1966, while at Doulton's) the east wall decoration of the same architect's Church of Our Lady of the Rosary, City of Westminster, opened in 1963. The hand-painting for all these commissions was done by Phyllis Butler in a special section set up by Carter's.[11] The St John Fisher reredos depicts the figure of St John Fisher surrounded by other saints significant in Rochester's history, including St Benedict and St Andrew.

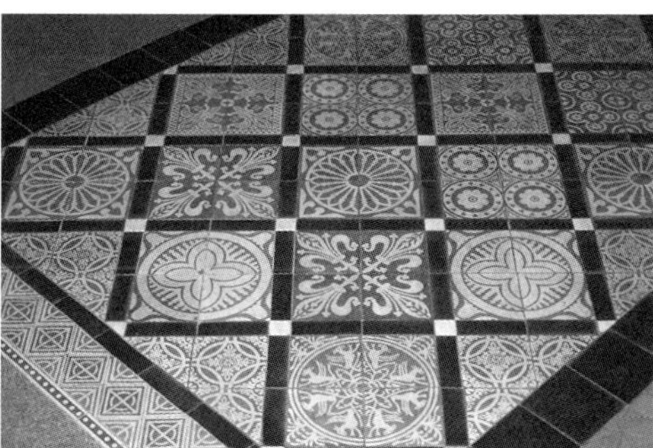

Fig 106.

TUNBRIDGE WELLS

The former children's ward of the **Kent and Sussex Hospital** (1932-4), MOUNT EPHRAIM, contains a contemporary tile scheme designed by Carter's of Poole. It comprised twenty separate panels showing a wide variety of animals running along the walls towards a large Noah's Ark panel at the end of the ward; the brightly-coloured panels were hand-painted on to a slip outline. Carter's were so proud of the scheme that these animal studies featured in their 1935 publicity leaflet *Carter Picture Tiles for Hospitals*. The panels were boarded over in 1965 but rediscovered in 1984 during building work.

WICKHAMBREAUX

St Andrew's Church, on THE GREEN, is best known for its American-designed east window, a dramatic art nouveau piece by Arild Rosenkrantz depicting the Annunciation. It dates from 1896 and was carried out in semi-opaque glass, which adds to the striking visual effect. Beneath the window, the altar is framed by rich, deep brown wall tiling that continues throughout the chancel. It probably dates from the 1868 restoration, along with the brightly coloured chancel tile pavement.

Kent Roundup

The thirteenth century floor tiles at Holy Innocents Church, **Adisham** have all been lifted and reset amongst plain black and red nineteenth century tiles; the chancel is dominated by late Victorian wall tiling, comprising repeats of two yellow, orange and grey floral motifs on rectangular tiles. The Victorian chancel encaustic pavement at St Mary's Church, **Bishopsbourne** includes a 'green man' and other designs copied from medieval Penn tiles, some of which remain in the church. In the churchyard of St Peter's Church in St Peter's village, **Broadstairs** is a First World War memorial comprising a panel of pale grey rectangular glazed tiles on which the names of the casualties appear in black. The fine sanctuary pavement at St Mary's Church, **Brook** consists of fourteenth century tiles forming circles and other patterns. In **Canterbury**, Tyler Hill medieval tiles may be found in the Jesus Chapel of the Cathedral, in a three-tile wide panel reset along a step. There is elaborate terracotta detailing on the former almshouses (1889), restored in 1980 as housing, in Lowfield Street, **Dartford**. The designs of the striking Victorian encaustic floor tiles at the Church of St John the Evangelist, **Ickham** are all based on medieval examples from Tyler Hill. There is ornate floor tiling in the chancel of Christ Church (1839-41), **Kilndown**, a favourite of the Ecclesiologists. There are nineteenth century floor tiles in the Queen's Room of **Leeds Castle**, brought from France by a former owner's wife; their motifs include a stag's head, representing St Hubert. The Victorian tile pavement in the chancel of St Clement's Church, Knightrider Street, **Sandwich** is copied from the designs of fourteenth century Tyler Hill and Penn tiles remaining in the church. There is a good display of glass tile and mosaic panels, mostly by Powell's of Whitefriars, at St James Church, **Staple**. The chancel decoration of St Mary's Church (1868-9, architect Arthur Blomfield), Vicarage Road, **Strood** includes polychromatic brickwork, Salviati mosaics and tiled floors. Inside the White Oak Indoor Bowls Centre, Hilda May Avenue, **Swanley** is a mosaic triptych (1992) of bowling scenes by Oliver Budd. In the chancel of All Saints Church, **West Stourmouth** is a good geometric pavement in red and yellow diamond-shaped tiles.

The following churches have small installations of medieval tiles: St Peter and St Paul, Appledore; St Lawrence, Bapchild; St Augustine, Brookland; St Mary Magdalene, Cobham; St Catherine, Preston, in Faversham; All Saints, Graveney; St John the Baptist, Harrietsham; St Mary, Lamberhurst; St Margaret, Lower Halstow; St Mary, Newington (near Sittingbourne); St Nicholas, New Romney; St Mary, Selling; St Mary the Virgin, Stone; St Mary the Virgin, Upchurch; St John the Baptist, West Wickham.

References

1. Rosemary Hill, 'Prior Commitment', *Crafts*, (2001) 172, pp28-31.
2. *Adam Kossowski: Murals and Paintings*, (Armelle Press, London, 1990).
3. *Image of Carmel: The Art of Aylesford*, (Carmelite Friars of Aylesford, 2000).
4. James H. Sephton, *The Friars Aylesford* (Sephton, Aylesford, 1999).
5. Desmond Eyles and Louise Irvine, *The Doulton Lambeth Wares* (Richard Dennis, Shepton Beauchamp, 2002).
6. Michael Ffinch, *Donald Maxwell 1877-1936* (Maxwell Estate, Kendal, 1995).
7. Catherine Arbuthnott, *E. W. Godwin and Ceramics*, in *E. W. Godwin: Aesthetic Movement Architect and Designer*, ed Susan Weber Soros, (Yale University Press, New Haven and London, 1999), pp297-311.
8. Libby Horner and Gill Hunter, *A Flint Seaside Church: St Augustine's Abbey Church, Ramsgate* (Pugin Society, Ramsgate, 2000).
9. Dennis W. Hadley, James Powell & Sons: A listing of opus sectile, 1847-1973, (2001).
10. Alison Kelly, *Mrs Coade's Stone* (Self Publishing Association, Upton-upon-Severn, 1990).
11. Jennifer Hawkins, *Poole Potteries* (Barrie & Jenkins, London, 1980), p190.

Lancashire

Although St George's Hall, Liverpool, has one of the finest Minton encaustic pavements in the world, the buildings of Lancashire are better known for their architectural ceramics than their decorative tiles. The so-called 'pot churches' of Edmund Sharpe at Bolton and Rusholme (Manchester), built in the 1840s, presaged the wider production and use of terracotta, but were seen at the time as poor substitutes for stone-built churches. Only a mile or so up the road from Sharpe's Rusholme church but over two decades later, terracotta was again introduced to church building in the Holy Name of Jesus R. C. Church, at the same time as it appeared in Waterhouse's Manchester Town Hall. After that, terracotta played a growing role in the townscapes of Lancashire. Much of it was supplied by Ruabon firms, although it was the Leeds Fireclay Company who eventually introduced faience on a large scale to the warehouses of Edwardian Manchester, clothing the city's mini-skyscrapers in gleaming Burmantofts ware.

Of course, the county's own ceramics manufacturers, Pilkington's (founded 1893) and Shaws of Darwen (founded 1897) had an important role to play. Two baths complexes, the Lister Drive Baths (1903), Liverpool and the Victoria Baths (1906), Rusholme, Manchester stand out amongst the work of Pilkington's, along with their unique war memorial reredos (1919-21) at the Albion United Reformed Church, Ashton-under-Lyne. The loss of the five Pilkington's tile panels commissioned for Liverpool Museum in 1913 is particularly sad.[1] Shaws of Darwen came to the fore in the 1930s when they gained an increasing number of faience contracts in Blackpool and for the Odeon cinema chain; the loss of their fine Derby Baths (1939), Blackpool in 1990 is deeply regrettable.

Lancashire is strong in post-Second World War ceramics, particularly those commissioned for the boom in Catholic church building during the late 1950s and early 1960s; Adam Kossowski's Leyland tympanum of 1963 is the outstanding example. Secular work includes the splendid Festival of Britain-style Carter's mural at Lewis's Store (1953), Liverpool, and works commissioned around 1960 by the University of Liverpool. In the latter part of the twentieth century, the county's hospitals were especially keen to include ceramic art in their new buildings.

Minor Lancashire highlights include the Minton pavement at Rochdale Town Hall and the same town's remarkable variety of pub tiling; two churches with tile pavements by Carter, Johnson & Co of Worcester (in Preston and Standish); the 'White Church' at Fairhaven, Lytham St Anne's; tiles and faience inside Blackpool Tower Buildings; and the Mersey Brewery, Liverpool, whose terracotta exterior and tiled interior is a match for any brewery in the country. Suggested reading: Kevin Gannon, 'Refuge Assurance Company Offices, Manchester', *Glazed Expressions*, 1990, vol 3, pp11-14; Robert Jolley, 'Edmund Sharpe and the 'Pot' Churches', *Architectural Review*, December 1969, vol 146, pp426-31; TACS Tour Notes *Blackpool* (1984), *Liverpool* (1994), *Manchester* (1985) and *Rochdale* (1991).

The *Gazetteer* entry for Lancashire covers the administrative areas of Blackburn with Darwen Borough Council, Blackpool Borough Council, Bolton Metropolitan Borough Council, Bury Metropolitan Borough Council, Knowsley Metropolitan Borough Council, Lancashire County Council, Liverpool City Council, Manchester City Council, Rochdale Metropolitan Borough Council, St Helens Metropolitan Borough Council, Salford City Council, Sefton Metropolitan Borough Council, Tameside Metropolitan Borough Council, Trafford Metropolitan Borough Council and Wigan Metropolitan Borough Council.

ASHTON-UNDER-LYNE

Ashton **Central Library and Art Gallery**, OLD STREET was built in 1893 as the Heginbottom Library and Technical College. Its reconstruction in 2000-1 included the formation of a fine gallery space on the first floor and the restoration (carried out by the Heritage Tiling & Restoration Company) of its mosaic floor and the pale brown relief tile dado which runs through the ground floor and stairwell. Just round the corner in OLDHAM ROAD is a pub now known as the **Theatre Tavern**; its light and dark green faience facade includes a sizeable plaque with good lettering in bronze-yellow faience reading 'Gartsides Famous Ales & Stout'. At the east end of Old Street, on the ST MICHAEL'S SQUARE roundabout, is a **former pub** with a striking facade made entirely of glass-like tiles, sky blue in colour above the dado and lime green below. On its fascia are brightly coloured small mosaic panels, some of which carry the letter 'S' on a red and yellow shield.

Cross the roundabout via the Memorial Gardens to reach the **Albion United Reformed Church**, marooned on the far side of the traffic island in STAMFORD STREET EAST. With its tall spire, the church (built in 1890-5, architect John Brooke) could easily be mistaken for the parish church, which stands much less visibly on the west side of the roundabout, nearer the town centre. The interior is very broad, reminiscent of Liverpool's Anglican Cathedral in its spaciousness and use of sandstone. The unexciting - and now rather worn - encaustic tiled pavement in the chancel dates from 1895.

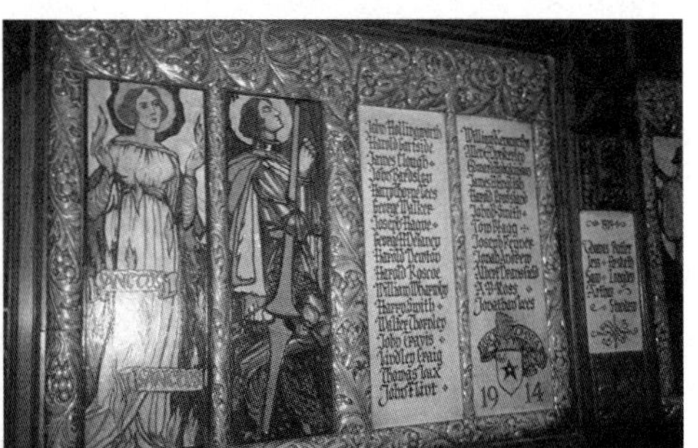

Fig 107.

At its east end is a surprising but fitting conclusion to this vast space: a ceramic war memorial reredos made by Pilkington's in 1919-21 (Fig 107). It comprises twelve panels, each around three feet high by a foot wide, set within a leafy scrolling border in typical Pilkington's orange vermilion. The four central panels and the pair at either end are figurative, while the remaining four bear the names of the fifty-seven fallen. All the figurative panels, which were designed by Gordon Forsyth, are tube-lined and vividly coloured. The central four-panel section depicts Christ offering the sacrament to those who made the supreme sacrifice in war; to its left is St George with an attendant angel, and to the right St Michael, also with an angel. The memorial's strong colours were thought to successfully complement the brilliance of the east window. Two small tablets were added to the memorial following the Second World War, but by the 1960s it was felt that their design was inadequate, and Pilkington's were asked to supply replacements. The resulting two black-and-white lettered panels were made by James Plenderleith, a craftsman who had been an apprentice to the maker of the original memorial, and were mounted in between the three large panels.[2]

Crowhill

The **March Hare PH**, CROWHILL ROAD, was designed in 1959 and opened in 1960; the pub remains unaltered and the toilets have tiles showing two different designs of hare.

Guide Bridge

On the altar wall of **St Paul's Church**, 285 STOCKPORT ROAD, Guide Bridge is large, irregularly-shaped ceramic relief of the Conversion of St Paul, made by the artist Adam Kossowski and dating from 1966.

BLACKBURN

There is much ornate buff Burmantofts terracotta ornamentation on the **College of Technology and Design** (c1888, architects Smith, Woodhouse & Willoughby of Manchester), BLAKEY MOOR. As Woodhouse & Willoughby, the same practice designed the equally huge Technical School (1900-3) at Barrow-in-Furness, Cumbria and a series of large-scale, often terracotta-detailed municipal buildings throughout Lancashire, culminating in the vast Manchester Police and Fire Station (1901-6), designed in collaboration with John Langham. John Henry Woodhouse (1847-1929) was in partnership with George Harry Willoughby from 1886 and was President of the Manchester Society of Architects in 1905-7.

BLACKPOOL

Blackpool's development as a resort began in the 1730s, but progress was slow until transport problems were overcome by the arrival of the railway, which reached the town in 1846 and soon had three large stations. The resulting influx of holidaymakers and daytrippers led to the first boom in building during 1860-80, but it was in the developments of the 1890s onward that terracotta began to be used widely as a building material. Buff and red terracotta supplied by firms in Accrington and Wigan had become popular throughout Lancashire in the 1890s, but in Blackpool it was the superior decorative capabilities of the Burmantofts branch of Leeds Fireclay that was exploited for the most prestigious contracts such as the Tower Building.

The borough surveyor set an example in the use of faience, especially for indoor and outdoor swimming baths, and a small group of local architects designed most of the hotels, guest houses, shops and offices which used blocks or slabs of glazed clayware. The architect Halstead Best was probably the most successful figure in the late 1920s, and the Hathern Station Brick and Terracotta Company won the contracts to supply many of his buildings. However it was the more local firm of Shaws of Darwen which gained the largest contracts in Blackpool. In 1929, having previously undertaken only small schemes in the town, they won the contract to supply the Winter Gardens; following this they supplied the largest schemes undertaken in the resort during the late 1930s.[3]

Terracotta and faience were used with bravura and indulgence in Blackpool, but many of the variations in colour and style previously visible have been destroyed or hidden by development during the last two decades of the twentieth century. However, travelling the length of the Promenade still provides an insight into the architectural use of faience. To begin at the north end of QUEEN'S PROMENADE, the stylish **Little Bispham Tram Station**, in brick with cream faience, was built in 1935. Its architect was the borough surveyor John C. Robinson (1879-1954), who had previously worked in Banister Fletcher's office. Shaws received a large number of orders relating to private hotels at Bispham and Norbreck during the mid and late thirties, while the vitreous glazed faience of the massive **Miners' Welfare Convalescent Home** (1927, architects Bradshaw, Gass & Hope) may have been supplied by the Bispham Hall Colliery Company. The **Cliffs Hotel**, with Shaws cream faience detailing, was begun after the First World War and completed in 1936-7 with the addition of the north wing and central section designed by Halstead Best. The **Savoy Hotel**, just north of Gynn Square, is one of the series of large red brick and red terracotta hotels built around the turn of the century. The architect was T. G. Lumb and the hotel opened in 1915; the sun lounge in Hathern's cream faience was added in 1935 by Lumb and Walton.

Before its demolition in May 1990 the Derby Baths stood on the Promenade to the south of Gynn Square; this exceptional modernist building, which opened in 1939, was designed by J. C. Robinson. Its yellow and lime green Shaws faience walls were cut through by porthole windows and decorated with fishy roundels. The loss of the Derby Baths was great in terms of architectural ceramics, environmental colour and seaside architecture, and followed the demolition of the South Shore Open Air Baths in 1983. The Open Air Baths, opened in 1923, were the largest in the world at the time and were completely clad in Shaws faience. But back to the present, and further down the PROMENADE is the **Princess Cinema** (1921-2, now a nightclub), one of Halstead Best's first major designs; its white faience facade was Hathern's second largest order in Blackpool. To the south of the North Pier is the **Savoy Café** (now a pub), carrying some of the nautical imagery fashionable in 1937 when Shaws supplied the cream faience to designs by Gorst and Crabtree.

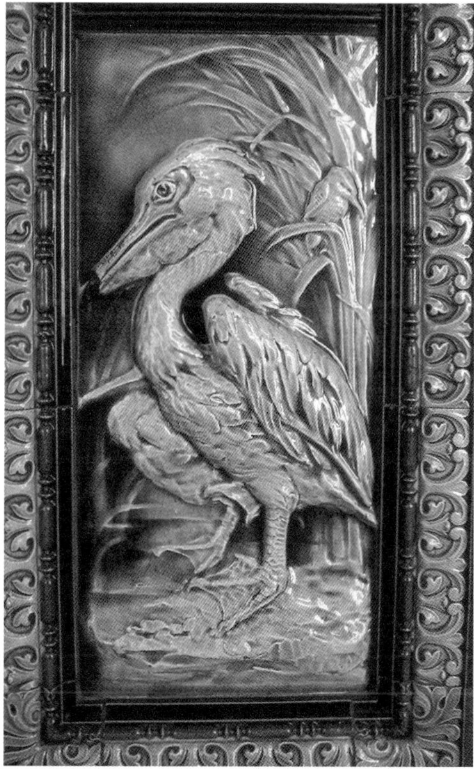

Fig 108.

The glory of Blackpool, and unusually in this resort a building which has retained most of its original ceramics, is **Blackpool Tower** (Fig 108). The Blackpool Tower Company began life in 1891, but the putative tower at first aroused little public enthusiasm, especially with residents who saw their tourist trade sliding downmarket. Only the influence of the Tower Company's chairman, John Bickerstaffe, Mayor of Blackpool, enabled the Company to continue with its plans. An architectural competition for the design of the

Tower Buildings was held in early 1891, the winners being the Manchester practice Maxwell & Tuke. The promenade site was almost rectangular; Maxwell & Tuke fitted the circus inside the Tower legs on the ground and first floors, located shops around much of the perimeter of the site, and filled the three-to-four-storey bulk of the Buildings with an aquarium, menagerie, restaurant, Grand Pavilion (later ballroom) and a winter garden on the roof, as well as the necessary services for both animals and humans. The Tower opened to the public on Whit Monday 1894 (Fig 109).

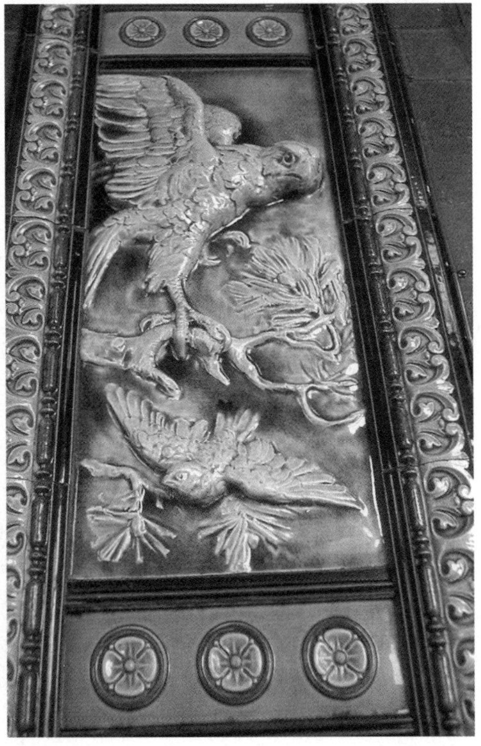

Fig 109.

The exterior design was conservative, using red brick and terracotta dressings supplied by the Ruabon Brick and Terra Cotta Company, but Tower Buildings made up inside for what it lacked in external flair, even mundane areas such as corridors and staircases sparkling with turquoise and grey low-relief Burmantofts faience panels set in terracotta by J. C. Edwards.[4] The panel designs, showing birds, fishes and children, were modelled by E. C. Spruce. Along the corridor leading to the Grand Pavilion were more Burmantofts faience panels in blue and buff, showing a winged figure bearing cornucopia, while the upper galleries of the ballroom were lined with brown and maroon tiles. The circus was unique, with the four legs of the Tower wrapped in cascades of gilded, scalloped moulding and glittering tiles forming the backdrop to the gallery seats. There was an Oriental feel to the decoration, and the entire building was a showpiece of structural and decorative skills, from the engineering of the Tower (by R. J. G. Reade) and the flooding mechanism of the circus ring to the brilliant interior detailing.

In 1898 the Tower's Grand Pavilion underwent conversion to the Tower Ballroom, Frank Matcham being engaged to outdo the decorations of the nearby Winter Gardens Empress Ballroom. It was completed in 1899 and was one of Matcham's most important and unusual works; it was burnt out in 1956 but was reconstructed to exactly the original design and reopened in 1958. A 1991 tile panel by Caroline Bilson showing 'World Towers' decorates its interior. In addition, a number of large mosaic panels of stylized circus scenes, commissioned for the front of the building around 1970, now line a staircase.

South of the Tower, the **Woolworth's Store** (now Pricebusters) represents one of the most dramatic uses of faience in Blackpool and a fully developed expression of the 'streamlined' style imported from America in the late thirties. It was rebuilt in 1936-7 by the Woolworth Construction Department employing direct labour. Over a steel frame and a brick cladding, cream faience was used to form a series of fin-like mullions, with dark brown panels imitating lead or copper and forming infills between each storey of windows. The corner tower was decorated with wave patterns and originally had a sign advertising the first floor café. In 1978 Shaws were commissioned to supply new faience to make good extensive deterioration; about ten per cent of the store was clad in new material.

Near the Central Pier, the **Lifeboat Station** (1937) is one of Halstead Best's most successful designs in faience, using material supplied by Hathern. Returning north and veering inland, it seems that the use of faience to clad building facades is almost as extensive away from the Promenade, although with less consistency in trying to create a seaside image or style. In

MARKET STREET is the elegant cream and blue thirties faience facade of **Leonard Dews Jewellers**, but this is only a trivial amount of faience in comparison to its dramatic use on the facade of the **Winter Gardens** in VICTORIA STREET. The Winter Gardens began life in 1878 and had a complex history of additions and alterations as its management attempted to compete with the Tower. The reconstruction scheme undertaken from 1929 (completed around 1939) to the designs of J. C. Derham provided a massive order of £22,638 to Shaws, who supplied 30,000 cubic feet of faience; this marked their establishment as a major manufacturer of the material. White marble-like faience is used for the exterior, with bright blue and yellow elements drawing attention to details (Fig 110). Inside, one of the many attractions is the Empress Ballroom (1896, architects Mangnall & Littlewoods), its original decoration including art nouveau Doulton faience panels of mermaids in rich, swirling blues, browns and greens.

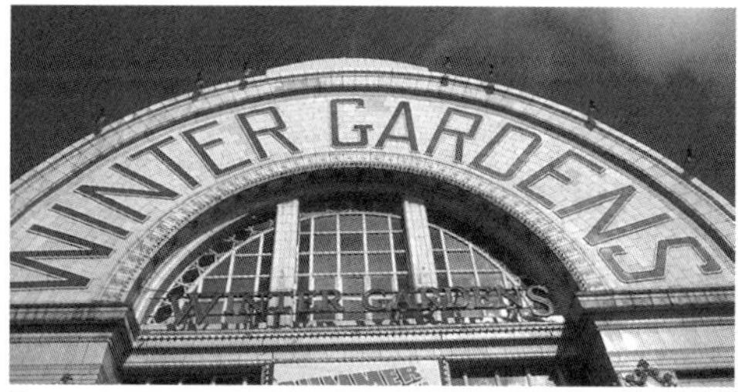

Fig 110.

One of the CHURCH STREET entrances to the Winter Gardens, dating from 1896, can be identified by its buff terracotta 'WG' above a blocked archway. Behind ran a corridor lined with a series of twenty-eight painted art nouveau Doulton tile panels designed by W. J. Neatby and showing female figures symbolising jewels; about eight of these panels still survive, although covered over. Further along Church Street is the former **Regent Cinema**, opened 1921, its large dome clad in white faience, actually Middleton Fireclay Company's 'Ceramo'. Stanley Buildings (1935, designed by J. C. Robinson), the municipal offices, on Church Street and Cookson Street, is clad in cream faience with reliefs of Viking ships. To the north is TOPPING STREET, with the best concentration of thirties slab faience away from the Promenade; most was supplied by Shaws with J. C. Derham being a recurring architect. **Don Chambers** has stylish red lettering round its doorway, while the former **Shakespeare Hotel** has the characteristic combination of cream slabs with a black plinth.

Further north in DICKSON ROAD is the **Duke of York Hotel** (1939, architect Halstead Best) clad in cream faience with circular plaques depicting the Duke of York. Finally to the former **Odeon Cinema** (1938-9, closed 1998), also in Dickson Road, which marks virtually the final development in the Odeon style of interwar cinema architecture. The majority of Odeons dating to the early or mid-thirties were designed by George Coles and used ceramics from Hathern, but it was the combination of Harry Weedon and Shaws which was the most ubiquitous just before the Second World War. The Blackpool Odeon, designed by Harry Weedon and W. Calder Robson, was the largest built by the circuit, seating over 3,000. The centre of its cream faience front is decorated with wave-like flutings, and set in a surround that aptly symbolises a proscenium; the cornice of red and black ribs is topped by a squat tower.

BOLTON

From the collection of buildings with terracotta facades in BRADSHAWGATE, right in the centre of Bolton, the buff terracotta frontage of **Yates Wine Lodge** (1906) is perhaps the most striking, although the former **Fleece Hotel** (1907, at number 28) comes a close second. Turning the corner into NELSON SQUARE is the red brick and terracotta **Prudential Building** of 1889, designed by a Bolton architect named Smith, although Alfred Waterhouse may have acted as consultant.[5]

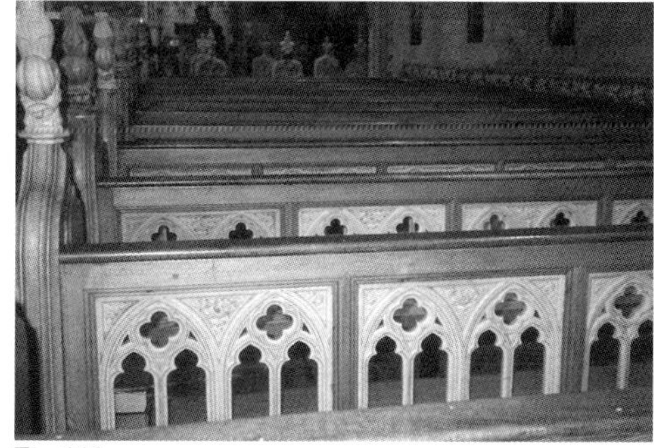
Fig 111.

Darcy Lever

The **Church of St Stephen and All Martyrs** (1844-5), RADCLIFFE ROAD, Lever Bridge was the first of three terracotta churches to be built by the architect Edmund Sharpe (1809-77) (Fig 111). It was mostly constructed from solid blocks of the material, unlike his second church, Holy Trinity (1845-6), Platt Lane, Manchester, which used a greater percentage of hollow blocks of terracotta, and his third, St Paul's (1876), Scotforth, near Lancaster, which was built from small, solid brick-like terracotta blocks. St Stephen and Holy Trinity became known as the 'pot churches' - a reference to the hollow blocks - and were derided by the architectural press for their apparent attempt to pass off terracotta as stone.[6]

St Stephen's came about through the initiative of Colonel John Fletcher, owner of the Ladyshore Colliery at Little Lever. He wanted to use fireclay, a by-product of coal mining, to build a church for which he would become the chief subscriber. Fletcher's venture necessitated the construction of new kilns and workshops, and the engagement of 'a capable and able modeller'. His prospective son-in-law, Edmund Sharpe, was commissioned to produce the design, in which five-inch deep blocks of terracotta (approximating to blocks of stone) were laid in courses. Their surface was scored in imitation of the tooling on ashlar masonry, and their buff, sandstone-like colour enhanced the sham stone effect. Sharpe had to prepare drawings for the entire church down to the tiniest detail to facilitate modelling and production, and had to devise techniques to overcome the novel problems of terracotta work, such as contending with warpage and differentials in shrinkage. To combat warpage he adopted the practice of hollowing out any large terracotta pieces which were necessary, and his solution to the problem of connecting the components of the spire and large windows was the manufacture of terracotta dowels. Despite criticism of the 'pot churches', Sharpe showed that the problems inherent in making terracotta and building with the material could be overcome; the same working practices were to be adopted by terracotta manufacturers and architects from the 1860s onwards.[7]

There is a profusion of ornament on the exterior of St Stephen, including an elaborate arched entrance with lettering, traceried windows and a pierced parapet, but the unique and intriguing interior is the most memorable part of the church, which has lost its tower and spire. The interior is almost totally terracotta, with a terracotta pulpit, organ-case, octagonal font and well-nigh unbelievable traceried pew-ends and backs, as well as much decoration on the terracotta blocks themselves. The interior terracotta work was splendidly restored in the late 1990s, with (amongst other items) replacement terracotta poppyheads being made for the pew ends. The repairs were carried out by Diana Hall, Axel Keim, John Winterbothom and Shaws of Darwen.[8]

Sharples

Two miles north of Bolton's centre on the BLACKBURN ROAD is **Sir John Holdens Mill** (1925-6, architects Bradshaw, Gass & Hope); its steel-framed structure is concealed by red brick and much terracotta detailing. There is no chimney as this was an innovative all-electric mill.

BURNLEY

Burnley **Town Hall** (1884-8, architects Holtom & Fox of Dewsbury), MANCHESTER ROAD, has an excellent interior decorative scheme running throughout its ground and first floors. It includes a Craven Dunnill mosaic pavement bearing the town's coat of arms, along with a colourful relief-tiled dado. A Craven Dunnill trade tile is set into the mosaic floor at the top of the stairs.

DARWEN

St Cuthbert's Church, BLACKBURN ROAD, was built in 1875-8 and designed by architects Paley & Austin of Lancaster; its sanctuary is floored with Godwin's impressed and encaustic tiles, mainly in alternating four-tile groups. This type of pavement is found in several of Paley & Austin's earlier churches.[9] The impressively large and colourful opus sectile reredos was installed in three parts, with the central Last Supper panel being supplied by Powell's of Whitefriars in 1887; the cartoon was by Frank Mann. In 1900 the same firm provided nine further opus sectile panels (as a memorial to Charles Greenway of Darwen) and the reredos was completed in 1912 when the ornate frame was added, again as a memorial (Fig 112).

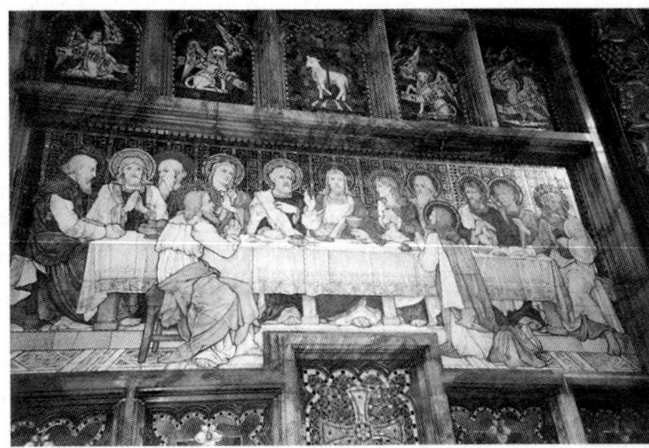

Fig 112.

ECCLES

The improbable setting of the R. C. Church of the City of Mary Immaculate, better known as **All Saints Church**, on REDCLYFFE ROAD, Barton upon Irwell, just south of the point where the Bridgewater Canal crosses the Manchester Ship Canal by means of a swing bridge, is one of its great attractions. However, construction of the Ship Canal in 1885-94 proved disastrous for the church, which was designed by E. W. Pugin and built in 1865-8, as most of its parishioners lived north of the new canal and could reach the church only by crossing the swing bridge. The first part of the church to be built was the de Trafford family chantry, in appearance a miniature church, in 1863. The de Trafford family provided the site and funded construction of the chantry and the church; of the seventy or more churches built by E. W. Pugin, this was his most lavish, and it shows. Inside, the nave arcade and chancel arch are starkly banded in red and white sandstone; the de Trafford chantry, north of the chancel, is screened off by a complex arcade and has a superlative Minton encaustic tile pavement.[10]

FARNWORTH

Artworks at the **Royal Bolton Hospital**, PLODDER LANE include a large glass and ceramic panel by artist in residence Gerald Buchanan of Bolton in the entrance hall. He was also responsible for a series of fourteen ceramic panels (each measuring 18″ by 24″), showing flora and fauna from a variety of natural habitats; these date from 1997. In addition, there are mosaic panels by Rachel Cooke on the ground floor pharmacy.

GREAT ALTCAR

The **Church of St Michael and All Angels** was designed by the Chester architect John Douglas (1830-1911) and built in 1878-9 at the expense of the Earl of Sefton. The tiny building itself is splendidly original, being entirely half-timbered, inside and out, and it has a very unusual tiled reredos, also of 1879. This has a central panel of Christ breaking bread, with St Michael to the left and Euphrasia to the right; it was painted and fired by Craven Dunnill from cartoons by Heaton, Butler & Bayne. The reredos is angled forward at the top, apparently to prevent reflections.

HALE

The Manchester architect Edgar Wood (1860-1935) built **Royd House**, 224 HALE ROAD for his own use in 1914-16 (Fig 113). The house, made from reinforced concrete and brick, was approached by a patterned brick path, and the centre part of its concave brick frontage was set with Pilkington's tiles in colourful zig-zag geometric patterns.[11] This bold use of lozenge and zig-zag shapes continued inside the house, with mosaic panels in the hall floor and stencilling on several doors. This was a precursor of what became known as the art deco style, and certainly a departure from the decorative norms of the time in terms of materials and motifs.

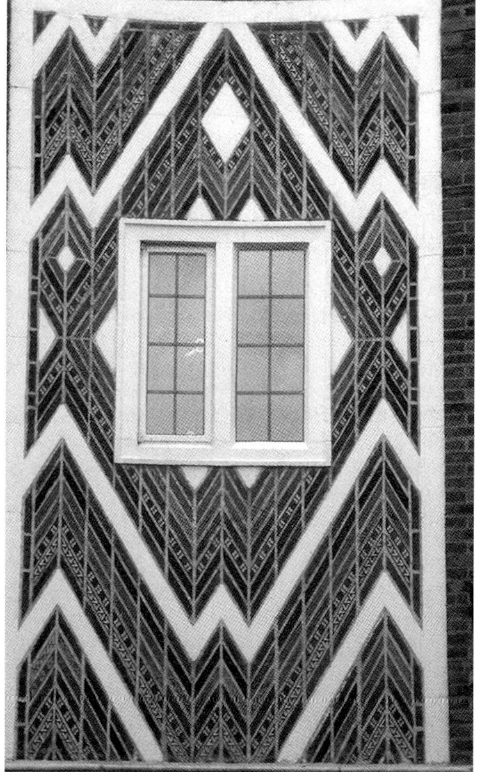

Fig 113.

HORWICH

St Catherine's Church, RICHMOND STREET was built in two phases to the design of the architect Frank Freeman. The nave and part of the chancel were put up in 1897-1902, then the chancel was completed in 1931-2. The interior is remarkable for its art nouveau fittings, including two unusual 3′ by 2′ high-quality glazed, tube-lined ceramic panels at the west end. They were installed around 1916 in memory of Catherine Ainsworth, who helped found the church, and show the flower garden at her home and a fiery scene of destruction with a quotation from Romans 16.20: 'The God of Peace shall bruise Satan under your feet shortly'.

LANCASTER

St Paul's Church (1874-6), Scotforth was the third terracotta church to be built by the architect Edmund Sharpe, although it can hardly be called a 'pot church' as it was constructed using small solid terracotta blocks, in effect bricks, as well as stone and yellow brick. The terracotta was supplied by Joseph Cliff & Sons of Wortley, Leeds. The surround of the south door is made entirely of buff terracotta, while inside the church the terracotta details include scalloped capitals and wall brackets supporting the roof timbers. Sharpe, who lived in Lancaster, died in 1877; his memorial is in the chancel, beneath blank terracotta arcading.

LEYLAND

The Polish-born artist Adam Kossowski's gigantic *Last Judgement* high relief ceramic tympanum (1963), shaded by a broad canopy, dominates the exterior view of **St Mary's R. C. Church**, BROADFIELD DRIVE (Fig 114). The church was commissioned in 1959 by the Benedictines of Ampleforth and opened in 1964, and was one of a large number of Catholic churches built throughout Britain between around 1953 and the mid-1960s. Its architects were Weightman and Bullen (project architect J. Faczynski), who produced a drum-shaped nave defined by fourteen Y-shaped concrete piers; the inner walls are lined with small relief tiles.[12] There is abstract glass by Patrick Reyntiens, a tapestry by Faczynski and bronze Stations of the Cross by Arthur Dooley, as well as a steel-framed monumental ceramic cross (1963) by Kossowski which is suspended above the centrally-placed altar. But it is the great rectangular tympanum, with its powerful figurative images, which remains longest in the mind. Christ the Judge is depicted in the centre, with the saved to his right and the devils and the condemned to his left.[13] Kossowski used a wide range of glaze colours for the tympanum, although golden-yellow, pale blue and red stand out, particularly the red of the stark, staring devils. The St Mary's tympanum is one of his most important works (apart from his masterwork at The Friars, Aylesford, Kent, which took over twenty years), and is all the more significant in art historical terms because of its setting, with other artworks created for the postwar Catholic church.

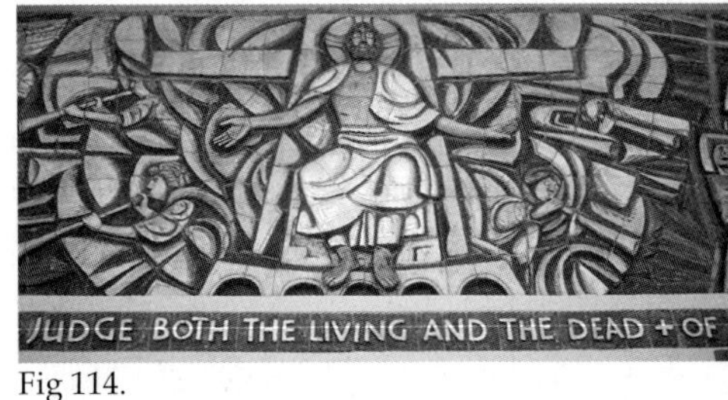

Fig 114.

LIVERPOOL

Situated on the east bank of the Mersey, Liverpool occupies one of the most dramatic locations of any British city, with a centre about a square mile in size. It runs in a series of plateaux rising from the waterfront to a ridge in the east, on which the two Cathedrals stand. The city centre is essentially a nineteenth century creation, as earlier development was swept aside by the explosion of economic activity in the Victorian period, when the city was one of the biggest ports in the world. This description begins at St George's Hall, opposite Lime Street Station, and continues west to the waterfront before returning through the main shopping area and finishing on and around the campus of the University of Liverpool; a list of suburban locations follows.

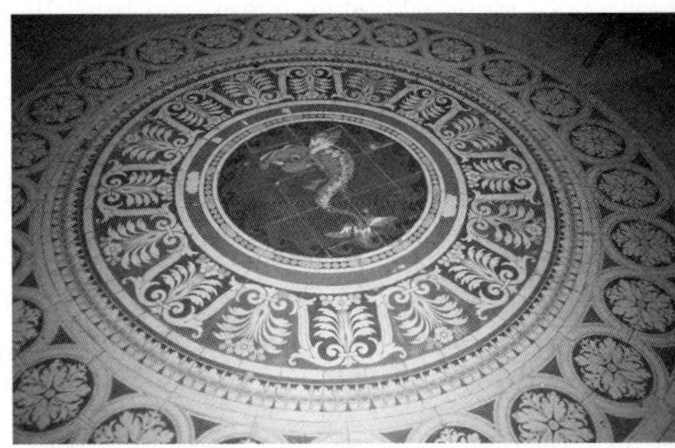

Fig 115.

The sublimely classical **St George's Hall**, LIME STREET was designed as a concert hall by the architect Harvey Lonsdale Elmes in 1839, with a later revision of the plans to incorporate law courts. Work began in 1841, but following the death of Elmes in 1847, construction was continued by the building's engineer Sir Robert Rawlinson in collaboration with the Corporation Surveyor. Initially, the floor of the Great Hall was to have been of stone, but after the appointment of C. R. Cockerell as architect in 1851, the decorative scheme planned by Elmes was changed to incorporate a tiled floor, which was in place when St George's Hall was opened in 1854, although the building was only finally completed in 1856 (Fig 115).

The general form of the vast interior spaces, with their fine sculpture and plasterwork, is due to Elmes, but the Great Hall's sumptuous tile pavement was commissioned by Cockerell and made by Minton's in 1853 (Fig 116). The Great Hall is almost 170 feet long and 74 feet wide at its maximum, and the tile pavement occupies most of this area, as a sunken floor with raised walkway all around. Over 30,000 tiles were used in a complex arrangement based on interlocking circles with figurative borders, the basis of the design being provided by George Eyre (1816-87), superintendent of the drawing office at Minton's.[14] He appears to have been the 'superintendent from Mr Minton', referred to in the Law Courts committee minutes of 1852, who produced two designs under Cockerell's direction.[15] However, the architect found these 'unsatisfactory and commonplace' and brought in the sculptor Alfred Stevens, who designed a figurative band depicting Neptune amongst sea nymphs, dolphins and other nautical imagery.[16] According to Stevens' biographer, this border was the 'redeeming feature' of the floor whose general design was 'unquiet and ill-suited to the architecture'.[17]

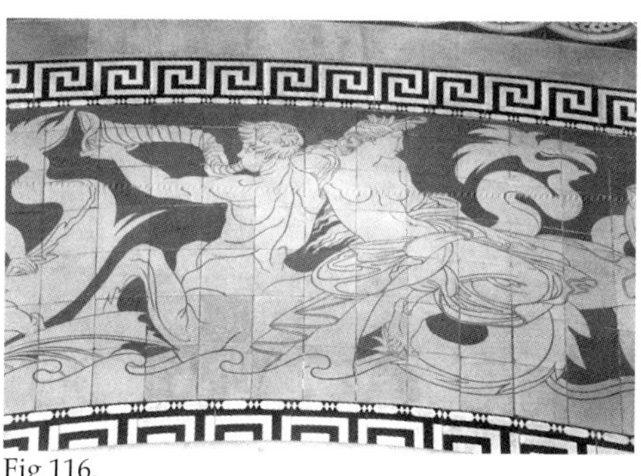
Fig 116.

Stevens' near semi-circular band, with buff figures on a warm red ground, appears four times over, twice in the centre of the floor and once at each end. The floor's major feature is the large circular arrangement, within which is the royal coat of arms, while two smaller circles contain the city's arms; beneath the organ gallery is a circular panel bearing the crest of the Prince of Wales. It was (and remains) one of the finest tile pavements in the world, but within a few years of its installation it was found to be unsuitable for dancing and the central well was covered with a raised wooden floor, fitting flush with the tiled walkway. This has had the happy side-effect of preserving the main pavement in pristine condition, as may be seen on the rare occasions when the wooden decking (which was modernised in the early 1990s) is taken up.[18] In comparison the walkway tiles, which include geometric and encaustic tiles with lettered inscriptions and several circular dolphin panels, are very worn in places and some are to be renewed.[19] After the court elements of St George's Hall became redundant in 1984, the whole building was closed and suffered years of neglect before restoration began in the 1990s; work continues in 2004.

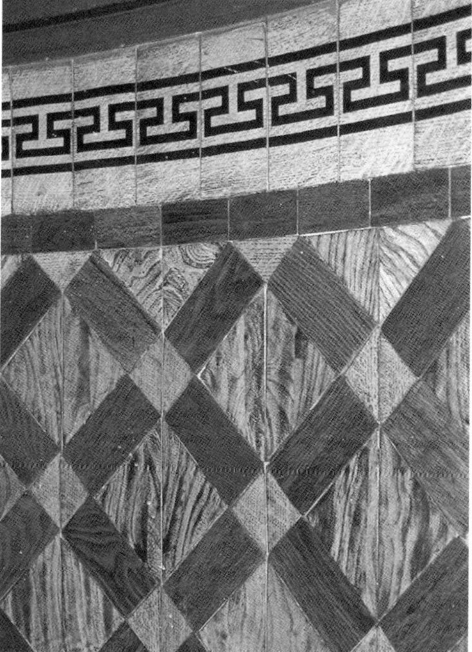
Fig 117.

North of St George's Hall is WILLIAM BROWN STREET with its monumental parade of classical civic buildings, the easternmost being the **County Sessions House** (1882-4, architects F. & G. Holme, disused in 2003). There is dado tiling throughout, in an unusual design of alternating maroon and green squares, Burmantofts wall tiling in one courtroom, and in the barristers' room is a Doulton tiled fireplace. The good mosaic flooring was laid by the local tile fixer and mosaic layer George Swift, whose own Swan Tile Works opened around 1900 at Binns Road, four miles east of the centre of Liverpool.[20] To the south, on the far side of the gardens at the rear of St George's Hall, is ST JOHN'S LANE and the former **Pearl Life Assurance** office, its ground floor used as Doctor Duncan's public house since 1999. The building was designed by Alfred Waterhouse and largely built in 1896-8; it has a Portland stone exterior, possibly to differentiate it from the rival (and earlier) Prudential Assurance building nearby in Dale Street. The interior of the lofty room which was the company's public office is entirely clad, ceiling and all, with unusually colourful Burmantofts faience in brown, green, yellow and blue. There is also a large brown faience fire surround and a mosiac floor, the latter by Rust & Co.

Turn west into VICTORIA STREET past the flat-iron shape of **Imperial Buildings** (1879, now Scottish Legal Life Asurance) at number 70. It was designed by E. & H. Shelmerdine and is faced in ornate grey terracotta by Gibbs & Canning, including two allegorical female figures of 'Industry' and 'Commerce' and - near the roof - a profile of Queen Victoria. This is a relatively early use of terracotta. In DALE STREET, a block to the north, is the towered, rather French Renaissance form of the **Municipal Buildings** (1860-6), designed by the Corporation Surveyor John Weightman (although completed by his successor). The walls of the entrance corridors are lined with brown and ochre tiles decorated with what appears to be a printed wood grain design, the whole creating the effect of genuine wood panelling (Fig 117). These curious tiles were probably identical to samples shown by Minton's at the 1866 Staffordshire Industrial Exhibition, held in Hanley. These tiles, 'apparently converted into blocks of wood', were produced by a process called nature printing, patented in 1865 by William Scarratt and William Dean of Longton, Stoke-on-Trent. It allowed a wood grain pattern, derived directly from an impression of the wood involved, to be printed on tiles or other surfaces. In the case of tiles, it would allow the substitution of nature printed wall tiling for expensive wood cladding, but it seems to have been a short-lived novelty, as the process was somewhat laborious.[21]

Further west at 30-38 Dale Street is the landmark former **Prudential Assurance Building**, designed by Alfred Waterhouse and built in 1885-8, with later alterations by Paul Waterhouse. The hard red terracotta of its gothic exterior was supplied by J. C. Edwards of Ruabon; a terracotta figure of *Prudentia* stands in a niche above the slightly art nouveau main entrance. The subdued interior faience work by Burmantofts is mostly overpainted. A diversion of a further block north via MOORFIELDS is required to visit the **Lion Tavern**, which stands on the corner with Tithe Barn Street. The pub, which was built about 1865 and remodelled around 1905, has good art nouveau dado tiling, in bright colours on white ground.

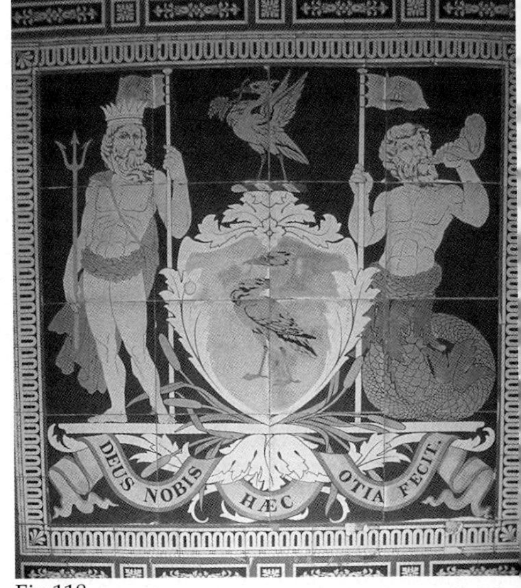

Fig 118.

Return to DALE STREET and continue west to find the **Town Hall**, the city's third, designed by John Wood the Younger of Bath and built in 1748-55. The ground floor was originally open and was intended to act as an exchange for merchants to transact business, while the upper floor was used for civic purposes. The building was severely damaged by fire in 1795, after which James Wyatt and John Foster Senior reconstructed the interior, then added the impressive dome on its high drum (1802) and the two-storey portico (1811). The dome is crowned by a Coade stone figure of Britannia, sometimes referred to as Minerva as she lacks trident and shield. The figure, made in 1801-2 by J. C. F. Rossi at a cost of £4295, was fired in pieces and delivered in several shipments; it is covered in 87,000 square inches of gold leaf. The entrance hall has an excellent Minton tile pavement dating from the 1860s, which was restored by H. & R. Johnson during the early 1990s (Fig 118). The design, by George Eyre and reminiscent of his St George's Hall floor although rather less complex, includes blue hand-painted pictorial roundels of Neptune and the Liver birds, and the city's coat of arms.[22] The gentlemen's toilets, in the basement, have lavish ceramic work with a dado, fireplace and columns in green and pale green relief decorated tiles. The ladies toilet merely has a fireplace with yellow lustre glazed tiles.

Head westward along Water Street to THE STRAND and **Tower Buildings** (1906-10, being converted to apartments in 2004), designed by the architect W. Aubrey Thomas, who was also responsible for the Royal Liver Building (1908-11) which stands opposite. Thomas was a highly individual architect whose buildings show stylistic variety and unconventional use of materials; the greyish-white Doulton faience of Tower Buildings was self-cleaning. Its battlements refer the ancient Tower of Liverpool which once stood on the site. Hidden away at the back of this massive block, and facing on to TOWER GARDENS, is **Ma Boyle's PH**, which retains its early 1960s interior ceramic mural by Rhys and Jean Powell; the partly abstract design shows nearby buildings and the Mersey. Rhys and his wife Jean Powell trained at Wallasey School of Art, producing their first tile murals as early as 1954. Opposite the pub is **Reliance House**; in its Tower Gardens side entrance are two colourful mosaic panels of ships (galleons of 1492 and steamers of 1905), both dating from around 1905 and about 15 feet in length. They were salvaged from Colonial House, which formerly stood on the site but was destroyed by enemy action in 1941. Just south along the Strand, with its entrance in JAMES STREET, is **Albion House**, the former White Star Line offices (1895-8, Richard Norman Shaw), its Portland stone and red brick bands a notable landmark. The ground floor general office has a fireproof ceiling - now mostly hidden - of terracotta panels by J. C. Edwards of Ruabon; the building was mentioned in their 1903 catalogue.

Return to the centre via Water Street, Castle Street and HARRINGTON STREET, which once contained John Sadler's printing premises. Sadler and his assistant Guy Green discovered a method of printing on tiles in 1756 and rapidly built up an extensive trade in printing on earthenware tiles and vessels which carried on until shortly after 1780. Harrington Street incorporates the rear elevation of **Cavern Walks**, MATHEW STREET, which stands near the site of the Cavern Club (demolished 1973), the venue which launched the Beatles. The present structure was designed by the Liverpool architect David Backhouse and built in 1982-4. It contains a rebuilding of the Cavern Club in the basement, shops, offices and an internal nine-storey atrium. The slightly tacky post-modern facade includes individually sculpted terracotta reliefs of doves and roses (symbolising peace and love) designed by Cynthia Lennon and made by Hathernware. The terracotta keystone in the archway over the Harrington Street car park entrance depicts a 'gorilla applying lipstick'; the inspiration for this image was the aphorism 'Art is to architecture like lipstick to a gorilla'. The building has a high craft content, with stained glass and cast iron as well as terracotta; this type of detail was then almost revolutionary in the context of plain modernist architecture. More visually interesting is the **Cavern Wall of Fame**, also in Mathew Street and opposite the site of the original Cavern Club. The Wall, in highly fired deep reddish-purple bricks, was opened in 1997 to celebrate the fortieth anniversary of the Cavern Club. It bears the name of every band that played there during 1957-73 as well as some of the bands who played at the club in the 1990s.

Just south along Dorans Lane in LORD STREET is an attractive turn-of-the-century shopfront with white, orange and brown glazed and matt bricks in patterns, as well as much terracotta enrichment including initials in the gable; the architect was Edmund Kirby. Continue east into Church Street; leading north from it is TARLETON STREET and the **Conway Castle** public house. This was formerly a branch of Yates's Wine Lodge. It had been a run-down pub and was bought by Yates's in 1931. The original plan was to 'preserve the old world exterior', but in 1933 consent to rebuild was obtained and a restrained art deco design adopted. The cream slab faience of the facade, with its high relief coloured panel of the castle, was supplied by Shaws of Darwen during 1935-6.[23] Further east along Church Street is the junction with HANOVER STREET; at its far end, turning the corner with Paradise Street, is **Church House** (1885), with multicoloured brick and good red and yellow terracotta decoration including terracotta mullions; the architect was George Enoch Grayson. Opposite is **12 Hanover Street** (1889-90, refurbished in the 1990s), which makes the curve round into Duke Street; the building was designed by Edmund Kirby as offices and warehouses for shipowners Eills & Co, and features rich terracotta detailing from the Ruabon Brick & Terra Cotta Company.[24] Leading east from Church Street is BOLD STREET, where

Coopers has a jazzy interwar faience facade and an interior tile panel by Catherine Smyth dating from 1966. A block east on RENSHAW STREET is the huge, multi-domed former **Central Hall of the Liverpool Wesleyan Mission** (Bradshaw & Gass, 1905, now a nightclub) with much buff terracotta ornament.

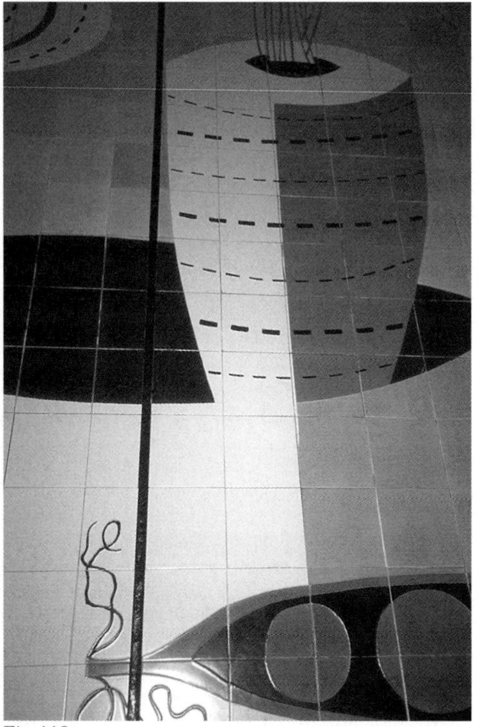

Fig 119.

Almost opposite, occupying the corner site on Renshaw Street and RANELAGH STREET is **Lewis's Store**, rebuilt in the early 1950s after its predecessor was destroyed in a 1941 air raid. On the fifth floor were three restaurants opened in 1953 and decorated in varying degrees of luxuriousness; one, designed by Misha Black, was widely publicised but the largest, the cafeteria, recived little notice at the time. The fifth floor is now used as a storage area and is not open to the public, but the restaurant spaces remain. The best-preserved is the cafeteria, a stunning space complete with original light fittings (a colourful horizontal grid) and tiling by Carter's of Poole; to enter is to step back into the world of the Festival of Britain.[25] The largest area of tiling is a mural, some 65 feet long and 10 feet high, originally situated behind the servery counter (Fig 119). This slip-outlined mural includes hand-printed and hand-painted tiles with strong, colourful imagery of outsize items of food, drink and cooking utensils, and was probably designed by A. B. Read; it appears to be the earliest extant postwar Carter's mural and is in pristine condition. The seating area and supporting columns are also tiled, the columns in a mainly grey and white horizontal-striped design, which is also used on the walls in another colourway, where a single red or yellow stripe is introduced. Another design features a knife and fork, the motif running across two tiles and being mostly black and white (one tile is the reverse of the other) or a more complex red, black and white; there is only one small area of the latter. The tiling has survived very well, with only a few tiles on a single column having become detached; the reverse of one of these patterned tiles carries the date 1953 and the Carter's name.

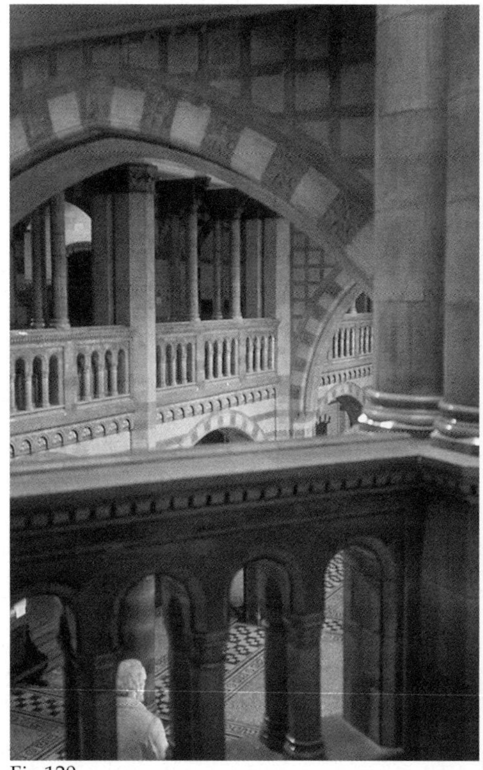

Fig 120.

The **University of Liverpool** campus lies east of Lewis's, up BROWNLOW HILL. Towards the far (eastern) edge of the campus is the **Mathematical Sciences Building** (1959-61, on Peach Street). In its foyer are five reliefs designed by the sculptor John McCarthy and installed in the year the building was opened. Their theme is the essence of mathematics and the material is terrossa ferrata, that is clay strengthened with resin. Each of the panels, a uniform turgid brown in colour, comprises several mostly rectangular segments depicting a mathematical idea in visual terms. The installation is impressively large but visually uninspiring, a result of its colour and perhaps its too-literal imagery.

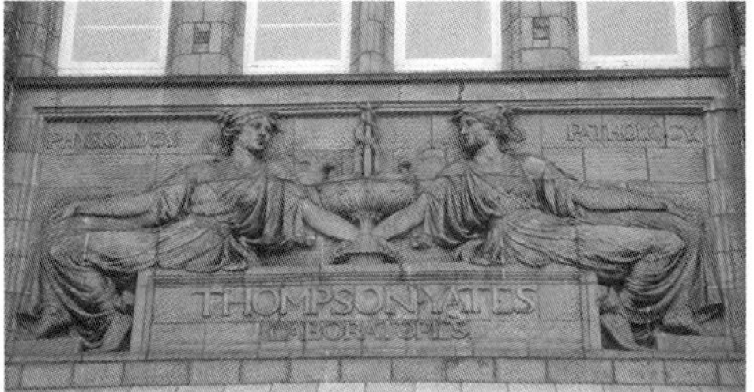

Fig 121.

At the heart of the University Precinct is the landmark tower of the **Victoria Building** on Brownlow Hill, designed by Alfred Waterhouse and built in 1889-92 (Fig 120). The building originally contained a hall, library and lecture rooms as well as the Jubilee Tower, which is resplendent in red brick and bright red Ruabon terracotta; the terracotta detailing on the tower's exterior was modelled by Farmer & Brindley, church furnishers and suppliers of architectural sculpture, and includes a fine coat-of-arms. The interior has a breathtaking Burmantofts faience-clad hall, brown up to dado level and pale green and yellow above in chequerwork and stripes. The hall leads on to an equally fine faience staircase with sturdy brown faience balusters. Across the Quadrangle is the **Thompson Yates Building** (1894-8), also by Waterhouse; on the exterior is an elegant terracotta relief panel dated 1896 and designed by Charles John Allen (1862-1956). Allen worked for Farmer & Brindley during 1879-89 and was instructor of sculpture at Liverpool's School of Architecture and Applied Art from 1894. This large (over 6 feet high and 16 feet long) panel showed flowing female figures representing 'Physiology and Pathology' and was made at the Ruabon terracotta works of J. C. Edwards (Fig 121).[26]

West of the Quadrangle on Brownlow Street is the **Civil Engineering Building** (1958-9, architect E. Maxwell Fry), instantly recognisable by the gigantic concrete mural of the names of engineers covering the whole vertical slab face of the structure. Covering one wall of the foyer is a large enamelled tile mural by the St Ives artist Peter Lanyon (1918-64) entitled 'The Conflict of Man with the Tides and the Sands' (Fig 122). Lanyon, a painter of landscape-inspired abstracts, did many months of investigation into hydraulics before designing the mural, which is a visualisation of research into fluids and solids; an early sketch of the design was shown in the exhibition *Mural Art Today* held at the Victoria and Albert Museum in 1960.[27] Lanyon also had to familiarise himself with the technique of enamelling tiles, the medium having been suggested by the building's architect as one which would stand up to university life better than a conventional canvas.[28] The mural consists of 750 standard six-inch white glazed tiles, which were set out on a 30° ramp to be painted after which they were fired in a small kiln at St Ives. Many of the resulting tiles were found to be unusable due to cracking, shattering and poor paint quality; the work was eventually completed over six months during 1959-60.[29] The mural is strongly coloured and the design very powerful, but the dull quality of the low-fired enamelled surface detracts from its impact.

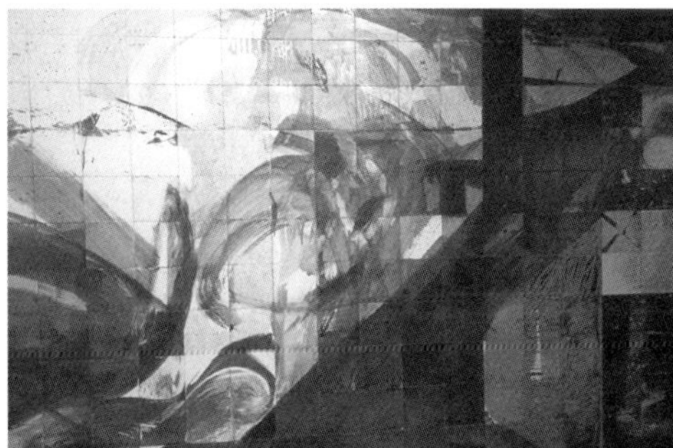
Fig 122.

At the north end of Brownlow Street, on PEMBROKE PLACE, is the former Liverpool Royal Infirmary (1886-9, architect Alfred Waterhouse), to which a new outpatients' department was added in 1909-11 (architect James Francis Doyle); its centrepiece was a galleried hall lit from above and clad in cream and deep green Craven Dunnill tiling. The hospital closed in 1978 and was vacated completely in 1981. Several development proposals were put forward but eventually the University of Liverpool and the North West

Regional Health Authority joined forces in 1992 and came up with a scheme which retained all the Waterhouse buildings along with Doyle's outpatients' department.

The buildings, which were in an advanced state of decay, were renovated from 1994, the former outpatients' department becoming part of the University of Liverpool's **Foresight Centre**. Restoration of the galleried hall involved the construction of a new entrance arch in MDF, which was then painted by John Hogg, a local sculptor, to resemble tiling. Some moulded plaster replacements were made for damaged tiles, while substitute ceramic tiles were obtained from H. & R. Johnson; the original tiles were 12mm thick, whereas the Johnson replacements were mostly 5 or 6mm. The large number of different sizes and shapes of tiles in the building made restoration difficult, and resin moulds were made for several of these specials. Overall, the restoration is certainly a visual success, giving an impression of a totally ceramic-clad room, although the pre-existing loss of the whole height of the main hall, due to the insertion of upper-level rooms, was unfortunate. Even though ceramics were not used throughout due to the prohibitive cost, the renovated building is now popular and so distinctive as to be remembered by those who use it. This one is not for purists, however. The restoration of Waterhouse's neighbouring Infirmary **Chapel** was much more successful. It has a Moorish feel, with large areas of grey, blue and green relief tiling and a roof supported by a series of circular cross-section columns. There were faced in unusual triangular tiles which curve three ways; replacements for some were made by Johnson's.

Back on PEMBROKE PLACE, note the green and yellow tiled facade of **Galkoff's** kosher butcher's shop, complete with Hebrew lettering. Nearby is the **Dental Hospital** (1965-9); in its entrance hall is a large, low-relief abstract ceramic mural by Rhys and Jean Powell. Finally, and slightly west, on the corner of LONDON ROAD and Hart Street, is the elaborate bright red terracotta form of the **NatWest Bank** (1899, W. Hesketh & Co), erected for the Liverpool Furnishing Company. The terracotta was supplied by Jabez Thompson of Northwich, makers of bricks, chimney pots and ridge tiles as well as terracotta of all hues.

To explore the area south of the city centre, begin at the **Metropolitan Cathedral of Christ the King** (1962-7, architect Sir Frederick Gibberd), MOUNT PLEASANT; in the Lady Chapel is a statue of the *Madonna and Child* by Robert Brumby (b1934) which dates from the 1960s. The basement below the main foyer has a buff and brown tiled floor in a geometric design by David Atkins, who was also responsible for the layout of the marble flooring of the Cathedral itself. Then south to HOPE STREET and the **Philharmonic Hotel**, designed by Walter W. Thomas and built around 1898-1900. Its interior is one of the most lavish in Britain, with lashings of mahogany, copper, plaster and stained glass, although little in the way of ceramics apart from in the fairly decorative gentlemen's toilets. Just south-east is the **R. C. Church of St Philip Neri** (1914-20) in CATHARINE STREET; its richly decorative, domed interior includes several mosaics. Chinatown lies to the west, past the Anglican Cathedral, and centres on NELSON STREET. Its **Chinese Arch** (completed 2000) has ceramic bronze-yellow roof tiles with figures and animals worked into them; the arch was designed and made in China by the Shanghai Linyi Garden Building Co Ltd, and erected in Liverpool by Chinese craftspeople (Fig 123).[30] The nearby **Golden Yuen** restaurant sports a large Chinese-themed tile panel.

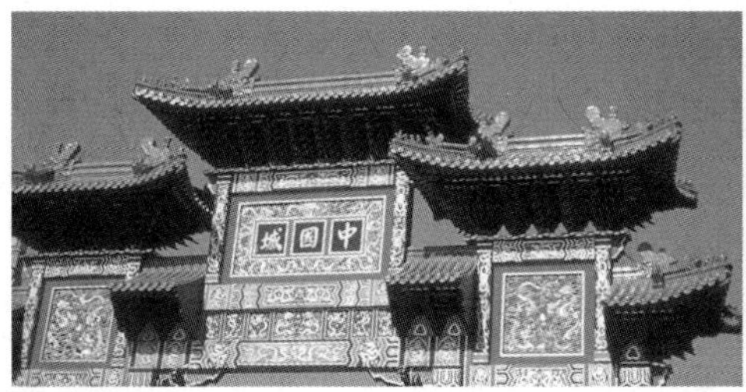

Fig 123.

But the great ceramic surprise of the Cathedral area stands slightly further to the south: the mighty red terracotta towers and stack of the **Mersey Brewery** in STANHOPE STREET (Fig 124). Like many Victorian breweries this is a complex structure erected over several years, although bright red Ruabon terracotta and red brick covers most of its exterior. The rear section was begun for the brewer Robert Cain around 1875 and completed in 1887; the terracotta bears repeats of one of Cain's symbols, hops above five crosses (a unicorn was also used by Cain's). The front section was completed in 1902, and its interior faced throughout with glazed bricks, all now overpainted apart from those in the top floor hop store, which is a wonderful showpiece. Its wall surfaces are completely of glazed brick, basically in white but with a pale blue dado and arched openings picked out in brown. The brewery was sold to Higson's in 1923, and the new owners changed the terracotta work to include their name; this can easily be seen from the side elevation where plain bricks have been substituted for the previous lettering. But Higson's could not get rid of all the Cain's symbolism, as three unicorns remain, one over the gateway and two high up on the facade. These red terracotta unicorns, which must have been very difficult to make, are beautifully preserved with their horns intact. There is also good terracotta lettering for the Grapes Inn, the brewery tap, which forms one corner of the brewery. Altogether this is an outstanding building, which still performs its original function.

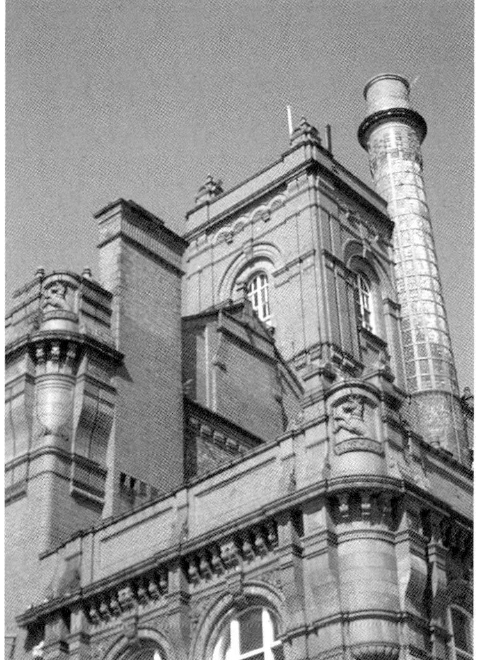

Fig 124.

Aigburth

St Mary's Church, ST MARY'S ROAD, Grassendale was built in 1853-4 and designed by the architect Arthur Hill Holme; the church has a Minton tile pavement.

Anfield

St Columba's Church (1932), PINEHURST ROAD was designed in art deco style (hence its nickname the 'Anfield Odeon') by the Liverpool architect Bernard Miller. It was built from small, handmade grey bricks, a favourite of Miller's, and roofed in bright green pantiles. Inside are several works by the Liverpool potter Julia Carter Preston, who first collaborated with Miller when she was a student during the 1950s.[31] The wall plaques in the sanctuary, the door to the aumbry in the Lady Chapel, and the bowl of the font and its ewer were all carried out in sgraffito by Julia Carter Preston, who also designed one of stained glass windows. The plaques commemorate the golden and diamond jubilees of the church, while a further plaque installed during 2002 marks the seventieth anniversary of the consecration of the church, as well as its recent restoration. The latter plaque is located in the entrance hall, which links the church with its new community centre.

Edge Hill

Liverpool Women's Hospital, CROWN STREET opened in 1995; its wide range of artworks includes three ceramic installations by Gerald Buchanan dating from around 2002. The lozenge-shaped 'Rock Pool' and seven lancet-shaped panels can be found in the central corridors of the building, while a further eight lozenge-shaped abstract panels hang in the rear entrance. All use brightly coloured glazes in mainly greens and blues, along with small glass insets; the overall theme is water. To the east in SMITHDOWN ROAD, opposite Toxteth Park Cemetery, is the **Royal Hotel** with ornate exterior tilework by Maw & Co, mostly in floral relief patterns including a pomegranate design which appeared in the firm's 1883 catalogue.

Garston

Bryant & May's match factory (architects Mewes & Davis) on Speke Road is an art deco structure dating from the 1920s; it has a colourful frieze of six-inch tiles running along its entire length between the ground and first floor windows. The factory closed in 1994 and was partly refurbished as offices - the **Match Works** - around 2001 by Urban Splash.

Mossley Hill

Sudley House, MOSSLEY HILL, was built in the early 1800s and was the home of the shipping magnate and art collector George Holt and his family. In 1944 his daughter Emma Holt bequeathed the house and the collection of paintings assembled by her father to the City of Liverpool. Sudley is now part of the National Museums and Galleries on Merseyside, and houses a unique survival, a Victorian picture collection in its original domestic setting. There are several tiled fireplaces: in the Library fireplace are panels depicting Music and Painting by W. B. Simpson, while other fireplaces have (mainly Dutch) tin-glazed earthenware tiles and the Classical Ladies series by Minton China Works.

Speke

Speke Hall (NT), which dates from about 1530, stands on the north bank of the Mersey at the end of The Walk. It is home to a large Delft tile panel conserved in 1999 at the NMGM Conservation Centre in Liverpool. On the far side of Speke in Heathgate Avenue is **St Ambrose R. C. Church**, designed by Weightman & Bullen and built in 1959-61. Its rectangular openwork tower is as dramatic as its lofty interior, which houses Stations of the Cross (1960) by the artist Adam Kossowski. The colourful, unglazed ceramic plaques are all about three feet square.

Toxteth

The **Princes Road Synagogue** was opened in 1874 and designed by the Audsley brothers, the architects George Ashdown Audsley (1838-1925) and William James Audsley (1833-1907), who practiced as partners in Liverpool from 1860. Its vestibule is floored by an excellent geometric tile pavement whose layout is based around repeats of the six-pointed Star of David, while a strip of brown tiles bearing white Hebrew lettering - 'Blessed Art Thou Who Enter Here' - forms the border between the vestibule and the synagogue proper (Fig 125). Inside, the sumptuous Moorish decoration, restored after damage by fire in 1978, is the best remaining example of the decorative work of the Audsleys, who were also leading pattern designers. The slightly earlier restoration by the Audsleys of Bebington parish church in Cheshire (reopened 1872) featured Prussian-made tiles designed by the architects.[32]

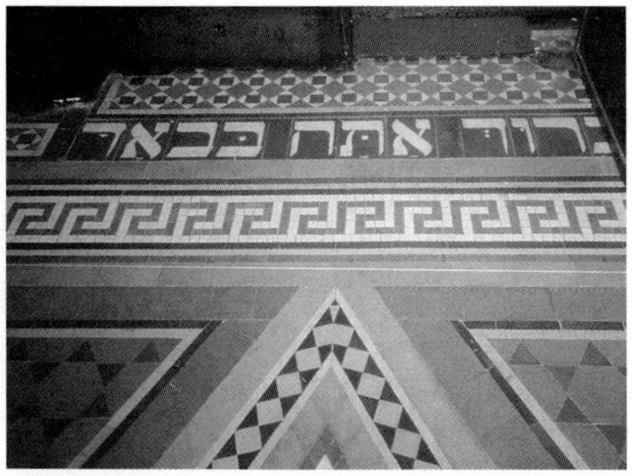

Fig 125.

Next door to the Synagogue at 5 Princes Road is **Streatlam Tower** (1871), a Scottish Baronial-style pile designed by the Audsleys with an interesting (if small) encaustic tile pavement in the circular entrance hall. Just north of the house is **St Margaret's Church** (1868-9, G. E. Street); its rich anglo-catholic interior, which includes an opus sectile reredos, was undergoing renovation in 2003.

Tue Brook

The Public Baths on Lister Drive opened in 1903; it was one of a number of baths and washhouses built in the city around the turn of the century. The baths closed in the early 1980s, but after six years of neglect restoration began and the building was eventually reopened by businessman Bob Allen in 1992 as the **Lister Drive Fisheries and Pet Centre**. Nearly 2,000 koi carp now swim contentedly in the thirty-metre pool, while songbirds inhabit the changing cubicles and all around are pet accessories, crammed into every nook and cranny of the superb Pilkington's faience and tile interior, shown in the firm's trade literature and a precursor of Manchester's Victoria Baths (see below).[33] The facade is in unremarkable red brick, but the entrance hall is all green and yellow faience, with a good green faience stair ascending to the rear. Repeats of the *Fish and Leaf* tile, designed by the architect C. F. A. Voysey for Pilkington's, in two shades of green feature on the tile and faience arcade surrounding the pool, while more fish appear as motifs in the stained glasswork.[34] Low lights, glistening tiles, reflections from the water and the presence of the fish, from regal carp to mere goldfish, make for a uniquely atmospheric setting.

West Derby

Inside **St James Church**, Mill Lane is an impressive war memorial which includes an image of the *Lusitania*; it is one of only two such memorials in the country to depict the liner. This unusual memorial, which measures around 15 feet high by 6 feet wide, is made from a glazed ceramic, possibly opus sectile, and glass mosaic. It records the dead of the First World War in a roll of honour topped by a female head, and includes images of a soldier and sailor as well as the liner; beneath is an additional section recording names of the fallen in the Second World War. Its maker is unknown; it is not in the style of Powell's of Whitefriars, who made many opus sectile memorials. The memorial is in poor condition and the church hopes to be able to fund its conservation.

Woolton

Twenty-four glazed ceramic relief panels were made by the artist Adam Kossowski in 1962 for the courtyard of **St Francis Xavier's College**, BEACONSFIELD ROAD. They are all about six feet in height and eighteen inches wide and their designs represent religion (ten panels), art (seven panels) and science (seven panels). The three themes also have different combinations of glaze colours.

LYTHAM ST ANNE'S

The town of Lytham St Anne's stretches round the Fylde coast from the suburb of St Anne's in the north-west through Fairhaven to Lytham at its eastern end. The main road running through the town, parallel to but a little inland from the coast, is Clifton Drive.

Fairhaven

Fairhaven Congregational Church (now United Reformed Church), CLIFTON DRIVE SOUTH and Ansdell Road South, is often referred to as the White Church because of its striking white faience exterior; a 90 feet high domed, octagonal campanile adds to the exotic effect. It was built in 1904-11 and designed in vaguely Byzantine style by the architects Briggs, Wolstenholme and Thornley of Blackburn, who were also responsible for the Palatine Bank, Manchester, put up in 1908-9. Its banking hall had a remarkable interior faced with white Doulton Carraraware and including several pictorial tile panels. It was not Doulton, however, who supplied the faience for the White Church but the Middleton Fireclay Works, founded as an offshoot of the Leeds Fireclay Co Ltd in 1909; the faience, tradename Ceramo, has already required substantial restoration and is still in poor condition. Inside the church is unusual stained glass by the Lancaster firm Abbott & Co, featuring a portrait of Oliver Cromwell and showing his part in the history of the reformed tradition, as well as attractive arts and crafts style furnishings.

St Anne's

The St Anne's Hotel used to stand on ST ANDREW'S ROAD NORTH, close to St Anne's railway station; it has been replaced by the Crescent PH but the original basement bar, once known as Burlington Bertie's, still remains as a nightclub by the name of **Tiles**. The bar, which can be seen from the street, is an excellent example of complete fitting out by Craven Dunnill, and includes a good geometric tiled floor, moulded wall tiling (some plain, some flowers and patterns) and an exceedingly long ceramic barfront in one of the firm's two standard designs. It is identical to the barfront at the Red Lion, Erdington, Birmingham and in colour is mostly yellow, brown, green and pink, with some floral motifs.

MANCHESTER

Manchester is not such a ceramic city as Birmingham or Leeds. The only local tile factory - Pilkington's, whose works are four miles north-west of the city centre at Clifton Junction, Pendlebury - was established near the turn of the century and quarries producing durable stone were nearer to the city centre than any major terracotta works. But two suburban churches provide significant examples of the early use of terracotta: Holy Trinity Church, Platt, Rusholme (1844-6), one of Edmund Sharpe's 'pot churches', albeit something of a false start, and Holy Name of Jesus, Chorlton on Medlock (1869-71), one of several 1860s churches where experimentation with the material resumed. Manchester saw many terracotta and faience buildings erected in the Edwardian era, with Burmantofts faience in particular coming to the fore as cladding for the city's mini-skyscrapers; in addition, tiled entrance halls from this period are almost ten-a-penny. The otherwise unspectacular **Albert House** (1903) for instance, in BLOOM STREET just west of Piccadilly Station, has a lovely glazed faience foyer in deep lime green and rich turquoise. This description follows a broadly circular route around the city, beginning and ending at Piccadilly railway station, and is followed by a listing of suburban locations.[35]

From platform level at Manchester Piccadilly, descend through the brick-arched bowels of the station to the Metrolink platforms and thence the pedestrian exit; once across London Road, the towers of WHITWORTH STREET beckon. The first of the monumental structures which inhabit this grand terracotta canyon is the former **Police and Fire Station** (1901-6, architects Woodhouse, Willoughby and Langham). Here Renaissance forms are modelled on a Baroque scale with enormous sculptural figures and corner cupolas; the buff terracotta and darker brown faience is by Burmantofts, the various symbolic pictorial panels - on judicial and firefighting themes - being modelled by J. J. Millson of the Manchester firm of architectural sculptors.[36]

Next in line is the Main Building of the **University of Manchester** (1895-1902, architects Spalding and Cross). Another behemoth, its exterior is lavishly endowed with tawny-red Burmantofts terracotta panels with Renaissance motifs. Inside, stairs with terracotta balustrades lead down to the main hall, which has large, square cross-section terracotta columns ending in massive brackets, and there is yet more terracotta on the main staircase at the rear. The architects Bradshaw, Gass and Hope, who made extensive use of architectural ceramics through the Edwardian and interwar periods, designed the extension (behind the Main Building) in 1927; its red brick and terracotta must have appeared quite outlandish by the time the block was completed in 1957. Continue a few blocks west to find **Asia House** (1906-9, architect I. R. E. Birkett, now apartments) at 82 PRINCESS STREET; the warehouse's complex of entrance passages are lined with much green faience while a fabulous relief-tiled frieze of art nouveau trees and fruits runs up the stairwell.

Still further west, past the junction with Princess Street, is a series of warehouses built for Lloyd's Packing Warehouses Ltd, a firm which built some of Manchester's largest warehouses in the first three decades of the twentieth century, before the cotton trade began to decline. Lloyd's offered space to individual merchants and supplied the necessary loading and packing machinery. The Blackburn architect Harry S. Fairhurst moved his practice to Manchester in 1905 after gaining his first Lloyd's commission, and went on to build most of their warehouses.[37] Those in Whitworth Street, with their facings of Burmantofts faience and their steel frames, are probably the nearest English equivalent to the skyscrapers being built in New York and Chicago just after the turn of the century. Fairhurst designed **Lancaster House**, with its glazed terracotta wedding-cake style tower on the Princess Street corner, in 1907-10; the 150 feet high tower made the warehouse the tallest building in Manchester. Just beyond is **India House** (1905-9, also by Fairhurst) with its yellowy-buff vitreous glazed terracotta and red brick, while opposite is Fairhurst's **Bridgewater House** (1912-14), clad in Burmantofts Lefco. When complete, Bridgewater House was the tallest building in Britain and the largest packing house in the world. At this point, a diversion south into CHARLES STREET (via Princess Street) will bring you to the **Lass O'Gowrie**, a pub built on almost as grand a scale as the nearby warehouses. It has a facade (probably late Victorian) of rich dark brown faience, mostly plain but with good lettering and improbably tall doorcases.

Return to Whitworth Street for its culmination, the former Refuge Assurance Building, now the **Palace Hotel**, much of it clad in dark red Doulton terracotta.[38] The massive towered structure was built in three phases: firstly the Oxford Street and Whitworth Street corner (1891-5, Alfred Waterhouse), then a second building on Oxford Street (1910-12, Paul Waterhouse) including the tower above the main entrance, and finally the third element on Whitworth Street (1932, Stanley Birkett). Burmantofts wares decorate the interior of the first building. Its corner entrance is now closed but the excellent golden-brown, cream and green faience arcaded vestibule is still visible, and there is a miniature turreted castle - symbolising a refuge - in terracotta on the facade above. After the death of Alfred Waterhouse in 1905 his practice turned to J. C. Edwards of Ruabon for terracotta supplies, and ceramics for the building's interior decorative scheme were supplied by Edwards along with Burmantofts and Doulton. The main entrance courtyard is in buff glazed material and parts of the slightly disappointing interior are richly decorated with cream, red and green faience.[39]

A little south of the Palace Hotel, and across OXFORD STREET, is the former Regal Cinema (1929-30, architects Pendleton & Dickenson), now the **Dancehouse Theatre**. Its classical buff faience facade has orange highlights and the letters 'EN' for Emmanual Nove, for whom the cinema was built. Turn north again to find **J. & J. Shaw's warehouse** in NEW WAKEFIELD STREET, just before the railway bridge; its fine ceramic doorcase incorporates the date 1924 and the firm's name. The manufacturer was probably Carter's of Poole, to judge from the distinctive blue glaze and the style of lettering. Return to Oxford Street, turning left to find the **Palace Theatre** (1891), its facade of pale yellow Shaws of Darwen faience being an addition of 1956 by architects Wilfred Thorpe and H. Hirst Smith. A close inspection of the facade reveals that the Shaws 'Sunshine' mottled faience has a rich variety of surface patterning, a type of finish popular in the fifties. Frank Matcham's 1896 internal redecoration (not in a publicly accessible area) included extensive glazed tiling featuring plaques of nymphs. The faience cladding is described as 'ugly beige tiles' in Clare Hartwell's Pevsner *Manchester* (2001), while Parkinson-Bailey's *Manchester* (2000) suggests the facade looks 'like a public lavatory'. Clearly appreciation of twentieth century architectural ceramics is still lacking amongst some architectural historians.[40]

Across Oxford Street is **Churchgate House**, all red brick striped with buff glazed terracotta; it was built in 1896-8 (architect J. Gibbons Sankey) as warehouses and offices for the Bolton firm of textile manufacturers Tootal, Broadhurst and Lee. Briefly left into GREAT BRIDGEWATER STREET for **Canada House** (now offices), a packing warehouse built in 1905-9 (architects W. & G. Higginbottom) with acres of shining, ornate buff faience. Just beyond is the **Peveril of the Peak** public house, a little ceramic jewel on a triangular site, refaced around 1900 with much yellow glazed brick in two shades with some relief patterning. Its completely ceramic exterior includes good lettering, green faience window surrounds and colourful relief-tiled doorcases. Further along, near the Bridgewater Hall, is the **Britons Protection**, a pub remodelled in the 1920s with an unusual amount of tiling in the bar and corridors. Return to OXFORD STREET for all that remains of **Prince's Building** (1903, I. R. E. Birkett), the facade in shiny dark buff terracotta with a scalloped roofline, and the nearby Picture House (1911, now **McDonalds**), an early cinema for Provincial Cinematograph Theatres by architects Naylor and Sale, with pretty buff terracotta dressings.

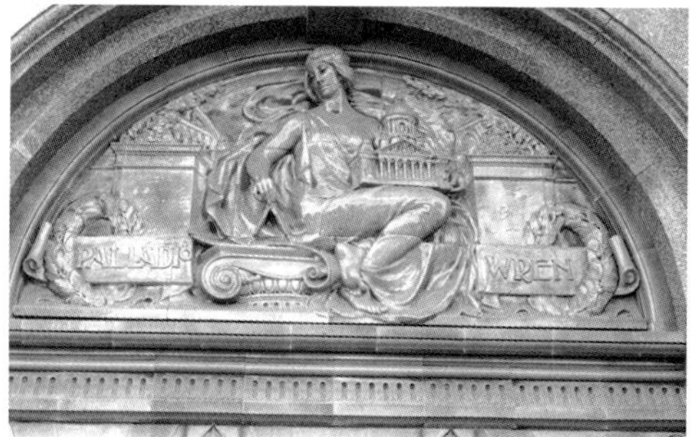

Fig 126.

Oxford Street runs into Peter Street where the **Midland Hotel** (now Crowne Plaza), a gargantuan essay in terracotta and faience, stands on the south side of ST PETER'S SQUARE (Fig 126). This massive block, in red brick and Leeds Fireclay's brown vitreous faience (even the chimney pots are glazed), was built for the Midland Railway in 1898-1903 to designs by their architect Charles Trubshaw (1841-1917), an enthusiast for terracotta which can also be seen on his slightly earlier London Road station in Leicester. The Midland Hotel provided accommodation in the form of 400 bedrooms for the adjacent Central Station (1880, now GMEX) to which it was linked by a glazed canopy. The hotel was the counterpart of the Grand Hotel at London's St Pancras Station, where Midland trains from Manchester terminated. Unlike St Pancras, the Central Station never had a proper frontage; wooden offices were erected as a temporary measure, but after the hotel was put up across the street, the ramshackle offices continued to disfigure the great trainshed, which closed in 1969.

The frontages of the Midland Hotel use French Renaissance forms, such as pediments and arcades, but worked to a huge scale with a range of figurative sculpture including several of the Midland Railway's wyverns on the north facade. On the Lower Mosley Street side are four high relief semicircular panels in golden-brown Burmantofts faience signed by E. C. Spruce, showing female figures representing the Arts; architecture is illustrated by a figure holding a pair of dividers over an ionic capital and holding in her left hand a Renaissance building. Along with a stained glass window, these tympana are the last vestiges of the hotel's first floor concert hall, which was reconstructed to provide more bedrooms in 1922. On the Mount Street side is a pitch-roofed and double-arched secondary entrance, again in ornate brown faience, which leads to a spiralling stairwell lined with unusual, probably continental, glittering white rectangular tiles with a delicate floral motif. This area was originally the entrance to the German Restaurant. In the St Peter's Square entrance is a red terracotta wall plaque (1999) by the sculptor Lynda Addison depicting the meeting of Charles Rolls and Henry Royce at the hotel in 1904.

Northward across St Peter's Square is the **Town Hall** (1868-77, architect Alfred Waterhouse), a hollow triangle in plan with its main entrance on ALBERT SQUARE. The magnificent interiors have a complexity in part resulting from the triangular site, but also from the use of a wide range of decorative materials and finishes, including tiles and terracotta. The main entrance and the waiting hall are dominated by a variety of stone finishes, but the walls of the waiting hall have a six feet high dado of tiles in two colours, capped by a stone moulding and carried up to terracotta arches. Some of the ground and first floor corridors have a groined roof covered by ribs of moulded terracotta manufactured by Gibbs & Canning of Tamworth; the walls down to within about five feet of the floor are also of terracotta, in blue and buff bands, below which is a dado of glazed tiles. The design and colour of the tile dados varies throughout the building, giving identity to the important but otherwise rather gloomy circulation areas. The buff and pale blue colours of the terracotta supplied by Gibbs & Canning present a fascinating antecedent for the facade of Waterhouses's Natural History Museum, completed in 1881. It seems likely that the architect's experience of working with Gibbs & Canning, and in achieving a blue colour through the use of a cobalt slip over the buff body at Manchester, gave him the confidence to use this supplier for the polychromatic terracotta on the facade and the interior of the Museum.

Alfred Waterhouse is known to have designed tiles for Craven Dunnill, and these probably include the encaustics of the Town Hall's first floor corridor and possibly the more elaborate designs in the reception room chimneypiece. There is a very wide range of designs and forms in the chimneypiece tiles of the state rooms and mayoral apartments. Some of the best tiles are in the banqueting hall, in blue and white colours and depicting fruit; the nearest equivalent to these designs are those in the Poynter room at the Victoria and Albert Museum.[41] The **Town Hall Extension** (1934-8, E. Vincent Harris) stands to the south of the Town Hall, fronting on to St Peter's Square. Its facing is mostly of sandstone but there are decorative faience panels by Shaws of Darwen below the top storey windows; these were mentioned in the firm's list of contracts executed during 1935-6. Their designs, complex tree-like forms, seem rather too detailed for distant viewing.

Return to PETER STREET for a contrast to both the gothic Town Hall and slightly overblown Midland Hotel, the gaudy facade of the YMCA Building (now **St George's House**), which is almost unique in its exploitation of the decorative possibilities of faience in a modernistic manner. Designed by Woodhouse, Corbett and Dean and built in 1907-11, it represents an attempt to combine a structure of reinforced concrete (the first in the city) with appropriate facings by Burmantofts. The faience blocks and slabs were fixed directly to the reinforced concrete, which was used for both frame and walls. The ground floor is of deep chocolate coloured material, rusticated with rounded corners appropriate for moulded rather than carved material. Brown and buff material is used for the upper floors, with the decoration at second floor level being in vertical strips of spiralling acanthus set between plain blocks of faience. When the building was converted to offices in 1993 by Austin Strzala Turner and Ove Arup & Partners, many faience blocks with distinctive spirals of fruit and vegetation were lost, as incursions were made to treat rusted reinforcements. However, replacement blocks by Shaws of Darwen proved a good match for the colour and gleaming surface of the originals.[42]

Turn north now to head for Victoria Station, which can be reached by Metrolink tram as an alternative to the walk along Deansgate. The tram route takes in the HIGH STREET and the **Arndale Centre** (1972-9, Wilson & Womersley), once the largest covered shopping mall in Europe, which was damaged but not completely destroyed by a terrorist bomb in 1996. The Arndale's tower and external walls were faced with pre-cast panels of Shaws Twintiles in a deep buff, almost bronze, colour. Twintiles, manufactured during the 1960s and 1970s, were 9 inch by 3 inch tiles made specifically to be used on a concrete surface, either prefabricated or in situ. The vast tiled walls of the Arndale almost inevitably gave rise to its nickname, 'the largest public lavatory in the world', and its 1998-9 refurbishment banished tiling from the most popular pedestrian routes.

The walking route to Victoria Station continues along Peter Street, passing the former Albert Memorial Hall, a methodist hall built in 1910 for the local Wesleyan Mission. The exterior includes some decent Burmantofts buff terracotta detailing, while the fine art nouveau tiled foyer seems quite appropriate for its present use as **Brannigans**, a public house; the building underwent conversion in 1999. Turn right into DEANSGATE, coming almost immediately to the red brick and buff terracotta **Onward Buildings** at 205-9 Deansgate. It was designed by the architect Charles Heathcote, best known for his lavish bank interiors, and built in 1903-5 for a wealthy temperance organisation, the Band of Hope. No expense was spared on the Onward Buildings interior (no public access), which includes an unusual top floor meeting room with completely tiled walls and faience-lined porthole windows. The dado, about nine feet in height, is of relief tiles in shades of green, possibly made by Pilkington's; they record the names of towns throughout Lancashire, beginning with Accrington, presumably wherever the temperance societies had a presence.

At the crossing with John Dalton Street is the **Sawyer's Arms** pub, its elaborate early twentieth century red and yellow faience facade including grotesque capital heads. Slightly west on BRIDGE STREET is the former **Manchester and Salford Street Children Mission** (1896, W. & G. Higginbottom); its pretty green and cream faience facade has good lettering and panels of children's heads. Return to Deansgate, turning left then right along King Street to reach CROSS STREET and **Mr Thomas's** pub (formerly the Chop House), its rear facade refaced in buff terracotta in 1901. Inside is an unusual green-tiled archway dividing two rear rooms. To the east at 10 NORFOLK STREET, on the corner with Brown Street, is the former **Palatine Bank** (1908-9, architects Briggs, Wolstenholme and Thornley), recognisable by its massive circular towers. The street is now something of a backwater and the bank's exterior gives no clue as to the existence of three superb Doulton pictorial panels in the domed banking hall; they came to light during the building's conversion to offices in 1991-3. This remarkable interior had walls faced in Doulton's Carraraware, into which were set, at a high level, three semicircular painted tile panels, each about ten feet wide and five feet in height. The panels, by the Doulton designer Arthur E. Pearce (who worked for Doulton of Lambeth during 1873-1930, becoming chief draughtsman at the Lambeth Pottery) and the artist John Henry McLennan, are on the themes of shipping, trading and the arts. The basic form of the banking hall was retained during the conversion work, with the addition of a high-level circular walkway to allow access to the panels.[43]

At the north end of Cross Street is EXCHANGE SQUARE and the former Corn Exchange, rebuilt after damage from the 1996 bomb blast as **The Triangle** shopping mall. The original building, which was put up in two phases, 1889-90 and 1904-14, had a large interior tiling scheme of which a substantial amount survives. At the south (Hanging Ditch) entrance plain, highly glazed wall tiles, mostly in shades of green, can still be seen running upward through several floors of the stairwell, with some relief tiles on the upper floors.

A block north, past the glass block of Urbis, is **Victoria Station** on VICTORIA STATION APPROACH. With Piccadilly Station having been rebuilt and Central Station closed, Manchester Victoria is the only station to survive in much of its original form. It is something of a conglomeration, partly due to the fact that it was located adjacent to Exchange Station which is now closed; it was also altered during the 1990s to provide for the Metrolink trams. Victoria Station was given a lengthy stone frontage block in 1909 when the Lancashire & Yorkshire Railway employed William Dawes to bring some order to a rather rambling collection of platforms and offices. Much of the concourse is still lined with glazed bricks, with faience blocks being used as signs for the offices. Other signs, such as for the lavatories, are executed in gold and turquoise mosaic, and the ladies toilet has interior tiling featuring a relief of the Tudor rose. One wall of the station, in the double-height opening to Victoria Station Approach, is almost completely covered with a railway map showing the routes of the Lancashire & Yorkshire Railway. The lines (in red) appear to have been painted on white glazed bricks rather than fired into the glaze. The most impressive ceramic feature of the station is the refreshment room which was originally the first class restaurant and grill room. Above its glazed bricks is a cornice of vitreous buff faience with mosaic lettering and sweeping acanthus decoration in green and white; the interior is also highly decorative.

To return to Piccadilly, head east along HANOVER STREET, passing the ice blue and cream Baroque faience facade of **Holyoake House** (architect F. E. L. Harris), built in 1911 for the Co-operative Union, one of several Co-op buildings in this area. Continue south-eastward, eventually crossing TIB STREET after about a quarter mile. Centred on Tib Street is a **public art trail** including pavement poetry, ceramic birds perched on window ledges (a reminder of eighteenth-century bird sellers) and new ceramic street signs - white on blue for east-west streets and blue on white for north-south - which help give the district its own identity. The artworks continue at 1-5 DORSEY STREET, where small blue and gold ceramic insets decorate a new building, and along VILLAGE WAY, where tiles depict historical images. Finally there are ceramic murals in FOUNDRY LANE - Mr Tib (1997) by Stephen Dixon, in glazed stoneware and reduction-fired red earthenware, occupies a building niche - and on the SILVER JUBILEE WALK and Tib Street corner, whose gable end displays Duck and Potts Mill (1997), a ceramic mural by Liz Scrine who based the design, which shows the ghost of the old mill, on textile patterns. At the top of Tib Street, on the east corner with SWAN STREET, is an interwar office building with an excellent white faience facade including green decorative elements; just west, at 8 and 10 Swan Street (the latter the former office of the print union NATSOPA), are two more interwar buildings with mostly yellow faience facades and egyptianate detailing.

Slightly east on OLDHAM STREET is the **Castle Hotel**, a small pub with a brown faience facade dating from around 1897 and including white 'Castle Hotel' lettering with an emphatic full stop; the entrance mosaic shows a castle while a colourful, curved faience barfront survives inside.

Nearby is the overpowering interwar white faience facade of the former **Dobbins** store. Turn left into Dale Street, heading towards Piccadilly, but for an interesting diversion go left into Port Street then right into HILTON STREET; here **Hilton House**, a 1960s office block, displays prodigious areas of bluish-purple twintiles, as facing on its Port Street facade and as a huge rectangular mural on its Tariff Street side. Continue east along Tariff Street, crossing the Rochdale Canal to see, standing alone in LAYSTALL STREET, the former warehouse (1880, M. Seanor) of **Armstrong's**, a firm of terracotta and firebrick manufacturers established in 1838, whose works stood near the site of Piccadilly Station.[44] Not surprisingly, its facade has much terracotta enrichment.

Return to DALE STREET; near the Rochdale Canal Basin is **Langley Buildings** (1909, R. Argile) in gleaming brown faience, bloated neoclassical in style with much ornate decoration. Take Lena Street to reach PICCADILLY; on the corner, at **107 Piccadilly**, is the former office and warehouse of Sparrow, Hardwick & Co (1899, Charles Heathcote) with an open tiled entrance in typical Burmantofts colours, pale browns and greens, including a good shell niche. Almost opposite is the flamboyant red brick, buff terracotta and olive green faience facade of the **Malmaison Hotel**, which incorporates Joshua Hoyle's steel-framed warehouse (1904, Charles Heathcote). Piccadilly Station is straight ahead along Station Approach.

Ancoats

The **Marble Arch** at 73 ROCHDALE ROAD (the junction with Gould Street), less than a mile north of the city centre, was built in 1888 for the local brewers, McKenna's Harpurhey Brewery. McKenna's were taken over by Walker & Homfrays of Salford in 1903, and the pub went through further changes of ownership before closing in the early 1980s and being sold off, by which time its interior was a mass of plasterboarding. It eventually reopened and the interior was slowly restored, a process which took until the late 1990s and revealed a magnificent ceramic interior. The pub, which was designed by architects Darbyshire & Smith, has a sloping, patterned mosaic floor over huge cellars, which extend beyond the confines of the pub and were used for maturing casks of McKenna's porter. The walls are of glazed brick in shades of brown, with a top-level frieze of floral relief tiles bearing the words 'Gin', Porter', 'Brandy' and so forth. The unusual jack-arched ceiling has exposed cast-iron beams supported on faience-clad brackets; Darbyshire was an expert in fireproof construction.

Ardwick

The **Apollo Theatre** (1938, architects Peter Cummings and A. M. Irvine), originally a 'super cinema', STOCKPORT ROAD, is now a concert hall. Its modernist white faience facade has rounded front corners and some art deco ornament.

Chorlton on Medlock

Just south of the city centre, on OXFORD ROAD at its junction with Grosvenor Street, is the neoclassical green and white faience facade of the former **Grosvenor Picture Palace** (1913-15, now a pub); its canted corner tower, open at top and bottom, is a minor landmark. The cinema was designed by the architect Percy Hothersall and said to be the largest outside London; it seated almost 1,000. Hothersall went on to design the Piccadilly 'super cinema' (opposite Piccadilly Gardens) in 1922, which was faced in Doulton's Carraraware; this closed prior to the Second World War although part of the facade remains.

Across Oxford Street is Grosvenor Square and the campus of Manchester Metropolitan University. On the south side of the square is the Grosvenor Building, part of which was originally the **Municipal School of Art**, and to the rear in HIGHER ORMOND STREET its 1897 red brick and salmon-pink Doulton terracotta extension designed by J. Gibbons Sankey (architect of Churchgate House). A range of nine semicircular-headed windows each comprise a pair of lancets with an angel spandrel; the angels, designed by W. J. Neatby, hold shields on which is a date or image, including a coat of arms. The chimneys are corbelled out on delightful angel heads, and green men lurk in foliage. A large plaque records the gift of £10,000 towards the erection of the new wing by the council and guarantors of the Manchester Royal Jubilee Exhibition held in 1887. Inside is more Neatby detailing on terracotta arcades in the upper floor corridors. Opposite is the **Righton Building** (1905), built as a draper's shop in rich ochre terracotta and white brick, but impossible to enjoy because of the hideous replacement corner section.

Slightly north, on the west side of Grosvenor Square in LOWER ORMOND STREET, is the **Ormond Building**, built in 1881 as offices for the Poor Law Commissioners, and now part of Manchester Metropolitan University; the architects were Mangnall & Littlewoods of Manchester, who later became well known for their seaside buildings. Its extensive interior wall tiling, some (possibly all) by Minton's, was overpainted in the 1930s and revealed during its 1996-7 refurbishment.

Immediately north of the Ormond Building is **St Augustine's R. C. Church**, the Catholic parish church of Chorlton on Medlock and the chaplaincy of Manchester Metropolitan University. The parish was established in 1820; the previous church was destroyed in the Blitz of 1940, and the present St Augustine's was built in 1967-8. The architects were Desmond Williams & Associates. Inside this dark brick box is a massive *Christ in Glory* reredos by Robert Brumby, a huge floor to ceiling installation centred on the grey figure of Christ amidst manic whirls of blue, green and brown stoneware tiles, set on edge and at all angles; there are also some glazed elements (Fig 127). Despite the muted colours this is a very powerful piece, but its method of construction, with the individual pieces jammed together higgledy-piggledy, may cause conservation problems eventually as some tiles have already become loose.

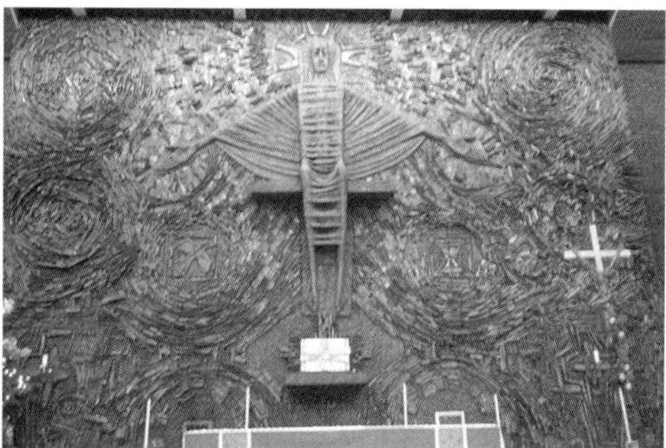

Fig 127.

About half a mile further south along Oxford Road, just south of Dover Street, is the vast **Holy Name of Jesus R. C. Church** (1869-71), a Jesuit foundation notable for its internal use of terracotta by Gibbs & Canning. Experimentation with terracotta in a church context had almost ceased after the criticism of Edmund Sharpe's two 'pot churches' in the 1840s, but by the 1860s a few architects were prepared see what possibilities were offered by the material. The Holy Name of Jesus was designed by the architects Joseph Aloysius Hansom and his son Joseph Stanislaus Hansom, who used lightweight polygonal blocks of terracotta to form the rib-vaulting which runs throughout the church (Fig 128). The rib-vaults were very like those of Manchester Town Hall, being put up by Waterhouse at much the same time and using terracotta by the same manufacturer. In the church, the supporting piers were thinner than normal stone piers, and as a result the church seems airy and open; the tracery is noticeably more delicate than stonework, with an almost frilly feel. Terracotta was also used as an internal facing material, for instance in the diamond-patterned columns of the baptistery. The interior lightness extends to the colour of the terracotta, which was sandblasted in 1972, taking off its buff surface and rendering it much paler.

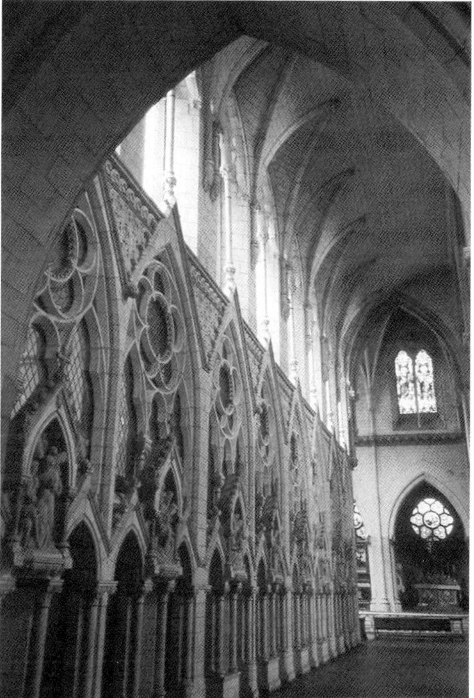

Fig 128.

A further half mile south on the east side of Oxford Road is the **Royal Eye Hospital** (1886), which has much bright red terracotta with unremarkable decoration. The exception is a well-modelled relief panel high up at the north end of the facade, entitled *The miracle of Jesus healing a blind man*; the subject and style suggest this may be by George Tinworth of Doulton's.[45] Almost opposite the hospital is the **Whitworth Art Gallery**, built between 1894 and 1908; the architects were J. W. Beaumont & Sons. Again red terracotta (here by J. C. Edwards) dominates, with yards of hefty balustrading and runs of large, semicircular decorative panels in arcading on the north and south sides of the building.

Hulme

Stretching along the front of **Hulme Library and Adult Education Centre**, STRETFORD ROAD (just south of the city centre) is the Hulme Millennium Mural, an irregularly-shaped ceramic mural over ninety feet in length. Its bold, colourful images, including the nearby Hulme Arch of 1997, show the history of Hulme and its regeneration. The mural, which was unveiled in 2002, took two and a half years to make and used over two tonnes of clay; it was the work of Hulme Urban Potters, a collective of students and tutors based at the Centre.

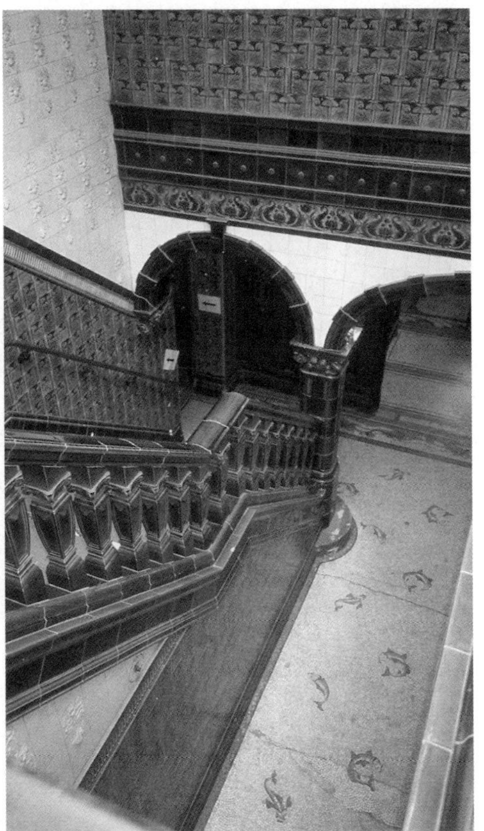

Fig 129.

Rusholme

The **Victoria Baths**, HATHERSAGE ROAD, was a luxurious bathhouse built by Manchester Corporation in 1903-6 to serve the whole of the city; it was designed by the City Architect, Henry Price (Fig 129). The building cost £59,000 and was described by the Lord Mayor on its opening day as a 'water palace'. The exterior, with its fine clock turret, makes a strong statement in red brick with buff terracotta dressings by J. C. Edwards including a mermaid relief and signs for 'Males 1st Class', 'Males 2nd Class' and 'Females'. Inside are three swimming pools (the first-class males bathed in the water before it was recycled for other users!), a complete Turkish Baths suite, a laundry and much tiling and stained glass. The most lavishly tiled entrance was for the first-class males, with floor-to-ceiling art nouveau relief patterned tiling in green and yellow, a wonderfully fishy mosaic floor and a green faience balustrade on the main staircase. Pilkington's were almost certainly responsible for the faience; they supplied a similarly elaborate faience staircase for Liverpool's Lister Drive Baths, completed in 1903 (see Liverpool, Tue Brook, above).[46] There is also tiling in the second-class male entrance, but the female entrance is rather more basic, although still with a tiled dado. The tiles were made by Pilkington's and designed by Frederick C. Howells, who was taken on by the firm to carry out large-scale tiling contracts.[47] The unusual stained glass windows include some with images of sportsmen by William Pointer of Manchester. The Baths closed in 1993 and since then has been cared for by the Victoria Baths Trust, which is hoping to re-open the main swimming pool and restore as many of the building's original features as possible.

About half a mile south of the Victoria Baths is PLATT LANE and **Holy Trinity Church**, Platt, the second of the architect Edmund Sharpe's terracotta 'pot churches'; his first was built on the outskirts of Bolton in 1844-5. In 1844, well before the Bolton church was complete, Sharpe was commissioned by Thomas Worsley of Platt Hall to design a second terracotta church. Holy Trinity was erected in 1845-6 using (as before) terracotta from the Ladyshore Colliery, Little Lever; it was much less profusely decorated than the Bolton church, although almost twice the size with a handsome tower and tall spire. Sharpe encountered fewer difficulties in its construction, partly due to the experience gained at Bolton, but also to the fact that the Platt design called for less detailing; the decoration was designed to be worked in smaller pieces, thus ensuring the wall blocks were properly fired. Also, owing to the earlier experience where underfired and porous blocks had to be cut out and replaced, more of the Platt terracotta was hollow, leading to *The Builder*'s comment that 'Every piece is hollow, being as it appeared, afterwards filled or backed up with concrete. They are nothing more than pots...'.[48] Unfortunately neither Sharpe nor *The Builder* had the imagination to see that this method of construction would become standard practice; Sharpe's main concern was authenticity rather than innovation.

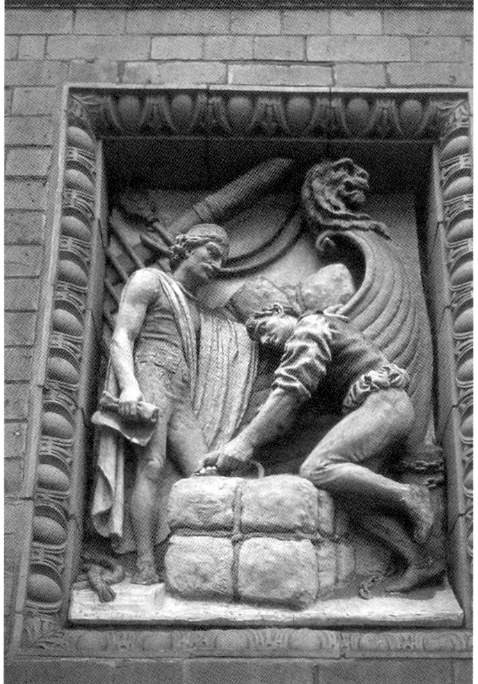

Fig 130.

Whalley Range

St Bede's R. C. College (now St Bede's Preparatory School), ALEXANDRA ROAD SOUTH, was built in 1878-84 incorporating the former Manchester Aquarium; the architects were Dunn & Hansom (Fig 130). This eleven-bay Italianate structure of red brick and bright orangey-red Doulton terracotta has some unusual decorative features including giant terracotta bees (a Manchester symbol) buzzing about on the upper part of the facade, modelled terracotta heads in the window pediments, and a pair of blue glazed Doultonware columns supporting the porch. The main entrance is flanked by four vitreous enamelled terracotta panels representing scholarly and academic disciplines and modelled in high relief by John Broad; these are the only known examples of this striking technique.[49]

MORECAMBE

The **Victoria Pavilion** was built on MARINE ROAD CENTRAL, right at the centre of Morecambe's seafront, in 1897. The architects of the music hall, which was an extension of the Winter Gardens (1878, demolished 1982), were Mangnall & Littlewoods of Manchester, who had just completed the Empress Ballroom in Blackpool's Winter Gardens; Frank Matcham was a consultant. The music hall has a distinctive bright red brick facade with terracotta detailing and a broad crow-stepped gable. In the tile and faience-lined entrance are a pair of pictorial panels - cornucopia figures in pale green and yellow glazes - above a mosaic floor (Fig 131). The exterior of the music hall, which is often known as the Winter Gardens, was restored in 1997 by Lancaster City Council. The currently inaccessible interior has dado tiling and stairs with faience balustrades.

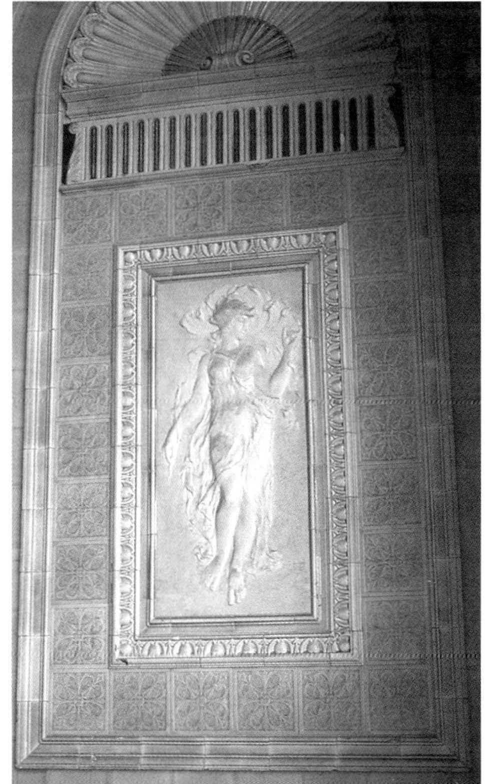

Fig 131.

Close to the Victoria Pavilion is a good pair of interwar white faience facades, those of **Woolworths** and the former **Burtons**, while inland on the corner of THORNTON ROAD and Euston Road is the unmistakable brick-built slab tower of the former **Odeon** (now a DIY store). It was built in 1937 (architect W. Calder Robson of Harry Weedon's office) and closed in 1976. The facade - partly in white faience with green stripes, probably by Shaws of Darwen - has a strange glazed protuberance, in fact a pier-like observation deck at third floor level.

OLDHAM

The tiled floor of the hexagonal gazebo at Parklands House, opened in 1999 and part of the **Royal Oldham Hospital**, was made by Jane Knowles with the assistance of the Occupational Therapy Pottery Group. Its design, which depicts various herbs, was created by rolling thin white clay images of the plants on to a red clay base. After biscuit firing, copper carbonate was rubbed in and then the tiles were fired at 1280°C; vitrifying clays were used to ensure that the floor was frostproof.[50]

Hollinwood

The **Grey Horse Inn** at 723 OLDHAM ROAD has a pretty blue-tiled facade probably dating from the early interwar years. Beside the front door is a fine polychrome plaque depicting a flat-capped chap contemplating a pint of ale from the local brewer J. W. Lees; the legend reads *Mine's a "John Willie"*.

PENDLEBURY

Tile production began in 1893 at the CLIFTON JUNCTION works erected by the Pilkington family of colliery owners. The firm was incorporated in 1891 under the name Pilkington's Tile & Pottery Co Ltd, and made encaustic and other floor tiles, printed, majolica and hand-decorated tiles and panels, as well as Lancastrian pottery. In 1937 production of pottery ceased and the firm became known as **Pilkington's Tiles Limited**. Tile production still continues on the site (at the end of Rake Lane), which is about four miles north-west of Manchester in the beautiful rural setting of the Irwell valley, albeit with the railway and other factories close by and the M60 in the distance.

The first floor stairwell of the office block is lined with cream tiles incorporating a handpainted tile panel showing a map of the works and the immediate area. This jolly pictorial panel, which is framed by step moulded tiling, was designed by T. B. Jones (Head of the Design Department following the retirement of John Chambers), painted by G. Ormrod and installed in 1948. The remainder of the cream wall tiling is of a later date, but the curved, faience-clad wall at the head of the stairs probably also dates from 1948 or earlier. The black and white matt faience centres on an opening which was originally the receptionist's window. Set on the black ground are eight small white relief figures depicting different stages in tile making. There are also several small tile panels by John Chambers and Gordon Forsyth in the firm's conference centre.

PRESTON

Right in the centre of Preston is the **Miller Arcade**, a cross-plan arcade with its southern entrance on FISHERGATE. The architect was Edwin Bush, who won a competition for its design in 1895; the building, which included turkish baths below the ground floor shops and a hotel above, was completed in 1901 and restored in 1972. There is faience and buff terracotta by Gibbs & Canning on its exterior, while the upper floor of the interior is clad in ornate green and cream faience. Almost opposite the arcade at 6 Fishergate is **Waterstone's**, formerly Booth's grocery store; the upper floors of the shop were refaced with heavily decorated white faience in 1915. Just off the south side of Fishergate in CHAPEL STREET is the basilica-style **St Wilfrid's R. C. Church**, rebuilt in 1879-80 but with a hugely elaborate Ruabon terracotta facade added in 1892.

Slightly north of Fishergate in FRIARGATE is the **Black Horse** public house, its interior dating from around 1900 with a fine curved faience barfront in cream, brown and yellow, whose manufacturer is something of a puzzle. The earliest of these rare faience bars were produced by Burmantofts in the early 1890s; they were fairly plain, and by the mid-1890s Craven Dunnill were making an elaborate polychrome floral barfront, followed by (from around 1902), a simpler version with grotesque heads for decoration. Doulton and Minton's also produced the occasional ceramic bar, but none of the designs resemble the Black Horse bar, which could perhaps be attributed to Burmantofts on grounds of colour alone. Another possibility is the nearest faience manufacturer, Pilkington's.

A quarter mile north-east and just beyond the ring road is **St Ignatius R. C. Church**, MEADOW STREET, designed by J. J. Scoles and built in 1833-6. Its chancel was added by J. A. Hansom in 1858 and further alterations were made in 1886 by the practice M. E. Hadfield & Son of Sheffield. These latter alterations must have been supervised by Charles Hadfield, as his father, Matthew Ellison Hadfield, died in 1885. The works included the installation of a very fine chancel encaustic pavement made by Carter, Johnson & Co of Worcester.[51] This rare pavement displays a wide range of buff and brown designs and large *IHS* monogram panels.

ROCHDALE

Rochdale's main claim to fame - apart from Gracie Fields, who was born in a small room over a fish and chip shop in Tweedale Street on the 8th January 1898 - is as the birthplace of the Co-operative Movement. The Rochdale Equitable Pioneers Society opened its first shop in Toad Lane on the 21st December 1844. In the nineteenth century Rochdale was a major textile centre in its own right, its status reflected in the size and grandeur of the **Town Hall**, which stands on THE ESPLANADE. The Town Hall was built in 1866-71 and designed by William H. Crossland, once a pupil of Sir George Gilbert Scott. Its interior has lavish painted and sculpted decoration, with a rich Minton encaustic tile pavement in the main ground floor hall, originally known as the Exchange (Fig 132).

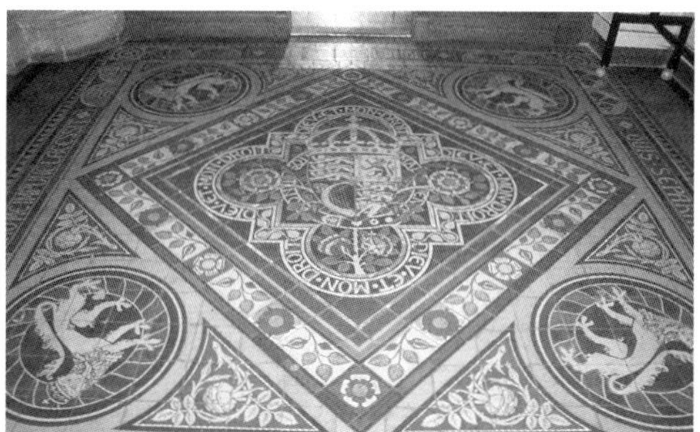

Fig 132.

The entire floor is tiled, mainly with elaborate panels of specially-made tiles including the Royal Arms, lions, roses, thistles and shamrocks, all laid out in an arrangement designed by Heaton, Butler and Bayne; fifteen panels of tiles show either the Royal Arms, the arms of the County of Lancaster or the Borough of Rochdale. The latter includes a ceramic spelling error, with Rochdale's motto *Crede signo* (Believe in the sign) rendered as *Credo signo* (I believe in the sign).[52]

South of the Town Hall on DOWLING STREET, opposite the railway station, is **St John Baptist R. C. Church**, a concrete-domed edifice built in 1924 by architects Hill, Sandy & Norris. Inside, its tall apsidal chancel is covered by a brightly coloured mosaic centred on the figure of Christ; this was designed by Eric Newton (1893-1965) and executed by L. Oppenheimer Ltd of Manchester in 1933. Newton was born Eric Oppenheimer but later changed to his mother's maiden name. Oppenheimer's, a tile importing business, was set up by Eric Newton's grandfather; Newton designed mosaics for the firm from around the early 1920s.

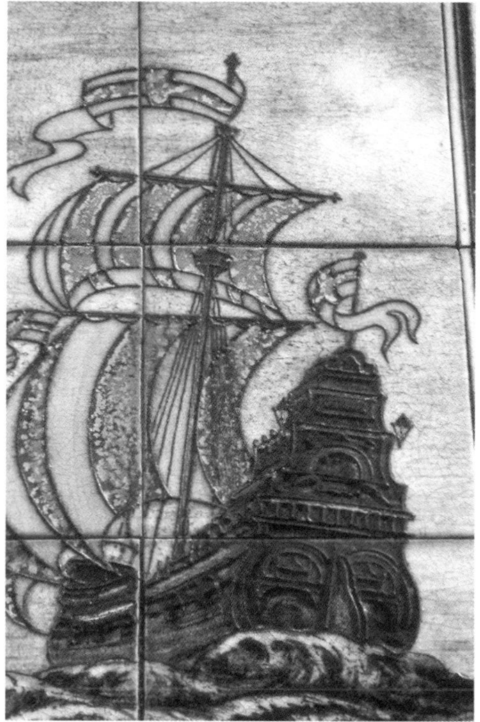

Fig 133.

Rochdale has retained a good variety of tiled shops and pubs dotted about the area to the north and west of the Town Hall. The town's inter-war pubs developed a local style of decoration: the tiny lobby has wall tiles giving a visual rendition of the pub name or brewery logo, and the doorway mosaic shows the pub name. Examples are the **Merry Monk**, 234 COLLEGE ROAD, with the Phoenix Brewery logo in its lobby wall tiling; and the **Globe**, WHITWORTH ROAD and Princess Street, with tiling showing delightful floating globes. Other good tiled pubs are the **Cemetery Hotel**, 470 BURY ROAD, where the art nouveau tiles appear in a Maw & Co catalogue dating from around 1907; the **Healey Hotel**, 172 SHAWCLOUGH ROAD, redecorated in 1920 and including unusual speckled, lustred mosaic panels highlighted in reds; the **Brown Cow**, EDENFIELD ROAD, Norden, with Craven Dunnill handpainted panels of local rural scenes; and the **Two Ships Hotel** (now Tap and Spile), HOPE STREET and Goose Lane, built during the 1920s for the Bury Brewery Company with an external tile panel of two galleons with orange-yellow sails (Fig 133). This last could be by Pilkington's, who produced several panels with similar ship motifs.[53] There are fewer tiled shops to choose from, but **The Bouquet**, SPOTLAND ROAD has two good tube-lined panels showing fruit and fish, and there are handpainted pictorial tile panels at the **butcher's** on MARKET STREET, Whitworth.

SALE

The **Church of St Mary Magdalene**, HARBORO ROAD, Ashton upon Mersey was built in 1874 but its surprisingly lavish chancel decoration was not completed until the installation of a reredos, supplied by Powell's of Whitefriars, in 1923. The reredos includes a figure of Christ carried out in opus sectile and designed by the draughtsman W. Read. Powell's also provided ten opus sectile panels of saints for the chancel walls in 1905; these were designed by Read and Frank Mann.[54]

SALFORD

To explore Salford on foot, begin near Salford Crescent railway station and walk eastward through the centre; four rather more distant locations are also described. The route runs along THE CRESCENT past Salford University's **Peel Building**, built in 1896 as the Royal Technical College by the architect Henry Lord and refurbished in 1999. Its elaborate red Dennis Ruabon terracotta facade includes several large high-relief figurative plaques by the architectural sculptors Earp, Son and Hobbs, while inside is tall dado tiling in olive green and turquoise.[55] Just east of the Peel Building on the lawn is a little domed **gazebo**, also of red terracotta and built around 1895; its original purpose was to hide a ventilation outlet.

Directly opposite is the **Working Class Movement Library** at 51 The Crescent, a Queen Anne Revival style house with a large red terracotta cartouche reading '1897 Queen's Jubilee Nurses Home'. Continue into CHAPEL STREET for the **R. C. Cathedral of St John Evangelist** (1844-8), from which much of the decoration has been removed, although encaustic tile pavements remain in two chapels, notably the Blessed Sacrament Chapel in the south transept, where the 1884 fittings by Peter Paul Pugin include large tiles depicting a pelican in her piety.[56] Next door is the huge buff Doulton terracotta facade of **Salford Education Offices**, built in 1895 as a Board School by the architects Woodhouse & Willoughby, who later designed Manchester Police and Fire Station. There are several panels of elaborate scrollwork and masks by W. J. Neatby. Just east is the **Town Hall** (1825-7) in BEXLEY SQUARE; its entrance hall has bright geometric paving and good dado tiling, all by Craven Dunnill and perhaps installed when the Town Hall was extended around the turn of the century. Continue east along Chapel Street to the former **Salford Cinema** (1912, now New Harvest Christian Fellowship) on the corner with ST STEPHEN STREET; its jolly buff terracotta facade is topped by an open cupola. After passing beneath the railway bridge turn right into BLACKFRIARS STREET (towards Manchester's centre) for the former **Crown Hotel**, with a pleasant Craven Dunnill facade of green and yellow tiles, mostly plain but with details including the pub's name.

Higher Broughton

The rather plain nave of the **Church of St John Evangelist**, MURRAY STREET, Higher Broughton was privately-endowed and erected in 1836-9, with the chancel, in contrasting ecclesiological style, being added in 1846. This was probably a memorial to the patron of the church, the Rev. John Clowes, a noted gardener and botanist, who died in that year; his monument is in the church. The architect of the chancel was the Dumfries-born Manchester architect John Edgar Gregan (1813-55). The design of the colourful Minton encaustic tile pavement, which was probably installed when the chancel was built, centres on a circular tile showing a pelican in her piety. The stone-traceried reredos is flanked by a pair of Minton tile panels, nearly twenty feet in height, edged with decorative border tiles and bearing the ten commandments and the apostle's creed. The lettering is in white on brown ground, while the relief moulded tiles are coloured with majolica glazes in yellow, green, brown, black and white.[57] Although ceramic text panels are not uncommon in churches, the sheer size of these examples is out of the ordinary.

Kersal

St Paul's Church, MOOR LANE, Kersal Moor was built in 1851-2 then reordered in the mid-1880s and early 1900s. The original ornate wall decorations were overpainted in 1924, but the following year two murals depicting scenes from the life of St Paul were installed, one at either side of the east window. The murals were designed and supplied by Walter J. Pearce Ltd of Manchester, who specialised in 'Vitremure' mosiac made from glass tiles embedded in concrete; this was very similar to the opus sectile work produced by Powell's of Whitefriars. The murals survived the dramatic fire of 31st January 1987, following which the church was rebuilt and the restored murals returned to their positions flanking the east window.

Ordsall

In the chancel of **St Clement's Church** (1877-8, architects Paley & Austin, normally no public access), HULTON STREET, Ordsall are Doulton murals of religious scenes. These may have been installed some years after the church was built, as Paley & Austin generally did not work in the High Anglican decorative style, which often included lavish tilework.[58]

STANDISH

St Wilfrid's Church, MARKET PLACE, is a rare late sixteenth century church, with equally unusual encaustic floor tiles by Carter, Johnson & Co of Worcester; these probably date from 1878 when alterations were made to the chancel. There is also a colourful opus sectile reredos of the *Baptism of Christ*, probably by Powells of Whitefriars.

TOTTINGTON

Tottington has two pubs of ceramic interest, the **Old Dungeon Inn** at 9 TURTON ROAD and the nearby **Hark to Towler**. The Old Dungeon has porch tiling by Pilkington's, tiled fire surrounds, ceramic doorframes and a complete tiled staircase and landing, while the Hark to Towler, which also has Pilkington's porch tiling, boasts an unusual ceramic barfront with large panels in imitation of dressed stone.

WHISTON

In **Whiston Hospital**, on WARRINGTON ROAD, is a long, irregularly-shaped ceramic mural by Robert Nicholson and Magdalene Al Tayyr; it was commissioned by Whiston Hospital Trust installed in 1993. The colourful mural shows the sun shining brightly on various local scenes including the Mersey, the Dee, Formby, Crosby, Liverpool, the Wirral, Chester and North Wales.

Lancashire Roundup

The extensive Coppull Mills (1906, architects Joseph Stott & Sons), at **Coppull**, south-west of Chorley, have yellow glazed brick and buff terracotta decoration with a good Byzantine-style tower; some of the building materials were supplied by Dennis Ruabon.[59] At St Joseph's R. C. Church, Warren Road, Blundellsands, **Crosby** is a baptismal font (1970) with ceramic reliefs by Adam Kossowski, and a ceramic plaque of the same date. There is extensive interior tilework at the Victoria PH (1905), St John's Street, **Great Harwood**. The font of All Hallows Church, **Great Mitton** stands on a large platform paved with Victorian encaustic tiles. A tile panel showing a woman spinning is mounted in the foyer of the Town Hall, Market Place, **Leigh**; it came from a shop in Spinning Jenny Street, Wigan and was restored during the 1990s by the Jackfield Conservation Studio. The parade of three shops at 33-37 Manchester Road, **Middleton**, designed by Edgar Wood and built in 1908, are decorated with Pilkington's 'Parian faience' in green and white chevrons; to the north in the Cemetery on Boarshaw Road is the chevron-tiled grave designed by Wood for his friend, the Middleton artist Frederick William Jackson (1859-1918).[60] Tilework at Gawthorpe Hall (1600-5, NT), **Padiham** includes an encaustic pavement in the vestibule, probably dating from the 1849-51 restoration, and De Morgan tiles in the long gallery fireplace. The wrought iron gates, with their inset ceramic plaques, of St Helen's Church, **Sefton** were designed in 1997 by the potter Julia Carter Preston. The office building at the **Waterside** works of Shaws of Darwen was built in 1927 using the firm's own grey and white faience. There is elaborate red terracotta detailing on the former Technical College (now Municipal Buildings), Library Street, **Wigan**, which was built in 1901-3; the architects were Briggs and Wolstenholme.

References

1. Barry Corbett and Angela Corbett, *Tiles Tell the Tale* (Pilkington's Lancastrian Pottery Society, 2004).
2. Information from Pilkington's Lancastrian Pottery Society Newsletter, 1998, vol 1, pp41-4; and Albion United Reformed Church guidebook.
3. Michael Stratton, *Shaws of Darwen and a Ceramic Tour of Blackpool* (TACS, 1984).
4. Michael J. Dillon, *Bricks, tiles and terracotta from Wrexham and Ruabon* (Wrexham Maelor Borough Council, Wrexham, 1985).

5. Colin Cunningham and Prudence Waterhouse, *Alfred Waterhouse, 1830-1905: Biography of a Practice* (Clarendon Press, Oxford, 1992).
6. Robert Jolley, 'Edmund Sharpe and the 'Pot' Churches', *Architectural Review*, 146 (1969) December, pp426-31.
7. Alan Swale, *Architectural terracotta - a critical appraisal of its development and deployment*, 1998, MA dissertation, History of Ceramics, University of Staffordshire.
8. Diana Hall, 'The Terracotta Restoration Work at the Church of St Stephen and All Martyrs, Lever Bridge, Bolton', *Glazed Expressions*, (2001) 43, pp7-9.
9. Philip and Dorothy Brown, 'Lancaster architects - church terracotta and tiles', *Glazed Expressions*, (1990) 21, pp8-10.
10. Paul Atterbury and Clive Wainwright, *Pugin: A Gothic Passion* (Yale University Press, New Haven and London, 1994), pp264-7.
11. *Pilkington's Lancastrian Pottery Society Newsletter*, vol 2, p105.
12. Elain Harwood, 'Liturgy and Architecture: The Development of the Centralised Eucharistic Space', *Twentieth Century Architecture*, 3 (1998), pp49-74.
13. *Adam Kossowski: Murals and Paintings*, (Armelle Press, London, 1990).
14. Paul Atterbury and Maureen Batkin, *The Dictionary of Minton* (Antique Collectors' Club, Woodbridge, 1998), p266.
15. Loraine Knowles, *St George's Hall, Liverpool* 2nd ed (Liverpool City Council, Liverpool, 1995), p33.
16. Kenneth Romney Towndrow, *Walker Art Gallery Monograph Number 1: Alfred Stevens* (University Press of Liverpool, Liverpool, 1951).
17. Hugh Stannus, *Alfred Stevens and His Work* (The Autotype Company, London, 1891).
18. Donald Insall, *Historic floors at risk: St George's Hall, Liverpool*, in *Historic Floors: Their history and conservation*, ed Jane Fawcett, (Butterworth-Heinemann, Oxford, 1998) pp194-197.
19. Tony Herbert and Kathryn Huggins, *The Decorative Tile in Architecture and Interiors* (Phaidon Press, London, 1995), pp165-6.
20. Penny Beckett, 'George Swift and Liverpool's Swan Tile Works', *TACS Journal*, 10 (2004), pp24-31.
21. Lance S. Fuller, 'Nature Printing', *Glazed Expressions*, (2002) 44, pp2-4.
22. Atterbury and Batkin, *Dictionary of Minton*, p266.
23. Shaws Glazed Brick Co Ltd, Darwen, *List of Contracts executed 1935-1936*.
24. Joseph Sharples, *Liverpool*, Pevsner Architectural Guides (Yale University Press, New Haven and London, 2004).
25. Lynn Pearson, 'Postwar Tile Panels: An Endangered Species?' *Glazed Expressions*, (2003) 46, pp3-5.
26. Terry Cavanagh, *Public Sculpture of Liverpool* (Liverpool University Press, Liverpool, 1997), pp228-9.
27. *Mural Art Today*, (Victoria and Albert Museum, London, 1960).
28. Margaret Garlake, *Peter Lanyon* (Tate Publishing, London, 2001).
29. Mo Enright, *Peter Lanyon: The Mural Studies* (Gimpel Fils, London, 1996).
30. Sharples, *Liverpool* (2004).
31. E. Myra Brown, *Julia Carter Preston* (National Museums & Galleries on Merseyside, Liverpool, 1999).
32. *Building News*, 12th April 1872, p303.
33. Pilkington's Tile & Pottery Co. Ltd., Clifton Junction in British Library, Trade Literature, OM06y. This brochure, comprising twelve photographs of interiors with Pilkington's faience and tilework, was probably produced shortly after the opening in 1903 of two buildings featured: Corporation Baths, Lister Drive, Liverpool and the Stock Exchange, Bristol. It includes two photographs of Lister Drive Baths, one showing the entrance hall and staircase which is captioned 'Faience Balustrade & Wall Tiling'; the other shows the main baths. Seven out of the twelve photograph captions mention faience, suggesting that Pilkington's was a major producer of coloured slab faience during the early 1900s.
34. A. J. Cross, *Pilkington's Royal Lancastrian Pottery and Tiles* (Richard Dennis, London, 1980), p22.
35. The Pevsner City Guide for *Manchester* by Clare Hartwell (Penguin, London, 2001) has provided much useful general information for this section.
36. Clare Hartwell, *Manchester*, Pevsner Architectural Guides (Penguin Books, London, 2001), pp168-9.
37. Simon Taylor, Malcolm Cooper and P. S. Barnwell, *Manchester: The Warehouse Legacy* (English Heritage, London, 2002).
38. Paul Atterbury and Louise Irvine, *The Doulton Story* (Royal Doulton Tableware, Stoke on Trent, 1979), p80.
39. Kevin Gannon, 'Refuge Assurance Company Offices, Manchester', *Journal of the Tiles and Architectural Ceramics Society*, 3 (1990), pp11-14.
40. John J. Parkinson-Bailey, *Manchester: An Architectural History* (Manchester University Press, Manchester, 2000).
41. Michael Stratton, *Tour of Manchester* (TACS, 1985).
42. Michael Stratton, *Clad is bad? The relationship between structural and ceramic facing materials*, in *Structure and Style: Conserving Twentieth Century Buildings*, ed Michael Stratton, (E. & F. N. Spon, London, 1997), pp164-92.
43. John Malam, 'A newly recognised Doulton interior, Manchester', *Glazed Expressions*, (1993) 27, pp1, 12.
44. Hartwell, *Manchester* (2001).
45. Rosemary Cochrane and Alex McErlain, *Architectural Terracotta* (Manchester Metropolitan University Slide Library, Manchester, 1999).
46. Lynn Pearson, 'Faience at the Victoria Baths, Manchester', *Glazed Expressions*, (2004) 51.
47. Prue Williams, *Victoria Baths: Manchester's Water Palace* (Spire Books, Reading, 2004), pp73-5.
48. *The Builder*, vol 3, 29th November 1845, pp571-2.
49. Atterbury and Irvine, *Doulton Story*, pp78-80.

50. Ruth Pavey, 'Parklands House, the Royal Oldham Hospital', *Crafts*, (1999) 159, pp20-23.
51. *The Builder*, vol 51, 2nd October 1886, p482.
52. Herbert and Huggins, *Decorative Tile*, p167.
53. *Pilkington's Lancastrian Pottery Society Newsletter*, vol 3, September 2003, p132.
54. Dennis W. Hadley, *James Powell & Sons: A listing of opus sectile, 1847-1973*, (2001).
55. Terry Wyke and Harry Cocks, *Public Sculpture of Greater Manchester* (Liverpool University Press, Liverpool, 2004), pp179-81.
56. Clare Hartwell, Matthew Hyde and Nikolaus Pevsner, *Lancashire: Manchester and the South-East* (Yale University Press, New Haven and London, 2004), p618.
57. Peter Skinner, 'Wall Tiles in Churches', *Glazed Expressions*, (1987) 14, p6; Hartwell, *Lancashire: Manchester and the South-East* (2004), pp630-1.
58. James Price, *Sharpe, Paley and Austin: A Lancaster Architectural Practice, 1836-1942* (Centre for North-West Regional Studies, University of Lancaster, Lancaster, 1998), p46.
59. *Dennis Ruabon Catalogue*, (1908).
60. *Pilkington's Lancastrian Pottery Society Newsletter*, vol 2, pp36-7; Hartwell, *Lancashire: Manchester and the South-East* (2004), p513.

Leicestershire

Until its closure in summer 2004, Leicestershire had its own terracotta and faience manufacturer, originally known as the Hathern Station Brick & Terra Cotta Company, at whose works near Loughborough terracotta manufacture began around 1883. Notable locations where the firm's products may be seen include Leicester, with its massive Odeon, and of course the Hathernware heaven of Loughborough itself. Despite having a ceramics firm based in the county, the wares of other manufacturers have probably contributed more to Leicestershire's architectural history. Hathern's production was modest until the late 1890s, and then much of it was directed outside the county, for instance to Birmingham for turn-of-the-century public house construction. In addition, the faience products of Hathern's interwar years can be found country-wide, for instance on the facades of the Odeon cinema chain, rather than locally.

Nationally important locations for Burmantofts wares can be seen in Leicester at the Alexandra House warehouse and the Church of St James the Greater, while in the same city Doulton's were responsible for the delightful facade of the Turkey Café. Leicestershire was not enthusiastically anglo-catholic, so although much church building was carried out in the late Victorian period, highly decorative interiors are at something of a premium. Leicestershire is, however, the county where the greatest concentration of Queen Victoria terracotta plaques can be found. These were manufactured by Stanley Brothers of Nuneaton to mark the 1887 and 1897 jubilees, the latter being much more commonly seen; a good example is at Witherley.

The interwar years are represented in the county by several super-cinemas, but early postwar work is sparse; the most significant site is St Aidan's Church (1957-9), Leicester, which has a large mural by William Gordon, probably his sole extant architectural work of any size. Soon afterwards, ceramic history was changed as the University of Leicester's Engineering Building (1959-63) provided a great impetus to the use of tile cladding. After the generally lean years of the seventies and eighties, when restorations were much more common than new installations, in the late 1990s ceramic public artworks became an accepted means of emphasising town regeneration, marking the presence of cycleways and footpaths, and establishing company identity. Suggested reading: Jean Farquhar and Joan Skinner, *The History and Architecture of the Turkey Café* (Sedgebrook Press, Leicester, 1987); TACS Tour Notes *Leicester* (1997) and *Loughborough* (2003). The *Gazetteer* entry for Leicestershire covers the administrative areas of Leicester City Council, Leicestershire County Council and Rutland County Council.

IBSTOCK

The **Ibstock Landmark Sculpture** (unveiled 1998) stands on the HIGH STREET, at the corner with Hinckley Road. It is a glazed stoneware column bearing images related to Ibstock and topped by a stubby tree representing the National Forest and the town's regeneration. The sculptor was Ailsa Magnus, Ibstock's artist-in-residence during 1997, who worked with local children on the project. They also produced tiles and 'Welcome' plaques which decorate the Youth Centre, the Community College and the town's Junior and Infant Schools. Materials for the Landmark Sculpture were donated by Ibstock Building Products Ltd.[1]

LEICESTER

Leicester is not as well endowed with decorative claywork as other Victorian cities, but it does have a few outstanding examples, notably the Burmantofts interior at the Church of St James the Greater, along with many minor uses of tiles, terracotta and faience. The main locations are listed here on a two-mile circular route, beginning and ending at London Road railway station and extending west to Bede Park; a few sites south of the central area and in the suburbs are also described. The identity of the manufacturers and designers is often difficult to discover; the nearest works is that of Hathern, near Loughborough, but no Hathernware earlier than that of the 1937-8 Odeon has yet been identified in a Leicester building.

LONDON ROAD **Railway Station** was rebuilt for the Midland Railway in 1892; the design was by Charles Trubshaw (1841-1917), the company architect. A long screen broken by massive archways culminates in a clock tower, the whole being decorated with much orangey-brown

Burmantofts terracotta (Fig 134). Inside, the walls of the booking hall have cream embossed tiles combined with various patterns of moulded tiles by Minton Hollins. (In 2003 it was proposed to redevlop the station site while retaining the frontage.) From the station, head north-west along GRANBY STREET, passing **Balmoral House** with its buff and brown-tiled name strip; the building was designed by Shenton and Baker in 1873 for boot and shoe manufacturers Charles Bruin & Son. The flamboyant buff terracotta of the former **General News Rooms** (corner with Belvoir Street) is rather more impressive, and indeed featured in a Burmantofts catalogue of 1902. The building was designed by the Leicester architectural practice Goddard & Co in 1898, and the terracotta sculptures are allegorical male and female figures designed and modelled by E. C. Spruce.

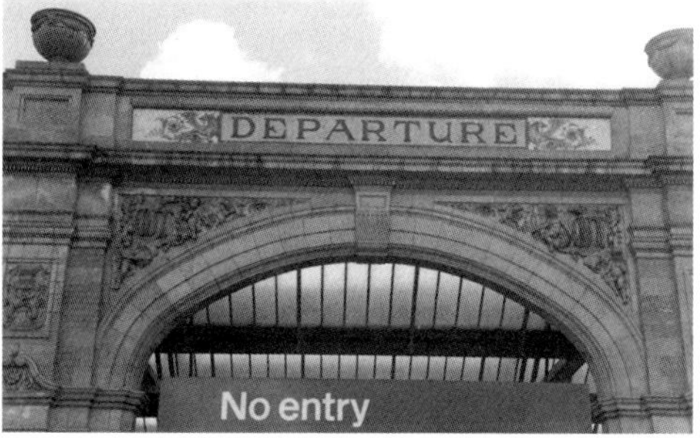

Fig 134.

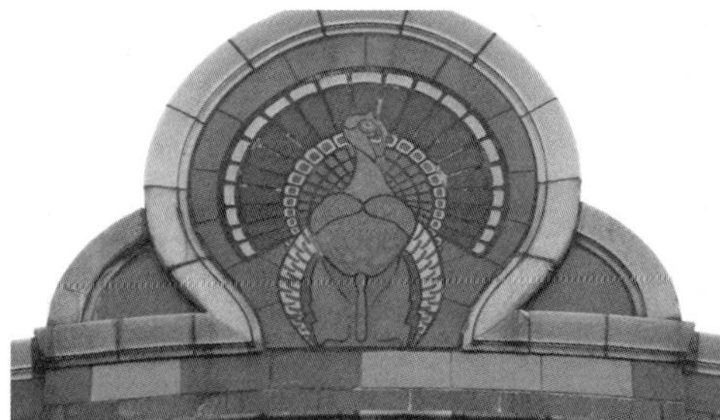

Fig 135.

The highlight of Granby Street is the **Turkey Café**, designed by the local architect and developer Arthur Wakerley (1862-1931) and built in 1900-1 (Fig 135). Its narrow Moorish-style facade in coloured Doulton Carraraware is topped by a huge fan-tailed turkey at whose feet are the words 'Doulton' and 'Dimsie 1901'; it appears that Dimsie may have been the model for this handsome turkey (Fig 136). The Turkey Café was one of a series of popular cafés built for John Winn around the turn of the century, each of which followed the stylistic impulse of its name: Oriental, Sunset, Café Royal. The ground floor frontage of the Turkey Café has been altered at least twice. Brucciani's bakery installed a turkey-patterned tile mural in 1968, but this was later covered over and the café was restored in 1984, although not exactly to the original design; some replacement ceramic blocks were obtained from Hathernware.[2]

Left into HORSEFAIR STREET for the 1978 extension to the Victorian **Fish Market**. Inside, near the steps on the south-east, is a tile panel full of colourful fishy motifs and dating from 1998; it was made by Louise Skinner of De Montfort University. Continue through the market to Market Place and thence HOTEL STREET for the **County Rooms** (now City Rooms), intended to be an hotel but opened as assembly rooms; it was built in 1792-1800 and designed by the architect John Johnson. Ornamentation on the facade includes a pair of Coade stone bas reliefs, a popular design known as *The Borghese Dancers*, reminiscent of the three (rather higher) relief panels on Johnson's slightly earlier Shire Hall, Chelmsford. The figures of *Dancing* and *Music* in their niches are in artificial stone (not Coade stone) or possibly terracotta and are by J. C. F. Rossi and John Bingley, with whom Rossi was in partnership for a short time.

Continue west along Friar Lane to SOUTHGATES for the **Southgate Subway Mural**, an extensive mosaic mural designed by Sue Ridge with Christopher Smith (an expert on roman mosaic), and made by Hamilton Smith Associates in 1991. As well as references to Leicester's roman history, the complex design also involves representations of air, earth, water and fire; it is one of the largest areas of mosaic in the world. Leave the subway at the western exit, almost immediately turning right into Castle View to reach **St Mary De Castro Church** in CASTLE YARD. Around the font (beneath the tower) are fourteenth century heraldic tiles in twenty-seven different designs.

Return along Castle View to THE NEWARKE and **Trinity Hospital Almshouses**. The hospital was founded in 1331 by Henry, Earl of Lancaster and Leicester, to care for the poor and infirm. Henry gave four acres of land next to his castle for the hospital buildings and gardens, and endowed it financially. Many changes have been made to the structure, most of which now houses the offices of De Montfort University, although the late fourteenth century chapel still remains. It has a tile pavement of sixteen different designs including the arms of the founder, which appear in four-tile groups. The Nottingham-type tiles, which appear to be in their original position, include three designs not found elsewhere that seem to be printed rather than inlaid. The chancel pavement has been repaired with modern tiles, but the medieval arrangement and a large proportion of the tiles have been retained.[3]

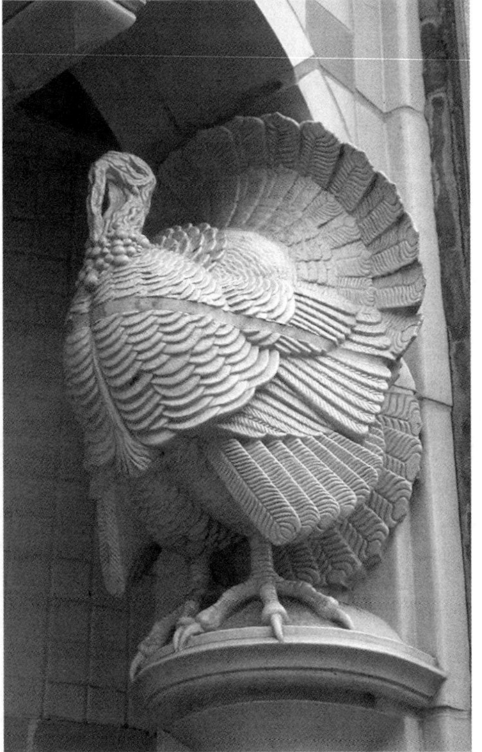

Fig 136.

Almost opposite the Almshouses is GATEWAY STREET and the former **Harrison & Hayes** hosiery factory (1913, architect S. H. Langley, now flats). The external walls of this turn-of-the century building are all of glazed-brick in creamy yellow, green and brown. Ahead in MILL LANE, which crosses Gateway Street, is the red brickfest of the **Queens Building** (1989-93, architects Short & Ford), De Montfort University. This low energy-consuming structure with its towering ventilation stacks has won several architectural awards. Mill Lane leads on to Western Boulevard, which gives access to BEDE PARK, opened in 1999 as part of Leicester's twelve-mile Riverside Park green corridor. Bede Park, a transformation of the previously industrial Bede Island, is flanked by the River Soar and the Grand Union Canal. The park includes a footpath and a Sustrans cycle route marked by the landmark sculpture **Making a Place**, a glazed ceramic map of Leicester designed and made in 1999 by Rory McNally and Chloe Cookson; it comprises 180 separate sections in the form of a column resting on a circular plinth. Nearby is the **Wildlife Map** (1999) by the same artists working with local schoolchildren; the ceramic map features images of wildlife common in the surrounding area and tops a broad circular plinth which acts as a roundabout for cyclists and walkers.

From the park head north to WEST BRIDGE and the terracotta spandrels of the **Mermaids Archway**. This pair of rather manly mermaids, embraced by coils of swirling water, were designed by William Neatby in 1900 and executed by Doultons. They were the spandrels in the entrance to the Wholesale Market in Halford Street, but were removed when the market was demolished in 1972 and reset on the West Bridge in 1980. Just east is ST NICHOLAS CIRCLE, the site of the Wathes Building, originally a nineteenth century cheese factory, until its demolition in 2003. Mounted on its facade were sixteen panels of mostly inlaid tiles by various manufacturers including Maw's and Mintons China Works; these are now on display inside the **BBC Radio Leicester** building, which opened on the site in 2005. Left in HIGHCROSS STREET (across the dual carriageway) is the redundant **All Saints Church** with fourteenth century heraldic tiles in around forty different designs.

Back to the HIGH STREET for the lengthy form of **Coronation Buildings** (1902-4, architect Arthur Wakerley), clad in Doulton's blue-grey Carraraware and their grey and cream terracotta. The building was designed to celebrate the coronation of Edward VII and is packed with pictorial references to the British Empire. A series of faience cartouches at first floor level each enclose a coloured Union Jack and are topped by name panels for the Empire's constituents along with a representative animal, for instance Australia with its kangaroo. Below the large fanlight, really too high up to make much of a showing, are three ceramic panels, two of which still have their original tiles showing galleons. The building was the main showroom of the Singer Sewing Machine Company from 1904 until the 1960s, and is commonly known as the Singer Building. Also in the High Street is Butler's chemist's shop (now **Joseph's**) which dates from the 1890s and bears a pictorial tiled advertisement for 'Sea Breeze' liver salts. Samuel Butler's Sea Breeze Factory once stood nearby, and a mosaic image of an imposing chemist is also part of the shop facade.

At the east end of the High Street is GALLOWTREE GATE and the former **Thomas Cook Building** (1894, architects Goddard, Paget & Goddard) with its ornate terracotta facade and puzzling set of four relief panels located between first and second floors. The pictorial panels commemorate Cook's first excursion, by train to Loughborough (1841); an excursion to the Great Exhibition (1851); General Gordon's voyage along the Nile (1884); and the firm's golden jubilee (1891). All show suitable forms of transport in splendid detail, but the material from which they are made is unclear. They each appear to have been manufactured in several sections, and could be of terracotta with a metallic or vitreous finish. Continue east into HUMBERSTONE GATE to find the **Old Black Lion** and its pair of outsize black ceramic lions (overpainted in gold during 2003), a Delft mark clearly visible. Nearby is the **Secular Hall** (1881) and its quintet of red terracotta busts of free-thinkers by the London sculptor Ambrose Louis Vago; much offence was caused by the inclusion of Jesus in such company as Robert Owen, Thomas Paine, Voltaire and Socrates.[4]

Turn south into RUTLAND STREET to see the opulent decoration of **Alexandra House** (1895-8, architect Edward Burgess), a massive warehouse built for Faire Brothers and partly clothed in buff Burmantofts terracotta so ornate that it was featured in the 1902 catalogue of the Leeds firm. There are many Faire symbols including 'F' motifs and their trademark elephants by the main door; the vestibule has a vaulted ceiling in blue mosaic. Opposite is the huge **Odeon** (1937-8, architect Robert Bullivant for Harry Weedon, closed 1997), a striking contrast to Alexandra House with two bold brick slab towers and its curving, winged green and white mottled vitreous Hathernware faience frontage on a black faience base. To return to London Road railway station, turn left into Granby Street.

Before looking at the suburbs of Leicester, there are four sites of interest just south of the central area. The basilica-style **Church of St James the Greater** stands about half a mile south of the railway station on the LONDON ROAD, at its junction with Victoria Park Road. It was built in 1899-1901, although the west end was not completed until 1914 due to lack of funds. The architect was Henry Langton Goddard, who originally suggested a gothic design, but - following a visit to northern Italy, where he saw the Cathedral at Torcello, amongst others - produced a plans for a basilica church including faience panels in the sanctuary inspired by the majolica work of della Robbia.[5] The proposed campanile was never built, leaving the west facade looking rather unfinished, but the interior is beautifully spacious, with much use of pale buff terracotta in the arches and the pulpit. A frieze of buff on dark blue majolica angels helps divides the chancel from the nave, and similar figures decorate the apse (although these may date from 1938). The terracotta was by Burmantofts, who had also supplied the terracotta for the Goddard-designed General News Rooms of 1898; Burmantofts featured St James the Greater in their 1902 catalogue.[6] Church folklore suggests that the Hathern Station Brick and Terracotta Company was the source of the terracotta, but the firm - although local and presumably less expensive - was then relatively newly-established; as Hathern were definitely sent some of the church plans, perhaps they were simply asked for a quotation as to the cost.

To the west, bordering on VICTORIA PARK ROAD, is the campus of the University of Leicester. The unmistakable red-tiled **Engineering Building** (1959-63), designed by James Stirling & James Gowan, was crucial to the increasing use of tile cladding for concrete as its Dutch-tiled, boxy, geometric form was generally well-received by the architectural press.[7] About half a mile north-west on REGENT ROAD is **Holy Trinity Church** (1838 and 1871-2), internally remodelled during the 1960s but still retaining its opus sectile reredos of the Last Supper supplied by Powell's of Whitefriars in 1901. The drawing was by the artist Ada Currey (1852-1913), who worked for Powell's from 1890 until 1901; it took her 196 hours.[8] Just west is the **Leicester Royal Infirmary** on INFIRMARY CLOSE; in the Balmoral Building is a bronze lustre glazed stoneware sculpture by Jim Robison. Entitled *Voyages of Discovery*, it was inspired by standing stone circles and dates from 1980.

Belgrave

At seven feet high by six feet wide, the faience relief of Cardinal Wolsey over the entrance to the **Sangra Building**, ABBEY PARK STREET, Belgrave is surprising in its scale as well as its colour, the Cardinal's portrait being set on a blue circular ground within a yellow frame. The building, formerly Wolsey's warehouse, was built in 1922-3 and designed by W. Riley. The source of the faience is likely to be either Carter's of Poole or Burmantofts.

New Parks

St Aidan's Church, NEW PARKS BOULEVARD was designed by Basil Spence & Partners and built in 1957-9. In the porch is a large (24 feet by 17 feet) contemporary stoneware mural by William Gordon depicting scenes from the life of St Aidan.[9] This was the first major tile commission obtained by Gordon, who produced studio pottery at the Walton Pottery in Chesterfield throughout the 1950s, when he also experimented with salt-glazed porcelain tiles. Following the closure of the Walton Pottery in 1956, William Gordon concentrated on tile production; amongst other architectural commissions, he designed the Carter & Co abstract tile mural (now lost) installed at Basildon Bus Station in 1958.

LOUGHBOROUGH

Loughborough was a hosiery town that expanded in the nineteenth century from a population of 4,500 in 1801 to 21,000 a century later. During Edwardian times and the interwar years, when street widening and new building took place, the wares of the Hathern Station Brick & Terra Cotta Company, based at Normanton on Soar, three miles to the north, contributed in large measure to the townscape. The Hathern works was founded by George Hodson, the sanitary inspector for Loughborough Board of Health; designs for architectural forms in terracotta, such as window surrounds, were published in 1883 and the terracotta section developed rapidly from 1896.

The earliest Loughborough projects supplied by the firm, including the Great Central Hotel, date to 1898. Grey terracotta became increasingly popular just before the First World War, but glazed finishes dominated into the twenties and thirties. The company was particularly successful during the interwar years in supplying shopfronts and cinema facades, and was responsible for some striking polychromatic schemes. Loughborough became a major showcase for Hathern's ceramics and the firm fought hard to ensure that no other manufacturer gained contracts on their home patch. Most of the buildings are relatively modest in scale and in the lavishness of their decoration, but they provide a remarkable three-dimensional catalogue of twentieth century terracotta and faience. This ceramic profusion makes the town a very special place; as a brewery tap is to a brewery, so Loughborough is to Hathern.

As there are so many ceramic locations, only the highlights can be described here, beginning at the north end of the main shopping area with the Echo Press (now **Loughborough Echo**) building in SWAN STREET; the white faience frontage dates from 1931-2 when street widening took place. Its design was by the local architect E. J. Allcock; elegant Hathernware details include the Echo Press logo topping the pediment and colourful egyptianate column capitals. Opposite the Market Place is BAXTER GATE and the streamlined form of the **Odeon Cinema** (1936, now Beacon Bingo), small but still a corker, and looking rather out of place in downtown Loughborough. It was possibly the largest contract that Hathern ever gained in their home town. The facade was designed by Arthur J. Price of the Harry Weedon practice, who gave it stylish cream fins in mottled vitreous faience above a base of black and green faience banding. The buff faience slabs in the upper part of the facade were set in pairs with the joint at right angles to that of the adjacent pair, the resulting visual effect imitating a woven pattern.

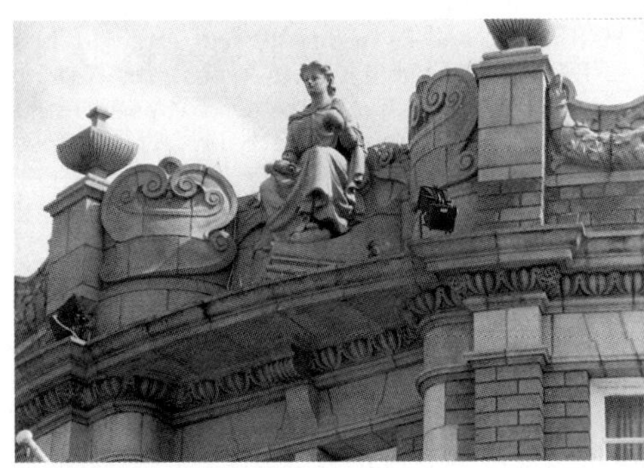

Fig 137.

Back to the HIGH STREET for **Lloyds Bank** (1907), on the corner with Market Place (Fig 137). Hathernware decoration on this well-handled, commanding corner site includes a pair of dolphins and an elaborate parapet with pilasters carrying urns, all topped by an allegorical female figure enthroned on the skyline. Further along the High Street the variety of Hathernware facades takes in **Argos** (probably 1980s) with its series of deep chestnut brown slabs at first floor level; these unusual but little-noticed ceramic squares proved to be a major design challenge for Hathern. Return to the MARKET PLACE where the first floor facade of **Etam** (early twentieth century) sports three semicircular terracotta reliefs of nude children dancing and playing music in woodland settings - a rampant Bacchanalia. The style is similar to that of the Hathern frieze on the NatWest Bank (1903-4), Shepshed which was modelled by George Harry Cox. Continue into CATTLEMARKET for the jazzy, towered white faience facade of the New Empire Cinema (now **Curzon**), remodelled from its predecessor the Empire Palace of Varieties in 1936 by the Birmingham architect A. Hurley Robinson. Its Hathernware facade includes green, blue and yellow art deco detailing; the multi-angled tower holds the water tank.

Opposite the Curzon is GRANBY STREET, at the far end of which is the **Central Library** (1903-5), a Carnegie Library in Edwardian baroque style with much terracotta. The design was selected by competition, the winners being architects Barrowcliff & Allcock; the builder was William Moss & Sons, the bricks were supplied by Tucker & Son, and the tawny unglazed terracotta was supplied by Hathern, of whom George Hodson, the assessor of the competition, was a founder member. All these firms were local. The library extension (1965-6) in the CLASP prefabricated system has bright red tile hanging. Finally into MARKET STREET, mostly rebuilt in the 1930s, with a variety of Hathern faience and terracotta, mainly at first floor level. Best is a run of three stylish thirties buildings on the north side, which use brick and Hathern faience in inventive combinations with much emphasis on the horizontal.

Further from the centre, on the the exterior walls of **Burleigh Community College** (no public access), THORPE HILL is a series of polychrome tin-glazed earthenware reliefs of the *Signs of the Zodiac* by the Austrian-born sculptor Willi Soukop (1907-95), all executed around 1957; for similar sets, see Anstey and Wigston.

LUTTERWORTH

In the MARKET SQUARE is the **Lutterworth Market Place Sculpture**, a tapering ceramic tower about nine feet in height, designed by Martin Williams and unveiled in 1997. Motifs on the glazed tiling mostly relate to the town's medieval history. The Godwin encaustic pavement in the chancel of nearby **St Mary's Church** dates from its restoration of 1867-9 by George Gilbert Scott.

OAKHAM

The interior of **All Saints Church**, CHURCH STREET underwent a no-expense-spared restoration at the hands of George Gilbert Scott in 1857-8. The somewhat unimpressive Minton tiles forming the chancel pavement were designed by Lord Alwyne Compton, chairman of the Architectural Society of the Archdeaconry of Northampton, a man felt by Scott to exceed Pugin in terms of skill in the overall arrangement of tile pavements (although not in pattern design).[10] On the facade of **Somerfield**, WESTGATE is a 1984 stoneware tile relief by Martin Minshall, then Director of Art and Design at Oakham School. It depicts a scene of old Oakham and was modelled and fired at Oakham School.[11]

SHEPSHED

In the BULL RING, right at the centre of Shepshed, is the **NatWest Bank**, built for the Nottingham and Nottinghamshire Banking Company in 1903-4 and designed by A. E. King. Its size is such that local lore suggests the bank was intended for a site in Derby until the plans were mixed up. The buff Hathern terracotta decoration is exceedingly ornate, and includes the long, high-level 'Four Seasons' frieze by the Leicester-based modeller George Harry Cox in which putti carry out the relevant labours.

THEDDINGWORTH

All Saints Church was restored in 1857-8 by George Gilbert Scott at the same time as he was working on All Saints, Oakham. As at the Oakham church, Minton tiles designed by Lord Alwyne Compton, chairman of the influential Architectural Society of the Archdeaconry of Northampton (ASAN), were introduced, perhaps understandably as Theddingworth's rector was the Rev. Thomas James, secretary of ASAN.[12]

THRINGSTONE

Grace Dieu Manor (now a school) was built in 1833-4 for Ambrose Lisle March Phillipps, and quickly became a centre for the revival of Catholicism; Phillipps and A. W. N. Pugin met at Grace Dieu in 1837. Pugin worked for Phillipps on the design of nearby Mount St Bernard Abbey in 1839-44, and also extended the house and chapel at Grace Dieu from 1841. The chapel, although much altered during the 1960s, retains its original floor tiles.

TUR LANGTON

St Andrew's Church was built in 1865-6 by Henry Goddard & Son of Leicester, with Henry's son Joseph Goddard taking responsibility for its unusual design. It is mostly of brick, the interior being of red brick banded with black; there is frequent use of shaped brick. The floor tiles are strongly patterned.

WALTHAM ON THE WOLDS

Although Pevsner's *Leicestershire* suggests that the Powell's of Whitefriars 'tile and mosaic' reredos of **St Mary Magdalene Church** dates from 1872, the firm's records state that at least part of the reredos, an opus sectile panel of the Last Supper, was supplied in 1918 at a cost of £60.[13] The later panel may have been a replacement for or an addition to an earlier reredos.

WHITWICK

In 1835 Ambrose Lisle March Phillipps of Grace Dieu, near Thringstone, donated land at Mount St Bernard, two miles south-east of the manor house, for the building of a Cistercian monastery which opened in 1837. A. W. N. Pugin met Phillipps at Grace Dieu in 1837, and agreed to design a much larger abbey just north of the original site; this was partly funded by the Earl of Shrewsbury and construction began in 1839. The first monks occupied the **Mount St Bernard Abbey** buildings in 1844. There were many subsequent alterations including an octagonal chapter house designed by E. W. Pugin and opened in 1860. Although converted to a library (the Abbey is still a monastic foundation), this retains its elaborate encaustic tiled floor.

WIGSTON

The weird, wave-like brick frontage of **Sainsbury's** (1977), BELL STREET was designed by the sculptor George Pickard. Nearly a mile west of Bell Street, on the the exterior walls of **Guthlaxton Community College** (no public access), STATION ROAD is a series of polychrome tin-glazed earthenware reliefs of the *Signs of the Zodiac* by the sculptor Willi Soukop (1907-95), all executed around 1957; for similar sets see Anstey and Loughborough.

WITHERLEY

On a house in CHURCH ROAD is a two-foot square red terracotta commemorative plaque showing a relief bust of Queen Victoria and produced by Stanley Brothers of Nuneaton. Initially these plaques were made to mark the Queen's fiftieth jubilee in 1887, but the design was later adapted for the 1897 Diamond Jubilee, as in this example. Although the plaques were sold throughout the country, they tend to be found mainly in central and southern England, and Leicestershire has a particularly high concentration. The reason for this appears to have been a connection between Stanley's and Broadbent's, a Leicester builder's merchants, who probably acted as agents for the Nuneaton firm.[14]

Leicestershire Roundup

On the the exterior walls of the Martin High School (no public access), Link Road, **Anstey** is a series of polychrome tin-glazed earthenware reliefs of the *Signs of the Zodiac* by the sculptor Willi Soukop (1907-95), all executed around 1957; for similar sets see Loughborough and Wigston. At St Peter's Church, **Barrowden** is a majolica tile reredos by Maw & Co, dating from the 1875 restoration when the chancel floor was also paved with Maw's tiles.[15] Coade stone statuary in the gardens of Coleorton Hall (1804-8), **Coleorton** includes busts of Milton and Shakespeare. St Andrew's Church, **Hambleton** stands on a peninsula protruding into Rutland Water; the remodelling of its chancel in 1892 included the installation of wall tiling. A Minton tiled floor and dado were installed at the Church of theAssumption of St Mary, **Hinckley** during 1880-1.[16] The encaustic tile pavement at All Saints Church, **Husbands Bosworth** dates from restoration during the 1860s. On the Market Bosworth Hall estate, **Market Bosworth**, the former Home Farm (1888) buttery, Barton Road has blue and white pictorial tiling showing farm work. The brick relief (on the theme of the former cattle market) on the side of Sainsbury's (1993), St Mary's Place, **Market Harborough** was designed and executed by the letter-cutter Richard Kindersley. There is an encaustic tile pavement in the sanctuary of Christ Church (1848-9), **Smeeton Westerby**, which was designed by the gentleman architect Henry Woodyer.

References

1. Terry Cavanagh, *Public Sculpture of Leicestershire and Rutland* (Liverpool University Press, Liverpool, 2000), pp63-5.
2. Jean Farquhar and Joan Skinner, *The History and Architecture of the Turkey Cafe* (Sedgebrook Press, Leicester, 1987).
3. Norma R. Whitcomb, *The medieval floor-tiles of Leicestershire* (Leicestershire Archaeological and Historical Society, Leicester, 1956), p21.
4. Cavanagh, *Leicestershire and Rutland*, pp132-4.
5. Alan McWhirr, 'The building of St James the Greater, Leicester', *Transactions of the Leicestershire Archaeological and Historical Society*, 60 (1986), pp63-77.

6. Burmantofts Catalogue (1902), Ironbridge Gorge Museum Trust Library, accession number 1900.3736.
7. Michael Stratton, *Clad is bad? The relationship between structural and ceramic facing materials*, in *Structure and Style: Conserving Twentieth Century Buildings*, ed Michael Stratton, (E. & F. N. Spon, London, 1997), pp164-92.
8. Dennis Hadley, 'Ada Currey (1852-1913): a forgotten artist', *The Journal of Stained Glass*, 24 (2000), pp29-37.
9. 'Tiled Church Wall', *Architectural Review*, 126 (1959), p287.
10. Geoffrey K. Brandwood, *Bringing them to their knees: church-building and restoration in Leicestershire and Rutland 1800-1914* (Leicestershire Archaeological and Historical Society, Leicester, 2002), p30.
11. Cavanagh, *Leicestershire and Rutland*, p298.
12. Brandwood, *Bringing them to their knees*, p31.
13. Dennis W. Hadley, *James Powell & Sons: A listing of opus sectile, 1847-1973*, (2001).
14. Arthur Sadler, 'Victorian Commemorative Plaques', *Leicestershire Historian*, (1999) 35, pp1-2.
15. Brandwood, *Bringing them to their knees*, p75.
16. Brandwood, *Bringing them to their knees*, p93.

Lincolnshire

Although the manufacture of tiles was well established in Lincolnshire by the early fourteenth century, only a few examples of medieval tiles survive in situ, for instance at Thornton Abbey and Frampton Church. From the early nineteenth century the county offers the sad remnant of the massive Coade stone statue of George III which once topped a land lighthouse, but is now to be found in the grounds of Lincoln Castle. Indeed it is the Victorian restoration and rebuilding of churches which provides much of Lincolnshire's ceramic interest, in the form of encaustic pavements and other decoration. In the Diocese of Lincoln, about £600,000 was spent on church restoration during 1840-74, with a huge increase in the number of restorations from the late 1850s, and in the same period over £230,000 was spent by the diocese on the construction of new churches.[1] James Fowler of Louth was one of the locally-based architects most involved in this work, his commissions often including the installation of encaustic pavements, as did those of the rather less prolific Edward Browning of Stamford, who was probably responsible for the excellent early Minton pavement at St Martin's Church, Stamford.

Terracotta was produced in Lincolnshire by John Blashfield, who transferred his architectural terracotta works from London to Stamford in 1859 to be nearer the clay beds. A wide range of wares was made and the firm was active until 1875, but the best remaining Blashfield work is outside the county rather than within, at Castle Ashby (Northamptonshire) and Dulwich College, London. The architect William Watkins of Lincoln made much use of terracotta from the mid-1880s, but had to obtain his supplies from a variety of non-local sources. In the domestic context, the use of porch tiles was widespread in turn-of-the-century Cleethorpes and Lincoln. Aside from the occasional interwar cinema and shop, the use of architectural ceramics in Lincolnshire petered out almost completely in the early twentieth century; even in modern times there is hardly anything of note apart from the large terracotta plaque above the entrance to Lincoln Magistrates' Court (1990). Public ceramic artworks do not appear to have seeped into the county from neighbouring Leicestershire. Suggested reading: David Kaye and Sam Scorer, *Fowler of Louth* (LNALS, 1992); *The Victorian Facade: W. Watkins and Son, Architects, Lincoln 1859-1918* (Lincolnshire College of Art & Design, Lincoln, 1990). The *Gazetteer* entry for Lincolnestershire covers the administrative areas of Lincolnshire County Council, North East Lincolnshire Council and North Lincolnshire Council.

AMBER HILL

The red brick, neo-Norman former **Church of St John Baptist** was built in 1867 and designed by Edward Browning (1816-82), who succeeded to the Stamford architectural practice of his father Bryan Browning (1773-1856). Edward Browning's youger brother Henry Bailey Browning (1822-1907) worked in the office briefly before being ordained in 1851; he held the living of St George's with St Paul's in Stamford from 1862 until 1890.[2] Amongst his other works, Edward Browning built, rebuilt and altered around sixteen Lincolnshire churches, and at Amber Hill experimented with decorative brickwork and terracotta. The porch has terracotta capitals while the interior is of yellow brick with a red brick dado and black brick band; the chancel arch has a small amount of terracotta decoration. The manufacturer of the terracotta is not known, but could well have been John Blashfield, whose works in Stamford opened to a welter of publicity in 1859 and supplied the terracotta for the massive, lettered balustrade at Castle Ashby, Northamptonshire around 1867, when the Amber Hill church was under construction. Blashfield specialised in the intricate design of terracotta, with undercutting and applied detailing, so it is possible that the deeply moulded terracotta at Amber Hill was his work. As well as the terracotta detailing, St John Baptist also has a high-level fleur-de-lys tile frieze in the chancel and a majolica tile reredos. As the church is now a private house, there is no public access.

BIGBY

All Saints Church was restored in 1878 by the architect James Fowler (1828-92) of Louth, the most prolific church architect of the time in the north of the county. His work at Bigby included the installation of a Minton tile pavement in the chancel, along with terracotta floral reliefs on the east wall.

BURRINGHAM

The **Church of St John the Baptist** (1856-7, now in the care of the Churches Conservation Trust), HIGH STREET, was designed by the London architect Samuel Sanders Teulon who obtained a series of commissions for church building and restoration in Lincolnshire, possibly because of his low churchmanship.[3] Burringham's interior is typical Teulon in its unremitting polychromy; yellow brick walls have red and black brick patterning, there is a colourful encaustic tiled floor and even the octagonal font is decorated with blue and yellow encaustics. The church was a close precursor of Teulon's better-known St Mark's Church (1860-2), Silvertown, Newham, east London, in which the architect combined polychromatic brickwork with hollow grey terracotta 'bricks' in an aggressive display of architectural imagination.

CLEETHORPES

The growth of Cleethorpes as a seaside resort was boosted by the arrival of the railway in 1863, and the town enjoyed a boom towards the end of the nineteenth century and into the early years of the twentieth. Decoration of houses built in this period was correspondingly lavish, and there are porch tiles throughout the central area, for instance in ST PETER'S AVENUE and ISAACS HILL; further south, the pseudo-half timbered **Tudor Terrace** in BRADFORD AVENUE provides another good example. In addition, on Isaacs Hill, near the station, there are also larger houses which combine porch tiling with plaster reliefs above. Of course, some porch tiles are now hidden behind outer doors, whilst others have been painted over or removed, but many are still easily visible; there is a good variety of designs in this pleasant little town of tiles, albeit no picture panels. Also popular in Cleethorpes were tile pavements in porches and extending into hallways, and black and white geometric tiled pathways to front gates.

Other highlights in the town centre include **Gresham's Fisheries**, HIGH STREET, with its full height 'Fresh Fish Daily' exterior tile panel; the replacement stall riser of 1992 by Wilton Studios shows a Grimsby scene featuring the famous Dock Tower. South in OXFORD STREET is the former **Co-op** with greyish faience detailing, centred on a beehive, high up on the canted corner. Turning back towards the sea, the substantial **Queens** pub on CAMBRIDGE STREET and Seaview Street has a good interwar white faience facade; its side garage entrance has excellent detailing of bunches of grapes.

DONINGTON ON BAIN

At **St Andrew's Church** is an unusual tiled wall memorial dating from about 1910 and made by Jones & Willis of London. The matt glazed tiles are cream in colour and carry red gothic-style lettering; the surround is of opaque glass in various colours. A very similar memorial, by the same firm but dating from 1920, may be seen at Selby Abbey, North Yorkshire.

DUNSTON

St Peter's Church was mostly rebuilt in 1874-6 (architect R. H. Carpenter), the new chancel having a good encaustic pavement. The works were largely paid for by the Marquess of Ripon from nearby Nocton Hall, itself rebuilt in 1841 following a fire. Sir Francis Dashwood of High Wycombe had been a visitor to the original house, having married the widow of Sir Richard Ellis of Nocton in 1745. In the mid-eighteenth century Nocton Heath was so difficult for travellers to cross that Sir Francis had a huge column erected in 1751, on which was placed a lantern; this land lighthouse, over 100 feet in height, was known as the Dunston Pillar, and its remains still stand on the A15 about four miles west of Dunston (six miles south-east of Lincoln). The light was lit for the last time in 1808, and the lantern fell from the pillar during a storm in 1809. It was replaced the following year by an almost three-times life-size Coade stone figure of George III, modelled by Joseph Panzetta and given by the Duke of Buckingham to mark the King's golden jubilee. During the Second World War the statue was removed and the column shortened, the statue breaking into fragments which found their way to Lincoln Castle. The head and shoulders of this enormous piece of Coade statuary, perhaps one of the largest ever made, have been reconstructed and are now on display in the Castle grounds.[4]

FRAMPTON

There are decorated medieval tiles on the floor of the south aisle chapel of the parish church, **St Mary's Church**. Just over a mile to the west is **St Michael's Church**, built in 1863 as a private chapel for the Tunnards of Frampton House. The architect was James Fowler, whose work included the design of the Minton-tiled sanctuary.[5]

GREAT CARLTON

St John Baptist Church was mostly rebuilt in 1860-1 by James Fowler. The strongly polychromatic interior has lozenge-shaped panels of colourful encaustic tiles in the spandrels along either side of the nave arcade; above are strings of tiles bearing texts. The pulpit comes in for its share of decorative motifs, with more tiled lozenges set into its brick base, and there is an ornate encaustic pavement in the sanctuary. Most lavish of all is the opus sectile reredos of the Last Supper, from a new cartoon by Frank Mann, which was supplied by Powell's in 1889; its richness of colour is enhanced by mosaic side panels in gold and turquoise.

GRIMSBY

In the centre of Grimsby is the FRESHNEY PLACE shopping centre, where the backdrop to **Boaters Tea Garden** is provided by a large tile mural of Grimsby including the town's coat of arms, the inescapable Dock Tower and a portrait of Queen Elizabeth II. The mural, which was designed by J. N. Freear, was installed in 1977 to mark the Queen's silver jubilee. Outside in VICTORIA STREET is the former **Savoy Cinema** (now McDonalds), built in 1920 for Savoy Picture House Ltd and designed by Chadwick & Watson. Its neo-classical white faience facade is topped on the curving corner by a figure of a female dancer.

Away from the main shopping area in VICTORIA STREET NORTH is something of an oddity, the pretty tiled wall of a car park belonging to the **Palace Buffet** public house, in the lee of the huge Victoria Flour Mills. This unexpected full-height wall tiling, in mainly browns and pale greens with classical motifs, turns out to be the remains of the Palace Theatre, built in 1904 and mostly demolished in 1979. In FREEMAN STREET, east of and running parallel to Victoria Street North, is the **ABC Cinema** sporting a tall 1960s abstract tile mural. Although the colours - mauves, browns - are not bright, the overall effect is quite striking. The tiles were probably made by Malkin Tiles or H. & R. Johnson, who worked together during the 1960s and produced this type of geometric relief design.

LINCOLN

To explore Lincoln, begin at 358 HIGH STREET, towards the south end of this long thoroughfare, with the **Magistrates' Court** (1990). Stationed above the entrance on the front of this low-rise, buff brick building is a large, circular red terracotta plaque of the British coat of arms. Further along the High Street is the terracotta territory of local architect William Watkins (1834-1926), 'the father of Lincoln architects'. He was attracted to terracotta as a building material in the mid-1880s, and used it with brio on the renaissance facade of the former **Peacock & Willson's Bank** (1897) at 190-1 High Street.[6] Watkins produced sixty to seventy drawings of the detailing alone for Doulton's, who supplied the distinctive salmon-pink terracotta from their Lambeth works. It was the first use of terracotta on a public building in Lincoln. The ground floor had been altered, but this part of the facade was reinstated during 1993 using Hathernware products.[7] Close by is another Watkins building, the former **Brown and Hewitt** shop at 185-6 High Street, the tallest building in the street when it was put up in 1900. In this case the flamboyant buff terracotta was supplied by the Hathern Station Brick & Terra Cotta Company.

Onwards up Steep Hill to reach the **Cathedral**, where two small panels of encaustic floor tiles in the sanctuary, beside the high altar, date from 1857-8 and were probably made by Maw & Co. Just west of the Cathedral is **Lincoln Castle**, where the remains of a massive Coade stone statue of George III (1810) may be seen in the grounds. The fifteen-foot high statue originally topped the Dunston Pillar, a land lighthouse erected in 1751 six miles to the south-east of Lincoln (for details see entry for Dunston). Return towards the centre of Lincoln, taking Greestone Place, near the east end of Minster Yard, and descending into LINDUM ROAD to see the first major essay in terracotta by William Watkins, the **Girls' High School** (1893, extended 1911), now part of Lincolnshire College of Art & Design; its blast of red Ruabon terracotta dominates the hillside below the Cathedral. There is a whole range of small-scale detailing including dolphins and flaming torches. Continue south into BROADGATE to see more of Watkins in the form of his domed **Constitutional Club** (1895), on the corner of Silver Street, where he combined bright red terracotta (supplied by J. C. Edwards of Ruabon and mentioned in the firm's 1903 catalogue) with much Tudor-style rubbed brick. Watkins moved on to experiment with the fashionable, paler coloured terracottas in his later High Street buildings, just west of Broadgate.

Finally, away from the centre in the MOUNT STREET area, developed when the city was undergoing a period of growth in late Victorian and Edwardian times, are more than sixty examples of tiled porches, some with full-height tiling. Mount Street itself comprises a row of thirty-six terraced houses which all have different porch tiling, some with individual art nouveau motifs and others with complex arrangements including up to sixteen different tiles.[8]

LOUTH

The Maw & Co floor tiling in the south porch of **St James Church** was installed by the architect James Fowler during his restorations of 1860 and 1868-9, as were the superb Minton tiles in the chancel and sanctuary pavements. There is good tiling in the **Church of St Michael and All Angels** (1863), Church Street, which was also designed by Fowler; the interior is polychromatic brickwork.

REVESBY

In the tower of **St Lawrence Church** is a panel (about 4′ by 6′) of thirteenth century tiles made up from those found during excavations at the Cistercian foundation of Revesby Abbey, about half a mile south of the church. The black, green and light brown tiles, which came from the cloister and south choir aisle, are set in bands of star forms. The extensive mosaic pavements of the Abbey had ten different layouts in long panels.

RISEHOLME

The Bishop of Lincoln, Dr John Kaye, became rector of **St Mary's Church** in 1847 and rebuilt the little church during 1850-1. His chosen architect was S. S. Teulon, who produced a design on strictly Ecclesiological principles; the proposed tower and spire were never built. The nave is paved with red and black Broseley tiles forming triangular patterns, while the chancel is much more decorative, with an elaborate Minton encaustic tiled pavement; the tiled risers bear inscriptions.[9]

SPALDING

So impressive is the white faience facade of the former **Savoy Cinema** (1937, now bingo), Sheepmarket, that it could almost pass muster for an Odeon. The cinema was built for the Spalding Picture House Company by the Nottingham architect Alfred J. Thraves, who used faience supplied by Hathern in his design which features a series of almost full-height green fins.[10] Thraves also specified Hathernware in his design for the Regal Cinema (1937), Boston, which was demolished in 2002.

STAMFORD

Begin at the centre of Stamford, Red Lion Square. On the north side, and facing away towards All Saints Place, is medieval **All Saints Church**, restored in 1857 by Edward Browning, who added the Minton encaustic tile pavement in the sanctuary. Scotgate runs north-west from the church, and at number five is the **Scotgate** public house (known disgustingly in 2002 as Doctor Thirstys). The red brick facade dates from 1871 and is topped by a splendid grey terracotta parapet bearing the lettering 'P & R. Phipps. Brewers.'; above is a magnificent crest, a tiny castle with two supporting lions, the Phipps trademark (Fig 138). There is other terracotta (as well as stone) detailing. The brewers were based in Northampton, about 30 miles to the south-west, and perhaps felt they had to stump up for such a striking facade in order to compete with the local brewers, one of whom brewed close by in All Saints Street, while another (a potential source of loss-making confusion) was Phillips Stamford Brewery, based near the river in Water Street.

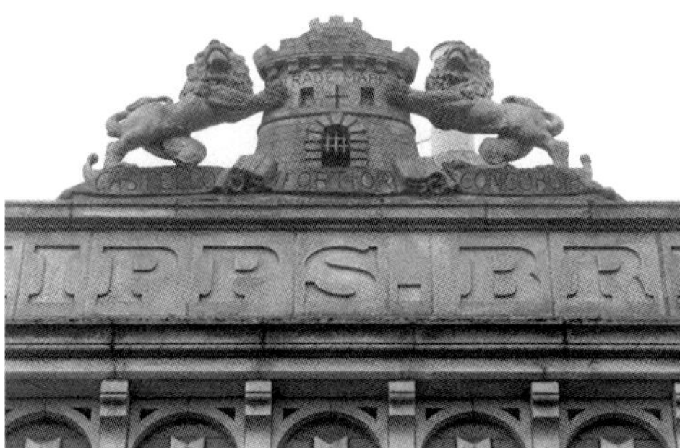

Fig 138.

The Scotgate's terracotta was supplied locally, by John Marriott Blashfield, a London tilemaker who was making architectural terracotta at Millwall by the end of 1851. He transferred production to Stamford in 1859 to be nearer the clay beds, and made a range of wares from classical ornaments to architectural dressings. Blashfield liked to create unusual forms in terracotta, and also employed major sculptors; he ceased production in 1875. The major Blashfield sites of Dulwich College (London) and Castle Ashby (Northamptonshire) apart, surprisingly little evidence of his terracotta remains extant, even in Stamford, where the Scotgate is one of only two minor locations. To see the other, head back across Red Lion Square and into the HIGH STREET; at number thirty, on the north side, is the strange 1873 frontage of a shop (currently **Cottage Frames**), mostly of brick and stone but including five red terracotta panels amongst its detailing. For Blashfield enthusiasts, this is really rather disappointing.

Turn south towards the river Welland, eventually crossing the Town Bridge at the foot of St Mary's Hill and continuing up into HIGH STREET ST MARTIN'S. On the left is **St Martin's Church**, which - apart from its many monuments to the Cecils of nearby Burghley House - has a superb early Minton encaustic tile pavement running throughout the chancel. The overall design focuses on a six-feet long tile cross sited just in front of the altar; the cross is made up from buff and brown specials, but the tiles in the rest of this exquisite pavement come direct from Minton's *First Printed Catalogue* of 1842. Around the cross are a number of four-tile groups, with the 'rose window' design, number 21 in the *Catalogue*, featuring heavily. In the centre of the choir is a series of nine-tile groups, mostly made up from three different tile designs, but with a more complex asymmetric group needing five separate tiles. At least twenty-four designs from the *Catalogue* are used, along with various border tiles and the specials.[11]

Pevsner suggests that the probable date of the St Martin's pavement is 1865, but given that Edward Browning designed fittings for the church in 1845, soon after the *Catalogue* became available, the latter date would seem much more likely.[12] In 1845 such tiles would have been seen as suitable for an important church, as well as being fashionable; a date of 1865 would have provided a much broader choice of design and manufacturer. This may even have been the first time that Browning, who eventually became an enthusiastic user of encaustic tiles, specified a tile pavement. Also to be seen at St Martin's, on the north wall of the nave, is an unusual ceramic plaque, a wall memorial to Thomas Cooper Goodrich (d1885), 'A Rare Cricketer and a Good Man'.

Further along High Street St Martin's is **Stamford High School for Girls** (1876, architect Edward Browning) with an encaustic-tiled entrance hall, possibly by the Campbell Brick & Tile Company.

SUTTERTON

The chancel of **St Mary's Church** was rebuilt in 1861-2 by Edward Browning, who installed its pavement of Maw's encaustic tiles.[13] James Fowler, who restored the chancel in 1879, probably added the brightly colourful wall tiling and the fine tile and mosaic reredos.

TATTERSHALL

On the north side of the churchyard of **Holy Trinity Church** is the sandstone tombstone of Frances Dryland (d1872), the wife of William Turner. Set into it is an inlaid quatrefoil-shaped ceramic plaque in red, buff, white and blue, with a central motif of the Pascal Lamb.

THORNTON ABBEY

Thornton Abbey (EH) was founded as a priory in 1139 for Augustinian canons; it was raised to the status of an abbey in 1148. Beyond the vast, fourteenth-century gatehouse lie the remains of the church and the monastic quarters. The refectory was in the south range, which was built in 1326-8; its undercroft retains an area measuring about 3' by 4' of much-broken rhombic tiles with eleven recognisable designs. The rhombic shape was unpopular with medieval tilers as tiles of other shapes were required in order to form arrangements other than herringbone or chequerwork, and their production ceased during the 1340s.[14]

WAITHE

St Martin's Church was mostly rebuilt in 1861 by James Fowler. The work was funded by the Haigh family of Yorkshire mill owners, who moved into now-demolished Grainsby Hall, a mile or so to the south, during the 1840s. The result of their generosity was a richly decorative interior, including a Minton fleur-de-lys relief tiled dado in the chancel, which also has an elaborate encaustic pavement. Lozenge-shaped memorial tablets in the apse record Haigh family burials in the vault beneath the chancel. The church is now in a poor state of repair and has been closed to worship for some time.

WEST DEEPING

The restoration of **St Andrew's Church** in 1874-7 was one of the later works of William Butterfield; his refit of the interior emphasised colour, with much tiling and an especially ornate mosaic reredos.

Lincolnshire Roundup

There is good tile and mosaic work of 1867 in the chancel of St Stephen's Church, **Careby**. The Church of St Lawrence and Bishop Edward King (the dedication dates from 1960), **Dalby** was rebuilt by James Fowler in 1862; the interior is typical Fowler polychromatic brickwork with a tiled reredos. The Church of St Cornelius, **Linwood** has interesting majolica and encaustic east wall tiling, the scheme including lettering beneath symbols of the evangelists. St Helen's Church, **Little Cawthorpe** (now in the care of the Churches Conservation Trust), built in 1860 by the London architect R. J. Withers, has an encaustic tiled reredos. James Fowler's 1862 work at St Thomas, **Market Rasen** included the installation of a Minton reredos with roundels of the evangelists. All Saints Church, **Snelland**, restored and rebuilt by Edward Browning in 1862-3, has a good tile pavement throughout. At St Hilary's Church (1875), **Spridlington** is a gothic-lettered six-tile wall memorial dating from about 1920; there is also an encaustic tile pavement in the sanctuary.

In addition, the following churches have encaustic tile pavements: St Peter and St Paul, Algarkirk; St Peter and St Paul, Caistor; St Mary and the Holy Rood, Donington; All Saints, Friskney; St Peter, Great Limber; St Stephen, Hatton (also reredos); St Andrew, Heckington; St Luke, Holbeach Hurn; All Saints, Holton Beckering (also excellent mosaic reredos); Holy Trinity, Horncastle; St Mary, Long Sutton (Minton); St John the Baptist, Nettleton; All Saints, Nocton; St Mary, Old Leake (also reredos); St Mary, Pinchbeck; St Lawrence, Sedgebrook; St Botolph, Skidbrooke (in the care of the Churches Conservation Trust); St Michael, South Hykeham (east wall only); St Martin, Stubton.

References

1. Chris Miele, '*Their interest and habit': professionalism and the restoration of medieval churches, 1837-77*, in *The Victorian Church*, eds Chris Brooks and Andrew Saint, (Manchester University Press, Manchester, 1995), pp151-172.
2. Howard Colvin, *A Biographical Dictionary of British Architects, 1600-1840* 3rd ed (Yale University Press, New Haven and London, 1995), p172.
3. Anthony Symondson, *Theology, worship and the late Victorian church*, in *The Victorian Church: Architecture and Society*, eds Chris Brooks and Andrew Saint, (Manchester University Press, Manchester, 1995), pp192-222, see p199.
4. David Start, 'Dunston Pillar', *Lincolnshire Past & Present*, (2003) 52, pp10-11.
5. David Kaye, Sam Scorer and David N. Robinson, *Fowler of Louth: The Life and Works of James Fowler, Louth Architect 1828-1892* (Louth Naturalists', Antiquarian and Literary Society, Louth, 1992).
6. Michael Stratton, *William Watkins and the Terracotta Revival*, in *The Victorian Facade: W. Watkins and Son, Architects, Lincoln, 1859-1918*, (Lincolnshire College of Art & Design, Lincoln, 1990), pp24-28.
7. Paul McAuley, *Terracotta Facades in Lincoln*, in *Architectural Ceramics: their history, manufacture and conservation*, ed Jeanne Marie Teutonico, (James & James (Science Publishers) Ltd, London, 1996), pp122-7.
8. Ian Bayne, 'Tiled Porches in Lincoln', *Glazed Expressions*, (1997) 34, pp6-7.
9. *The Builder*, vol 9, 23rd August 1851, p534.
10. Kevin Wheelan, *The History of the Hathern Station Brick & Terra Cotta Company* (Mercia Cinema Society, Birmingham, 1982).
11. The tile designs used in the pavement of St Martin's Church, Stamford are numbers 1, 9, 12, 20-1, 31, 35, 51-2, 54, 61, 63-5, 67-75 and 81 from Minton's *First Printed Catalogue* of 1842.
12. Nikolaus Pevsner, John Harris and Nicholas Antram, *Lincolnshire* 2nd ed. Buildings of England (Penguin, London, 1989), p692.
13. *The Builder*, vol 20, 6th September 1862.
14. G. K. Beaulah, 'Tiles of rhombic shape at Thornton Abbey, with notes on some others', *TACS Journal*, 1 (1982), pp23-27.

London

'Westminster' tiles, along with Penn (Buckinghamshire) tiles the most common types of decorated medieval floor tiles found in the London area, were named after Westminster Abbey, where there are still several extant groups. At least some of the 'Westminster' tiles were made in London, but they were technically of much poorer quality than the thirteenth century Chertsey-Westminster tiles found in Westminster Abbey's Chapter House. The production of 'Westminster' tiles ceased around the beginning of the fourteenth century, when the initial demand for floor tiles had been largely satisfied.

The next phase of London's tile making began when the Antwerp potter Jacob Jansen (d1592) established a pottery at Aldgate in 1571, and was assisted there by six other Flemish potters; this produced tin-glazed earthenware, including floor tiles, and continued until about 1615. Other potteries making tin-glazed floor tiles were set up in Southwark around this time, the best known being the Pickleherring pottery, which acquired exclusive rights to the manufacture of tin-glazed tiles and earthenware for a twenty-one year period from 1628. Demand for fashionable delftware wall tiles led to the establishment of a works in Vauxhall by the Delft potter Jan Ariens van Hamme in 1676, and by the early eighteenth century tiles were being produced at several delftware potteries on the south bank of the Thames.[1] They were used mainly for fireplaces but few remain *in situ*, even in London, whereas Dutch-made tiles of the same period do survive in several London locations.[2]

In the early sixteenth century relatively small amounts of decorative terracotta had been used in the construction of Hampton Court (Richmond upon Thames), setting off a short-lived enthusiasm for the material, especially in East Anglia. However, London's earliest large-scale producer of architectural ceramics was Coade's, manufacturers of Coade stone, a type of stoneware. The business was established in Lambeth in 1769 by Eleanor Coade and her daughter Eleanor, the latter normally known as Mrs Coade (1733-1821). By 1799 her cousin John Sealy had become a partner, the firm then being known as Coade and Sealy, but after Sealy's death in 1813 the business name reverted to Coade. The firm considered its best work to be the Nelson pediment (1810-12) on the King William Building at the Royal Hospital for Seamen in Greenwich, but there are many other examples of Coade ornament in London. J. C. F. Rossi, who at one time worked for Coade's, modelled the terracotta caryatids at St Pancras New Church (1819-22, Camden); this early appearance of terracotta was followed from the 1860s by its use, along with faience, in the seminal buildings of South Kensington (Kensington & Chelsea). The terracotta of the Charing Cross Hotel (1863-5, Westminster) represents an early and extensive use of the material in a commercial building.

The first significant encaustic tile commission carried out by the Stoke-on-Trent tile manufacturer Herbert Minton was in the City of London at the Temple Church. Most of the designs of the pavement laid during the 1841-3 restoration of the church were based on those of the newly-rediscovered medieval tiles in Westminster Abbey Chapter House; the installation won general acclaim and resulted in much publicity for the firm. Equally influential in the secular rather than the ecclesiastical context was the encaustic tiling carried out at the Palace of Westminster, where the best of the Pugin-designed Minton pavements date from 1847 and 1852.

Although Minton tiles were used in a significant number of London buildings, the city's major tile and architectural ceramics manufacturer was Doulton's, established when John Doulton bought the Vauxhall Pottery in 1815. He went into partnership with John Watts, initially the pottery's manager, and the firm traded as Doulton & Watts during 1820-58; they began producing terracotta building components in the 1820s, and by 1828 had moved to High Street, Lambeth. After the death of Watts, John Doulton continued in business with his sons John and Henry as Doulton & Co. The Lambeth Pottery finally closed in 1956, and only one corner of the works - Doulton House (1878, Lambeth) - survives, complete with a terracotta tympanum modelled by George Tinworth which shows Henry Doulton amongst his artists. The company's headquarters between 1939 and 1971 was the art deco Doulton House (1938, architects T. P. Bennett & Son), which stood on the Albert Embankment. After the firm moved out, the building remained empty, still sporting its immense polychrome stoneware frieze modelled by Gilbert Bayes and entitled *Pottery Through the Ages* (1939). When the building faced sudden demolition in 1978 the frieze, comprising over 300 stoneware blocks, was taken down (in wintry conditions) by volunteers from Ironbridge Gorge Museum; it was restored at the Museum and eventually returned to London where it is on display at the Victoria & Albert Museum (Fig 139). Mounted on the side of Doulton House was the much smaller *Dutch Potters* stoneware panel, also by Bayes; this can now be seen at the Jackfield Tile Museum.

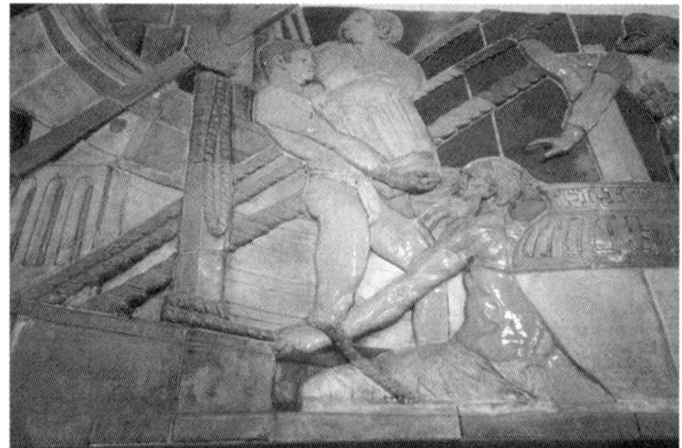

Fig 139.

Burmantofts of Leeds produced large blocks and slabs of glazed and unglazed faience from the early 1880s, but this was intended for internal work, as the material was not resistant to frost damage. Their coloured faience made frequent appearances in London's clubs and restaurants during the 1880s, but the first major interiors were at the National Liberal Club (1884-7, Westminster). The same material appeared on the exterior of 47 Maddox Street (1892, Westminster), but it was really Doulton's development of frost and pollution-resistant Carraraware in 1888 which allowed faience to emerge into the daylight, an early example of its use, and the most extensive ever, being the polychrome Carraraware-clad Birkbeck Bank (1895-6, demolished 1965) near the north end of Chancery Lane.[3]

From the mid-nineteenth century Doulton's had a close relationship with the licensed trade. This resulted in the installation of hand-painted pictorial tile panels in many turn-of-the-century London pubs, for instance the St James's Tavern (Westminster); similar work from the tile-decorating firm W. B. Simpson & Sons survives at the Ten Bells (Tower Hamlets). Simpson's was founded in 1833 and from 1868 was based at premises in St Martin's Lane, where the upper floors were used as a tile painting studio and for the production of stained glass and opus sectile panels. The stained glass firm Powell's of Whitefriars were the most important producers of opus sectile work, which was generally found in churches such as St Mary's, Balham (Wandsworth). Outstanding examples of ecclesiastical tile murals are at All Saints Margaret Street (Westminster) and St Augustine (Kensington & Chelsea), both by William Butterfield.

Into the twentieth century, colourful faience made up the facade of a series of London Underground stations, but as these share many characteristics they are summarised below, along with the London-wide Blue Plaques scheme, a pleasing ceramic byway. It is interesting to note that the use of decorative ceramics on the Underground network never appealed to architectural critics, despite its success in creating a brand image for the various lines. The Dutch modernist faience-clad Holland House (1914-16, City of London) proved uninfluential, and it was cinemas such as Southall's Palace (1928-9, Ealing) which kept architectural ceramic innovation alive between the wars. Victor Pasmore's groundbreaking 1951 mural at the Regatta Restaurant was lost along with all the other Festival of Britain buildings, apart from the Festival Hall, although the Susan Lawrence School (1951, Tower Hamlets), part of the Festival's 'Live Architecture Exhibition', survives with its well-publicised Peggy Angus pattern-making tiles.[4] In the capital, postwar ceramic mural work tended towards corporate imagery and public art projects of varying degrees of sophistication; a notable example of the latter is Jean Powell's mural at Stepney Green School (2002, Tower Hamlets).

Blue Plaques

The Blue Plaques scheme for the erection of plaques to commemorate famous people was founded by the Society of Arts in 1866, their first ever plaque, to Lord Byron, being erected in 1867.[5] This was lost due to demolition in 1889, and the oldest surviving plaque is for Napoleon III (1808-73), which was put up in 1867 in King St, St James's, Westminster. It is a circular, sky blue encaustic plaque with white lettering, but the manufacturers, Minton Hollins, found these hard to produce and most pre-1901 plaques were chocolate-brown in colour, as these could be made more easily and cheaply; an example is the Michael Faraday plaque at 48 Blandford Street,

Westminster, which dates from 1876. The Society of Arts erected 35 plaques (of which only 13 remain) before the scheme passed into the hands of London County Council (LCC) in 1901.

The first LCC plaque was put up in 1903, and the Council continued erecting plaques at a rate of about eight per year until the First World War. Although retaining Minton Hollins as manufacturers, the LCC made many experiments with design and materials, and some of the most distinctive examples date from the Edwardian period, for instance William Wilberforce at 111 Broomwood Road (Wandsworth, 1906). This is a square, encaustic-tiled plaque in white on brown with an ornate border. By 1921 the LCC's architect had decided that glazed Doulton stoneware would be cheaper and easier to clean than the encaustic plaques, and a circular Doulton plaque in blue with a wreath surround became the norm, for instance William Ewart Gladstone at 11 Carlton House Terrace (Westminster, 1925). A simpler design, minus the wreath border, was proposed in 1938 and continues in use today. Doulton's produced the plaques until 1955, when their Lambeth factory was on the point of closure, after which Carter's of Poole took on the job. Doulton's made over 200 blue plaques for the LCC, each costing around eight guineas.[6] In numerical terms, some of the rarest surviving plaques are those made by Carter's for the LCC, which was only putting up a handful every year by 1965, when the scheme was taken over by the Greater London Council (GLC). Two such are to Sir Charles Stanford, 56 Hornton Street, Kensington (1961) and the plaque marking the historical associations of Essex Street, off the Strand (Westminster, 1962, re-erected 1964).

The GLC installed an average of 13 plaques per year; Carter's produced them in their Faience Department at Hamworthy until 1977, when the work was transferred to the East Quay site where over 70 slip-trailed faience plaques were decorated by Cynthia Bennett, Julie Williams and Hilda Smith before 1981, when Carter's ceased making them.[7] The Gerald Du Maurier plaque at 14 Cannon Place, Hampstead (Camden, 1967) was made by the Faience Department, while the East Quay was responsible for Wilfrid Scawen-Blunt's plaque at 15 Buckingham Gate (Westminster, 1979) and George Orwell's at 50 Lawford Road, Kentish Town (Camden, 1980).

After 1981, production of the blue plaques, with their distinctive lettering designed by Harry Hooper, was taken over by independent craftspeople; the first was Alan Dawson, who had previously worked for sanitaryware manufacturers Armitage Shanks. By 1985 the number of commissions had increased to the point where Dawson could not fulfil them alone, and some of the work went to Frank and Sue Ashworth of Blackheath, London. In 1986 the scheme itself passed from the GLC to English Heritage (EH), who produced their own font for the plaques and commissioned Dawson to make them. Following Dawson's death in 1994, the Ashworths continued the work, with Richard Wildblood of Burton upon Trent being brought in to share production.

An example of an EH design is the Jimi Hendrix plaque at 23 Brook Street, Mayfair (Westminster, 1997), made by Frank and Sue Ashworth; on average it takes two months to produce a standard glazed ceramic plaque, which is 50mm thick and 495mm in diameter. By 2004, EH had erected about 400 new plaques in London at a rate of around 20 per year, bringing the total to over 760, with the scheme being extended into the English regions from 2004. Bloomsbury (Camden), particularly Bedford Square and the adjoining section of Gower Street to the north, is an excellent area for plaque-spotting with 11 ranging in date throughout the whole of the twentieth century and erected by the LCC, GLC and EH. There are plaques by all three of the major manufacturers as well as the post-1981 makers, including a rare LCC/Carter's - Thomas Wakley, 35 Bedford Square (1962) - and William Butterfield's 1978 plaque at 42 Bedford Square.

London Underground Stations

The world's first underground passenger railway was opened by the Metropolitan Railway in 1863, its steam-operated track connecting Paddington and Farringdon Street; what is now the Circle line was completed in 1884. The development of electric traction and improved tunnelling techniques led to the construction of deep-level 'tube' lines, the first of which - the City & South London Railway - opened in 1890. In 1900 came the Central London Railway (CLR), running between Shepherd's Bush and Bank (now part of the Central line), the surface buildings at each station being designed by architect Harry Bell Measures (1862-1940) and faced in pinky-brown terracotta produced by J. C. Edwards of Ruabon.[8] It seems that the terracotta was only partly fired in order to achieve the colour required; this led to the relatively rapid deterioration of what one critic described as 'wretched terracotta structures, apparently cast from one badly detailed mould'.[9]

The CLR platform tunnels were lined with functional white tiles, unlike those of the deep-level tube lines built in 1906-7 by four companies which eventually came under the control of the Underground Electric Railways Company of London, normally known as the Underground Group; these now make up the central sections of the Bakerloo, Northern and Piccadilly lines. The architect Leslie William Green (1875-1908) designed over 40 stations for the Underground Group, using bright, fully glazed Burmantofts oxblood red faience for the exterior of the surface buildings, green wall tiles for the booking hall and coloured tiling in distinctive geometric patterns on the platforms; it seems, however, that Green had little influence on the design of the subterranean areas, with the tile fixing contractors probably taking much of the responsibility.[10] The wall tiling came from several firms including George Wooliscroft & Sons, Craven Dunnill and Maw's, the latter products being supplied by W. B. Simpson & Sons, who fixed the tiles. About 1.5 million 9" by 3" tiles were used along 94 platforms at 43 stations, the general scheme comprising a white or cream ground with horizontal bands of different coloured tiles at bottom, top and waist level. Vertical coloured bands were introduced at fairly regular intervals, and the station name was generally shown in 15" high letters on three panels.[11]

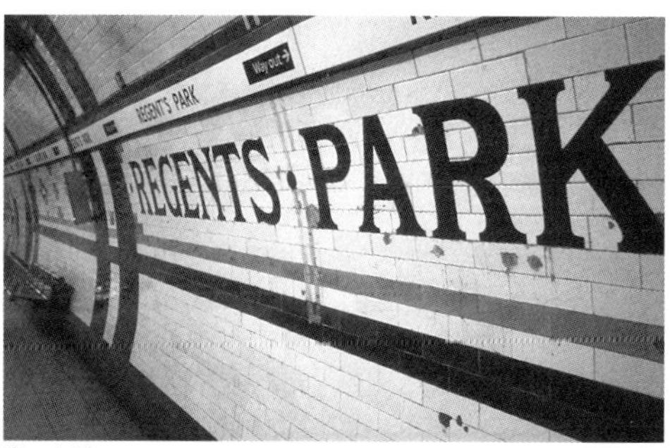

Fig 140.

Of Green's 43 stations, 12 are still operational but have lost most of their original features, while 6 are disused but retain largely intact facades. The 25 operational stations with original features include Tufnell Park (1907), where the tiling - as at the disused Aldwych (1907) - was by the Permanent Decorative Glass Company, a small concern which ceased to function in 1913. The best of Green's surviving stations is Russell Square (1906), where the tiling is by Wooliscroft's, with several original direction signs and a trade tile on one of the bridges connecting the lower lift landing with the platforms. Regent's Park (1906) is the oldest station to have survived at platform level, and a Maw's/Simpson's trade tile can be seen at the lower lift landing (Fig 140).

In conjunction with Green's work on the Piccadilly line, several stations on the District Railway were rebuilt by the architect Harry Ford (1875-1947), who also specified faience for the station facades, but in more muted brown shades. Hathern's light brown vitreous faience was used by Ford at Earl's Court (1906), its duller finish now sometimes being confused with that of Burmantofts oxblood faience following cleaning with hydrofluoric acid, which destroys its glazed surface. The deep buff and chocolate coloured faience frontage of Ford's Barons Court (1905) has also lost most of its glazed finish through over-zealous cleaning.[12] The Metropolitan Railway and its architect Charles W. Clark began modernisation of its stations in 1914, the work being interrupted by the First World War. Farringdon (1923), Edgware Road (1928) and Great Portland Street (1930), amongst others, were rebuilt in conservative neo-classical style using pale buff Gibbs & Canning faience.

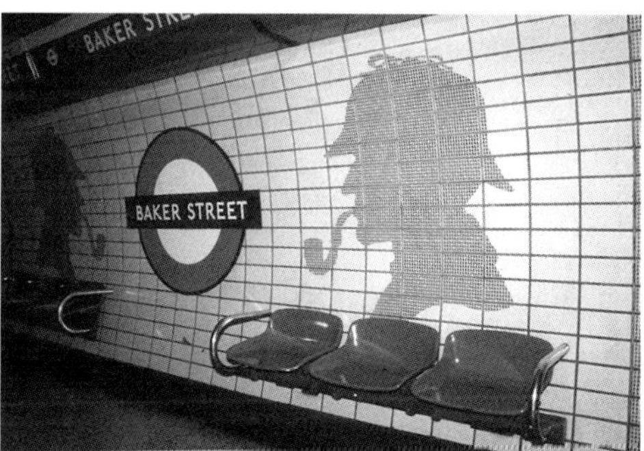

Fig 141.

Interwar platform tiling tended towards the relatively bland, with large areas of white or cream tiles and minimal coloured banding which often highlighted entrances and exits; much of this was supplied by Carter's of Poole.[13] A variation was introduced at the instigation of the administrator and design reformer Frank Pick (1878-1941), who began working for the Underground Group in 1906 and ended his career in 1940 as vice-chairman of the London Passenger Transport Board. In 1936 Pick commissioned Harold Stabler (1872-1945) to design a series of eighteen London-themed tiles with low-relief moulded decoration which were produced by

Carter's. These were installed as random ornamental insets at Aldgate East and St Paul's (where they can still be seen today) in 1938 and were in use until 1947; the Aldgate East tiling is the most complete remaining scheme, but was threatened by proposed refurbishment in 2005. *The Builder* considered the tiles to be 'an excellent notion, and one which will certainly arouse popular interest', but the architectural critic J. M. Richards felt they represented 'a kind of arti-craftiness' out of character with the Underground's modern standardised detailing.[14]

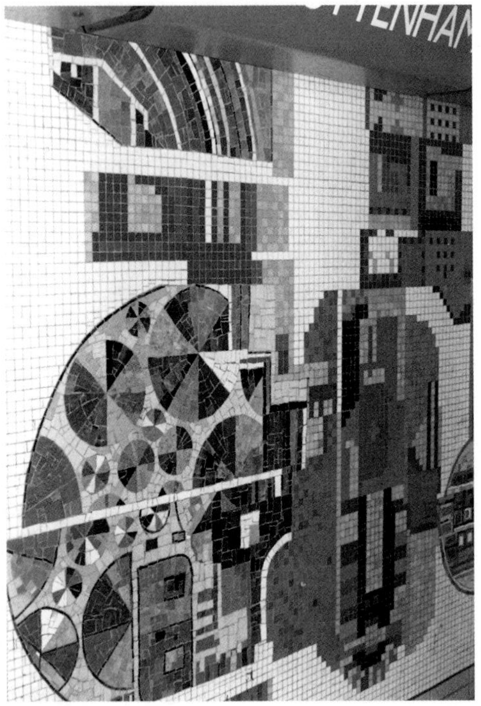

Fig 142.

The Victoria line, connecting Victoria and Walthamstow, was first mooted in the 1930s and finally opened in stages during 1968-71. Its twelve stations were designed 'in-house' under the direction of the London Transport Design Panel, one of whose members was the industrial designer Misha Black. Apparently at Black's suggestion the platform tiling (by Carter's) was largely grey, but with colourful seat-back alcoves whose designs reflected the locality; the artists involved were Julia Black (Walthamstow), Hans Unger (Blackhorse Road, Seven Sisters, Oxford Circus and Green Park), Edward Bawden (Tottenham Hale, Highbury & Islington and Victoria), Tom Eckersley (Finsbury Park, King's Cross and Euston) and Alan Fletcher (Warren Street). Platform tiling on the Jubilee line (opened 1979), connecting Baker Street to Charing Cross, was altogether brighter, and included a leaf pattern on red ground for Green Park. This was designed by June Fraser (b1930) and fired by Michael Douglas, and - in a different colourway - was also used in 1979 to replace the badly faded Hans Unger abstract panels on Green Park's Victoria line platforms.[15] The Bond Street Jubilee line platforms were tiled with a stylish hat box motif designed by Tom Eckersley.

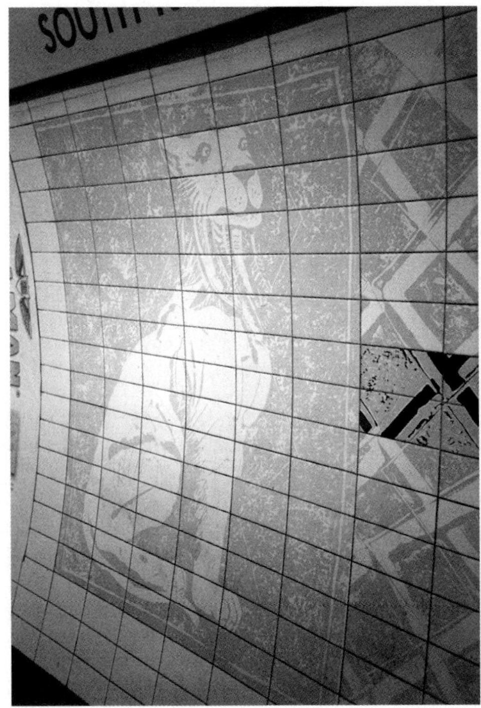

Fig 143.

During the 1980s the Underground's design strategy changed from one of overall uniformity to emphasis on individual station identity; specific artists worked with the architects on every updated station.[16] Bond Street's Central line platforms were tiled with a 'wrapping paper' motif in 1982, Baker Street's Sherlock Holmes silhouette tiling (designed by Michael Douglas and over-glaze printed by Pamela Moreton) was installed around 1983 (Fig 141), and the spectacular Eduardo Paolozzi (1924-2005) glass mosaic mural scheme at Tottenham Court Road dates from 1983-5 (Fig 142). The 1984-6 Piccadilly Circus refurbishment used specially-made German tiles with high-gloss glazes, and the 1984-7 works at Paddington included the construction of a new ticket hall with tiling designed by David Hamilton depicting early tunnelling machines. At Waterloo (Northern line, 1987) jazz-themed tiling by Avril Toplee Tipping delineates the exits, while the South Kensington (1988, Piccadilly line) platform tiling design by Mary J. Woodin was inspired by inhabitants of the Natural History Museum (Fig 143).

The outcome of the race to refurbish the network was called into question in 1987 when the Victorian Society and the Thirties Society published their joint report *End of the Line?* which described lost and endangered features, particularly tiling, in splendid detail.[17] The authors were not keen on new tiling 'of strident and often lurid colours' and shared this view with other architectural critics, including Colin Amery of the *Financial Times*, who described Baker Street's tiling as 'meretricious'.[18] The report created a storm of publicity, and although modernisation continued, there has since been a stronger input from the conservation lobby, and many stations are now listed buildings. The policy of individualisation became more conservative, with installations such as the 1993 Tessera Designs full-height tiling in the Elephant & Castle booking hall, which reproduces an early twentieth century local street scene. Replacement tiling was still being introduced during the 1990s, notably at Mornington Crescent and Earl's Court, in the latter case using tiles made at H. & E. Smith's Britannic Works, Stoke-on-Trent.

It is unfortunate that one unforeseen result of the otherwise totally laudable *End of the Line?* appears to have been to inhibit experiments with modern ceramic tiling on the Underground network. The only relatively recent tiling tends to take the form of reproductions, not even always exact copies, for instance the Edwardian-style booking hall at Edgware Road with its ticket window faience surrounds. The Jubilee line extension stations of 2000 featured much attractive mosaic work but no ceramic tiling. However, enough remains of the Leslie Green stations - especially their platform tiling, which is still not fully published - along with the 1930s Stabler tiles and the 1960s-1980s artist-designed installations to make every underground journey a ceramic adventure.

Suggested London-wide reading: Paul Atterbury and Louise Irvine, *The Doulton Story* (Royal Doulton Tableware, Stoke-on-Trent, 1979); Ian M. Betts, *Medieval 'Westminster' floor tiles* (Museum of London Archaeology Service, 2002); Emily Cole, *Blue Plaques: A Guide to the Scheme* (English Heritage, Swindon, 2002); Desmond Eyles and Louise Irvine, *The Doulton Lambeth Wares* (Richard Dennis, Shepton Beauchamp, 2002); David Lawrence, *Underground Architecture* (Capital Transport Publishing, Harrow, 1994); David Leboff, *The Underground Stations of Leslie Green* (Capital Transport Publishing, Harrow, 2002).

The *Gazetteer* entries for London are listed alphabetically by borough; within each borough entries are listed by area and then alphabetically by street.

References

1. Alun Graves, *Tiles and Tilework of Europe* (V & A Publications, London, 2002).
2. Personal communication, Ian Betts, Museum of London Specialist Services, 12th August 2004.
3. Lynn Pearson, 'Lost - A Ceramic Extravagance', *Glazed Expressions*, (2004) 49, p10.
4. Lynn Pearson, 'To Brighten the Environment: Ceramic Tile Murals in Britain, 1950-70', *TACS Journal*, 10 (2004), pp12-17.
5. Emily Cole, *Blue Plaques: A guide to the scheme* (English Heritage, London, 2002).
6. Desmond Eyles and Louise Irvine, *The Doulton Lambeth Wares* (Richard Dennis, Shepton Beauchamp, 2002), p234.
7. Leslie Hayward, *Poole Pottery: Carter & Company and their Successors, 1873-2002* 3rd edition, ed Paul Atterbury (Richard Dennis, Shepton Beauchamp, 2002), p177.
8. *J. C. Edwards, Ruabon: Catalogue*, Ruabon (1903).
9. David Lawrence, *Underground Architecture* (Capital Transport, Harrow, 1994).
10. David Leboff, *The Underground Stations of Leslie Green* (Capital Transport Publishing, Harrow Weald, 2002).
11. M. A. C. Horne, G. Jasieniecki, J. Liffen and D. Rose, 'A preliminary study of tiling on certain London Underground railway platforms', *Glazed Expressions*, (1982) 3, pp4-5.
12. Michael Stratton, *Clad is bad? The relationship between structural and ceramic facing materials*, in *Structure and Style: Conserving Twentieth Century Buildings*, ed Michael Stratton (E. & F. N. Spon, London, 1997), pp164-92.
13. Jennifer Hawkins, *Poole Potteries* (Barrie & Jenkins, London, 1980), p138.
14. 'Decorative tiles on the Underground', *The Builder*, 157 (1939), p163.
15. Lawrence, *Underground Architecture* (1994).
16. Hans van Lemmen, 'New tiles and mosaics in London Underground stations', *Glazed Expressions*, (1986) 12, pp6-8.

17. Alan Powers, ed, *End of the Line? The Future of London Underground's Past* (Victorian Society and Thirties Society, London, 1987).
18. Colin Amery, 'Tube design has hit the buffers', *Financial Times*, 13th April 1987.

BARKING AND DAGENHAM

Barking

Barking Magistrates Court (1893-4, architect C. J. Dawson), EAST STREET, has extensive dado tiling throughout its interior, which includes an impressive stair hall.

BARNET

Finchley

College Farm, FITZALAN ROAD, was erected as a model farm for the Express Dairy Company in 1883. Its ornamental dairy is lined with Minton tiles including some from the 'rustic figures' series, and there was tiling elsewhere in areas where animals were housed. The dairy was used as a tea house for some years.

Golders Green

Golders Green Crematorium, HOOP LANE, was opened by the London Cremation Society in 1902, the buildings dating from between 1905 and 1939. In the main cloister (1912-16), amongst the multitude of memorials, is a series of glazed polychrome ceramic plaques, mostly in the form of wreaths; there is also an ambitious terracotta monument to Ethel Watkins, dating from around 1920 and featuring two angels.[1] The West Chapel (1905), leading off the cloister, has a Jones & Willis opus sectile panel of 1915. In the east end of the Ernest George Columbarium (1922-8) is a superb Doulton polychrome stoneware funerary casket designed by Gilbert Bayes and made for Basil Edwin Lawrence and Mary Lawrence, who both died in 1928.

High Barnet

St John the Baptist Church, WOOD STREET, was rebuilt by William Butterfield in 1871-5, with the fittings being installed during 1878-85; these included a fine hand-painted tiled reredos depicting the *Nativity*. Butterfield went 'to meet Standish for the reredos painting' in 1880 and charged for 'superintendance of the picture'.[2] The stained glass of the east window (1880-2) was supplied by Alexander Gibbs, who had worked with Butterfield on the tile paintings at All Saints, Margaret Street, Westminster during the mid-1870s. Most of the actual painting had been carried out by his younger brother Isaac Alexander Gibbs, who set up a stained glass and tile painting business in the early 1880s with W. W. Howard. The style of the Margaret Street and High Barnet paintings are very similar indeed, and it is possible that the otherwise unknown Mr Standish worked for Gibbs & Howard.

Holders Hill

The chapel at **Hendon Cemetery**, HOLDERS HILL ROAD, was built in 1899 but later re-ordered when it became the north chapel of the crematorium complex; its monumental glazed ceramic reredos is therefore at the rear of the current lay-out. The reredos was made at the Fabrica Cantagalli of Florence, established in the fifteenth century and used by William De Morgan in the late nineteenth century.[3] The firm, which specialised in majolica ware, was probably responsible for the production of most of the small, highly-glazed reliefs with religious themes, often copies of della Robbia originals, popular in England during the mid to late nineteenth century as church decoration. The unusually large Hendon example is a copy of a Luca della Robbia *Resurrection* relief in a sacristy of Florence Cathedral.

References

1. Peter C. Jupp and Hilary J. Grainger, eds, *Golders Green Crematorium, 1902-2002: a London centenary in context* (London Cremation Company, London, 2002).
2. Paul Thompson, *William Butterfield* (Routledge & Kegan Paul, London, 1971), p458.
3. Bridget Cherry and Nikolaus Pevsner, *London 4: North*. Buildings of England (Penguin, London, 1998).

BEXLEY

Bexleyheath

The **Red House** (NT), RED HOUSE LANE, was commissioned by William Morris in 1859 and designed by Philip Webb; it was Morris's home for five years. The most interesting of the remaining tiles, some of which post-date Morris's occupation of the house, are two groups of Morris tiles, possibly the first made by the firm. One hundred tiles of three different designs survive as a lining to a garden porch seat; these were designed - and reputedly painted by William Morris himself - around 1861. Original tiles may also be seen in two bedroom fire surrounds, but the identity of the designer is unclear.[1] The Dutch tiles in the dining room fireplace date from around 1880.

References
1. Richard Myers and Hilary Myers, *William Morris Tiles - The tile designs of Morris and his Fellow-Workers* (Richard Dennis, Shepton Beauchamp, 1996).

BRENT

Kensal Green

The interior decoration of the **Paradise PH**, 19 Kilburn Lane, includes a late 1880s Burmantofts faience panel showing a woman in classical dress gathering grapes; it was marketed as one of a pair entitled *The Gatherers*.[1]

Kensal Rise

There is good, varied porch tiling (and terracotta roofware) on many of the houses occupying the slopes above Kensal Green, notably in Clifford Gardens NW10, developed in the 1890s, and the half-dozen or so roads running parallel and to the north.

Kilburn

The passageway at 275 Kilburn High Road, on its west side between the **Tricycle Theatre** and Brondesbury Medical Centre, is faced with a tile mural designed and produced around 1998 by Clifford Strong and Richard Wells (Fig 144). The design, based on the local street map, successfully combines small-scale silk-screened images with bold visual impact. Nearby on the High Road are the Cock Tavern, rebuilt in 1900 with (just inside the door) a fine tube-lined plaque showing a cockerel; shops near the market with 1960s wall tiling; and the former Gaumont State Cinema (1937, architect George Coles), its cream and black faience supplied by the Hathern Station Brick and Terra Cotta Company.[2]

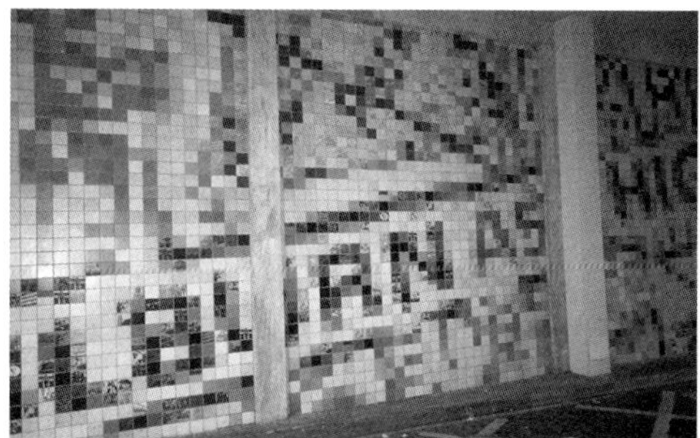

Fig 144.

References
1. *Burmantofts Pottery*, (Bradford Art Galleries and Museum, Bradford, 1983), p62.
2. Kevin Wheelan, *The History of the Hathern Station Brick & Terra Cotta Company* (Mercia Cinema Society, Birmingham, 1982).

BROMLEY

Beckenham

The glazed faience relief in the tympanum of the west door on the exterior of the **Church of St Michael and All Angels** (1955-6, architects Hobday & Maynard), Ravenscroft Road, was made by Carter's of Poole. It was designed for the architects by Jessie Bayes and depicts St Michael with a dragon and figures of angels. Jimmy James, the Deputy Decorating Department Manager, carried out some of the filling-in painting, and the background tiles were by A. B. Read and Peggy Angus.[1]

Bromley

The thirteen hand-made relief tile panels on the exterior of **Sainsbury's**, Walter's Yard and West Street, were designed and made by Kenneth Bright. The high-fired panels show aspects of the local townscape and were installed around 1993-4.

Chislehurst

In exile from France, Emperor Napoleon III (1808-73) and his wife, the Empress Eugénie, came to live in Chislehurst in 1870. After the Emperor's death, the Empress ordered the construction of a mortuary chapel (1874, architect Henry Clutton) as an extension of **St Mary's R. C. Church**, Hawkwood Lane; however, the Emperor's grand tomb was removed from Chislehurst to Farnborough Abbey in 1887, following the Empress Eugénie's 1881 purchase of the mansion Farnborough Hill (see Farnborough, Hampshire) and the construction, from 1886, of the associated abbey and mausoleum. The pavement of the Chislehurst mortuary chapel includes decorative encaustic tiles made by the French firm Boulenger, established near Beauvais in 1848 (Fig 145).[2] One of its founding brothers, Jean-Baptiste Aimé Boulenger (1825-87), specialised in the manufacture of encaustics, and was commissioned to make the Chislehurst tiles, some of which bear Napoleonic motifs.[3]

Fig 145.

Orpington

The splendid faience ram, about three feet in height, on the outer end wall of **Hillside Primary School** (formerly Orpington-Ramsden County Primary School), DYKE DRIVE, was made by Carter's and probably dates from the 1960s. The black-glazed ram is incised with white lines to the design of the school's architect, Oliver E. Steer.[4]

References

1. Carter Archive, Poole Museum Service, 3D-27 (Religion).
2. Hans van Lemmen, 'Napoleonic Tiles at Chislehurst', *Glazed Expressions*, (1985) 10, p12.
3. Tony Herbert and Kathryn Huggins, *The Decorative Tile in Architecture and Interiors* (Phaidon Press, London, 1995), p80.
4. Carter Archive, Poole Museum Service, CP45.

CAMDEN

Belsize Park

The **Washington PH**, 50 ENGLAND'S LANE has a floor mosaic reading 'Washington Hotel Billiards' and an unusual, delicately painted tiled wall panel showing George Washington in a pseudo-classical surround, with the name W. Holman (probably the then-proprietor) in a prominent position above. This late Victorian panel is signed 'Carter, Johnson & Co London & Worcester'. There is an abundance of interesting and varied late Victorian porch tiling in Belsize Park, with good architectural detailing, including the use of tiles and terracotta on facades, continuing north into Hampstead.[1]

Bloomsbury

The offices of the publishing company Thames & Hudson formerly occupied 30-34 BLOOMSBURY STREET, and could be identified by the three sets of tiled steps sporting the firm's logos; one set has been removed, but the tiles at 32 and 34 are extant (Fig 146). The tiles were designed by William Gordon and probably produced by Carter's.

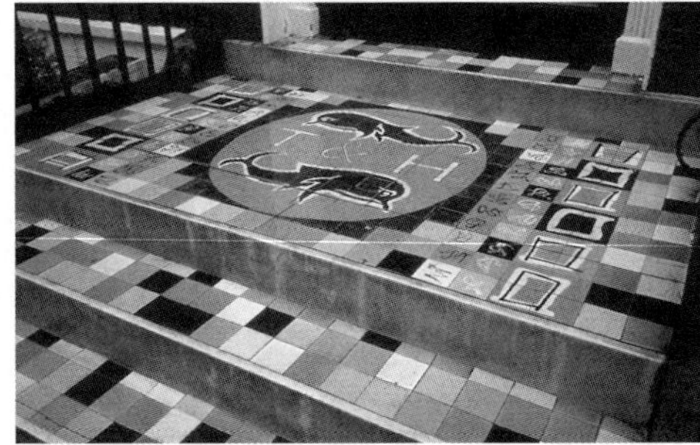

Fig 146.

Hathernware terracotta was used in the late 1990s in the restoration and conversion of Alfred Waterhouse's massive red brick and terracotta University College Hospital (1894-1903), GOWER STREET, to a research and teaching centre known as the **Cruciform Building** from its cross-shaped plan. The Hospital was one of only two buildings where Waterhouse specified painted tile panels for the interior, in this case for the children's ward, where twenty-four Doulton nursery rhyme and fairy tale panels were installed, some signed by Margaret Thompson.[2] Many of these were covered or removed during earlier alterations, and one is in the collection of the Bethnal Green Museum of Childhood (Tower Hamlets).[3]

Waterstone's bookshop, on TORRINGTON PLACE (between Gower Street and Malet Street) is a frilly, pale buff terracotta confection built in 1907 and designed by the architect Charles Fitzroy Doll (1851-1929); its detailing includes figurative gargoyles and diminutive turrets. The terracotta may have been supplied by Doulton; Doll certainly used the firm for his nearby but earlier **Russell Hotel** (1896-1900), RUSSELL SQUARE, a chateau-like pile with excellent terracotta detailing including portrait busts, cherubs and sculptures by Henry Charles Fehr (1867-1940).[4]

The former J. Evans dairy (now **Fitzroy Tiles**), on the corner of Conway Street and WARREN STREET, dates from the early twentieth century. The exterior is faced with blue and white glazed brick and tiles, and inside the walls are white tiled with some blue-framed blank panels; the marble-topped counter (is this original?) is fronted by three pictorial tile panels of rural scenes.

Hampstead

The former Congregational Church (1883-4, architect Alfred Waterhouse), LYNDHURST ROAD, was converted to house a concert hall and recording studios in 1991-2, and is now known as **Lyndhurst Hall**. The dark red terracotta of its exterior came from J. C. Edwards of Ruabon.[5]

Holborn

The spectacular interior of the **Princess Louise PH**, 208-9 HIGH HOLBORN, dates from its refurbishment in 1891 by the architect Arthur Chitty. The lavish - although non-pictorial - tilework, including full-height tiling in the gents' toilets, was supplied by W. B. Simpson & Sons and is most probably by Maw & Co (Fig 147).

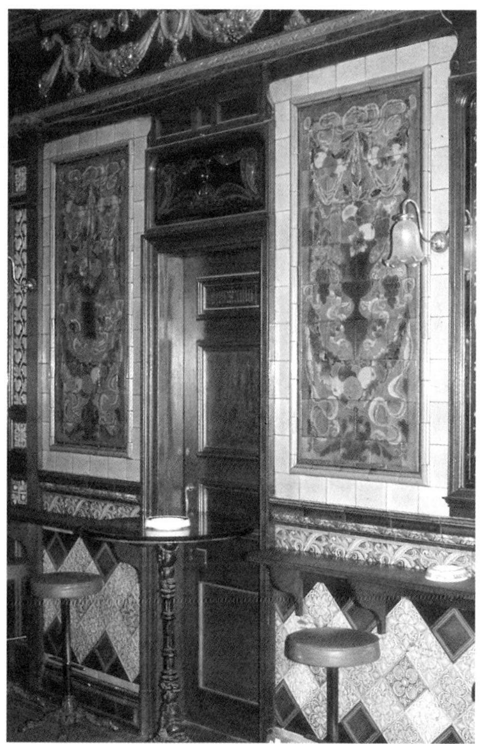

Fig 147.

The massively red **Prudential Assurance** building, on the north side of HOLBORN, was erected in four stages over 1876-1905 to the designs of Alfred Waterhouse; it was the first of twenty-seven commissions received by Waterhouse from the Prudential. The vast scale of the building can best be seen from the semi-public Waterhouse Square - a reminder of the great court of Furnival's Inn, previous occupier of the site - reached through an imposing archway from Holborn. The company's new head office of 1876-9 was the first section to be built, and was faced in red brick and buff terracotta, the latter from Gibbs & Canning who also supplied the red terracotta used in the later phases of construction. The colour red, a contrast to stone and London stock brick, was the choice of the Prudential rather than Waterhouse.[6] The present appearance of the building results from demolition of the 1876-9 block in 1930; its replacement, complete by 1932, used red terracotta from the Hathern Station Brick and Terra Cotta Company.

The building as a whole offers little in the way of external terracotta decoration apart from an allegorical figure of *Prudence* (1898) by the Scottish sculptor William Birnie Rhind (1853-1933) above the entrance arch. Ward-Jackson suggests that this was made by Edwards of Ruabon, apparently because the rather different *Prudentia* at Liverpool's Prudential Assurance building (1885-8, terracotta by Edwards of Ruabon) predates the London statue.[7] It seems far more likely that Gibbs & Canning supplied all the terracotta for the pre-1930 Holborn building, including the figure. Internally, the 1895-1905 range, fronting on to Holborn, has much Burmantofts faience decoration including arcades, cream and ochre facing on columns and a lavish multi-coloured stairway. Ibstock Hathernware made over 500 terracotta blocks for the building's 1990 restoration and redevelopment.

On the exterior of **Sir John Soane's Museum**, 12-14 LINCOLN'S INN FIELDS, are Coade stone caryatids of 1812. Set into the fire surround of the second floor front room are 42 early eighteenth century Chinese blue and white decorative porcelain tiles, with another 32 in the fireplace of an adjoining room; over 200 more such tiles are held in storage by the museum. The tiles may have been added to the fire surrounds in 1891 by the then-curator, James William Wild, who had a strong interest in oriental art.[8]

The architect Percy Westwood was a personal friend of the tailor Austin Reed, commuting daily with him to London. Reed naturally turned to Westwood and his partner Joseph Emberton for a new headquarters office building, and the result was **Summit House** (1925), RED LION SQUARE.[9] The steel-framed block is faced in smooth Gibbs & Canning amber-coloured faience, with minimal decoration in the form of repeated oblongs.[10] The architects were much influenced by Berlage's strange faience-clad Holland House (1914-16, see City of London), indeed Summit House may be its sole British progeny; it was certainly a sophisticated contract for Gibbs & Canning.

SICILIAN AVENUE (1906-10, architect Robert J. Worley), off Southampton Row, was a purpose-built classical-style pedestrianised shopping street; the facades and terminating screens are clad in Doulton's Carraraware.[11] Even the central lamp-posts have blue faience pedestals.

Kentish Town

The Egyptian-style black and cream faience of the former **Forum Cinema** (1934, architect John Stanley Beard, interior by W. R. Bennett), HIGHGATE ROAD, was probably supplied by Shaws of Darwen; Beard used the firm for his very similar Forum Ealing, also 1934.

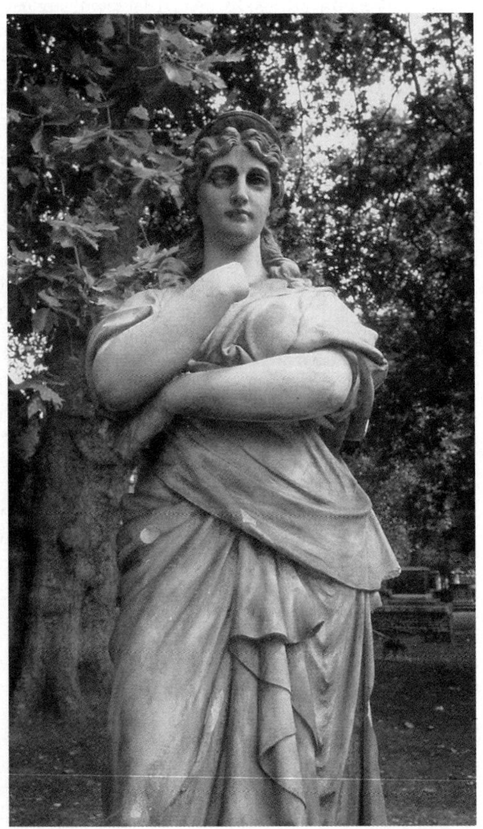

Fig 148.

St Luke's Church (1867-9, architect Basil Champneys, now in the care of the Churches Conservation Trust), OSENEY CRESCENT, has a rich encaustic pavement in its sanctuary including distinctive sixteen-tile groups designed for Maw & Co by the architect George Goldie. The same group can also be found in Chester Cathedral, where they were installed in the 1860s, and at St Asaph Cathedral, where they date from 1867-75.

St Pancras

The entrance hall of **St Pancras Chambers** (1868-76, architect George Gilbert Scott, formerly the Midland Grand Hotel), EUSTON ROAD, was complete in time for the opening of the hotel on 5th May 1873; its floor is of Minton geometric tiling with mosaic insets.

In **St George's Gardens**, HEATHCOTE STREET, stands the Doulton buff terracotta figure of *Euterpe* (sculptor John Broad) which was originally part of the decoration of the Apollo and the Muses PH on Tottenham Court Road (1898, C. Fitzroy Doll); the pub was demolished in 1961 and the figure presented to the Mayor of St Pancras (Fig 148).

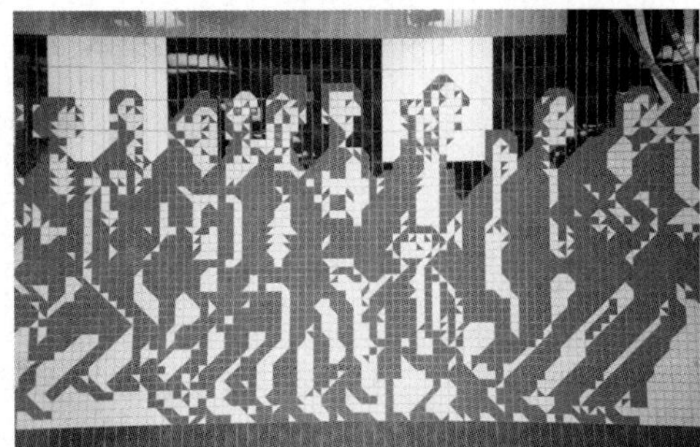

Fig 149.

In the entrance of **Thameslink Station**, PENTONVILLE ROAD, is a full-height modern tile mural installed by W. B. Simpson & Sons showing hurrying passengers; the mural is under threat as the station is due to be moved by 2007 as part of the Channel Tunnel Rail Link works (Fig 149).

St Pancras New Church (1819-22), UPPER WOBURN PLACE, was designed in Greek Revival style by the London architect William Inwood and his son Henry William Inwood (1794-1843). During 1818-19 Henry Inwood travelled in Italy and Greece, later publishing what became the standard work on the Erechtheion, an Ionic temple on the Acropolis in Athens. The north and south porticos of St Pancras are based on the Porch of the Caryatids at the Erechtheion; Henry took complete casts of the Greek caryatids, which John Rossi then copied in terracotta. The colossal grey terracotta caryatids are load-bearing and have cast iron cores (Fig 150).

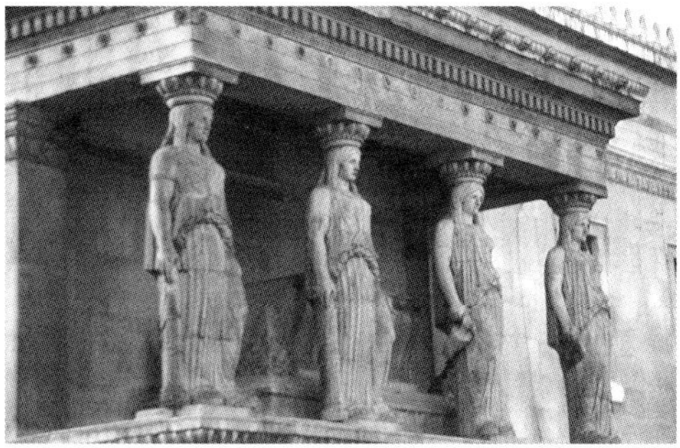

Fig 150.

Somers Town

The anglo-catholic priest Basil Jellicoe founded the St Pancras Home Improvement Society (now St Pancras & Humanist Housing Association) in 1924, declaring a 'war on slums' in Somers Town; the intention was to provide high quality homes with facilities such as nursery schools for the poorest tenants. The Sidney Street Estate, now known as the **Sidney Estate**, lies west of Chalton Street and is bounded by Werrington, Bridgeway and Aldenham Streets (Fig 151).

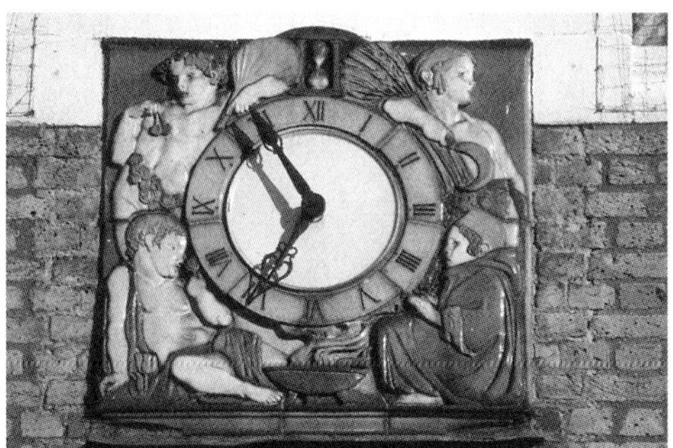

Fig 151.

This compact area formed the final phase of the Society's second major scheme in Somers Town, planned in 1929 and completed in 1939. Its flats, which are arranged around a central courtyard, were designed by the Society's architect Ian B. Hamilton. The great delight of the development is the Doulton polychrome stoneware decoration by Gilbert Bayes (1872-1953), who - as a result of his concern with the role of colour in sculpture - had experimented with designs in Doultonware from the early 1920s.[12] Bayes worked with Hamilton during the 1930s on decorative features for all the Society's Somers Town estates, but the Sidney Street scheme was the most complex and varied, originally including sculptured finials, many of their designs inspired by nursery rhymes, on the washing-line posts; these did not survive beyond the 1970s (Fig 152). Still extant, however, are the low relief lunettes showing fairy tale scenes and the *Four Seasons* clock overlooking the courtyard.[13] The housing association is currently (2004) undertaking a major programme to renovate the Somers Town estate courtyards and to install replica washing-line posts and finials.

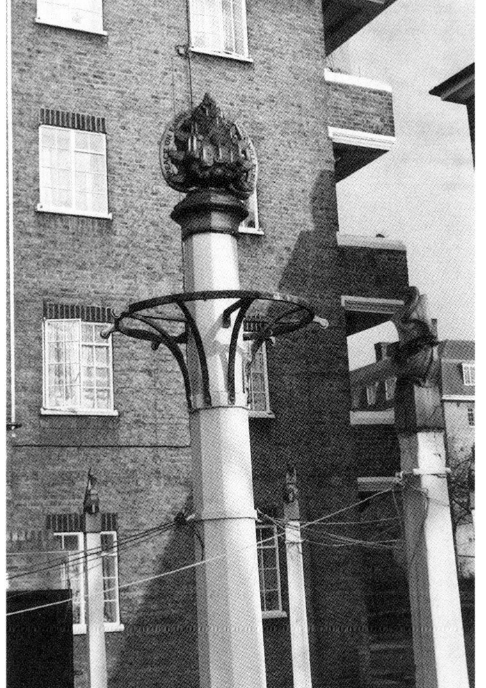

Fig 152.

Less than a quarter mile south of the Sidney Estate is Doric Way and the **Drummond Estate**, with the earliest flats put up by the St Pancras Home Improvement Society, three five-storey blocks erected between 1926 and 1936; the architect was Ian B. Hamilton. Decoration includes the cast stone *Eagles and Fish* balcony panel by Gilbert Bayes, and on St Mary's (completed 1930) are hand-painted Dunsmore tiles showing assorted fish and crustaceans (Fig 153).

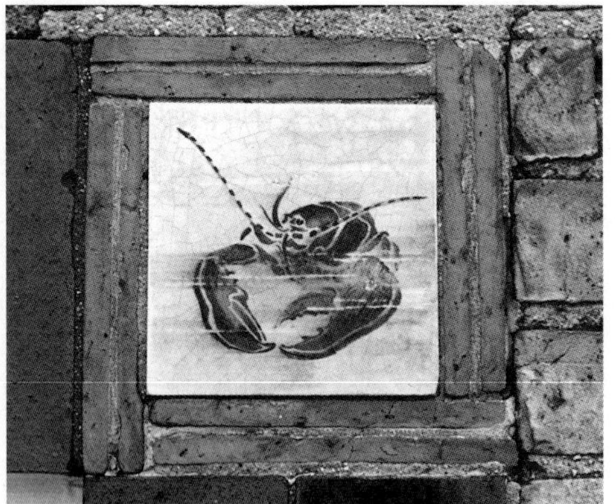

Fig 153.

On EUSTON ROAD, in front of Euston Station, is the former **London, Edinburgh & Glasgow Assurance** building (1906-7, architect Beresford Pite) which retains its original decorative scheme in the currently disused entrance hall. The walls are clad with Doulton's Parian ware in pale yellow and sage green, and the floor mosaic, by Rust's Vitreous Mosaic Co of Battersea, incorporates the signs of the zodiac; Doulton's Parian ware, developed by W. J. Neatby, was earthenware with a dull, eggshell-like finish. The brown and yellow dado tiling in adjoining corridors is also by Doulton's.[14]

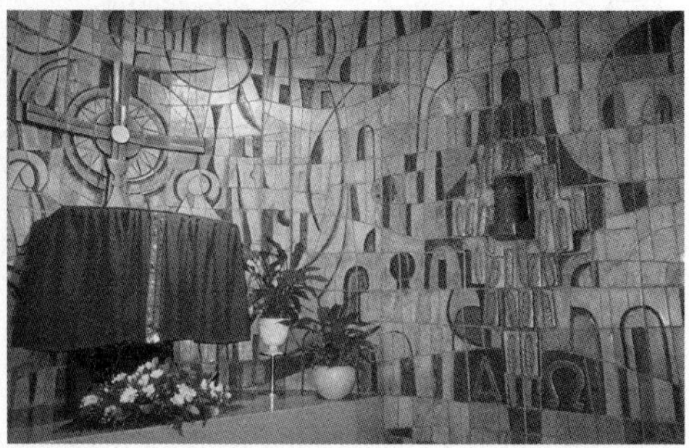

Fig 154.

St Aloysius R. C. Church (1966-8, architect John Newton), PHOENIX ROAD (between the Sidney and Drummond Estates) has an elliptical interior with striking abstract stained glass by Whitefriars Studios. The apsidal recess of the Blessed Sacrament Chapel is faced with a brightly coloured ceramic mural by Adam Kossowski (Fig 154).

References

1. Bryan Diamond, 'Architectural details on Hampstead houses', *Camden History Review*, 25 (2001), pp32-6.
2. Colin Cunningham and Prudence Waterhouse, *Alfred Waterhouse, 1830-1905: Biography of a Practice* (Clarendon Press, Oxford, 1992), p98.
3. John Greene, *Brightening the Long Days* (Tiles and Architectural Ceramics Society, 1987).
4. Paul Atterbury and Louise Irvine, *The Doulton Story* (Royal Doulton Tableware, Stoke on Trent, 1979).
5. *J. C. Edwards, Ruabon: Catalogue*, Ruabon (1903).
6. Cunningham, *Alfred Waterhouse* (1992), p116.
7. Philip Ward-Jackson, *Public Sculpture of the City of London*. Public Sculpture of Britain (Liverpool University Press, Liverpool, 2003).
8. Rose Kerr, 'Hidden treasure at Sir John Soane's Museum', *Apollo*, 156 (2002) November, pp23-9.
9. Rosemary Ind, *Emberton* (Scolar Press, London, 1983).
10. Information from Angella Streluk.
11. Tara Draper-Stumm and Derek Kendall, *London's Shops: the world's emporium* (English Heritage, London, 2002).
12. Philip Ward-Jackson, *Gilbert Bayes - Essays in the Study of Sculpture* (Henry Moore Institute, Leeds, 1998).
13. Louise Irvine and Paul Atterbury, *Gilbert Bayes, Sculptor, 1872-1953* (Richard Dennis, Shepton Beauchamp, 1998).
14. 'The London, Edinburgh, and Glasgow Assurance Building, London', *Architectural Review*, 23 (1908) March, pp169-176.

CITY OF LONDON

Twentieth century ceramic tablets erected by the Corporation of the City of London to mark sites of demolished buildings can be found throughout the City; the manufacturer is unknown, although Doulton of Lambeth produced very similar plaques. The twenty-one site description boards of the London Wall Walk, created in the 1980s to follow the route of the medieval wall between Tower Hill and the Museum of London, have blue ceramic surrounds and tile numbers by Maw & Co (then part of H. & R. Johnson).

In **Postman's Park**, just west of ALDERSGATE STREET, is an open lean-to sheltering the Memorial to Heroic Sacrifice, instigated by the artist George Frederic Watts, designed by the architect Ernest George and opened in 1899; the first memorial tablets, recording the name of the victim and details of their fate, were installed in 1900 (Fig 155).[1] In all there are 53 memorial tiles, the first 24 of which were made by William De Morgan at Sands End; the first four of these comprise just two large tiles, rather than the cheaper and smaller tiles used in all the other memorials. The tiles installed from 1908 onward (apart from the final tile) were manufactured by Doulton's of Lambeth; the Doulton name appears at the bottom left of the lowest row of tiles. The last memorial, added in early 1931, was a replacement for a De Morgan tile bearing incorrect information. It was made by the tile painter Fred Passenger, one of De Morgan's partners at Sands End, who in 1931 was working at the Bushey Heath Pottery. The De Morgan tiles can be identified by their slightly greenish glaze, flowing lettering and occasional ornament (including a ship motif), while the Doulton tiles are whiter and more regulated in appearance.[2]

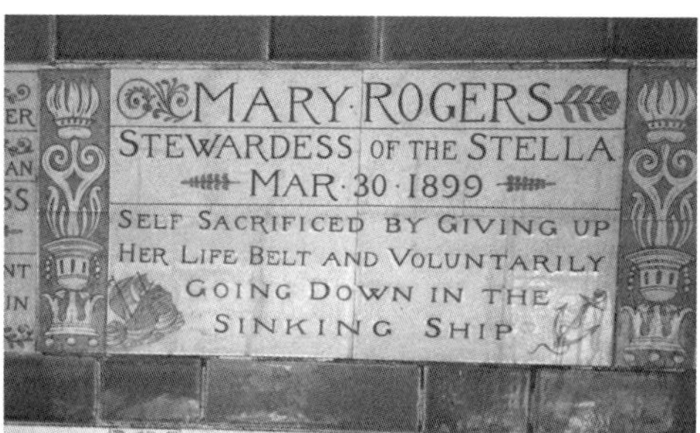

Fig 155.

The **Bishopsgate Institute** (1892-4), BISHOPSGATE (on the corner with Brushfield Street) was designed by the arts and crafts architect Charles Harrison Townsend, who produced a highly original design with twin towers and cupolas above an arched entrance. The facade is entirely constructed of Gibbs & Canning's buff block terracotta, with some decoration including a *Tree of Life* motif stretching across the narrow frontage; this was modelled by William Aumonier. The Institute's facade demonstrated terracotta's great ability to provide naturalistic decoration combined with plain walling. The tiled dado in the entrance hall is by Maw & Co.[3] Just south at 178 Bishopsgate is the 1930s **Sir Robert Peel PH**, (opposite the entrance to Liverpool Street station) retains the upper part of its facade with blue and yellow Carter's tiling including a large figure of the man himself.[4] The almost adjacent police station dates from the late 1930s.

The peculiar little glazed brick and terracotta structure protruding from BISHOPSGATE CHURCHYARD was the entrance kiosk of **Nevill's New Turkish Baths**, built in 1894-5 on a very cramped site, thus the tiny surface building through which bathers passed on their way to the complex of rooms below (Fig 156). The architect was the little-known Harold Elphick, who employed Craven Dunnill in 1894 to make several ranges of Islamic-style interlocking tiles to his own designs; these were used, along with other Craven Dunnill products, in an elaborate scheme which runs throughout the surviving rooms.[5] The building ceased to function as a Turkish baths in 1954 and was converted to its present restaurant use during the 1970s.

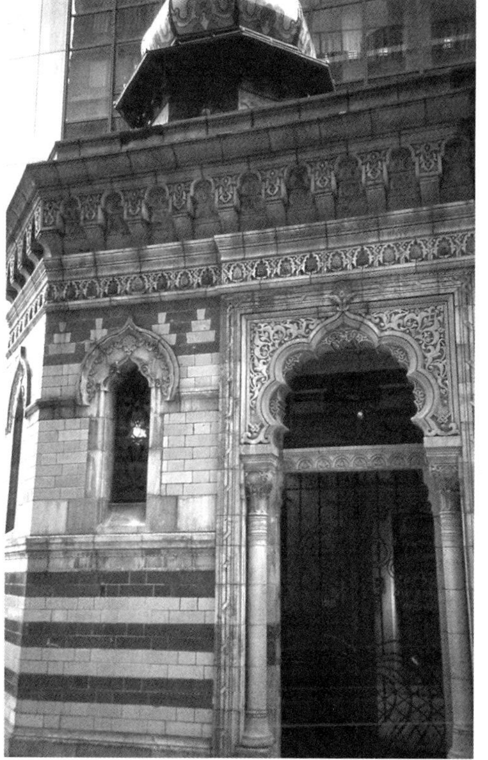

Fig 156.

The **pedestrian underpass** at the south end of BLACKFRIARS BRIDGE, still within the City of London, was decorated in 1995-6 with an overglazed mural showing a series of historical images from the Guildhall Library; the tiles were designed and supplied by Langley Architectural.[6]

Holland House (1914-16), 32 BURY STREET, was designed by the Dutch architect Hendrick Petrus Berlage (1856-1934) for a Dutch shipping firm run by A. G. Kröller-Müller, who wanted a landmark commercial building to impress the City; most of the building materials were brought over from Holland in the company's own ships, although some white glazed brickwork is by the Leeds Fireclay Company. Apart from its black granite plinth, Holland House was clad in semi-matt blue-green faience made by the Delft factory De Porceleyne Fles, which often worked with Berlage and specialised in ceramic cladding (Fig 157). Porceleyne Fles products were normally supplied in Britain through the agency A. Bell & Co of Northampton, and were used for facing commercial premises.[7] Berlage's design for Holland House was slightly compromised by an argument with his client, resulting in the interior work (1916), by the Dutch artist Bart van der Leck, being completed under the supervision of the Belgian architect Henri van der Velde.[8] The walls of the entrance lobby are faced in white glazed brick with string courses made by De Porceleyne Fles, and the ceiling is mosaic work.

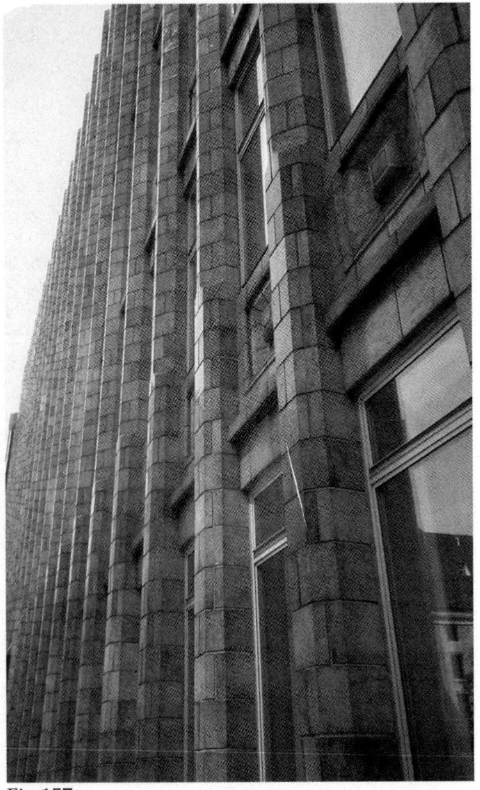

Fig 157.

The windows of Holland House are set so closely that - when viewed at an angle - the outer wall becomes a flat plane. This use of faience as cladding for an overtly modern steel-framed structure inspired the design of Summit House (1925, see Camden) but little else, as faience became associated with external decoration, on interwar cinemas for instance, and modernist architects tended to prefer other facing materials. In 1931 the architectural critic Christopher Hussey picked out Summit House and Spicer Brothers' warehouse (1913-17, see New Bridge Street, below) as examples of 'outstanding experiments in the application of faience to modern designs'; Holland House was probably omitted as Hussey appears to have only considered the work of English architects.[9] Hussey's vision of faience providing a route to increased colour in architecture had, however, become something of a curiosity just fifty years on, when a Building Centre exhibition on modernist building materials described these faience-clad structures as 'the very last flowerings of a great tradition'.[10] The use of architectural faience in twentieth century Britain emphasised decorative mouldings rather than expression of structure.

The **Law Society's Hall** in CHANCERY LANE was extended in 1902-4; the architect was Charles Holden (1875-1960), who was then chief assistant to Percy Adams and later became famous for his work with London Underground. Holden was always keen to collaborate with artists, and commissioned tiles from Conrad Dressler's Medmenham Pottery for the Grand Staircase. The Persian-enamelled ceramic reliefs (1904) by Dressler in the first floor Common Room, however, were commissioned by the Law Society and installed against Holden's wishes.[11] The polychrome frieze comprises two large panels, depicting Human Justice and Divine Justice, and eleven smaller panels representing various attributes including Truth and Prudence. The Common Room also has a fire surround with tiles by William De Morgan.

On the south side of CORNHILL at 39-41 is the former **Union Discount Company** (1889-90, now part of Union plc), designed by the architect John Macvicar Anderson (1835-1915), which retains its banking hall with elegant cream and white tiles and faience, including the ceiling, by Burmantofts, the firm he normally used for such schemes; it was shown in their 1902 catalogue. Also on the south side at **54-55 Cornhill** is a good salmon-pink Doulton terracotta facade of 1893 by architect Ernest Runtz; the sculptural details, including two devilish finials, are by W. J. Neatby.[12]

Bolton House (1907), 14-16 CULLUM STREET, has a white faience facade with green and turquoise decoration including the heraldic device of Prior Bolton, after whom the building was named; Bolton House was renovated in 1984.

On the FARRINGDON STREET facade of the **Fleet Building** (1956-60, architect W. S. Frost for the Ministry of Works), a huge slab block which originally housed a telecommunications centre and telephone exchange, are nine 7′ by 5′ abstract stoneware tile panels (1960) with a 'communications' theme designed by the mural painter Dorothy Annan (Fig 158).[13] They were intended to 'add interest at street level to Farringdon Street ' and may have been made by Hathernware, who were credited with the building's decorative ceramic tiles.[14] The panels remain in good condition, although their future must be in doubt as the building is empty in 2004 and the site may be redeveloped. Nearby, the **stairwell** connecting Farringdon Street and Holborn Viaduct is lined with tiling (2002) depicting the construction of the viaduct, which was completed in 1869. The tiles were supplied by the London firm World's End Tiles, and designed and made by July Ceramics of Newcastle under Lyme.

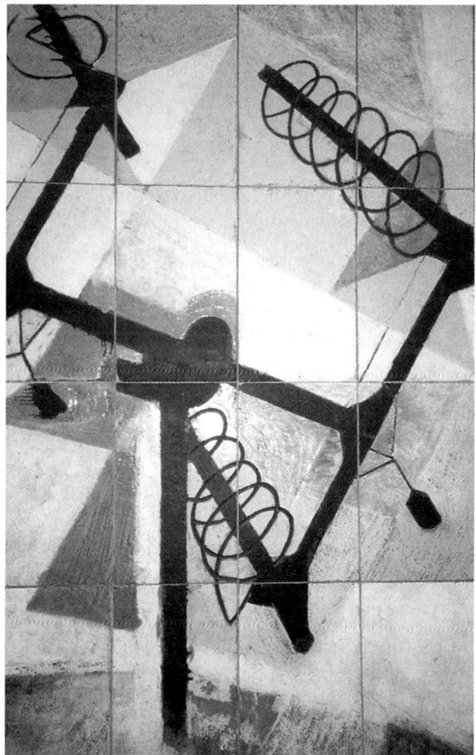

Fig 158.

The **Lamb Tavern** in Leadenhall Market (1880-1), GRACECHURCH STREET, has full height porch tiling with a pictorial panel by W. B. Simpson & Sons depicting Sir Christopher Wren and the construction of the Monument; the panel is faintly dated 12th March 1882 (possibly 1889). The Lamb's cellar bar is also fully tiled, in cream and shades of green, and there is wall tiling on the stairway to the dining room.

In GREYSTOKE PLACE are the former **offices** (1961) of architects Yorke, Rosenberg & Mardall, clad in the firm's trademark white Twintiles. Eugene Rosenberg advocated tiles rather than exposed concrete as a modernist response to the British climate, and experimented with them on the Greystoke Place offices; the dimensions of the building were such that no tiles needed to be cut.[15]

The **Temple Church**, INNER TEMPLE LANE, was consecrated in 1185. Early works carried out during the 1841-3 restoration by Sydney Smirke and Decimus Burton included the excavation of its floor, when traces of the original medieval tile pavement came to light.[16] It was decided to replace the floor with modern encaustic tiling, and to ascertain an appropriate layout, the architect and restorer Lewis N. Cottingham was asked to investigate the medieval pavement of the Chapter House at Westminster Abbey, which had lain unseen for many years beneath wooden boarding while the room was in use as a store; access was via one of two trapdoors let into the boards.[17] Cottingham made tracings of the tiles, and Herbert Minton agreed to undertake the manufacture of the new pavement, carrying out the work on this prestigious project at nominal cost.[18] This was the first significant encaustic tile commission carried out by Minton; the tiles for the encaustic pavement at Kilmory Castle, Argyll & Bute, had been supplied by Minton in 1837 out of stock taken over from Samuel Wright. The designs for the Temple pavement were mostly copies of those in the Chapter House, and the commission turned out to be a huge success; Smirke described the tiles as 'a new manufacture of great beauty'. However, a century after its installation, the pavement was badly damaged in a bombing raid of 1941, and some of the remaining tiles were eventually taken up and relaid in the triforium of the circular nave (normally no public access) (Fig 159). Aside from the Chapter House designs, there are four-tile groups bearing the Agnus Dei (symbol of the Middle Temple) and Pegasus (for the Inner Temple).

Oriental figures sculpted by John Broad form part of the white Doulton Carraraware facade of **Asia House** (1912-13), 31-3 Lime Street.

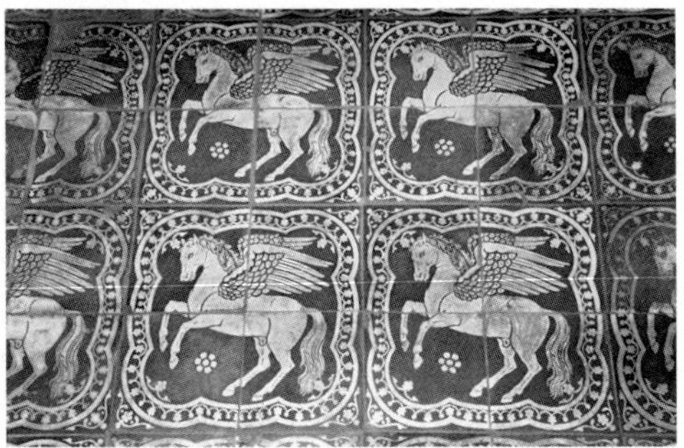

Fig 159.

The streamlined moderne **Ibex House** (1935-7, Fuller, Hall & Foulsham), 41-7 Minories, a six-storey office building, is faced in creamy-yellow and black faience, mostly standard slab blocks apart from those which curve around its pair of towers. Restoration in 1994-5 involved replacing the faience of its north tower, where many blocks had become crazed or suffered frost damage. New faience blocks were supplied by Gladding McBean of Lincoln, California.

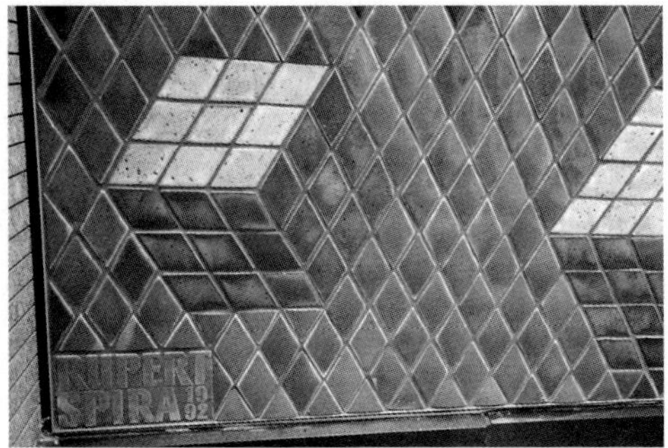

Fig 160.

On the west side of New Bridge Street is the former Spicer Brothers warehouse and office, **Blackfriars House** (1913-17, F. W. Troup), a proto-modernist eight-storey grid faced in white Doulton Carraraware. Across the street is **100 New Bridge Street**; its rear facade - actually in Waithman Street, approached from the main street by Pilgrim Street - springs a surprise with a series of twenty-three large hand-made stoneware tile panels of 1992 by the potter Rupert Spira (b1960), all with different Escher-like patterns (Fig 160). The glazes are a mix of beautifully mottled reds, blues, turquoise, green and grey, and it is hard to believe the panels are flat rather than three-dimensional. In the early 1990s Spira was producing pots at Lower Froyle, Hampshire, when he was offered a commission for tiles.[19] At Swallow Tiles in Cranleigh he discovered how to produce tiles by hand, in interlocking shapes and with a full palette of glaze colours; he then made 18,000 tiles for a garden in Paris (1991) and carried out the 1992 commission from developers Rosehaugh Stanhope for 100 New Bridge Street. Financially secure from the tile making, Spira returned to making pots, experimenting with simpler forms and monochrome glazes, totally different from the New Bridge Street panels, his sole British tile commission.

The complex of former GPO offices just north of St Paul's Cathedral takes in **King Edward Buildings** (1907-11), on Newgate Street and King Edward Street. The site (no public access) includes an older cellar with a large nineteenth century brick-built water tank lined with tin-glazed tiles of unusually varied design, including parts of four tile pictures, letter tiles and designs by Sadler & Green of Liverpool; they date from around the middle of the seventeenth to eighteenth centuries.[20]

The gentlemen's cloakroom in the basement of the City Club (now **City of London Club**), Old Broad Street, has retained its floor-to-ceiling Burmantofts tile and faience decorative scheme of 1907.

The three walls above the central circular lightwell at **No 1 Poultry**, a complex of shops and offices completed in 1998 (architects James Stirling, Michael Wilford & Associates), are lined with startling blue faience cladding from Hathernware. The site was formerly occupied by assorted late-Victorian buildings, notably Mappin & Webb's; one result of the bitter fight over its redevelopment was the retention of a few Victorian decorative elements, notably the red terracotta *Reliefs of Royal Progresses* of 1875, sculpted by Joseph C. Kremer, which can now be seen above the archway on Poultry. Each panel comprises up to ten separate terracotta sections.[21]

On the Primrose Street and Appold Street corner of **Exchange House**, part of the Broadgate development, is a recessed hand-painted tiled fountain (1990) several storeys in height. The artist was the Spanish ceramicist Joan Gardy Artigas (b1938), who worked with Joan Miró for many years, collaborating on works such as the ceramic mural at Barcelona airport. The fountain's concave surface is pleasingly colourful but the waters appear to have ceased flowing some years ago, and the installation is looking increasingly shabby.

The banking hall of the former British Linen Bank (1902-3, John Macvicar Anderson, now **Bank of Scotland**), THREADNEEDLE STREET, retains its striking pastel-coloured Burmantofts faience ceiling, which extends into a subsidiary hall.[22]

The bright red high-relief terracotta frieze (1887) on the exterior of **Cutlers' Hall** (1886-7), WARWICK LANE, realistically depicts late Victorian cutlery production; the sculptor was Benjamin Creswick (1853-1946) of Sheffield, Ruskin's protégé and once a cutler himself (Fig 161). Creswick, who opened his London studio in 1884, was Master of Modelling and Modelled Design at Birmingham School of Art during 1889-1918, and carried out several terracotta commissions in Birmingham. The frieze was made by E. Goodall & Co of Manchester.[23]

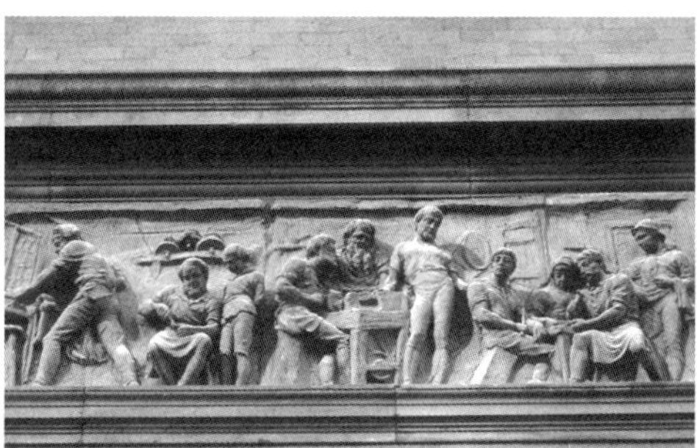

Fig 161.

On the exterior of the former **Nordheim Model Bakery**, WIDEGATE STREET, are four blue and white glazed faience reliefs (1926) of bakers in action, rare ceramic works designed by the London sculptor Philip Lindsey Clark (1889-1997) and made by Carter's of Poole.[24]

References

1. Philip Ward-Jackson, *Public Sculpture of the City of London* Public Sculpture of Britain (Liverpool University Press, Liverpool, 2003).
2. John Price, ''Everyday heroes': The Memorial Tablets of Postman's Park', *TACS Journal*, 10 (2004), pp18-23.
3. *The Builder*, vol 67, 24th November 1894.
4. Carter Archive, Poole Museum Service, CP348.
5. *The Builder*, vol 68, 9th February 1895, p98. G. H. Elphick registered three interlocking tile designs (numbers 241167-9) on the 29th September 1894.
6. *Tile UK*, October 1996, vol 1, no 2, p17.
7. *Tour Notes: Holland House and the City of London*, (TACS, 1990).
8. Simon Bradley and Nikolaus Pevsner, *London 1: The City of London*. Buildings of England (Penguin, London, 1997).
9. Christopher Hussey, 'Faience as a Medium for Modern Architecture', *Architectural Review*, 70 (1931), pp101-4.
10. Russell Wright, *Signs of the Times: a guide to the materials of modernism 1927-1933* (Building Centre, London, 1981).
11. Finch Allibone and Lynn Quiney, *The Law Society's Hall: An architectural history 1823-1995* (The Law Society, London, 1995).
12. Paul Atterbury and Louise Irvine, *The Doulton Story* (Royal Doulton Tableware, Stoke on Trent, 1979).
13. 'Two new telephone exchanges in London', *Architects' Journal*, 129 (1959) 12th February, p256.
14. 'Office building, Holborn', *Architect and Building News*, 220, 16th August 1961, pp245-50.
15. Michael Stratton, *Clad is bad? The relationship between structural and ceramic facing materials*, in *Structure and Style: Conserving Twentieth Century Buildings*, ed Michael Stratton (E. & F. N. Spon, London, 1997), pp164-92.
16. Tony Herbert and Kathryn Huggins, *The Decorative Tile in Architecture and Interiors* (Phaidon Press, London, 1995), pp73-7.
17. Jane Cochrane, 'Medieval Tiled Floor Patterns', *TACS Journal*, 5 (1994), pp11-19.
18. Joan Jones, *Minton: The first two hundred years of design and production* (Swan Hill Press, Shrewsbury, 1993), p161.
19. Emmanuel Cooper, 'Signature Pieces', *Ceramic Review*, (2004) 208, pp18-21.
20. Personal communication, Ian Betts, Museum of London Specialist Services, 12th August 2004.
21. Ward-Jackson, *City of London* (2003).
22. *Burmantofts Pottery*, (Bradford Art Galleries and Museum, Bradford, 1983).
23. *British Architect*, 29, 6th April 1888, pp243-4.
24. 'A Modern Bakery', *Architect and Building News*, 119, 10th February 1928, pp219-21, 230.

CROYDON

Croydon

St John the Baptist Church (rebuilt 1870, architect George Gilbert Scott), CHURCH STREET, has a fine display of Godwin's encaustic floor tiling in the chancel, which was reconstructed in 1892-3.

South Norwood

The Stanley Works in South Norwood, founded by the inventor and philanthropist W. F. R. Stanley (1829-1909), manufactured and exported scientific instruments. Stanley relinquished control of his firm in 1900 and thereafter devoted his time and fortune to the betterment of South Norwood, initially by the construction of a public hall. He designed, financed and supervised the building of the Stanley Hall and its art gallery in 1901-3, later adding a smaller hall (1904), the Trade Schools (1907) and several additional rooms, the whole being completed only after his death in 1909.[1] The **Stanley Halls** complex on SOUTH NORWOOD HILL has been owned by the Borough of Croydon since 1944. Although some of the original elaborate decoration has disappeared, much remains including the odd earthenware flowerpots mounted above the gable end and a pair of green-glazed cherubs on the facade. Inside, there is extensive wall tiling and a stunning ceramic stair, all by Burmantofts, as confirmed where their trademark 'propellor blade' tile back has made an impression on the wall. The Halls were refurbished in 1987 and English Heritage installed a blue plaque on the facade in 1993.

References

1. J. Steele, ed, *Croydon's Built Heritage* (Croydon Society, 1995).

EALING

Ealing

Sir John Soane bought **Pitzhanger Manor**, Walpole Park, MATTOCK LANE, in 1800, replacing much of the existing building in 1801-3. The figures topping the four grand Ionic columns of the facade are of Coade stone; Soane is known to have ordered more than three dozen Coade caryatids, also using them on his home in Lincoln's Inn Fields (see Camden).[1] There is more Coade ornament inside the Manor, whose Victorian wing is now a museum, the PM Gallery; it holds a large collection of pottery by the Martin Brothers, who moved their works from Fulham to Southall in 1877. The collection includes a Martinware fire surround (1891) designed by the architect William Aitken Berry, and the upper part of an elaborate fountain designed and made by Robert Wallace Martin in 1901-6 which was originally located in Southall Park.

Also on Mattock Lane is the **Questors Theatre**, part of its facade comprising the faience fascia saved from the demolished Walpole Picture Theatre (1912, architect John Stanley Beard), which stood in Ealing's Bond Street. Beard designed several other cinemas with eccentric faience facades including the Forum Cinema (1934, now **UGC Cinema**) just north on NEW BROADWAY (part of Uxbridge Road), which has an impressive colonnaded faience frontage by Shaws of Darwen. The building is due to be redeveloped as a sixteen-screen cinema opening in 2006; its facade is to be retained.

Half a mile east along UXBRIDGE ROAD, opposite Ealing Common underground station (at 2 The Bridge) is **Mo's Fisheries**. Its splendid interior, dating from the early 1900s and complete with marble display fittings, has six hand-painted tile panels, four of fish and game birds, the others showing Calais Harbour and the Royal Yacht Britannia. The latter pair are marked Malkin Tile Works Co Ltd, but designs for the fish and bird panels, some by the artist Albert H. Wright, are held in the Minton archives. It appears that Wright was a freelance who sold his work to several manufacturers.[2]

East Acton

St Aidan's R. C. Church (1958-61, architect John Newton), stands amidst an interwar shopping parade on OLD OAK COMMON LANE, south-west of East Acton tube station. Its fine collection of contemporary furnishings includes ceramic reliefs of angels and a dove (representing the Holy Ghost) by Adam Kossowski on the baptistery wall.[3]

Hanwell

The dark green faience facade of the **Forester PH** (1909), LEIGHTON ROAD, is typical of the style of its architect T. H. Nowell Parr (see Hounslow).

Perivale

The white concrete and glass facade of the art deco **Hoover Factory** (1931-5, architects Wallis, Gilbert & Partners), WESTERN AVENUE, is enlivened by Carter's tiling in brilliantly coloured strips. Supposedly Egyptianate in style, it was the fanciest in the series of Wallis, Gilbert 'Fancy Factories' which included Firestone (1928), a few miles south on the Great West Road in Brentford; its partial demolition in 1980 aroused great protests.[4] The rear of the Hoover Factory was rebuilt as a supermarket in 1992, and the front section serves as offices.

Southall

The exterior of the former Palace Cinema (1928-9, architect George Coles), SOUTH ROAD, is a Chinese fantasy with a pagoda-style pantiled roof, dragon finials, ornate ridge tiles and a multicoloured faience facade, the ceramics being supplied by the Hathern Station Brick & Terra Cotta Company.[5] The Palace was converted to house an indoor market before being gutted by fire in 1998; after complete restoration, it reopened as the **Himalaya Palace Cinema** in 2001.

Twelve of the Carter's tile panels (1934) from the children's ward of Ealing's King Edward Memorial Hospital have been restored and re-sited at **Ealing Hospital**, UXBRIDGE ROAD, on the eastern fringe of Southall. The panels, most of which depict nursery rhymes, were decorated by Phyllis Butler, senior paintresss at Carter's during 1927-72, and fired four times to provide the required detailing.[6]

References

1. Alison Kelly, *Mrs Coade's Stone* (Self Publishing Association, Upton-upon-Severn, 1990).
2. Robert Walker, 'Finding Mr Wright', *Glazed Expressions*, (1986) 13, pp4-5.
3. *Adam Kossowski: Murals and Paintings*, (Armelle Press, London, 1990).
4. Joan S. Skinner, *Form and Fancy: Factories and Factory Buildings by Wallis, Gilbert & Partners, 1916-1939* (Liverpool University Press, Liverpool, 1997).
5. *Modern Practice in Architectural Terra Cotta*, (Hathern Station Brick & Terra Cotta Co Ltd, Loughborough, 1930).
6. John Greene, *Brightening the Long Days* (Tiles and Architectural Ceramics Society, 1987).

ENFIELD

Enfield

The elaborate encaustic tile pavement in the sanctuary and chancel of **St Mary Magdalene Church** (1881-3, William Butterfield), WINDMILL HILL, was made by Godwin's and includes their 'Green Man' design.

GREENWICH

Charlton

The Jacobean mansion **Charlton House** (now a community centre), CHARLTON ROAD, was built around 1607-12 and contains many fireplaces, some of extremely elaborate design; most of them include hand-painted tin-glazed tiles with polychrome floral or geometric patterns. Two fireplaces have eighteenth century Spanish or seventeenth century Dutch tiles, but the majority of the fireplace tiles were produced in Millwall by Frederick Garrard, who made copies of Spanish cuenca tiles and early polychrome Delftware designs towards the end of the nineteenth century. The ground floor 'Delft Corridor' is lined with nineteenth century machine-made blue and white tiles.[1]

Eltham

The luxurious mansion on BEXLEY ROAD rebuilt by the nitrate speculator Colonel John Thomas North in 1889-91 was mostly destroyed during the Second World War, but the remainder, with its splendid winter garden, is now part of the **Avery Hill Campus of the University of Greenwich**. The Colonel's villa included a spectacular private three-roomed Turkish bath (lost in the war), with an octagonal frigidarium (cold room) featuring red and white Burmantofts faience arcading.[2] The same firm's faience in shades of blue, green, grey and white was used for the walls and ceiling of the tepidarium (warm room), and on the walls of the calidarium (hot room).[3] Still surviving in the entrance hall is a fireplace with tiling which bears the W. B. Simpson & Sons 'WBS' mongram; the tiles show allegorical female figures and the matching hearth tiles depict a pair of heads. The room (of around 1890) which now serves as the women's staff locker room and toilet is a Burmantofts tour-de-force with relief patterned floral wall tiles in yellow ochre, a patterned faience dado, cream faience panelled ceiling and an elaborate olive-green faience mirror fitment.[4]

Greenwich

The most southerly of the structures on the **Royal Observatory** site (now part of the National Maritime Museum) on BLACKHEATH AVENUE in Greenwich Park are the Altazimuth Pavilion and the South Building, both put up in 1894-9 to the designs of the eighth Astronomer Royal, William Christie, and the London architect William Crisp. The Altazimuth Pavilion, which held a small telescope, is mainly brick with a terracotta porch and entrance. The larger South Building, originally the New Physical Observatory, currently houses a Planetarium and has much external terracotta ornament including the names of famous astronomers and instrument makers, and a bust of the astronomer John Flamsteed above the entrance. There are also allegorical figures with symbols of the Zodiac; these were modelled by W. J. Neatby for Doulton's of Lambeth, their marks appearing on the buff terracotta.

On CROOM'S HILL, which runs along the western edge of Greenwich Park, is the **R. C. Church of Our Lady Star of the Sea** (1851, architect W. W. Wardell), with a mildly decorative Minton encaustic tiled chancel pavement. Its lay-out was planned by A. W. N. Pugin, whose detailed drawing survives, complete with identification of the tile designs and the quantities required.[5]

In the middle of Greenwich on ROMNEY ROAD is the former Royal Hospital for Seamen, now largely the **Maritime Greenwich Campus of the University of Greenwich**. Its construction began in 1696, and the Queen Mary Building (now Queen Mary Court), which included the Chapel, was completed in 1751. The Chapel was gutted by fire on the 2nd January 1779; its refitting and redecoration carried on until 1789, and included the use of a significant amount of Coade stone: 32 pilaster capitals and bases, 32 cherub heads, the Hospital arms, 6 angels supporting the communion table, 4 oval medallions of prophets and 6 circular medallions of apostles. The medallion designs were provided by the artist Benjamin West, who also designed the four Coade stone statues in the Chapel's entrance vestibule. Following the death of Lord Nelson in the Battle of Trafalgar in October 1805, his body lay in state in the Hospital's Painted Hall in early January 1806. Soon afterwards, Benjamin West produced several paintings and sketches on the theme of Nelson's death, including *The Immortality of Nelson*, in which Neptune delivers the heroic figure of Nelson to Britannia; he chose this image for the Nelson pediment of the King William Building (now King William Court). This huge pediment sculpture, 40 feet wide and 10 feet high at its apex, was modelled in Coade stone by West and Coade's Joseph Panzetta in 1810-12 (it is marked 1813), and was considered by the firm to be its finest achievement (Fig 162). The Nelson pediment was intended to be the first in a series of Hospital pediment sculptures commemorating naval actions, but was the only one executed. West had seen and been much impressed by the Elgin Marbles when they were first displayed in London in 1807, and felt that in regard to the Nelson pediment, both his artistry and the sculptural qualities of Coade stone, particularly its durability, were at least the equal of the Greeks.[6] The final Hospital order from the Coade works (in 1814) was for a frieze of the Hospital arms for the west front of the Civic Offices or Trafalgar Quarters (1813-15), just east of the main site on Park Row; the building required suitable decoration as it terminated the eastward view through the grounds.

The **Greenwich Mural** (1972), in WOOLWICH ROAD, was commissioned from Philippa Threlfall and Kennedy Collings by the architects of Greenwich District Hospital, which was completed in the late 1970s but closed in 2001; the 60′ long mural, however, remains *in situ* (Fig 163). The mural, whose theme is the maritime history of Greenwich, is made from glazed and unglazed ceramics and stone; it was one of the earliest large-scale murals to be produced by Threlfall and Collings.[7]

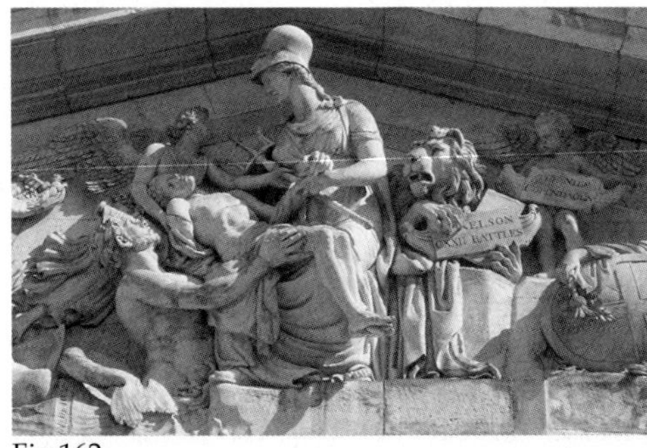

Fig 162.

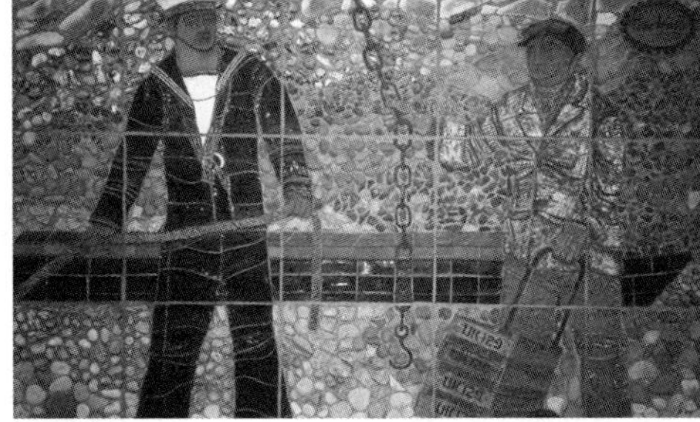

Fig 163.

Woolwich

On the south platform of **Woolwich Arsenal** railway station, in the centre of Woolwich on WOOLWICH NEW ROAD, is a large high-relief terracotta mural entitled *Workers of Woolwich* (1993) by Martin Williams. Just west of the station at 15 THOMAS STREET is the **Earl of Chatham PH** (1903); the impressive floral tile panels on its facade were supplied by tile merchant Alfred Carter (a son of Jesse Carter of the Poole firm Carter's) from his Brockley works, a few miles south-west of Woolwich. Slightly north in the main shopping area, POWIS STREET, is the massive former **Central Store** (rebuilt 1903, now offices) of the Royal Arsenal Co-operative Society; the design was by the Society's architect Frank Bethell. Its elaborate red brick and pale brown terracotta facade includes a statue of Alexander McLeod, one of the founders of the Society, by the well known sculptor Alfred Drury (1856-1944).[8]

At the west end of Powis Street is JOHN WILSON STREET and the former Odeon Cinema

(1937, architect George Coles, now **New Wine Church**) with its sensational curved wall and fin of buff mottled Hathernware with black highlights.[9] Continue about a quarter mile west, crossing the main road; take Leda Road northward, then Venus Road which leads to the river and RESOLUTION WALK to see the colourful **Sealife** tile mural (1987) by Charlie Pig, installed as part of the Elfrida Rathbone Society's 1980s Riverside Walk Project. Just west in DEFIANCE WALK (off Antelope Road) is the **Clockhouse Community Centre**, home to two large pictorial tile panels which were part of the decoration in the Clarence Arms PH in Plumstead Road, near Woolwich Arsenal, until its demolition in 1980. One shows sailors manning a machine gun, the other a muzzle-loading gun, and both are signed by W. Lambert, dated 1896 and marked 'G. W. & S. Ltd'. William Lambert was a glass and tile painter who set up his own firm in the early 1890s but went bankrupt in 1895, after which he designed and painted tiles for George Wooliscroft & Sons of Stoke-on-Trent.

References

1. Personal communications, Chris Blanchett, 5th August 2004; and Ian Betts, Museum of London Specialist Services, 12th August and 2nd September 2004.
2. David Shorney, *A Brief History of the Mansion at Avery Hill* (Thames Polytechnic, London, 1990).
3. 'Turkish Bath, Avery Hill', *The Builder*, 63, 26th November 1892, p420.
4. *Burmantofts Pottery*, (Bradford Art Galleries and Museum, Bradford, 1983).
5. Paul Atterbury and Clive Wainwright, *Pugin: A Gothic Passion* (Yale University Press, New Haven and London, 1994), pp147-8.
6. John Bold, *Greenwich: An Architectural History of the Royal Hospital for Seamen and the Queen's House* (Yale University Press, New Haven and London, 2000), pp176-9, 185.
7. Penny Beckett, 'The Ceramic Murals of Philippa Threlfall', *Glazed Expressions*, (1999) 39, pp2-4.
8. Michael Stratton, *The Terracotta Revival* (Victor Gollancz, London, 1993), p132-3.
9. Kevin Wheelan, *The History of the Hathern Station Brick & Terra Cotta Company* (Mercia Cinema Society, Birmingham, 1982).

HACKNEY

Dalston

The interior wall tiling at the former **Cooke's Eel, Pie & Mash** shop (now a Chinese restaurant), 41 KINGSLAND HIGH STREET, dates mostly from its opening in 1910, although the rear dining room was added in 1936. The plain tiling has maritime-themed pictorial insets.

Hackney

The **Dolphin PH**, 165 MARE STREET, was remodelled around 1900 with elaborate tiling by W. B. Simpson & Sons including two large hand-painted panels near the original entrances, one showing the Greek poet Arion who was saved from drowning by a dolphin. Further north on Mare Street is the **Hackney Empire** (1901, architect Frank Matcham), with an exuberant buff terracotta exterior (by the Hathern Station Brick and Terra Cotta Company) including twin domes, taken down for safety reasons in 1979 along with the Doulton statue of *Euterpe*, the muse of music. All were reinstated in 1988 after a public enquiry report insisted on their restoration in terracotta rather than substitution with another material or removal, and Shaws of Darwen produced all the new terracotta work; the building, used for bingo for many years, was returned to theatre use in 2003.[1] At the road junction just to the north, facing AMHURST ROAD, is **Hackney Central** railway station, marked by its streamlined 'BR' leaning tower forecourt sign in pale blue, white and red tiles; it probably dates from around 1980.

Haggerston

The **Suleymaniye Mosque** (1993-8, architect Osman Sahan), 212-6 KINGSLAND ROAD, is decorated with much Iznik-style tiling (1999) made by the Guven Cini factory at Kutahya in western Turkey. The firm, which has produced art tiles since 1940, has supplied tiles for many recent mosques in Germany and Turkey.

Homerton

The 1915 frontage of the **Adam and Eve**, HOMERTON HIGH STREET, is in purple faience with Doulton Carraraware above, the latter including a large pub sign modelled by John Broad.[2]

Hoxton

In CHARLES SQUARE, off Old Street, is the **Charles Square Mural** (1999) designed by Neil Irons and made at Hackney City Farm by Irons and S. Bird. The ceramic mural, commissioned by Hackney Council, is nearly 70 feet long and about 6 feet high, and uses on-glaze enamels to portray local scenes.

Lea Bridge

The *Rise and Shine Magic Fish* (1990-1, designed and made by Kate Malone) protrude from the waters of the **Hackney Marshes Nature**

Reserve, part of the Lea Valley Park off LEA BRIDGE ROAD. The massive stoneware forms of two carp, a pike and a rudd, all English freshwater fish, are between three and four feet in height and were intended to educate and entertain visitors to the Reserve.

Stoke Newington

Inside the **Rochester Castle** (1892-3, architects G. R. Crickmay & Sons), 143-5 Stoke Newington High Street, is lavish wall tiling including several pictorial panels of allegorical figures.

References

1. Julia Abel Smith, 'Decorating a Revival', *Country Life*, 184, 1st November 1990, pp94-96.
2. Philip Ward-Jackson, *Public Sculpture of the City of London*. Public Sculpture of Britain (Liverpool University Press, Liverpool, 2003), p452.

HAMMERSMITH AND FULHAM

Hammersmith

Six hand-painted tile panels of domestic and agricultural scenes by W. B. Simpson & Sons (two given by the Simpson family) installed at the former **Charing Cross Hospital** during the 1890s were removed in 1978-9, restored and resited on the first floor of the hospital's main entrance area at its new site in FULHAM PALACE ROAD.[1]

The **Church of St John the Evangelist** (1857-9, William Butterfield), GLENTHORNE ROAD, has typically elaborate east wall decoration including yellow zigzag tiling; there are also two memorial tiles, one by the font and the other near the choir steps. The Craven Dunnill encaustic tile pavement in the Lady Chapel (1898, J. F. Bentley) includes a four-tile 'green man' group.

The **Salutation Inn** (1910, by the London architect A. P. Killick), 154 KING STREET W6, with its strange blue and mauve faience and red brick facade, was a showpiece pub for the local brewers, Fuller, Smith & Turner, whose Griffin Brewery still stands under a mile away in Chiswick.

In an office on the first floor of **Hammersmith Library** (1904-5), SHEPHERDS BUSH ROAD, is a ceramic fireplace made at the Fulham Pottery (see below, Parsons Green) in 1879 for the Pines, the Putney home of the novelist Theodore Watts-Dunton (1832-1914). The fireplace was one of matching pair; both were removed from the house in the late 1930s and returned to the pottery, where one was re-erected. The other was kept in parts until being donated to the Library in 1970.

William Morris (1834-96) moved to a Georgian house on UPPER MALL in 1878, naming it **Kelmscott House** after his country retreat, Kelmscott Manor. There is no public access to the main part of the house, which has two fireplaces with Morris & Co *Poppy* tiles in a first floor room, but the basement - the headquarters of the William Morris Society - is opened regularly to the public, and has a fireplace with Dutch tiles commissioned by Morris and probably designed by Philip Webb (1831-1915).[2]

Parsons Green

Inside the **Duke of Cumberland PH** (1892-3), 235 NEW KINGS ROAD (on the south edge of Parsons Green itself), is a large area of mostly floral wall tiling by the Brierley Hill firm Gibbons, Hinton & Co; it is split into three main areas centred on figurative relief panels, above a dado including three panels of nesting birds. Almost at the west end of New Kings Road, on the corner with BURLINGTON ROAD, is an unusual survivor: a brick-built nineteenth century **bottle kiln**, the last remnant of the Fulham Pottery, which occupied the site from around 1672 until 1986. John Piper was one of the artists involved with its production of art ceramics during the late 1940s and early 1950s.

References

1. John Greene, *Brightening the Long Days* (Tiles and Architectural Ceramics Society, 1987).
2. Richard Myers and Hilary Myers, *William Morris Tiles - The tile designs of Morris and his Fellow-Workers* (Richard Dennis, Shepton Beauchamp, 1996).

HARINGEY

Crouch End

The **Queen's Hotel**, 26 BROADWAY PARADE (1899-1901), was built as a combined pub and hotel by the Scottish developer and architect John Cathles Hill (1858-1915), who was responsible for the construction of much local housing and an even more spectacular suburban pub in nearby Harringay (see below). The facade of the Queen's includes art nouveau tiled stall risers.

Harringay

The interior of the **Salisbury PH** (1898-9, designed and built by John Cathles Hill), 1 Grand Parade, GREEN LANES, is relatively untouched and retains extensive mosaic flooring and good wall tiling.

Highgate

Highpoint Two (1935-8), NORTH HILL, was the second of two modernist blocks of flats in Highgate designed by Berthold Lubetkin and the Tecton group; the entrance vestibule is lined with plain Carter's tiles.

Muswell Hill

The cream and black faience forming the stepped facade of the **Odeon Cinema** (1936, architect George Coles), FORTIS GREEN ROAD, was made by the Hathern Station Brick and Terra Cotta Company.[1] The former shop, possibly a florist's (now **Prickett & Ellis**, estate agents), on PARK ROAD at the corner with Etheldene Avenue has a tiled facade and pretty interior tiling by T. & R. Boote dating from around 1910. This complete decorative scheme includes a tiled dado and high level frieze with panels of patterned tiles in between.

References

1. Kevin Wheelan, *The History of the Hathern Station Brick & Terra Cotta Company* (Mercia Cinema Society, Birmingham, 1982).

HARROW

Canons Park

The ceramicist Philippa Threlfall (b1939), who went on to produce many large-scale mural works from the late 1960s onward, spent her early teaching career at the **North London Collegiate School**, CANONS DRIVE, where her head of department was the designer Peggy Angus (1904-93), who taught at the school during 1947-65.[1] An early Threlfall construction, a freestanding wall made from concrete blocks, glazed ceramic ware and pebbles brought in by the pupils, still remains in the school grounds.[2]

Harrow on the Hill

The Chapel (1854-7) of **Harrow School**, HIGH STREET, has an opus sectile reredos (1899) and wall panels designed by Sir Arthur Blomfield and made by Powell's of Whitefriars. The firm's principal designer John W. Brown (1842-1928) also had a hand in the designs, as he was paid £42 for his work on the commission.[3]

Wealdstone

On the first floor landing of **Harrow Civic Centre** (1966-72), MILTON ROAD, is the Kodak Mural (1974), a brilliantly colourful wall comprising nearly 1,000 different 6" tiles designed by Pentagram and made by Kenneth Clark Ceramics; Kodak Ltd have been associated with Harrow since 1890. All the tiles show Harrow-related images, which were either screen-printed or decorated by a photographic process in a bravura display of the art of tile making. The original design of the Civic Centre complex included a raised piazza, which was never built, leaving the proposed entrance area stranded on the present first floor; it would seem that the Kodak Mural was intended to be seen in the main entrance.[4]

References

1. Katie Arber, 'Peggy Angus, designer of modern tiles for a modern Britain', *Decorative Arts Society Journal*, 26 (2002), pp120-134.
2. Carolyn Trant, 'The Red Angus - Peggy the teacher and inspirer', (2002). Paper given at study day 'Peggy Angus, Mid-Century Designer', 9th November 2002, Museum of Domestic Design and Architecture, Middlesex University, Barnet.
3. Dennis W. Hadley, *James Powell & Sons: A listing of opus sectile, 1847-1973*, (2001).
4. Jonathan Clarke, Peter Guillery and Joanna Smith, *Gazetteer of London Town Halls*, in *London's Town Halls: The architecture of local government from 1840 to the present*, (English Heritage, Swindon, 1999), pp34-77.

HAVERING

Rainham

Rainham Hall (NT), in the centre of Rainham on THE BROADWAY, was built in 1729 for the merchant and ship owner John Harle; its interior includes six delft-tiled fireplaces, with many of the tiles depicting nautical subjects. The majority of the tiles were Dutch-made (others were produced in London), and despite the Hall's interior being generally unaltered, most of the fireplace tiles are not original but later replacements. The basement room appears to have been used as a dairy, and has four (re-ordered from five) panels of plain and decorative delft tiles.[1] Just north of the Hall is the **Church of St Helen and St Giles**, restored between 1892 and around 1902 by the Essex architect-priest Ernest Geldart, who was responsible for the striking patterned floor in red, black and yellow tiles.[2]

Wennington

A couple of miles south-east of Rainham is Wennington and the **Church of St Mary and St Peter**, where Ernest Geldart added a new south aisle in 1883-6. This work was recorded on one of

Geldart's trademark glazed tiles, which formed part of the decorative scheme.[3]

References
1. Personal communication, Ian Betts, Museum of London Specialist Services, 12th August 2004.
2. James Bettley, ''The Master of Little Braxted in his prime': Ernest Geldart and Essex, 1873-1900', *Essex Archaeology and History*, 31 (2000), pp169-194.
3. Lynn Pearson, 'Memorial and Commemorative Tiles in Nineteenth and Early Twentieth Century Churches', *TACS Journal*, 9 (2003), pp13-23.

HILLINGDON

Hayes

The London ceramicist Lubna Chowdhary was commissioned by Hillingdon Council to produce a tile installation for the walls of the pedestrian underpass at **Hayes and Harlington Railway Station**, STATION ROAD, Hayes. The resulting work, installed in 2003, combined hand-glazed and industrially-made tiles, with designs based on stylised plant forms.[1]

References
1. Claudia Clare, 'Constructive Dialogue', *Ceramic Review*, (2004) 208, pp24-7.

HOUNSLOW

Bedford Park

The overmantel in the rear bar of the **Tabard Inn** (1880, architect Richard Norman Shaw), BATH ROAD, includes a pair of two-tile panels depicting *Nursery Rhyme* scenes hand-painted in blue enamel on plain Dutch tin-glazed tiles. These were most probably designed by Walter Crane and decorated in the Morris & Co workshops.[1] The front bar's high-level frieze of tiles by William De Morgan runs on into the porch.

Brentford

The architect T. H. Nowell Parr (see below, Hounslow) often used coloured Doultonware for his pub facades, as at the **Beehive** (1907), 227 HIGH STREET; only the colour is unusual here, a mottled bluish-green.[2] South of Brentford's centre is **Syon Park**, PARK ROAD, where the ornamental dairy, built after 1847 by Decimus Burton, has internal Wedgwood encaustic tiling; the earliest Wedgwood encaustic tiles were produced in the late 1860s.

Hounslow

The **Treaty Centre** (1984-7), a combination of shopping mall and library on the HIGH STREET, occupies the site of the library, baths and council house complex of 1904-5 designed by Thomas Henry Nowell Parr (1864-1933), architect to Brentford Urban District Council during 1897-1907. The old group of civic buildings was rich in faience, terracotta and internal tiling, and a single pathetic remnant has been preserved above the High Street entrance of the new structure.[3] T. H. Nowell Parr also worked privately from around 1900, and was appointed architect to two local breweries, Fuller, Smith & Turner's Griffin Brewery, Chiswick, and Brentford's Royal Brewery. His pubs, mainly in the west London suburbs, tended towards the domestic in scale and were often faced with dark green or brown Doulton faience at ground floor level (see above, the Beehive, Brentford; and the Forester, Ealing).[4]

Isleworth

The **Church of St Mary the Virgin**, WORTON ROAD, was designed in 1937 by the architect H. S. Goodhart-Rendel and built during 1952-5. It has a colourful tile reredos (1955) measuring about 20' high by 10' wide which was designed by Joseph Ledger for Carter's of Poole; the tiles were hand-painted by Phyllis Butler directly on to raw glaze and fired at around 1100°C.[5] The reredos depicts a series of scenes centred on the Virgin and Child. Ledger designed two other large-scale Carter's ceramic reredoses for Goodhart-Rendel, both at Roman Catholic churches: St John Fisher, Rochester, Kent (1955) and Our Lady of the Rosary (Westminster, 1966).

References
1. Richard Myers and Hilary Myers, *William Morris Tiles - The tile designs of Morris and his Fellow-Workers* (Richard Dennis, Shepton Beauchamp, 1996), p126.
2. Paul Atterbury and Louise Irvine, *The Doulton Story* (Royal Doulton Tableware, Stoke on Trent, 1979), p90.
3. Bridget Cherry and Nikolaus Pevsner, *London 3: North West*. Buildings of England (Penguin Books, London, 1991).
4. A. Stuart Gray, *Edwardian Architecture: A Biographical Dictionary* (Gerald Duckworth, London, 1985).
5. TACS Location Index.

ISLINGTON

Clerkenwell

The art nouveau pale green and white faience facade of the **Fox and Anchor PH** (1898, architect

Latham Augustus Withall), CHARTERHOUSE STREET, is signed by both Doulton's and their designer W. J. Neatby; its motifs include a fox, an anchor and assorted gargoyles.

The exterior of the late nineteenth century former **dairy** (now studio spaces) at 30a GREAT SUTTON STREET is decorated with a frieze of framed Minton China Works picture tiles of rural scenes designed by William Wise.

Finsbury Health Centre (1935-8, architects Berthold Lubetkin and Tecton), PINE STREET, had plain tiles lining its internal walls in accordance with Lubetkin's views on the positive effects of clean and bright surfaces. Its exterior was partly clad with cream tiles, which by the early 1990s had become cracked and filthy. Restoration by Avanti Architects during 1994-5 included the replacement of some tiling on the left hand entrance wing; after trials with samples from Shaws of Darwen, the architects finally used tiles glazed in northern France, which were blander and not an ideal match.[1]

Inside the George and Dragon PH (now **Peasant**), 240 ST JOHN STREET, is good turn-of-the-century tilework including a depiction of St George and the dragon.

Finsbury Park

In the café of the **Centre for Lifelong Learning**, City and Islington College, which is housed in a renovated nineteenth century school building on BLACKSTOCK ROAD, is a wall of around 3,000 ceramic tiles made by the London textile designer Kate Blee (b1961); the wall is in shades of white and its design was inspired by Victorian institutional tiling.

Islington

The red terracotta ornament of the huge former **Leysian Mission** (1901-6, architect J. J. Bradshaw, now lofts and flats), CITY ROAD, was supplied by Dennis Ruabon; the building was mentioned in the firm's catalogue.

The faience of the temple-like Egyptian facade of the former Carlton Cinema (1930, architect George Coles, now **Mecca Bingo**), ESSEX ROAD, was made by the Hathern Station Brick and Terra Cotta Company and included much polychrome decoration.[2]

The architect and speculative builder Herbert Huntly-Gordon (1864-1926) used terracotta for several of his (now mostly demolished) London buildings including the combined shops and offices at 140-3 UPPER STREET (1891, on the corner with Almeida Street), which has a terrifically ornate salmon-pink terracotta facade. Huntly-Gordon worked in association with Doulton's to produce a rough-faced brown terracotta specifically suited to renaissance architectural ornament.[3]

Pentonville

Inside the **Killick Street Health Centre**, 77 KILLICK STREET, is a large W. B. Simpson & Sons hand-painted tile panel entitled 'Playing Bowls on Copenhagen Fields in the Reign of George III'; this was originally at the Star & Garter PH in adjacent Caledonian Road, and was restored by the Jackfield Conservation Studio in 1996.

Upper Holloway

The former **William Plumb's butcher's shop** at 493 HORNSEY ROAD has a magnificent turn-of-the-century art nouveau tiled interior by Burmantofts including two pictorial panels of pastoral scenes on the front of the marble-topped counter; the building underwent conversion to living and working spaces during 2003-4.

References

1. Michael Stratton, *Clad is bad? The relationship between structural and ceramic facing materials*, in *Structure and Style: Conserving Twentieth Century Buildings*, ed Michael Stratton (E. & F. N. Spon, London, 1997), pp164-92.
2. Kevin Wheelan, *The History of the Hathern Station Brick & Terra Cotta Company* (Mercia Cinema Society, Birmingham, 1982).
3. Walter R. Jaggard, 'Obituary: Herbert Huntly-Gordon', *RIBA Journal*, 34, 4th December 1926, p116.

KENSINGTON AND CHELSEA

Brompton

The monumental domed pile of **Harrods** store, which occupies a site near the north end of BROMPTON ROAD, originated as a small grocery shop owned by Charles Henry Harrod in 1853. As the business grew, adjoining properties were purchased, and the architect C. W. Stephens was appointed in 1894 to oversee the complete rebuilding of the four and a half acre site. The first stage included the erection in 1902-3 of the elaborate salmon-pink Doulton block terracotta Brompton Road facade, which is topped by a high relief figure of Britannia modelled by John Broad, along with the Harrods motto *Omnia Omnibus Ubique* - All things, for all people, everywhere. The same shade of terracotta continues on the south (Hans Road) elevation, also by Stephens and mostly dating from 1910-12, although the entrance to the flats which originally comprised four of the upper floors was built in 1895. Stephens was also responsible for the east (Basil Street) facade, but this was rebuilt in 1929-30 by Louis D. Blanc, who was the Harrods house architect during 1920-35. Blanc chose matching unglazed brown Doulton terracotta and the same firm's stoneware in a new bronze finish for the neo-classical facade.[1] The north (Hans Crescent) side of the block was largely rebuilt in 1939 by the architect John L. Harvey.

The store's original internal plan was cellular, with a series of separate units lit by light wells, which continued through to the flats above; the flats were replaced by sales floors in the early 1930s. One relatively unchanged - although restored - survivor is the ground floor Meat Hall (1902-3), which centres on its infilled lightwell and is decorated in Doulton's Parian ware with a delightful scheme including twenty medallions of stylised images of farming and hunting scenes designed by W. J. Neatby. Further tiling was provided for the Meat Hall in 1911 by the Art Pavements & Decorations Co, a London firm founded by Conrad Dressler.[2] Next door to the Meat Hall is the Tea, Coffee and Chocolate Hall (originally the Bakery) of 1902-3, where the wall tiling, with its floral frieze and flowered dado, was supplied by Malkin Tile Works.[3] The two adjoining halls, Floral and Charcuterie, were built in 1925 and have some (restored) Doulton tile decoration. Other minor pieces of ceramic decoration inside Harrods include a modern panel showing polo players; this can be found in the fifth floor Riding Department.

The open porch of 1 CADOGAN GARDENS (built in the 1890s) has a tall and elaborate dado of mainly late nineteenth century Spanish *cuerda seca* tiles whose designs are mostly copies of fifteenth to sixteenth century Spanish motifs. There are also some earlier Spanish tiles, a four-tile group of Moorish design and a few small painted tiles. Set into the wall are two tile plaques bearing crowns and lettering; they were made in Seville around 1700 and were originally fixed to a property which belonged to the city's Royal Hospital.[4]

At 52 CADOGAN SQUARE (1885) is an example of the typically flamboyant use made of terracotta by the architect Ernest George (1839-1922) of George & Peto; its buff Doulton terracotta ornament includes a group of three grotesque figures above the main window, the central one being a jester playing a violin.

Chelsea

The large hand-painted, tin-glazed tile installation depicting Chelsea scenes completed for the interior of the **Waitrose** store at 196 KING'S ROAD in 1999 was designed and made by Reptile (Edward Dunn and Carlo Briscoe of Carmarthen); it was Reptile's thirty-third commission from the supermarket chain, which has their tiling in about 40% of its branches.

The former dairy, at the rear of the house now known as the **Old Dairy**, 46 OLD CHURCH STREET, was rebuilt in 1908 and has a terracotta bull's head protruding just below its pediment. Another such head ornaments the house itself, along with three tile panels, two on the front and a larger pastoral scene on the side; all seem likely to date from 1908. The front panels show a dairymaid and 'The early mower whets his scythe'; in fact he is about to take a drink from his flask.

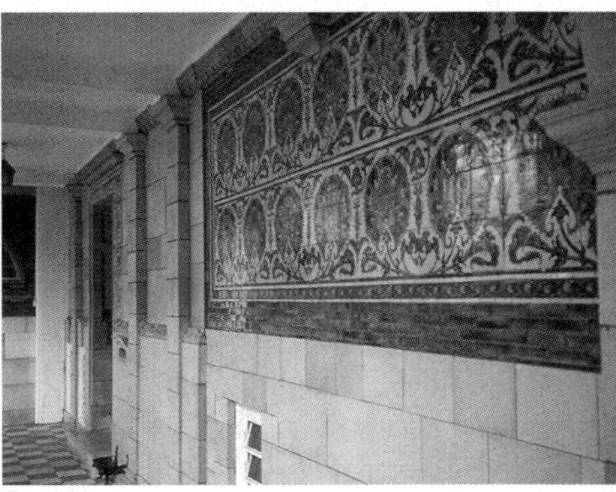

Fig 164.

Kensington

The **Debenham House** (1904-7), 8 ADDISON ROAD, allowed the theories of its architect, Halsey Ricardo, their fullest expression. He was an enthusiast for colour in the townscape, for building materials which could resist the corrosive effects of city air, and rejected elaborate external ornament in favour of polychromy (Fig 164). The facade of his villa designed for Ernest Ridley Debenham, chairman of the department store Debenham & Freebody, combined cream Doulton Carraraware with glazed bricks by Burmantofts in shades of deep green, reflecting the colours of the garden, and light blue, to mirror the sky.[5] The brick backs carry the Leeds Fireclay Company mark. The house is approached through a covered walkway decorated with tiles by William De Morgan; Ricardo was the architect of De Morgan's Sands End Pottery (1888) and was De Morgan's business partner during 1888-98. De Morgan shared Ricardo's views on colour and architecture, and the remaining stock of the Pottery, from which De Morgan retired in 1905, was used up in and around the Debenham House. The walkway has some of the best tiles, including trial runs for De Morgan's P&O liner panels, which can also be seen to the rear of the house in the loggia and breakfast room, while a peacock design appears in the vestibule.

The focal point of the interior is the central domed hall, clad in richly coloured mosaics which were commissioned separately after completion of the house. The design, by George Jack (1855-1931), better known as principal furniture designer for Morris & Co, included mythical and legendary figures, signs of the Zodiac and small portraits of the Debenhams and their children; Gaetano Meo supervised the execution of the mosaic work.[6] The main rooms of the house contain a starry array of arts and crafts fittings, notably a series of De Morgan tile panels of wonderfully varied design; the strange beasts populating the lustre tiles of the several bathrooms are especially memorable. Whether or not De Morgan ever saw the house is unknown, although he did describe it as a 'beautiful palace' after having read an article about it sent to him by Ricardo.[7] It is certainly the most wide-ranging architectural use of De Morgan tiles in Britain. The tiling was restored in 2002-3 by conservator Clare Spicer, after Debenham House had reverted to private domestic use following its stint as an institutional base.

The Jacobean mansion **Holland House**, at the centre of HOLLAND PARK, was damaged during the Second World War and mostly demolished in the 1950s, leaving just a shell and some interesting outbuildings. Running in front of the house is an unusual pierced block wall, probably part of the 1839-46 alterations to the gardens, which uses an early form of buff terracotta from Broseley; terracotta was being made in the East Shropshire coalfield by the mid nineteenth century.[8] Connecting the house with the stables, to the south-west, is the covered arcaded Causeway (1890); its ground floor is decorated with panels of large tiles depicting grapes, while above are more tile panels and benches with brightly coloured heraldic tiles. The Causeway - now part of the tea garden - would look equally at home in Spain or southern Italy, which is where the tiles may have originated.[9]

Many pubs originally in the estate of the London brewers Charrington's have white faience facades, most likely in Doulton's Carraraware, but the **Castle**, on the corner of HOLLAND PARK AVENUE and Clarendon Road, is an exception, with an interwar facade of olive green faience including good lettering. On the Clarendon Road side, above a doorway, is large, unsigned, pictorial panel of a castle on a hill.

Leighton House (1866, now a museum), 12 HOLLAND PARK ROAD, was designed for the artist Frederic Leighton (1830-96) by his friend George Aitchison, who later added the Arab Hall (1877-9), which was intended to house Leighton's collection of Middle Eastern tiles brought back from his travels through Damascus, Cairo, Jerusalem and Rhodes in the 1860s and 1870s. He also bought tiles from others who visited the same areas, and the tiles became so popular with European collectors that large panels were often split up. Leighton commissioned Walter Crane to design a mosaic frieze for the Arab Hall, and asked William De Morgan to make additional tiles to fill gaps in panels where tiles were broken or missing. The majority of the tiles in the Arab Hall were produced in Damascus during the sixteenth and seventeenth centuries, and De Morgan was able to create replacements which can only be distinguished from the originals by their slightly yellow ground and crackly glaze.[10] Leighton's collection, with its De Morgan additions, extends elsewhere on the ground floor, but the centrepiece is the exotic Arab Hall with its marble pool.

The creation of the Arab Hall was the high point of the fashion for eastern-style interiors which followed the publication of Owen Jones's books on the Alhambra during the 1840s. Home-produced versions of Moorish, Iznik, Persian or even Alhambra styles varied considerably in quality, and after initial adoption by the wealthy, often for smoking or billiard rooms, the style became watered down and appeared more frequently in Turkish baths and public houses. One of the more successful of these interiors, still extant in 1971, was at 12 KENSINGTON PALACE GARDENS, which the architect Matthew Digby Wyatt (1820-77) redecorated for its new owner, city merchant Alexander Collie, around 1866.[11] Digby Wyatt's work included a Moroccan billiard room incorporating the fireplace he had designed for London's International Exhibition of 1862. It was adapted from the 'style of the Alhambra' and set with Maw's majolica tiles; the same firm supplied tiles in similar style for the billiard room dado.[12]

William Burges built the **Tower House** (no public access), 29 MELBURY ROAD, for himself in 1876-8. Its ambitious interior decorative scheme - the architect's own 'Palace of Art' - which mostly remains in place, included a tile frieze in the dining room showing scenes from fairy tales and folk stories; the style is very like that of the Nursery tile frieze at Cardiff Castle, which was executed around 1878-9 by Horatio Walter Lonsdale, who often worked with Burges.

Notting Hill

The **Church of St John the Evangelist** (1844), on the corner of LANSDOWNE CRESCENT and Ladbroke Grove, at the top of Notting Hill, has a Doulton terracotta reredos of 1890 designed by Aston Webb. It depicts the life of St John in a series of high relief (almost three dimensional) panels within a perpendicular gothic framework; the sculptor was Emmeline Halse (1853-1923).

The flat-iron shaped combined florists and **public lavatories** (1991-3) at 222 WESTBOURNE GROVE was designed by architects CZWG and clad in a specially produced shade of green glazed brick from Ibstock Brick.

South Kensington

The **Victoria and Albert Museum**, CROMWELL ROAD, occupies the south-easternmost portion of the estate purchased for educational purposes from the proceeds of the 1851 Great Exhibition, but it was not the first structure to be put up on the estate; this was the garden of the Horticultural Society. The notion of constructing a garden, surrounded by buildings, on the site had originally been promoted by Sir Henry Cole, one of the committee members of the 1851 exhibition and later Secretary of the Department of Science and Art (DSA). With the assistance of his architect, Captain Francis Fowke (1823-65) of the Royal Engineers, and the artist Richard Redgrave (1804-88), adviser to the DSA, Cole produced a site plan into which the Horticultural Society's garden was incorporated. Sydney Smirke was appointed as architect although all the DSA planning team, which from 1859 also included the artist Godfrey Sykes (1824-66), contributed to the design. The garden, which included a series of brick and terracotta arcades designed by Fowke and decorated by Sykes, was opened in 1861; Sykes's slender, twisted terracotta columns - inspired by Italian renaissance models - won much praise. The terracotta, which was supplied by Mark Henry Blanchard, the leading British manufacturer at the time, was carefully tested by the DSA for its load-bearing capacities. The Horticultural Society garden was largely demolished between 1889 and 1892, but its design had already established the essential characteristics of the later South Kensington style, and showed that terracotta was a structurally sound and cost-effective means of providing decoration.[13]

Work on Fowke's designs for the South Kensington Museum, now the V&A, began with the construction of the North (1860-2) and South (1861-2) Courts, on the east side of what is now the central quadrangle. These inward-facing facades were decorated with Blanchard's pale buff terracotta, its forms designed and modelled by Sykes; the frieze running between first and second floor windows was designed by James Gamble (1835-1911) of the DSA team. The more elaborate north range, intended as the main entrance, followed in 1864-6, although work on decorative details continued until 1872; its facade used glazed ceramics on a scale not seen before in Britain. Topping its prominent pediment is a terracotta putto designed by Gamble; the two other high-level sculptural groups were designed and modelled by Percival Ball of Doulton's and made from their 'best imperishable material'. Beneath the terracotta cornice is a ceramic mosaic commemorating the 1851 exhibition by Reuben Townroe (1835-1911), also of the DSA team, and above the lecture theatre entrance are two faience panels designed by Sykes and supplied by Minton Hollins. The Blanchard terracotta columns, which enclose iron stanchions, were designed and modelled by Sykes on the theme of the stages of human life; these 15' high columns were probably Sykes's last work. The identical columns on the outside of the Science Schools (1867-74, architect Henry Scott), now known as the Henry Cole Wing, were modelled by Gamble in terracotta supplied by A. Wilson of Dunfermline. Much of the terracotta used on the Science Schools, to the north-west, was supplied by Blanchard, but the second floor windows came from James Pulham & Son of Broxbourne, Hertfordshire (a firm better known for the artificial stone Pulhamite), and the street-level balustrading from Doulton's. Minton's and Gibbs & Canning supplied majolica tiling or panels. Finally, the south side of the quadrangle was built from 1874, with the terracotta contract being awarded to Doulton's, but its facade was not finished until 1901, as part of Aston Webb's 1899-1909 scheme to complete the main Cromwell Road frontage.

Inside this complex building are some of the finest products of British nineteenth century ceramic design, installed to display the possibilities of contemporary building materials. The decorative scheme of the Ceramic Staircase (on the north-west edge of the quadrangle) was designed by Frank Moody (1824-86) in 1866 and completed around 1877. Two of its three flights are clad with Minton Hollins majolica, the themes being arts on the first flight and science and manufacture on the second; much of the work was modelled by Moody, assisted by R. Lunn, Albert Gibbons and E. Wormleighton. Moody, with the assistance of William Wise and Owen Gibbons, also painted the ceilings and spandrels, using Colin Minton Campbell's newly-developed vitrified ceramic painting process. The tiles of the stair risers are by Minton Hollins, and on the lower landing is a memorial to Henry Cole designed by Moody, a majolica panel with a mosaic portrait of Cole executed by Florence Cole.[14]

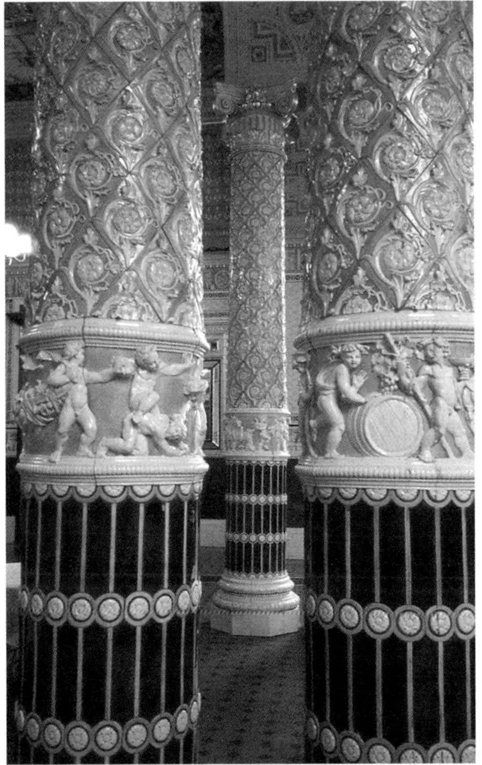

Fig 165.

Leading off the Ceramic Staircase was the first floor Ceramic Gallery, where the original late 1860s decorative scheme included ten Minton Hollins majolica-clad columns in grey and white featuring the names of famous ceramicists lettered in the pictorial alphabet designed by Sykes. The columns were dismantled in 1914 but the tiles were stored, and two columns (including some new tiles faithfully copied by Charlotte Hubbard of the V&A) were reinstated when the rooms reopened as the Silver Galleries in 1996. Similar columns first appeared in the Centre Refreshment Room (Gamble Room), opened in 1868 but whose thoroughgoing ceramic decoration, possibly inspired by the Royal Dairy, was not completed for some years. The design was by James Gamble and includes Minton Hollins majolica-clad columns, a Sykes letter frieze (also Minton Hollins), Maw's majolica panels above the doors, and mirror frames by Gibbs & Canning (Fig 165).

East of the Gamble Room is the Grill Room, where a series of large tile panels depicting the seasons and months, designed by Edward Poynter, is arranged above a dado of blue and white floral and landscape tiles painted in 1867-71 on Minton blanks by female students from the National Art Training School. Much else of ceramic interest remains in the frequently altered V&A, including - in the Henry Cole Wing - a grand staircase whose terracotta balustrade was designed by the London architect James William Wild (1814-92).[15]

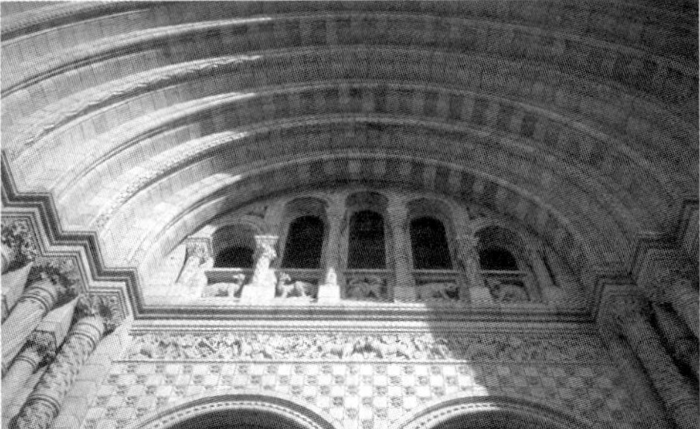

Fig 166.

Just west of the V&A on Cromwell Road is the **Natural History Museum**, built in 1873-81 on the site of the 1862 International Exhibition (Fig 166). The 1863 competition for its design was won by Francis Fowke, but following his death in 1865 the project was taken on by Alfred Waterhouse, who changed the appearance of the elevations from renaissance to romanesque whilst retaining the spirit of Fowke's original plan. Waterhouse specified terracotta block construction for the whole of the interior and exterior walling, because of its resistance to atmospheric pollution and its relative cheapness, and was largely responsible for the appointment of Gibbs & Canning as the suppliers; he had been working with them since 1868 on the construction of Manchester Town Hall, completed 1877. Building work on the

Museum began in 1873, but severe difficulties in obtaining sufficient quantities of the buff and pale blue terracotta led to delays, and Waterhouse never again used block terracotta as his main constructional material.[16]

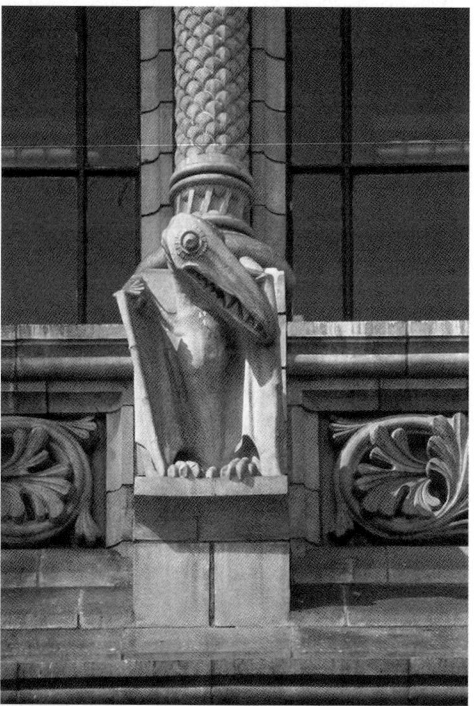
Fig 167.

Not only was the Natural History Museum the first major public building in Britain to be built with an entire facing of terracotta, the scale and richness of its decoration was unmatched (Fig 167). Beasts peer down from the parapet, clamber around windows and are entwined with foliage, while monkeys skitter up arches in the entrance hall and the ornament continues on a smaller scale throughout both wings. The driving force behind the use of 'objects of natural history' as decorative features was the Museum's founder and first superintendent, Richard Owen (1804-92), who also suggested the division of species between living (west wing) and extinct (east wing). Owen, who in 1842 had been first to coin the term 'dinosaur', was a creationist at a time when this view was seen as somewhat old-fashioned following the publication of *On the Origin of Species* in 1859. Waterhouse produced detailed drawings for all the ornamental features, which tread a path between scientific correctness and artistic freedom. They range from low relief to completely three-dimensional and comprise some 272 species. To model his designs, Waterhouse - having rejected sample models from three firms - turned to the architectural carvers Farmer & Brindley, who took on a young Frenchman, Monsieur Dujardin, to carry out the contract. Little is known about Dujardin, who appears to have returned to France after completing work on the Natural History Museum. Once the clay models were made, at one-twelfth over size, they were passed to Gibbs & Canning, who made plaster of Paris moulds and thence the final terracotta blocks.[17] The end result of this collaborative process was a magical architectural bestiary, which initially pleased the critics but was then generally ignored until cleaning in 1975 effected a transformation of the facade; this, however, was achieved with the use of hydrofluoric acid, which scored and bleached the surface of the terracotta. Replacements for some of the parapet sculptures, including a lion and a wolf, were made in 1998 by Hathernware.

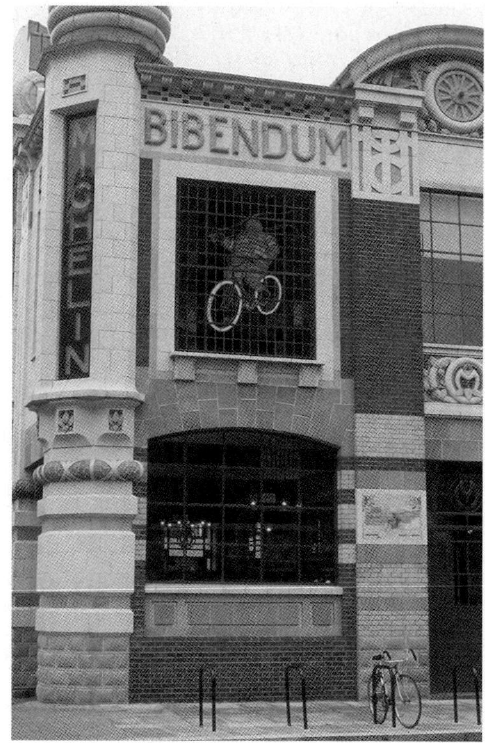

Fig 168.

The **Michelin Building** (1910), on the corner of FULHAM ROAD and Sloane Avenue, was commissioned in 1909 as the British headquarters of the Michelin Tyre Company; this three-dimensional advertisement for the pneumatic tyre opened in 1911 (Fig 168). It was designed by Michelin's own engineer-cum-architect, François Espinasse, probably with substantial input from the brothers André and Edouard Michelin, who both had artistic backgrounds. Hiding its reinforced concrete frame is mostly white Burmantofts Marmo cladding with blue, yellow and green highlights, and a series of high relief faience blocks with assorted tyre-related imagery from rubber plants to interlocking wheels. This eccentric structure is replete with decoration, including stained glass and mosaics depicting Bibendum (the Michelin man), glass cupolas in the form of piles of tyres, and thirty-four tile panels, most of which show motor racing scenes (Fig 169). These were replicas of a set originally made for the Michelin headquarters in Paris by the architectural tile painting firm Gilardoni Fils et Cie, also of Paris, with images largely taken from drawings by the poster artist Ernest Montaut. Gilardoni Fils et Cie went out of business shortly after making the second run of tile panels, which are of rather more mixed quality than the first set. One panel, made of smaller, more detailed tiles with a richer glaze, celebrates the royal warrant granted to the firm in 1908; it was made, probably in England, near the end of 1910.[18] Michelin left the building in 1985; following restoration, completed in 1987, the Michelin Building reopened as an office, shop and restaurant (Bibendum) complex.

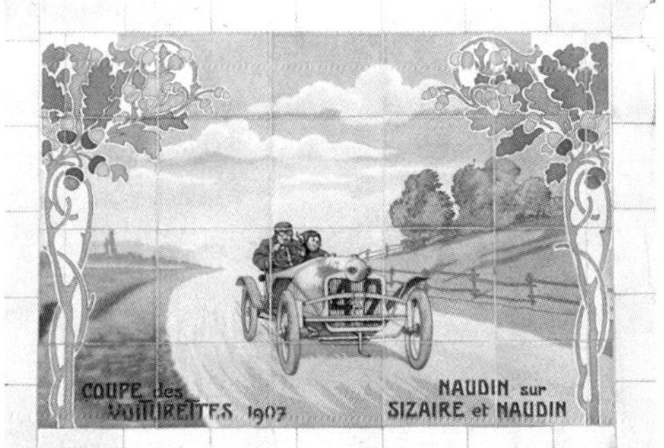

Fig 169.

The typically polychromatic interior of **St Augustine's Church** (1870-7, William Butterfield), QUEEN'S GATE, was further decorated in 1889-91 with the addition of an astonishing series of pictorial tile paintings running around the entire nave and culminating in a large east wall mural (Fig 170). Towards the end of his career, Butterfield came to prefer the more permanent medium of tile paintings to mural decoration, and favoured the London stained glass firm Bell & Beckham, whose James Sinclair Beckham (1838-1930) would have prepared cartoons under Butterfield's direction from the architect's designs; Butterfield's final two tile paintings at All Saints Church, Margaret Street, Westminster, were executed in 1888 and 1890-1 by the firm. The St Augustine series, which also includes three pairs of small murals in the spandrels of the nave arches, depicts scenes from Genesis to the Ascension. Amongst the north aisle murals are Adam and Eve, Noah and the Tower of Babel; the style is bold, with black lines delineating the figures, almost as if in stained glass. The more delicate south aisle murals begin with the baptism of Jesus and end with the Ascension. All the murals were designed by Butterfield, but only those in the south aisle are known to have been executed by Beckham; some of the north aisle murals have been fired unevenly.[19] The paintings have not always been popular - one turn-of-the-century critic thought their colours 'puerile in the extreme' - and they were whitewashed during the 1920s, when the reredos, which still hides the east wall mural, was added.[20] However, the other murals were revealed during a restoration programme which began in the mid 1970s.

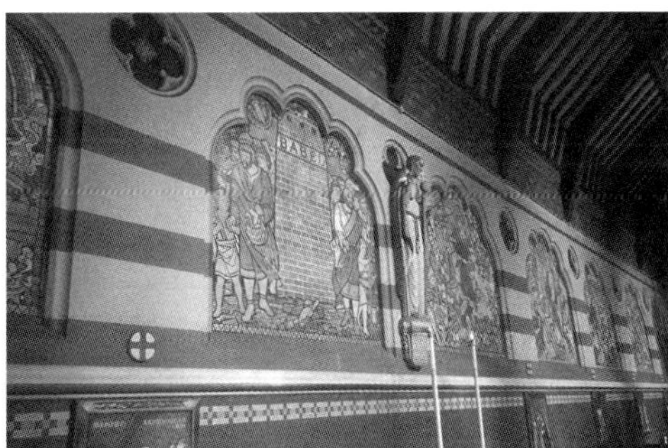

Fig 170.

References

1. Paul Atterbury and Louise Irvine, *The Doulton Story* (Royal Doulton Tableware, Stoke on Trent, 1979). However, the listed building description for Harrods, written in 1969, suggests that the stoneware or faience of the 1929-30 Basil Street facade was by Hathernware.

2. Williamson Art Gallery and Museum, *Della Robbia Pottery, Birkenhead, 1894-1906: An interim report* (Metropolitan Borough of Wirral, Department of Leisure Services, Birkenhead, 1980).
3. *Tactile*, Newsletter of the Tiles and Architectural Ceramics Society, June 2001, no 55, p4.
4. With thanks to Anthony Ray for information on these tiles.
5. Graham Scott, 'The Dream of City Architecture Expressed in Colourful Ceramics - the theories and architecture of Halsey Ralph Ricardo', *TACS Journal*, 7 (1998), pp11-17.
6. Amy Clarke, 'George Jack (1855-1931): Arts and Crafts architect and designer-craftsman', paper given at House of Falkland Study Day, 23rd October 2004, Falkland, Fife. Jack's mosaic designs for Debenham House, dated 1913, are held by the William Morris Gallery.
7. Mark Hamilton, *Rare Spirit: A life of William De Morgan, 1839-1917* (Constable, London, 1997).
8. Michael Stratton, *The Terracotta Revival* (Victor Gollancz, London, 1993).
9. Personal communication, Tony Herbert, 24th July 1997.
10. Venetia Porter, 'William De Morgan and the Islamic Tiles of Leighton House', *Decorative Arts Society Journal*, 16 (1992), pp76-9.
11. Mark Girouard, 'Gilded preserves for the rich', *Country Life*, 150 (1971) 18th November, pp1360-4.
12. Tony Herbert and Kathryn Huggins, *The Decorative Tile in Architecture and Interiors* (Phaidon Press, London, 1995), pp143-6.
13. Alan Swale, *Architectural terracotta - a critical appraisal of its development and deployment*, 1998, MA dissertation, History of Ceramics, University of Staffordshire.
14. John Physick, *The Victoria and Albert Museum: The history of its building* (Phaidon - Christie's, Oxford, 1982).
15. Bridget Cherry and Nikolaus Pevsner, *London 3: North West*. Buildings of England (Penguin Books, London, 1991).
16. Swale, *Architectural Terracotta* (1998).
17. Colin Cunningham, *The Terracotta Designs of Alfred Waterhouse* (Wiley-Academy, Chichester, 2001).
18. Wendy Hitchmough, *The Michelin Building* (Conran Octopus, London, 1995).
19. Michael Kerney, 'All Saints', Margaret Street: A Glazing History', *Journal of Stained Glass*, 25 (2001), pp27-52. However, Laura Trelford, *A Discussion of the Figurative Tile Panels in the Nave of All Saints', Margaret Street, designed by William Butterfield, 1873-91* (2004, MA dissertation, Courtauld Institute of Art), pp18, 56-65, states (without offering supporting evidence) that all the St Augustine tile panels date from 1871-6, with Bell & Beckham being responsible for the execution of those in the north aisle and Minton's for the south aisle and west wall panels.
20. T. Francis Bumpus, *London Churches Ancient and Modern* (T. Werner Laurie, London, 1908).

KINGSTON UPON THAMES

Kingston upon Thames

High up in the lofty atrium of the **Bentall Centre**, a massive shopping centre which opened in 1992 on CLARENCE STREET, is the *Bentall's Clock*, signalling the location of the Food Court. The clock, which features ceramic number markers in the form of edible items like cakes and fruit, was designed by the ceramicist Kate Malone; the number markers were made under her direction by Jola Spytkowska. Just east along Clarence Street is **Pizza Hut** with its colourful, pizza-themed ceramic mural designed by Scurr & Partners using mostly Portuguese commercially-manufactured tiles supplied and hand-cut by Paul J. Marks, a mosaics firm. Similar tilework was installed in about sixty British Pizza Hut branches from 1998 onward, with the standard format being varied to suit site requirements. On the right at the end of Clarence Street is WHEATFIELD WAY, where there is a large, highly-textured external tile mural of local historic scenes, probably dating from the 1980s and made by the North Wales (now Shropshire) ceramicist and painter Maggie Humphry.

LAMBETH

Clapham

St Mary's R. C. Church, CLAPHAM PARK ROAD, built in 1849-51 to the design of Pugin's pupil, William Wardell, has extensive encaustic tiling, notably the Godwin pavement in the Lady Chapel (1883-6 by the architect J. F. Bentley, a parishioner) and tiles bearing the letters 'G' and 'M' in the St Gerard Majella Chapel (1910 by Bentley's son, Osmund Bentley).

Kennington

On the west side of **Kennington Park**, KENNINGTON PARK ROAD, is a buff Doulton terracotta column, the remains of a fountain made for an exhibition held in Kensington in 1869 and donated to the park in the same year by Sir Henry Doulton. It was designed by John Sparkes, head of the Lambeth School of Art, and the central shaft includes an early sculpture by George Tinworth, the *Pilgrimage of Life*.[1] The column was originally topped by a family group in medieval costume, also by Tinworth.

Lambeth

The expanding firm of Doulton & Watts moved its pottery works from Vauxhall to

Lambeth High Street during 1826-8 and continued to grow, building two kilns in 1829-30 and larger kilns three years later. Properties were bought up around the factory to create room for growth and the end result, when Doulton's production was at its height towards the end of the nineteenth century, was a Doulton estate extending over a quarter mile south from near the present Lambeth Bridge.[2] Increased demand for Doultonware and architectural terracotta and faience led to the construction of three ornate buildings, along with a 233' tall Italianate chimney stack, in 1876-9. The two most striking structures (A and B blocks), completed by 1879 and designed by Doulton's regular architects Waring & Nicholson in a rather Frenchified Gothic style, faced the Albert Embankment and included a large showroom and production facilities for sanitaryware and faience. Naturally they were showpieces for quantities of terracotta detailing designed by Wilkinson & Tarring, some of which had already been used on the firm's profusely decorated Doultonware studios and showroom, a slightly smaller building (later known as Southbank House or **Doulton House**) put up in 1876-8 on the corner of BLACK PRINCE ROAD and Lambeth High Street.[3] It appears that Doulton's used Waring & Nicholson for the more mundane factory structures while Robert Stark Wilkinson (1844-1936) and Frederick William Tarring (1847-1925) were responsible for the appearance of the showier buildings. The firm's growth continued: five kilns jammed into a 35 metre square area operated, with shared chimneys, during 1890-1923, and a radically modern headquarters went up on the Embankment in 1939.[4] However, A and B blocks were demolished in 1952, along with the great stack, and the Lambeth Pottery closed in 1956; the headquarters building survived until 1978. Now, the last lonely remnant of Doulton's presence in Lambeth is Doulton House (currently vacant), its decoration an excellent and early example of the use of Doultonware in an architectural context (Fig 171). Although it has lost its original balustraded parapet, it has retained the high-relief terracotta tympanum by George Tinworth over the canted corner entrance, which shows Henry Doulton and several of his artists including Hannah Barlow (and her cat Tommy) and Tinworth himself.

Near Doulton House at 39 Black Prince Road is the former **Beaufoy Institute** (1907, F. A. Powell), whose trustees included members of the Beaufoy and Doulton families. Its interior has much plain tilework and an unusual ceramic stair in rich brown glazed bricks, with an elegant curved handrail formed from specials; Doulton's would seem the most likely manufacturer. It is possible the firm were experimenting with glazed bricks in an attempt to replicate the faience interiors produced by Burmantofts, although by 1907 demand for these was in decline.

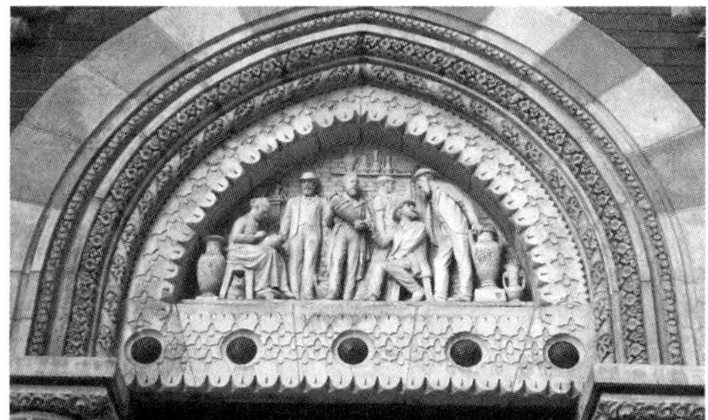

Fig 171.

Another Tinworth relief, a *Crucifixion* of 1888-9, can be seen inside St Mary's Church (now the **Museum of Garden History**), LAMBETH PALACE ROAD, just to the north of Doulton House. The buff terracotta panel, on the north aisle wall, is the remaining central part from a war-damaged three-section reredos designed by J. O. Scott and erected by Sir Henry Doulton in memory of his wife Sarah (d1888). Two smaller Tinworth reliefs are in the south aisle: *Christ among the Doctors* and *Christ Blessing the Little Children*. In front of the church is the Coade stone tomb of the Sealy family from 1800, including Coade's partner John Sealy, while in the main churchyard is the Coade sarcophagus of William Bligh (1754-1817).

The chapel of **Lambeth Palace**, immediately north of the Museum of Garden History on Lambeth Palace Road, was built around 1214-25 and has one of only two major *in situ* medieval tile pavements in London (the other is at Westminster Abbey); it includes twenty different 'Westminster' floor tile designs, and the main part of the layout has a chevron pattern of alternating plain and decorated tiles.[5] Part of the pavement, which probably dates from the 1270s or 1280s, is visible beneath the restored stalls and screen.[6]

Further north along Lambeth Palace Road is **St Thomas's Hospital** (1868-71, architect Henry Currey), which originally comprised seven brick pavilions on the riverside, although only the three southernmost and the Chapel remain. In the first floor Chapel is a large, three-panel figurative terracotta reredos modelled by George Tinworth and presented to the chapel in 1899 in memory of Sir Henry Doulton, who was a governor of the hospital; there is also a salmon-pink Doulton terracotta panel of *Spring* in the north aisle. Following war damage, the north end of the hospital was rebuilt from 1962, the second stage of the work being designed by architects Yorke, Rosenberg & Mardall and completed in 1969-76; their large ward block was clad in the practice's trademark Shaws Twintiles. Around thirty early 1900s Doulton tile panels, designed by William Rowe and depicting nursery rhymes, originally formed part of the decoration of two of the old children's wards. After their closure for rebuilding, most of the panels were eventually resited in the new hospital, along with a few panels of similar date from the Royal Waterloo Hospital for Children and Women; three may be found in the café by the main riverside entrance, and another two are mounted in the Central Hall, beneath the Chapel.

The former Royal Waterloo Hospital for Children and Women (1903-5, Waring & Nicholson) stands on WATERLOO ROAD at the south end of Waterloo Bridge; the building now houses **Schiller International University** and is known as Royal Waterloo House (Fig 172). Its green Doultonware porch was donated by Henry Lewis Doulton, who had followed his father Henry Doulton as head of the firm, and the facade has much elaborate Doultonware ornament including lettering.

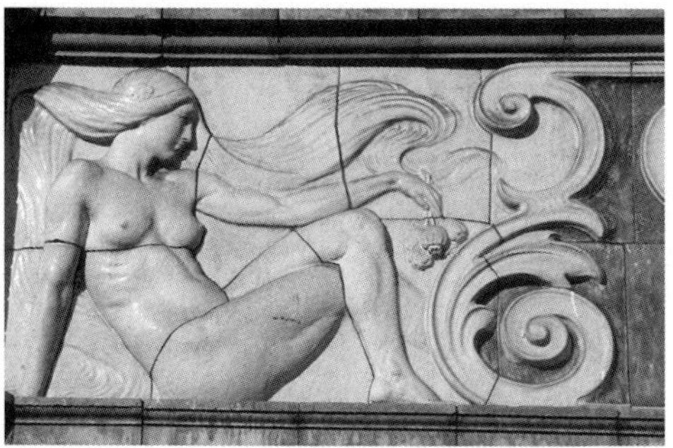

Fig 172.

The massive Coade stone **South Bank Lion** at the east end of WESTMINSTER BRIDGE originally stood on the riverside parapet of Goding's Lion Brewery (1836-7), demolished in 1949 during site clearance for the Festival of Britain. The lion, modelled in 1837 by the sculptor William Woodington (1806-93), was one of the last products of the Coade factory, which stood a little way to the north of the bridge; the Coade exhibition gallery opened at the east end of the bridge in 1799. The lion was initially relocated near Waterloo Station before being moved to Westminster Bridge in 1966.

Streatham

Streatham Hill Theatre (1928-9, W. G. R. Sprague & W. H. Barton, now used for bingo), 110 STREATHAM HILL, was the last theatre designed by Sprague and has a fine neoclassical Doulton Carraraware facade.

West Norwood

A chancel was added to **St Luke's Church** (1822), NORWOOD HIGH STREET (at the junction with Knights Hill), in 1872-3 by G. E. Street, and the blind windows above its altar were filled in 1885 with four large memorial panels in Doulton's new Vitreous Fresco ware painted by John McLennan to the designs of the architect J. F. Bentley and the artist William Christian Symons. This technique involved painting terracotta slabs in a wide range of colours which fired to a matt surface resembling fresco, and was intended for large figurative compositions in public buildings, especially churches.[7] The St Luke's panels measure about 10′ high by 2′ 6″ wide and show Christ and St George, both with an angel; above each pair is a small semicircular panel. The church has been subdivided and the memorial panels can now (improbably) be seen in an upper floor community room.

Close by the church is **West Norwood Cemetery**, off NORWOOD ROAD. On the far side of the cemetery, at the top of the hill and just beyond the crematorium, is the Tate family mausoleum, built around 1883 and designed by the architects George & Peto using bright orange-red Doulton terracotta blocks. The interior includes decorative terracotta blockwork, a frieze of red and white glass tiles, and an opus sectile figure of Christ. Just south of the Tate mausoleum, on the Doulton path, is the Doulton family mausoleum built in 1899 by George & Peto, who also designed Doulton's country house at Ewhurst (see Surrey). This had just been completed when Sarah Doulton died in October 1888; Doulton then asked the architects to design a mausoleum for him on a similar scale to their earlier Tate mausoleum. The Doulton mausoleum is built from salmon-pink terracotta blocks and miniature bricks; the external low relief panels and other ornament were by the Doulton artist Mark Marshall (Fig 173). Other ceramic memorials in the cemetery include (on the east side) the Ibbotson tomb, a blue and buff Doultonware cross and slab dating from around 1904, and an ornate terracotta memorial of 1885 to James Baldwin Brown, minister of Brixton Independent Church; this is down the slope just north of the Tate mausoleum. North-west of the crematorium, downhill and off the path, is the monumental tomb of London draper Alexander Berens (d1858), designed by E. M. Barry with a double frieze of Minton tiles, one of them carrying the letter 'B' and a bear (the Berens rebus), the other an inscription (Fig 174).[8]

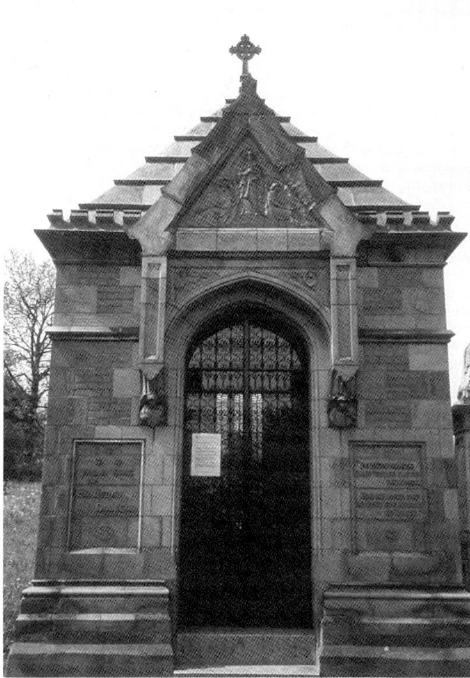

Fig 173.

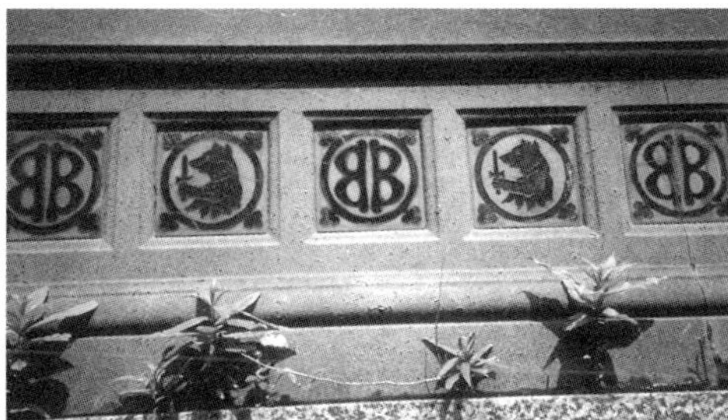

Fig 174.

References

1. Miranda F. Goodby, 'George Tinworth: an Artist in Terracotta', *Journal of the Tiles and Architectural Ceramics Society*, 3 (1990), pp15-21.
2. Desmond Eyles and Louise Irvine, *The Doulton Lambeth Wares* (Richard Dennis, Shepton Beauchamp, 2002).
3. *The Builder*, vol 34, 9th December 1876, pp1192, 1195; *The Builder*, vol 37, 2nd August 1879, pp856, 859.
4. Kieron Tyler, 'Doulton in Lambeth', *Archaeology Matters*, 18th July 2002.
5. Susan Degnan and Derek Seeley, 'Medieval and later floor tiles in Lambeth Palace Chapel', *London Archaeologist*, 6 (1988) Winter, pp11-18.
6. Ian M. Betts, *Medieval 'Westminster' floor tiles (MoLAS Monograph 11)* (Museum of London, London, 2002), p24.
7. Paul Atterbury and Louise Irvine, *The Doulton Story* (Royal Doulton Tableware, Stoke on Trent, 1979).
8. *The Builder*, vol 16, 20th November 1858, pp778-9.

LEWISHAM

Brockley

The interior of **Talents Music**, a former fish and game shop at 9 BROCKLEY RISE, is completely tiled and dates from the early part of the twentieth century. There are two pictorial panels, one showing a fisherman, the other a delicately painted portrayal of game birds which occupies a semicircular recess.

The oldest of the three buildings making up the **Lewisham College** campus on LEWISHAM WAY is a plain brick structure put up in 1927-30 by London County Council. Its facade is enlivened by a series of heraldic plaques in Doulton's polychrome stoneware designed by Gilbert Bayes and the sculptor Stanley Nicholson Babb.[1]

Lee

In the entrance of the **Old Tiger's Head** (1896), 351 LEE HIGH ROAD (at its east end, on the corner with Lee Road), is a large hand-painted Craven Dunnill tile panel showing a tiger's head. Opposite, at 159 LEE ROAD, is the **New Tiger's Head**, with an elaborate facade including a terracotta tiger's head at parapet level.

References

1. Louise Irvine and Paul Atterbury, *Gilbert Bayes, Sculptor, 1872-1953* (Richard Dennis, Shepton Beauchamp, 1998).

MERTON

Merton

The **Nelson Arms**, on the south side of MERTON HIGH STREET, has excellent exterior tilework including ceramic lettering on its brown-tiled ground floor facade and three pictorial panels signed by Carter's of Poole; these date from 1910. There are two small panels of the *Victory* and Nelson on the main frontage, with a large panel of the *Victory* on the Abbey Road elevation. The pub's site marks the entrance to Merton Place, where Nelson lived during 1801-5.

Wimbledon

The Jacobean mansion **Eagle House** (1613), HIGH STREET, was restored by its current owners, the Yamani Cultural and Charitable Foundation, in 1989. In Pitt's Room (first floor) is a fire surround with London-made delftware figurative landscape tiles dating from 1740-60.[1] There is also a fire surround with De Morgan tiles and another with 10″ by 14″ Chinese-style tiles, which probably date from the late nineteenth century or after.

References

1. Personal communication, Ian Betts, Museum of London Specialist Services, 12th August 2004.

NEWHAM

East Ham

In 1898 East Ham Urban District Council decided to collect all its civic buildings together on one site, the result being the four grand structures, each with a terrific display of external terracotta, standing at the junction of Barking Road and HIGH STREET SOUTH. The first to be put up was **East Ham Town Hall** (1901-3), designed by Henry Cheers, who specialised in municipal buildings, and Joseph Smith. Its dominant feature is an elaborate clock tower around 150′ in height, and the pale red terracotta was supplied by Doulton's. Next to be built was the **Technical College** (1903-4, Cheers & Smith), which also used Doulton's terracotta; Maw's provided some internal faience decoration designed by John Windsor Bradburn, then the head of the firm's faience department.[1] The **Library**, an extension of the Town Hall which opened in 1908, was designed by A. H. Campbell, the borough engineer. Here, and in the **Fire Station** (1913, now offices), by the borough surveyor J. E. W. Birch, the buff terracotta came from Gibbs & Canning.

Silvertown

The former **St Mark's Church** (1860-2, S. S. Teulon), CONNAUGHT ROAD, was one of a series of 1860s churches in which architects experimented with the use of terracotta in the context of the gothic revival. Its interior is lined with hollow, interlocking blocks of pale buff terracotta which also feature on the polychromatic exterior. The church was gutted by fire in 1984; its restoration was completed in 1989 using terracotta blocks from Shaws of Darwen. The church is now a theatre and is home to Brick Lane Music Hall.

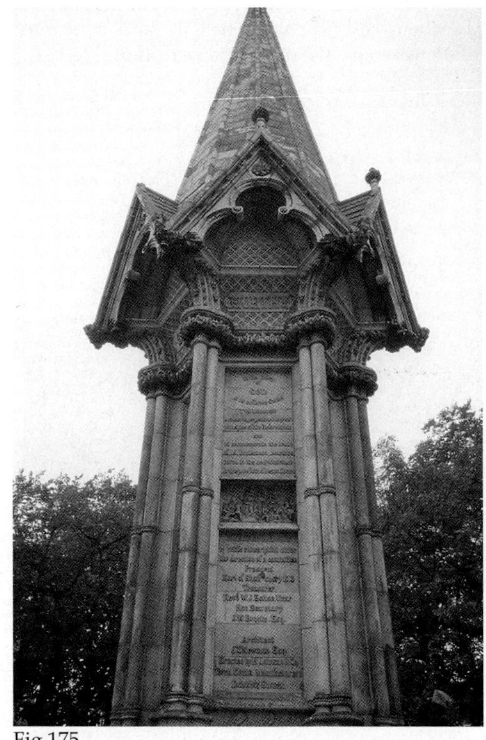

Fig 175.

Stratford

Mary I (1516-58), a catholic, was Queen of England during 1553-8. She attempted to return the country to catholicism and was committed to burning protestants for heresy; on her orders, eleven men and two women were burnt to death at a single stake in Stratford on the 27th June 1556 for their protestant beliefs. This event was commemorated in 1878-9 by the erection of the **Martyrs' Memorial**, which stands towards the south end of St John's churchyard on the BROADWAY. The 65′ high hexagonal terracotta column is in gothic style and was designed by the London architect John T. Newman (Fig 175). It was built by H. Johnson & Co of Ditchling, East Sussex, who also manufactured the fine buff terracotta, which has hardly weathered and carries impressively crisp lettering; every full stop is a miniature cylinder of terracotta. Johnson's, who were active from the 1870s, made terracotta, bricks, tiles and pottery, and also had a works a mile west of Ditchling at the brickmaking centre of Keymer (West Sussex). The firm was present at the Philadelphia Centennial Exhibition of 1876.

Stratford's HIGH STREET runs south-west of the Broadway. **Essex House**, at 375-7 High Street, has good late Victorian terracotta including two large salmon-pink figurative panels and three griffins on its parapet. Much further south, at 137 High Street (near the junction with HUNTS LANE), is a late 1960s **factory** designed by the architect Desmond C. Skells; on its facade is a Carter's tile panel measuring about 8′ long by 4′ high which shows a cheerful Dalmatian dog.

References

1. Lezli Richer, 'Training for Industrial Design and the Decline of Maw & Co', *Glazed Expressions*, (1996) 33, pp3-5.

REDBRIDGE

Woodford

In the churchyard of **St Mary's Church**, HIGH ROAD, Woodford, is an excellent collection of monuments including several Coade stone table tombs; a Coade & Sealy sarcophagus of 1812 with lion's paw feet stands opposite the south porch. The ornate Coade tombchest of Edward Keepe (d1782) was designed in 1784 by the architect Samuel Robinson (1752-1833), who is better known for his warehouse designs.

RICHMOND UPON THAMES

East Sheen

Inside **R. Chubb & Son**, a butcher's shop at 350 UPPER RICHMOND ROAD WEST (a little east of Clifford Avenue) are five pictorial tile panels showing varieties of fowls.

Ham

Ham House (NT), HAM STREET, was built in 1610, altered internally in 1637-8 then enlarged during 1672-4. A hefty Coade stone *River God* by John Bacon stands in the forecourt to the north of the house, and twelve Coade pineapples (a symbol of hospitality) of 1799-1801 decorate the forecourt railings (Fig 176). Inside the house are several plain-tiled fire surrounds dating from the 1670s, and two fire surrounds with Dutch blue and white landscape and figurative tiles of around the same date or slightly earlier. The dairy, refurbished in the early nineteenth century, is lined with plain and ivy-leaf patterned Wedgwood creamware tiles; the marble worktops are supported by cast iron cow legs.

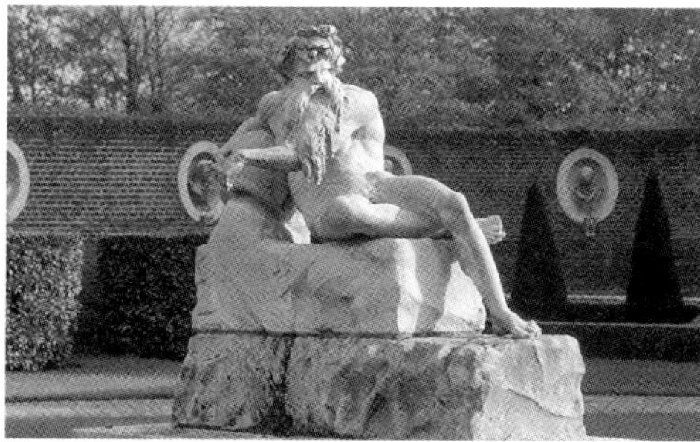

Fig 176.

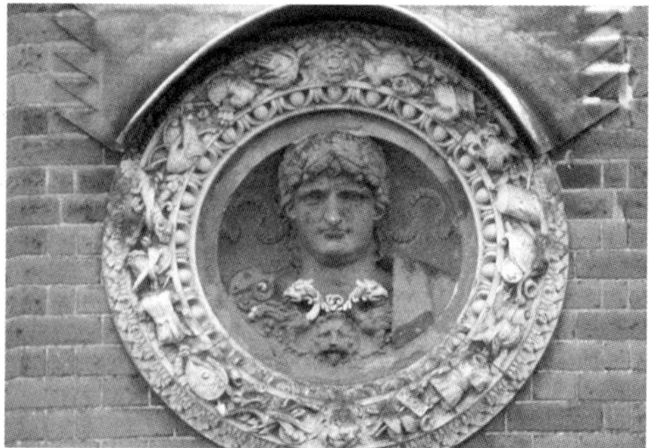

Fig 177.

Hampton Court

Thomas Wolsey was appointed Archbishop of York in 1514 and shortly afterwards signed a ninety-nine year lease on **Hampton Court** (now entered from HAMPTON COURT WAY), intending to turn it into a country seat fit for entertaining royalty; building work began almost immediately. Wolsey's Long Gallery, built around 1515-16 and demolished in 1689, was one of the first buildings in England, possibly the very first, to have classical pilasters on its exterior. These newly fashionable decorative elements were made from terracotta, and may have been produced locally. The ten ornate terracotta roundels of 1520-1, each displaying the head of a Roman emperor, which remain at the Palace today were imported from Italy and made by the sculptor Giovanni da Maiano (Fig 177). Items of high fashion at the time, they can be seen on the walls of the Great Gatehouse, the inner gate and George II's Gate, although they may not all be in their original positions. A terracotta plaque of Wolsey's arms also survives on the east side of the inner gate.[1]

Hampton Hill

There is a fine display of tiled flooring in **St James's Church**, ST JAMES'S ROAD (at the junction with Park Road), which was begun in 1864, enlarged during the 1870s and completed in 1888 with the erection of its tower. A geometric pavement in the choir leads on to more decorative paving in the sanctuary, and there are mostly geometric tile panels on the east wall to either side of the altar, as well as a tiled niche. Nothing unduly decorative but a good example of a complete scheme, with all the tiling still visible.

Hampton Wick

At the junction of Park Road and SANDY LANE (opposite Vicarage Road, which leads to Hampton Wick station) is the colourful Doultonware **monument** (1900) to the shoemaker Timothy Bennet (1676-1756), who undertook a lengthy campaign to open the adjoining footpath, Cobbler's Walk, for public use; the slab shows a relief of a shoemaker at work.

Richmond

Overlooking THE GREEN is **Richmond Theatre** (1899, Frank Matcham), an elaborate twin-towered red brick and buff terracotta pile. Most of its terracotta was made by the Hathern Station Brick and Terra Cotta Company, but the figure of *Euterpe*, the muse of music, is in material of a slightly different hue and probably came from Doulton's.[2] The same combination of firms supplied the terracotta for Matcham's 1901 Hackney Empire, which has an identical *Euterpe* on its facade; the figure was probably modelled by John Broad, who executed a similar statue for the Apollo and the Muses PH on Tottenham Court Road (1898). This latter *Euterpe* now stands in St George's Gardens (see Camden).

The former dairy of **J. Clarke & Sons** (now a hairdresser's) on HILL RISE, south of the centre, retains its complete early twentieth century tiled interior including half a dozen excellent but unsigned pictorial panels of pastoral scenes.

Strawberry Hill

During 1749-66 Horace Walpole transformed Strawberry Hill (now **St Mary's College**, part of the University of Surrey), WALDEGRAVE ROAD, turning it from a cottage into a little castle in true Gothic (or Gothick) taste. There were extensions in 1790 but the house eventually became derelict before being inherited by Lady Frances Waldegrave, who restored it in 1855-6 and added a new wing in 1860-2. She enlarged the entrance hall, replacing its hexagonal stone tiles with a five-colour carpet-pattern Minton encaustic tile pavement, and installed tiled fire surrounds throughout the house, mostly with 8″ printed tiles; particularly notable are those in the Smoking Room, which are partly gilded. Strawberry Hill is currently on English Heritage's Buildings at Risk Register.

Twickenham

Above the Rowland Hill Memorial Gate at the entrance to the Twickenham headquarters of the **Rugby Football Union**, WHITTON ROAD, is a gilded Coade stone lion, which like its counterpart the South Bank Lion (see Lambeth) came from Goding's Lion Brewery (demolished 1949); it was given to the RFU by the chairman of the Greater London Council and installed at Twickenham in 1972.

References

1. Simon Thurley, *Hampton Court: A Social and Architectural History* (Yale University Press, New Haven and London, 2003), pp22-5.
2. John Earl, *The London Theatres*, in *Frank Matcham: Theatre Architect*, ed Brian Walker (Blackstaff Press, Belfast, 1980), pp36-61.

SOUTHWARK

Camberwell

Mounted on the south gable end of the former **Public Library**, WELLS WAY, is a 20′ by 14′ Doulton tile mural of a Camberwell Beauty butterfly, which originally decorated the nearby 1920s factory of the stationers Samuel Jones & Co, once known for their Butterfly Brand goods. The panel was rescued in 1980, just before the Jones's building was demolished, and resited on the library in 1983.

Dulwich

Charles Barry (1823-1900), son of the architect Sir Charles Barry (1795-1860), was appointed as Architect and Surveyor to the Dulwich College Estate in 1858, in succession to his father. Sir Charles Barry had been involved with J. M. Blashfield in the experimental manufacture of terracotta at Canford in Dorset in 1839, and the young Barry, who entered his father's office in 1840 at the age of seventeen, had worked up the detail of his father's designs for Blashfield's terracotta ornaments.[1] The New Buildings of **Dulwich College** (1866-70), COLLEGE ROAD, West

Dulwich, were designed by Barry junior in a hybrid Italianate style with lavish external terracotta decoration, mostly in buff but with contrasting areas of blue-grey and red, all supplied by Blashfield from his Stamford works. Barry himself assisted with the modelling of much of the terracotta.[2] The result was a triumph for the architect and for Blashfield, who proved himself to be an efficient large-scale manufacturer.

Nunhead

The Stearns mausoleum, a little romanesque shed of Doulton's salmon-coloured terracotta, stands beside the path running up the hill on the west side of **Nunhead Cemetery**, LINDEN GROVE. The mausoleum, which is lined with brown and yellow glazed brick and ornamented with Celtic motifs, was put up for Laura Stearns (d1900) of Twickenham, although her remains are now buried elsewhere in the cemetery (Fig 178).

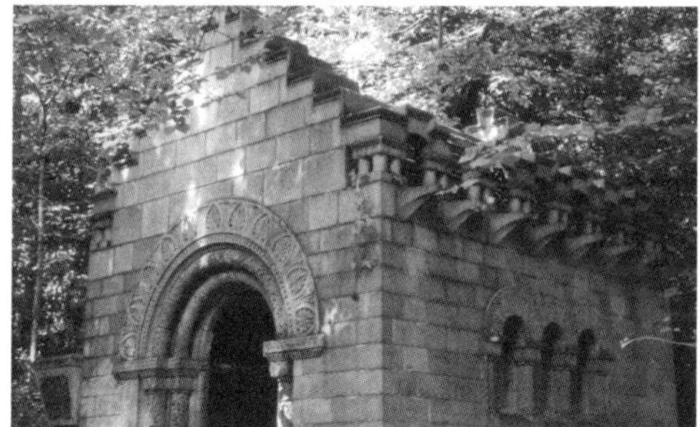

Fig 178.

Peckham

On the exterior of the former North Peckham Civic Centre (1962-7, Southwark Borough Architect's Department, now known as the Civic and home to the pentecostal church **Everlasting Arms Ministries**), OLD KENT ROAD on the corner with Peckham Park Road, is the largest secular work of the sculptor Adam Kossowski (1905-86). Indeed, at 1,000 square feet, it is probably the largest of any of his works (Fig 179). The polychrome ceramic frieze, which depicts local historic scenes in high relief, was designed in 1964 and completed in 1965; the traditional Cockney figures of the Pearly King and Queen are especially striking. The art historian Benedict Read suggests that it was the only point of Kossowski's career in which he approached the idealistic nationalist spirit of the secular works carried out in his native Poland before coming to Britain in 1942.[3]

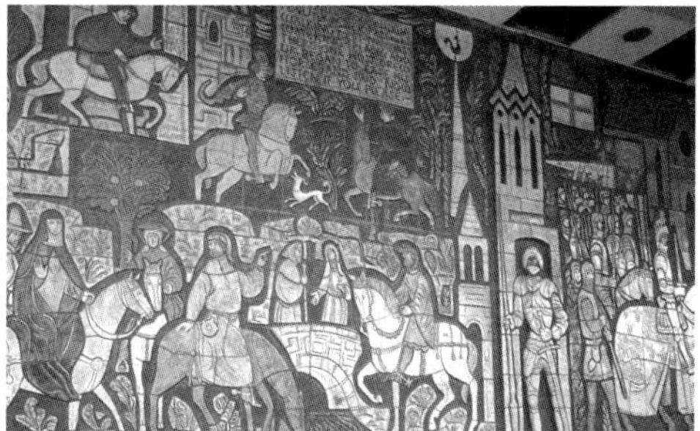

Fig 179.

Rotherhithe

The modern tube-lined tile Stations of the Cross at the parish church of **St Mary Rotherhithe**, ST MARYCHURCH STREET, came from the Bruges-based Kunstateliers Slabbinck, an art studio and clerical suppliers founded by Hendrik Slabbinck in 1903.

Southwark

Inside the **Paper Moon PH**, 24 BLACKFRIARS ROAD, is a turn-of-the-century pictorial tile panel by Carter's of Poole depicting Shakespeare enjoying the hospitality of an inn.

On QUEEN ELIZABETH STREET, at the south end of Tower Bridge, is **The Circle** (1989, architects CZWG), an apartment block notable for its curving elevation of royal blue glazed brick by Shaws of Darwen.

Just west at 88 TOOLEY STREET, before London Bridge Station, is the **Shipwrights Arms**; inside, in what was originally the pub's entrance lobby, is a large, square tile panel dating from around 1900 and showing shipwrights working in the Pool of London. It is signed Charles Evans & Co, a west London concern which produced tiles, mosaic and stained glass; Charles Evans (1828-64), the son of noted Shrewsbury stained glass painter David Evans, assisted his father before moving to London to set up on his own account, probably during the 1850s, and the firm continued until at least the end of the nineteenth century.[4] An earlier Charles Evans & Co panel can be seen at Whitechapel Library (Tower Hamlets). Further west on Tooley Street, almost at London Bridge itself, is the art deco classic **St Olave's House** (1931-2, architect H. S. Goodhart-Rendel), converted from a warehouse to be the stylish offices of the Hay's Wharf Company. On its river frontage, delineating the tall windows of the main rooms, is a unique large-scale modernist relief in gilded Doulton stoneware set into black granite. It was designed and modelled by the sculptor Frank Dobson (1886-1963), and symbolises the activities of the riverside.

References

1. Alan Swale, *Architectural terracotta - a critical appraisal of its development and deployment*, 1998, MA dissertation, History of Ceramics, University of Staffordshire.
2. Jan Piggott, *Charles Barry, Junior and the Dulwich College Estate* (Dulwich Picture Gallery, London, 1986).
3. *Adam Kossowski: Murals and Paintings*, (Armelle Press, London, 1990), p17.
4. Joyce Little, Angela Goedicke and Margaret Washbourn, eds., *Stained Glass Marks & Monograms* (NADFAS, London, 2002).

SUTTON

Carshalton

Little Holland House, 40 BEECHES AVENUE, was designed, built and furnished by the artist and craftsman Frank Reginald Dickinson (1874-1961) in 1902-4. Unable to afford the arts and crafts style home of his dreams, Dickinson - who was employed by Doulton's at their Lambeth works - determined to build his own house. He was assisted by two of his brothers, a labourer, and his fiancée; the couple moved in on their wedding day and spent their honeymoon completing their ideal home. The furnishings include arts and crafts tiles in several fireplaces, most probably designed by Dickinson and perhaps made by Doulton. Little Holland House was bought by the Borough of Sutton in 1972.

The **Water Tower**, WEST STREET, is a brick-built entertainment building put up in the pleasure garden of Sir John Fellowes's Carshalton House around 1716-21; Fellowes was Sub-Governor of the South Sea Company. Inside the Tower is a suite of rooms including a pump room, saloon and orangery. The bathroom, with its huge and probably cold water bath, is lined with blue, manganese and white tin-glazed tiles; all the decorated tiles show flowers in vases (Fig 180). It is unclear whether the tiles were Dutch-made or imported (Skelton refers to them as Anglo-Dutch), and their date is uncertain, as the first reference to the tiled bath is in 1839.[1] However, it is possible that they were installed when the Water Tower or Water House was built, and in any case they constitute an unusual *in situ* survival of early tin-glazed tiles. The building is now administered by the Water Tower Trust and the Friends of Carshalton Water Tower.

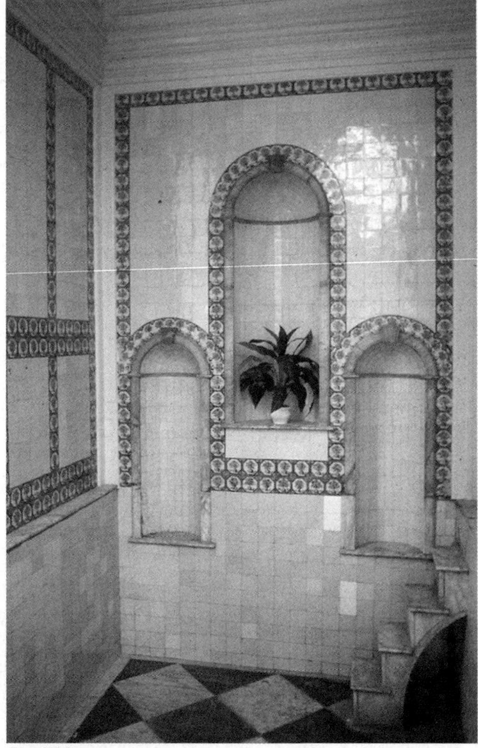

Fig 180.

References

1. Andrew Skelton, 'The Carshalton Water Tower Tiled Bath - a study in Anglo-Dutch tiles', *TACS Journal*, 7 (1998), pp31-4.

TOWER HAMLETS

Bethnal Green

Inside the former **Unitarian Church** (1871, now Chalice Foundation), at the south end of MANSFORD STREET, is a 1903 opus sectile panel symbolising charity. It was designed by Henry Holiday (1839-1927) and made in his own workshop, which he set up in 1891 soon after leaving Powell's of Whitefriars, where he had been the principal designer. Just across Mansford Street from the church, on the outer wall of **Lawdale Junior School**, is a jolly Millennium tile panel (2000) with a lively depiction of the Dome (Fig 181).

On the outside of the little chapel (1904) attached to **St Margaret's House** (originally a women's settlement), OLD FORD ROAD, is a colourful semicircular majolica relief of the

Annunciation, a memorial to P. R. Buchanan; it was probably imported from one of the Italian factories which made copies of della Robbia ware.

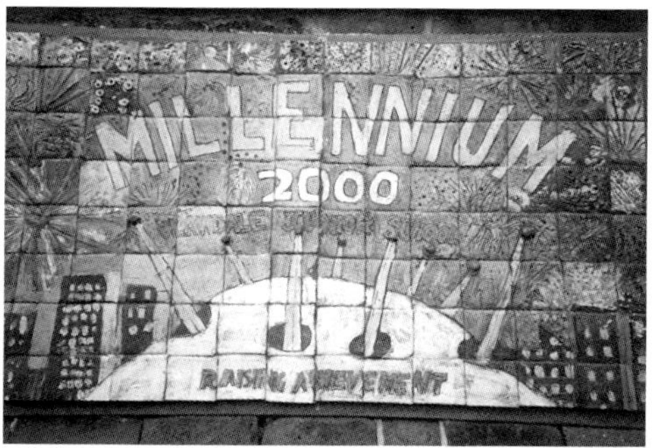

Fig 181.

St Matthew's Church, St Matthew's Row, was built in 1743-6 but its interior was destroyed by fire in 1859; although reopened in 1861, bombing during 1940 left the church as a roofless shell. The present church was rebuilt in 1958-61 by architect Antony Lewis, who commissioned several young artists to produce work for its interior. The ash-glazed stoneware Stations of the Cross were made by the sculptor Donald Potter (1902-2004) using a wood-burning kiln he built at Bryanston School, Blandford, Dorset, where he taught art during 1940-84 while continuing with his own commissions.[1]

Limehouse

Behind the bar of the **George Tavern**, 373 Commercial Road, is a complete tiled wall including three pictorial panels painted by W. B. Simpson & Sons, the largest of which shows the tavern in 1654

Mile End

Carter's of Poole produced the interior tilework for the foyer of the new Engineering Building at **Queen Mary College** (part of the University of London), Mile End Road, in 1958 (Fig 182). Although some of the stairwell tiling has disappeared, two tube-lined murals remain beside a lecture theatre entrance: a coat of arms and *Forces of Nature*, an engineering-inspired design by A. B. Read which incorporates letters from the Greek alphabet.[2] In 1960-1 Carter's made six large pictorial panels on highly technical themes for the exterior of the Physics Building, just east of Engineering; the firm described these attractive and still-extant works as part of 'a particularly interesting contract for us' (Fig 183).[3]

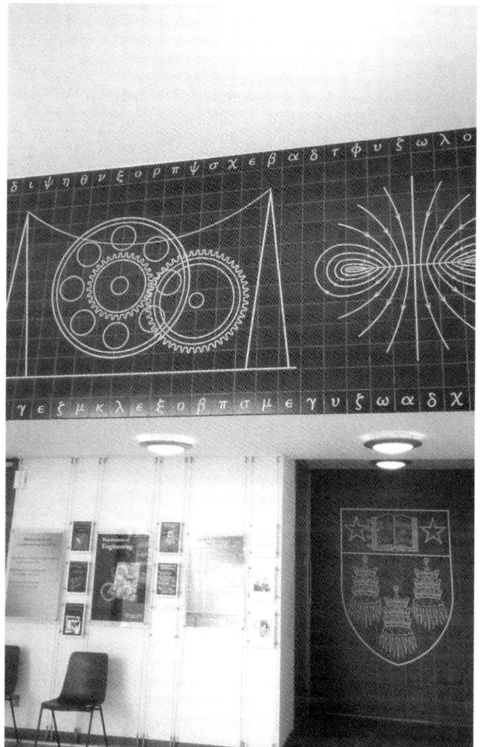
Fig 182.

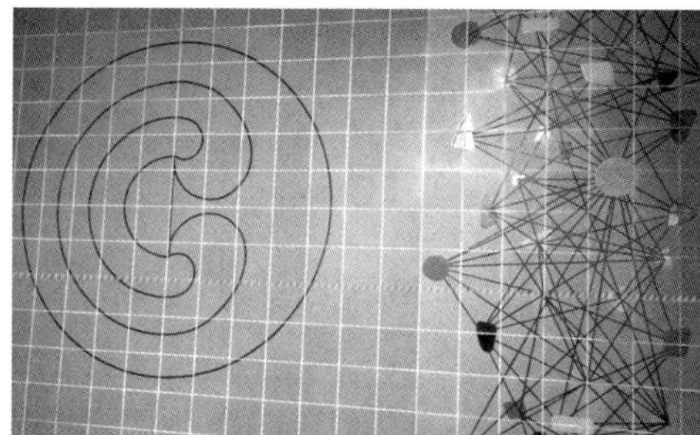
Fig 183.

Not far from the College is the Three Crowns (now **L'Oasis**), 237 Mile End Road, with good interior tiling by W. B. Simpson & Sons including a panel of the *Field of the Cloth of Gold* just inside the front door.

Poplar

Screen-printed tiles designed by Peggy Angus and made by Carter's of Poole were used as mural decoration inside the **Susan Lawrence**

School (1951), Cordelia Street, and the adjoining Elizabeth Lansbury Nursery School (1952). The schools (no public access), now merged, were designed by architects YRM, the earlier building being part of the Festival of Britain 'Live Architecture Exhibition' in Poplar's Lansbury Neighbourhood. Specially-commissioned pattern-making tiles line the rear wall of the double-height hall at the Susan Lawrence School, where only three different tiles, including the well-known *Wave* and *Circle* motifs, appear in repeats of eighteen; other Angus tiles were used in the school's dining hall. Critics approved of the school and it was published widely, and influentially, in the architectural press; the tiles were considered to combine practicality with a craft-based appearance which added texture to the relatively severe lines of the modern buildings.[4]

Shadwell

Between the Thames and THE HIGHWAY is the **King Edward VII Memorial Park**; towards its south-west corner is the Navigators' Memorial (1922), a tablet and three-tiled Carter's semicircular polychrome plaque showing galleons in full sail. It was erected by London County Council to commemorate a group of merchant adventurers who set sail from Shadwell in 1553.

Spitalfields

The facade of the former **Jewish Soup Kitchen** (1902, architect Lewis Solomon, now apartments), BRUNE STREET, is largely of buff terracotta by Edwards of Ruabon; lettering in curling script includes English and Hebrew dates, and a relief of a soup tureen hovers above the entrance.

Inside the **Ten Bells**, 84 COMMERCIAL STREET, is lavish late Victorian tiling by W. B. Simpson & Sons including a large pictorial panel entitled 'Spitalfields in ye Olden Time - Visiting a Weaver's shop'. The pub, which stands near Christ Church Spitalfields, is famed for its connections with Jack the Ripper.

On the chancel beam inside **Christ Church Spitalfields**, FOURNIER STREET, is an unusually highly detailed Coade stone representation of the royal arms as it appeared during 1816-37. It is dated 1822 and signed by William Croggon, who bought the business after Mrs Coade's death in 1821.[5]

Stepney

Stretching along the front wall of **Stepney Green School**, BEN JONSON ROAD, is a fabulous tile mural designed by Jean Powell with the school's pupils and made around 2002 by Powell's firm, Craig Bragdy Design (Fig 184). Individual tiles by the schoolchildren form the central section but above and below are the brilliant swirls of colour so characteristic of Powell's own work, which is rarely seen on this scale in Britain as most of Craig Bragdy's murals are now commissioned by foreign clients.

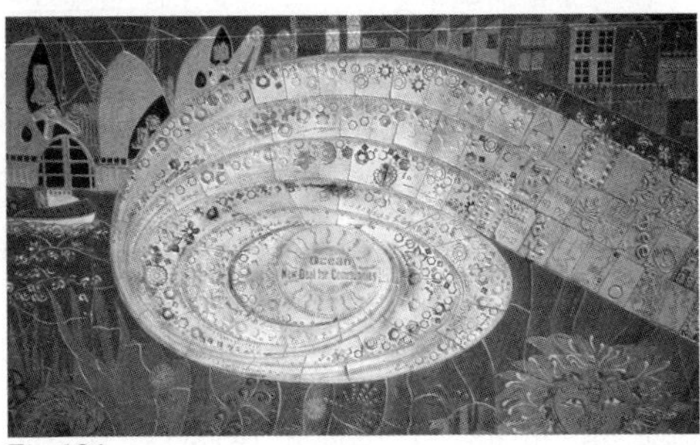

Fig 184.

Faience for the massive, faintly art deco cream facade of the former Troxy Cinema (1931-3, architect George Coles, now **Mecca Bingo**), COMMERCIAL ROAD, was supplied by the Hathern Station Brick and Terra Cotta Company.

Whitechapel

Whitechapel Library (1891-2, architects Potts, Son & Hennings), 77 WHITECHAPEL HIGH STREET, has dressings of buff Burmantofts terracotta; inside the lobby is a pictorial tile panel of 'Whitechapel Hay Market 1788' which was originally at the Horns, a nearby pub demolished in 1963. The panel dates from 1889 and was painted by Charles Evans & Co, the west London firm of art tile and glass designers. The Library was funded by the newspaper editor and philanthropist John Passmore Edwards (1823-1911), who was also responsible for its close neighbour the **Whitechapel Art Gallery** (1898-1901, architect Charles Harrison Townsend); the upper part of its unusual art nouveau facade is clad in buff terracotta by Gibbs & Canning of Tamworth.[6] The Gallery is undergoing redevelopment work which should be completed in 2007.

References

1. Vivienne Light, 'An Inspiring Century', *Ceramic Review*, (2003) 199, pp22-3.
2. Carter Archive, Poole Museum Service, CP720.

3. Lynn Pearson, 'To Brighten the Environment: Ceramic Tile Murals in Britain, 1950-70', *TACS Journal*, 10 (2004), pp12-17.
4. Katie Arber, 'Peggy Angus, designer of modern tiles for a modern Britain', *Decorative Arts Society Journal*, 26 (2002), pp120-134.
5. *Columns*, Newsletter of the Friends of Christ Church Spitalfields, 21, Autumn 2003, p1.
6. *Architectural Review*, vol 9, 1901, pp129-30.

WALTHAM FOREST

Leyton

In the **Coronation Gardens**, off HIGH ROAD LEYTON at the junction with Buckingham Road, is the Coronation Fountain, a double-bowled Doulton fountain dating from the park's opening in 1903. It was designed by Joseph Pritchard of the Kidderminster architects Meredith & Pritchard, who collaborated with Doulton's on several memorials and fountains in the early 1900s. Nearby at 275 High Road Leyton is **Galaxy Travel**, housed in a former butcher's which still retains an excellent and complete, probably Edwardian, tiled interior.

WANDSWORTH

Balham

The lavish chancel decoration of **St Mary's Church**, BALHAM HIGH ROAD, includes a series of large Powell's opus sectile panels added during 1897-8.[1]

Battersea

The name of the **Old Imperial Laundry**, a late Victorian building now functioning as offices and galleries at 71-3 WARRINER GARDENS, is shown on its exterior in terracotta lettering. There is much terracotta ornament straight from the manufacturer's catalogue as well as a series of small panels showing a washerwoman.

Earlsfield

The mostly red brick **Church of St Andrew** (1889-90, architect E. W. Mountford), on GARRATT LANE at Waynflete Street, originally had a Minton tile pavement. Its Doulton terracotta font includes several reliefs modelled by George Tinworth and depicting biblical scenes relating to children.

Putney

The **Elliott School** (1955-6), PULLMAN GARDENS, a comprehensive school designed by London County Council's in-house architects, has much decorative detailing including a large external tile mural beside an entrance. The design shows stylised sunflowers and birds on a pale ground.

Roehampton

Holy Trinity Church, PONSONBY ROAD, near the south end of Roehampton Lane in the old village of Roehampton, was designed by the architect George Fellowes Prynne (1853-1927) and built in 1896-8. Inside is polychrome brickwork and an unusual encaustic tile pavement with nine-tile groups depicting symbols of the Passion Cycle. The opus sectile Stations of the Cross are by the architect's brother, the artist Edward Fellowes Prynne (1854-1921), who also painted three panels in the oak altar.

Southfields

The jolly facade of the former **Frame Food** confectionery works (1903-4, architects C. E. Dawson & W. T. Walker, now flats), 59 STANDEN ROAD, includes blue, green and white glazed bricks and a Doulton faience frieze. The architectural style of the factory has been described as arts and crafts, art nouveau and art deco.

Tooting

Jubilee Villa (1887), 156 LONGLEY ROAD, is something of a showpiece for Maw & Co's products with seven tile panels on its facade including transfer-printed pictorial tiles by Owen Gibbons, who had worked on the decoration of the South Kensington Museum during the 1870s and produced many designs for Maw's during the 1880s.[2]

About a quarter mile north of Longley Road is MITCHAM ROAD and **Tooting Library** (1902, William Hunt), with its elaborate Doulton terracotta porch. Also on Mitcham Road is the overbearing Shaws of Darwen faience facade of the **Granada Cinema** (now Gala Bingo), built in 1930-1 with an outer shell designed by the architect Cecil Masey and a spectacular interior by Theodore Komisarjevsky.

There is extensive wall tiling, although no pictorial panels, inside the **King's Head** (1896), 84 UPPER TOOTING ROAD, which was designed by the specialist pub architect W. M. Brutton. He was also responsible for the St James's Tavern (1896), Shaftesbury Avenue, Westminster, with its Doulton picture panels.

Vauxhall

The polychrome terracotta relief of the **River God** (1988) at ELM QUAY COURT, off Nine Elms Lane, is by the sculptor and poet Stephen Duncan.

Wandsworth

A Doulton buff terracotta panel of the *Last Supper*, modelled by John Broad and shown at the Royal Academy in 1896, was soon afterwards built into the newly constructed apsidal east end of **St Anne's Church**, ST ANN'S HILL.[3] The panel is a copy of Leonardo da Vinci's *Last Supper* fresco.

To the east on TRINITY ROAD, Wandsworth Common, is the **Church of St Mary Magdalene** (1887-8), where a Tinworth-designed Doulton terracotta relief of the *Ascension* formed part of the original aisle decoration; it was intended to be the first of a series.[4]

References

1. Dennis W. Hadley, *James Powell & Sons: A listing of opus sectile, 1847-1973,* (2001).
2. Kathryn Huggins, 'Owen Gibbons - London to Ironbridge', *Glazed Expressions,* (1985) 9, pp1-2.
3. Paul Atterbury and Louise Irvine, *The Doulton Story* (Royal Doulton Tableware, Stoke on Trent, 1979).
4. *The Builder*, vol 55, 15th December 1888, p441.

WESTMINSTER

Covent Garden

The **Covent Garden Fountain** was made by Somerset stone carver Philip Thomason for Westminster City Council around 2000; the material is a recreation by Thomason of the Coade stone formula (Fig 185). The fountain features a massive indented shell and is sited beside St Paul's Church; access from COVENT GARDEN or the churchyard.

The grey block terracotta facade of the **London Coliseum** (1902-4, Frank Matcham), ST MARTIN'S LANE, was the largest contract ever undertaken by the Hathern Station Brick and Terra Cotta Company. Interior decoration restored by RHWL Architects during major refurbishments of 2000-4 included the tiled floor of the foyer and terracotta ornament in the auditorium.

Knightsbridge

On BREMNER ROAD, immediately south-west of the Albert Hall, is **Queen Alexandra's House** (1884, architect Caspar Purdon Clarke), built as a hostel for women studying at the schools of music, art and science in South Kensington. It has retained much of its original high quality interior decoration, as well as Doulton terracotta reliefs of *Art* and *Music*, modelled by the Burslem artist Richard Ledward (1857-90), in the double height porch. The entrance hall, altered but still impressive, is lined with ornate, mainly grey-green faience tiles designed by Doulton artists and supplied at cost price by Henry Doulton, who undoubtedly saw the publicity value in his work at the hostel. In the drawing room-cum-library is a massive faience chimneypiece given by Doulton, who also donated the twelve pictorial tile panels in dining room. These comprise two views of Lambeth and ten allegorical panels depicting art and music; all were designed by John Eyre and painted by Esther Lewis, Walter Nunn and John McLennan.[1]

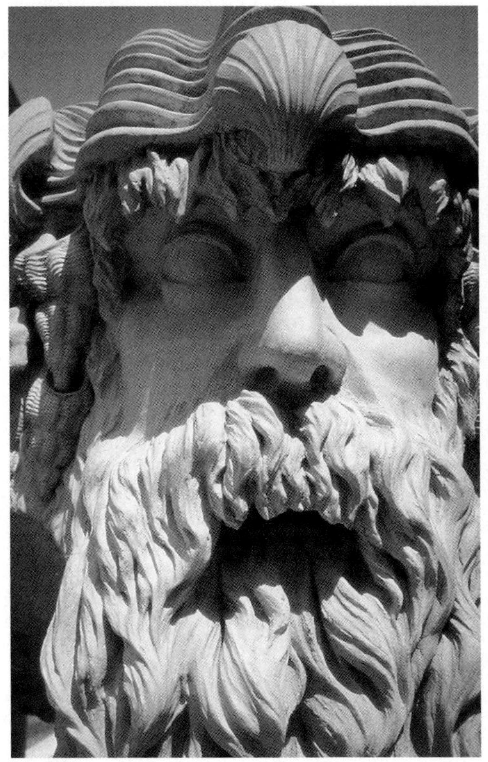

Fig 185.

Queen Victoria laid the foundation stone of the **Albert Hall** (properly the Royal Albert Hall of Arts and Sciences), KENSINGTON GORE, in 1867, while the Albert Memorial (1863-72) was still under construction just to the north. The Hall's huge elliptical brick drum had been planned by Captain Francis Fowke, architect of the South

Kensington Museum (now V&A, see Kensington & Chelsea), but following his death in 1865 the project was taken on by Henry Scott, who was responsible for the Hall's exterior, although Reuben Townroe designed the decorative features of its buff terracotta cladding, which came from Gibbs & Canning of Tamworth. This was the first time such a substantial terracotta contract had been awarded to a single supplier, rather than to a number of smaller firms; however, late delivery of the terracotta caused delays in construction.[2] Townroe undertook much of the modelling, which was supervised by Scott's assistant Gilbert Redgrave; Scott and Redgrave ensured that the blocks were not smoothed over, the result being a rough-textured finish which was intended to add spontaneity to the rigorous repetition of sculptural detail. This effect is now impossible to see as the fireskin and much of the Hall's decorative detailing were sandblasted away in 1971.[3]

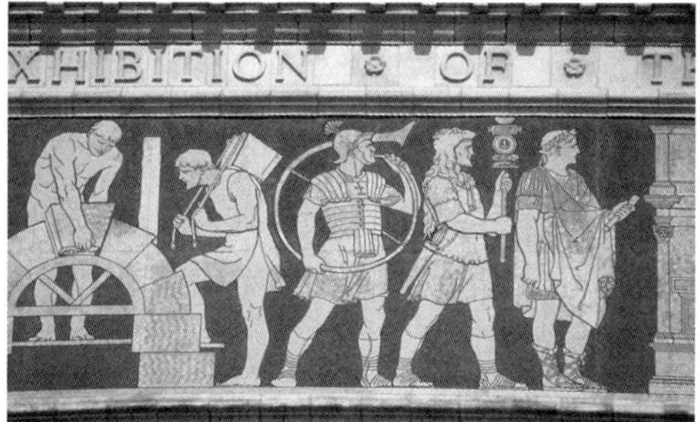

Fig 186.

Encircling the outside of the Hall, high up above the balustraded balcony, is an 800′ long terracotta mosaic frieze depicting artistic and scientific activities; above it runs an inscription in moulded terracotta capitals (Fig 186). The format of the frieze was decided by Scott in conjunction with the artists Henry Stacy Marks (1829-98), Frederick Richard Pickersgill (1820-1900) and William Frederick Yeames (1835-1918), the latter pair being joined by Edward Poynter (1836-1919), Edward Armitage (1817-96), John Callcott Horsley (1817-1903) and the sculptor Henry Hugh Armstead (1828-1905) in completing detailed designs of the various sections. The chocolate and ochre tesserae were produced at the adjacent and recently established Minton Hollins workshop, which supervised the execution of the panels by the Ladies Mosaic Class of the National Art Training School.[4] During the 1970s part of the terracotta balcony was found to be damaged, probably by water ingress causing cracking, and some concrete substitute sections were introduced. These were replaced with terracotta blocks supplied by Hathernware in the early 1990s, at the start of the Hall's long-term restoration programme, which was completed in 2004. Above the new south porch, opened in 2003, is a 60,000 piece glass mosaic designed by Shelagh Wakely and made by Trevor Caley; its abstract design was inspired by the Hall's terracotta frieze.

St Paul's Church (1840-3), WILTON PLACE, was the first parish church in London to put into practice the teachings of the Oxford Movement. The influence of tractarianism is reflected not in its architecture but in its anglo-catholic interior decoration, which dates from the latter part of the nineteenth century. Running round the nave is an outstanding series of eighteen large tile panels depicting scenes from the life of Christ, executed mainly in sepia and shades of green and purple; at the west end of the nave are two additional sets of three lancet-shaped panels showing St Peter and St Paul (Fig 187). These were all painted during 1869-79 by the stained glass designer and fresco artist Daniel Bell (b1840), younger brother of Alfred Bell (1832-95) of the stained glass makers Clayton & Bell.[5] Daniel initially worked for his brother's firm, but began the St Paul's panels when in partnership with Richard Almond (b1841) as stained glass artists and church decorators Bell & Almond.[6] Daniel Bell worked independently from 1875 and appears to have concentrated on frescoes towards the end of his career, his latest known work being the frescoes begun in 1896 at St Matthias, Stoke Newington, Hackney.[7] These paintings were lost - the fate of much of Bell's work - when the church interior was severely damaged during the Second World War. The St Paul's panels appear to be his only ceramic works.[8]

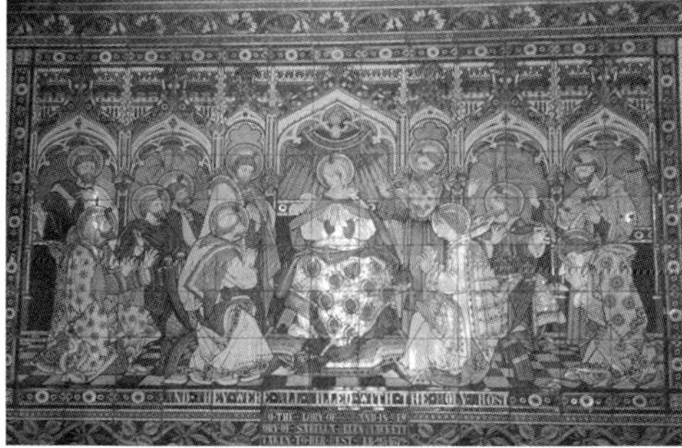
Fig 187.

Maida Vale

The **Chippenham**, a late Victorian pub at 207 SHIRLAND ROAD, retains some of its original full height interior wall tiling; the elaborate entrance of the turn-of-the-century **Warrington Hotel**, 93 WARRINGTON CRESCENT, mostly comprises standard tile and faience elements supplied by Craven Dunnill.

Marylebone

Just inside the entrance of the **Waitrose** store at 98-101 MARYLEBONE HIGH STREET is a tile mural (1999) by Reptile Tile & Ceramics showing local people and scenes including Lord's Cricket Ground. On the rear facade of the store, in Cramer Street, is a five-panel ceramic installation designed and executed by the artist Robert Dawson entitled *Tyburn, Lethewards has sunk* (2000), which was part of Westminster City Council's Hidden Rivers public art project.

The huge Great Central Hotel (1897-9, now **Landmark Hotel**), 222 MARYLEBONE ROAD, has much intricate Doulton terracotta ornament on its facade; the figures of *Night* and *Day* in the spandrels of the main entrance were modelled by John Broad.

The **R. C. Church of Our Lady of the Rosary** (1959-63), 211 OLD MARYLEBONE ROAD, is the third of the trio of churches designed by the architect H. S. Goodhart-Rendel in which the chancel decoration includes Carter's tiling designed by Joseph Ledger and painted by Phyllis Butler. Rather than a reredos, as at Rochester (Kent) and Hounslow in 1955, here Ledger designed fifteen individual hand-painted tile panels depicting the *Mysteries of the Rosary* (1966) which are mounted between the narrow lancets of the east wall (Fig 188). Carter's also supplied geometric-patterned blue and grey glazed tiling for the chancel dado.[9]

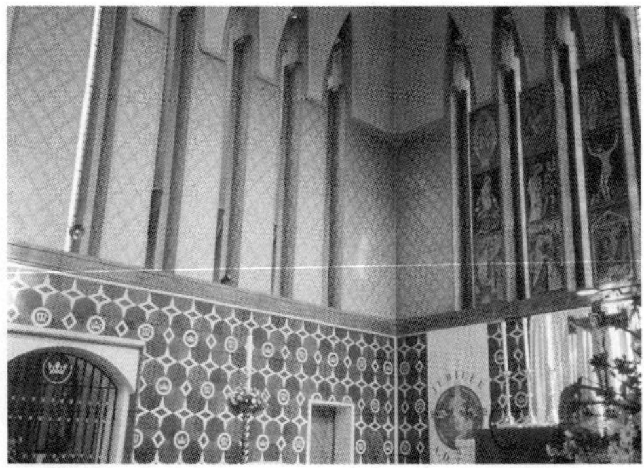

Fig 188.

In the conservatory (no public access) of 33 WEYMOUTH STREET (now a dental practice, 1894-5, architects H. D. Davis & B. Emanuel) is an extensive trompe l'oeil slip-trailed tile mural of a landscape; it is signed Marcel Logeat, Paris and dated 1905. There are also two smaller hand-painted murals by the same firm, who were probably tile decorators (Fig 189).

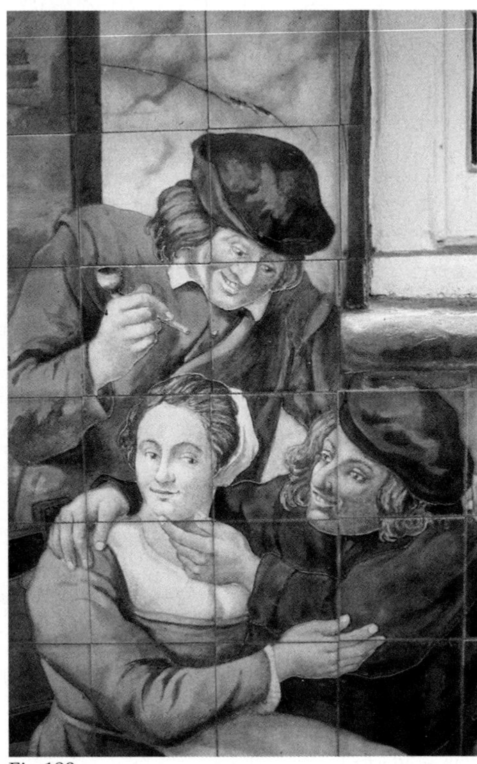

Fig 189.

Mayfair

The **Handel House Museum** at 25 BROOK STREET was the home of the composer George Frideric Handel during 1723-59. The Museum is entered from Lancashire Court, a narrow alleyway lined with a long ceramic mural by the London sculptor and tile designer Michael Czerwinski (assisted by Ray Howell) entitled *London* (2001); it shows hand-painted and relief scenes of the ancient and modern city.

Beside the altar on the east wall of **Christ Church** (generally no public access), DOWN STREET, is a First World War memorial by William Glasby. The panel, one of Glasby's most impressive and earliest works in opus sectile, dates from about 1920 and depicts Christ.

The former nonconformist King's Weigh House Chapel (now **Ukrainian Catholic Cathedral**), DUKE STREET, was put up in 1889-93 by the architect Alfred Waterhouse with a wealth of buff Burmantofts terracotta dressings; the firm's faience is used inside as cladding on four columns. Alterations of 1903 by J. J. Burnet included the addition, at the east end, of a Burmantofts terracotta screen bearing figurative decoration, but a new screen was installed around 1980.

The art deco apartment block **Carrington House** (1936, architects W. & E. Hunt), HERTFORD STREET, has strings of cream and mottled grey-green faience cladding which swoop beneath its rows of window boxes. A carriage entrance leads into the courtyard, where more faience ornament takes the form of large mouldings and great zigzags. These ceramics are unusual in colour and form, and possibly came from the Delft factory De Porceleyne Fles, which was well known for its architectural faience. The architects, William Hunt (1854-1943) and his son Edward Hunt (1877-1963), who was articled to his father and became a partner in 1905, designed several town houses and business premises in Mayfair. William Hunt was the architect of Tooting Library (1902, Wandsworth), which has an elaborate Doulton terracotta porch, but Edward Hunt was probably responsible for Carrington House.

The extensive pedestrian subways at HYDE PARK CORNER are lined with tiling completed in 1995 by the Hackney-based Free Form Arts Trust; the project's art director was Alan Rossiter. The historical images, which cover 900 square metres of subway wall, were painted on-glaze by a team of six artists using brushwork, spraying, stencilling and sponging.[10]

The tailors Messrs Cooling Lawrence & Sons, specialists in military and naval uniforms, had new premises built at 47 MADDOX STREET (now **Browns Restaurant**) in 1892. Their architect was Walter Williams (1863-1954), who produced a shiny brown Burmantofts glazed faience facade with good detailing including dragon finials. The shop is said to have the earliest complete faience facade in London.[11] Burmantofts produced large blocks and slabs of glazed and unglazed faience from the early 1880s, but this was intended for internal work, as the material was not resistant to frost damage; coloured faience made frequent appearances in London's clubs and restaurants during the 1880s, for instance lining the walls of the buffet and grill rooms at the First Avenue Hotel (1883), Holborn. It was Doulton's development of frost and pollution-resistant Carraraware in 1888 which allowed faience to emerge into the daylight, an early example of its use - and the most extensive ever - being the polychrome Carraraware-clad Birkbeck Bank (1895-6, demolished 1965) near the north end of London's Chancery Lane. The Cooling Lawrence shop, opened four years before the bank, was an early and daring external use of Burmantofts faience. By the turn of the century Burmantofts had improved the glazing and body of their coloured faience so that it could be used safely externally; however, it was 1908 before the firm developed Marmo, their response to Doulton's Carraraware.

Redevelopment of MOUNT STREET, part of the Duke of Westminster's Grosvenor Estate, began in the early 1880s and continued until 1897, the result - especially on the south side of the street - being a high-spirited concentration of terracotta ornament which even the Duke, a keen proponent of the material, found overdone in parts. The first of the mostly shops-cum-flats went up at the east end in 1880-2, but the ceramic story begins with numbers 104-8 (1886, George & Peto), entirely faced in buff block terracotta from Doulton's.[12] Its even colour contrasts with that of 109-11, where George & Peto obtained the richer buff to pink terracotta from J. C. Edwards of Ruabon.[13] The section was completed by the same architects with number 113 (1891-2). James Trant Smith designed 115-6, a smaller, single block with a grey terracotta finish, and the outrageously intricate numbers 117-21, all built in 1886-7. Behind the blousy buff terracotta columns on the facade of butcher's **Allen & Co**, 117 Mount Street, the contemporary interior is still complete with extensive tilework and original fittings, although no pictorial panels. The most easterly of the street's terracotta structures are numbers 125-9 (1886-7, W. H. Powell), where Doulton's buff terracotta is combined with 'streaky bacon' style banded bricks in buff and red. Last in date, largest and most heavily decorated is the range at 87-102 (1889-95, Arthur J. Bolton) at the west end, reaching round into South Audley Street, with mostly buff terracotta supplied by Edwards of Ruabon. Apart from the visual impact of architectural ceramics in such profusion, there is much interest in Mount Street's detailing, from the shades of terracotta produced by different manufacturers to subtle variations in depths of courses and widths of terracotta blocks.

The 11' high *Queen of Time* clock above the main entrance of **Selfridges** (1908-28), 400

OXFORD STREET, was planned in 1926 and completed in 1931. The sculptor was Gilbert Bayes, who originally intended the entire group to be made from Doulton's polychrome stoneware, but eventually it was cast in bronze, overlaid with gold and inset with stoneware panels.

The tall corner block, notable for its bright green and white striped Doulton Carraraware gable, which occupies 137 PICCADILLY and 148-50 Old Park Lane is a former car showroom, **Gloucester House** (1905, T. E. Collcutt & S. Hamp); its ground floor now houses the Hard Rock Café.

Thomas Goode founded his china retailing business in 1827 and came to South Audley Street in 1845, when Minton's were already the firm's major supplier. Goode's son, the designer William James Goode (1831-92), took over the running of the business in 1867 and from 1875 began to expand the **Thomas Goode & Co** premises at 17-22 SOUTH AUDLEY STREET, retaining Ernest George as his architect. The new shop went up in three sections: central in 1875-6, south (which extends into South Street) in 1876-7 and north in 1890-1. The South Street block is a five-bay single-storey gallery with a blind arcade defined by six delicately painted Japanese-style pictorial panels, each of twenty-seven tiles. The shop retains most of its lavish Victorian interior decoration including Minton tiles in twelve different designs displayed on the six piers of an open arcade.

The gigantic former **Debenham & Freebody's** (1907-8) at 27-37 WIGMORE STREET is entirely faced in Doulton's Carraraware, which was also used on the facade of the Debenham House (see Kensington & Chelsea), built in 1904-7 for the store's chairman Sir Ernest Debenham.

Paddington

The **Porchester Centre**, PORCHESTER ROAD, is a complex consisting of a public baths (1923-5, architect Herbert Shepherd) and Turkish baths and library (1927-9, Shepherd & Thomerson), all still in use and lined throughout the baths areas with pale brown glazed faience by the Hathern Station Brick and Terra Cotta Company.[14]

Piccadilly

The pilasters of **Harvie & Hudson**, 97 JERMYN STREET, are decorated with Pugin-designed polychrome block-printed tiles made by Minton's around 1850 using the technique invented by Alfred Reynolds (1818-91), who was associated with the firm's tile department from 1848.[15]

The former Albemarle Hotel (1887-8, George & Peto, now **Albemarle House**), 60-1 PICCADILLY, is constructed from pinkish-brown block terracotta supplied by Doulton's. The facade includes a series of large relief portrait medallions similar to those shown in the firm's catalogue and designed by George Tinworth; they were based on coins in the collection of the British Museum.

The **Criterion**, PICCADILLY CIRCUS, was designed by Thomas Verity and built in 1874; it was partially reconstructed by Verity in 1884, since when the subterranean auditorium has remained largely unchanged. The walls around the stairs leading down to the theatre are extensively tiled in a sumptuous scheme which alternates mirrors and pictorial panels by W. B. Simpson & Sons, with figure designs by A. W. Coke and possibly W. S. Coleman. Below the Simpson tiling is a lower dado of plainer Maw & Co relief-moulded tiles. Restoration in 1992 extended the decoration into new bar areas using original Simpson's tiles and material with matching images.[16]

Inside the **St James's Tavern** (1896, W. M. Brutton), SHAFTESBURY AVENUE (near Piccadilly Circus at Denman Street), are six Doulton pictorial tile panels. Four, measuring about 6′ by 3′, show Shakespearian scenes with Falstaff, Prince Hal, Bardolph and Touchstone, and may have been painted by John McLennan; the two smaller panels depict hops and grape vines.

The restaurant now known as **Destino**, 25 SWALLOW STREET, opened in 1921 and was the first in London to serve Spanish food. The King of Spain, a friend of the original owners, donated the profusion of Seville tiles which can be seen in the main restaurant, where there are several splendid pictorial panels and a fountain, and in the private room, which has a *cuenca* tile dado.

St John's Wood

The salmon-pink terracotta of the Pavilion (1889-90, Thomas Verity) on the west side of **Lord's Cricket Ground**, ST JOHN'S WOOD ROAD, was supplied by J. C. Edwards of Ruabon, who mentioned it in their 1903 catalogue. One curious feature of the facade is the series of terracotta corbel-head portraits of cricketers which runs above the balcony.

Soho

The extensive wall tiling inside the front and back bars of the **Dog & Duck PH** (1897, architect Francis Chambers), 18 BATEMAN STREET, includes repeats of a single tile showing the eponymous dog grasping a duck.

All Saints Church, MARGARET STREET, the 'model church' of the Ecclesiological Society, was designed by William Butterfield and erected in 1850-2, although decoration of the interior continued piecemeal up to its consecration in 1859 and for many years afterwards (Fig 190). A Butterfield-designed Minton tile pavement runs throughout, with mainly geometric tiles in a pattern which increases in intensity towards the chancel. Frescoes were originally planned for the lower parts of the nave walls, but tile murals were installed instead from the 1870s, Butterfield by then preferring a more permanent medium. The north wall panels of 1874-5, a memorial to the first vicar of All Saints, were designed by Butterfield, commissioned from Alexander Gibbs and fired in his Bloomsbury Street kilns, although the figure painting was executed by his younger brother Isaac Alexander Gibbs (1849-89), with background work by the French artist Alexander Gravier. The five large panels carry images of the *Adoration of the Magi* with characters from the old and new testaments. Fixing was carried out by Henry Poole & Sons of Millbank, who also provided the north and south aisle tile dados in 1876. The tile mural beneath the west window shows *Moses and the Brazen Serpent* (1888) and was probably designed by Butterfield. It was executed by the London stained glass firm Bell & Beckham, who also carried out the final tile mural on the adjacent south wall; this shows the *Ascension* (1890-1) and is known to have been designed by Butterfield.[17]

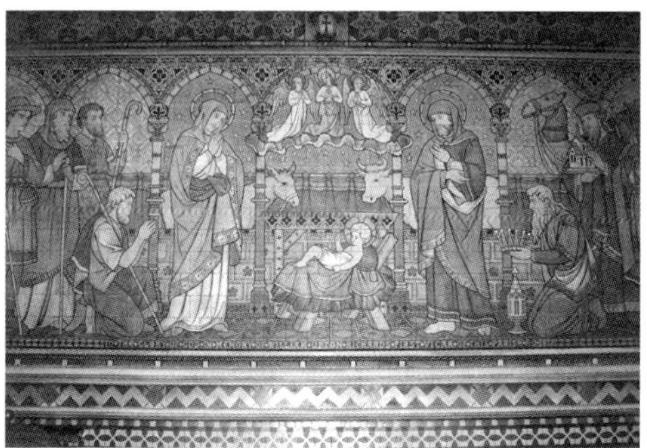

Fig 190.

Paul Thompson, the architect's biographer, feels the All Saints tile panels are not easy to assess, and is unconvinced of their quality; certainly they came towards the end of Butterfield's architectural career, during which he rarely used painted decoration.[18] His interest in permanent mural decoration began in 1867 with the use of mosaics, and the tile panels of All Saints, Margaret Street and St Augustine (1889-91), South Kensington, represent its culmination. However, despite their visual importance in this most significant of churches, the All Saints tile mural sequence now receives minimal critical comment; for instance, the mural historian Clare Willsdon mentions only William Dyce's original fresco painting (1854-5) in the chancel, ignoring the tile murals altogether.[19] The relationship of ceramic decoration in Victorian churches with 'trade' in the form of the ecclesiastical decorating companies perhaps induces critical uncertainty; in addition, the mass industrial connotations of tile manufacture and the necessarily collaborative processes of ceramics design, production and installation are quite different from the working patterns of 'fine' artists. In this context, the rediscovery of the St Augustine panels should encourage the consideration of ceramic murals as serious artworks.

Much Doulton terracotta is in evidence inside and on the outside of the **French Protestant Church** (1891-3, Aston Webb), near the north-west corner of SOHO SQUARE. Most interesting is the interior, with buff and brown terracotta appearing in bands on the walls; the pulpit and font are also of terracotta.

Strand

Lloyds Bank, 222-5 STRAND (at the east end), was built in 1882-3 (architects Wimble & Cuthbert) as the restaurant of the Royal Courts of Justice, opposite which it stands; an earlier occupant of the site was the Palsgrave Head Tavern, frequently visited by the dramatist Ben Jonson. The exotic entrance lobby is completely lined in Doultonware and unglazed Silicon ware mosaic, its elaborate modelling including water bowls, flying fish and crazily twisted columns (Fig 191). In the original restaurant, now the banking hall, are Doulton pictorial tile panels by John McLennan showing characters from Ben Johnson plays, Frederick Palsgrave (once King of Bohemia), and chrysanthemums as grown in nearby Temple Gardens in the early 1880s.[20]

Just west on the corner of the Strand and ARUNDEL STREET is **Abbey Life House** (1963-5) whose entrance is marked by a large ceramic relief (1963) by the sculptor Geoffrey Earle Wickham; it is made up from irregular sections and shows the area as it was in the seventeenth century.

Further west on the Strand beyond Somerset House is the frontage of the 1903-4 extension to the **Savoy Hotel**, known as Savoy Court (architect

T. E. Collcutt) and clad in cream Carraraware; it was an important commission for Doulton's which also included much sanitaryware. The arts and crafts **Coal Hole PH** at 89 Strand is part of the complex; inside is a grape-themed terracotta fire surround.

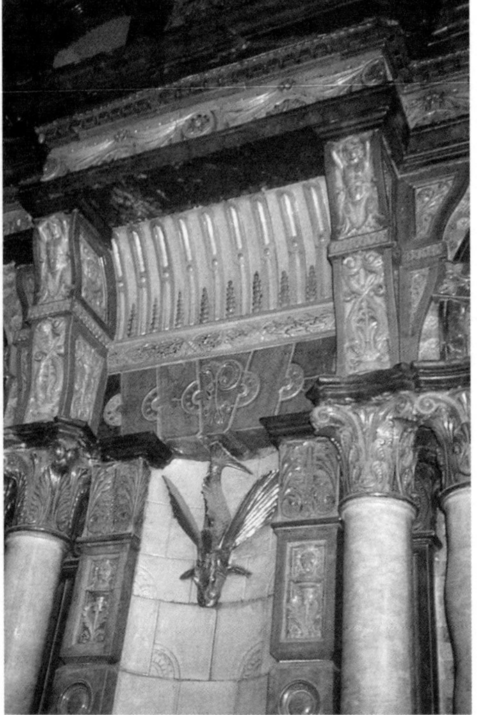

Fig 191.

Towards the west end of the Strand is the **Charing Cross Hotel** (1863-5, E. M. Barry), at the terminus of the South Eastern Railway. Blanchard's, who supplied the terracotta used in the Horticultural Society's successful 1861 garden at South Kensington, provided the hotel's elaborate terracotta detailing, all of which was non-structural. This early use of the material for a commercial building is comparable with its less extensive appearance on Plymouth's Duke of York Hotel and Scarborough's Grand Hotel, both of 1863-7. Although terracotta had been used for a complete building, the first of the 'pot churches' at Lever Bridge, Bolton, as early as 1844-5, its large-scale use at Charing Cross, as commercial architecture in the capital, was undoubtedly more influential.[21]

Whitehall

The **Foreign & Commonwealth Office** (1861-75, George Gilbert Scott) complex on KING CHARLES STREET comprises four sections, each with its own courtyard, all arranged around a central quadrangle. The India Office (for which Matthew Digby Wyatt provided the interior decoration) and Foreign Office were open by 1868, with the Home and Colonial Offices being completed in 1875. Scott designed the Foreign Office's lavish interiors with the intention of impressing visitors from abroad. His work included immense corridors with geometric tiled floors and the Locarno Conference Room, whose coffered ceiling is supported by brackets bearing majolica roundels depicting emblems of twenty countries. In the India Office, the loggia and one balcony of Matthew Digby Wyatt's Durbar Court (1866) have polychrome majolica friezes and coved tiled ceilings in Maw's new majolica glazes. The Maw's geometric tiled pavements were executed by W. B. Simpson & Sons.[22]

The former smoking room of the old **Whitehall Club** (1864-6, now an annexe of the House of Commons Library), 47 PARLIAMENT STREET, is lined with original block-printed Minton wall tiling; its three main designs were shown in the Mintons China Works catalogue of around 1885.

The opulent club room interiors of the **National Liberal Club** (1884-7, Alfred Waterhouse), WHITEHALL PLACE, are lined throughout with Burmantofts faience, which also makes up the ceiling of the smoking room. This was Waterhouse's first major use of the newly-available glazed faience, and his enjoyment at exploring its possibilities is evident; his overall scheme provided different combinations of colours - from brown through green and gold to ivory and grey - and finishes for every room, including the seven lower ground floor billiard rooms.[23] Also notable are a first floor billiard room with a huge faience fire surround, and the faience-clad oven of the grill room.[24] The David Lloyd George Room's faience was restored in 2001 by the Conservation Unit of the University of Lincoln.[25]

Westminster

The facade is all that remains of the original **Orchard House** (1898), 14 GREAT SMITH STREET, but this retains its Doulton buff terracotta ornament including good lettering and peacocks modelled by W. J. Neatby.

The medieval floor tiles known as the 'Westminster' type were first recognised at

Westminster Abbey, PARLIAMENT SQUARE, where there are still several extant groups, for instance in the Pyx Chamber, St Faith's Chapel, St Benedict's Chapel and most notably the Muniment Room, which has one of the only two major *in situ* medieval tile pavements in London; the other is in the chapel of Lambeth Palace. At least some of the 'Westminster' tiles were made in London at a kiln in what is now Farringdon Road, and they have a wide distribution; they were often laid in unusually decorative patterns but their technical quality is generally poor. The Muniment Room floor dates from the late 1250s or early 1260s, just before the 'Westminster' tile industry went into decline, towards the end of the thirteenth century. The most technically advanced medieval tiles at the Abbey are in the Chapter House (1246-50), whose Chertsey-Westminster pavement probably dates from the early to mid 1250s and includes a rich array of human, architectural, animal and floral motifs. The Chapter House was used for storing official records from the late sixteenth century and the floor was boarded over, thus preserving the tiles, which could be seen through two trapdoors but aroused little interest until the architect Lewis N. Cottingham investigated them in the early 1840s in connection with the restoration of the Temple Church (see City of London) and made tracings of the designs. George Gilbert Scott restored the Chapter House in 1866-73 and relaid the pavement, incorporating some replacement tiles made by Minton using Cottingham's tracings; Minton's also made the reproductions of 'Westminster' tiles which form part of the pavement of the entrance way to the Chapter House.[26]

On Parliament Square just north of the Abbey is **St Margaret's Church**, with an ornate chancel pavement of highly glazed encaustic tiles given in 1878 by Colin Minton Campbell (1827-85), who became MP for North Staffordshire in 1874 and founded the Campbell Brick & Tile Company in the following year. *The Builder* was disdainful: 'It is surprising that people cannot apparently be happy or devotional in church now without the glitter of glazed tiles, which form really a very commonplace and tawdry source of effect'.[27] On the wall at the east end of the south aisle are two large Powell's opus sectile memorial panels of 1893 and 1894, each in three sections; the cartoons were by George Parlby.[28]

The **Palace of Westminster** (Houses of Parliament), between Parliament Square and the river Thames, was rebuilt after a fire in 1834 destroyed most of the old Palace; building began in 1840 and was substantially complete by 1870.[29] The architectural competition for the New Palace was won by Charles Barry with assistance from A. W. N. Pugin, who provided him with sets of fine drawings and was eventually to be responsible for all the internal detailing including tile designs; Barry and Pugin visited the Minton factory in Stoke together on the 2nd October 1845.[30] The first encaustic floor tiles, designed by Pugin and made by Minton's, were laid in the Peers Lobby in early 1847; over the years, further tiling was installed, resulting in the most complex series of elaborate secular pavements in the world.[31] Their creation acted as an important encouragement to the nascent British encaustic tile industry, and was the inspiration for the introduction of encaustic pavements into prestigious civic and public buildings around the world.

Tiles seen on the normal public route through the Palace, the Line of Route, are described here first, followed by those in non-public areas. Beginning at the Victoria Tower, the Royal Staircase - whose tiled risers are normally hidden by carpet - leads to the Norman Porch; the vault mosaics and other decoration in these areas date from the 1860s. In the Queen's Robing Room is a fireplace by E. M. Barry with block-printed Minton tiles depicting the fleur-de-lys, a portcullis and the VR monogram. The fine encaustic tiled floor of the Royal Gallery was designed by Pugin around 1851; the arrangement features large blocks of patterned tiles delineated by broad strips of letter tiles bearing Latin inscriptions almost a foot high. Although Minton's own employees probably installed the early floors, by July 1851 tile pavements throughout the Palace were being laid by the London Marble & Stone Working Company of Esher.[32] Next comes the Prince's Chamber, where the Pugin-designed fireplace, with foot-square red and blue encaustic tiles bearing the three lions motif and the royal monogram, was installed in 1847 with the Peers Lobby pavement, which lies beyond the House of Lords; its tiles, which measure about 12" square, run parallel with the walls.

The Peers Corridor, with replacement tiling from the 1970s, connects the Peers Lobby with the octagonal Central Lobby and its fabulous Pugin-Minton encaustic pavement, whose arrangement is based on an eight-pointed star and includes roundels of national emblems (Fig 192). After the Commons Corridor, where the tiling was renewed in the 1970s, come the Commons Lobby, the House of Commons and then St Stephen's Hall, with a long encaustic pavement including many armorial and letter tiles. This was completed, along with the Central Lobby, by early 1852. In the most heavily used areas of the Palace the floor tiling has become worn, and a programme of recording, protection and restoration is now in place.[33]

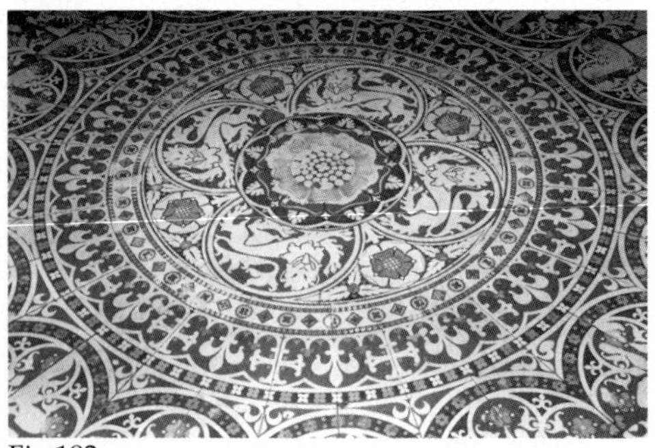
Fig 192.

Minton tiles in other parts of the Palace include those of the Lower Waiting Hall (early 1850s) and the Speaker's House (1858). Tiling for the floor of the Chapel of St Mary Undercroft (Crypt Chapel) was supplied by the contractor William Field during restoration by E. M. Barry in the 1860s.[34] Replacement encaustic tiles were made for the Chapel by Carter's of Poole soon after the Second World War.[35] The early Minton block-printed wall tiles of the Strangers' Smoking Room, now the Terrace Cafeteria, were restored during 1994-6 by Jackfield Conservation Studio and the Decorative Tile Works.[36]

Original Minton chancel encaustic floor tiling at **St Stephen's Church** (1847-50), ROCHESTER ROW, includes nine-tile groups in a mixture of red, blue and buff showing symbols of the Evangelists and a pelican in her piety.

A mostly geometric tile pavement by Maw's forms but a small part of the conclusively polychromatic interior of **St-James-the-Less Church** (1859-61, G. E. Street), VAUXHALL BRIDGE ROAD; the *Last Judgement* mosaic above the chancel arch is by G. F. Watts, who carried out the design as a fresco in 1861 but replaced it with mosaic in the 1880s following its deterioration.[37]

There is Doulton terracotta latticework tracery in the sanctuary dome's semicircular windows at **Westminster R. C. Cathedral** (1895-1903, J. F. Bentley), Ashley Place, off VICTORIA STREET. As well as the Cathedral's extensive mosaics, there is early twentieth century opus sectile work in the Chapel of St Gregory and St Augustine, where the panels were by J. R. Clayton of Clayton and Bell, and in the Chapel of the Holy Souls, where its design was by the artist William Christian Symons (1845-1911), a friend of the architect.[38]

At the west end of Victoria Street is **Victoria Station**; on the wall of the narrow central passageway connecting the trainshed with the forecourt are two large unsigned tile maps of the London, Brighton & South Coast Railway network, one showing the company's suburban lines, the other their entire system and a coat of arms within an elaborate cartouche; they probably date from 1906-8 when the Brighton (western) side of the trainshed was rebuilt.

References

1. Louise Irvine and Deborah Lambert, '"For present comfort and for future good" - Queen Alexandra's House, Kensington', *Decorative Arts Society Journal*, 21 (1997), pp27-34.
2. Alan Swale, *Architectural terracotta - a critical appraisal of its development and deployment*, 1998, MA dissertation, History of Ceramics, University of Staffordshire.
3. Michael Stratton, *The Terracotta Revival* (Victor Gollancz, London, 1993), pp62-3,236.
4. John Physick, *Albertopolis:The Estate of the 1851 Commissioners*, in *The Albert Memorial*, ed Chris Brooks (Yale University Press, New Haven and London, 2000), pp308-38.
5. Katy Carter, *St Paul's Church, Knightsbridge, 1843-1993: The first 150 years* (St Paul's Church, Knightsbridge, London, 1993).
6. Joyce Little, Angela Goedicke and Margaret Washbourn, eds, *Stained Glass Marks & Monograms* (NADFAS, London, 2002).
7. T. Francis Bumpus, *London Churches Ancient and Modern* (T. Werner Laurie, London, 1908), p223.
8. Lynn F. Pearson, 'The TACS Gazetteer Project: Tile discoveries in London and Newcastle upon Tyne', *Glazed Expressions*, (1998) 36, pp1-2.
9. Jennifer Hawkins, *Poole Potteries* (Barrie & Jenkins, London, 1980).
10. Hannah Wingrave, 'Art of Cladding', *Studio Pottery*, (2000) 39, pp21-4.
11. Simon Bradley and Nikolaus Pevsner, *London 6: Westminster* Buildings of England (Yale University Press, New Haven and London, 2003), p539.
12. Paul Atterbury and Louise Irvine, *The Doulton Story* (Royal Doulton Tableware, Stoke on Trent, 1979).
13. *J. C. Edwards, Ruabon: Catalogue*, Ruabon (1903).
14. *Modern Practice in Architectural Terra Cotta*, (Hathern Station Brick & Terra Cotta Co Ltd, Loughborough, 1930).
15. John S. Reynolds, 'Alfred Reynolds and the Block Process', *TACS Journal*, 5 (1994), pp20-26.
16. John Earl and Michael Sell, eds., *The Theatres Trust Guide to British Theatres, 1750-1950: A Gazetteer* (A. & C. Black, London, 2000).
17. Michael Kerney, 'All Saints', Margaret Street: A Glazing History', *Journal of Stained Glass*, 25 (2001), pp27-52.

18. Paul Thompson, *William Butterfield* (Routledge & Kegan Paul, London, 1971), pp459-60.
19. Clare A. P. Willsdon, *Mural Painting in Britain 1840-1940: Image and Meaning* (Oxford University Press, Oxford, 2000), pp213-20.
20. *The Builder*, vol 44, 2nd June 1883, p753
21. Stratton, *Terracotta Revival* (1993), p67
22. Tony Herbert and Kathryn Huggins, *The Decorative Tile in Architecture and Interiors* (Phaidon Press, London, 1995).
23. Colin Cunningham and Prudence Waterhouse, *Alfred Waterhouse, 1830-1905: Biography of a Practice* (Clarendon Press, Oxford, 1992), pp163-4.
24. Julie Gillam Wood, 'Burmantofts' stories in faience: The National Liberal Club, 1 Whitehall Place, London', *Glazed Expressions*, (2004) 50, pp14-16.
25. Rachel Faulding and Susan Thomas, 'Ceramic tiles in historic buildings: examination, recording and treatment', *Journal of Architectural Conservation*, 6 (2000) March, pp38-55.
26. Ian M. Betts, *Medieval 'Westminster' floor tiles (MoLAS Monograph 11)* (Museum of London, London, 2002).
27. *The Builder*, vol 36, 6th and 13th July 1878, pp509, 720.
28. Dennis W. Hadley, *James Powell & Sons: A listing of opus sectile, 1847-1973*, (2001).
29. Alexandra Wedgwood, *The New Palace of Westminster*, in *The Houses of Parliament*, eds Christine Riding and Jacqueline Riding (Merrell, London, 2000), pp113-135.
30. Alexandra Wedgwood, *The New Palace of Westminster*, in *Pugin: A Gothic Passion*, eds Paul Atterbury and Clive Wainwright (Yale University Press, New Haven and London, 1994), pp219-36.
31. Clive Wainwright, Hans van Lemmen and Michael Stratton, *TACS Tour Notes: Tiles and Terracotta in London* (Tiles and Architectural Ceramics Society, 1981).
32. *The Builder*, vol 9, 26th July 1851, p461 and 2nd August 1851, p486
33. A. T. Jardine, *Encaustic pavements, conservation, protection and replacement issues: The Palace of Westminster*, in *Historic Floors: Their history and conservation*, ed Jane Fawcett (Butterworth-Heinemann, Oxford, 1998), pp187-193.
34. Bradley and Pevsner, *London 6: Westminster* (2003), p229.
35. Hawkins, *Poole Potteries* (1980), p170
36. Lesley Durbin, 'Conservation and restoration of Pugin tiles at the House of Commons', *Context*, (1997) 54, pp24-5.
37. *The Builder*, vol 19, 1861, p410 and vol 20, 15th March 1862, p187.
38. Peter Howell, 'John Francis Bentley: Homage for his Centenary', *The Victorian*, (2002) 9, pp12-15.

Norfolk

Norfolk's most significant contribution to the history of architectural ceramics was made during the early sixteenth century, when the fashion for Italian-style terracotta resulted in the construction of the Ferrers monument at Wymondham (which Henry Cole visited prior to the construction of the seminal South Kensington Museum), the Jannys tomb in Norwich, the Berney monument at Bracon Ash and the extraordinary Bedingfield monuments at Oxborough. There is also a group of early sixteenth century north-west Norfolk halls - Denver, East Barsham, Great Cressingham, Great Snoring and Wallington - sporting terracotta decoration with gothic or renaissance motifs. This was a short-lived and expensive fad, and Norfolk displays its built consequences better than any other English county. Norwich was also briefly home to the Antwerp potters Jasper Andries and Jacob Jansen during 1567-70. They produced colourful tin-glazed floor tiles (none survive *in situ*) before Jansen established his works at Aldgate in London.

The home-grown firm Gunton's carried on the county's association with baked clay, manufacturing Cosseyware on the outskirts of Norwich from 1827; the idiosyncratic local architect George Skipper used this material, along with a variety of other architectural ceramics, in several of his turn-of-the-century Norwich buildings. Pugin worked in Norfolk, some of his best tiles now being marooned at West Tofts Church in the Army's Stanford Training Area; in addition there is the curious tale of the Pugin chantry which moved from West Tofts to Santon.

A very unusual sequence of late nineteenth to early twentieth century memorial tiles can be found at Southery, in the far west of this large and varied county, and there is a connection here with the similar memorial tiles at Brightlingsea, Essex. Rather different is Great Yarmouth's seafront, a ceramic showpiece where excellent early twentieth century buildings show faience being used innovatively by local architects. There is little of any note to report in Norfolk from the late twentieth century apart from the visually disappointing County Hall, Norwich (1966-8), which is partly faced in traditional Hathernware faience slabs. Suggested reading: TACS Tour Notes *Norwich & Norfolk* (1991). The *Gazetteer* entry for Norfolk covers the administrative area of Norfolk County Council.

BRACON ASH

The doorway of the Berney Mausoleum at **St Nicholas Church** is surrounded by part of the front of an early renaissance style terracotta monument dating from around 1525. It was very probably executed by the same local craftsmen who worked on the terracotta tombchests of the Bedingfield Chapel, Oxborough, the fashionable material having sprung into brief and brilliant prominence in Norfolk by way of its use at Hampton Court and Layer Marney Tower in Essex.

CASTLE RISING

In the upper part of the archway leading into the Norman keep of **Castle Rising** (EH) is a panel of attractive medieval tiles made at the Bawsey kiln, a few miles south of the castle. The relief and counter-relief tiles were inserted in the archway in the mid-Victorian period. Nearby, on the east range of **Trinity Hospital** almshouses (1609-15) is a terracotta lion plaque.

EAST BARSHAM

Much-restored **East Barsham Hall** is a red brick manor house built in the 1520s, almost certainly by Sir Henry Fermor. In addition to lavish renaissance style brick detailing, the terracotta decoration on its multiplicity of chimney shafts includes fleurs-de-lys and diapers, while the detached gatehouse has the arms of Henry VIII executed in cut brick above the main arch; it also bears Sir Henry Fermor's coat of arms. East Barsham is the most sumptuous of the group of Norfolk halls with gothic or renaissance terracotta detailing, its splendid heraldic display reflecting the alliances of this rising Tudor family whose town house in Norwich sported some identical motifs.[1]

GORLESTON ON SEA

The genteel resort of Gorleston lies just to the south of Great Yarmouth's harbour mouth. Beachmen and pilots were established in

Gorleston by the eighteenth century, and development moved to Cliff Hill, overlooking the harbour, during the early nineteenth century. The beach companies, formed in the 1820s to supply shipping and assist in rescues, built warehouses along the quayside. Roads of terraced houses appeared south of the original centre in the 1860s, then from the 1880s grander houses were put up nearer the cliffs; resort development took place from the 1890s. Significantly, Gorleston was home to the Cockrill family of architects and builders, who had a great influence on the development of Great Yarmouth and Gorleston in the late nineteenth and early to mid twentieth centuries. One of the family, the architect J. W. Cockrill, was the inventor of a patent wall facing tile; for details of the Cockrill family, please see the Great Yarmouth section.

Cockrill tiles may be glimpsed during a brief exploration of Gorleston, beginning above the pier in BELLS ROAD, where the **Fishmonger's**, at number 59, is completely tiled internally in Carter's tiles (Fig 193). They are mostly turquoise with a dark green and yellow dado, and an excellent frieze in blues and white shows fishes of many varieties. Head eastward, passing the end of MARINE PARADE, where the **shelters** are partly built with Cockrill tiles. Then down to sea level for the **Pavilion** (1901, J. W. Cockrill), PIER GARDENS, a domed music hall in red brick with terracotta panels and mouldings. In addition, well west of the river and beyond the unpleasant barrier of the Inner Relief Road, is **Gorleston Cemetery Chapel** (1889), CRAB LANE, again designed by J. W. Cockrill; its south porch has red terracotta columns.

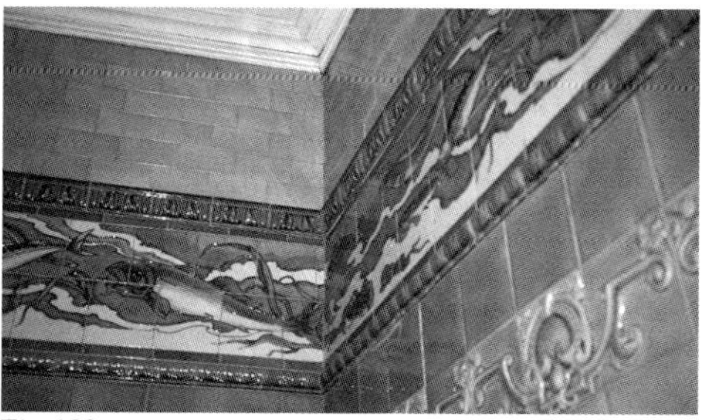

Fig 193.

GREAT CRESSINGHAM

The remaining fragment of the **Manor House**, put up around 1545 for John Jenney, has superb terracotta facing on its first floor, basically a pattern of blank lancets in moulded brick surrounding long, narrow terracotta panels with motifs including Jenney's hawk and hand crest, and a monogram roundel with two 'J's and an 'E', for Jenney and his wife Elizabeth. Amongst the Norfolk halls displaying terracotta detailing, Great Cressingham is the most medieval and least renaissance in its imagery.[2]

GREAT SNORING

The **Old Rectory** is part of the manor house built for the Shelton family around 1525 or shortly before; its terracotta detailing takes the form of bands above the ground and upper floor windows. In this example of the group of terracotta-decorated Norfolk halls, the motifs are both gothic and renaissance: the lower, gothic, frieze combines panels and lettering (repeats of 'MR IHS' for Christ and the Virgin Mary), while the upper, renaissance band includes profile heads.

GREAT YARMOUTH

Great Yarmouth was an important medieval port, providing almost double the number of ships London could manage for Edward III's navy in 1347. The Town Walls, emphasising Yarmouth's concentration on the River Yare rather than sea, were begun in 1285 and completed by 1893; the gates were demolished in the late eighteenth and early nineteenth centuries, but almost two-thirds of the length of the Walls survive. The unique town plan within the Walls also remains: the Rows, narrow medieval alleys which connected the three main north-south streets, escaped the Second World War almost unscathed. The town remained within its Walls until the nineteenth century; outside the Walls lay the open denes, used for grazing and the racecourse, in the middle of which was raised the Nelson Monument in 1817-19.

The first of Yarmouth's resort hotels, the Royal, was built near the beach in 1840. In contrast to many other resorts, commercial developments were funded by outside, often London money; in other areas, resort companies used either local capital or capital provided from the catchment area. The Midlands provided most of Yarmouth's visitors, but London initially provided the finance. Later, locals took over, rapidly followed by the Borough Council in the early years of the twentieth century. In terms of seaside architecture and architectural ceramics, the sea front remains one of Britain's best and least altered.

Yarmouth's own architects were in large part responsible for the buildings of the sea front, two major early cinemas - the Gem and Empire, both with ceramic facades - being designed by Arthur Samuel Hewitt, a rather shadowy figure who was articled to John Bond Pearce of Norwich, the designer of Yarmouth's Town Hall, and was practising in Yarmouth by 1886. However, Yarmouth's major turn-of-the-century architectural practice was begun by John William 'Concrete' Cockrill (1849-1924), son of Gorleston builder William Cockrill, whose four sons (along with several of the third generation) became architects or builders. J. W. Cockrill attended Yarmouth School of Art and began practising as an architect in 1869, becoming borough engineer in 1874, a post which he held until 1922. His younger son, Ralph Scott Cockrill (b1879), was articled to his father in 1896-9 then remained as an assistant, designing many buildings in and around Yarmouth.[3]

The Cockrills were keen users of architectural ceramics in their buildings, although 'Concrete' Cockrill was, of course, a concrete enthusiast. His scheme to concrete Yarmouth's unpaved Rows, half the cost to be paid by the Borough and half by the property owners, was one reason for his sobriquet. He invented the Cockrill wall facing tile, which he patented with Doulton's of Lambeth in 1893; this L-shaped tile obviated the need for shuttering during the building of concrete walls by acting as a retainer for the concrete.[4] The tour of Great Yarmouth begins on the Fishwharf, towards the south end of the quayside, then makes its way northward into the commercial centre of the town and out to the sea front, finishing near the Pleasure Beach and the Nelson Monument.

Begin at the **Dolphin** public house on the FISHWHARF; this was built as the Fish Wharf Refreshment Rooms in two phases (1901 and 1904) to a design by J. W. Corckrill. Its facade is of red brick with buff and deep orange terracotta, as well as green Cockrill patent tiles. Fishy imagery abounds, with dolphins and Neptune motifs in terracotta and fish in the stained glass. Now head northward along the quay (Southgates Road) towards the first sight of the Town Walls in the form of Palmer's Tower, just north of MARINER'S ROAD, on which stands the **Blackfriars Tavern**. This pub was part of the 376-house tied estate of the local brewer Lacon's, who had brewed at the Falcon Brewery on Church Plain, in the centre of Yarmouth, since the seventeenth century; the firm was taken over by Whitbread's in 1966 and the brewery closed in 1968. Between the wars, Lacon's was one of the few brewers who continued to use decorative ceramics on their pubs, partly because of the enthusiasm of their in-house architect A. W. 'Billy' Ecclestone, who designed pubs in both neo-vernacular and modern styles. For the traditional-style pubs he had two-inch bricks and tiles specially handmade by the Somerleyton Brick Company and Tucker's of Loughborough respectively. His pubs almost always sported a tile panel by Carter & Co of Poole, which acted as the pub sign; these panels continued to be manufactured for Lacon's into the 1950s.[5] The small Blackfriars tile panel is signed by Carter's and shows two monks taking wine from a barrel. A couple of streets north in FRIAR'S LANE is another former Lacon's pub, the **Clipper Schooner** (1938, A. W. Ecclestone) where the rather larger Carter's tile panel shows a ship.

Further along SOUTH QUAY, between Nottingham Way and Yarmouth Way, is **Row 111 House** (EH), an early seventeenth century merchant's house reconstructed following the Second World War and opened in 1954. It has a fine eighteenth century Dutch-tiled fire surround whose nautical motifs include sea horses, ships, whales and sea monsters. At the end of South Quay, opposite Haven Bridge, is HALL QUAY and the **Midland Bank**, which opened in 1939 as the Yare Hotel. A tall fin was removed from its grey and white faience facade during remodelling as a bank in 1968. Another good faience facade is to be found nearby at 85 NORTH QUAY, a richly-ornamented former pub. Turn eastward into REGENT STREET, soon passing (at 30-31) the odd facade of **Fastolff House** (1908, Ralph Scott Cockrill), an office building with lively Germanic Art Nouveau decoration and oriel bays in an unusual, almost vitreous, buff faience. Next is the white faience neo-classical frontage of the **Central Arcade** (1925-6). Our route continues toward the seafront, along King Street and Trafalgar Road, but a diversion north at this point, beyond the Market Place, brings the visitor to the **Garibaldi** public house on the corner of ST NICHOLAS ROAD and Factory Road. This enormous pub was rebuilt by Lacon's in 1957, and a Carter's tile panel of Garibaldi was installed on its exterior the following year; the 5′ by 3′ panel was hand-painted by Phyllis Hunter.[6] There is also a tile panel bearing the pub name.

Nearing the seafront in NELSON ROAD CENTRAL is the **Norfolk Institute of Art and Design**, built as the School of Arts and Crafts by J. W. Cockrill in 1912; the pepper-pot finials are of buff terracotta. It is a fairly early example of a steel-framed building, about which 'Concrete' Cockrill said that everything was concrete except the doors, but he was working on that.[7] Now to the seafront, MARINE PARADE, which is explored from the north end - the **Royalty** - to the south. The Royalty has a complex history, originating as the incomplete Aquarium (1875-6) which closed in 1882 but reopened as the Royal Aquarium the following year, having been reconstructed by local architects Bottle & Olley; it is now a cinema. The renaissance facade uses buff stone, Gibbs & Canning terracotta and moulded brick by Gunton's of Costessey; there is some partially hidden tilework in the foyer.[8] Next is one of the stars of the seafront, the former **Empire Cinema** (1911), a chunk of crushing ceramic classicism by Arthur Hewitt (Fig 194). This early cinema, with its massive Leeds Fireclay Co vitreous terracotta facade (which originally carried a segmental arch), was built for the Yarmouth & Gorleston Investment & Building Co; the dado and marble floors were by Art Pavement and Decorations Ltd.[9] The lush interior plasterwork is extant but dilapidated.

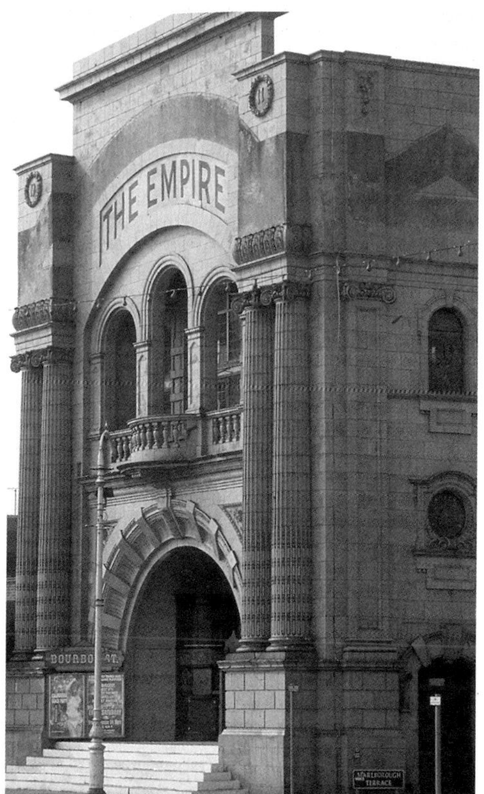

Fig 194.

Close to the Empire are the **Marine Arcades**, built in 1902 and 1904 by Arthur Hewitt for the local solicitors and developers Ferrier & Ferrier. Their orangey-red terracotta facades include dated pediments. In the yard of the **Maritime Museum**, on the corner of York Road, may be found the remains of the Coade stone head of Britannia, which originally topped the Nelson Monument (see below). Further south, almost opposite the Jetty and now largely obscured by the Flamingo amusement arcade, is the **Hippodrome** (actually on ST GEORGE'S ROAD). This purpose-built circus, for entrepreneur and circus entertainer George Gilbert, was designed by Ralph Scott Cockrill and opened on the 20th July 1903. The delightful towered and curved main frontage is faced with pinky-brown terracotta whose Art Nouveau motifs include birds, foliage and elongated faces (Fig 195). Although the interior has been altered, the original ring flooding mechanism is still in action, making the Hippodrome one of only a handful of such venues in the world. It is also one of only two surviving purpose-built circuses in Britain, the other being at Blackpool Tower. Despite the loss of chariot-racers from its three stained glass windows, and the closing off of direct access from the promenade, the facade retains a magical quality which heightens expectations of the show itself; fortunately, the dramatic introduction of water to the ring is as satisfying as ever.

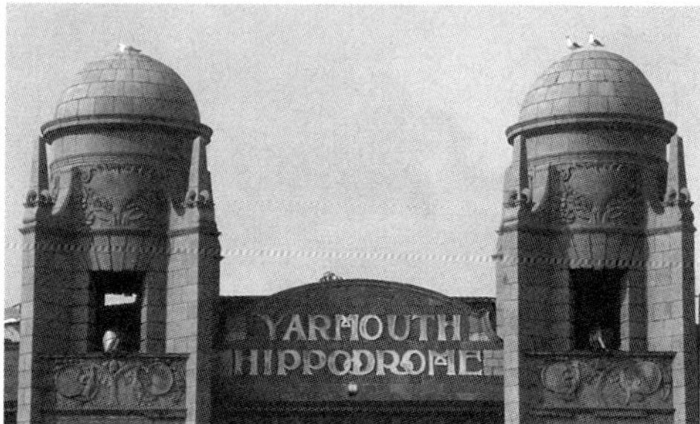

Fig 195.

Towards the south end of Marine Parade is the **Windmill**, built as the Gem Cinema by Arthur Hewitt for entrepreneur Charles B. Cochran in 1908. It is a jolly Edwardian baroque affair in buff faience, with twin towers, ogee roofs and globe finials (Fig 196). At night it was transformed into the 'Palace of 5000 Lights' by means of 1,500 electric light bulbs fixed to almost every surface; the windmill sail in the centre of its facade was a later addition. Across Marine Parade, Wellington

Pier and the adjoining Winter Gardens (bought from Torquay by Yarmouth Borough Council in 1904) mark the end of the main seafront. The Wellington Pier Pavilion (1903, J. W. Cockrill) is a splendidly idiosyncratic design in a style reminiscent of European exhibition pavilions; it was originally clad in metallic uralite, but was reclad - and somewhat diminished by the removal of most decorative elements - in the 1950s. There is much use of tiles and terracotta on the steps at the sides of the **Wellington Pier approach**, the terracotta work bearing the town's coat of arms. Indeed, all along the seaward side of Marine Parade there are small-scale terracotta features including urns and bases, and even a pinky-red terracotta toilet block dated 1900.

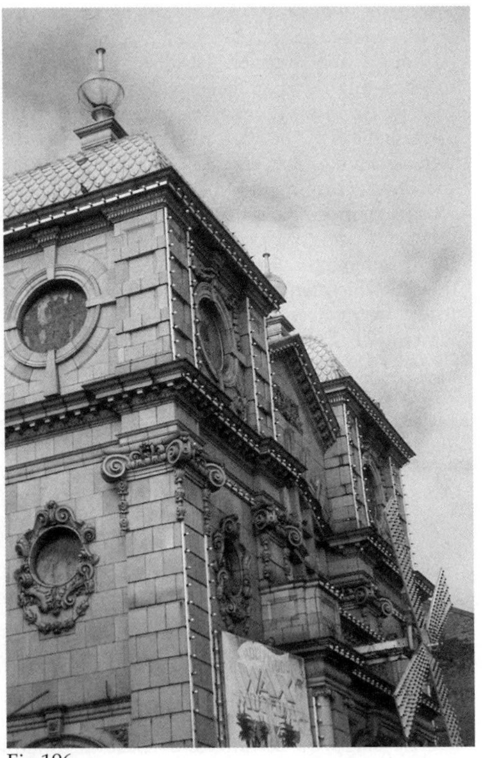

Fig 196.

Finally, and almost at the southern tip of Great Yarmouth, to the **Nelson Monument** on MONUMENT ROAD, put up in 1817-19 at the then-racecourse. It was designed by William Wilkins junior and is 144 feet in height, only a foot shorter than the rather later Nelson's Column in Trafalgar Square. At its top a ring of six caryatids holds up a figure of Britannia. All these figures were originally of Coade stone, but the caryatids were replaced by concrete copies in 1896 at the behest of J. W. Cockrill.[10] Britannia herself was replaced by a largely fibreglass replica in 1982-3, along with the caryatids. The figure, sculpted by Joseph Panzetta, had been filled with concrete at some point, probably 1896, and the removal of the concrete reduced the Coade stone surface to rubble.[11] However, the head and helmet, both of which had escaped the concrete, were intact allowing moulds to be taken, and the remains of Britannia's Coade stone head may now be seen at the Time and Tide Museum of Great Yarmouth Life in Blackfriars Road. The Monument is due to be fully restored by 2005.

HILGAY

All Saints Church, which was restored by G. E. Street in 1862, has a series of memorial tiles to departed communicants dating from around 1898 to 1902. The church lies only a few miles north of Southery (see below), where there is a much longer sequence of such tiles.

HOLKHAM

Although the restoration of **St Withburga's Church**, in the park of Holkham Hall, was apparently carried out by the London architect James K. Colling in in 1868-71, it was described in *The Builder* of 1876 as recently restored. The strongly coloured tile pavement, shown in an engraving, was by Maw & Co.[12] Colling had been a pupil of the Norwich architect John Brown during 1836-40.

KING'S LYNN

The major ceramic attraction in King's Lynn is **Clifton House**, on the corner of QUEEN STREET and King's Staithe Lane, near the quayside. Behind its 1708 brick facade is the remains of a medieval merchant's house and an intriguing Elizabethan watchtower, the last survivor of a series of look-out towers beside the river. The floors of the hall and solar are laid with commercially produced 'Westminster' tiles, mostly light and dark glazed but with a few decorated specimens. The tiles, which probably date from the second half of the thirteenth century, are 4¾" square and laid in a pattern of bands and blocks. After being hidden beneath floorboards in the 1580s, they were rediscovered in the early 1960s, then relaid (allowing a damp-proof floor to be installed) in exactly their original positions. The Clifton House pavements are rare examples of *in situ* secular tiling.[13]

Turn eastward into SATURDAY MARKET; on its south side is **St Margaret's Church** with a rich encaustic pavement laid during the 1875 restorations of the nave, by George Gilbert Scott, and chancel, by Ewan Christian. The tiles, which are mostly by Godwin (with some Minton work in the chancel) include four-inch tiles around the font and nine-tile groups leading to the altar. There are eight different four-tile patterns and seven different sixteen-tile patterns in this excellent display. Continuing east into ST JAMES' STREET, at number thirty is a **butcher's shop** whose doorways are flanked by sets of three late nineteenth-century pictorial tiles of farm animals, including an excellent pig.

NORTH BARNINGHAM

In the nave floor of **St Peter's Church** is an unusual and attractive mosaic arrangement of tiles and stone in a rose window formation. This small medieval church, now in the care of the Churches Conservation Trust, was restored in 1893.

NORTH TUDDENHAM

The medieval **Church of St Mary** was restored in 1868, but the unusual encaustic tiled dado, which stretches around nave and chancel, dates from the 1880s. The tiles were overpainted in 1978 but later revealed.

NORWICH

The buildings of Norwich display a remarkable range of building materials, with flint and plaster being particularly characteristic. For the ceramic enthusiast, the city is perhaps best known for the decorative brickwork produced by the firm of Gunton's, and for a remarkable series of turn-of-the-century buildings designed by the architect George Skipper, with rich terracotta or faience decoration. Norwich was also the home of the firm Barnard, Bishop & Barnard, established 1851, who made cast iron fireplaces at their riverside metalworking site. They also supplied a range of tiles for use in the fireplaces, notably the William De Morgan design 'BBB' with its floral motif, named after the firm and probably his most popular design.

An estate yard supplied moulded bricks used in the rebuilding of Costessey Hall, on the north-western edge of Norwich, in 1827. Subsequently, George Gunton, son of the original foreman, started working the Costessey yard and selling decorative brickwork and small solid blocks of terracotta; by 1851 he was offering ornamental chimneys, turrets, cornices and copings. Costessey brickwork and terracotta was used in the 1870s and 80s for hotels round the coast of East Anglia, and for the window tracery of numerous chapels. The works at Costessey closed about the time of the First World War, but production continued elsewhere until the Second World War.

John Betjeman described George Skipper (1856-1948) as being 'to Norwich rather what Gaudi was to Barcelona'.[14] He was one of the most inventive of the late Victorian architects and gave Norwich a series of remarkable buildings which use polychromy and art nouveau detailing to bring colour and animation to the city's streets. Skipper was the son of an East Dereham building contractor. Following a year at Norwich School of Art and pupilage with an architectural practice in London, he set up practice in East Dereham in 1879, moving to Norwich the following year. During the 1890s he undertook a series of major commissions in Cromer, erecting the three largest hotels in the resort and the town hall. Several of his major works in Norwich feature in this tour of the city, which starts north of the River Wensum at St George Colegate (about a quarter-mile north-west of the Cathedral). For a shorter version, which still includes the Skipper buildings, begin in London Street and finish at Red Lion Street.

In **St George's Church**, COLEGATE is the early renaissance terracotta tombchest of Robert Jannys, mayor of Norwich in 1517 and 1524. Jannys died in 1530 and the tall tombchest dates from 1533-4, making it slightly later than Norfolk's three other similar terracotta monuments at Oxborough, Wymondham and Bracon Ash, although probably carried out by the same hand. Decorative motifs on the tombchest include pairs of dolphins, each with a tiny ball in its mouth.

To reach the city centre, walk south along St George's Street, cross the river and continue up St Andrew's Hill, turning right into LONDON STREET. The small building at **7 London Street** (1896) was George Skipper's architectural office; it is now part of Jarrold's department store. The facade expresses his indebtedness to renaissance design and his love of decorative ceramics. The six relief panels above the windows were produced by Gunton at his Costessey Works in a fine clay termed 'Cosseyware'. The main reliefs show Skipper on site with his wife and a young boy, inspecting the work of stonemasons, and Skipper debating plans with a client and his family. The smaller flanking panels show carpenters, smiths, bricklayers and plasterers at work. Next door, on the corner of London Street and Exchange Street, is **Jarrold's** store, designed by Skipper and built in 1903-5 (with later alterations); it was his first use in Norwich of the neo-baroque style. Sadly the dome which Skipper had proposed for the corner was never erected. The London Street elevation, begun in 1903, was given Doultonware panels bearing the names of celebrated authors first published by Jarrolds; these have now been painted over.

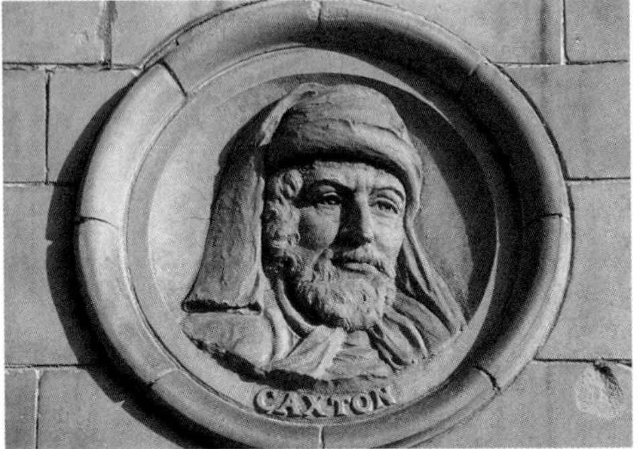

Fig 197.

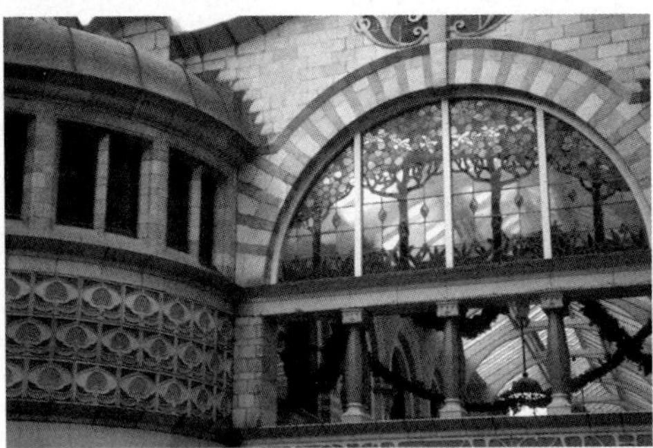

Fig 198.

Continue west up Guildhall Hill and into St Giles Street to see the former **Norfolk Daily Standard Offices** (1899-1900, G. Skipper), on the corner with Upper Goat Lane (Fig 197). This small building demonstrates the way in which Skipper used ceramics and a medley of fashionable styles to produce a striking frontage which made the most of a small corner site. The Standard offices are in a honey-coloured terracotta over a granite base, and the elevation includes reliefs of Caxton and Defoe. Return to the Market Place; directly across it is Gentleman's Walk and Skipper's best-known building, the **Royal Arcade** (1898-9), built on a site occupied by the stables and stableyard of the Royal Hotel (Fig 198). It was put up for a consortium of seaside hoteliers and its appearance was so colourful and exotic that the press likened it to a 'fragment from the Arabian nights dropped into the heart of the old city'.[15] Skipper worked with W. J. Neatby, the head of the architectural department at Doulton's, to produce the ceramic decoration in which a variety of fashionable forms, including wide arches and bulging polygonal columns, were given art nouveau detailing (Fig 199). Most of the patterns were created by glazes being poured into indentations formed in the blocks when they were pressed. Carraraware was used for the exterior, while inside the arcade are friezes of Parian ware decorated with zodiac symbols, peacocks and foliage. The rear entrance incorporated the rebuilt White Rose public house, but this elevation was mutilated during conversion to a butcher's shop in 1963. The floor of the arcade dates from restoration work carried out in 1986-91.

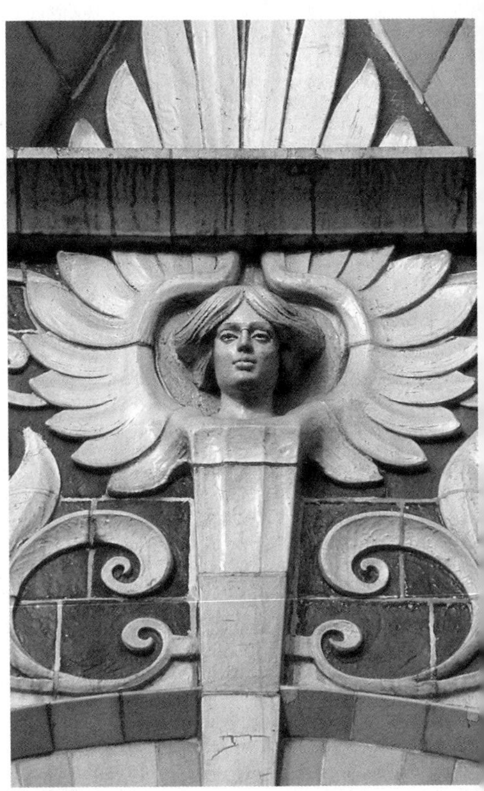

Fig 199.

Continue south along Gentleman's Walk, which soon becomes HAYMARKET; look out for the former **Haymarket Chambers** (1901-2, G. Skipper), where diminutive turrets top an elevation with dolphin-like figures and small decorative panels. The facade is given increased interest through the use of three colours of terracotta: red, cream and grey-brown. Backtracking slightly, take White Lion Street eastward to RED LION STREET for Skipper's **Commercial Chambers** (1901-3). The rustication and banding give added weight to the elevation, and the terracotta caryatids have a serious task in supporting the first floor balcony.

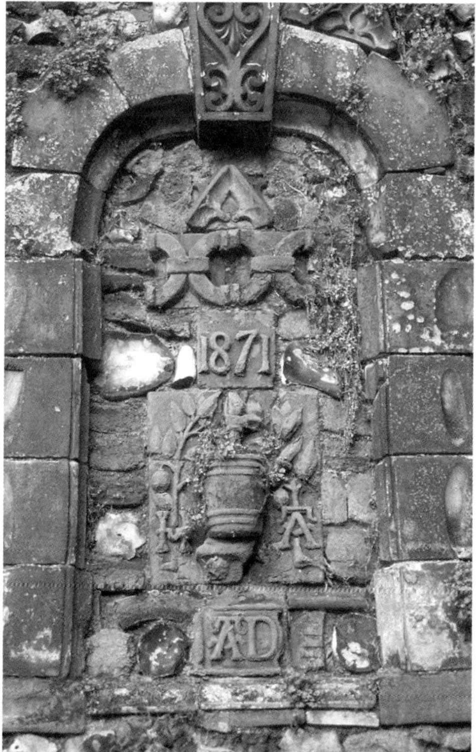

Fig 200.

The city's other ceramic locations are further from the centre. On its south-western fringe is the **pedestrian underpass** beneath CHAPEL FIELD ROAD, linking Chapelfield Gardens with Vauxhall Street. Here the walls have been lined by colourful mass-produced industrial tiles which have been cut and arranged to form abstracted shapes representing local buildings, including the Royal Arcade; this mural work is by Melanie Strank and dates from 1988.

To the west of the centre, just beyond the inner ring road at 4 EARLHAM ROAD, is the **Plantation Garden**, created by the wealthy Norwich upholsterer and cabinetmaker Henry Trevor from 1856 onward in a former chalk quarry (Fig 200). Over a period of forty years Trevor built ornate medieval-style walls, ruins and follies using local brick, laid out serpentine paths and balustraded terraces, and added a rustic bridge, a palm house and a gothic fountain, the latter partly made from Cosseyware. The garden, with its dramatic changes of level, became something of a tourist attraction but was eventually abandoned following the Second World War. It is currently undergoing restoration by the Plantation Garden Preservation Trust, and visitors are once again able to see some of Trevor's wickedly inventive brick and terracotta work.

Just over half a mile further west is the entrance to **Norwich (Earlham Road) Cemetery**, opened 1856. The Soldiers' Monument (1878) is a column with a Doulton terracotta figure depicting the 'Spirit of the Army'. It was designed by the sculptor John Bell, who had been responsible for the marble figures symbolising *America* (1865-71) which formed part of the Albert Memorial. Bell persuaded Henry Doulton to allow his sculptor George Tinworth to work with him to reproduce *America* in Doulton terracotta; this immense group was shown at the Philadelphia Centennial Exposition of 1876, where it attracted much attention. Bell commented that 'Nobody before has ever dared to produce terracotta on a really heroic scale'.[16]

Finally, on the southern edge of the city is **County Hall** (1966-8, Uren & Levy), MARTINEAU ROAD, a massive reinforced concrete-framed block set in parkland. It was one of the last substantial buildings to use the traditional style of faience cladding, in this case slabs of russet Hathernware faience combined with red brick. Unfortunately, at a distance the effect is simply an undifferentiated dull brown mass.[17]

OXBOROUGH

The great brick pile of **Oxburgh Hall** (NT) was built by Edmund Bedingfield in the 1480s; Henry VII visited in 1487, by which time Bedingfield had been knighted. The moated hall was damaged in the Civil War and rebuilt from about 1835 by the sixth baronet, Sir Henry Richard Bedingfield. His architects were J. C. Buckler and A. W. N. Pugin, although there is little which can directly be attributed to the latter. Buckler's restoration was the making of the picturesque house of today, and included the addition of red terracotta oriel windows. In the library (now dining room) his neo-tudor chimneypiece, which dates from the 1850s, has blue, white and gold tiles bearing the arms and monogram of the sixth baronet. Their design refers to late fourteenth-century floor tiles used in the palaces of Burgundy.[18]

Sir Edmund Bedingfield (d1496) was married to Margaret (d1513), sister of Lord Marney, the builder of Layer Marney Tower in Essex, which was intended to rival Wolsey's Hampton Court in size and grandeur, although only its massive gatehouse was built, around 1520. Both Hampton Court and Layer Marney were decorated with newly fashionable Italian renaissance terracotta, and the terracotta tombchests of Lord Marney (d1523) and his son John (d1525) were in the same style.

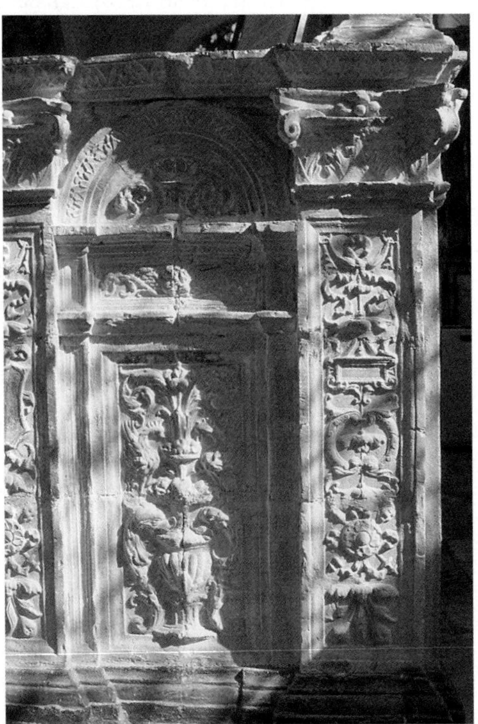

Fig 201.

In her will, dated 1513, Margaret Bedingfield ordered that her body be laid to rest in a chapel - yet to be built - at the **Church of St John Evangelist**, Oxborough. The construction date of the Bedingfield Chapel is unknown, but it contains two monumental and identical terracotta tombs, the paleness of the terracotta combining with their billowing canopies to achieve an unearthly lightness (Fig 201). It seems that connections between the Marney and Bedingfield families ensured that Italian-style terracotta was introduced to Norfolk, the date of the tombs probably being about 1525. The Oxborough terracotta work was possibly carried out by local craftsmen rather than Italian workers, as at Layer Marney, where there is no documentary proof that the craftsmen were Italian.[19] Certainly the Oxborough craftsmen appear to have worked on the three other Norfolk tombs executed in terracotta around the same time and in the same style: the Berney monument at Bracon Ash, the Ferrers monment at Wymondham Abbey and - dating from 1533-4 - the Jannys monument at St George Colegate, Norwich.[20] After this, and its use on a number of Norfolk houses, the spurt of interest in terracotta died out as the country became more insular following the dissolution of the monasteries; intense religious and political nationalism would have been intolerant of a material so obviously derived from Italy.

SANTON

On the 26th April 1857, the Revd William Weller-Poley preached twice at West Tofts Church, about four miles north of the now-redundant **All Saints Church**, Santon, of which he had recently become rector. West Tofts Church had just been completely restored for the Sutton family by E. W. Pugin, although partly to his father A. W. N. Pugin's design; in the process, the elder Pugin's 1846 chantry chapel had been demolished. At the time of Weller-Poley's visit, it lay dismantled. In contrast to West Tofts, All Saints was a small church with no chancel, and its wealthy new rector appears to have seized the chance to remedy this state of affairs, as much of the old Pugin chantry now forms the chancel of All Saints, complete with the elaborate reredos of fleur-de-lys and incised yellow tiles and the large, patterned floor tiles. Much the same tiles remain at West Tofts (see below).[21]

SOUTHERY

St Mary's Church (1858) contains an extremely unusual collection of ceramic memorial tiles, similar to those at All Saints Church,

Brightlingsea, Essex, although lacking their maritime theme.[22] Southery's rector during 1895-1932 was G. C. M. Hall, who had previously been a curate at Brightlingsea, where the architect-priest Ernest Geldart occasionally preached.[23] Geldart, whose views on church decoration strongly influenced the use of tiles at Brightlingsea, designed the north porch and some fittings for Southery Church over the period 1899-1919. He often used small tile plaques to record his building works, and at Southery there are two such tiles in the porch, dating from 1904 and recording the names of its builders. Another Geldart tile marks the dedication of the organ in 1899. In addition, a long sequence of tiles begun by G. C. M. Hall runs through the entire nave and into the chancel, and records the names of deceased communicants. Other tiles are used to mark events such as the floods of 1915 and 1916, and gifts of money for repairs.

WALLINGTON

Wallington Hall dates from the late fifteenth century, but was partly rebuilt soon after its sale in 1525 to Sir William Coningsby. His works included the addition of the north porch, in brick with lavish terracotta detailing such as friezes of blank tracery and lozenges, and egg-and-dart motifs.

WELLS-NEXT-THE-SEA

Inside the **Robert Catesby** pub (converted from a georgian house in the late 1990s) on STAITHE STREET is a 6′ by 3′ tile panel of Catesby (1573-1605), one of the conspirators in the Gunpowder Plot. The panel, which is in poor condition, was saved from the Robert Catesby pub in London's Tottenham Court Road, demolished in the 1970s.

WEST TOFTS

A chantry was added to the medieval **Church of St Mary** by A. W. N. Pugin (1812-52) in 1846, in memory of Lady Mary Sutton (d1842) of nearby Lynford Hall. Following Sir Richard Sutton's death in 1855, the new baronet Sir John Sutton, who had been a friend and patron of Pugin, was able to fully restore the church. Demolition of the old chancel, along with Pugin's chantry, began in March 1856; the chantry was eventually removed to Santon (see above).[24] The works, which were carried out by E. W. Pugin but partly to the 1850 designs of his father, were completed around the end of 1856. The chancel was by the younger Pugin, but the new and much grander chantry, the Sutton Chantry, was by A. W. N. Pugin. Here the Sutton tombchest is surrounded by lavish Pugin-designed Minton floor tiling, some of which bears the Sutton emblem, a barrel combined with the letter 'S'.[25] Please note that St Mary's Church stands within the Army's Stanford Training Area, and access is only by Ministry of Defence permit. Further information from Headquarters Stanford Training Area, West Tofts Camp, Thetford (01842 855235).

WYMONDHAM

In **Wymondham Abbey** is the the Ferrers monument, a renaissance-style terracotta structure dating from around 1525. It comprises three spectacular half-cylinders mounted above canopies and niches, the cylindrical parts made from the same moulds by the same craftsmen as those of the Bedingfield Chapel at Oxborough.[26] Henry Cole saw the Ferrers monument in 1864; it was one of many visits he made at home and abroad to study the use of terracotta while overseeing the design development of the Victorian and Albert Museum.[27]

Norfolk Roundup

In the sanctuary pavement of St Andrew's Church, **Barton Bendish** are some fourteenth century patterned tiles. At St Nicholas Church, **Blakeney** is a Godwin pavement of uncommon black and yellow relief tiles. There are reused Roman tiles in the north porch of St Edmund's Church, **Caistor St Edmund**, which stands within the brick and tile walls of the Roman town Venta Icenorum. Several cottages in **Costessey** High Street have unusually tall and ornate chimneys made locally by Gunton's; one cottage is dated 1852 in terracotta. On the crow-stepped east gable (c1520) of Denver Hall, **Denver** is a series of terracotta tablets bearing letters and decorative motifs; a similar series resides at the foot of the wall. In the Church of St Andrew and St Mary, **Langham** is a Second World War memorial in terracotta and decorated tiles, giving thanks from the Netherlands Forces. The summerhouse (1915) in the gardens of **Sandringham House**, overlooking the lake, contains large spreads of Dutch tiles of contemporary date including two panels of galleons. New Hall (1878-80), **Snettisham** has several contemporary fire surrounds of William De Morgan's lustre tiles.

References

1. Jeremy Musson, 'East Barsham Manor, Norfolk', *Country Life*, 198 (2004), pp52-57.
2. Jane A. Wight, *Brick Building in England from the Middle Ages to 1550* (John Baker, London, 1972), p184.
3. Lynn F. Pearson, *The People's Palaces - Britain's Seaside Pleasure Buildings* (Barracuda Books, Buckingham, 1991), pp83-4.
4. Patent No. 23,230, 4th December 1893; J. W. Cockrill and H. L. Doulton.
5. Lynn Pearson, 'Decorative ceramics in the buildings of the British brewing industry', *TACS Journal*, 8 (2000), pp26-36.
6. Carter Archive, Poole Museum Service, 3D/7.
7. Michael Stratton and Lynn Pearson, *Tour Notes: Norwich & Norfolk* (TACS, 1991).
8. Tamworth Castle, Gibbs & Canning Archive; information from Angella Streluk.
9. *Burmantofts Pottery*, (Bradford Art Galleries and Museum, Bradford, 1983).
10. Nikolaus Pevsner and Bill Wilson, *Norfolk 1: Norwich and North-East* 2nd ed. Buildings of England (Penguin, London, 1997), p159.
11. Alison Kelly, *Mrs Coade's Stone* (Self Publishing Association, Upton-upon-Severn, 1990), pp237-8.
12. *The Builder*, vol 34, 22nd April 1876, pp387, 389.
13. Ian M. Betts, *Medieval 'Westminster' floor tiles (MoLAS Monograph 11)* (Museum of London, London, 2002).
14. David Jolley, *Architect Exuberant: George Skipper, 1856-1948* (Norwich School of Art, Norwich, 1975).
15. Rosemary Salt, *Plans for a Fine City* (Victorian Society East Anglian Group, Norwich, 1988).
16. Desmond Eyles and Louise Irvine, *The Doulton Lambeth Wares* (Richard Dennis, Shepton Beauchamp, 2002), p78.
17. Michael Stratton, *Clad is bad? The relationship between structural and ceramic facing materials*, in *Structure and Style: Conserving Twentieth Century Buildings*, ed Michael Stratton (E. & F. N. Spon, London, 1997), pp164-92.
18. Hans van Lemmen, *Tiles in Architecture* (Laurence King Publishing, London, 1993), p117.
19. Wight, *Brick Building*, p181.
20. Nikolaus Pevsner and Bill Wilson, *Norfolk 2: North-West and South*. Buildings of England (Penguin, London, 2000), p582.
21. Anthony Barnes, 'Pugin Rediscovered?' *Ecclesiology Today*, (2001) 26, pp30-33.
22. Lynn Pearson, 'Memorial and Commemorative Tiles in Nineteenth and Early Twentieth Century Churches', *TACS Journal*, 9 (2003), pp13-23.
23. The editor is grateful to James Bettley for information on Southery Church.
24. Barnes, 'Pugin Rediscovered?'
25. Paul Atterbury and Clive Wainwright, *Pugin: A Gothic Passion* (Yale University Press, New Haven and London, 1994), pp146-7.
26. Pevsner, *Norfolk2*, p797.
27. Michael Stratton, *The Terracotta Revival* (Victor Gollancz, London, 1993), p54.

Northamptonshire

Although it cannot be said that Northamptonshire is a major ceramic county, it has a number of interesting locations, notably those with Minton tiles designed by Lord Alwyne Frederick Compton (1825-1906), bishop of Ely 1886-1905 and chairman of the influential Architectural Society of the Archdeaconry of Northampton. His work deserves more attention, for Sir George Gilbert Scott remarked that 'No one has equalled (Pugin) in the designing of patterns, though I think Lord Alwyne Compton greatly excels him in arrangement.'[1] In Northamptonshire his tiles may be seen at the churches of Castle Ashby, Easton Maudit and Northampton (Holy Sepulchre), with possible attributions at Cotterstock and Pilton; in Leicestershire, they may be found at Theddingworth and Oakham (Rutland). Lord Alwyne's family home was Castle Ashby, itself one of the best two surviving locations in England for Blashfield's terracotta, produced over the Lincolnshire border in Stamford.

In addition, Northamptonshire can offer late Coade stone at Easton Neston, a tile pavement donated by Herbert Minton at Winwick, fine Powell's work at Kelmarsh, and the massive Barratt's works at Northampton with its gargantuan terracotta lettering by Gibbs & Canning. Modern locations are scarce apart from the tile pavement of Northampton's Guildhall, which was recreated in the early 1990s. The *Gazetteer* entry for Northamptonshire covers the administrative area of Northamptonshire County Council.

ALTHORP

The dairy built in 1786 at **Althorp**, near Great Brington, is one of the most important survivors from a group of eighteenth-century tiled dairies put up for aristocrats on their country estates. It has an original Wedgwood tiled interior, mostly in white but with some decoration in the form of a trailing ivy motif, with fittings also by Wedgwood. The dairy was erected for Lavinia, Lady Spencer, on her return from France, where she had seen Marie Antoinette's dairy at Versailles under construction.[2]

CASTLE ASHBY

The four linked terraced gardens lying to the east and north of **Castle Ashby**, an Elizabethan and Jacobean mansion, are defined by terracotta balustrades made at the works of John Blashfield in Stamford. The gardens were completed in 1864, to the designs of W. B. Thomas, and the ornate balustrades added about two years later; the whole project was supervised by Sir Matthew Digby Wyatt for the 3rd marquess of Northampton. The outer balustrades, which separate the terraces from the park, have continuous lettering in imitation of the south parapet of the house itself, the text being as follows: 'The grass withereth and the flower fadeth but the word of the Lord endureth for ever' and 'Consider the lilies of the field how they grow they toil not neither do they spin and yet I say unto you that Solomon in all his glory was not arrayed like one of these'. Finally comes a Latin dedication to Theodosia, the 3rd marchioness, who died in 1865 before the terraces were complete.

Completing this excellent display of early terracotta are two terracotta fountains (east terrace) and a large terracotta urn to the north-east. Almost adjoining the balustrades east of the house is the **Church of St Mary Magdalene**, whose rector during 1852-78 was the high churchman and antiquarian Lord Alwyne Compton, son of the second marquess of Northampton. The church, which was restored in 1870 by G. E. Street, has Minton tiles designed by Lord Alwyne Compton, whose skill in the design of tile arrangements was admired by Sir George Gilbert Scott.[3]

EASTON MAUDIT

The **Church of St Peter & St Paul** has an exceptional Minton pavement running throughout the church; motifs include the motto of the marquesses of Northampton, a mitre and pairs of birds. The tiling dates from 1859-60 and was designed by Lord Alwyne Compton while he was rector of Castle Ashby, a couple of miles to the west.

EASTON NESTON

The grand gateway screen of **Easton Neston** house, which now forms the entrance to Towcester Racecourse, dates from around 1822 and was made by William Croggon, who bought Mrs Coade's business following her death in 1821 (Fig 202). The single-storey Coade stone archway, which is signed Croggan rather than Croggon, is crowned by a coat of arms while the two lodges are each topped by recumbent hinds.[4]

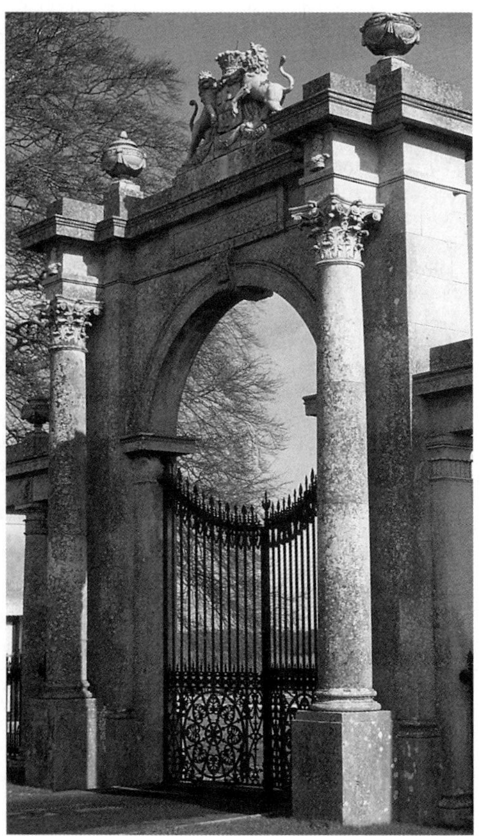

Fig 202.

KELMARSH

The lavish high Victorian interior of the **Church of St Dionysius** (also known as St Denys) results from work undertaken by the architect J. K. Colling in 1874. Its chancel wall decoration includes a Powell's opus sectile panel designed by H. E. Wooldridge and depicting the Four Evangelists with St Denys; it cost just over £77, about £20 more than the east wall opus sectile panel of St Peter and St Paul, also by Wooldridge.[5]

NORTHAMPTON

Northampton's gothic **Guildhall** in St Giles's Square was built in 1861-4 to the designs of the young architect E. W. Godwin, later to become one of the leading figures in the aesthetic movement. The building was greatly extended in 1889-92 and again in the early 1990s; the latter work, completed in 1992, included the refurbishment of Godwin's original gothic structure under the direction of the architect Roderick Gradidge.[6] Godwin's designs for the tiled floor and wall tiling of the council chamber have survived in the Victoria and Albert Museum. They include Godwin's earliest known individual tile design, dating from around 1863, which was intended to be used in a band of glazed tiles on the lower part of the wall. These were not executed, probably due to financial constraints in the fitting-out phase of construction; it is unclear whether the pavement was unexecuted or had simply not survived.[7] Gradidge therefore worked with H. & R. Johnson's to recreate the pavement from Godwin's drawings, which show the tiles forming a mostly geometric border in black, buff and red around a central oak floor. The major decorative element was the inclusion of the town's coat of arms.

To the north of the Guildhall in Abington Square is the Doulton terracotta statue of the MP **Charles Bradlaugh** (by George Tinworth, 1894). A little to the west in Sheep Street is the ancient Church of the Holy Sepulchre, with its rare circular nave. Sir George Gilbert Scott's additions of 1860-4 included a semicircular apse with tiles by Lord Alwyne Compton of about 1861.

Much the most impressive of Northampton's ceramic locations lies on the northern edge of the town: the ornate neo-baroque form of **Barratt's Footshape Bootworks** (1913), Kingsthorpe Hollow, Kingsthorpe Road. This three-storey red brick and terracotta factory building proudly displays the words 'Footshape' and 'Bootworks' in Gibbs & Canning's tawny terracotta as larger-than-life parapet lettering.

THORPE MANDEVILLE

The chancel of the medieval **Church of St John Baptist** was restored by the architect Albert Hartshorne in 1872. Powell's of Whitefriars supplied several windows for the rebuilt chancel as well as an early example of opus sectile work for the reredos, which, unusually, was to the architect's own design. It includes figures of St Mary and St John, and cost £30.[8]

WINWICK

The chancel of **St Michael's Church** was added around 1853 to the design of the architect E. F. Law. Its pavement comprises tiles donated to the church in August 1852 by their manufacturer, Herbert Minton.[9]

Northamptonshire Roundup

Inside All Saints Church, Blakesley Lane, **Adstone** are nineteenth-century ceramic tablets bearing religious texts. The expensive reconstruction of the chancel of St Mary's Church, **Ashley** by Sir George Gilbert Scott in 1867 included the installation of a marble and encaustic tile pavement. St Mary's Church, **Benefield**, a lavish Tractarian building of 1847, has an encaustic tile pavement throughout. In the drawing room of **Canons Ashby House** (NT) is a magnificent fire surround which includes some delft tiles. The chancel tiles at St Andrew's Church (restored by G. E. Street in 1877), **Cotterstock** may have been designed by Lord Alwyne Compton. Maw & Co supplied the chancel pavement at St Peter's Church, **Deene**, which was restored in 1868-9 and is now in the care of the Churches Conservation Trust. Maw's were also responsible for the pretty chancel pavement at St Mary's Church, **East Haddon** restored in 1878 by E. F. Law & Sons.[10] There are mid-fourteenth century tiles in the chancel of St Mary's Church, **Higham Ferrers**. In West Street, **Oundle**, near the market square, is the butcher's shop of Johnson & Sons, its tiled stall risers displaying a good pair of animal panels. The chancel pavement (probably 1864) at St Mary and All Saints, **Pilton** includes tiles with bird and animal motifs, and could well be the work of Lord Alwyne Compton. There is a patterned Minton tile pavement in the sanctuary of St John Evangelist, **Whitfield**, rebuilt by the architect Henry Woodyer in 1869-70.[11] The sanctuary of St Mary the Virgin, **Woodford Halse** has a roof lined on the interior with encaustic tiles; this perhaps dates from the 1878 restoration of the church.

References

1. Geoffrey K. Brandwood, *Bringing them to their knees: church-building and restoration in Leicestershire and Rutland 1800-1914* (Leicestershire Archaeological and Historical Society, Leicester, 2002), p39.
2. Alison Kelly, *Decorative Wedgwood in architecture and furniture* (Country Life, London, 1965), p121.
3. Nikolaus Pevsner and Bridget Cherry, *Northamptonshire* Buildings of England (Penguin Books, London, 1973).
4. Alison Kelly, *Mrs Coade's Stone* (Self Publishing Association, Upton-upon-Severn, 1990), pp207, 366.
5. Dennis W. Hadley, *James Powell & Sons: A listing of opus sectile, 1847-1973*, (2001).
6. Michael Hall, 'Modern Gothic', *Country Life*, 187, 4th February 1993, pp48-51.
7. Susan Weber Soros, ed. *E. W. Godwin: Aesthetic Movement Architect and Designer* (Yale University Press, New Haven and London, 1999), pp301-5.
8. Hadley, *James Powell & Sons*, 2001.
9. 'The Late Herbert Minton, Esq.' *Annals of the Diocese of Lichfield, past and present: being a Supplement to the Lichfield Church Calendar*, (1859) Crewe, Newcastle-under-Lyme, pp83-88. Reprinted in *Glazed Expressions* 32, Spring 1996, pp3-6. This encomium, published in the year following Minton's death, details the 173 gifts made by Herbert Minton to churches and other institutions.
10. *The Builder*, vol 36, 6th July 1878.
11. John Elliott and John Pritchard, eds, *Henry Woodyer: Gentleman Architect* (Department of Continuing Education, University of Reading, Reading, 2002).

Northumberland

The north-east is tile rather than terracotta country. The local clay did not have the specific properties required for terracotta production, and it never became a part of Newcastle's Victorian townscape in the manner of other northern cities. There is however, despite the lack of any significant local tile manufacturers, a wealth of late Victorian ceramic interiors in Newcastle, and some unusual tiles in the county as a whole, notably at Brinkburn Priory, Morpeth and Stamfordham. Of course, in this hard-drinking area, many turn-of-the-century ceramic pub facades have survived, but no interiors. The current revival of Newcastle's fortunes has led to the restoration of some important buildings - most recently the first class refreshment room at the railway station - while several present-day ceramicists have large installations in and around the city. And there is the unique underwater ceramic experience of the 1950s Tyne Tunnels! Suggested reading: apart from the Maling Pottery, the county's ceramic history has not been well-documented; it is difficult to recommend anything other than TACS Tour Notes *Newcastle upon Tyne* (1990, 1993, 2002). The *Gazetteer* entry for Northumberland covers the administrative areas of Newcastle upon Tyne City Council, North Tyneside Borough Council and Northumberland County Council.

BELSAY

Belsay village clings to a sharp bend in the main road between Newcastle and the Scottish Borders, its precise stone arcade proclaiming the existence of a noble neighbour. A winding lane swings away across the fields, soon revealing the awesome silhouette of **Belsay Hall** (EH), a crushingly severe Greek temple set amidst the Northumbrian countryside. It was designed and built by Sir Charles Monck in 1807-17, the inspiration coming from the architectural wonders viewed during his honeymoon tour of Europe in 1804-6. Its golden sandstone, pitted with flecks of iron ore, was dug from a site beside the house, now an idyllic quarry garden leading to the ruins of the original Belsay Castle. The Hall itself is entered between a pair of vast and chilling fluted columns, and the visitor is then deposited in the central hall, a cool and perfect space of naked stone. Beyond is a series of secondary rooms, some floorless due to rot; in the strange setting of one of these cavernous holes, a Dutch-tiled fireplace still adheres to the wall. The tiles of this pretty little piece came from the Tjallingii works in Harlingen between 1870 and 1910, the motifs being mainly maritime scenes. The fireplace was probably introduced by Sir Charles Monck's grandson, Sir Arthur Middleton; Monck himself built the model village.

BLTYH

The **Harbour Commissioners' Offices** on BRIDGE STREET is a reminder of this sad little town's industrial past, when shipbuilding and coalmining brought a sort of prosperity. Its architects were the well-known Newcastle firm of Cackett & Burns Dick, who were also responsible for the unusual concrete pleasure dome of Whitley Bay's Spanish City. In 1913 they housed the Commissioners in a solid and substantial corner block, its circular entrance lobby leading to stairs giving access to the boardroom, which is decorated by panels of Dutch tiles (mostly showing landscapes) taken from the S.S. *Walmer Castle*, built in 1902 and broken up at Blyth in 1932. Blyth also sports a couple of typically north-eastern brown and yellow faience pub facades, probably by Burmantofts: the **Blyth & Tyne Hotel**, REGENT STREET, and the **Masons Arms**, PLESSEY ROAD. Both have decent lettering while the latter has a nice bay window.

BRINKBURN PRIORY

To reach **Brinkburn Priory** (EH) one must descend a craggy, winding path from the road; below, the Coquet slithers over its rocky bed whilst alongside tree roots like elephant trunks curl across the rocks, gripping tight to avoid plunging downward. At the bottom of the hill is the Priory, set in a tiny glade partly bordered by the river and hemmed in by verdant woodland. Erection of the church for its Augustinian community began just before the end of the twelfth century and took about thirty years, with additions in the fourteenth century. From the early seventeenth century decay set in, and it was not until the mid nineteenth century that restoration was contemplated; work began in

1858, with the structure completed in 1859, although furnishing took a further eight years. The architect was Thomas Austin of Newcastle, a pupil of John Dobson who practised on his own account from around 1855, and eventually took over Dobson's substantial practice in 1865.

The Priory is almost Norman in style, its arched windows having the merest of points; the squat tower hardly rises above the roof-ridges. Inside is a wonderful ethereal space, with a tiled floor as strange as the surroundings, though not unattractive. The pavement - which dates from 1858 and extends throughout the church - is a geometric mosaic of small, now-unglazed tiles, ranging in colour from black to a pale buff, with one or two royal blue examples near the altar. These latter, which have retained their glaze, form a star-shape. The tiles are laid in various geometric patterns, notably a chequerboard formation beneath the crossing. All the tiles were made specially for the restoration, and the designs are likely to have been based on those of the few remaining original medieval tiles, now reset beneath the high altar. Altogether it is a curiosity.

It has been suggested that the tiles were a product of a local brickworks, whose inexperience resulted in the glaze flaking off most of the tiles; however, the restoration of Ponteland Church, a few miles north-west of Newcastle, in 1861-2 included the installation of 'an encaustic-tiled pavement from the tileworks at Brenckburn'. Perhaps tilemaking was a short-lived experiment at a brickworks near Brinkburn, an alternative to buying in tiles from afar for the new floor. Certainly Minton tiles had already been used locally for both new churches and restorations, for instance at Meldon, where Dobson (possibly with the assistance of his pupil Austin) restored the medieval church in 1849.[1] Austin's restoration of the Priory was seen as sensitive and restrained; perhaps he simply disliked the bright, modern Minton tiles, and set up the Brinkburn tileworks to provide what he saw as a more appropriate alternative.

BYWELL

The seemingly remote churches of **St Andrew** and St Peter stand barely one hundred yards apart, between the grounds of Bywell Hall and the north bank of the Tyne. Their idyllic and unusual situation results from their erection either side of the boundary of a pre-Conquest division of lands, which eventually came to be adjoining Norman baronies. The mainly thirteenth century body of St Andrew's was altered in 1830, then in 1850 by John Dobson of Newcastle, and again in 1871; these latter works included stained glass by William Wailes of Newcastle, who is buried at St Peter Bywell. The glory of the church, apart from the fine Saxon tower and the many early grave covers, is the decorative scheme of its sanctuary, which is in the style favoured by the artist and designer Walter Crane (Fig 203).

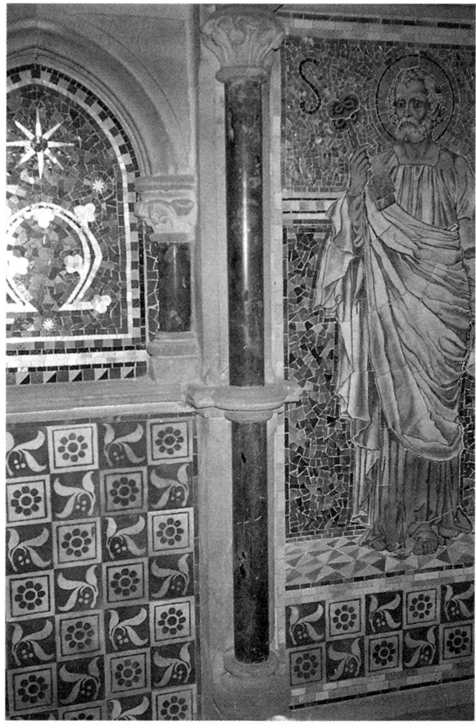

Fig 203.

Crane visited Bywell in 1871, during a sketching tour commissioned through Somerset Beaumont of Bywell Hall, but it was not until the early 1880s that the new scheme was begun.[2] As well as stained glass in the north transept and chancel, it included a wonderful reredos which combines mosaics (mainly in gold and shades of blue), attractive red and white glass tiles - quartered, with a floral design - and opus sectile depictions of Saints Andrew and Peter. The whole was designed, like the east window, by John W. Brown of the manufacturers James Powell & Sons, Whitefriars, London. St Andrew's was declared redundant in 1973; it is normally open to the public.

CRAMLINGTON

In the first floor café of the **Concordia Leisure Centre** in MANOR WALKS SHOPPING CENTRE is a large (about 5′ by 4′) and colourful tile panel, installed in 1995 to mark European Nature Conservation Year. It was designed and painted for CONE - the Cramlington Organisation for Nature and the Environment, a group comprising local business, wildlife and council interests - by the Gateshead-based ceramist Christine Constant. The intricate and detailed images, including Cramlington landmarks and an assortment of flora and fauna, were based on designs suggested by local schoolchildren; the mole in the bottom right-hand corner is especially jolly.

HOWDON

The northern entrance to the **Tyne Pedestrian and Cycle Tunnels**, an elegant circular structure known as the Howdon Rotunda, lies off BEWICKE STREET just west of the Tyne Vehicle Tunnel entrance. In 1937, just nine years after the opening of the Tyne Bridge, Durham and Northumberland Councils put forward a scheme for a road tunnel between Howdon and Jarrow; this was approved in 1943. The intention was to build a vehicle tunnel and two smaller tunnels, for pedestrians and cycles, but post-war restrictions on capital expenditure meant work went ahead only on the smaller tunnels, beginning in 1947. The tunnels were completed in 1951 and were used by 18,000 people a day at their peak. The foot tunnel has a wooden-tread escalator with a vertical rise of 85′ through a 200′ long tunnel, one of the longest in the world at the time of construction; the tunnels were awarded grade II listed status in 2000.

Both the pedestrian tunnel (900′ long, 10′ 6″ diameter) and the cycle tunnel (900′ long, 12′ diameter) are lined throughout with yellow and - mainly - pale green tiles produced by Carter's of Poole.[3] There are tiled signs near the tunnel entrances for 'Pedestrians' and 'Cycles', and in the centre of the tunnel, about 40′ below the River Tyne, are boundary plaques for the counties of 'Northumberland' and 'Durham'. A walk or cycle beneath the Tyne provides a unique ceramic experience.

Returning to the surface, just to the east is the **Tyne Vehicle Tunnel**, opened in 1967; its pedestrian walkways (no public entry), running above and beside the road, are partly faced with Italian marble mosaic in pale pastel colours. The later tollbooths, which replaced the original and inefficient conical models, have white vitreous tiling (now overpainted) on the underside of their curved flying canopies. Escape from traffic noise at the **Duke of Wellington**, close to the tunnel entrance in NORTHUMBERLAND DOCK ROAD. Its facade is a typical example of the local style in early twentieth century pub fronts: severely classical yellow and brown faience enlivened with elegant lettering.

LONGHIRST

St John's Church is a perfect, barely changed example of a church given to a village by local landowners, in this case the Lawsons of Longhirst Hall, which is hidden in the trees to the west of the church. St John's was built in 1876 by Sir Arthur Blomfield and embellished in the early twentieth century by the Joicey family, then resident in the Hall; memorials to various Joiceys who met untimely ends are scattered around the nave. The church is small but attractive, with interesting stained glass and an intricate wooden rood screen, an Edwardian addition carved by the Reverend Proctor and his villagers, who produced it as an evening class exercise. The fussily patterned sanctuary tiling is very probably by Maw & Co.

MINSTERACRES

The approach to Minsteracres, once the home of the Silvertop family but now a retreat, is unforgettable: an avenue of monstrous Californian Redwoods leads toward the house, their trunks appearing to swirl as one progresses between them - shades of Pinocchio and the magic broomsticks. Escaping into daylight at the end of this weird lane, one sees the house, built in 1758 but much modified during the following century, to which the family's private chapel is attached. This is now the **R. C. Church of St Elizabeth of Hungary**, put up in 1854 by Joseph Hansom, founder of *The Builder*. The little church has an unusual openwork clock tower, while the interior sports a highly (and lovingly!) polished floor of red, yellow and black geometric tiles, set in a striking hexagonal pattern which repeats throughout the church.

MORPETH

St James the Great, NEWGATE STREET, is a neo-Norman church built in 1844-6 by the architect Benjamin Ferrey for the Reverend Francis Richard Grey (the sixth son of Earl Grey of Reform Bill fame). Reverend Grey, who had spent his honeymoon in Italy during 1840, wanted his new church to be similar in style to the cathedral at Monreale near Palermo, Sicily. Ferrey obliged, designing a thoroughly Norman building which could seat 1,030 people. The elaborate tiled pavement in the chancel and sanctuary was donated by Herbert Minton in 1845; Italian craftsmen were brought to Morpeth to lay the tiles (Fig 204). A letter dated 2nd June 1844, from Minton to the Building Committee of St James, tells how he felt it to be 'a privilege in helping forward the good and holy work in which you are engaged'.[4]

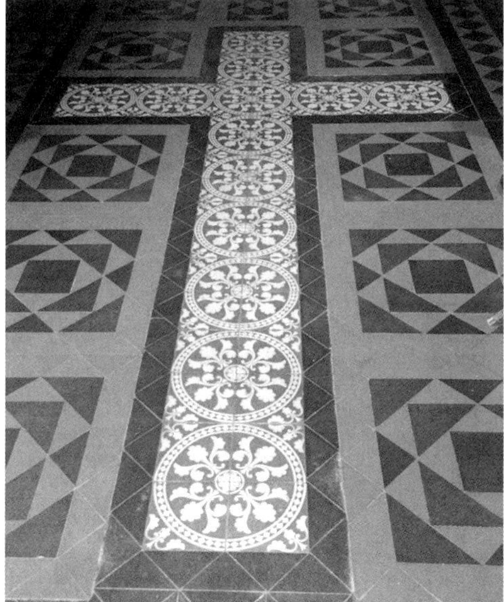

Fig 204.

The Reverend's sister-in-law was Harriet, Duchess of Sutherland, an early patron of Herbert Minton; Minton tiles were used extensively at her home Trentham Park, Staffordshire, built during 1833-42. The brother of the Duchess was George Howard, the seventh earl of Carlisle; as Viscount Morpeth, he was MP for the town during 1826-30 and his father, the Earl of Carlisle, donated part of the site for the new church. The web of personal connections between Herbert Minton and this particular church appears to have encouraged him to give a donation of the highest design quality. The motif of the choir pavement is a large Latin cross comprising blue and cream foliage pattern tiles, within a red and black geometric pavement. Tiled risers lead up to a further pavement, where a Greek cross bearing lines of biblical text divides roundels of the evangelists. The sanctuary pavement, which includes a variety of repeat patterns, is reached via more lettered risers. A series of painted murals in the apse, executed by artists from the London firm of Clayton & Bell in 1875, completes the decorative scheme of this extraordinary church.

NEWCASTLE UPON TYNE

This description of Newcastle begins with the railway station, sited high on the north bank of the Tyne at the critical junction between the river gorge, with its unique collection of bridges, and the clean-cut stone-built lay-out of Graingertown, Richard Grainger's redevelopment of the 1820s and 1830s. The medieval city's centre was the quayside, but by the eighteenth century new squares and streets were being built well above the river, and now the centre of activity is the 135' high Grey's Monument (1838), near the southern end of Northumberland Street, Newcastle's peerless gift to northern shoppers. Most routes from quayside to Monument offer wonderful views due to the steepness of the river bank, the sheer number of bridges, the constant changes of level and the survival of many narrow passageways and stairs. Late twentieth-century reconstruction of the quayside has opened up the river promenade, but added little in the way of good building.

The **Central Station**, NEVILLE STREET, with its stunning curved trainshed, was built in 1845-50 by Newcastle architect John Dobson, although the grand porte cochère was a later addition. As part of an 1892-3 scheme by North Eastern Railway architect William Bell, which included extensions to the neighbouring Station Hotel, Dobson's original waiting room was clad in faience and became the First Class Refreshment Room, now the Centurion Bar (Fig 205). A ceramic interior was chosen partly to cut the costs of cleaning the smoke-filled rooms of the time.[5] It is decorated with Burmantofts faience in baroque style from floor to ceiling, and top-lit by a faience-clad lantern. The main colours are browns, yellows and greens, with columns of circular and square cross section at either end of the room. A semi-circular faience-fronted bar, originally sited at the western end of the room, was removed many years ago (and replaced by a concrete police cell, itself now demolished), but a wooden replacement was introduced during restoration in 2000. This work included stripping overpainted tiles, revealing the lantern and repairing damaged areas of faience with fibrous plaster; if not a full restoration, at least this amazing room - one of the best-remaining railway interiors in the country - is now in use once again.

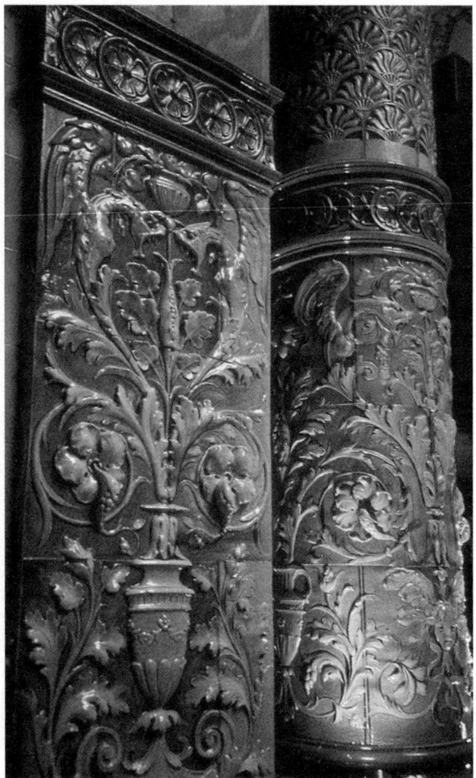

Fig 205.

Almost opposite the front of the station is **St Mary's R. C. Cathedral**, CLAYTON STREET WEST. The church was designed by A. W. N. Pugin and built in 1842-4; it became the cathedral in 1850. The spire was added in 1872 by local architects Dunn & Hansom. The floor has many plain tiles interspersed with patterned encaustic designs, probably dating from the original period of construction, although some retiling took place in 1901. Around the font is a small square dais tiled with repeats of a gothic 'M' design in buff and red. The most interesting and unusual tiles - the frieze which runs at window-sill level around the body of the cathedral - were added in 1901-2, when the baptistery (now the entrance porch) was built (Fig 206). The frieze, mainly in mauve and yellow, carries names of Northumbrian saints (south) and English martyrs (north) on scrolls and within canopies. Most of the martyrs were priests and many have now been canonised. The frieze also includes the names of relatives of the benefactors who paid for this idiosyncratic tiling, which was made by the local stained glass and church decorating firm Atkinson Brothers; the name Atkinson features amongst the benefactors. There is also wall tiling in the north (Blessed Sacrament) chapel and in the confessionals to the south of the altar.

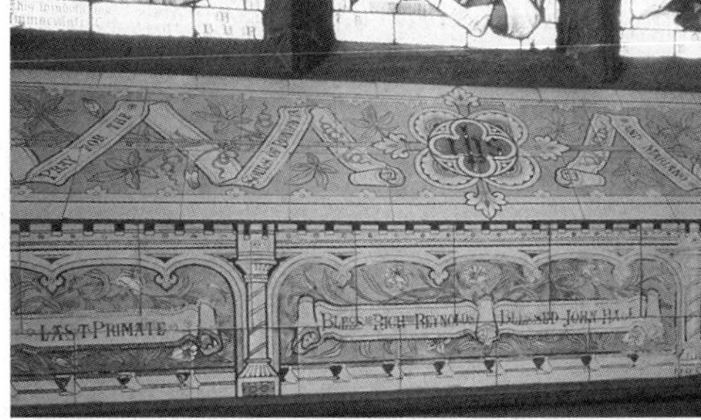

Fig 206.

Fig 207.

Just north is **Newcastle Arts Centre**, WESTGATE ROAD, where what has been described as the largest handmade tile project of the twentieth century took place during 1982-8. Changing teams of community programme workers, funded by the Manpower Services Commission and known as the Newcastle Arts Centre Tile Workshop, designed and made the geometric terracotta floor tiles and brilliantly colourful wall mosaics which line the floor and walls of the rambling Art Centre; some tiles were even made from clay dug on site. The mosaics in the ladies' loo are especially good! Further west is **Newcastle Discovery Museum**, BLANDFORD SQUARE. This grandiose structure was built as a warehouse and offices for the Co-operative Wholesale Society in 1897-9 by Oliver, Leeson and Wood. Apart from great views over the city, the top floor Great Hall (originally the Co-op staff restaurant) has a ceramic frieze in a highly glazed, rich deep blue and white relief pattern involving urns and foliage with repeats of a grotesque face; it was probably made by Burmantofts (Fig 207). Alterations to the building in the 1920s included two stylish Art Deco tiled toilets: the larger, for the board of directors, has blue tiles and fittings throughout, while the smaller - for the chairman - has a yellow theme.

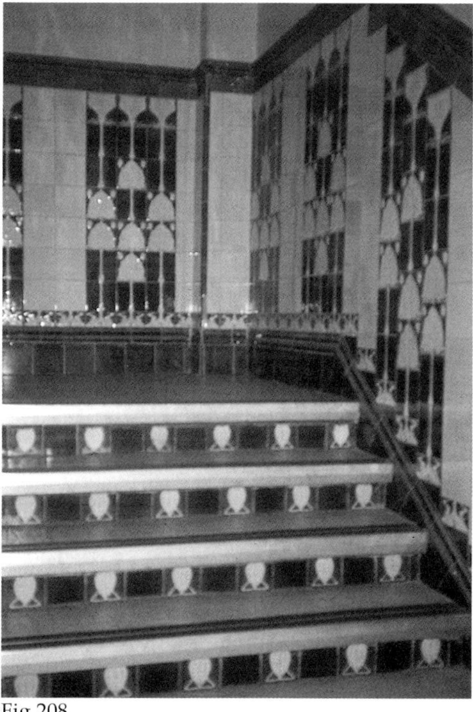

Fig 208.

East of the station in DEAN STREET, **Milburn House** is the massive corner office block built in 1902-5 on a sloping site by Oliver, Leeson and Wood. Its six entrances, on all sides and varying levels, lead into a baffling maze of corridors tiled art nouveau-style in mainly green and yellow (Fig 208). The Dean Street entrance lobby is especially impressive, with its painted leather panels and high-level tiled frieze; this combines primrose yellow and deep green in a swirling floral design. Also visible from the lobby are exquisite stair risers with a heart motif. The tiles were manufactured by H. & R. Johnson of Stoke-on-Trent, who were also responsible for their restoration in 1991, when the firm found that variations in size and colour of the originals made for some difficulties with production of replacements.

Fig 209.

A little way up Dean Street is another tall office block, **Cathedral Buildings** (1901), with a turquoise-pattern tiled dado winding throughout its stairwell. On the corner of Dean Street and MOSLEY STREET is the former **Prudential Assurance Building**, now a café. Built in 1891-7 by Alfred Waterhouse, the ground floor interior has a sparkling Burmantofts faience scheme, including open arches; the colours are mainly pale green and yellow.[6] Heading north into CLOTH MARKET, the **Bee Hive** appears at the junction with High Bridge (Fig 209). The pub was rebuilt by Newcastle Breweries in 1902, using their regular local architects Joseph Oswald & Son. Its ground floor facade is decorated with green and yellow faience in a floral pattern with bees and beehives hidden in the leaves; it is likely to be by Burmantofts, as the Oswalds often used this firm.

At the top of GREY STREET is the **Central Arcade**, created when the interior of Exchange Buildings was burnt out around 1904. Its replacement, designed by Joseph and Harold Oswald and completed in 1906, was the glorious Central Arcade, its two storeys of shops faced entirely in brown and yellow Burmantofts faience (Fig 210). This contract appears to be the last substantial interior completed in Burmantofts faience.[7] The brightly unpleasant floor, which replaced the worn original 'vitreous imitation marble mosaic' in 1990, is of American Olean mosaics; the excuse was that no English supplier could be found. Just west of the Monument on BLACKETT STREET is **Parsons Polygon**, a rugged hexagonal rocket cone sculpted in brick and tile cladding by David Hamilton in 1985. Its subject is Sir Charles Parsons, creator of the turbine-powered *Turbinia,* and the structure is actually a ventilator shaft for the Metro station beneath. The designs of the tiles were taken from Parsons' engineering drawings.[8]

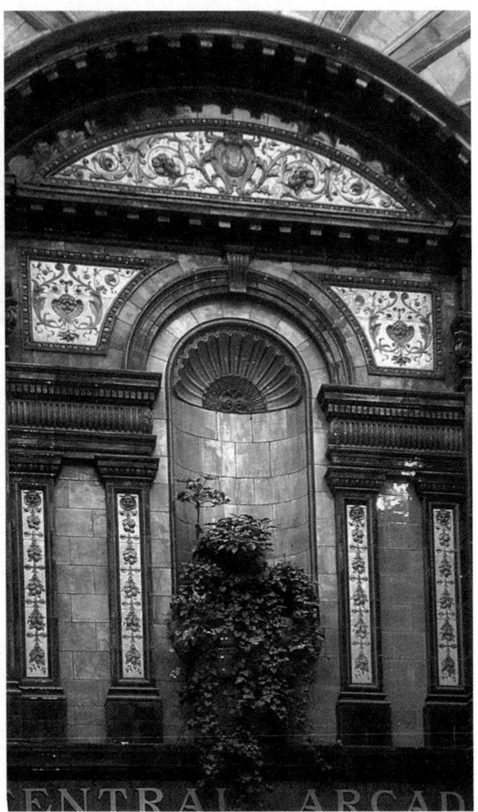
Fig 210.

Further west of the centre on GALLOWGATE is **Magnet House**, built for the General Electric Company around 1938. Its facade includes thirteen 3' square art deco low relief terracotta panels (in four different designs) showing human figures symbolic of power generation. Similar motifs were used on the interior of Battersea Power Station in the first stage of its construction in 1929-35.[9] North on HAYMARKET, the former **Newcastle Breweries Offices** were erected by Oswald & Son in 1896-1901 (Fig 211). The entrance hall, the arcaded clerks' and accountants' room, and an upper corridor were all faced in faience - almost certainly Burmantofts - mainly in turquoise, buff and pale yellow; the Newcastle Breweries logo panels are particularly fine. This type of interior tile scheme, often included in late nineteenth-century bank, insurance company and utilities offices, is a rarity in a brewery context.

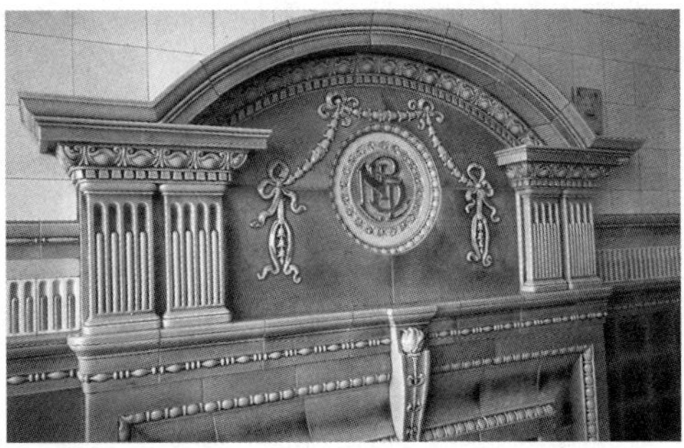
Fig 211.

Nearby is the **Royal Victoria Infirmary**, QUEEN VICTORIA ROAD. The RVI, designed by W. L. Newcombe and Percy Adams, was built during 1900-6 and features much plain tiling by Maw's in its opulent entrance hall and corridors; the beautiful little chapel also has gold and blue mosaics.[10] The Building Committee was convinced that bright, colourful decoration was necessary for the children's wards, and sample tile panels were obtained from Doulton and W. B. Simpson; Doulton's designs were selected in 1904. The scheme, comprising 61 nursery rhyme and fairy tale panels, is almost completely intact, with only a handful of panels now hidden from view. This is probably the most complete set of such panels still in existence; they were made at the Lambeth works and signed by the artists William Rowe, John McLennan and Margaret Thompson.[11] Welcome additions to the hospital's artworks in 1998 were the three ceramic panels by Paul Scott sited in the Opthalmology reception area (Fig 212).[12] The large, vibrant installations burst with colourful local images, while a snake-like motorway winds through the largest panel. The designs resulted from consultation with hospital users, who wanted to include city landmarks, particularly the football ground, thus ex-England centre forward and local hero Alan Shearer features prominently on this ceramic St James's Park.

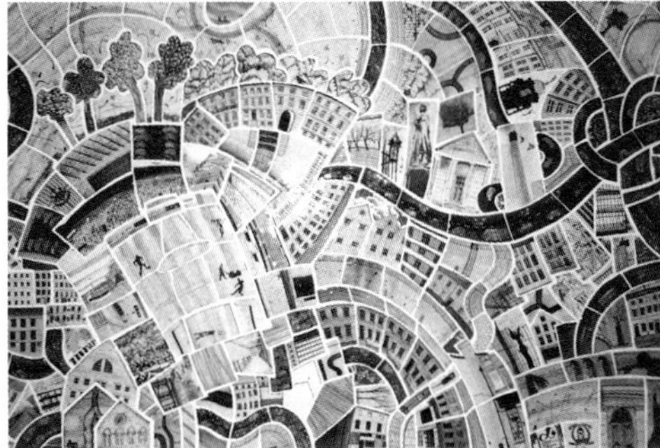

Fig 212.

East of the Monument at the **Laing Gallery**, JOHN DOBSON STREET is the Blue Carpet, an outdoor public square floored with 22,500 purpose-made tiles made from white resin and recycled glass shards; it was created by the artist Thomas Heatherwick and installed during 2001-2. The Blue Carpet looks stunning at night, when the neon lighting beneath the seats - chunks of turned-up carpet - is seen to best effect. Further east on NEW BRIDGE STREET is the **Gibson Street Centre**, a complex of baths and wash-houses designed by the city architect F. H. Holford and opened in 1907 (Fig 213). They were considered to be the latest thing in bath design, and included a glazed brick entrance hall with five Carter's pictorial tile panels, each around 4′ high by 2′ wide. Four show aquatic scenes - jolly water-polo players, nubile mermaids - while a less inspiring fifth lists the members of the Baths and Wash-houses Committee.[13]

In NORTHUMBERLAND STREET, just north of the Monument, is the heavily classical facade of **Fenwick's** department store, one of the last surviving historic shopfronts in this famous shopping street. The monster white faience facade, designed by shop-fitting specialist Cyril Lyon, was added to Fenwick's 1885 building in 1913. When restored and extended in 1996 by Shaws of Darwen, it was the largest-ever British faience contract. Further north in NORTHUMBERLAND ROAD is a real joy, a collection of grotesque bright red terracotta gargoyles peering down from the equally bright red terracotta parapet of the **Sutherland Building**,

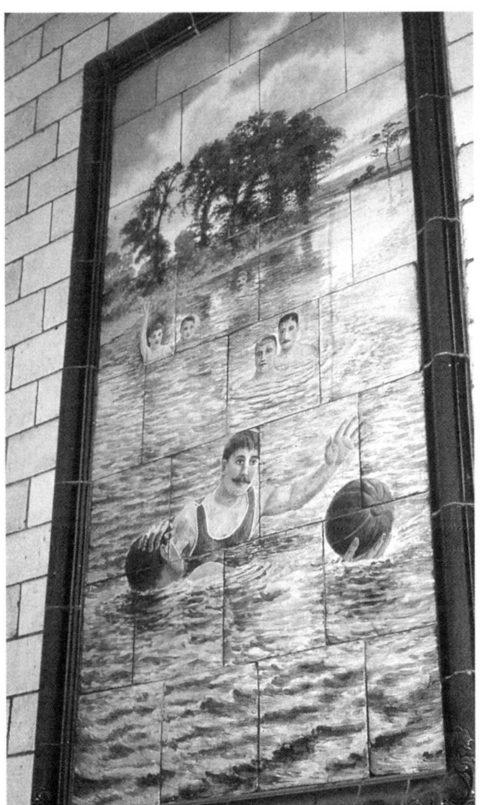

Fig 213.

University of Northumbria. As the lettering 'DUMS' announces, this was once the Durham University Medical School, erected in 1887 by Dunn, Hansom & Dunn. Were the weird animals meant to inspire the Victorian tyro medics? The terracotta was probably manufactured by Doulton's, as this architectural practice used the firm for their slightly earlier St Bede's College, Manchester (which also has strange, high relief detailing).[14] North again to the University of Newcastle's campus and the **Robinson Library**, off JESMOND ROAD. The lengthy issue desk carries seventeen tile panels installed in 1997 and designed by local tilemaker Charles Allen of Newcastle Delft. The design - a John Ruskin quotation in black Gothic lettering with illuminated letters in blue, red, black and gold - was inspired by a typeface from the fifteenth century *Sarum Missal*, one of the earliest books in the library's collection. Seen from a distance, and preferably minus student queues, the effect is intriguing, but on closer inspection it is disappointing to find the quotation simply repeated several times over (although this was at the express wish of the client).

Byker

Thomas Miller auctioneers in Algernon Road has an excellent cream faience facade dating from 1926; the building was formerly occupied by the tea supplier's Rington's, their logo being displayed in coloured faience above the doorway.

Gosforth

Unique in Britain is the Doulton-tiled proscenium arch in the Jubilee Theatre at the old **St Nicholas Hospital**, JUBILEE ROAD, which was built around 1896 (Fig 214). The stage is 16′ high and 21′ wide, and the arch is outlined in white faience slabs with coloured insets. The full-height tube-lined tile surround was designed by W. J. Neatby, whose signature it bears, along with the date 1896. The flowing motifs include birds, flowers, elegantly curving trees and two languid female figures; the whole is very highly glazed in lustrous shades including a memorable iridescent purple. This awesome art nouveau scheme, with its kaleidoscopic colours, is the only one of its kind in any hospital. Doulton's also supplied the sanitary fittings for what was then the city asylum.

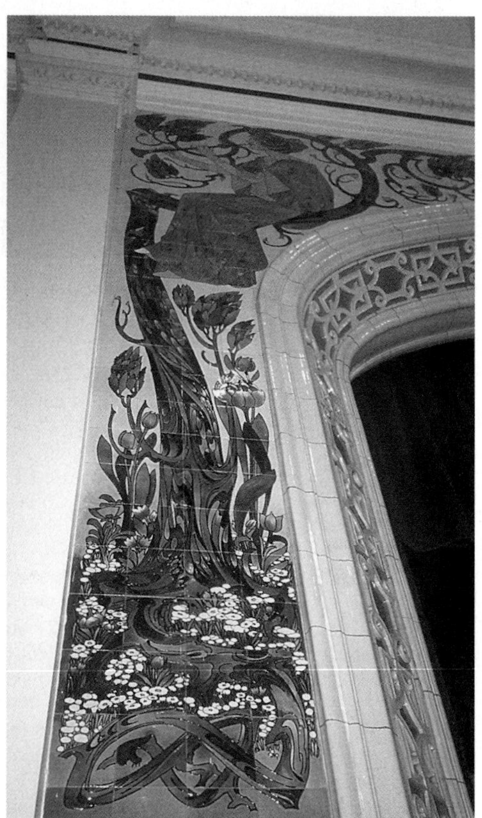

Fig 214.

One of the largest tile installations in Newcastle (a veritable city of grand gestures) is the mural 'Metro Morning' which spans the front of the **Regent Centre Metro Station**, GREAT NORTH ROAD. About three yards high by thirty yards long, it was installed in 1988 and depicts travellers on Metro trains (Fig 215). The artist was Anthony Lowe, who photographed his subjects during morning rush hours, then incorporated their life-size portraits into the final work using photographic silk-screening. The mural is one of several 'Art on the Metro' commissions to be found throughout the network, and includes much intricate and colourful detail of trains and track as well as the easily recognisable passengers; it was made at Ceramic Prints of Brighouse, near Huddersfield. Almost opposite the Metro station is **Asda**, where the Gosforth Community Mural, a high-relief interior ceramic panel showing local scenes, was installed in 1990.

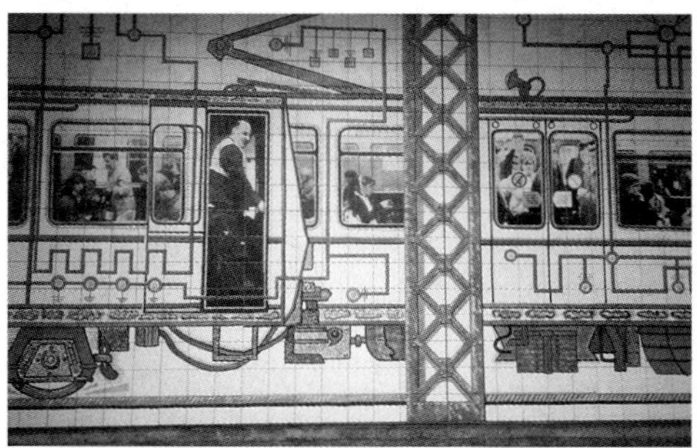

Fig 215.

Jesmond

A tall campanile signals the presence of a very unusual church in leafy Jesmond: **St George's Church**, OSBORNE ROAD was built in 1887-90 to the design of the architect Thomas R. Spence for the industrialist Charles Mitchell (1829-95), partner of Lord Armstrong. Mitchell had moved to Jesmond from the shipbuilding area of Walker, and it soon became clear to him that a new church was required for the expanding suburb. First he purchased a temporary iron church, then in 1886 offered to finance the construction of a new church, providing he was allowed a free hand in its design. He then engaged as his architect Spence, who specialised in lavish interiors and had previously enlarged Mitchell's house, Jesmond Towers; his son, the artist Charles William Mitchell (1854-1903), was deeply involved with the decoration of the church. The resulting interior, an essay in arts and crafts bordering on art nouveau, was expensive and stylish, and included a breathtaking chancel lined with tiles and mosaics which focused on a stunning white marble altar (Fig 216).

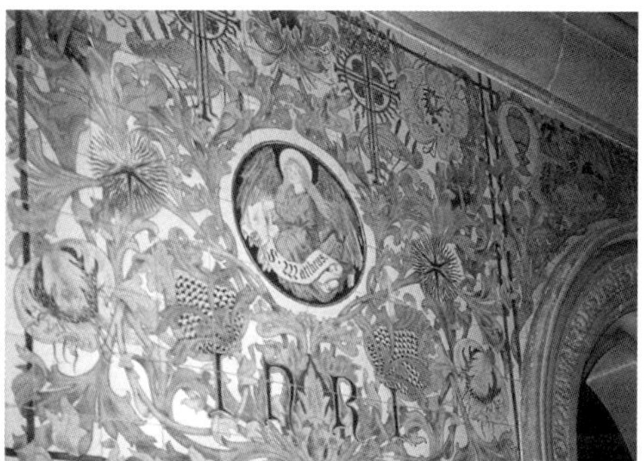
Fig 216.

Running round the sanctuary is a frieze of astonishing highly-glazed tiles: roundels of the evangelists are set in a surround of almost abstract luxuriant, curving foliage in bronze-yellow, gold and green. Christian symbols, including those of the Passion Cycle, are interwoven with huge blooms and fleshy leaves. Spence was responsible for this anarchic foliage, while the roundels were designed by George Woolliscroft Rhead (1854-1920), an artist and designer in many media who occasionally worked for Doulton's and Wedgwood; Spence, the younger Mitchell and Rhead were all early members of the Artworkers Guild. These superbly designed and executed tiles are underglaze painted on thin dust-pressed buff bodies; their manufacturer may be Craven Dunnill, for whom Spence is known to have designed faience around the turn of the century.[15]

Above the frieze are mosaics executed by Jesse Rust & Co depicting saints and apostles; these tall, colourful figures are said to have been the work of C. W. Mitchell, while the adjoining foliate ornament is by Spence, who also designed - and apparently executed - the mosaic dado below the tile frieze, installed in 1894 to replace the original marble dado. Rust & Co were responsible for the main wall mosaics and the mosaic floors throughout St George's, while most of the windows came from the innovative Gateshead Stained Glass Company, one of whose founders, in 1879, was Spence.[16] Altogether the church fulfils the aims of the Artworkers Guild, in that its spectacular arts and crafts decoration encompasses many art forms, as well as being an indication of the radical thinking of Charles Mitchell, one of a group of north-eastern patrons who saw the arts and crafts as a modern art movement rather than a return to craft-based utopianism.[17]

Also in Jesmond, the interior of **Acorn Fisheries** (a former Maypole Dairy), Acorn Road has two pictorial panels of eighteen six-inch tiles showing arcadian scenes which probably date from the 1920s and are signed 'JE'.

Walker

The **County Hotel**, Walker Road (on the eastern edge of Newcastle), rebuilt 1906, has a very colourful and ornate classical faience facade (Fig 217).

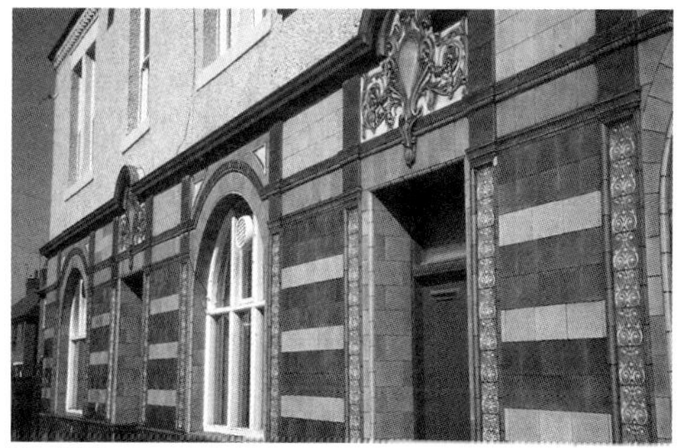
Fig 217.

NORTH SHIELDS

North Shields was a major fishing port by the end of the first decade of the twentieth century, with 76 steam trawlers based there in 1909 and more than 600 herring boats appearing for the summer harvest in the years before the First World War. The quayside area in particular was packed with pubs, and although many have disappeared, enough remain to give an impression of turn-of-the-century Shields.[18] The typical pre-1914 pub was small, built on a corner site and faced with highly glazed faience in shades of brown and yellow; the best remaining example is the **Berwick Arms**, TRINITY STREET. It was rebuilt by local architects Oswald & Son in 1891, although the faience facade dates from around 1913; its motifs include yellow dragon heads worked into the floral decoration of the green spandrels.

On display in the engine shed of the **Stephenson Railway Museum**, MIDDLE ENGINE LANE, is a Doulton tile panel, measuring 98" by 44", showing George Stephenson and Edward Pease with Stephenson's *Rocket* in the background. This panel, and three others (showing Thomas Bewick, the building of Hadrian's Wall, and Henry III conferring a licence to dig coals at Wallsend), were exhibited in Newcastle in 1887 by Doulton's at the Royal Mining, Engineering and Industrial Exhibition on the Town Moor. They then appeared (although possibly minus the Wallsend panel) in 1895 at the new premises of Townsend & Co, glass and china merchants, in Northumberland Street. All the panels were designed by John Eyre and painted by W. J. Nunn.[19]

ROTHBURY

All Saints Church, rebuilt 1850, has a chancel pavement of red, buff and black dust-pressed Godwin tiles; many of the designs are shown in the firm's catalogue issued around 1860, including a nine-tile group of 'pattern 483'. However, the main ceramic interest of this busy little town lies in the hills just to the north-east, at **Cragside** (NT), Lord Armstrong's country seat. As originally built by Armstrong in 1864, Cragside was a relatively unremarkable villa, but the transformation wrought by Richard Norman Shaw during the 1870s and 1880s produced a breathtaking vision of Englishness - all half-timbering, bulging bay windows and piled-up gables - which protrudes through the tall pines on the hillside above Debdon Burn. Lord Armstrong (who was buried at All Saints Church) first visited Rothbury as a small child, and decided to make Cragside his main home in 1869. The first tranche of work on the house took place in 1870-2 and included innovative bathing and heating arrangements, with hot and cold running water, central heating, water closets, a shower cabinet and luxurious bathing arrangements. The plunge bath, first used in 1870, is lined with blue and white Delftware tiles in a floral pattern, with a top border row of tiles featuring a variety of horsemen (Fig 218). A mahogany-framed set of these contemporary Dutch tiles, probably made in Utrecht, also forms a splashback behind the bath.

These basement baths are reached via stairs from the inner hall passage, which is lined with cuenca tiles - which have coloured glazes separated by moulded ridges - patterned in green, blue, white and orange, to dado level; cuenca tiles of a slightly different design, but also on plastic clay bodies, line the walls of the first floor landing. The hall tiles were probably installed during the first building campaign, which added a library and dining room (both with tiled fireplaces) at the far end of the inner hall, although they may have been part of the subsequent set of alterations conducted during 1872-7, which included a new entrance hall.[20] The landing tiles appear to have been added in 1877, when Shaw remodelled the staircase; all these colourful dado tiles were made by Frederick Garrard of Millwall, London, a manufacturer favoured by Norman Shaw.

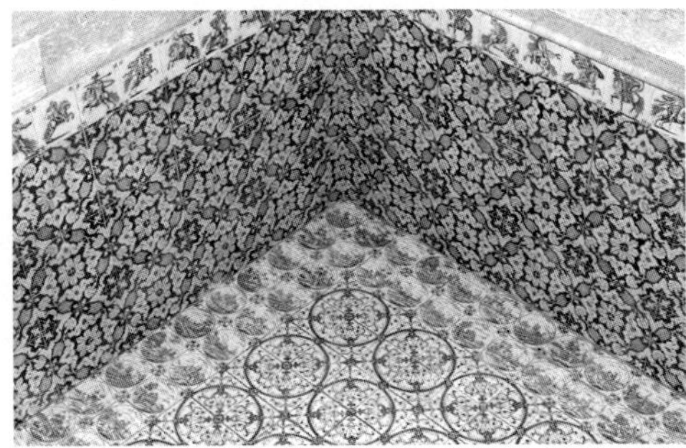

Fig 218.

STAMFORDHAM

The **Church of St Mary the Virgin** stands at the far end of Stamfordham's village green. A walk through the churchyard reveals the site to be on the edge of a broad ridge, as an unexpected westward panorama greets the visitor on the way to the south porch. Benjamin Ferrey partly took down and rebuilt the medieval church in 1848 (not long after his work at Morpeth), apparently cleaning and replacing the stonework exactly as he found it. Inside are several unusual wall paintings and a colourful organ painted Burges-style, but the trio of lancets attracts the eye to the chancel and thence the particularly striking sanctuary tiles (Fig 219). The pavement, by Chamberlains of Worcester, whose 1844 catalogue shows many of the designs, is formed of highly glazed brown and buff tiles, with motifs including the evangelists - a startling grimacing lion for St Mark - and at least two cases of reversed colourways in one of a four-tile group; these reversed designs do not appear in the catalogue. The overall arrangement is forceful and very lively, and made all the more interesting by the fact that these tiles must have been some of the last produced by the firm before being sold to J. H. Maw in 1850; indeed, they may even have been supplied by Maws from old factory stock.

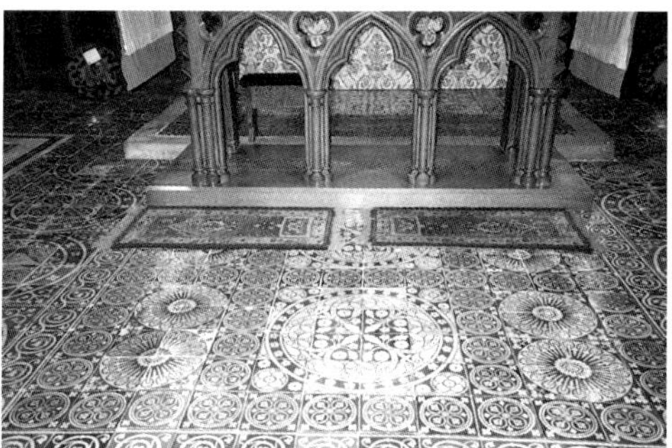

Fig 219.

TYNEMOUTH

It is easy to be distracted from the sad remains of the medieval floor tiles in the warming house at **Tynemouth Priory** (EH) by the vastly expansive views over river and sea; open to the weather on the tip of a blustery promontory, it is no wonder these tiles - a roughly ten foot square area, probably dating from the fourteenth century - have not survived intact. Nor, for that matter, have many of the sandstone headstones in the atmospheric graveyard just east of the priory, beyond the fifteenth century Percy Chantry, where John Dobson's restoration of 1852 included a pavement of Minton tiles; Dobson normally used Minton's for his restoration work. The tiles, themselves needing restoration after water damage, are geometrics in the nave with a tiny sanctuary pavement of red, blue and cream patterned encaustics; overhead is an intricate scheme of sculptured roof bosses.

Tynemouth itself is reached through the Castle gatehouse, a reminder of the importance of the site as both barracks and defensive position, although latterly the town's major role has been as a resort. To gauge the one-time importance of this traffic, pass the stern late 1930s white faience facade of the **Turks Head Hotel** on FRONT STREET to reach **Tynemouth Station**, whose acres of glass canopies have been beautifully restored; they once sheltered huge numbers of Newcastle day trippers. The station, with its ornate ironwork, was built by the North Eastern Railway's architect William Bell in 1882; it is now part of the local Metro network. The NER attached such importance to the station that the company put up one of its ceramic map panels on the eastern platform (Fig 220). These large, framed panels were manufactured by Craven Dunnill, and show the entire NER network at the turn of the century; the first (of fourteen) was installed at York Station in 1900.[21] The Tynemouth map was restored by Maw's in 1973 and is one of the best preserved of the nine remaining examples.

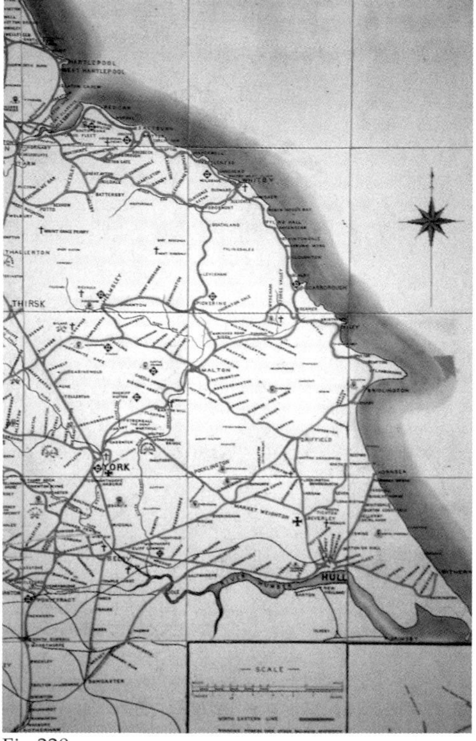

Fig 220.

Northumberland Roundup

The walls of the Tower Room at **Ford Castle** are lined with unusual blue and white patterned tiles, which may be nineteenth century Portuguese in origin; perhaps they were part of the alterations made by Louisa, Marchioness of Waterford, when she was in residence during 1861-5. St John's Church, West Lane, **Killingworth** (north-eastern edge of Newcastle), built in 1869, has a decorative tiled chancel pavement, but the church is normally closed. The delightful and interesting Church of St John at **Meldon** stands on a hill in beautiful surroundings near Meldon Park, home of the Cooksons, who are much commemorated here (excellent modern glass in the east window); the sanctuary pavement by Minton, probably installed during the 1849 restoration by Dobson, includes roundels of St John the Evangelist. Inside the Anglers Arms at **Weldon Bridge**, near Longframlington, are some unusual hand-painted wall tiles. The New Coliseum, Whitley Road, **Whitley Bay** (now a shop) has a cream interwar Hathernware facade. **Whittingham** village fountain (near the church) is a Gothic creation of 1874, commemorating the virtues of the vicar's wife. On its four sides it carries very battered but unusual incised tiles depicting ladies' heads and birds; the colour is brown with line drawing in red, but the maker is unidentified.

References

1. Catalogue of the Kenneth Beaulah Collection of Tiles and Related Material, TACS, 1993, vol 1, tile number 1967; *The Builder*, vol 20, 12th July 1862, p336; A. B. E. Clark, *Brinkburn Priory* (English Heritage, London, 1992), p21.
2. *Bywell St Andrew, Northumberland*, (Redundant Churches Fund, London, 1990).
3. Carter Archive, Poole Museum Service, 3E 29.
4. Marilyn N. Tweddle, *An historical guide to the Church of St James the Great, Morpeth* (Tweddle, Morpeth, 1994).
5. John Addyman and Bill Fawcett, *The High Level Bridge and Newcastle Central Station* (North Eastern Railway Association, Newcastle upon Tyne, 1999), p105.
6. Colin Cunningham and Prudence Waterhouse, *Alfred Waterhouse, 1830-1905: Biography of a Practice* (Clarendon Press, Oxford, 1992), p266.
7. Mark Anders, *Burmantofts Architectural Faience*, in *Burmantofts Pottery*, (Bradford Art Galleries and Museums, Bradford, 1983), pp28-37; see p33.
8. Paul Usherwood, Jeremy Beach and Catherine Morris, *Public Sculpture of North-East England* (University of Liverpool, Liverpool, 2000), pp98-9.
9. John Grundy, *et al.*, *Northumberland* Buildings of England (Penguin Books, London, 1992), p461.
10. *Architectural Review*, vol 20, July 1906, p30 states that the tiles were by Maw & Co and H. Walker & Sons, Newcastle upon Tyne; Walker's may have been tilers.
11. John Greene, *Brightening the Long Days* (Tiles and Architectural Ceramics Society, 1987), p46.
12. Germaine Stanger, *Opthamology Department Arts Lottery Project* (Royal Victoria Infirmary, Newcastle upon Tyne, 1998).
13. Lynn F. Pearson, 'The TACS Gazetteer Project: Tile discoveries in London and Newcastle upon Tyne', *Glazed Expressions*, (1998) 36, pp1-2.
14. Paul Atterbury and Louise Irvine, *The Doulton Story* (Royal Doulton Tableware, Stoke on Trent, 1979), p78.
15. Personal communication, Neil Moat, 3rd March 2005; *Magazine of Art*, 1903, pp80-4. See also *The Builder*, 30th March 1888, vol 56, p243.
16. Joyce Little, Angela Goedicke and Margaret Washbourn, eds. *Stained Glass Marks & Monograms* (NADFAS, London, 2002).
17. *William Morris and the Arts & Crafts Movement in the North-East*, (Bowes Museum, Barnard Castle, 2003).
18. Lynn F. Pearson, *The Northumbrian Pub - An Architectural History* (Sandhill Press, Warkworth, 1989), pp110-4.
19. John Greene, 'Doulton Panels from the Premises of Townsend & Co., Newcastle upon Tyne', *Glazed Expressions*, (1993) 27, p6.
20. *Cragside*, (National Trust, London, 1985), pp17, 39.
21. 'Railway Map in Tiles', *Brickbuilder*, (1900) June, ppxxii-xxiii.

Nottinghamshire

Nottinghamshire has two early sixteenth century terracotta locations at Kneesall and Rampton, although here the material is not used in such a lavish manner as at the better-known group of contemporary Norfolk hall houses. From the late nineteenth and early twentieth centuries, there are good Powell's opus sectile panels at Hucknall, Lenton (Nottingham) and St Mary Magdalene, Newark, where there are also some unusual Victorian memorial tiles; in addition, there is a rare tiled reredos by the stained glass makers Shrigley & Hunt at St Edmund, Holme Pierrepoint. However, the bulk of the county's sites are in Nottingham, where the local architect Watson Fothergill produced a series of showy buildings with tile and terracotta decoration, and the recently restored Prudential Assurance building has an excellent Burmantofts interior. Not surprisingly, considering the city's proximity to the former Hathern works (about ten miles to the south, near Loughborough), Nottingham also has a good variety of interwar faience facades. Modern work is in fairly short supply in the county. Suggested reading: Ken Brand, *Watson Fothergill, Architect* (Nottingham Civic Society, 1997); Ken Brand, *Ornamental Nottingham* (TACS Tour Notes, 1992). The *Gazetteer* entry for Nottinghamshire covers the administrative areas of Nottingham City Council and Nottinghamshire County Council.

HOLME PIERREPOINT

The hand-painted tile reredos (1877) in **St Edmund's Church** is a rare example of tiling in a church context by the Lancaster stained glass firm Shrigley & Hunt; their tiles were very popular in the 1870s and 1880s, but were mostly used in furniture and fire surrounds. The tile panels show emblematic plants - vine leaves and a corn on the cob - on either side of an inscription.[1]

HUCKNALL

Three fine Powell's opus sectile panels may be seen at the **Church of St Mary Magdalen**, burial place of the poet Lord Byron. A panel showing angels with musical instruments is on the north wall of the church, between two of the twenty-five Kempe windows. This dates from 1897, while 'The return of the prodigal son' was supplied by Powell's in the following year. The third panel, including angels bearing a scroll, dates from 1905.[2]

KNEESALL

Old Hall Farm was probably built as a hunting lodge around 1515-40; its significance resides in its early use of constructional terracotta, which can be seen in the terracotta blocks of the staircase and in the remains of the mullioned windows. There are two other sites in Nottinghamshire with early sixteenth century terracotta: the gateway near Hill's Farm at Rampton, which bears terracotta coats of arms, and All Saints Church at Granby, where the east window of the chancel was of terracotta (replaced by stone in 1888, although fragments remain). However, none of these buildings had such lavishly decorative terracotta as the Norfolk hall houses of the same date.[3]

MANSFIELD

H. & R. Johnson's provided two tube-lined murals for the Mansfield **Safeways** store around 1990; made by the firm's Minton Hollins section, the murals depicted Robin Hood and Nottingham Castle. In contrast is the faience facade of the shop at 11 LEEMING STREET, which was built for Boot's the Chemists and dates from about 1900. Its decoration includes roundels bearing the letter 'B'.

NEWARK

The parish church of **St Mary Magdalene**, CHURCH WALK, is the third on its site, an impressive spire signalling its presence at the centre of Newark (Fig 221). The present tower was begun by 1230, while the remainder of the church was rebuilt in the two centuries after 1310. The galleries accumulated during the eighteenth century were swept away in the mid-nineteenth century, when most of the stained glass was installed. A very fine Powell's opus sectile panel depicting 'The Adoration of the Lamb' was installed in the Lady Chapel in 1912, to mark the seventy-eighth birthday of Newark's vicar during 1880-1907, Marshall Wild (who also has a memorial tile in the choir). The design of this

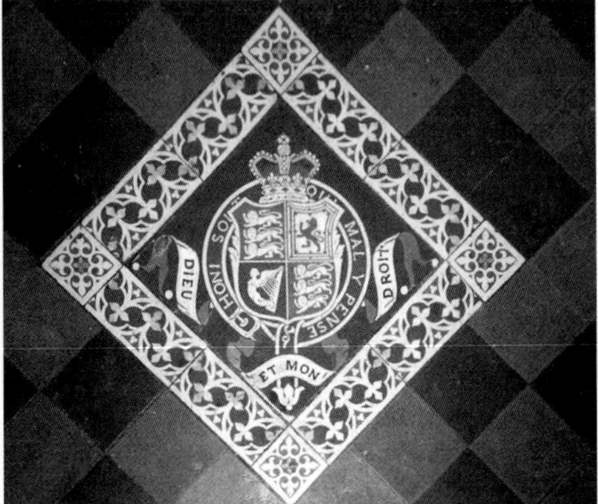

Fig 221.

costly panel, one of Powell's more expensive opus sectile contracts at £256, combines angels from cartoons used previously by the firm with a new central feature by Charles Hardgrave.[4] The angel wings in deep reds, greens and blues are vibrant, as is the flowing water of life. The choir has a Minton pavement and there are lozenge-shaped memorial tiles dotted about throughout the church, dating from between 1885 and 1916. These commemorate individuals, including the Borough Surveyor, but - more unusually - also events such as the installation of glass in the tower (1887) and clerestory (1890) windows. There is also a handsome royal coat of arms in an ornate border set into the red and black pavement just inside the west door.

There is little else in Newark of ceramic interest apart from a couple of minor locations, each close to one of the town's pair of railway stations. The **Waitrose** store in OSSINGTON ROAD (opposite Newark Castle station) sports two large tile panels by Reptile behind its meat and fish counters, while near Newark Northgate station is **Jabez House** (1880), 51 ALLIANCE STREET, with a strip of pretty green and white floral-motif tiles set into the doorcase at either side of its front door.

NOTTINGHAM

Central Nottingham has a slightly foreign air, with lofty, bright red brick buildings layered upward like inverted wedding cakes and topped by half-timbering. Tiles and terracotta feature mainly as decorative additions in these late Victorian structures, particularly in the work of the architect Watson Fothergill. The only complete faience interiors were introduced to Nottingham by organizations based outside the city, the railway companies and Prudential Assurance. There is also much interwar faience to be seen, of varying quality, on this circular tour which begins and ends at the railway station, to the south of the centre, with an optional extension to the west and a few items from the suburbs.

Nottingham's first railway station, the terminus of the Midland Counties Railway branch from Derby, opened on Carrington Street in 1839. Their through station came into operation in 1848, just to the east, but despite enlargements this appeared totally inadequate in the face of direct competition from the Great Central Railway, whose Victoria Station, on the northern edge of the central area, opened in 1900. Victoria Station was designed by a local architect, A. E. Lambert, who provided the Great Central with an imposing renaissance-style structure complete with a clock tower over 100 feet in height. The interior was also impressive, with its dining room and refreshment room decked out with Burmantofts faience; they were both shown in the Leeds firm's catalogue of 1902.

The Midland Railway responded by hiring Lambert to design a new station of their own, a rebuilding of the through station on the CARRINGTON STREET site. The **Midland Station** (1904) is now the sole functioning passenger station in the city, as the Victoria Station was closed in 1967 and mostly demolished, although the clock tower remains, near the Victoria Centre (see below). For the Midland, Lambert produced a long, red sandstone facade dominated by a central, orangey-brown terracotta-domed clock tower. There are masses of ornate terracotta dressings, and the airy booking hall behind the outer screen is lined with bottle-green glazed faience blocks; on the floor is a modern mosaic portraying local industries. Down at platform level, the small buffet (formerly refreshment room) between platforms two and three has a nicely tiled interior in pale yellows and greens, with some relief pattern tiles and a chunky brown fireplace surround, all probably by Burmantofts.

Directly north of the station on CANAL STREET is **Broad Marsh Bus Station**. Inside, running across the width of this long, low space at both ends are large murals of Shaws Twintiles, probably dating from the early 1970s. The western mural shows a townscape of Nottingham while the portrayal of the Goose Fair at the opposite end includes a huge white goose. Continue northward through the grim Broad Marsh shopping centre, whose 1970s wall tiling - including one mural believed to be the largest permanent work of computer art in the world in 1974 - disappeared during later refurbishments.[5] Leave the shopping centre at the LISTER GATE exit and pass the complex interwar white faience facade of **Marks & Spencer**, topped with strange mushroom-like finials. Its next-door neighbour **W. H. Smith's** also has a good white faience facade with black faience columns at first floor level.

Head directly north through the pedestrianised area to reach the Old Market Square; on its far side, LONG ROW, is the unusual green and white striped interwar faience facade of **Namco**. Turn right along CHEAPSIDE, which runs along the southern face of the massive classical Council House, to pass more white faience in the form of the neo-Baroque offices above **Poultry Arcade**. Just to the right, on the corner with BRIDLESMITH GATE, is the **County Club** (1869, now American Express), designed by one of the city's two most notable Victorian architects, Thomas Chambers Hine (1813-99); it sports horizontal strings of buff and brown terracotta tiles which alternate the club motif and the entwined letters 'NC' for Nottinghamshire Club. Turn left into HIGH STREET, which is dominated by the beautifully preserved shopfront of the former **Boots the Chemists** store (1903-4, now a fashion shop), a wonderful domed Edwardian baroque structure clothed in deep buff terracotta; it was designed by the local architect Albert Nelson Bromley and became the model for Boots stores throughout the country. There is some good detailing, especially the pair of figures supporting the clock on the corner tower, and more figures almost hidden beneath the semicircular balcony. The store was restored by the Architects Design Group in 1974 and by Hathernware in 2000.

To inspect the **Lion Hotel**, a turn-of-the-century essay in yellow and green faience, go directly ahead into CLUMBER STREET; now return to the High Street and turn east into Pelham Street, then left into THURLAND STREET for the red brick **Corn Exchange** (1849-50), on the right; this was T. C. Hine's first major building in Nottingham. Its facade displays a string course of encaustic tiles with a guilloche motif in brown, buff and black. Continue along Thurland Street, then right into Lincoln Street; at the T-junction go a few yards to the right to see the architect **Watson Fothergill's office** (now a shop and gallery) at 15 GEORGE STREET. Fothergill (1841-1928) had been turfed out of his previous office accommodation just to the west in Clinton Street as a result of demolition work caused by railway construction. His new office, put up in 1895 and which he designed himself, was a model of his architectural attitudes: it was a confident and eclectic stylistic mix with much ornament, including a canopied figure of a medieval architect holding a bundle of plans, surely based on Fothergill. Over the entrance is a stone bearing the words 'Watson Fothergill Architect', close to the names of his mentors George Gilbert Scott, William Burges and Richard Norman Shaw, and unnamed busts of G. E. Street and A. W. N. Pugin. The major terracotta decoration is in the form of four panels, each about a foot high and two feet across, depicting the construction of classical, medieval and Elizabethan buildings. Inside is some unusual wall tiling, possibly of terracotta, with motifs including a multi-rayed sun.

Turn back northward along George Street, going left into LOWER PARLIAMENT STREET and soon reaching another Fothergill extravaganza, the shop and warehouse of **Furley & Co**, high class provision merchants, built in 1896-7. There are a few strings of art nouveau tiling on the side elevation and four terracotta panels on the main facade; these have an oriental theme and show *Five men plying sampans, A Far Eastern market, Cutting sugar cane* and *Boiling sugar cane*. Across the road is the **Victoria Centre**, and a brief diversion northward along its MILTON STREET boundary brings into sight a dramatic printed-tile mural designed and made by the London artist Robert Dawson (Fig 222). Entitled *Cycle*, it was installed in 2001 during the John Lewis Partnership's redevelopment of the Jessop & Son's store. The mural is almost 50' long and about 8' in height, and shows highly convincing computer-manipulated images of moving bicycles, entirely appropriate for its site behind a set of bicycle racks. Return to Lower Parliament Street and continue west into UPPER PARLIAMENT STREET to see the offices of the **Nottingham Express**, built by Fothergill Watson in 1876; the extensions of 1899 are by the same architect, who by that time was known as Watson Fothergill, having changed his name by deed poll in 1892. There are eight tiles, four of them portraits, set into the inside wall of its open corner porch, which also has a rather worn encaustic tile pavement.[6]

The circular route now goes left into King Street; for the longer route, which continues along Upper Parliament Street, please see below. On the corner of Upper Parliament Street and KING STREET is the soaring white Hathern faience facade of the former **Elite Picture Theatre** (now Paul Davey), with its series of statues - figures representing art, drama, music and so forth - crammed into niches along the parapet. This cinema development of 1919-21 was designed by Adamson & Kinns and incorporated a four-storey office block, restaurants and masonic lodges in assorted historical styles.[7] Further south, the triangular site at the junction of King Street and Queen Street is occupied by the towering pile that is the former **Prudential Building** (now the Hard Rock Café), designed by Alfred Waterhouse and built in 1893-8. The rich, deep red terracotta of its facade and the ornate faience of its recently restored interior - including a pitched-roofed faience clock - were supplied by Burmantofts. At the corner of King Street and Long Row is **Queen's Chambers** (1897), another typical Watson Fothergill building with much terracotta decoration.

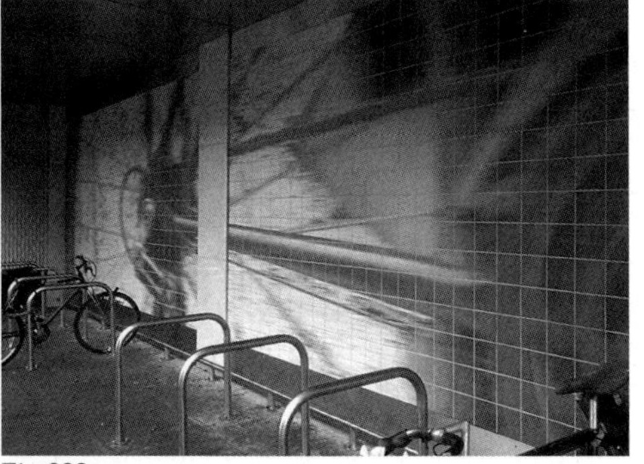

Fig 222.

Opposite is the Council House; from here, the return route to the railway station lies directly south, past St Peter's Church and through the Broad Marsh Shopping Centre. However, to explore the western fringe of the city centre, return via Queen Street to UPPER PARLIAMENT STREET and continue west, passing the **Blue Bell** public house on the north side of the road. It was designed by Hedley Price and built in 1904; the decorative ground floor facade is in matt olive green faience. Just before the pub is a sixties shopfront with several high-relief abstract turquoise panels which are probably ceramic. Next, on the south side, is the pub now known as **Number 10**, with a good interwar faience facade including lettering for the local Home Brewery and the date 1928. Further along, and back on the north side, is the rather larger form of **Co-operative House**, the former Nottingham Co-operative Society store, with a fine terracotta frontage dating from 1916 (architect W. V. Betts); this featured in a Hathern Station Brick and Terra Cotta Company publication issued around 1930.[8] The facade is particularly notable for its three colourful relief panels above the main entrance, showing giant-size figures in the shipbuilding, textile manufacturing and railway engineering industries. It is unclear whether Hathern or another manufacturer was responsible for these panels, which are probably ceramic.

West of Co-operative House, across the broad road junction, is the landmark domed tower of the **Albert Hall** on NORTH CIRCUS STREET. It was built in 1907-9 to the designs of A. E. Lambert and includes much buff terracotta. Opposite on DERBY ROAD is the **R. C. Cathedral of St Barnabas** (1842-4, A. W. N. Pugin), which - after St Chad's Cathedral, Birmingham - was Pugin's second great church commission in the Midlands. Some of its Puginian character has been lost during frequent internal rearrangements, but original encaustic floor tiles remain in several areas, notably the Blessed Sacrament Chapel to the south of the retrochoir. Here, in intensely Puginian surroundings reminiscent of St Giles Cheadle, are floor tiles with large *Agnus Dei* motifs. The rather stark nave pavement dates from the Cathedral's 1994 re-ordering. West of St Barnabas, via Upper College Street, is 19 PARK TERRACE (1881), one of the many houses on the Park Estate designed by T. C. Hine; it bears a large terracotta plaque with the date and the initials 'TCH'.[9]

A diversion about a third of a mile north of the Cathedral, via Clarendon Street, leads to the former **College of Art and Design** (1863-5, architect Frederick Bakewell of Nottingham) on the corner of PEEL STREET and Waverley Street. Now known as the Waverley Building of Nottingham Trent University, it carries an encaustic tile frieze. In the **General Cemetery**, immediately south on WAVERLEY STREET, is the Bright family memorial, a white faience tabernacle on an octagonal shaft with an hexagonal pedestal and plinth. This dates from about 1908 and can be found on the south side of the cemetery; it commemorates members of the family who died between 1871 and 1928.

From the Cathedral, return to the railway station via Long Row and the main shopping area, or alternatively by taking in the **Castle Museum**, about a third of a mile south of St Barnabas. Here tiles by Joanna Veevers, made in the late 1990s, are set above the handbasins in the lavatories. The tiles, which depict scenes from Nottingham's history, were designed using a monoprint technique in which images were drawn in slip on a plaster slab then cast in semi-porcelain.

Just east of the city centre in Sneinton a wide range of porch dado tiling may be found in an area taking in over thirty streets. Here the housing generally dates from between 1900 and 1914, and over 250 different tile designs have been recorded including striking art nouveau flowers. In the western suburb of Lenton is **Holy Trinity Church**, CHURCH STREET, where the cigarette manufacturer W. G. Player worshipped; the John Player & Sons tobacco factories were built just to the north, on Radford Boulevard, from 1883. The present reredos was given to the church by W. G. Player in 1911. It is a handsome Powell's piece which combines opus sectile work with green and gold glazed tiles; it shows the figure of Christ holding a chalice, with the cross in the background and angels at his feet. This was a costly commission at £310.

RAMPTON

The **gateway** between the churchyard and the yard of Hill's Farm is a splendidly showy piece of early sixteenth century work in terracotta and brick, the panels of terracotta bearing coats of arms. The gateway originally formed part of the route between the now-demolished manor house and the church.

RAVENSHEAD

Papplewick Pumping Station, in LONGDALE LANE, Ravenshead (just over a mile east of Papplewick), was built in 1881-5, and was one of three such water pumping stations serving Nottingham. Its 1884 twin beam-engines still occupy palatial surroundings with much ornate cast ironwork, tiling, stained glass and lacquered brass. The decorative theme is water-based and naturalistic, including motifs of fish, water birds, plants and fauna, as well as a terracotta phoenix which guards the pump house entrance. The phoenix was stolen around 2002 but a replacement was soon made by Hathernware, who were also responsible for the restoration of the building's terracotta decoration. The stamp of the Hathern Station Brick and Terra Cotta Company has been found on some of the original terracotta, identifying it as an early example of the firm's production.

Nottinghamshire Roundup

The spectacular octagonal dairy (no public access) at Dairy Farm, Mansfield Road, **Arnold** has wall tiling showing scenes of dairymaids throughout the world. The architect G. F. Bodley's 1864-5 decoration of the chancel at All Saints Church, **Coddington** included the installation of an encaustic tile pavement. In the chancel of All Saints Church (1875, architect J. T. Lee of London), **Harby** is an encaustic tile pavement whose design incorporates texts. The colourful Minton encaustic tile pavement in the chapel (the former chapter house) at **Newstead Abbey** dates from its redecoration in the 1860s; the Pugin-type designs include some on an unusual pale green ground. All Saints Church (1886-8), **Winthorpe** has an encaustic tiled pavement in its chancel and baptistery. The French Horn Hotel (architect F. Hopkinson), 15 Potter Street, **Worksop** has a good Burmantofts faience facade of 1906.

References

1. William Waters, *Stained Glass from Shrigley & Hunt of Lancaster and London* (Centre for North-West Regional Studies, University of Lancaster, Lancaster, 2003), pp26-7, 81.
2. Dennis W. Hadley, *James Powell & Sons: A listing of opus sectile, 1847-1973*, (2001).
3. Nikolaus Pevsner and Elizabeth Williamson, *Nottinghamshire* Buildings of England (Penguin, Harmondsworth, 1979).
4. Hadley, *James Powell & Sons*, 2001.
5. 'Mural expresses computer art', *Ceramic Industries Journal*, 84 (1974) 989, p9.
6. Ken Brand, *Watson Fothergill* (Nottingham Civic Society, Nottingham, 1997).
7. Richard Gray, *Cinemas in Britain: One Hundred Years of Cinema Architecture* (Lund Humphries Publishers, London, 1996).
8. *Modern Practice in Architectural Terra Cotta*, (Hathern Station Brick & Terra Cotta Co Ltd, Loughborough, 1930).
9. Ken Brand, *Thomas Chambers Hine: Architect of Victorian Nottingham* (Nottingham Civic Society, Nottingham, 2003).

Oxfordshire

Medieval tiles, often made outside Oxfordshire, can be found in many of the county's churches and most notably at West Hendred, where there is a large expanse of fourteenth century tiling; however, the pavements in the Muniment Tower at New College, Oxford are in rather better condition. There are fine late eighteenth century Coade stone panels at the Radcliffe Observatory in Oxford, the city which was to be at the heart of the anglo-catholic Oxford Movement in the mid-nineteenth century. Examples of highly decorative Tractarian church interiors are therefore relatively easy to find, although the inclusion of substantial amounts of tiling in these schemes is less common. Even in Keble College Chapel (1873-6), William Butterfield's visualisation of a neo-medieval setting for collegiate worship, mosaic work is predominant with tiles making only a minor contribution.

Perhaps the most unusual ceramic location in Oxfordshire is Sunningwell Church (1877), where the encaustic pavement includes Godwin tiles designed by the architect John Pollard Seddon; their wonderful gothic imagery is based on Revelations, the last chapter of the New Testament. Sunningwell appears to be the sole English site where these 'Revelations' tiles survive *in situ*, although they are present in at least another three churches in Wales, where Seddon built and restored many churches. Finally, as with many of England's more rural counties, modern ceramic work is in fairly short supply. Suggested reading: Chris Blanchett, 'The Tiles of Dorchester Abbey' *TACS Journal* 6, 1996, pp13-22. The *Gazetteer* entry for Oxfordshire covers the administrative area of Oxfordshire County Council.

BROUGHTON

Broughton Castle, which originated as an early fourteenth century fortified manor house, occupies a beautiful moated site just east of the church. A licence was granted to John de Broughton for worship in his tiny private chapel in 1331; it retains many mid-fourteenth century tiles, although the pavement may have been relaid during 1860s alterations by George Gilbert Scott.

BUCKLAND

The Barcote Aisle, a once-private chapel in the south transept of **St Mary's Church**, is a lasting memorial to Clara Jane West (d1888), wife of William West of nearby Barcote Manor, director of the Great Western Railway. Beneath the gold stars of its sky-blue ceiling the walls are almost completely faced with shining Powell's opus sectile work, ordered from the firm in late 1890 along with stained glass and other furnishings and fittings including wrought iron lamp standards. There are brilliantly colourful and complex groups of angels and archangels, along with figures of prophets and apostles; the decoration even extends above the north entrance archway, where rose-winged angels swirl on mosaic ground. A stained glass window of the Ascension looks down upon this unusually complete decorative scheme, to which the Powell's artist George Parlby contributed a sketch, although the principal draughtsmen were Sharp and Charles Hardgrave. Ada Currey also had an input to the Barcote Aisle, being paid for 119½ hours of work on it, but none of the final design can definitely be attributed to her. The overall cost was £1,000 plus £46 for the paving.[1]

CHASTLETON

St Mary's Church has a good set of fourteenth century floor tiles in its south aisle as well as an encaustic pavement throughout the chancel, which was rebuilt by C. E. Powell in 1878-80. Beside the church is **Chastleton House** (NT), built for Walter Jones, a Witney wool merchant, and completed in 1612. In the Great Parlour is a fire surround decorated with a mixed bag of sixty-four Dutch tin-glazed tiles, all but four of them blue and white, the others being manganese and white. They date from between 1630 and 1800, and show a wide variety of images including the Three Kings, swans, sailing vessels and mythical beasts.

CHECKENDON

There are some fourteenth century tiles in the sanctuary of the **Church of St Peter and St Paul**; in addition, Powell's made opus sectile panels for the church in 1919 and 1932. Just over a mile south-east of the village is **Wyfold Court** (no public access), a madly gothic country house built in 1874-84 for Edward Hermon, Conservative MP for Preston during 1868-81 and a partner in the cotton spinners Horrocks, Miller & Co of the same town. He was one of the richest of the cotton magnates and an enthusiastic patron of contemporary artists. His architect George Somers Clarke (1825-82) provided him with a series of vast internal spaces including a stone-vaulted main corridor floored with black and white tiles, a huge stairwell and a picture gallery. The house was used as a hospital from 1932 until the early 1990s, after which it was restored and converted to luxury apartments by P. J. Livesey Rural Heritage Ltd, opening in 1999. Many of the original decorative features still remain, including several tiled fire surrounds and, most importantly, one of a series of large tile paintings which originally hung in the main corridor. It measures around 7′ across by 5′ high and shows Christ preaching in a crowded temple. The highly detailed and colourful scene is signed by I. A. Gibbs & Howard, 64 Charlotte Street, Fitzroy Square, London, a firm of church decorators.[2]

DORCHESTER

The **Abbey of St Peter and St Paul** originated as an early Christian shrine. St Birinius, a Benedictine monk, was granted land at Dorchester to build a cathedral in 634; shortly after its refoundation as an Augustinian abbey in 1140, the present church was built. The monastic buildings were almost entirely demolished following the Dissolution, and the church itself was much altered during the seventeenth century. It had been paved with inlaid tiles during the mid to late fourteenth century, but the remaining fragments of the pavement were relaid in 1747 or later as patches in the main body of the church; these tiles were recorded in the mid-Victorian period. All that now remains of the medieval tiling is a strip comprising pieces of Penn and Late Wessex designs beside the screen dividing the nave and south aisle.

William Butterfield worked at Dorchester during 1846-53, installing tiling on the east wall of the chancel - an arrangement of plain and majolica glazed geometric and inlaid tiles and marble - and the nearby tile pavement. The tiling was all supplied by Herbert Minton, but the unusual inlaid wall tiles were probably made by Samuel Wright of Shelton. Minton used Wright's patent inlaid tile production method under licence from 1835, and appears to have bought at least some of Wright's stock of tiles, which he then sold as his own products.[3] George Gilbert Scott continued the restoration of the Abbey during 1859-74, adding the Godwin tile pavement which covers the floor and steps of the People's Chapel in 1863.[4] Most of the designs of these plastic clay inlaid tiles were based on medieval examples from the Abbey. Finally Godwin's dust-pressed inlaid tiles, again with designs mostly drawn from Dorchester's medieval paving, were installed in the Lady Chapel, the Requiem Chapel and St Birinius Chapel during the 1870s and 1880s. Altogether the Abbey provides an interesting vision of the way in which Victorian architects and tile manufacturers used medieval exemplars as the basis for contemporary pavements.

EWELME

Remote **St Mary's Church** was rebuilt and endowed by William de la Pole, later Duke of Suffolk, and his wife Alice from about 1432. The chancel's south chapel, dedicated to St John the Baptist, is lavishly decorated, the motifs including much heraldry. In the tile pavement may be found the wheel of the Roet family (the name was the French word for wheel) and the fine two-tailed lion of the Burghersh family (the arms of Alice's grandmother). Originally there were probably further tiles in the body of the church, with heraldry for the de la Poles, but only a few fragments remain around the font.[5]

GORING

On the vestry walls in the **Church of St Thomas of Canterbury** are around ninety mostly thirteenth century tiles which probably came from the nuns' church erected following the building of an Augustinian Priory (as an extension to the parish church) in the late twelfth century. They have bird, animal and foliage designs as well as the double-headed eagle of the patron, Richard of Cornwall.

HAILEY

The original design of the **Church of St John the Evangelist** (1868-9) was criticised by the diocesan architect G. E. Street as being 'needlessly eccentric', but in its built form even the revised version is genuinely odd, with strong colours and improbably large detailing. Its architect was Clapton Crabb Rolfe (1845-1907), who was only twenty-one years of age when appointed to the job in 1866 by his father, the Revd. George Crabb Rolfe, vicar of Hailey. The young Rolfe also designed the furnishings, including the encaustic tiling flanking the altar; in addition, the sanctuary is paved with tiles.[6]

HORTON-CUM-STUDLEY

St Barnabas Church was built in 1867-8 by William Butterfield. The exterior is attractive, with hand-made yellow brick (from the nearby south Oxfordshire grey brickfields) banded in red and blue; inside, the Butterfield-designed reredos is a colourful geometric pattern of cut tiles.

KELMSCOTT

Kelmscott Manor was the summer home of William Morris from 1871 until his death in 1896. The fireplace in the Green Room is covered with a combination of Morris-designed tiles made and decorated in Holland (*Swan, Sunflower* and *Artichoke* patterns, incorrectly arranged and probably installed in 1873) with a few traditional Dutch 'tulip and carnation' tiles, possibly introduced in the 1960s. In the Panelled Room, the fireplace tiling is Dutch and dates from around 1880 to the 1900s; the designs were copied from sixteenth century Iznik tiles, probably as special commissions for the London tile importers Murray Marks (later Thomas Elsley & Co).[7] Also at Kelmscott are cast-iron grates probably supplied by Elsley & Co with Iznik-patterned six-inch tiles made by the Dutch firm Ravesteijn.[8]

KIDMORE END

The **Church of St John the Baptist** was built in 1852 to the design of the London architect Arthur Billing. Its polygonal apse is floored with unusual glazed tiling, and the stone pulpit has mosaic panels by Salviati.

NUFFIELD

There are several medieval tiles in the chancel of **Holy Trinity Church**, outside which is the grave of William Richard Morris (1877-1963), Lord Nuffield, the founder of Morris Motors. His home from 1933 until his death was **Nuffield Place**, just off the A4130 which runs to the north of the village (about two miles west of Nettlebed). The house was built in 1914 and enlarged for Lord Nuffield in 1933. Its interiors still reflect typical upper middle class taste of the thirties, with tiled bathrooms (by Carter's of Poole and H. & R. Johnson) and several tiled fire surrounds, including - in the drawing room - one with tiles designed by Reginald Till for Carter's.

OXFORD

There is much of ceramic interest to see in the city, from medieval to modern locations, although access to sites within individual colleges is often difficult and may require an appointment. Begin right at the centre with the **Ashmolean Museum** (1841-5, C. R. Cockerell) in BEAUMONT STREET; high up on its fine classical facade, of Portland and Bath stone, runs a series of pale grey terracotta consoles. These may have been produced in adjacent St Giles Street at the works of Thomas Grimsley, who manufactured terracotta in Oxford between around 1837 and his death in 1875, after which the business was carried on by his sons.

Take Cornmarket to the south, which leads into ST ALDATE'S; on the left is the **Town Hall**, just past the busy junction with the High Street. This expensive and lavish structure was put up in 1893-7 to the designs of the young architect Henry T. Hare, who won the commission in a competition held following Oxford's elevation to county borough status in 1889. The building showed that the city could, for once, match the University as an architectural patron. The room directly above the entrance, reached via the very grand main staircase, is the Assembly Room, which has a large stone fire surround dated 1895 and an iron fireback dated 1896; to either side of the fireback are red lustre tiles designed by William De Morgan. These are variants on the 'BBB' design, named after the Norwich metalworking firm Barnard, Bishop and Barnard, who probably made the fireback; they also supplied a range of tiles for use in their fireplaces, notably the 'BBB' with its floral motif.

Across St Aldate's and a little to the south is the **Bradford & Bingley Building Society**; in the main office is a large ceramic panel showing the buildings of the *City of Oxford* and signed by Philippa Threlfall (Fig 223). This richly modelled mural with its colourful glazes dates from the early 1970s, and was one of a series of about twelve made by Threlfall and her husband and partner Kennedy Collings for the Bradford & Bingley during the 1970s. The materials were high fired ceramics glazed with natural oxides and lustres then bedded into fibreglass backing.

Head back towards the Town Hall and turn right into the High Street, just south of which stands **Merton College**, MERTON STREET. In its fourteenth century library, the oldest in Oxford, are medieval tiles which, however, were bought and laid in 1623 when other alterations were made to the building. Merton's Chapel, restored in 1849-56 by William Butterfield, was the first of the college chapels to be restyled in the anglo-catholic taste of the Oxford Movement; fittings included a colourful and extensive tiled floor with many decorative nine-tile groups. Return along the HIGH STREET to the **Covered Market** on the north side; at its far end is Lindsey's butcher's stall, with modern tiling by Von Ellis showing traditional butcher's imagery.

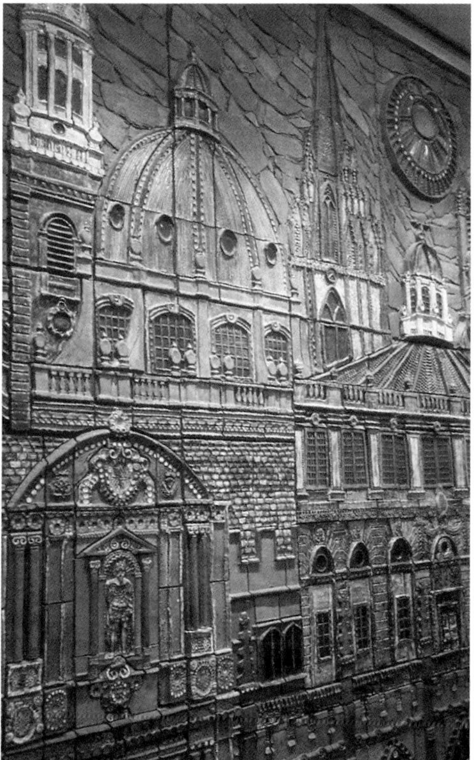

Fig 223.

Emerge on to Market Street, turning right then left into TURL STREET for **Jesus College**, where the Chapel, restored by G. E. Street in 1864, has a complex floor of alabaster, marble and Minton encaustic tiles.[9] Across Turl Street is **Exeter College**; in the Morris Room are fire surrounds with tiles by William De Morgan, and in the Chapel, built in 1856-9 by George Gilbert Scott to replace the expanding college's seventeenth century Chapel, is a good encaustic tile pavement including a Greek cross arrangement, as well as Salviati mosaics around the polygonal apse. William Morris and Edward Burne-Jones were undergraduates at Exeter College durings the 1850s.

At the north end of Turl Street turn right into Broad Street, continuing past the Sheldonian Theatre into HOLYWELL STREET; the entrance to **New College** is on its south side. In the Muniment Tower (the treasury, now used for college archives) are four rib-vaulted rooms with tiled floors dating from around 1386, the upper two pavements being largely undamaged; the need for strict security led to limited access and thus little wear on the glazed floor tiles. The ground floor pavement includes tiles bearing the New College arms, and the first floor tiling was relaid around 2005, as the bricks beneath had begun to disintegrate.[10] Next, head east to the end of Holywell Street, going left into ST CROSS ROAD; on the rght, at number ten, is the tile-hung **Old School House** (no public access), formerly a lodge house for the adjacent Holywell Cemetery. It was built in 1848 by Thomas Grimsley using structural terracotta beams made at his St Giles Street workshop; the beams may be seen protruding beneath the eaves. This is an early date for such use of terracotta and a most unusual method of construction; replacement of wood by terracotta was intended to improve the building's fireproofing qualities.[11]

On the northern edge of the centre in PARKS ROAD is **Keble College** (1868-82), the first complete college to be built in Oxford since the seventeenth century; the architect was William Butterfield. In a revival of the medieval ideal of a college propounded by the anglo-catholic Oxford Movement, Keble was intended to attract poorer scholars, many of whom might eventually enter the anglican priesthood.[12] Butterfield's design used locally-available red brick in place of the traditional stone, and the polychromatic walls of the quadrangle are a feast of red, blue and white brick. The Chapel (1873-6), all spiky pinnnacles outside and transcendent gloom within, cost £40,000 and was paid for by the anglo-catholic guano magnate William Gibbs of Tyntesfield in Somerset, itself a house replete with ceramic decoration. Butterfield based the Chapel's decorative scheme on an iconography of 'the successive dealings of God with his church'; it was executed in mosaics and stained glass by Alexander Gibbs (c1831-86, no relation), a frequent collaborator of Butterfield's.[13] Beneath the high-level band of stained glass windows runs a series of strongly coloured mosaic panels depicting scenes from the Old Testament, and below these is blank arcading enclosing polychromatic banding. The sanctuary steps are paved with a combination of marble and encaustic tiles. The tiles, which are mostly buff and brown with yellow glaze covering the buff sections, were made by Minton Hollins and are marked on the reverse; the twin bird design has an unusual black body.

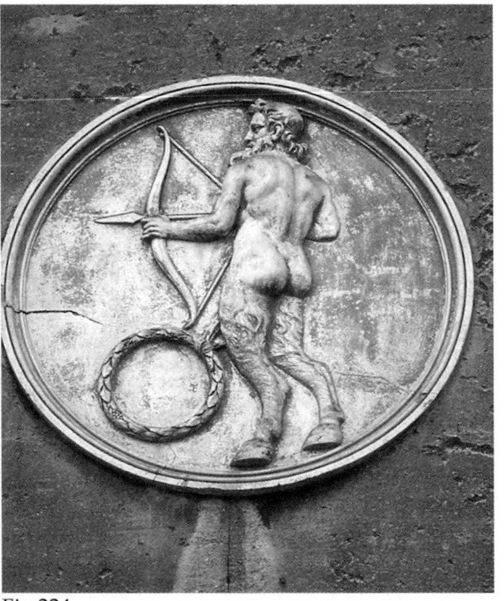

Fig 224.

Slightly north-west of Keble College on the west side of BANBURY ROAD is the former **High School for Girls** (1879, architect T. G. Jackson, now the University's Department of Materials), in Queen Anne Revival style with an ornate Doulton red terracotta facade; the detailing, designed by Jackson, includes columns with strapwork.[14] West again to the WOODSTOCK ROAD; in the forecourt of the **Radcliffe Infirmary** is the rugged Triton Fountain (1857), designed by John Bell and made from terracotta produced by J. M. Blashfield at his Millwall workshop.[15] Just north-west is the remarkable **Radcliffe Observatory**, in the grounds of Green College (Fig 224). The construction of an observatory tower was suggested by Thomas Hornsby, Savilian Professor of Astronomy, and plans were drawn up in 1772 by the London architect Henry Keene. Work began in 1773 but after Keene's death in 1776 the project was taken on by the young architect James Wyatt, and the final design - inspired by the Hellenistic Tower of the Winds in Athens - is largely due to Wyatt. Building was finished by 1779 but decoration of this stunning neoclassical tower was not completed until 1794. Its exterior is rich with Coade stone ornament including a series of beautiful plaques of the *Signs of the Zodiac*, some impressed with the Coade mark, and bas-relief panels symbolising *Morning*, *Noon* and *Night*, all modelled by J. C. F. Rossi. Even the dome's interior has Coade ribs and capitals, although these have been overpainted.[16]

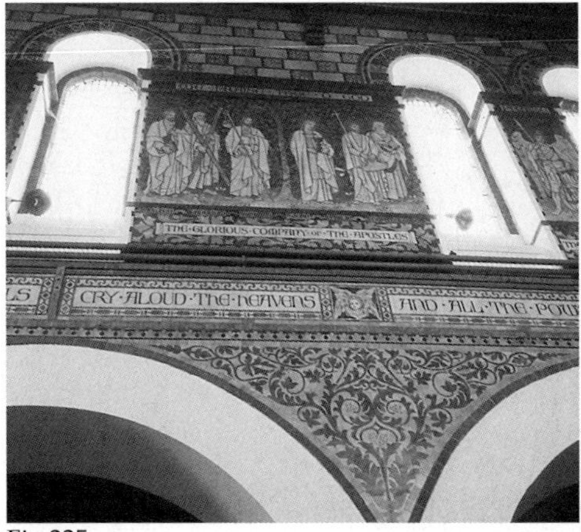

Fig 225.

Now turn southward into Jericho for the **Church of St Barnabas** (architect Arthur Blomfield, 1869-72), its landmark campanile overlooking the Oxford Canal from ST BARNABAS STREET (Fig 225). Construction was at the expense of the staunch anglo-catholic Thomas Combe of the nearby University Press, whose workers lived in the surrounding area, then an 'unsavoury slum'. The foundation of the church was thus an expression of the church's mission to the poor, one of the ideals of the anglo-catholic tradition. The bland walls of its exterior (rubble faced with Portland cement) leave the visitor unprepared for the wealth of colourful detailing within, including a good geometric tile pavement in the sanctuary. The highlight of the decorative scheme, begun in 1893 and never completed, is the combination of opus sectile, blue glass tiles and ceramic tiles on the wall above the north aisle arcading; permission for this nave decoration was requested in 1905.[17] Powell's of Whitefriars then supplied the church with a total of eighteen opus sectile figures of apostles and others during the period 1905-11.[18] The murals were intended to represent a Ritualist vision of heaven, while the theme of the east end decoration, with its seven hanging lamps, was the fourth chapter of Revelations (see Sunningwell, below). Thomas Hardy began writing *Jude the Obscure* (published 1895) in 1893, and may have seen the partly-decorated interior of St Barnabas, which features in the book as St Silas, Christminster, the 'Church of Ceremonies'.

Finally, return eastward to Walton Street, Jericho's main thoroughfare, heading north to find **St Sepulchre's Cemetery** (founded 1849), which is accessed via a gravel path leading from a gateway just north of JUXON STREET. Thomas Combe's grave is here, as well as a good selection of terracotta headstones made nearby at the St Giles Street workshop of Thomas Grimsley. Most of them are impressed with the firm's mark, and there is an example of the most ornate of his sixteen different designs, a jewelled cross.

SUNNINGWELL

St Leonard's Church was restored by the architect John Pollard Seddon (1827-1906) in 1877.[19] He designed the Pre-Raphaelite style east window, which portrays the Adoration of the Magi, and the very unusual encaustic floor tiles whose theme is the fourth chapter of Revelations, the last book of the New Testament (Fig 226). The tile and mosaic pavement includes a nine-tile group centred on a winged figure above a globe, surrounded by seven lamps with lettering - Scientia, Consilium, Sapientia, Fortitudo, Timor, Intellectus, Pietas - beneath. This refers to Revelations 4.5:

'And out of the throne proceeded lightnings and thunderings and voices: and *there were* seven lamps of fire burning before the throne, which are the seven Spirits of God.'

There are also four-tile groups showing six-winged versions of an ox, a lion, an eagle and a man; these are the 'four beasts' round about the throne (Revelations 4.6). Another four-tile group depicts one of the 'four and twenty elders' who sat near the throne and 'cast their crowns' before it, while yet another shows a complex lamp, in fact a Duplex (twin-wick) burner oil lamp, a rare non-traditional image for a Victorian tile.[20] Similar pavements, containing most of the above elements, can also be found in three Welsh churches restored by Seddon: St Padarn (1868-9, 1878-80 and 1882-4), Llanbadarn Fawr, near Aberystwyth, where the tiles are mostly covered by carpet; Christ College Chapel, Brecon, Powys (1861-4) and St Jerome, Llangwm Uchaf, near Usk, where the tiles form part of a larger pavement and date from around 1866-8. The British Museum holds panels of the six-winged ox and lion, and the elder casting the crown; some of these have Godwin's backmarks, suggesting that several sets of the 'Revelations' tiles were made by the firm to Seddon's designs.[21] In addition, drawings by Seddon in the collection of the Victoria and Albert Museum show the 'Revelations' designs in a detailed plan of a tile pavement, but name no specific church.[22] It seems likely that further 'Revelations' pavements may be found at churches restored or built by Seddon, a most inventive designer. Certainly the 'casting crowns' tiles appear at St Oudoceus, Llandogo, north of Chepstow; the church was built by Seddon in 1859-61 but much of the decoration is of a slightly later date.[23]

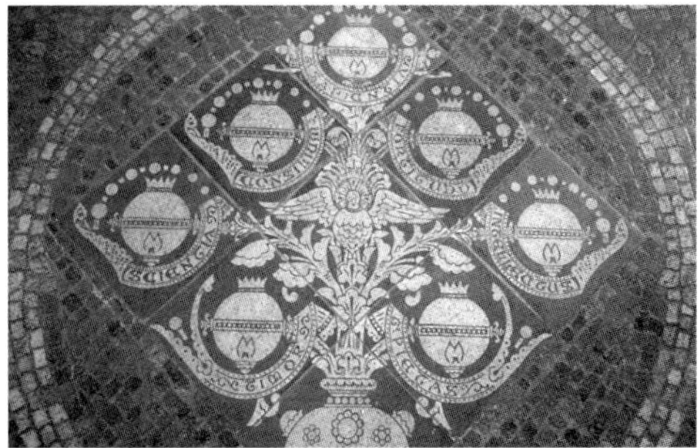

Fig 226.

WEST HENDRED

Holy Trinity Church has not been altered a great deal since it was built in the fourteenth century, and amazingly still retains a large expanse of its original medieval tiling on the floors of the chancel and the nave, although the upper step to the sanctuary is paved with Victorian encaustics. The chancel tiles, which have been relaid in panels divided by bands of newer plain tiling, have only two patterns, a fleur-de-lys and a geometric motif of two half circles. The fleur-de-lys tiles also cover most of the nave floor, with some plain yellow and green tiles near the font. Despite the fact that many different patterned tiles were available, pavements comprising only three or four different basic designs appear to have been common.[24]

Oxfordshire Roundup

In the south transept of St Mary's Church, **Adderbury** are black and white tiles dating from the fourteenth century. The little Church of St Mary, **Adwell** (rebuilt 1865, architect Arthur Blomfield) has a tiled reredos. The Ardington Pottery occupies the nineteenth century dairy of Home Farm, School Road, **Ardington**; the dairy's walls are completely tiled with Minton panels by

Henry Stacy Marks and others, all framed by an elaborate floral frieze. There are some well-preserved fifteenth century floor tiles in the chancel of St Lawrence Church, **Besselsleigh**. In St Mary's Church, **Childrey** are about one hundred rather worn late fifteenth century floor tiles, mostly with geometrical and floral designs along with a green man. A good collection of fourteenth century patterned floor tiles is set into the west end wall of the south aisle at St Peter's Church, **Great Haseley**. There are fifteenth century tiles on the floor of the chapel to the north-west of Thame Park House, **Thame**. The encaustic tile pavement in the sanctuary of St Lawrence Church, **Toot Baldon** dates from its restoration in 1863-6 by Henry Woodyer. The little-altered interior of St Lawrence Church (1844-7), **Tubney** - a rare anglican commission for A. W. N. Pugin - includes an encaustic tile pavement. The chancel of St Leonard's Church (rebuilt 1846), **Woodcote** has an encaustic tile pavement and a glazed relief tile dado. The diminutive porch added to Wood Eaton Manor (1775), **Wood Eaton** by the architect Sir John Soane in 1791 has Ionic capitals of Coade stone as well as bases and - unusually - shafts of the same material.[25]

In addition, there are small numbers of medieval tiles at the following churches: St Helen, Berrick Salome; St Michael, Blewbury; St Bartholomew, Brightwell Baldwin; St Mary, Charlton-on-Otmoor; St Andrew, Chinnor; St Mary, Cholsey; St Mary, Crowell; St Leonard, Drayton St Leonard; St Peter, Easington; St Mary, Great Milton; St Margaret, Harpsden; St Mary, Kidlington; St Mary, Long Wittenham; St Nicholas, Marston; St Giles, Newington; St Mary, North Stoke; St James, Somerton.

References

1. Dennis Hadley, 'Ada Currey (1852-1913): a forgotten artist', *The Journal of Stained Glass*, 24 (2000), pp29-37.
2. John Greene, *Brightening the Long Days* (Tiles and Architectural Ceramics Society, 1987).
3. Chris Blanchett, 'The Tiles of Dorchester Abbey', *Journal of the Tiles and Architectural Ceramics Society*, 6 (1996), pp13-22.
4. *The Builder*, 26th December 1863, vol 21.
5. Jane A. Wight, *Mediaeval Floor Tiles* (John Baker, London, 1975).
6. Andrew Saint, 'Three Oxford Architects', *Oxoniensia*, 35 (1970), pp53-102.
7. Richard Myers and Hilary Myers, *William Morris Tiles - The tile designs of Morris and his Fellow-Workers* (Richard Dennis, Shepton Beauchamp, 1996), pp104, 116, 140.
8. Hans van Lemmen, *Delftware Tiles* (Laurence King, London, 1997).
9. *The Builder*, vol 21, 24th October 1863.
10. Jane Cochrane, 'Medieval Tiled Floor Patterns', *TACS Journal*, 5 (1994), pp11-19.
11. Information from John Ashdown.
12. Geoffrey Tyack, *Oxford: An Architectural Guide* (Oxford University Press, Oxford, 1998), pp229-31.
13. Peter Howell and Ian Sutton, eds, *The Faber Guide to Victorian Churches* (Faber and Faber, London, 1989).
14. Information from John Ashdown.
15. Jennifer Sherwood and Nikolaus Pevsner, *Oxfordshire* Buildings of England (Penguin, Harmondsworth, 1974), p305.
16. Alison Kelly, *Mrs Coade's Stone* (Self Publishing Association, Upton-upon-Severn, 1990).
17. Anne Abley, *St Barnabas, Oxford: Some notes on the mosaics* (Oxford, 1993).
18. Dennis W. Hadley, *James Powell & Sons: A listing of opus sectile, 1847-1973*, (2001).
19. Lynn Pearson, 'The 'Revelations' tiles of John Pollard Seddon at Sunningwell Church, Oxfordshire', *Glazed Expressions*, (2003) 48, p18.
20. Tony Herbert and Kathryn Huggins, *The Decorative Tile in Architecture and Interiors* (Phaidon Press, London, 1995), p83.
21. Personal communication, Imogen Loke, Special Assistant, Department of Medieval and Later Antiquities, British Museum, 21st June 1995. The British Museum's 'Revelations' tiles are known to have been purchased in 1994 at a sale of Godwin tiles in Stroud, Gloucestershire.
22. Michael Darby, *John Pollard Seddon* Catalogues of Architectural Drawings in the Victoria and Albert Museum (Victoria and Albert Museum, London, 1983), p116; see also p74 for the similar tile pavement at Llangwm Uchaf Church. Of the Seddon drawings held by the V&A, D.2096-1896 includes most of the 'Revelations' series in a plan for a pavement (a few are shown in several other drawings) and D.1669-1896 is a handpainted design for the six-winged lion.
23. John Newman, *Gwent/Monmouthshire*. Buildings of Wales (Penguin, London, 2000).
24. Wight, *Mediaeval Floor Tiles*, p135.
25. Alison Kelly, 'Sir John Soane and Mrs Eleanor Coade', *Apollo*, (1989), pp247-253.

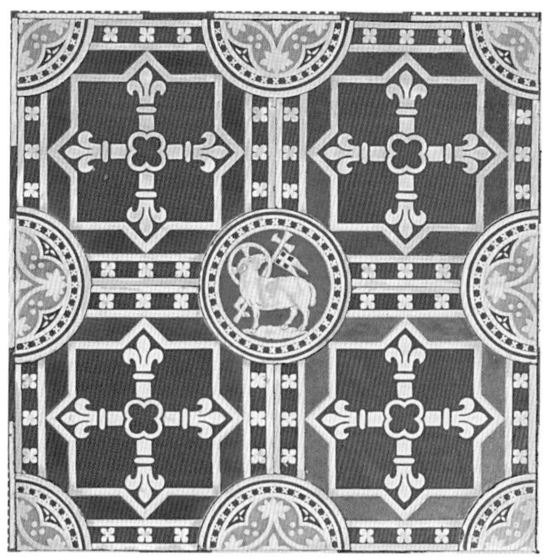

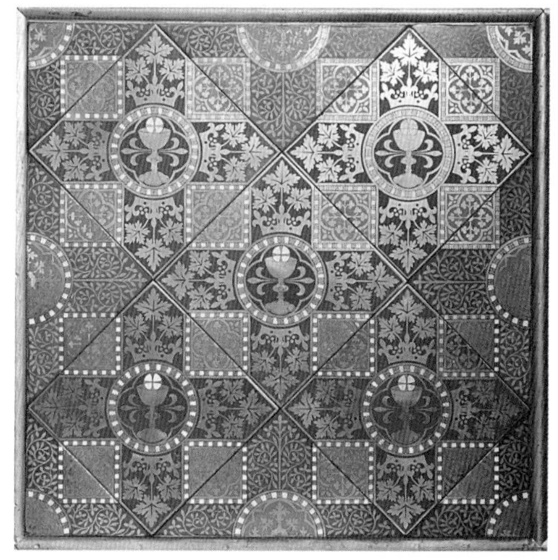

St Giles R. C. Church, Cheadle,
Staffordshire.

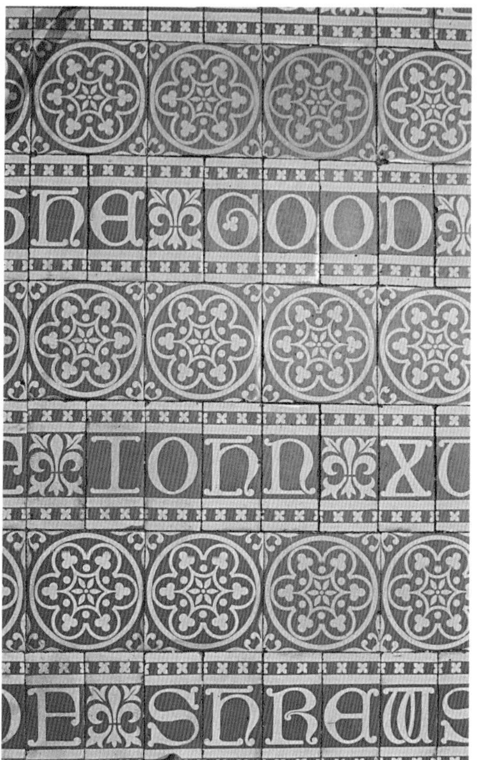

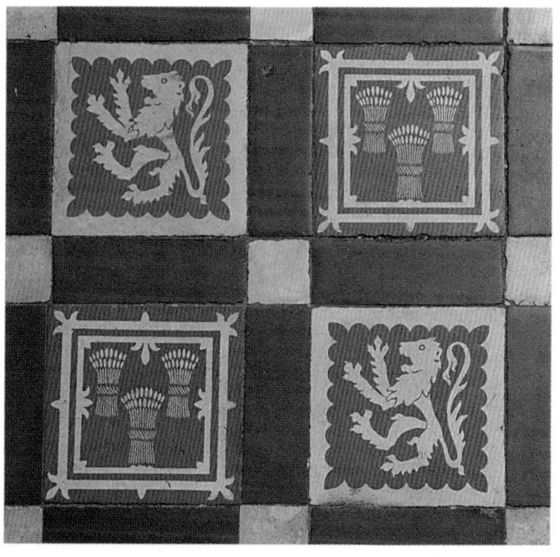

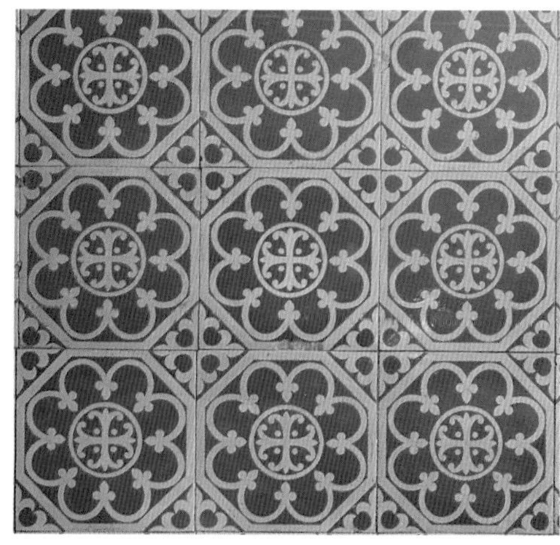

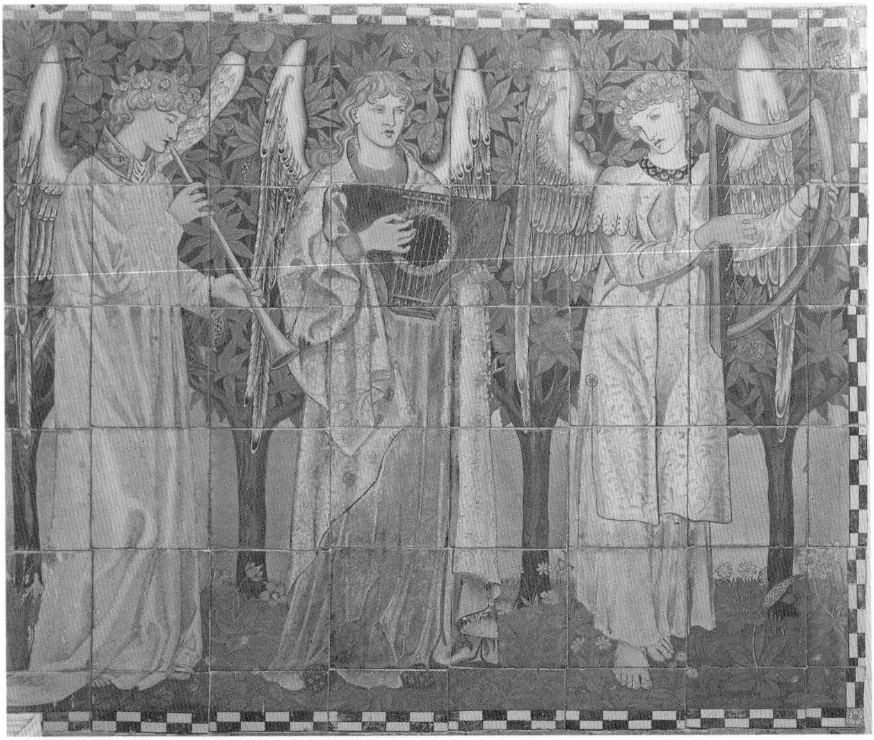

Church of St John the Baptist, Findon, West Sussex.

St Peter's Church, Ayot St Peter, Hertfordshire; detail from the chancel arch by the Martin Brothers, and tiles from the 'Revelations' series designed by J. P. Seddon.

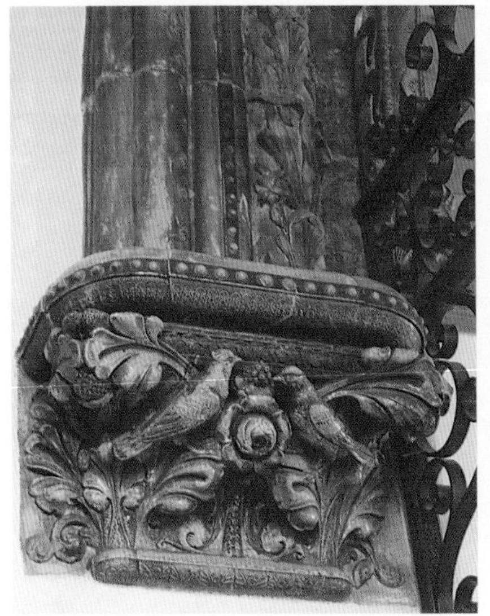

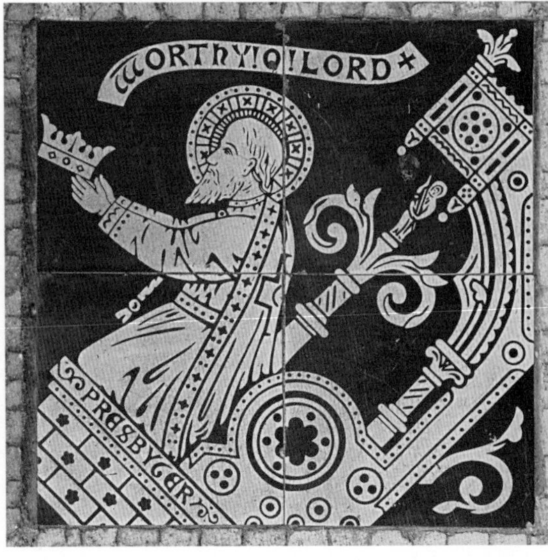

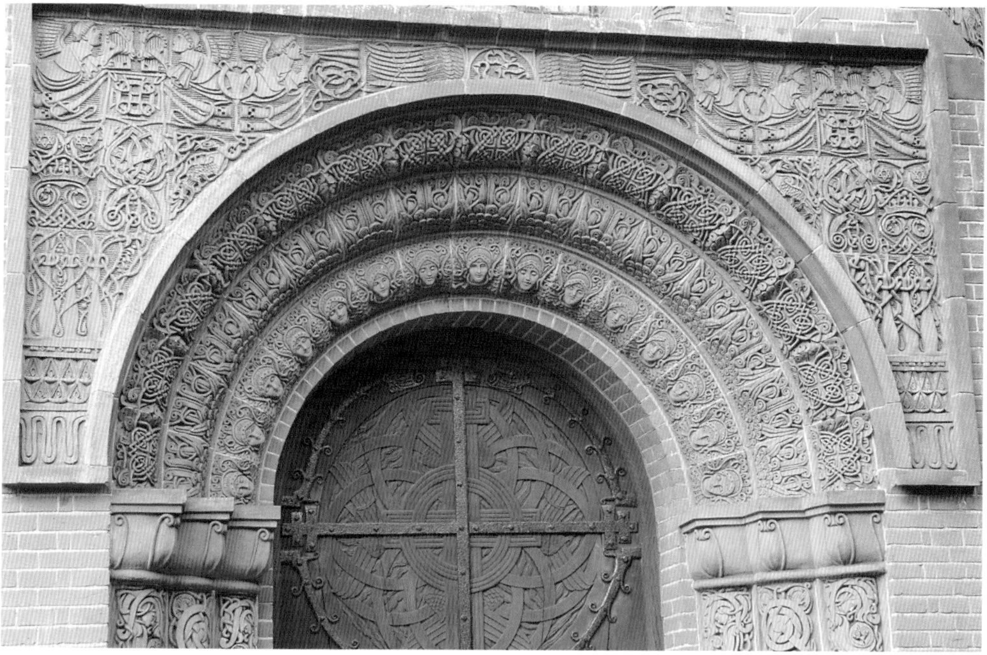

Watts Chapel, Compton, Surrey.

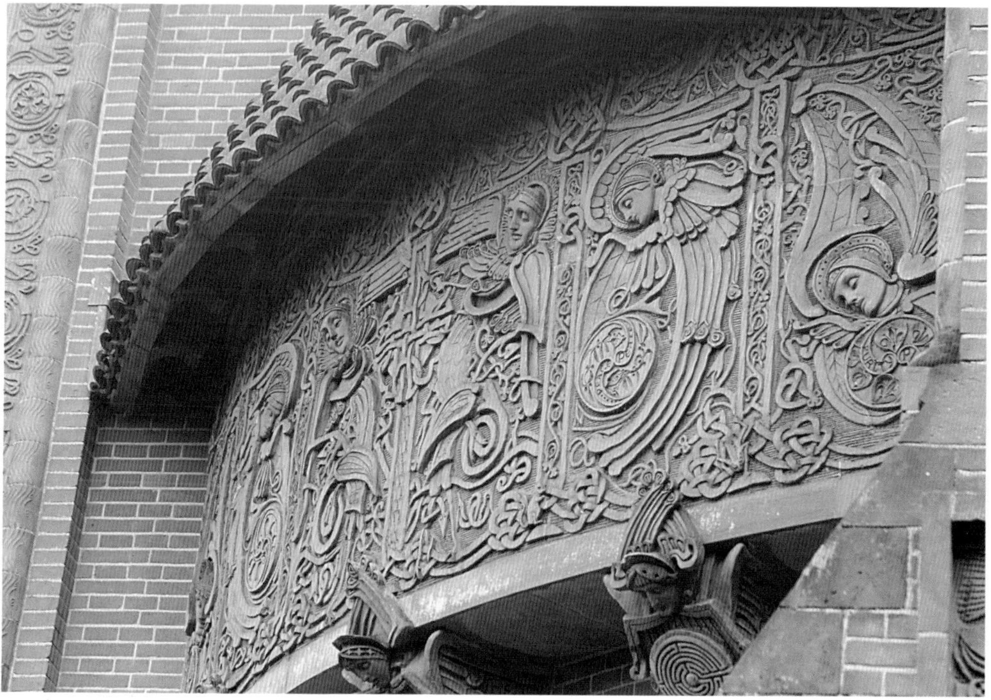

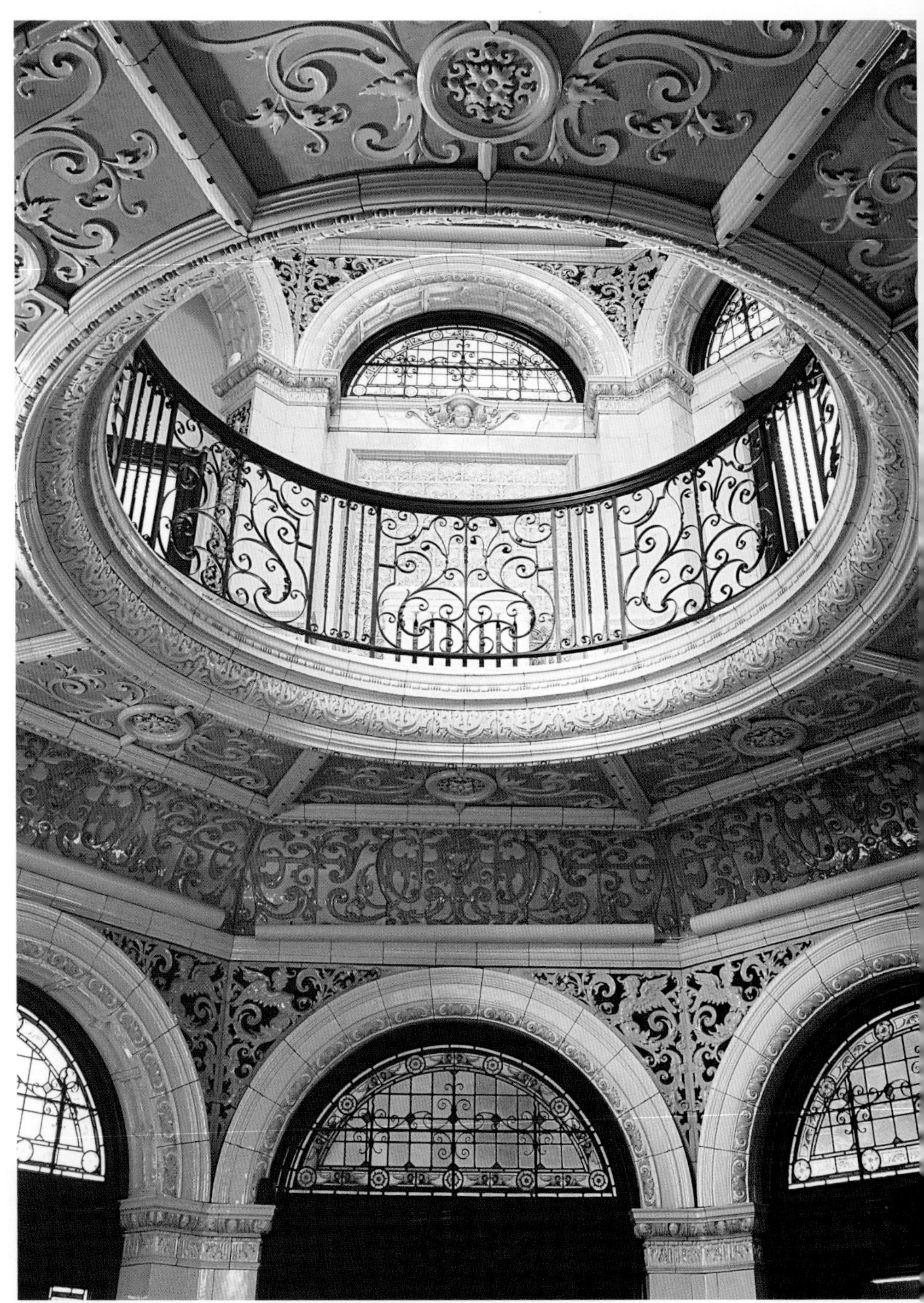

St Vincent's Works, Bristol, Gloucestershire.

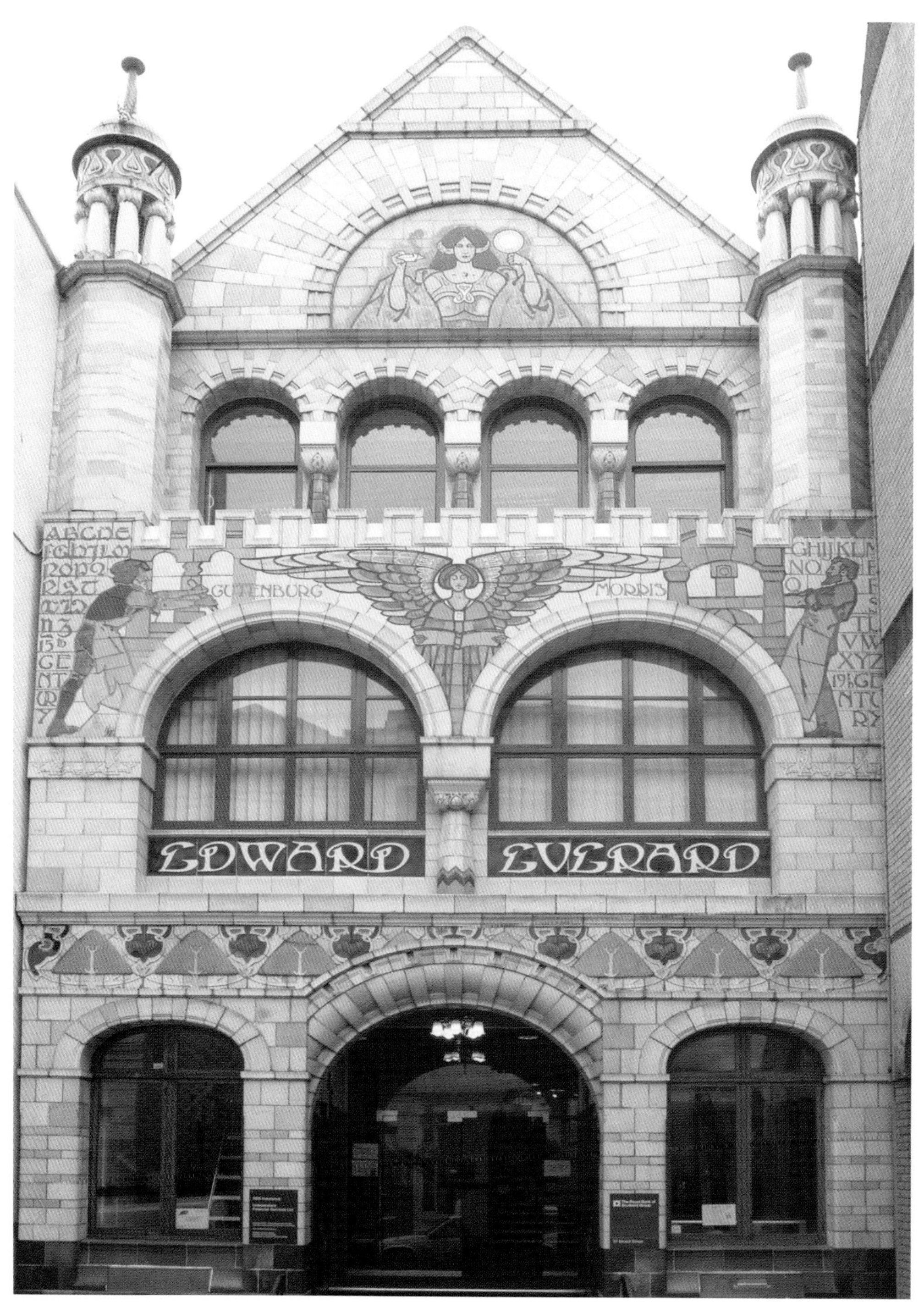

Everard Building, Bristol, Gloucestershire.

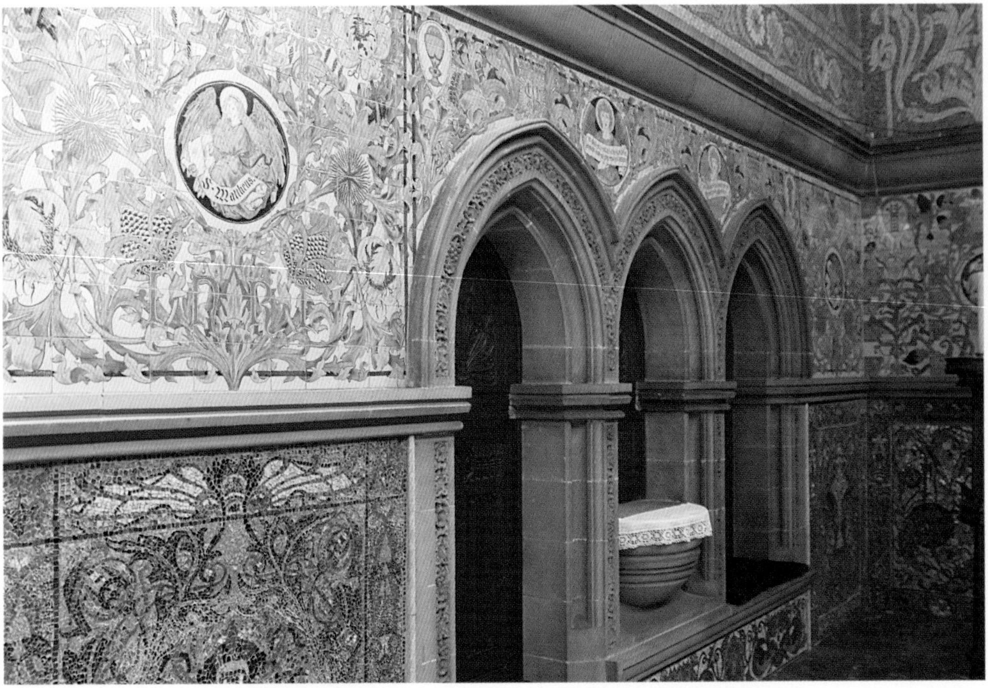

St George's Church, Jesmond, Newcastle upon Tyne, Northumberland.

St Augustine's Church, Queen's Gate, Kensington & Chelsea, London.

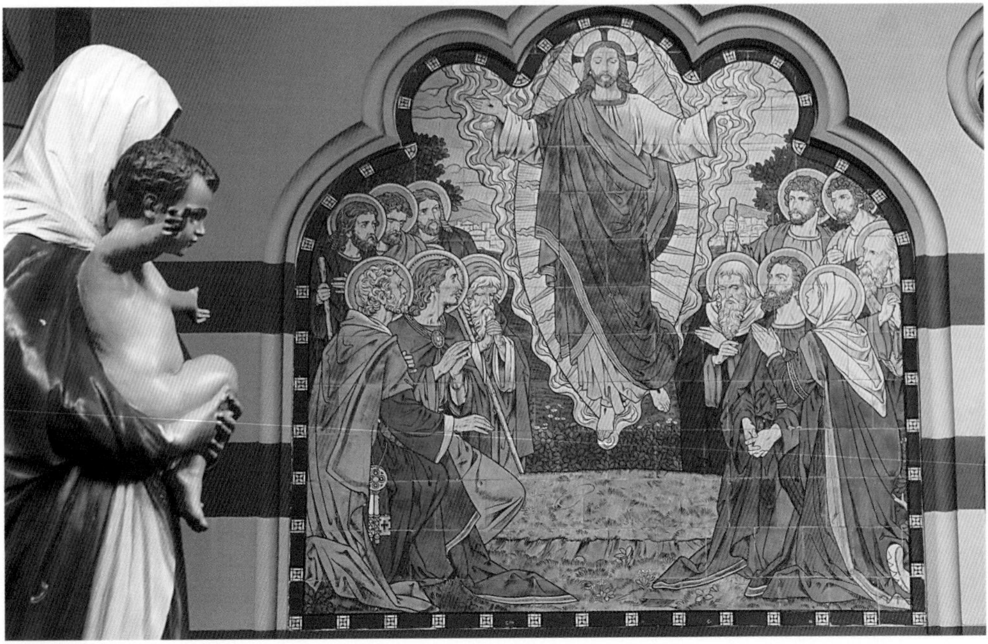

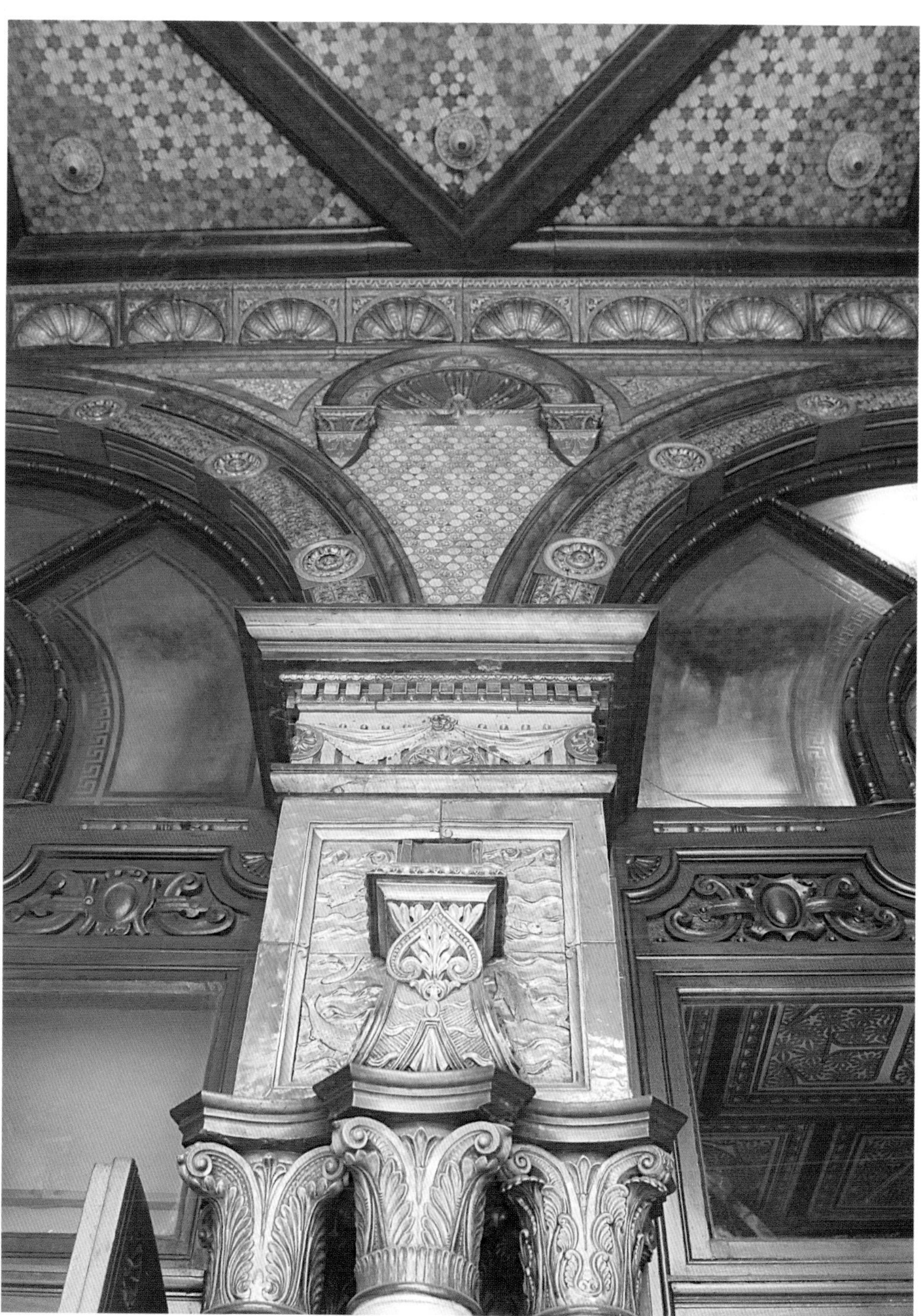

Lloyds Bank, Strand, Westminster, London.

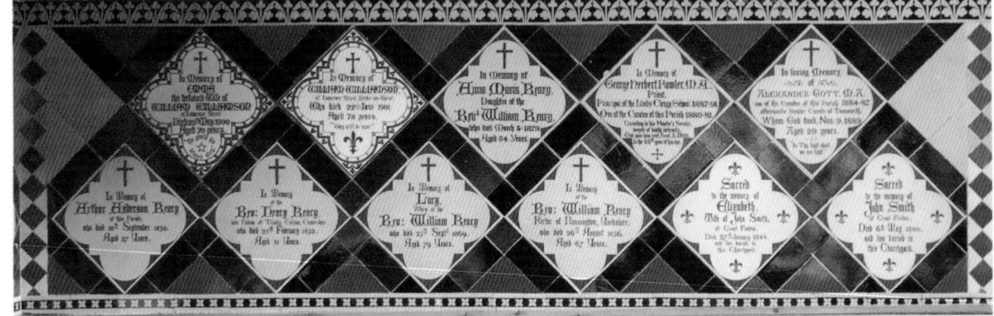

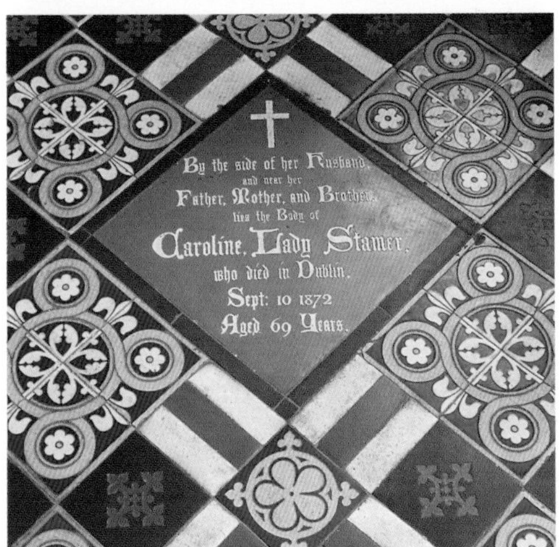

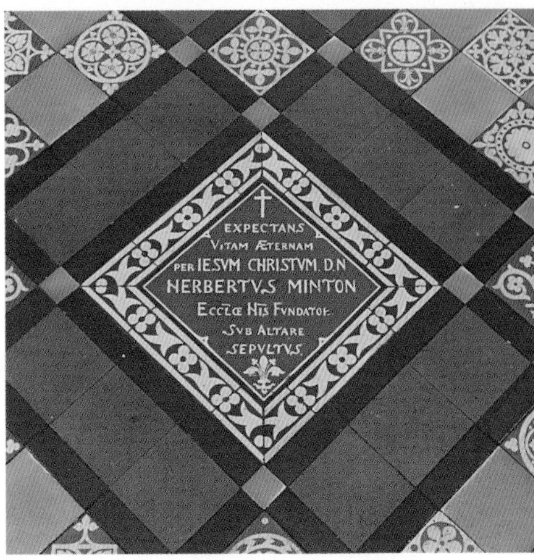

Memorial tiles from Holy Trinity Church, Hartshill and St Peter ad Vincula, Stoke, Stoke-on-Trent, Staffordshire.

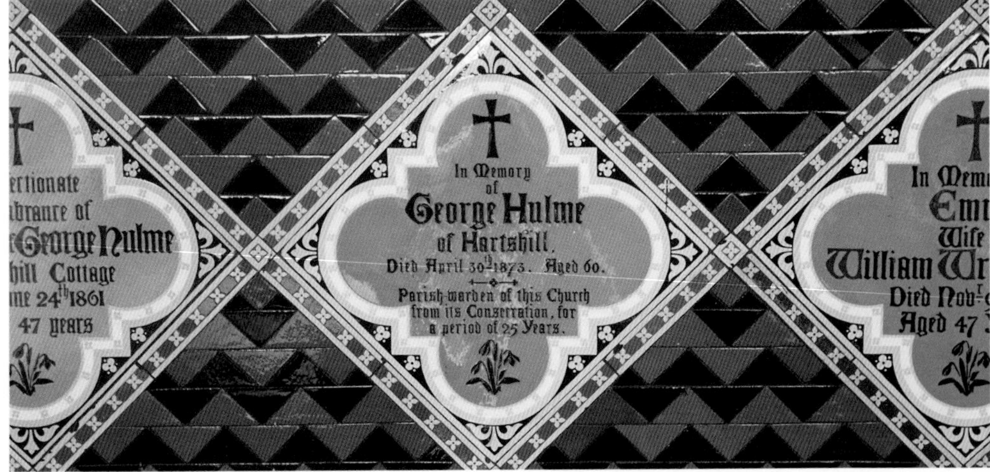

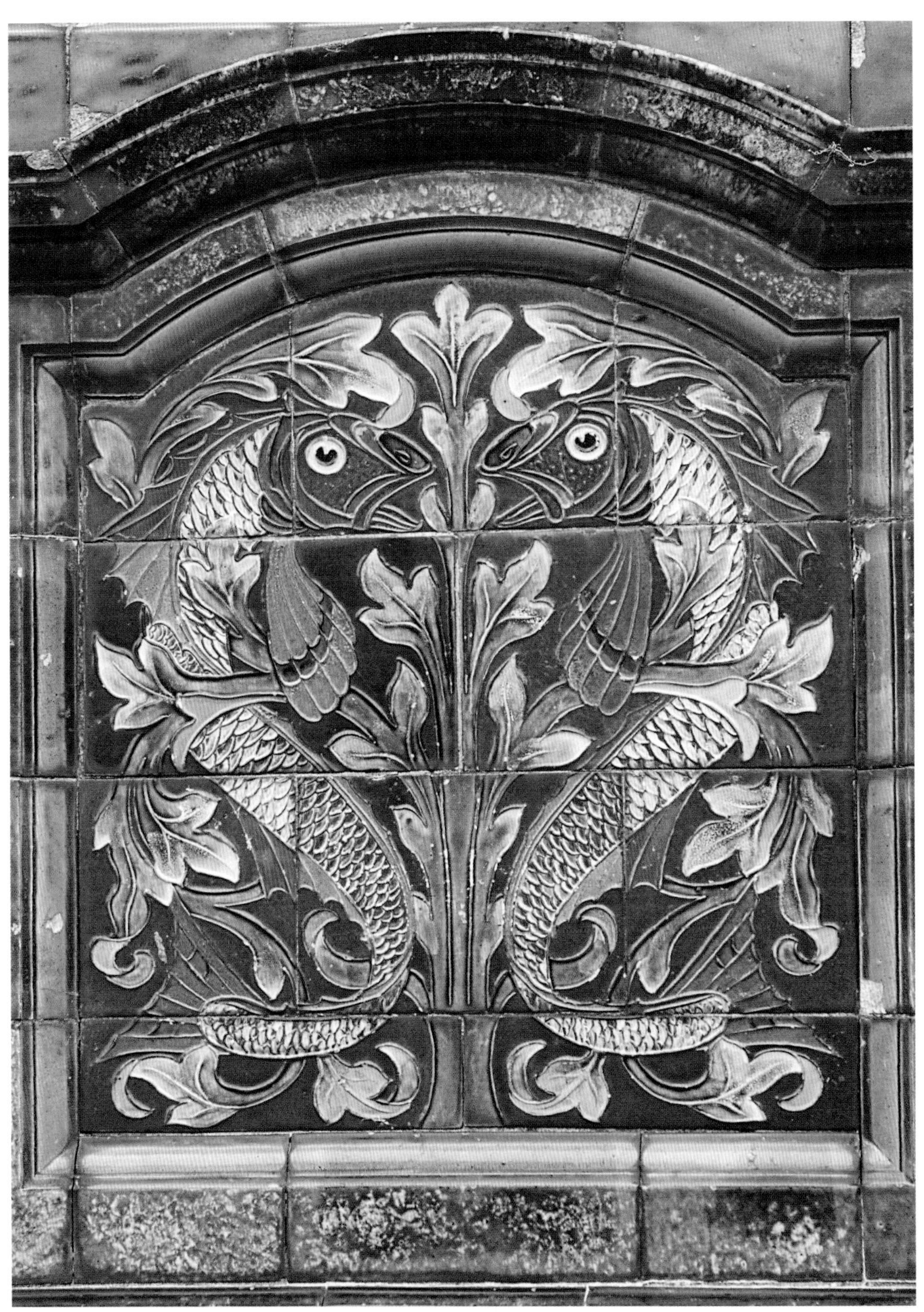

Richard Eve Memorial, Kidderminster, Worcestershire.

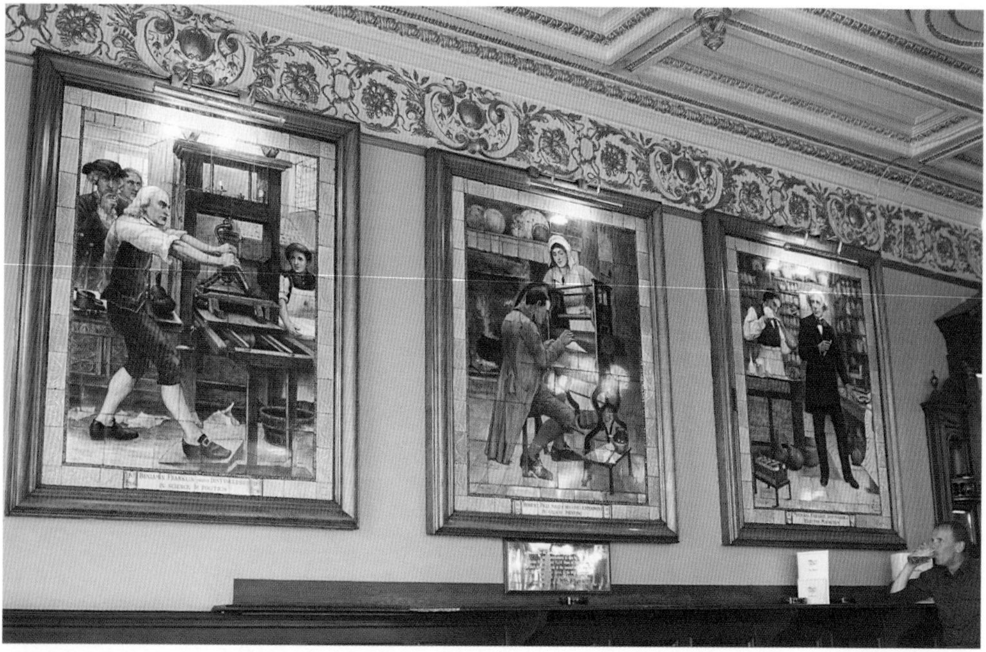

Café Royal, Edinburgh.

St Marie's R. C. Cathedral, Sheffield, South Yorkshire.

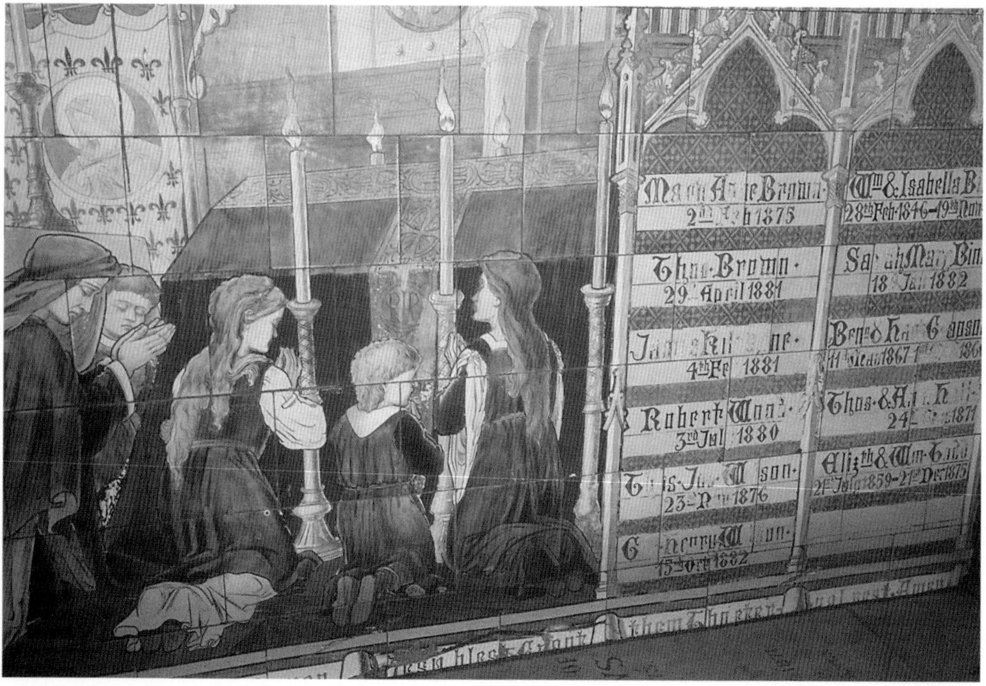

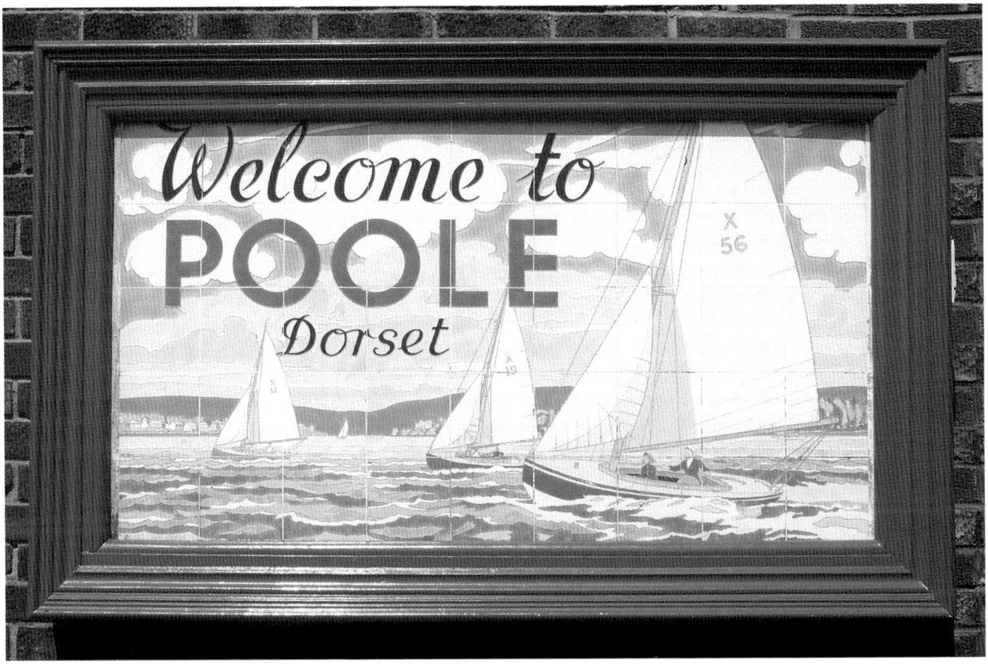

Welcome to Poole' panel by Carter's near the former site of the Poole Pottery, Dorset.

Church of St Mary the Virgin, Isleworth, Hounslow, London.

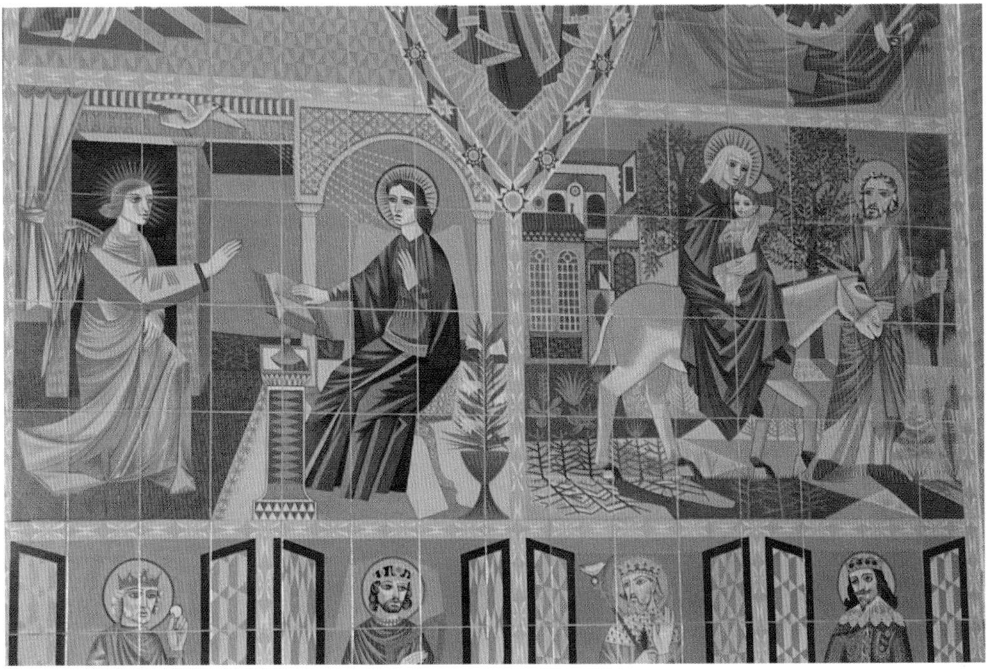

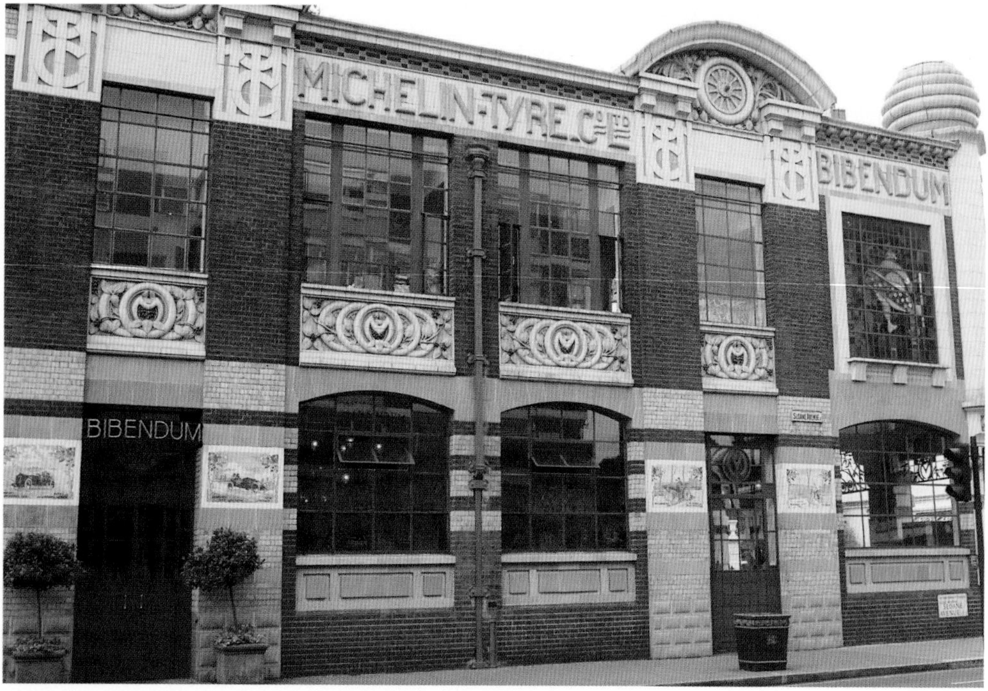

Michelin Building, Kensington & Chelsea, London.

Mo's Fisheries, Ealing, London.

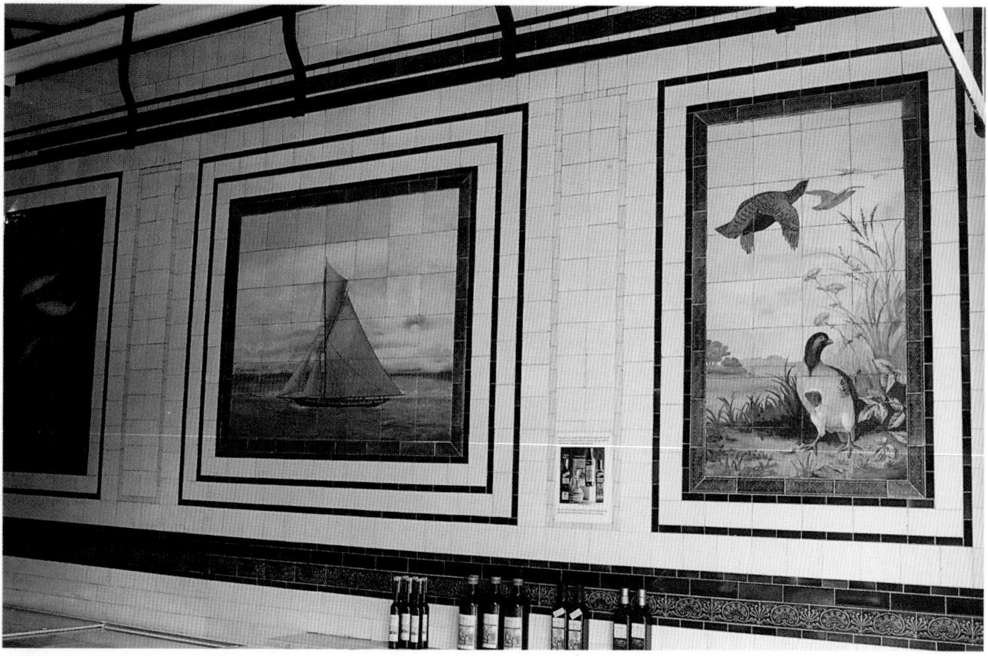

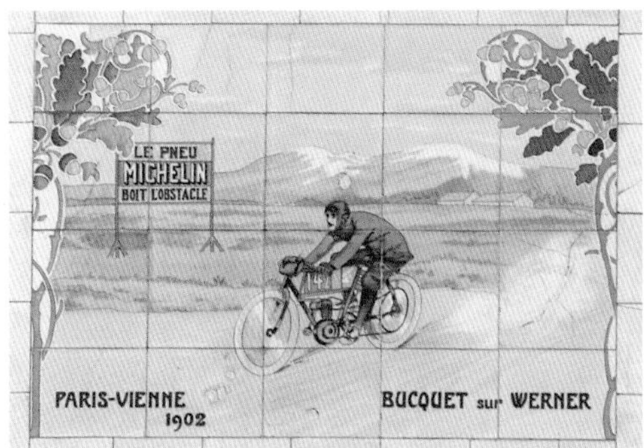
LE PNEU
MICHELIN
BOIT L'OBSTACLE
PARIS-VIENNE
1902
BUCQUET sur WERNER

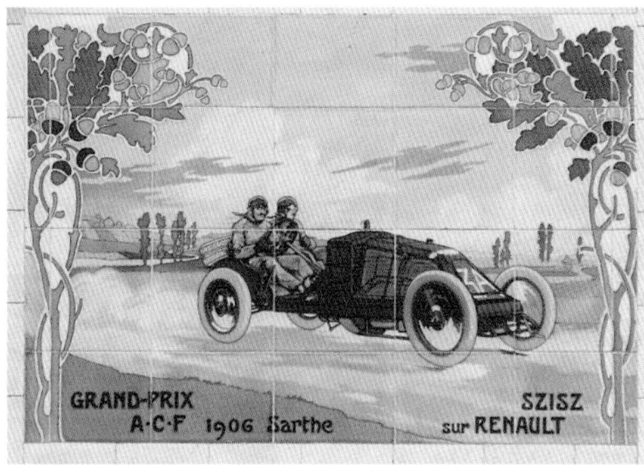
GRAND-PRIX
A·C·F 1906 Sarthe
SZISZ
sur RENAULT

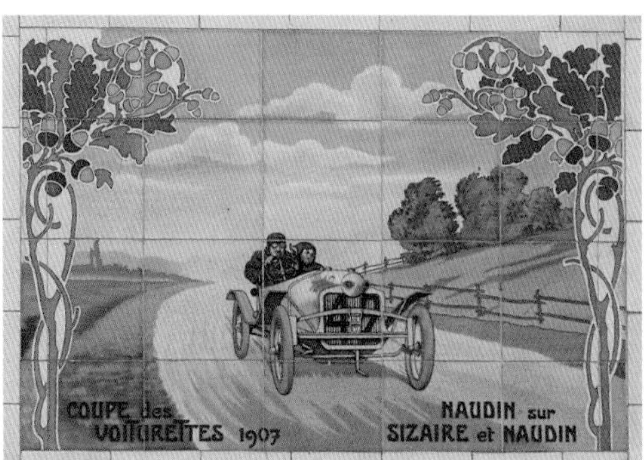
COUPE des
VOITURETTES 1907
NAUDIN sur
SIZAIRE et NAUDIN

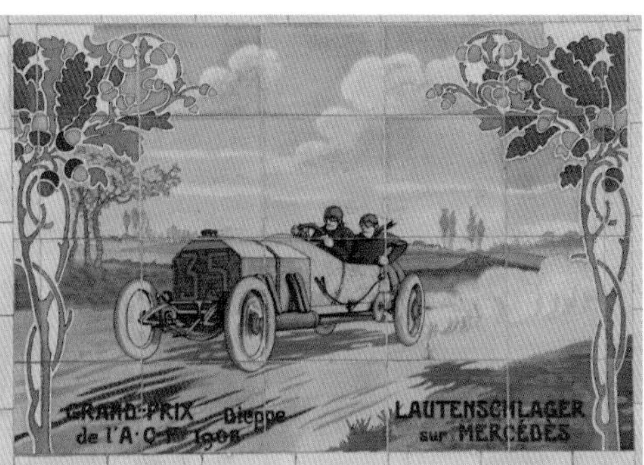
GRAND-PRIX Dieppe
de l'A·C·F 1908
LAUTENSCHLAGER
sur MERCÉDÈS

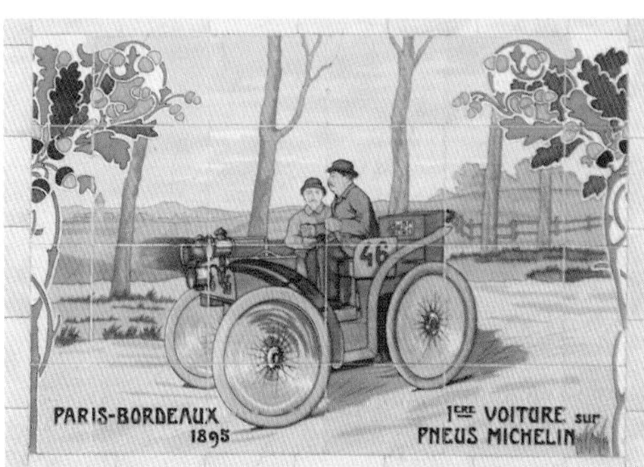
PARIS-BORDEAUX
1895
1ère VOITURE sur
PNEUS MICHELIN

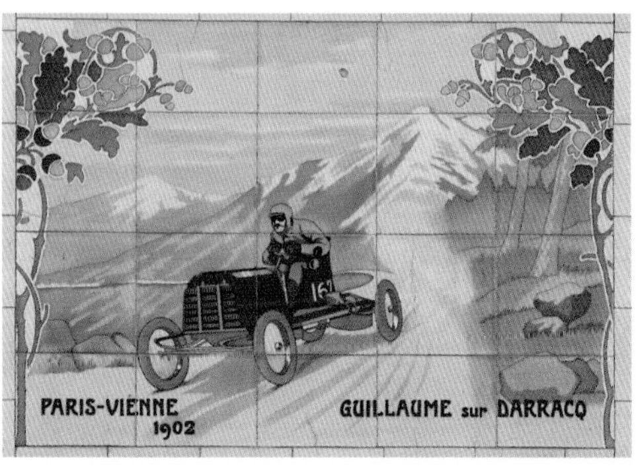
PARIS-VIENNE
1902
GUILLAUME sur DARRACQ

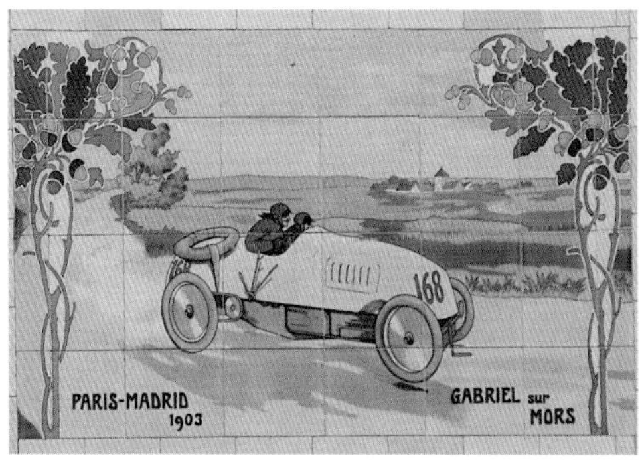
PARIS-MADRID
1903
GABRIEL sur
MORS

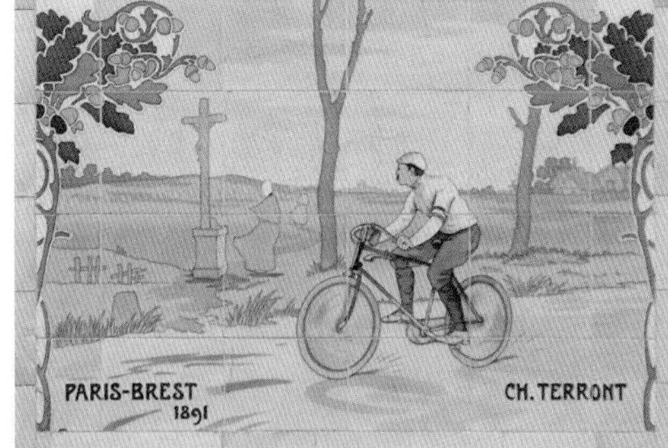
PARIS-BREST
1891
CH. TERRONT

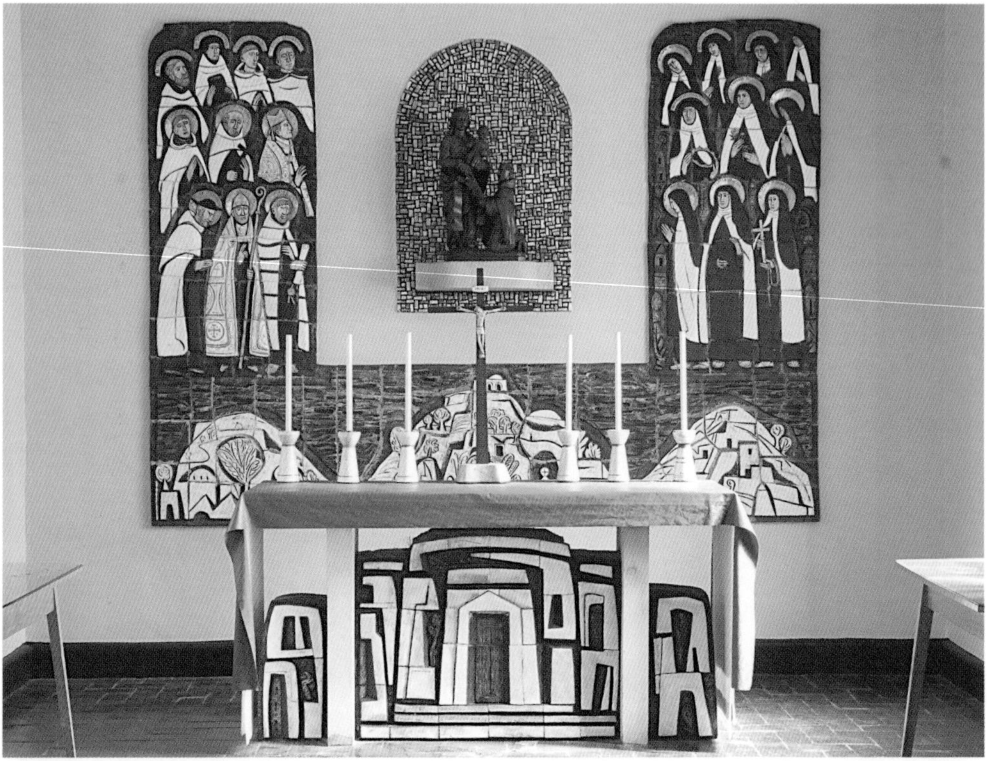

The Friars, Aylesford, Kent.

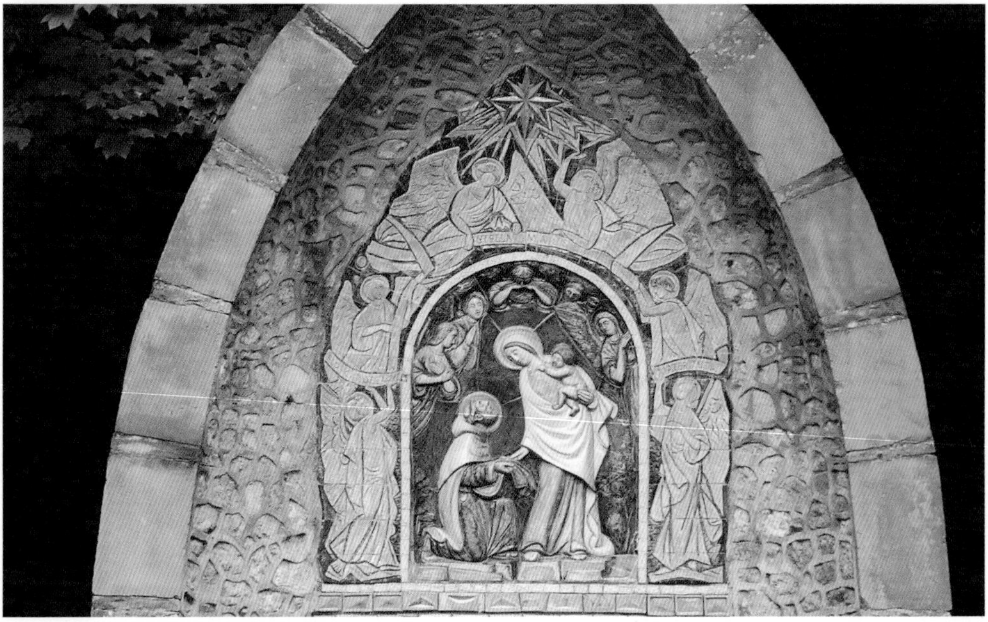

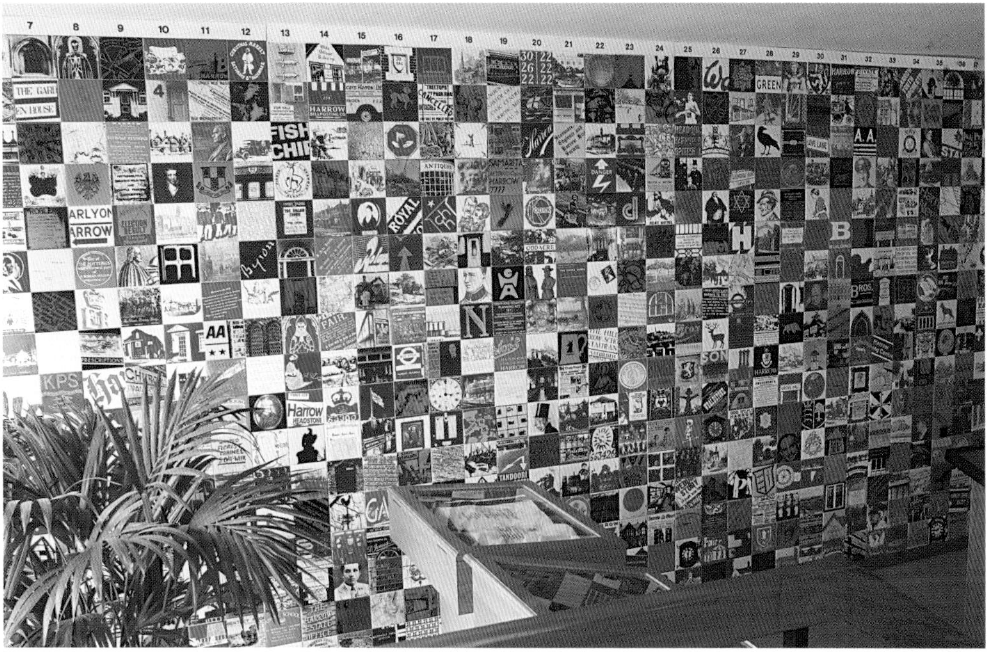

Harrow Civic Centre, Wealdstone, Harrow, London.

Gateshead Leisure Centre, County Durham.

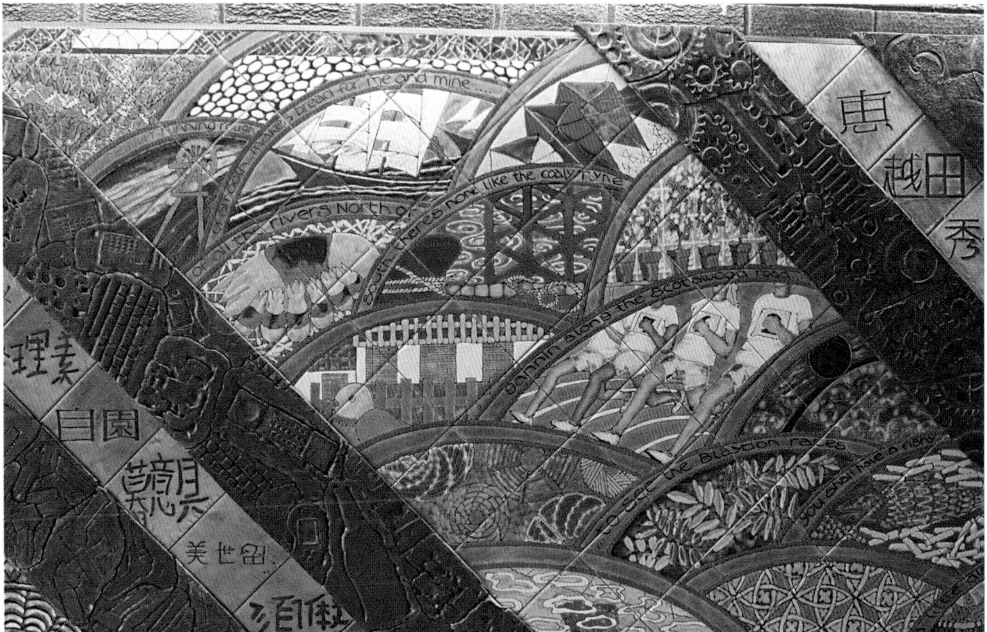

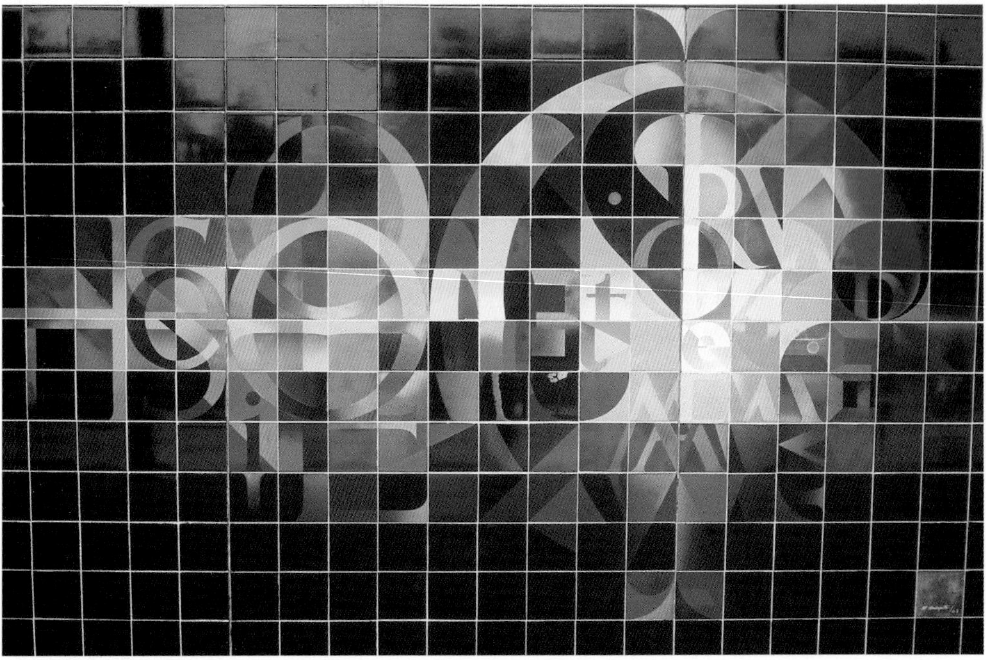

Sunderland Museum and Winter Gardens, County Durham.

Motherwell Theatre, Civic Centre, Motherwell, North Lanarkshire.

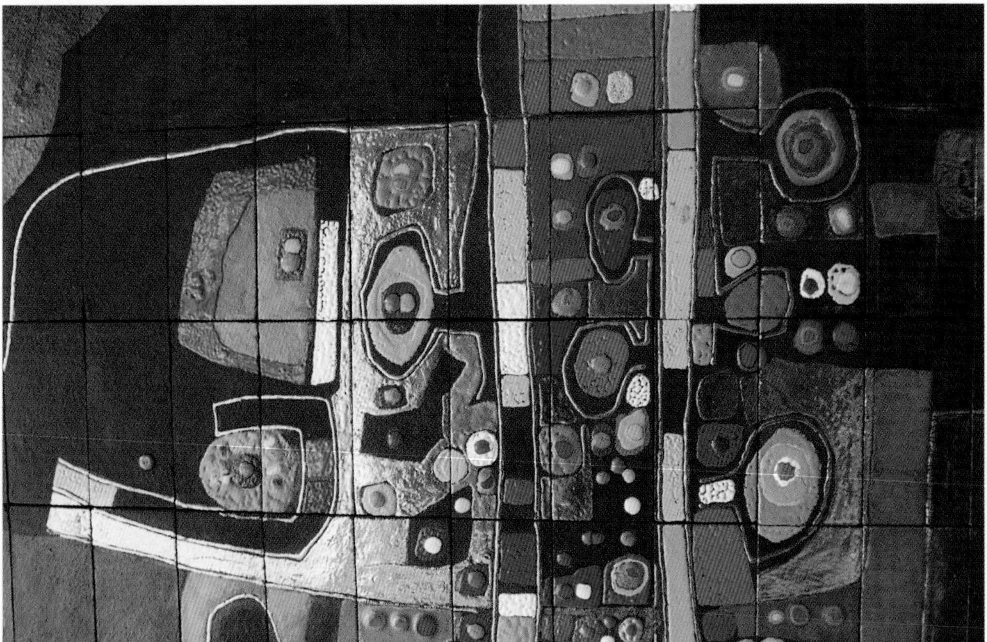

Shropshire

Shropshire offers many minor locations with medieval tiles still in situ, notably the large pavement at Acton Burnell Church, and a memorable Coade stone site in the form of the colossal statue which tops Lord Hill's Column in Shrewsbury. Dating from only thirty years after the Column, Llanymynech Church (1844-5) is an example of the experimental and generally unpopular use of terracotta for church construction during the 1840s. This was a phenomenon of two areas where terracotta was available locally, Lancashire - the 'pot churches' - and the Welsh borders, with four locations in Wales and one in Shropshire. Indeed the county's clay, especially the 'heavy clay' of Broseley, has been of huge significance in encouraging the development of so many brick and tile makers around Ironbridge, their activities peaking during the period 1870-1910.

With two of the country's (and the world's) most important tile manufacturers, Maw & Co and Craven Dunnill, situated in the heart of Shropshire at Jackfield in the Ironbridge Gorge, it would be surprising if the county did not have a wealth of interesting ceramic locations. Maw's opened their works at Benthall, near Broseley, in 1852, moving to their Jackfield factory in 1883, not far from Craven Dunnill's Jackfield works which had opened in 1874. The products of these two firms, as well as some early Minton work, can be found throughout the county, although the locations, which include many churches, are often less dramatic than contemporary sites in urban areas, and are sometimes a touch idiosyncratic. The lavish floor at Battlefield Church, with its strange coffin-shaped design by Maw's, is a real oddity. Other highlights include the early Minton floor at St Mary's Church in Shrewsbury, and of course Jackfield, with its church and tile factories. Also of interest are the homes of George and Arthur Maw, Benthall Hall and the Valley Hotel, Ironbridge respectively, and aside from locally-made ceramics, in a beautiful setting on the Welsh border is St Michael's Church, Stowe, with a superb decorative scheme by Powell's of Whitefriars.

Finally, a piece of innovative modern work is the early 1980s Shaws of Darwen scheme alongside the road at Nabb Hill, Telford; this is tiling on a dramatic scale. The *Gazetteer* entry for Shropshire covers the administrative areas of Shropshire County Council and Telford & Wrekin Council.

ACTON BURNELL

St Mary's Church stands close to the romantic ruins of Acton Burnell Castle, a fortified house dating from the thirteenth century. The north transept of the church is paved with about 900 four-inch square fourteenth century tiles, mainly line-impressed and counter-relief with a few inlaid. A nice range of motifs includes oak leaves, a hunter blowing his horn, and a griffin, the latter design being quite common in this area. In addition, the sanctuary has a Victorian dust-pressed encaustic tile pavement. Just over a mile south of the village, in the tiny hamlet of Langley, is **Langley Chapel** (EH) with a complete set of early seventeenth century fittings and furniture. At its east end are some thirteenth or fourteenth century tiles which were laid in their present positions during the seventeenth century.

BATCHCOTT

All Saints Church, in the hamlet of Batchcott, is set high above the village to which it belongs, Richards Castle, which lies across the county border in Herefordshire. It was designed by Richard Norman Shaw and built in 1890-3. The interior has relatively little decoration, but there is a good opus sectile figure of Christ, the *Light of the World*, designed by James Hogan (1883-1948) in 1924 and supplied by Powell's of Whitefriars at a cost of £130; Hogan was the firm's principal in-house designer. The panel is a memorial to Richard Betton Betton-Foster of nearby Overton Grange.

BATTLEFIELD

The medieval **Church of St Mary Magdalene** at Battlefield, out in the countryside on the northern fringe of Shrewbury, was in the ownership of the Corbet family of now-demolished Sundorne Castle (just over a mile to the south-east of the church) from 1638. The church was restored at the family's expense in 1861, their architect being Samuel Pountney Smith (1812-83) of Shrewsbury. An elaborate encaustic pavement, including tiles by Maw & Co and Minton, runs throughout the church, with eighteen royal coats of arms on the chancel floor and an extraordinary coffin-shaped arrangement by Maw's in the Corbet family chapel (Fig 227). Altogether, with its Corbet symbols and several splendidly large Maw trade tiles, this is a church floor to rival any in Britain. St Mary Magdalene is now in the care of the Churches Conservation Trust.

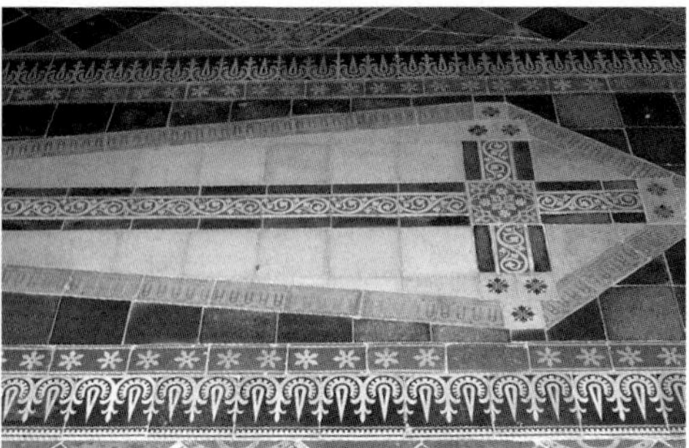

Fig 227.

BENTHALL

St Bartholomew's Church, Benthall (a mile west of Broseley) was damaged during the Civil War and rebuilt in 1667. Thirteenth century tiles from the original church survive in the sanctuary and near the font; the latter, lozenge-shaped tiles are very similar to those displayed in the porch of neighbouring **Benthall Hall** (NT). The Hall, which dates from the sixteenth century, was leased by the brothers George and Arthur Maw (of Maw's Benthall tileworks) from 1853 to 1886; initially the house was divided into two dwellings, but later Arthur moved to a neighbouring house to make room for their growing families. In 1859 the flagstones of Benthall Hall's entrance hall were repaced by a colourful Maw's geometric and encaustic pavement, probably designed by George Maw himself. Although the tiles were covered by an oak floor in 1918, a trapdoor ensures that a small section of this attractive pavement can still be seen.

BROSELEY

In KING STREET, right in the middle of Broseley, is an astonishing former **butcher's shop** completely tiled inside and out with products from the Maw's factory, only a mile or so away beside the Severn at Jackfield (Fig 228). The shop's owner was Matthew Davis, whose name appears on the facade; he emigrated to South America in the 1890s but returned shortly afterwards and purchased the little shop, which he enlarged. He then bought a substantial number of tiles from Maw's, perhaps getting them at a good price as they were taken from a pile stored outside the factory, and hired a local man (who had a reputation as something of a drunkard) as a tile fixer.[1] The result is happily eccentric.

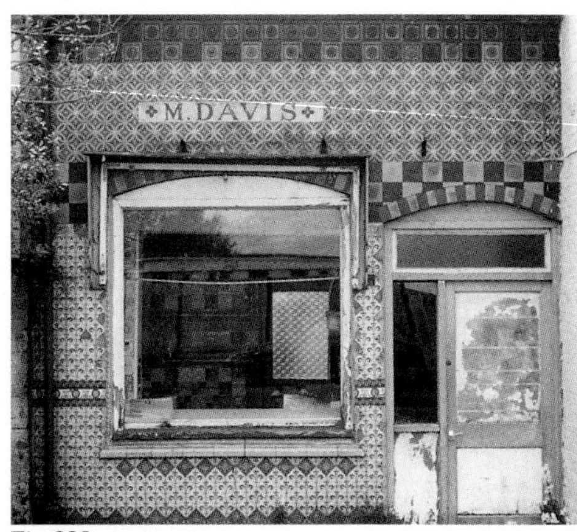

Fig 228.

BUILDWAS

There are several areas of medieval tiling visible amongst the ruins of the Cistercian foundation **Buildwas Abbey** (EH), which lies on the south bank of the Severn opposite the village; some of the best are in the chapter house, where there are relaid tiles from the thirteenth and fourteenth centuries (Fig 229).

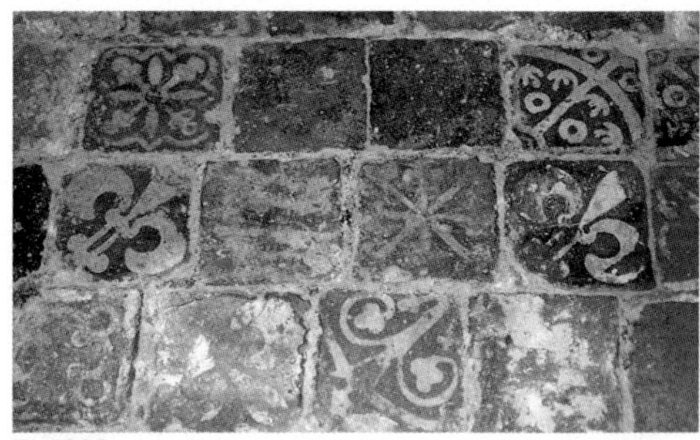

Fig 229.

CARDINGTON

The east wall of **St James Church** is faced with decorative tiling which reaches up to the lower edge of the east window. Its main features are four pictorial panels depicting biblical figures, and the lettering 'Do this in remembrance of me' above the altar. This colourful scheme, with its chevron-style arrangement of tiles, probably dates from restoration work carried out during the 1860s; the maker is unknown. The church also displays a ceramic panel made by local people and installed in 2000; it shows St James at the centre of the community.

CHETWYND

The **Church of St Michael and All Angels** (1865-7, architect Benjamin Ferrey) stands about two miles north-west of Newport, not far from Chetwynd Hall. Most of the east wall tiling dates from 1867, although the majolica reredos was installed in 1880; it shows the Symbols of the Passion in rich colours and is probably by the Campbell Brick & Tile Company.

CHIRBURY

There are some relaid medieval floor tiles in the south aisle of **St Michael's Church**, which was restored in 1871-2. The Powell's opus sectile reredos, which includes a pair of kneeling angels, dates from 1878 and is one of the earliest designs attributable to Suter, a Powell's cartoonist.[2]

IRONBRIDGE

The **Valley Hotel**, BUILDWAS ROAD is a Georgian building previously known as Severn House when it was the home of Arthur Maw, the tile manufacturer. Its ceramic decoration, much of which can be seen in the hotel's reception area and main staircase, includes a Maw's geometric and encaustic pavement, a tiled dado and a high-relief majolica-tiled archway. Beside the hotel is a cottage with unusual diaper patterned polychrome roof tiling.

JACKFIELD

St Mary's Church (architect Arthur Blomfield, 1863), its exterior an essay in the use of polychromatic brick, predates the two tile factories which now dominate the visitor's impression of Jackfield (Fig 230). It was built from 'Broseley' bricks, made from high-quality local clay, their colours ranging through two shades of red to yellow and blue. The bricks and roofing tiles were made at the works in Calcutts Road, Jackfield established by Theophilus Doughty in 1840, and are reputed to have been supplied free of charge.[3] Inside, the encaustic and geometric tile pavement is by Maw & Co, in muted colours but with some interesting motifs; the Maw's wall tiling around the apsidal east end is in the same vein.[4] The pictorial tiled reredos, a colourful triptych of the crucifixion, is by Craven Dunnill, and stood for many years in their works showroom before being presented to the church in the early 1950s when the firm left Jackfield.

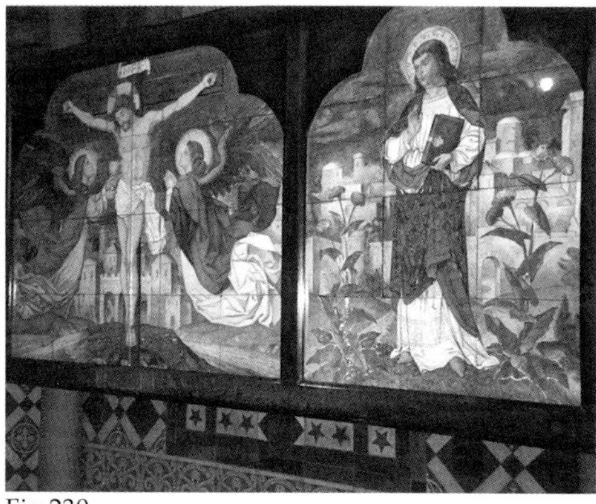

Fig 230.

Round the corner from the church is the **Jackfield Tile Museum**, formerly Craven Dunnill's factory, designed by the architect Charles Lynam and built in 1871-4. The Jackfield Encaustic Tile Works was the second tileworks to be designed by Lynam, the first having just been completed for Michael Daintry Hollins in Stoke-on-Trent. For Craven Dunnill, a firm which had been in existence in the Severn valley from the 1860s, Lynam supplied a model tile factory in which the production processes were logically arranged and the neighbouring railway line was used for the import of raw materials and the export of finished tiles. Aside from its spire, exterior decoration was far from lavish, being restricted to decorative panels of unglazed geometric tiles above the windows, in a similar manner to the earlier Minton Hollins factory; inside, an original tiled washroom remains on the first floor. Tile manufacture ceased in the early 1950s and the works was bought by the Ironbridge Gorge Museum in 1983.

A few hundred yards east along the valley is **Maw's Craft Centre**, housed in what remains of Maw & Co's Benthall Works, which opened in 1883 and was the largest tileworks in the world by the turn of the century; it was Charles Lynam's third tile factory design (Fig 231).[5] The long, narrow complex of buildings stood beside the railway line, with a row of bottle kilns at one end. The factory closed in 1970, and two-thirds of the site was demolished during the 1970s before conversion of some of the remaining buildings into flats, small business units and shops in the early 1980s; Maw's Craft Centre opened in 1988. As with Lynam's previous two tileworks, there was not a great deal of external decoration, although the broad tile panel above the main entrance, which records key dates in the firm's history, is still extant. In the courtyard is a small tile pavement including oddments of letter tiles, and a wall tile panel shows a hand pointing to the foreman's office. Rather more lavish is the entrance and stairs which originally led to the showrooms, with a good mosaic floor, a large ceramic First World War memorial plaque and a tile dado including panels of classical figures. Restoration work on the hallway tiling was carried out by Lesley Durbin and Su Turner of the Jackfield Conservation Studio around 1991.

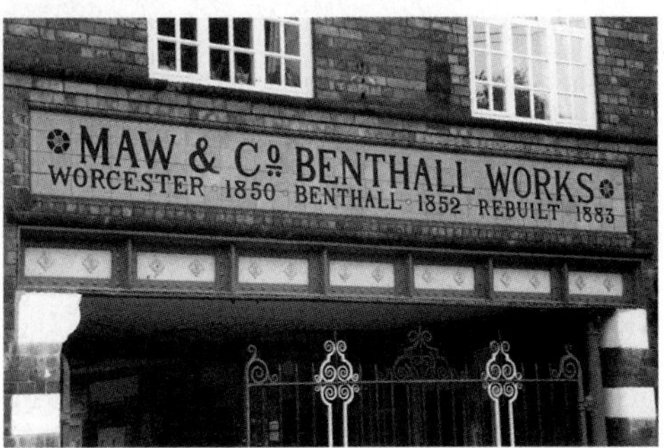

Fig 231.

KEMBERTON

St Andrew's Church, High Street, stands on a medieval site although the church itself mostly dates from 1882; the architect was Joseph Farmer of Kemberton. Only the nave of the church is dedicated to St Andrew; the chancel dedication is to St John the Baptist. The Craven Dunnill encaustic pavement in the chancel includes tiles depicting hunting scenes, the designs being derived from fourteenth century tiles, examples of which can still be seen at Neath Abbey (Neath Port Talbot, Wales).[6]

LLANYMYNECH

Llanymynech is a village of two halves, with the border between England and Wales (Powys) running for about half a mile along its main street. **St Agatha's Church**, designed by the architect Thomas Penson of Oswestry and built in 1844-5, lies on the Shropshire side of the divide. It is one of five churches built in the borders (the other four are in Powys) during the 1840s in which yellow terracotta or 'firebrick' was used in combination with buff brick to give rich decorative features at a lower cost than carved stone. Penson was responsible for three of these churches, his first being at Welshpool (1839-44), where brick and terracotta were used only on the inside of the building. At St Agatha, his second church of this group, he added elaborate external terracotta in the neo-norman style with zigzag patterning and many modelled heads. Penson's third terracotta church - St David, Newtown (1843-7) - took the use of this material to its logical end point, with brick and terracotta completely replacing stone. The source of the Llanymynech terracotta was probably the firebrick works at Trefonen, four miles to the north.

The Lancashire 'pot churches' designed by the architect Edmund Sharpe were being put up at the same time as these Welsh border churches, although Sharpe's use of terracotta was rather more innovative in structural terms. His Holy Trinity (1845-6), Rusholme, Manchester used a higher percentage of hollow blocks than his first terracotta church, St Stephen (1844-5), Lever Bridge, Bolton. As far as the critics of *The Ecclesiologist* were concerned, however, any use of terracotta in church architecture was beyond the pale. They felt its only theoretically sound use would be for building in the classical idiom, with which Coade stone had been associated, but clearly this would be unacceptable for the gothic revival churches being promoted by the Camden Society. Terracotta ornament was seen as second rate and unworthy, lacking the authenticity bestowed upon stone by medieval churches. Sharpe was pleased to find that visitors to Lever Bridge had not realised they were looking at terracotta, mistaking it for stone; Penson, on the other hand, may have been more concerned with originality than imitation. In any case, the use of terracotta in church construction had reached a dead end with these 1840s buildings; it was to be a generation before ecclesiastical architects were again prepared to experiment with the material.[7]

St Agatha's Church was listed grade II in 1987. Echoing Lever Bridge, it is interesting to note that despite Michael Stratton's comments in *The Terracotta Revival* that these Welsh border churches incorporate 'dressings of 'firebrick', large blocks too yellow in colour to be mistaken for stone', the lengthy list description does not mention terracotta, instead referring to 'yellow sandstone'!

LUDLOW

In the **Cotswold** fashion shop on CHURCH STREET, formerly a Maypole Dairy, is a pretty pictorial panel showing a rural scene with a maypole; it is part of a larger decorative scheme, the rest of which is now hidden. Most of these Maypole panels were produced around 1920-30 by Pilkington's, and may have been painted by the artist T. F. Evans, who joined the firm in 1894 and remained with them until his death in 1935.[8] However, the Ludlow panel, which could well have been transfer printed then hand-coloured, is not in Pilkington's style and was probably made by another firm; the Maypole chain is known to have commissioned many panels of differing designs.[9]

MUCH WENLOCK

There are medieval tiles in the scriptorium and south aisle of **Wenlock Priory** (EH), a large Cluniac property; these are mainly fourteenth century tiles relaid in the twentieth century. There is also a recent replica medieval floor by tilemaker Diana Hall. In the town itself, the font (1874) of **Holy Trinity Church** is ornamented with four large hand-painted tiles.

SHREWSBURY

Begin at the neo-tudor **Railway Station** (1849, 1855 and 1903) on CASTLE GATES; its 1985-6 renovation included the removal of the Craven Dunnill encaustic and geometric tile pavement from the refreshment room and its reinstatement (in part) in the ticket office, where a trade tile can be seen on the far left as one enters from the street. There is also a small but well-preserved tile pavement in the gentlemen's toilet on the island platform.

From the station, turn left and climb Castle Street; at the junction with pedestrianised Pride Hill, go left into ST MARY'S STREET to find **St Mary's Church**. This superb medieval church offers an insight into early Victorian encaustic tile design, with contrasting pavements by Minton's, Godwin and Maw & Co, as well as a reredos of Powell's opus sectile work (Fig 232). Beneath a roof in which timber angels hover, tiles occupy almost the whole of the floor area, the grid-patterned pavement in the nave (1864) being by Minton and the font dais by Godwin. The chancel and sanctuary tiling, also Godwin and dating from around 1868, has a wide variety of designs including symbols of St Mary and the four evangelists. To the south is the Trinity Chapel, where rebuilding was completed in 1888. Its tile pavement is by Maw while the reredos, with two delicate blue angels in opus sectile work and much subtly-patterned red glass tiling, was supplied by Powell's in 1908. There is still more: the most unusual pavement in the church is that of St Catherine's Chapel, north of the choir. This tiny area, which functions as a foyer for the well-hidden café to the rear, has an excellent display of Minton tiling laid during the 1840s (relaid 1865), including many of the designs from the *Earliest Pattern Book* which just pre-dated the firm's first printed catalogue of 1842. St Mary's Church has been in the care of the Churches Conservation Trust since 1987, and the entire floor of their 'cathedral' was cleaned and restored in 1998; this involved the replacement of around 120 tiles with copies produced by H. & R. Johnson's.[10]

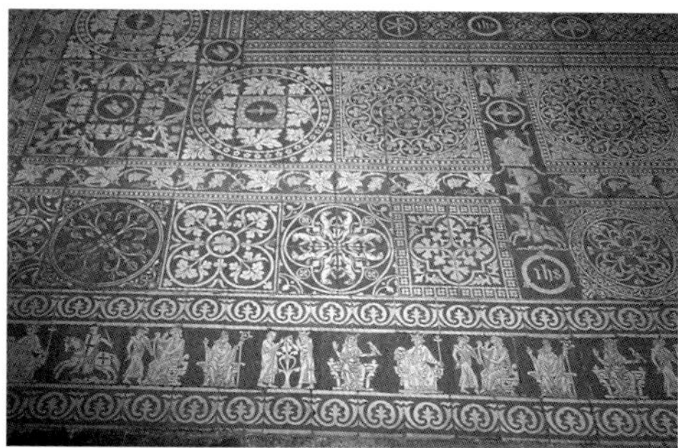

Fig 232.

Just south of the church in St Mary's Place is the Elizabethan **Drapers Hall** (now a restaurant), where a medieval tile floor was relaid after its removal from Shrewsbury Abbey in the sixteenth century; there are also three fireplaces surrounded with eighteenth century delft tiles. Continue down Dogpole and turn left into Wyle Cop, heading for the Abbey. In ST JULIAN FRIARS, on the right just before the bridge, is the **Hop and Friar** pub, with a colourful modern tile panel of 'olde worlde' figures inside the entrance. It is good to see a revival of this traditional form of tied estate branding.

After crossing the Severn, **Shrewsbury Abbey** lies ahead on ABBEY FOREGATE. There are groups of medieval tiles near the south porch (relaid) and in the adjacent vestry (a framed panel), but the Abbey's most important medieval tiles are in a small relaid pavement, low down on the north side of the chancel; it is here that the famous St Agatha tile can be found. Its inscription, given in the lesson for St Agatha's Feast, was used as a charm to protect against fever and fire. The Abbey's tiles, a mixture of line-impressed, counter-relief and inlaid designs, date from the thirteenth to late fifteenth century and may have been made at a local kiln. In addition, on the north wall of the Abbey's nave, towards its east end, is a highly glazed lozenge-shaped memorial tile bearing the date 1887.

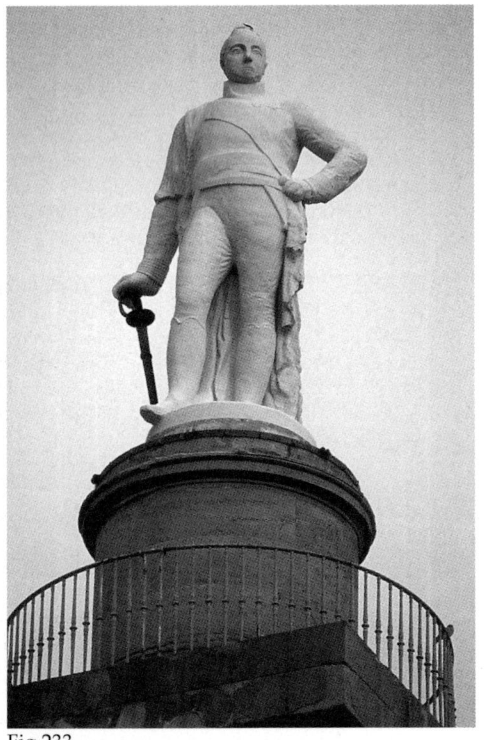

Fig 233.

Now for the long trudge up ABBEY FOREGATE, which culminates in **Lord Hill's Column**, reputed to be the tallest Doric column in the world at 133′ 6″ (Fig 233). This monumental column was put up in 1814-16 to commemorate the soldier Viscount Rowland Hill (1772-1842), whose 17′ 6″ Coade stone statue looks out over Shrewsbury from its top.[11] The Viscount fought at Waterloo in 1815, and the column was unveiled on the first anniversary of the battle. Joseph Panzetta modelled the statue, which was put on show at Coade's Lambeth Manufactory in August 1816; it is said to be the largest Coade stone statue in the world. It has, however, proved troublesome. Frost caused parts to fall off in 1879, an arm fell in 1945, and in 1967 its complete replacement by a fibreglass replica was proposed. Instead the hollow figure was filled with cement, but in the 1970s a concrete replica was substituted for the right leg, while wood was used for the right hand. Finally, in 1994-5 the statue was lowered to the ground, repaired and restored.

Just beyond Lord Hill's Column in WENLOCK ROAD is the the **Peacock** public house, its facade displaying a highly glazed ceramic panel of a peacock, mostly in attractive shades of blue and green. This dates from 1980 and is by Lee Cox of Liverpool. To return to the Railway Station simply reverse the route, although a diversion via MURIVANCE (take Beeches Lane on the left soon after the bridge, then continue around Town Walls) will allow an inspection of the fine red brick and terracotta facade of the former **Eye, Ear and Throat Hospital** (1879-81, architect C. O. Ellison of Liverpool). The brick and terracotta, which includes some good figurative work, came from the Ruabon works of J. C. Edwards.[12] The entrance hall decoration included three panels of twelve six-inch tiles depicting female figures of Faith, Hope, and Charity. These were drawn by one Mr Weatherstone for Maw & Co, who originally intended to use the finished panels in a church reredos. However, the drawings were later modified by the artist Charles Henry Temple (1857-1940), who worked for Maw's during 1887-1907.[13] Temple then painted the underglaze panels, which - following the closure of the old hospital in the late 1990s - were moved to the **Royal Shrewsbury Hospital**, MYTTON OAK ROAD, on the western edge of Shrewsbury, where they are now on display in the foyer of the Head and Neck Unit. From Murivance, return to the centre of Shrewsbury via St John's Hill.

STOWE

St Michael's Church has a beautiful setting, in the remote hills of south Shropshire looking across the River Teme into Wales. Its chancel decoration is mostly by Powell's, with a red glass tile dado, an opus sectile figure of Faith (1913) on the north wall, complementing Faith and Charity in the south windows, and an elaborate reredos (1902) in marble, copper and mother of pearl including opus sectile figures of St Michael and St George.

TELFORD

Inside the TELFORD SHOPPING CENTRE, dominating Sherwood Square, is the **Telford Time Machine**, a massive novelty clock topped by a huge green frog. Designed by Kit Williams and unveiled in 1996, the casing of the intricate machine is faced with colourful hand-made tiles produced by the Decorative Tile Works at nearby Jackfield. There is another ceramic surprise to be found in a business park well away from the new town's centre, in the form of the **ENTA** office building in STAFFORD PARK. This 1990s pagoda-style structure has an astonishing display of Chinese ceramics including dragons and other deeply-moulded forms.

On a rather larger scale, over 2,000 square metres of a retaining wall alongside the road at **Nabb Hill** were faced with bands of coloured tiles during its construction in 1982-3. The effect is akin to geological strata, faults and all, and twenty-two tilers were needed to fix the Shaws of Darwen tiles in place. The project designer was Kenneth Budd for the Telford Development Corporation.

Wellington

Sunnycroft (NT), 200 Holyhead Road, Wellington is that rare survivor, an almost unaltered example of a late Victorian suburban villa, in its own spacious grounds and complete with most of its contents. It has Maw & Co tiled floors and tiled Coalbrookdale fireplaces.

Wrockwardine Wood

The **Bull's Head** pub has a good Maw's glazed brick and tile facade dating from around 1904, as well as an interior tile scheme. The faience and tiled chancel walls of **Holy Trinity Church**, CHURCH ROAD, were shown in a Craven Dunnill catalogue dating from around 1890.

WHITCHURCH

There are several minor ceramic locations in Whitchurch, notably four tiled **street names**: Bargate, Highgate, High St and Church St. These name panels, which are made from very early Minton letter tiles, probably dating from the late 1830s or early 1840s, were restored in 1995 by Lesley Durbin of the Jackfield Conservation Studio. Many of the HIGH STREET shops have tiling below or around their windows, although most are overpainted. Inside the former butcher's at **31 High Street** is a good blue and white bull's head frieze, while the interior of Bradbury Brothers butcher's at **42 High Street** was retiled in 1999 (covering 1928 tilework) with a scheme incorporating historic photographic images.

Shropshire Roundup

There is a complete set of original fittings, which included an encaustic tile pavement, in Holy Trinity Church (1885-7), **Bicton**, about four miles north-west of Shrewsbury. The extensive encaustic tile pavement at St Leonard's Church (1860-2), **Bridgnorth** is by Maw & Co; the church is in the care of the Churches Conservation Trust.[14] There are several fourteenth century line-impressed tiles on the floor of the bell tower at St Peter's Church, **Cound**. St Peter's Church, **Diddlebury** has several groups of memorial tiles set in a Godwin encaustic tiled pavement; these Victorian tiles are a memorial for an earlier death and include dates involving the change from the Julian to the Gregorian calendar, which took place in September 1752. There is a good set of late fourteenth century line-impressed tiles at the Church of St John the Baptist, **Hughley**. Adcote (1879, Richard Norman Shaw), the country house (now a school) built about a mile east of **Little Ness** for the Darbys of Coalbrookdale, has two large fireplaces with tiles by William De Morgan. There is pleasant art deco inter-war tiling in the ladies' toilets on Church Street, **Market Drayton**. Most of the fittings inside Holy Trinity Church (1843), **Middleton** (near Chirbury), including the mosaic altar, are by the Revd. Waldegrave Brewster, vicar 1872-1901. In the side chapel of St Bartholomew's Church, **Moreton Corbet**, is a cast iron fireplace lined with tiles from the Minton China Works 'Old Testament' series designed by John Moyr Smith and produced from the early 1870s. The original chancel decoration of the Church of King Charles the Martyr (1869-70), **Newtown**, included a Maw encaustic pavement and a majolica and enamelled tile reredos.[15] A tile above the south doorway of St Chad's Church, **Prees** records its 're-edifying' (restoration) in 1864. St Andrew's Church, **Shifnal**, restored in 1876-9 by Sir George Gilbert Scott, has a good Craven Dunnill tile scheme including a ceramic reredos. In St Bartholomew's Church, **Tong** is a Coade stone coat of arms of King George III, dating from 1814. Holy Trinity Church (1856, S. Pountney Smith), **Uffington** has a Maw's sanctuary pavement with Chamberlain tiles around its ceramic font. The chancel of the Church of St John the Baptist, **Whittington** dates from 1861, although much of its interior decoration - which includes a tile panel showing Christ with three saints - dates from 1894, when the entire building was restored by the architect Eustace Frere, who added much red terracotta to the exterior.

References

1. Information from the Michael Stratton Archive.
2. Dennis W. Hadley, *James Powell & Sons: A listing of opus sectile, 1847-1973*, (2001).
3. A. J. Mugridge, *The Broseley Heavy Clay Industry* (Mugridge, Telford, 2001).
4. *The Builder*, 5th September 1863, vol 21.
5. Geoffrey Kay, 'Charles Lynam - an Architect of Tile Factories', *Journal of the Tiles and Architectural Ceramics Society*, 4 (1992), pp21-28.
6. Tony Herbert and Kathryn Huggins, *The Decorative Tile in Architecture and Interiors* (Phaidon Press, London, 1995), p28. Craven Dunnill mentioned their Kemberton Church tiling in a catalogue dating from around 1892 which is held by Shropshire Archives, Shrewsbury (F. C. Howells, M77, acc 5724).
7. Michael Stratton, *The Terracotta Revival* (Victor Gollancz, London, 1993), pp50-1.
8. A. J. Cross, *Pilkington's Royal Lancastrian Pottery and Tiles* (Richard Dennis, London, 1980).
9. 'Tiles - John Eyre - Pilkington Designer?' *Newsletter of Pilkington's Lancastrian Pottery Society*, 3 (2003) June, pp105-8.
10. Peter Williams, 'Floor tiling in Saint Mary's Church, Shrewsbury', *TACS Journal*, 8 (2000), pp16-25. Williams suggests (p16) that the floor tiles in St Catherine's Chapel were donated by Herbert Minton, but this seems unlikely as there is no mention of such a gift in the list of Minton's tile donations to churches which was published in the *Annals of the Diocese of Lichfield* in 1859, and reprinted in *Glazed Expressions* 32, Spring 1996, pp3-6. See Lynn F. Pearson, *Minton Tiles in the Churches of Staffordshire* (TACS, 2000) for further discussion of Minton's donations.
11. Alison Kelly, *Mrs Coade's Stone* (Self Publishing Association, Upton-upon-Severn, 1990).
12. *The Builder*, 20th September 1879, vol 37, p1050.
13. *The Builder*, 10th February 1894, vol 66.
14. *The Builder*, 29th November 1862, vol 20.
15. *The Builder*, 24th April 1869, vol 27, p332.

Somerset

There are excellent thirteenth century tiles to be seen at Cleeve Abbey (Washford) and Muchelney Church (from its adjoining Abbey), but the great strength of Somerset lies in its Victorian church tiles. Research by Philip and Dorothy Brown has provided detailed information on the many churches in the county with encaustic tile pavements and also wall tiling, which appears to have been especially popular in Somerset; even with an extended roundup section, there are many more churches with substantial ceramic interest than it is possible to list here. Hornblotton Church, with its rare - in an ecclesiastical context - Aesthetic Movement interior, is the outstanding example of wall tiling with its De Morgan reredos. Local tile production is represented by Sir Edmund Elton's turn-of-the-century Sunflower Pottery at Clevedon; some of the few examples of Eltonware in architectural use are the Jubilee Clock Tower at Clevedon and East Clevedon Church. From the twentieth century, one of the county's highlights is the seminal 1931 mural by Sylvia Packard at the Royal High School, Bath, which was followed by the formation of the tile manufacturers Packard & Ord. From the postwar period, in what might be seen as a continuation of the anglo-catholic tone set by Tyntesfield's ornate Victorian chapel, comes the ceramic triptych (1956) by the artist Adam Kossowski in the Sacred Heart Chapel of Downside Abbey, Stratton-on-the-Fosse. The county's ceramic tradition is currently being upheld by several contemporary makers including Rosie Smith (based in Weston-super-Mare), Bronwyn Williams-Ellis (Bath), and Philippa Threlfall (Wells). Suggested reading: Philip Brown, TACS Tour Notes *Somerset* (1995). The *Gazetteer* entry for Somerset covers the administrative areas of Bath & North East Somerset Council, North Somerset Council and Somerset County Council.

BARROW GURNEY

Barrow Minchin Nunnery was founded around the end of the twelfth century on land about a mile west of Barrow Gurney. Following the Dissolution the site was eventually sold and the domestic buildings converted into a residence, Barrow Court, which was acquired in 1881 by Antony Gibbs of Tyntesfield House, about three miles to the north west (see below, Wraxall). The estate was sold on to Antony's younger brother, Henry Martin Gibbs (1850-1928) in 1883 and the house carefully restored by the gentleman architect Henry Woodyer, who was already known to the Gibbs family. Woodyer also restored the parish church, **St Mary and St Edmund**, BARROW COURT LANE, which originated in the twelfth century but had been mostly rebuilt in 1825. Woodyer's work, carried out during 1886-91, resulted in the creation of an elaborate, neo-medieval interior including the Gibbs family chapel in the south aisle; a covered passage connects it to Barrow Court.[1] The altar in the Gibbs chapel has a ceramic inlay.

By 1897, the only remaining part of Barrow Minchin Nunnery was a stone barn, but during work on the grounds west of the church an area of early fourteenth century Wessex tiling was found. This appeared to be the covering of a tomb, possibly that of an unnamed prioress who died in 1316. The tiles, many bearing coats of arms, were left exposed and began to deteriorate, so in 1911 they were relaid and a small building was erected to shelter the pavement. The tiles were rediscovered in 1995, beneath matting in a rarely used room of the church.[2]

BATH

Sylvia Packard (1881-1962), founder with Rosalind Ord of the tile manufacturers Packard & Ord, later Marlborough Tiles, created her first tile mural at the **Royal High School**, LANSDOWN ROAD. Packard retired from her post as art teacher at the school in 1929 (she was succeeded by Ord), and immediately began work on designs for the mural, which was to cover a wall joining the Memorial Hall (opened 1925) and the domestic economy wing (opened 1930).[3] The hand-painted figurative mural, installed in 1931 and almost seventy feet long, represented the occupations of the 'Virtuous Woman' of *Proverbs* 31: 'her price is far above rubies'; the school magazine called it 'the Bayeux Tapestry of our day'. Mural painting had once again become popular between the wars, and the scale of this mural, as well as the use of staff and students as life models, places the work directly in the arts and crafts tradition, although the imagery is rather more modern in style. It comprises nearly 1,000 tiles, probably Carter's blanks which were fired in Poole. The mural is of great significance in the history of twentieth century British tile manufacturing, as it led to the start of the Packard & Ord collaboration around 1933, but was in poor condition by the mid-1990s.[4] There is no public access to the mural, which it is hoped will eventually be restored and housed in the Holburne Museum of Art, Great Pulteney Street, Bath.

Nearly a mile south of the school, right in centre of Bath, is **St John's R. C. Church** (1861-3), SOUTH PARADE, which has a Minton tile pavement. Continuing south, in **Perrymead R. C. Cemetery**, off BLIND LANE, is the mortuary chapel of the Eyre family (1861, architect C. F. Hansom), which has a porch pavement incorporating Eyre armorial tiles by Minton's.

Twerton

The ceramicist Bronwyn Williams-Ellis designed a brilliantly colourful floral-themed tile installation for the jacuzzi and shower areas of the RNID's **Poolemead Centre**, WATERY LANE, in 1997.

CHARLTON MACKRELL

St Mary's Church was heavily restored around 1847 by Benjamin Ferrey; the chancel has a lavish Minton polychrome encaustic tile pavement including many heraldic symbols. Nearby is **Charlton Mackrell School** (1852), built in memory of the Revd. W. T. Parr Brymer, who died in 1852 and set up a trust for the school in his will. The main school hall and an adjoining room have unusual block-printed dust-pressed wall tile decoration by Minton Hollins, including plain tiles in white, buff and red, patterned tiles in red/white and blue/white, and horizontal strings of texts.

CHEDZOY

The tile pavement in the chancel of **St Mary's Church** (restored 1884-5) combines inlaid tiles designed by Carter, Johnson, & Co with plain tiles having a glistening, almost scintillating, glaze. The tiles were chosen by the architect Spencer Slingsby Stallwood (1842/3-1922).[5]

CLEVEDON

On the seafront, almost opposite Clevedon Pier in ALEXANDRA ROAD, is the splendid little Doulton glazed stoneware **drinking fountain**, erected by Mr T. Sheldon in 1895 and restored in 1992 (Fig 234). This colourful fountain was one of a number of standard designs available from Doulton's, and is marked 'Doulton Lambeth' near its bottom right corner. Inland, over the hill and down in the commercial centre of Clevedon, all life revolves around the Eltonware-decorated **Jubilee Clock Tower** in THE TRIANGLE. It was presented to the town in 1897 by the local artist potter Sir Edmund Elton of Clevedon Court to mark the Diamond Jubilee of Queen Victoria. Sir Edmund began experimenting with mosaics in 1879 and was producing pottery, known as Eltonware, at his Sunflower Pottery by 1881. The Jubilee Clock displays a roundel of Father Time and strings of rich ornament featuring birds, beasts and fishes in deep greens and reds.

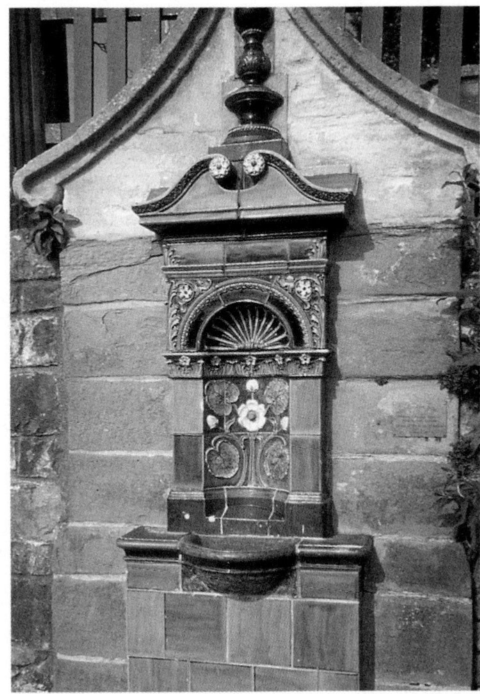

Fig 234.

East Clevedon

Sir Edmund Elton's ancestral home, Clevedon Court (NT), a fourteenth century manor house wedged into the hillside just beyond the eastern edge of the town, has a good collection of Eltonware. About half a mile west of the house is **All Saints Church** (1860), ALL SAINTS LANE, built and endowed by Dame Rhoda Elton and Sir Arthur Hallam Elton. The tiling on its baptistery wall appears to be Eltonware.

DUNSTER

During G. E. Street's restoration of **St George's Church** in 1875-7, inlaid medieval tiles were relaid in a small chapel. The east end of the church was paved by Godwin's with a lavish arrangement of their own plain and inlaid tiles, some of which were copies of medieval tiles found on the site.[6]

EAST WOODLANDS

St Katherine's Church, Woodlands, on the ridge west of Longleat Park, was mostly rebuilt by the architect John Loughborough Pearson in 1880. Its tile pavement includes an enlarged version of the Bishop Ken monogram tile usually found as a single four-inch or six-inch tile, but here designed for multiple tile settings.

FELTON

St Katherine's Church (just east of Bristol International Airport) was designed by the Revd. J. Hardman. There are polychrome inlaid tiles on the face of the stone chancel screen, as well as memorial tiles, some painted and some inlaid.

FROME

St John's Church, BATH STREET was almost totally rebuilt in 1844 (chancel) and 1852-66. Its fine anglo-catholic interior has an assortment of tile pavements, some including a twelve-inch polychrome tile bearing the monogram of Bishop Ken (d1711). These tiles also cover the grave of Bishop Ken, which is in the churchyard immediately east of the church; its canopy was designed by Benjamin Ferrey and added in 1844. Also in Bath Street, at number 19, is a good **butcher's shop** with a tiled facade dating from the 1920s.

HORNBLOTTON

St Peter's Church was rebuilt in 1872-4 to the designs of the architect Sir Thomas Graham Jackson (Fig 235). Its Aesthetic Movement interior is spectacular, with walls covered in pink sgraffito work by Heywood Sumner and contemporary furnishings decorated with natural forms such as sunflowers. Sumner (1853-1940) was an artist, illustrator and wallpaper designer who decorated eleven churches with sgraffito between 1887 and 1897.

The chancel pavement is an elaborate mosaic of opaque glass, some elements of which are rectangular pieces in two sizes: a 4½ inch square with a running interlacing pattern in white on a dull red background, and a rectangle a little over 6x8 inches which borders the choir pavement and is decorated in blue and grey with paired fish. The reredos and east wall have tiles by William De Morgan: the central cross is made up of strips of tile glazed in red lustre, and around this are tiles painted in blue, white and yellow with leaves and flowers or the sacred monogram and, at the sides, unusual figurative panels of the Evangelists in mostly blue and white. The accounts for the rebuilding of the church contain bills from James Powell & Sons in 1873 and 1874 for the 'Chancel pavement in opaque glass', and a bill from William de Morgan for 'Execution on earthenware of Reredos painting for Hornblotton Church'.[7]

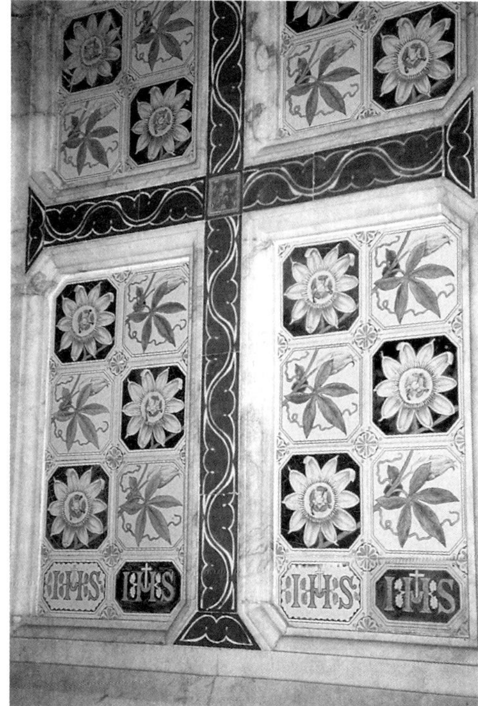

Fig 235.

MUCHELNEY

The present remains of **Muchelney Abbey** (EH) date mostly from the twelfth century, although the best-preserved element, the Abbot's Lodging, was completed in 1539. There are a few thirteenth and fourteenth century tiles still *in situ* at the Abbey, but a more impressive display may be found at the adjoining parish church of **St Peter and St Paul**.[8] Near the font are two re-set arrangements (concentric circles) of mid-thirteenth century tiles found in the cloisters of the Abbey during the 1880s (Fig 236). The tiles were probably made by tilers who had worked on Henry III's new chapel at Clarendon Palace before moving on to Somerset.[9]

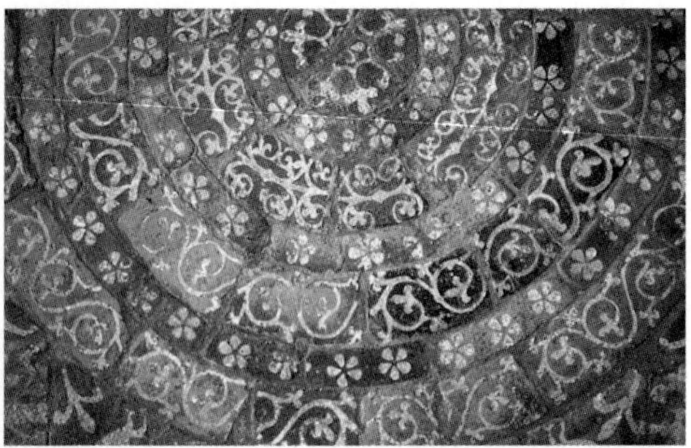

Fig 236.

NYNEHEAD

Inside **All Saints Church** are two plaques of the Virgin and Child attributed to the Florentine della Robbia workshop, one sited near the former rood stair, the other in the south aisle. They were given to the church by the Revd. John Sanford, vicar of Nynehead, resident of Florence and a notable art collector; the Sanford family home was Nynehead Court. In addition, the reredos includes two Powell's opus sectile panels dating from 1881-2.

PRISTON

The attractive east wall tiling at the **Church of St Luke and St Andrew** comprises four nine-tile groups, two either side of the stone reredos (which dates from after 1863), each showing a multicoloured angel, above a dado of mainly floral patterned tiles. They are painted over-glaze and are probably the work of a church decorating company, quite likely Heaton, Butler & Bayne, the London stained glass house which is known to have produced tiles for churches and is said to have been responsible for the stained glass of St Luke and St Andrew's post-1869 east window.[10]

STOGUMBER

St Mary's Church was restored in 1873-5 by the architect J. D. Sedding; the cost of £2,400 was borne by Prebendary Edward Jones, vicar of Stogumber during 1871-1907 and a follower of Wiliam Morris. The design of the chancel wall tiling is attributable to Sedding, although Jones was responsible for the stencilled decoration of the roof and walls; the chancel floor is also tiled.[11]

STRATTON-ON-THE-FOSSE

Downside Abbey, also a school, stands just to the west of Stratton-on-the-Fosse; it occupies the former Mount Pleasant estate at Downside, which was bought by the Benedictine community in 1814. Extensions were made to the existing Downside House from 1823, then new and larger buildings including part of the church were erected from 1872. The present chancel dates from 1901-5 and the nave from around 1923-5; the 166′ high tower was completed in 1938. In the Sacred Heart Chapel, immediately to the right of the Lady Chapel, is a colourful ceramic relief triptych by Adam Kossowski installed in 1956. The central and smallest section, above the altar, shows the crucifixion, while the two adjoining parts combine inscriptions, four small reliefs and larger pictorial panels.

WASHFORD

The Cistercian foundation of **Cleeve Abbey** (EH) dates from 1198, although the remaining buildings date from between the thirteenth and sixteenth centuries. The Abbey had extensive tile pavements, laid from the mid-thirteenth century, when locally-made tiles were used to pave the east end of the church, to the early fourteenth century.[12] The major visible pavement is that of the former frater (refectory), which may have been laid as early as the 1270s; it was relaid during the 1960s (Fig 237). This Wessex pavement includes large (about 8″ square) heraldic tiles bearing the arms of England, Cornwall and de Clare, probably made to commemorate the 1272 marriage of Henry III's nephew Edmund of Cornwall to Margaret de Clare.

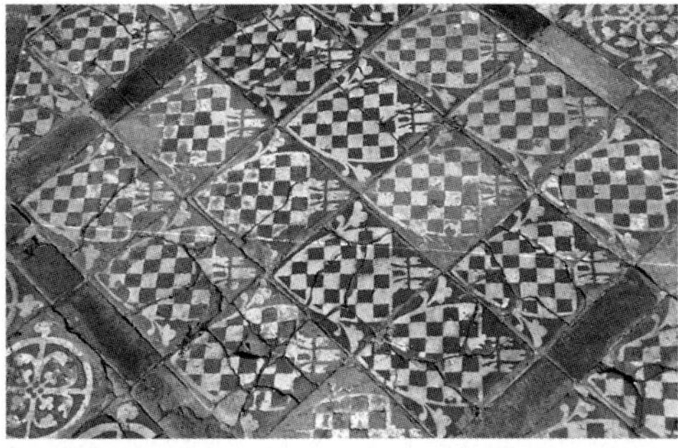

Fig 237.

WELLS

The thirteenth century floor tiles relaid in the Corpus Christi Chapel (north quire aisle) of **Wells Cathedral** show heraldic images associated with Richard of Cornwall (1209-72), younger brother of Henry III, including the coats of arms of the Count of Poitou and the Clare family. On a rather larger scale are the early Minton encaustic tile pavements in the (partly carpeted) quire and Lady Chapel. The quire pavement comprises diagonally-set 36-tile blocks, formed of either single designs or nine 4-tile groups, with the dais pavement including monogrammed and fleur-de-lys designs. The Lady Chapel has an unusual pavement arrangement based on an eight-pointed star, with letter tiling on three step risers and roundels of the evangelists.

Immediately east of the Cathedral in TOR STREET is the terracotta workshop of **Black Dog of Wells** (set up by Philippa Threlfall and Kennedy Collings in the 1960s), with a Threlfall-designed ceramic relief in the gable end dating from around 1999.

WESTON-SUPER-MARE

The brutal **Odeon Cinema** (1935, architect T. Cecil Howitt) stands plumb in the centre of Weston-super-Mare on the corner of LOCKING ROAD and Walliscote Road. This huge structure is made up from rectangular forms topped by a tower whose flat roof is supported by twelve stubby columns. The whole is clad in faience by Shaws of Darwen, all buff with the exception of four thin parallel green bands tracking around the top of the facade.[13]

With the exception of some minor sites, such as tiled stall risers and the like, the remainder of Weston's ceramic locations are modern and produced by local tile decorator Rosie Smith, who undertook a series of commissions for Weston's public buildings beginning in the mid 1980s. Smith's work normally involves the production of large-scale tile panels using the painstaking technique of building up colours with on-glaze enamels applied over several firings to standard white glazed tiles; the result is akin to a watercolour painting. At the **Winter Gardens Conference Centre**, on the seafront at ROYAL PARADE, are five of her tile panels of panoramic landscapes (1991), while just inland at the **North Somerset Museum**, BURLINGTON STREET, is a series of three panels (1986) by Smith showing the historical development of Weston's swimming pools. In GROVE PARK, on the northern edge of the town, is **Jill's Garden**, created in 2001 in memory of the murdered television presenter and journalist Jill Dando, who grew up in Weston; it features a nine-tile panel by Rosie Smith on the theme of forget-me-nots.

Back in the town centre is the **Churchill Sports Centre**, CHURCHILL GROVE, where a 1994 refurbishment of the swimming pool included the addition of over 1,600 of Smith's hand-stencilled tiles on a theme of the 'formal garden'. Out in the southern suburb of Uphill, in the main entrance of the **Weston General Hospital** (1986), GRANGE ROAD, is a tile panel by Rosie Smith showing the 1928 Queen Alexandra Memorial Hospital; there is another Smith panel, of Weston's Winter Gardens, in the outpatients waiting area. The hospital's Long Fox Unit (1992) has a large tile scheme developed by Smith in collaboration with its architect, David Gould of Bristol's Kendall Kingscott Partnership; there are twelve works in all, mainly seascapes and landscapes, with border tiles having a common colour theme reflected in the palette used by the architect throughout the unit. Finally, in the main reception area of the Quantockhead Rehabilitation Unit (1993) is a Smith tile panel showing a view of Weston's promenade.

WEST QUANTOXHEAD

The **Church of St Ethel Dreda** (or St Audrey) was put up in 1856 and designed by the architect John Norton (1823-1904), best known for his lucrative country house practice although he was also involved, with his partner Philip Masey, in a series of rather shady attempts to build seaside winter gardens during the 1870s. The Minton encaustic pavement in the chancel includes tiles with coats of arms of the Aclands, for whom the church was built; Norton also designed their nearby mansion, St Audries.[14]

WRAXALL

Tyntesfield House (NT), just east of Wraxall in a beautiful setting overlooking the Yeo Valley, was extensively remodelled by John Norton in 1863-5 for the successful merchant William Gibbs (1790-1875), who made his fortune in the guano trade. The tiled pavements of the porch and entrance corridor probably date from the 1860s, although they could have been added during alterations made by the architect Henry Woodyer in 1887-90 for William's son Antony Gibbs (1841-1907), which included installing new floors throughout the house. Off the entrance corridor is the library, which has Minton-tiled window seats. The main ceramic interest of Tyntesfield is its magnificent chapel, added in 1873-5 and designed by Arthur Blomfield. Gibbs, an enthusiastic high churchman, had already funded the construction of several new churches as well as contributing to the restoration of Exeter and Bristol Cathedrals; Butterfield's Keble College Chapel (1873-6), Oxford, was built entirely at his expense. The stone-vaulted Tyntesfield chapel is very different from Keble, but still strongly anglo-catholic, with ornate decoration including Powell's mosaic and opus sectile work, and mosaics by Salviati & Co (designed by Henry Wooldridge) at the east end. Also in the chapel is one of the first opus sectile panels produced by Powell's, a *Head of Christ*, which was made in 1864 and sold to Gibbs in 1865. Outside, in the Old Rose Garden, are two summerhouses, both in poor condition and with internal pale green and floral glazed wall tiling, probably by Minton's.

YEOVIL

There are several installations by Rosie Smith, a tile decorator based in Weston-super-Mare, at **Yeovil District Hospital**, HIGHER KINGSTON. The Queensway Day Hospital (1995) has tile panels which act as entrance signs and show images of the countryside, while in the main hospital are five panels of tiles (1996) with the winning designs from a children's art competition. The reception area of the Children's Unit has a tile scheme (1998) by Smith incorporating delightful flying pigs, and more tiling in the adjacent roof garden shows views of Yeovil.

Somerset Roundup

The nave aisles of St John Baptist, **Ashbrittle** are laid with a crazy paving of mixed Victorian inlaid tiles. The tiled stall riser of the butcher's at 9 High Street, **Axbridge** has a blue bull's head at its centre. There is a nineteenth century tin-glazed tile mural of a biblical scene at Barrington Court (NT), **Barrington**; the tiles are probably Portuguese.The east wall of St Michael's Church, **Brent Knoll** is decorated with a strange mixture of tiles.[15] The tile pavement, perhaps by Maw's, at St Mary's Church, **Bridgwater** was probably laid in 1878 and is unusual for its inclusion of line-impressed tiles in a region without medieval examples of this type. St Mary's Church, **Cannington** has an encaustic tile pavement in the chancel and a Powell's opus sectile reredos (1893) of *Christ in Glory*, which includes portaits of its donors, Mr and Mrs Philip and Joanna Pleydell Bouverie; the cartoon was by E. Penwarden. Holy Trinity Church, **Chantry** (1846, Scott & Moffat) has an encaustic tile pavement throughout the chancel. St Mary Magdalen Church, **Chewton Mendip** has Victorian east wall tiling including Maw's majolica. St Mary's Church, **Clatworthy** has excellent tile pavements by the Architectural Pottery Co. St Thomas Church, **Cothelstone** has a nave encaustic pavement and a Maw's mosaic of curvilinear plain tiles in its chancel.[16] Christ Church (1839), **Coxley** has pavements of plain and inlaid tiles with notably rich orange glaze; they were made by Craven Dunnill and probably laid in 1884.[17] The Powell's opus sectile and glass tile reredos at St John's Church, **Cutcombe** dates from 1896. St Michael's Church, **East Coker** has a reredos including lettered tiles and symbols of the Evangelists. The east wall decoration of All Saints

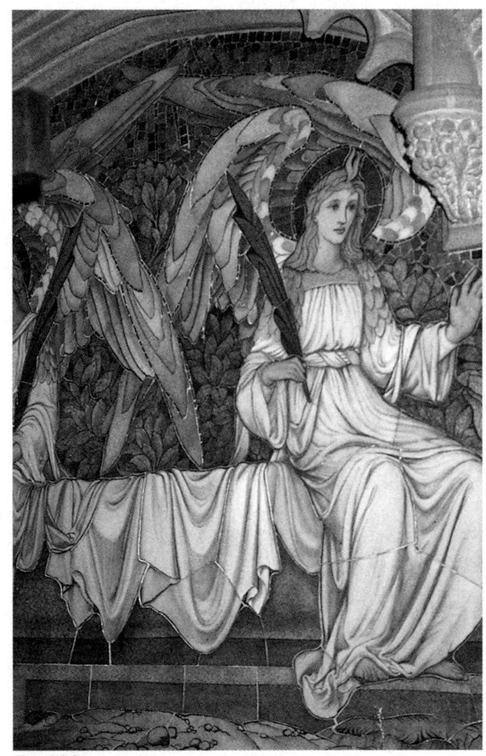

Fig 238.

Church, **East Pennard** includes mosaic along with plain and inlaid tiles in soft colours. Some thirteenth century two-colour tiles still remain *in situ* at the Abbey in **Glastonbury**; they are protected by hinged wooden boxes. St John Baptist, **Heathfield** has majolica tiles on its east wall, possibly dating from the 1870 restoration by

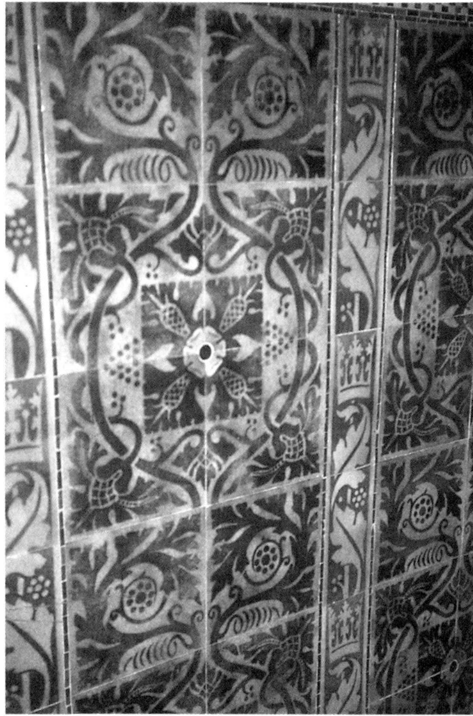

Fig 239.

the Exeter architect Edward Ashworth.[18] Striking majolica tiles flank the reredos of St Peter's Church, **Huish Champflower**. St Mary's Church (restored 1893), **Leigh Woods** has lavish Godwin tile pavements. The Church of St Peter and St Paul, **Maperton** and St Catherine's Church, **Montacute** have very similar east wall tiling including Minton roundels; they were restored by Henry Hall in 1869 and 1870-1 respectively.[19] The Tesco store (2002) on Stockway North, **Nailsea** has a pair of large ceramic murals by Ned Heywood which show historical scenes of the local glass industry. The tiles, including some with a large angel motif, on the curtained east wall of **Norton St Philip** parish church probably date from its 1847-8 restoration by George Gilbert Scott. St Andrew's Church, **Old Cleeve** has inlaid medieval tiles around the font (and framed on the wall) as well as rich, possibly Minton, encaustic pavements with designs unlike those of the medieval tiles. The children's pool (1996) at the Parish Wharf Leisure Centre, **Portishead** has ceramics designed by Rosie Smith on a nautical theme including pirates, sea creatures and hidden treasure. St Barnabas Church, **Queen Camel** has an elaborate chancel tile pavement (1886), probably by Godwin, and a lavish reredos of around 1907 with a Powell's opus sectile panel (Fig 238) and glass tiling (Fig 239).[20] Many worn decorated medieval floor tiles, some with unusual designs, have been relaid in the main doorway of St Michael's Church, **Raddington**. Some Chamberlain tiles from a larger scheme survive around the font at Christ Church, **Redhill**.[21] The *Central Somerset Mural* (1978) by Philippa Threlfall and Kennedy Collings occupies the wall of the High Street walkway connecting a car park and a supermarket in **Street**; in shows local architectural and landscape features in ceramics and slate. On the floor of the chancel at the Church of St Decuman, **Watchet** are several medieval tiles, relaid in 1886; others are framed on the north aisle wall. St Mary's Church, **Witham Friary** was rebuilt in 1875 by the architect William White; there are good Maw encaustic pavements. St Mary's Church, **Yarlington** was mostly rebuilt in 1878; its opus sectile reredos of the Annunciation dates from 1921.[22]

References

1. John Elliott and John Pritchard, eds, *Henry Woodyer: Gentleman Architect* (Department of Continuing Education, University of Reading, Reading, 2002).
2. Barbara J. Lowe, *Decorated Medieval Floor Tiles of Somerset* (Somerset Archaeological and Natural History Society and Somerset County Museums Service, Taunton, 2003).
3. Susan Rasey, 'Sylvia Packard and the tile mural at the Royal School, Bath', *Glazed Expressions*, (1997) 35, pp2-3.
4. Tony Herbert, 'Tile Mural at the Royal School, Bath', *Glazed Expressions*, (1997) 35, p1.
5. Somerset Archive and Record Service: P/D/chedz 6/1/1.
6. *Building News*, vol 31, 1876, p299; *The Builder*, vol 34, 1876, p959; Somerset Archive and Record Service: D/D/Cf 1875/3.
7. Somerset Archive and Record Service: D/P/horn 8/2/3.
8. 'Tiles in Muchelney Abbey', *The Builder*, 37 (1879), pp1075-8.
9. Elizabeth Eames, *English Tilers* (British Museum Press, London, 1992).
10. Information from John Wilkinson, Priston, 18th April 2002.
11. *Building News*, vol 34, 1878, p641.
12. Jane Harcourt, 'The Medieval Floor-tiles of Cleeve Abbey, Somerset', *Journal of the British Archaeological Association*, 153 (2000), pp30-70.
13. Shaws Glazed Brick Co Ltd, *List of Contracts executed 1935-1936*, Darwen, (1936).
14. *The Builder*, vol 14, 1856, p608.
15. Somerset Archive and Record Service: D/P/brent k 6/1/1.

16. A sketch of the Cothelstone chancel pavement is amongst the Maw's material held by Shropshire Archives, Shrewsbury. Information from Philip Brown.
17. *Bath & Wells Diocesan & Parochial Magazine*, 1884, p75.
18. Somerset Archive and Record Service: D/P/heath 6/1.
19. *The Builder*, vol 28, 1870, p291; Somerset Record and Archive Service: D/D/cf 1869/5.
20. Philip Brown, *Tour Notes: Tiles in a group of Somerset Churches* (Tiles and Architectural Ceramics Society, 1995).
21. *The Ecclesiologist*, vol 3, 1844, 23.
22. Dennis W. Hadley, *James Powell & Sons: A listing of opus sectile, 1847-1973*, (2001).

Staffordshire

Staffordshire is a county of great scenic contrasts, from the rolling moorlands of the north to the urban dreariness of the south, and - in between - the Potteries, the cradle of the ceramics industry. It is also the county of Minton and Pugin: St Giles Church, Cheadle, is the country's outstanding example of Pugin's medieval vision of modern worship. Although Minton's were pre-eminent, there were many other tile (rather than terracotta) producers based in Stoke-on-Trent, including Johnson's, Richard's and Wooliscroft's. However, despite this multitude of tile producers, these products at their creative peak are generally found *in situ* elsewhere in the country, in the great cities which Staffordshire lacks. Exceptions to this rule are those churches to which Herbert Minton donated tiles during the 1840s and 1850s; these early encaustic tile church pavements are a tribute to the inventiveness of the factory's artists and designers. Minton's own Hartshill Church, of course, is one of the best examples. This idiosyncratic county has also retained, in its southern sprawl, numerous ceramic pubs, their survival a testament to the lack of development of these areas, although Wolverhampton's excellent Elephant and Castle, with faience by Burmantofts, was demolished in March 2001 (Fig 240). Other outstanding sites in the county are the Wedgwood Institute, Burslem, the outcome of early enthusiasm for terracotta, which sadly set no local precedents; Lichfield Cathedral, Trentham Church and Wightwick Manor, the latter a supreme display of hand-made tiles, quite different from anything else Staffordshire has to offer. Suggested reading: TACS Tour Notes *Cheadle* (1984), *East Staffordshire* (2001), *Lichfield* (1991), *Stoke-on-Trent* (2000) and *Wightwick* (1986); Lynn Pearson, *Cumming Report: Minton Tiles in the Churches of Staffordshire* (TACS, 2000); Lynn Pearson, 'Memorial and commemorative tiles in nineteenth and early twentieth century churches', *TACS Journal*, 9 (2002); and Alan Swale, 'The Terracotta of the Wedgwood Institute, Burslem', *TACS Journal*, 2 (1987), pp21-7. The *Gazetteer* entry for Staffordshire covers the administrative areas of Sandwell Metropolitan Borough Council, Staffordshire County Council, Stoke-on-Trent City Council, Walsall Metropolitan Borough Council and Wolverhampton City Council.

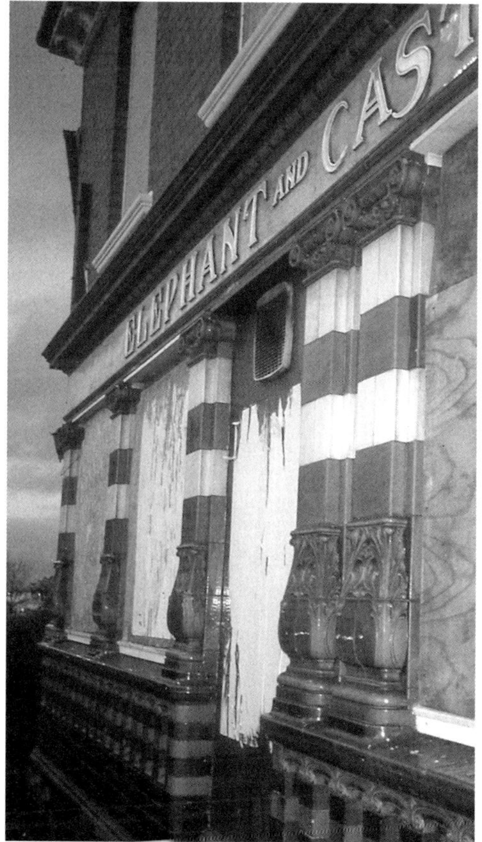

Fig 240.

ALTON

Beyond the parish church in the gothic paradise of Alton is the **Hospital of St John** and St John's Chapel, now the R. C. Church of St John; its little north chapel (1840-2) has a pavement of Minton encaustic tiles decorated with emblems of the Earl of Shrewsbury, its founder (Fig 241). A. W. N. Pugin was the architect of the Hospital, a term then used in the medieval sense to describe an almshouse with communal facilities such as the chapel. Pugin described the Hospital tiles in a letter to Shrewsbury dating from December 1841: 'The tiles produce a most glorious effect and are certainly a cheap decoration. The floor of the hospital is exceedingly rich and most durable'. The cost was just under £34.[1] Across the moat from the Hospital is **Alton Castle**, also designed by Pugin for the Earl, on which work began in 1844. The steeply-pitched roof of its chapel is clad in yellow and green ceramic tiles, specially requested by Pugin from Herbert Minton, who was asked to experiment with the production of coloured roofing tiles. By autumn 1848 Minton had succeeded, and Pugin wrote to the Earl of Shrewsbury saying 'Minton has perfectly succeeded with the tiles....and I have ordered them for the chapel'.[2] This was the only building where Pugin used coloured tiles to make a patterned roof. Since 1996 the Castle has been run by the Roman Catholic Archdiocese of Birmingham as a residential youth centre, and the chapel roof has been restored with coloured tiles replicating the Minton originals.[3]

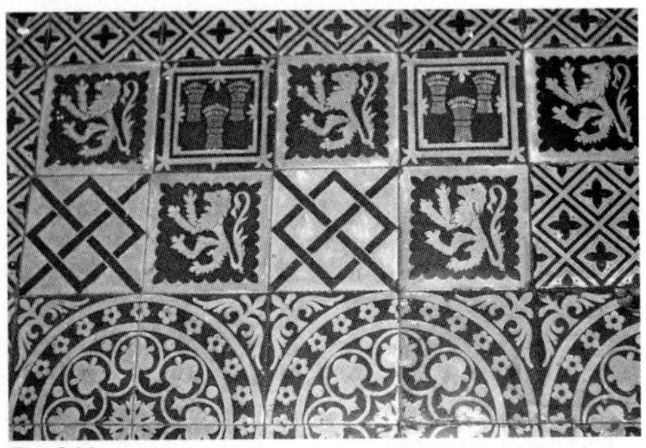
Fig 241.

ARMITAGE

In this odd industrial village - home of Armitage ceramic sanitary ware - and perched above the Trent, stands the neo-Norman **St John's Church**, built in 1844-7 by the architect Henry Ward of Stafford to replace a genuine Norman building. Herbert Minton made three separate donations of tiles to the church during 1845-7, and the result is a spectacular but gloomy interior. The tiling is elaborate: in the chancel is a large Latin cross composed of roundels of the evangelists, while the main nave aisle has a mass of different geometric designs - many from Minton's first printed catalogue of 1842 - along with an unusual knotted design of border tile. There are also blue, buff and black fleur-de-lys tiles in the sanctuary.

AUDLEY

The **Church of St James** dates from around 1300 and was partially rebuilt by Gilbert Scott in 1846-7, with restoration continuing until 1856. It is an imposing structure which occupies a good vantage point, with views from the churchyard stretching back towards Newcastle. There are tiles throughout the church, resulting from four donations of tiles by Herbert Minton around 1846-54. The nave aisle tiles have been completely carpeted over, and the real ceramic interest lies in the sanctuary; its steps have tiled risers with lettering in white on blue ground. The sanctuary pavement combines tiles with four fleur-de-lys on each, in blue and brown, with a variety of designs showing symbols of Christ, the Passion Cycle and the Resurrection. The reredos has a vine leaf border, then the basic pattern is a tile with a single fleur-de-lys, on red or green ground, alternating diagonally with red and green blanks. The overall impression is one of great richness.

BLITHFIELD

The medieval church of **St Leonard's** lies deep in Blithfield Park and immediately north of Blithfield Hall, home of the Bagot family for 600 years. Its chancel was restored by Pugin in 1851 and Herbert Minton donated the chancel pavement in July 1852. The chancel roof was constructed to a Pugin design which supposedly recreated the thirteenth-century roof, and the east window also followed the exact pattern of the original. The tradition that Pugin reproduced faithfully what was there before does not seem to extend to the tiling, which is far from lavish, although there are colourful Pugin-style red, buff and blue patterned tiles bordering the altar. Most strange, however, are the fleur-de-lys floor tiles in which ragged ventilation holes seem to form an intrinsic part of the design. It is difficult to say whether these holes were formed at the factory, and the tiles made specifically for ventilation purposes, or whether the tiles were pierced at a later date.

BREWOOD

The tall spire of **St Mary and St Chad** looks over the little town of Brewood ('Brood' to the natives) and out towards the Shropshire border. The expansive Godwin encaustic tile pavement was probably installed in the parish church around 1860-70; it is at its most attractive in the chancel, where a tide of decorative tiling laps around four substantial alabaster monuments to the Giffards of nearby Chillington Hall. Brewood was the centre of a strongly Catholic area, and **St Mary's R. C. Church** was built on the edge of the town by

A. W. N. Pugin in 1844; it has a Minton encaustic tile pavement in its chancel and north aisle.

BROOKHOUSES

On the south side of THE GREEN (A521) in Brookhouses, on the western edge of Cheadle, stands the **Huntsman** pub, both its gable ends boasting impressive tiled panels showing rural scenes with a red-coated huntsman and his hounds (Fig 242). The expressions of the dogs in the larger of the pair, on the west side of the pub, are particularly well captured, while the glaze on the brown-framed, tube-lined panels has unusually rich combinations of colours. They probably date from between the wars, but the manufacturer is unknown; perhaps they were locally produced.

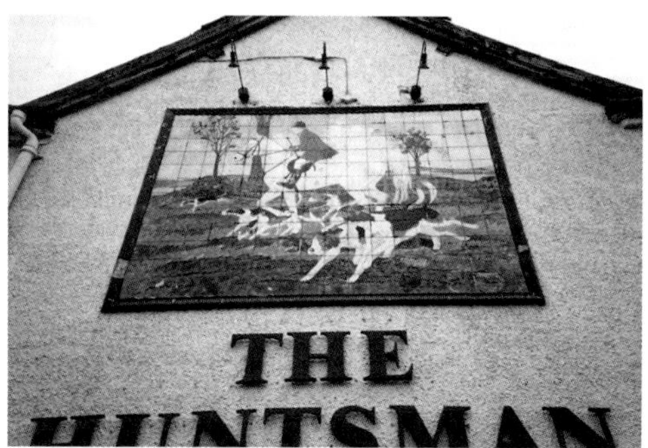

Fig 242.

CHEADLE

On CHAPEL STREET, wedged into the tightly-knit back alleys of Cheadle, is A. W. N. Pugin's awesome **St Giles R. C. Church**, a revelatory vision of colour, decoration and delight (Fig 243). For Pugin, who was received into the Catholic Church in 1835, the structure of a church was religion in built form, and the intent behind St Giles was to produce a modern version of a fourteenth-century country parish church.[4] The true church - pre-reformation Catholicism - would thus be housed in its true home, a Gothic church. His patron was John Talbot, sixteenth Earl of Shrewsbury and the leading Catholic layman of the time, whose seat lay a few miles to the east at Alton Towers; Pugin began work there on a banqueting hall and chapel in 1837. The church itself was built in 1841-6, part of the multitudinous decorations on its soaring steeple being twin Talbot hounds; below it are the striking west doors, each bearing the family symbol, a golden lion within a scalloped border on bright red ground.

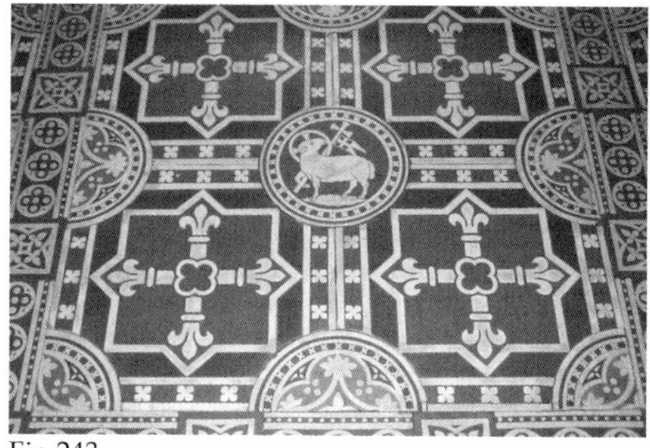

Fig 243.

Inside the church, all is colour, ornament and pattern, from the encaustic tiles, which cover the entire floor area as well as the nave dados, to the gilded and painted roof. Work began on the interior decoration in 1844, and Pugin himself was responsible for the design of many of the church furnishings, including the majority of the tiles, which were manufactured by Minton's. The tile pavement, ornate even at the west end where it includes several inscriptions, increases in complexity and lavishness to culminate in the Chapel of the Blessed Sacrament with its golden reredos of printed and painted tiles. The nave, porch and west tower floor tiles are all two-coloured encaustics (buff and red or buff and black) while those further east are multi-coloured; these latter are undoubtedly by Pugin. The tile designs used in the main body of the church appear in Minton's first printed catalogue of 1842, thus it might be argued that no direct connection exists between Pugin and these tiles. However, it appears likely that at least some of the nave designs were by Pugin's hand, including the Talbot symbol tile, number five in the 1842 catalogue.[5]

In sum, St Giles is a very English church; it was built by local men using local materials, all in the service of the only true church. With all its colour and richness, it was too English for the mid nineteenth-century Roman tradition of Catholicism; ironically, its influence - in architectural terms - weighed most heavily on the Church of England. As to its tiles, which saw Pugin's designs progress from the use of medieval motifs to a more individualistic and colourful approach, one can only echo the words of the future Cardinal Newman, overwhelmed by the sumptuous Chapel of the Blessed Sacrament at St Giles: 'This is the gate of heaven'.[6]

CHURCH LEIGH

The rebuilding of **All Saints Church** was completed in 1846 by the architect Thomas Johnson of Lichfield; the reconstruction was funded mainly by Richard Bagot of Blithfield, Bishop of Oxford (later Bishop of Bath and Wells) and former rector of All Saints. Another member of the Bagot family was the incumbent at the time of the rebuilding. The floor tiles, which run throughout the lofty church and have been attributed to Pugin, were donated by Herbert Minton in 1845; he also donated the reredos in 1851 (Fig 244). The aisles display repeats of common four-tile groups interspersed with single tiles showing an attractive griffin, while around the font are roundels decorated with the image of a pelican in her piety. The splendidly colourful chancel pavement comprises repeats of Richard Bagot's coat of arms as Bishop of Oxford; his arms lie within a frame including a bishop's mitre, and show a delightful picture of three medieval maidens in the dexter chief. In the rather less decorative sanctuary are tiles with the letters 'RB' and the bishop's mitre. The reredos is made up of moulded buff terracotta in a pattern of hexagonal and triangular pieces; the centres of the hexagons are overpainted in gold. This style of reredos is very similar to that produced soon after 1845 by Minton for St Stephen's in Westminster, and was based on the decoration of St Dunstan's shrine at Canterbury Cathedral.[7]

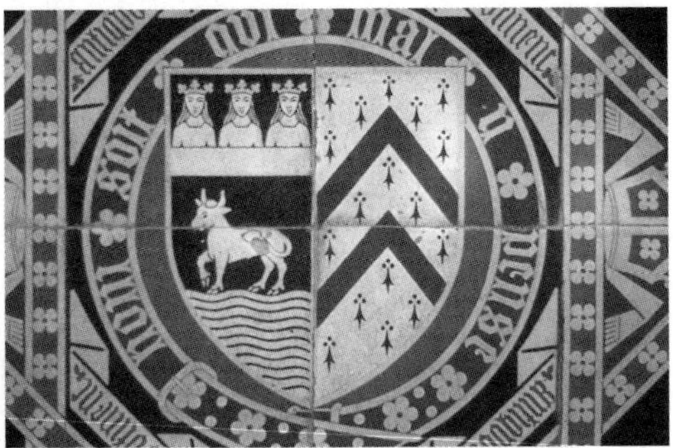

Fig 244.

COTTON

Deep in the moorlands to the north of Alton lies another element in Pugin's Gothic transformation of Staffordshire. **Cotton College** originated as Cotton Hall, given to the Brothers of the Will of God (a band of Anglican priests who had coverted to Catholicism) as a place of respite by the Earl of Shrewsbury in 1846. Pugin extended the buildings, erecting St Wilfrid's Chapel in 1846-8; its decoration includes Pugin-designed Minton tiles. The Brothers did not stay long at Cotton, eventually becoming absorbed in the Birmingham Oratory, and the site became a school in 1868.

DILHORNE

The sanctuary of thirteenth-century **All Saints Church** has a fine display of early Minton encaustic tiles donated by Herbert Minton to the church in 1851. Along with many familiar four-tile patterns from the firm's first printed catalogue of 1842 are roundels of the evangelists, altogether making an attractive sanctuary pavement.

ELFORD

Apart from its tower, **St Peter's Church** was rebuilt by Anthony Salvin in 1848-9; the south aisle and chapel were rebuilt by Street in 1869-70. Salvin's objective was to restore the church to its fourteenth century appearance. The nave aisles have unusual line-impressed tiles in buff or black with a circular relief pattern. These are described in a contemporary account of the church, which relates that Salvin:

'paved the floor with the buff and chocolate-coloured tiles, ancient specimens of which, arranged in the pattern carefully reproduced in the new pavement, had been discovered under the brick floor. These tiles, made by Messrs Minton, of Stoke-upon-Trent, have the advantage of being *indented,* instead of glazed, and so are much less slippery than the ordinary Church tiles.'[8]

Herbert Minton gave tiles to the church in April 1849, although it is not clear which tiles comprised the donation. At the east end of the centre aisle is a very ornate panel with roundels of the four evangelists in atypical frames, while the sanctuary is striking: the pavement is of blue and yellow tiles with a small star design, and the reredos is of moulded grey hexagonal terracotta tiles. These are partly painted in red and gold, with red and gold lettering above; this is very like the reredos at Church Leigh. Altogether this is a most unusual decorative scheme.

HEDNESFORD

There are two sites of ceramic interest in this little ex-colliery town, the first being a former Maypole Dairy, now **Images of Beauty** hair salon, in the

HIGH STREET. Inside is a 24-tile Pilkington's panel showing dancers whirling around a maypole, typical of the panels used in Maypole shops during the 1920s-30s and which were probably painted by T. F. Evans.[9] The panels were not all exactly alike, but the differences between them - which involved the type of maypole, the dress of the dancers, and the house and church in the background - were minor, not enough to identify the panels with an individual town. Not far away is **94 Market Street** where an unusual encaustic tile panel may be seen, apparently set in place of a window, on a wall of a house with startling polychromatic brickwork. In the centre of the panel is a good reproduction of the Royal arms; although there is no date, this probably commemorates a Royal event, perhaps the coronation of George V in 1910 (or even his popular Silver Jubilee in 1935).

ILAM

The village of Ilam, in beautiful Dovedale, was bought in the early nineteenth century by a wealthy manufacturer, Jesse Watts Russell. He rebuilt Ilam Hall in 1821-6 then added the spiky, octagonal memorial chapel (commemorating his father-in-law) to the **Church of the Holy Cross** in 1831. George Gilbert Scott thoroughly restored the church in 1855-6, adding the encaustic tile pavement in the chancel; there are also four majolica memorial tablets, with dates ranging from 1867 to 1878, on an inside wall. These lozenge-shaped ceramic plaques seem to have become popular towards the end of the 1860s and are found chiefly in Staffordshire and, to a lesser extent, Derbyshire. In the graveyard are several headstones incorporating single tiles, all probably by Godwin or Minton. They are a colourful collection, although some are becoming worn, while the grave of James Slaney, died 1874, has its own memorial plaque similar to those inside the church.

KNIGHTLEY

The odd little white-brick **Christ Church** was built in 1840-1 by Thomas Trubshaw, although its chancel was added in 1882 by Nicholas Joyce; it has a good tiled chancel pavement and east wall.

LEEK

The architect Richard Norman Shaw said that **All Saints Church**, which he built in 1885-7, was 'the best and most satisfactory piece of work I have ever had done'.[10] The church is long and low with a spacious interior, the decorative emphasis being on the chancel with its huge painted reredos; the partnership of architect and artists (including the Leek School of Embroidery) made this a crucial building in the history of the Arts and Crafts Movement. The ceramic interest here is relatively small, but unusual: a tiled memorial panel dating from 1902, made by Wooliscroft's and commemorating a member of the Wooliscroft family. Also notable is the terrace of houses (1877) immediately north of the church, which has some unusual terracotta decoration.

LICHFIELD

There is much to see in **Lichfield Cathedral**, which is fortunate in possessing important floor tiling schemes from both medieval and Victorian periods, as well as the most unusual hand-painted wall tiles of Bishop Selwyn's tomb. The most impressive medieval tiles are on the floor of the Library, which is an elongated octagon on the first floor above the Chapter House; this stands to the north-east of the crossing, but is not normally open to the public. The Library was built around 1246 and the tiles are thought to be c1290, the majority of the floor being as originally laid. The tiles are in a symmetrical arrangement of longitudinal bands, groups of patterned tiles alternating with plain red and black glazed tiles; a few tiles have some of their clear lead glaze still intact.[11]

Lichfield Cathedral suffered severe damage during the Civil War and this may help to explain the poor survival of medieval tiles elsewhere in the building. Such medieval tiles as do remain are now mostly in the Consistory Court (south-east of the crossing). There are both line impressed and inlaid fourteenth-century tiles, although most are worn beyond recognition. They have been reset into an arrangement with Victorian red and black quarries; in the south-west corner of the room are several trade tiles impressed 'W Godwin Hereford', while a few large black tiles of Staffordshire coal complete this intriguing miscellany. George Gilbert Scott began major restoration work at the Cathedral in 1856, and the present floor of the Consistory Court probably dates from the very active period of work between 1856 and 1861. Scott was impressed with the quality of Godwin products and also used them in the restoration of Hereford Cathedral in 1857.[12]

But in the gloom of the choir is the complex pavement which presents the most spectacular display of Victorian floor tiles at Lichfield (Fig

245). A donation of tiles was made by Minton's to the Cathedral during its restoration, which ceased in 1861.[13] A contemporary account attributes all the choir tiles to Minton, claiming that their patterns are copied from ancient examples found in the Cathedral; there is certainly a similarity between the design of the line impressed tiles in the Consistory Court, and those in the choir pavement.[14] However, *The Builder* reported in 1862 that the incised pavement just west of the altar rail was by Clayton & Bell, a firm often associated with Scott but better known for its stained glass and general decorative schemes; it is possible that they had some supervisory role in the chancel's renovation.[15] In addition, it is known that the area of pavement in front of the high altar, depicting biblical scenes, was given by Colin Minton Campbell, who continued Minton's china business after the death of Herbert Minton in 1858. This would suggest that the date of the gift of tiles to the Cathedral was the late 1850s or very soon after, following the death of Herbert Minton.

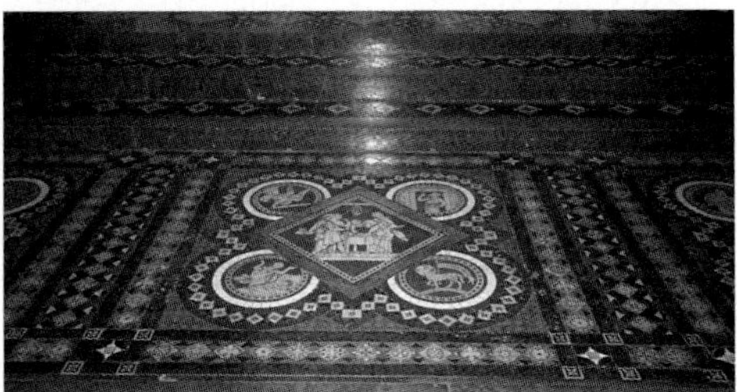

Fig 245.

The overall design of the complex tile and stone pavement is almost certainly by Scott, who produced plans for the choir in 1857-8, immediately prior to its excavation.[16] There are geometric and patterned encaustic tiles of a very elaborate nature, with inlaid medallions showing kings, bishops and scenes from the history of the diocese. Here, too, are bands of marble and large roundels of white stone inlaid with black mastic using the champlevé technique. This was developed in the Pas-de-Calais region of northern France in the second quarter of the thirteenth century; a resinous mastic composition is used to fill depressions or channels carved to form a design in a stone tile.

Last in the Cathedral's astounding array of tilework is Bishop Selwyn's Tomb, the middle of three tiny chapels to the south of the Lady Chapel (Fig 246). The Minton Hollins wall tiling of 1878 - hand-painted in overglaze enamels - in this confined space displays an unusual use of Victorian pictorial tiles.[17] The two panels showing Staffordshire miners in a pithead scene and Maoris are a tribute to Bishop Selwyn's work and links with both Staffordshire and New Zealand. George Augustus Selwyn (1809-78) became bishop of New Zealand in 1841, and was a great influence on the development of the colonial church; he became bishop of Lichfield in 1868. Selwyn College, Cambridge, was erected in his memory and his life is memorialised by ceramic plaques found in churches throughout Staffordshire.

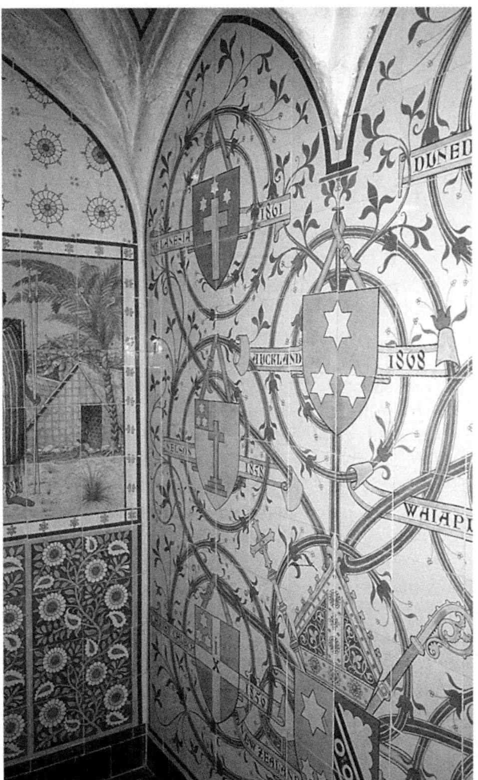

Fig 246.

In the city beyond the Cathedral is **Lichfield Library**, THE FRIARY, home to a stone fireplace from the original Tudor friary, which is decorated with blue and white seventeenth (possibly eighteenth) century Dutch tiles. Gregory Stonynge built a brick house on part of the site of the medieval Lichfield Friary about 1545; it had an elaborate fireplace ornamented with his name and other decoration. The fireplace was incorporated into the Friary School during the 1920s, and is now resident in the Children's Library. The tiles, which are somewhat battered, show street and working scenes, mainly centred on a single figure. In the entrance hall of the Library is a ceramic mosaic panel depicting a bull's head; this was reconstructed at a smaller scale than at its original location as a stall riser of a butchers shop in Tamworth Street.

MEERBROOK

Up in the north of the county, the little village of Meerbrook lies in the lee of the grim, millstone-grit Roaches, beside the Tittesworth Reservoir. The interior of **St Matthew's Church** is more cheering; the church was built in 1868-73 by Norman Shaw, and its chancel decoration, which includes a colourful Hispano-Moorish style east wall dado of cuenca tiles, dates from around 1870. The tiles, which feature different colour glazes run into depressions separated from each other by small moulded ridges, have a distinctive palette including orange, green, blue and brown, all on a white background. The bold, four-tile pattern stretches the entire width of the dado and is topped by a frieze also using cuenca tiles, but here with a floral motif; the tiles have a plastic clay (rather than dust-pressed) body. Cuenca tiles appeared to become fashionable as church furnishings during the 1870s despite their non-Christian origins, although Moorish craftsmen certainly decorated many Christian churches in Spain. Shaw was an enthusiastic user of these tiles as he liked their handmade look and feel. They were produced by several of the larger manufacturers, but the Meerbrook tiles were probably made by Frederick Garrard of London, whose products were often used by Shaw.

NEWCASTLE UNDER LYME

In ceramic terms, there is one outstanding site in this rather anonymous town, and that is **St George's Church**, QUEEN STREET. St George's was built as a Commissioner's Church in 1828 and was designed by Francis Bedford. Everything in this magnificent building seems to be on a large scale, from the height of the vaulted roof to the size of the organ, and it is tiled throughout, from west porch to sanctuary. Herbert Minton donated tiles to the church in 1854, although some of the tiles must have been re-sited or replaced, as the chancel was extended into the easternmost bay of the nave in 1879-81. The central aisle has an Escher-like border, in which reversed triangles of light and dark tiles almost induce an optical illusion. From the crossing eastward the tiling becomes more decorative, and the choir pavement is articulated by crossed bands enclosing nine-tile groups; at each crossing point is a fleur-de-lys tile. The tiles are notable by their sheer number and extent, and the use of general decorative motifs rather than the specific Christian symbols which appear in several nearby churches to which Minton donated tiles. Altogether, this is a very unspoilt example of Minton tiling in an unusual church. There is another encaustic tile pavement in the town, east of the centre at **St Paul's Church**, VICTORIA ROAD, which was built in 1905-8 and is tiled throughout. The tiles in the large, open interior probably originated from one of the three concerns spawned by Herbert Minton's firm: Minton Hollins & Co, Mintons China Works and the Campbell Brick & Tile Co.

OLDBURY

Outwardly, the **Waggon & Horses PH** in CHURCH STREET is just an ordinary - even rather dull - turn of the century pub, its red brick facade topped by a gable with a little buff terracotta decoration. However, its interior is richly tiled, using a combination of pale yellow, green and brown relief patterned tiles; in addition, the tile mosaic pavement still remains. No flashy picture panels or individualised tiles specific to the pub, but this is a good, relatively unspoilt example of an urban pub interior from around 1900.

PENSNETT

In the midst of the grim dross which passes for urban townscape west of Dudley, the setting of **St Mark's Church** is stunning, high on a hill in lush parkland with views all around. The church is reached either from VICARAGE LANE or through the park and then the churchyard, a mini-necropolis clambering up the steep hillside; the occupants include several chest tomb-type graves of black glazed brick, rather like massive black baths. This substantial, splendidly High Victorian church - known as the 'Cathedral of the Black Country' - was built in 1846-9 by John Macduff Derick (c1805-59), a relatively unimportant church architect from Ireland. He was a professional adviser to the Oxford Architectural Society, founded in 1839 by Oxford University undergraduates, many of whom later joined the ranks of the clergy; Derick probably obtained the Pensnett commission through these contacts.[18] The cost of the large, stone church was £6,700, which was provided by its patron, Lord Dudley. The extravagantly decorated chancel - *The Ecclesiologist* criticised St Mark's 'needless profusion of ornament' - was originally intended to contain the family pew.[19] Herbert Minton donated tiles for the church in 1849, and the well-preserved chancel tiles remain; there are also tiles around the font. Given the size and general grandeur of the church, the sanctuary tiles are a little disappointing, with no designs unique to the church, either letter or symbolic tiles. Altogether it is a rich if rather anonymous display, one which resulted, perhaps, from there being no personal connection between Minton and the church or its benefactor.

SMETHWICK

The **Waterloo Hotel**, SHIRELAND ROAD was built in 1907 as a flagship pub for the brewers Mitchells & Butlers, whose Cape Hill brewery stood less than half a mile away. The design was by the West Bromwich architects Wood & Kendrick, who built several Birmingham pubs for Mitchells & Butlers in the early 1900s. Behind the Edwardian baroque exterior, which includes good buff and red terracotta ornament, is a real ceramic heaven, with the public bar, hall and grill room all faced in Carter's tiles. The public bar has three green-tiled walls with a pink and cream frieze beneath a blue and cream-tiled ceiling, but much more memorable is the basement grill room, with its tiled, coffered ceiling and green-tiled walls around which floats a frieze of tube-lined galleons. The original cast iron grill is still in use, and the pub has also retained its tiled toilets with original Twyford's urinals.[20]

STAFFORD

Right at the very centre of Stafford is the **Collegiate Church of St Mary**, in ST MARY'S GATE. The church originated about 1190, and was extensively restored by George Gilbert Scott in 1842-4; this was one of his earliest church restorations, a commission which he obtained through his friendship with Thomas Stevens, the curate of Keele. Although Scott felt that 'a more careful restoration…never was made', his attempt to replicate the thirteenth-century appearance of the church caused much controversy. It seems he was not as satisfied with the interior of the church as with the exterior. He stated that 'the fittings of St Mary's were not very successful', but it is unclear whether this remark includes the tilework, to which much attention was paid, especially in the sanctuary.[21] The tiles were donated by Herbert Minton in 1844, and a contemporary report on the re-opening of the church describes the interior as follows:

'The greatest attraction among the internal decorations is the floor of the chancel, which is of magnificent encaustic tiles, gradually increasing in richness as they approach the eastern end. The portion of the east wall below the window is encased with still richer tiles enclosing different religious symbolical devices in gold, upon blue and other grounds. The designs, execution, and arrangement of these tiles is truly admirable - they are the work of Mr H. Minton, of Stoke-upon-Trent, by whom a large proportion of them has been munificently presented to the church.'[22]

It is indeed a wonderful display; the tile pavement covers the three broad steps leading to the sanctuary and the sanctuary itself, while there is also a gorgeous tiled reredos with gold symbols on mainly light blue grounds.

Ceramic attractions elsewhere in Stafford are rather thin on the ground, but include the massive bulk of the **Shire Hall**, now an art gallery, which dominates MARKET SQUARE. This Classical pile was built by John Harvey in 1795-9 and shelters a pair of elegantly draped Coade stone wenches within its pediment. They were modelled by J. C. F. Rossi, who worked for the Coades before leaving to start his own artificial stone business; the figures represent justice and mercy.[23] In the main shopping street, GREENGATE STREET, is **Burton's**, whose 1930s Classical white faience facade, probably Hathernware, turns a corner with elegance and ease. West of the town, less than a mile along Newport Road, is CASTLECHURCH, where **St Mary's Castle Church** lies below the remains of the nineteenth-century reconstruction of a medieval castle. Apart from its tower, the medieval church was pulled down and rebuilt by George Gilbert Scott in 1844-45, work beginning before his reconstruction of St Mary's in the centre of Stafford was complete. There is elaborate patterned Minton tile pavement throughout the tower, nave, aisles, chancel and sanctuary, with an east wall dado including gold letter tiles forming an inscription. The whole is similar in style to the tiling in the Collegiate Church of St Mary, although rather less lavish.

STOKE-ON-TRENT

Following the federation of Burslem, Fenton, Hanley, Longton, Stoke and Tunstall in 1910, Stoke-on-Trent became a city in 1925. However, this administrative fact has made little difference to the visitor's experience of the six towns. Busy roads criss-cross the hills which the collection of towns occupy, with Hanley (the uppermost) as the nominal city centre. There are several unique buildings in this low-density, low-rise city, and the gazetteer concentrates on the more substantial sites, although porch tile panels and indeed other small-scale ceramic detail can - unsurprisingly - be found throughout Stoke-on-Trent.

Burslem

The bright red brick and buff terracotta of the **Wedgwood Memorial Institute** materialised into the smoke-blackened gloom of Burslem in 1869, although its complete repertoire of external decoration was not fully revealed until 1872 (Fig 247).[24] The QUEEN STREET building, now a public library, was conceived with the intention of promoting the constructional use of terracotta, and was designed as a combination of library, museum and art school. Its original plan was by G. B. Nichols, although the facade was the result of a later competition, held to encourage the use of decorative ceramics and won by Robert Edgar and John Lockwood Kipling. The eventual result of this protracted design process was a remarkable building, wilfully ornate with beautifully modelled decoration including a series of figures representing the months of the year.

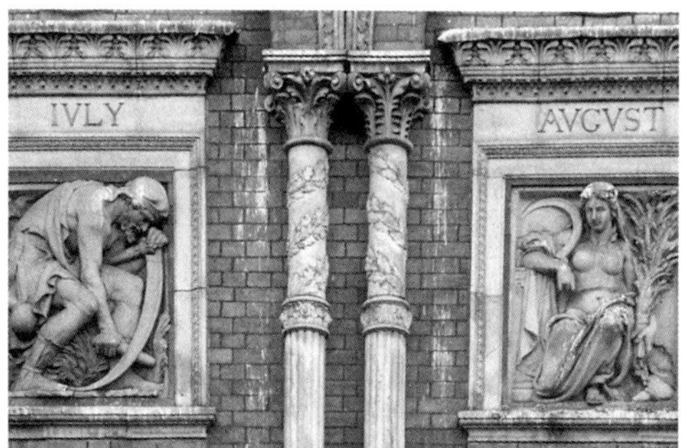

Fig 247.

The first pieces of terracotta for the facade of the two-storey building were produced by Blanchard & Co of Blackfriars, London, in 1866. In fact, Blanchards went on to manufacture all the Institute terracotta apart from the ten high-relief buff terracotta panels depicting the processes involved in pottery manufacture; these were provided by John Marriott Blashfield of Stamford, Lincolnshire. All modelling of the figurative panels was carried out by Rowland Morris, a Burslem man, although the design of the 'pottery process' panels was by Matthew Elden, a former Stoke School of Art student. The Institute, completed after tortuous delays, also displays a statue of Josiah Wedgwood, modelled by Morris and fired by Blanchard's.[25] The entire facade repays study; cats pursue birds through the terracotta foliage between windows, while the porch is tremendously ornate, using locally-produced tiles as well as terracotta. A success, then, as a building, but a failure in terms of the prime ambitions of its begetters: encouraging local production of terracotta and its wider use as a building material; although the latter did eventually come to pass, the Institute was not crucial to its development.

Just north of Queen Street is the imposing red brick and terracotta facade of the late Victorian **Liberal Club** (now offices) at 28 MARKET PLACE; its Dutch gable is topped by a colourful mosaic panel. Inside, the Snooker Room is completely tiled above dado level, but unfortunately the tiles - which include panels with floral designs - have been totally overpainted.

Half a mile east of Burslem's centre, on MOORLAND ROAD (opposite **Burslem Park** with its terracotta water fountain), is **Haywood House**, built in 1886-7 as the Howard and Richard Haywood Hospital following an endowment of £30,000 for the 'sick poor of Burslem' in Howard Haywood's will of 1875. The brothers Haywood owned a brick and tile factory at Brownhills in Burslem. Their hospital was expanded in 1891 and 1907, then relocated to a new site in 1930.[26] After proposals for its demolition, the original hospital building, complete with central pediment depicting the Haywood coat of arms in red terracotta, was taken over by the Burslem Community Development Trust during the 1990s. Inside is an unusual 70-tile monochrome brown panel measuring 5' by 3'6", set within a yellow-glazed moulded frame; it shows Jesus surrounded by children, beneath an arch inscribed 'Suffer little children to come unto me and forbid them not'. The panel was made by the Burslem firm Malkin, Edge & Co around the end of the nineteenth century, and painted by Frederic J. Harper, a local artist, teacher and shopkeeper; it won first prize in the Davis Testimonial Competition. The significance of the competition is lost to us now, but happily the panel has been rescued and restored, with the addition of new edging tiles donated by H. & R. Johnson.

At the end of Moorland Road is a complex junction where HANLEY ROAD leads off southward; the entrance to **Burslem Cemetery** is on the west side of Hanley Road. In the centre of the wooded burial ground is a small chapel, with encaustic tiling over its door, and just beyond is the dramatic - albeit rather battered - dark green

Doulton faience tomb of Thomas Hulm (1830-1905) of Longport. Hulm was organist of Burslem Sunday School for forty years, chairman of the school board for ten years, and a member of Staffordshire County Council; *He loved Burslem* reads one of its many inscriptions. This tomb, a rare survivor from a fairly small number of Doultonware memorials, was sculpted by John Broad and is unusually ornate; although its crowning urn has vanished there are reliefs of local buildings and even an upstanding angel holding what appears to be a musical instrument. It is, however, in poor condition and appears vulnerable (Fig 248).[27]

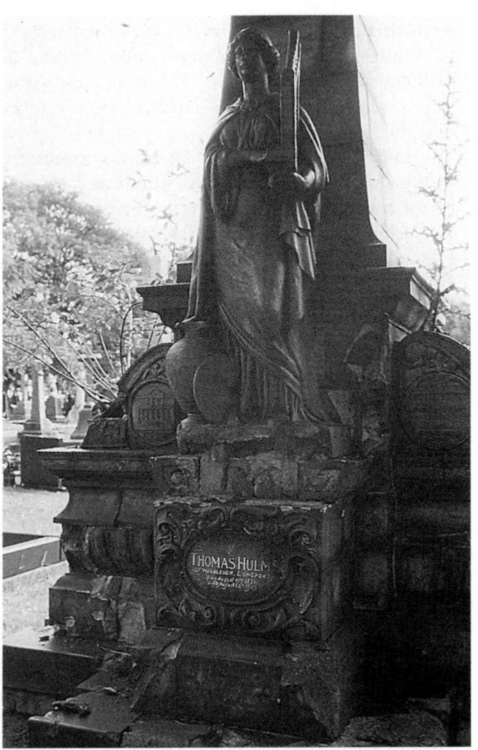

Fig 248.

Fenton

Fenton **Town Hall** (1888-9), in ALBERT SQUARE, has a tiled entrance hall; inside nearby **Fenton Library** (1905-7), GLEBEDALE ROAD, is much art deco tiling.

Hanley

In tune with Stoke-on-Trent's diffused nature, the ceramic attractions in its city centre, Hanley, are scattered widely. Beginning with the main shopping area, in STAFFORD STREET is a mid-1960s C&A store (now **Wilkinson's**) with an attractive full-height exterior ceramic panel, its abstract design based on squares (Fig 249). This little-noticed panel is composed of 6" surface-textured tiles in a variety of muted tones, mainly greens, purples and blues, some with geometric reliefs. The mural is unusual because it is one of the few surviving installations produced by Malkin Tiles; at least one of the motifs is from their 'Turinese' range marketed during 1961-8 and designed by Leonard Gladstone King, Malkin's art director.[28] Malkin's worked with H. & R. Johnson from 1964 before formally becoming a part of the company in 1968.

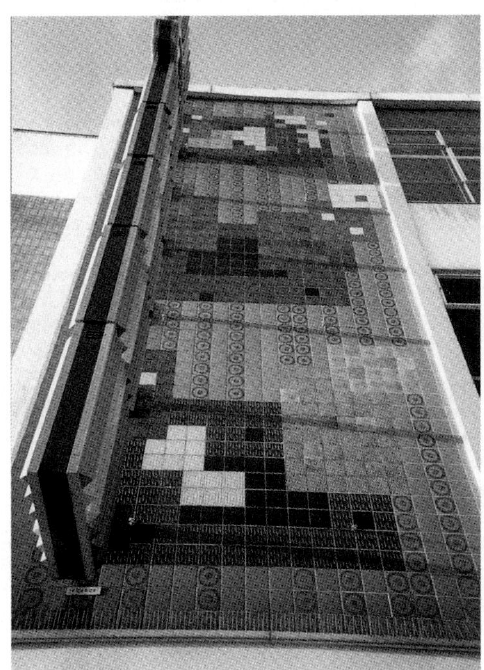

Fig 249.

Just east at 1 UPPER MARKET SQUARE is the **NatWest Bank**; inside, at the top of the escalators, is a brick relief entitled *Hanley Girl* by Walter Ritchie. It shows a languid female figure holding back a Staffordshire bull terrier, and was executed in 1976 using 10" handmade Shepshed bricks. Continue north across the ring road to OLD TOWN ROAD and the **Golden Cup** public house with its excellent 1912 ceramic facade. The basic dark green faience is enlivened by the words 'Bass Only' on the fascia, a cup and the pub name on a panel at first floor level, and lifebelt-style Bass symbols below the two front windows. The manufacturers of these facades are notoriously difficult to identify, but this one could well be the work of the Campbell Tile Co.

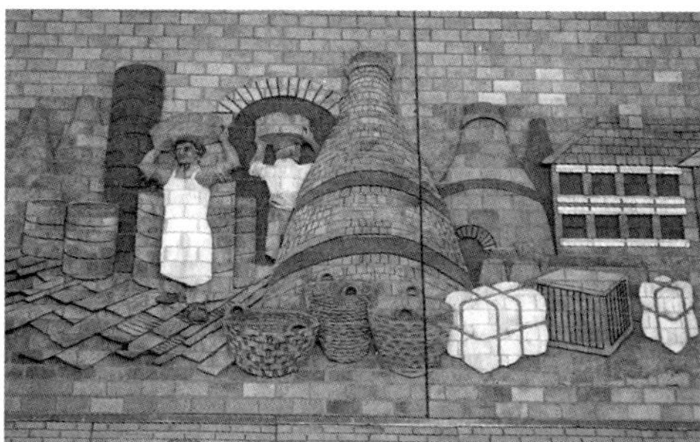

Fig 250.

In WELLINGTON ROAD, a quarter mile east of the ring road, is **Hanley St Luke's Church of England Aided Primary School**, a pair of uniquely tiled buildings put up in 1893 for the Hanley School Board, although the original Infant School is now in non-school use. The two large halls and seventeen classrooms have lavish wall tiling by Minton Hollins, remarkable both for its extent and its variety. There are over fifty different tile designs, ranging from stylised foliage and geometric motifs to birds and cherubs, the colour palette being a generally muted combination of browns, buff and cream. Within the dados are large panels of single tile designs, almost giving the impression of extracts from a manufacturer's catalogue. Despite much of the tiling in the Junior School being overpainted (four dado panels were revealed by a TACS working party in July 2002), the buildings are unusually complete, with good stained glass complementing the tilework.[29] The tiles play such a significant role in the life of the school that in the late 1990s the pupils were inspired to design and make two of their own multi-tile panels, colourfully depicting local scenes, which were fired by H. & R. Johnson's and mounted on the playground wall.

Back in Hanley's centre, running south from Stafford Street is PICCADILLY and the white faience Art Deco facade of the **Regent Theatre**, built in 1929 as a cinema for Provincial Cinematograph Theatres Limited; its architect was W. E. Trent. The well preserved faience, maker unknown, includes the letters 'PCT' and the cinema's name along with masks of comedy and tragedy. The cinema closed in 1989 but was lavishly transformed into a theatre, re-opening in 1999. To its rear in ALBION STREET is the **Victoria Hall**, where a circular hand-made tile mural was installed in 2003. The mosaic-style mural was the work of community artist Philip Hardaker and local schoolchildren, and colourfully depicts Stoke's creative and cultural activities. MARSH STREET runs north of Piccadilly, and at its junction with TRINITY STREET is **Telephone Buildings** (now a bar), built around 1900 as a telephone exchange with ornate terracotta detailing including floral motifs and lettering; the architect was L. A. S. Stokes. The interior decoration includes Minton Hollins wall tiling in the entrance foyer and stairwell. Southward beyond Piccadilly is Broad Street, where the striking brick and terracotta frieze which proclaims the presence of the **Potteries Museum & Art Gallery**, BETHESDA STREET comes into view (Fig 250). The frieze, ranging from pale buff to dark red in colour, was designed by the potter and sculptor Frank Maurier and installed in 1980; it runs across most of the Bethesda Street frontage and depicts work in the pottery industry, from mining clay to firing in bottle ovens.[30]

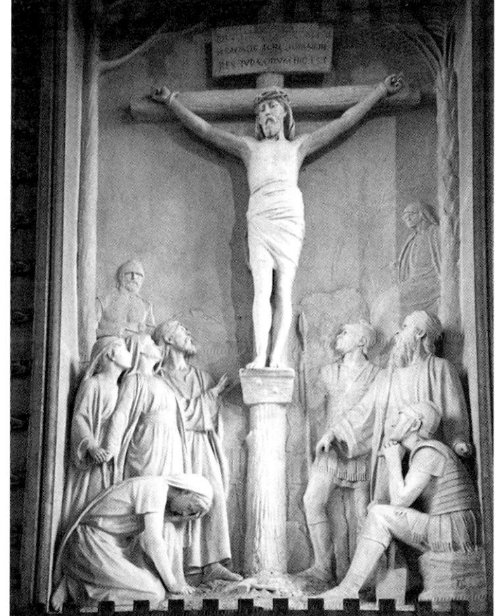

Fig 251.

Continuing down Broad Street, the tower of **St Mark's Church**, SNOW HILL, Shelton, beckons; it is a church full of ceramic interest, belied by its stark exterior (Fig 251). St Mark's was one of the 'Waterloo' churches, built in the aftermath of the

Napoleonic Wars to cater for the large number of people who had moved to new centres of industry in search of work. The ceremonial laying of the foundation stones, on St Mark's Day 1831 - 25th April - was accompanied by a display of ceramic tiles, two porcelain, one in ironstone, and one of earthenware, made at the pottery of Hicks, Meigh & Johnson in Broad Street. Each bore an inscription relating to the church and the dignitary laying the stone, and they were intended to be placed in niches beneath the four corner stones. However, one of the porcelain tiles escaped burial and has been preserved by the church. It shows a view of Shelton with Cliff Ville, the seat of John Tomlinson, patron of the church, in the distance. Clay dug from the foundations was used to produce items of pottery made by John Simpson at Dimmock's Pottery, and one of these jars is also retained by the church.[31]

The church, designed by the architect John Oates, was completed in 1834 and was one of the largest in the diocese, originally seating 2,100; it later underwent extensive alterations, including the rebuilding of the chancel in 1866-7. The sanctuary has a tiled floor by Minton & Co with several memorial plaques, including a small one to 'William Ireland choir boy' and another unusually decorative example to Bishop Selwyn of Lichfield. The three mainly gold pictorial mosaics on the front of the altar were the gift of Mary Ann Boothman in memory of her father Edward Duncan Boothman, vicar during the 1895 improvements.

But the glory of the church is its stunning reredos in the form of a massive Doulton terracotta triptych, a masterwork by George Tinworth. Its central panel, depicting *The Crucifxion,* measures 5′ by 10′ and weighs 1.25 tonnes; it is supported on steel girders and dates from 1896. The two side panels, each measuring 7′ by 3′, were added in 1902 and illustrate *The Visit of the Wise Men* and *The Visit of the Shepherds.* A smaller low relief panel by Tinworth entitled *The Holy Family in Egypt* can be seen in the Lady Chapel; this dates from 1899. The central triptych panel was unveiled in 1897, as part of Queen Victoria's Diamond Jubilee celebrations, while the side panels may commemorate the coronation of Edward VIII.[32] The sheer size and undoubted complexity of the reredos make it extremely unusual, as does the fact that it remains in the setting for which it was designed. It has been overpainted in grey, giving it a strange, dour appearance; the triptych is certainly staggering, but visually is somewhat unappealing.

Tiled porch panels are everywhere in Stoke-on-Trent, but those in the substantial late Victorian terrace of **The Parkway** (opposite HANLEY PARK and about half a mile east of St Mark's) are rather better than run-of-the-mill since they include picture panels as well as patterned tiling, along with paving tiles. The full height porch tiling has an inset low-relief deep yellow panel above the dado, showing a woman dancing in front of a shell-shaped niche; the immediately adjoining porch displays a complementary panel of slightly different design. The tiles were manufactured at the Minton Hollins Patent Tile Works, which included one of the panel designs in their 1903 catalogue.

Finally, on the western edge of Hanley in what remains of Etruria is the **Wesleyan Methodist Chapel** (1820), ETRURIA OLD ROAD. Inside is a substantial brown and white glazed ceramic wall memorial to James Mainwaring (d1891). The central panel of this unusual memorial is a relief bust of Mainwaring in brown faience; to either side are descriptive panels and above is a segmental section. The ornate classical frame, in white faience, features urns, ionic pilasters and an angel below.

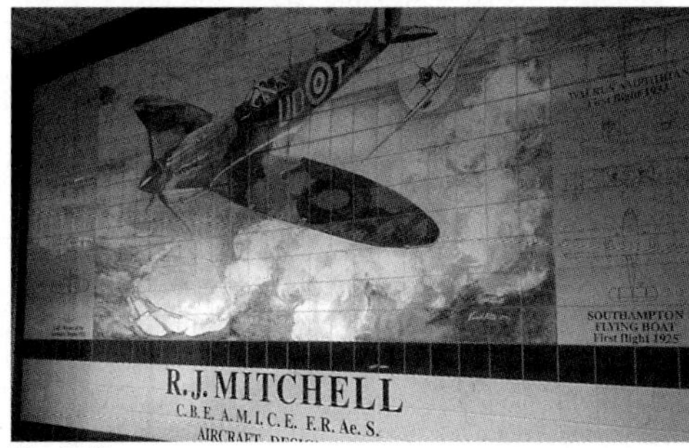

Fig 252.

Longton

Almost under the railway bridge in the cramped centre of Longton is the **Crown Hotel**, KING STREET, whose impressive and colourful porch tiles may be by Gibbons Hinton, or could even be of American origin; the designs include vivid golden-yellow sunflowers. Across TIMES SQUARE is the **Town Hall**, whose grand staircase has a green-tiled dado; immediately behind is the airy **Market Hall** and an unusual clock (1877) with an encaustic-tiled face. Leave the market by the TRANSPORT LANE exit to find a small block of 1970s **public conveniences** faced with Carter's industrial tiling and made to stand out from the dreary surroundings with a dark green geometric pattern on white ground; these relief tiles were designed by Ivor Kamlish. Turn right into the **Bennett Precinct** (1965) where a colourful 1994 tile panel by Kenneth Potts shows a Spitfire in full flight (Fig 252); it commemorates the aeroplane's designer, local man R. J. Mitchell (1895-1937).

To the south is the **Longton Centre**, formerly the Sutherland Institute, in LIGHTWOOD ROAD (Fig 253). The red-brick pile was built in 1897-9 by local architects Wood & Hutchings, and has a fine salmon-pink high-relief terracotta frieze stretching across its facade. This dates from 1908-9 and its subjects, not surprisingly, are the pottery and mining industries; it includes a total of 28 labouring workers centred on an enthroned figure.

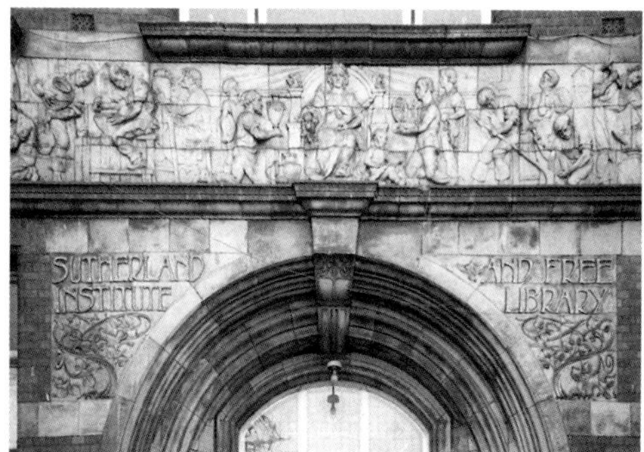

Fig 253.

Even further south on Lightwood Road is the junction with UPPER BELGRAVE ROAD; the **Church of the Holy Evangelist**, Normacot, is a quarter mile along (Fig 254). The little church was built in 1846-7 by George Gilbert Scott at the expense of the Duke of Sutherland. Herbert Minton donated the tiles, comprising a sanctuary pavement with fleur-de-lys tiles and evangelist roundels, and two coats of arms in the pavement at the rear of the nave. The arms, in buff and red encaustic tiles, are dated 1846 and 1847, and are those of the Duke of Sutherland and the Earl of Lichfield; they face the north doorway in what was originally the aisle between banks of pews.

A mile or so to the west in Blurton is **St Bartholomew's Church**, CHURCH ROAD; although there is now no sign of the tiles donated to the church by Herbert Minton in 1851, there is a fine collection of highly-glazed 12" square memorial tiles forming a dado on the south wall.

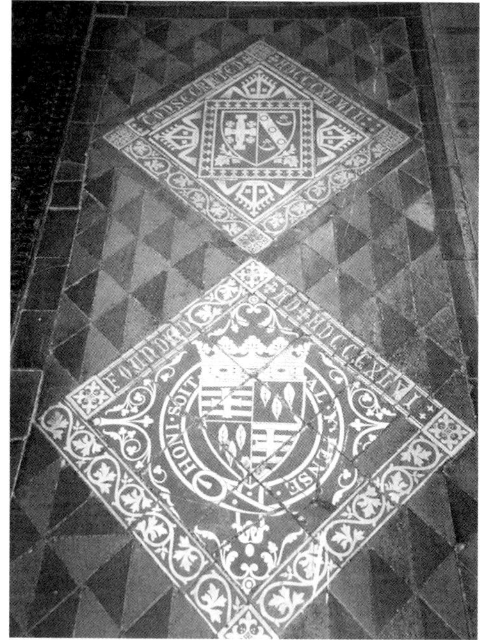
Fig 254.

Stoke

Trekking beneath the tracks at **Stoke-on-Trent Railway Station** is made immensley more attractive by the colourful tube-lined majolica murals beckoning the passenger at either end of the subway (Fig 255). They were installed in 1994 and were the result of a creative partnership between the railway company, local organisations including schools and the council, and H. & R. Johnson's, who produced the murals at their Highgate Tile Factory, Tunstall. The lively designs, featuring trains and all manner of Stoke people and places, were by artist Elizabeth Kayley in collaboration with local children.[33]

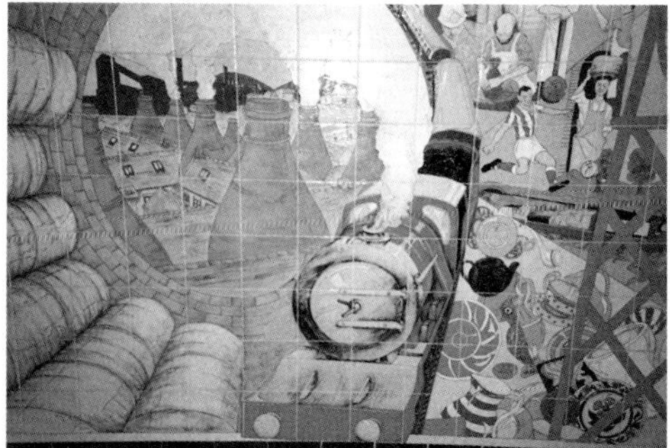
Fig 255.

Opposite the station in STATION ROAD is the **North Stafford Hotel**, where the abrupt tiled sign for 'Lavatory' points downstairs into a handsome fully-tiled Art Nouveau gent's, probably dating from the turn of the century; the scheme, mainly in green and white, runs down the stairs and throughout the toilets (Fig 256). The hotel itself, a Tudorbethan expression of railway self-confidence, opened a year after the station in 1849, and both were designed for the North Staffordshire Railway Company by architect H. A. Hunt of London. The pair define an exceptional station square, now blighted by continuous cross-traffic. The hotel was such a success that it was extended in 1878, and it later starred as the *Five Towns Hotel* in an Arnold Bennett novel, probably around the time that the gent's tiling was installed.[34] The remains of the **Minton Hollins & Co** factory, now converted to offices, can be found west of the station by the roundabout in SHELTON OLD ROAD. It was built soon after 1869 for Michael Daintry Hollins by the architect Charles Lynam, who incorporated the radical principle of linear production in its design.[35] The factory was also intended as a showpiece and included a museum as well as being decorated with the firm's wares; although only a small part of the original extensive building complex is extant, several panels of encaustic tiles - tiny vertical geometric pavements - can still be seen on the facade.

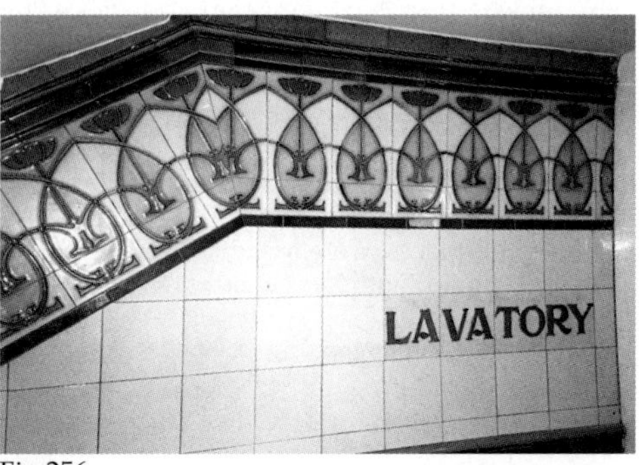

Fig 256.

The parish church of **St Peter ad Vincula** lies south of Stoke's centre in GLEBE STREET; it was built close to the site of its medieval predecessor in 1826-30. It was the first of the new nineteenth-century churches in the Potteries and was supported by many enthusiastic subscribers; the interior, renovated in 1888, is impressively colourful, with much visual interest (Fig 257). It is notable for the sheer quantity of its memorial wall tiles, commemorating parishioners and others connected in some way with Stoke, which form a dado around the nave. These tiles were first installed in 1859 by the rector, Sir Lovelace Tomlinson Stamer (1829-1908), grandson of John Tomlinson, patron of St Mark's Church, Shelton; this is the earliest known use of such memorial tiles. Stamer, whose uncle had been the previous rector, took up the Stoke living in January 1858 and moved to Stoke in March 1858; he remained at Stoke until 1892. He may have attended the funeral of Herbert Minton, who died on the 1st April 1858 and was buried at nearby Hartshill Church. There may have been wall memorial tiles at Hartshill Church, but there is no evidence on this point as the church was burnt out in 1872 (although rebuilt shortly afterwards). If memorial wall tiles were present at Hartshill, that may have been the source of Sir Lovelace Tomlinson Stamer's decision to introduce them at St Peter ad Vincula.[36]

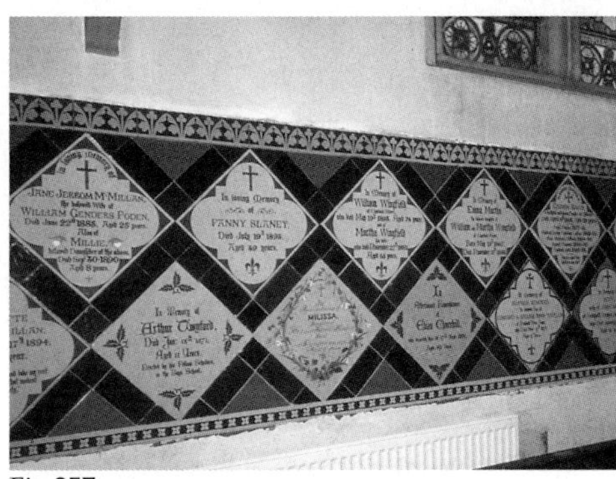

Fig 257.

Although some tiles have been removed from the south wall of the nave, 289 memorial tiles still remain at St Peter; a few are upright rectangles, but most are the typical lozenge shape, mainly in cream with red lettering. They date generally from the 1860s and 1880s, but some are as late as 1908. Occasional tiles are more decorative, for instance with a green floral band around the edge. The tiles were overpainted but have been cleaned and are now described in the church guidebook as being 'of some rarity and historic value'. Amongst the tiles at the rear of the church is an olive-green faience memorial plaque including two high-relief figures; this dates from around 1903. There is also an attractive tile pavement in the sanctuary, with many differing patterns and some unusual mauve tiles as well as striking armorials; there are several memorial tiles set in the floor, including at least two to members of the Stamer family, buried beneath. Out in the churchyard, near the tomb of Josiah Wedgwood, is a Gaudiesque blue ceramic bench installed to mark the Queen's Jubilee in 2000. Its design, by artists Helen Sayer, Philip Hardaker and Edgar Ruddock, was based on ideas suggested by local schoolchildren; the images, which include the footballer Stanley Matthews, relate to St Peter's and to Stoke's industrial history.

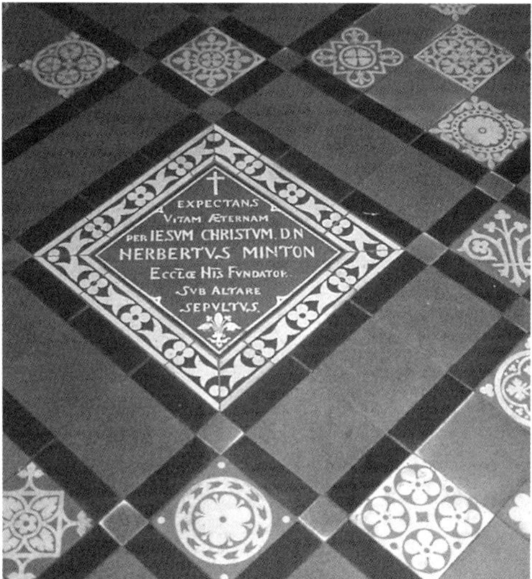

Fig 258.

Across Glebe Street, the old entrance to **Stoke-on-Trent Civic Centre** (formerly Stoke Town Hall) has good wall tiling and an imposing Boer War ceramic memorial panel of 1904 with a pronounced green faience frame. A little further south in LONDON ROAD is **Stoke Library**, purpose-built by the architect Charles Lynam in 1878. His innovative design featured a series of large, porthole-like windows with tile panels above and a continuous frieze of windows beneath the eaves. The tile panels, which show flowers in urns, are now very faded, making the building appear shabby; venture inside, however, and the basement - originally the Reading Room - is a revelation. Beneath the wallpaper, its walls turn out to be tiled with a near-comprehensive collection of the various, mostly twelve-tile, pictorial series produced by the prolific designer John Moyr Smith, who worked for both Minton & Co and Minton Hollins. Although only a few picture tiles are currently visible, there are probably about two hundred of them hidden in this fascinating room, which is now a toy library but may once have served as a canteen for council workers.

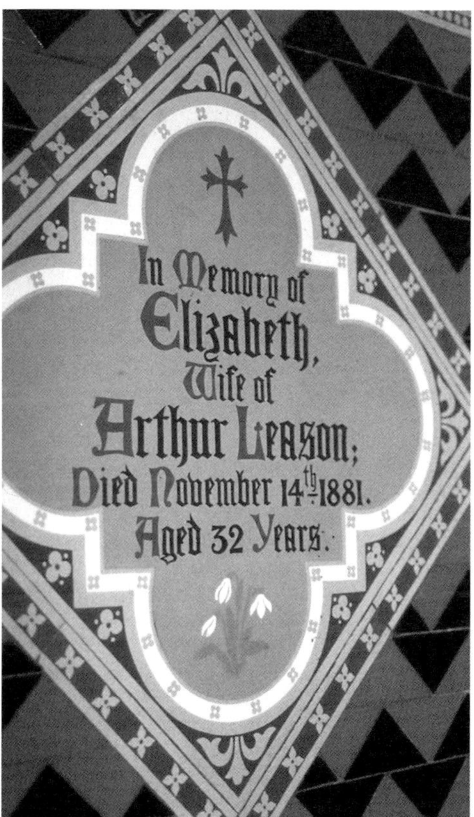

Fig 259.

HARTSHILL ROAD leads westward and upward from Stoke's centre to Hartshill and Herbert Minton's **Holy Trinity Church**, its hilltop spire a landmark for miles around (Fig 258). Minton also paid for the adjoining parsonage and school, and a group of houses near the church, as well as giving land for the churchyard. MINTON STREET runs to the rear of the church, which was designed in mid-1841 by George Gilbert Scott, and built in 1842. Much of the detailing, including the square-ended chancel, was taken - apparently at Minton's insistence - from Lichfield Cathedral. Colin Minton Campbell rebuilt the chancel in memory of his uncle, probably in 1862, but the church was almost entirely burnt out in 1872. It was then restored by Scott on much the same lines as his 1841 design, albeit with a longer apsidal chancel and a south chapel (Fig 259). Most of the chancel tilework, therefore, dates from 1862 or - rather more likely - 1872, although Holy Trinity's nave pavement is entirely original. Many of the nave designs appear in Minton's *Earliest Pattern Book*, itself a forerunner of Minton's first printed catalogue of 1842.[37]

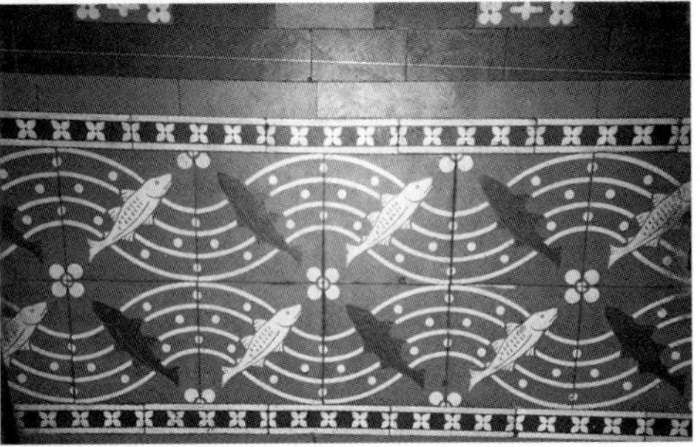

Fig 260.

Altogether it is an astounding ceramic display: tiles are everywhere, right from the little vestry by the north entrance to the remarkable chancel, and on the walls as well the floor (Fig 260). Beginning in the chancel, the east end wall, almost hidden by the altar, turns out to have vividly coloured, highly glazed tiles in a diagonal arrangement. It includes the twin bird design in buff on red ground, with yellow enamel over the inlay; these are by Minton & Co. The altar dais riser has letter tiles in red and buff: 'Do this in remembrance of me'. On the south wall, twin sedilia are set on highly glazed deep red tiling delineated with black bands. The surprisingly plain sanctuary pavement comprises black bands delineating green, buff and red geometric patterns. The choir is much more decorative, mixing buff and red patterned tiles with plain tiles in green and buff; in the centre of the choir is a lozenge-shaped memorial tile to Herbert Minton, who is buried beneath.

At the head of the nave is a large square of ornate buff and red designs including some armorial tiles. The entire nave floor is tiled using a huge variety of red and buff designs displaying much Christian symbolism. In the side aisles are four-tile groups including the rose window, but these aisles are dominated visually by the brilliantly glossy wall tiling, comprising a frieze of ornate memorial tiles above a largely red dado, the latter partly of the same design as the sedilia tiling in the chancel. The memorial tiles, added by Robert Minton Taylor from 1872 onward, are much more colourful and complex than those of St Peter ad Vincula in Stoke, leading to the suggestion that they were used initially at St Peter's; however, it is impossible to come to a firm conclusion on this point as there is no evidence concerning the existence of memorial tiles at Hartshill prior to the 1872 fire.

Finally, in this breathtaking array, at the west end of the nave are tiles showing delicate fish within undulating lines, representing waves; the fish are in both black and buff, and are so detailed that their scales are visible. These are of a later date than the main nave pavement, probably 1872, and were manufactured by the Campbell Brick and Tile Co. It is unfortunate that Holy Trinity, a monument to Minton and the industry he did so much to create, remains so little-known. Normally locked, as with most urban churches, its exterior gives no indication of the ceramic wealth inside. The interior is a revelation.

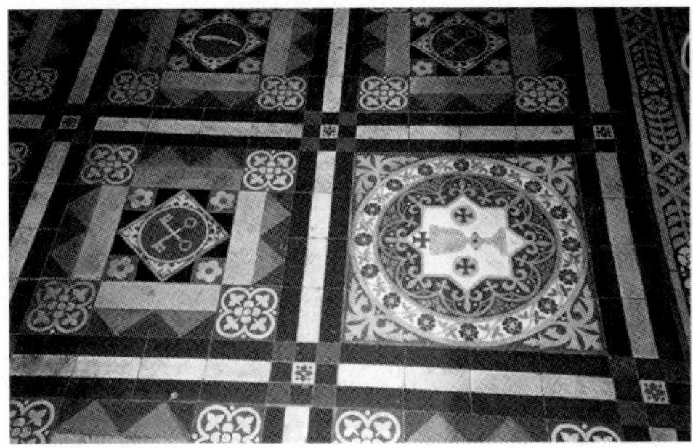

Fig 261.

Cross Hartshill Road, and heading towards Penkhull along QUEEN'S ROAD we find **Ceram Research**, built in 1947-50 as a research centre for the former British Ceramic Research Association. The lobby of this stripped Classical structure has very unusual large-scale cream relief cushion-style tiles within framed borders. There is also an encaustic tiled panel probably made by H. & R. Johnson around 1980, similar to those used in the refurbishment of the Palace of Westminster. In the centre of Penkhull, in the square off NEWCASTLE LANE, is the **Church of St Thomas**. It was built by Scott & Moffat in 1842, largely at the expense of Herbert Minton's brother, the Reverend Thomas Webb Minton. The incumbent was Samuel Minton, son of Thomas and nephew of Herbert Minton, who donated tiles for the church in 1845 and paid off the debt which Samuel had incurred during its construction. The tiling, in the choir and sanctuary, is unusual although relatively small in area (Fig 261). Large panels of an agnus dei and a pelican in her piety dominate the choir, while a series of small, sky-blue tiles bearing symbols of the Passion Cycle lie across the sanctuary. Behind the altar - and presumably intended to be seen by the incumbent alone - is a design which appears to be unique: a white, octagonal star-shaped tile showing a golden chalice. The tiling has been restored by the Heritage Tiling & Restoration Company.

Tunstall

Stoke-on-Trent's northern outpost is marked by its rather Germanic **Clock Tower**, which dominates the smaller-scale buildings beside it in TOWER SQUARE. The tower, erected in 1893 in commemoration of the local Smith Child family, is basically an octagonal column clad in buff terracotta; it is topped by a bellcote and carries large clock faces. Just east is the **Town Hall**, which has a good encaustic tiled floor. To the north on HIGH STREET is the **NatWest Bank** (ex-Manchester and Liverpool District Bank), a fine towered corner building in ornate buff terracotta, dating from 1899; next door is **Barclay's** (ex-Bank Chambers), built in 1893 and displaying a series of double-height bay windows faced in a slightly paler - but just as ornate - terracotta.

About half a mile south-west of Tunstall's centre is the HAREWOOD STREET works of **H. & R. Johnson Tiles Limited**, opened in 2002. In the foyer of the office block is a colourful 10' by 12' tile mural designed by interior design students Andrew Cheung and Alex Forster, winners of a 2001 competition to create a design for the site.

STONE

A substantial Catholic settlement was founded in Stone in the mid-nineteenth century, its various buildings standing on the corner of MARGARET STREET and the High Street. There is a large, towerless church, built in 1852-4 and dedicated to the **Immaculate Conception and St Dominic**, as well as a small chapel designed by A. W. N. Pugin in the garden of the convent. This is an example of the very simple type of church Pugin planned for newly-founded missions. St Dominic itself has a Minton sanctuary pavement, partly of plain tiles in buff or black but with additional blue, buff and black tiles displaying the initials 'SD' twice over. There is also a small Minton pavement near the chapel. An excellent array of Minton encaustic tiles may be found in **St Michael's Church**, CHURCH STREET, where symbols of the Passion Cycle are incorporated into an unusual chevron arrangement.

TAMWORTH

The local terracotta manufacturers, Gibbs & Canning, produced the faience facade of the **Tamworth Cooperative Society** building on COLEHILL, as well as its colourful tiled entrance and stairs.

Glascote

St George's Church, BAMFORD STREET was designed by the architect Basil Champneys and built in 1880 of brick with an interior including much (now largely overpainted) Gibbs & Canning brownish-red terracotta. This was donated by C. Canning, who gave the church £150 and terracotta worth a further £100. North across Bamford Street is **Glascote Cemetery**, where there are two terracotta memorials, one of which - a miniature Albert Memorial in style - was erected around 1902 by Gibbs & Canning workmen in memory of one of their fellows.

TRENTHAM

The **Church of St Mary and All Saints** was built by the architect Sir Charles Barry in 1842-4, soon after his completion of the adjacent and palatial Trentham Park, erected in 1833-42 for the second Duke of Sutherland and largely demolished in 1910-12. The Duke of Sutherland's visit to Minton's Works, then in the charge of Herbert's father Thomas Minton, led to the Duke and Duchess becoming enthusiastic patrons of Herbert Minton's products, and Minton donated tiles for the nave, aisles and chancel of Trentham Church in 1844 (Fig 262). The church is approached from the main road, where a hulking mausoleum reminds the visitor of the lost empire of the Sutherlands. Beyond is a dramatic bridge, and then the little church set amongst Italianate remains of some grandeur, both sad and magical. Behind its anonymous exterior, the church

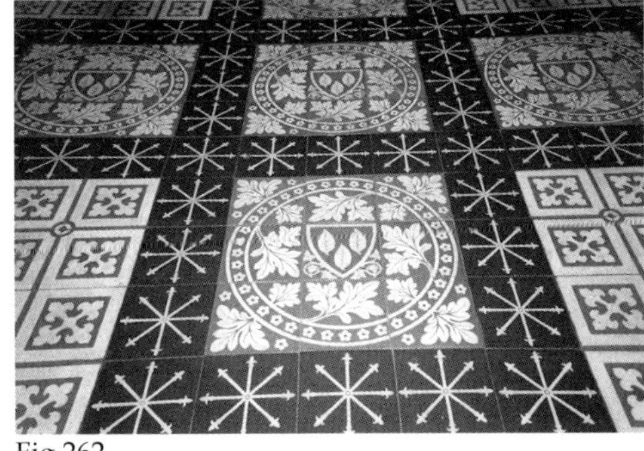

Fig 262.

exhibits a spectacular array of tiling. There are floor tiles (some now covered by carpet), memorial wall tiles and even a large Doulton terracotta panel by George Tinworth, dating from 1885, which is a memorial to the fourth Duke of Sutherland (Fig 263).

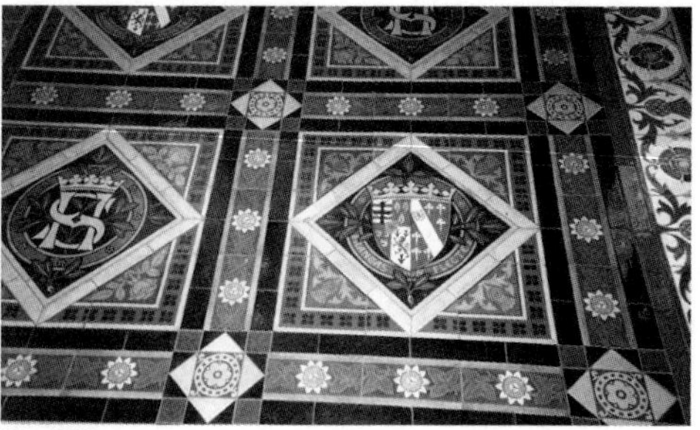

Fig 263.

In the Sutherland Chapel, the floor is of glazed tiles with very vibrant colours; the decorations appear to date from 1870, and the floor tiles have been attributed to Minton Hollins & Co. Here two distinct pattern elements repeat alternately, a coat of arms and a set of initials, while the border has a rose and thistle design. The sanctuary tiles, a striking combination of black, buff and red designs, include the Sutherland coat of arms, while in the choir are some memorial floor tiles, including one to the apparently ubiquitous Bishop Selwyn. The central nave aisle has some large memorial specimens; the most easterly, next to the chancel, is dedicated to Herbert Minton. Completing this sumptuous display is a frieze of highly glazed memorial tiles on the north wall, installed (at least partially) by 'Mr Minton's workmen' on the 22nd October 1860; this includes some uplifting lettering on its borders.[38] With the decorative elements of the church saved from its predecessor on the site, including a startling rood screen, the whole is pure delight.

WALSALL

The short twentieth century, as Eric Hobsbawm defined it, did not do much for the urban fabric of Walsall. Its centre became just another extrusion of identical facades from the sausage machine of corporate design, while good new architecture was rare. Gone was the confidence which saw the opening of the **Institute of Science and Technology** (now School of Art), BRADFORD PLACE, in 1888. On either side of the main gable, above lashings of ornate buff terracotta, stand the bear and ragged staff, Walsall's crest. This substantial building looks down on a typical turn-of-the-century pub, the **Tavern in the Town** (now 2 Toes), in BRADFORD STREET. It has an elaborate brown, green and yellow faience facade, probably by Burmantofts, with unusual scalloped sections in the ceiling of both porches, which presumably would have taken light fittings. If the ordinary pubs of the town were colourful, then so were the everyday offices: close by in BRIDGE STREET, both **Imperial Buildings** and **King's Court** (built in 1904) have tiled dados throughout ground and first floors, with the tiling in Imperial Buildings being especially elegant as it curves serenely up the stairwell. Also in Bridge Street, **Tudor House** (1926, architects Jeffries & Shipley) has an interesting Gibbs & Canning grey terracotta facade with much low relief decoration including Tudor roses.

But after years of relative decline, Walsall has a new image, and it is clad in grey terracotta tiles: the **New Art Gallery**. This monumental building, which overlooks the canal from GALLERY SQUARE, right in the town centre, was commissioned by the local council and funded by the national lottery; it opened in early 2000 and houses the Garman Ryan Collection as well as community facilities. Its architects, Caruso St John, clad the exterior with large terracotta panels in subtle grey tones, the panels being bolted to the inner skin of the building and diminishing in size towards the top. The effect is very cool, more like 1960s ribbed concrete or even wood shingles than traditional terracotta, but appealing, especially when viewed across the canal in winter gloom. The reflection dissolves the stark structure, leaving only bands of light floating on the water. And Walsall's sudden enthusiasm for the shock of the new has not stopped with the New Art Gallery; in 1999 the bus station was transformed into a dramatic soaring space roofed by a visitation of flying saucers, resting awhile on spindly white stalks. These are surely the iconic concrete mushrooms of Frank Lloyd Wright's Johnson Wax Building, revived by the organic architecture of the new millennium. Welcome to Walsall.

WALTON-ON-THE-HILL

The **Church of St Thomas**, Berkswich, in the parish of Walton-on-the-Hill, is about two miles south-east of the centre of Stafford; it stands just off the A513, a little way beyond its junction with the A34 at Weeping Cross. The church was originally a chapel of ease, built in 1842 by Thomas Trubshaw, and Herbert Minton donated of tiles for its altar space in 1844. The interior displays an excellent range of tiles, including many designs from Minton's first printed catalogue of 1842; the chancel tiles are particularly lavish and colourful. There are several memorials to the Levett family of nearby Milford Hall, whose initials can also be found in unusual blue and buff tiles.

WEDNESBURY

The *Shell Guide* called Wednesbury a 'shapeless, straggling town' while Pevsner described its art gallery as 'funny', but do not be deterred. **Richards Art Gallery** (1890-1, architects Wood & Kendrick), at the end of a row of substantial public buildings on the HOLYHEAD ROAD, turns out to have a striking and unusual facade dotted with busts and relief portraits by Doulton's George Tinworth. Just east is the former **Science School** (1896) with an ornate terracotta facade, and further along is the ex-**Birmingham Gas Board** offices (1899, by Wednesbury architects Joynson Brothers) with more terracotta.

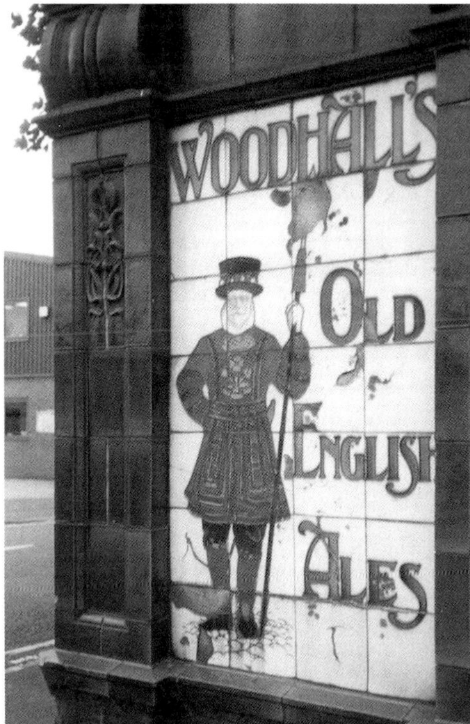

Fig 264.

Turn south into BRIDGE STREET to find the **Coachmakers** pub, with a fine dark brown Doulton faience facade featuring a colourful 28-tile panel on which an upstanding beefeater advertises Woodhall's Old English Ales (Fig 264). Samuel Woodhall's was a West Bromwich brewery active between the 1870s and the 1930s; the tile panel, which is in poor condition, probably dates from around 1910. Minton's also designed tile panels for Woodhall's, although probably at a later date.[39] Then north to the MARKET PLACE and the old **Talbot Hotel**, built in 1879 with yet another interesting terracotta facade; a further half a mile or so northward is the **Horse & Jockey** on WOOD GREEN ROAD, with a terrific art nouveau glazed ceramic bar counter in green, white and shades of brown.

WEST BROMWICH

The main ceramic interest in West Bromwich lies west of the market area, on the HIGH STREET. First in a series of memorable facades is the former offices of **Kendrick & Jefferson**, an 1883 structure fairly dripping with pinky-red terracotta detailing. Next is **Sandwell Central Library**, whose monumental classical facade hides one of the most spectacular interiors in the Midlands, or further afield for that matter (Fig 265). Once

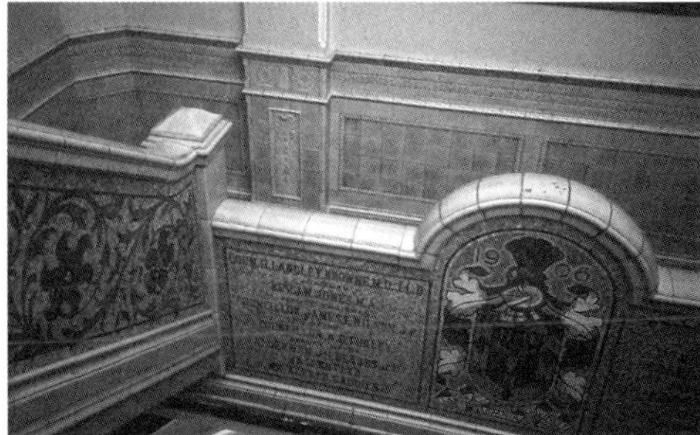

Fig 265.

through the grand ionic portico, the visitor is transported to a pristine world of faience and mosaic, resulting from a 1993 renovation of this Carnegie Library, designed by the little-known Birmingham architect Stephen J. Holliday and opened in 1907. The foyer is lined with glistening pale green and yellow faience, some in relief designs, which stretches up the curving stairway and along the first floor gallery; chunky, brightly coloured ceramic mosaics are set into the faience. Borrowers pass beneath a ceramic lintel as they enter the library proper, itself lined to dado level with faience, which also covers the supporting columns; the whole effect is bright and airy, if rather surprising for a library.

Next door to the Library is the **Town Hall** (1874-5, architects Alexander & Henman of Stockton-on-Tees), its germanic tower a landmark amongst the clutch of civic buildings at the western end of the High Street. A rather dull, albeit patterned, Maw & Co encaustic tile pavement runs throughout its ground floor.[40] A more decorative tile pavement can be found across Lodge Road at the **West Bromwich Institute**, built in 1886 and designed by West Bromwich architects Wood & Kendrick, best known for their ornate turn-of-the-century Birmingham pubs. The institute's tudorbethan exterior is richly ornamented with dark red terracotta.

At the northern end of the High Street on Carters Green stands the **Farley Clock Tower**, unfortunately now overlooking a grim road junction (Fig 266). This red brick gothic tower was built in 1897 and bears a series of pinky-red terracotta relief panels, signed A. Hopkins, which show local buildings - the Town Hall and sixteenth-century Oak House - and a bearded gentleman. This is, in fact, Alderman Reuben Farley, three times mayor of West Bromwich. He saved the Oak House from decay, employing Wood & Kendrick to oversee its restoration, and in 1898 presented the building to the town for use as a museum.

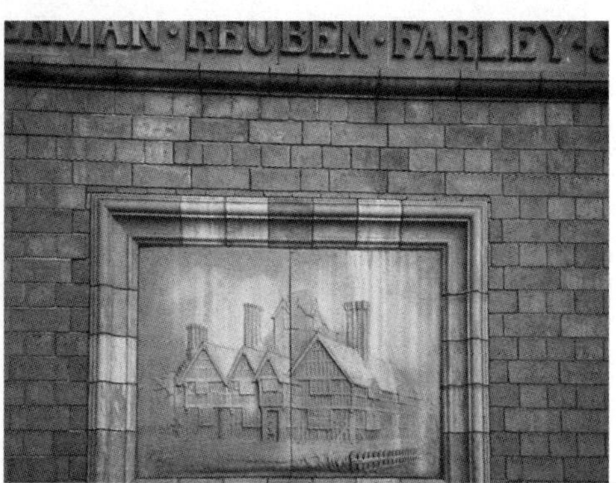

Fig 266.

Well to the east of central West Bromwich, the **Hawthorns Metro Station**, Halford's Lane, has decorative red terracotta tiling (1998) by David Mackie set into the north platform retaining wall. The tiles have a relief of leaves and appropriate lettering in six designs: palmate, pinnate, cordate, truncate, ovate and needle. The theme relates to the variety of trees planted along the Metro tracks, and the manufacturer was Ibstock Cattybrook (Bristol).

WHITMORE

The medieval church of **St Mary and All Saints** was restored and partly rebuilt around 1880, leaving its interior very much a testament to late Victorian taste. Unusually, a glazed tile dado runs throughout the church, and in addition there is a tiled reredos; all this is probably by Minton Hollins & Co, given that there is a Hollins family connection with the church. The little estate village is attractive, with only a tree-lined avenue separating the church from Whitmore Hall, home of the Mainwaring family, who are commemorated by several monuments inside the church.

WOLVERHAMPTON

We begin in the densely-packed centre at Lichfield Street, where the University of Wolverhampton now inhabits the old **Post Office** building, a three-storey mass of brick encrusted with pale buff terracotta by Dennis, Ruabon. It was completed in 1898 by Sir Henry Tanner of the Office of Works, an architect responsible for many post offices. The string courses are very thin, emphasising the bright, pinkish-red colour of the immaculate brick facade. Decorative terracotta detail includes several Classical motifs in crisply modelled reliefs, seen most conspicuously on the imposing, heavily ornate entrance. Further west on Lichfield Street is the **Posada**, a pub with an excellent faience facade in the form of a single curving bay; it also sports the pub name in vertical lettering on pilasters in the twin porches. Almost opposite is **St Peter's Church**, set back from Lichfield Street in St Peter's Close; at the rear of the church, set on a wall above the stairs, are six memorial tablets of the 1860s and 1870s, five typical lozenge-shaped plaques and one smaller, glazed square tablet in green and white. Returning eastward, on the corner of Lichfield Street and Stafford Street is the **Royal London Building**, built in 1902, with three interesting blue and buff relief terracotta plaques by Carters above the entrance; their maker's mark and date has been incised into the base of the plaques, where it can still be seen clearly. Across Stafford Street, the **Hogshead** (ex-Vine) and the old **Drill Hall** both display unusual amounts of terracotta enrichment, notably on the pub's pilasters.

Broad Street leads from Stafford Street towards the infernal ring road, but as the traffic looms ahead we reach the junction with Fryer

STREET and **Amar House**; its completely improbable interior was probably designed as a showroom for the hardware merchants John Shaw & Sons. Through arches, up stairs and around corners, highly glazed cream and yellow faience with delicate sky blue floral relief panels make a spectacular scheme which looks very Burmantofts and probably dates from around 1890, when the Leeds firm is known to have supplied Shaw's with ceramics for their Wolverhampton premises (Fig 267).[41]

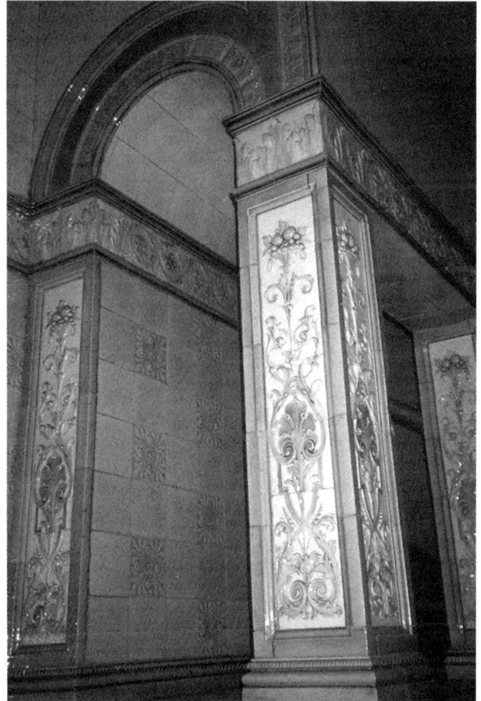

Fig 267.

South of the city centre in SKINNER STREET is the former **Odeon Cinema** (1937, architect P. J. Price of the Harry Weedon practice, now Mecca Bingo) which still retains its unusually colourful finned facade with faience in black, red, green and cream. Further south in SNOW HILL is the **Central Library**, completed in 1902 and designed by the architect Henry T. Hare, who specialised in public buildings. Built from bright red brick and buff Doulton terracotta, the greatest mass of the latter is employed at ground floor level, where it serves to form the massive corner entrance. Above is a terracotta frieze including the royal and municipal arms, while at first floor level terracotta panels bear the names of prominent authors. Far outside the northern bounds of the dual carriageway on CANNOCK ROAD is the **Waggon & Horses**, a 1950s pub with a large tile panel of the waggon and two white horses above its front entrance.

But away from the centre, two star attractions lie far out in the western suburbs of Wolverhampton; the first is **Wightwick Manor** (NT), temple of the Arts and Crafts movement, standing just off the Bridgnorth Road at WIGHTWICK BANK. Wightwick Manor was built for the industrialist Samuel Theodore Mander, partner in a varnish and paint manufacturing concern. It was erected in two phases, the main house in 1887 and the east wing six years later; both were by Edward Ould of Liverpool, an ex-pupil of John Douglas of Chester, grand protagonist of the half-timbered revival. It is therefore no surprise to find that Wightwick's exterior is emphatically black and white neo-Tudor; indeed, Girouard describes the 1893 extension (built to cater for house parties) as 'an anthology of half-timbering'.[42] While the external appearance was intended to reflect the style of the early sixteenth century, the internal decoration is a Victorian vision of early seventeenth century taste, full of pattern and artistic eclecticism. Morris & Company and C. E. Kempe are particularly well represented in this Old English interior.

At the time the Manor was built there was a fashion, particularly among the artistic middle-classes, to decry the mass-produced tiles of the Staffordshire potteries in favour of the products of craft workshops, such as William De Morgan's designs and hand-made tiles imported from Holland.[43] The largest range of Dutch tiles was available from Thomas Elsley's shop in London. Elsley was primarily an iron and brassfounder, but at some time during the 1880s he acquired the rights to a range of Dutch tiles previously marketed by Marks & Durlacher Brothers. Elsley's catalogue showed fireplaces, tiled and untiled, and nearly one hundred Dutch hand-painted tiles in both 5″ and 6″ sizes. The domestic market in Holland would have had no requirement for the larger size, which was made specifically for export, to fit British cast-iron grates. The tiles in Elsley's catalogue are a mixture of traditional Dutch designs and those inspired or commissioned by the British Arts and Crafts Movement. There is no firm evidence that the Dutch tiles at Wightwick were obtained from Elsley, although all but two of them appear in his catalogue.[44]

The fireplaces throughout the house include not only the well-known tiles by William de Morgan, but also other good quality English and Dutch wares. Best known of the William De Morgan tiles are those set in the Italian Renaissance chimneypiece of the drawing room.[45] They are the potter's typical fantastic animals, the forms of which, in an Oxford fireplace, are said to have inspired the characters in Lewis Carroll's *The Hunting of the Snark*. De Morgan tiles are also found in a bedroom, its adjoining boudoir, the morning room and possibly the hall, where the plain green oblong tiles arranged in a chevron pattern in the fireplace may also be De Morgan's work. Tiles in the library fireplace, one of Maw & Co's Anglo-Persian patterns, also show his influence. The inglenook fireplace in the Billiard Room is furnished with Dutch tiles with a design derived from Morris's *Daisy* pattern; however, this version is certainly Dutch, and was probably made by either Ravesteijn of Utrecht or Tjallingii of Harlingen. The majority of the fireplaces contain Dutch tiles illustrated in the Elsley catalogue.[46] Although the tiles in themselves are exceptional, the essence of the Wightwick experience is the overall vision, the expression of contemporary taste through furnishings and decoration, a very English pastime.

Finally to **St Bartholomew's Church**, CHURCH HILL, PENN; the steep hill allows an unexpected and welcome view of open country to the south. Although this medieval but much-altered church was presented with a reredos by Herbert Minton in 1851, the only surviving tiling is the sanctuary pavement. The lower part has a fish design in buff on red ground along with smaller, triangular, buff and green tiles. The upper area provides a real puzzle: here is a large and attractive group of picture tiles, clearly five of the Minton designs copied from the Westminster Abbey Chapter House floor. In Minton's first printed catalogue they are numbered 14-18 and show St Edward the Confessor giving his ring to a beggar, an abbot, King Henry III, Queen Eleanor holding her falcon, and two minstrels. The tiles were originally laid in the sanctuary, but were moved to the vestry following alterations in 1871, then relaid in the sanctuary in 1928. These tiles pose several questions: could they have been an unrecorded donation to the church by Herbert Minton, or were they simply purchased from Minton's? When were they installed? Were the designs chosen (by Minton or the purchaser) because of the association of the name Penn Church with the medieval tilery at Penn in Buckinghamshire? And what was the design of the Minton reredos, lost when the chancel was extended in 1871? There appear to be no archival sources which can provide information on these matters, so Penn Church remains an enigma.

Staffordshire Round-Up

There is rich terracotta decoration (including a nicely moulded cherub) on the facade of the former Technical School, Mount Pleasant, **Bilston**, while the town's otherwise anodyne 1960s Jobcentre, High Street, has an excellent exterior panel packed with references to the local steel industry; it appears to be made mainly of sculpted brick. A mile east of **Cheadle** on the B5417 is the Les Oakes architectural salvage centre, where several buildings erected in the 1980s and 1990s include substantial rescued terracotta panels and ornament. In remote **Gratwich**, the tiny Church of

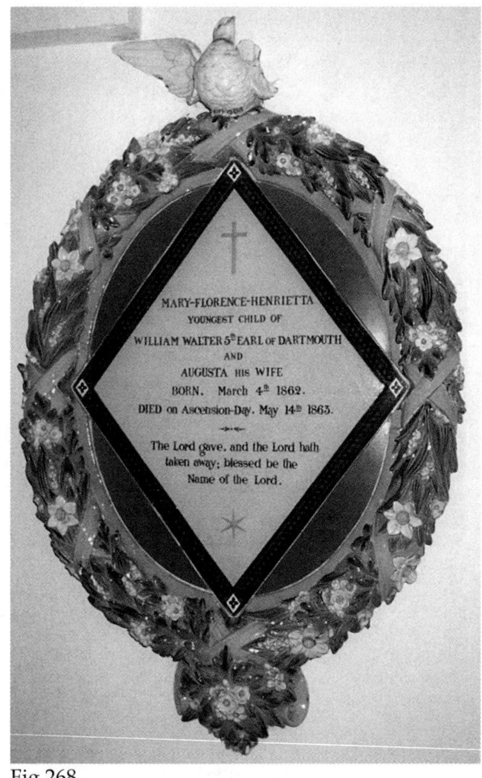

Fig 268.

St Mary has an impressive display of tiles donated by Herbert Minton; motifs include the Latin cross and evangelist roundels. The choir vestry, beneath the tower of St Werburgh's Church, **Hanbury**, has colourful 1883 Minton tiling showing symbols of the Passion Cycle. Dunwood Hall (1871, architect Robert Scrivener), **Longsdon**, was built for Thomas Hulme, a partner in the Burslem pottery of James Macintyre & Co; its double-height galleried hall has an elaborate and extensive Minton encaustic tile pavement. St John's Church, **Marchington Woodlands** has a brightly coloured sanctuary pavement, again donated by Minton; it was laid on the diagonal. Inside **Patshull** Church (SJ801006, access by footpath only) is an unusual 1863 wall memorial, an elongated diamond-shaped buff encaustic tile set within a colourful Minton majolica garland of flowers and topped by white dove; the tile pavement is by Maw & Co (Fig 268). A pair of unusual, highly-glazed tile panels decorate the east wall of St John the Baptist, **Stowe-by-Chartley**; the panels, and also the sanctuary pavement, are probably by Colin Minton Campbell. St John's Church, **Tixall**, was built for the Hon. John Chetwynd Talbot in 1848-9, with the intention that it should eventually become his mausoleum; the Minton floor tiles include a group of nine different specials (mainly monograms) at the nave crossing which commemorate the consecration of the church in 1849. The 1877 chancel of St Mary the Virgin, **Uttoxeter**, has an oddly coloured glazed encaustic tiled reredos by Maw & Co, including an image of Judas and symbols of the Passion Cycle (Fig 269). St Peter's Church, **Yoxall**, restored by the architect Henry Woodyer in 1865-8, has a patterned Minton encaustic tile pavement in the sanctuaryy.[47]

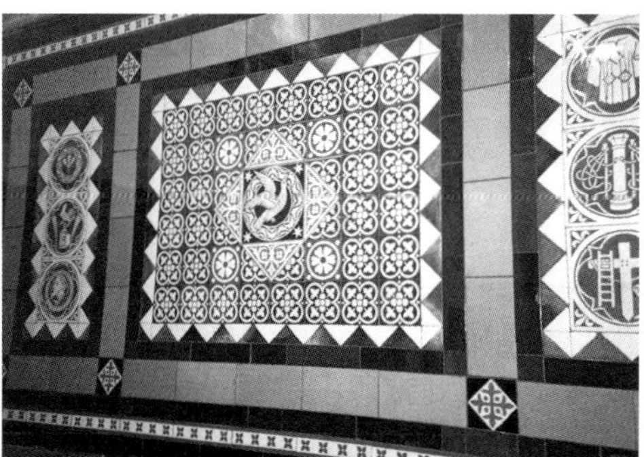

Fig 269.

References

1. Margaret Belcher, ed., *The Collected Letters of A. W. N. Pugin: Vol 1, 1830-1842* (Oxford University Press, Oxford, 2001), p297.
2. Michael Fisher, *Pugin-Land* (Fisher, Stafford, 2002), p71.
3. Timothy Brittain-Catlin, 'Pugin's Perfect Priestly Palaces', *Country Life*, 198 (2004), pp68-71.
4. Paul Atterbury and Clive Wainwright, *Pugin: A Gothic Passion* (Yale University Press, New Haven and London, 1994), p68.
5. Carol Maund and Hans van Lemmen, *Encaustic Tiles in St Giles, Cheadle, Staffordshire* (Tiles and Architectural Ceramics Society, 1984).
6. Michael Fisher, *A Vision of Splendour: Gothic Revival in Staffordshire, 1840-1890* (Fisher, Stafford, 1995), pp94-101.
7. Philip Brown, *Tour Notes: Tiles in a group of Somerset Churches* (Tiles and Architectural Ceramics Society, 1995).
8. Francis E. Paget, *Some account of Elford Church: Its decays, and its restorations, in ancient and recent times* (Lomax, Lichfield, 1880).
9. A. J. Cross, *Pilkington's Royal Lancastrian Pottery and Tiles* (Richard Dennis, London, 1980), p23.
10. Michael Fisher, *A Vision of Splendour* (1995), p144. Fisher adds that one of the masons working on the construction of the church was George Rhead; it is possible that he was a member of the Rhead family of potters who were related to the Wooliscrofts.
11. Jane Cochrane, 'Medieval Tiled Floor Patterns', *TACS Journal*, 5 (1994), pp11-19.
12. Betty Greene, 'The Godwins of Hereford', *TACS Journal*, 1 (1982), pp8-16, see p9.
13. VCH *Staffordshire*, vol 3, 1970, p194.
14. J. C. Woodhouse, *A short account of Lichfield Cathedral* 8th ed, Lichfield, 1862), pp51-2.
15. *The Builder*, vol 20, 8th March 1862.
16. David Cole, *The Work of Sir Gilbert Scott* (Architectural Press, London, 1980), pp64-6.
17. Tony Herbert and Kathryn Huggins, *The Decorative Tile in Architecture and Interiors* (Phaidon Press, London, 1995), p229.
18. Chris Brooks and Andrew Saint, eds., *The Victorian Church* (Manchester University Press, Manchester, 1995), p168.
19. Phil Mottram, 'John Macduff Derick (c.1805/6-59): A Biographical Sketch', *Ecclesiology Today*, (2004) 32, pp40-52.
20. Alan Crawford, Michael Dunn and Robert Thorne, *Birmingham Pubs 1880-1939* (Alan Sutton, Gloucester, 1986).
21. George Gilbert Scott, *Personal and Professional Recollections* (Da Capo Press, New York, 1977), pp97-8, 100; Cole, *Gilbert Scott* (1980), p32.
22. *Re-opening of St Mary's Church, Stafford*, 21st December 1844, Staffordshire Record Office D834/4/1/3
23. Robert Gunnis, *Dictionary of British Sculptors 1660-1851* (Abbey Library, London, 1951), p328.
24. Alan Swale, 'The Terracotta of the Wedgwood Institute, Burslem', *Journal of the Tiles and Architectural Ceramics Society*, 2 (1987), pp21-27.
25. Michael Stratton, 'Science and Art Closely Combined: the organisation of training in the terracotta industry, 1850-1939', *Construction History*, 4 (1988), pp35-51.
26. VCH Stafford vol 8, pp118,128, 330; *TACS Newsletter* 12, 1990, pp2-3.

27. Lynn Pearson, 'The First Five Thousand: TACS Database reaches 5,000 entries', *Glazed Expressions*, (2002) 45, pp6-7.
28. Lucien Myers, 'Variety and vitality in ceramic tiles', *Design*, (1965) 195, pp28-35.
29. Tony Herbert, 'All is Revealed!' *TACtile, Newsletter of the Tiles and Architectural Ceramics Society*, (2002) 61, p1.
30. Hans van Lemmen, *Architectural Ceramics* (Shire Publications, Princes Risborough, 2002).
31. Leonard Skinner, *Shelton and its Church* (Countryside Publications, Chorley, 1985).
32. Miranda F. Goodby, 'George Tinworth: an Artist in Terracotta', *Journal of the Tiles and Architectural Ceramics Society*, 3 (1990), pp15-21.
33. 'New murals for Stoke-on-Trent', *TACS Newsletter*, (1994) 29, p1.
34. Oliver Carter, *An illustrated history of British railway hotels* (Silver Link, St Michael's, 1990), p23.
35. Geoffrey Kay, 'Charles Lynam - an Architect of Tile Factories', *Journal of the Tiles and Architectural Ceramics Society*, 4 (1992), pp21-28.
36. Lynn Pearson, 'Memorial and Commemorative Tiles in Nineteenth and Early Twentieth Century Churches', *TACS Journal*, 9 (2003), pp13-23.
37. G. K. Beaulah, 'Samuel Wright of Shelton and his Tiles', *Journal of the Tiles and Architectural Ceramics Society*, 3 (1990), pp28-32.
38. June Steed, *Trentham: A church through history* (Panda Press, Stone, 1994), pp71, 89.
39. Joan Jones, *Minton: The first two hundred years of design and production* (Swan Hill Press, Shrewsbury, 1993), p295.
40. Anne Wilkins, *West Bromwich Town Hall* (West Bromwich Library User Group, 2003).
41. Information from Julie Gillam Wood.
42. Mark Girouard, *The Victorian Country House* (Yale University Press, New Haven and London, 1979), p377.
43. Hilary Myers and Richard Myers, *Wightwick Manor Tour Notes* (TACS, 1980).
44. Richard Myers, 'Murray Marks and Thomas Elsley, importers of Dutch tiles', *TACS Journal*, 2 (1987), pp3-9.
45. Hilary Myers and Richard Myers, *Tour Notes: Wightwick Manor* (TACS, 1986).
46. Hilary Myers, 'Wightwick Manor', *Glazed Expressions*, (1981) 2, pp1-2.
47. John Elliott and John Pritchard, eds., *Henry Woodyer: Gentleman Architect* (Department of Continuing Education, University of Reading, Reading, 2002), pp209-10.

Suffolk

Suffolk can hardly be recommended to tile enthusiasts. In terms of medieval tiles, Icklingham Church is the most notable site with a good display of plain and line-impressed designs, and there are several other churches with small numbers of medieval tiles on display. A handful of locations have good early sixteenth century Italian-style terracotta; however, better examples of this short-lived fashion in building materials exist to north and south of the county in Norfolk and especially Essex, where it first took root in East Anglia. Heveningham Hall and Great Saxham Hall (although access to both is difficult), and to a lesser extent Ickworth, have good Coade stone, while the Ancient House in Ipswich has an unusual delft tile panel. As to Victorian tiles, Suffolk had its share of church restorations, often carried out by the local diocesan architect Richard Phipson, and some new churches were built, but in most cases the tiles (usually by Minton or Maw) were pretty unremarkable; an exception is St Agnes, Newmarket, where the extensive Spanish-style tilework may be by Frederick Garrard. The pick of the few Victorian secular sites must be the lavish Maw's dairy at Easton Farm Park. The most modern of the substantial sites listed is Lowestoft's Boston Deep Sea Fisheries, with its pair of (probable) interwar Doulton murals; after 1950 there is nothing to report from this ceramic backwater. Suggested reading: David Sherlock, *Medieval floor tiles in Suffolk churches* (Suffolk Historic Churches Trust, 1980); Anne Riches, *Victorian church building and restoration in Suffolk* (Boydell Press, Woodbridge, 1982). The *Gazetteer* entry for Suffolk covers the administrative area of Suffolk County Council.

BARHAM

The large, four-light window in the vestry of **St Mary's Church** is made from terracotta and dates from about 1525. Its style, early Italian renaissance, is similar to that of other Suffolk windows at Barking and Henley churches and at Shrubland Old Hall, Coddenham. These four sites are grouped together just a few miles north of Ipswich and lie about twenty miles north-east of Layer Marney in Essex, where Sir Henry Marney began to build a palace on his country estate around 1520; the gatehouse is notable for its use of near-renaissance style terracotta decoration. The Layer Marney terracotta workshop was broken up around 1523-5, after which the craftsmen appear to have been responsible for creating a series of Italian-style terracotta structures in Suffolk (the windows of the Barham area) and Norfolk (the north-west Norfolk halls and four related church monuments).[1]

BARKING

A window on the north side of **St Mary's Church** has early Italian renaissance style terracotta mullions and jambs, with decoration made from the same moulds as used at Barham (see above).

BARSHAM

In **Holy Trinity Church** is the fine terracotta tombchest of Sir Edward Eckingham (d1527), its early renaissance decoration identical to that found on the Oxborough Church tombchests in Norfolk. There are also plain black and yellow glazed medieval tiles by the church's north doorway (and do not miss the extraordinary flint latticework east wall exterior).

CODDENHAM

In the grounds of Shrubland Park, south-west of Coddenham, is **Shrubland Old Hall**, which has a pair of three light terracotta windows in early Italian renaissance style. They date from around 1525 and have decoration made from the same moulds as used at Barham and Barking (see above).

EASTON

The octagonal dairy in the grounds of **Easton Farm Park** was built in 1870 for the Duke of Hamilton; the floor tiles surrounding its octagonal marble fountain incorporate the family crest, while stained glass in the doors shows the Hamilton monogram. The wall tiling includes vertical panels of flowers and birds in low-relief white slip on buff ground in the manner of the hand-made French pâte-sur-pâte technique, but in this case created by means of a mechanical process devised by Maw & Co. This lavish dairy was built during the aristocratic vogue for such buildings following the completion of the Royal Dairy at Windsor in 1861.[2]

HENLEY

The large, three-light south nave window in **St Peter's Church** is made from terracotta and dates from around 1525; it is in early Italian renaissance style and was made by the same craftsmen who worked at Barham, Barking and Shrubland Old Hall, Coddenham (see above).

HEVENINGHAM

Heveningham Hall (no public access), about a mile north-east of the village, is one of England's most important country houses. The twenty-five bay Palladian exterior of the Hall was designed about 1778 by Sir Robert Taylor, while the interior, completed in 1784, is the work of James Wyatt. The stuccoed brick exterior has a fine display of Coade stone including urns, recumbent lions, caryatids and griffin plaques. There is more Coade ornament on the orangery, designed in the 1780s by Wyatt.[3] The east wing of the Hall suffered extensive fire damage in 1984; restoration of the Hall and its parkland began in 1994 and still continues.

ICKLINGHAM

All Saints Church, now in the care of the Churches Conservation Trust, has attractive early fourteenth century plain and line-impressed tiles on the floor of its chancel. The tiles vary in shape, colour and design forming a complex mosaic, while individual motifs include a lion's face and an earless man wearing a coronet. Some tiles are pseudo-mosaic, in that they appear to be two tiles but are in fact a single tile. The tiles were supplied by Ely Cathedral, about fifteen miles to the west, where the ornate floor of Prior Crauden's Chapel was probably completed around 1324.[4]

IPSWICH

Behind the unmistakable seventeenth century pargetted facade of the **Ancient House** (now a shop), in the centre of Ipswich on BUTTERMARKET, are two Dutch delft tiled fireplaces dating from the seventeenth or eighteenth centuries. The images on one have an equestrian theme while the other displays mostly landscapes and animals. However, the main ceramic attraction of this unusual building is a 6′ by 4′ Dutch delft tile panel in dark blue and off-white showing the Greek gods Pallas and Mars; it was possibly originally intended for a country house. Just north in TOWER STREET is the **Church of St Mary-le-Tower**, which was completely rebuilt in 1863-7 by Richard Phipson (1827-84), who was to be diocesan architect during 1871-84. Although the nave wall tiling has been removed, there is lavish chancel tiling and the floor tiles bear the boar symbol of local banker Edward Bacon, who funded part of the rebuilding. The floor of the tower was laid with Minton's encaustic tiles during the restoration.[5]

Further from the centre, **St Pancras R. C. Church** (1861-2, architect George Goldie), ORWELL PLACE has panels of embossed majolica tiles, possibly by Maw's, below its reredos. To the north-west at 46 NORWICH ROAD is the **Maharani Restaurant**, which started life as a fishmonger and purveyor of game and has an excellent pictorial tile panel to prove it. The 8′ by 4′ mural, which shows a hunting scene and is signed 'Carter & Co., Poole, Dorset, 1897', is set on a wall of relief pattern tiling in grey, blue and green with brown border tiles. It is known that Carter's provided three murals for the shop, but two have been lost. Further out on CHEVALLIER STREET - the inner ring road, which crosses Norwich Road - is **All Saints Church** (not normally open), built in 1886-7 and designed by the Morecambe architect Samuel Wright, who won the commission in competition; its interior, with terracotta columns and much red brick, has been described as a 'clayworkers' paradise'. Wright's use of terracotta may have been influenced by his proximity to the third of Edmund Sharpe's terracotta churches, St Paul's (1874-6), Scotforth, Lancaster.[6]

LANGHAM

St Mary's Church (not normally open) stands in the grounds of Langham Hall. The Essex architect-priest Ernest Geldart rebuilt its nave and restored its chancel in 1886-9, installing encaustic floor tiles supplied by W. B. Simpson & Sons of London; they were most likely to have been made by Maw & Co, for whom Simpson's were London agents.

LOWESTOFT

The **Boston Deep Sea Fisheries** building (architects Dalton & Cockrill) in WAVENEY ROAD, overlooking the harbour from the north, is a little gem amidst the general dross of Lowestoft's built environment (Fig 270). It was put up by Consolidated Fisheries, probably between the wars but possibly a little earlier, and taken over by Boston Deep Sea Fisheries around 1945. Its original name was Columbus Buildings, which explains the presence of two large, colourful (perhaps tube-lined) murals showing galleons - presumably the *Nina*, the *Pinta* and the *Santa Maria* - on its otherwise white faience facade, which could be of Doulton's Carraraware or Carter's Ceramic Marble.[7] The panels do not feature in the catalogue of Carter's photographs of their installations, thus are more likely to be by Doulton.

Fig 270.

NEWMARKET

St Agnes Church (not normally open), BURY ROAD, was built in 1886 as a private chapel for Agnes, Duchess of Montrose; her architect was R. H. Carpenter. The red brick structure sports an unusual tower, while the high church interior is almost exotic in its decoration, with a huge marble reredos, much Salviati mosaic, windows by Clayton & Bell and a dado throughout in what *Pevsner* describes as 'Spanish tiles'; these may well be the cuenca tiles made by Frederick Garrard of Millwall.

SOMERLEYTON

Somerleyton Hall was designed by John Thomas and erected during 1844-57 for the building magnate Sir Morton Peto. The entrance hall is paved with panels of Minton encaustic tiles set between marble strips. Although this floor is relatively early, dating from around 1850, it incorporates green and bright blue tiles as well as the more usual buff, red, brown, black and white. Several passages in the Jacobean-style house have early Minton dust-pressed geometric pavements which include tiny and very decorative tiles. In the ballroom, colourful 12" square transfer printed dust-pressed Minton tiles (using the technique developed in 1851 by Minton's in conjunction with Collins & Reynolds) adorn several fire surrounds, and there are more of these in the winter garden along with further encaustic and geometric tiles.

Suffolk Roundup

Mustow House, 1 Mustow Street, **Bury St Edmunds** has an encaustic tiled floor (designed specifically for this site) with rich classical motifs. The east wall decoration of St John Baptist (1894-5, architect Sir Arthur Blomfield), Orwell Road, **Felixstowe** was supplied by Powell's in 1899; it includes alabaster, opus sectile, mosaic and stencilled glass tiles.[8] The moorish gothic garden building in the grounds of Great Saxham Hall, **Great Saxham** is made from Coade stone and marked Coade and Sealy. There are Victorian and medieval floor tiles in the sanctuary of St John's Church, **Great Wenham**. St Mary's Church, **Harkstead** (restored 1867, architects Slater & Carpenter) has a Minton encaustic pavement and a mostly mosaic reredos by Powell's.[9] Part - it is not clear exactly which part - of the top frieze on the rotunda of Ickworth House (NT), **Ickworth** is of Coade stone, as are the capitals and bases (1821) of four columns in the library. Inside All Saints Church, **Lawshall**, on the west wall of the nave close to the tower, is a blue and white-tiled war memorial plaque dating from 1947; it commemorates a Dutch pilot killed nearby in 1945. St Nicholas Church, **Oakley** has a tile and mosaic reredos (1882) of the *Last Supper*. In the churchyard of St Edmund's Church, **Southwold** is a substantial tomb decorated with encaustic tiles whose lettering includes the names and dates of the deceased. Medieval tiles have been reset in a piscina in the chancel of All Saints Church, **Sudbourne**; restoration of the church in 1878 included the installation of tiled floors throughout. There is a terracotta reredos (1883) of the *Last Supper* by George Tinworth of Doulton's at St Mary's Church, **Walsham-le-Willows**; there are also medieval floor tiles at the east end of the south aisle.

In addition, there are medieval tiles at the following churches: All Saints, Acton (behind north-east altar); St Michael, Boulge (reset in niche in north wall of chancel); St Mary, Brent Eleigh (east end of south aisle); St Mary, Coney Weston (reset in north-west corner of nave); St Mary, Dennington (reset beside Bardolf tomb, south chapel); and All Saints, Drinkstone (east end of nave).

References

1. Nikolaus Pevsner and Enid Radcliffe, *Suffolk* Buildings of England (Penguin, London, 1974).
2. Tony Herbert and Kathryn Huggins, *The Decorative Tile in Architecture and Interiors* (Phaidon Press, London, 1995), pp96-7.
3. Alison Kelly, *Mrs Coade's Stone* (Self Publishing Association, Upton-upon-Severn, 1990).
4. Laurence Keen and David Thackray, 'A fourteenth century mosaic tile pavement with line-impressed decoration from Icklingham', *Proceedings of the Suffolk Institute of Archaeology*, 33 (1974), pp153-167.
5. *The Builder*, vol 25, 2nd February 1867.
6. Anne Riches, *Victorian church building and restoration in Suffolk* (Boydell Press, Woodbridge, 1982).
7. Diana Clegg and Peter Clegg, 'Tile Panels at Lowestoft', *Glazed Expressions*, (1985) 10, p9.
8. Dennis W. Hadley, *James Powell & Sons: A listing of opus sectile, 1847-1973*, (2001).
9. *The Builder*, vol 25, 21st December 1867.

Surrey

Surrey is a county with its own reserves of clay but only a relatively small number of tile and architectural ceramic locations; however, their quality makes up for their lack in quantity. The medieval tiles made on the site of Chertsey Abbey were some of the most technically sophisticated and ornate of the period, although few can still be seen *in situ* and most of these have been relaid. Compensating for the lack of medieval tile locations is the lavish renaissance-style terracotta ornament of Sutton Place (1521-5), near Guildford, which is comparable with Layer Marney in Essex and shows how quickly the techniques of terracotta production were learned by English craftsmen following the example of Hampton Court.

There is a good (although small) Pugin encaustic pavement at Albury Old Church, while tile pavements, often by Minton, are the norm in the many churches built or restored by the gentleman architect Henry Woodyer (1816-96), who ran his practice from his home at Grafham, south of Guildford. Surrey is fortunate to have two churches with magnificent opus sectile decoration by Powell's of Whitefriars: Christ Church, Epsom Common and St Martin's, Dorking; the latter has a memorial to Arthur Powell, senior partner in the firm and local resident. Finally, the unique Watts Chapel (1896-1904), Compton, is a site of international ceramic significance, and is a thoroughgoing practical display of the arts and crafts ethos, albeit with its distinctive brand of Celtic art nouveau ornament designed and carried out by Mary Seton Watts. In architectural terms it led nowhere but the Compton Potters' Arts Guild, which produced the chapel's terracotta, flourished for half a century. Five or six miles away, on the western fringe of the county, home-grown production of ceramics continues on the site of the Farnham Pottery, established in 1872, while Redhill's Belfry Shopping Centre (1991-2) represents the largest use of faience in a postwar building project. Suggested reading: John Elliott and John Pritchard (eds), *Henry Woodyer: Gentleman Architect* (Department of Continuing Education, University of Reading, 2002); Veronica Franklin Gould, *The Watts Chapel: An Arts & Crafts Memorial* (Watts Gallery, Compton, 1993). The *Gazetteer* entry for Surrey covers the administrative area of Surrey County Council.

ALBURY

The banker Henry Drummond (1786-1860) bought the much-altered Tudor manor house in Albury Park in 1819. Originally the manor house, church (**St Peter and St Paul Old Church**) and village stood close together, but by 1800 many of the cottages had been demolished and the population encouraged to move a mile or so west to the hamlet of Weston Street, now known as Albury. By the time of Drummond's arrival, little remained of the old village, although St Peter and St Paul still functioned as the parish church. By the mid-1820s however, Drummond had become deeply involved with the teachings of the Scottish preacher Edward Irving, which were to form the basis of the Catholic Apostolic Church, established in London in 1832; Drummond withdrew from Albury parish church in that same year. Members of the Irvingite movement frequently met at his mansion, only a few hundred yards from the church, whose fabric was increasingly difficult to maintain. This odd state of affairs continued until the late 1830s, when Drummond conceived a plan to keep both villagers and Irvingites happy: he would build a parish church in the village and provide a new building near Albury Park for the Catholic Apostolic Church.

Thus the the Irvingite Church arose just north of the park in 1840 and the Church of St Peter and St Paul, a red brick romanesque structure, was put up in Weston Street, Albury in 1842; both were designed by William McIntosh Brookes. As to the Old Church, it must still have held some religious or historic significance for Drummond, as he brought in A. W. N. Pugin around 1846-7 to convert its south transept into a family mortuary chapel, the Drummond Chantry. Much of the decoration is by Pugin's own hand, including the exquisite Minton encaustic floor tiles, but he also employed some of the best craftsmen of the time, including William Wailes (stained glass) and Thomas Earley, who was responsible for the striking red, blue and gold stencilling of the roof and walls; this atmospheric chamber is one of Pugin's best works. There is no direct access to the chapel, and no electric lighting, but peering through the screen it is possible to see armorial tiles in red, white and blue representing the Drummond family and their ancestors, as well as more common buff and brown designs featuring wavy stripes, lion heads, floral spirals and shields (Fig 271).

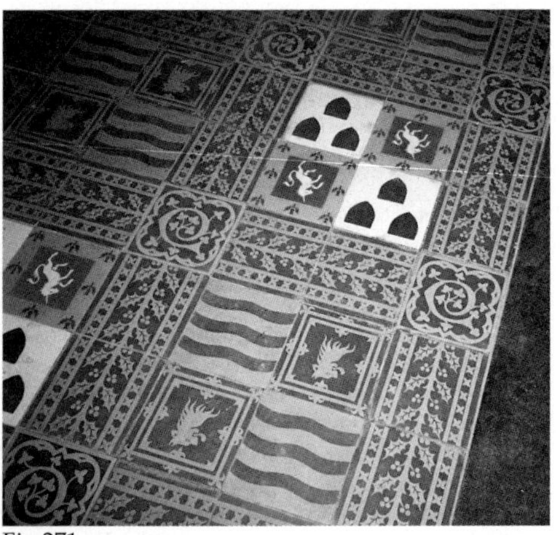

Fig 271.

Having resolved the problem of the parish church, Henry Drummond brought in George Myers, the building contractor regularly used by Pugin, who transformed the mansion around 1847-56; he topped the red brick gothic exterior with sixty-three ornate chimneys, all different and all copies of Tudor designs.[1] Drummond represented West Surrey in parliament from 1847 until his death in 1860, after which he was buried in the vault below the Drummond Chantry. It is ironic to note that of the three churches in which Henry Drummond had a hand, the new Albury church is still very much in use, while there have been no services at his own Irvingite Church since 1950, and the last regular services at the Old Church were held in 1861. It was then closed and left to decay, but since 1921 annual services have been conducted and from 1974 the building has been in the care of the Churches Conservation Trust. Drummond's home, now known as Albury Park House, has been converted to apartments.

BANSTEAD

The tile decorating firm **W. B. Simpson & Sons** was founded in 1833, becoming well-known for its hand-painted tiles in the late nineteenth century. They moved from central London to Camden Town in 1936, then Wandsworth in 1945; three further moves took place within London before the firm (now part of a larger group) moved to what is now St Martins House, Banstead Goods Yard, BANSTEAD ROAD in 1999. In the offices are several Simpson's tile panels, including *Harvest Time* (1905), a pair of medieval-style figures painted on cast earthenware bodies, and an intricate hunting scene.

COMPTON

Mary Seton Fraser-Tytler was born in 1849 and brought up in Scotland, in her family's castle on the shore of Loch Ness.[2] Unusually, her father encouraged his daughters to follow their artistic inclinations, and Mary went on to study at the South Kensington Art Training School and the Slade. She was taught clay modelling by the French sculptor Aimée-Jules Dalou, who emphasised the sculptural properties of the material rather than its surface values, and she eventually went on to teach the subject, although she generally preferred easel painting as an art form. In 1887, when nearly thirty-seven, she married the well-known painter George Frederic Watts, then aged sixty-nine. This alliance of like minds allowed her creativity to flow in pursuit of the expression of complex ideas through symbolic decoration; they felt that art could be used to uplift and improve whilst bearing a spiritual message.

They soon moved to Compton, deep in the tree-lined hills of Surrey, where their new home was Limnerslease (1891, now flats), designed by the architect Ernest George. Mary proceeded to decorate much of the house with Celtic-inspired panels of what she described as gesso but should more accurately be called stucco, as her method was to mix steeped felt with plaster and apply it by hand rather than with a brush.[3] The couple were greatly concerned with handicrafts, seeing such work as bringing beauty to the lives of those otherwise deprived of such stimulation. Mary's chance to put theory into practice came in 1895, when the parish council bought land on Budburrow Hill to provide a new burial ground, Compton's old graveyard being almost full. Almost immediately Mary offered to build a mortuary chapel at the new cemetery; within months she had produced a model of her design and located a seam of gault clay at Limnerslease. In November 1895 she began to teach the villagers how to model clay and by 1898 the chapel's structure was complete; it was consecrated on the 1st July 1898. Everything had been made locally, including the little 1¾" red bricks, which came from Messrs E. and A. Miles at Guildford.

Looking at the **Watts Chapel**, standing tall above the winding path leading up through the cemetery from DOWN LANE, is a unique experience, from the brilliance and crisp cutting of its orangey-red terracotta to the copious Celtic art nouveau forms of its decoration (Fig 272). The whole was designed by Mary Seton Watts, although it is possible that an architect may have been involved at some stage. The plan is simple, a Greek cross superimposed on a circle, but unravelling the pantheistic symbolism could be a lifetime's task. Fortunately Mary Seton Watts (always, after her marriage, known as Mrs G. F. Watts) produced a key to this 'world of enchantment' in her book *The Word in the Pattern* (1904).[4] The domed chapel is unexpectedly lofty, the major decorative element on the exterior being a frieze symbolising the *Path of the Just.* This encircles the building but is split into four sections, the Spirits of Hope, Truth, Love and Light, each section resting on three angel corbels, each holding a maze (for The Way), a boat (The Truth) or a tree (The Life). The maze is a copy of the early Christian labyrinth found on the floor of the Church of San Vitale in Ravenna.[5] Within the terracotta frieze, and bound together by a seemingly endless 'Celtic cord of unity', is a myriad of small animals and birds as well as much lettering. The Celtic theme continues on supporting columns and around the ornate doorway, where a semicircle of fifteen angel heads dares one to enter.

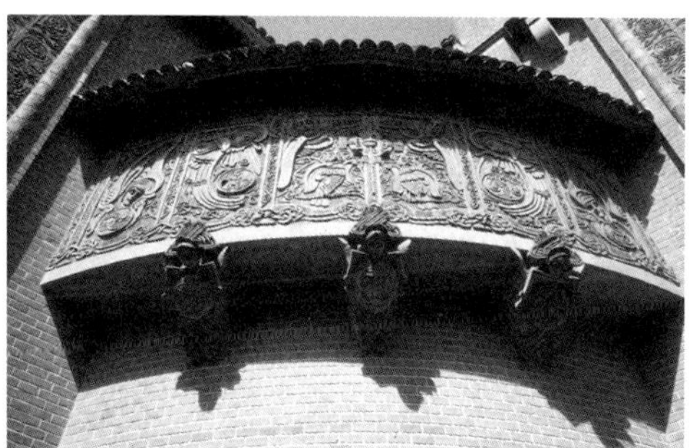

Fig 272.

Inside is a dark, cool space; a stone bench curves around the wall, allowing one to sit and look upward at the mysterious and unsettling decorative scheme devised and carried out by Mary Seton Watts and her assistants. Her chosen material was gesso (as she termed it) covered with a ground of white metal leaf, on which she painted in tempera; the addition of yards of swirling, gold-lustred piping cord resulted in vibrant, barely believable colours. The forms of angels - elongated, drifting heavenward - dominate this outstanding Arts & Crafts interior which was completed in 1904. After G. F. Watts inspected the chapel in May 1904, Mary commented that 'He had not before realized what I had aspired to in the matter of this glorified wallpaper'.

This unique chapel was far from the sole product of these talented villagers, all seventy-two of whom were individually named in Mary's *The Word in the Pattern*. Some of them became highly skilled and, after the fashion of a medieval guild, Mary set up the Compton Potters' Arts Guild which was based at the Watts Gallery, a few hundred yards north of the Watts Chapel; this combined a display space for the paintings and sculptures of G. F. Watts with a hostel for the apprentice potters. The Gallery was designed by a local amateur architect, Christopher Turnor, and completed in 1904. The Guild successfully made terracotta wares incuding Celtic crosses, sundials, garden ornaments (note the fountain plaque on the gatepost opposite the Watts Gallery), frost-proof pots and headstones, continuing in production up to 1951. A wide range of the Guild's wares was shown at the 'Modern Celtic Art' exhibition of 1903, including a design by Mary Seton Watts for 'Tiles for a Sanctuary Floor', but it appears that this was never carried out. Several examples of the Guild's headstones may be seen in the Compton cemetery garden, where there is also a Celtic-style terracotta wellhead and the Cloister (1907), designed by Mary Seton Watts to house a memorial to her husband, who died on the 1st July 1904 (Fig 273).

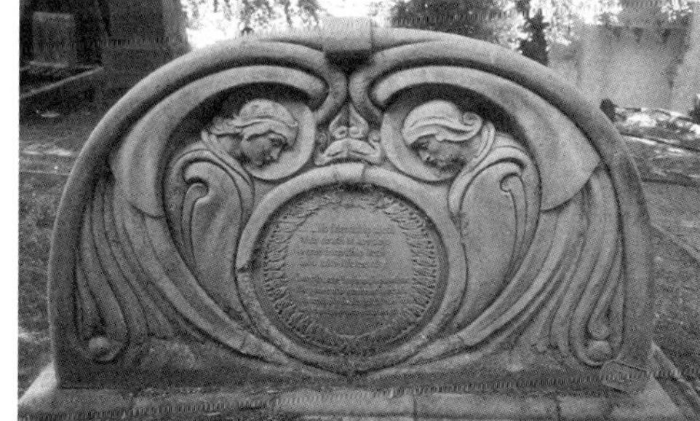

Fig 273.

The present pristine appearance of the chapel is, in fact, due to a programme of repairs and restoration work undertaken by the architect

Nigel Hammett during 1995-7.[6] Fifteen 'River of Life' blocks forming part of the pilasters were replaced by matching blocks made by Mick Pinner of West Meon Pottery, replacements for about half the roof tiles were required, and the bell turret had to be completely re-assembled to incorporate steel supports. The curving terracotta seat outside the Watts Chapel is a perfect spot to contemplate this wonderfully renewed marriage of art and pantheism, clay and Celtic mythology, possibly in the company of the cemetery's two cats, devoted guardians of Mary's spirit.

DORKING

Arthur Powell (1812-94), senior partner in the glassworks James Powell & Sons of Whitefriars, lived in Dorking from 1858 until his death; his firm was responsible for much of the internal decoration of **St Martin's Church**, its stone spire a landmark in the centre of town. The church was rebuilt in 1866-77 by Henry Woodyer and its series of opus sectile panels date from between 1891 and 1921. The great *Crucifixion* (1891-2) above the chancel arch was designed by George Woolliscroft Rhead (1854-1920), who had previously worked for Minton's and Doulton's. The flanking panels of archangels were installed in 1901-2 as a memorial to Queen Victoria, and are probably the work of Charles Hardgrave, who is known to have visited the church twice. Arthur Powell's own opus sectile memorial (1894) is at the east end of the north aisle. Other Powell's works include the Duchess of Marlborough's memorial (1910), designed by A. F. Coakes (who also visited the church) and a series of large panels in the south chapel.[7]

EPSOM

The Delaforce family of port wine merchants lived at Abele Grove (now the **Haywain**, 2-4 ST MARGARET'S DRIVE, off the A24 Leatherhead road) from 1920 until 1928; the building was used as a convent school during 1928-1992 before opening as a pub in 1997 (Fig 274). In the porch is a blue and white tile panel of the Virgin Mary, and inside are two larger panels, also blue and white, showing images of a merchant ship and grape harvesting; this pair are signed Fca Do Carvalhinho, Porto and dated 1920. The Carvalhinho factory was established in the late 1840s in Porto and flourished until the late 1920s. These panels, an unusual sight in Britain, were probably bought by the Delaforce family from stock, as the company specialised in this type of work.

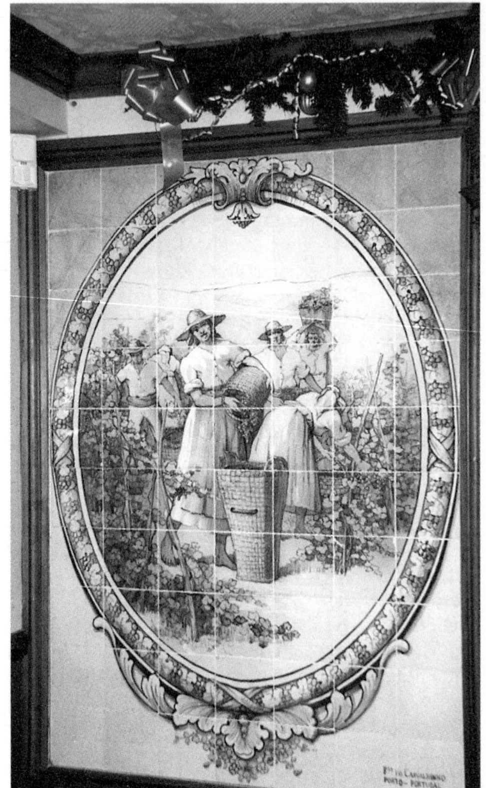

Fig 274.

Epsom Common

Christ Church (1876, architect Arthur Blomfield), Epsom Common has a Godwin tile pavement and a fine display of Powell's opus sectile work, glass tiles and mosaic on its east wall (Fig 275). The three-panel reredos (1885) of the *Transfiguration* was designed by Charles Hardgrave, as were the four evangelists (1887), two either side of the east window, which are shown within ornate canopies; the decorative scheme continues above the window, filling the remainder of the east wall.

EWELL

Henry VIII began building Nonsuch Palace in 1538; although construction was finished in 1541, its elaborate decorative scheme was still not complete at the time of the King's death in 1547, and the Palace was demolished in 1682-3. **Nonsuch Mansion House** (1802-6, architect Jeffry Wyatt) now stands in Nonsuch Park, EWELL ROAD, on the north-eastern edge of Ewell. Soon after the house was acquired in 1936 by a consortium of local authorities, a small outbuilding - until recently used as a toilet - was decorated internally with Delft wall tiles, originally 500 in number (reduced to 480 by theft) and with 180 different design types. They include Dutch tiles from the mid seventeenth to the mid nineteenth centuries, London designs from around 1700-40 and Liverpool designs from 1740-90. The house is now used for functions and weddings.[8]

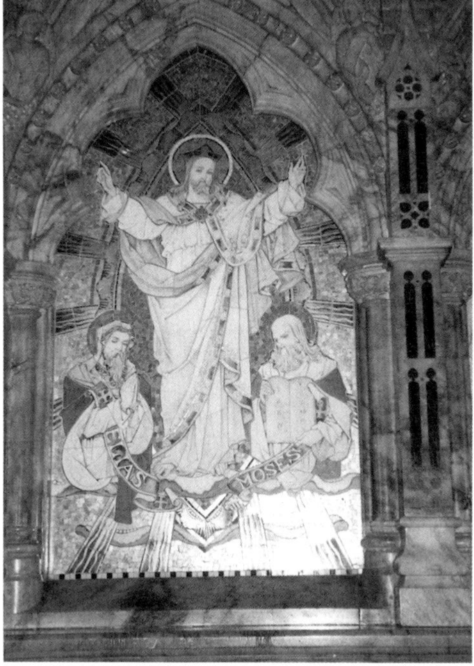

Fig 275.

EWHURST

The mansion Woolpits (now the **Duke of Kent School**), PEASLAKE ROAD, was designed by the architects Ernest George & Harold Peto for the ceramics manufacturer Henry Doulton and built during 1885-8. Doulton, who was knighted before its completion, used the full range of his firm's skills, allied to George's enthusiasm for terracotta, in the construction of the house. Much buff terracotta detailing remains, along with a single relief panel by George Tinworth and a tiled bathroom, but the rest of the lavish ornament, including pictorial panels painted by John Eyre and a faience billiard room by Arthur Pearce (who designed most of Doulton's exhibition pavilions), have long since disappeared.

FARNHAM

The **Farnham Pottery** was established at QUENNELLS HILL, Wrecclesham (on the south-west edge of Farnham) by Absalom Harris in 1872. Initially the wares were horticultural and domestic, but from around 1880 until the First World War green-glazed wares were produced and marketed as Farnham Green-ware. From the 1920s production concentrated on large terracotta horticultural wares; the Harris family were still working the pottery in the late 1990s, although about two-thirds of the site had been sold. The Farnham (Building Preservation) Trust now cares for this fine example of a Victorian country pottery, much of which was built using Harris's home-produced terracotta, bricks and tiles; even the window frames were terracotta. The best of the remaining structures are the bottle kiln, the carved brick chimney stacks and a weird faience arch depicting an owl with outstretched wings.

LINGFIELD

On the north wall of the lady chapel in the **Collegiate Church of St Peter and St Paul** are two unusual monuments, a pair of rather worn incised effigial slabs made from what appears to be a ceramic material with a pale buff body.[9] The design, with each figure beneath a canopy, is reminiscent of brasses, and indeed incised slabs were developed at least a century before brasses. The better preserved of the two is about 3′ 6″ high and shows a fashionably dressed male who is likely to have been a lesser member of the local gentry. The slabs, which probably date from around 1500-10, were originally laid on the floor but were moved in order to protect them from damage; some of their red, black and yellow colouring remains.[10]

PEPER HAROW

A. W. N. Pugin worked at **St Nicholas Church** around 1847, adding the north aisle and mortuary chapel for Lord Midleton. The church is partly floored with Pugin-designed Minton & Co encaustic tiles, some of which bear the Midleton arms while others have 'M' for the Virgin Mary. In the churchyard is a terracotta grave memorial (1914) for a child, in the form of a diminutive angel.

REDHILL

The **Belfry Shopping Centre** in Redhill was built in 1991-2 for the Burton Property Trust; the design was by Leslie Jones Architects. One inspiration behind the use of faience as cladding for this large complex was the traditional use of faience on many Montague Burton stores during the interwar years. For the Belfry, Shaws of Darwen supplied about 9,000 units of block and 50mm thick slab faience in nine different shades of glaze, mimicking the colour variation of older ceramic facades; the project was thought to constitute the largest single postwar use of faience in Britain. Despite all the attention to detail, the overall effect is bland and very unlike typical thirties faience facades with their combination of uncompromisingly modern design and inventive decoration; here all we have is overblown postmodern detailing.

REIGATE

The **shop** at 27 LESBOURNE ROAD was built in 1907 as the dairy for the Reigate Industrial and Provident Society; the architects were Baker & Penfold. Its tile-lined interior features two pictorial wall panels by Carter's of Poole, one showing a rural scene with cattle, the other depicting a milkmaid. This unusually well-preserved shop has also retained its free-standing marble counter and marble shelving, along with its red terrazzo mosaic floor.

STAINES

The **Watermans Buildings** office development on the Thames riverside at Staines was completed in 1991; the architects were Twigg Brown and Partners. In the washrooms are twenty-seven 3' by 4' tile panels showing local heroes and institutions. These murals were an early commission for Tiles of Stow - Odette Wells and Sebastian John - who used a combination of hand-painting and stencilling to produce the series.

SUTTON PLACE

Sutton Place, about three miles north of Guildford, was built in 1521-5 for Sir Richard Weston, a protégé of Henry VIII, who had been granted the Sutton estate in 1521. The house shares with Layer Marney in Essex, built from around 1520, the early and lavish use of renaissance terracotta ornament. Work on these two great houses began about seven years after the start of construction at Hampton Court, where terracotta roundel busts were commissioned from the Italian sculptor Giovanni da Maiano in 1521. The walls of Sutton Place are of load-bearing brick with elements such as window mullions, transoms and door surrounds of terracotta; it is almost certain that the terracotta window components at Sutton Place were made at the same (probably English) workshop as those of Hampton Court.[11] The 'antique' terracotta ornament of Sutton Place includes a total of thirty-eight winged cherubs. Courtiers of the time vied to build ostentatious houses in imitation of Hampton Court, although a statute of 1522 prohibited men below a particular rank from employing foreign craftsmen, inadvertently ensuring that foreign-style decoration became a sign of the elite. Sutton Place is now known to have reached its final form in 1720, when original and copied materials were used in combination.[12]

By the late 1980s the terracotta was showing signs of decay, and a five-year programme of conservation began under architect Julian Harrap, who had to deal with irregular block sizes and colours, and coarsely mixed clay bodies pierced by air hoiles, as well as blocks which had been overpainted or relocated. Replacement terracotta blocks were supplied by Hathernware, who produced eighteen different colour blends to reflect the original work, much of which was cream in colour; the total cost of restoration was over £12 million.

WOKING

The pedestrian bridge connecting the town centre with **Woking Railway Station** is lined with a Shaws Twintile mural showing railway engines and probably dating from the 1960s or 1970s. Just west of the centre on VICTORIA WAY is another ceramic mural, in this case celebrating the town's links with the writer W. G. Wells and featuring scenes from his *The War of the Worlds*.

Nearly a mile east of the station is the **Shah Jahan Mosque**, 149 ORIENTAL ROAD; it is set in its own grounds, to which there is restricted access. The Shah Jahan (or Shah Jehan) Mosque, in appearance a tiny Moghul pavilion, was the first purpose-built mosque in Britain; it was erected in 1889 and designed by the architect W. I. Chambers to serve Muslim students studying at the nearby Oriental Institute, Maybury. On its facade are unusual six-inch square 'tiles' - actually hollowed-out 'bricks' nearly three inches thick - in green and buff (originally red and blue) with a fan-shaped motif, which form a pattern of overlapping circles when laid together. The mosque, which was restored during the late

1990s, stands next to a modern building with tiling of a similar design.

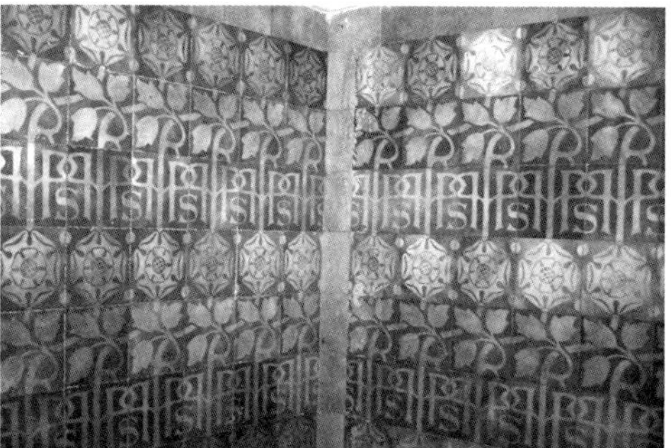

Fig 276.

Surrey Roundup

Grinsteads butcher's shop in High Street, **Bramley** has a tiled stall riser, probably interwar, with three pictorial panels of farm animals. Henry Woodyer's 1859-60 rebuilding of St Mary's Church, **Buckland** included the addition of floral tiling on the east wall and a Minton tile pavement. St Peter's Church, Guildford Street, **Chertsey** has Coade stone aisle window tracery (1806) stamped Coade and Sealy, and a few Chertsey Abbey tiles in the chancel. St Mary's Church, **Chiddingfold** was rebuilt by Henry Woodyer in 1869-70, the Minton tile pavement in the nave being a part of these works; in the chantry chapel are two Doulton terracotta panels designed by George Tinworth. There is a rich Minton tile pavement in the sanctuary of the chapel (1868-9, architect Henry Woodyer) at Cranleigh School on the northern edge of **Cranleigh**. Either side of the reredos at St Lawrence's Church, **Effingham** are pictorial panels of mosaic and terracotta (1911) by Caesar Czarnikow. On **Egham** High Street are two shops with ceramic interest: the facade of number 65 (formerly Clarke's butcher's) sports two majolica cow's heads, while number 72 has tiling inside and out. The Church of St Peter and St Paul, **Godalming** was restored by George Gilbert Scott in 1880; the works included the installation of a reredos and dado of Powell's glass tiles and mosaics in the north chapel, where there is also a Godwin tile pavement (Fig 276). The Powell's opus sectile reredos of the *Last Supper* at St Margaret's Church, **Ockley** dates from 1873 and was designed by Harry Burrow. In St Mary's Church, **Stoke D'Abernon** is a Powell's opus sectile panel of three angels playing musical instruments; it was designed by Gerald P. Hutchinson (b1876) and dates from 1902. St James Church (1860-1, architect John Loughborough Pearson), **Titsey**, has a good Minton encaustic tiled pavement. At Sainsbury's, Limpsfield Road, **Warlingham** are two mosaics (2000) designed and made by Oliver Budd; these replaced his original 1994 mosaics, lost when the store was enlarged in 1999-2000.

References

1. Paul Atterbury and Clive Wainwright, *Pugin: A Gothic Passion* (Yale University Press, New Haven and London, 1994), pp89, 189-90, 286.
2. Veronica Franklin Gould, *The Watts Chapel: An Arts & Crafts Memorial* (Watts Gallery, Compton, 1993).
3. Veronica Franklin Gould, 'The symbolic bas-relief designs of Mary Watt', *Journal of the Decorative Arts Society*, (1997) 21, pp9-21.
4. Mrs George Frederick Watts, *The Word in the Pattern* (facsimile edition, first published 1904, Society for the Arts & Crafts Movement in Surrey, 2000).
5. Robert Field, *Mazes Ancient & Modern* (Tarquin Publications, Diss, 2001).
6. Jeremy Musson, 'When Mary came to the Temple', *Country Life*, 191, 19th June 1997, pp52-53.
7. Dennis W. Hadley, *James Powell & Sons: A listing of opus sectile, 1847-1973*, (2001).
8. Personal communication, Ian Betts, Museum of London Specialist Services, 12th August 2004.
9. F. A. Greenhill, *Incised Effigial Slabs: A Study of Engraved Stone Memorials in Latin Christendom, c.1100 to c.1700* (Faber & Faber, London, 1976).
10. Nigel Saul, *The Collegiate Church of St Peter and St Paul Lingfield* (Collegiate Church of St Peter and St Paul, Lingfield, 2001).
11. Richard K. Morris, 'Architectural terracottas at Sutton Place and Hampton Court Palace', *British Brick Society Information*, (1988) 44, pp3-8.
12. Nicholas Cooper, *The Gentry House in the Age of Transition*, in *The Age of Transition: the archaeology of English culture 1400-1600*, eds David Gaimster and Paul Stamper (Oxbow Books, Oxford, 1997), pp115-126.

Sussex

Although brick and roof tiles were famously made from Sussex clay, there is little use of decorative architectural ceramics in the county, apart from some surviving early renaissance terracotta at Laughton Place (E), the extraordinarily high-relief Coade stone plaques at Castle Goring near Worthing (W), and Jonathan Harmer's terracotta bas-relief plaques on gravestones in the Heathfield (E) area, produced during 1799-1819. There is ample evidence in Ditchling (E) of roof tiles and red terracotta wares produced by the Ditchling Potteries over a two hundred year period from the mid-eighteenth century, but there is nothing on the scale of the Martyrs' Memorial, Stratford, East London. This buff terracotta gothic column was made by Messrs H. Johnson & Co, 'Terra Cotta Manufacturers', of Ditchling in 1878. Perhaps clay was just too commonplace in Sussex to be generally desirable in the form of a top quality building material such as highly-moulded terracotta; certainly the Edwardian terracotta villa at Bexhill (E) comes as a surprise on the seafront.

Sussex may lack terracotta in any quantity, but it has several nationally important tiled locations including an unusual sixteenth century Flemish tile pavement at Boxgrove (W). The Brassey Institute (1877-80), Hastings (E) is one of the few surviving British buildings with external pictorial tile panels, in this case by W. B. Simpson & Sons. There are superb William Morris tiles (1873-4) at Findon (W) and especially Clapham (W); these are the only two remaining churches in the country with Morris tile installations. One of the best turn-of-the-century pub interiors in Britain is the Havelock (1889-90) in Hastings, with four excellent Doulton picture panels, and there is a fine Moorish-style Craven Dunnill tile and faience scheme of 1906 at Brighton Museum and Art Gallery (E). Not to be missed from between the wars is the Carter's Ceramic Marble bandstand at Eastbourne (E), while for 1960s style (and Pilkington's tiles) a visit to Chichester (W) railway station is essential. Suggested reading: TACS Tour Notes *Tiles in the Churches of West Sussex*, 1998. The *Gazetteer* entry for Sussex covers the administrative areas of Brighton & Hove City Council, East Sussex County Council and West Sussex County Council.

East Sussex

ALCISTON

Charleston, a modest eighteenth century farmhouse about a mile north-west of Alciston, became the home of the writer David Garnett and the artists Vanessa Bell and Duncan Grant in 1916. The house had been found by Bell's sister Virginia Woolf, who lived with her husband Leonard Woolf about four miles to the west, near Beddingham; the Woolfs moved across the River Ouse to Monk's House, Rodmell, in 1919. In the three years following their arrival at Charleston, Bell and Grant decorated the entire house, with painted murals on every available wall surface as well as ceramics and painted furniture. Charleston became a focus for the Bloomsbury Group of artists and intellectuals including the critic and painter Roger Fry, founder in 1913 of the Omega Workshops in which young artists designed and made a wide range of domestic wares. Bell and Grant were co-directors of Omega as well as being prolific producers. Omega tiles were available from 1914, and after the demise of the Workshops in 1919, Bell and Grant continued to paint tiles in their bold, modern style, decorating them at a south London pottery. The tiles were used on furniture and in fireplace surrounds, notably at Monk's House and Charleston, where vivid fireplace tiles can still be seen in Duncan Grant's studio (1925).

BEXHILL

The **De La Warr Pavilion** (1934-5), MARINA, one of Britain's most memorable seaside buildings, was designed in modern movement style by the architects Erich Mendelsohn and Serge Chermayeff. Its brown floor tiles and cream wall tiles were supplied by Carter's of Poole, then the ceramics maker of choice for modern architects. Restoration of the Pavilion in the early 1990s included replacing the 12" x 3" buff-glazed facing tiles which corrosion had forced off the concrete-encased steel columns along the seaward balcony.

On the landward side of Marina is **Oceania**, a large, strident Edwardian Baroque villa completely faced in rich, deep ochre terracotta. Perhaps - as with the Pavilion - this ceramic covering was an attempt to combat the salty air of Bexhill. Turning inland, at 56 SEA ROAD, on the way to the town centre, is a butcher's tiled stall riser with two good black and white lozenge-shaped pictorial panels of a bull and a sheep.

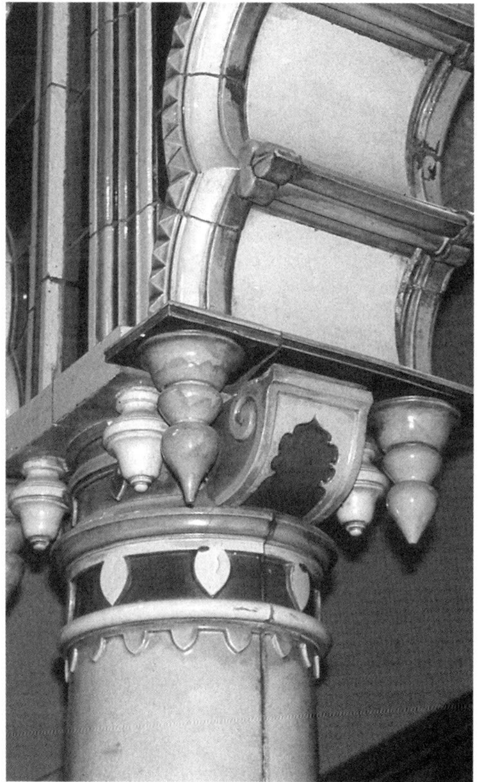

Fig 277.

BRIGHTON & HOVE

Begin at Brighton's **Railway Station**, TERMINUS ROAD, where the palatial subterranean toilets have a fabulous 1932 tile and mosaic scheme in which pearly-white tiling is complemented by yellow (Ladies) and black (Gents) tiled trimmings. Just west of the station is the **Railway Bell PH**, SURREY STREET. Its tiled sign, which probably dates from the interwar period, shows a handbell above an old-fashioned engine. Head south along Queen's Road then left into North Road to find Jubilee Street and the **Jubilee Library** (architects Lomax, Cassidy & Edwards with Bennetts Associates) which opened in 2005 and forms the focal point of JUBILEE SQUARE. Its west wall is clad with several thousand dark blue and green hand-glazed ceramic tiles, similar to the mathematical tiles sported by many local buildings. Inside, the back wall of the Children's Library is given over to Kate Malone's *Wall of a Thousand Stories* featuring a myriad of ceramic objects.

Continue south to CHURCH STREET; just to the left is **Brighton Museum and Art Gallery**, reopened in May 2002 after restoration and now entered from the Royal Pavilion gardens. An elaborate Moorish-style Craven Dunnill tile scheme of 1906 runs throughout the building and includes scalloped faience surrounds to doorways and archways in the Dome Theatre section of the building (Fig 277). The dado comprises turquoise and pale green interlocking tiles designed by the London architect Harold Elphick and illustrated in Craven Dunnill's catalogue (Fig 278). The pattern is made using a single tile - basically an oblong but with an indented centre and pointed ends, like a bow tie - set in two directions. Elphick was the architect of Nevill's New Turkish Baths (1894-5) in the City of London, where the tiles were also used. Restoration work on the tiles and faience was carried out by tilemakers Craven Dunnill of Jackfield, revived in 2000 after the original firm ceased production in the early 1950s.

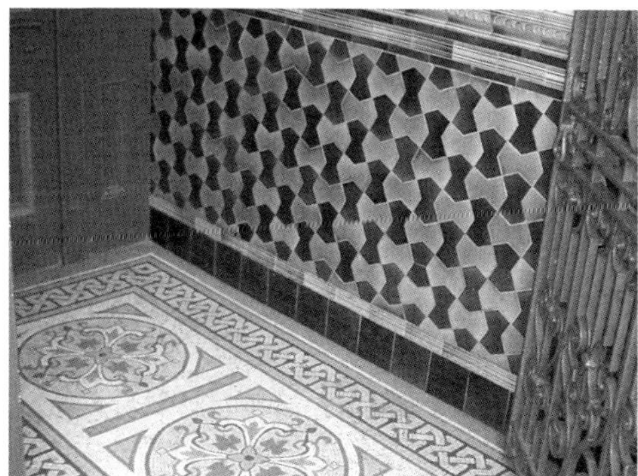

Fig 278.

From Church Street, turn south down NEW ROAD to see the **Colonnade Hotel**, its bar being part of the nearby Theatre Royal. On either side of the entrance is an area of colourful full height tiling including two handpainted tile panels bearing the words 'The Colonnade Hotel'; both are signed 'Painted by Webb & Co, 294 Euston Rd, London NW'. Continue seaward via North

Street and WEST STREET, where the anglo-catholic **St Paul's Church** (1846-8, architect R. C. Carpenter) has much Pugin-designed stained glass and other ornate funishings with a rather anticlimactic early Minton tile pavement in the chancel.[1] The church was built by Henry Michell Wagner, Vicar of Brighton during 1824-70, for his son Arthur Wagner (1824-1902); the church was completed prior to the ordination of Arthur, who was also a follower of the Oxford Movement. Return to the station along West Street and Queen's Road.

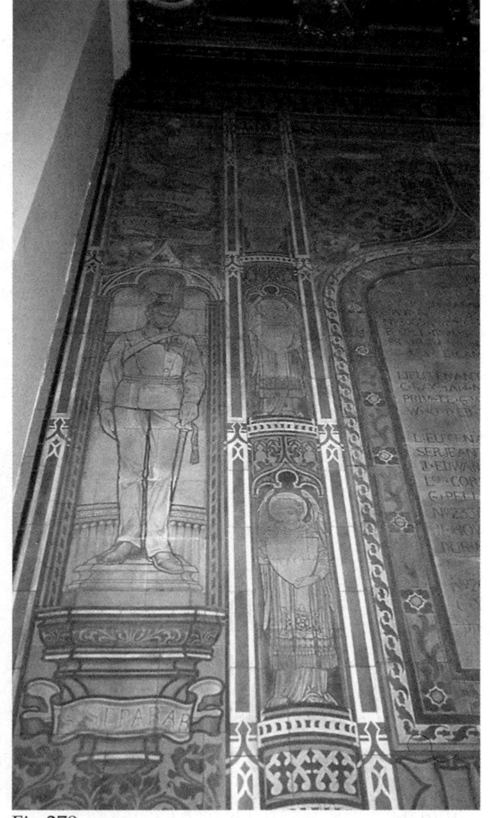

Fig 279.

An excursion north-eastward begins just off the southern end of Lewes Road in MALTHOUSE LANE, at the former offices (1893) of **Tamplin's Phoenix Brewery**; the company ceased to brew in 1973, but the building is still topped by their terracotta phoenix symbol, which rises from some unusually vivid flames. Head north along the east side of Lewes Road to find the former **Municipal Technical College** (1897-8) on RICHMOND TERRACE. The exterior features much buff terracotta ornament including a coat of arms, and the entrance foyer has a full-height Craven Dunnill tile scheme, restored in the late 1990s. The building was undergoing conversion to apartments (known as '1897') in 2004, with much of the tiling being retained.

Further along LEWES ROAD, on the corner of St Martin's Place, is **St Martin's Church** (1874-5, architect Somers Clarke, now St Martin's with St Wilfrid's), one of five Brighton churches built by Arthur Wagner (Fig 279). In this case he shared the cost with his family, as the church was a memorial to his father as well as serving the local barracks. There is a red terracotta relief above the porch door, and the ornate interior decoration, all planned by Arthur Wagner, includes a large, sombre three-part tiled memorial panel for the 5th Lancers in their 1884-5 campaigns; it was painted by W. B Simpson & Sons and designed by Somers Clarke.[2] The Stations of the Cross are also ceramic, and there are three glazed ceramic reliefs, one almost semicircular, the others being smaller plaques. The three reliefs were probably imported from Florence and made by the Cantagalli factory, who produced copies of della Robbia ware in the late nineteenth century. These majolica plaques - holiday souvenirs in the form of correct ecclesiastical decoration - seem to have been especially popular in Brighton; others may be seen at the **Church of St Michael and All Angels**, VICTORIA ROAD (just west of Brighton's centre), and at the **Church of the Annunciation**, WASHINGTON STREET (uphill to the east of Lewes Road), where two plaques form part of the east wall decoration.[3]

EASTBOURNE

There are three major ceramic attractions in Eastbourne, the most modern being the seafront **Bandstand** and shelter on GRAND PARADE, built in 1931-5 (Fig 280). This elegant structure provides a fine display of Carter's Ceramic Marble, a material developed by the Poole firm around 1909 in order to compete with Doulton's Carraraware and similar products. It was made in several shades of white as well as blue and green, and was craze-proof, thus resistant to seawater and weathering, and ideal for building at seaside resorts.[4] The roof of the circular bandstand is gleaming turquoise faience, and there is a mass of intricate detailing on the column heads and around the broad, colonnaded shelter, the latter in mottled Ceramic Marble.

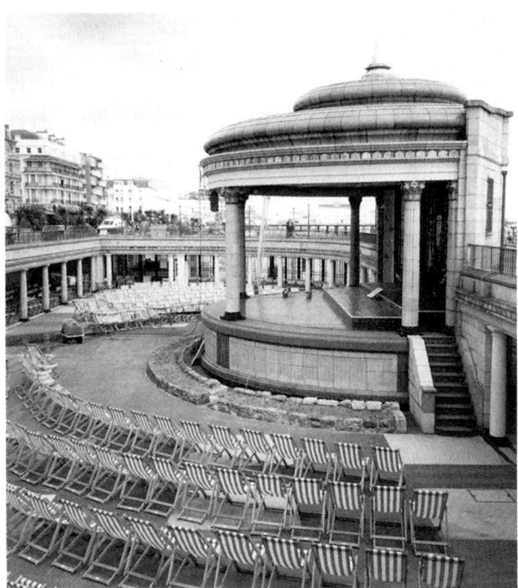
Fig 280.

Almost a mile west of the bandstand and slightly above the seafront in DARLEY ROAD is the former **All Saints Hospital**, founded by Harriet Brownlow Byron, Mother Superior of All Saints' Sisters of the Poor from Margaret Street in Westminster, where Butterfield's All Saints Church had been completed in 1859. The convalescent hospital was built in 1867-70 to the design of the gentleman architect Henry Woodyer, who added its Chapel in 1873-4; its breathtaking interior appears completely unchanged since the day it was dedicated (Fig 281). The walls are of red and black brick with stripes of white stone and yellow and black tiles, as well as a series of deep red terracotta lettered medallions. The floor is laid with superb geometric tiling in complex radiating patterns which rise across several broad steps into the sanctuary, where there is an elaborate encaustic pavement with unusual colouring. With its rich stained glass and wonderful ironwork, especially the font cover, this is a uniquely memorable space.

Back to the centre of Eastbourne for **All Souls Church**, SUSAN'S ROAD, built in 1881-2 for Lady Victoria Wellesley and designed by the London architect Alfred Strong of Parr & Strong. Its rather unexpected Byzantine style, with a campanile and much ornate buff and red terracotta (especially the west rose window tracery), was copied from an Italian church. Inside, there is much painted and mosaic decoration, and - stretching across the width of the church above the west door - a tile panel bearing a biblical quotation 'The souls of the righteous are in the hand of God, and there shall no torment touch them' (Wisdom 3.1) in red on cream ground.

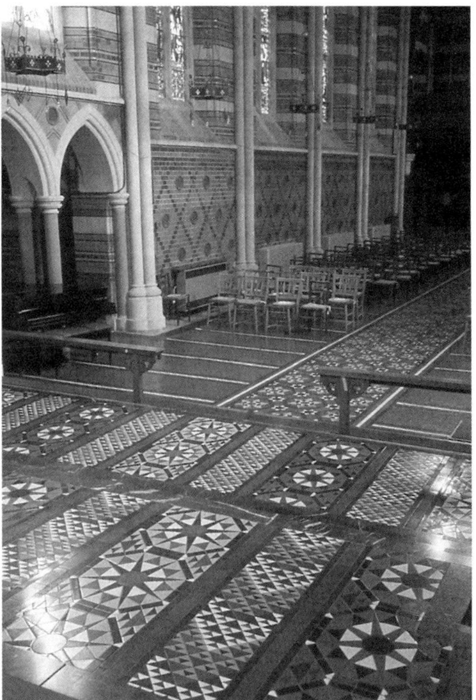
Fig 281.

EAST HOATHLY

East Hoathly Church was restored in 1856, although much of its stained glass (by Shrigley & Hunt) dates from around the 1890s; on either side of the east window are Powell's opus sectile panels designed by John W. Brown. In the churchyard are two headstones with terracotta plaques by Jonathan Harmer of Heathfield; a third terracotta plaque, a good reproduction dating from the 1980s, was made by a local potter.

Halland Park Farm lies about a mile south-west of East Hoathly, but more significant is the proximity of Laughton Place, a couple of miles to the south, which was the home of the Pelham family. Laughton Place was rebuilt around 1534, then the family moved to a new mansion near Halland in 1595. All that remains of the Halland courtyard house is part of the outer brick wall, chimneybreasts and the walled garden, but in the farmhouse there is a fragment of early renaissance terracotta, which probably originated at Laughton.

HASTINGS

Handily placed on HAVELOCK ROAD, on the direct route between Hastings railway station and the seafront, is the **Havelock PH**, its colourful exterior tiling doubtless intended to entice day trippers away from pier and beach (Fig 282). The pub was built in 1857 but its magnificent set of Doulton pictorial panels date from a refit carried out during 1889-90 by a local architect named Ward.[5] The porch panel, easily visible from the street, shows General Havelock, hero of the Indian Mutiny, and advertises not only the pub but the supplier of the tiles, its inscription reading 'This tiling was executed by A. T. S. Carter Brockley London. S. E.'. Alfred T. S. Carter, a son of Jesse Carter of Carter's of Poole, set up in London as a builders' merchant after the mid 1870s. He soon became a tile merchant, but although the firm did make mosaic, they probably did not manufacture tiles, which they seem to have bought in from larger firms, Doulton in the case of the Havelock. Inside the pub is rich wall tiling including three pictorial panels showing Hastings Castle and the town's pier, the Battle of Hastings, and a sea engagement including a pirate ship; the artist is likely to have been John Eyre or John H. McClennan. Below is a relief-tiled dado while the floor is black and white geometrics. This wonderful interior must be amongst the candidates for the best turn-of-the-century pub tile scheme in Britain. It certainly stands comparison with Sunderland's Mountain Daisy, where the 1900-2 tiling (with seven picture panels and a ceramic bar counter) is by Craven Dunnill.

Not far west of the Havelock on CLAREMONT is a most peculiar building, put up by Thomas Brassey (created Lord Brassey in 1886), railway entrepreneur and MP for Hastings, in 1877-80 as his town house. Only a hundred yards or so from the sea, it was no ordinary house: a suite on the second floor was for the use of the Brasseys, but the remainder was for the townsfolk, with accommodation for a library, assembly room, school of art and science, and assorted local societies. The design, by Hastings architect W. L. Vernon, was an interpretation of the merchant palaces of Venice. The Brassey Institute was integral with its neighbour, a printing works and shop, and together they formed **Claremont Buildings**. In the narrow street the Institute's tower soars above its neighbours, and decoration - including upwards of seven large pictorial tile panels by W. B. Simpson & Sons - covers a large part of the facade.[6] Although these have faded, the detailing of local historical scenes may still be deciphered and the colours glow. The building was restored in 1992 and now houses Hastings Library; its porch has a floor mosaic, terracotta wall decoration with fleur-de-lys motifs, and a glass mosiac frieze by Antonio Salviati showing scenes from the Bayeux Tapestry. The neighbouring structure, the office of the *Hastings Observer*, also had lavish ceramic decoration but much of the tiling has come away, leaving clear impressions of backmarks identifying the tiles as products of the Campbell Brick & Tile Co.

Finally, down on the seafront at WHITE ROCK, almost opposite the pier, is the White Rock Pavilion (1913-27, architect C. Cowles Voysey), now known as the **White Rock Theatre**. Its surprisingly dull Spanish Colonial style exterior is enlivened by a frieze of eight relief-modelled roundels in Doulton's polychrome stoneware. The sculptor was Gilbert Bayes and there are four designs representing Drama, Romance, Adventure and Terpsichore, the muse of dancing.[7]

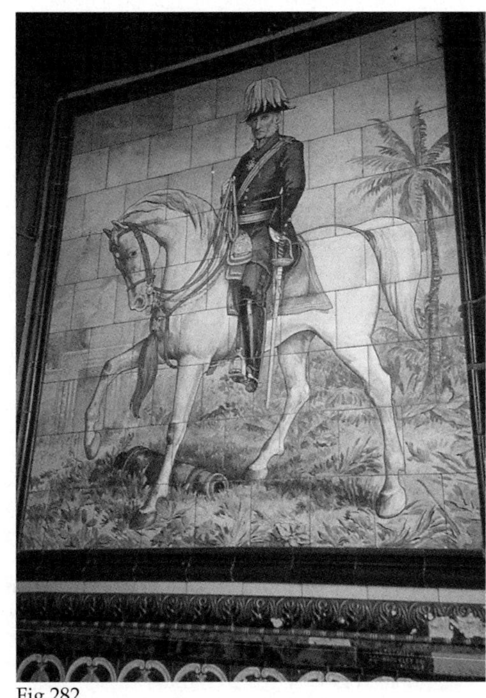

Fig 282.

LAUGHTON

Laughton Place was the main home of the Pelham family from around 1400; its drastic remodelling by

Sir William Pelham from 1534, which was completed before his death in 1538, included the addition of fashionable renaissance-style terracotta decoration. Terracotta was used to face a splendid turreted entrance building, now gone, as well as for the surviving window surrounds.[8] The reliefs on the vertical terracotta window mouldings include winged cherub-heads, showing the influence of continental design on native terracotta manufacturing.[9] The family moved west to Halland (see East Hoathly) in 1595, driven out by the damp, and all that remains of the mansion is its sturdy brick tower, along with a Gothick extension of 1753. After the tower was sold by the Pelhams in 1927 it suffered from neglect until rescued by the Landmark Trust, who bought it in 1978. The Trust successfully cleaned the terracotta window surrounds using Johnson's baby shampoo, and the tower is now in use as holiday accommodation.[10]

RODMELL

Monk's House (NT) was the home of the author Virginia Woolf and her husband Leonard from 1919. To help with its decoration, Virginia called on the expertise of her sister, the artist Vanessa Bell, who lived at Charleston (see Alciston), about six miles to the east, with the artist Duncan Grant and the writer David Garnett. Bell and Grant were co-directors of the Omega Workshops, founded by Roger Fry in 1913. Omega tiles were available from 1914, and after the demise of the Workshops in 1919, Bell and Grant continued to paint tiles which were used on furniture and in fireplace surrounds, notably at Charleston and Monk's House. Virginia built an extension to Monk's House in the early 1920s, and her new bedroom has brightly coloured fireplace tiles by Bell, who took as their theme her sister's novel *To The Lighthouse*. Back in the village, **St Peter's Church** has colourful early Minton encaustic tiles dating from around 1850.

East Sussex Roundup

In and near to the chancel of the Church of the Assumption and St Nicholas, **Etchingham**, are original fourteenth century floor tiles with good animal designs. There are tile and mosaic wall murals beside the altar at St Augustine's Church (1839, architect Decimus Burton), **Flimwell**, whose chancel was built in 1879. The three Coade stone panels representing Wisdom, Justice and Mercy on County Hall (1808-12, architect John Johnson), High Street, **Lewes**, are identical to those used at the same architect's Shire Hall (1790-2), Chelmsford, Essex. There are Powell's glass tiles of various designs on the chancel walls of St Mary's Church (restored 1886-7), **Newick**. The 1867 restoration of St Peter's Church, **West Firle** included the installation of a Maw & Co tiled chancel pavement and reredos.[11]

There are terracotta plaques by the potter Jonathan Harmer (1762-1849) of Heathfield on gravestones in the churchyards at Ashburnham, Brightling, Burwash, Cade Street (near Heathfield), Chiddingly, East Hoathly, Glynde, Hailsham, Hellingly, Herstmonceux, Salehurst, Wadhurst, Waldron and Warbleton.

West Sussex

AMBERLEY

St Michael's Church has very unusual geometric floor tiles which date from its 1864 restoration; their arrangement is based on a circle rather than the more common square. The tiles were made by Maw & Co and the receipts are still retained in the church records; their cost was £27 14s 4½d including carriage.

BOXGROVE

The Benedictine Priory of Boxgrove was founded in 1105 and was a daughter house of Lessay Abbey in Normandy. It was suppressed by Henry VIII and eventually fell into disrepair, the surviving part of the priory church now functioning as the parish church, **St Mary and St Blaise**. On the floor of its south chapel, in front of the altar, is an area of medieval and later tiles including a number of Flemish inlaid tiles dating from the sixteenth century. These incorporate the inscription 'Die tijt is cort - die doot is snel - wacht u va sonde - soe doedi wel' (Time is short - death is swift - beware of sin - so do you well). There are also a number of relief tiles which appear to be German in origin, and a number of larger tiles, probably of a later date, with inlaid designs featuring cockerels, stags and lions. These designs are poorly executed and seem to have been stamped with a block which was narrower than the tile, leaving a ridge on the surface. In addition, there is a ceramic memorial plaque on the south wall just to the right of the chapel; it dates from 1937 and was made by Carter's of Poole.

CHICHESTER

There is a major surprise at Chichester's **Railway Station**, SOUTHGATE, where the booking hall remains blissfully unchanged from its opening in 1961; design was by British Railways Southern Division. The elongated rods of the light fittings, pastel hexagonal-coffered ceiling, Festival of Britain-style clock and Pilkington's pattern-making tiles below the ticket office counter all appear - aside from a thick coating of dust - as if just installed. The tiles were shown (in a different colourway) in Pilkington's September 1962 *House Journal*, the Chichester arrangement being made up from pale cream-coloured blanks and a tile with a flowing red-on-cream sideways 'W' motif, which can be used facing right or left. This is a fine interior, but lack of appreciation of sixties architecture is shown by the fact that it does not rate a mention in Gordon Biddle's otherwise magisterial gazetteer *Britain's Historic Railway Buildings* (OUP, 2003). The station certainly deserves statutory protection.

Half a mile or so north of the station, in the centre of Chichester, is the **Cathedral**. Beyond the high altar, and John Piper's stunning 1966 tapestry depiction of the Holy Trinity, is the Lady Chapel with a small but very fine pavement of Godwin's encaustic tiles, installed during the chapel's 1871-2 restoration; the circular arrangement includes beautiful roundels of the Signs of the Zodiac (Fig 283).[12] There is also floor tiling, featuring several good sixteen-tile groups, in the former chapel of St Pantaleon on the east side of the south transept; however, this is now a vestry with no public access.

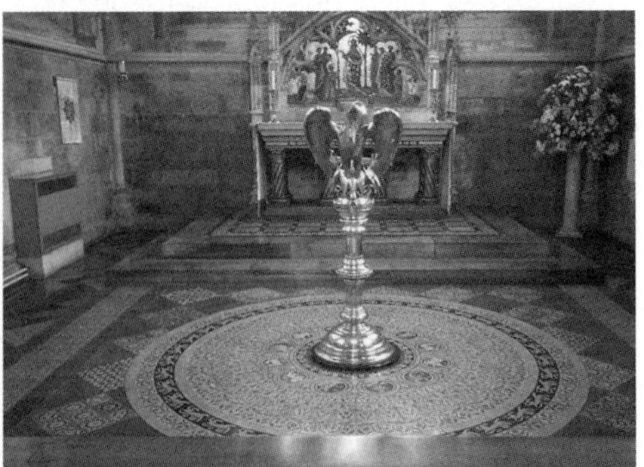

Fig 283.

CLAPHAM

The **Church of St Mary the Virgin** contains some of the finest surviving examples of tiles painted by Morris, Marshall, Faulkner & Co (Fig 284). The tiles form part of a major restoration carried out in 1873-4 by George Gilbert Scott with the assistance of his son, George Gilbert Scott junior (1839-97), who had finished similar work at Findon Church, two miles to the north-east, in 1868. Morris tiles were specified at Findon, and supplied by the firm despite their doubts about taking the commission, following the disastrous technical problems experienced at St Peter's Church, Bournemouth, where their six pictorial panels eventually had to be removed. Scott must have been convinced that the Findon tiling had been a success, as the Clapham scheme includes a full-scale reredos and flanking tiling.

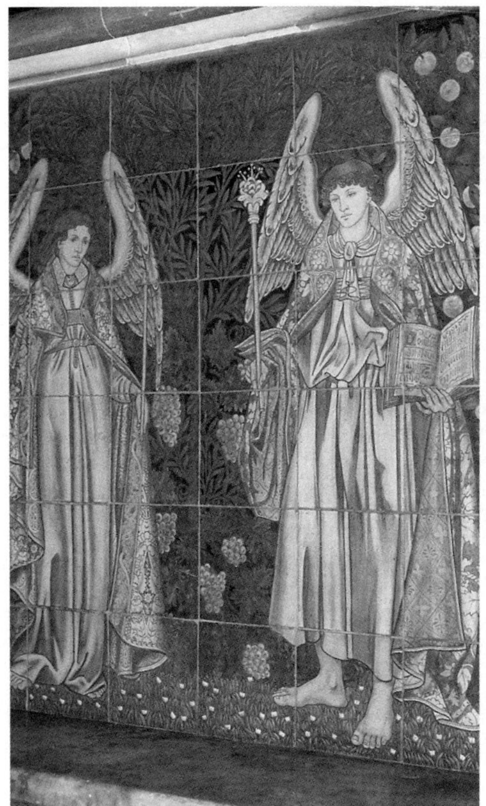

Fig 284.

The tiling is in three sections: the central section, designed entirely by William Morris, depicts the four archangels *Gabriel, Michael, Raphael, and Uriel* standing before a background of fruit trees, willow, roses and vines. This panel is the largest produced by Morris's firm as a single unit and probably represent the technical zenith of the firm's tile production. Unlike many other Morris tiles this panel is almost perfectly preserved, the only damage of note being a few stress cracks caused by movement of the church wall. At the sides of the main panel are two areas of a vine pattern probably designed by William Morris and known as the *Clapham Vine*.[13]

Also probably dating from Scott's restoration are the fine panels of tiles depicting the twelve apostles which are situated between the chancel windows. These are by W. B. Simpson & Sons and are signed with the 'WBS&S' logo.

FINDON

The medieval **Church of St John the Baptist** was restored by George Gilbert Scott junior (1839-97) in 1867-8, the commission having been passed on to him by his father, George Gilbert Scott; the cost - over £2,400 - was mostly born by the Dowager Marchioness of Bath, a member of the local Wyatt family (Fig 285). The restoration included stained glass by various firms although not Morris, Marshall, Faulkner & Co, despite the fact that Scott junior was an early patron of the firm and was close to Morris's circle in the 1860s.[14] Morris's firm seem only to have been asked to provide a tiled reredos; this form of decoration may have been suggested to Lady Bath by Dante Gabriel Rossetti, one of the partners in the firm.[15] Not only was Rossetti's aunt employed by Lady Bath, but in June 1866 Lady Bath's brother-in-law (and auxiliary patron at Findon) Lord Charles Thynne visited Rossetti at his studio. The request for a tiled reredos, which appears to have been made in mid-1866, came at a difficult time for the firm, who were in the process of completing the installation of six tile pictures on the chancel walls of St Peter's Church, Bournemouth. Technical difficulties caused the tiles to deteriorate rapidly, and they were removed in 1899. Warington Taylor, the firm's business manager, was very much against the production of any tiling other than basic patterned tiles, perhaps because of the Bournemouth experience; he was very reluctant to undertake the Findon reredos. In November 1866 he wrote to Philip Webb:

'About this Findon tile reredos - we cannot do it - *see this is settled at once.* Must write Lady Bath saying circumstances have compelled us to discontinue the manufacture. Bournemouth was a disgrace - and only half done now.'[16]

However, the firm eventually did supply the tiling for the east wall, if not the entire reredos. Parish records state that Lord Henry Thynne paid for the 'encaustic tiles within the altar rails', which could well have been the Morris tiles.[17]

The tiling remaining at Findon comprises two tile panels flanking the south aisle altar; there were originally two further rows of floral tiles framing a small reredos, but these were removed to make room for a larger reredos, itself now gone. The tile panels depict six minstrel angels from a series of twelve designed by Morris probably before 1865; these appeared in a number of the company's stained glass commissions. Below the angels are panels with floral designs. The Findon tiles, one of the only two surviving Morris commissions for church tiles (the other is Clapham, two miles to the south-west), have survived in relatively good condition although the wall on which they are set was deemed to be too damp to be painted.

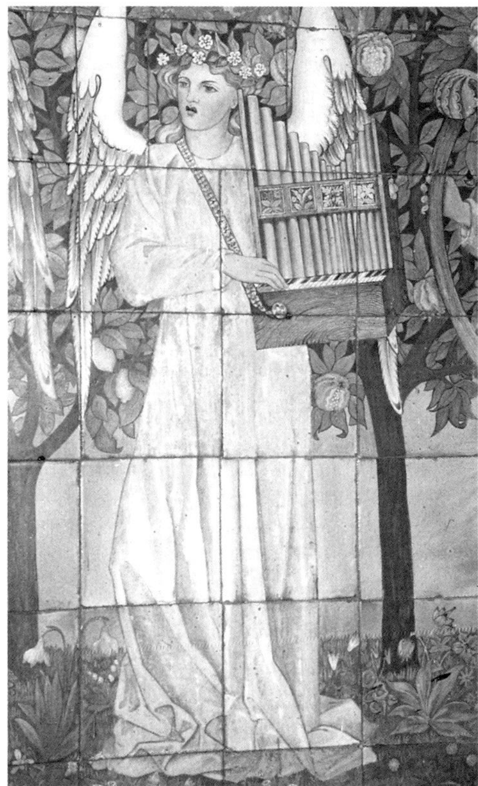

Fig 285.

FULKING

Beisde the famous stream on Fulking's main street is a little nineteenth century brick **pump house** bearing a brown and buff encaustic letter-tiled plaque; the words are from Psalms 104 and 107: 'He sendeth springs into the valleys which run among the hills. Oh that men would praise the Lord for His Goodness'. Nearby is a small **drinking fountain** (1866) with a tiled surround; its tube-lined tiles, restored by Maw's Specialist Products Department, combine a floral motif with quotations from Psalms 78.

WORTHING

Just beyond the north-western edge of Worthing, about a couple of miles north of the suburb of Goring-on-Sea, is **Castle Goring** (no public access), ARUNDEL ROAD, an idiosyncratic and little-known folly castle less than a hundred yards from the A27; in fact the nearest village is Clapham, about a mile away northward across the main road. It was designed by the Worthing architect John Biagio Rebecca (d1847) around 1795 for Sir Bysshe Shelley, grandfather of the poet, and is a combination of gothic castle on the entrance side and classical mansion to the rear; indeed the rooms change style half way through. The garden front is adorned with three large Coade stone plaques of 1797-8 whose figures - *Bacchus*, *Ceres* and a *Satyr* - lean out precipitously from their frames, as though in disbelief at their situation. The castle, which took thirty-four years to complete, also has Coade capitals, balusters and a coat of arms. Castle Goring, although listed grade I, is only partly occupied and is in such poor condition that in 2003 it was on English Heritage's *Buildings at Risk Register*.[18]

West Sussex Roundup

Restoration and repair of the extensive late nineteenth century Godwin encaustic tile pavement at St Nicholas Church, **Arundel**, was completed in July 2000 by tilemakers Diana Hall and Chris Cox. On the floor of the choir of St Mary's Church, **Binstead**, is an elaborate Powell's glass mosaic panel probably dating from about 1890, when the firm is known to have made a small number of such installations; it includes several designs not found elsewhere. Standen (NT), West Hoathly Road, **East Grinstead**, was designed by Philip Webb and built in the 1890s; its arts & crafts interior includes tiles made at the Cantagalli factory in Florence. Ann Clark designed several tile murals on the theme of 'summer' for the Princess Royal Hospital, Lewes Road, **Haywards Heath** around 1991. St Peter's Church, **Henfield**, has encaustic tiles by Chamberlain & Co on its sanctuary steps. Holy Trinity Church (1843-5, architect Sir Charles Barry), **Hurstpierpoint** has Chamberlain & Co encaustic floor tiles including some with symbols of the evangelists. On the seafront at **Littlehampton** is one remaining 1950s kiosk still faced with tiles by H. & G. Thynne; other kiosks have lost their original tiles. A Minton encaustic tile reredos was installed during restoration of St Andrew's Church, **Nuthurst** in 1867.[19] Knightscroft (1879, architect Richard Norman Shaw), Sea Lane, **Rustington**, has several fireplaces with tiles by William De Morgan.[20] The dairy at Uppark (NT), a mile south of **South Harting**, has white Wedgwood wall tiles, some hand-painted with ivy tendrils.

References

1. Gordon O'Loughlin and D. Robert Elleray, eds., *Saint Paul's Brighton, 150 Years: A Celebration* (Optimus Books, Worthing, 2000), p20.
2. 'Military Memorials at Brighton', *The Builder*, 51 (1886), pp42.
3. Peter F. Anson, *Fashions in Church Furnishings 1840-1940* 2nd ed (Studio Vista, London, 1965), pp258-9.
4. Jennifer Hawkins, *Poole Potteries* (Barrie & Jenkins, London, 1980), pp117-8.
5. Ian Murray, 'Pub honoured for knight on the tiles', *The Times*, 25th October 1996.
6. 'Hastings School of Art and Public Institution', *The Builder*, 35, 26th May 1877, pp533-6.
7. Paul Atterbury and Louise Irvine, *The Doulton Story* (Royal Doulton Tableware, Stoke on Trent, 1979), p103.
8. Maurice Howard, *Civic Buildings and Courtier Houses: new techniques and materials for architectural ornament*, in *The Age of Transition: the archaeology of English culture 1400-1600*, eds David Gaimster and Paul Stamper (Oxbow Books, Oxford, 1997), pp105-113.
9. David Gaimster and Beverley Nenk, *English Households in Transition c1450-1550: the ceramic evidence*, in *The Age of Transition: the archaeology of English culture 1400-1600*, eds David Gaimster and Paul Stamper (Oxbow Books, Oxford, 1997), pp171-195.
10. Julia Abel Smith, 'Decorating a Revival', *Country Life*, 184, 1st November 1990, pp94-96.
11. *The Builder*, vol 25, 28th December 1867
12. Mary Hobbs, ed., *Chichester Cathedral: An Historical Survey* (Phillimore, Chichester, 1994).
13. Richard Myers and Hilary Myers, *William Morris Tiles - The tile designs of Morris and his Fellow-Workers* (Richard Dennis, Shepton Beauchamp, 1996), pp98-9.
14. Gavin Stamp, *An Architect of Promise: George Gilbert Scott junior (1839-1897) and the Late Gothic Revival* (Shaun Tyas, Donington, 2002), pp210, 377.
15. Jan Marsh, 'The Tiles at Findon Church', *Journal of the William Morris Society*, 14 (2000) 1, p82.
16. Myers, *William Morris Tiles*, pp74-8, 146.
17. Tessa Kelly, 'The Morris Reredoses at St. John the Baptist Church, Findon, and The Church of The Blessed Virgin Mary, Clapham, West Sussex', *Journal of the William Morris Society*, 13 (2000) 4, pp30-34.
18. Alison Kelly, *Mrs Coade's Stone* (Self Publishing Association, Upton-upon-Severn, 1990).
19. *The Builder*, vol 25, 29th June 1867.
20. Chris Blanchett, *William De Morgan Tiles at Knightscroft House, Rustington, West Sussex* (Buckland Books, Tring, 1992).

Warwickshire

Local terracotta production was crucial to the appearance of Warwickshire's, and especially Birmingham's, buildings. Just north of the city in Tamworth, Staffordshire, Gibbs & Canning pioneered the manufacture of terracotta for large architectural contracts by works located in coalfields. Their works was established in 1847, and the firm's terracotta was used for a series of major contracts in the Midlands - notably the Victoria Law Courts, Birmingham - during the 1880s. Gibbs & Canning was one of the four major British producers of terracotta. In addition Stanley Brothers of Nuneaton, established by Reginald Stanley, made terracotta in the form of simple architectural details and garden ornaments from 1881; the firm also specialised in finials, including the well-known dragon design. Stanley Brothers manufactured two-foot square terracotta plaques showing a relief bust of Queen Victoria to mark the Queen's Golden Jubilee in 1887; the design was adapted to mark the 1897 Diamond Jubilee, the later version being much more common. George T. Noszlopy's *Public Sculpture of Warwickshire, Coventry and Solihull* (2003) suggests the relief of Queen Victoria may have been designed by the sculptor Henry Hugh Armstead (1828-1905), but gives no grounds for this attribution. Stanley's Jubilee plaques can be found throughout the country but the greatest concentration is in central and southern England; in Warwickshire, examples may be seen in Atherstone, five miles north-west of Nuneaton, and Knowle.

Apart from the all-pervading terracotta, also seen on the many Birmingham 'tile and terracotta' pubs, other Warwickshire highlights include a significant late fourteenth century secular tile pavement which was revealed in 2000 at Warwick Castle; the tiles came from the Chilvers Coton tilery near Nuneaton. One of the best of the few extant early postwar ceramic murals in Britain can be found in Coventry's Lower Precinct, and in the same city are the iconic 1960s buildings of the University of Warwick, the loss of whose Twintile cladding became a sorry story for the ceramics industry. In contrast, and just around the corner from the University, is the innovative blue Hathernware faience roof of the 1993 Cable & Wireless College.

Suggested reading: Alan Swale, 'The Gordon Cullen Ceramic Murals: Lower Precinct, Coventry', *Glazed Expressions* (2003), 46, pp14-15 and 47 pp14-15; *Birmingham Terracotta* (Birmingham City Council Planning Department, 2001); George T. Noszlopy, *Public Sculpture of Birmingham* (Liverpool University Press, 1998); TACS Tour Notes *Birmingham* (1989); Alan Crawford, Michael Dunn & Robert Thorne, *Birmingham Pubs 1880-1939* (Alan Sutton, Gloucester, 1986). The *Gazetteer* entry for Warwickshire covers the administrative areas of Birmingham City Council, Coventry City Council, Solihull Metropolitan Borough Council and Warwickshire County Council.

ATHERSTONE

On the facade of **Primrose Cottage**, 176 LONG STREET (which runs south-east from the railway station) is a good example of the 1897 Queen Victoria Diamond Jubilee terracotta plaques made by Stanley Brothers of Nuneaton; the plaques are about 2′ square and 3½″ thick.[1] Just to the north, outside the office of **Warwickshire Probation Service** in MARKET STREET, is a 1998 ceramic tile mural by Justin Sanders entitled *We are here*; it measures about 5′ by 4′ and the design, incised in in grey and white on a dark ground, shows local scenes.[2] Further north on Sheepy Road is St Mary's Church, where the Minton tile pavement was donated by Herbert Minton himself in 1850.[3]

BIRMINGHAM

Birmingham exemplifies, as much as any city or town in Britain, the rich contribution which 'fired earth' - bricks, tiles, terracotta and faience - made to Victorian and Edwardian building. Lacking a suitable local source of good stone in sufficient quantities to meet the growing needs of the city, developers turned to terracotta, initially to supply the dressings for buildings but ultimately for complete facades of block terracotta. Even before the completion in 1891 of Birmingham's most impressive terracotta edifice, the Victoria Law Courts, the city already possessed quite a display of terracotta on buildings designed by local architects such as Martin & Chamberlain and Essex, Nichol & Goodman. Martin & Chamberlain first used the material in 1879, and a whole spate of municipal buildings - libraries, public baths and schools - followed during the 1880s and 1890s. The excesses of some of the later terracotta buildings resulted in the publication of a letter headed 'The bane of modern Birmingham' in the *Daily Mail* of the 3rd November 1908; the writer pointed out that:

'Terracotta has a painfully hard effect, and lends itself so easily to cheap surface ornamentation that few architects can resist the temptation of covering their terracotta buildings with meretricious, meaningless and tasteless 'decorative' detail.'

Although there have been significant losses, the city centre retains a high density of terracotta facades, while several of the suburban libraries and baths have also survived along with good examples of the city's renowned turn of the century 'tile and terracotta' public houses. Some architectural practices tended to specialise in pub design, notably James and Lister Lea, who generally specified Hathernware terracotta (from Loughborough) and Minton tiles (from Stoke-on-Trent), and a house style is discernable amongst a number of pubs built for individual breweries such as Mitchells and Butlers.

This tour of Birmingham concentrates on major ceramic locations in the central area, beginning and ending in VICTORIA SQUARE - next to the Town Hall and just south of the Council House (1874-9), whose main facade sports a Salviati mosaic - then looks at sites in the suburbs, taken alphabetically. There are many more buildings with decorative ceramics than can be described here, particularly in the intensely terracottary sectors around Newhall Street and the Law Courts. On the south-west edge of Victoria Square is **Queen's Chambers**, PARADISE STREET, refronted - possibly in 1904 - by architects Mansell & Mansell; its tudor-gothic facade is entirely in shades of buff terracotta supplied by Doultons. The hooded central doorway features a bold relief of Queen Victoria seated on her throne, flanked by a lion and unicorn, while grotesque demons decorate the ground floor piers. Head north into CHAMBERLAIN SQUARE to find **Birmingham Museum and Art Gallery** (1884-9) on the right, with its fine collection of tiles. Mosaics dominate the museum's entrance hall, then geometric tile flooring runs from the impressive Round Room through the Ceramics Gallery to the restaurant, in a real showcase of municipal ceramics. The tiles complement their surroundings perfectly, although the airy ironwork of the galleries provides a welcome contrast to the huge acreage of muted ruddy-browns and fawns.

Turn right along Edmund Street, soon reaching MARGARET STREET; just to the left is the **Birmingham School of Art**, built in 1883-5 (architects Martin & Chamberlain), now part of the University of Central England; the CORNWALL STREET extension was added in 1891-3.[4] The exterior of the original section features an array of architectural ceramics, from glazed tiles and mosaics by Craven Dunnill to blocks of foliated terracotta tiles below the roof. Most conspicuous is the large rose window in buff terracotta with a pattern of lilies on a lattice background; this was modelled by the sculptor Samuel Barfield of Leicester and made by King & Co of Stourbridge. In the same Ruskinian gothic spirit, the Cornwall Street wing sports decorative tiling and terracotta putti, the latter representing the arts and modelled by Benjamin Creswick (1853-1946), Master of Modelling and Modelled Design at the School of Art during 1889-1918.

Continue along Edmund Street to meet NEWHALL STREET; at 19 is **The Exchange**, built in 1896 as a telephone exchange for Bell Edison by the architect Frederick Martin. The richly ornamented terracotta was supplied by J. C. Edwards of Ruabon, and the porch retains its tiling showing the Bell Edison logo. High up on the facade of **56-60 Newhall Street**, built for Birmingham Office Co Ltd in 1899-1900, are four buff Doulton terracotta panels designed by W. J. Neatby; they all show a figure engaged in conflict with a serpent. Now turn south to COLMORE ROW: at 166 is **Victoria House**, an office building put up around 2000 on the site of a Victorian hotel. Much of the facade is red brickwork, but contrasting decorative detail on the ground floor arches and columns is in Hathernware's architectural terracotta. Looking south, at 44 TEMPLE ROW WEST is the late nineteenth century tudor gothic fantasy of the **Birmingham Midshires Building Society**, originally Ocean Assurance, with well detailed buff terracotta including fish swimming beneath the architraves. Continue northward along Colmore Row; those wishing to visit the Jewellery Quarter (see below) should take Church Street, on the left. At the end of Colmore Row is Colmore Circus and the opportunity for a diversion north to **St Chad's R. C. Cathedral**, whose stark red brick facade overlooks ST CHAD'S CIRCUS. The cathedral is the work of A. W. N. Pugin and was mostly erected in 1839-41; the original and extensive Pugin-designed Minton pavement was removed during reordering in 1967, but some tiles from the chancel and Lady Chapel were relaid in the former baptistery, now Chapel of the Oils, in the north aisle.[5]

Return to Colmore Circus and go left into STEELHOUSE LANE to see the former Birmingham General Hospital (1892-7, architect William Henman); the **Children's Hospital** took over the site in 1998. The original E-shaped complex was constructed of bright red brick and deep red terracotta supplied by Doulton's from their local Rowley Regis works. Unfortunately the open courts facing Steelhouse Lane were filled by later extensions and much of their terracotta elaboration has disappeared, including a Doultonware fountain and a series of female figures treading upon the Serpent of Death. However, a great deal remains, including terracotta ornament on the boundary walls, and some of the regrettable additions are now being removed.

Turn the corner into CORPORATION STREET, passing **Ruskin Buildings** (1899) then **Coleridge Chambers** (1887-1904) on the right. These two adjoining buildings are constructed of red brick with mostly light buff terracotta enrichment, although Ruskin Buildings, designed by Ewan Harper, has sturdy red terracotta columns guarding its central entrance; Coleridge Chambers has an attractive majolica-tiled interior with an elaborate mosaic floor. Ruskin Buildings was restored in 2000, the replacement terracotta being provided by Ibstock Hathernware. Across the road is the unmistakeable vertiginous tower (from whose balcony sprouts a small tree) of the **Methodist Central Hall**, designed by the brothers Ewan and James A. Harper and built in 1899-1903 using rich red terracotta probably supplied by Gibbs & Canning, although as G. King of Stourbridge are known to have produced a series of detailed drawings for the supply of the material, there is some doubt about this attribution.[6] The grand entrance has a deeply recessed moulded arch, and high relief red terracotta groups of a female figure with children, in fact allegories of teaching. These reliefs may have been modelled by the chief modeller at Gibbs & Canning, John Evans, who could also have been responsible for the pair of buff terracotta relief panels in the porch; these show events in the life of John Wesley.[7] The building was unoccupied in 2002 and may be undergoing conversion.

Almost facing the Central Hall is the is red, red bulk of the **Victoria Law Courts** (1887-91, architects Aston Webb and Ingress Bell), its almost carmine terracotta replete with decoration emphasising the building's concern with law and order (Fig 286). It was the first major public building in Britain to be faced entirely in red terracotta, in this case supplied by J. C. Edwards of Ruabon; ochre terracotta blockwork by Gibbs & Canning provided the surfaces of most of the important interior walls. Much consideration was given to the design and execution of the modelling and sculpture, undertaken by a team of designers and decorative sculptors under the guidance of the architects. William Aumonier (1841-1914) and his London firm, which included his sons William and Percy Aumonier, carried out most of the decorative modelling, with Aumonier himself contributing some of the more important terracotta sculpture. In the course of this he had scaffolding raised to the height of sixty feet at the Ruabon works, thus enabling him to work on a gallery then view the effect of the modelling from ground level. A few of the more prestigious works were carried out by specialists including the London sculptor Harry Bates, who was responsible for the statue of Queen Victoria over the main entrance, and W. S. Frith, who sculpted the figure of *Justice* on the main gable, and also undertook figurative modelling to the designs of Walter Crane.

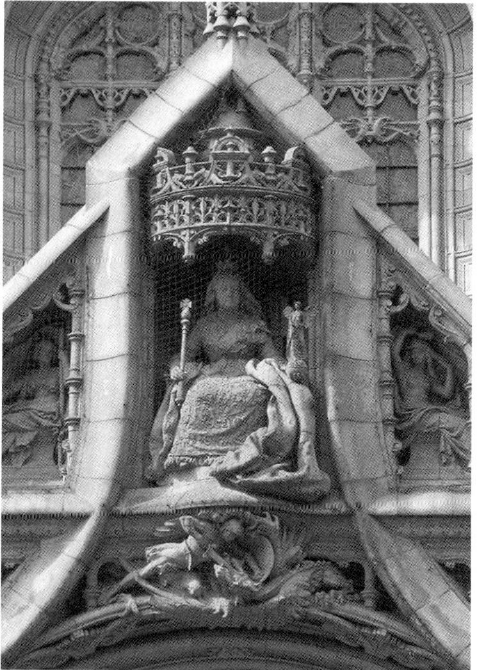

Fig 286.

The grand entrance is somewhat compromised by the usual security precautions, but once inside, the Great Hall is a breathtaking space dominated by two matching, ornate arched entrances massively surmounted by lions and unicorns supporting the Royal Arms. The window tracery is of course red, which makes for interesting junctions with the ochre terracotta of the interior. Decoration is mainly at the level above the entrance, and continues around the walls with a series of oriel-like openings separating the huge stained glass windows. Low passageways, defined by ochre terracotta arches receding into the distance, lead on to a square toplit crossing whose terracotta bears the words: 'Thou shalt not bear false witness against thy neighbour'. This is a truly powerful building, the force of law made palpable.

From the Law Courts, head south along the west side of Corporation Street, crossing Newton Street, to find (at 153-161) **County Buildings**, also known as the Dean & Pitman Building or Murdoch & Pitman Chambers. Of pale red brick with light red and buff terracotta by Gibbs & Canning, County Buildings (1896-7) was designed by Joseph Crouch and Edmund Butler to cater for A. R. Dean, furnishers, and Pitman's Birmingham Vegetarian Hotel and Restaurant Limited. The activities of the occupiers are reflected in the main feature of the facade, a buff terracotta frieze over the ground floor depicting diners at table to the right, and carpenters at work to the left. This was by Benjamin Creswick, as was the buff terracotta allegorical figure group (representing Birmingham and Industry) on the gable.

Continue southward along Corporation Street, looking for UNION STREET on the left, which is connected to Union Passage by the **City Arcade** (1898-1901, architects Newton & Cheatle); originally there were four covered alleyways but the other three were demolished in 1971. Its external decoration includes a frieze of fantastic creatures in Doulton's buff terracotta, and within is a green and blue faience balustrade formed of entwined beasts; the sculptor throughout was W. J. Neatby. At the bottom of Corporation Street turn right into NEW STREET; the second block on the right (at 41-42a) is **Newton Chambers** (or Central Buildings), bordering Cannon Street. It was built in 1899 by architects Essex, Nichol and Goodman using buff block terracotta from the Hathern Station Brick and Terra Cotta Co. Interior tiling and murals from the original Kardomah café appear to have been lost in a 1998 refurbishment.

Further along New Street on the right is TEMPLE STREET and the **Trocadero** pub, built in 1883 but with a pretty, creamy-yellow faience and mosaic facade dating from soon after 1902 when the premises were sold to The Trocadero Ltd. The faience was made by Maw & Co and designed by John Windsor Bradburn, Head of the Faience Department at Maw's.[8] The Trocadero was shown in the firm's catalogue published around 1905, which referred to the frieze bearing the pub's name as being of 'lustrous mosaics, richly iridescent'. Just across New Street is the bold white faience facade of the **Piccadilly Arcade**, built in 1909-10 as the Picture House and converted to a shopping arcade in 1926. Continue west along New Street to return to the start of the central tour, Victoria Square.

Aston

In the best chamber (red room) of the Jacobean mansion **Aston Hall** (1618-35), Aston Park, TRINITY ROAD, is a fire surround containing 45 Liverpool tin-glazed tiles in purple and white. It probably dates from the redecoration and refurbishment of the Hall carried out between the 1740s and the 1760s by Sir Lister Holte, and could therefore be a rare surviving example of an original installation. The fireplace in the green Kidderminster-stuff chamber also has a tiled surround from the same period. Just west of Aston Park in WITTON ROAD is the **R. C. Church of the Sacred Heart and St Margaret Mary** (1922, architects Harrison & Cox), built in red and purplish brick with lavish grey terracotta trimmings; a campanile-style tower was added to the church in 1934. On the tower is a seven feet high grey terracotta statue of Christ designed by the architect George Cox and modelled by John Evans, chief modeller at Gibbs & Canning; it was his last major work for the firm.[9]

In the centre of Aston, close to the railway station, is the **Britannia PH**, 287 LICHFIELD ROAD. It was rebuilt in 1898-1900 by the architects Wood & Kendrick for Mitchells & Butlers, its facade combining rich brown faience and buff terracotta, with a terracotta figure of Britannia topping the central pediment. The tiling, by Maw & Co, can be seen in the public bar, on the stairs and in the passages, where Lewis F. Day designed the frieze tiles.[10] On the far side of the railway bridge is the **Swan & Mitre PH**, Lichfield Road, built in 1898-9 by architects James and Lister Lea for the Holt Brewery Company. Although the pub has been altered, a substantial amount of original tiling, probably by Minton Hollins, is still in place and has been restored. Also on Lichfield Road are the

Prince of Wales, with much wall tiling, and (just north of the station at the junction with Waterworks Street) the remains of the brown faience facade of the now-derelict **Church Tavern** (1900-1). Its colourful tiled interior, by Maw's, was one of the best in Birmingham.

Finally to the most famous of Birmingham's ceramic pubs, the **Bartons Arms**, 152 High Street, Aston (actually the A34, on the cusp between Aston and Lozells). It was built in 1899-1901 for Mitchells & Butlers, the architect being one Mr Brassington from the James and Lister Lea practice (Fig 287). The opulent tiled interior, once populated by customers of the nearby Aston Hippodrome, includes a tile painting depicting a hunting scene (in the staircase hall); there is a Minton Hollins trade tile on the wall to the right of the bar in the smoke room, where replacment tiles dating from alterations made around 1969 may also be seen. Wonderful ironwork, woodwork and stained glass complete this magnificent interior. Following many years of uncertainty about its future, and nearly two years of closure, the Bartons Arms was bought by Oakham Ales of Peterborough in 2002; after restoration work, the pub reopened in early 2003.

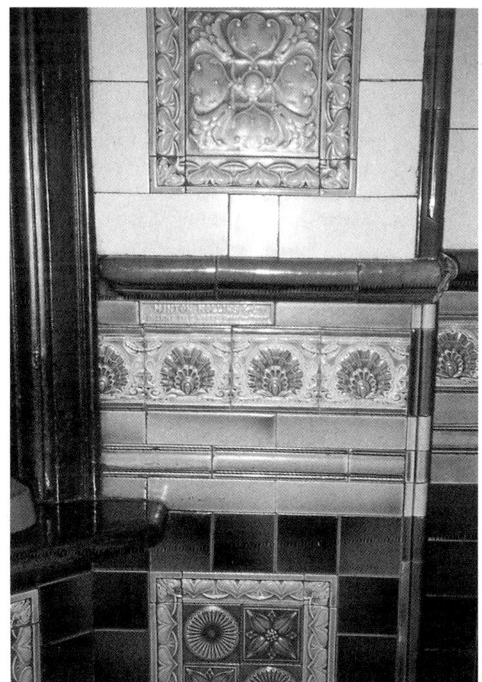

Fig 287.

Balsall Heath

On Moseley Road is **Moseley Road Swimming Pool**, opened as the Public Baths in 1907 and currently in poor condition; the architects were William Hale & Son. Terracotta for the ornate exterior was provided by Jabez Thompson & Co, a firm of brick, roof tile and terracotta manufacturers from Northwich in Cheshire. The interior is rich in glazed brickwork, much of it patterned; this was supplied by Rufford & Co and the Stourbridge Glazed Brick Co, and Doulton faience was also used in the building.

Digbeth

The works of custard makers Alfred Bird & Sons (now known as the **Custard Factory**) on High Street Deritend (A41) was built around 1901 using red brick and, unusually, Doulton's buff Carraraware dressings. There is some good detailing including much lettering.[11] On Alcester Street, running south of this major highway, is the red brick cliff of the **Chamberlain Hotel**, built in 1903 as a working man's hostel. It became a Rowton House, providing accommodation for the homeless, before conversion to an hotel in 1993. Buff terracotta dressings include two large cherubs on the porte cochere; inside, the original dining room retains its pale blue and white glazed brick geometric-patterned dado.

The hotel is at the junction with Moseley Street, on which stands (at number 210) the **Market Tavern**, built in 1899-1900 by James and Lister Lea for the Holt Brewery. There is much Minton wall tiling inside, and the pub is very similar to the **White Swan**, two blocks north at 276 Bradford Street. This was built by the same architects in 1899-1900, but for Ansells Brewery, and also features floor-to-ceiling Minton tiling. Terracotta dressings for both pubs were supplied by the Hathern Station Brick and Terra Cotta Co. There is more Minton work at the **Woodman**, 106 Albert Street, which lies north of the A41, just on the eastern edge of the city centre and close to Millennium Point; the pub was built by James and Lister Lea for Ansells in 1896-7. The striking polychrome sculpture above the doorway of the nearby Gun Barrel Proof House, Banbury Street, is apparently of stone rather than Coade stone.

Edgbaston

The **Church of St Mary and St Ambrose** (1897-8, architect J. A. Chatwin) stands on the Pershore Road just north of the major junction with Edgbaston Road. It has excellent bright red terracotta dressings, manufacturer unknown, and a spire in what appears to be glazed red brick. The **Edgbaston Cricket Centre** (2000), on the Warwickshire County Cricket Ground site in EDGBASTON ROAD, can be seen just to the east of the church. The artwork for its terracotta rain screen, which forms the end wall, was designed by Mark Renn and Mick Thacker, and includes a poem by Simon Rae and an image of the globe. A quarter-mile north-east of the cricket ground, almost in Balsall Heath, is the **Edward Road Baptist Church** (1899), with excellent ochre terracotta ornament almost Moorish in its elaboration.

Erdington

The **Red Lion** (1899, architects Wood & Kendrick), STATION ROAD, Erdington B23 has a fine Craven Dunnill bar front, with intricate floral relief moulded tiles, wreaths and ribbons in pink, green, mustard and soft grey on a beige background (Fig 288). The whole design, with the upper part curving outward, is identical to the bar front at the Crown, Belfast; both were shown in an early twentieth century Craven Dunnill catalogue.

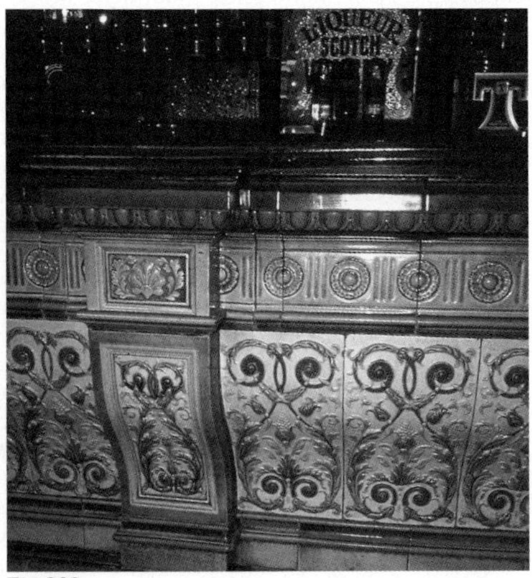

Fig 288.

Five Ways

Just beyond Five Ways, on the south-western fringe of the city centre, is the **Birmingham Chamber of Commerce and Industry** (1958, architect John Madin), a T-shaped office block at the junction of HARBORNE ROAD and Highfield Road; in the entrance foyer is a richly coloured abstract mosaic mural (1960) designed by John Piper; it measures around 10′ high by 16′ wide, and is signed by the artist on a single tessera near the bottom right hand corner. Although still very much in use, the building is currently (2004) under threat of demolition.

Handsworth

The **Red Lion** (1901-2), 270 SOHO ROAD, built by James and Lister Lea for the Holt Brewery Company, has a Hathernware facade and a spectacular tiled staircase hall. To the west is the **New Inns** (1881, extended in the early 1900s), HOLYHEAD ROAD, with tiling by Maw's including some De Morgan-style tiles set into the panelling of the staircase hall.

Hodge Hill

The **Church of St Philip and St James** (1967-8, architect Martin Purdy), HODGE HILL COMMON, built to act firstly as a social centre, has an unusual cubic font with glazed ceramic panels on each side. The floor and wall tiling was supplied by Cotswold Tile.[12]

Jewellery Quarter

Throughout the Jewellery Quarter, which lies about half a mile north-west of the city centre, there are numerous buildings with bits and pieces of ceramic decoration, for instance the faience-clad entrance to the **Gwenda Works** (1913), LEGGE LANE, and the (supposedly) terracotta pelican topping the **Pelican Works**, GREAT HAMPTON STREET, which was built around 1868.[13] However, the major ceramic locations are near the Jewellery Quarter Metro Station and clustered around Constitution Hill (just north of Snow Hill Station), where this mini-perambulation begins.

One of the best-known buildings in the Jewellery Quarter is **Sale's Works** (1895-6) at 1-7 CONSTITUTION HILL. This flat-iron shaped former die-sinking works, with its domed openwork corner tower, has a tremendous range of bright red terracotta ornament. On Constitution Hill itself is the **Bismillah Building**, a former electroplating works, with a good red brick and terracotta facade. Now go left into Henrietta Street to pass beneath the Snow Hill Viaduct, turning right on to LIVERY STREET to see the **Vaughton Gothic Works** (1902, architect Sidney H. Vaughton) with its excellent terracotta details, especially the lettering. Turn left down Cox Street to reach St Paul's Square, then head west via Caroline Street and Warstone Lane to find the Jewellery Quarter Clock Tower.

Opposite, on the corner of WARSTONE LANE and Vyse Street, is the **Rose Villa Tavern** (1919-20, by architects Wood & Kendrick for Mitchells & Butlers), with a fine tile and faience interior by Carter's of Poole illustrating a midway point in the transition from vivid Victorian and Edwardian colour to the restrained decor of the interwar years. The theme is classical, with multicoloured swags along the frieze, hefty chunks of cream faience and a single pictorial panel (there were more) showing a group of dancing maidens.

King's Heath

Highbury Hall (1879-80), YEW TREE ROAD was designed for Joseph Chamberlain, MP and Mayor of Birmingham, by the unrelated John H. Chamberlain of the practice Martin & Chamberlain. It was Joseph Chamberlain's home during 1880-1914, and is now a conference centre. There are a few encaustic tiles dotted about the exterior, but it is in the hugely rich interiors where the real ceramic interest lies, with transfer printed dust-pressed tiles set into the panelled walls of the Great Hall and above the dado in the stairwell, and a variety of tiled fire surrounds throughout the house, some with hand-painted tiles.[14]

Kingstanding

One of the most spectacular and architecturally significant interwar cinemas was the former **Odeon** (1934-5, now Mecca), at the junction of KING'S ROAD and Kettlehouse Road, Kingstanding. It was designed by the architect J. Cecil Clavering of the Harry Weedon practice, and was the first Odeon to display all the elements which became associated with the Odeon style including a faience facade, rounded corners and a prominent vertical feature, in this case a triple fin. The buff and polished black faience was supplied by Shaws of Darwen.

Ladywood

In an isolated position on the middle ring road roundabout at the top of Ladywood Middleway is **Spring Hill Library** (1893), ICKNIELD STREET. One of the city's many municipal buildings by Martin & Chamberlain, its striking red terracotta detail includes traceried windows, coats of arms, angels and winged lions, as well as an extravagant clock tower. About a mile south in Ladywood proper is **St George's Church of England School**, PLOUGH AND HARROW ROAD, where Jeffrey Salter's buff and grey abstract ceramic cross (1970) overlooks the playground.

Lozells

The **Gunmakers Arms**, GERRARD STREET (not far west of the Bartons Arms, see Aston) was designed by the architect Matthew Butcher and built in 1902-3 for Ansells. Apart from some relatively run-of-the-mill wall tiling, its outstanding feature is the curving Craven Dunnill bar front of relief moulded tiles featuring grotesque heads, ribbons and garlands.

Half mile to the west is **St Mary's Convent of Mercy**, 98 HUNTER'S ROAD, designed by A. W. N. Pugin and built during 1840-1. There are Minton tiles in two locations: a pavement dating from 1860-2 in an aisle of the main chapel and, more significantly, tiles installed in the chapel in 1840-1 which have been relaid in the McAuley Oratoria (named after Catherine McAuley, founder of the Sisters of Mercy). Several designs in the latter pavement appear in Minton's *Earliest Pattern Book* (which just pre-dated the firm's first printed catalogue of 1842), and there are also armorial tiles relating to John Talbot, 16th Earl of Shrewsbury, a benefactor of the foundation.[15] The tiles are mentioned in a rare surviving letter from Pugin to Herbert Minton, dated 19th September 1840.[16]

Moseley

Right in the middle of Moseley is the tall terracotta clock tower of the **Fighting Cocks PH**, ST MARY'S ROW; it was built in 1898-9 for the Holt Brewery Company by architects Newton & Cheatle, and is now known as the Goose. Inside is standard Craven Dunnill wall tiling; two large hand-painted tile panels of local scenes, thought to have been lost during 1980s alterations, were revealed again during 1991 restoration work.

Nechells

Allegorical terracotta relief panels by Benjamin Creswick run along the facade of **Bloomsbury Public Library** (1891-3, Cossins & Peacock), NECHELL'S PARKWAY. Another Creswick terracotta panel, in this case a coat of arms, can be seen on the former **Nechells Public Baths** (1910, now a community centre), NECHELLS PARK ROAD.

New Oscott

St Mary's College, New Oscott, the seminary for the R. C. Diocese of Birmingham, was founded in 1794 and moved to its present parkland site (on the junction of Chester Road and COLLEGE ROAD, south-west of Sutton Coldfield) in 1835, the early buildings being designed by the architect Joseph Potter of Lichfield. A. W. N. Pugin was associated with the College from 1837, furnishing and decorating the chapel, which was consecrated in 1838, and creating several magnificent interiors which included early Minton encaustic tile pavements dating from around 1840. Pugin's work at Oscott was crucial to the development of his career; exposing the seminarians to the power of gothic revival architecture and decoration allowed his influence to spread rapidly throughout the Catholic church.[17]

Winson Green

The exterior of the grade II* listed **Bellefield PH**, 36 WINSON STREET, is completely unremarkable, but its interior is a revelation, with colourful tiling in the public bar (by Carter's of Poole and possibly dating from 1913 or 1922) and the smoke room, where the green floor-to-ceiling Minton's tilework (probably installed in 1910) includes moulded frames for a series of engravings. In autumn 2003 the Bellefield was closed and boarded up, and the Victorian bar back was stolen in spring 2004; however, the pub has changed ownership and the interior is to be fully restored.

COVENTRY

Much of central Coventry was devasted during the Blitz of 1940, the Cathedral itself being burnt out on the night of the 14th November 1940. Following this, Coventry was the first English city to embark on a comprehensive scheme for rebuilding its centre and suburbs, the plan for the city centre being produced in 1941 and revised in 1952. Its hub was a new shopping precinct, whose axis was pedestrianised in 1955, just before construction work began on the new **Cathedral of St Michael** (architect Sir Basil Spence, 1956-62) in PRIORY STREET, to the east of the precinct. The staggering display of decorative artwork in the Cathedral includes a mosaic-decorated ciment fondu panel (1960-1) by Steven Sykes, behind the altar in the Gethsemane Chapel, but no tilework as such.[18] In contrast, the shopping precinct boasts two tiled installations, the earlier in BROADGATE, the central square, its 1950s proportions still clear (as are those of the entire shopping precinct) despite later alterations. High on the wall of **Broadgate House**, on the south side of the square, is the *Godiva and Peeping Tom Clock* (sculptor Trevor Tennant, 1953). On the hour, Godiva emerges astride a white horse and reveals nearly all to Peeping Tom, who pops out cuckoo-clock style above, beneath a clockface; Godiva's backdrop is a panel of Carter's blue and white pattern-making tiles.[19]

Head downhill and west to the far end of the LOWER PRECINCT (1957-60). Just inside the Lidice Place entrance is the **Cullen Mural**, a superb pictorial tile mural designed in 1958 by the architect and town planner Gordon Cullen (1914-94) and made by Carter's of Poole (Fig 289).[20] It was commissioned in 1957 by the City Planning & Redevelopment Committee on the recommendation of Arthur Ling, chief architect to the corporation, to illustrate the spirit in which the reconstruction of the city was undertaken, and was originally sited on the ramp entrance to the Lower Precinct.[21] Redevelopment of the Lower Precinct in 2002 resulted in the mural, which had suffered from neglect (as well as the loss during the 1970s of the part showing a map of medieval Coventry), being restored and relocated. The restoration was supervised by Lesley Durbin of the Jackfield Conservation Studio, and involved cutting the mural into sections complete with its heavy concrete backing, then cleaning; matching replacement tiles for the base of the mural were supplied by Craven Dunnill.[22] The mural, which combines tube-lined and screen-printed tiles, is one of the best early British postwar tile murals still extant, and is certainly the most accessible of the few remaining, its strong colours and powerful forms dominating the brightly-lit entrance walkway.[23] It shows images relating to Coventry from prehistoric times up to the 1950s, culminating with the city's postwar masterplan on a detached section; especially attractive are an assortment of beady-eyed dinosaurs and a variety of bicycles representing the cycle industry.

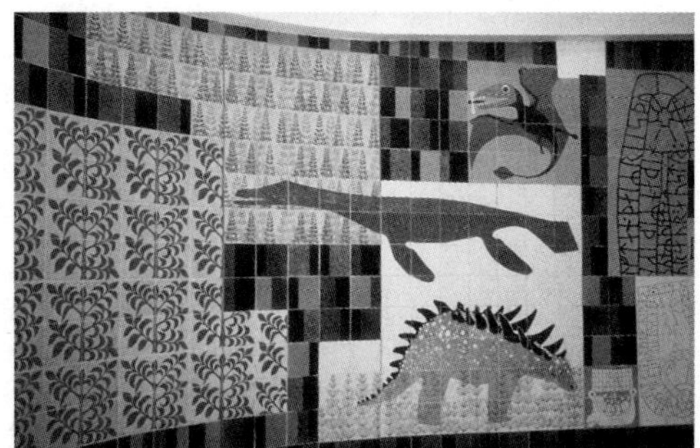

Fig 289.

Return through the precinct to find medieval **Holy Trinity Church**, which stands between Broadgate and the Cathedral off PRIORY ROW. There is a good Minton encaustic tile pavement in the sanctuary, with letter tiles in gold on royal blue fronting the risers of the three steps up to the altar; all this tiling dates from the 1854-6 restoration by Sir George Gilbert Scott. Running north from Holy Trinity and Priory Row is the walkway created during 2001-3 as part of the Phoenix Initiative, Coventry's millennium project. This involved the excavation of the medieval site of St Mary's Priory and the construction of the Priory Visitor Centre; finds on display include a well-preserved section of fourteenth century floor tiling from the refectory.[24] Some of the locally-made tiles show armorial motifs.

South of Holy Trinity in BAYLEY LANE is **St Mary's Guildhall**, with medieval floor tiles in the oriel window on the west of the spectacular Great Hall. Upstairs, the Treasury is floored with re-laid medieval tiles which probably came from the Great Hall, and thus would date from the late fourteenth or early fifteenth century. Just south-east in JORDAN WELL is the former Odeon Cinema, which was built in 1928-30 and opened as the Gaumont Picture Palace in 1931; it is now Coventry University's **Ellen Terry Building**. The architect was Percy Bartlett, chief assistant in the Bristol practice of William Henry Watkins, which designed four Gaumonts during 1931-2.[25] Bartlett's impressive, basically white, modernist faience facade has colourful egyptianate pilaster capitals and a green faience frame to the large central area of fenestration. Next to the old cinema - and in contrasting Edwardian baroque style - is an ornate white faience facaded shop, topped with a balustrade and gleaming dome.

Rowley's Green

About a mile and a half of the walls bounding the dual carriageway PHOENIX WAY, about three miles north of the city centre, are faced with over 1.5 million bricks to a design by Derek Fisher. The colours and patterns, which reflect local history and culture, have a vertical emphasis in order to be seen clearly by drivers passing at speed.

Westwood Heath

In its early years, the site of the **University of Warwick**, GIBBET HILL ROAD, was a sea of red mud into which white Twintiles fell from the modernist, tile-clad Library and Science Buildings, erected by the progressive architectural practice Yorke, Rosenberg & Mardall (YRM). This was not how it was meant to be. Shaw-Hathernware's 9"x3" Twintiles were widely used in the 1960s to face concrete structures such as railway stations and shopping centres. White Twintiles became a YRM hallmark and the iconic University of Warwick Library won an RIBA award in 1967, the year before completion of the initial phase of building on the Warwick campus. In February 1969, however, the first signs of distress appeared when an area of Twintiles on the YRM-designed Rootes Hall was seen to be bowing out. Worse was to follow. A large slab of tiles and backing soon fell from the Library, and a survey of the campus - which had been intended as a showcase for tile-clad architecture - revealed numerous areas of concern.

For some time students and staff went about their business in buildings hung with scaffolding, fencing and safety nets, as remedial work was delayed by disputes over liability and the campus became a prime test-case. Litigation dragged on until 1988 and the University eventually had to fund most of the remedial work itself. After overcladding in 1987-8, all that can be seen today of the white-tiled grid blocks, the original architectural conception, is the pristine pair of the Humanities Building and the Physics Building. The latter, completed in 1969, was given special aluminium copings to prevent water accumulation around windows; its appearance shows that properly fixed and protected Twintiles could survive in good condition.[26]

A mile or so north-west of the University at 320 WESTWOOD HEATH ROAD is the **Cable & Wireless College** (1993, architects MacCormac Jamieson Prichard), whose concrete facade is topped by a wave-contoured roof of Hathernware's high-gloss mottled blue faience slabs. This unique roof, which comprises over 27,000 extruded slabs, reflects the changing colours of the sky.

GALLEY COMMON

St Peter's Church in Galley Common, a few miles west of Nuneaton, was built in 1909 to the design of the influential arts and crafts architect Percy R. Morley Horder (1870-1944). Sir Alfred Hickman, owner of Haunchwood Colliery, partly funded the building, which is an aisled hall with rendered walls of hollow terracotta blocks apparently made in Italy at Rimini (rather than local Stanley Brothers terracotta). The blocks were left bare on the inside walls. The building has been under repair since 2001; amongst other constructional defects, the walls have cracked and distorted.

LAPWORTH

The Ireton Bathroom at **Packwood House** (NT) is lined with mainly seventeenth and eighteenth century blue and white Dutch tiles depicting children's games, soldiers, landscapes and biblical scenes, along with a few English eighteenth century delftware tiles. The tiles were probably installed during the 1930s.

LOWER SHUCKBURGH

St John the Baptist Church was built for George Shuckburgh of nearby Shuckburgh Hall in 1864, soon after he returned from the Crimean War, which ended in 1856. The architect was John Croft, who seems to have been asked to provide a colourful, orientally-inspired building, a contrast to the existing church at Upper Shuckburgh (see below), near the Hall, with its collection of family monuments. Croft's polychromatic interior combined limestone, blue brick and red terracotta, the latter also appearing as coffering in the vaulting; the tower and chancel vaults were clad in mosaic tiling. The Moorish arches, with their serrated edges, are of red brick and hollow red terracotta blocks, making this something of a 'pot church'. Croft may have come across architectural terracotta in Lincolnshire (John Blashfield's works moved to Stamford in 1859), where he built All Saints Church, Cold Hanworth in 1861-2; this had Minton tile pavements as well as much exposed brick. It appears that Lower Shuckburgh Church is an example of the sporadic use of terracotta which occurred in the 1860s and 1870s, between the 'pot churches' of the 1840s-1850s and the later vogue for terracotta decoration.[27]

NUNEATON

Stanley Brothers produced terracotta at their Nuneaton works between 1881 and around 1920. On the southern edge of Nuneaton in HEATH END ROAD are **Sunflower Cottages**, the last remaining pair of several cottages built for Stanley's workers, with much red terracotta ornament including a lion below each finial and the terracotta equivalent of bargeboards. A good example of ornamental buff terracotta can be seen in the town centre at **Barclays Bank** (1896), 7 MARKET PLACE, which was probably built by Stanley's themselves; the architects were the West Bromwich practice Wood & Kendrick, best known for their public house work.

The home of Reginald Stanley (1838-1914), founder of the firm, was **Manor Court** (now a nursing home), MANOR COURT ROAD, which has much Stanley's terracotta decoration, some of which is illustrated in the firm's catalogue. Most attractive is a horse's head on the stables (now a flat in the grounds), supposedly modelled on one of Reg Stanley's favourite horses. Off the same road is **Manor Hospital** (1893), also with a good display of Stanley's terracotta wares, while the chancel pavement of **St Mary's Church**, Manor Court Road, includes fragmental remains of medieval tiles in the form of a wheel of fortune. Finally at ABBEY GREEN, at the north end of Manor Court Road, is a **ceramic column** (of blue glazed bricks and terracotta sunflowers) by Tracey Heyes dating from 2002; it was put up as part of the regeneration of the Abbey Green area.

STRATFORD-UPON-AVON

Right in the centre of Stratford, on the corner of CHAPEL STREET and Ely Street, is the **HSBC Bank**, built for the Birmingham Banking Company in 1885 (architects Harris, Martin & Harris). Its elaborate external decoration includes fifteen red terracotta relief panels showing detailed scenes from Shakespeare plays; these were designed by the sculptor Samuel Barfield of Leicester, who produced terracotta reliefs for the Leicestershire Banking Company's building in Leicester during the early 1870s and worked on the Birmingham School of Art in the early 1880s. In **Red Lion Court**, a modern shopping precinct, is a set of three tile murals showing the former Flower's Brewery (closed 1968); further from the centre, carved into the wall of the **Fire Station** in MASON ROAD, is a brick relief of a fireman (1951) by the local artist Walter Ritchie (1919-97).

To the south is **Holy Trinity Church** (the burial place of William Shakespeare, restored 1888-92 and 1898), OLD TOWN, where several eight-inch armorial tiles are set into the encaustic tile pavement of the sanctuary. Continue by the river along WATERSIDE to the **Royal Shakespeare Theatre** (1932, architect Elizabeth Scott), which has five allegorical brick reliefs by the artist Eric Kennington (1888-1960) on its front facade; the bricks were made by S. & E. Collier's of Reading. Nearby is the old theatre (1874-9), now the **Theatre Museum**; a wing containing a library and art gallery was added in the early 1880s, and on its facade are three terracotta reliefs dating from 1886 and portraying *Comedy*, *History* and *Tragedy*; the sculptor was Paul Kummer (1882-1913).

SUTTON COLDFIELD

Half a mile south of the town centre is the Odeon Cinema, Birmingham Road, a mountainous faience-clad structure built in 1935-6 and designed by J. Cecil Clavering, assistant in the Harry Weedon practice which produced ten new Odeons for Oscar Deutsch's circuit during 1936.[28] Its buff faience cladding was supplied by Shaws of Darwen and covered most of the facade, apart from a huge brick slab tower from which a faience fin protruded. The Sutton Coldfield contract was one of thirty-one cinema commissions (including seven Weedon-designed Odeons) carried out by Shaws during 1935-6.[29]

WARWICK

There are late fourteenth century tiles, probably originating from the Chilvers Coton tilery near Nuneaton, in the apartments of Guy's Tower (completed 1394), **Warwick Castle**. Many of the tiles, which have a distinctive pinkish body, bear heraldic designs including the emblem of Warwickshire. The pavement, which was revealed in 2000 and has been conserved by the Jackfield Conservation Studio, is one of the few such intact floors to have been found at a secular site. In the town itself, there is a Godwin tile pavement in the Beauchamp Chapel of **St Mary's Church**.

Warwickshire Roundup

The chancel of St John Baptist Church, **Brinklow** has unusual Victorian tiling. There are three medieval tiles on the ledge of the north-east nave window at the Church of St Nicholas and St Peter, **Curdworth**; one tile bears the alphabet (with lines running right to left), another a king's head and the third a flower. A Stanley Brothers 1897 Queen Victoria Diamond Jubilee terracotta plaque may be seen on the outside of Jubilee House, 17 Kenilworth Road, **Knowle**. There are decorative wall tiles either side of the wooden reredos at St John the Baptist Church, **Lea Marston**; there is also a Coade stone monument to Mrs Adderley (1784). On the east wall of St George's Church, **Lower Brailes**, are six memorial tiles of a slightly smaller size than normal. There is a brick sculpture entitled *Rugby's Industrial Heritage* (2000) by John McKenna on the outside of the public toilets in North Street, **Rugby**. The interesting sanctuary pavement of the Church of St John the Baptist in the Wilderness, **Upper Shuckburgh**, is probably by Minton's.

In addition, medieval tiles may be found at the following churches: All Saints, Burton Dassett; St Mary and St Bartholomew, Hampton in Arden; St Nicholas, Kenilworth; St Michael, Maxstoke; Our Lady, Merevale; St Botolph, Newbold-on-Avon; St Editha, Polesworth; St Mary Magdalene, Tanworth-in-Arden; All Saints, Weston-on-Avon and St Peter, Wormleighton.

References

1. Arthur Sadler, 'Victorian Commemorative Plaques', *Leicestershire Historian*, (1999) 35, pp1-2.
2. George T. Noszlopy, *Public Sculpture of Warwickshire, Coventry & Solihull*. Public Sculpture of Britain (Liverpool University Press, Liverpool, 2003).
3. Lynn Pearson, *Minton Tiles in the Churches of Staffordshire* 2000, Tiles and Architectural Ceramics Society.
4. John Swift, *Changing Fortunes: The Birmingham School of Art Building, 1880-1995* (Article Press, Birmingham, 1996).
5. Brian Doolan, *The Pugins and the Hardmans* (Archdiocese of Birmingham Historical Commission, Birmingham, 2004).
6. Alan Swale, *Tour Notes: Birmingham and District* (TACS, 1989).
7. George T. Noszlopy, *Public Sculpture of Birmingham* (Liverpool University Press, Liverpool, 1998).
8. Lezli Richer, 'Training for Industrial Design and the Decline of Maw & Co', *Glazed Expressions*, (1996) 33, pp3-5.
9. *Birmingham Post*, 1st June 1935.
10. Alan Crawford, Michael Dunn and Robert Thorne, *Birmingham Pubs 1880-1939* (Alan Sutton, Gloucester, 1986).
11. Paul Atterbury and Louise Irvine, *The Doulton Story* (Royal Doulton Tableware, Stoke on Trent, 1979), p99.
12. 'Church and youth centre', *Architects' Journal*, 150, 8th October 1969, pp875-886.
13. John Cattell and Bob Hawkins, *The Birmingham Jewellery Quarter* (English Heritage, London, 2000).
14. Deborah Skinner, *Tour Notes: Highbury and Birmingham* (TACS, 1986).
15. Willem Irik, 'An 1840 letter from Augustus Welby Pugin to Herbert Minton', *Glazed Expressions*, (2002) 44, pp11-12.
16. Willem Irik, 'An 1840 letter from Augustus Welby Pugin to Herbert Minton', *Glazed Expressions*, (2001) 43, p4.
17. Paul Atterbury and Clive Wainwright, *Pugin: A Gothic Passion* (Yale University Press, New Haven and London, 1994), pp79-80.
18. Louise Campbell, ed., *To Build a Cathedral: Coventry Cathedral, 1945-1962* (University of Warwick, 1987).
19. Carter Archive, Poole Museum Service, CP637.
20. Carter Archive, Poole Museum Service, CP153.

England

21. Alan Swale, 'The Gordon Cullen Ceramic Murals: Lower Precinct, Coventry. Part 1: Background to the removal and reinstallation of the mural', *Glazed Expressions*, (2003) 46, pp14-15.
22. Alan Swale, 'The Gordon Cullen Ceramic Murals: Lower Precinct, Coventry. Part 2: The removal, re-installation and restoration of the mural', *Glazed Expressions*, (2003) 47, pp14-15.
23. Lynn Pearson, 'Postwar Tile Panels: An Endangered Species?' *Glazed Expressions*, (2003) 46, pp3-5.
24. Margaret Rylatt and Paul Mason, *The Archaeology of the Medieval Cathedral and Priory of St Mary, Coventry* (City Development Directorate, Coventry City Council, Coventry, 2003).
25. Richard Gray, *Cinemas in Britain: One Hundred Years of Cinema Architecture* (Lund Humphries Publishers, London, 1996).
26. Michael Stratton, *Clad is bad? The relationship between structural and ceramic facing materials*, in *Structure and Style: Conserving Twentieth Century Buildings*, ed Michael Stratton (E. & F. N. Spon, London, 1997), pp164-92.
27. Michael Stratton, *The Terracotta Revival* (Victor Gollancz, London, 1993), p66.
28. Allen Eyles, *Odeon Cinemas 1: Oscar Deutsch Entertains Our Nation* (Cinema Theatre Association, London, 2002).
29. *List of Contracts executed 1935-1036*, (Shaws Glazed Brick Co Ltd, Darwen, 1936).

Wiltshire

Wiltshire was of crucial importance in the history of English tiles as it was at Clarendon Palace, near Salisbury, that the earliest two-colour tile pavement was manufactured between 1240 and 1244; a pavement was ordered from a Westminster tiler in 1237 but it is unknown whether this was actually made. The surviving tiles from the Clarendon Palace pavement are now in the British Museum, but an important Wessex pavement dating from around 1260 remains in the muniment room of Salisbury Cathedral; however, its preservation beneath boarding means access is difficult. The delightful but much later renaissance-inspired tile pavement at Lacock Abbey was taken up in the nineteenth century and is in storage at the house, whose entrance hall sports a series of unusual terracotta sculptures executed in 1755-6.

Wiltshire has many churches with Victorian tiling, notably those of the architect Thomas Henry Wyatt (1807-80), who became consulting architect to the Salisbury Diocesan Church Building Association in 1836, and William Butterfield, who restored many churches in the county, installing his typical brand of bright, geometric tile arrangements on floors and walls. There is an exceptional Minton armorial pavement at Wyatt's Cholderton Church (1841-50) and equally exceptional Powell's opus sectile work, some of the best in Britain, at St John the Evangelist, Warminster. However, Wiltshire has little to inspire twentieth-century tile enthusiasts. Suggested reading: TACS Tour Notes *Warminster* (2004). The *Gazetteer* entry for Wiltshire covers the administrative areas of Swindon Borough Council and Wiltshire County Council.

BAVERSTOCK

The 1880-2 restoration by William Butterfield of **St Edith's Church** included the addition of east wall tiling in typical late Butterfield style, with striking colours and a strong geometric pattern.

BRITFORD

St Peter's Church was restored in 1872-3 by G. E. Street; his lavish east wall decoration included Spanish-style tiles below painted murals flanking the window. At Hilmarton, in a similar scheme combining tiles and murals, the cuenca tiles were made by Street's one-time assistant Frederick Garrard (c1838-93) at his Millwall works; it therefore seems likely that the Britford tiles were also by Garrard.

CALNE

For over thirty years, up until 1865, Calne had an evangelical vicar, but his high church successor was not popular with all the congregation and around eighty parishioners, led by members of the Harris family, owners of the town's large bacon factory, eventually left the parish church. The foundation stone of their own **Calne Free Church** in CHURCH STREET was laid in 1867, and the first service was held in 1868; their architect was William Jervis Stent of Warminster. Pevsner's description of the gothic exterior includes the one-word sentence 'Terrible' and the interior would probably have been just as unacceptable: the apse has a geometric tiled pavement and a brown relief-tiled dado around six feet in height, and there are also tile panels bearing hand-painted mottos on scrolls.

CASTLE COMBE

Much of **St Andrew's Church**, MARKET PLACE was pulled down and rebuilt in 1850-1; chancel fittings dating from this period include an encaustic tile pavement with Scrope family armorial tiles and an east wall of colourful glazed tiling.

CHOLDERTON

The Reverend Thomas Mozley, a convinced Tractarian who was also a *Times* leader-writer, became rector of Cholderton in 1836 and soon decided to rebuild **St Nicholas Church**. The work was carried out during 1841-50 by the architect T. H. Wyatt entirely at Mozley's expense; so great was the financial burden, in fact, that Mozley had to resign as rector in 1846, although he continued funding the project until the church was consecrated in 1850. Lavish Minton floor tiles run thoughout the church in a design shown by the firm at the 1851 Great Exhibition; there is a fine representation of the royal coat-of arms in the ante-chapel.[1] The motifs for the modern hassocks were inspired by the tile designs.

DEVIZES

In the MARKET PLACE is the **Bear Hotel**, where over a hundred Bristol-made delftware tiles, dating from around 1750 and including many landscape motifs, are situated behind the main bar. Originally they probably formed the lining of a pantry or buttery.

DITTERIDGE

In 1859-61 the architect and designer E. W. Godwin (1833-86) restored **St Christopher's Church**, most of the work comprising an internal refit. The geometric and encaustic tile pavement, manufactured by Minton Hollins to a design by Godwin, includes triangular black tiles of different sizes and results in a striking overall pattern. E. W. Godwin first specified encaustic tiling in 1854 (for a Bristol church), but his ledgers do not cover the period 1853-8, making Ditteridge his earliest identifiable pavement.[2]

EAST KNOYLE

The chancel decoration of **St Mary's Church** is astounding, with relief plasterwork of biblical scenes designed by the ardent royalist Dean Christopher Wren (father of the architect of St Paul's Cathedral) and executed around 1639 by a local plasterer. In 1876, Sir Arthur Blomfield introduced into this setting a Minton tiled reredos - now found so abhorrent by the congregation that it is covered by curtains - and a Minton encaustic tiled pavement, which is still visible.

FONTHILL GIFFORD

Holy Trinity Church (1866, architect T. H. Wyatt) was built for the local landlord, the Marquess of Westminster, who bought the Fonthill Abbey estate following the collapse of William Beckford's gothic folly tower in 1825. It replaced the church built by Beckford's father in 1748, which had fallen into disrepair. The attractive encaustic tile pavement, featuring mostly nine-tile groups divided by plain black bands, is by Maw & Co; a broken fragment held in the church reveals the 'Benthall Broseley' backmark.

HEYTESBURY

The **Church of St Peter and St Paul** was restored by William Butterfield in 1865-7. The works included paving the nave with Peake's plain Staffordshire tiles, while coloured tiles by Minton's were used as inlays on some walls and the reredos; the encaustic pavement in the chancel was also by Minton's.[3]

HILMARTON

St Laurence Church was restored by G. E. Street during 1879-81; from this period date the panels of cuenca tiles flanking the reredos, with wall paintings above. The tiles were made for Street by Frederick Garrard of Millwall.[4]

LACOCK

Lacock Abbey (NT) was founded in 1229 for Augustinian canonesses; most of its buildings were complete by 1247, although there were later additions. The abbey was dissolved in 1539 and bought by William Sharington (d1553) in the following year; his niece married into the Talbot family, with whom the house remained until 1958. Much of the nunnery survives, with some medieval tiles still *in situ* in the sacristy and the chapter house. The most interesting tiles of this period, however, were those made for William Sharington in the early 1550s, possibly at Lacock itself, and used in conjunction with some traditional designs from the Bristol and Malvern tileries to floor his newly-built south gallery.[5] This pavement was taken up in the nineteenth century but most of the tiles, which reflect Sharington's advanced tastes in design, are still stored at the house.[6] The two-colour tiles, which had their white clay applied as a shallow inlay rather than poured slip, had delicate renaissance-inspired motifs including Sharington's scorpion badge and initials. These high-quality examples are the latest two-colour tiles to which a date can be ascribed, after which the industry declined due to its unfashionably gothic products, rather than a lack of expertise.[7]

The entrance hall of Lacock Abbey was created in 1754-5 for John Ivory Talbot by the gentleman architect Sanderson Miller. Its decoration included a series of canopied gothick niches which were filled with theatrical terracotta statuary by Victor Alexander Sederbach, an otherwise unknown Austrian or German who worked at Lacock during 1755-6. The obscure figures include the foundress of the Abbey, *Death*, and the scapegoat (from the Old Testament).

MARLBOROUGH

The medieval **Church of St Peter and St Paul**, HIGH STREET, was made redundant in 1974 and is now a crafts and exhibition centre. Its chancel was refitted in 1862-3 by the architect T. H. Wyatt, who introduced an elaborate Minton encaustic tiled pavement and lavish east wall decoration including encaustic, majolica and plain tiles (possibly by Maw & Co) with glass and ceramic mosaic and inlaid and painted stone. The east wall scheme was overpainted during the 1960s but cleaned completely in the early 1990s. There are also a few relaid fifteenth century two-colour tiles.

SALISBURY

Salisbury Cathedral was once richly tiled throughout its east arm and into the octagonal chapter house, the latter tiling dating from around 1266 and having an arrangement of wedges radiating out from the central column. The medieval designs and overall layout were replicated in the Minton pavement laid in 1855-6 during the restoration of the chapter house by Henry Clutton and William Burges, thus at least enabling the present-day observer to study a facsimile of the complex medieval arrangement with its eight adjoining mirror-image sections.[8] Most of the original tiling, still apparently in good condition, was simply thrown out, although a group of reset medieval tiles, probably from the chapter house, has been reset in the chapel at the east end of the north presbytery aisle.[9] The Godwin encaustic pavement of 1876 installed by George Gilbert Scott in the choir was destroyed in 1969.

However, one of the best-preserved medieval tile pavements in Europe remains within the Cathedral, mostly out of sight beneath protective boarding in the muniment room (no public access); there are also patches of tiles on the staircase leading up to the muniment room.[10] This octagonal, inlaid tiled floor dates from around 1260 and comprises fifteen different designs of Wessex tiles including lions, griffins and fleur-de-lys; the contrast in appearance between these glazed tiles and the worn tiles of the north presbytery aisle is arresting. The tiles of the muniment room are similar to the Wessex tiles commissioned by Henry III for Clarendon Palace, whose site was just a few miles east of Salisbury. The earliest two-colour tile pavement for which there is both documentary and archaeological evidence was made between 1240 and 1244 at Clarendon Palace for its new chapel.

Opposite the west door of the Cathedral in the King's House at 65 THE CLOSE is the **Salisbury and South Wiltshire Museum**. On the first floor, at the entrance to its ceramics gallery, is a specially-commissioned earthenware tile panel (1985) by designer-makers Wendy Barber and John Hinchcliffe of Charlton Marshall in Dorset. It shows a selection of objects from the Museum's collection; much of the tile painting was carried out by Wendy Barber in the Museum.

Just beyond the east side of the Cathedral Close on EXETER STREET is **St Osmund's R. C. Church**, designed by A. W. N. Pugin and built in 1847-8 to replace the tiny Salisbury chapel where Pugin had been received into the Roman Catholic Church in 1835. Pugin lived in the city during 1834-7, and retained many friends there even after leaving to better his career in London. His vision for St Osmund's was that it should replace the Cathedral, which held the shrine of St Osmund, as the true centre of Catholic faith in Salisbury. His drawings for the church survive, and include a plan which shows designs for three different encaustic floor tiles, one a fleur-de-lys, and their arrangement in the chancel and south aisle.[11] Despite many changes to this pretty little church, most of the tiles, which were manufactured by Minton's, still remain.

WARMINSTER

The **Church of St John the Evangelist**, BOREHAM ROAD, lies on the south-eastern edge of Warminster in Boreham (Fig 290). It was designed by the architect G. E. Street and built in 1864-5 to relieve the pressure of numbers on the parish church; the land was endowed by a local farmer, William Temple, and the funds were raised by public subscription. Following the consecration of St John, gifts of furnishings and other items continued for many years, with Temple's son donating the reredos in 1868 and his daughter, Elizabeth Rule, funding the construction of the baptistery in 1925-6. Its architect was Charles Edwin Ponting (1850-1932), who became Diocesan Surveyor for the Wiltshire part of the Salisbury Diocese in 1883. Ponting was also Diocesan Surveyor for a section of the Bristol Diocese from 1887 and the Dorset half of the Salisbury Diocese from 1892, giving him a district larger than any other diocesan surveyor in England. He became well known for his sympathetic church restorations and the introduction of high-quality arts and crafts fittings; Ponting resigned from the Salisbury Diocese in 1928.[12]

C. E. Ponting appears to have had a strong influence on planning the most notable feature of St John's Church: its collection of opus sectile panels made by Powell's of Whitefriars and donated to the church between 1888 and 1930. The first panels were acquired for the north aisle in

1888, five years after Ponting took over responsibility for the church, and 1893, but the project expanded into a complete decorative scheme in 1911, when the Reverend Brocklebank paid for the opus sectile work in the chancel. He asked C. E. Ponting to plan for similar panels, mainly representing scenes from the life of Christ, on the south and west walls, but following 1915 the impetus behind the scheme appears to have faltered, to be replaced by the idea of building the baptistery at the west end. The final panel, a madonna and child, was installed in 1930 in memory of Elizabeth Rule.[13]

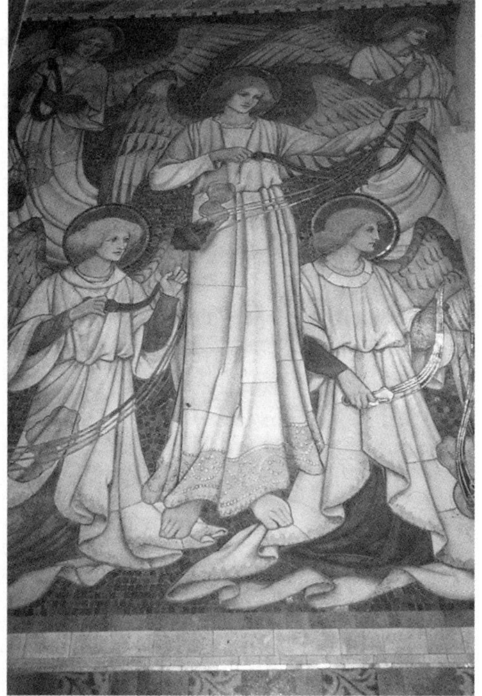

Fig 290.

The sketches and cartoons for most of the substantial panels were supplied by Charles Hardgrave, for many years Powell's highest paid in-house designer, whose speciality was opus sectile and mural decorations. The major panels include the *Annunciation* (1914), the *Nativity* (1912), the *Presentation in the Temple* (1893) and the four archangels flanking the east window. The scenes run from the west end of the north aisle into the chancel roughly in chronological order, although this was not the order in which they were supplied by Powell's, for whom this was clearly a lucrative contract.[14] The interior of this unpretentious church is a revelation, with one of the best displays of opus sectile work in Britain.

On the western edge of Warminster in SAMBOURNE ROAD is a cottage displaying a real curiosity, an 1897 Queen Victoria Golden Jubilee plaque made by Stanley Brothers of Nuneaton; it is of the standard design but has a pale chocolate coloured glaze rather than being the usual plain buff or red terracotta. The *British Clayworker* reported in April 1897 that the firm was making the plaques in glazed ware as well as terracotta, and this is a rare example of the glazed (and presumably more expensive) variety.[15]

Wiltshire Roundup

Polychrome east wall tiling, dating from William Butterfield's 1852-3 restoration, is hidden behind a curtain at the Church of St Mary and St Melor, **Amesbury**. The late nineteenth century reredos at St Mary's Church, **Burton** (actually Nettleton Church) is a Doulton terracotta panel of the *Last Supper* by George Tinworth. The encaustic tile pavement in the chancel of All Saints Church (1861-2), **Chitterne**, was supplied by Minton's.[16] On the porch floor of St Andrew's Church, **Donhead St Andrew**, are medieval tiles with a star motif, and there is a Godwin pavement (probably dating from the 1875 restoration) in the chancel. St Nicholas Church (1844, architect Benjamin Ferrey), **East Grafton**, has a Chamberlain tile pavement. There is a Minton tiled reredos at St Nicholas Church, **Fisherton de la Mere** (now in the care of the Churches Conservation Trust); it may date from the 1861 rebuilding. St John the Baptist Church (1878-81, architect William Butterfield), **Foxham**, has a colourful tiled dado. In the chancel of St Margaret's Church (1846, architect James Thomson), **Leigh Delamere**, is a fine Minton encaustic tile pavement, and there is another Minton pavement at St Katherine's Church (rebuilt 1876-7, architect William Butterfield), **Netherhampton**. The architect G. E. Street restored the chancel of St John Baptist Church, **Pewsey**, in 1861, installing a tile pavement by Maw & Co.[17] The tiled reredos at St Peter's Church, **Pitton**, probably dates from the 1878-80 restoration by Ewan Christian. There are good armorial floor tiles in the mausoleum of J. L. Phipps (d1871) at the Bratton Road Cemetery, **Westbury**. St Mary Magdalene Church, **Winterbourne Monkton**, was rebuilt by William Butterfield in 1877-9 and displays his typical chancel and reredos tiling.

In addition, medieval tiles survive at the following sites: St James Church, Avebury; St Nicholas Church, Huish (on display only, none *in situ*); Malmesbury Abbey (on display only, none *in situ*); St Michael's Church, Mere; St Mary's Church, Stapleford; and St Peter's Church, Winterbourne Stoke.

References

1. RCHME, *Churches of South-East Wiltshire* (HMSO, London, 1987).
2. Catherine Arbuthnott, *E. W. Godwin and Ceramics*, in *E. W. Godwin: Aesthetic Movement Architect and Designer*, ed Susan Weber Soros (Yale University Press, New Haven and London, 1999), pp297-311.
3. *The Builder*, vol 25, 5th October 1867.
4. Philip and Dorothy Brown, 'Cuenca tiles and Frederick Garrard', *Glazed Expressions*, (1993) 26, pp10-11.
5. Elizabeth S. Eames, *Catalogue of Medieval Lead-Glazed Earthenware Tiles in the Department of Medieval and Later Antiquities, British Museum* (British Museum Publications, London, 1980), vol 1, p266.
6. Jane A. Wight, *Mediaeval Floor Tiles* (John Baker, London, 1975), pp153-4.
7. Elizabeth Eames, *English Tilers* (British Museum Press, London, 1992).
8. Christopher Norton, *The Decorative Pavements of Salisbury Cathedral and Old Sarum*, in *Medieval Art and Architecture at Salisbury Cathedral*, eds Laurence Keen and Thomas Cocke (British Archaeological Association, 1996), pp90-105.
9. Jane Cochrane, 'Medieval Tiled Floor Patterns', *TACS Journal*, 5 (1994), pp11-19.
10. Sarah Brown, *Sumptuous and Richly Adorned: The Decoration of Salisbury Cathedral* (HMSO, London, 1999).
11. John Elliott, 'Pugin, St Osmund and Salisbury', *Sarum Chronicle*, 2 (2002), pp45-53.
12. A. Stuart Gray, *Edwardian Architecture: A Biographical Dictionary* (Gerald Duckworth, London, 1985).
13. Personal communication, Sheelagh Wurr, 23rd February 2004.
14. Dennis W. Hadley, *James Powell & Sons: A listing of opus sectile, 1847-1973*, (2001).
15. Arthur Sadler, 'Victorian Commemorative Plaques', *Leicestershire Historian*, (1999) 35, pp1-2.
16. *The Builder*, vol 20, 29th November 1862.
17. *The Builder*, vol 20, 11th January 1862.

Worcestershire

Inside many Worcestershire churches are still significant numbers of medieval tiles made at the Great Malvern tilery. Great Malvern Priory itself has a superb display, including wall tiles which retain their original glaze, and there are interesting medieval armorial tiles at St Giles Church, Bredon, altough these were made at Droitwich. Notable Victorian and turn of the century sites in the county include the Harris and Pearson office building (1888) in Dudley, where the firebrick manufacturers put on an excellent show of their own ceramic building materials. The Richard Eve Memorial (1902, Doulton) in Kidderminster is the country's best extant example of a polychrome faience memorial. In Worcester, George Gilbert Scott's 1864-74 restoration of the Cathedral included the installation of a beautiful Signs of the Zodiac pavement by Godwin's, while the unique Maw's cuenca-tiled waiting room exteriors at the city's Shrub Hill Station date from 1865. Indeed, apart from the Eve memorial and Dudley's massive 1937 Shaws faience Odeon, there is little of ceramic interest in Worcestershire from the twentieth century. Suggested reading: Nicholas A. D. Molyneux and John E. McGregor, *The Medieval Tiles at Great Malvern Priory* (Friends of Great Malvern Priory, 1997). The *Gazetteer* entry for Worcestershire covers the administrative areas of Dudley Metropolitan Borough Council and Worcestershire County Council.

BREDON

St Giles Church has a fine collection of floor tiles, including 86 fourteenth-century heraldic tiles on the sanctuary steps; some of the 39 different coats of arms are clearly visible on the risers. There are also groups depicting the months of the year, and all were probably fired at the Droitwich tilery.[1] The nave is paved with an attractive lozenge tile patchwork in red, yellow and black, the arrangement producing a three-dimensional effect; these tiles are identical to examples found over the border in Gloucestershire at Oxenton Church and nearby Tredington Court. The latter tiles have been found to date from the mid seventeenth to early eighteenth century, thus a probable date of around the late seventeenth century seems appropriate for the Bredon nave pavement.[2]

CALLOW END

Benedictine nuns moved to **Stanbrook Abbey** in 1838; their red-brick church, designed by E. W. Pugin, was built in 1869-71. Originally a Minton & Co tile pavement, which took E. W. Pugin and John Hardman Powell (1827-94) two days to design, ran throughout the church, but only the choir floor survives following re-ordering in 1971.[3] Although the church is a listed building (grade II), the future of the site is in doubt as in 2002 the nuns decided to sell the Abbey and leave Callow End.

DROITWICH SPA

In the centre of Droitwich at **Salters Shopping Centre** (next to the Droitwich Carpets shop) is a 1975 ceramic mural by Philippa Threlfall and Kennedy Collings which depicts the town's historic buildings; it is about 5' high and 12' long.

Witton

The **Church of St Peter de Witton**, ST PETER'S CHURCH LANE, has fifteenth century tiles around its font and late nineteenth century encaustic tiling by Godwin's.

DUDLEY

The former **Odeon Cinema** (since 1977 a church), CASTLE HILL, was designed by the Harry Weedon practice (job assistant Budge Reid) and opened in 1937. Its massive buff faience facade, by Shaws of Darwen, is broken up in the centre by a series of tall windows between rounded piers.[4]

Brierley Hill

The **Harris and Pearson** office building (1888), BRETTELL LANE, was saved from demolition by Dudley Metropolitan Borough Council and listed grade II in 1996; from 2003 it has been in the care of the West Midlands Historic Buildings Trust. Harris and Pearson moved to the site in 1852; the firm made firebricks, used to line furnaces and kilns, from the high quality Stourbridge clay. Their office building, its every brick made at the works from local clay, uses a remarkable variety of architectural ceramics on its facade. There are glazed and unglazed materials in a variety of colours, unusual glazed fireclay sills to the windows and bold white glazed lettering reading Harris and Pearson, the latter a rare example of Victorian architectural graphics still *in situ*. Inside there are coloured glazed brick walls and good mosaic floors. All the ceramics were made by the company, thus the building acted as a piece of advertising architecture for the ceramics industry. In this respect it is rather more forceful than earlier examples such as the factories of Minton Hollins (1869) in Stoke-on-Trent, Staffordshire and Craven Dunnill (1871-4) at Jackfield, Shropshire, and more akin to Doulton's 1878 Lambeth Pottery.

EVESHAM

There are extensive Victorian tile pavements at **St Lawrence Church**, which is in the care of the Churches Conservation Trust. Unusual hexagonal tiles and uncommon motifs are visible, and some designs are very similar to those of tile pavements in Dorchester Abbey, Oxfordshire. As the Dorchester tiles are by Godwin's, this suggests the same manufacturer was responsible for the St Lawrence pavements.

GREAT MALVERN

Great Malvern Priory was founded in 1085, but most of the original structure was swept away during the rebuilding of the church which took place between about 1440 and 1500. Around 1,300 tiles survive from this period, made by the tilers who set up their workshops and kilns in the precinct east of the priory church in the 1450s. Altogether there are at least ten different sizes of tile and over 100 different designs, some of tremendous beauty and complexity.[5] The floor was paved with plain and two-colour tiles made from local clay; the decoration, including intricate heraldic motifs, was designed specifically for the Priory. During the nineteenth-century restoration of the church these decorated tiles were mounted on the wall to the rear of the high altar, where they may still be seen today.[6] The tilers also produced the rectangular wall tiles which flank the high altar's reredos, some of whose decoration featured the dates 1453, 1456 and 1458/9. As their glazed surfaces are still intact, they provide a rare glimpse of how the original floor must have appeared.

The Priory also illustrates the Victorian approach to church refurbishment. Following the discovery of the Priory's medieval kilns in 1833, the antiquarian and architect Harvey Eginton, County Surveyor of Worcestershire, attempted to find modern copies of the tiles. He supplied patterns traced from medieval tiles to his friend Walter Chamberlain of Worcester, who began the manufacture of inlaid tiles in 1836. Chamberlain's exact replica tiles, with their medieval-style rough finish, were used in the refurbishment of several religious institutions including Great Malvern Priory, where they are mounted on the back wall of the sanctuary (Fig 291). These Chamberlain & Co tiles date from the early 1840s. The spectacular Minton tile pavement on the steps leading up to the high altar probably dates from the 1860 restoration work undertaken by George Gilbert Scott. The opus sectile reredos, showing the *Adoration of the Magi*, was supplied by Powell's of Whitefriars in 1884 and is flanked by the same firm's glass tiles.

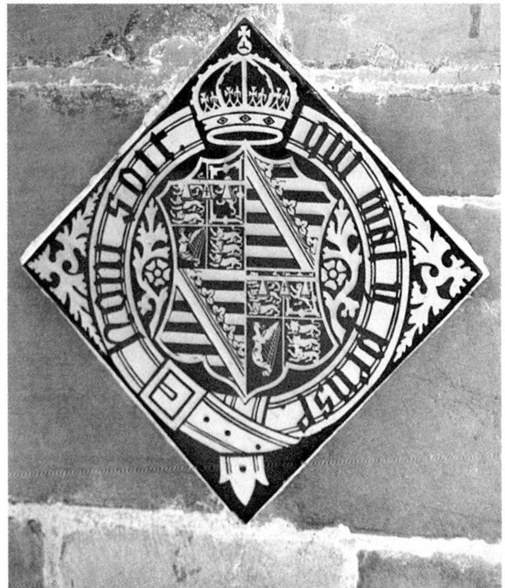

Fig 291.

HALLOW

Just south of the village is the **Parkfield** estate, which was centred on a now-demolished nineteenth century country house. Parkfield's garden is listed in the UK Database of Historic Parks and Gardens, and several estate buildings remain, including two with ceramic interest, the former summer house and games pavilion, both built around 1870-80. The summer house has some exterior tiling, completely tiled interior walls and a patterned tile floor; some of the wall tiling bears images of faces of the gods. The games pavilion is in similar style but even more decorative, with three interior tile panels showing archery, badminton and croquet.

HANLEY SWAN

St Gabriel's Church was designed by George Gilbert Scott and built in 1872-4. Its reredos, showing Gabriel and Michael in opus sectile, was supplied by Powell's of Whitefriars in 1873 although the figures were drawn by Clayton & Bell, the London church decorating firm; this was the first of several Clayton & Bell orders received by Powell's. Flanking the reredos are large areas of unusual glassy floral tiling, probably also supplied by Powell's.[7] Nearby, in what was once the grounds of Blackmore Park, is the **R. C. Church of Our Lady and St Alphonsus** (1844-6, architect Charles Hansom). The excellent metalwork was designed by A. W. N. Pugin, as was the fine Minton encaustic tile pavement.[8]

KIDDERMINSTER

BRINTON PARK, a public park on the southern side of Kidderminster, was given to the town in 1887. Following the death of Richard Eve (1831-1900), a prominent local freemason, a committee was convened to recommend a suitable memorial, and suggested a drinking fountain to be sited at the highest point of the park, near the bandstand. The Kidderminster architectural practice begun by J. T. Meredith (1834-98) and Joseph Pritchard provided a design which was commissioned from Doulton's of Lambeth. The sculptor John Broad provided the portrait roundel of Eve which sits within a magnificent polychrome faience fountain, and the **Richard Eve Memorial** was unveiled in 1902 (Fig 292). The structure is basically square in cross-section and 29 feet in height, with four inset relief panels depicting stylised fish and further panels giving details of Eve's life; the predominant colours are brown, green and gold.[9] The cost of the memorial was £540.

Joseph Pritchard designed several other memorials in conjunction with Doulton's, but this appears to have been the first in the series. They collaborated on the Coronation Fountain at Leyton, which probably dates from 1903, and the Queen Victoria Memorial Fountain in Malacca, produced in 1904. It is certainly the most lavish of the extant Doultonware memorials, although other good examples remain at Burslem Cemetery, Stoke-on-Trent (Hulm Memorial, 1905) and Hartlepool, County Durham (Henry Withy Memorial Fountain, 1902). These memorials are smaller in size than Doulton's large-scale water fountains, notably their Victoria Fountain (Glasgow, 1888), but much more colourful. Given the significance of the Eve memorial, it is unfortunate that it has now fallen into disrepair and stands cordoned off behind metal barriers.

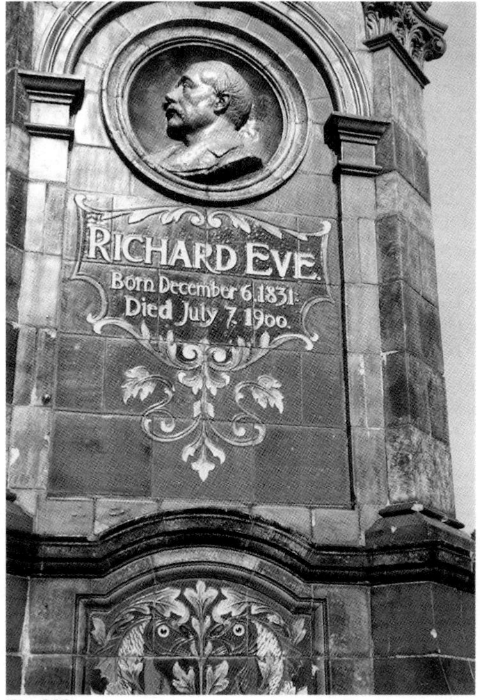

Fig 292.

LITTLE COMBERTON

Amongst the collection of about 150 reset fifteenth century tiles in the sanctuary at **St Peter's Church** are two unusual square memorial floor tiles to Richard Neale (d1753) and William Neale (d1754), rector. They may have been produced by Godwin's, who made the encaustic tile pavement in the choir which was installed around 1886 when the original tiles were relaid. It has good four-tile and sixteen-tile groups reproducing medieval tile patterns (Fig 293).

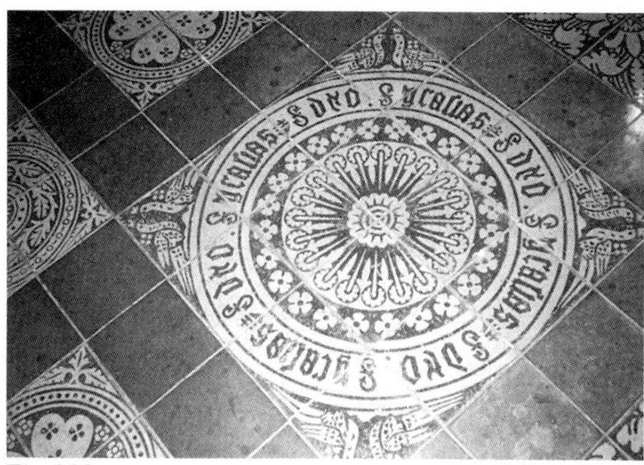
Fig 293.

NEWLAND

The architect Philip Charles Hardwick began work at Madresfield Court near Great Malvern in 1863, adding the chapel in 1867 (its arts and crafts decoration dates from the early twentieth century) and making alterations to the house for the Lygon family, the Earls Beauchamp. A mile north-west of the house in the village of Newland, Hardwick had started building **St Leonard's Church**, next to the Beauchamp Almshouses, in 1862; the church was completed in 1864. Its opulent interior is little changed, and includes a complete scheme of wall paintings as well as a striking geometric and encaustic tiled pavement running throughout.

TENBURY WELLS

Oldwood Common

The **Church of St Michael and All Angels** (1854-6) and its associated music college were built for the musician and composer Sir Frederick Gore Ouseley, who found most of the £20,000 cost himself. The architect for all the works was Henry Woodyer, who provided his patron with a large church, its dramatic Minton floor of blue, black and white tiles becoming increasingly complex towards the east end; the sanctuary floor is mosaic.[10] Although the college closed in 1985, the church continues as a parish church; it is situated in the hamlet of St Michaels, two miles south-west of Tenbury Wells, on the A4112 to Leominster at Oldwood Common.

WORCESTER

Worcester Cathedral, on COLLEGE GREEN beside the River Severn, dates back to the seventh century; although the present building was begun in 1084 and the crossing tower was rebuilt in 1374, much of its external appearance is strongly Victorian. The fine medieval tile pavement which floored the Old Singing School was recorded and published in 1858, but now the carpet pattern - a typical Malvern combination of foliage and heraldic designs - has completely worn away.[11] However, some inlaid tiles probably dating from the second half of the fourteenth century can still be seen in the passage leading to the Old Singing School. George Gilbert Scott restored the Cathedral in 1864-74, introducing a choir pavement of Godwin tiles set between bands of marble and stone. In the sanctuary is a superb circular Signs of the Zodiac tile scheme, also by Godwin, but which may be covered by carpet.[12]

From the Cathedral, head north along FRIAR STREET. At the junction with Pump Street is the ornate mostly brown and green faience facade of the **Eagle Vaults PH**, built for the brewers around the turn of the century; good lettering and heavy doorcases ensure this little pub makes the most of its corner site. Turn left along Pump Street then right into HIGH STREET to see another attractive and eye-catching building occupying a corner site, the former Cadena Café (probably early twentieth century, now **Alliance and Leicester Bank**) at 59-60 High Street; dark red terracotta dressings emphasise the entrance. In 1999 it was converted to flats and offices by DJD Architects, using replacement terracotta from Hathernware. On the right in CORNMARKET is the **Exchange PH**, another essay in brown faience for Mitchells & Butlers albeit slightly less flamboyant than the Eagle Vaults. Continue northward along High Street to the corner of Sansome Street and THE FOREGATE, where the red brick and pinkish terracotta of the huge **Hop Market Hotel** towers above the road. It was put up in 1900 by a local building firm, Bromage & Evans; the terracotta has good lettering, swags and figurative plaques. Slightly west in THE BUTTS is the **Paul Pry PH** (1901, architect Frederick Hughes), its splendid central hallway tiled from floor to ceiling.

Just north of the centre in THE TYTHING, a continuation of Foregate Street, is **St Oswald's Hospital**, built in 1873-4 at the site of an ancient almshouse and designed by the local architect Henry Rowe, the city surveyor. The interior walls of the chapel (1878, also by Rowe), were finished in brick with bands of red and buff tiles, with the addition of porcelain tiles supplied by Messrs Grainger in the chancel; an encaustic tile pavement ran throughout.[13]

Shrub Hill

In what was the industrial eastern suburb of Shrub Hill is **Shrub Hill Railway Station**, where two linked waiting rooms of 1865 on platform two were built of cast iron framing (by the local Vulcan Iron Works) with colourful inset panels of cuenca tiles by Maw & Co, who left Worcester for the Ironbridge Gorge in 1852. Originally there were similar exotic structures on platform one.

Worcestershire Roundup

The mid-nineteenth century pavilions in the wall surrounding the forecourt of Hanbury Hall (NT), **Hanbury**, have colourful inner wall dados of Minton's majolica-glazed tiles. Godwin's manufactured the colourful 1867 encaustic tile pavement at St Michael's Church, **Little Witley**.[14] Fifteenth century tiles from the site of the north transept were relaid in the south-east chapel of **Pershore Abbey** in 1862. St Nicholas Church (restored 1884-5), **Pinvin**, has a fine Godwin encaustic pavement including unusual four-tile and sixteen-tile groups; the squirrel motif is particularly notable. St Mary's Church, **Sedgeberrow**, was restored by the architect William Butterfield in 1866-8 and has colourful chancel wall tiling (even brighter than his usual work) and a pavement by Godwin's. There is elaborate terracotta decoration on the Hagley Road Centre of Stourbridge College, built as a library and technical college in 1903-4 and 1908-9; it stands on Hagley Road, **Stourbridge**. There is a large collection of fifteenth century Malvern tiles in the nave of St John the Baptist Church, **Strensham**, which is in the care of the Churches Conservation Trust.

In addition there are numerous medieval tiles at the following churches: St James, Bredicot (porch); St Mary Magdalene, Broadwas (chancel); St Michael, Churchill, near Worcester (chancel); St John Baptist, Claines (displayed in north porch); St Leonard, Cotheridge (armorial tiles in chancel floor); St John the Baptist, Fladbury (also Victorian pavement); St Peter, Flyford Flavell (tower, also Victorian pavement); St John the Baptist, Halesowen; St James, Hindlip; St Martin, Holt; St James, Huddington; St Edburga, Leigh (also 1855 pavement); St Giles, Little Malvern (also known as Little Malvern Priory); St Nicholas, Middle Littleton; St Peter, Pirton; St Andrew, Shelsley Walsh; St Michael, South Littleton; St Nicholas, Warndon; and St Anne, Wyre Piddle.

References

1. Jane A. Wight, *Mediaeval Floor Tiles* (John Baker, London, 1975).
2. Betty Greene, 'Some unusual tiles at Bredon, Oxenton and Tredington', *Glazed Expressions*, (1992) 24, p8.
3. Roderick O'Donnell, *The Pugins and the Catholic Midlands* (Gracewing, Leominster, 2002).
4. *List of Contracts executed 1935-1036*, (Shaws Glazed Brick Co Ltd, Darwen, 1936).
5. Nicholas A. D. Molyneux, *TACS Tour Notes: Great Malvern Priory* (TACS, 1984).
6. Nicholas A. D. Molyneux and John E. McGregor, *The Medieval Tiles at Great Malvern Priory* (Friends of Great Malvern Priory, Great Malvern, 1997).
7. Dennis W. Hadley, *James Powell & Sons: A listing of opus sectile, 1847-1973*, (2001).
8. Peter Howell and Ian Sutton, eds., *The Faber Guide to Victorian Churches* (Faber and Faber, London, 1989).
9. Paul Atterbury and Louise Irvine, *The Doulton Story* (Royal Doulton Tableware, Stoke on Trent, 1979), p90.
10. John Elliott and John Pritchard, eds., *Henry Woodyer: Gentleman Architect* (Department of Continuing Education, University of Reading, Reading, 2002).
11. Jane Cochrane, 'Medieval Tiled Floor Patterns', *TACS Journal*, 5 (1994), pp11-19.
12. Betty Greene, 'The Godwins of Hereford', *TACS Journal*, 1 (1982), pp8-16.
13. *The Builder*, vol 36, 23rd February 1878.
14. *The Builder*, vol 25, 20th July 1867.

Yorkshire

Yorkshire's major producer of tiles and architectural ceramics was the Leeds Fireclay Company, based at Burmantofts in Leeds, whose first catalogue was published in 1882. Their large blocks and slabs of architectural faience, with the brand name Burmantofts Faience, were used widely until the early 1900s. From 1908 Burmantofts produced Marmo faience, in direct competition with Doulton's Carraraware; the works closed in 1957. The firm specialised in brightly coloured tile and faience for both interiors and exteriors, and York retains one of the few remaining late nineteenth century complete Burmantofts faience rooms in its Royal York Hotel. The city also offers a wide range of high quality ceramic locations within its walls, from the early Minton pavement in York Minster's chapter house to rare hand-painted exterior tile panels (1887) on the City Art Gallery.

Kenneth Beaulah's 1979-81 survey of around 250 parish churches in the East Riding revealed that encaustic tiles dating from the period 1842-98 were present in about one hundred of them. He identified the products of seven tile manufacturers, with Minton's being the only tiles used in the area before 1862. For churches where the pavements dated from after 1870, tiles by Godwin's were found in over twenty-six and by Maw's in over a dozen. The architect George Edmund Street, who designed or restored fourteen East Riding churches (as well as being consultant architect to York Minster between 1868 and 1881) particularly favoured Godwin's products.[1] Many of his churches were designed for Sir Tatton Sykes, fifth baronet, of Sledmere House, one of the great Victorian church builders. The entries for East Yorkshire reflect this preponderance of churches, other highlights mainly being in Kingston upon Hull (hereinafter referred to as Hull), with some excellent pub tiles, including two rare faience barfronts, a wealth of porch tiles and good ceramic interiors at Holderness Road Baths (1897-8) and Beverley Road Baths (1903-5). Finally for the east there is the unique tiled house *Farrago* in Hornsea, erected by the Hull master builder David Reynard Robinson in 1908-9.

As well as its share of Victorian church tiles, North Yorkshire has a broader range of ceramic locations including Britain's earliest medieval pavements, relaid at Fountains Abbey, and the best *in situ* pavements, at Byland Abbey. Other highlights are the early terracotta dressings of Scarborough's Grand Hotel (1863-7), and a series of fine ceramic interiors from the late nineteenth and early twentieth centuries: spectacular but little-known Craven Dunnill tiling at the Zetland Hotel (1893), Middlesbrough; masses of glazed brick at Harrogate Turkish Baths (1894-7); extensive wall tiling combined with colourful Powell's opus sectile panels at the Brunswick Room (1895-8), Whitby; and the Burmantofts faience of the former Pump Room at Ripon Spa Baths (1904-5). Lastly for the north, the unusual Burmantofts terracotta facade of Richmond's Fleece Hotel (1897) brings Scottish Baronial style to North Yorkshire. Apart from the Brunswick Room, which was used for Methodist teaching, all these turn-of-the century sites are associated with commercialised leisure and pleasure buildings, mostly in the north's resort towns.

South Yorkshire is rather different, with an almost exclusive emphasis on urban areas - Barnsley, Doncaster, Rotherham and Sheffield - and several interwar sites, notably Doncaster's array of white faience shop facades. The Cooperative movement provides some memorable buildings, the pick of their facades being Barnsley's hulking baroque Burmantofts faience store (1911) and Doncaster's 1936-49 modernist Co-op. The best Co-op interior is their early sixties Sheffield store, which retains fine Carter's geometric-patterned tiling on the stairwells; unlike the Doncaster and Barnsley Co-ops, the Sheffield store is still in use by the Co-op. The undoubted ceramic star of South Yorkshire is also in Sheffield: St Marie's R. C. Cathedral has extensive encaustic, pictorial and memorial tiling, a display of Victorian ecclesiastical ceramics unrivalled in Britain yet little known outside the city itself.

Tile and architectural ceramic locations in West Yorkshire are dominated by the products of the Burmantofts works in Leeds, which began to produce tiles and architectural faience from about 1880; by the late 1880s the firm was making large blocks and slabs of architectural faience under the brand name Burmantofts Faience. From 1889 the company was known as the Leeds Fireclay Company Ltd; it developed into the largest clay-working business in the north of England, its best-known designers being W. J. Neatby, the main artist from around 1880 to 1890, and the sculptor E. C. Spruce, principal designer and modeller by the late 1890s. Brightly coloured tile and faience went out of fashion in the early 1900s, and from 1908 Burmantofts began the production of Marmo faience, continuing until the early 1950s; the works closed in 1957 and was demolished. Good examples of Burmantofts architectural wares in West Yorkshire include the Midland Hotel (1890), Bradford; the Garden Gate (1903), Hunslet, Leeds; Atlas Chambers (1910), Leeds; and the Public Library (1905-6), Morley.

Another local producer of architectural wares was the Clayton Fireclay Works in Bradford, whose owner's house, The Towers, was built in the 1880s partly as a ceramic advertisement for the firm. St Bartholomew's Church, Armley, Leeds and Christ Church, Todmorden have two of the best displays of Powell's opus sectile work in Britain, but the future of the latter is threatened by plans to convert it for residential use. Already lost is the 85' long ceramic mural *Life in West Riding* by Philippa Threlfall and Kennedy Collings, which was installed at Leeds-Bradford Airport, Yeadon, in 1969 but perished during 2002-3 rebuilding work. Also currently (2004) at risk is Queensgate Market (1969-70), Huddersfield, with its huge external stoneware mural by Fritz Steller.

Suggested reading: Hans van Lemmen and Jose Montgomery, *Dutch Tiles at 'Farrago' and A History of the House and its Tiles* (Leeds Polytechnic, 1990); Christopher Ketchell and Jose Montgomery, *Tiles Tour - Hull* (Hull College of Further Education, 1990); Hans van Lemmen, *TACS Tour Notes: Tiles, Terracotta and Faience in Leeds* (2003); Jennie Stopford, *Medieval Floor Tiles of Northern England: Pattern and purpose - production between the 13th and 16th centuries* (Oxbow Books, Oxford, 2004); and *Burmantofts Pottery* (Bradford Art Galleries and Museums, 1983).

The *Gazetteer* entry for York covers the administrative area of York City Council. The *Gazetteer* entry for East Yorkshire covers the administrative areas of East Riding of Yorkshire Council and Kingston upon Hull City Council. The *Gazetteer* entry for North Yorkshire covers the administrative areas of Middlesbrough Council, North Yorkshire County Council and Redcar & Cleveland Borough Council. The *Gazetteer* entry for South Yorkshire covers the administrative areas of Barnsley Metropolitan Borough Council, Doncaster Metropolitan Borough Council, Rotherham Metropolitan Borough Council and Sheffield City Council. The *Gazetteer* entry for West Yorkshire covers the administrative areas of Bradford City Council, Calderdale Metropolitan Borough Council, Kirklees Metropolitan Borough Council, Leeds City Council and Wakefield Metropolitan Borough Council.

York

YORK

York's **Railway Station**, with its dramatically curved iron-and-glass trainshed, was built in 1871-7; those responsible were the North Eastern Railway's architect Thomas Prosser and engineer T. E. Harrison, with Prosser's successors Benjamin Burleigh and William Peachey. On the wall just left of the main exit from the trainshed is a Craven Dunnill tiled map of the North Eastern Railway's network, installed in 1900 and showing the company's lines as they were at that time, apart from the addition of the Beverley to North Frodingham line. This was the proposed North Holderness Light Railway, which was never built but which is shown on the map.[2] These tiled maps, comprising sixty-four tiles within a substantial ceramic frame, were later installed at fourteen other NER stations. Apart from the York example, eight other maps remain *in situ*: those at Beverley, Bridlington, Hartlepool, Middlesbrough, Saltburn, Scarborough, Tynemouth and Whitby. The maps from Hexham, Hull, Morpeth, Normanton and Tyne Dock have been removed, two of them now being on display at the National Railway Museum in York and Jackfield Tile Museum in the Ironbridge Gorge. The status of the fifteenth map, at South Shields, is unclear.

Adjoining the station to the north is the **Royal York Hotel**, STATION ROAD, built as the Royal Station Hotel for the NER in 1877-8 to the designs of Thomas Prosser and William Peachey. It was extended in 1896, and although most of the massive structure is of yellow brick, some terracotta dressings are visible on the east (garden) front. The octagonal foyer which forms the direct entrance from the station has a pretty geometric and encaustic tile pavement. Inside, a tiled stairwell leads down to the basement and a splendid ceramic room by Burmantofts, where faience in browns, cream, yellow and green covers the walls and ceiling; the chunky fire surround is particularly ornate (Fig 294). It seems likely that the room dates from around the time of the 1896 building work, as the firm only began to supply this type of faience in the early 1880s, with ceiling fittings being later still.[3] Originally the room would probably have been a public restaurant or refreshment room. It was later used as a bar, necessitating some alteration, but damage to the faience was made good, using a surprisingly convincing mixture of wood and resin, during restoration in 2004. Unfortunately the floor level has also been raised, thus obscuring the bottom few inches of faience; however, it remains a fine room.

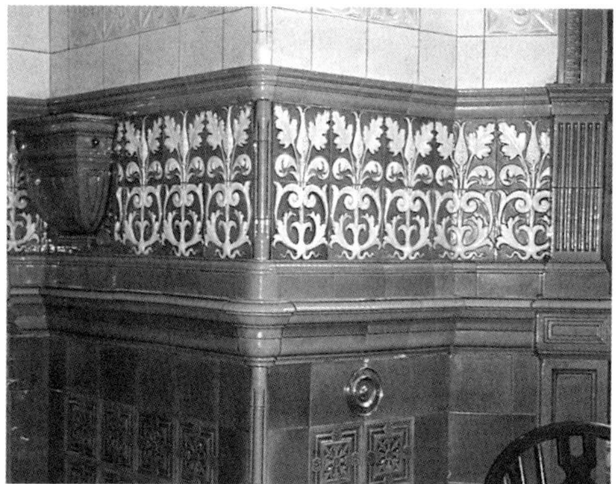

Fig 294.

From the hotel, head towards the Minster, crossing Lendal Bridge to reach MUSEUM STREET; on the right is **Pizza Express**, housed in a former gentlemen's club (the Yorkshire Club) built in 1868-70. The toilets are decorated with superb turn-of-the-century Medmenham Pottery tiles with a distinctive fish motif. At the end of Museum Street turn left into St Leonard's Place, soon reaching the **City Art Gallery** (1879, architect Edward Taylor) in EXHIBITION SQUARE. On its facade are two overglaze-painted tile panels, one depicting Leonardo da Vinci dying in the arms of Francis I, the other showing Michelangelo with his statue of Moses for the tomb of Pope Julius II. Poor cleaning technique has resulted in the images becoming faint. The facade was originally to have had seven tile panels, two large and five small, all of historical subjects relating to art and science. In 1883 the London firm Gibbs & Howard provided an estimate for this work of £250, the addition of carved reliefs over the panels bringing the total to £425. Alderman Agar of York provided £100 to purchase two large tile panels, the Leonardo and the Michelangelo, which were ready in 1887, but no further decoration of the facade was ever undertaken. The stained glass and tile painting business Gibbs & Howard had been set up around 1878 by Isaac Alexander Gibbs (1849-89) and William Wallace Howard (b1856).[4] Gibbs was the younger brother of Alexander Gibbs (c1831-86), who supplied a series of tile panels designed by William Butterfield for All Saints Church, Margaret Street, Westminster, in the mid-1870s; although Alexander Gibbs took full responsibility for the Margaret Street panels, the actual painting was mostly carried out by Isaac Alexander Gibbs.[5] Gibbs & Howard also produced a series of large tile paintings for Wyfold Court (1874-84), Oxfordshire.

Further west along BOOTHAM is **Bootham Park Hospital** (no public access), a purpose-built psychiatric hospital which opened in 1777 and is still fulfilling its original function. The hospital has a complex building history: the main block was designed by John Carr and built in 1772-7, but additions and alterations were made throughout the nineteenth century, especially during the 1880s and into the 1890s when the fine Minton floor tiles were laid. These unusually extensive tile pavements, and the tiled dados lining many corridors, form part of the impressive public spaces within the hospital. The most elaborate pavement is in the main corridor, with encaustic tiles in the area below the light well having up to seven different types of coloured clays. The floors were restored and relaid during 1990-1, when a small number of modern replacement tiles were introduced.

Return to the centre along High Petergate, soon approaching **York Minster**, where the main ceramic interest lies in the large octagonal chapter house, built around 1275-91 and notable for its lack of a central pier. Restoration by the architect Sydney Smirke in 1844-5 included the installation of its Minton tile pavement. The tiles have a red body (some black) and the buff inlaid decoration has been covered with yellow enamel; many of the designs appear in Minton's first printed tile catalogue of 1842. The complex layout of the floor - which was ignored by the 1995 *Pevsner* and is sometimes covered by seating - begins with an octagonal outer rim of four-tile groups within floral border tiles. Inside this are eight segments, narrowing towards the centre, with nine-tile and sixteen-tile groups tiles laid on the diagonal, that is not square to either the outer border or the segmental dividers. The central octagonal section includes green, blue and white tiles with floral motifs.

Apart from the chapter house pavement, there are also medieval tiles in the crypt and the former treasury (now consistory court, near the south transept). In St Stephen's Chapel, at the east end of the north aisle, is a Doulton reredos by George Tinworth set in an elaborate wooden surround designed by G. E. Street in 1875. The grey terracotta reredos, made in 1876 and showing The First Hour of the Crucifixion, was Tinworth's first major architectural commission. It has been overpainted to resemble carved wood.[6]

North of the Minster in MINSTER YARD is the **Treasurer's House** (NT), originally home to the treasurers of York Minster but restored for the local industrialist Frank Green around 1898-1900. This work involved the addition of decorative fittings dating from the sixteenth century onward, including the late nineteenth century Dutch delftware tiles which line the kitchen walls (Fig 295). The blue and white tiles, made by Ravesteijn of Utrecht, show children's games and landscapes; at least ninety-six different children's games have been featured on Dutch tiles and many of these can be seen in the kitchen. The green landscape tiles running along the top border were made by the firm Van Hulst of Harlingen, Friesland.

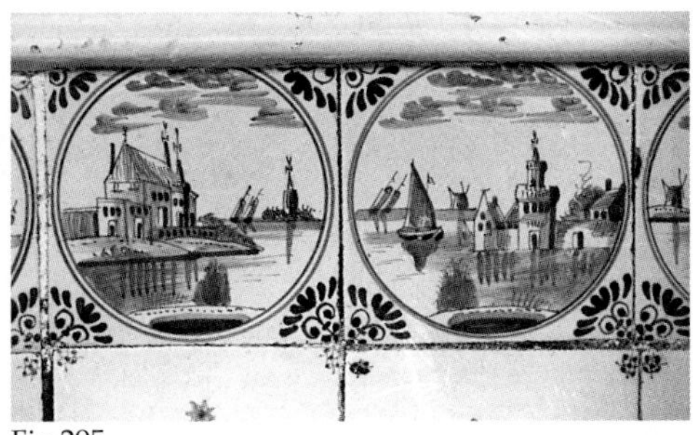

Fig 295.

Just south of the Minster is STONEGATE, a long and narrow street with many good shop fronts. The facade of **10 Stonegate** dates from about 1875 and is covered with encaustic and geometric tiles made by Maw & Co; this is an unusually complete and early attempt to add colour to buildings by using ceramic cladding (Fig 296). At the end of Stonegate turn left into Davygate which leads to ST SAMPSON'S SQUARE and the **Three Cranes PH**, which has an interesting ceramic pub sign panel above its entrance, probably dating from the 1930s. Continue south-east to the end of PARLIAMENT STREET, where the striking, pinky-red terracotta **Barclays Bank** occupies a corner site. It was put up in 1901 and designed by the Liverpool architect Edmund Kirby (1838-1920), who was a keen user of terracotta in his home city. Turn left into Pavement then right along FOSSGATE to see the former **Electric Theatre** (1911, now Macdonalds furniture shop), the city's first purpose-built cinema. The yellowy arched Doulton faience facade was designed by local architect William Whincup for the London chain National Electric Theatres.

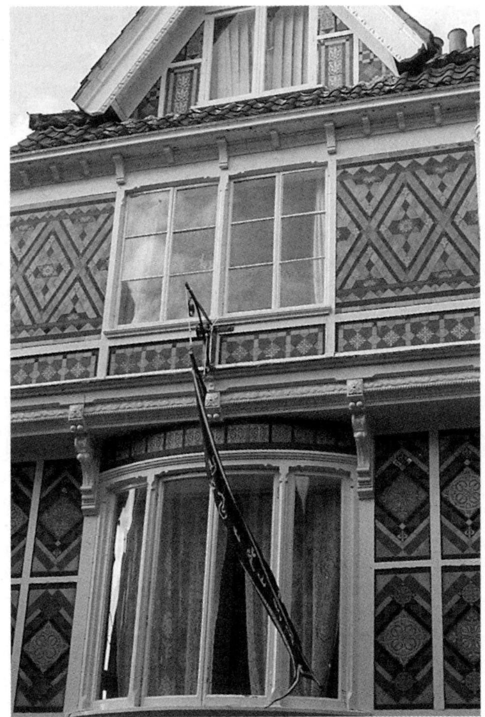

Fig 296.

Continue east along WALMGATE to **St Denys Church**, whose sanctuary has unusual late nineteenth century hand-painted wall tiling including symbols of the evangelists and panels bearing the commandments and the Lord's Prayer, all probably carried out by a church decorating firm (Fig 297). From St Denys Road turn right along Piccadilly, heading left down

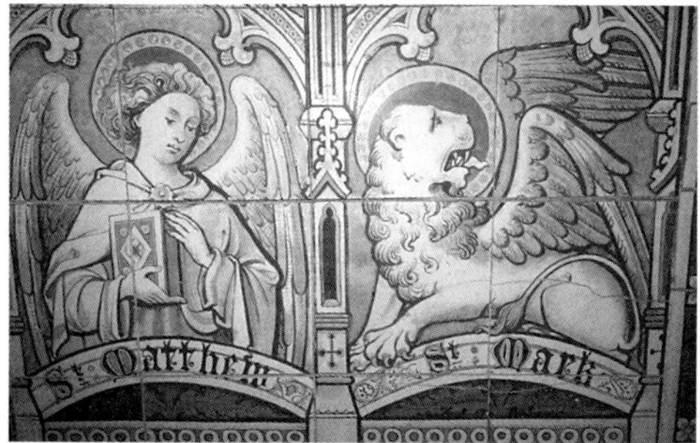

Fig 297.

COPPERGATE just before Barclays Bank. The facade of **5 Coppergate** (1908) is of Burmantofts Marmo and shows fine architectural detailing and classical figures. Left on CASTLEGATE, beside Fairfax House, is the remains of the ornate, classical mottled browny-grey faience facade of the former St George's Hall Cinema (1921). At the end of Castlegate go right into Tower Street and then CLIFFORD STREET where the former **Technical College** (1883-4, architect Walter G. Penty) is now a bar. It was built for the York Institute of Art, Science and Literature and the mixed motifs on the impressive greyish-buff terracotta columns of its entrance appear to have been inspired by the Natural History Museum, which was completed only a few years before the Technical College in 1881.[7]

Turn left along Low Ousegate to cross the Ouse Bridge and continue on Micklegate, passing through Micklegate Bar, the gateway in the city wall. The **Bar Convent**, opened in 1686 for the education of Catholic girls, stands on the far side of the crossroads in BLOSSOM STREET. Flooring the glazed courtyard is a mosaic and encaustic tile pavement by Maw & Co dating from around 1870; it has an especially ornate central motif (Fig 298).

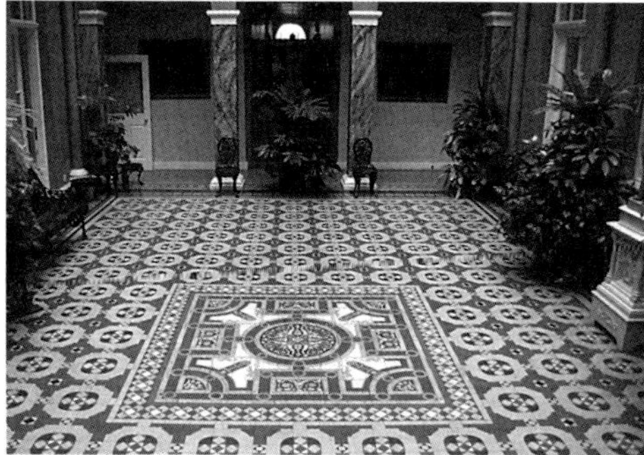
Fig 298.

Clementhorpe

The reredos of **St Clement's Church** (1872-4, architects J. B. & W. Atkinson), SCARCROFT ROAD is a terracotta relief of the *Last Supper* by Mr Thrupp.[8]

Dringhouses

The **Church of St Edward the Confessor** (1847-9, architects Vickers & Hugall of Pontefract), TADCASTER ROAD, was put up by Mrs Frances Leigh in honour of her husband, the late Reverend Edward Trafford Leigh, local Lord of the Manor. The church, which was consecrated on Edward Leigh's birthday and dedicated to St Edward the Confessor in his memory, has good glass by William Wailes and a Minton tile pavement.

York Roundup

Seven miles south-east of York is **Wheldrake**, where St Helen's Church has a tile pavement by Robert Minton Taylor dating from 1875, just before his firm was bought out by his cousin Colin Minton Campbell.

East Yorkshire

ANLABY

St Peter's Church is the only one in East Yorkshire with a tile pavement by Craven Dunnill, in this case chancel tiling of 1885 including armorials of the donors.[9] Two other churches in the former East Riding - Thorpe Bassett and Willerby (near Filey) - both now over the border in North Yorkshire, also have Craven Dunnill pavements dating from the early 1880s. The Thorpe Bassett is much more restrained in colour than Anlaby's, using mostly line-impressed tiles.

BARMBY MOOR

St Catherine's Church was the recipient of gifts of tiles from Herbert Minton in 1849 and 1851, the latter comprising tiles for the nave and aisles; the chancel is also paved. The church was medieval, but was rebuilt in 1850-2 to the designs of R. D. Chantrell. The incumbent in 1850 was the Reverend Robert Taylor, brother-in-law of Herbert Minton, and the church contains inscribed tiles recording Minton's donation and commemorating members of the family, including Catherine (1805-61), the wife of Robert Taylor; she was Herbert Minton's youngest sister. There is also a Minton-tiled Royal arms dating from 1850. Robert Minton Taylor - who went into partnership with Michael Daintry Hollins in 1863 before setting up his own tile business at Fenton in 1869 - was the child of Catherine and the Revd. Robert Taylor, and was probably born in the 1830s. His father appears to have assumed the name Minton, as he was referred to as Revd. Robert Minton Taylor at Fangfoss Church, for which he was also responsible.[10]

BEVERLEY

The best of Beverley's ceramic locations is the 1867 Godwin sanctuary tile pavement at **St Mary's Church**, which stands almost in the centre of the town on NORTH BAR WITHIN. It was installed by Sir George Gilbert Scott after his refitting of the nave in 1864-7. East in SATURDAY MARKET is the former **Corn Exchange** (1886) with good red terracotta dressings; continue east to the **Railway Station**, STATION SQUARE, where there is one of the series of Craven Dunnill NER tile maps, installed shortly after 1900. Also of interest is the Maw pavement at **St Nicholas Church** (1879-80, architect F. S. Brodrick), HOLME CHURCH LANE.

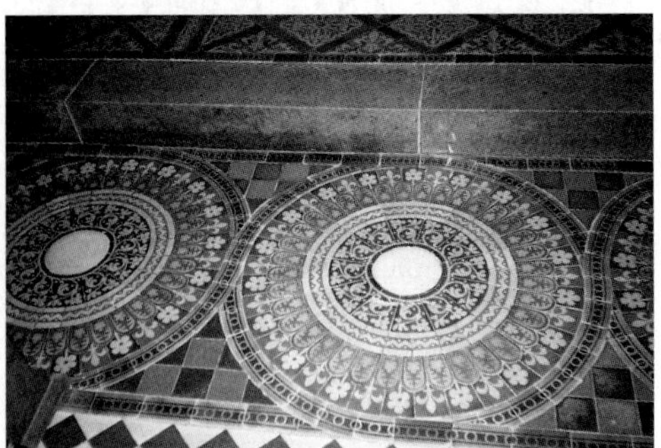

Fig 299.

BISHOP WILTON

St Edith's Church was restored by the architect John Loughborough Pearson in 1858-9 for Sir Tatton Sykes, fourth baronet, of Sledmere House. It was one of a handful of churches built or restored by Pearson for Sir Tatton during the 1850s, although the impetus behind the work may have been due to his son, Sir Tatton Sykes (1826-1913), fifth baronet, who succeeded to the Sledmere estates in 1863 and became one of the greatest of the nineteenth century English church builders. St Edith's Church has an elaborate interior, its flooring being part mosaic and part tiling; the mosaic, by Salviati and dating from 1902, was designed by the architect Temple Moore. The rich sanctuary tile pavement of 1859 is by Godwin's and includes a row of interconnected circular arrangements based on medieval tiles found at Jervaulx Abbey in North Yorkshire (Fig 299).

FANGFOSS

The Minton encaustic floor tiles (1849) in the sanctuary of **St Martin's Church** are of interest largely because they were, according to the church guidebook, 'provided for the Church by a relative of the Revd. Robert Minton Taylor, whose photograph is located in the vestry'. Fangfoss is about four miles north of Barmby Moor, and the two village churches share the same vicar. St Martin's was rebuilt in 1849-50 by the architect R. D. Chantrell, who rebuilt St Catherine's, Barmby Moor, shortly afterwards; there, the tiles are known to have been donated by Herbert Minton, brother-in-law of Revd. Robert Minton Taylor.

FIMBER

Within two years of Sir Tatton Sykes, fifth baronet, succeeding to the Sledmere estates in 1863, the architect J. L. Pearson - who had worked for Sir Tatton's father, the fourth baronet - was commissioned to prepare plans for new churches at Thixendale and Wansford. However, it seems the designs did not please Sir Tatton, who dispensed with Pearson and brought in the rather more Tractarian architect G. E. Street, who made his first visit to Sledmere in autumn 1865.[11] St Mary's Church (1869-71), Fimber, was the third new church built by Street for Sir Tatton on the Sledmere estates, and the smallest. Its decorative tilework includes Godwin's dust-pressed tiles with black body and yellow inlay.[12]

GARTON-ON-THE-WOLDS

St Nicholas Church was restored for Sir Tatton Sykes, fourth baronet, in 1856-7 by J. L. Pearson, but it is the unparalleled decorative scheme, designed by G. E. Street for Sir Tatton's son, the fifth baronet, in 1872-8 and completed by Pearson in 1879-81, which makes this church one of the wonders of the Victorian age (Fig 300). A unique series of wall paintings (restored in 1987-91) carried out by Clayton & Bell illustrates the creation story and relates to the images of the stained glass, made by the same firm. It seems this theme was chosen to combat increasing public disbelief in the biblical version of the creation.[13] The ceramic interest in this superlative interior is provided by the Spanish-style *cuenca*-tiled dado, the tiles having been supplied and fixed by Frederick Garrard of Millwall at a cost of £166.12.0; the tiles are now known to have been made by Garrard himself rather than imported.[14] The church is floored with Cosmati marble work and mosaics, the latter made by George Trollope & Sons of London.

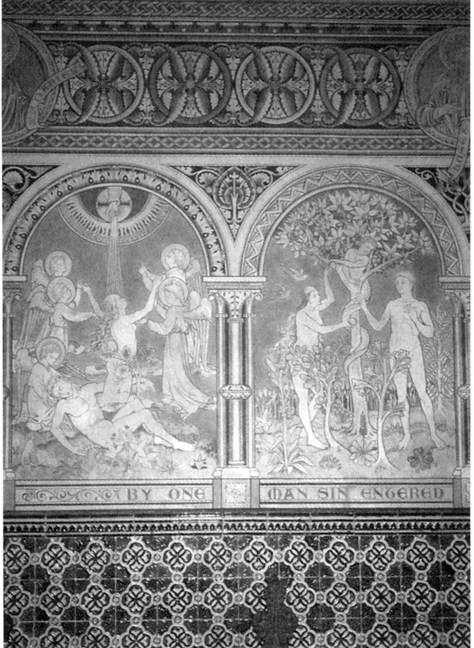

Fig 300.

HORNSEA

Farrago, at 6 WILTON ROAD, roughly halfway between Mere and sea, is indescribably odd. The house (no public access) was designed and built by the Hull master builder David Reynard Robinson (1843-1913) in 1908-9 as his own retirement home, and is more artwork than architecture.[15] The bolted steel frame, brick walls and mass-concrete floors were run of the mill, but the cladding and layout of the rooms were most definitely not: what appears to be the front door leads into a garage (into which it is impossible to drive a car), the bathroom projects from the front of the house, there is an upstairs back yard complete with outside toilet, and almost every internal surface - apart from the walls of the octagonal drawing room, which are stencilled - is clad in ceramic tiles or glazed bricks. The front facade has bright, polychrome zigzags of glazed brick, while the tiles used internally are Dutch, Spanish and English, some broken and laid in wild patterns on the floors, others used more decorously in dados and wall panels (Fig 301). Robinson himself remains an enigmatic figure about whom little is known, apart from the fact that he was a successful commercial builder whose major contract was Hull's City Hall (1903-9). He was born at Skirlaugh, about eight miles south-west of Hornsea, and he died at Farrago in 1913; he was buried at Skirlaugh Church. Farrago was listed, although only at grade II, in 1985. The house is a monument to Robinson's creativity, skill at improvisation and sense of constructional fun; and perhaps also to a profitable City Hall contract.

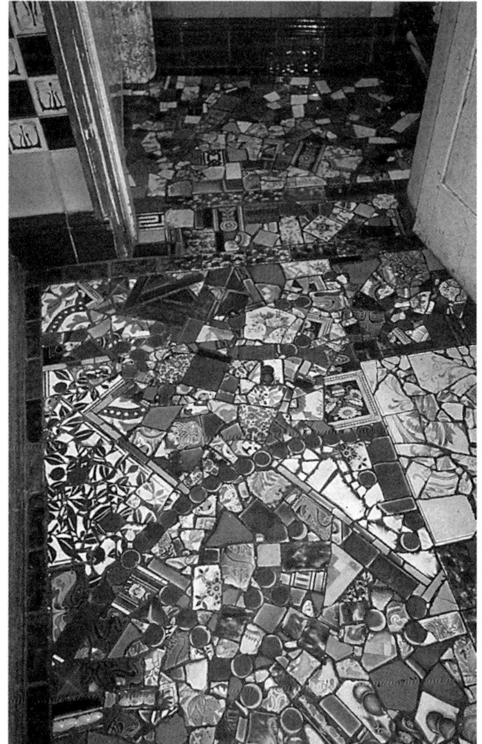
Fig 301.

HULL

There were significant losses from Hull's stock of ceramic locations during the 1980s and 1990s. The

Hull Daily Mail Building (1923), with an interesting assortment of mostly Dutch tilework inside and out, closed in 1989 and was demolished shortly afterwards. The Madeley Street Baths (1885), off Hessle Road, had fine Craven Dunnill art nouveau tiling, but was demolished in the early 1980s, and several of the city's tile, glazed brick and faience pubs were lost around the same time. However, much remains, including two of only fourteen turn-of-the-century curved ceramic bar counters left in England, at the White Hart and the Polar Bear. Many of the city's tiled street names have also survived, as have most of the amazing array of Victorian, Edwardian and interwar porch tiles; this is probably the best collection of *in situ* porch tiles in Britain, only rivalled by those of Crewe, Cheshire.

This tour begins on the west of the city centre at **Paragon Station**, PARAGON SQUARE, and ends in the Old Town near Holy Trinity Church in the Market Place. The railway reached Hull in 1840, terminating at the Humber Dock, with the first station on the present site being completed in 1848. William Bell, the North Eastern Railway's chief architect, made large extensions to the station, including the construction of a new booking hall, in 1903-4. This unusual space has arcaded walls in cream, green and brown Burmantofts tiling, and centres on the large oak-panelled former ticket office, whose window labels include '1,000-mile Tickets' and 'Pleasure Parties'.[16] The booking hall tiling was carried out by Whitehead of Leeds, and the terrazzo mosaic floor, with its NER motif, is by Hodkin & Jones Ltd of Sheffield.[17]

From the station, before crossing Paragon Square, turn right into ANLABY ROAD to see the now-disused **Tower Cinema** (1914), a notably early purpose-built cinema designed by the Hull architect Horace Percival Binks (Fig 302). The jolly classical faience facade is topped by twin golden, glass mosaic-covered domes, between which is a female figure - claimed to be Mary Pickford - holding a cinematograph camera and a roll of film. The surface of the green and white faience, which was probably made by Burmantofts, has been damaged by over-zealous cleaning. Now cross Paragon Square, heading into PARAGON STREET where one of the local chain of **William Jackson's** shops stands on the corner with South Street; it was probably designed by the local architectural practice begun by Sir William Alfred Gelder (1855-1941). Its 1920s white faience facade includes blue mosaic advertising panels. Many of the Jackson's shops in Hull have similar mosaic advertisements for 'Wedding Cakes' and the like.

Just north on JAMESON STREET is the brick and white faience **King Albert Chambers** (1923, architect T. Beecroft Atkinson); its foundation stones - actually glazed faience blocks - bear the builder's and architect's names. Inside the entrance hall are four hand-painted tile panels (on dust-pressed 6" blanks) depicting Belgian scenes including Bruges, Brussels and King Albert of Belgium. These tiles were probably produced by the firm Les Majoliques de Hasselt (also known as Manufacture de Céramiques Décoratives) from Hasselt in north-east Belgium, as one of the boats shown has 'MH' as its registration letters.

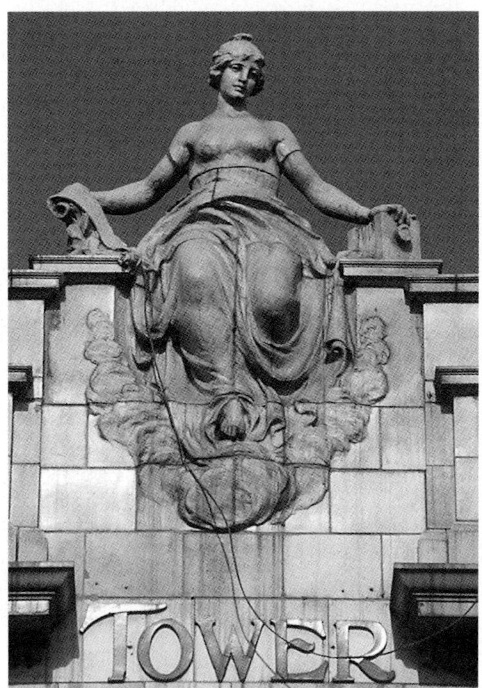

Fig 302.

The junction to the east, where Jameson Street joins KING EDWARD STREET, is dominated by a vast mosaic mural, occupying the concave, square 'gable end' above the entrance to the **BHS store** (1963, formerly the Hull & East Riding Co-op). The mural was designed by the Wolverhampton artist Alan Boyson and its theme is ships and the sea. Follow King Edward Street south to QUEEN VICTORIA SQUARE; on the north side is the **Yorkshire Bank** (1898, architect B. S. Jacobs, originally the Yorkshire Penny Bank). Its renaissance-style terracotta was a warm orangey-pink until cleaning removed the terracotta fireskin, and it is now a paler yellow. Jacobs was responsible for several similar terracotta buildings in Hull.

The west side of the square is occupied by the City Hall (1903-9), built by David Reynard Robinson, creator of the tiled house Farrago in Hornsea and builder of the nearby **Punch Hotel** (1896). Its extravagant, mock Tudor Burmantofts terracotta facade was designed by the local architects Smith, Brodrick & Lowther, a practice begun by the Hull-born Cuthbert Brodrick (1821-1905) in 1845 (Fig 303). Brodrick is best known for his 1852 competiton-winning design for Leeds Town Hall, and for Scarborough's Grand Hotel (1862-7). Brodrick ceased to practice in 1869 but the firm was continued by his nephew, Frederick Stead Brodrick, in partnership with Richard George Smith by 1875 and Arthur Lowther from the early 1890s, after which the firm produced some of Hull's most memorable ceramic pubs.[18] As well as good lettering, the Punch Hotel has decorative panels above its entrance by the Burmantofts artist E. C. Spruce.

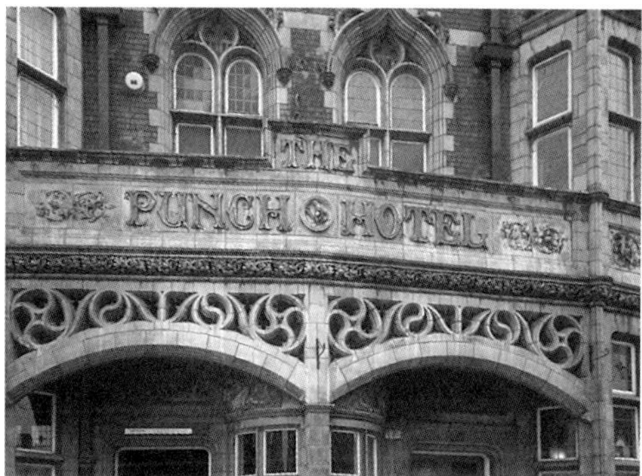

Fig 303.

From Queen Victoria Square, head east into the Old Town along Whitefriargate; at its end, on the right, is TRINITY HOUSE LANE and the **Bonny Boat Inn**. Its green-tiled exterior by David Reynard Robinson features a small panel depicting a punt-like craft. Return to Whitefriargate, turning right into SILVER STREET to find (down an alley on the north side) the **Old White Harte** pub. Around the fireplace are late nineteenth century Dutch tin glazed tiles showing landscapes and biblical scenes; they were probably made by Ravesteijn of Utrecht. Two blocks north on ALFRED GELDER STREET is the **White Hart PH** (1904, architects Freeman, Son & Gaskell); it was built by David Reynard Robinson. Although its tiled back room and blue Minton Hollins ceramic barfront were destroyed in 1981, a semicircular bow-fronted olive green and yellow ceramic bar remains in the front room. It is one of only fourteen such faience barfronts left in Britain, and is almost identical to the Burmantofts example at the Garden Gate PH, Leeds.

Continue east towards the River Hull along Chapel Lane, turning right into HIGH STREET. At 40 High Street is the red brick and buff terracotta facade of the former **Pacific Club** (1899), whose architect Benjamin S. Jacobs of Hull was an enthusiastic user of architectural ceramics; here the lintels are made of faience blocks fitted together jigsaw-puzzle style. Nearby at 25 High Street is the mid-seventeenth century facade of the **Wilberforce House Museum**, birthplace of the anti-slavery campaigner William Wilberforce. Inside are several fireplaces with Dutch tin-glazed tiles, mostly showing landscapes, biblical scenes and animals; the majority date from the eighteenth century but some are from the seventeenth and nineteenth centuries.

To the south in the MARKET PLACE is the massive **Holy Trinity Church**; its transepts, built in the early fourteenth century, represent the earliest substantial use of brick for church construction in England. The Godwin tile pavement in the sanctuary was installed in 1870 as part of Sir George Gilbert Scott's restoration. Just south-east, in the shadow of the church and almost beneath the gilded statue of King William III on horseback (1734, Peter Scheemakers), is the gentlemen's public convenience known as the **'King Billy' toilets**. A glazed brick stairway leads down to this lavish art nouveau underground gents, which was built in 1902 and designed by the City Engineer W. H. Lucas; it has hardly been altered. J. C. Edwards of Ruabon supplied the terracotta, the tile and faience work - including friezes and ornate columns with scalloped and swagged capitals - is by Burmantofts, and the shield on the coping came from the Accrington Brick & Tile Company.[19] Even the urinal stalls are of transfer-printed ceramics. The sanitary fittings were provided by B. Finch & Co of Lambeth, sanitary engineers. To return to Paragon Station, head west past Prince's Dock and along Paragon Street.

Of the many interesting ceramic locations in Hull's suburbs, the **Beverley Road Baths** (1903-5, designed by the first City Architect, Joseph H. Hirst) is the best-known; it stands about a mile north of the city centre at 250 BEVERLEY ROAD. The baths survived threats of partial demolition during the early 1990s, and after a two-year closure for refurbishment around 2002, now functions as a swimmimg centre. It has a magnificent art nouveau tiled entrance hall by the Campbell Tile Co, as well as good tiling and mosaic work along the corridors and in the baths, where the individual cubicles still retain their tiles.[20] There are several good ceramic pub facades nearby on the Beverley Road, notably the **Bull** (1903, architects Freeman, Son & Gaskell).

North-west of the centre in SPRING BANK is the **Polar Bear PH**, which has a semicircular brown faience bow-fronted barfront. It might well have been made by Burmantofts, as it resembles their earliest known example, which was installed at Newcastle upon Tyne's Station Hotel in 1892-3. On the right at the end of Spring Bank is PRINCE'S AVENUE, the four streets running west from it being known as **The Avenues**, an area of broad tree-lined streets of middle class housing laid out from 1874; here there are many tiled porches, dados, steps, entrance halls and paths. On the corner of Prince's Avenue and THORESBY STREET is a **former butcher's shop** with four animal heads on its stall riser and an excellent tiled interior.

There are more ceramic pubs west of Hull's centre along HESSLE ROAD. First, near the east end, is the turn-of-the-century **Alexandra Hotel** (Smith, Brodrick & Lowther) with a lower facade of nicely detailed glossy baroque Burmantofts faience in brown and yellow, set off by glazing bars in unusual star-shapes.[21] Just over a mile further west near the junction with Hawthorn Avenue is the **Dairycoates Inn** (1874), its green-tiled exterior featuring an elegant panel of an anchor; this refers to the pub's original owners, Hull's Anchor Brewery, known from 1888 as the Hull Brewery Company. Many Hull Brewery pubs were built or rebuilt by the builder and tile enthusiast David Reynard Robinson, which probably explains their profusion of tilework, particularly the unusually high number of ceramic barfronts, of which there were at least eight in the city's pubs.

From the north-east edge of the city centre, North Bridge leads across the River Hull into WITHAM. On the south side at 119-127 Witham are the livery stables (now shops) of **T. S. Annison & Sons**, built around 1900 and still retaining the ususual upper floor stabling; the facade is of red brick with white brick and faience dressings. Further along is the polychrome Burmantofts faience lower facade of the **Windmill Hotel**, which includes reliefs of windmills and dates from 1902. The continuation of Witham is the HOLDERNESS ROAD; about a quarter-mile along is **East Hull Pools**, built as the Holderness Road Baths in 1897-8 and probably designed by J. H. Hirst. There is much red and yellow brick outside and a superb tile and faience interior, with ornate cream, buff and pale green mouldings. Just over a mile along Holderness Road in the **East Park** area are many houses with tiled porches; those in WESTMINSTER AVENUE (east of the park) are notable for their use of Spanish tiles.

RUDSTON

The extensive tile pavements at **All Saints Church** were installed during the 1861 restoration by the architect G. Fowler Jones, who was also responsible for the unusual reredos: a stone arcade on marble columns, behind which is very bright Minton wall tiling with lots of red and blue geometrics. A mile to the east of the village is **Thorpe Hall**, where the octagonal dairy (1821, no public access) is faced with coloured glazed tiles.

SLEDMERE

Sledmere House was begun by Richard Sykes in 1751 then much enlarged by Sir Christopher Sykes during 1783-1800; seven armorial and figurative Coade stone plaques from the late 1780s still ornament the exterior. A fire in 1911 nearly destroyed the house, which was rebuilt for Sir Mark Sykes, sixth baronet, and his father Sir Tatton Sykes (1826-1913), fifth baronet, in 1912-17, its appearance being maintained almost exactly as before. Some changes were made to the interior, including the installation of the Turkish Room for Sir Mark Sykes (d1919), who was a noted orientalist. The Turkish Room, whose walls are completely tiled, was designed by an Armenian artist, David Ohanessian, and based on a room in the mosque of Yeni Valideh Djami, Istanbul; it was intended as a cooling room for a Turkish bath. The tiles were made in Damascus under the supervision of Ohanessian.

East Yorkshire Roundup

Ayres butcher's shop at 25 Prospect Street, **Bridlington**, has a stall riser (probably interwar) sporting two fancy blue pig heads. In the north chapel of the exuberantly classical R. C. Church of St Mary and St Everilda (1836-9), **Everingham**, are good encaustic tiles; the church stands next to Everingham Hall in Everingham Park. In the churchyard of St Augustine's Church, **Skirlaugh** (south-west of the church) is the grave of David Reynard Robinson (1843-1913), builder of 'Farrago', Hornsea; around the low, stone tomb runs a band of pseudo-mosaic tiles.

In addition the following churches have tile pavements: St Margaret, Beswick (Minton, 1871);

All Saints, Brantingham (Godwin, 1872); St Oswald, Flamborough (Minton, 1869); St Augustine, Hedon (Minton, 1844 and Godwin, 1869); All Saints, Hessle (Maw, 1870); St Peter, Hutton Cranswick (Minton, 1877); St Andrew, Kirk Ella (Minton, 1860); St Andrew, Middleton-on-the-Wolds (Minton); St Stephen, Newport (Godwin, 1898); All Saints, North Ferriby (Minton, 1848); All Saints, Rise (Minton, 1844); St Leonard, Scorborough (Minton, 1859) and St Mary, South Dalton (Maw, 1861).

North Yorkshire

BALDERSBY ST JAMES

The architect William Butterfield built much of the village of Baldersby St James for his frequent patron, the seventh Viscount Downe of Baldersby Park, including the **Church of St James the Greater** (1855-7). Encaustic tiles in the chancel, probably by Maw & Co, include four-tile armorial groups of Viscount Downe's family, the Dawnays. Also in the chancel is a monument to the Viscount, who died shortly before completion of the church.

BARTON

Inside **North Hall** (no public access), SILVER STREET, is an unusually extensive series of tile murals by Carter's dating from 1913. The finely-detailed medieval hunting scene was designed and painted by James Radley Young (1867-1933).

BOLTON-ON-SWALE

The architect William Eden Nesfield (1835-88) restored **St Mary's Church** around 1877. His work included the installation of a *cuenca* tiled dado which runs from the sanctuary into the Carpenter Chapel. Spanish-style tiling was popular with several architects during the 1870s and into the early 1880s, notably G. E. Street (1824-81), whose *Some account of Gothic Architecture in Spain* was first published in 1865. Street's chief assistant in 1859 was Richard Norman Shaw (1831-1912), who worked with Nesfield from 1863; Shaw and Nesfield were in a formal partnership during 1866-9. All three architects used very similar *cuenca* tiles in church restoration work.[22] Street stated that the tiles which he specified for Christ Church Cathedral, Dublin, during his 1868-78 restoration were made by Frederick Garrard of Millwall, who was described by the architect as 'that most exact and perfect maker of majolica - my old assistant and friend, Mr Garrard'.[23] The tiles were copies of original Spanish majolica wall tiles found during the restoration work. It is almost certain that the *cuenca* tiles used by all three architects were manufactured by Garrard.

The Carpenter Chapel is also of interest for its series of 1905-6 cement reliefs by the sculptor Mary Ellen Rope, who also designed for Birkenhead's Della Robbia Pottery from 1896 until the firm closed in 1906. The reliefs were commissioned as a memorial to Admiral Talbot Carpenter and his wife; the Admiral was naval aide-de-camp to Queen Victoria and one of Rope's most distinguished patrons. The design, based on psalm 104, shows farming and seafaring scenes.[24]

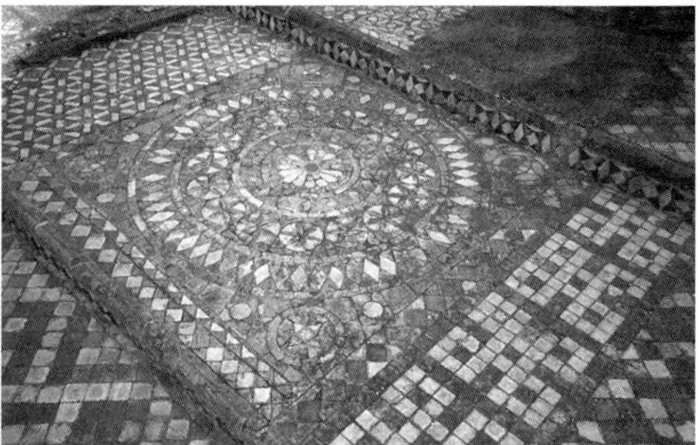

Fig 304.

BYLAND ABBEY

The Cistercians moved to **Byland Abbey** (EH) in 1177. The monastery prospered until the end of the thirteenth century, but was pillaged by the Scots in 1322 and only twelve monks remained by 1381; its dissolution took place in 1538. The site today is dominated by the remains of the great west front and its wheel window. The whole church was originally tiled in green and yellow geometrical patterns, and some tiles remain in the south transept chapels and parts of the crossing; although other Yorkshire abbeys had similar tiling, these are some of the finest medieval pavements which remain *in situ* (Fig 304). The tile pavement in the nave was divided into east-west bands two to three yards across, but in the south transept chapels the design is in smaller sections of differing patterns, including a complete roundel. The risers of the steps in the chapels and presbytery are faced with unworn tiles which show how bright the pavement would have looked when originally laid, either at the end of the twelfth century or near the middle of the thirteenth century. The tiles were probably made at the nearby Old Byland tilery, or possibly in Ryedale, near Rievaulx.[25]

COVERHAM

The architect Christoper George Wray, sometime chief architect to the Government of Bengal, restored **Holy Trinity Church** in 1878, installing two striking but rather different areas of wall tiling (Fig 305). The reredos is by Minton & Co and includes much highly glazed pink, green and yellow tiling centred on an agnus dei tile. The majolica tiles by Maw & Co which cover the east wall of the south aisle are mostly in pink, blue, green and white with scroll and anthemion patterns, and were presented by the patron of the church, Thomas Topham, who also gave the chancel's encaustic tile pavement. The nave and aisle flooring was of patent polished concrete bordered by glazed encaustic tiles.[26] This remote church is in the care of the Churches Conservation Trust.

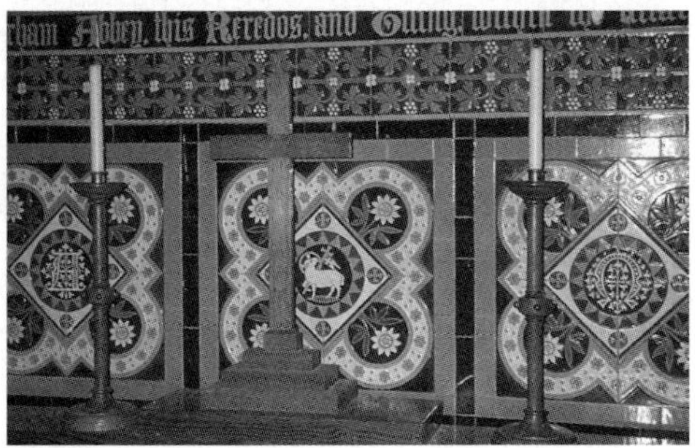

Fig 305.

COXWOLD

The terracotta tombstone of Michael Stratton (1953-99), author of *The Terracotta Revival* (1993) and founding secretary of the Tiles and Architectural Ceramics Society in 1981, stands in the churchyard of **St Michael's Church**. It was designed by the architect Ptolemy Dean and made by Shaws of Darwen (sculptor Norman Scanlon), its production taking around four weeks in order to avoid warping. The headstone was erected in 2002, after a long battle with the Church of England concerning the use of terracotta rather than stone.

FOUNTAINS ABBEY

By the end of the twelfth century there were more than fifty Cistercian monks and at least two hundred lay brothers at **Fountains Abbey** (NT), and much building work took place in the first half of the thirteenth century; the site is now the largest monastic ruin in Britain. It is probable that the decorative tile pavements at the abbey were the first in Britain; they were laid between 1220 and 1247 and were probably made at Fountains by tilers from Cistercian houses on the continent. Some of the tiles, which are unusually thick, have been relaid near the site of the high altar of the abbey church, where they can still be seen.[27]

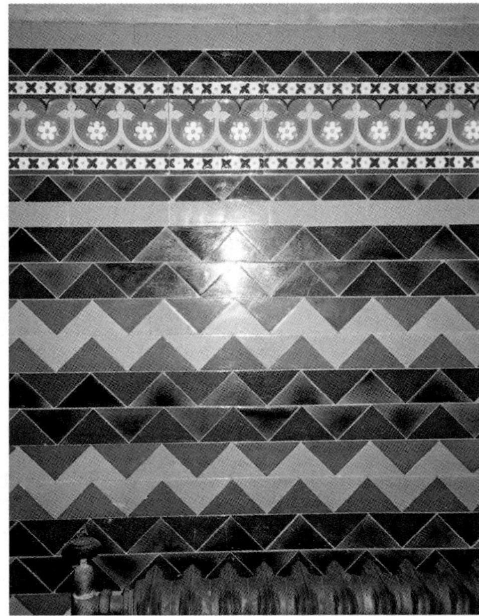
Fig 306.

FOXHOLES

St Mary's Church was rebuilt in 1866 by the York architect George Fowler Jones. The floor is of unremarkable, mostly geometric, tiling but the apsidal chancel has a dado of zigzag tile bands in bright blue, red and green, topped by a pretty yellow and green floral frieze (Fig 306). The whole is certainly a shock, but attractive; was it a case of trying to outdo Butterfield? The church records show that Minton & Co were paid £32.1s.6d for the chancel tiling.

HARROGATE

Harrogate developed as a spa town after the discovery of medicinal springs in 1571, but by the 1880s the town's bathing facilities were seen as less attractive than those of competing British and Europan resorts. A competition was held in 1889-90 to produce a design for a completely new baths establishment; from twenty-six entries, the winners were the architects Frank Baggallay and Fred Bristowe of London. Their plans were amended to include Turkish baths, which in England comprised three progressively hot rooms where dry heat was interspersed with cold showers or dips in a plunge pool. The true Turkish bath uses wet heat (steam) and is normally referred to in England as a Russian bath. The foundation stone of what was intended to be the finest hydrotherapy treatment centre in Europe was laid in 1894, and the Royal Baths was opened in 1897; the cost was around £120,000. It is now known as **Harrogate Turkish Baths and Health Spa**, and stands on CRESCENT STREET and Parliament Street.

The interior, where Turkish baths and more than a dozen other types of treatment were available, was a glazed brick nirvana with Moorish-style arches, columns and screens, terrazzo floors and walls of colourful brickwork. The tiled walls of the inhalation room were by Wedgwood, who featured the scheme in their catalogue, but the extensive glazed brickwork, which ran throughout a series of rooms in varying patterns, would have been supplied by another manufacturer, possibly Craven Dunnill.[28] Initially the Royal Baths were hugely successful, but changing fashions resulted in the closure of the treatment rooms in 1969, after which the complex became known as the Assembly Rooms. However, a revival in the popularity of hydrotherapy led to its refurbishment in two stages, during 2002 and 2004, the latter works including complete restoration of the Turkish baths.

Also in Harrogate, on EAST PARADE, is the **Odeon Cinema**, opened in 1936 and designed by W. Calder Robson of the Harry Weedon practice. Its design, with a finned facade and much buff faience by Shaws of Darwen, was almost exactly the same as that of the Odeon, Sutton Coldfield, Warwickshire, whose architect J. Cecil Clavering had left the Weedon practice in 1935, soon after completing the iconic Odeon, Kingstanding, Birmingham, which combined streamlining, faience and the vertical feature or fin.[29]

HELMSLEY

All Saints Church was rebuilt in 1866-9. Immediately afterwards a new vicar, Charles Norris Gray, arrived in Helmsley. At the time church attendances were small and the village a rural backwater, but Gray rapidly changed this, starting a parish magazine, studying the history of the town, and rebuilding local churches; he also became famous as a trainer of clergy. Gray gave All Saints its extravagantly colourful interior, which includes dramatic wall paintings (notably a dashing dragon), stained glass and encaustic tiles (Fig 307). The tiled floor is fairly plain but in the choir is a cross-shaped installation of decorative glazed encaustics centred on a mosaic of a pelican in its piety.

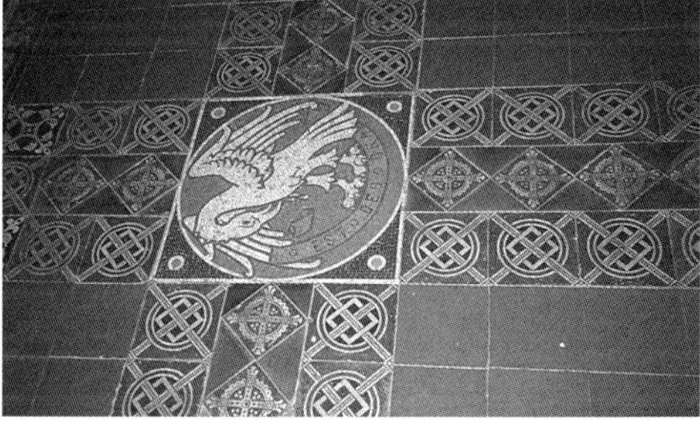

Fig 307.

LOW BENTHAM

St John the Baptist Church was restored by Richard Norman Shaw in 1876-8; it has a chancel dado of *cuenca* tiles made by Frederick Garrard of Millwall. (See above, Bolton-on-Swale, North Yorkshire.)

MIDDLESBROUGH

At the **Railway Station** on ZETLAND ROAD is a Craven Dunnill tile map of the North Eastern Railway network dating from soon after 1900 (for further details, see above, York Railway Station). Opposite the station at 9 Zetland Road is the **Zetland Hotel**; its 1893 back bar extension (by local architect John M. Bottomley) has spectacular polychrome wall tiling by Craven Dunnill including pictorial panels of local scenes, a variety of classical mouldings and faience-framed mirrors.[30] Nearer the centre of Middlesbrough on CORPORATION ROAD is the eclectic salmon pink Doulton terracotta facade of the former **Empire Theatre** (1897-9, now a pub); its architect was the theatre specialist Ernest Runtz.

MOUNT GRACE PRIORY

The entrance to **Mount Grace Priory** (EH), the fourteenth-century remains of a Carthusian foundation, is through the manor house built in 1654 in the ruins of the fifteenth-century monastery guest house. In 1900-1 the manor house was carefully rebuilt, using traditional techniques, by the Middlesbrough industrialist Sir Lowthian Bell and his architect Ambrose Poynter. The tiles of the fire surrounds in the entrance hall and the northernmost room of the upper floor date from this rebuilding work, and were probably made at the Garrard & Co works in Millwall, which produced copies of Delft tiles during 1895-1920. The polychrome tiles in the upper room have colours different from the Delft originals on which they are based, and their fleur-de-lys corner motifs are broader and truncated.[31]

OLD BYLAND

The tiled altar platform at All Saints Church is the only known example of a medieval tile pavement in a Yorkshire parish church; it has a circular geometric pattern.[32]

RICHMOND

The **Fleece Hotel**, FRIARS WYND (just off the market place) is a miniature castle in yellowy-brown terracotta, all turrets and battlements. The pub was built in 1897 and designed by G. Gordon Hoskins, once clerk to Alfred Waterhouse. Hoskins had just completed work on Darlington Technical College (1893-6), which used quantities of buff Burmantofts terracotta; it therefore seems likely that the same firm supplied the terracotta wares for the Fleece, including plaques bearing the date and the brewer's arms. The pub was put up for the Sunderland brewer Robert Fenwick, whose brewery had become a limited liability company as R. Fenwick & Co in 1896, with an estate of sixty-three houses. Possibly the Fleece, which must have been expensive to construct, proved too great an investment for the brewery, as the firm was acquired by the Alloa brewer George Younger in 1878.

RIEVAULX

The magnificent ruins of **Rievaulx Abbey** (EH), the first of the northern Cistercian foundations, lie deep in the valley of the River Rye about three miles west of Helmsley. The site was granted in 1131 and colonised the following year by monks from Clairvaux. The church, which was completed in the thirteenth century, was built on a north-south axis due to the constraints of the site. In the remains of the nave chapels and elsewhere are small areas of mosaic tiles dating from the mid-thirteenth century; they were probably made nearby in Ryedale (Fig 308). These were first exposed to view in the 1920s and are in fairly good condition, some still retaining their original glazed surface.

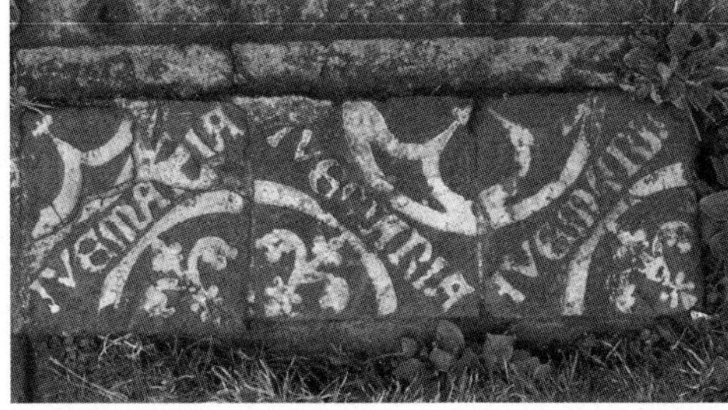

Fig 308.

Rievaulx Abbey was dissolved in 1538. After several changes of hands, the site was bought by Sir Charles Duncombe, a London banker, in 1687. After his death in 1711 the estate was inherited by his brother-in-law, Thomas Brown, who changed his name to Duncombe and began to build Duncombe Park, just south-west of Helmsley, which was completed in 1713. He also laid out a gently curving terrace to the east of the house and erected a temple at each end. Duncombe's grandson inherited the estate in 1746 and set about making his own terrace overlooking Rievaulx in 1751-61; he may have intended to connect it with the Duncombe terrace using a viaduct. His **Rievaulx Terrace** (NT, access from the B1257), on the valley top, well above the abbey, has a rectangular Ionic temple at its north end and the circular Tuscan temple, built about 1758, at the south end. The interior of the Tuscan temple has rich plasterwork decoration and is floored with part of a medieval tile pavement supposedly found near the high altar of Rievaulx Abbey in 1821; alternatively the tiles may have come from Byland Abbey. By the early 1990s the tiles were in poor condition and suffering from salt action.

RIPON

The elaborate, almost pale orange terracotta facade of the **Spa Baths** (1904-5, architect S. Stead) in PARK STREET is vaguely art nouveau in style (Fig 309). Inside is an even more splendid Burmantofts faience and tile-lined foyer,

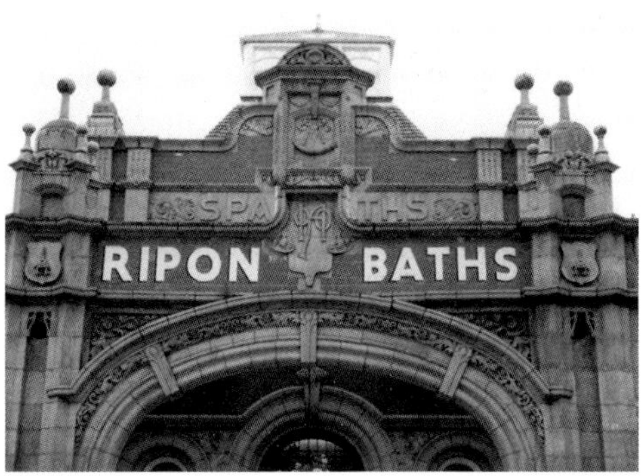

Fig 309.

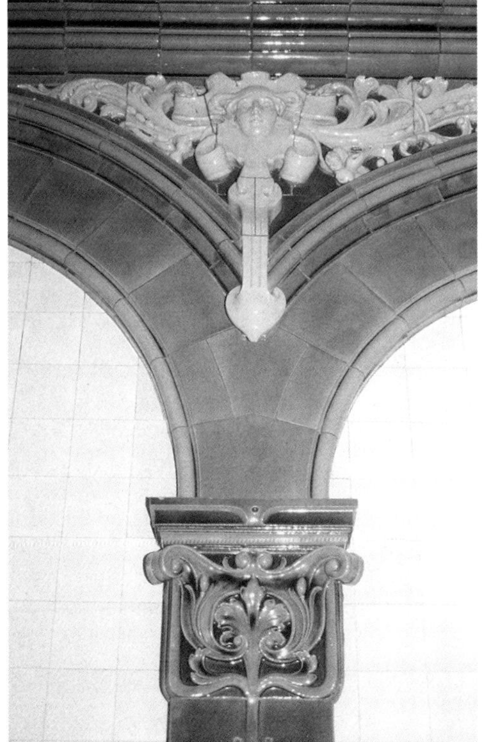
Fig 310.

originally the Pump Room, with good stained glass windows showing scenes from Ripon's past (Fig 310). The faience is mainly olive green but with rich ornament - scrollwork, female heads, fabulous monsters - in bright red and yellow. There is also a faience fountain supported on corbels in the form of female heads.

SALTBURN

At Saltburn's **Railway Station** is one of the Craven Dunnill tile maps of the North Eastern Railway network; it dates from soon after 1900. Just seaward of the railway station, on the corner of MILTON STREET and Ruby Street (one of the 'jewel streets') is **Gosnay's butcher's shop**, with a fully tiled 1920s interior including a colourful ornate frieze with swags and scrollwork in menu-like motifs.

SCARBOROUGH

Scarborough was a flourishing spa resort by the late seventeenth century, and its sea bathing season had begun to develop by the 1730s. The arrival of the railway in 1845 was followed by weekend invasions of trippers in the early 1850s, and by 1881 Scarborough was the sixth largest resort in England and Wales. A jolly clock tower of 1883 marks out the much-extended **Railway Station** on WESTBOROUGH, which still retains a Craven Dunnill tile map of the NER network dating from soon after 1900. Opposite is the **Stephen Joseph Theatre**, formerly the Odeon Cinema (1935-6), designed by J. Cecil Clavering and Robert Bullivant of the Harry Weedon architectural practice. The ground floor is clad in black faience, with cream faience, picked out in red and black, above and on the tall fin. Conversion to a theatre during the early 1990s entailed the loss of much of the interior, but the exterior was changed only slightly, with alterations to the signage and replacement or repair of a few previously damaged faience slabs.

Continue along Westborough towards the sea. Shortly on the left is ALBEMARLE CRESCENT and the **Capitol Cinema** (1928-9, now Mecca Bingo) with an ornate classical white faience facade including figures, musical instruments, fish shells and other motifs. Further along Westborough, and again on the left, is ABERDEEN WALK and the **Scarborough Evening News office**. Inside, but just visible from outside when closed, is an exquisite frieze of Pilkington's galleon tiles interspersed with plain lustre tiles, all probably dating from renovation of the building around 1900.

Now for the seafront. Head south along Huntriss Row (almost opposite Aberdeen Walk), emerging on to ST NICHOLAS CLIFF, where the massive bulk of the **Grand Hotel** (1863-7, architect Cuthbert Brodrick) obscures most of the sea view. This mountainous structure is said to be a calendar building, in that it has four towers (the seasons), rises twelve floors above the promenade (the months), has 52 chimneys (the weeks) and 365 bedrooms (the days). In fact the number of rooms is debateable, but the hotel was certainly the most advanced in Europe once complete. Its construction took around 6.25 million bricks, all made at Malton's brickworks, about a mile west of the hotel on the Scalby road.[33] In addition the Grand's facings include much tawny terracotta, mostly used as string courses and in unusual spiralling dressings around the doors and windows. These have worn well, in contrast to the red sandstone of its ornate porch, which has decayed badly; the source of the terracotta is unknown. The Grand Hotel is an example of the increasing use of terracotta during the 1860s; another is the Duke of Cornwall Hotel in Plymouth, also built in 1863-7, where Blashfield's provided the terracotta dressings.[34]

South of the hotel is the Cliff Bridge, beneath which stood the Aquarium (1874-7), an extravagant entertainment centre designed by Eugenius Birch and demolished in the late 1960s. Most of the floors and dados of its exotic interior were tiled: there were red, buff and black encaustics with a hawthorn blossom pattern, and floor tiles with shells, seaweed, starfish and dolphin motifs. Still surviving, however, below the Esplanade on South Bay, is the **Spa Complex**, which can be seen from Cliff Bridge. A new ballroom, clad in faience from the Hathern Station Brick and Terra Cotta Company, was added to the 1877-80 spa building in 1925.[35]

The view north from Cliff Bridge is dominated by the Castle, just west of which, overlooking the North Bay, is the **Castle by the Sea**, MULGRAVE PLACE, off Castle Road. This low, castellated house (now an hotel) was built for the painter John Atkinson Grimshaw (1836-93), and was his home during 1876-9. In the dining room is a composite fireplace built by Grimshaw from found architectural elements. Its two tiled panels were painted by Grimshaw, and are probably the only tiles he ever painted. They show medieval figures, flowers, birds and insects in great and colourful detail, and in true Grimshaw style.

THIRKLEBY

All Saints Church (1849-50) was designed by the architect E. B. Lamb and built for Lady Louisa Frankland-Russell as a family mausoleum and memorial to her husband Sir Robert, seventh baronet, of Thirkleby Park. The buff, blue and brown encaustic tiles flooring the Frankland Chapel bear complex, intertwined Frankland monograms and were designed by Lamb, as were most of the furnishings.[36]

WEETON

St Barnabas Church (1851-3) was designed by George Gilbert Scott for the third Earl of Harewood (Fig 311). This lavishly appointed church benefited from several donations: Scott provide the star-spangled chancel roof, while Herbert Minton gave the reredos tiles, a brilliant display in red, blue and yellow featuring repeats of the Pugin-designed agnus dei roundel.[37] The sanctuary encaustic pavement, with roundels of the evangelists, is also by Minton.

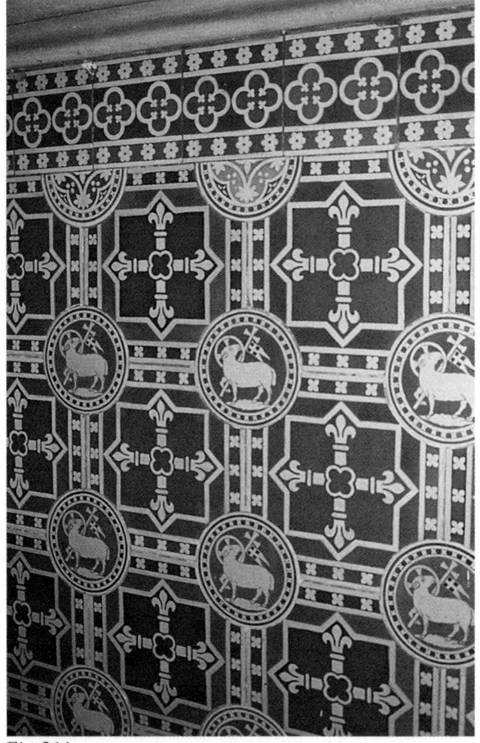

Fig 311.

WHITBY

On the east side of the River Esk, below the Abbey, there are many minor ceramic locations, particularly in Church Street and Sandgate. Most notable are the **Black Horse PH**, CHURCH STREET, which has late nineteenth century embossed tiles on its exterior, and the interwar tiled shopfront of **J. Storr Jet Manufacturer** at the top end of the street; in SANDGATE is a former butcher's shop with tile panels of bull and sheep heads. Across the bridge, the **Railway Station**, NEW QUAY ROAD, has one of the Craven Dunnill tiled maps of the North Eastern Railway network, dating from soon after 1900.

Just west of the station is **Bagdale Hall**, BAGDALE, built in 1516 as a manor house and now an hotel and restaurant (Fig 312). It has many fireplaces with Dutch tiles, either consisting of a mixture of seventeenth century and eighteenth century tiles, or a more homogeneous arrangement of what appear to be early twentieth century tiles. The most interesting examples are in the dining room, where one large fireplace has early twentieth century Dutch tiles painted in green (an unusual colour) and made in Harlingen, Friesland, while another has English tiles made by Carter, Stabler & Adams of Poole around 1920, with blue hand-painted scenes designed by the Belgian refugee Joseph Roelants. Near Bagdale Hall at the rear of **4 Bagdale**, now a solicitor's office, is an entrance tiled from top to bottom with late seventeenth and eighteenth century Dutch tiles, showing landscapes and biblical scenes. This is probably a nineteenth century installation and is still in good condition.

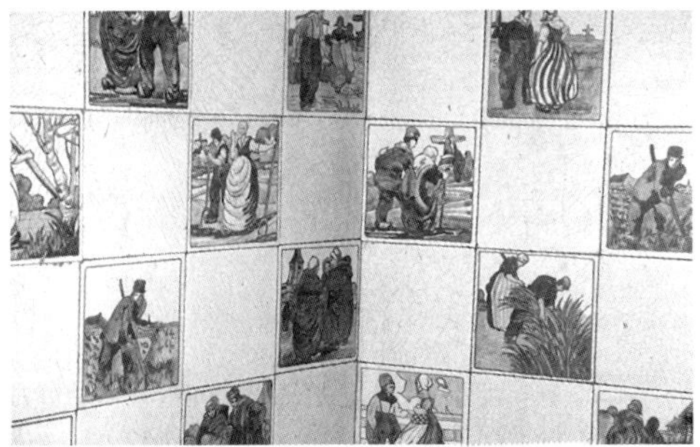

Fig 312.

Immediately north on BRUNSWICK STREET, also accessible from Baxtergate, is the **Brunswick Methodist Church**, designed by architects Waddington & Son of Burnley and opened in 1891; the adjoining Brunswick Room opened the following year. In 1895 Alderman Robert Elliott Pannett of Whitby, who believed that an air of reverence was best created in a place of beauty, paid for the interiors of the Brunswick Room and the associated spaces (including a smaller classroom known as the Pannett Room) to be lavishly decorated with tiles; the tile-lined walls are mostly pale green and primrose, with elaborate borders and a frieze of relief angel heads with wings.[38] In the Brunswick Room, on either side of the organ, which was finally installed in the 1920s, are tall, lancet-shaped panels of Powell's opus sectile work dating from 1898. They show Christ blessing children and Christ healing the sick; the cartoons were by John W. Brown and the cost was £150.[39] The combination of these large and colourful panels with the fine wall tiling is impressive and attractive, and is a rare example of the use of decorative ceramics within a Methodist building. Despite this, in 1996 the church was the subject of a planning application which would have involved demolition of the Brunswick Room. However, this was rejected following objections by many heritage bodies, and the room is now used for events such as antique fairs and the like.

North Yorkshire Roundup

The four-panel tiled reredos of St Oswald's Church, **Askrigg**, includes biblical quotations and is probably by Minton Hollins. As well a magnifient Minton encaustic pavement, the Church of St Thomas the Apostle, **Birstwith**, has a Powell's reredos of 1883 with mosaic panels flanked by glass tiles. The encaustic tile pavement in the sanctuary of St James Church, **Boroughbridge**, was donated by Herbert Minton in 1852; the tiles are a mixture of brown/buff and blue/buff designs. The chapel of **Giggleswick School** (1897-1901, architect Sir Thomas G. Jackson) has a copper-covered dome made of terracotta and faced internally with Powell's mosaics to a design by Jackson including the four evangelists; the cost of the mosaics was over £3,150.[40] Thirteenth century mosaic tiles from the adjacent Guisborough Priory have been relaid in St Nicholas Church, **Guisborough**. St Paul's Church (1854, William Butterfield), **Hensall**, built for the seventh Viscount Downe, has Minton encaustic floor tiles including Downe armorials and a very ornate tile and mosaic reredos (restored 1970), also by Minton's, featuring symbols of the passion. The sanctuary walls of All Saints Church, **Kirk Deighton**, are decorated with a broad band of Minton tiling including a series of roundels showing Christian symbols including those of the evangelists; it probably dates from 1874. The excellent green and white classical faience facade of the butcher's shop (formerly Freer's) on Commercial Street, **Norton**, dates from 1912, and includes a three-dimensional bull's head above the doorway; inside, the tilework features lozenge-shaped panels of animal heads (Fig 313). A tiled war memorial of 1920 by Jones & Willis of London may be seen at Selby Abbey, and there are interwar tiles by Candy & Co at the nearby New Inn on the main street of **Selby**. The Minton sanctuary tile pavement at Holy Trinity Church, **Skipton**, includes roundels of the four evangelists and probably dates from the 1850s or 1860s. The odd purple and green tiled reredos at St John the Baptist Church, **Stanwick St John**, was probable installed during its 1868 restoration by Anthony Salvin. The Craven Dunnill tile pavement at All Saints Church, **Thorpe Bassett**, was installed by Lancaster architects Paley & Austin during 1879-80 restoration work, and like many of their churches features line-impressed designs, which they first used in 1873.[41] There is dado tiling throughout the Church of St John the Evangelist (1858-60, architect G. E. Street), **Whitwell-on-the-Hill**. In St Martin's Church, **Womersley**, on the wall by the font, is a Spanish tile panel measuring about 5' by 3' and showing the Last Supper; it probably dates from the eighteenth century and was bought in Barcelona by Cassandra, Countess of Rosse, whose family held the Lordship of the Manor.

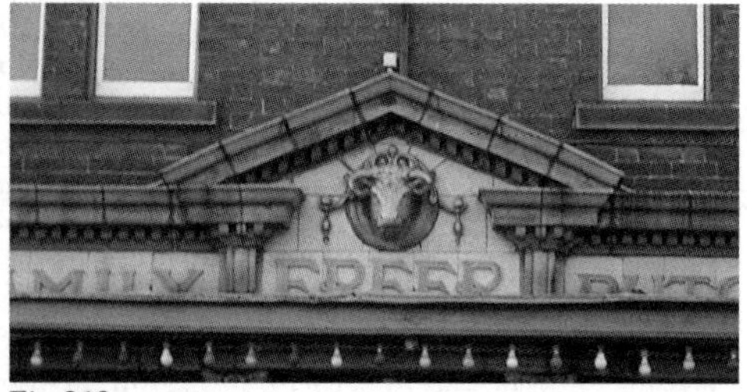

Fig 313.

South Yorkshire

BARNSLEY

In the centre of Barnsley, on WELLINGTON STREET and New Street, is the massive faience-clad form of the former **Barnsley Cooperative Store** (1911, architect A. H. Walsingham, listed II but disused in 2001). Its aggressively baroque facade is strongly articulated with shiny buff and matt green faience, the latter having a buff body and appearing so odd that it could simply have been overpainted (Fig 314). The ground floor was ruined by the insertion of new shopfronts during the 1970s, but above this, all is intact, with numerous cartouches, some with female heads and one bearing the words 'Barnsley British Co-operative Society Ltd'; a reclining lion looks down from the corner. While this is not a pretty building, it is a fabulous example of the external use of Burmantofts wares.[42]

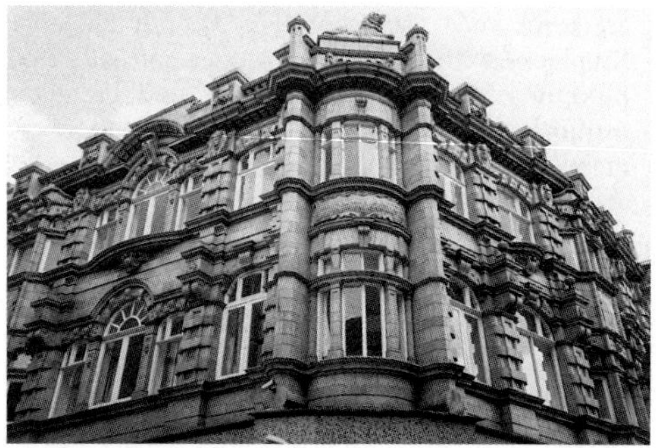

Fig 314.

To the north in SHAMBLES STREET is the mid-1960s **Central Library**; its dark brick walls were brightened in 1999 by the addition of three pictorial tile panels, the *Barnsley Banners* by Ailsa Magnus. They each measure about 4' high by 2' wide and are mounted well above ground. To the south of the old Co-op, in GEORGE STREET, is **Holy Rood R. C. Church**; its Lady Chapel has several ceramic wall panels.

DONCASTER

Marooned on the north side of the ring road, CHURCH WAY, is the cathedral-like **St George's Church**, built by George Gilbert Scott in 1854-8 to replace the ancient parish church burned out in 1853. The Forman Chapel - the lady chapel on its south side - was paid for by the wealthy landowner and property speculator William Henry Forman and has an elaborate Minton encaustic tile pavement. Beyond the ring road an alleyway leads into the shopping centre on Baxter Gate, where there are several shops with good interwar white faience facades, the two best being **Burton's**, with its ceramic name intact, and the larger but duller **Binn's**. At the south end of Baxter Gate turn left into the pedestrianised HIGH STREET; along the length of its pavements runs the **Doncaster Time Line**, a series of bricks and tiles with reliefs of historic local events and personalities. At 40 High Street is the bizarre **Westminster Offices**, with a 1920s facade of little bright blue glazed bricks with highlights in blue and gold mosaic, and other mosaic ornament. At the end of the High Street, just north in SILVER STREET, is a **jeweller's shop** of 1910 with massive white faience corbels propping up an overhanging oriel window.

From the end of High Street go south into Cleveland Street then right along PRINTING OFFICE STREET; the overpainted interwar faience facade of **Nelson's PH** includes two reliefs depicting Nelson and a galleon in full sail. Opposite is the little red brick and terracotta frontage of the former works of **Harold Arnold, Builder**, the name picked out in a string of encaustic letter tiles at first floor level. Finally, rounding the corner with ST SEPULCHRE GATE (the continuation of Baxter Gate) is the former Cooperative Store (1936-49), now partly known as **Danum House**. Its huge, modernist white faience facade includes a pair of bulging windows and a glazed stairwell which itself contains a glass brick tower and curving stair. Doncaster's interwar architecture is certainly impressive although much neglected.

SHEFFIELD

Begin at the **Railway Station** (1870, extended 1904) on SHEAF SQUARE, which has retained its original decoration in several public spaces, including the well-hidden tile-lined former first class refreshment room. Next head north up POND STREET, passing some bulky examples of Sheffield's 1960s rebuilding, notably the **Epic Development** (1968-9), which housed the Odeon and Roxy cinemas and is clad in acres of white Shaw-Hathernware Twintiles; it was the subject of redevelopment proposals in 2004.

At the top of Pond Street is FITZALAN SQUARE; on the left is the **White Building**, put up around 1908 and designed by the Sheffield architects Flockton & Gibbs, who built and owned it. The creamy-white Burmantofts Marmo facade includes a series of fine high-relief studies known as *The Sheffield Trades*, designed by the brothers Alfred Herbert Tory (b1881) and William Frank Tory, normally known as Frank Tory junior; the Tory brothers were sons of Frank Tory senior, who established the local firm of architectural stonemasons.[43] The Torys modelled the tradesmen's figures which were then sent away to Leeds to be replicated in faience. From left to right the trades shown are a silversmith, a steel roller and a file cutter, a grinder and a cutler (the initials of the artists are beneath this pair), a chaser and an engineer, and a steel crucible teemer.[44]

Turn left on to the High Street then right at Castle Square to find the monumental Cooperative store, **Castle House** in ANGEL STREET. This wonderful example of sixties architecture, christened 'the building of the future' by a local paper, was opened on the 13th May 1964. It was built for the Brightside & Carbrook (Sheffield) Co-operative Society Ltd following the destruction of their City Stores on Exchange Street by bombing during December 1940. The stairwells of the Castle Street (north) entrance and the Angel Street (west) entrance retain their exciting full-height geometric abstract Carter's tile murals, although the black and white relief-tiled lift surrounds by Lucien Myers have been replaced.[45]

Punched dramatically through the Co-op store's centre is a spiral stair, connecting the top-floor restaurant with the lower floors. At ground level in the Angel Street corner is a post office, whose entrance is now host to a First World War memorial to Sheffield's postal workers. The panel, showing a roll of honour between two classical columns, was moved from a nearby post office due to its closure in 1999. It was made by a local firm, Robertson & Russell, from an apparently ceramic material called morsatile; its opus sectile-like sheen and curving, cut forms suggest it contains some glass. The firm produced several other morsatile war memorials for local churches during 1920-1, including the example still extant at Wadsley Parish Church, Worrall Road, to the west of the city centre, where Jeremiah Robertson of Robertson & Russell was a parishioner.[46]

Opposite the Co-op's CASTLE STREET entrance, which is marked by a single mosaic-clad piloti, a drab gable end has been transformed by a 1986 brick mural, the ***Steelworker*** by the artist Paul Waplington. It was constructed by Sheffield's City Works Department using eighteen different types of brick from eight manufacturers, the total number of bricks being about 30,000. Just east of Castle House Co-op is **Castle Hill Market**, its WAINGATE entrance leading to a stairwell with a geometric tile mural comprising cut 6" tiles in black and dark gold, very effective in this gloomy space. Another modern installation is a short diversion east, through the Victoria Quays canal basin and across the bridge to the South Quay; just beyond is the BLAST LANE **pedestrian underpass** at the start of Sheffield Parkway. It is faced with an abstract tile mural, made in 1996 by local ceramicist Tracey Heyes (b1964), which uses a wide range of coloured mass-produced tiles (on white ground) in standard rectangular shapes; there are over 5,000 tiles. However, the vibrant colours are partly masked by much graffiti and the subway, part of a still-unfinished cycle route, is clearly neglected.

If Blast Lane is a step too far, head west along the High Street from Castle Square, turning left into pedestrianised Fargate just before the Cathedral. Soon on the left is NORFOLK ROW, leading to the theatres, Winter Garden and **St Marie's R. C. Cathedral** (1847-50), the highlight of any ceramic tour of Sheffield (Fig 315). Here the tile memorial has been transformed into a work of art. In the north aisle Mortuary Chapel one is invited to pray for the souls of the clergy who have served this parish, whose names and anniversaries are recorded month by month on an entire wall of glazed tiles; there is also a fine pictorial panel showing the death of a priest, and the floor comprises strips of brown encaustic tiles, some with lettering in buff recording those passed away. But this is far from all: there is a memorial floor tile inscription just north of the Mortuary Chapel, further tiling in the Blessed Sacrament Chapel and an encaustic pavement upstairs in the Lady Chapel (1878-9). In the south transept are more wall tiles requesting prayers for the deceased, with dates ranging from the 1860s to the 1880s, along with another long pictorial panel. Finally in the nearby Norfolk (or St Joseph's) Chapel, the excellent encaustic tiled floor shows emblems (the lion flying over the hat) of the Duke of Norfolk. Six pictorial tile panels on its south wall show female saints, and on the north are two more large tile panels depicting scenes relating to the Sisters of Notre Dame, who taught in Sheffield. This is a superb display of Victorian ecclesiastical tilework; all the hand-painted panels were probably produced by a local church decorating firm.

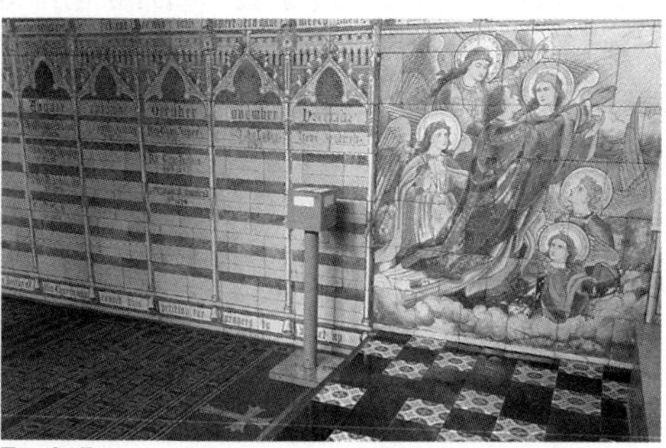

Fig 315.

Back on Fargate, continue south into PINSTONE STREET; just past the Town Hall is the **Peace Garden** (1999). This circular garden centres on a fountain, towards which the waters flow from eight coloured ceramic cascades and along eight channels lined with ceramics: these *Aquatic Plantforms* are by Tracey Heyes. She used press moulded and repeated forms in mostly blues and greens to achieve this unusual effect, which depicts the plant life which has returned to local rivers after years of industrial pollution. On the corner south of the Peace Garden is the rather undistinguished former Prudential Assurance building (1895-8, architect Alfred Waterhouse), now a **Laura Ashley** shop; its red terracotta is by J. C. Edwards of Ruabon.[47]

Attercliffe

In the centre of Attercliffe, on the south side of ATTERCLIFFE ROAD just east of the junction with Effingham Road, is **Spartan Works**, a small industrial complex dating from around 1880 which is decorated with ornate terracotta supplied by the Wharncliffe Fireclay Works (see Devonshire Quarter). A little further east, beyond Staniforth Road, is **Banners Store** (1926-8, extended 1933-4), an essay in white Doulton Carraraware and one of the best of several early twentieth century faience-faced commercial developments on the outskirts of the city centre.

Broomhill

Etruria House (1876, now an hotel), CROOKES ROAD, in the western suburb of Broomhill, was built for John Armitage of the Wharncliffe Fireclay Works (see Devonshire Quarter); the main building material was yellow brick, but with lavish use of terracotta ornament from the Works.

Devonshire Quarter

The Devonshire Quarter lies about a quarter-mile west of the city centre; on WEST STREET, near the tram stop, is the brown and yellow faience facade of local brewer Greaves & Co's **Hallamshire Hotel** (1903), with some fine lettering. A little south-west at 140-6 DEVONSHIRE STREET is the elaborately decorated former warehouse and showroom of the Wharncliffe Fireclay Works (1888), owned by John Armitage & Sons; the works themselves were sited at Deepcar, about ten miles north-west of the city.

Netherthorpe

The south-east gateway to **Weston Park** (opened 1875), WESTERN BANK, has piers of unpleasantly overpainted terracotta supplied by Blanchard's and designed by James Gamble; they include decorative panels based on earlier designs by the Sheffield-trained artist Godfrey Sykes (1824-66) for South Kensington Museum. Within the park is a monument to Sykes, a tall, white-painted six-section terracotta column set upon a stone base; it was made in 1871 and erected in 1875.

Norton Woodseats

St Chad's Church, LINDEN AVENUE, was built in 1912, although its chancel was added in 1933 (architects C. & C. M. Hadfield); it has an unusual ceramic chancel screen wall.

Shalesmoor

On the northern fringe of the city centre at 312 SHALESMOOR is the **Ship Inn**, with a splendid exterior display of 1920s golden brown faience; its good lettering is complemented by a colourful semicircular tiled plaque of a galleon above the entrance.

South Yorkshire Roundup

There is a Minton tile pavement in the entrance hall of Brodsworth Hall (1861-3, EH), **Brodsworth**. In the Methodist Chapel of **Hollow Meadows**, a hamlet about seven miles west of Sheffield on the A57, is a hand-painted six-tile First World War memorial, with six names listed beneath a canopy. As well as polychromatic brickwork (including a mural) on the low-energy Magistrates' Courthouse (1992-4), The Statutes, there is much good interwar faience in central **Rotherham**, particularly a former Burton's and a nearby stripped classical facade. On the main road through **Royston**, Midland Road (B6428), the Salvation Army building has buff terracotta dressings with good lettering.

West Yorkshire

BATLEY

On HICK LANE, near the centre of Batley and marking the entrance to a conservation area, is the ***Batley Bats*** gateway, a landmark sculpture installed in 1995 as part of the Brighter Batley project. The designers were Chloe Cookson and Rory McNally, and the 150 ceramic components in the 30′ high structure were made at Shaws of Darwen, where McNally spent an eight month residency. The gateway is crowned by a pair of 5′ high terracotta bats, wings outstretched, which were the most difficult pieces to produce.[48] Well north-west of the town centre in Upper Batley, off BRADFORD ROAD, is the **Bagshaw Museum** in Wilton Park. This gothic mansion was built in 1875-6 and still appears as a lavishly furnished late nineteenth century home. The unusual decorative scheme involved woodwork and wallpaper as well as interesting tiling in several rooms, including Maw & Co encaustics in the entrance hall; there are also several tiled fireplaces, one with pictorial panels of the *Seasons* by Burmantofts.

BRADFORD

Begin outside Bradford's Forster Square railway station, a shadow of its former self following rebuilding in 1990. Opposite is the **Midland Hotel**, CHEAPSIDE, built with the original Midland Railway station in 1890 and designed by the company architect Charles Trubshaw. The hotel entrance on the former station concourse is a splendid timepiece: a tile-lined, ramped, curving passageway used by passengers and - once upon a time - porters with handcarts going straight into the bowels of the hotel. The floor and pavement are covered by wooden boards, and the pavement has iron kerbs to protect it from damage by carts. The walls are completely tiled; turquoise relief tiles with an entwined knot motif form the dado, while above is a decorative border and then mostly pale amber tiles reaching up to the ceiling. The manufacturer was Burmantofts.[49]

Just south in the main shopping area is **Waterstone's**, MARKET STREET, built as the Wool Exchange (1864-7, architects Lockwood & Mawson of Bradford). The walls of the north entrance stairs are lined with Maw's tiling including a series of colourful lozenge-shaped majolica panels.[50] On the corner with SUNBRIDGE ROAD is the former **Prudential Assurance** (1893-6, architect Alfred Waterhouse) with a fine pinky-red terracotta exterior by J. C. Edwards of Ruabon.

Cross the main square, passing the Town (now City) Hall, to reach PRINCES WAY and the **National Museum of Photography, Film & Television**. It was founded in 1983 then much expanded during 1996-9, when the rich, dark royal blue brickwork curving around the lower part of the main stair tower was installed; the maker was Shaws of Darwen. Just north of the museum is the former **Odeon Cinema** (1930, architect William Illingworth, originally the New Victoria) whose white faience facade was also produced by Shaws; the building is disused and at risk.[51] Almost adjacent is the **Alhambra Theatre** (1914, architects Chadwick & Watson of Leeds, altered 1986), occupying the triangular site bounded by Princes Way, Morley Street and Great Horton Road. The buff faience for its classical MORLEY STREET elevation was supplied by Gibbs & Canning.

Now to Bradford's more distant locations. Take Great Horton Road to the west, then after less than half a mile turn right into RICHMOND ROAD; this is the campus of the **University of Bradford**, an institution created in 1966. Just down the hill on the right is the Richmond Building, an unlovely slab block dating from the late 1960s (Fig 316). Its entrance is oversailed at first floor height by a single-storey lecture theatre whose main frontage is decorated by a big, bold ceramic mural, about 45' long by 15' high. The abstract geometric design is carried out in rectangular and circular amber, brown, grey and generally sludgy-coloured relief tiles. The artist is unknown, as is the manufacturer, but the mural survives in good condition, although - perhaps because of its glum colour mix - it is visually rather less successful than others of its era.

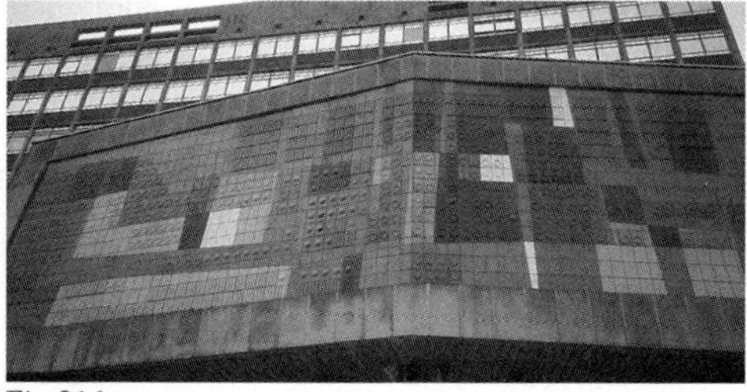

Fig 316.

Allerton

A couple of miles west of the city centre in OAKS LANE is **Rhodesway School**, a secondary school built in 1957-9 and designed by Scherrer & Hicks with Bradford's City Architect, W. C. Brown. The materials used have a strongly industrial feel, with much whitewashed brickwork; the main external decorative feature is the full height ceramic mural beside the entrance. Its abstract geometric design was by Joe Mayo, using a range of tiles designed by Kenneth Clark in collaboration with Malkin Tiles Ltd.[52] The brightly coloured hand-made tiles have rich glazes, mostly red, yellow and shades of blue.

Bolton

About a mile north of the city centre on the BOLTON ROAD is **St James's Church** (1876-8, architects Andrews & Pepper of Bradford), where the mosaic pavement in the porch and the fabulous wall mosaics of the sanctuary were provided by W. B. Simpson & Sons of London.[53] A tiled reredos by Heaton, Butler & Bayne has been reported at this church, but this appears to have been replaced by an alabaster relief of the *Last Supper*; the window above is the work of Shrigley & Hunt.[54]

Clayton

Julius Whitehead founded the Clayton Fireclay Works at Clayton, on the south-western fringe of Bradford, in 1880. The firm produced sanitary ware, glazed bricks and chimney pots using locally-extracted clay; the works closed in 1970 and most of the buildings have been demolished. Still remaining, however, is the house Whitehead designed and built for himself in the 1880s on a hillside overlooking the site: **The Towers** (no public access), BROW LANE. A rectangular mini-castle, with corner towers connected by balustraded parapets, the whole acts as an advertisement for the firm's products, including their reddish-brown salt-glazed brick from which it is mostly built (Fig 317). There are pretty ceramic plaques on the exterior, and the interior has a wealth of home-produced detail including tilework and ceramic stair treads, while an array of decorative salt-glazed wares, from urns to reclining lions, may be found in the garden.

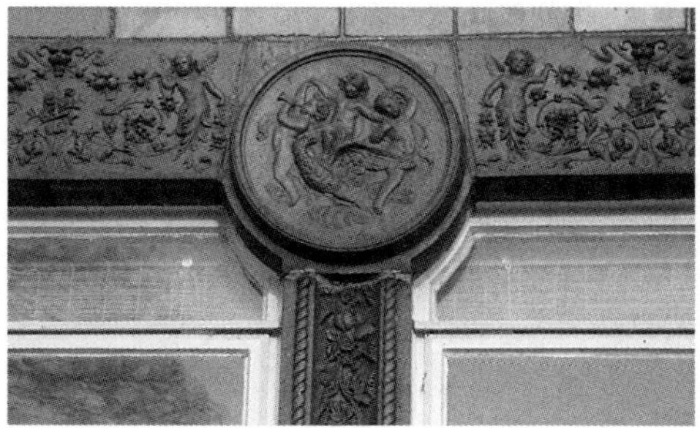

Fig 317.

The lodge to The Towers (now known as **The Elders**, no public access), also on Brow Lane, was built at the same time and in the same spirit. The small terrace has deep red brickwork with fine salt-glazed cherubic medallions and decorative bands above the windows, and glazed brick panels in blue and white. These latter are replicated on the sole surviving remnant of the Clayton Fireclay Works, its elaborate, square-sectioned **chimney stack**, which stands about fifty yards south-west of The Towers; it was put up by Julius Whitehead's son around 1890.

Little Horton

Under a mile south of the University of Bradford campus is the landmark tower of **All Saints Church** (1861-4), LITTLE HORTON LANE, on Little Horton Green; the church has extensive encaustic tile pavements.

CASTLEFORD

In the centre of Castleford on STATION ROAD is the **Picture House**, a former cinema opened in 1921 and closed in 1964. Its white faience facade includes two insets showing female figures. Two streets south, on the walls of houses in GLEBE STREET, is the ***Glebe Street Forest*** (1994), a series of glazed brick trees by Lyndele Fozard.

On the western edge of Castleford in METHLEY ROAD (A6032) is the long, curving form of **Three Lane Ends School**, built as Whitwood Mere Infant School in 1937-9 by the idiosyncratic modernist architect Oliver Hill. It was his only school; he designed a companion secondary school for the West Riding Education Authority, but this was never built.[55] Part of the north side of this single-storey structure is faced with a long ceramic frieze, where the life-size outlines of leaping deer are incised on rectangular jade green faience slabs. The artist was John Skeaping (1901-80), who worked in a variety of mediums and was best known for his modernist depictions of wild and domestic animals; the manufacturer was Carter's of Poole.[56] The design of the school was so unusual that it was featured in several architectural journals including *Country Life*, which reported the head-mistress as likening the school to 'the promised land'.[57]

HALIFAX

In the centre of Halifax there is good turn-of-the-century pub tiling in the **White Horse**, 33 SOUTHGATE (porch tiling includes pub name), the **Sportsman**, CROWN STREET (refronted 1904, porch wall tiles) and the **Plummett Line**, 17-21 BULL CLOSE LANE, where the tiled interior features a pictorial panel. To the north, up on HALEY HILL, is the landmark spire of **All Souls Church**, built in 1856-9 by local mill owner Edward Akroyd for his model village Akroydon; the architect was George Gilbert Scott. Its richly furnished interior includes extensive Minton tile pavements.

HOLMFIRTH

The three ceramic reliefs entitled *Holmfirth* in the foyer of **Holmfirth Civic Hall**, HUDDERSFIELD ROAD, were made by the American-born sculptor and ceramicist Jim Robison (b1939) and installed in 1998; Robison has lived and worked near Holmfirth since 1973.

HUDDERSFIELD

Begin at Huddersfield's impressively classical **Railway Station** (1847-50) on RAILWAY STREET for a short stroll through this stone-built Victorian town, ending at Queensgate Market. First, the station booking hall (1938) retains its original counter, with an unusual frontage of small - about one and a half inch square - mottled greeny-brown tiles. Note the brass bag-rests, a nice touch. From the station, head past the hurrying figure of former Prime Minister Harold Wilson (1999, sculptor Ian Walters) south along Railway Street, turning left into WESTGATE for the **Byram Arcade** (1880-1) with its encaustic tiled string course of alternating four-tile groups with tudor rose and fleur-de-lys motifs. Now right into John William Street, the main shopping street, which continues as New Street. Off to the right in CLOTH HALL STREET is the neo-classical white faience facade of **King's Head Buildings** (1924), probably in Burmantofts Marmo; round the corner at 25-7 MARKET STREET is another interwar white faience facade (overpainted sky blue), which in contrast is more modern in style with good detailing. Return to New Street; on the corner with RAMSDEN STREET is the red terracotta former **Prudential Assurance** (1899-1901, architect Alfred Waterhouse), complete with a statue of *Prudentia* in a high-level niche.

Opposite is **Ramsden House** (1967), on which is a full-width ceramic mosaic mural by Harold Blackburn (1899-1980), who vividly depicted the woollen industry using colourful, larger-than-life figures. Ramsden House seems to have been a landmark building in the town's extensive sixties redevelopment, as its south end sports another, almost equally large, mosaic mural showing a lively Huddersfield townscape. Yet more mosaics - a sparky 1969 abstract by Richard Fletcher entitled *Systematic sequence in line and shade* - decorate the **flats** across New Street in BUXTON WAY. Return to Ramsden Street for the **Library and Art Gallery** (1937-43), a fine stripped classical stone building with sparse but good relief decoration. Just inside, hung above the double stairwell, is a pair of large pictorial tile panels commissioned in 1987 to mark the fiftieth anniversary of the gallery. A third and larger panel, showing the town's buildings, was sited on the landing above until 2003, when it was removed (to store) as part of improvement works.

Just south of the Library is the New Market Hall (1969-70, architects J. Seymour Harris Partnership), now known as **Queensgate Market** (Fig 318). The interior is stunning, as the roof structure is based on twenty-one asymmetric concrete hyperbolic paraboloids, which loom over the market stalls like giant mushrooms. The east facade, facing the inner ring road on QUEENSGATE, is just as remarkable, with its extraordinary series of massive ceramic murals entitled *Articulation in Movement* by the German-born sculptor Fritz Steller (b1941). The work, which was made from Stourbridge fireclay, is about 4,500 square feet in size with nine large panels and a free-standing 32 foot high sculpture pierced by a staircase to the market. A special kiln had to be built at Steller's Square One Design Workshop in the village of Snitterfield, near Stratford-upon-Avon, to fire the panels at around 1300°C, thus producing stoneware which was intended to weather better than Huddersfield's local stone. The rusty-brown colouring of the panels came from a combination of their reduction firing and their iron and manganese oxide content, and their design reflects the structure and use of the market hall.[58]

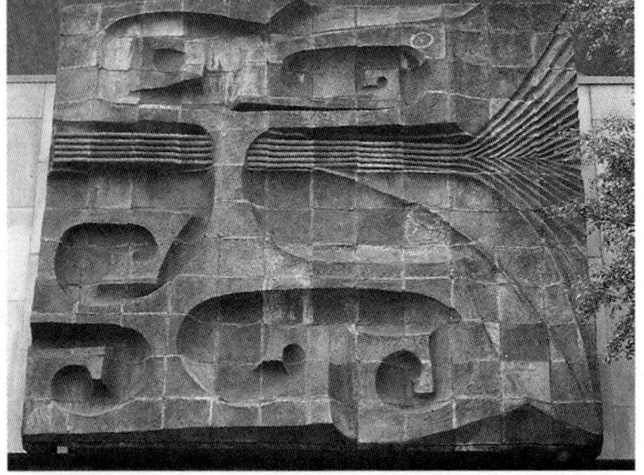

Fig 318.

The Steller sculpture is unusual in that most postwar British external architectural decoration was carried out in materials such as concrete, ciment fondu, metal or fibreglass rather than the difficult medium of ceramics. In terms of ceramic history the mural's precedents are large-scale architectural works such as the Natural History Museum (completed 1881), whose terracotta flora and fauna celebrated the activities within, and the stoneware frieze *Pottery Through the Ages* (1939) which adorned Doulton House in Lambeth. In postwar Britain, ceramic murals were generally on a much smaller scale than the Queensgate Market panels; only a few installations, for instance the six-storey tile mural on Transport House (1956-9) in Belfast, approach it in size. Although *Articulation in Movement* is a significant landmark in ceramic history, it was not followed by other similar sculptures, probably because of a combination of cost constraints, growing lack of enthusiasm on the part of architects for external decoration, and the sheer complexity of producing monumental ceramic works. All the more worrying, then, that several options announced by the local council in 2004 for the redevelopment of Huddersfield's central area included the demolition of Queensgate Market.

LEEDS

In ceramic terms Leeds is almost synonymous with the Burmantofts works of the Leeds Fireclay Company, as it was known from 1889; it was initially the works of William Wilcock and John Lassey, later Wilcock & Co. The works stood just over a mile east of the city centre from the 1840s, when brickmaking began, until closure in 1957. The firm produced a huge range of decorative bricks and tiles, and colourful architectural ceramics under the brand name Burmantofts faience; their white glazed ware Burmantofts Marmo was launched in 1908. This easy availability of terracotta and faience meant that by around 1900 the use of stone to face commercial buildings had been almost abandoned in Leeds; the colours of the resulting facades - not all made from local materials - varied from white and cream through pink to orange and bright red, and occasionally included polychrome faience and mosaic.[59]

There are numerous Burmantofts locations within Leeds, including lavish displays like the faience-lined walls of the Great Hall of the University of Leeds, and a plethora of public houses. These range from the relatively mundane to the spectacular, in the form of the Garden Gate in Hunslet, one of the country's best ceramic pubs. But there is another side to Leeds, with ceramic locations including Godwin encaustics at the parish church, St Peter, and excellent terracotta and astounding mosaics by Frank Brangwyn at St Aidan's Church, Harehills; indeed, the suburbs are particularly rewarding. This tour of the city centre takes in the area bounded by the inner ring road loop to the north, and the River Aire to the south; the extensive suburbs are then taken alphabetically.

Begin at the massive, iconic **Town Hall** (1853-8, architect Cuthbert Brodrick), which stands about a quarter mile north of the railway station on the main thoroughfare, THE HEADROW. The vestibule was originally paved with Minton & Co encaustic floor tiles with classical patterns, but in 2001 these were replaced with exact replicas made by H. & R. Johnson. The staircases leading off from the vestibule are tiled with plain blue and white tiles with a border of majolica tiles by Minton, Hollins & Co.[60]

Just to the east on The Headrow is the **Central Library** (1876-84, architect George Corson), built as the Municipal Buildings. Its lavish fittings include a tremendous ceramic display, with tiles made by Edward Smith & Co of Coalville on the walls of the staircases, corridors and many rooms. The most spectacular area is the original reading room, to the right of the entrance, whose walls and ceiling are entirely covered in Smith & Co tiles. The vaulted ceiling is faced with coloured hexagonal tiles, some of which are hollow and form part of the room's ventilation system, and there is also a series of terracotta busts of literary figures, including Milton and Shakespeare, modelled by the London artist Benjamin Creswick. Almost opposite the Library is the former **Jubilee Hotel** (1904) at 167 The Headrow; the pub was designed by Thomas Winn, a local commercial architect. Its salmon-pink terracotta may have been supplied by J. C. Edwards of Ruabon, who made the terracotta used in several Leeds buildings around the turn of the century.

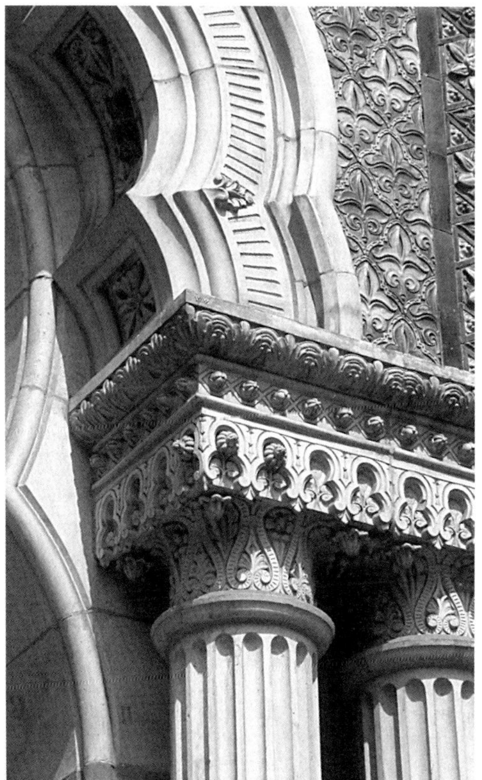

Fig 319.

Continue another block west along The Headrow, turning left into Park Square East to find **St Paul's House** (1878, architect Thomas Ambler) on the far side of PARK SQUARE (Fig 319). This Moorish warehouse and factory (now offices) was built for Sir John Barran, pioneer of the ready-made clothing trade. Its original entrance, on the corner of Park Square East and St Paul's Street, has an arch of scallop-shaped terracotta, with Moorish-style salt-glazed stoneware tiles, known as Doultonware, above; 'Doulton Lambeth' can be seen stamped on the blocks of the archway. St Paul's House was the first major application of Doulton's architectural products. The building's interior was gutted during the late 1970s; when its outer shell was restored, the terracotta minarets and much of the ornate parapet decoration were replaced with fibreglass, as the requisite manufacturing skills had been lost.

Head east along St Paul's Street and turn right into KING STREET. On the corner is **Atlas Chambers** (1910, architects Perkin & Bulmer), built from white Burmantofts Marmo; Thewlis & Co modelled its imposing sculptural embellishments including the figure of Atlas over the main entrance, and window keystones representing the continents. Further along is the magnificent pink terracotta facade of the **Metropole Hotel** (1897-9) by local architects Chorley & Connon; the terracotta was made by J. C. Edwards of Ruabon. The same combination of architects and terracotta suppliers were responsible for the former **Liberal Club** (1890, now Quebecs hotel), QUEBEC STREET, which leads east from King Street (Fig 320).[61] It would appear that Chorley & Connon went to the Ruabon works specifically to obtain the bright red and pink terracotta used on this pair of buildings, in contrast to the more muted tones available from Burmantofts.

Quebec Street ends at CITY SQUARE; occupying its western side is the curved, classical frontage of the former **Majestic Cinema** (1921-22, architect Pascal J. Steinlet), built entirely from Burmantofts Lefco (a later variation of Marmo), with moulded swags and elaborate panels of musical instruments. To the north is PARK ROW, a narrow street flanked by a series of towering offices and banks including, on the east side, the former **Prudential Assurance** building (1890-4, architect Alfred Waterhouse), in which the Leeds Fireclay Company had an office.[62] The facade, of pinky-red brick and buff Burmantofts terracotta, was partly restored by Shaws of Darwen in the early 1990s. On the west side of Park Row is the

Burmantofts Marmo facade of the Scottish Union and National Insurance Company (1909, architects Perkin & Bulmer, now **Royal Bank of Scotland**). Its sculptural decoration includes a figure of *Wisdom* carried out by Thewlis & Co.

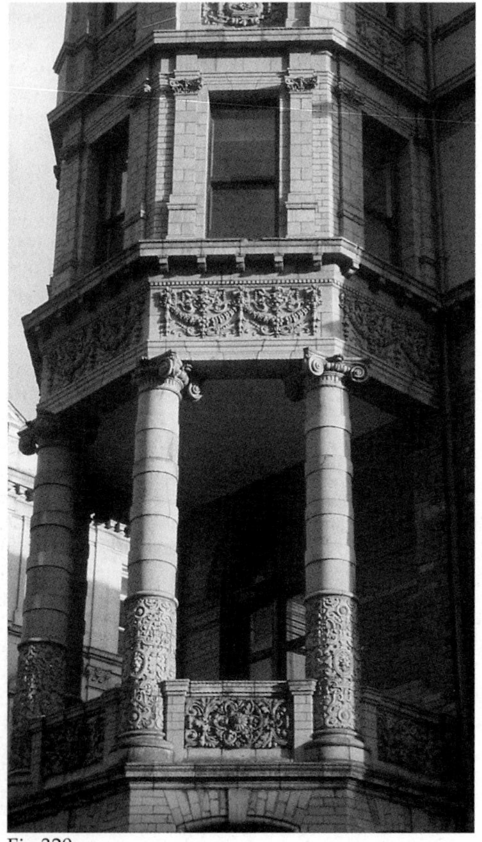

Fig 320.

To visit the city's Victoria Quarter, head east along pedestrianised Bond Street and Commercial Street, emerging on to Briggate just north of the alley which leads to **Whitelocks** in the TURKS HEAD YARD. This eighteenth century pub was rebuilt in 1886 and has an excellent tiled barfront, with brown faience framing green and yellow floral tile panels, plus interesting brass fittings and glass. The barfront is flat rather than bowed out, but does curve round a protruding section of the bar; it was probably by Burmantofts, as the brown faience was a typical local product. From the early 1890s the firm produced more complex curved barfronts, initially in brown faience. Return to the main street to see the former premises of **Thornton & Co**, India Rubber Manufacturers, at 50 BRIGGATE. It was built just after the First World War and has an imposing classical facade with well-detailed lettering, and columns and pilasters of Burmantofts Marmo; the architect was Sydney Kitson.

To the north, the sumptuous **County Arcade** runs east off Briggate. With the **Cross Arcade**, which leads south from its centre, the arcade was part of a comprehensive redevelopment of an area of yards and slaughterhouses undertaken in 1898-1900; the architect was Frank Matcham. The County Arcade in particular is extensively decorated with Burmantofts faience and terracotta, and the pendentives of its glass domes have figurative mosaics in art nouveau style.[63] The buff terracotta of its exterior has been given a thin coating of transparent glaze to improve its weather resistance. The arcades were refurbished by Shaws of Darwen in the 1990s. A diversion to NEW BRIGGATE, directly north across The Headrow, is required to see the **Grand Arcade** (1898, architects Smith & Tweedale). The entrances on New Briggate and Vicar Lane have colourful Burmantofts faience decoration, while J. C. Edwards of Ruabon also supplied brick or tiles for this arcade.[64] The stalls bar of the adjacent **Grand Theatre** (1878) has an extensive tiled dado.

Continue through the County Arcade and turn right into Vicar Lane, passing Kirkgate Market and reaching the Corn Exchange at the end of New Market Street. Opposite in CROWN STREET is **Crown Street Buildings** (2004), an apartment block partly faced in polychrome slab faience ranging in colour from a brilliant, yellowy lime green to rich royal blue. Finally for the city centre, a little way east on KIRKGATE, beyond the railway, is **St Peter's Church** (1837-41), the parish church of Leeds. The sanctuary was remodelled in 1876 when the Salviati mosaics of the Apostles were added around the east end; the Godwin encaustic tile pavement, which includes many twelve-tile cross-shaped groups, probably dates from this period. The tiles were donated by a former curate.

Armley

Inside **St Bartholomew's Church**, WESLEY ROAD, is a superb display of opus sectile work by Powell's of Whitefriars.[65] The first seven pictorial panels were installed on the apsidal wall of the east end in 1878-9, and were followed in 1884 by a mosaic and opus sectile panel, 5′ high and over 28′ in length, on the baptistery wall. It shows the *Baptism of Christ by St John*, with a procession of saints, angels and elders of the church which includes (in the top right-hand corner) Dean Hook, the former Vicar of Leeds. It was to be almost forty years until the next panels were added. The pair of angels to either side of the altar date from 1925; nearby are St Luke and St John (1929), and the final panel, appropriately of St Bartholomew, was installed in the apse in 1934. Almost all the panels were gifts made as memorials to the dead.

Beckett Park

Beckett Park, now part of the campus of Leeds Metropolitan University, was originally the grounds of The Grange (1752); it is approached from OTLEY ROAD via Churchwood Avenue. Lurking in its wooded depths is the **Victoria Arch**, an ashlar structure which probably dates from 1766 and comprises four Ionic columns supporting a pediment; it is likely to have been built as an eye-catcher for The Grange.[66] In celebration of Queen Victoria's visit to Leeds in 1858, when she opened the Town Hall, it was elaborately decorated with Minton encaustic tiles (Fig 321). The somewhat anticlimactic arch stands in Queen's Wood, just past the south-western edge of the central buildings.

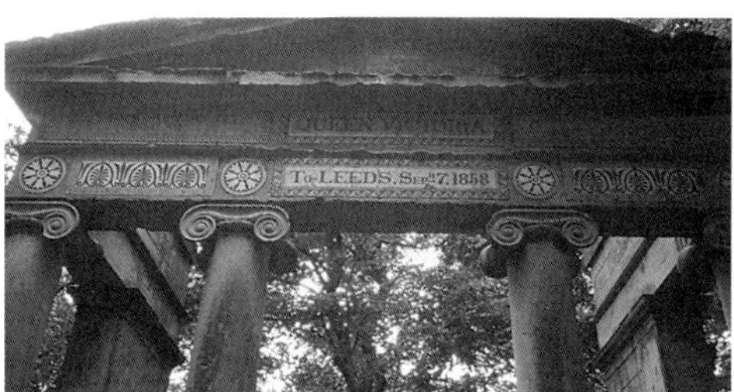

Fig 321.

Bramley

Bramley Baths (1904, architect H. A. Chapman), BROAD LANE, was one of a series of baths built in Leeds around the turn of the century. These included Kirkstall Road (1895), Union Street (1895), Holbeck (1898), Hunslet (1898), Meanwood Road (1899) and York Road (1905); Chapman also designed the York Road Baths.[67] Bramley Baths, which was restored in 1992, has a lavish interior with fine stained glass and wall tiling.

Burmantofts

Nothing remains *in situ* of the Leeds Fireclay Company's Burmantofts works, which closed in 1957 and was demolished in 1967. Its site is marked by a Leeds Civic Trust plaque mounted on the wall of a seventeen-storey block of flats in the Ebor Gardens estate, off TORRE ROAD. Just north of the flats on STONEY ROCK LANE is **St Agnes Church** (1886-7, now St Stephen and St Agnes); its Burmantofts tile and faience reredos dates from 1891, but has been overpainted. At the rear of the church is a ceramic wall memorial erected by Burmantofts workers in memory of James Holroyd (1839-90), works manager from 1879, who began the production of art pottery, tiles and architectural faience.

Chapel Allerton

Inside **Chapel Allerton Library** (1904), HARROGATE ROAD, by the Leeds architect W. H. Thorp (1852-1944), the green-tiled walls bear the 'LPL' logo for Leeds Public Library. Almost opposite in STAINBECK LANE is the **Mustard Pot PH**, which has a nineteenth century fireplace set with early delftware tiles dating from around 1650 and showing children's games. The area is also notable for its profusion of distinctive Victorian chimney pots, many made at the Burmantofts works or at Whitehead's Clayton Fireclay Works near Bradford.[68] On the south-west edge of

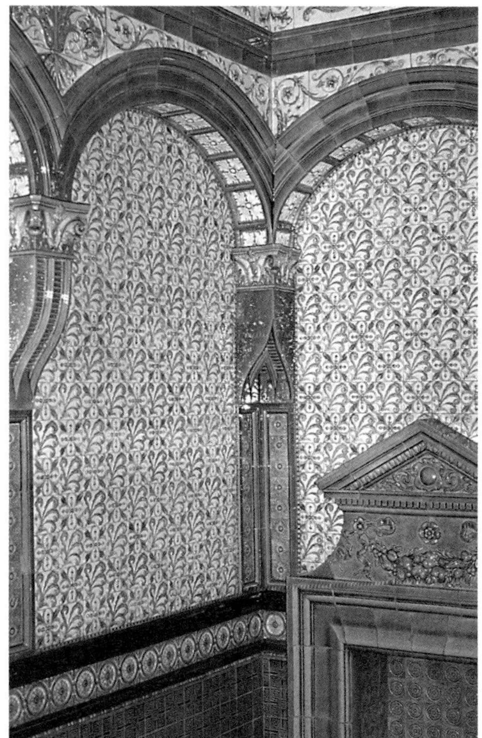
Fig 322.

Chapel Allerton, off HAREHILLS LANE, is **Chapel Allerton Hospital**; its redevelopment during 1992-3 led to the installation of several ceramic works by artists Maggie Angus Berkowitz, Marion Brandis, Cynthia Harrison and Kate Malone.[69]

Chapeltown

Inside **Gledhow Hall** (completed around 1766, now flats and offices with no public access), GLEDHOW LANE, is a bathroom of about 1885 with sumptuous wall tiling and faience by Burmantofts; even the ceiling is ceramic (Fig 322). It was part of the alterations and extensions to the mansion commissioned from architects Chorley & Connon - designers of the Metropole Hotel (1897-9) and the Liberal Club (1890) in the centre of Leeds - by James Kitson (1835-1911), Lord Airedale, during 1885-90. Kitson, the second son of James Kitson (1807-85), a locomotive manufacturer, wanted to expand the house so that it could be used for frequent entertaining. Chorley & Connon's bathroom was so unusual that a drawing of it, complete with serving maid, was published in *The Builder*.[70] The accompanying text emphasised that the glazed porcelain walls and ceiling ensured 'the utmost degree of cleanliness'.

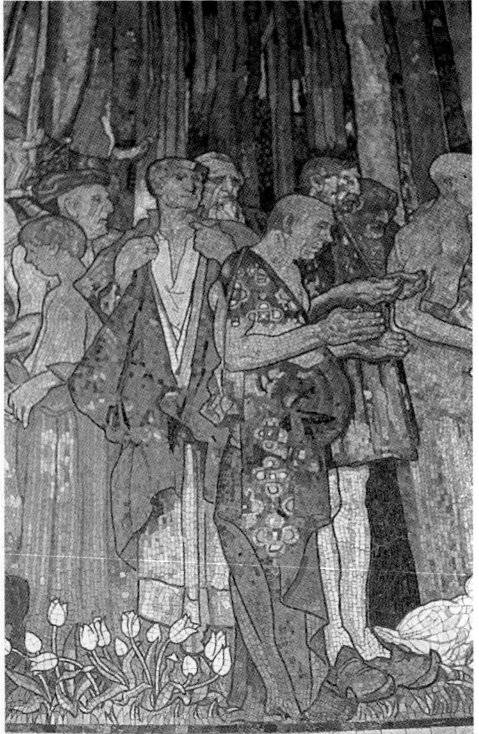
Fig 323.

Crown Point

The **Adelphi**, a multi-roomed pub on HUNSLET ROAD, just south of Leeds Bridge, was designed by Thomas Winn and built in 1901. It has an ornate staircase and many original fittings including good decorative wall tiling.

Harehills

St Aidan's Church, ROUNDHAY ROAD (at Elford Place) was built in 1891-4; the red brick, romanesque design was by the Newcastle upon Tyne architectural practice of R. J. Johnson & A. Crawford-Hicks, and its exterior features bright red terracotta decoration on the apsidal west end, above the main road. Arthur Swayne, who became vicar in 1897, was married to Eva Kitson, daughter of James Kitson and sister of Lord Airedale (see Gledhow Hall, Chapeltown, above). The Kitson family became parishioners at St Aidan's, with Eva's brother, the architect Sydney Kitson, designing fittings for the church and handling repairs.

In 1908 the Rev. Swayne appealed for a benefactor to assist with decorating the chancel, and his wife's nephew, Robert Hawthorne Kitson (1873-1947), an accomplished amateur painter, came forward.[71] He was a friend of the artist Frank Brangwyn (1867-1956), and in 1909 commissioned him to paint a series of tempera frescoes at St Aidan's; the work was eventually carried out in Rust's vitreous mosaic, a laborious process which was not completed until 1916.[72] The result was a spectacular and nationally important work of mural decoration, the best but probably the least known of Brangwyn's nineteen mural projects, and his only large-scale mosaic (Fig 323). The theme of the apse mural is the life of St Aidan, and apart from the multitude of highly detailed figures, the strongest impression is conveyed by the blue horizontals of the sky and the green verticals of the trees.

Headingley

At the north end of HEADINGLEY LANE, by St Michael's Road, is the **Church of St Michael and All Angels** (1886), where there is a Godwin encaustic tile pavement. Headingley Lane continues as Otley Road; shortly on the left in NORTH LANE is the **Lounge Cinema** (1918), with a facade of Burmantofts Marmo. About half a mile further north on the right at 114-120 OTLEY ROAD is a terrace of four houses (1885) with elaborate buff terracotta decoration; the houses appear to have been designed specifically to show off the products of the Burmantofts works. Further along Otley Road on the right is **Spenfield House** (1875-7, architect George Corson, now an hotel), with splendid encaustic floor tiles, including the 'JWO' monogram of the owner James Walker Oxley, in the entrance hall.

Holbeck

The former **Holbeck Free Library** (1901, architect William Bakewell), Nineveh Road, has a facade of red brick and bright red terracotta by J. C. Edwards of Ruabon; the building was mentioned in the firm's 1903 catalogue. About half a mile to the north is the Tower Works, Globe Road; the factory, built in the 1860s, produced pins for wool, flax, cotton and silk combing and for carding cloth. Its 1899 extensions designed by William Bakewell include the **Giotto Tower** (or Big Tower), a dust extraction chimney of square cross-section with panels of gilded tiles in recesses near the top; it was based on the fourteenth-century campanile of Florence Cathedral, designed by Giotto. The gilded tiles may have been produced locally, or could have come from Edwards of Ruabon; the Tower Works features in their 1903 catalogue, but this might refer solely to the brickwork.

Hunslet

The **Garden Gate** (1903), 3 Whitfield Place, just off the south end of Hunslet Road, is one of the country's foremost ceramic pubs, with a fine two-tone brown faience facade, a wealth of corridors tiled floor to ceiling, a chunky green faience fire surround and a bow-fronted ceramic bar; it is lacking only in pictorial panels (Fig 324). It seems inconceivable that the tiles, faience and barfront could be by anyone but Burmantofts, given the colour of the faience, the large scale of the slabs, and the proximity of the works, but no archival evidence has been found. The olive green and yellow ceramic bar, one of only fourteen remaining in Britain, is almost exactly the same design as the 1904 bar of the White Hart in Hull.

North on Hunslet Road is the entrance to the metal pressings works (1888) of **T. F. & J. H. Braime**; the doorway has a fine buff faience surround, with columns, swags and a cartouche, which is most likely by Burmantofts. A mile or so south-west of the Garden Gate, on the far side of the motorway and almost in Beeston, is the **New Inn**, 259 Dewsbury Road (opposite Stratford Street). This turn-of-the-century pub has an ornate white faience facade, with twin oriel windows and good detailing; it is probably by Burmantofts.

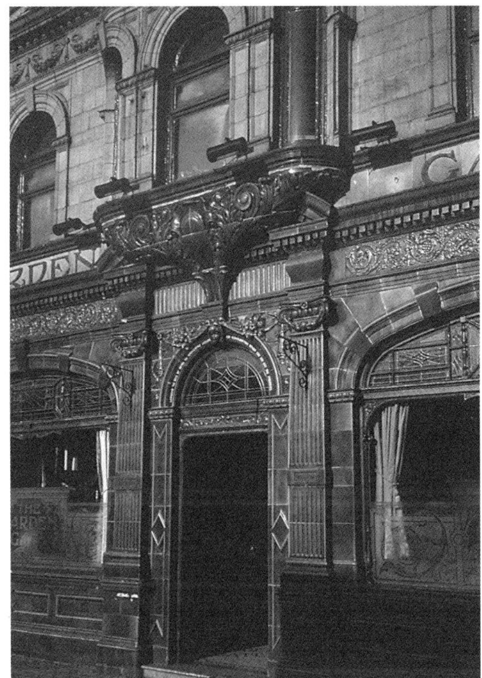

Fig 324.

Hyde Park

The **Hyde Park Picture House**, on the corner of Brudenell Road and Queen's Road, dates from around 1914 and has a facade of Burmantofts Marmo; the architects were Thomas Winn & Sons. Further west along Brudenell Road at Thornville Road is the green dome of the **Almadina Jamia Mosque** (2002-3), designed by the Bradford-based architectural practice Archi-Structure, which was set up in 1999 by Al Samar raie (Fig 325). The mosque is of buff stone with

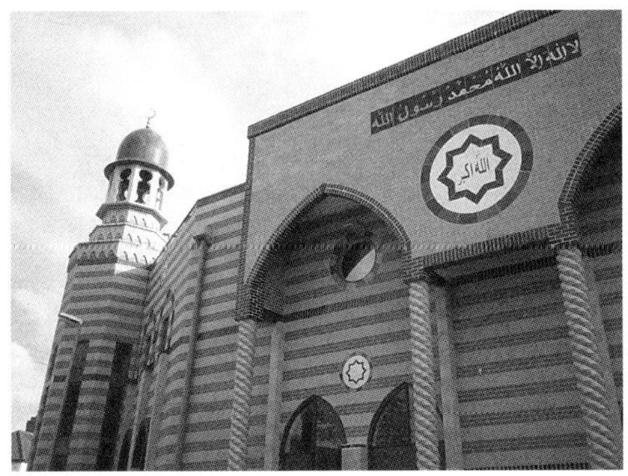

Fig 325.

red brick stripes and a series of dark blue and green ceramic horseshoe motifs. On the west side four double-height spiral pillars of buff brick support a large rectangular area of pale green glazed brick, on which is a ceramic panel with Islamic inscription. This is an unusually attractive and confident design for a British mosque.[73]

Kirkstall

Inlaid tiling survives in the fifteenth century refectory and in the side chapels to the left of the main altar in the church of the Cistercian foundation of **Kirkstall Abbey**, ABBEY ROAD.[74] A substantial fragment of a large circular arrangement of reset thirteenth century mosaic floor tiles has also survived in the refectory.[75]

New Town

The **Thackray Medical Museum**, BECKETT STREET, is housed in the former Leeds Union Workhouse (1861), which was part of St James's University Hospital until 1995. The entrance hall retains its art nouveau Burmantofts wall tiling, which dates from the early 1900s, and there is further tiling in the main stairwell and corridor.

Roundhay

In the chancel of **St John's Church**, WETHERBY ROAD, is a large First World War memorial of 1921-2 carried out in Powell's opus sectile; its pictorial panels (cartoons by Wilfred Edwards) show six soldier saints.

Swarcliffe

Adam Kossowski designed a large ceramic relief of Our Lady for **St Gregory's R. C. Church**, SWARCLIFFE DRIVE, in 1969.

Woodhouse

St Mark's Church, ST MARK'S ROAD, Woodhouse, has a sanctuary encaustic tile pavement by the Campbell Brick & Tile Co dating from around 1880; some of the elaborate four-tile groups show the 'IHS' monogram.

Around half a mile to the south on UNIVERSITY ROAD is the campus of the University of Leeds, originally Yorkshire College; many of its buildings were designed by Alfred Waterhouse from the mid-1870s onward. His **Great Hall** (1892-5), much delayed due to lack of funds, has an imposing entrance hall with a dado and staircase decorated in pale buff Burmantofts faience.

Slightly south at 23 CLARENDON ROAD is **Claremont** (West Yorkshire Archaeological Society) with late nineteenth century Maw encaustic tiling in the hallway and four Maw faience roundels depicting the *Seasons* in the library. Take the footbridge east over the inner ring road to find **Leeds General Infirmary**, CALVERLEY STREET; in front of the late 1990s Jubilee Building is Jubilee Square, with extensive brick landscaping by Tessa Jaray in collaboration with Tom Lomax.

MORLEY

Morley's **Public Library** (1905-6) in COMMERCIAL STREET was given to the town by Andrew Carnegie; the architect was the Borough Engineer, W. E. Putman.[76] Like some other early twentieth century Carnegie Libraries, for instance Sandwell (1907, West Bromwich, Staffordshire), its classical exterior hides an interior elaborately decorated with ceramics, in this case full-height wall tiling probably manufactured by Burmantofts. Above a tall, mostly bottle-green dado is a very unusual art nouveau frieze depicting literary figures; additionally, in tiled aedicules are details relating to the building, Carnegie and members of the Leeds Library Committee. There is also a good mosaic floor.

OTLEY

The little five-cottage, turn-of-the-century terrace at 1-5 GUYCROFT is faced in an exhilarating mix of coloured glazed bricks. It was probably intended as an advertisement for a local brickmaker, perhaps Julius Whitehead & Sons, whose Clayton works was a few miles to the south on the outskirts of Bradford.

OXENHOPE

The neo-Norman **Church of St Mary the Virgin** (1849) was designed by the Durham architectural practice of Ignatius Bonomi and his junior partner, John Augustus Cory.[77] The sanctuary floor was originally laid with colourful Minton encaustic tiles; although these have been taken up, some are still visible in the vestry. The underside of the chancel arch is still decorated with printed or stencilled tiles designed specially for the church by J. A. Cory, who was something of an antiquarian, using motifs taken from illuminated manuscripts held in the Chapter Library of Durham Cathedral. The tiles were made by Wilson & Co at their Tyne-Maine Pottery in Gateshead.[78]

PONTEFRACT

In the centre of Pontefract on SALTER ROW is the former Carnegie Free Library (1904, architects

Garside and Pennington) which reopened as **Pontefract Museum** in 1978. Its strange exterior, with pairs of truncated towers on either side of the entrance, combines ochre terracotta - possibly by Edwards of Ruabon - and red brick in a style which has elements of aesthetic movement and Viennese Secessionist, with overtones of Mackintosh and art nouveau touches like the sinuous leaf forms. Just as unexpected is the interior, with apple green and blue art nouveau tiled walls, mosaic floor and a dramatic bottle green faience-lined oval opening leading to the stairs.

At the east end of Salter Row is the **Windmill PH**, its grey interwar faience facade brightened by a green and yellow windmill above the entrance. Opposite is the 1983 **Salter Row Shopping Centre**, marked by a large ceramic plaque of local scenes displayed at first floor level; the artists were Sue King and James Robison. Just to the left in GILLYGATE is the former **Pineapple PH**, now a shop, but retaining the upper part of its white faience facade including a delightfully sculpted pineapple. Adjacent is the MARKET PLACE where **W. H. Smith**, formerly England's Furniture Store (1894), has an ornate pale buff terracotta facade by the Leeds Fireclay Company..

About a mile south of the centre at 22 CARLETON CREST is the **Holy Family R. C. Church** (1965, architect Derek Walker); on the east wall, behind the altar, is a ceramic depiction of *Christ in Majesty* by Robert Brumby. His work may also be seen at St Augustine's R. C. Church (1967-8), Chorlton on Medlock, Manchester.

TODMORDEN

Christ Church (1830-2) acquired a new chancel in 1885; its architect was Jesse Horsfall, a local man. It may be that there was some competition between Christ Church - the parish church - and Todmorden's landmark building, the lavishly furnished Unitarian Church, which was erected on the hillside above the town in 1865-9 (and probably contains a tile pavement). Between 1893 and 1925 the chancel walls of Christ Church were decorated with a hugely elaborate and complete scheme comprising mosaic, tilework and opus sectile pictorial panels, all supplied by Powell's of Whitefriars. The artists involved included George Parlby, John W. Brown, James Hogan and Charles Hardgrave, a specialist in opus sectile and mural decorations, who visited the church in 1904.[79] The result was one of the best examples of opus sectile work in Britain. The church, however, closed in 1992 and is redundant; it was saved from demolition around 2000 only to be threatened in 2003 by an application to convert it to a single house, with little consideration given to its unique interior.

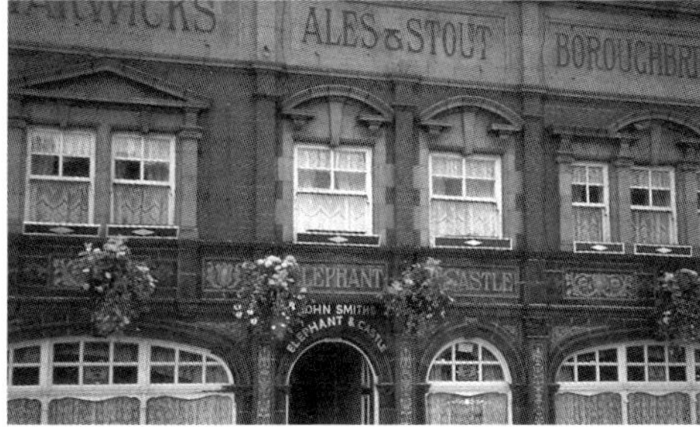

Fig 326.

West Yorkshire Roundup

About two miles north-east of **Aberford** is Hazlewood Castle, the home of the Vavasour family since the thirteenth century but now an hotel and restaurant; in the private graveyard is the substantial tomb of William Joseph Vavasour (d1860), with insets of colourful encaustic tiles including some armorials. Over the chancel arch of St Paul's Church (1876-8, architect William Swinden Barber of Halifax), **Drighlington**, is a tile mosaic panel of St Paul. The chancel walls of St Michael's Church (1848), **Mytholmroyd**, are completely covered in mosaics supplied by Powell's of Whitefriars in 1928 at a cost of £3,500; images include the Nativity, the Ascension, the Twelve Apostle and the Northern Saints, and the artist was James Hogan (1883-1948). There are patterned Minton encaustic tiles on the floor of the Salt family mausoleum, which was added to **Saltaire** Congregational Church (1858-9) in 1861. The Elephant and Castle PH, Westgate, **Wakefield** (opposite the railway station) has a good turn-of-the-century ceramic facade including lettering for Warwick's Anchor Brewery of Boroughbridge (Fig 326).

References

1. G. K. Beaulah, 'Church tile survey in Yorkshire', *Glazed Expressions*, (1981) 1, pp2-3. Of around 250 parish churches in the East Riding, the survey - which took two years - covered all but fifteen. Of around 100 churches using decorated tiles, eighteen used Minton's.
2. 'Railway Map in Tiles', *Brickbuilder*, (1900) June, ppxxii-xxiii.
3. Mark Anders, *Burmantofts Architectural Faience*, in *Burmantofts Pottery*, (Bradford Art Galleries and Museums, Bradford, 1983), pp28-37.

4. Joyce Little, Angela Goedicke and Margaret Washbourn, eds. *Stained Glass Marks & Monograms* (NADFAS, London, 2002).
5. Michael Kerney, 'All Saints', Margaret Street: A Glazing History', *Journal of Stained Glass*, 25 (2001), pp27-52.
6. Miranda F. Goodby, 'George Tinworth: an Artist in Terracotta', *Journal of the Tiles and Architectural Ceramics Society*, 3 (1990), pp15-21.
7. Lynn Pearson, *Building the East Riding* (Smith Settle, Otley, 1995).
8. Nikolaus Pevsner and David Neave, *Yorkshire: York and the East Riding* 2nd ed. Buildings of England (Penguin, London, 1995).
9. Kenneth Beaulah and Hans van Lemmen, *Church Tiles of the Nineteenth Century* 2nd ed (Shire Publications, Princes Risborough, 2001).
10. Lynn Pearson, *Minton Tiles in the Churches of Staffordshire* 2000, Tiles and Architectural Ceramics Society.
11. John Hutchinson and Paul Joyce, *George Edmund Street in East Yorkshire* (Department of the History of Art, University of Hull, Hull, 1981).
12. Kenneth Beaulah, *Catalogue of the Kenneth Beaulah Collection of Tiles and Related Materials* (Tiles and Architectural Ceramics Society, 1993), vol 1, number 547.
13. Jill Allibone, *The Wallpaintings at Garton-on-the-Wolds* (Pevsner Memorial Trust, London, 1991).
14. Philip and Dorothy Brown, 'Cuenca tiles and Frederick Garrard', *Glazed Expressions*, (1993) 26, pp10-11.
15. Hans van Lemmen and Jose Montgomery, *Dutch Tiles at 'Farrago' and 'Farrago' - A History of the House and its Tiles* 2nd ed (Leeds Polytechnic, Leeds, 1990).
16. Gordon Biddle, *Britain's Historic Railway Buildings: An Oxford Gazetteer of Structures and Sites* (Oxford University Press, Oxford, 2003).
17. Christopher Ketchell and Jose Montgomery, *Tiles Tour - Hull* (Local History Archives Unit, Hull College of Further Education, Hull, 1990).
18. Pevsner and Neave, *York and the East Riding* (1995), pp91-2.
19. Pevsner and Neave, *York and the East Riding* (1995), pp540-1.
20. Tiles and Architectural Ceramics Society *Newsletter* 15, May 1991, p3.
21. *Burmantofts Pottery*, (Bradford Art Galleries and Museum, Bradford, 1983).
22. Philip and Dorothy Brown, 'Spanish flavour in church tiles', *Glazed Expressions*, (1992) 25, pp9-10.
23. George Edmund Street, *The Cathedral of the Holy Trinity, commonly called Christ Church Cathedral, Dublin* (Sutton Sharpe, London, 1882).
24. *Ellen Mary Rope: The Poet Sculptor*, (Joanna Barnes Fine Arts and H. Blairman & Sons Ltd, London, 1997).
25. Jennie Stopford, 'The Yorkshire Medieval Tile Project', *TACS Journal*, 4 (1992), pp11-14.
26. *The Builder*, vol 36, 16th November 1878, p1206.
27. Elizabeth Eames, *English Tilers* (British Museum Press, London, 1992).
28. Maureen Batkin, *Wedgwood Ceramics 1846-1959* (Richard Dennis, London, 1982), p117.
29. Allen Eyles, *Odeon Cinemas 1: Oscar Deutsch Entertains Our Nation* (Cinema Theatre Association, London, 2002).
30. David Gamston, ed., *CAMRA National Inventory of Historic Pub Interiors* (CAMRA, St Albans, 2003).
31. Personal communication, Chris Blanchett, 27th August 1999.
32. Stopford, 'Yorkshire Medieval Tile Project', (1992).
33. Jack Binns, *The History of Scarborough* (Blackthorn Press, Pickering, 2001).
34. Alan Swale, *Architectural terracotta - a critical appraisal of its development and deployment*, 1998, MA dissertation, History of Ceramics, University of Staffordshire.
35. *Modern Practice in Architectural Terra Cotta*, (Hathern Station Brick & Terra Cotta Co Ltd, Loughborough, 1930).
36. Peter Howell and Ian Sutton, eds., *The Faber Guide to Victorian Churches* (Faber and Faber, London, 1989).
37. 'The Late Herbert Minton, Esq.' *Annals of the Diocese of Lichfield, past and present: being a Supplement to the Lichfield Church Calendar*, (1859) Crewe, Newcastle-under-Lyme, pp83-88. Reprinted in *Glazed Expressions* 32, Spring 1996, pp3-6. This encomium, published in the year following Minton's death, details the 173 gifts made by Herbert Minton to churches and other institutions.
38. Maggie Goodall, 'Whitby Gem', *Victorian Society News*, (1996) Autumn, p7.
39. Dennis W. Hadley, *James Powell & Sons: A listing of opus sectile, 1847-1973*, (2001).
40. Hadley, *James Powell & Sons* (2001).
41. Philip and Dorothy Brown, 'Lancaster architects - church terracotta and tiles', *Glazed Expressions*, (1990) 21, pp8-10.
42. *Burmantofts Pottery* (Bradford, 1983).
43. *Burmantofts Pottery* (Bradford, 1983).
44. Public Art Research Archive, Sheffield Hallam University (online, cited 22nd January 2005), <http://public-art.shu.ac.uk>. See also Ruth Harman and John Minnis, *Sheffield* (Yale University Press, New Haven and London, 2004), pp150-1.
45. Carter Archive, Poole Museum Service, 3C (Shops) 101.
46. Personal communication, Anne Diver, 21st April 2003.
47. Colin Cunningham and Prudence Waterhouse, *Alfred Waterhouse, 1830-1905: Biography of a Practice* (Clarendon Press, Oxford, 1992).
48. Alan Swale, 'The Batley Bats', *Glazed Expressions*, (1999) 39, pp4-5.
49. *Burmantofts Pottery* (Bradford, 1983).
50. *The Builder*, vol 25, 26th January 1867 and 23rd March 1867.
51. *The Builder*, 24th October 1930, p709.
52. 'Rhodesway Secondary School, Bradford', *RIBA Journal*, 68 (1960) November, pp14-15.
53. *The Builder*, 12th January 1878, vol 36.

54. William Waters, *Stained Glass from Shrigley & Hunt of Lancaster and London* (Centre for North-West Regional Studies, University of Lancaster, Lancaster, 2003), pp27, 84.
55. Alan Powers, *Oliver Hill: Architect and Lover of Life, 1887-1968* (Mouton Publications, London, 1989).
56. 'School at Castleford, Yorkshire', *Architects' Journal*, 94, 18th December 1941, pp398-402, xxiv.
57. Christopher Hussey, 'The School-Building Programme', *Country Life*, 94 (1943) 13th August, pp288-9.
58. '"Movement" panels for market hall', *Huddersfield Daily Examiner*, 9th October 1969, p16.
59. Derek Linstrum, *West Yorkshire: Architects and Architecture* (Lund Humphries, London, 1978), pp22-3.
60. Hans van Lemmen, *Tiles, Terracotta and Faience in Leeds* (TACS, 2003).
61. *J. C. Edwards, Ruabon: Catalogue*, Ruabon (1903).
62. Cunningham and Waterhouse, *Alfred Waterhouse* (1992), p114.
63. Hans van Lemmen, *Architectural Ceramics* (Shire Publications, Princes Risborough, 2002).
64. Margaret MacKeith, *Shopping Arcades: A gazetteer of extant British arcades 1817-1939* (Mansell Publishing, London, 1985).
65. Hadley, *James Powell & Sons* (2001).
66. George Sheeran, *Landscape Gardens in West Yorkshire, 1680-1880* (Wakefield Historical Publications, Wakefield, 1990).
67. Marcus Binney, Hana Laing and Alastair Laing, *Taking the Plunge: The architecture of bathing* (Save Britain's Heritage, London, 1981).
68. Hans van Lemmen, *Tiles, Terracotta and Faience in Leeds* (TACS, 2003).
69. Gail Bolland, 'New Tiles at Chapel Allerton Hospital, Leeds', *Glazed Expressions*, (1994) 28, pp6-8.
70. *The Builder*, vol 49, 18th July 1885, p101.
71. Janet Douglas, 'Patronage and Politics in a Leeds Parish - The Story of the Brangwyn Mosaics in St Aidans Church, Harehills', *Journal of the Tiles and Architectural Ceramics Society*, 6 (1996), pp23-28.
72. Libby Horner, 'A masterpiece in Leeds: Brangwyn and St Aidan's mosaics', *Ecclesiology Today*, (2000) 21, pp17-22.
73. Lynn Pearson, 'Ceramic decoration in modern British mosques', *Glazed Expressions*, (2003) 48, p11.
74. Stopford, 'Yorkshire Medieval Tile Project', (1992).
75. Elizabeth S. Eames, *Catalogue of Medieval Lead-Glazed Earthenware Tiles in the Department of Medieval and Later Antiquities, British Museum* (British Museum Publications, London, 1980), vol 1, pp132-3.
76. *The Builder*, vol 91, 3rd November 1906, p518
77. J. H. Crosby, *Ignatius Bonomi of Durham: Architect* (City of Durham Trust, Durham, 1987).
78. *St Mary's Church, Oxenhope, Centenary Souvenir Booklet*, Oxenhope (1949).
79. Hadley, *James Powell & Sons* (2001).

Isle Of Man

As befits an island with its own government, the prime ceramic locations in the Isle of Man have connections with the Tynwald - the Minton encaustic pavement at the national church - and the Bishop of Sodor and Man, whose former home, Bishopscourt, has another Minton pavement. Many of the island's churches (which are generally open) have encaustic pavements of lesser importance, but several house lozenge-shaped ceramic memorial tiles dating from around the 1880s. A selection of shops and entertainment venues (the Waterloo Hotel in Douglas is especially striking) rounds off the island's sites, although the most unusual location is St Olave's Church in Ramsey, where two Maw & Co trade tiles form part of the sanctuary pavement, in full view of the congregation. Suggested reading: *The Grand Tour* (Isle of Man Victorian Society).

BALLAUGH

The sanctuary tile pavement at **Ballaugh Church** (1832, architects Joseph Hansom and Edward Welch) is now hidden by carpet; all that remains is the teasing inscription on the chancel step recording that it was laid by James Daugherty in 1892 in memory of his parents. However, the church, which was restored during 1892-3, still has five lozenge-shaped ceramic memorial tiles, one for a naval officer and four commemorating local clergy, including Rowley Hill (1836-87), Bishop of Sodor and Man from 1877 until his death; Rowley Hill tiles, all of the same basic design, appear in several of the island's churches.

BISHOPSCOURT

Extensive works were carried out at **Bishopscourt**, the home of the Bishop of Sodor and Man, during 1854-60 to improve the living accommodation, rebuild the chapel and extend the premises to form a theological school. The Chapel of St Nicholas, consecrated in 1858, has a rich Minton & Co tiling with a buff and brown geometric pavement at the entrance, a sanctuary pavement in red, blue, gold and white encaustics; and the altar dais in red, blue and buff foliate patterned encaustic tiling.[1] The chapel was designated a pro-cathedral around 1895 and served as such until 1980 when the house was sold. Although the chapel is still consecrated, Bishopscourt is now a private house and there is no public access to the chapel.

DOUGLAS

Begin in the financial district on PROSPECT HILL, where a distinctive terracotta dragon corbel strikes an unusual pose high on **Kissacks Building**. Originally the dragon was not merely ornamental, but supported a structural member relating to a now-demolished tower. The rear of the building faces ATHOL STREET, where bulky **St George's Chambers**, built in 1898, displays ornate bright red Ruabon terracotta dressings on its

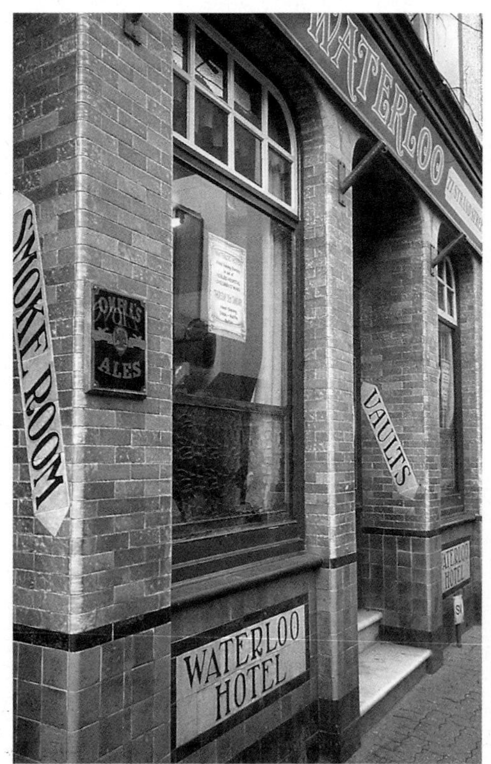

Fig 327.

complex corner site. Downhill into VICTORIA STREET to find a typical **Burton's** (1928, nowOffice World), designed by the Leeds architect Harry Wilson, who used Burmantofts white faience for its two-sided corner facade.

Turn north into STRAND STREET, one of the town's main shopping streets (running behind the Promenade), to see the ornate white faience facade of the **Strand Cinema** (1913). This little gem was designed by George K. Timperley of Manchester, who maximised the potential of a very narrow site: a pair of balconies, set one above the other, is flanked by angular, spindly turrets bearing brightly coloured leaded windows. The Strand (its auditorium demolished) now functions as the entrance to Littlewood's, and the change of use has resulted in a slightly characterless appearance. Also in Strand Street is the **Waterloo Hotel**, with an excellent facade of small, grey glazed bricks and green tiling, in which the pub's name is set in black on white ground; similar tiled lettering on the architraves directs customers to the smoke room or vaults (Fig 327). This facade probably dates from the interwar period but could even be 1950s.

Overlooking Douglas Bay from HARRIS PROMENADE is the **Gaiety Theatre**, reconstructed by Frank Matcham from an existing music hall and opened in 1900; there is a mainly geometric pavement in the foyer, while a green and brown relief tiled dado slopes down the auditorium. The dado tiling was made by Minton Hollins & Co and installed by Thomas Quayle, a local monumental mason and tiler. A little further north on CENTRAL PROMENADE is the imposing **Castle Mona Hotel**, built in 1801-4 by George Steuart as a residence for the Duke of Atholl and bearing four round heraldic Coade plaques. Nearby on the promenade is the **Crescent Leisure Centre**, designed by the local architects Lomas & Barrett in 1930 as the Crescent Cinema and again faced with sparkling white classical Burmantofts faience. Finally, above the town centre is the **Manx Museum and Art Gallery** on CRELLINS HILL. It was built in 1886-7 as Noble's Isle of Man Hospital, using Ruabon bricks supplied by J. C. Edwards; the architects were Cubbon & Bleakey of Birkenhead. At its side entrance is a pretty little encaustic and geometric tile pavement; this was part of the original building, although the mosaic section bearing the Museum's name was inserted in 1922 when the building was converted to its present use. Above this colourful pavement the entrance is marked by a terracotta archway topped by the Manx arms.

LAXEY

On NEW ROAD, within sight of the great wheel and near the Manx Electric Railway Station, is a former butcher's shop, originally part of the Laxey Industrial Co-operative Society premises (Fig 328). It is decorated inside and out with mainly plain blue and white tiles, although pictorial tiling in the open porch shows a good bull's head within a blue wreath. The manufacturer of the tiles, which date from around 1920, was probably J. & W. Wade of Burslem.

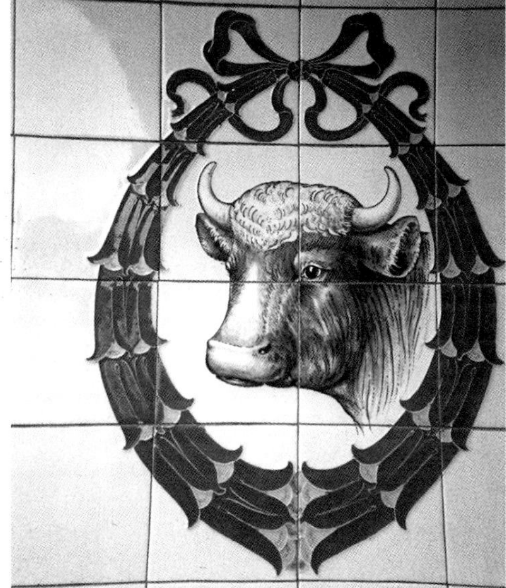

Fig 328.

PEEL

Paradise & Gell, MICHAEL STREET has an ornate red terracotta facade, with a pair of lion heads on its parapet; the shop was designed by the Ramsey architect J. T. Boyde. **St German's Cathedral**, TYNWALD ROAD, was built in 1879-84 (architects T. D. Barry & Son of Liverpool), although it was awarded cathedral status only in 1980; the sanctuary has a complex encaustic tiled pavement by Maw & Co.

RAMSEY

There are two most unusual tiles in the sanctuary pavement of **St Olave's Church**, BOWRING ROAD, North Ramsey: a pair Maw & Co trade tiles, about six feet apart and set directly in front of the altar. These 2″ square plain tiles, one black, one dark brown, are both marked 'Maw & Co Broseley' in low relief, and lie within an encaustic and geometric pavement which includes several repeats of a fleur-de-lys design encaustic tile. Although it is not unknown for trade tiles to appear in a church, the position in the sanctuary is most peculiar. The church was built in 1861-2 (architect M. P. Manning of London), although it was not consecrated until 1881; there is also a memorial tile to Bishop Rowley Hill.

St Paul's Church (1818-22) stands in the MARKET PLACE at the centre of Ramsey. It has a Minton Hollins (trading as Minton & Co) encaustic tiled pavement (1884) in its sanctuary, the design including an alpha and omega, symbols of the four evangelists, and another symbol now hidden by carpet; there is also a tiled pavement around the font, at the rear of the church.

ST JOHN'S

The **Royal Chapel of St John the Baptist** is the national church, used for the annual Tynwald Ceremony every July. It was built in 1847-9 and designed by the Manchester architect Richard Lane (1795-1880); the island's records confirm that Minton's encaustic tiles were supplied for this prestigious location.[2] The designs, many of which come from Minton's first catalogue, include symbols of the four evangelists and a pelican in its piety in the sanctuary pavement, while the chancel pavement has groups of four and nine decorative encaustic tiles separated by diagonals of plain black tiles.

Isle of Man Roundup

Tony Brown Electrics (formerly Cubbons'), 5 Arbory Street, **Castletown** has a pair of amber-tiled stall risers with strong lettering in brown. In **Port St Mary** High Street the lustrous black tiled facade of the former chemist's (now Dorian Hill Classic Cars) probably dates from the 1930s, while Corrin's butcher's shop has a fully tiled interior by Carter's of Poole with a coloured relief pattern frieze (possibly 1890s); its doorway mosaic reads T. Clague.

References

1. *Manx Sun*, 4th September 1858.
2. Manx Society, 'Records of the Tynwald and St John's Chapels', 19 (1858).

Scotland

Stone is the predominant building material in Scotland, and locations of terracotta and architectural faience are relatively few, apart from the iconic India of Inchinnan offices (1929-30), Renfrewshire, and at Dumbarton, West Dunbartonshire, where art deco faience facades were popular in the 1930s, but these are exceptional. However, compensations include the unparalleled collection of Doulton's ceramic fountains in Glasgow, ranging from the newly restored Doulton Fountain (1887-8), now stationed outside the People's Palace Museum on Glasgow Green, to the sad remains of the Hamilton Fountain, posing as a flowerbed in Maxwell Park, Pollokshields. There are also two outstanding Scottish locations for Coade stone: Gosford House (1790-1800), East Lothian, where there is a unique range of specially made and mostly figurative Coade stone ornament, and Dalmeny House (1814-17), Edinburgh, with its huge collection of gothic Coade ware, mainly in the form of architectural elements such as chimneys and turrets.

Floor tiles were produced in medieval Scotland, although hardly any remain *in situ*. The industrial-scale manufacture of decorative tiling was not a Scottish speciality, although rare delftware tiles of about 1755 from Glasgow's Delftfield Pottery can be seen in a fire surround at Pollok House, Pollokshaws, Glasgow. When tiles were required they were often imported from England, as at Kilmory Castle, Argyll & Bute, which has the only known floor (1837) of Samuel Wright's encaustic tiles, and at St John's Episcopal Church, Jedburgh, where there is an excellent early Minton scheme of 1844. The architect Alexander Ross used Minton tiles bearing unusual Old Testament motifs at his Episcopal churches in Inverness (1869) and Fort William (1880), both Highland; indeed, tile pavements in Episcopal churches throughout Scotland merit further investigation. Minton's and other manufacturers were involved in the display of sample floor designs of 1861 at the Royal Scottish Museum, Edinburgh.

There are fine examples of art tilework throughout Scotland, for instance the nine Doulton pictorial tile panels at the Café Royal, Edinburgh, which date from shortly before the turn of the century; fire surrounds possibly by Daniel Cottier in Montrose, Angus; tiles and faience (1887) by the Dunmore Pottery in the former works manager's house at Dunmore, Falkirk; and a superb pictorial frieze (1899) by Copeland & Sons at Park Circus, Kelvingrove, Glasgow. Scotland's best-known supplier of pictorial panels is James Duncan Limited of Glasgow, a firm of tile decorators established in 1865 which specialised in tube-lining. In the 1920s and 1930s they were responsible for many spectacular shop interiors throughout Scotland and beyond, and worked on chains of shops including the Buttercup Dairies; production ceased around 1965. A major puzzle concerning Scotland's, and in particular Glasgow's, tile heritage is the survival of so few James Duncan locations, given that the firm was the city's major supplier of shop tile panels for a century.

Of later work, the most significant is the series of ceramic murals carried out by the Scottish artist Robert Stewart (1924-95) during the 1960s and 1970s; these were made largely for public buildings and many have already been destroyed along with the buildings in which they were installed, but his superb abstract panels survive at Motherwell Theatre (1966), North Lanarkshire. Finally, one curiosity is the fate of the circular Doulton stoneware view indicators or toposcopes which were erected on the tops of Ben Macdui (1925), Moray; Lochnagar, Aberdeenshire; and Ben Nevis, Highland.[1] The Ben Nevis example was vandalised in the 1940s and removed, and it would be surprising if the other two have survived in such a harsh environment.

Service times and opening details of members of Scotland's Churches Scheme are given in the 2004 edition of *Churches to Visit in Scotland* (National Museums of Scotland and Scottish Christian Press, Edinburgh, 2003). Suggested reading: Liz Arthur, *Robert Stewart: Design 1946-95* (A. & C. Black, London, 2003); Gilbert T. Bell, *The Monument That Moved: Springburn's Ornamental Column* (Springburn Museum Trust, Glasgow, 1999); Rudolph Kenna and Anthony Mooney, *People's Palaces: Victorian and Edwardian Pubs of Scotland* (Paul Harris Publishing, Edinburgh, 1983); Elspeth King, *People's Pictures: The story of tiles in Glasgow*

(Glasgow Museums, 1991); Ray McKenzie, *Public Sculpture of Glasgow* (Liverpool University Presss, Liverpool, 2002); Christopher Norton, 'Medieval Floor Tiles in Scotland', pp137-173 in John Higgitt (ed), *Medieval Art and Architecture in the Diocese of St Andrews* (British Archaeological Association, 1994); Deborah Skinner, *TACS Tour Notes: Architectural Ceramics in Glasgow* (TACS, 1986). Scotland's *Gazetteer* entries are listed alphabetically by unitary council; there are no entries for the area of Shetland Islands Council.

Aberdeen

ABERDEEN

Throughout the city of Aberdeen there are tiled street names, which originally involved a total of about 8,000 Minton's encaustic tiles; these were replaced with replica encaustics during the late 1990s. In a prominent position about a quarter-mile north-west of the railway station is **His Majesty's Theatre** (1904-8, architect Frank Matcham), ROSEMOUNT VIADUCT; the interior is surprisingly restrained, but at the rear of the circle is a shoulder-height maroon-tiled dado with a flowery art nouveau frieze. The tiles were restored in 1982 by the Jackfield Conservation Studio as part of the theatre's £3 million refurbishment. The ceramic Stations of the Cross (1963) by Adam Kossowski at **St Peter's Catholic Church**, Chapel Court, JUSTICE STREET, (off Castlegate), were installed as part of a series of postwar embellishments of the church including new stained glass and an extension of the sanctuary. Down to the harbour to see a pretty piece of interwar seaside architecture, the **Beach Ballroom** (1926, extended early 1960s), ESPLANADE, with its cream faience facade; the original architects were Thomas Roberts & Hume, who won the commission in competition.[2] Although still a popular entertainment venue, the future use of the building remains uncertain.

Aberdeenshire

ELLON

The **Church of St Mary on the Rock** (1871, architect G. E. Street), Craighall, at the south end of Ellon, has floor tiles by Minton's.

Angus

ARBROATH

Just south of the railway station at 16 KEPTIE STREET is **Smithies**, a delicatessen whose complete tiled interior originated as a turn-of-the-century Lipton's. The tiles are mainly pale yellow with a frieze of green thistles and an unusual dado. To the east of the A92, which runs north-south through the town, are the ruins of **Arbroath Abbey** (HS), a Tironensian monastery founded in 1178. In the upper room of the abbot's house are the badly eroded remains of a medieval mosaic pavement of green and yellow tiles.

DUN

The **House of Dun** (NTS), off the A935 three miles west of Montrose, was designed by William Adam and built in 1730. The Dutch tiles of the saloon fireplace, purchased for the house in the early 1740s, have been carefully restored with replicas based on the original designs.

DYKEHEAD

Glen Prosen was one of the favourite haunts of the Antarctic explorers Robert Falcon Scott and Edward Adrian Wilson; indeed, Captain Scott planned his final expedition - during which both men died, in March 1912 - whilst staying in the glen. A monument to the pair, a terracotta fountain, was produced by the Compton Potters' Arts Guild in 1919 and erected in the glen, but was later demolished by a car.[3] The remains have been incorporated into a **cairn** which stands on a bend beside the minor road up the eastern side of the valley, about a mile west of Dykehead at NO372606.

MONTROSE

The **Links Hotel** (originally Links House), MID LINKS, is a mid eighteenth century mansion which was once the home of the owner of Montrose Linen Mill. Its interior has high quality mid Victorian decoration including stained glass by the aesthetic movement pioneer Daniel Cottier and several interesting tiled fire surrounds. It is not clear if Cottier & Co were responsible for the Links House fire surrounds, but the firm is known to have included tiles designed by John Moyr Smith and Albert Moore and others manufactured by Simpson & Sons in fireplaces at Coll-Earn House (1869-71), Auchterarder, Perth & Kinross.[4]

Argyll & Bute

DUNOON

The splendid interior of **St John's Church** (built 1876-7 as Dunoon Free Church by architect Robert A. Bryden), ARGYLL STREET, includes a small polychromatic Minton tile pavement in the sanctuary.

HELENSBURGH

The construction of **St Michael and All Angels Episcopal Church**, WILLIAM STREET, was begun in 1867 and completed, apart from the tower (1930), in 1882; its architect was Robert Rowand Anderson (1834-1921), who carried out a series of Episcopalian commissions from the 1860s onward.[5] At Helensburgh, with its relatively wealthy congregation, he was able to produce a lavish interior including *cuenca*-style wall tiling in the chancel.

INVERARY

There is a colourful chancel tile pavement at **All Saints Episcopal Church** (1885-6, architects Wardrop & Anderson of Edinburgh), THE AVENUE.

KILMODAN

The library of **Kilmodan Primary School**, deep in rural Glendaruel (Cowal), is the location of one of Robert Stewart's last site-specific ceramic murals, which he presented in 1975 in appreciation of the school's education of his six children. The 6′ square abstract panel is highly textured and includes many local details.[6]

KILMORY

Kilmory Castle, just south of Lochgilphead, was much enlarged by Sir John Powlett Orde (1803-78) after he bought the estate in 1828. The London architect Joseph Gordon Davis, who carried out several commissions in the Lochgilphead area during the 1830s, extended the house between 1828 and 1836, decorating the main rooms in lavish Chinese style; further extensions were made around 1860. The estate was sold in 1949 and Kilmory Castle became the headquarters of Argyll and Bute Council in 1974. The original entrance hall (south of the present entrance) has a floor of encaustic tiles made by Samuel Wright of Shelton, Staffordshire, who patented his inlaying process for paving tiles in 1830 (Fig 329). Wright sold his moulds and equipment to Herbert Minton in 1835, but retained the patent rights; the Kilmory Castle floor was supplied by Minton in 1837 out of the stock taken over from Wright. The unglazed tiles are pale buff inlaid with black clay, and are of vaguely Moorish rather than gothic design.[7]

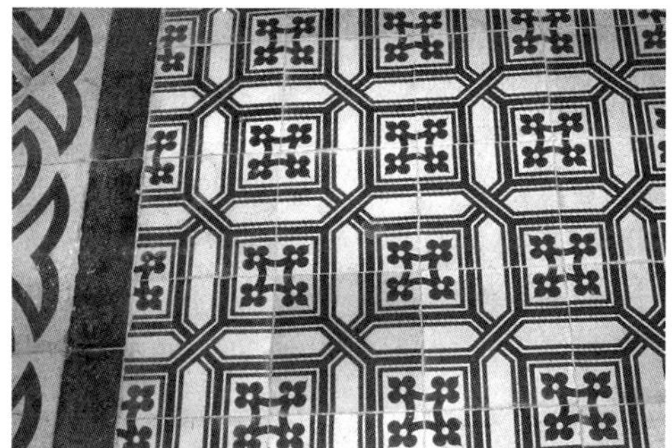

Fig 329.

MOUNT STUART, BUTE

The third Marquess of Bute was nearing the end of creating his neo-medieval vision of Cardiff Castle (with his architect William Burges) when the family seat, **Mount Stuart**, about three miles south of Rothesay, was largely burnt out in 1877. The Marquess consulted the Edinburgh architect Robert Rowand Anderson, with whom he had previously collaborated, and it was decided to build a vast mansion, almost a palace; construction began in 1879 and took over three decades. Burges, whose 1873-5 Mount Stuart oratory survived the fire, was not involved in the rebuilding but his team of Cardiff craftsmen were responsible for the hugely rich interiors, strong on marble rather than the pictorial tiling of Cardiff Castle.[8]

The third Marquess died in 1900 and was succeeded by his son John, also a keen builder. He added a faience-vaulted, tile-lined, heated gothic swimming pool to Mount Stuart in the early 1900s; it is reached via a stone spiral staircase descending from the great hall. Replacements for some damaged tiles in the pool were made in the early 1990s by Susan and Douglas Dalgleish of Edinburgh Ceramics, who also designed a tube-lined tile frieze, showing plants and animals, for a refurbished pantry at Mount Stuart.

ROTHESAY, BUTE

Once ashore, the first building passed by passengers leaving the ferry from Wemyss Bay is Rothesay's famous **public convenience**, built on the PIERHEAD in 1899-1900 when the resort was at its peak of popularity with day-trippers from Glasgow (Fig 330). This gentlemen's lavatory was designed by the Rothesay architect John Russell Thomson (1841-1910), and the brown glazed bricks of its exterior were supplied by James Craig & Co of Kilmarnock; one of the bricks bears the firm's name. Inside, the walls are lined with tiles, mainly yellow with some green, and on the ceramic mosaic floor, which includes the town's coat of arms, stand twenty Twyfords imitation marble ceramic urinal stalls, six of them on a central island. The marble effect was achieved by the use of transfer printing. After being out of use for several years, the gents was restored and improved (a modern ladies toilet was created using outbuildings) during the early 1990s by Strathclyde Building Preservation Trust and the Jackfield Conservation Studio at a cost of almost £300,000; it reopened in 1994.

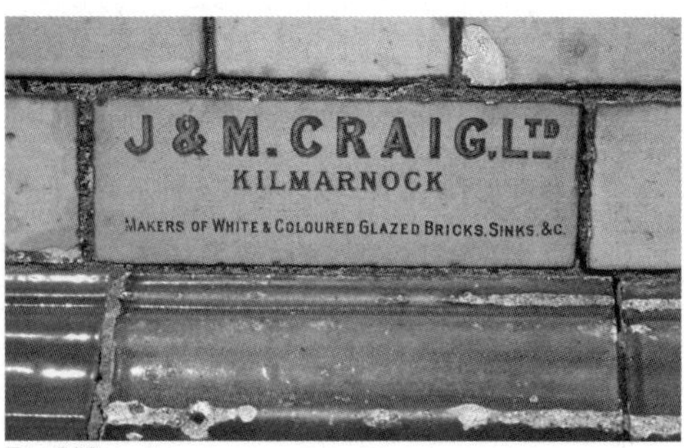

Fig 330.

Just west of the pierhead on the ESPLANADE is the domed former **Winter Garden** (1923-4), now the Isle of Bute Discovery Centre; its ironwork was prefabricated at Glasgow's Saracen Foundry. Inside, at the centre of the great dome, is a large and unusual light fitting in deeply moulded pale blue, brown and cream faience, most probably by Burmantofts. The twenties is very late for this type of colourful faience, suggesting that the light fitting originally belonged to the octagonal Victorian bandstand which was incorporated into the Winter Garden.

Clackmannanshire

ALLOA

East of the main shopping area on PRIMROSE STREET is the red sandstone **Speirs Centre**, built as the Public Baths and Gymnasium in 1895-8 by architects John Burnet, Son & Campbell. Originally the building (now a leisure centre) had swimming and plunge pools as well as Turkish and Russian baths, but the Turkish baths were destroyed by fire during refurbishment in 1966. Much has been altered internally with most of the tiling overpainted, but the dark green tiled lobby remains impressive, while almost full-height emphatically broad stripes of dark green and white tiling run throughout the entrance hall and stairwell.

Dumfries & Galloway

ANNAN

The colourful, clock-themed tile frieze above the windows of **Jopson's Jewellers**, 83 HIGH STREET, was installed around 1990 as part of the town's regeneration scheme; the tiles were made in Jackfield by the Decorative Tile Works.

CASTLE DOUGLAS

The mostly white-tiled, early twentieth century interior of **Henderson's** butchers at 64 KING STREET includes a fine blue and white Wedgwood frieze in which animal heads alternate with rural scenes.

CHALLOCH

All Saints Episcopal Church (1871-2) stands a couple of miles south of Penninghame House, the home of Edward J. Stopford Blair, for whom the church was built by the London architects Habershon & Pite as a private chapel. The rich interior includes a tile pavement which becomes increasingly elaborate towards the sanctuary, and decorative wall tiling either side of the altar. The *Buildings of Scotland* gives the manufacturer of the floor tiles as Colla, but as they appear to be standard products of one of the large English manufacturers, perhaps this may have been the supplier.[9] Stopford Blair died in 1885 and his grave lies outside the east end of the church.

DUMFRIES

The ornate encaustic tile pavement in the sanctuary of **St John the Evangelist Episcopal Church** (1867-8), LOVERS WALK, was designed in 1872 by Slater & Carpenter of London, architects of the church.[10] At the west end are two turn-of-the-century Powell's opus sectile memorial wall panels; the cartoon for the *Good Shepherd* (1899) was by Percy James.

South of the centre on BANKEND ROAD is the **Dumfries and Galloway Royal Infirmary** where the *Cairt Frieze* ('cairt' meaning a chart or map) was installed in the Macmillan Unit in 2004. The cartographically-inspired artwork, which includes hand-glazed porcelain tiles, was designed and made by the potter Will Levi Marshall (b1969) whose studio is near Auchencairn, about fifteen miles south-west of Dumfries.

GLENLUCE

In the late fifteenth century chapter house of **Glenluce Abbey** (HS), a Cistercian foundation whose remains stand in Dunragit, about two miles north-west of Glenluce, about 150 plain medieval glazed floor tiles survive around the central pier. Others may be found in the refectory and in the Abbey's small museum.

PARTON

Parton is the Edwardian estate village built by B. Rigby Murray of Parton House (demolished 1964); it includes an L-shaped terrace of arts and crafts houses, an octagonal communal lavatory (now a summerhouse), a village hall and the **Parish Church** (1832-3), inside which is a fine Doulton tiled wall memorial to Ebie Gray (1863-92), the wife of John Rigby Murray. The tiles, which are set in a brown faience frame, show an angel in flowing pink robes on gold ground.

SANQUHAR

The ruined Victorian office of the **Sanquhar & Kirkconnel Coal Co** was still extant in the centre of Sanquhar on CHURCH ROAD, just beyond the Tolbooth, in 2000. It was built from the firm's own terracotta bricks.[11] North of the main street and across the railway line stood the Buccleuch Terracotta Works, which was in operation from the late nineteenth century until the 1960s.

Dundee

DUNDEE

Dundee's most impressive ceramic installation overlooks the Firth of Tay from EARL GREY PLACE, close to the railway station but separated from it by a discouraging network of busy roads and walkways. To the west front of the **Olympia Leisure Centre** (1974) was added in the mid-1980s a huge abstract ceramic mural stretching across the whole width of the building; it was part of a refurbishment carried out by DDC Architects.[12] The mural is made up from Twintiles in shades of blue, pink and black, the combination resulting in a pleasing rippling appearance.

North-east at 36-40 SEAGATE is **Robertson's Bond** (1897, architects Johnston & Baxter), a former bonded whisky warehouse which later became the Seagate Gallery; inside is a good tiled ceiling. Further from the centre in the suburb of Hilltown (at the Carnegie Street end of CHURCH STREET) is **St Salvador's Episcopal Church** (1865-75, architect G. F. Bodley), with a spectacularly colourful interior including a tile pavement. Still further north-east on the corner of ARBROATH ROAD and Morgan Street is the monumental form of the mid twentieth century **Tay Spinners Jute Mill**, now disused. Its Odeon-like facade includes much buff faience with grey-blue string courses, the square-arched canted corner being most impressive.

East Ayrshire

CUMNOCK

Dumfries House (about three miles west of Cumnock), the eighteenth century mansion which was the Bute family home for many years, has several tiled fire surrounds.

GALSTON

St Sophia's R. C. Church (1885-6), BENTINCK STREET, is a Byzantine-style, brick-built domed church designed by the architect Robert Rowand Anderson for the third Marquess of Bute as a memorial to his mother. The dark red brickwork was restored in 2003 using bricks specially made by the Errol Brick Company of Errol, near Perth.

East Dunbartonshire

MILNGAVIE

A tube-lined abstract mural by Robert Stewart was installed at **Douglas Academy**, CRAIGTON ROAD in 1966. It was Stewart's third mural for a school site, and the design was based on the sight of a seagull passing in front of the sun; the tiles were fired several times to achieve the required density of colour and texture. The school may be rebuilt as part of a 2004 improvement plan.

East Lothian

DUNBAR

A well-preserved Buttercup Dairy trademark tile panel by James Duncan of Glasgow is still *in situ* in a HIGH STREET shop; see Edinburgh (Bruntsfield) for details of the Buttercup Dairy chain. **Dunbar Castle** (1790-2), which dominates the view from the High Street, was designed by Robert Adam for the Eighth Earl of Lauderdale; on its cornice is a large Coade stone winged sphinx.

LONGNIDDRY

Gosford House, two miles north-east of Longniddry, was built in 1790-1800 by Robert Adam for the Earl of Wemyss (Fig 331). It is decorated with a uniquely wide range of Coade stone ornament, some from the standard Coade catalogue but much figurative and specially made including medallions, plaques, sphinxes, and heraldic swans and lions.[13] Coade stone plaques and sculptures can be seen on the exterior of the house, the stable block and the boathouse on the lake.

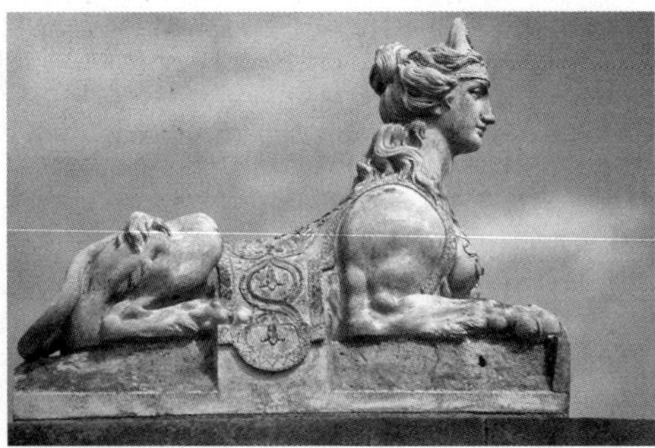

Fig 331.

East Renfrewshire

CLARKSTON

Holmwood House (1857-8, architect Alexander 'Greek' Thomson) stands at 61-3 NETHERLEE ROAD, Clarkston, really a suburb of Glasgow but administratively in East Renfrewshire. It was built for James Couper, owner of a nearby paper mill, and is decorated in a picturesque version of classical Greek style; there is tiling in the entrance hall and elsewhere.

NEWTON MEARNS

An abstract ceramic mural by Robert Stewart measuring almost 7′ by 21′ was installed at the newly-built **Eastwood High School**, CAPELRIG ROAD, in 1965; the school still occupies the same building.

Edinburgh

DALMENY

Dalmeny House, which overlooks the Firth of Forth two miles north-east of the village of Dalmeny, was designed by the architect William Wilkins and built in 1814-17; it was Scotland's first gothic revival house (Fig 332). Its numerous Coade chimneys, battlements, plaques, coats of arms and pinnacles make it the most extensive collection of gothic Coade ware surviving on a private house.[14] Unusually, Wilkins supplied the designs himself rather than ordering from Coade's catalogue, a fact which undoubtedly contributed to the Dalmeny decorations costing nearly £5,000, probably the firm's most lucrative domestic order.[15]

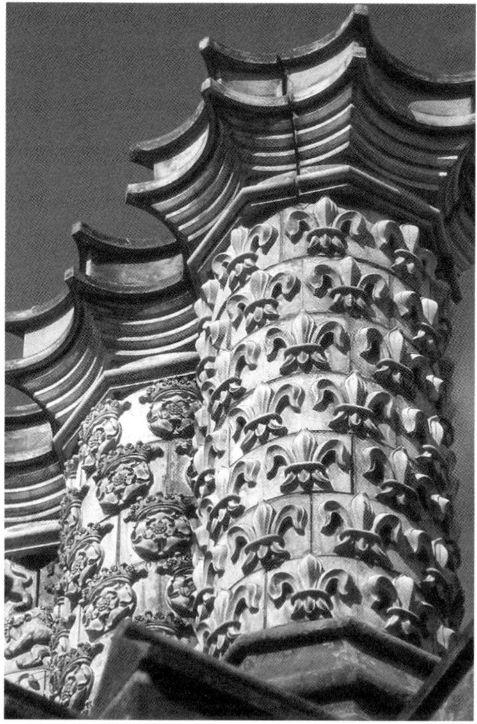

Fig 332.

EDINBURGH

Close to Edinburgh Waverley railway station, on the north (New Town) side just beyond Princes Street, is the **Café Royal**, WEST REGISTER STREET, its classic interior boasting no fewer than nine Doulton pictorial panels; despite this it narrowly escaped demolition during the late 1960s to make way for a car park. The Café Royal has occupied its present site since 1863, and from the 1890s underwent a series of alterations culminating in 1900-1 with a scheme by the architect James MacIntyre Henry which created the large Circle Bar (the public bar) and a buffet bar, now the Oyster Bar, both with opulent decoration.[16] In the Circle Bar are six panels designed by John Eyre which depict famous inventors; they were executed by Walter J. Nunn assisted by Katherine Sturgeon, and were shown at the International Inventions Exhibition held in London in 1885.[17] A seventh inventor panel by Eyre is in the Oyster Bar, along with two panels painted by the seascape specialist Esther Lewis; these show a Liverpool paddle steamer and the Cunard liner Umbria, and were shown at the 1891 Royal Naval Exhibition held at Chelsea's Royal Hospital, probably in the marine art section. All the inventor panels are said to have appeared at Edinburgh's 1886 International Exhibition of Science, Art and Industry, following which they were bought for the Café Royal. The Oyster Bar also has colourful relief wall tiling and a series of stained glass windows of sportsmen by the local firm Ballantine & Gardener (the designer was Thomas Wilson), while small tiled ovals showing putti are set into the bar counter.[18]

Bear left out of the Café Royal and turn right into ST ANDREW SQUARE; the **Bank of Scotland**, with its distinctive array of parapet statuary, soon appears on the right. It was built for the British Linen Bank in 1846 (architect David Bryce) and retains its original elaborate Minton tiled floor, which is still visible in the entrance hall and the passageway leading to the banking hall. On the south side of the square is the former Prudential Assurance (1895-9, architect Alfred Waterhouse & Son), now the **Tiles** bistro, with a spectacular Burmantofts faience interior in pale buff, brown and green with an unusual blue and white thistle frieze. The faience and tiling was restored during 1990-1 by Susan and Douglas Dalgleish of Edinburgh Ceramics, who had to produce several hundred replacement tiles of varying shapes and sizes; much experimentation was required to match the original glazes as closely as possible.

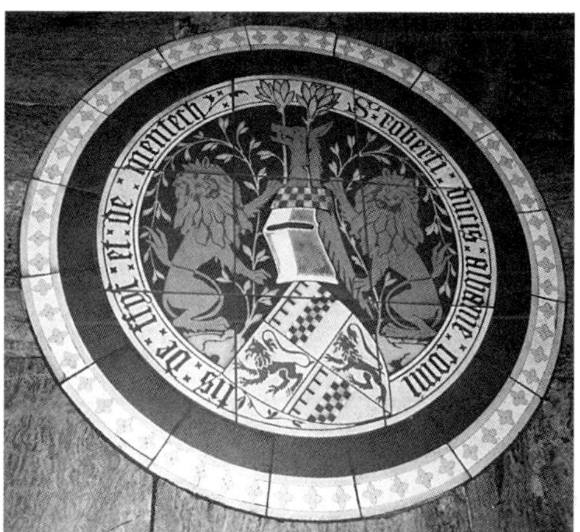

Fig 333.

Take George Street west from St Andrew Square; at the first junction a diversion is possible (northward via Hanover Street) to see **Unicorn Antiques**, a former dairy at 65 DUNDAS STREET. The fully-tiled interior includes three hand-painted blue and white panels of pastoral scenes, one signed Maw & Co. Otherwise, go south along

Hanover Street then next right to find the **Kenilworth** at 152-4 ROSE STREET; the pub was completed around 1904 (architect Thomas Purves Marwick) and has lashings of wall tiling and an island bar. Take the next major left turning, which leads on to PRINCES STREET; at its west end is **St John's Episcopal Church**. Its stone reredos (1889, carved by James Kerr) is set with three large tile and mosaic panels of Christ, St John and St Mary by W. B. Simpson & Sons.

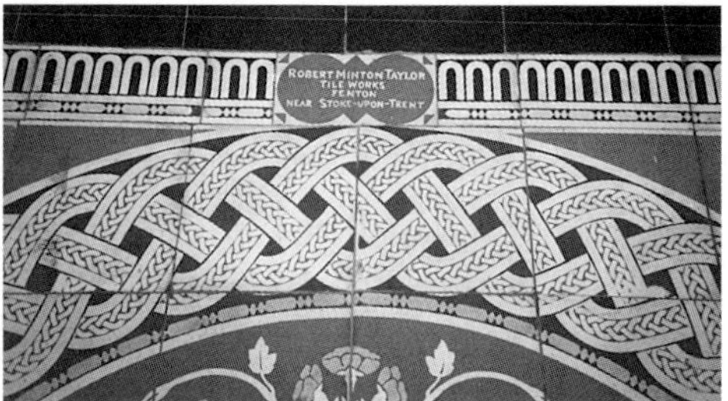

Fig 334.

Now return along Princes Street and head south via The Mound to the Old Town, climbing Bank Street to reach the Royal Mile; here, turn left to see **St Giles Cathedral** on HIGH STREET. Fairly ornate encaustic tile pavements, probably by Maw & Co, remain in chapels to either side of the organ (the Chepman Aisle and the Holy Blood Aisle) and near the Thistle Chapel, though clearly much tiling has been removed. In the Albany Aisle (just left of the entrance), rearranged as war memorial chapel in 1951, two superb heraldic tiled roundels are set into the floor (Fig 333). It is possible to continue directly east along the Royal Mile to Holyroodhouse, but for a more ceramically interesting route, turn south along George IV Bridge (just west of the Cathedral), soon reaching the **Royal Scottish Museum** (1861-74) on the left in CHAMBERS STREET. Inside is the soaring ironwork of the Great Hall (1861), its original plain geometric tile flooring removed in 1971, but in the adjacent arcade a remarkable display remains, as this area was set aside for major manufacturers to submit sample pavements of their best designs (Fig 334). The most elaborate sections are by Robert Minton Taylor (including a trade tile) and Minton's, with fine blue roundels of sea creatures, while Maw's and the Patent Architectural Pottery of Poole are amongst the other firms represented..

At the east end of Chambers Street turn right into Nicholson Street, which becomes Clerk Street; **St Peter's Episcopal Church** (1857-65), on the left in LUTTON PLACE, has an elaborate scheme of Minton & Co encaustic tiles in its chancel.[19] The architect was William Slater of Slater & Carpenter, who designed an encaustic pavement for a Dumfries church in 1872 (see above, Dumfries & Galloway). Return along CLERK STREET, passing the impressive white Hathern faience facade of the **Odeon**, opened as the New Victoria Cinema in 1930; the design was by the cinema architect William Edward Trent.[20] Back at the Royal Mile, turn right on to HIGH STREET for the mostly sixteenth century **John Knox House**, where several fire surrounds are decorated with late eighteenth or early nineteenth century Dutch tiles made in Rotterdam (Fig 335). The first floor fireplace has three floral panels, a speciality of Rotterdam's De Bloempot factory, while other fireplace panels show religious scenes.[21]

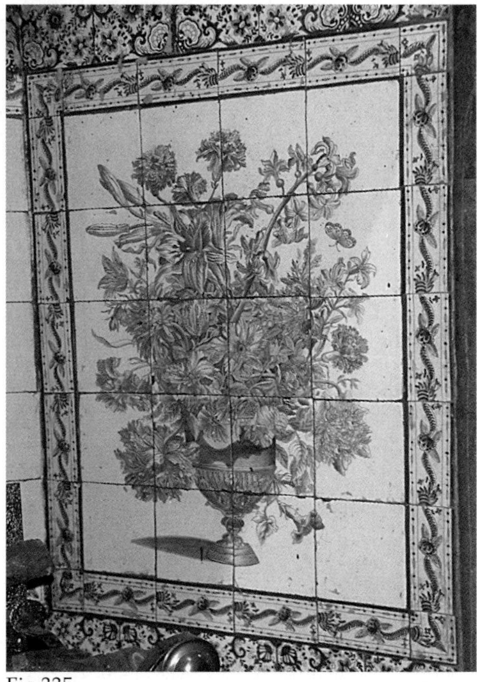

Fig 335.

Now to the east end of the ROYAL MILE for the **Palace of Holyroodhouse**, its complex building history beginning with the founding of Holyrood Abbey in 1128; it may have been a royal residence as early as the fourteenth century. James IV built a new palace on the site in 1501-5, and many alterations and extensions followed, including those made for Queen Victoria on and after her first visit in 1842. Ten rooms of the palace contain fireplace tiles, largely seventeenth and eighteenth century Dutch delftware tiles made at places such as Rotterdam, Utrecht and Amsterdam; in the King's Closet there are a few eighteenth century English delftware tiles set amongst the Dutch tiles. The tiles were probably put into the fireplaces during the nineteenth century. Some of the most attractive tiles are in the two rooms associated with Mary Queen of Scots; in her Inner Chamber are Dutch tiles with landscapes and pastoral scenes of the second half of the seventeenth century, alternating with eighteenth century biblical scenes painted in cobalt blue. In her Outer Chamber are Dutch tiles depicting animals, children's games, landscapes and seascapes of the second half of the seventeenth century, alternating with eighteenth century biblical tiles.[22]

To complete this circuit of inner Edinburgh, return to Waverley station via Calton Road and Princes Street. Above Calton Road and to the north (actually on REGENT ROAD) is the **Burns Monument** (1830), a monumental circular temple which originally housed a statue of the poet Robert Burns. The 20′ diameter internal chamber has a floor of encaustic tiles with a floral motif.

Bruntsfield

On the south side of the Old Town, just beyond Toll Cross at 8 LEVEN STREET, is **Bennet's Bar**, its interior designed by the architect George Lyle and dating from 1891, with alterations by Lyle in 1906. The latter probably included the unusual arcade of recessed, round-headed mirrors which runs along the wall opposite the serving counter; framing each mirror are narrow pictorial tile panels by W. B. Simpson & Sons which depict cherubs and female figures. Nearby at 23 Leven Street is **Millars** fish shop; the interior has suffered some damage but retains most of one good pictorial tile panel showing a variety of fish; this may be the work of Craven Dunnill.

Just to the south - bear left along Bruntsfield Place and Whitehouse Loan - is the **Meadows Lamp Gallery** at 48 WARRENDER PARK ROAD. The shop was formerly one of the Buttercup Dairy chain which had over 400 premises throughout Scotland, and has their trademark tube-lined pictorial panel - a girl in a pink dress offering a buttercup to a large brown cow - in the doorway. The source of the image was a Victorian painting which hung in the firm's head office at Leith.[23] These oval panels are normally signed 'J. Duncan Ltd Glasgow', the firm that was responsible for tiling all the chain's shops.[24] James Duncan's were tile decorators, using blanks supplied by large manufacturers such as T. & R. Boote. The suppliers for several Buttercup Dairy shops during the First World War were Maw & Co, who sent tiles to Duncan's for the outlet at 48 Warrender Park Road in 1917.[25] It is probable that Maw's also supplied some of the plain, mostly green, tiling for the dairies, leaving Duncan's to concentrate on designing and painting the picture panels.

Coates

St Mary's Episcopal Cathedral, PALMERSTON PLACE (a little way north of Haymarket station) was designed by George Gilbert Scott and built in 1874-9, although the chapter house and western spires were added later. The chancel is floored with an intricate pavement of 1878 combining Godwin encaustic tiles and marble.

Leith

The **Central Bar**, at the junction of LEITH WALK and Duke Street, was built in 1898-9 to replace its predecessor, demolished when the North British Railway Company built Leith Central Station (1898-1903, disused) at the foot of the Walk. The bar's architect was Peter Lyle Henderson (1848-1912), known throughout

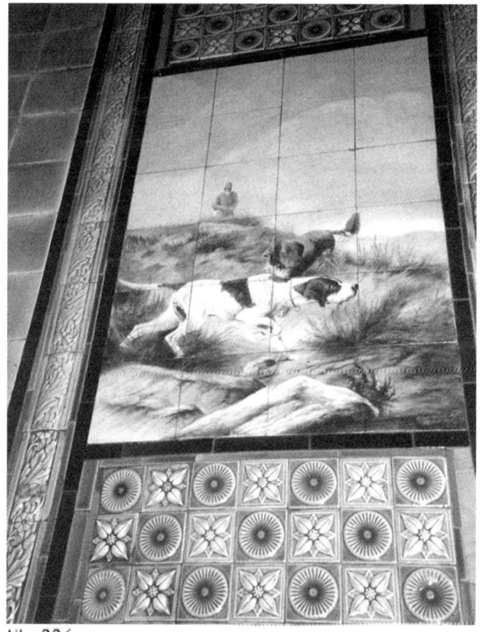

Fig 336.

Scotland as 'the brewers' architect'; he was reputed to have the largest workload of new pub commissions of any Edinburgh architect. In both his pub and, more surprisingly, his brewery architecture he was noted for ornamental designs, specialising in tiled pub interiors. The Central Bar is an excellent example, its walls completely tiled from floor to ceiling and including four tiled murals of sporting activities by Minton Hollins; the tiles have been restored by Susan and Douglas Dalgleish of Edinburgh Ceramics (Fig 336).

Newhaven

Starbank Park, STARBANK ROAD, was laid out around 1890; its **Devlin Fountain** (1910), in the lower part of the park near Laverockbank Road, was designed by George Simpson and is thought to have been made by Kilmarnock's Southhook Potteries. The terracotta fountain, which was commissioned by Newhaven merchant Thomas Devlin, has been badly vandalised. Southhook Potteries, a sanitary ware firm who later branched out into art tiles, became a limited company in 1935.[26]

Ravelston

A six-panel tile mural entitled *The Physic Garden*, designed and produced by Margery Clinton and her assistant Evelyn Corbett, was installed in the dining room of the **Mary Erskine School**, RAVELSTON DYKES ROAD, in 1994. The mural commemorates the founding of the school in 1694, and comprises earthenware tiles of various sizes with complex lustre glazes and some tube-lining.[27]

Falkirk

DUNMORE

Pottery was made on the estate of the Earl of Dunmore from the 1790s, but after Peter Gardner (1835-1902) took charge of the works following the death of his father in 1866, production moved over to art pottery. Gardner experimented with unusual shapes and brightly coloured glazes, and the **Dunmore Pottery** prospered, even becoming a tourist attraction. After Gardner's death the Pottery was sold and continued in production until around 1914, but all that remains today is the manager's house and a range of workers' cottages; the last bottle-kiln was destroyed in 1974. The pottery also produced tiles and colourful faience, some of which can still be seen in the manager's house. In one room tiles made to commemorate the visit of the Prince of Wales in 1887 covered the ceiling and walls, but now only remain on the doors and fireplace.

FALKIRK

In the front bar of the **Woodside Inn**, 76 HIGH STATION ROAD, Woodside, Falkirk (not far from Falkirk High railway station) is a small Minton tile pavement; the pub also has good stained glass and mirrors.[28]

Fife

DUNFERMLINE

The philanthropist Andrew Carnegie was born in Dunfermline in 1835, and donated the Free Swimming Baths to his native town in 1875. A new Carnegie Centre was built at a cost of around £45,000 on an adjacent site in PILMUIR STREET during 1902-5; the architect was Hippolyte J. Blanc (1844-1917) of Edinburgh. The building, now known as the **Carnegie Leisure Centre**, was modernised and extended in 1979-91. It retains some of its original polychrome wall tiling and Moorish-style faience archways in the Turkish baths.

GLENROTHES

The first houses at Glenrothes, Scotland's second new town, were built in 1951 and its central shopping mall, the **Kingdom Centre**, was begun in 1961. Just inside, at ALBANY GATE, is a large terracotta tile mural showing local people and activities. It looks to date from the early 1980s, after the departure of David Harding (b1937), who occupied the post of Town Artist at Glenrothes during 1968-78. He oversaw the installation of many sculptures and other artworks in the town, including the early 1970s Celtic-inspired tiling by Pilkington's which covered the entire outer wall of a Glenrothes school.[29]

KIRKCALDY

The interior decoration of the **Feuars Arms PH**, in Bogies Wynd, off COMMERCIAL STREET, Pathhead, dates from 1904. Most impressive is the long, art nouveau brown-tiled bar counter, which is three-sided - although flat rather than bow-fronted - and has white glazed bricks on the serving side; the tiling is mostly plain but with some relief tiles. The front bar's deep dado tiling is of the same colour and design, and includes two delicately painted ceramic panels (single slabs rather than tiles) of the *Shepherdess* and the *Fool*, both signed 'Doulton & Co. Lambeth'. Just downhill from the pub in Flesh Wynd (off MID STREET) is **Ravens Craig**, a development of three fifteen-storey tower bocks built by Wimpey in 1964-5. The outer wall at the entrance to each block of flats is faced with a colourful abstract mosaic mural.

Glasgow

GLASGOW

Glasgow is predominantly a stone city, but there are some good examples of the use of tiles, terracotta and faience in building schemes dating from the late nineteenth century. The city's architectural ceramics originate from major English manufacturers as well as local companies, notably the Glasgow tile decorating firm James Duncan Limited, which was established in 1865 and continued in business for a century. Duncan's were responsible for designing many of the tube-lined wall tiles used in the entrance stairways of Glasgow's tenement buildings, especially between about 1904 and 1910; these tiled communal areas were known as wally closes, from the word 'wally', meaning something made of white china. The tiling varied from mostly plain cream tiles with a simple coloured border to complex arrangements with pictorial elements; the more superior the tenement, the further the tiles were continued up the stairwell. Much of this tiling is still in existence, but is difficult to see as most closes are now have security gates. North of the river there are wally closes in Partick (G11) on Caird Drive, Crow Road, Havelock Street, Laurel Place, and Marlborough Avenue; in Hyndland (G12) on Falkland Street, Hyndland Road, Lauderdale Gardens and Queensborough Gardens; in North Kelvin (G20) on Avenuepark Street, Fergus Drive, Hotspur Street, Kelbourne Street, Oban Drive and Queen Margaret Drive; and south of the river in Pollokshields (G41) on Bellwood Street, Darnley Road, Deanston Drive, Kirkcaldy Road, Mount Stuart Street and Trefoil Avenue. Elspeth Gardner, a Glasgow designer and maker of tiles, has produced replica tiles for one of the closes in Bellwood Street.

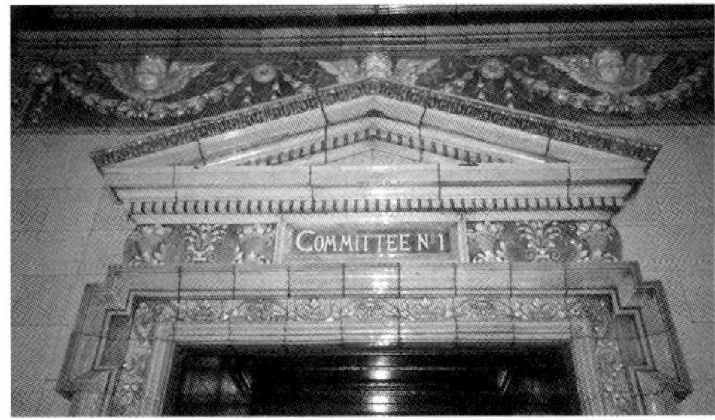

Fig 337.

Very few of the large number of Glasgow shop interiors tiled by James Duncan Limited survive, although occasional rediscoveries occur when shops are being refitted. The best remaining is the **Nimmo General Store** at 126 NITHSDALE ROAD, Pollokshields; when Duncan's supplied the tiling in 1894 this was Alex Reid's fishmonger's shop, and the interior has a continuous frieze incorporating ships and mermaids. There are also Duncan's pictorial panels at a shop in Tollcross, on the south side of TOLLCROSS ROAD just east of Braidfauld Street. Duncan's tiled many of the Glasgow branches of the Buttercup Dairy, which had over 200 shops in the city, but all the interiors have disappeared.

To explore the ceramic locations of Glasgow's centre, begin in GEORGE SQUARE at the **City Chambers** (1883-8, architect William Young). The interior, which dates from 1887-90, is a fine example of late nineteenth century civic grandeur with lavish stonework, plasterwork, mural painting and - originally - an elaborate tiling scheme from various factories, including Doulton's and Burmantofts (Fig 337). The surviving ceramic highlight is the Councillors' Corridor (or Faience Corridor), linking the committee rooms beneath a series of domes; it is elaborately clad with relief-moulded and pierced Burmantofts faience and majolica tiles in yellow, green, blue and white (Fig 338). There are faience labels for the comittee rooms and a thistle motif appears in the decoration. The refreshment room, which once opened off the Councillors' Corridor and whose decoration included Doulton pictorial medallions, has gone, but much Burmantofts plain tiling along corridors and stairwells remains, along with some red lustre tiles in the fireplace of the Council Chamber.[30]

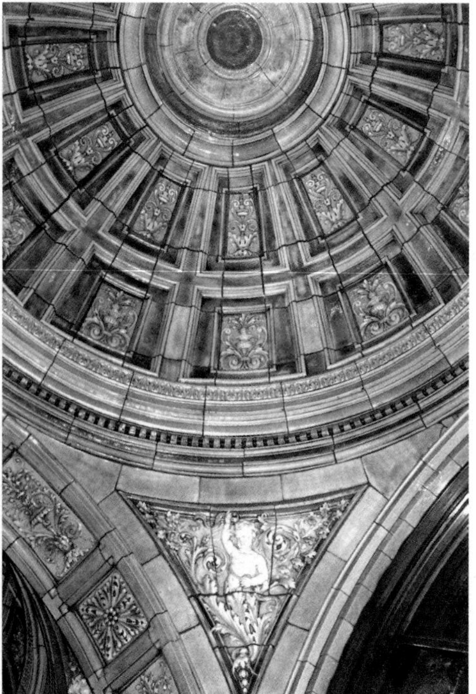

Fig 338.

At 12-16 ST VINCENT PLACE, leading off the south-western edge of George Square, is the ornate white Doulton Carraraware facade of the former **Anchor Line Building** (1905-7, architect James Miller), restored by Ibstock Hathernware in 1994. Miller was the first Scottish architect to experiment with faience, but used it only once more, for the facade of Cranston's Tearoom (1914-16) in Renfield Street, which has now been replaced with concrete.[31] On the pediment above the main entrance of **Fraser's Department Store**, 45 BUCHANAN STREET (at the west end of St Vincent Place), are life-size terracotta figures of 1884-5 representing *Art* and *Industry* below the royal coat of arms. Two blocks west on the corner of West Regent Street and RENFIELD STREET is the former Prudential Assurance building (1888-90, architect Alfred Waterhouse & Son), now housing the restaurant **Bouzy Rouge** in the original Burmantofts tile-lined telling room, which also has a ceramic ceiling. Return to George Square via a southward loop taking in the **Gallery of Modern Art** in QUEEN STREET. On the top floor, in the public facilities adjacent to the Air Gallery, are nine large ceramic panels of 1996 depicting stars, planets and galaxies by Susan and Douglas Dalgleish of Edinburgh Ceramics; two panels were recreated in 2001 following a fire.

Charing Cross

On the western fringe of the city centre, just beyond the motorway at the junction of WOODSIDE CRESCENT and Sauchiehall Street is the partly terracotta, octagonal **Cameron Memorial Fountain and Clock Tower** (1895-6), commemorating Sir Charles Cameron (1841-1925), newspaper editor, popular Member of Parliament and a leader of the Temperance Movement. The overall design was by the architect Robert Bryden and Mr Lightbody of Doulton's, who provided the buff and red terracotta; the bronze portrait medallion was by George Tinworth. The edifice has leant precariously for some years, and restoration was being considered in 2002.[32]

Garnethill

On the northern edge of the city centre at 25 ROSE STREET is **St Aloysius R. C. Church** (1908-10); the architect was Charles Menart from Belgium. Decoration of the interior, which has many mosaics, began in 1927 but was never completed; it was undergoing restoration in 2004. There are fourteen rectangular Stations of the Cross panels, each measuring about 2′ 6″ across by 3′ 6″ high and made from an opus sectile-like material which could be polished, painted glass or a ceramic. One is signed 'J. M. McG.', for Jessie M. McGeehan (1872-1961), an Airdrie-born painter of mainly figurative oils and watercolours who lived in Glasgow.

Glasgow Green

Glasgow Green, the finest open space in the city, lies by the riverside on the eastern edge of the centre. The main approach is from SALTMARKET, just north of Albert Bridge, through the McLennan Arch, salvaged from the Ingram Street Assembly Rooms (1796) and moved here in 1991-2. Between 1890 and 2001 the path eastward from the arch led straight to the **Doulton Fountain**, originally known as the Victoria Fountain (1887-8), which was made by Doulton & Co as the central feature of their exhibit at the Glasgow International Exhibition of 1888 held in Kelvingrove Park (Fig 339). Following the exhibition, Sir Henry Doulton presented the pink and buff terracotta fountain to the City of Glasgow, and in 1890 it was re-erected on Glasgow Green. The extravagant, three-storey structure, topped by a standing figure of Queen Victoria, was said to be the 'largest thing of the kind ever executed in terracotta'.[33] The diameter of the outer basin was 70 feet, the overall height 46 feet; the body of the fountain was made from terracotta blocks filled with brick, stones and cement.[34]

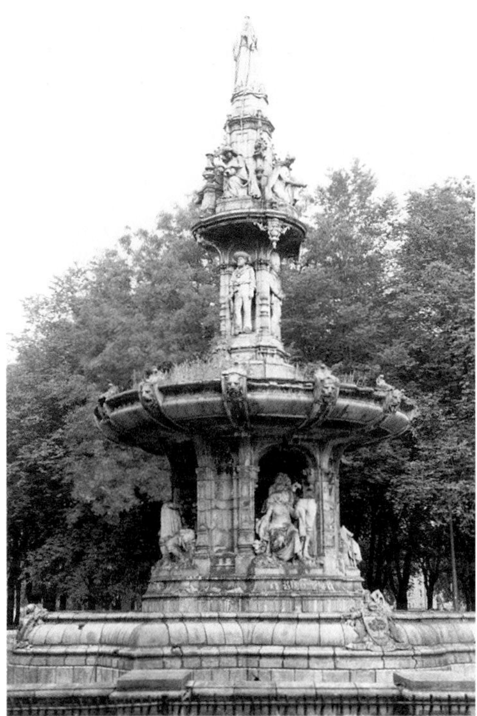

Fig 339.

The complex sculptures, which are symbolic of the British Empire, include four large allegorical figures: India, modelled by John Broad, who was also responsible for the figure of Queen Victoria; South Africa, modelled by Herbert Ellis; Canada, modelled by William Silver Frith; and Australia, modelled by Frederick Pomeroy. In addition there were figures of a sailor and Scottish, English and Irish soldiers, and four female water carriers. The overall design of the fountain was by Arthur Edward Pearce, and the modelling was supervised by Frith.[35]

Problems with the fountain began soon after it was moved to Glasgow Green; a lightning strike destroyed the statue of Queen Victoria in 1894, one of the basins sprang a leak in 1896, and vandalism was a constant difficulty. The internal hydraulic system ceased to function in 1965, and by 1990 the fountain had become severely decayed and needed scaffolding for support. However, in 1999 the City Council decided to restore the fountain and commissioned Ibstock Hathernware to carry out the work, which began in 2001; the estimated cost was about £1.2 million. After the fountain had been measured and dismantled, the buff terracotta was found to have a pink underbody, indicating that it was not fired thoroughly; this may explain why it weathered so badly. About 40% of the structure required replacement, including the four water carriers, for which new figures were modelled by Jez Ainsworth in 2002-3. The Doulton Fountain was re-erected on a new site in front of the People's Palace Museum, on the east side of Glasgow Green, in 2005.

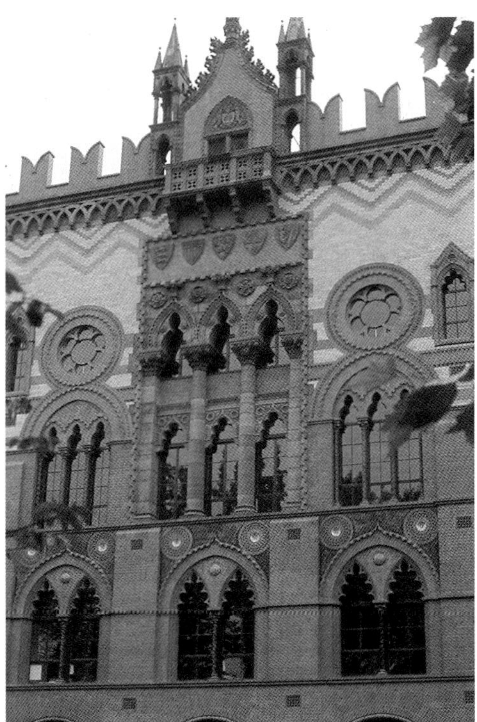

Fig 340.

It is a perfect architectural complement to Templeton's Carpet Factory (1888, now the **Templeton Business Centre**) just east on TEMPLETON STREET, with its colourful array of amazing barley-sugar faience mullions facing out on to Glasgow Green (Fig 340). The facade of this fantasy factory, based on Venice's Doge's Palace, was designed by William Leiper for the carpet manufacturer John Stewart Templeton, and makes full use of elaborate polychrome brickwork (some marked Carmichael Alloa) and terracotta, some of which was supplied by J. C. Edwards of Ruabon and the Leeds Fireclay Company; the interior is purely functional.[36] Extensions were added in the 1920s and in 1936-7 (architect George A. Boswell), when some effort was made to match the splendour of the earlier building with the use of coloured glazed bricks and mosaic. It was bought by the Scottish Development Agency in 1979 and converted to a business centre.[37]

Gorbals

The former **Scotland Street Public School** (1904-6, architect Charles Rennie Mackintosh), 225 SCOTLAND STREET, is the only Mackintosh building where tiles are used on a large scale, notably on the first floor near both staircases, where there are stubby, blue-tiled square cross-section columns with green tiled capitals.[38] To the east, on the waterfront in ADELPHI STREET, is the former **Adelphi Street School** (now a business advice centre), where the 47′ long abstract tile mural by Robert Stewart installed in 1965 is still extant.

Hillhead

The extravagant Moorish style interior of the **Western Baths Club** (1876-81), a private swimming club in CRANWORTH STREET, close to Hillhead underground station, includes much tiling. At the north end of the street is VINICOMBE STREET and the arched vanilla and pistachio striped faience frontage of the **Botanic Gardens Garage** (1912, architect D. V. Wylie).

Kelvingrove

Land for a park in Glasgow's west end was purchased by the Corporation in 1852, and Joseph Paxton was commissioned to design West End (now Kelvingrove) Park in 1854. The architect Charles Wilson then completed the adjoining residential layout begun in the 1830s with a series of terraces centred on PARK CIRCUS, designed in 1855 and built in 1857-8. On its south-west, where the circus meets Park Street South, is **22 Park Circus** (now used for marriage ceremonies and as offices), built in 1872-4 as the town house of the local ironfounder Walter MacFarlane (1817-85). Its interior design was by the architect James Boucher, who had already built two foundries for MacFarlane. The *Art Journal* of 1875 reported that Copeland & Sons supplied tiles for the bathroom and billiard room which were painted by R. J. Abraham (son of Copeland's art director at the time), Lucien Besche, who also worked for Minton's, and C. F. Hurten. The stunning three foot deep frieze in the former billiard room is painted with narrative designs of the four sporting ages of a gentleman: Health, Strength, Courage and Fortitude; it includes scenes of tiger hunting with elephants.[39]

The ironfounder's adopted son - actually his nephew - Walter MacFarlane (1853-1932) moved to Park Circus in 1898, and the interior was redecorated soon afterwards by the Glasgow Style architects James Salmon (1873-1924) and his partner John Gaff Gillespie. Their additions include tile and mosaic fire surrounds. The glass mosaic in the anteroom fireplace portrays two girls reading, and was made in 1898 by the stained glass designer Stephen Adam Junior (1873-1960), who was best known for his domestic work.[40]

Below Park Circus, down in the south-east part of Kelvingrove Park, is the **Stewart Memorial Fountain** (1872), a structurally and symbolically complex design by the architect James Sellars. Around its upper basin runs a series of faience roundels showing the Signs of the Zodiac. The fountain was restored to working order in 1988 but has since deteriorated.

Partick

A three-panel representation of *The Kingdom Come* by ceramicist Katie Cuddon, a graduate of Glasgow School of Art, was installed in **St Peter's R. C. Church** (1903), HYNDLAND STREET, Partick, in 2003; the panels were made from a ceramic composite material and sheet glass.

Pollokshaws

Pollok House (NTS), in Pollok Park (off POLLOKSHAWS ROAD), was built around 1747-52 for the Maxwell family. In the Keir Bedroom, the principal guest room, is a fireplace with rare *in situ* tin-glazed tiles probably made by Glasgow's Delftfield Pottery and dating from about 1755. The Pottery was set up in 1748 and produced delftware tiles right from the start, their advertisements of 1752, 1757 and 1760 listing 'chimney tiles' amongst other products available.[41]

Pollokshields

On the east side of Maxwell Park, GLENCAIRN DRIVE, Pollokshields (a mile or so north-east of Pollok Park) is the sad remnant of the **Hamilton Fountain**, its 40′ wide lowest basin now doing service as a flower bed. The 35′ high white Carraraware fountain was designed by Frank Burnet and made by Doulton's in 1907; it was topped by a statue of Thomas Hamilton, a local merchant. Although renovated in 1953, the superstructure was dismantled in the late 1980s.[42]

Springburn

In the centre of Springburn Park, BALGRAYHILL ROAD, is an **ornamental column** topped by a unicorn, in fact the remains of a much larger Doulton Carraraware fountain of 1912 which originally stood nearby in Balgray Pleasure Ground; Hugh Reid, chairman of the North British Locomotive Company, had presented both Pleasure Ground and fountain to the people of Springburn in 1912. The ornate base of the fountain incorporated a relief of a Springburn-built locomotive as well as several grotesque dolphin water-spouts. The Pleasure Ground was closed around 1970 and the unicorn column moved to Springburn Park; the fate of the body of the fountain is unknown, as is its designer.[43] The unicorn is of particular interest, as its horn turns out to be made of bronze. There are few nineteenth or twentieth century terracotta unicorns in existence, possibly because of the difficulty of manufacturing a satisfactory horn. Two red terracotta unicorns dating from about 1902 look down from the upper part of the facade of the Mersey Brewery, Liverpool, but the material from which their horns are made is unclear.

Highland

DINGWALL

Set into the canted corner of **Mansefield House**, HIGH STREET, is an unusually colourful faience plaque marking Queen Victoria's 1897 Diamond Jubilee; within its floral frame, the letters 'HA' appear below a portrait of the Queen.

FORT WILLIAM

In the elaborate sanctuary of **St Andrew's Episcopal Church** (1879-84, architect Alexander Ross), HIGH STREET, is a Minton encaustic tile pavement (1880) with Old Testament motifs.[44]

INVERNESS

St Andrew's Episcopal Cathedral, NESS WALK, was designed by the Inverness architect Alexander Ross (1834-1925) and built in 1866-9. As at his later St Andrew's, Fort William (see above), Ross used Minton encaustic tiles with images from the Old Testament in the sanctuary pavement (1869). Here they depict the Passover, the bronze serpent and the Sacrifice of Abel.[45]

LOCHINVER

Highland Stoneware was established in 1974, opening its first factory at Lochinver the following year. The first tile panel was painted at Highland Stoneware in 1980, but it was not until the late 1990s that the firm produced them in significant numbers. However, an extruder bought in 1993 made tile production easier, and in that year tiles were used for 'Welcome to Highland Stoneware Pottery' signs outside the potteries at Ullapool (opened 1981) and Lochinver.[46] The facades of both potteries are decorated with large-scale mosaics made from their own waste ceramic materials; the designs were created by Highland Stoneware artists in collaboration with Kaffe Fassett and Brandon Mabley. On Loch Inver shore, close to the pottery, mosaic boulders have been created by decorating rocks in the same manner.

ULLAPOOL

For details of the mosaic facade (2002) of **Highland Stoneware**, MILL STREET, and the 'Welcome to Highland Stoneware Pottery' sign, see Lochinver, Highland, above.

Inverclyde

GOUROCK

Original Artists, a former butcher's shop at 25 KEMPOCK STREET, has one of the few remaining tiled interiors by James Duncan Limited of Glasgow; it includes a frieze showing a panoramic view of countryside and steamers on the Clyde. There are also some tiled tenement entrances in the same street.

GREENOCK

The gargantuan form of Greenock Municipal Buildings (1879-86, architects H. & D. Barclay), now **Inverclyde Council Offices**, looms over the pedestrian plaza at the centre of Greenock. Its north-western entrance, on WALLACE PLACE, is faced with hexagonal, pale yellow wall tiles. The pedestrian underpass connecting Wallace Place and the **Bullring Car Park** is lined with a full-height tile mural (1964) by Robert Stewart showing Clyde paddle steamers; the detailed design was screen-printed on to plain white tiling. Compared to Stewart's abstract murals with their innovative, richly coloured glazes, the work is somewhat uninspiring. Following damage by contractors, the mural was restored by the artist Bill Brown.

Midlothian

DALKEITH

St Mary's Episcopal Church was built in 1843-5 as the private chapel for Dalkeith House by the architects William Burn and David Bryce; it stands at the north end of the HIGH STREET by the Town Gates, in what is now Dalkeith Country Park. There is an heraldic Minton encaustic pavement in the chancel. Dalkeith's town centre, in the area where High Street meets SOUTH STREET, was redeveloped in the early 1960s; the large, multicoloured Carter's tile panel on the High Street side of the central block dates from this period and mixes textured with plain tiling. **St David's R. C. Church** (1853-4, architect Joseph Hansom), ESKBANK ROAD, is the southernmost of the town's splendid array of spired churches; its Lady Chapel has a glazed, relief-tiled dado.

Moray

CULLEN

The entrance gateway to **Cullen House** (now flats), about a mile south-west of Cullen, was designed by Robert Adam and carried out in Coade stone in 1816; the archway is topped by three lions.

North Ayrshire

MILLPORT, GREAT CUMBRAE

During the mid nineteenth century the island of Great Cumbrae, which lies off Largs, was owned by George Boyle, sixth Earl of Glasgow, a great benefactor of the Episcopalian Church. He commissioned William Butterfield to design a chapel and college at Millport, the chapel being built during 1849-51 and designated the **Cathedral of the Isles** in 1876; it stands on COLLEGE STREET, on the edge of the town. Its Tractarian interior includes chancel wall tiling with large diamond patterns in green, black and red.

North Lanarkshire

MOTHERWELL

Chunky, concrete **Motherwell Theatre** was built in the 1960s as part of the Civic Centre development, well east of the town centre on Windmillhill Street; access to the theatre is via CAMP STREET. Entry to the Scandinavian-style interior is through a lobby defined by two sets of glass doors; on either side of this small space are voluptuous abstract tile murals measuring over 6′ by 8′ and made by Robert Stewart in 1966 at his Loch Striven Studio in Argyll (Fig 341). Their fabulous lustre glazes and eye-boggling colours

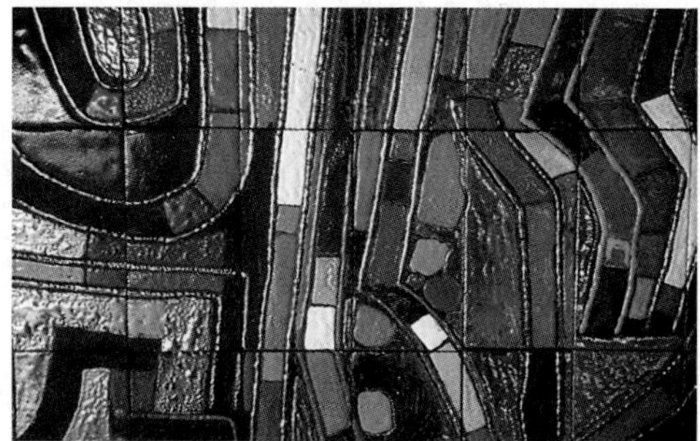

Fig 341.

are a huge contrast to Stewart's 1978 mural in the town's shopping centre, in the subway at the end of the BRANDON ARCADE. Here he used photographic images of old shops (printed by Peter Anderson) along with a sequence of silvery-grey to black pop art tiles which form a large oval motif when seen from a distance.[47] This unusual mural was in poor condition in 2004.

Orkney

KIRKWALL, MAINLAND

St Magnus Cathedral, BROAD STREET, dates from the mid twelfth century; its chancel was much rebuilt between 1913 and 1930, the work including the installation of an extensive encaustic tile pavement by Craven Dunnill during 1913-19. There are some unusual motifs, especially on the larger tiles, and the whole has a distinct Celtic feel.

Perth & Kinross

ERROL

The **Errol Brick Company** is based at Errol, eight miles east of Perth. Its 'leaping salmon' symbol may be seen at the works in the form of a brick sculpture near the beehive kiln.

Renfrewshire

INCHINNAN

The India Tyre & Rubber Company bought a parcel of land and old industrial buildings at Inchinnan in 1927; the architects Wallis, Gilbert & Partners were commissioned to produce designs for a modern office block and warehouse in 1929. The classic art deco **India of Inchinnan** building, which then stood beside the main Glasgow to Greenock road, was complete by 1930. The long, low, mainly white two-storey office block, designed to be seen from fast-moving vehicles, used green, black and red Carter's faience on its capitals, bases and door surrounds, and string courses in green faience, all creating a memorable company image. Inside, the entrance hall was a minor art deco masterpiece, with terrazzo flooring bearing the company logo, red and black faience inlaid in archways, and angular glazing bars.[48]

In 1932, only two years after the building was finished, the company was taken over by Dunlop Ltd. The office block was extended in 1956, but the site was vacated in 1982 and the factory was eventually demolished, leaving the office block to deteriorate until Graham Technology plc commissioned its restoration in 1999; the Glasgow architect Gordon Gibb supervised the work, which included an unusual rear extension. Some of the original faience, including much from the 1956 building, required replacement; after much experimentation with glazes, Shaws of Darwen managed to replicate the faience in the requisite colours and forms, and restoration was completed in 2003.[49]

PAISLEY

The J. & P. Coats textile business was founded in Paisley in 1828. One of the members of the family firm was the younger brother of J. & P. Coats, the philanthropist Thomas Coats. Following his death in 1883, the family held an architectural competition for the design of a memorial church. It was won by Hippolyte J. Blanc, and the vast, gothic revival **Thomas Coats Memorial Baptist Church**, HIGH STREET, was opened in 1894. The interior is hugely lavish with much marble, alabaster and mosaic; even the toilets could be described as sumptuous, with Doulton's floral sanitary ware, mosaic floors and wall tiling.

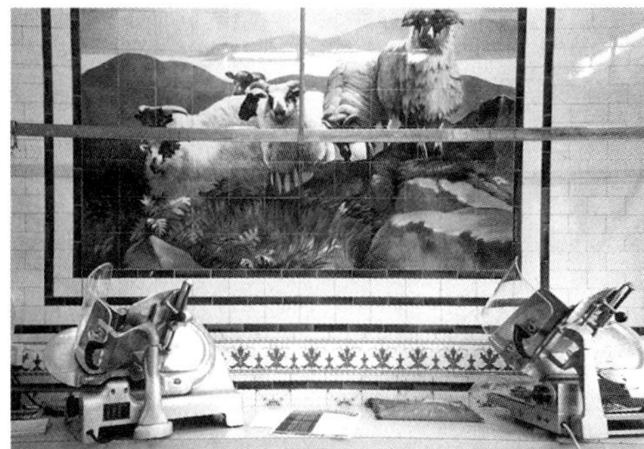

Fig 342.

Scottish Borders

COLDSTREAM

The turn-of-the century interior of **Telford's** butcher's shop, 59 HIGH STREET is completely tiled, mainly in white with blue bands, but on the wall behind the counter is a 5′ by 3′ pictorial panel of sheep in rural setting, its colours mostly blue tones (Fig 342). The individual tiles measure 150mm square, suggesting they were manufactured in the Netherlands.

INNERLEITHEN

A well-preserved Buttercup Dairy trademark tile panel is still *in situ* in what is now an electrical goods shop on the north side of the HIGH STREET (Fig 343).

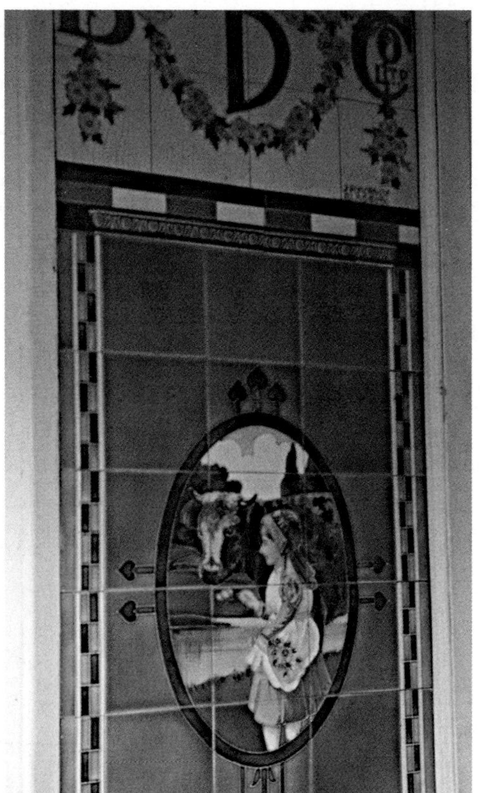

Fig 343.

JEDBURGH

Built in 1843-4, **St John's Episcopal Church**, PLEASANCE, was the first substantial Scottish church to be designed in the Tractarian manner, with lavish decoration. Its architect was John Hayward of Exeter and the funds were provided by John Kerr, seventh Marquess of Lothian, and his devout Anglican wife Cecil, daughter of the

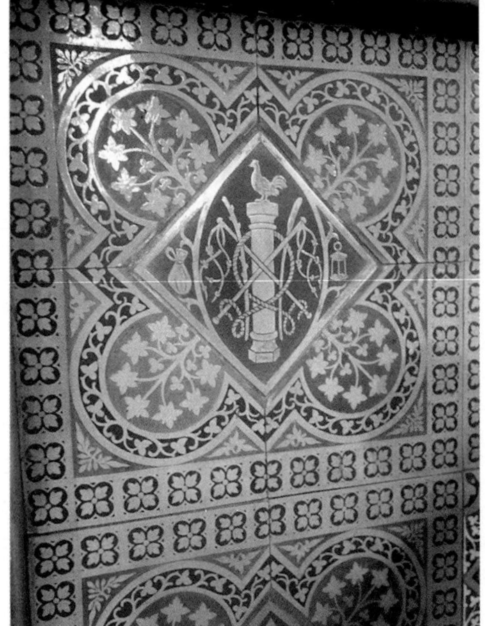

Fig 344.

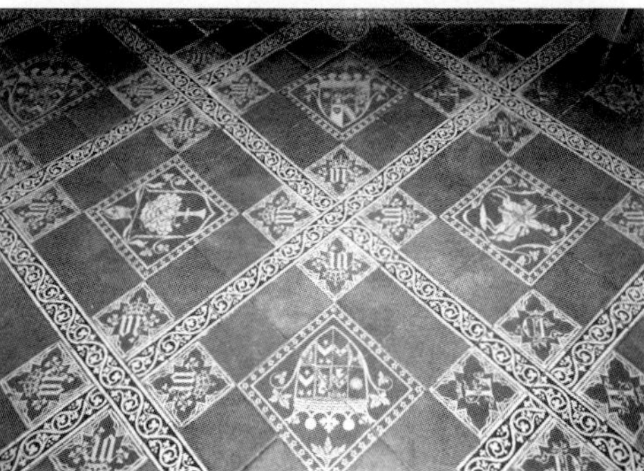

Fig 345.

Marquess of Bath. Much of the original wall painting has been lost, but the 1844 encaustic tile pavement, which runs throughout the church, remains intact; Minton's designs for these tiles have survived in Scottish archives.[50] In the south porch are specially-commissioned arms of the Lothian family and the diocese of Glasgow, and with a four-tile group of a knight on horseback. The nave pavement has repeats of ten different date and mongram tiles, while at its head is a sixteen-tile group centred on the royal arms. The two chancel step risers bear biblical inscriptions, leading up to the elaborate choir pavement, where the arrangement is in the form of a saltire; the sanctuary wall tiling includes enamelled plaques with symbols of the instruments of the passion in gold and deep blue (Fig 344). Even the ceiling is ceramic, being faced with tiles designed and presented by Herbert Minton; his blue porcelain tiles bear gilt stars and red quatrefoils showing sacred motifs. Because of the number of heraldic and other special designs, the Jedburgh scheme has few equivalents, and is a very unusual and complete example of early Minton tiling (Fig 345).[51]

LAUDER

The former dairy (1840) at **Thirlstane Castle**, now used to display laundry equipment, has peculiar black and white wall tiling which gives an impression of outsize spiders' webs and was apparently intended to repel flies.

PAXTON

The main gateway to **Paxton House** is marked by a pair of Coade stone lions, probably dating from 1789. In the grounds, down by the River Tweed, is a large-scale modern glazed brick sculpture.

TWEEDSMUIR

An excellent art deco tile scheme of 1936 survives in the ladies' and gentlemen's toilets of the **Crook Inn** (on A701).

South Ayrshire

AYR

A mural comprising nearly 1,000 tiles designed and made by Susan and Douglas Dalgleish of Edinburgh Ceramics was installed in the public dining room of **Ayr Hospital**, DALMELLINGTON ROAD, in 1997. The shaped, tube-lined and hand-painted tiles show local scenes.

PRESTWICK

Robert Stewart produced a ceramic mural for the international departure lounge of **Glasgow Prestwick International Airport** in 1973; it depicted the airport and Orangefield House, a seventeenth century mansion which was used as the main terminal building in the 1950s and early 1960s.

South Lanarkshire

BOTHWELL

In the graveyard of the **Parish Church**, MAIN STREET, is the superb yet little-known buff Doulton terracotta monument to the poet and dramatist Joanna Baillie (1762-1851), who was born in Bothwell. The memorial is about 4′ in height, with a domed canopy sheltering a square cross-section central core, on which is a delightful mosaic depicting the poet and details of her life.

Stirling

KINBUCK

Just over a mile north-west of Kinbuck is **Cromlix House** (1874), now an hotel; in the chapel are sanctuary floor tiles of 1883 by the Campbell Tile Company bearing religious motifs and texts.[52]

West Dunbartonshire

DUMBARTON

Unusually for Scotland, Dumbarton's HIGH STREET has a series of good art deco thirties faience facades, for instance the former **Burton's** (1937-8) and the former **City Bakeries** at 55-59 with black, green and orange highlights. The later **Royal Bank of Scotland** (1972) at 37 continues the theme, using bands of cream tiling.

West Lothian

LINLITHGOW

Inside **T. D. Anderson's** butcher's shop at 163 HIGH STREET are several fine pictorial tile panels, probably Edwardian, set in unusual scrollwork frames; one shows a railway viaduct, an unusual subject for such panels.

TORPICHEN

On the main road through the village, in THE SQUARE, stands the octagonal **Jubilee Fountain** (adapted from an old wellhead) which bears a Queeen Victoria 1897 Diamond Jubilee terracotta plaque made by Stanley Brothers of Nuneaton (Fig 346). This is the most northerly location yet confirmed for a Stanley's plaque; one has been reported to exist in Inverness, Highland, but its exact location (if extant) is unknown.

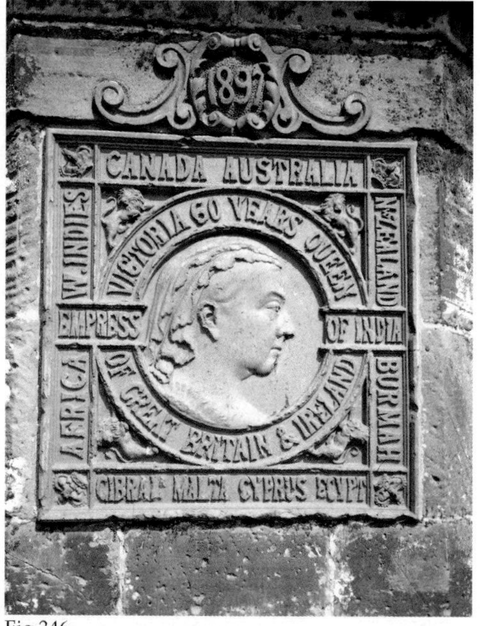

Fig 346.

WEST CALDER

The interior of the Carnegie **Public Library** (1903, architect William Baillie), HARBURN ROAD, has good original stained glass and tiling.

Western Isles

STORNOWAY (STEORNABHAGH), LEWIS

Stornoway Museum (Museum nan Eilean) opened in 1995 in the converted Secondary Department of the Nicolson Institute (1898), FRANCIS ROAD (Sraid Fhrangain). The tiles lining the walls of its lobby, staircase and landing are well-known block-printed designs by Minton Hollins.

References

1. Desmond Eyles and Louise Irvine, *The Doulton Lambeth Wares* (Richard Dennis, Shepton Beauchamp, 2002), p234.
2. W. A. Brogden, *Aberdeen: An Illustrated Architectural Guide* 2nd ed (Rutland Press, Edinburgh, 1998).
3. Gilbert T. Bell, *The Monument That Moved: Springburn's Ornamental Column* (Springburn Museum Trust, Glasgow, 1999).
4. Max Donnelly, 'Daniel Cottier, Pioneer of Aestheticism', *Decorative Arts Society Journal*, 23 (1999), pp32-51.
5. Frank Arneil Walker, *Argyll and Bute* Buildings of Scotland (Penguin, London, 2000), p38.
6. Liz Arthur, *Robert Stewart: Design 1946-95* (A. & C. Black, London, 2003).
7. G. K. Beaulah, 'Samuel Wright of Shelton and his Tiles', *Journal of the Tiles and Architectural Ceramics Society*, 3 (1990), pp28-32.
8. Frank Arneil Walker and Fiona Sinclair, *North Clyde Estuary: An Illustrated Architectural Guide* (RIAS, Edinburgh, 1992).
9. John Gifford, *Dumfries and Galloway* Buildings of Scotland (Penguin Books, London, 1996).
10. Gifford, *Dumfries & Galloway* (1996).
11. John R. Hume, *Dumfries and Galloway: An Illustrated Architectural Guide* (RIAS, Edinburgh, 2000).
12. Charles McKean and David Walker, *Dundee: An Illustrated Architectural Guide* (RIAS, Edinburgh, 1984).
13. Alison Kelly, *Mrs Coade's Stone* (Self Publishing Association, Upton-upon-Severn, 1990).
14. Kelly, *Mrs Coade's Stone* (1990).
15. Michael Stratton, 'Science and Art Closely Combined: the organisation of training in the terracotta industry, 1850-1939', *Construction History*, 4 (1988), pp35-51.
16. Rudolph Kenna and Anthony Mooney, *People's Palaces - Victorian and Edwardian Pubs of Scotland* (Paul Harris, Edinburgh, 1983).
17. Paul Atterbury and Louise Irvine, *The Doulton Story* (Royal Doulton Tableware, Stoke on Trent, 1979).
18. Michael Donnelly, *Scotland's Stained Glass: Making the Colours Sing* (Stationery Office, Edinburgh, 1997).

19. John Gifford, Colin McWilliam and David Walker, *Edinburgh* Buildings of Scotland (Penguin, Harmondsworth, 1984).
20. Kevin Wheelan, *The History of the Hathern Station Brick & Terra Cotta Company* (Mercia Cinema Society, Birmingham, 1982).
21. Wilhelm Joliet, 'Tiles from Rotterdam in John Knox House, Edinburgh', *Glazed Expressions*, (1999) 38, pp10-11.
22. Hans van Lemmen, 'Delftware tiles at the Palace of Holyroodhouse, Edinburgh', *Glazed Expressions*, (1991) 22, p4.
23. Hans van Lemmen, *Tiles: A Collector's Guide* (Souvenir Press, London, 1979), p134.
24. Elspeth King, *People's Pictures: The story of tiles in Glasgow* (Glasgow Museums, Glasgow, 1991).
25. Shropshire Archives, Shrewsbury: Maw & Co Abstract Book no 28, 10th September 1913 - 13th March 1919; 6001/5242. Job number 2557.
26. Bell, *Monument That Moved* (1999); *British Clayworker*, vol 45, 16th November 1936, p250.
27. Margery Clinton, 'A Physic Garden Mural', *Ceramic Review*, (1996) 159, pp42-3.
28. David Gamston, ed., *CAMRA National Inventory of Historic Pub Interiors* (CAMRA, St Albans, 2003).
29. Julian Barnard, *The Decorative Tradition* (Architectural Press, London, 1973), p126.
30. *Journal of Decorative Art*, February 1890, p26.
31. Audrey Sloan and Gordon Murray, *James Miller, 1860-1947* (RIAS, Edinburgh, 1993).
32. Ray McKenzie, *Public Sculpture of Glasgow* (Liverpool University Press, Liverpool, 2002).
33. Deborah Skinner, *TACS Tour Notes: Architectural Ceramics in Glasgow* (TACS, 1986).
34. *British Architect*, 1888, vol 30, p456.
35. McKenzie, *Public Sculpture of Glasgow* (2002).
36. *J. C. Edwards: Catalogue of Patterns*, (1890).
37. 'Templeton's commercial break', *Architects' Journal*, 21st November 1984, pp50-55.
38. Hans van Lemmen and Bart Verbrugge, *Art Nouveau Tiles* (Laurence King, London, 1999), pp65-7.
39. Skinner, *TACS Tour Notes: Glasgow* (1986).
40. Raymond O'Donnell, *The life and work of James Salmon, Architect, 1873-1924* (Rutland Press, Edinburgh, 2003).
41. Jonathan Kinghorn and Gerard Quail, *Delftfield: A Glasgow Pottery 1748-1823* (Glasgow Museums and Art Galleries, Glasgow, 1986).
42. McKenzie, *Public Sculpture of Glasgow* (2002).
43. Bell, *Monument That Moved* (1999).
44. John Gifford, *Highlands and Islands* Buildings of Scotland (Penguin, London, 1992).
45. Gifford, *Highlands and Islands* (1992).
46. Malcolm Haslam, *Highland Stoneware: The first twenty five years of a Scottish pottery* (Richard Dennis, Shepton Beauchamp, 1999).
47. Arthur, *Robert Stewart* (2003).
48. Joan S. Skinner, *Form and Fancy: Factories and Factory Buildings by Wallis, Gilbert & Partners, 1916-1939* (Liverpool University Press, Liverpool, 1997).
49. Joan Skinner, 'India of Inchinnan: The delights and demons of restoration', *Glazed Expressions*, (2002) 45, pp10-12.
50. Tristram Clarke, 'A display of Tractarian energy: St John's Episcopal Church, Jedburgh', *Records of the Scottish Church History Society*, 27 (1999).
51. Lynn Pearson, 'St John's Episcopal Church, Jedburgh', *Glazed Expressions*, (2003) 47, pp10-11.
52. John Gifford and Frank Arneil Walker, *Stirling and Central Scotland* Buildings of Scotland (Yale University Press, New Haven and London, 2002).

Wales

The only two examples in Wales of medieval pavements exposed and in use since they were laid are at St David's Cathedral (Pembrokeshire) and Old Radnor Church (Powys); however, relaid medieval pavements are visible at several other sites, notably Neath Abbey (Neath Port Talbot) and Strata Florida Abbey (Ceredigion).

The elaborate Coade archway at Tremadoc Church (Gwynedd) was completed in 1811, while during 1839-51 Powys was the site of early experiments in the use of terracotta in church construction, with examples at Dolfor, Newtown, Penrhos and Welshpool. The border churches are rich in mid to late Victorian encaustic pavements, and merit further research. Most of the major suppliers were involved, although it was Godwin's who made the 'Revelations' tiles designed by the architect J. P. Seddon and which may be seen in the churches at Llanbadarn Fawr (Ceredigion), Llandogo and Llangwm Uchaf (Monmouthshire) and Christ College Brecon (Powys). Superlative encaustic pavements and equally fine pictorial wall tiling form an integral part of the William Burges-designed medieval fantasy which is Cardiff Castle.

Ruabon (Wrexham), the 'terracotta town' of north Wales, is the source of much of the terracotta used in the construction of the great Victorian cities of England. Although this hard-wearing, colourful material was produced in Wales, many of the best examples of its use are outside the country, and only minimal amounts remain in Ruabon itself. There were two main Ruabon firms, established by Henry Dennis and J. C. Edwards, and many smaller works; Henry Dennis produced terracotta at the Hafod Brick & Tile Works during 1890-1933. The Trefynant Fireclay Works of J. C. Edwards manufactured buff and pink terracotta, while Edwards' trademark bright red terracotta was made at the Pen-y-bont Brick & Tile Works. The firm, reputed to be the world's largest terracotta manufacturer, also produced interesting tiles and faience around the turn of the century. Cardiff's Pierhead Building (1896-7), its ornate red terracotta supplied by Edwards, is probably the best-known building in Wales made from Welsh terracotta; Wrexham County Borough Museum has a good collection of J. C. Edwards material.

Wales had its share of early twentieth century cinemas, for instance the Carlton (now a bookshop), Swansea, with its Doulton Carraraware facade, but it was really after the Second World War that ceramic installations became popular again in Wales. Examples include the series (1975-91) of large-scale broken-tile mosaics by Kenneth and Oliver Budd at Newport, Gwen Heeney's massive 1990s carved brick sculptures in Cardiff, and Penny Hampson's Millennium Mural in Wrexham. Mention must also be made of the home-grown firm Craig Bragdy Design of Denbigh (Denbighshire), founded by Jean and Rhys Powell, who trained at Wallasey School of Art from 1948. They began making pottery and decorative tiles in the 1950s and went on to produce murals in the 1960s, eventually gaining contracts for large-scale murals in the Middle East and the USA; however, there appears to be only a single publicly-accessible Powell mural in Wales, at Denbigh Library (1989).

Suggested reading: Andrew Connolly, *Life in the Victorian brickyards of Flintshire and Denbighshire* (Gwasg Carreg Gwalch, Llanwrst, 2003); Michael J. Dillon, *Bricks, tiles and terracotta from Wrexham and Ruabon* (Wrexham Maelor Borough Council, 1985); Ifor Edwards, 'Claymasters and Clayworkers in the old parish of Ruabon', *Transactions of the Denbighshire Historical Society*, vol 35 (1986), pp83-98; J. M. Lewis, *The medieval tiles of Wales* (National Museum of Wales, Cardiff, 1999). The *Gazetteer* entries for Wales are listed alphabetically by unitary council.

Blaenau Gwent

EBBW VALE (GLYNEBWY)

The 1992 Garden Festival Wales was held at a site in Victoria, at the southern end of Ebbw Vale.

Although most of the artworks have long since gone, and the site was developed from the mid-1990s as the **Festival Park Factory Shopping Village**, Gwen Heeney's carved brick sculpture *Mythical Beast* remains. The 98′ long spiral form incorporates seats and planting, and comprises 30,000 pieces initially carved by Heeney (b1952) from wet brick; the materials were supplied and fired by Ibstock Bricks.

Bridgend

MERTHYR MAWR

The little **Church of St Teilo** (1849-51, Benjamin Ferrey) has Minton floor tiles throughout, including - on the font dais - blue and yellow designs representing the Holy Spirit.[1]

PONTYCYMER

The **bus shelter** on PONTYCYMER SQUARE was lined with screen-printed tiles in 2000 as part of the Garw Valley Project which involved the community in producing decorative street furniture; the artists were Maureen O'Kane and Anne Gibbs.

Caerphilly

PONTLOTTYN

St Tyfaelog Church was built in 1862-3 by the architect Charles Buckeridge of Oxford for the Rev. Gilbert Harries, rector of Gelligaer, some five miles to the south. Harries attempted to prevent those wishing for adult baptism by total immersion (a procedure popular in the mining communities of South Wales) from turning to the Baptist Church by promoting the construction of immersion fonts.[2] His own church at Gelligaer has such a font, installed by Buckeridge during restoration in 1867-8, and the similar Pontlottyn example is near the west end of the church. It is approached by steps and lined with Godwin's tiles, and there is a large white tiled cross on the floor of the baptistery.[3]

Cardiff

CARDIFF (CAERDYDD)

Cardiff Castle has occupied its present site since Roman times, but Cardiff itself only began to grow in size significantly when the second Marquess of Bute (1793-1848) developed the docks in what became known as Butetown, south of the Castle, from the 1830s. The docks provided an export outlet for iron and coal from the Valleys, and created much wealth for the Bute Estate. The third Marquess of Bute, who was only six months old when the second Marquess died, became fascinated by medieval art, ritual and religion, and eventually converted to Catholicism. His father had carried out very few works on the Castle, and after meeting the architect, designer and medievalist William Burges in 1865, the third Marquess set about transforming it into his vision of a truly medieval castle. The great Clock Tower was begun in 1869 and building continued until Bute's death in 1900, with William Frame taking over after the death of Burges in 1881. The result was a dizzying sequence of elaborately decorated rooms within the towering western apartments, four of which include stunning displays of unique floor or wall tiles, merely one element in an overwhelmingly rich medieval fantasy. Be warned, though, that visitors on the generally available guided tours of the Castle do not see all the tiled rooms.

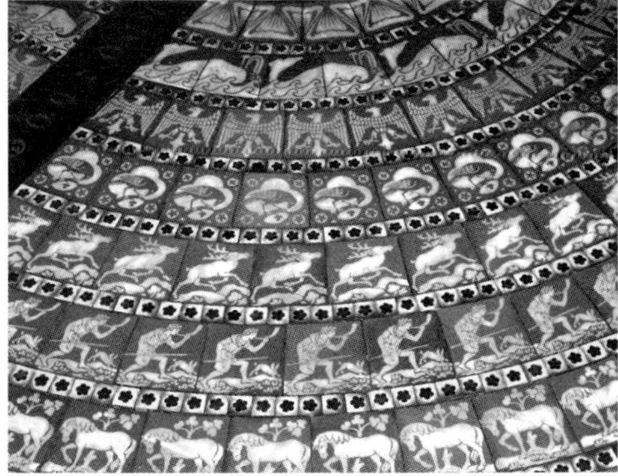

Fig 347

Burges based his interior decorative scheme for the Clock Tower on 'The passing of time between January and December', with the tile panels in the Summer Smoking Room, at the top of the tower, portraying legends of the zodiac.

The wall tiling appears to have been completed in 1874; the designs were probably painted on Maw's nine-inch square blanks by the artist Frederick Smallfield (1825-1915) using cartoons by Fred Weekes.[4] The room is floored with a magnificent encaustic tile pavement whose circular arrangement centres on a map of the ancient world inlaid with silver, bronze and copper. The tiles, laid in concentric bands of the same motifs, depict symbols of the five continents and the Holy City, and life patterns of birds and beasts (Fig 347).[5] Although all the Cardiff Castle tiles seem to have been supplied by W. B. Simpson & Sons, the firm did not make encaustic tiles, so these would have been obtained from manufacturers such as Maw's (for whom Simpson's were London agents), Craven Dunnill, or Godwin's, who produced sophisticated pavements incorporating the Signs of the Zodiac at Rochester Cathedral around 1870 and Chichester Cathedral in 1871-2.

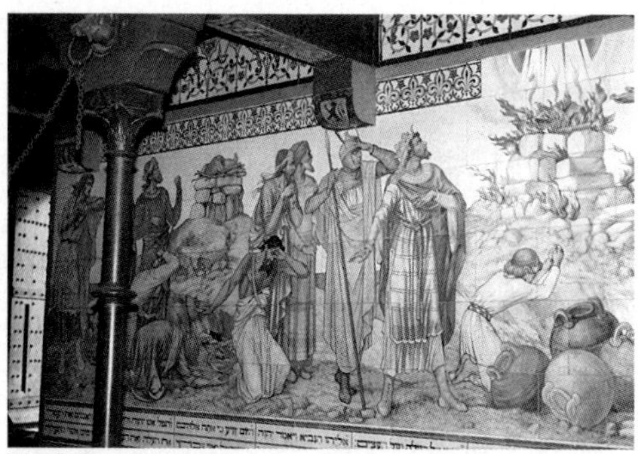

Fig 348.

At the north end of the apartments is the Bute Tower, topped by the Roof Garden (Fig 348); this was completed in 1876 but Burges decided on the introduction of its painted narrative tiling in 1873, asking his friend and frequent collaborator, the Mexican-born architectural artist Horatio Walter Lonsdale (1844-1919) to prepare cartoons on the biblical theme 'Elijah and the Prophets of Baal' (Kings 1/18).[6] Lonsdale is also believed to have carried out the painting, which may have been his first attempt at tile decoration. Charles Campbell was probably responsible for the tiled calligraphic frieze which runs beneath the panels. In the Guest Tower (1877-8), reached via a corridor running north from the Clock Tower, is the Nursery, with a tile frieze showing images of fables and fairy tales; the tiles were painted by Lonsdale and the work was complete by 1879 (Fig 349). To the north is the Beauchamp Tower; the Chaucer Room, at its top, was decorated in 1879-89 as a sitting room for Lady Bute. Alphabet tiles line the fire surround and the floor has an octagonal encaustic and plain tile pavement in the form of a Burges-designed maze, possibly inspired by the labyrinth on the floor of Reims Cathedral, with which the architect was familiar.

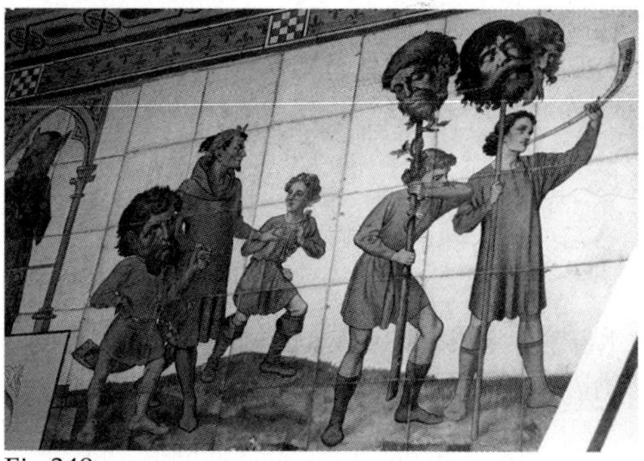

Fig 349.

Once reconstruction of the castle was in progress, Burges persuaded the Marquess to begin rebuilding Castell Coch (see Tongwynlais), a medieval castle lying about seven miles to the north-west, and in 1887-8 Bute's passion for building and restoration extended to the archaeological excavation of the site of the thirteenth century Dominican priory Blackfriars. This lies immediately north-west of Cardiff Castle in Cooper's Fields, part of Bute Park. Many late fifteenth century glazed two-colour tiles were found, and during the 1890s the Marquess had the nave and chancel of the former priory church laid out with Godwin's encaustic tiles, all copies of the medieval designs with the addition of some bearing the Bute arms. Sadly over half of these tiles, including some with unique designs, had been lost to weather and theft by 1976, and those remaining were taken up and put into storage in 1984; there is little to be seen today.[7]

After the death of the third Marquess in 1900, his son John continued with the restoration of Cardiff Castle, but following the sale of the Glamorgan estate in 1938 and the death of the fourth Marquess in 1947, the fifth Marquess presented the Castle and grounds to the city in the same year. Cardiff Castle is currently (2004) in the middle of a five-year conservation programme.[8]

For a brief tour of tile locations in Cardiff's centre, begin at the **National Museum & Gallery**, a quarter mile or so north-east of the Castle in CATHAYS PARK. Beneath the stairway leading to the archaeology section is a large ceramic installation in bright primary colours; it dates from 1994 and was designed by the artist Patrick Caulfield (b1936). The title *Flowers, Lily Pad, Pictures and Labels* refers to nearby Monet paintings. The commission was executed in handmade tiles by Jean Paul Landreau (b1953), who has lived in Wales since 1987. From the Museum, walk south along Park Place, turning right into Queen Street and quickly left into CHARLES STREET to find **St David's R. C. Cathedral**, built in 1884-7 but reconstructed during the 1950s after bomb damage. The high-relief stations of the cross (1959), each with a distinctive red-glazed cross on an otherwise unglazed ground, are by Adam Kossowski; the differing shapes of the plaques are determined by the form of their subject matter. Also in 1959, Kossowski executed another set of ceramic stations of the cross, which can be found in the western suburb of Ely at **St Francis R. C. Church**, COWBRIDGE ROAD WEST (1960), where they are mounted on a sgraffito frieze.[9]

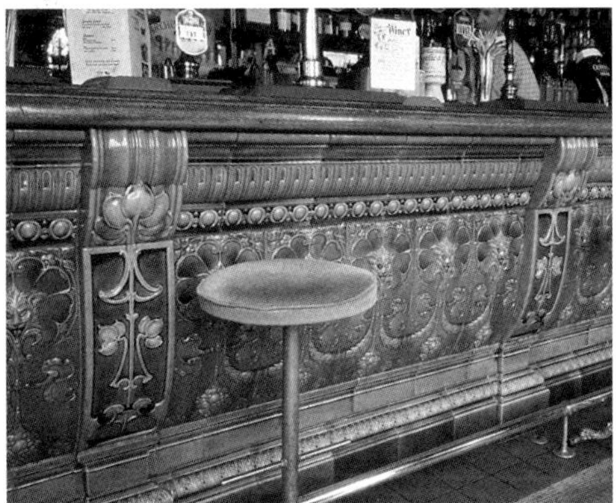

Fig 350.

At the far end of Charles Street turn right into Bridge Street, which curves round into HAYES BRIDGE ROAD. Here the **Golden Cross PH** has excellent Brain's Brewery lettering on its faience exterior as well as a complete Craven Dunnill tiled interior of 1903 including two hand-painted pictorial panels, showing Cardiff Castle in 1903 and the Old Town Hall in 1863 (Fig 350). The star of this ceramic show is the long L shaped ceramic bar counter featuring grotesque heads. Craven Dunnill were specialists in the production of these counters, which they made in two formats, a complex polychrome floral design dating from the mid-1890s, and the slightly later and relatively plain bar, as at the Golden Cross. Both types - floral and grotesques - appeared in the early twentieth century Craven Dunnill catalogue. The Golden Cross also has a post-1980 tile panel of Brain's Old Brewery in St Mary Street, Cardiff, around 1890.

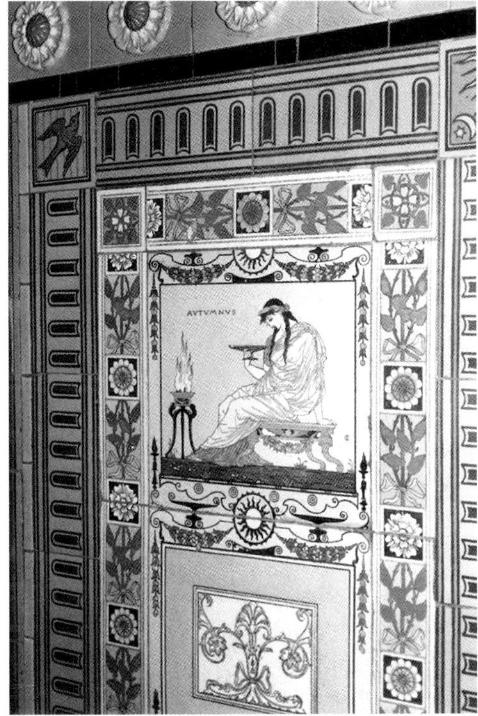

Fig 351.

Now head north toward the main shopping area, along The Hayes. As the road broadens out into Victoria Place, the former **Free Library** (1880-2 and 1893-6, architect Edwin Seward of James, Seward & Thomas) can be seen, with its entrance to the left on TRINITY STREET (Fig 351). The earlier, northern section of this building is now a pub, while the southern part - in which there remains an unusual Burmantofts drinking fountain in green, brown and buff faience with two low relief female figures - has had varying short-term municipal functions. The main ceramic interest lies in the entrance corridor of 1882, which can be seen from the pub doorway on Trinity Street. This lavish vaulted passageway is lined with majolica, printed and painted tiles by Maws including designs by Walter Crane depicting the *Seasons* and the *Times of Day*. The floor is paved with patent mosaic tiles and even the barrel-vaults of the roof are clad in faience; the entire scheme cost £465 in 1882. Immediately north of the old library is the

Church of St John the Baptist, ST JOHN STREET; its Godwin encaustic tiled chancel pavement dates from restoration in 1884-9.

Further from the centre to the west is the **Queen's Vaults PH** (now Flyhalf & Firkin), WESTGATE STREET, just north of the Millennium Stadium; its tiled facade has elaborate lettering reading 'Ind Coope & Co Entire', 'entire' being better known as porter. To the south, across CENTRAL SQUARE, is **Cardiff Central Station** (1932-4, Great Western Railway Architects' Department) with much pale cream slabbed Doulton Carraraware featuring pointing fingers and platform numbers in amber. The faience underwent restoration in 2000.[10]

Now to the suburbs, which expanded from the 1870s until just after 1900, with local landowners, notably the Bute Estate, retaining estate architects to ensure high quality designs.[11] The housing is well known for its abundance of late Victorian and Edwardian porch tiles, plain and pictorial, as well as multicoloured tiled hall floors. The variety of designs, of both floors and porch tiling, was remarkable, and elaborate flooring could be found even in smaller houses.[12] The best of the porch tiles can be seen in Pontcanna, just west of Bute Park, for instance in CATHEDRAL ROAD; in Maindy, north of Bute Park, for instance in COLUM ROAD where tiling by Gibbons, Hinton & Co of Brierley Hill, who supplied several builders in Cardiff, has been recorded; and in Roath (Y Rhath), about three miles north-east of the centre. Here there are especially good examples in NINIAN ROAD, which was built between 1891 and around 1910 by the Bute Estate and is adjacent to Roath Park, and in nearby streets such as KIMBERLEY ROAD (east of the park) and - west of the park -ALFRED STREET (1891-6), DIANA STREET (1891-5) and ANGUS STREET (1891-5).

Cardiff Bay

Next to the site of the National Assembly of Wales on HARBOUR DRIVE, looking out over Cardiff Bay, is the **Pierhead Building**, built in 1896-7 to the designs of William Frame, assistant to Burges at Cardiff Castle and Castell Coch. This landmark red gothic structure, entered at the base of its forceful clock tower, once housed the offices of the Bute Dock Company but now serves as an information centre for the National Assembly (Fig 352). Its bright red brick and terracotta was supplied by J. C. Edwards of Ruabon; the building is mentioned in the firm's 1903 catalogue. The ornate terracotta detailing includes much heraldic work and an image of a steam train. Inside, red terracotta arches run throughout the central hall, and the colourful relief-tiled dado (probably also by Edwards) continues up the part-terracotta stairwell.

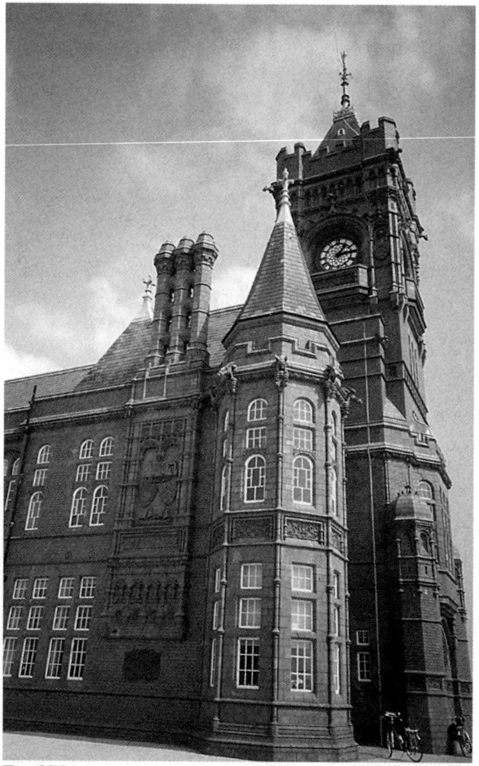

Fig 352.

Head south along Harbour Drive towards the Norwegian Church, turning left into BRITANNIA QUAY, which runs alongside Roath Dock. Here there is a series of nine carved red brick seats - the **Beastie Benches** - made in 1994 by the ceramic artist Gwen Heeney. They were commissioned by Cardiff Bay Arts Trust and sponsored by Dennis Ruabon, who supplied the bricks. The designs were inspired by the mythical creatures described in the Dylan Thomas poem *Ballad of the Long-Legged Bait* and by the terracotta reliefs on the Pierhead Building. Another example of Heeney's carved brick sculptures, **Rhiannon**, stands on ATLANTIC WHARF, just over half a mile to the north, beyond Cardiff Bay railway station.[13]

Llandaff

Llandaff still feels very much like a self-contained village, and only became part of Cardiff in 1922. From the main Cardiff road, take the HIGH STREET - where there is a **tile map** of the locality designed and made by Angela Davies in 1981 for the Llandaff Society - to reach THE GREEN and **Llandaff Cathedral**, set well down towards the river. The first sight of its interior is dominated by a blast of the twentieth century, the Jacob Epstein statue *Christ in Majesty* (1957) set upon a nakedly powerful parabolic concrete arch. It sits well in its medieval surroundings, as do the six Della Robbia Pottery plaques, *The Six Days of Creation*, given to the Cathedral in 1945 and now mounted in their original frame, designed by Frank Roper, behind the altar of the Dyfrig Chapel (Fig 353). The Pottery produced several versions of this series, based on the Edward Burne-Jones designs of 1893-8 for a similar set of stained glass windows, made by Morris & Co for the chapel of Manchester College, Oxford. On each of the six low-relief panels an angel holds a roundel, illustrating one of the six days. Various members of the Pottery are known to have worked on the *Creation* series including Harold Rathbone, Carlo Manzoni, Cassandia Annie Walker, Alice Maud Rathbone, Ruth Bare and Marianne de Caluwé. The panels, which use thin glazes, appear to have been produced from around 1901.[14]

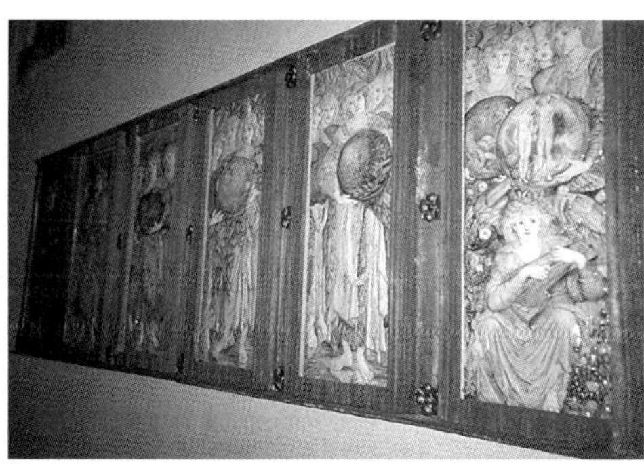

Fig 353.

TONGWYNLAIS

The architect William Burges and his patron the third Marquess of Bute rebuilt medieval **Castell Coch** (Cadw), a mile north up the wooded hillside from Tongwynlais, in 1875-9. The decoration of its interior was carried out during the 1880s to detailed designs left by Burges, who died in 1881; it was completed in 1891. The tiled fire surround in the drawing room, which probably dates from around 1886-7, includes pretty zodiac designs produced by W. B. Simpson & Sons.[15]

Carmarthenshire

LLANGATHEN

There is a decorative encaustic tile pavement in the area surrounding the main tombs inside **St Cathen's Church**.

Ceredigion

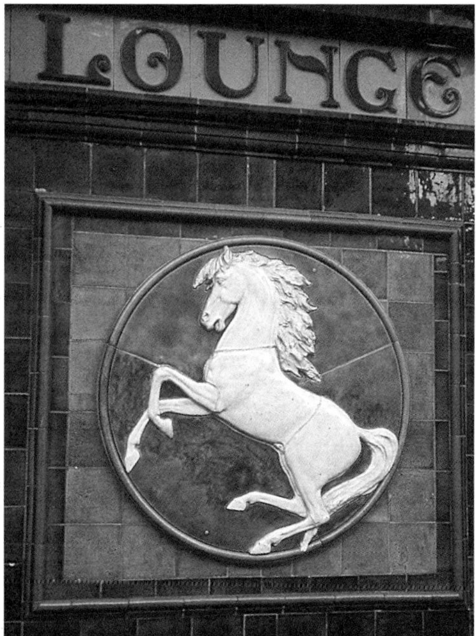

Fig 354.

ABERYSTWYTH

At 26 TERRACE ROAD (which runs between the railway station and the sea front) is **Dewhurst's** butcher's with six Carter's four-tile panels from the *Farmyard* series of animals and birds designed by E. E. Stickland around 1922 and used by Dewhurst's over many years. Further seaward, on the corner of Terrace Road and PORTLAND STREET, is the **White Horse Hotel**, with a splendid tile and faience facade including good lettering and a superbly modelled rearing white horse on circular green ground (Fig 354). The facade is said to date from shortly after the First World War, but looks rather earlier.

On reaching the seafront, turn left and continue to the **Old College**, part of the University of Wales, Aberystwyth, on NEW PROMENADE. This began life as the Castle Hotel (architect J. P. Seddon) in 1865, but reopened in 1872 as a university college, the first university institution to be established in Wales. A fire destroyed the south wing in 1885 and high on a turret of its 1888 replacement are three large mosaic panels designed by C. F. A. Voysey, showing Archimedes and symbols of modern science and industry.

CARDIGAN

Near the centre of Cardigan there is good turn-of-the-century porch tiling in PRIORY STREET, where several porches display a pheasant design, and also in MORSE STREET, NORTH ROAD and GWBERT ROAD, where there are floral relief tiles.

ELERCH

St Peter's Church (1865-8, architect William Butterfield) has a tiled reredos.

LLANBADARN FAWR

The **Church of St Padarn** is almost immediately on the left after the Llanbadarn Fawr village turning off the A44 from Aberystwyth. The monastery founded by St Padarn on this site dates back to the sixth century, and parts of the present building date from around 1200; by the Dissolution, the parish was the most extensive in Wales. After the building of a new church in Aberystwyth, St Padarn fell into disrepair, and restoration was begun in 1868 under the architect J. P. Seddon. Three periods of restoration followed, 1868-9, 1878-80 and 1882-4. William Morris, founder in 1877 of SPAB, the Society for the Protection of Ancient Buildings, wrote to the vicar of St Padarn on the 29th September 1877 protesting at the proposed rebuilding of what was then the best thirteenth century church in Wales. Although he had previously produced glass for Seddon, and knew Seddon was to be the restorer, Morris made no mention of the architect in his letter. Seddon was mightily offended, and vitriolic correspondence ensued in the pages of the *Ecclesiastical Art Review*. Seddon eventually rebuilt the church using glass by Jesse Rust rather than Morris; he also used Rust's mosaic in the choir pavement.

Seddon's work included the introduction of Godwin's encaustic tiles to his own design, athough at the time of writing (2004) most of these were covered by carpet. The four-tile groups show a Duplex or twin wick burner oil lamp (below the chancel arch), while those in the transepts show a figure on a throne, in fact an elder casting a crown; these tiles are from the 'Revelations' series designed by Seddon and used by him in the restoration of Llangwm Uchaf Church, Monmouthshire, around 1866-8; Christ College Chapel, Brecon, Powys (1861-4); and Sunningwell Church, Oxfordshire (1877). At St Padarn and Sunningwell the tiles are set in a mosaic pavement.[16]

PENRHYN-COCH

An unusual feature of **St John's Church** (1880, architect R. J. Withers) is its colourful ceramic lectern in the form of an eagle and dragon.[17] Near Penrhyn-coch is **Crosswood Park (Trawsgoed)**, a vast mansion which was the ancestral home of the Earls of Lisburne. In its 1891 wing, which is now holiday accommodation with no public access, is an apartment with a tiled indoor water fountain installed for the Sixth Earl of Lisburne's retriever. In another room is a Spanish tile panel depicting an elaborately-dressed Virgin Mary, which dates from the late nineteenth or early twentieth centuries and was almost certainly made at one of the many factories in Triana, Seville.

STRATA FLORIDA ABBEY

Strata Florida Abbey (Cadw), about a mile south-east of Pontrhydfendigaid, was established by the Cistercians on its present site in 1166 and rebuilt following a fire in 1285. Early fourteenth century floor tiles still survive in the south transept chapels and in a small area against the west wall of the north transept. The tiles, which once paved a large part of the abbey church, were probably produced at a tilery in the upper Severn valley, around Shrewsbury.[18] One unusual motif is a figure of a man wearing a doublet and apparently peering into a mirror; it is thought he may symbolise pride or vanity. The south transept pavements were restored in 1890 and the 1930s using fragments found in other areas of the church.[19]

Conwy

CONWY

St Mary's Church, the town's parish church in the centre of Conwy, was originally the church of the Cistercian abbey of Aberconway. It was rebuilt during the fourteenth century and 110 medieval floor tiles - possibly dating from the early sixteenth century - found there during restoration around 1872 are now mounted on the south wall of the chancel.[20] Just north of the church on the HIGH STREET is the **Castle Hotel**, an ancient coaching inn refaced in 1885 by Douglas & Fordham in broken limestone and red Ruabon brick and terracotta from J. C. Edwards.[21] The architect John Douglas (1830-1911) frequently used the products of the Edwards works, his practice's testimonial appearing in an Edwards price list of 1896; the Castle Hotel was mentioned in the 1903 Edwards catalogue.[22] The hotel's terracotta includes ornate fenestration and panels of Jacobean-style strapwork.

LLANDUDNO

The **Oriel Mostyn** (1901, George Alfred Humphreys), VAUGHAN STREET, has an excellent red terracotta facade by J. C. Edwards including several modelled figures. The Llandudno architect G. A. Humphreys (1865-1948) was surveyor to Lord and Lady Mostyn, whose family were responsible for the development of Llandudno by the Mostyn Estates from 1849. Nearby **Imperial Buildings** (1898) also has the remains of a good red terracotta facade above first floor level.

Denbighshire

BODELWYDDAN

A previously gloomy lobby area of **Glan Clwyd Hospital (Ysbyty Glan Clwyd)** was brightened up considerably by the introduction of a series of tile panels by Bronwyn Williams-Ellis in 2001. The panels show colourful scenes of parrots in flight, and were carried out using cuerda seca outlines and several layers of glazes. The hospital stands about half a mile north of the main road through Bodelwyddan, the A55.

BODFARI

St Stephen's Church, rebuilt by T. H. Wyatt in 1865, has a colourful encaustic tile pavement in the chancel and an extensive glazed tile reredos by Maw & Co, including alpha and omega symbols and lettering.

DENBIGH

In the stairwell of **Denbigh Library, Museum and Art Gallery**, HALL SQUARE, is a large ceramic mural (1989) by the local firm Craig Bragdy Design; it depicts local scenes and can be viewed from several levels. The encaustic tile pavement in the lavishly fitted chancel of **St David's Church** (rebuilt 1894-5, architect R. Lloyd Williams), ST DAVID'S LANE, was supplied by Carter's of Poole.[23]

LLANDYRNOG

The medieval **Church of St Teyrnog** was expensively restored by the architect William Eden Nesfield (1835-88) during 1876-8, at the same time as he was working on St Mary's Church, Bolton-on-Swale, North Yorkshire. In both churches he installed fashionable Spanish-style *cuenca* tiling almost certainly manufactured by Frederick Garrard of Millwall; at Llandyrnog it forms a dado on the east wall of the sanctuary.

LLANGOLLEN

At **Plas Newydd**, BUTLER HILL, the home of the famous Ladies of Llangollen from 1780, are four complete Dutch delft-tiled fire surrounds which were probably installed during the nineteenth century. The tiles themselves variously date from the first half of the seventeenth century, in two of the first floor fireplaces, to around 1800 in a ground floor fire surround.

PRESTATYN

On the seafront at Prestatyn, just off BEACH ROAD at its junction with Bastion Road (which runs seaward from the railway station), is the **Wavey Ceramic Mural** by Teena Gould; it was made around 1999 and is one of the artworks on the Sustrans National Cycle Network. The mural covers two large gable ends, one of which appears to depict a giant cockerel in tiles and mosaic.

RHYL

At the entrance to **Rhyl Library, Museum and Arts Centre**, CHURCH STREET, is a mural by the ceramicist Maggie Humphry, who lived and worked in north Wales from around 1970 until 1999, after which she moved to Shropshire. The design of the main panel, which is seven feet in diameter, is based on the mythical tale of the bard Taliesin.

ST ASAPH

George Gilbert Scott's 1867-75 restoration of **St Asaph Cathedral** included the introduction of a glazed inlaid tile pavement by Maw & Co into the chancel; some of the motifs are said to be based on those of medieval tiles found during the restoration work. The rich sixteen-tile groups repeated in the sanctuary were designed for Maw's by the architect George Goldie, one of their regular designers. The same group can also be found in the Lady Chapel of Chester Cathedral, where they were installed in the 1860s. The Chester and St Asaph tiles were supplied by W. B. Simpson & Sons, who were the sole agents for Maw's products in London from 1858.

Flintshire

Encaustic tile pavements were installed at several Flintshire churches in the late Victorian period, for instance Emmanuel Church, Mold Road, Bistre, Buckley (manufacturer J. C. Edwards, fitted 1881); St David's Church, Chester Road, Pentre, Flint (Minton, 1872) where the tiling included references to the builders of the church, and there is also yellow terracotta detailing; St Mary the Virgin, Halkyn (Campbell Brick & Tile Co, 1878) designed by John Douglas for the Duke of Westminster's Flintshire estate; St Mary's Church, Nannerch (Minton, 1853); and St John Evangelist, Rhydymwyn (Minton, 1863).[24]

QUEENSFERRY

In Queensferry but not of it, the former **General Office Building** of Shotton Steelworks (now the headquarters of Corus Colors) stands isolated on the north bank of the River Dee, opposite the town and close to Hawarden Bridge railway station (Fig 355). The works, which originally made corrugated galvanised iron sheets, was established in 1896 by John Summers & Sons, a clog-nail making firm from Stalybridge, and expanded rapidly during the early years of the twentieth century. Production at Shotton soon outstripped that of Stalybridge and it was decided to move the head office to Shotton; the General Office Building was erected in 1907-8 to the designs of the architect James Harold France (b1872) of Manchester, a friend of the family.[25] France was in partnership with the Blackburn-based architect Harry Smith Fairhurst from around 1901; the partnership was dissolved in 1905, after which Fairhurst immediately began designing some of Manchester's most notable buildings, including several of the massive Whitworth Street warehouses.

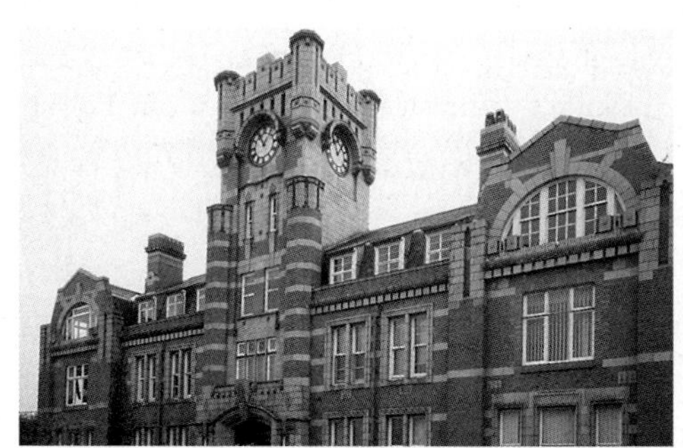

Fig 355.

Perhaps the Summers & Sons commission was the opportunity for France to show his erstwhile partner (who had been articled to Maxwell & Tuke of Blackpool Tower fame) that he could also build on a grand scale, for the General Office Building is a tour-de-force in ochre terracotta, most likely by J. C. Edwards of Ruabon, with unusual art nouveau detailing and a gloriously confident turreted facade. The imposing porch, above which the terracotta bears the legend 'JSS 1907', is reached by a terracotta bridge over what could easily be interpreted as a moat. Inside, the little-altered entrance hall is lined with green-glazed and tube-lined tiles, perhaps by Wooliscroft's, with some hand-painted tiles on the stairwell. The stained glass and other fittings are equally ornate. The building was wholly appropriate for a company which was one of the world's largest manufacturers of galvanised sheeting by the 1920s. Ownership of the works was transferred to the British Steel Corporation in 1967, and then to Corus in 1999, following British Steel's merger with Koninklijke

Hoogovens. The General Office Building, with its feast of ceramic decoration, is currently (2004) unprotected by listing.

Gwynedd

BANGOR

The **Cathedral of St Deiniol** was restored in 1868-73 by George Gilbert Scott and further work was carried out during 1879-80. Medieval tiles were discovered in both phases, and tiles found in the latter period had been relaid by 1892 at the west end of the north aisle, where they remain today, albeit hidden by carpet in the bookshop. These tiles probably date from the first quarter of the fourteenth century.[26] The extensive Craven Dunnill floor tiling installed around 1875 includes very unusual line impressed and relief glazed tiles in mainly green, red and yellow, their designs probably drawing on those of their medieval predecessors. Maw & Co also supplied tiles to Bangor; some border tiles bear their mark, and the Cathedral is mentioned in their 1906 catalogue.[27]

Near the Cathedral, on the exterior of St Deiniol's Shopping Centre, is the three-part ceramic **St Deiniol's Mural** (1992) by Maggie Humphry showing local and historical scenes.

CRICCIETH

The **Chapel of Art**, 8 Marine Crescent, is a former chapel built in 1878 and converted to an arts centre in 1989-95. Leading up to it is the International Potters' Path, a pathway comprising thousands of hand-made tiles by individual potters around the world. Its first phase was completed at the end of 1999, and tiles are still being added.

PORTMEIRION

In the washrooms of the **Portmeirion Hotel** are colourful tiled panels (1989) by Bronwyn Williams-Ellis, some depicting exotic mermaids.

TREMADOC (TREMADOG)

The churchyard of the former **St Mary's Church**, Church Street, is entered through a Coade stone archway, a wonderful castellated gothic revival structure ornamented with elephant heads (Fig 356).[28] Both church and arch were completed in 1811 and paid for by the local woollen mill owner William Alexander Maddocks. The archway was repaired in the late 1960s but has since deteriorated; restoration is currently being undertaken by the local buildings preservation trust, the Friends of Tremadog (Cyfeillion Cadw Tremadog).

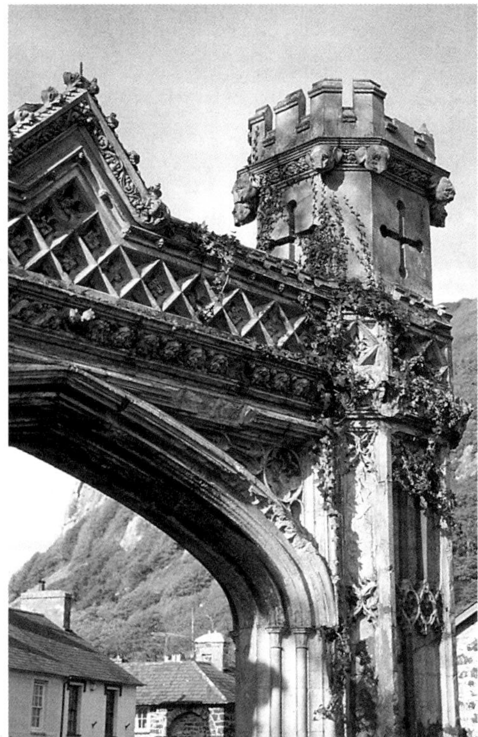

Fig 356.

Isle of Anglesey

LLANBADRIG

Ancient **Llanbadrig Church**, just east of Cemaes Bay, was restored in 1884 at the expense of the 3rd Lord Stanley of Alderley (1827-1903), a diplomat and orientalist who succeeded to the peerage and estates in Cheshire and Anglesey in 1869. He stipulated that Llanbadrig's interior decorative scheme should include elements repesenting his adopted Muslim faith, thus there is much red, blue and white in the stained glass, and a pretty blue glass-tiled dado in the sanctuary. The custom-made Powell's tiles show a variety of mainly floral motifs.

LLANFAIRPWLLGWYNGYLL

The dairy (now tea room) at **Plas Newydd** (NT), on the banks of the Menai Strait, has almost fully tiled walls in a geometric pattern of white and dark green.

PENRHOS

The Tower (no public access) was built in the early nineteenth century to house workers on the Penrhos estate on Holy Island. The former dairy, which was added around 1885, has a complete Minton Hollins interior tile scheme of blue and white printed tiles as well as four pictorial panels, three probably based on designs by William Wise. The largest panel, showing a milkmaid, was painted by W. B. Simpson & Sons, and the floor is also tiled in blue and white. The wall tiles had been hidden beneath layers of paint and wallpaper for many years, but were rediscovered in the 1980s.

Merthyr Tydfil

MERTHYR TYDFIL

The **Old Town Hall**, HIGH STREET, was built in 1896-7 to the designs of local architect E. A. Johnson. The exterior displays much terracotta ornament and the main staircase hall is a real ceramic treat, with stylish faience and tiling. The grade II listed building was last in use in 2001, when it functioned as a nightclub, but firm plans to redevelop it as a media and arts centre were unveiled in 2004.

Monmouthshire

ABERGAVENNY (FENNI)

On the facade of the interwar **Burton's** in the HIGH STREET is a black ceramic panel measuring about 7′ by 9′ which bears orange-glazed lettering reading: 'Let Montague Burton The Tailor of Taste Dress You'.

CHEPSTOW (CAS-GWENT)

On the exterior of the **Tesco** store in STATION ROAD is a pair of ceramic tile panels (1998) by the potter Ned Heywood (b1947) of Chepstow; they show local historical scenes including the Severn Bridge.[29]

LLANDOGO

The chancel of **St Oudoceus Church** (1859-61, architect J. P. Seddon) was decorated in 1889 with a scheme by Seddon & Carter which includes wall paintings and Powell's opus sectile work on the east wall with figures designed by Harry Wooldridge and Frank Mann.[30] In the sanctuary there are also Godwin's encaustic tiles to Seddon's design showing an elder casting a crown; these tiles are from the 'Revelations' series also used in Seddon's restorations of Christ College Chapel, Brecon, Powys (1861-4); Llangwm Uchaf Church (around 1866-8), Monmouthshire; St Padarn (1868-9, 1878-80 and 1882-4), Llanbadarn Fawr, Ceredigion; and Sunningwell Church (1877), Oxfordshire.

LLANFAIR KILGEDDIN (LLANFAIR CILGEDIN)

Although the main attraction of the **Church of St Mary the Virgin**, now in the care of the Friends of Friendless Churches, is the 1888-90 scheme of sgraffito wall decoration by the artist Heywood Sumner, there is also decorative floor tiling throughout, installed by the architect J. D. Sedding during his 1873-6 reconstruction of the church.[31]

LLANFOIST (LLANFFWYST)

The **Church of St Ffwyst** was restored in 1872, probably by the architect J. P. Seddon; a decorative tile pavement runs throughout.

LLANGATTOCK NIGH USK (LLANGATWG DYFFRYN WYSG)

The village is also known as The Bryn. Tiles dating from around 1455-80 have been relaid as panels in the west wall of **St Cadoc's Church**; they are Malvern-type designs probably made at the Cadogan House kiln in Monmouth.

LLANGATTOCK-VIBON-AVEL (LLANGATWG FEIBION AFEL)

The encaustic tile pavement (1866) at **St Cadoc's Church**, which includes biblical texts on the sanctuary steps, was installed by church decorators and furnishers Cox & Son.[32]

LLANGWYM UCHAF

St Jerome's Church, which stands about a quarter mile up the valley from St John's Church, Llangwym Isaf, was partly rebuilt in 1863-9 by J. P. Seddon. The extensive nave (red and yellow plain tiles) and chancel tiling dates from around 1866-8, and includes patterned tiles by Maw & Co as well as examples of the 'Revelations' series designed by Seddon and made by Godwin's. The focus in the chancel is on a patriarchal or two-barred cross in black and green triangular tiles, into which are set several four-tile groups including, at the intersections, an agnus dei with the Book of Seven Seals, one of the 'Revelations' motifs. Either side of the cross are other 'Revelations' groups including the nine-tile set showing a winged figure surrounded by seven lamps. The Duplex (twin-wick) burner oil lamp group is also present, on the step leading to the tower, north of the chancel. All this elaboration lies behind a fantastic rood screen of about 1500, partly reconstructed by Seddon in 1876-8.[33]

MAGOR (MAGWYR)

The architect John Norton's restoration of **St Mary's Church** in 1861-8 included the installation of a decorative encaustic tile pavement in the chancel.

MONMOUTH (TREFYNWY)

In the centre of Monmouth on CHURCH STREET is **St Mary's Church**, which has a good collection of medieval tiles, some thirteenth century but mostly fifteenth century, relaid in the floor and walls of the south aisle. The later tiles have Malvern-type designs and were produced just north of the church at the Cadogan House kiln on Monk Street; this is the only first-floor kiln to have been found in Wales. The wide range of designs includes several armorial tiles and a St Agatha tile, whose inscription was said to provide protection against fire.

South-west of the church, at the far end of MONNOW STREET, is Monnow Bridge and its fortified gate, Britain's only surviving example of a medieval gate-tower on a bridge at the entrance to a town. Adjacent is the **History Wheel** (2002) a ceramic installation by the Chepstow potter Ned Heywood, with forty stoneware segments showing local historical images on a circular platform.

TINTERN ABBEY (ABATY TYNDYRN)

A Cistercian foundation was established at Tintern in 1131. Almost nothing remains of the earliest church; the ruins of **Tintern Abbey** (Cadw) as seen today date from the early thirteenth to the mid fourteenth centuries. A few plain medieval floor tiles remain in the Chapter House. Outside the main site, at the foot of the hillside to the south, lies the early thirteenth century St Anne's House, incorporating the gatehouse and chapel. Inside are relaid late thirteenth century tiles from the abbey church.

Neath Port Talbot

NEATH (CASTELL-NEDD)

A mile west of Neath is the Cistercian foundation of **Neath Abbey** (Cadw), which originally had extensive and elaborate fourteenth century tile pavements. Their deteriorating condition led to them being lifted during the 1980s, and they are now preserved under cover at the site, laid out in the vaulted undercroft of the dormitory. The designs include a rectangular tile showing knight on horseback. A few tiles also remain in the ruined abbey church, in the south choir aisle.

Newport

NEWPORT (CASNEWYDD)

Dominating the view from the train entering Newport is the smoothly white and vaguely Italianate Civic Centre, its tower looming over the town from Godfrey Road, west and uphill from the station; the architect was T. Cecil Howitt (1889-1968) of Nottingham. The first phase of building was carried out in 1937-9, but it was 1964 before the Civic Centre was complete; Howitt's Home Brewery in Nottingham, another towered structure, suffered similar war-related delays. The upper part of the Civic Centre's stair hall was painted in 1961-4 with a series of eleven history murals by Hans Feibusch; set into the ground floor, below this breathtaking scheme, is a marble mosaic of the town's coat of arms by the artist Kenneth Budd.

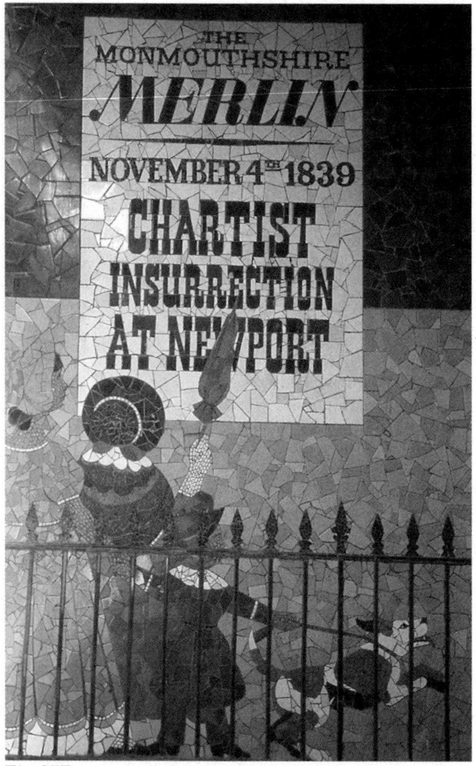

Fig 357.

Buoyed with confidence from this hugely successful venture into municipal decoration, it seems Newport developed something of an obsession with mural art. To see the results, head east from the railway station towards the remains of the medieval castle, crossing the north end of the main shopping area to reach the OLD GREEN roundabout. The descent to the pedestrianised centre is brightened considerably by a 1990 shopping-themed mural, the work of Kenneth Budd (d1995) and his son Oliver Budd. Highly coloured rectangular industrial tiles flank a large tile and mosaic mural, while smaller mosaic panels run through the adjacent subway. Kenneth Budd produced large-scale mosaic works from the early 1960s, with Oliver joining his father's Kent-based firm in 1982. Their work often involved the use of cut tile along with other elements, the tiles normally being imported from Germany. On the far side of the roundabout, on the curving wall below the castle ruins, is **The Monmouthshire Railway and Canal Company** (1975) a large, partly mosaic installation by Kenneth Budd depicting the part played by the canal and railway in Newport's growth. Continue on through the subway leading to Baltic Wharf, above the River Usk, to see yet more mosaics of local scenes (1991) by Kenneth and Oliver Budd.

Now return to the town centre and go south to find JOHN FROST SQUARE, the centrepiece of the town's 1970s redevelopment. Its tunnel-like northern entrance is much enhanced by the **Chartist Mural** (Kenneth Budd, 1978), a 120′ long tile and mosaic mural (made from around 200,000 pieces) commemorating the 1839 Chartist uprising in Newport, when the Chartists, headed by John Frost, marched to the nearby Westgate Hotel and were fired upon (Fig 357).

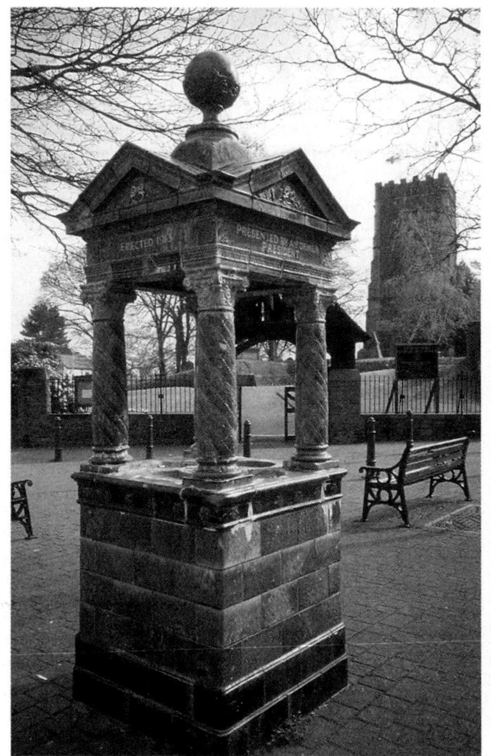

Fig 358.

Newport's other ceramic locations are more distant, the closest being the **drinking fountain**

(1913) near the west end of the Cathedral of St Woolos on STOW HILL, nearly half a mile south - and up - from the centre. This elaborate olive green and mottled dark blue faience fountain was most probably made by Doulton's, who produced several such monumental fountains in the early years of the twentieth century; the date of the Newport example is unusually late (Fig 358). It was presented to the town by the British Women's Temperance Association and moved to Stow Hill from nearby **Belle Vue Park** in 1996. The Park itself, a little south of the Cathedral on BELLE VUE LANE, was designed by Thomas Mawson and opened in 1894; its 1910 terraces and tea pavilion (undergoing restoration in 2004) have rich red terracotta dressings. On the southern edge of Newport in the suburb of Pillgwenlly, nearly a mile south-east of Belle Vue Park and close to the famous Transporter Bridge (1901-6), is the **Waterloo Hotel**, at the south end of ALEXANDRA ROAD. It retains half of its Doulton faience barfront of 1904, the other half having been exported to the USA.[34]

Christchurch

On the north-eastern edge of Newport, nearer junction 24 of the M4 than anything else, is the **Celtic Manor Resort Hotel** at Coldra Woods. Its foyer is graced by a suspended ceramic panel showing local scenes designed and made around 2001 by the potter Ned Heywood of Chepstow.

Duffryn

The suburb of Duffryn is now best-known for its collection of late twentieth century factories, offices and housing, developed from 1974 in the vast parkland of **Tredegar House**, a grand mansion owned by the Morgan family. The town of Tredegar, near Ebbw Vale, took its name from the house; the family were major landowners in the area. The Victorian kitchen of Tredegar House has fairly plain and functional wall tiling by Maw & Co, but of more interest are the Dutch tiles found in fire surrounds throughout the house, particularly the eighteenth century tiles in the Best Room which show figures on horseback.[35]

Pembrokeshire

Pembrokeshire has an abundance of churches with mid to late Victorian encaustic tile pavements and other ceramic decoration. Churches with worthwhile tile pavements include those at Angle, Cosheston (also tiled dado), Hodgeston (Minton with arms of incumbent), the impressive Monkton, Prendergast (a fine Godwin floor) and St Bride's (Godwin, arms of local landowner Lord Kensington). Slebech Church (closed 1991) has an excellent and extensive Chamberlain encaustic pavement dating from around 1843-4 with specially-made armorial tiles.[36] At Nevern, geometric tiling by Minton Hollins flanks the reredos, and there are tiled reredoses at Llanychaer and Meline.

John Frederick Campbell, first Earl Cawdor, restored all the churches on his south Pembrokeshire estate during the 1850s, beginning with Stackpole (1851-2 by George Gilbert Scott), near the now-demolished family home, Stackpole Court.[37] As at Bosherton (restored 1856), Castlemartin (1858), St Petrox (1855), St Twynnells (1858), and Warren (1856), the tile pavement is by Minton and bears Cawdor heraldic motifs.

CAREW CHERITON

The sanctuary pavement of **St Mary's Church** includes relaid fifteenth and sixteenth century heraldic tiles, some originally used at Carew Castle. There are a number of square Malvern-type designs as well as unusual rectangular tiles which may have been made locally.[38]

ST DAVID'S (TYDDEWI)

On the three steps leading to the high altar in the choir of **St David's Cathedral** is one of the best surviving medieval tile pavements in Wales. Some of these sixteenth century tiles were relaid during George Gilbert Scott's restoration of the Cathedral in the 1860s, but others remain *in situ;* all were made in the Severn Valley, many probably originating at a kiln in the Worcester area. The designs were copied by Godwin's for the extensive (and still extant) encaustic tile pavement installed in the Cathedral as part of Scott's restoration work (Fig 359).

Half a mile south of St David's itself, on the road to St Non's Bay, is an 1865 gothic villa, now the **Warpool Court Hotel**, which was occupied by the Williams family during the late nineteenth and early twentieth century. Mrs Ada Lansdown Williams raised six children at the house, and on becoming a widow, took inspiration from Howel the Good (Hywel Dda), King of Wales in the tenth century, who ruled that a genealogical record of each family should be preserved in imperishable material in their own home. From 1893 she meticulously painted the detailed history of her family on around 3,000 eight-inch square white tiles, all of different design; there are armorial motifs, tiles resembling illuminated manuscripts and others showing events from her life. The tiles were sent to England for firing then mounted on walls throughout the house, where they remain as a unique genealogical mural. She also found time to copy Walter Crane's *Flower Fairies* series for the nursery.

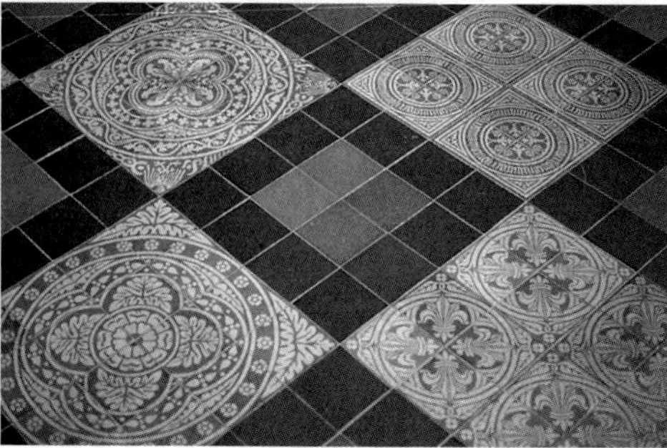

Fig 359.

Powys

Patterned Victorian encaustic tile pavements are common in the churches of Powys, with a wide range of manufacturers responsible for supplying the tiles including, in central Powys or Radnorshire, Chamberlain (at St Mary, New Radnor, 1845), Craven Dunnill, J. C. Edwards, Godwin, Maw and Webb's Worcester Tileries.[39] Godwin's provided wall tiles for St Meilig, Llowes, in 1891-2, although most of this ornate sanctuary dado was removed in 1931, as it had deteriorated and was disliked.[40]

The mid-Victorian period in the Welsh borders also saw a brief experiment with the use of terracotta in church construction. For reasons of economy - terracotta was available locally - and originality the Oswestry architect Thomas Penson (c1790-1859), County Surveyor of Denbighshire and Montgomeryshire for over thirty years, used yellow moulded bricks and terracotta rather than stone for the arches and vaulting of Christ Church (1839-44), Welshpool, quickly following this with limited external use of the material at St Agatha (1844-5), Llanymynech, Shropshire. At his final brick and terracotta church, St David (1843-7), Newtown, there was no stone whatsoever. Sidney Smirke used yellow brick and a sprinkling of terracotta at Holy Trinity (1845), Penrhos, and lastly there is St Paul's Church (1851, architect T. G. Newenham), Dolfor, where the ornate window tracery and much else is of terracotta. However, with no medieval precedent for the use of terracotta in gothic revival churches, there was little enthusiasm from architects or critics.[41]

BRECON

Christ College, BRIDGE STREET, was founded in 1541, but by 1837 its attendance had fallen to just seven boys. A new governing body decided to rebuild the school, and the architects Prichard & Seddon won a competition for its new design in 1859; this included the conversion of part of the medieval friary to form the College Chapel. Building work began in 1861 and was almost finished by mid 1864, but the Chapel's wall decoration was still incomplete in 1885. The surviving Christ College drawings, including designs for tiles and tile arrangements, indicate that John Pollard Seddon was largely responsible for the restoration of the Chapel.[42] Its sanctuary encaustic pavement includes two sets of nine-tile groups showing seven lamps, part of Seddon's 'Revelations' series manufactured by Godwin's, which were later used at Llangwm Uchaf Church, Monmouthshire (around 1866-8), Llanbadarn Fawr Church, Ceredigion (1868-9 at the earliest) and Sunningwell Church, Oxfordshire (1877). Assuming the pavement of Christ College Chapel was installed during the main period of construction, 1861-4, this could be first use of 'Revelations' tiles; however, part of the series appears at St Oudoceus, Llandogo, Monmouthshire, built in 1859-61 but with decoration of a slightly later date.

CAPEL-Y-FFIN

The eccentric visionary and preacher Joseph Lyne, known as Father Ignatius (d1908) founded the monastery of Capel-y-ffin in 1869. Building work continued on the church until 1882, but the vaulting collapsed around 1920; Eric Gill set up a self-sufficient religious community at the monastery during the 1920s. The **tiled grave** of Father Ignatius, restored around 1970, stands in the centre of the ruined church, to which there is no public access.

HAY-ON-WYE (Y GELLI)

Richard Booth's bookshop, 44 LION STREET, occupies a former agricultural suppliers; its two pilasters display cow and sheep tiles from

Wedgwood and images of farming activities from T. & R. Boote.

LEIGHTON

The spire of **Holy Trinity Church** (1851-3) can be seen for miles around, which was probably the intent of its patron, the Liverpool banker John Naylor whose **Leighton Hall** (no public access), a mile to the south, was put up around 1850-6; Naylor bought the Leighton estate in 1849. The architect for both church and hall was W. H. Gee of Liverpool. A Minton tile pavement, with some designs by A. W. N. Pugin, runs throughout the church, and the same manufacturer's tiles were also used in the Hall, which Pugin and J. G. Crace had been asked to decorate following the success of the Medieval Court at the Great Exhibition.[43] The estate, with its spectacular gardens, was broken up in the 1920s and the Hall remained largely unused, falling into a state of great disrepair until restoration began in 1995.

NEWTOWN

Just north of Newtown railway station is the monumental form of **St David's Church**, NEW ROAD, completed in 1847 and the last of Thomas Penson's terracotta churches. His apse was replaced by a yellow brick chancel in 1874-5, when the internal galleries were also removed. The internal terracotta was painted with a colourful scheme in the early 1960s. Head north along New Church Street to reach the town centre, turning right into HIGH STREET to find the delightful **W. H. Smith's**, opened in 1927 and restored to its original state in 1975 as the company's contribution to European Architectural Heritage Year.[44] Although the shop was modernised around 1960, none of the many tile panels was removed, and the shop is now a treasure trove of ceramic advertisements (Fig 360). Products and services featured in panels on the facade, in the front bookstall and in the first floor museum include 'Newspapers regularly delivered', 'Guide books and maps of all parts' and 'Books on architecture', each with an appropriate image. The panels, with lettering designed by Eric Gill, were produced by Carter's of Poole for the W. H. Smith chain during the 1920s. This timewarp of a shop is even stranger when entered via the modern shopping development at its rear.

Returning to the present day, terminating the view at the east end of the High Street is the red brick and buff terracotta clock tower of **Barclay's Bank**, actually Cross Buildings, BROAD STREET, put up by the Birmingham architects Wood & Kendrick (best known for their pubs) in 1898-1900. It was erected at the cost of local landowner Sarah Brisco and intended to commemorate Queen Victoria's Golden Jubilee. This outstanding example of terracotta modelling, with its ornate plaques and strapwork, is mentioned in the 1903 catalogue of J. C. Edwards of Ruabon.

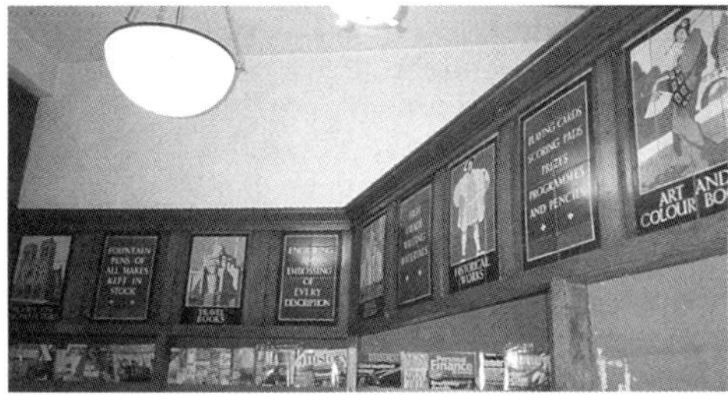

Fig 360.

OLD RADNOR (PENCRAIG)

St Stephen's Church, rebuilt during the fifteenth and late sixteenth centuries, retains four groups of medieval tiles, most with relief and counter-relief decoration. These *in situ* tiles and the repaired pavement at St David's Cathedral are the only two examples in Wales of medieval pavements exposed and in use since they were laid.[45] St Stephen's was restored in 1882, when Godwin's plain and encaustic tiles were introduced, but their designs do not appear to have been derived from their medieval predecessors (Fig 361).[46]

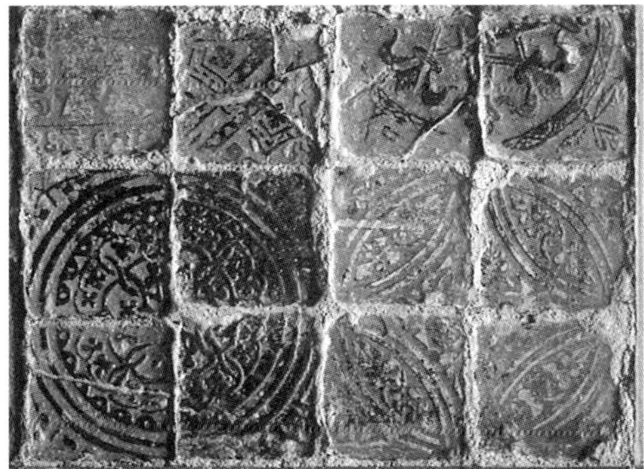

Fig 361.

WELSHPOOL (Y TRALLWNG)

Welshpool lies immediately north-east of Powis Castle (NT), whose grounds are accessible on foot from a path leading off the High Street, the town's main shopping street. Beyond this point, climb west along the High Street, which becomes Chapel Street and then MOUNT STREET; at its top, look left for a narrow lane which winds upward to the former **Christ Church** (now a private house, no public access), built for the Earl of Powis in 1839-44 by Thomas Penson; this was the architect's first terracotta church, where the material was used internally in arches and vaults. There is a fine view from the churchyard, on the edge of the great park.

Back in the centre of town, off Broad Street to the south is NEW STREET and the turn-of-the-century **Welsh Independent Baptist Church**, its facade a feast of yellow dog-tooth terracotta. At the east end of Broad Street is CHURCH STREET; on the left is the **Past Times** shop, formerly I. & M. Morris agricultural implement suppliers, with good red terracotta ornament including head-shaped keystones.

Rhondda Cynon Taff

PORTH

Porth Public Library, PONTYPRIDD ROAD, was built around 1912 as a pair of shops, with rich red terracotta ornament including figures as corbels; the building was restored around 1999 by Shaws of Darwen.

Swansea

SWANSEA (ABERTAWE)

The twin-towered former Carlton Cinema, OXFORD STREET, was built in 1912-14 to the designs of Swansea architect Charles Tamlin Ruthen for the Swansea Electric Cinema Company. Having survived the Second World War almost intact, the Carlton closed as a cinema in 1977, re-opening as **Waterstone's** bookshop in 1995 after a long planning battle which almost resulted in its demolition. The fine Edwardian baroque Doulton Carraraware facade includes four friezes of dancing cherubs.[47]

Torfaen

PONTYPOOL (PONTYPWL)

Inside **St Alban's R. C. Church** (1844-6), GEORGE STREET, are several works carried out in 1955-6 by the artist Adam Kossowski. There are fourteen glazed ceramic Stations of the Cross, a mahogany altar crucifix with ceramic inlay, and two glazed ceramic holy water stoups. The exterior of **Pontypool Rugby Club** features a colourful 45 square yard mosaic mural entitled *Try and Try Again!* which was designed and made by Oliver Budd in 1992-4; the materials included cut tile.

Vale of Glamorgan

EWENNY (EWENNI)

In the priory church of **Ewenny Priory** (Cadw), at the crossing, is a frame containing relaid early sixteenth century tiles taken up from the north transept. The presbytery was floored with Godwin tiles in the late nineteenth century, their lay-out possibly being derived from the medieval pavement. In the adjoining churchyard are several low-lying grave surrounds, dating from the 1940s to the early 1960s, made from a ceramic material which successfully imitates grey or black ganite.

PENARTH

Sadler's fish and game shop in VICTORIA ROAD, almost opposite Penarth railway station, has one fully-tiled interior wall with two large Minton Hollins pictorial panels, one of fish and one of game; they were probably designed by Albert Slater. Nearer the shore, several houses on MARINE PARADE and BRIDGEMAN ROAD have two, three or even four red terracotta dragon finials.

Wrexham

BETTISFIELD

The *cuenca* wall tiles either side of the reredos at **St John Baptist Church**, restored by G. E. Street in 1872-4, were almost certainly made by Frederick Garrard of Millwall.

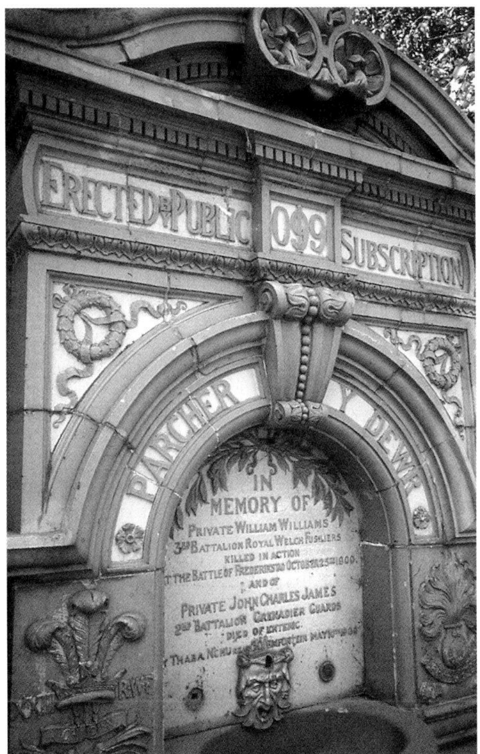

Fig 362.

CHIRK (Y WAUN)

Very little of the interior decorative scheme designed by A. W. N. Pugin and J. G. Crace for **Chirk Castle** (NT) in 1845-8 survives, although there are Pugin-designed Minton-tiled fire surrounds of 1847 in the Long Gallery, along with other Minton fireplaces in areas not normally open to the public. After Pugin's death in 1852, his son Edward Welby Pugin carried out further works at Chirk, most probably including the design of tiles with motifs of a hand and the letter 'M' for Robert Myddelton Biddulph (1805-72) in 1858. These were manufactured by Minton's but none remain *in situ* at the Castle.[48]

FRONCYSYLLTE

Above and beyond the southern end of the Pont Cysyllte aqueduct, at the side of the main road through Froncysyllte (the A5), is a wonderfully intact war memorial **fountain** of 1909 in cream and grey-green faience, almost certainly by Doulton (Fig 362).

RUABON (RHIWABON)

The boom in the development of brickworks in Flintshire and Denbighshire began in the 1860s, driven by the easy availability of workable clay and coal, and often finance from English entrepreneurs. By the turn of the century there were nearly 130 such works - about thirty in the Ruabon area alone - ranging in size from small country brickyards to industrial-scale brick and terracotta works such as J. C. Edwards, which exported their wares around the world. Clayholes, some of huge dimensions, coal pits and spoil heaps were common. Brickmaking enjoyed its most prosperous times between the 1880s and the early years of the twentieth century, following which came a long decline due to lack of investment and difficulties with clay supplies. Even in the 1960s there was still much physical evidence of this industrial past, but today very little remains, with only a single firm, Dennis Ruabon (see Johnstown below), still maintaining production in Denbighshire.[49]

In terms of visible architectural terracotta, central Ruabon is now something of a disappointment, with only odd pieces of decorative ware, for instance the red terracotta lettering on the **County Constabulary** building of 1896, to be seen. In fact most locally-produced terracotta was used in the construction of Victorian cities, at home and abroad, but enough may still be seen around the outskirts of Ruabon to give an intriguing flavour of the town's appearance when the industry was at its height, when Ruabon was Terracottapolis and J. C. Edwards said to be the largest manufacturer of terracotta in the world, producing buff and pink wares (as well as tiles) at Trefynant, on the south-western edge of Ruabon, and their trademark bright red terracotta at the Pen-y-bont works in Cefn-mawr, down in the valley to the south.

Cefn-mawr

The **Pen-y-bont Brick & Tile Works** of James Coster Edwards (1828-96) was established in 1865. J. C. Edwards instigated the annual Edwards Terracotta Competition in 1880, to promote the use of terracotta in architectural design, and several prizewinning entries appeared in the firm's 1890 catalogue. In 1882 he built a block of four model cottages near the entrance of the Pen-y-bont Works; they were designed by George Canning Richardson, head of J. C. Edwards' design department, and acted as advertisements for the firm's products. The occupants were the works managers of the terracotta, encaustic tile, blue brick and roofing tile departments.[50] Along with terracotta blocks lying amidst the overgrown ruins, these cottages and a few office buildings (on the east side of the B5605, opposite Newbridge) are all that remain of the vast works, which finally ceased to function in 1961.

Johnstown

The works which became **Dennis Ruabon** was established by Henry Dennis (1825-1906) at the Hafod Colliery, Johnstown, in 1879; access is via a signposted by-road running north of the B5426 just west of its junction with the A483. Although the works is much diminished, with many kilns being demolished during the 1980s, it continues to produce quarry tiles and clay pavers. There is still a good deal of architectural work to see, including two turn-of-the-century red terracotta plaques set into the walls, one a coat of arms, the other figurative and bearing the words 'Terracotta Works' (Fig 363). The paving outside the offices includes a fine welsh dragon in cut brick, and there is external, probably 1960s, wall tiling in bright geometric patterns of yellow, brown and orange.

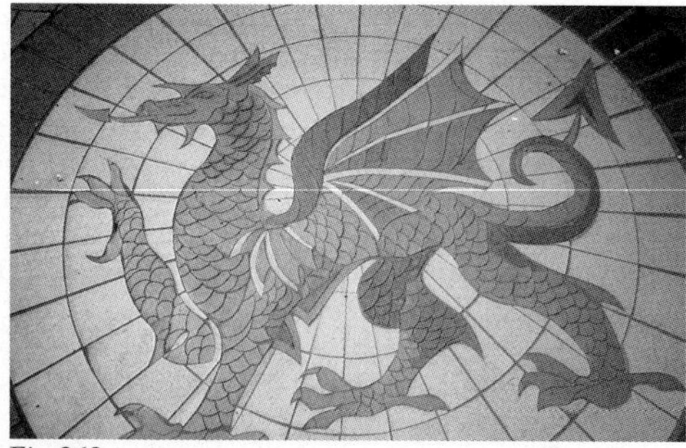

Fig 363.

Rhosllanerchrugog

Protruding from the gable of the **Nag's Head PH**, HALL STREET, is a well-modelled red terracotta horse's head.

Rhosymedre

St John's Church, CHURCH STREET (just north of the B5605) was rebuilt and refitted in 1887-8, partly at the cost of the claymaster J. C. Edwards, whose Pen-y-bont and Trefynant Works lay within a mile or so of St John's. The *Wrexham Advertiser* recorded that Edwards supplied encaustic tiles, made at his own works, for the pavement which ran throughout the church; this includes five unusual four-tile groups, one depicting three fishes.[51] Edwards died in 1896, and an elaborate tiled reredos was erected in his memory in 1906. It was made at the Trefynant Works by members of the congregation and that of a nearby church, and combines encaustic, relief moulded and plain tiles. In the churchyard is headstone with two inset relief tiles dating from the 1880s.

Trefynant

J. C. Edwards had established his works, eventually known as the **Trefynant Fireclay Works**, at Trefynant, just east of Trevor, by 1856. Almost nothing remains today apart from the gateposts of the company's main office building, which stood on the south side of the Ruabon-Llangollen road, the A539 (immediately east of the turning to the Pont Cysyllte aqueduct). The red brick and terracotta piers are marked 'J C Edwards' and 'Offices'. Opposite is an ornate pinky-red brick and terracotta villa, which must surely display local wares even if having no connection with the old works.

Trevor (Trefor)

The former methodist chapel (1902), STATION ROAD, now an **antiques centre**, has colourful glazed wall tiling in its foyer, along with unusual pierced ventilation tiles, all probably local products. Just over a mile west of the village is the eighteenth century mansion Trevor Hall, home of the claymaster J. C. Edwards and his family from the 1860s until his death in 1896. Edwards had been in the process of building a country house for his retirement in the valley to the south; it was completed in 1896 and is now the **Bryn Howel Hotel** (off the A539, three miles east of Llangollen). It was occupied by the Edwards family until the 1850s, but due to alterations during conversion, little of interest other than Edwards-made red brickwork, roof tiling and some terracotta tracery is visible externally as the original entrance has been hidden.

WREXHAM (WRECSAM)

Right in the centre of Wrexham, in RHOSDDU ROAD, is the **Library and Arts Centre**, whose external wall has been decorated since 2001 by the Millennium Mural, a nine metre by five metre work made in 1999-2000 under the direction of tile and mural maker Penny Hampson of Hebden Bridge.[52] The mural was the result of a fifteen-month project which involved local artists working with 1,200 schoolchildren aged between three and eleven. Each child made a tile, contributing to the overall theme of 'Wrexham Past and Present'; the tiles were dried and fired at the North East Wales Institute of Higher Education, and fixing was carried out by the Clitheroe Tile Company.[53]

Out on MOLD ROAD, north-west of the centre, is the **North East Wales Institute of Higher Education** campus, formerly Denbighshire Technical College. The entrance hall of the main building (1950-3) retains its original pattern-making wall tiling designed by Peggy Angus for Carter's; the lay-out incorporates a six-tile red dragon group and two different tiles showing leeks, all by Angus.[54]

References

1. Geoffrey O. Orrin, *Church Building and Restoration in Victorian Glamorgan* (University of Wales Press, Cardiff, 2004).
2. John Newman, *Glamorgan* Buildings of Wales (Penguin Books, London, 1995).
3. *The Builder*, vol 21, 21st November 1863.
4. Pauline Sargent, 'Painted tiles by William Burges', *Antique Collector*, 58 (1987) March, pp101-108.
5. J. Mordaunt Crook, ed., *The strange genius of William Burges* (National Museum of Wales, Cardiff, 1981).
6. *Horatio Walter Lonsdale, 1844-1919: Architectural Artist*, (Gallery Lingard, London, 1984).
7. Nigel M. Adams, 'Encaustic Tile Pavement, Blackfriars Priory, Cardiff', *Glazed Expressions*, (1986) 13, pp7-9.
8. John Edwards, 'Conserving Cardiff Castle', *Journal of Architectural Conservation*, 8 (2002) March, pp6-22.
9. *Adam Kossowski: Murals and Paintings*, (Armelle Press, London, 1990).
10. Gordon Biddle, *Britain's Historic Railway Buildings: An Oxford Gazetteer of Structures and Sites* (Oxford University Press, Oxford, 2003).
11. Newman, *Glamorgan* (1995).
12. Helen C. Long, *The Edwardian House: the middle-class home in Britain, 1880-1914* (Manchester University Press, Manchester, 1993).
13. Gwen Heeney, *Brickworks* (A & C Black, London, 2003).
14. Williamson Art Gallery and Museum, *Della Robbia Pottery, Birkenhead, 1894-1906: An interim report* (Metropolitan Borough of Wirral, Department of Leisure Services, Birkenhead, 1980).
15. David McLees, *Castell Coch* (Cadw, Cardiff, 1998).
16. Lynn Pearson, 'The 'Revelations' tiles of John Pollard Seddon at Sunningwell Church, Oxfordshire', *Glazed Expressions*, (2003) 48, p18.
17. Peter Howell and Ian Sutton, eds., *The Faber Guide to Victorian Churches* (Faber and Faber, London, 1989).
18. J. M. Lewis, *The medieval tiles of Wales* (National Museum of Wales, Cardiff, 1999).
19. David M. Robinson and Colin Platt, *Strata Florida Abbey* (CADW, Cardiff, 1998).
20. Lewis, *Medieval tiles of Wales* (1999).
21. Edward Hubbard, *The Work of John Douglas* (Victorian Society, London, 1991).
22. J. C. Edwards, Ruabon, Prices of Mediaeval Encaustic, Incised, and other Glazed and Unglazed Tiles, for Floors, etc. (1896); British Library YA.2002.a.12217.
23. *The Builder*, vol 68, 18th May 1895, p381.
24. For Buckley, Flint and Nannerch see Edward Hubbard, *Clwyd* (Penguin Books, London, 1994); for Halkyn see *The Builder*, vol 36, 16th November 1878; for Rhydymwyn see *The Builder*, vol 21, 24th October 1863.
25. Gordon Smith, *A Century of Shotton Steel (1896-1996)* (British Steel Strip Products, Shotton, 1996).
26. Lewis, *Medieval tiles of Wales* (1999).
27. Shropshire Archives, Shrewsbury, Maws Tiles 6001/4112, Tiling by Maw & Company Limited, 1906.
28. Alison Kelly, *Mrs Coade's Stone* (Self Publishing Association, Upton-upon-Severn, 1990).
29. Ned Heywood, 'New Ceramic Art', *Glazed Expressions*, (2004) 50, p11.
30. Dennis W. Hadley, *James Powell & Sons: A listing of opus sectile, 1847-1973*, (2001).
31. John Newman, *Gwent/Monmouthshire* Buildings of Wales (Penguin, London, 2000).
32. Newman, *Gwent/Monmouthshire* (2000).
33. Pearson, 'Sunningwell Church', 2003.
34. 'Waterloo Hotel', *Licensing World & Licensed Trade Review*, 10th December 1904, p421.
35. Wilhelm Joliet and Hans van Lemmen, 'Dutch Tiles with figures on horseback in Tredegar House, Wales', *Glazed Expressions*, (2003) 47, pp6-7.
36. Chris Cox, 'Chamberlain floor tiles at Slebech Church, Wales', *Glazed Expressions*, (1994) 28, pp9-11.
37. Thomas Lloyd, Julian Orbach and Robert Scourfield, *Pembrokeshire* Buildings of Wales (Yale University Press, New Haven and London, 2004).
38. Chris Cox, 'The medieval tiles of Carew Cheriton Church, Pembrokeshire', *Glazed Expressions*, (1996) 32, pp6-7.
39. Margaret A. V. Gill, 'A survey of floor-tiles in the churches of Radnorshire: Parts I and II', *Transactions of the Radnorshire Society*, 72 (2002), pp26-83.
40. Margaret A. V. Gill, 'Victorian floor tiles from the parish churches of the Wye Valley Group',

Transactions of the Radnorshire Society, 68 (1998), pp64-95.

41. Michael Stratton, *The Terracotta Revival* (Victor Gollancz, London, 1993), pp50-1.
42. Michael Darby, *John Pollard Seddon* Catalogues of Architectural Drawings in the Victoria and Albert Museum (Victoria and Albert Museum, London, 1983). Drawing D.943.96 (at 94.J.3, V&A Prints and Drawings Study Room) relating to Christ College Chapel shows a design for a tile arrangement including a group labelled 'Seven lamps'.
43. Paul Atterbury and Clive Wainwright, *Pugin: A Gothic Passion* (Yale University Press, New Haven and London, 1994), p58.
44. 'Newtown - heart of oak', *Newsbasket*, 68 (1975) 6, pp4-6.
45. Lewis, *Medieval tiles of Wales* (1999).
46. Jane Kent, 'Church Tiles at Old Radnor', *Glazed Expressions*, (1999) 39, pp8-9.
47. John Skinner, 'The Carlton Swansea: The Very Best Bookshop in Wales', *Picture House*, (2000) 25, pp27-34.
48. John Malam, 'Minton/Pugin Tiles at Chirk Castle, Clwyd', *Glazed Expressions*, (1993) 26, p3.
49. Andrew Connolly, *Life in the Victorian brickyards of Flintshire and Denbighshire* (Gwasg Carreg Gwalch, Llanrwst, 2003).
50. Edward Hubbard, *Clwyd* Buildings of Wales (Penguin Books, London, 1994).
51. Derek Jones, 'St John the Evangelist Church, Rhosymedre, Clwyd and J. C. Edwards', *Glazed Expressions*, (1987) 14, pp7-8.
52. Penny Hampson, 'A Millennium Tile Mural at Wrexham', *Glazed Expressions*, (2000) 40, pp8-9.
53. Penny Hampson, 'Millennium Mural', *Ceramic Review*, (2001) 188, pp44-5.
54. Katie Arber, 'Peggy Angus, designer of modern tiles for a modern Britain', *Decorative Arts Society Journal*, 26 (2002), pp120-134.

Appendicies

Appendix 1

Biographical Directory of Tile, Terracotta and Faience Artists, Designers and Manufacturers

This selective biographical directory concentrates upon individuals and firms whose work was used in an architectural context. Cross-references are indicated by an asterisk.

Accrington Brick and Tile Company
The Accrington Brick and Tile Company, one of the pioneers in exploiting the Lancashire shales for ceramics, was active during 1890-1939 at Accrington, Lancashire. The firm produced decorative plaques and other components for use in houses; after it was reconstituted around 1925 its main output became facing and engineering bricks.

Adams & Co
Adams & Co bought the Scotswood Road, Newcastle upon Tyne works of W. C. Gibson in 1902, continuing with the Gibson name for several years but eventually making sanitaryware under the trade name Adamsez; from 1904 until the First World War the firm also made Adamesk art pottery. Alan H. Adams, who joined the firm in 1912, introduced Elan ware and designed (in addition to sanitaryware) decorative plaques and tiles; the latter were large, thick and rather rustic in appearance. None has yet been seen in an architectural context. The firm went into receivership in 1975 and the Adamsez trade name was purchased by Anderson Ceramics; the Scotswood factory closed in 1980.

Adams and Cartlidge
See Cartlidge, George.

Architectural Pottery Co
See Patent Architectural Pottery Co.

Art Pavements & Decorations Co
The firm (a brainchild of Voysey*) was established by Conrad Dressler* in 1904, just before the demise of Medmenham Pottery*; it had a London office and acted as agents for Medmenham tiles. The firm provided some tiling for Harrods Meat Hall in 1911. In 1928 it amalgamated with Carter & Co London Ltd and the parent company, Carter and Co* of Poole. From 1936 until 1960 the firm's London base was in Camden Town; it was responsible for the tilework in several London Underground stations. The firm moved to Stockwell in 1960, remaining in London until Art Pavements & Decorations Ltd became a separate company once again in 1984, when the factory was moved to Kimbolton in Cambridgeshire. The company was dissolved in 1994.

Atkinson Brothers
This firm of church decorators, designers and stained glass makers of Newcastle upon Tyne probably produced the tiles installed in 1901-2 at the city's St Mary's R. C. Cathedral. They took part in the Trades Exhibition which accompanied the Second National Catholic Congress held in Newcastle during 1911.

Bagshaw, S.
S. Bagshaw painted six tile panels in 1928 for Sidney Fitton's butcher's shop in Middlewich, Cheshire; the pictures are now hidden.

Bale, Thomas Sanders
See Patent Architectural Pottery Co.

Barratt, J. H. & Co
John Hayes Barratt's Boothen Tile Works, Stoke-on-Trent was active from around 1895 until the late 1930s, making printed and majolica tiles. The works produced some of Cartlidge's* portrait tiles. G. J. V. Bemrose designed and painted tiles for the firm during the late 1930s.

Bayes, Gilbert
The sculptor Gilbert Bayes (1872-1953) trained first at Finsbury City and Guilds Technical College and then the Royal Academy (1896-1900). He always felt that his sculptures had an architectural function, and worked in concrete and cast stone as well as more traditional materials. During 1923-39, in conjunction with Doulton & Co*, he experimented with coloured glazes and their application to architectural stoneware, the best-known result being the 1939 low-relief frieze in polychrome stoneware for Doulton House on the Albert Embankment (now in the Victoria and Albert Museum).

Birmingham Tile & Pottery Works
See Ruskin Pottery.

Appendix 1

Bispham Hall Colliery Company

The Bispham Hall Colliery Company of Wigan was established around 1901 and functioned until 1933. Bispham specialized in making grey terracotta, and faience with white and cream-glazed finishes.

Blanchard, Mark Henry & Co

Mark Henry Blanchard worked at Coade's* in its later years, then set up on his own account in Westminster Road, London by 1850; he probably bought some of the Coade moulds. He emerged as the leading British terracotta manufacturer, his most important early contracts being for the Victoria and Albert Museum. Around 1883 the Mark Henry Blanchard & Co works moved to Bishop's Waltham, Hampshire and eventually concentrated on producing bricks and roofing and paving tiles; the firm was still active in 1898.

Blashfield, John

John Marriott Blashfield (1811-82), of Blackfriars and Millwall, was an early user of Copeland and Garrett's* plain red and black floor tiles (1836), and in 1839 laid a mosaic floor at Deepdene. *Designs for Mosaic Pavements* by Owen Jones* was produced for the firm in 1842. Blashfield manufactured his own tiles from around 1840, after an association with Herbert Minton*, and by the end of 1851 he was making architectural terracotta at Millwall. Production was transferred to Stamford, Lincolnshire in 1859 to be nearer the clay beds, and a range of wares from classical ornaments to architectural dressings was made both to order and to be sold from the catalogue. The firm was active until 1875.

Boote, T. & R.

Thomas Latham Boote (d1893) and Richard Boote (d1891), the youngest sons of a Cheshire farmer, were set up in business as potters at the Waterloo Pottery, Burslem, Stoke-on-Trent in 1842; they began to manufacture tiles in 1851. They started making encaustic tiles under a patent taken out by Minton Hollins*, and improved upon it with a patent of their own, hence the Patent Tile Works, one of 13 factories in and around Burslem and Longport owned and operated by T. & R. Boote in 1860; the Waterloo Pottery was the firm's head office. The four sons of Richard Boote eventually succeeded to the business, as Thomas Boote died without issue. This substantial firm tiled the Blackwall Tunnel in the late 1890s and carried out many tiled shop interior schemes; it was about the sixth biggest tilemaking company in the country between the wars. T. & R. Boote joined Richards Tiles* in 1963.

Bradburn, John Windsor

The tile and faience designer John Windsor Bradburn (1861-1947) became a trainee designer at Maw & Co* in 1872; he studied in London during 1882-5 then travelled to Paris and possibly Berlin before returning to Maw's by the end of 1886. His employment in the early 1890s is unknown, but in 1899 he became Head of the Faience Department at Maw & Co, then Head of Design in 1907, before being made redundant in 1911. Following this, he may have moved to Liverpool, and indeed is known to have produced at least one design for George Swift's Swan Tile Works* of Liverpool.

Brannam's North Devon Art Pottery

Charles Hubert Brannam (1855-1937) took over the Litchdon Street, Barnstaple, premises of his father's pottery in 1879. His Barum Ware (often in blue and chocolate) appeared in 1881, and Queen Victoria ordered four pieces in 1884, thus ensuring the success of the enterprise. A wide range of material - including tiles - was produced, and in 1884 William Leonard Baron (1863-1937), assistant decorator at Doulton's* Lambeth Pottery from at least 1881, was recruited by C. H. Brannam as a decorator. The Litchdon Street premises were expanded and rebuilt to include a new showroom in 1886-7, and Liberty's became Brannam's sole agent in 1889. From the late 1880s many grotesque designs were featured, these being influenced by the political cartoonist Francis Carruthers Gould, son of Barnstaple's Borough Surveyor. William Baron left in 1893, and set up on his own account in 1895 as Baron's Barnstaple Pottery, producing Baron Ware. This resulted in strong rivalry between Brannam and Baron. C. H. Brannam handed over the business to his sons C. W. Brannam and J. W. Brannam in 1913, and the company continued in production until it was sold to Candy & Co* in 1979. Manufacturing was moved to the Roundswell Industrial Estate, Barnstaple, in 1989 and continues under the name Brannam's. The Litchdon Street Pottery buildings were converted to offices, although one bottle kiln has been preserved along with the excellent decorative facade.

Broseley Tileries

The firm was founded in 1828 by the Broseley ironmaster John Onions II, the works being sited at what is now 'The Tileries' housing estate,

Coalport Road, Broseley; it was reconstituted as Broseley Tileries Co in 1877. The company made bricks, roofing tiles, encaustic and glazed decorative tiles and glazed faience, the latter often being attributed to better-known manufacturers. Broseley Tileries Co made floor tiles for the Royal Academy as well as other London buildings. The works was sold in 1919, and operated as Prestage & Broseley Tileries Co Ltd until acquisition by Coalmoor Refractories in 1938, after which it produced mainly refractory products until closure in the early 1950s.

Brown, John W.
John William Brown (1842-1928) was born in Newcastle upon Tyne and moved to London about 1870, joining Powell's* of Whitefriars as a painter in September 1874. By 1879 he was their highest paid painter, and by 1880 he had transferred to the design studio. He left the firm in 1886, but continued to supply designs for a further thirty-seven years. From 1891 onwards, Brown became Powell's principal designer; he retired in 1922.

Brown, Robert & Co
Brown's Paisley Earthenware Works was active during 1876-1933, manufacturing earthenware and tiles; the firm may have made the Brown's patent tiles (with a hop motif) used on the Clarence Street Brewery, Burton upon Trent, in 1883.

Brown-Westhead Moore & Co
Brown-Westhead Moore, makers of earthenware and fine bone china, was based at Cauldon Place, Hanley, Staffordshire from 1862; some of the firm's tiles are marked 'Ravenscroft Patent'. During the 1870s the firm supplied many letter tiles (in white on burgundy or deep blue ground) to the Great Western Railway for use on station nameplates. The name of the firm changed to Cauldon around 1895; in 1904 it became Cauldon Ltd, then in 1920 Cauldon Potteries Ltd. In 1936 the firm moved to the George Jones factory in Stoke and became part of the George Jones Group, ceasing to trade in 1961 when Richards Tiles Ltd* acquired Cauldon Tile Ltd.

Burgess, John
John Burgess began making encaustic and glazed decorative wall tiles in 1984 as John Burgess Tiles at what is now Maw's* Craft Centre, Jackfield. His tiles were used for restoration of the floors at the Foreign and Commonwealth Office; the business closed in 1999.

Burmantofts Pottery
See Leeds Fireclay Co Ltd.

Burne-Jones, Sir Edward C.
The Pre-Raphhaelite painter Sir Edward Burne-Jones (1833-98) designed and decorated tiles for Morris, Marshall & Faulkner and Morris & Co*.

Burrow, H. J.
Harry John Burrow (1846-1882) was a freelance artist who designed many windows for Powell's* of Whitefriars from 1872. Although his aspirations were far superior to his artistic capability and technical competence, Burrow's work was surprisingly popular.

Campbell Brick & Tile Co
Colin Minton Campbell (1827-85), a nephew of Herbert Minton, was in charge of Minton & Co's* china business from 1849 and greatly expanded production of printed wall tiles. When his cousin Robert Minton Taylor was looking for capital to realise the full potential of his floor tile business, Campbell offered to buy his Fenton, Stoke-on-Trent concern, retaining Taylor as manager. A new company was launched in 1875 as the Minton Brick & Tile Company, but when the name was disallowed by a court case, it was changed to the Campbell Brick & Tile Company. In 1876 the firm moved to a new factory at Stoke, and was known as the Campbell Tile Co from 1882. The firm manufactured wall and floor tiles; mosaic of variously shaped plain tiles was a speciality. By the late 1930s, Reginald G. Haggar worked for Campbell's as a designer and Leslie Sillitoe as a modeller. Campbell's acquired Maw & Co* in 1961 and Minton Hollins* the following year, continuing until 1965 when it merged with Richards Tiles* to form Richard-Campbell Tiles; this firm was absorbed by H. & R. Johnson* in 1968

Candy & Co
Frank Candy established Candy & Co's Great Western Pottery around 1875 at Heathfield, Newton Abbot, Devon, to exploit local white ball clays suitable for both bricks and buff terracotta. By about 1882 the firm had been incorporated as Candy & Co Ltd. Terracotta production ceased around 1914, and in the twentieth century the major growth was in the manufacture of tiles and glazed bricks for fireplaces (the 'Devon' fire). From 1963 production concentrated on glazed wall tiles; the name of the firm was changed to Candy Tiles in 1964. Candy produced the fish tiles used in the Harry Ramsden's chain of fish and chip shops in the 1990s. Candy Tiles ceased

production in the late 1990s and the works was demolished shortly afterwards.

Cantagalli

The Fabrica Cantagalli was established in Florence in the fifteenth century. By the late nineteenth century it was being run by the brothers Ulisse and Romeo Cantagalli, when William De Morgan* used the firm's kilns. Their products were sold by Liberty's during the late 1880s and 1890s, and they specialised in majolica ware; the works were still extant in 1911. They were probably responsible for the production of most of the small, highly-glazed reliefs with religious themes, often copies of della Robbia originals, popular in England during the mid to late nineteenth century as church decoration.

Carter, Alfred T.S.

Alfred T. S. Carter (b1849) was a son of Jesse Carter of Carter & Co*, Poole. After the mid 1870s he set up in London as a builders' merchant, developing into a tile merchant; it is uncertain whether the firm actually manufactured tiles, although their advertisements stated that they made ceramic or tile mosaic. In 1893 the firm's main address was the Encaustic, Tile, Marble and Ceramic Mosaic Works, Brockley, London SE. Apart from plain tiles, they stocked hand painted tiles and tile panels designed by well-known ceramic artists; these landscape and figurative panels were intended for decorating hotels, dairies, shops and suchlike. The Havelock Arms PH, Hastings, has several large pictorial panels executed by Carter. His son, Alfred Owen Carter (1874-1956), ran a London branch of Carter's of Poole from 1906, acting as a contractor; he retired in 1947.

Carter & Co

James Walker, chief technician at the Patent Architectural Pottery* of Hamworthy in Dorset, left the firm in 1861 to open T. W. Walker's Patent Encaustic and Mosaic Ornamental Brick and Tile Manufactory on Poole's East Quay. Despite the splendour of the nomenclature the firm did not prosper and Jesse Carter (1830-1927), a Surrey builders' merchant, took over the works in 1873. In 1880 he bought out the Worcester St George's Encaustic Tile Co*.

By the 1880s the East Quay works was firmly established, being well known for its tile murals, and in 1895 the Hamworthy works of the Patent Architectural Pottery was purchased. By the start of the twentieth century Carter & Co had become one of the country's leading firms making tiles, faience and pottery. Most of the larger architectural schemes used a single-fired faience, often glazed in strikingly original colours. The firm produced architectural faience, encaustic and other floor tiles, hand-painted, printed and majolica tiles. Jesse Carter retired in 1901 leaving the business in the hands of his sons Charles (b1860) and Owen (1862-1919).

In 1906 Carter & Co London Ltd was set up and in 1921, with the designers Harold Stabler and John Adams, the firm Carter, Stabler & Adams (often referred to as CSA) was formed as a wholly-owned but independent subsidiary to produce ornamental and domestic wares. The name CSA was retained until 1963 when it was replaced by Poole Pottery Limited; Carter & Co, including all the subsidiary companies, became part of Pilkington's Tiles* in 1964. The entire group was taken over in 1972 by Thomas Tilling Ltd, but a management buy-out in 1992 allowed Poole Pottery to become independent again. Redevelopment of the Pottery's quayside site began in 2000, with the Pottery itself being demolished in 2001; production moved to a new site in Sopers Lane, on the outskirts of Poole. Further management restructuring also took place, but problems affecting its corporate ownership resulted in Poole Pottery going into administration in 2003. The business was bought by a new company in November 2003, and remains a going concern, but the contents of the Pottery's museum and archive, including several tile panels and tile designs, were sold at auction in March 2004.

Artists and designers involved with the firm during its long history include Edwin Turner, James Radley Young and William Unwin, who all joined in the 1890s; Owen Carter, son of the firm's founder, who specialised in lustre wares; Phoebe Stabler, Truda Adams, Alfred (A. B.) Read (1898-1973), Cecil Aldin, Edward Bawden, Reginald Till, Dora Batty, Phyllis Butler, Susan Williams-Ellis*, Arthur Nickols, E. E. Stickland, Truda Carter; and from the 1950s Peggy Angus (1904-93), Ivor Kamlish and Robert Nicholson.

Carter, Johnson & Co

The firm took over the St George's Patent Brick & Pottery Works, Worcester, from David Barber in 1871 and functioned as Carter, Johnson's St George's Tile Works until 1895 making encaustic tiles.

Carter, Stabler & Adams

See Carter & Co.

Cartlidge, George
George Cartlidge (1868-1961) trained at Hanley School of Art then became an apprentice artist at Sherwin & Cotton* in 1882; he became the firm's art director in the early 1890s and introduced low-relief photographic-style portrait tiles. After leaving Sherwin & Cotton in 1911 he set up the firm of Adams & Cartlidge, producing wall tiles (portrait and tube-lined) at the old Sherwin & Cotton works in Vine Street, Hanley; the firm continued until 1915, after which Cartlidge designed tiles for other companies in Britain and America.

Cattybrook Brick Company
The Cattybrook Brick Company (1877-1972, a limited company from 1889) of Aldmondsbury near Bristol primarily produced red facing bricks and engineering bricks. The firm broadened its output in the late 1880s to include terracotta ornament, made from liquid clay poured into plaster moulds; these wares may be found on suburban houses and older factory buildings in the Bristol area.

Cauldon Ltd
See Brown-Westhead Moore & Co.

Caws, Frank
The architect Francis Edward Caws (1846-1905) was born in the Isle of Wight and served articles in Ryde; after a course at South Kensington he worked in Wolverhampton and for the North Eastern Railway in Darlington before beginning practice on his own account in Sunderland in 1870. His idiosyncratic buildings, designed in what he referred to as the Hindoo Gothic style, used quantities of colourful terracotta and faience. One judgement on his work was 'Caws and effect'.

Chamberlain & Co
This Worcester firm was founded by Robert Chamberlain in 1786. In 1836 Walter Chamberlain was encouraged by his friend Harvey Eginton, a Worcester architect and antiquary, to take up the manufacture of inlaid tiles by Samuel Wright's* process. Eginton supplied some original designs as well as tracings from old examples. In sympathy with the rough finish of medieval work, Chamberlain did not strive after mechanical perfection and so was able to offer his tiles to church architects two or three years before Herbert Minton*. In 1840 Chamberlain & Co amalgamated with Flight, Barr & Barr of Palace Row, Worcester. The new company, trading under the Chamberlain name, moved tilemaking over to Palace Row, where two partners, George Barr and Fleming St John, took over management and issued a first catalogue of 77 tile designs in 1844. Chamberlain tiles are found mainly in Wales, the midlands and the south of England; the firm ceased to make tiles in 1848 and the works was sold to J. H. Maw* in 1850.

Clark & Rea
Terracotta manufacturers Clark & Rea of Wrexham (active 1890-8) supplied a large number of major contracts in Lancashire, the midlands (including some Birmingham board schools) and London, most of them executed in red, pink or orange terracotta.

Clark, Kenneth
The Kenneth Clark Pottery (with work undertaken jointly by Kenneth and Ann Clark) started life in London during 1952, later moving to its present base in Lewes, East Sussex, where the firm eventually became known as Kenneth Clark Ceramics; amongst other commissions, the firm has designed many large mural panels.

Clayton & Bell
John Richard Clayton (1827-1913) worked as an apprentice sculptor at the New Palace of Westminster when aged 17, later being employed by Anthony Salvin as Clerk of Works for the restoration of Wells Cathedral. He became a freelance draughtsman and designer during the 1850s, and was also trained as a stained glass cartoonist. He was making stained glass for George Gilbert Scott from 1854, and went into partnership with Alfred Bell (1832-95) as Clayton & Bell in 1855. The firm, based in London, specialised in stained glass painting and general church decoration. Glass tiles sometimes formed a part of their decorative schemes, and from 1924 they made up their own glass tile panels, using tiles supplied by Powell's* of Whitefriars, rather than contracting the work out to Powell's as had previously been their policy.

Cliff, Joseph & Sons
Joseph Cliff & Sons of Wortley, Leeds, active during 1849-89, was one of the earliest firms to use the Leeds fireclay for making firebricks. They developed a strong reputation for their glazed ware, but in 1889 the business became part of the Leeds Fireclay Co Ltd*.

Appendix 1

Coade's Artificial Stone Manufactory
Coade Stone was an artificial ceramic stone, a type of stoneware, used for architectural work and for sculptures; Coade's was the most important of the artificial stone manufacturers. The works was started in 1769 at King's Arms Stairs, Narrow Wall, Lambeth, London by Eleanor Coade (d1796) and her daughter Eleanor, the latter normally known as Mrs Coade (1733-1821); the elder Eleanor's husband George Coade (1706-69) apparently died just before the establishment of the Coade works. John Sealy (1749-1813), Mrs Coade's cousin, had been brought into the business by 1792, and became a partner by 1799; Coade and Sealy were at the height of their success in the early nineteenth century. After Sealy's death, Mrs Coade took on her distant relative William Croggon (d1835) to manage the factory, but he was not taken on as a partner and the firm reverted to being known as Coade. Croggon bought the business following Mrs Coade's death in 1821, but went bankrupt in 1833 and died two years later. His son Thomas John Croggon refounded the firm in 1835 and a small amount of Coade stone was produced up to about 1840. Among the sculptors who worked for Coade's were John Bacon (1740-99) and Joseph Panzetta, who first worked for the firm around 1804.

Collier, S. and E.
S. & E. Collier of the Grovelands Potteries, Reading, Berkshire was the only firm to use Reading clays for making terracotta on a large scale. It was founded in 1848 and produced bricks, roofing tiles, finials (including dragons and dogs) and a variety of terracotta decorations. Some constructional forms of terracotta were made at the end of the nineteenth century; production ceased in 1929.

Collings, Kennedy
See Threlfall, Philippa.

Compton Potters' Arts Guild
Mary Seton Fraser-Tytler (1849-1938) and her husband the artist George Frederic Watts (1817-1904) lived at Compton in Surrey. In 1895 they offered to donate a motuary chapel, designed by Mary Seton Watts, to the local parish council, and Mary decided to train local residents to decorate the chapel using clay found on the Watts estate. Some of these workers became highly skilled, and after completion of the Watts Chapel exterior a studio was built for their use; as the Compton Potters' Arts Guild, they began work commercially in 1901 producing mostly terracotta wares. The Guild continued in production up to 1951 when it was bought out, carrying on as Compton Potteries Ltd until 1956 when the business closed.

Constant, Christine
By the late 1990s Christine Constant, based in Gateshead, had become known as one of Britain's foremost community ceramicists.

Copeland & Garrett
Copeland & Garrett's Spode Works, Stoke-on-Trent made earthenware and porcelain. Some plain floor tiles were manufactured from around 1834, encaustic tiles about 1837-40, and wall tiles around 1840-1903. The firm became W. T. Copeland in 1847; adding '& Sons' in 1867.

Corn, W. & E.
See Richards Tiles.

Craig Bragdy Design Limited
Jean and Rhys Powell trained at Wallasey School of Art from 1948 and married in 1950. They began making pottery, including decorative tiles, in the 1950s and went on to produce larger murals in the 1960s, their initial commissions being in the Liverpool area. They then gained contracts for large murals in the Middle East and the USA, with Rhys Powell gradually taking on responsibility for running the business while Jean Powell concentrated on design. Although Rhys Powell died in 1994, the firm - based in Denbigh, north Wales, and known as Craig Bragdy Design (after the old Rock Brewery) - continues to flourish with Jean Powell as designer-in-chief and their sons Nick and Shon Powell involved. From around 2000 Jean Powell has also produced smaller mural works, notably in north-west England, as well as designing exotic, large-scale ceramic works for the world market.

Crane, Walter
The author, illustrator and painter Walter Crane (1845-1915) designed tiles for Maw & Co* from 1874 and for Pilkington's Tile and Pottery Co* from 1900. His interior design schemes often included fireplace tiles.

Craven, Dunnill & Co Ltd
This firm was the last of several makers of encaustic tiles to be established in the Severn valley. It grew out of the partnership of Hawes and Denny, active in the 1860s; Hawes then left, while Hargreaves and Craven joined the firm, which traded as Hargreaves & Craven. Henry

Powell Dunnill (1821-95) managed the business from 1867, and when Hargreaves and Denny left, Craven took him into partnership, the firm becoming Hargreaves, Craven & Dunnill Co in 1870; the name changed to Craven, Dunnill & Co in 1871. The firm built a new factory - the Jackfield Encaustic Tile Works, designed by Charles Lynam* - in 1871-4 at Jackfield in the Ironbridge Gorge.

Geometric and encaustic tiles formed the major part of their production during the 1880s and 1890s, mainly using local clay. They aimed, very successfully, for an authentic medieval look to their encaustics, reproducing the lumpy surface and deviations from perfect symmetry of the originals. They made wall tiles and glazed faience during the 1890s, as well as hand-painted tiles including some pictorial panels (for instance those of the North Eastern Railway); they specialised to some degree in fitting out turkish baths. By the inter-war period faience manufacture had ceased and the firm reverted to concentrating on tile making; the production of tiles ceased in the early 1950s, although the business continued in existence as a distribution company based in Bridgnorth. Craven Dunnill tile making was revived in 2000 when the firm took over production at the Decorative Tile Works* which operated at the Jackfield Tile Museum, actually the old Craven Dunnill works, which had been bought by the Ironbridge Gorge Museum in 1983.

Day, Lewis F.

Lewis Foreman Day (1845-1910) worked for the stained glass manufacturers Lavers & Baraud, then as keeper of cartoons for Clayton & Bell*, before setting up on his own account as a designer in 1870. He designed tiles for Maw & Co*, Wedgwood* (in the Marsden* Patent range), Craven Dunnill*, Pilkington's* and J. C. Edwards*. From 1899 he designed tiles solely for Pilkington's.

Decorative Tile Works

The Decorative Tile Works began operating at Jackfield Tile Museum (the old Craven Dunnill* works) in 1989; the firm was one of the first to use computer technology in tile design, and its products were used in Harrods food hall and the malls of Telford Town Centre. It ceased to function in 2000 and production was taken over by Craven Dunnill.

Delftfield Pottery

Delftfield Pottery of Glasgow was Scotland's first industrial pottery and the country's sole producer of delftware. It was set up in 1848 on a site west of the present Central Station which is now known as James Watt Street, then standing in open country on the north bank of the Clyde. Delftware tiles were made at the Delftfield Pottery right from the start, and production continued until about 1775, although the Pottery itself continued in business until 1823.

della Robbia, Luca and Andrea

Luca della Robbia (1399/1400-1482) was the most important member of the della Robbia family of Florentine renaissance sculptors who were first to use a ceramic medium for their work, and gave their name to a type of large tin-glazed earthenware relief, normally of a religious subject in a wreath-like frame. Luca's nephew Andrea della Robbia (1435-1528) worked only in tin-glazed earthenware; he was assisted by his son Giovanni della Robbia (1469-1529) and there were several assistants in the workshop. Della Robbia reliefs became very popular in the mid-nineteenth century, when reproductions abounded, many of them produced by the Cantagalli* factory in Florence.

Della Robbia Pottery

The Della Robbia Pottery of Birkenhead, Cheshire was founded in late 1893 by Harold Steward Rathbone (1858-1929) and Conrad Dressler*. It opened in 1894, the intention being to use local clay and local labour to produce ornamental architectural pieces, in the manner of the fifteenth century Florentine della Robbia* potters, to sell to the rising business classes. However, local clay and local labour proved unsuitable, so Rathbone - against Dressler's wishes - brought in clay and hired a thrower from Doulton*; Dressler then left the pottery in 1896. The Della Robbia Pottery produced glazed panels, tiles, figures, and fountains; the domestic flat and hollow wares were successful, but the decorative, arts and crafts-inspired wares were not, and the pottery closed in 1906. In situ examples of Della Robbia architectural wares are rare.

De Morgan, William

William Frend De Morgan (1839-1917) trained at the Royal Academy, turning his attention from art to stained glass (and later ceramics) around 1863. He did occasional designs for Morris, Marshall, Faulkner & Co*. In 1872 he moved to Cheyne Row, Chelsea, where at his second set of premises he perfected lustre techniques and began to make large tile panels such as those used on P&O liners. In 1882 De Morgan moved his works to Merton Abbey, and then in 1888 to Sands End Pottery, Townmead Road, Fulham. In that year he entered a partnership with the architect Halsey Ricardo* which lasted until 1898, when a new partnership was set up with Frank Iles, De Morgan's kiln man at Chelsea, and the tile painters Charles and Fred Passenger; De Morgan retired in 1905 (the partnership ceased two years later) but his partners carried on producing De Morgan-style wares until 1911.

De Porceleyne Fles

The history of the Dutch firm De Porceleyne Fles in Delft goes back to the 'golden age' of Delftware production in the seventeenth century. The firm was reorganized under the directorship of Joost Thooft in 1876 and began to produce tiles alongside their pottery. Soon they also began the manufacture of architectural ceramics. Their tiles and architectural ceramics were exported to Britain and America. In Britain firms like A. Bell & Co Ltd in Northampon acted as their agent during the interwar period. De Porceleyne Fles is still an active concern today.

Dennis Ruabon

Henry Dennis (1825-1906) was a Cornish engineer who first pursued a career in building railways and investing in coal and lead mines, before becoming the major industrialist in Wrexham in the late nineteenth century. He came to North Wales in 1850 and went into business on his own account in the late 1850s, buying the Hafod Colliery at Johnstown, just over a mile north of Ruabon, in 1879; the firm had gone into liquidation and Dennis then made it part of his Ruabon Coal & Coke Company. As demand, especially for terracotta, grew, a new works was added on the Hafod site in 1890. One of the Ruabon companies owned by Henry Dennis traded under the title of 'Dennis Ruabon' and undertook several large contracts for terracotta around the turn of the century, although output eventually became concentrated on red quarry tiles; terracotta was produced during 1890-1933. In 1960 Dennis took over the works of the Ruabon Brick & Terra Cotta Company* on the northern edge of Ruabon; this site closed in 1975 but production of bricks, clay pavers and quarry tiles still continues at the Johnstown site.

Dorincourt Potters

This Leatherhead firm was formed just after the Second World War to create employment for disabled men and women; Dorincourt Potters began to decorate commercial tiles in 1956 and survives to the present day.

Doulton & Co Ltd

John Doulton bought the Vauxhall Pottery in 1815; after he had gone into partnership with John Watts, initially the pottery's manager, the firm traded as Doulton & Watts (this name was retained during 1820-58). They began producing terracotta building components in the 1820s, and by 1828 had moved to High Street, Lambeth. After the death of Watts, John Doulton continued in business with his sons John and Henry as Doulton & Co. Henry Doulton (1820-97), an inventive and innovative businessman who was knighted for 'services to sanitation' in 1887, introduced sculptural terracotta work and attracted several decorative artists to the Lambeth Pottery; he also began the manufacture of stoneware pipes, later in great demand, in 1846.

The Lambeth Art Studio began life in the late 1860s and was firmly established by the mid 1870s; the Studio employed over 200 people by the 1880s. Henry Doulton bought a major share in the Nile Street Pottery, Burslem in 1877, later buying out the original owners, and opened a new works at Rowley Regis in 1889 to supply the Midlands and the north of England; this functioned until 1910. After Doulton's death in 1897 the firm was continued by his staff and heirs; the Lambeth Pottery closed in 1956 and the closure of the Nile Street factory was planned for 2005.

Doulton's production of terracotta and faience continued for well over a century; the firm was responsible for a unique variety of ceramic compositions, and collaborated closely with sculptors and decorative artists. Amongst the artists and designers working at or producing designs for the Lambeth Art Pottery were Gilbert Bayes*, George Tinworth*, John Eyre*, Hannah Bolton Barlow (1851-1916) who worked at Lambeth from 1871, Esther Lewis who specialised in painting tile panels, John Henry McLennan who specialised in tile panels and murals, W. J. Neatby*, the tile painter Walter J. Nunn, William Rowe who painted tile panels, and Margaret E. Thompson who decorated stoneware, faience and tile panels during 1889-1926. The sculptor John Broad (1873-1919) produced several statues of Queen Victoria for the Lambeth Studio.

Dressler, Conrad

The sculptor Conrad Dressler (1856-1940) was co-founder of the Della Robbia Pottery* and worked there during 1894-6, although his designs were used throughout its short life. He went on to become director of the Medmenham Pottery* around 1897, living at Marlow Common, Buckinghamshire, where the pottery was based. Although the Medmenham Pottery was initially successful, Dressler became disillusioned and founded the London-based firm Art Pavements & Decorations Co* in 1904; this firm acted as agents for Medmenham tiles, but production at the Medmenham Pottery had ceased by 1905. Dressler later invented the tunnel oven, a method of continuous firing; the first tunnel kiln was installed for tile firing by J. H. Barratt & Co* of Stoke-on-Trent around 1913.

Duncan, James

James Duncan Limited of Glasgow was established in 1865; the firm specialised in the tube-lining technique, and during the 1920s and 1930s created many spectacular individualised shop interiors throughout Scotland and beyond; they also worked on chains of shops such as the Buttercup Dairies. Duncan's were solely tile decorators, working with machine-pressed blanks made by Maw & Co* and T. & R. Boote*. The firm, which had a showroom on West Campbell Street, Glasgow, continued in production until around 1965.

Dunmore Pottery

Pottery was made at Dunmore on the estate of the Earl of Dunmore in Falkirk from the 1790s, but after Peter Gardner (1835-1902) took charge of the works following the death of his father in 1866, production moved over to art pottery using local clay from Dunmore Moss and superior clay imported from Devon and Cornwall. The pottery also produced tiles and colourful faience, some of which, perhaps dating from around 1887, has survived in the old manager's house on the site. The pottery continued in operation until around 1914.

Dunsmore Tiles

The London tile decorating firm Dunsmore was founded by Polly Brace and Miss Pilsbury, and was in business by 1928 at Campden Hill, Kensington. Dunsmore produced a substantial range of hand-decorated tiles, including unusual sets of stencilled and aerographed picture tiles, in the 1930s; after a dormant phase during and after the war, production began again by 1950, with the decoration of Minton* and other tiles, although the firm ceased trading in 1956.

Edwards, J. C.

James Coster Edwards (1828-96) had established the Trefynant Fireclay Works (initially the Trefynant Brickworks) at Trevor, two miles south-west of Ruabon, by 1856; by 1896 he was employing 270 men to produce buff brick and terracotta, sanitaryware and tessellated and encaustic tiles. His Pen-y-bont Brick & Tile Works, just over a mile south-east of Trevor, was established in 1865 and made the celebrated Edwards red terracotta as well as roof tiles and red and blue bricks; it employed over 500 workers. In addition, Edwards bought the Copi Works (also known as the Rhos Works), Rhosllanerchrugog, north of Ruabon, in 1878; the works was rebuilt in 1883 and made coloured and glazed bricks. Encaustic tiles were first made at Pen-y-bont around 1880, but production moved to Trefynant around 1890. Edwards also produced glazed earthenware at the Plas Kynaston Pottery, Cefn Mawr, just east of Trevor, from about 1874.

The firm became renowned in the late nineteenth century as the largest manufacturer of terracotta in the world, giving Ruabon its nickname 'terracotta town' or Terracottapolis, but also produced architectural faience, floor tiles, majolica, printed and lustre tiles. The ruby lustre tiles imitated De Morgan's* style and were designed by L. A. Shuffrey and Lewis F. Day*. William Davis (1857-1951) worked for Craven Dunnill* during 1879-89 before moving to J. C. Edwards, where he eventually became the manager, retiring in 1935 (although he returned to work during the war); he specialised in ceramic art and experimenting with glazes. Davis was also interested in terracotta production, working with the firm's master terracotta modeller Elias Jones. The head of J. C. Edwards' design department was George Canning Richardson.

The two sons of J. C. Edwards - James Coster Edwards junior (1864-1934) and Edward Lloyd Edwards (1860-1956) - took over the business before the death of J. C. Edwards in 1896, and it remained in the family until the death of Edward Lloyd Edwards in 1956, when the firm was sold. Production then continued at the Trefynant Works until 1958 and at Pen-y-bont until 1961; the Copi Works was demolished in the 1950s.

Elton, Sir Edmund

Sir Edmund Harry Elton (1846-1920), an artist and inventor from Clevedon Court, Somerset, decided to try his hand at mural mosaics in 1879. The initial attempt was a failure but he persisted with experiments and by 1881 produced the pottery known as Eltonware. The Sunflower Pottery was best known for its extraordinary pots, but tiles and architectural pieces (including the Clevedon Jubilee Clock Tower of 1897) were also produced, using a range of rather sombre glazes. Sir Edmund continued working until at least 1916; after Sir Edmund's death in 1920, his son Ambrose tried to keep the pottery going, but demand for Eltonware declined and the pottery closed in 1922.

Eyre, John

John Eyre (1847-1927) was a Staffordshire-born artist and designer who trained at South Kensington School of Art. He worked for Minton's* Art Pottery Studio around 1872-3 before being employed at Doulton & Co's* Lambeth works around 1883-97, where he specialised in designing and painting pictorial tile panels. He was the son of the designer George Eyre (1816-87), who was involved in the development of the encaustic tile process at Minton & Co*.

Fletcher, Colonel John

Colonel John Fletcher produced terracotta during 1842-51 at Bolton in Lancashire. He discovered seams of fireclay at his colliery near Bolton and commissioned the architect Edmund Sharpe to produce designs for a 'pot' church, made entirely of terracotta; the result was St Stephen's Church at nearby Lever Bridge, built in 1842-5. By the late 1840s Fletcher's Ladyshore Terracotta Works was advertising a range of decorative products.

Garrard, Frederick

The artist, art potter and tilemaker Frederick Garrard (c1838-93) initially worked as an assistant to the architect G. E. Street, sometimes installing colourful *cuenca* tiles during Street's church restorations; Spanish-style tiling was popular with several architects during the 1870s and into the early 1880s. Street's chief assistant in 1859 was Richard Norman Shaw, who worked with William Eden Nesfield from 1863; Shaw and Nesfield were in a formal partnership during 1866-9. All three architects used very similar *cuenca* tiles in church restoration work. Street stated that the tiles which he specified for Christ Church Cathedral, Dublin, during his 1868-78 restoration were made by Frederick Garrard of Millwall, who was described by the architect as 'that most exact and perfect maker of majolica - my old assistant and friend, Mr Garrard'. It is almost certain that the *cuenca* tiles used by all three architects were manufactured by Garrard at his Garrard & Co works in West Ferry Road, Millwall; Garrard was still designing tiles in the late 1880s. Churches with Garrard tiles include Garton-on-the-Wolds (East Yorkshire), Hilmarton (Wiltshire), Meerbrook (Staffordshire), Llandyrnog (Denbighshire, Wales) and Christ Church Cathedral (Dublin).

Gateshead Art Pottery

The Gateshead Art Pottery of East Street, Gateshead was active from about 1880 to about 1887 making wares which included earthenware and hand-decorated art tiles of contemporary design. The Pottery was connected with the Gateshead Stained Glass Company.

Gibbons, Hinton & Co

Owen Gibbons trained at South Kensington during the 1870s (assisting with the decorative schemes for the Victoria and Albert Museum) before moving to Shropshire to become head of the Coalbrookdale School of Art, which trained designers for many local tileworks. At the same time, as a freelance worker, he also created many tile designs for Maw & Co*. In 1885 the firm of Gibbons, Hinton and Co Ltd was established by Gibbons, his brother Francis Gibbons (1852-1918), who had been art director at Doulton's* Lambeth works, and his brother-in-law W. J. Hinton. The company, which was based at Brierley Hill, Staffordshire and supplied tiles for many houses in the Wolverhampton area, was active until around 1950 making printed and majolica wall tiles.

Gibbs & Canning

Gibbs & Canning of Glascote, Tamworth, Staffordshire, pioneered the transformation of terracotta manufacture from being largely of ornamental ware, made in potteries, to the undertaking of large architectural contracts by works located in coalfields. The works was established in 1847, and three main groups of products were developed: sanitaryware, bricks and tiles, and terracotta. Della Robbia style plaques were also produced. The firm's buff and grey terracotta was widely used in South Kensington (notably at the Natural History Museum during 1873-81) and for a series of major contracts in the Midlands during the 1880s. The firm also established a pottery in Deptford, London in the 1890s. Gibbs & Canning was one of the four major British producers of terracotta, the others being J. C. Edwards*, Leeds Fireclay Co* and Doulton's*. Gibbs & Canning began to lay off staff from 1932, as terracotta declined in popularity, and the terracotta department was shut in 1940; the firm closed completely in the 1950s.

Gibbs & Howard
Alexander Gibbs (c1831-86) offered stained glass, mosaics and hand-painted tiles from his London studio in Bloomsbury from 1858 onward; the firm continued as Alexander Gibbs & Co following his death in 1886. The stained glass and tile painting business Gibbs & Howard was set up in the early 1880s by Isaac Alexander Gibbs (1849-89), the younger brother of Alexander Gibbs, with whom he worked in the 1870s, and William Wallace Howard (b1856). Gibbs & Howard produced a series of large tile paintings for Wyfold Court, Oxfordshire.

Glasby, William
William Glasby (1863-1941) began work at Powell's* of Whitefriars at the age of twelve, becoming their highest paid glass-painter by 1890. He left Powell's to work as foreman glass painter for Henry Holiday* from 1891 until 1906, when Holiday closed his Hampstead stained glass studio, although Glasby continued to paint glass for Holiday. He began making stained glass windows and opus sectile panels on his own account soon after the First World War.

Godwin & Hewitt
See Godwin, William.

Godwin, William
The firm was founded in 1852 by William Godwin (1813-83), a brickmaker at Lugwardine, just north-east of Hereford. He was joined in the enterprise by his brother Henry Godwin (1828-1910), who had worked at Maw's* in Worcester for two years, making encaustic tiles. Production was in full flow by 1853, when they were making their first forays into modern (as opposed to medieval) design. In 1857 the firm provided tiles for Hereford Cathedral, and from 1860 the standard finish on the surface of Godwin tiles was random indentations in the manner of orange peel. By 1861 the factory needed space to expand, and a site at Withington (a few miles north-east of Lugwardine) was purchased on which was built an extensive factory. It opened in 1863, making encaustic and plain geometric tiles, and was known as Godwin's Encaustic Tiles, although Henry Godwin left to form his own company in 1876. The Withington firm was called W. Godwin & Son from around 1880, and William Godwin's son William Henry Godwin (1841-1910) inherited the works on the death of his father in 1883.

The business then gradually declined (the original Lugwardine works closed before 1906) until it was sold to G. H. Lloyd and Thomas Pulling in 1906, then sold again to T. E. Davies in 1912; the firm was still trading as William Godwin and Son, Lugwardine Tile Works Ltd. Eventually the Withington factory was sold to H. & G. Thynne*, who ceased trading in 1958, when the factory was taken on by Hereford Tiles Ltd* until 1980, then the Shaw Hereford Tile Company (making wall tiles) until 1988.

When Henry Godwin left the firm in 1876 he set up at the Victoria Tile Works, Hereford producing dust-pressed and plastic tiles under the name Godwin. He was joined in 1884 by William Hewitt (who had also worked at the parent company), and their firm, known as Godwin & Hewitt, specialised in glazed tilework. During 1884-98 Godwin & Hewitt registered 105 tile desings, compared with the five of W. Godwin and Son. Henry Godwin sold out to Hewitt in 1894, and the works continued as Godwin & Hewitt until 1909, when it was bought by Herbert and Geoffrey Thynne, who renamed it Godwin & Thynne. In 1925 it became H. & G. Thynne Ltd, who bought the Withington factory in 1927. They produced a wide range of encaustic and decorative tiles, as well as architectural faience and slabbed fireplaces, but went bankrupt in 1957 and ceased trading the following year. The factory was taken over by Hereford Tiles Ltd and used as a showroom.

Gordon, William
William Gordon (b1905) produced studio pottery at the Walton Pottery, Chesterfield throughout the 1950s; during this period he also experimented with salt-glazed porcelain tiles. Following the closure of the Walton Pottery in 1956, Gordon concentrated on tile production, his first major commission being a large mural for St Aidan's Church, Leicester; he also designed the Carter & Co* mural installed at Basildon in 1958.

Green, Guy
See Sadler & Green.

Grimsley, Thomas
The sculptor Thomas Grimsley was born around 1800 in Middleton Stoney, about ten miles north of Oxford. He moved to London, where he was associated with the former Coade* works under William Croggon during the 1830s, but returned to Oxford by 1837 and set up as a terracotta

manufacturer and modeller. His business employed up to eleven people, much of the production comprising terracotta headstones which often carry the firm's stamp mark. They occur most frequently in the churchyards of Buckinghamshire, Berkshire and Oxfordshire (the Diocese of Oxford). Grimsley died in 1875 but the business was carried on by his sons Henry and Frederick.

Grundy, George Henry
See Photo Decorated Tile Co Ltd.

Gunton Brothers
Costessey Hall, on the edge of Norwich, was rebuilt in 1827 using bricks made on the estate; the foreman of the estate brickyard was George Gunton. The foreman's son, also George Gunton, then began to work the Costessey yard, selling decorative brickwork and small solid terracotta blocks made as architectural components. By 1851 Gunton was offering ornamental chimneys, Tudor-style window frames, turrets, cornices and copings. A finer red and white 'Costessey ware' could also be made from the local clay. George Gunton retired in 1870 and the title of the firm was changed to Gunton Brothers, although George's son William Gunton was the firm's sole proprietor. During the 1870s and 1880s Costessey brickwork and terracotta was used throughout East Anglia, especially for window tracery in chapels and for hotels around the coast. About 1914 the red clay became exhausted and the Costessey works closed, but William Gunton had three other works in Norfolk and production of bricks continued at Little Plumstead until the Second World War.

Hall, Diana
Diana Hall established a hand-painted ceramic tile business with Peggy Angus (see Carter & Co*) in 1979. She has made replica medieval and Victorian encaustic tiles for many locations including Winchester Cathedral.

Hardgrave, Charles
Charles Hardgrave (b1848) was born in York, and joined Powell's* of Whitefriars in 1871; by 1880 he had become their highest paid in-house designer. He retired from regular work in 1908, but continued to supply designs to the firm for a further twelve years. Although he was a versatile designer his speciality appears to have been opus sectile and mural decorations. He died after 1920.

Harmer, Jonathan
The potter Jonathan Harmer (1762-1849) was the son of a stonemason of Heathfield, East Sussex. He created a method of attaching his bas-relief terracotta plaques (made from Heathfield clay) to gravestones by cutting a recess into the stone then fixing the plaque into the cavity using mortar. He took over the family firm in 1799 and from then until 1819 produced delicate, mainly oval plaques for church memorials; the colours vary from red to cream, while the designs often included cherubs and vases. The plaques can still be seen in several East Sussex and Kent churchyards.

Hathern Station Brick & Terra Cotta Company
George Hodson, sanitary inspector for Loughborough Board of Health, had discovered good beds of clay at Sutton Bonington, near Loughborough. In 1874 George and his brother James Hodson established their brickworks beside the railway at Sutton Bonington; the nearest station - Hathern Station - was just to the south, equidistant between Hathern itself and the brickworks. Over the next few years, purchases of land in Hathern and at Cliff, near Tamworth, assured the company of future clay supplies. By 1883 the enterprise had become known as the Hathern Station Brick and Terra Cotta Company and began to offer a wide variety of architectural terracotta. Designs for architectural forms, such as window surrounds, were published in 1883 and the terracotta section developed rapidly from 1896.

James Hodson died in 1899 and was succeeded by George Hodson's son G. A. Hodson; the firm became a limited company in 1903 and expanded considerably over the next decade, although George Hodson died in 1907. During the First World War chemical stoneware was introduced to compensate for the slump in demand for architectural work, while faience production grew considerably between the wars; the firm was one of the most successful British terracotta manufacturers during the inter-war period. G. A. Hodson died in 1938, his son G. N. Hodson taking over the running of the company, whose name was then changed to Hathernware Limited.

In 1961 Hathernware merged with rivals Shaws of Darwen* to form the Shaw-Hathernware Group, but this went into receivership in 1980 and the Hathern part of the group was then aquired by Loughborough Industrial Securities. This allowed the renamed Hathernware Ceramics Limited to continue as a family business until 1990, when Ibstock Building Products Limited acquired the firm, which then became Ibstock Hathernware Limited. Along with Shaws of Darwen, it was one of the only two companies in

Britain still manufacturing architectural ceramics on an industrial scale in the early twenty-first century, but closed in September 2004.

Heasman, Ernest
Ernest Heasman (1874-1927) was a stained glass artist who also designed and painted tiles at his studio in Harpenden, Hertfordshire. The tiles were used in domestic and church settings and for personal occasions; the architect W. H. R. Blacking commissioned tiles from Heasman for church settings. Heasman's tiles were often anniversary gifts for family and friends. Monograms used on his tiles were EH or AEH (for Alfred Ernest).

Heaton, Butler & Bayne
London stained glass house formed by Clement Heaton, James Butler (joined in 1855) and Robert Bayne (from Clayton & Bell*) to form Heaton, Butler & Bayne in 1862; also church decorators and tile painters. Several tiled reredoses are known to have been made by the firm, but where a more sophisticated product was required, it appears that Heaton, Butler & Bayne produced cartoons which were then sent to a specialist ceramics firm for painting and firing, for instance the reredos at Great Altcar, Lancashire (1879), made in collaboration with Craven Dunnill*.

Hereford Tiles Ltd
Hereford Tiles Ltd, owned by H. David, bought the two Herefordshire works of H. & G. Thynne* in 1958: the Withington works originally owned by William Godwin & Son* and the Victoria Tile Works, Hereford, previously owned by Godwin & Hewitt*; tile production continued at Withington while the Victoria Works was used as a showroom. The Withington factory was bought in 1980 by the Concrete Masonry Company, who allied this to another of their acquisitions, Shaws of Darwen*, creating the Shaw Hereford Tile Company which made wall tiles at Withington until 1988 when the firm was sold.

Holiday, Henry
Henry Holiday (1839-1927) was approached by Powell's* of Whitefriars to act as a designer of windows in 1863, and learnt much about the principles involved from William Burges, with whom he co-operated until 1870; their windows were usually made by Lavers & Barraud. He was a superb draughtsman and was the principal designer, mainly in stained glass, for Powell's until 1890; he also commissioned the firm to make up many of his own orders. He designed and at least partly executed several opus sectile panels, writing about opus work in his book *Stained Glass as an Art*. Following his work for Powell's, in his own workshop he produced opus panels for St Chad, Kirkby (from 1899); Bethnal Green Unitarian Church (1903); Kensal Rise RC Church (1908) and East Claydon First School, Bucks (1908-9). His foreman glass painter William Glasby* also did some opus panels. Holiday's only known tile designs date from the mid-1860s, when he produced watercolour designs for a set of six tiles depicting the story of the *Little Mermaid*.

Hollins, Michael Daintry
See Minton & Co.

Hudspith, W.
The artist W. Hudspith was responsible for the three large abstract tile panels installed at Sunderland Museum in 1963.

Ibstock Hathernware Limited
See Hathern Station Brick & Terra Cotta Company.

Jennings, George
The sanitary engineer George Jennings produced pale grey and yellow terracotta at his factory in Poole, Dorset from around 1860 until 1910. Terracotta made by Jennings was used extensively in Poole, on the nearby Canford estate and in south London, where Jennings was involved in property development. Designs for terracotta architectural elements by the architect T. E. Collcutt were featured in a catalogue issed by Jennings.

Johnson, H. & R.
The firm H. & R. Johnson of the Crystal Tile Works, Cobridge, Staffordshire was founded in 1901. The factory itself had previously belonged to the Cristal Porcelain Company, and was bought for Harry Johnson (1878-1955) in 1901 by his father Robert Johnson; the new company was named after father and son, although Harry Johnson was the sole proprietor. The Highgate Tile Works at Tunstall, established by Alfred Meakin Ltd, was acquired by Johnson's in 1907, and Sherwin & Cotton* of Hanley was acquired in 1911.

Jeffrey Tiles of Hereford and Trent Tiles of Hanley was acquired in 1958; Johnson's invested in Malkin Tiles (Burslem) Ltd* in 1964, finally taking them over in 1968 when Johnson's amalgamated with Richards Tiles*, thus incorporating the Campbell Tile Co*, Minton Hollins & Co*, T. & R. Boote*, Maw & Co* and Cauldon Tile Ltd*, all of which had previously been acquired by Richards. The new firm was called H. & R. Johnson - Richards Tiles Ltd; in

1979 this company was taken over by Norcros plc, becoming H. & R. Johnson Tiles Limited.

In early 1970s, following the merger with Richards, the company had eleven tile factories in the Stoke-on-Trent area, including Longport Mills, the Valley Works and the Pinnox Works in Tunstall (the latter now a supermarket site). However, since the mid 1990s the Highgate complex at Tunstall has been Johnson's only manufacturing unit in Stoke. In late 2001 the company moved to a new factory in Tunstall, adjacent to the existing Highgate factory. At the same time, in order to concentrate production on modern wall and floor tiles, Johnson's sold the business of their Specialist Products Department to Maw & Company Ltd*. From their foundation in 1901 Johnson's used the brand name 'Cristal', which is the company's oldest registered trademark (registered in 1911). 'Johnson' is used as a brand name, while other brands like 'Minton Hollins' result from mergers.

Jones, Owen
Owen Jones (1809-74), author of *The Grammar of Ornament* (1856), provided Herbert Minton* with many designs for encaustic tiles and mosaics in the early 1840s.

Juniper, Harry
The potter Harry Juniper of Devon, a specialist in the sgraffitto technique, made the 26 ceramic plaques for the 1994 Alphabet Parishes Project in North Devon.

Kossowski, Adam
Adam Kossowski (1905-86), a Polish artist and refugee from the Russian labour camps, came to Britain in 1942 and from 1950 worked at The Friars, Aylesford, Kent (now a pilgrimage centre) intermittently during a period of over twenty years, producing mainly ceramic works including an eleven-foot high reliquary (c1963). Kossowski generally worked in the context of catholic churches and schools. The exterior ceramic mural at the former North Peckham Civic Centre (1964-5), Southwark, is his largest secular composition, and his best-known work outside south-east England is the massive *Last Judgement* ceramic tympanum (c1963) at St Mary's R. C. Church, Leyland, Lancashire.

Lagan Vale Estate Brick and Terra Cotta Works
This Belfast firm was the only clayworks in Northern Ireland to make terracotta on a large scale. It was established by H. R. Vaughan and a local building contractor in 1898, and functioned until 1920.

Lambert, William
William Lambert, who had previously worked in the Potteries, was taken on by Shrigley & Hunt* in the mid-1870s to oversee their tile department. He was responsible for painting and firing tiles until 1891, after which he left to establish a rival stained glass firm, Lambert & Moore, where he worked as a glass and tile painter, but went bankrupt in 1895. It appears that Lambert went on to design and paint tiles for Wooliscroft's* around 1896-1904, following the failure of Lambert & Moore.

Lauder and Smith
Alexander Lauder (1836-1921) was a successful architect and accomplished artist when he established a business with his brother-in-law William Otter Smith to make bricks, tiles, architectural earthenware and other wares in 1876 at their Pottington Road, Barnstaple works. After overcoming difficulties caused by the Pottington clay, they developed a wide range of decorative tiles in the early 1880s; some were shown in the 1883 Lauder and Smith catalogue and Lauder used them in his house 'Ravelin' (1889). Smith left the business in 1889 but Lauder carried on until around 1900, then was able to leave the running of the pottery to the staff, who kept it going until 1914, when it closed.

Leach, Bernard
The celebrated potter Bernard Howell Leach (1887-1979) made tiles at his studio in St Ives, Cornwall from the late 1920s onward. His hand-made stoneware tiles were often used in fireplaces.

Leeds Art Pottery & Tile Co
The Leeds Art Pottery & Tile Co was owned by R. Hauptman and based in Hunslet, Leeds; it was active from around 1890 to 1901 making earthenwares, art pottery, architectural faience and decorated tiles.

Leeds Fireclay Co Ltd
William Wilcock and John Lassey acquired land for a colliery at Burmantofts, Leeds in 1842. Clay was found on the site and brickmaking had begun by 1845, then sanitaryware production by 1861. John Lassey died in 1858, his widow selling her interest to John Holroyd in 1863, when the firm became known as Wilcock & Co. Holroyd's son Ernest Etches Holroyd became joint manager in 1870, when the firm had begun to make architectural goods. John Holroyd died in 1873 and William Wilcock in 1878; in 1879, James Holroyd (1839-90) took the place of his brother Ernest as manager of the works and within

eighteen months had begun to produce art pottery, tiles and architectural faience. The architect Maurice B. Adams (1849-1933) designed architectural wares for the firm, many of which appeared in their first catalogue, published in 1882. The first terracotta to be produced was a range of stock architectural details, but by the early 1880s the firm was producing large blocks and slabs of architectural faience, under the brand name of Burmantofts Faience; this could be purchased either unglazed or glazed. Burmantofts Faience was widely used by the architect Alfred Waterhouse. Most Burmantofts tiles were made from plastic clay.

In 1887 the company was reconstituted as Wilcock & Co Ltd, the name changing the following year to the Burmantofts Co Ltd; in 1889 it amalgamated with five local fireclay companies to form the Leeds Fireclay Co Ltd. Along with Burmantofts, the constituent firms were Wortley Fireclay Company, Joseph Cliff & Sons*, William Ingram & Sons, Joseph Brooke & Son and Edward Brooke & Son. James Holroyd died in 1890, and was succeeded by his son James, from whom Robert Bond (an employee of the pottery since the 1870s) took over in 1896. The firm continued to produce architectural faience and terracotta, and developed into the largest clay-working business in the north of England, having works at Leeds, Halifax, Hipperholme and Huddersfield. Well-known Burmantofts designers include W. J. Neatby*, their main artist from around 1880 to 1890, and the sculptor E. C. Spruce*, who was the principal designer and modeller by the late 1890s.

Brightly coloured tile and faience exteriors went out of fashion in the early 1900s, and the Central Arcade, Newcastle upon Tyne (1906), was the firm's last major contract of this type. From 1908 Burmantofts began the production of Marmo faience, in direct competition with Doulton's* Carraraware. Burmantofts Marmo was covered with a matt egg-shell glaze and made to withstand the ravages of frost, rain and soot-laden air; it was used for many buildings throughout Britain between 1910 and 1940. In 1912 the firm began to make a coarse kind of Marmo under the name Lefco, which was used mainly for garden ornaments. The Leeds Fireclay Co Ltd continued production of Marmo, Lefco and faience into the 1950s, but the Burmantofts Works closed in 1957. The works were demolished and the land used for housing.

Leeds Pottery and Middleton Fireclay Works

The firm was founded as an offshoot of the Leeds Fireclay Co Ltd* in 1909, and became a significant competitor in the inter-war period; it was known as the Middleton Fireclay Company during 1925-39.

Lynam, Charles

Charles Lynam (1829-1921) established his architectural practice in 1849; his output included the design of three innovatory tile factories: Minton Hollins* Tile Factory, Old Shelton Road, Stoke-on-Trent (1869), Craven Dunnill* Tile Factory, Jackfield (1874) and Maw & Co's* Tile Factory, Jackfield (1883).

Malkin Edge & Co

James Malkin (1828-94), manager of a canal boat company, married Annie Edge, daughter of the Burslem potter Joseph Edge, around 1860. Malkin assisted Edge's firm for several years and then took a financial interest in 1865, when they began to manufacture encaustic, printed and majolica tiles. The company then became known as Malkin Edge & Co of the Newport Works, Burslem (the earthenware section company was Edge, Malkin); the partners were James Malkin and Joseph Edge. The firm bought Boulton and Worthington's patent for a machine to press powdered clay to make encaustic tiles, and Malkin visited the United States in 1876 to sell the company's products. Two of Malkin's eight children, Sydney and Elijah, joined the tile and earthenware works, Sydney taking over the tileworks after his father's death in 1894, in settlement of any claim by the Edge family. In the late nineteenth century, the Burslem artist Frederic J. Harper painted the 70-tile panel by Malkin Edge & Co which is still to be seen at Haywood House, Burslem.

In 1901, Sydney Malkin, in partnership with his brother Elijah Malkin, reformed the company as the Malkin Tile Works Company; Henry Wood, apparently owner of the Marsden Tile Co*, also joined the partnership at that time. Elijah Malkin retired just prior to 1914, and Sydney's son Roy Malkin (d1951) bought out Henry Wood's interest in Marsden Tiles just after the First World War. The company was floated on the stock exchange as Malkin Tiles (Burslem) Ltd in 1928, and continued to prosper during the early 1930s when they pioneered the first English automatic tilemaking machine. The firm worked with Johnson's* from 1964, finally joining the larger company (as the Special Effects division) in 1968 after their amalgamation with Richards Tiles*.

Leonard Gladstone King was art director of Malkin Tiles and the associated company Marsden Tiles for almost fifty years. He designed the 1937 and 1953 coronation plaques, and (with

James Rushton) the Malkin Tiles 'Turinese' range made during 1961-8.

Mann, Frank

Frank Mann (c1867-1909) joined Powell's* of Whitefriars direct from school in 1881. He drew many cartoons, often for major windows, in a highly competent but conventional manner. He died in service after a short illness.

Marks, Paul J.

The firm of Paul J. Marks was set up in 1996 to produce cut tile murals and mosaics. It supplied the series of colourful panels, designed by Scurr & Partners, installed at Pizza Hut sites throughout Britain from 1998.

Marlborough Tiles

See Packard & Ord.

Marsden Tile Co

In 1879 George Anthony Marsden invented a decorative technique which gave the appearance of hand-decorated barbotine. He sold this invention to Wedgwood's* in 1880, and it was registered as Wedgwood Patent Impressed; Lewis F. Day contributed designs to the first selection Wedgwood made by this method, which were sold from late 1881. An independent tile department was set up at Wedgwood's in 1882 to manufacture the Patent tiles, with Marsden as director. However, Wedgwood's found's it unprofitable and closed the department in February 1888.

Marsden was kept on as a decorator (and also appears to have used his technique on Doulton* of Lambeth blanks), until he established the Marsden Tile Co at the Fairfield Works, Dale Street, Burslem around 1890. This firm did not concentrate on the Patent tiles but made a wide range of tiles including printed and majolica wall tiles. It was the sole producer of a patent interlocking tile which was absolutely secure when fixed, and also patented a rainbow-effect glazing technique.

The Marsden Tile Co later appears to have been owned by Henry Wood, who went into partnership with Malkin Edge & Co* in 1901, the combined companies being known as the Malkin Tile Works Company. Marsden Tiles continued in production until just after the First World War, when Wood's interest was bought out by the parent company, although the Marsden's name continued in use for many years (until around 1956 as the New Marsden Tile Co).

Martin Brothers

Robert Wallace Martin (1843-1923), known as Wallace, worked with stonemasons and studied at Lambeth School of Art, where he became friendly with George Tinworth*. In 1872 he began work at C. J. C. Bailey's stoneware pottery in Fulham, setting up his own business in the same year and renting Pomona House, Fulham, in 1873 as a workshop for decorating pottery. He was joined there by Walter Fraser Martin (1857-1912), who had previously worked in the art pottery department of Doulton's* in Lambeth, and had taken drawing lessons at Lambeth School of Art. Their first stoneware was fired (at Bailey's) in July 1873, and soon Edwin Bruce Martin (1860-1915), who had also worked for Doulton's, joined the business which was known as R. W. Martin & Brothers. In their early years they produced mainly architectural wares including some tiles, their works moving to Southall in 1877. The fourth brother Charles Douglas Martin (1846-1910) managed the Martin Brothers showroom in Holborn from 1878, as well as looking after the firm's finances. They produced salt-glazed stoneware, and in addition to Martinware pots made exotic fantasy animals known as 'Wally' birds as well as a range of functional wares that included tiles and fireplaces. Wallace was responsible for modelling, Walter threw the hollow wares and was an expert in glaze colours, and Edwin carried out the incised decoration. Production at Southall continued until 1915.

Maw & Co

John Hornby Maw (1800-85) retired from a successful family business (a manufacturing chemists in London) in 1835. He moved to Hastings, where he was involved with the local artistic community, and then in 1849 to Devon. He lived in Bideford, where his interest in medieval tiles was aroused, and he began collecting tracings of medieval tiles as a hobby. When Chamberlain & Co* of Worcester gave up their tilemaking department in 1848, John Hornby Maw saw the possibility of setting his sons George (b1832) and Arthur (b1835) up in business, and in 1850 decided to buy the designs, moulds, stock and the disused tileworks. The Maws, no doubt employing some of Chamberlain's workmen, began manufacturing floor tiles at Worcester in 1850.

In 1852 Maw & Co moved to Benthall in the Ironbridge Gorge. The firm grew rapidly over the next decade, in the 1860s adding the production of wall tiling and architectural faience to their earlier output of floor tiling; the address stamped on their tiles was 'Benthall Works, Broseley'. Having outgrown the Benthall site, the firm moved again in 1883, buying land at nearby Jackfield for the new 'Benthall Works'. The firm was registered as a limited company in 1888, becoming Maw & Co Ltd. In general Maw's favoured more complicated floor tile patterns than other makers and by 1890 had introduced into their range of church tiles many new designs which showed only a slight trace of traditional gothic. In the late nineteenth century Maw's was possibly the largest manufacturer of decorative tiles in the world. During this period the firm supplied some dramatic schemes incorporating faience. Charles Henry Temple was Head of Design at Maw's until made redundant in 1907 and replaced by John Windsor Bradburn*. Edward W. Ball was an artist and designer who worked for Maw's around 1927.

Maw & Co was acquired in 1961 by the Campbell Tile Co*, who merged with Richards Tiles* in 1965 and then with H. & R. Johnson* in 1968, the firm eventually becoming known as H. & R. Johnson Tiles Ltd; production at Maw's Jackfield works ceased in 1969 (the works now houses various small craft businesses). However, the Maw's name was revived in late 2001 when Johnson's sold the business of their Specialist Products Department to Maw & Company Ltd, now located at the Sneyd Hill Industrial Estate in Burslem. The firm intend to continue work on restoration of historic floors and hand-painting tile murals.

Maxwell, Donald

The topographical artist Donald Maxwell (1877-1936) designed a series of tiles showing Kentish scenes (the 'Domesday tiles') which were produced in conjunction with Doulton's during 1933-6; two of the tiles are set into the wall of Kemsing Church, Kent.

Measham Terra Cotta Company

The Measham Terra Cotta Company supplied terracotta for the Maidenhead Technical School during 1895-6.

Medmenham Pottery

During 1895-6, the Sunlight Soap magnate Robert W. Hudson bought Medmenham Abbey, the remains of a Thames-side Cistercian foundation once used by Sir Francis Dashwood for meetings of his Medmenham Club (popularly known as the Hell-Fire Club). Hudson was an admirer of the Arts and Crafts theories of William Morris, and around 1897 put up pottery workshops and kilns by the clay pits of Marlow Common (two miles north-east of Medmenham) in order to foster rural crafts and encourage local talent. The clay pits had been in use by a brick and tile works since 1895.

The new concern became known as the Medmenham Pottery, and the sculptor Conrad Dressler*, who had previously been employed at the Della Robbia Pottery* in Birkenhead, was brought in as its director. The individuality and handmade look of Medmenham tiles soon attracted the attention of architects, and they were used in prestigious locations such as the Law Society's Hall in London and Sunlight Chambers in Dublin. Although the Medmenham Pottery was initially successful, Dressler became disillusioned with the entire project and by 1905 production at Medmenham had ceased.

Meo, Gaetano

Born in 1850, in his youth Meo travelled from Italy to London as a strolling minstrel, but never reached his intended destination of New York. He talked his way into becoming an assistant in Rossetti's studio and during the early 1890s provided Powell's* of Whitefriars with a few cartoons for windows. His major achievement was to take charge of the programme of mosaic decoration in St Paul's Cathedral. He later designed and executed the mosaics in the hall of Halsey Ricardo's Debenham House, Kensington. He died after 1920.

Middleton Fireclay Company

See Leeds Pottery and Middleton Fireclay Works.

Minton & Co

Thomas Minton established his earthenware factory at Boothen Lane, Stoke-on-Trent in 1793. Here, his son Herbert Minton (1793-1858) experimented with tilemaking during the 1830s, buying Samuel Wright's* equipment in 1835 and using Wright's patent inlaid tile production method under licence. Minton took control of the firm following his father's death in 1836, and established a commercially viable tile department by 1840, at first producing encaustic tiles as Minton & Co but then expanding into majolica, block printed and dust-pressed tiles, buying a share in Richard Prosser's 1840 patent for the manufacture of ceramic buttons from clay dust. Minton was in partnership with John Boyle during 1836-41, then with Michael Daintry Hollins (1815-98), his nephew, from 1845; Hollins took charge of wall tile production, trading as Minton Hollins & Co, while encaustic tiles continued to be produced by Minton & Co. Colin Minton Campbell (1827-85), another nephew of Minton, became a partner in 1849 and was responsible for china production.

In 1859, following Herbert Minton's death the year before, the china and tile works split into independent companies, with Campbell - as Mintons China Works - producing a large range of tiles including encaustics, although Campbell and Hollins remained partners until 1868. Campbell's cousin Robert Minton Taylor was also in partnership with Hollins during 1863-8. After the dissolution of the partnership, Taylor started a tileworks at Fenton in 1869, and had considerable success with some fine pavements; he was bought out by Campbell in 1875, the firm eventually becoming the Campbell Brick & Tile Co*. Campbell was also instumental in setting up Minton's Art Pottery Studio in Kensington in 1871; hand-painted tiles were produced there until 1875. William Wise (1847-89) was working for Minton's in Stoke by 1877 and his designs were very popular in the 1880s, while the artist and designer Léon Victor Solon (1872-1935) worked for Minton's during 1896-1905. Mintons China Works continued to manufacture tiles until 1918.

Hollins, as sole proprietor of Minton Hollins & Co, built a large new tile factory (designed by Charles Lynam*) at Stoke in 1869, producing all types of tile. The firm also produced impressive forms of majolica which were displayed at exhibitions and used within the Victoria and Albert Museum. By the turn of the century they were making fountains in both majolica and faience. The artist W. H. Dixon worked for Minton Hollins around 1872-83; his work included painting the tiles used in the second-ever branch of Sainsbury's (the firm supplied tiles for Sainsbury's up to the mid-1930s). Other artists were John Moyr Smith*, William Page Simpson (b1845), who did mainly transfer prints, Albert Slater, Gordon Forsyth (art director during 1903-5) and J. B. Buxton, who may be the artist for some picture tiles signed 'JB' in the print. Minton Hollins was acquired by the Campbell Tile Co in 1962, and after mergers with Richards Tiles* in 1965 and Johnson's* in 1968 became part of H. & R. Johnson Tiles Ltd; the brand name 'Minton Hollins' continued in use for some years.

Minton Hollins & Co
See Minton & Co.

Morris & Co
Morris, Marshall, Faulkner & Co was established in 1861 as a partnership between Ford Madox Brown, Charles Faulkner, Edward Burne-Jones*, P. P. Marshall, Dante Gabriel Rossetti, Philip Webb and William Morris (1834-96). Early tiles decorated by the firm were imported from Holland. All the Morris tile designers occasionally executed their own designs, but most were painted by Kate and Lucy Faulkner, sisters of Charles Faulkner. Several Morris designs were also made in Holland. Morris bought out his partners in 1875 and the firm became Morris & Co. Tile production declined although Burne-Jones continued to supply designs, and one new set of designs by Walter Crane* was produced as late as 1880 or thereabouts.

Morris, Marshall, Faulkner & Co
See Morris & Co.

Moyr Smith, John
John Moyr Smith (1839-1912) was the outstanding designer of mass-produced block printed tiles, and was a prolific designer in several fields including furniture and glass as well as graphic design. He grew up in Scotland, later making his name in England as a designer and illustrator. His best-known tile designs were produced by Mintons China Works and Minton Hollins*, and included several pictorial series with literary themes.

Neatby, W. J.
William James Neatby (1860-1910) initially practised as an architect then worked at Burmantofts as a tile designer, being their main artist from around 1880 to 1890. He them moved to London to become head of the architectural department at Doulton* of Lambeth during 1890-1907, where he combined art nouveau style with architectural polychromy. He worked with provincial architects on several colourful and unusual buildings including the Royal Arcade (1899) in Norwich and the Everard Printing Works (1901) in Bristol. He also designed many tile panels for Doulton but most of these - apart from the Harrods Meat Hall designs - have been lost. A prolific sculptor, Neatby left Doulton in 1907 to work as a freelance designer, but continued to act as a consultant to Doulton's on important commissions.

Omega Workshops Ltd
The painter and art critic Roger Fry established the Omega Workshops in Bloomsbury, London in 1913 to sell fabrics, pottery and decorative schemes by young English post-impressionist artists; tiles were also advertised. The workshop closed in 1919.

Packard & Ord
Sylvia Packard (1881-1962) was born in Ipswich and trained at the Slade, moving to Bath in 1916

where she taught art at the Royal School for the Daughters of Officers. She retired in 1929 and began designing a ceramic tile mural for the school, on the theme of 'virtuous women', which was installed in 1931. Following this, Packard was offered a series of small tile commissions on which she collaborated from around 1933 with E. Rosalind Ord (b1901), who had joined the staff in 1930, succeeding Packard as art teacher. Initially biscuit tiles were bought from Carter's of Poole, and returned to Poole for firing after decoration; after receiving a large commission in 1935 Packard bought her own kiln, which was located at the home of her neighbours Arthur and Kathleen Coote.

In 1936 the Packard & Ord business, along with the Cootes, moved to Marlborough in Wiltshire; Arthur Coote did the glazing and despatching while Kathleen Coote helped with the book-keeping. Sylvia Packard and Rosalind Ord carried out most of the design work, although Thea Bridges also contributed several tile designs. Work ceased in 1940 because of the war and Packard retired, selling her share of the business to Hugh Robb. Rosalind Ord began work again in 1946, with the new partnership initially retaining the old styling of Packard & Ord. The business expanded rapidly, at one point employing thirty painters; from around 1957 their hand-painted tiles were marked 'Marlborough Hand Painted Tiles by Packard and Ord Limited'. Rosalind Ord retired in 1961, her share of the buiness being acquired by the Robb family. Competition eventually meant the introduction of machine printing, the firm becoming known as Marlborough Ceramic Tiles and then Marlborough Tiles, as it still continues in the charge of the third generation of Robbs to be involved with the firm.

Patent Architectural Pottery Co

The Patent Architectural Pottery Co works was set up in 1854 at Hamworthy, near Poole, opening officially the following year. Thomas Sanders Bale, John Ridgway, Thomas Richard Sanders and Frederick George Sanders formed the Staffordshire and Dorset partnership behind the firm, although Ridgway and Bale left by 1861. Bale worked with Frederick George Sanders on an 1852 patent concerning grinding clay, but the 1856 patent relating to the use of pulverised clay for making squares that could be pressed into a mosaic pattern was in the name of Frederick George Sanders, even though it was mentioned later as being connected with Bale. The large Hamworthy works produced a wide range of products including encaustic, vitreous, and other glazed wall tiles, and Bale's patent tessellated and mosaic floor tiles. The company was bought by Carter & Co* of Poole in 1895.

Photo Decorated Tile Co Ltd

George Henry Grundy (1862-1937) was born and brought up in Derby. He became interested in printing and photography and by 1891 had become established as a printer, going into partnership with George Arthur Lingard in 1893. They initially worked from Grundy's home but moved to a shop in Derby's Strand Arcade in 1895; at this time Grundy began to experiment with the application of photographic images to pottery. Maw & Co*, Wedgwood* and Minton's* had already tried to apply photographs to ceramics, but Grundy and Lingard patented an improved method in 1896-7. Grundy began to advertise his 'photo-decorated tiles', often showing scenic views of towns, from 1896. Following their success, Grundy sold the patent to the Royal Castle Flint Glassworks, whose small works was at Hatton, near Tutbury, between Burton upon Trent and Derby. This firm, which advertised the tiles under the name of the Photo Decorated Tile Co Ltd, continued to produce photographically decorated tiles at the glassworks using the method patented by Grundy and Lingard until about 1902; they also made tiles decorated by more traditional methods. Having sold the patent, Grundy then went into business producing artificial manure before moving to Liverpool in 1907 to open an early cinema; he returned to Derby after the First World War.

Pilkington's Tile & Pottery Co Ltd

The Pilkington family of colliery owners found red marl clay at their Clifton Colliery near Manchester around 1888. Having ascertained that the clay was suitable for tile manufacture, a new works was erected at Clifton Junction and tile production began in 1893; four Pilkington brothers had incorporated the firm in 1891 under the name Pilkington's Tile & Pottery Co Ltd. They made encaustic and other floor tiles, printed, majolica and hand-decorated tiles and panels, as well as Lancastrian pottery.

Tile designers included the first chief designer John Chambers, who had previously worked as a freelance for Doulton* and Wedgwood*, and A. J. (Joseph) Kwiatkowski (1870-1955), who specialised in modelling architectural faience and tiles. Pilkington's also regularly used the services of Lewis F. Day*, Walter Crane* and the architect C. F. A. Voysey*. Pilkington's own artists, including Gordon

Mitchell Forsyth (b1879), art director at Minton Hollins during 1902-5 before working for Pilkington's in 1905-16 and 1919-20, were responsible for the design of several large tile murals. Edmund Kent, a specialist in tube-lining, joined the firm in 1910 and remained there until 1939. During the 1930s the firm produced many tile panels for Maypole Dairy shops; these were probably painted by T. F. Evans, who was at Pilkington's during 1894-1935.

In 1937 production of pottery ceased and the firm became known as Pilkington's Tiles Ltd in 1938. It acquired Poole Pottery* in 1964, then was taken over in 1972 by the Thomas Tilling Group which itself was bought out by British Tyre and Rubber in 1983. The 1996 management buy-out of Pilkington's Tiles Limited was followed by the acquisition of Pilkington's by the Stockport terrazzo firm Quiligotti in 1997; the group's name was changed to Pilkington's Tiles Group plc the following year. Wooliscroft Tiles Ltd* was acquired in 1999, and moved to the Poole manufacturing site. Pilkington's still continues to manufacture tiles.

Poole Pottery Limited
See Carter & Co.

Powell & Sons
In 1834 James Powell (1744-1840), a London wine merchant, acquired a small glassworks on the north bank of the Thames near Fleet Street; his intention was to secure the business for his three sons Arthur, Nathaniel and John Cotton. The firm, James Powell & Sons of Whitefriars, became world-renowned for its stained glass but also specialised in opus sectile work and church decoration schemes. Opus sectile reredoses, panels and tablets were made by Powell's from around 1864. This form of church decoration became fashionable towards the end of the nineteenth century, with opus sectile panels often being used in conjunction with the firm's glass tiles and mosaic; production of glass tiles and opus sectile ceased in the 1930s. The Powell's business closed in 1980.

Many artists and designers worked for Powell's, although not all produced opus sectile designs. They included: John W. Brown*, Harry Burrow*, William Glasby*, Charles Hardgrave*, Henry Holiday*, Frank Mann*, Gaetano Meo* and Harry Wooldridge*. The artist H. J. Strutt, who was born around 1872, joined Powell's in 1886 and remained until 1929, although he was never a senior member of the studio. Bladen worked for Powell's from 1883 or before, and his name soon became prominent amongst the cartoonists; he appeared to have resigned in 1886, but was then paid for providing cartoons twice in 1891, and again in 1896.

Powell, Jean
See Craig Bragdy Design Limited.

Powell, Rhys
See Craig Bragdy Design Limited.

Pritchett, Harry
Harry Pritchett was the most prominent figure in the architectural modelling of terracotta on the Isle of Wight in the early twentieth century. He had works just outside Cowes and at Carisbrooke by 1905, making bricks, tiles, pottery and terracotta, including some lively hand-crafted dragon finials. His work, especially the finials in all their variety, may still be found all across the island.

Pugin, A. W. N.
The architect and designer Augustus Welby Northmore Pugin (1812-52) met Herbert Minton* around 1840 while searching for a suitable manufacturer to produce medieval-style floor tiles. Pugin visited Minton's factory in 1842 and in the same year used Minton tiles in one of his buildings for the first time. By the late 1840s the two had established a strong relationship, with Pugin providing a wide range of designs for tiles, tableware and other products. Pugin designs, or versions of them, remained in production at Minton's long after the death of Herbert Minton in 1858. Pugin's encaustic tile designs often incorporated the initials, rebus or coat-of-arms of a client; his first wall tile designs were multicoloured, and he also designed massive majolica tiles. Pugin's own patterns and Pugin-related designs became a standard part of many tile manufacturer's catalogues during the latter part of the nineteenth century.

Ravesteijn
The Dutch firm Ravesteijn was situated in Utrecht, Holland. It was founded in 1845 and specialised in the production of tin-glazed tiles. During the second half of the nineteenth century they exported tiles to Britain, probably using the London firms Murray Marks and Thomas Elsley as agents. One of their specialities was a range of fifteen cm square tin-glazed tiles with hand-painted arts and crafts designs, some of which were designed by the firm Morris & Co for use in the homes of wealthy English clients. In 1907 the firm became known as Westraven and continued tile production until the early 1990s.

Reptile Tile & Ceramics
Reptile Tile & Ceramics, comprising Carlo Brisco and Edward Dunn, produced the decorative tile murals installed at about 40% of Waitrose shops during the 1990s. The firm is based near Whitland in Carmarthenshire.

Rhead family
George Woolliscroft Rhead (1832-1908), from north Staffordshire, was an artist at Minton's, rising to the position of heraldic gilder, and a talented art teacher. Four of his eleven children became artists or designers: George Woolliscroft Rhead (1854-1920), Frederick Alfred Rhead (1857-1933), Louis John Rhead (1858-1926) who became an illustrator in America, and Fanny Woolliscroft Rhead (1865-1931), a freelance ceramic designer.

George Woolliscroft Rhead junior was apprenticed to Minton's* in 1871 and worked as a faience artist at Doulton's* around 1882. He was a member of the Artworkers Guild during 1890-1915, and was responsible for the glazed tile roundels of the evangelists which formed part of the Arts and Crafts design scheme of St George's Church, Jesmond, Newcastle upon Tyne (1888-89). Frederick Alfred Rhead was an apprentice at Minton's before becoming art director at a series of potteries; he supplied tile designs to several manufacturers, including Sherwin & Cotton*, during the 1880s. With his brother George Woolliscroft Rhead junior he wrote *Staffordshire Pots and Potters* (1906). He formed a partnership with F. H. Barker in 1908, and as F. H. Barker & Rhead Ltd they opened the Atlas Tile Works in Stoke, but the venture failed and was sold in 1910.

Frederick A. Rhead married the daughter of the Copeland* painter C. F. Hürten, and four of their six children became ceramic artists or designers: Frederick Hürten Rhead (1880-1942), who emigrated to America in 1902 and worked for several well-known firms including the American Encaustic Tiling Co, Harry Rhead (1881-1950), who also worked in America, Charlotte 'Lottie' Rhead (1885-1947), who worked for T. & R. Boote* in the 1900s before becoming more famous as a pottery designer, and Adolphine 'Dolly' Rhead (1888-1981) who worked as a decorator. Three of Frederick A. Rhead's nieces, Frances, Minnnie and Daisy Leigh, worked for Henry Richards Tiles Co*. Frederick A. Rhead had a longstanding connection with Wooliscroft's*.

Ricardo, Halsey
The architect Halsey Ralph Ricardo (1854-1928) was the architect of William De Morgan's* Sands End Pottery, Fulham, which was built in 1888 - the year De Morgan and Ricardo entered into partnership - and demolished around 1930. The partnership ended in 1898, but Ricardo continued to champion the use of colourful tiles and architectural faience in city buildings. His design for the Debenham House (1905-6) in London's Addison Road exemplified his theories, being a ceramic tour-de-force with many De Morgan tiles decorating the interior and a glazed brick and faience facade; the mosaic dome in its central hall was designed by Gaetano Meo*. Sadly, Ricardo never saw a whole city built on similar principles.

Richards Tiles
In 1837 Edward Corn (1804-1869), formerly a dairy farmer, bought Hancock & Lithcoe's earthenware works at Burslem, where he had been an apprentice. In 1850 he moved the works to larger premises at Navigation Road, Burslem and around that time retired, leaving the business to his sons William Corn (who died around 1885) and Edward Corn. The sons became partners in the firm W. & E. Corn in 1864. In 1890 the firm moved to the Top Bridge Works, Longport. When Edward died in 1891 his two sons, Alfred Henry Corn (d1916) and Edmund Richards Corn (d1945) took over. The firm, which made printed and majolica wall tiles, had a large share of the art nouveau tile market by 1900.

W. & E. Corn Ltd moved to the Pinnox Works at Tunstall in 1903. As two other firms, Corn Bros and Corn Bros & Co, had similar names, the brothers Alfred Henry Corn and Edmund Richards Corn used their middle names to create the Henry Richards Tile Company Ltd, which replaced the styling W. & E. Corn around 1903; the name Richards Tiles Limited was used from 1931. Richards took over Cauldon Tile Ltd* in 1961, T. & R. Boote* in 1963 then merged with the Campbell Tile Co* in 1965 to become Richard-Campbell Tiles; a merger with H. & R. Johnson* followed in 1968, the styling changing to H. & R. Johnson-Richards Tiles Ltd.

Robinson, David Reynard
The architect-builder David Reynard Robinson (1843-1913) carried out private and municipal work in Hull and elsewhere, building Hull City Hall as well as many tiled public houses in the city. He was not a tile manufacturer or designer but his house 'Farrago' in Hornsea is decorated with a huge number of English, Spanish and Dutch tiles.

Rock Tile Works
The Rock Tile Works, Jackfield, began production of glazed wall tiles in the 1880s but ceased after the First World War.

Rossi, J. C. F.
The designer John Charles Felix Rossi (1762-1839) worked for Coade's* from the end of the eighteenth century, modelling several large pieces for the firm, before setting up on his own account in the early nineteenth century; the terracotta caryatids on St Pancras New Church were modelled by Rossi.

Ruabon Brick & Terra Cotta Company Limited
The Ruabon Brick & Terra Cotta Company (also known as the Ruabon Brick & Terra-Cotta Works) was founded in 1883, initially working from Tathams Brickworks on the northern edge of Ruabon then expanding to a further site at nearby Gardden (the Jenks Works) from 1888. The bulk of the production was in the form of bricks and tiles, but terracotta (using clays from the Ruabon Marl beds) was made during 1890-1939; their terracotta was used in the construction of Blackpool Tower buildings. The firm's telegraphic address was 'Bricks' Ruabon. The company was taken over by Dennis Ruabon* in 1960; the works closed in 1975 and the site was cleared.

Ruskin Pottery
William Howson Taylor (1876-1935) and his father, the artist and art teacher Edward R. Taylor (1838-1912), founded the Birmingham Tile & Pottery Works at Smethwick, near Birmingham, in 1899. John Ruskin's executor gave Taylor permission to use the name Ruskin Pottery in 1909. W. H. Taylor specialised in making vases of simple Chinese-inspired form decorated only with remarkable coloured glazes; his work became known internationally during 1901-14. The pottery officially closed in 1933, although it remained active until 1935, when Taylor burnt all his glaze recipes. Some tiles were also produced, with similar abstract glaze patterns to the vases.

Rust & Co
Jesse Rust & Co's famous Rust's Vitreous Mosaic was important during the 1880s-1920s; Rust's also made some tiles and stained glass for churches.

Sadler & Green
John Sadler (1720-89) used plain white glazed delftware tiles for printing experiments at his printing works in Liverpool; on the 2nd August 1756 he swore an affidavit with his assistant Guy Green claiming the discovery of printing on tiles. They stated that within six hours they printed more than 1,200 tiles with different patterns; a delftware decorator could typically paint only two tiles per hour. The firing time for printed tiles was also shorter because of lower temperatures. Sadler printed from wood blocks, mainly exporting the tiles to America, during 1756-7, then went over to printing from copper plates. Sadler & Green went into partnership in 1761, when printing on creamware was started for Wedgwood*. Sadler retired in 1770 and Green carried on the business until shortly after 1780.

Salviati, Antonio
The Salviati glasshouse of Venice was founded (with English support) as the Società Salviati e Compagni in 1866 by Antonio Salviati (1816-90), a lawyer who became interested in glass for mosaic work. The firm obtained several important commissions in England. In 1876 Salviati left his English associates and set up a new firm of his own.

Scott, Paul
Paul Scott is an artist, writer and curator based in Cumbria, well known for his large-scale porcelain wall paintings and his printed ceramics.

Shaws Glazed Brick Company Ltd
Arthur Gerald Shaw (d1951) founded the Shaws Glazed Brick Company in 1897 at Whitebirk, Blackburn. The firm began to manufacture architectural ceramics using the clay deposits at mines owned by Shaw's father to the south-east of Blackburn at Belthorn and Waterside. Beginning with glazed bricks and tiles, production expanded to include terracotta and faience in the early 1900s, and a new factory was built next to the mines at Waterside, near Darwen, in 1908. Shaws became particularly successful in the 1920s and 1930s in producing slab faience, the firm's style changing to Shaws of Darwen in 1935. Fireplaces and grave ornaments were also made in the 1930s, while chemical stoneware and porcelain insulators were introduced during the Second World War. In 1961 Shaws merged with rivals Hathernware* to form the Shaw-Hathernware Group, which went into receivership in the early 1980s. The company was split, with Shaws being purchased in 1980 by the Concrete Masonry Company, who had also bought Hereford Tiles*, the two forming the Shaw Hereford Tile Company. This was sold to Southmoor Holdings in 1988, and then sold on to the ceramics manufacturer Shires Limited in 1995. Shaws of Darwen is the only company in Britain still manufacturing architectural ceramics on an industrial scale.

Sherwin & Cotton
James Sherwin, Arthur Sherwin and Samuel Cotton formed the firm of Sherwin & Cotton in 1876; the works was in Vine Street, Hanley. They were joined by David Sherwin, who left in 1884 when their partnership was dissolved. Sherwin & Cotton made transfer printed and majolica wall tiles; they were well known for barbotine work and produced George Cartlidge's* portrait tiles; Cartlidge was the firm's art director, leaving around 1900. The firm moved to the larger Eastwood Tile Works, Hanley in 1900. Sherwin & Cotton was acquired by H. & R. Johnson's* in 1919, the works continuing in production until about 1930.

Shrigley & Hunt
The founder of this Lancaster-based firm, Arthur Hunt (1849-1917), was apprenticed from around 1867 to Heaton, Butler and Bayne*, where family tradition holds that he learnt the skills of tile design as well as stained glass. He bought the church decorating firm Joseph Shrigley of Lancaster, and in 1874 Shrigley & Hunt was born, acquiring a London office as the firm expanded. Stained glass was their main business but almost all forms of decoration were taken on, and art tiles were important right from the start; Hunt himself had a large collection of De Morgan tiles. At first the firm used Minton's blanks, but was able to make as well as decorate its own tiles, which were marked with an 'SH' device, from 1875; they were featured in the firm's 1879 catalogue. Hunt recruited William Lambert* in the mid-1870s to oversee the tile department, which used the skills of their stained glass designers, notably John Milner Allen, Carl Almquist, Edward Holmes Jewitt and William Tipping. The tiles were very popular in the 1870s and 1880s, mostly being used in furniture and fire surrounds; production declined markedly by the turn of the century.

Simpson, W. B. & Sons
The firm was founded in 1833 by William Butler Simpson (1798-1882), an artist. His two sons, William Fredrick and Edward Henry, were apprenticed to the firm in 1852, becoming partners in 1860; around this time the firm became known as W. B. Simpson & Sons. In 1868 they moved from West Strand to premises (built by the sons) at 100 St Martin's Lane, London, where the upper floors were used as a tile painting studio and for the production of opus sectile panels and stained glass, much of it for the ecclesiastical market. From 1858 Simpson's had an arrangement with Maw & Co* for the sole agency of Maw's products in London, although Simpson's also decorated their own tiles, usually on biscuit supplied by Maw's to their kilns at Vauxhall. Simpson's had a large trade in hand-painted tile panel decoration for theatres, restaurants and turkish baths; Philip H. Newman was one of the firm's artists and designers. Simpson's never made encaustic tiles, although the fact that they supplied customers with encaustics from other manufacturers has led to confusion on this point.

Fredrick Simpson retired in 1892, then Edward Simpson followed in 1894, handing the business on to Edward Graham Simpson and Fredrick Coleridge Simpson, who eventually reorganised the firm to enable it to supply large-scale plain tiling contracts. Simpson's became a private limited company after 1925, moving to Camden Town in 1936, then Wandsworth in 1945; three further moves took place within London before the firm (now part of a larger group) moved to Banstead in Surrey in 1999, where it continues to flourish; recent contracts include the British Library and Jubilee Line underground stations.

Smith, Edward & Co
The firm Edward Smith & Co of Coalville, Leicestershire was active during about 1885-1900 producing transfer printed tiles. Smith's also traded as the Midland Brick & Terra Cotta Co during 1859-1900, making terracotta and sanitaryware.

Smith, Rosie
Rosie Smith is a tile decorator based in Weston-super-Mare who carried out several large-scale public tile commissions during the late 1990s.

Spruce, E. C.
The sculptor Edward Caldwell Spruce was born in Knutsford about 1866. After early employment in a local tile factory, he eventually moved to Leeds where he lived and worked until his death in 1922. By the late 1890s Spruce was principal designer and modeller at the Burmantofts Works of the Leeds Fireclay Company*, where he modelled bas-relief panels and statues for several important new buildings, including the Midland Railway Hotel, Manchester (c1896), the Alhambra Theatre, Blackpool (c1898) and the General News Room, Leicester (c1898). After spending some time in Paris around 1901, he returned to Leeds where his career as a sculptor was much enhanced.

Stanley Brothers
Reginald Stanley (1838-1914) made his fortune in America during 1857-66 then returned to join his

brother Jacob Stanley in Nuneaton, Warwickshire. Reginald invested in Jacob's brickworks, which began to produce terracotta in 1881. Stanley Brothers terracotta wares were mostly in the form of simple architectural details and garden ornaments, the firm being best known for its engineering bricks. It also specialised in finials, including the well-known dragon design. Stanley Brothers also manufactured two-foot square terracotta plaques showing a relief bust of Queen Victoria to mark the Queen's fiftieth jubilee in 1887; the design was later adapted to mark the 1897 Diamond Jubilee. Around 1900 the firm had branch works at Burslem and Willenhall. Stanley Brothers was still in business in 1999, although production of terracotta appears to have ceased about 1920.

Stewart, Robert
The Scottish artist and designer Robert Stewart (1924-95) designed and manufactured a series of large-scale ceramic murals for public buildings during the 1960s and 1970s. Many of his works, which were often abstract panels using unusual metallic glazes, have already been destroyed as the buildings in which they were installed have been demolished.

Swan Tile Works
George Swift (d1919) moved from Coalbrookdale to Liverpool around 1880, soon becoming established in Liverpool as a worker in tiles and mosaics. He lodged a patent application for a tile back - 'Swift's Patent Keyed Back' - in 1890, which was accepted the following year. In 1890 Swift built his Swan Tile Works in Binns Road, Liverpool, to manufacture floor tiles, mosaic, glazed wall tiles and faience. There was also an office and showroom in the city centre at The Temple, Dale Street. The Swan Tile Works was active during 1900-8, but the factory was closed by 1910 (the site has been redeveloped) and Swift became a tile merchant working from his Temple office. After Swift's death in 1919, his tile fixing firm continued under the title George Swift and Edgar (Tiles) Ltd until at least the mid 1990s.

Taylor, Robert Minton
See Minton & Co.

Threlfall, Philippa
The Wells-based husband and wife partnership of artist and designer Philippa Threlfall (b1939) and historian Kennedy Collings (1933-2002) completed over one hundred major ceramic works, mainly highly textured murals on historical themes, in Britain and abroad from the 1960s onward. The family business continues to trade as Black Dog of Wells, largely producing small-scale terracotta plaques.

Thynne, H. & G.
In 1909 the Victoria Tile Works, Hereford (previously owned by Godwin & Hewitt*) was purchased by the accountant Herbert Thynne (d1953) and the pottery manufacturer Geoffrey Thynne, both of Bristol. The firm was then called Godwin & Thynne, and made slabbed fireplaces in tile or faience. In 1925 the firm became H. & G. Thynne, and production of wall tiles was increased. Thynne's bought the Withington factory, originally owned by William Godwin & Son*, in 1927. Thynne's became bankrupt in 1957 and was bought, with both the Withington factory and the Victoria Works, in 1958 by H. David to form Hereford Tiles Ltd*, which produced glazed wall tiles at Withington until 1980 and operated a showroom at the Victoria Works. The Withington works was sold in 1980 and continued in production until 1988 as the Shaw Hereford Tile Company.

Tinworth, George
George Tinworth (1843-1913) trained at the Lambeth School of Art and the Royal Academy Schools before obtaining employment at Doulton & Co*. The Doulton works were then producing solely stoneware utilitarian vessels, but Henry Doulton had aspirations to produce more ornamental wares and statuary for garden and architectural purposes. In Tinworth, Doulton had discovered a major asset, and he spent his entire working life at the firm. Amongst Tinworth's first important works was a fountain displayed at an exhibition in Kensington in 1869. His sculptural work was exhibited at various national and international exhibitions, resulting in a range of commissions for very large relief panels. He was a versatile artist with a huge output; his first ecclesiastical commission was from G. E. Street for the terracotta reredos panel at York Minster of 1876.

Van Hulst
The Dutch firm Van Hulst of Harlingen, Friesland was a well established business before Jan van Hulst took control in 1850. Between 1850 and the firm's closure in 1933 they exported tiles to Britain via the importers Martin van Straaten of London and William Lawton of Manchester, who often had tile designs made to their own specifications for the British market.

Voysey, C. F. A.
The architect and prolific designer Charles Francis Annesley Voysey (1857-1941) designed tiles for Maw & Co*, Pilkington's* and Wedgwood*. His designs for Maw's were shown at the Arts and Crafts Exhibitions of 1888 and 1889, while those for Pilkington's were shown at the 1896 and 1903 Arts and Crafts Exhibitions.

Wade, J. & W.
The firm J. & W. Wade & Co of the Flaxman Tile Works, Burslem was founded in 1867, becoming prominent in the 1890s and early 1900s for its manufacture of a wide range of wall and floor tiles, faience and mosaic. By the late 1920s tiles were still being made at the Flaxman Tile Works although the firm had then become known as A. J. Wade Ltd.

Watcombe Terra-Cotta Co
The Watcombe Terra-Cotta Company was established at St Marychurch, Torquay in 1869 by George Allen, who had discovered clay beds during the construction of foundations for his new mansion, Watcombe House. The firm was one of the later concerns established specifically to produce decorative rather than architectural terracotta. Classical-style vases and hand-painted plates were made in large numbers, although during 1872-90 architectural terracotta was made and some small-scale architectural contracts were undertaken. The firm was sold in 1900 and amalgamated with the Aller Vale Pottery of Newton Abbot in 1901, the new company being styled the Royal Aller Vale and Watcombe Pottery Co.

Webb's Worcester Tileries
This Worcester firm was active between around 1870 and the early 1900s manufacturing encaustic and transfer-printed tiles.

Wedgwood, Josiah & Sons
The firm of Josiah Wedgwood & Sons was founded by Josiah Wedgwood (1730-95) in 1759; his Etruria, Stoke-on-Trent works was opened in 1769. The making of cream-coloured earthenware tiles was initiated by Wedgwood's around 1761, when many of these creamware tiles began to be transfer-printed in Liverpool by Sadler & Green*. The creamware tiles were made in large quantities at Etruria for use in dairies and for domestic use, but tilemaking was discontinued soon after 1800. During the early 1860s Wedgwood produced a small amount of art tiles, while dust-pressed tile making was introduced in 1867; by 1870 cream coloured body, encaustic, transfer printed and majolica tiles were being made.

Block printing on tiles was introduced in the late 1870s and Thomas Allen (1831-1915) became art director in 1878, staying in the post until 1898. Wedgwood's bought the tile decorating technique invented by George Marsden* in 1880, producing the tiles as Wedgwood Patent Impressed during 1881-8. During the 1890s Wedgwood offered a wide range of tiles and carried out several substantial architectural contracts, but not all the tiles were manufactured at Etruria, for example Wooliscroft's* supplied encaustic tiles. The tile department was closed in 1902, although a few tiles continued to be printed on blanks supplied by T. & R. Boote* until 1929.

Whitehead, Julius & Sons
Julius Whitehead & Sons were situated at Clayton, near Bradford, West Yorkshire and were in operation by 1892. They made all kinds of salt-glazed ware such as sanitary pipes, chimney pots, bricks, garden ornaments and architectural ceramics. The works closed down in the 1970s.

Wilcock & Co
See Leeds Fireclay Co Ltd.

Williams-Ellis, Susan
Susan Williams-Ellis (b1918), daughter of the architect Clough Williams-Ellis, designed tiles for Carter & Co* in 1946 which were displayed in the *Britain Can Make It* exhibition at the Victoria and Albert Museum; she also designed their *Sea* series in the early 1950s. She went on to establish Portmeirion Potteries, for which she created many designs.

Wooldridge, Harry Ellis
Harry Ellis Wooldridge was a designer who worked on tiles and glass during the 1860s; he designed a window at Minley Church, Hampshire. He probably did freelance work for Powell's*, and worked with Henry Holiday*. Wooldridge ended his career as a writer of hymns.

Wooliscroft, George & Sons
George Wooliscroft (1825-1906) established a brickyard at Chesterton, Staffordshire in 1849, initially making only bricks but soon producing quarry and dust-pressed tessellated tiles. He had acquired works at Etruria (previously operated by Wedgwood's*) by 1887 and Hanley (the Patent Tile Works) by 1900, producing encaustic and plain floor tiles as well as a wide range of decorative wall tiles, including majolica and hand-painted art tiles. The firm was incorporated in 1894. Success in tile manufacture led to the

introduction of a single-fired faience, which was used for several architectural contracts during the Edwardian period; production of faience ceased in 1909.

The factories were almost completely rebuilt after 1919, the Etruria factory concentrating on tessellated floor tile production while Hanley made glazed fireplaces; production at Hanley ceased in 1965. The Etruria works was completely rebuilt during the mid 1990s and made industrial floor tiles as well as external cladding. Wooliscroft Tiles Limited was acquired by Pilkington's* in 1999 (Wooliscroft's 150th year) and the works moved to Poole.

Worcester St George's Encaustic Tile Co

The Worcester St George's Encaustic Tile Co began to make encaustic tiles for church use at their St George's Pottery Works about 1878; their tiles resembled Craven Dunnill* products. The firm was bought out by Carter's* of Poole in 1880.

Wright, Samuel

Samuel Wright (1783-1849), of Shelton, Staffordshire patented his inlaying process for hard-wearing paving tiles in 1830. He had experience of making plain quarries and started manufacturing encaustic tiles. He was unlucky in aiming at the domestic rather than the ecclesiastical market and, becoming discouraged, sold his moulds and equipment in 1835 to Herbert Minton* of the china works at Stoke-on-Trent, little more than a mile from his own works. However, he kept the patent rights and Minton used the process under licence. The only floor of Wright's tiles at present known is one at Kilmory Castle, Argyll, supplied by Minton out of the stock he had taken over. The tiles, laid about 1837, are of Moorish rather than gothic design.

Appendix 2

Glossary

Terms in *italics* refer to entries elsewhere in the glossary.

Aerography
The application of colours to a tile by spraying through stencils, or over natural materials such as leaves. Aerography is sometimes detectable by small speckles of colour adjacent to the main images.

Architectural ceramics
Broad term covering bricks, chimney pots, roof tiles, wall tiles, floor tiles, and terracotta and faience facings. However, the term is frequently used with reference only to decorative interior and exterior finishes, thus excluding bricks, roof tiles and the like.

Artificial stone
A term applied during the eighteenth and early nineteenth centuries to blocks moulded in forms and colours imitating fine carved stone, whether composed of aggregated stone or fired clay.

Barbotine
An extension of the *tube-lining* process whereby the extruded slip clay is then manipulated by a brush, one colour being overlaid on another.

Biscuit
Unglazed and incomplete ceramic articles, for instance a tile after initial firing but prior to decorating or glazing.

Block-printing
See *transfer printing*.

Carraraware
Trade name for a glazed stoneware, single fired to a matt (often white) finish, developed by Doulton's of Lambeth during the late 1880s and used from 1888 in architectural work; it was produced until 1939.

Champlevé
The technique whereby a resinous mastic composition is used to fill depressions or channels forming a design in a tile.

China clay
A highly refractory clay, also called kaolin; an essential ingredient of porcelain.

Coade stone
A high quality terracotta made in Lambeth by Eleanor Coade from 1769; it closely imitated stone in its colour and texture.

Counter-relief decoration
See *impressed decoration*.

Cuenca
From the Spanish, meaning bowl; a mould is used to form a pattern as hollows in the surface of a tile, leaving a raised outline to keep different glaze colours separate.

Cuerda seca
From the Spanish, meaning dry cord; decorative technique using wax and powdered manganese lines to separate glaze colours. The sunken manganese lines remain after firing as black outlines.

Delftware
Derived from the Dutch town of Delft but applied to Dutch and English wares decorated with opaque white tin glaze onto which a design is painted, frequently in blue. Tile designs invariably include corner motifs and a central subject; large tile panels were also made using this technique.

Doultonware
Colourful salt-glazed stoneware introduced by Doulton's in the 1870s; it was fired at high temperature and intended for external architectural use.

Dust clay
See *dust-pressing*.

Dust-pressing
The compacting of dust clay, a fine powder clay with low moisture content, in a tile press. The process was invented by the engineer Richard Prosser in 1840 and became the revolutionary breakthrough for industrial tile production. A tile press has a square metal mould with an adjustable plate at the bottom set at a certain depth for a required thickness. The cavity of the mould is completely filled with slightly moist dust clay and the surface levelled. By turning the great flywheel, the screw, with a square metal plate at its lower end, is brought down and compresses the dust clay slowly, allowing the air to escape. It is then

raised slightly only to be brought down again with great force compressing the clay and forming the tile. The tile is removed from the press and then fettled to remove the thin featheredge or burr along the edges of the tile. When dry, the tile is biscuit fired and is ready for decorating and glazing.

Earthenware
A term applied to ware having porous bodies which may or may not be covered by a glaze.

Email ombrant
Email ombrant (or shadowed glaze) refers to relief tiles with tinted translucent glazes which pooled in the hollows of the design, producing graduated tones; the glaze was designed to finish with a flat surface. Sherwin and Cotton were the chief exponents of this technique; they produced many portraits in this manner, the best known being of W. E. Gladstone. Sherwin and Cotton's modeller George Cartlidge later set up his own company bringing with him his technique of producing almost photographic likenesses.

Encaustic tiles
See *inlaid tiles*.

Faience
Originally a name for tinglazed earthenware, taken from the Italian town Faenza, a major centre for glazed pottery production. In the context of architectural ceramics, faience refers to large blocks or slabs of ware glazed following an initial firing. Glazes may be translucent, opaque monochrome or polychrome, the ware may be relief modelled or flat, and the resulting blocks or slabs may be used as trim (applied cladding) or may be structural. Structural faience is normally heavily flanged or made in the form of hollow three dimensional blocks which are infilled during construction of the building. The glaze hides the colour of the clay, and it is the colour of the glaze that dominates the appearance of the faience. However, there is clearly a continuum of materials, beginning with *terracotta* (unglazed) and ending with highly glazed wares, not all of which are easily distinguishable.

Fireclay
A clay commonly found in coal mining areas that is resistant to high temperatures; it was used for various types of architectural ceramics.

Fireskin
The fireskin of an unglazed terracotta block is achieved by smoothing over the block after extraction from the mould and then giving it a full, high-temperature firing. The fireskin is a protective shield and gives the block its distinctive colour and texture.

Geometric tile pavements
Combinations of plain tiles in assorted geometric shapes and colours forming geometrically-related patterns; see also *mosaic*.

Glass tiles
A variation of the technique used to produce *opus sectile* resulted in patterned wall tiles known as glass tiles.

Glaze
An impervious (usually vitreous) material used to cover a ceramic article to prevent it from absorbing liquids or to give it a more attractive appearance. Glaze is applied to a tile by dipping it into or spraying on to its surface a solution of powdered glaze suspended in water, then firing at a high temperature.

Glazed faience
Faience is now generally understood to be a glazed ware, but in the late nineteenth century Burmantofts (for one) advertised glazed faience, apparently to emphasise the reflective properties of the material; it may also have been a very highly glazed ware. Although it is tempting to use the term 'glazed faience' in a similar manner today, the adjectival use of glazed is strictly unnescessary.

Glazed terracotta
Similar to *terracotta*, but coated with transparent high temperature glaze before firing at around 1250°C. This fuses the glaze to the body and results in high frost resistance; only a limited range of colours can be produced using this method. Also known as vitrified terracotta. It was sometimes known as vitreous faience (especially in the early twentieth century), but as the clay colour can still be seen clearly through the transparent glaze, it seems preferable to refer to it as terracotta. In *faience* proper the glaze hides the colour of the clay; the glaze colour dominates.

Imitation tube-lining
See *tube-lining*.

Impressed decoration
Linear decoration impressed into a tile through the use of a metal mould bearing the design in raised outline. This form of decoration is sometimes known as counter-relief or line-impressed.

Inlaid tiles
An inlaid tile is one in which the design is reliant upon the contrast of coloured clays let into the body of the tile, rather than surface decoration. During the Middle Ages inlaid tiles were frequently used to pave the floors of cathedrals, churches, monastic buildings and royal palaces. Most medieval inlaid tiles consisted of a body of red clay with an inlaid design of white clay; a transparent glaze applied to the surface made the body look brown and the white inlaid clay honey-coloured yellow. During the first half of the nineteenth century the manufacture of inlaid tiles was revived. They were then known as encaustic tiles, and were made either of *plastic clay* with slip infills or wholly of *dust clay*. In the 1840s, Minton & Co and Chamberlain were the first firms to manufacture replicas of medieval tiles successfully. Chamberlain covered their encaustic tiles with a transparent glaze, but Minton devised a method of heightening the effect of the inlaid design with a yellow enamel glaze, leaving the body of the tile unglazed. From 1842 onward Minton began to introduce colours such as blue and green to augment the basic red and yellow. Initially encaustic tiles were used mainly in churches but during the second half of the nineteenth century their use was extended to civic, public and domestic buildings.

Line-impressed
See *impressed decoration*.

Lockback
Undercut indentations on the backs of *dust-pressed* tiles which helped to 'lock' the tiles more firmly to the cement to which they were fixed. Some firms, including T. & R. Boote and H. & R. Johnson, took out patents for their particular type of lockback.

Lustre
A rich iridescent sheen used as a decorative effect, achieved by depositing a thin film of metal derived from metallic salts mixed with the glaze on the surface of the tile, and firing in a reducing (low-oxygen) atmosphere. Ruby lustre, derived from copper sulphate, was the most common but other colours including gold, green and blue could be achieved through the use of different metal salts. De Morgan, Maw & Co, Pilkington, Craven Dunnill and J. C. Edwards used this technique, as did other manufacturers to a lesser degree.

Majolica/Maiolica
The term maiolica is used for decorated tin-glazed earthenware pottery and tiles made in Italy during the fifteenth and sixteenth centuries with intricate decorations and scenes painted in blue, yellow, green and orange. In the nineteenth century the term majolica became associated with relief tiles and pottery decorated with colourful opaque glazes.

Marmo
Trade term for a new type of faience with an almost matt glazed white finish developed by the Leeds Fireclay Co and launched as Burmantofts Marmo around 1908. The firm's advertisements compared Marmo to white marble in colour surface and effect, and stated that an eggshell glaze was used in its manufacture.

Marsden's patent
Marsden's patent (or Wedgwood's patent impressed tile) was a process used in the 1880s. Tiles decorated in this manner show a finish similar to *barbotine*, only with sharp edges to the relief decoration; stencils were an essential part of the method of manufacture (although they are not mentioned in the patent). Most tiles decorated in this way have a stippled background applied before the relief decoration; some show the use of up to three stencils laid one after another.

Mosaic
A mosaic is a design achieved by fitting together, usually without interlocking, a number of small pieces of material known as tesserae; the term tessera is also sometimes applied to an individual unit of a tile pavement. Roman mosaic floors were made from marble, stone and glass tesserae. Medieval mosaic floors were made from geometrically cut pieces of fired clay covered with slips and glazes; alternating light and dark tiles were employed to create intricate floor patterns. This technique was used for large geometric tile pavements in many Cistercian abbeys.

During the 1840s Minton & Co made mosaic floors from small dust-pressed tesserae; Owen Jones made this type of floor popular in his book *Designs for Mosaic Pavements* (1842). Later in the century geometric pavements made from variously shaped and coloured plain geometrical tiles came into vogue. The phrases 'tile mosaic' and 'mosaic panel' are sometimes - and rather misleadingly - used to describe nineteenth century and early twentieth century pictorial wall panels comprising painted designs on (normally) square tiles.

There were many attempts at manufacturing simulated mosaic floors. In the 1860s, Maw & Co took out a patent for the production of a type of pseudo-mosaic tile made from *dust-pressed* clay, known as patent mosaic. The surface of the tile was indented with a linear pattern simulating a mosaic design, while the tiles sometimes had irregular edges. Once the tiles were laid, the linear impressions were filled with cement, creating a convincing illusion of mosaic, although the process was cheaper and less time-consuming than laying real mosaic.

The Architectural Pottery Company made a kind of tessellated tile by bonding small thin plastic clay tesserae, in the form of various rectilinear shapes, to the surface of a tile body. The tesserae were arranged on the face of a tile which had reached the same degree of plasticity as the tesserae, then an oiled plate was pressed down on the tesserae, bonding them to the tile body.

Maw & Co and Craven Dunnill made simulated mosaic, in which thin tesserae of various shapes were fused to the surface of the tile, but - unlike the tessellated tile technique - gaps were left between the tesserae. After the tiles were laid, cement was brushed over the surface then cleaned off, the cement remaining in the gaps helping to create the appearance of a tessellated pavement. The tiles themselves were sometimes given an irregular shape which further helped the illusion of real mosaic. Finally, transfer printed tiles with mosaic patterns were also made.

On-glaze decoration
In this process the decorator works on a ready-glazed blank; this enabled individuals and firms to buy glazed blanks and decorate them. Nineteenth-century tiles with on-glaze decoration are easily identified because the hand-applied colours were fired at a lower temperature and have a duller finish than the glaze they were painted on, and occasionally stand a little proud of it; there was also a much enhanced palette of colours.

Opus sectile
Literally translated as work made by cutting with a knife, the term was originally used in the early fourteenth century for a special type of mosaic work. In modern usage, opus sectile normally suggests tile pieces of varying shapes assembled in jigsaw-like designs; the resulting tile panels are often (and confusingly) referred to as mosaics. A specific and fairly common type of opus sectile was made chiefly by Powell's of Whitefriars from the 1860s until the mid-1930s. Their opus sectile material was produced from waste glass contaminated with impurities deriving from clay crucibles. The glass was ground to a powder and baked, yielding a solid, durable material with an eggshell surface suitable for opus sectile, wall tiles and mosaic, with an almost unlimited range of colours. The opus sectile pieces were shaped by filling a mould with the powder and heating until the material fused. In some cases, an area of coloured glass was placed in the mould using a thick stencil, the remainder of the area being filled with the background colour. More detail was added to the opus sectile pieces by using glass-based pigments that required firing at a temperature high enough for the colour to fuse with the base material. This sometimes resulted in the colour flaking away after only a few months, a process described as 'gone bad'; firing at too high a temperature caused discolouration, with the material said to be 'burnt'. Powell's made more than a thousand reredoses, pictorial panels, blind windows and memorial tablets from opus sectile.

Parian ware
Earthenware with matt finish developed by W. J. Neatby for Doulton's; intended for interior architectural work.

Patent mosaic
See *mosaic*.

Pâte-sur-pâte
From the French, meaning paste-on-paste. The process involved building up thin layers of slip using a brush, until the intended decoration was achieved; often white slip was layered on a black ground. A mechanically formed and less subtle version of the process was also available.

Photographic decoration processes
George Grundy patented a means of transferring a photographic image to a ceramic surface in 1896; he then formed the Photo Decorated Tile Company. Although his process was effective in reproducing a photographic image, it proved unprofitable. Grundy's method was to lay down a sensitised layer on a rubber pad, on which the subject could be printed from a photographic negative. This image, in vitrifiable ink, was transferred direct to the tile through pressure from the rubber pad. In the twentieth century the halftone dot process, as used in newspaper illustrations, has been used to convey a photographic image to ceramic. Halftone printing has also been applied to tiles by a photogravure process not relying on dots. Such printing has also been produced by the silkscreen process.

Plastic clay
Soft and easily mouldable clay.

Polychrome stoneware
See *stoneware*.

Relief tiles
Tiles bearing a raised design; the design is formed when clay is pressed into a mould.

Salt glaze
A glazing process actually carried out in the kiln. The ware is fired up to 1100 -1200°C and salt is then thrown on the fire, where it volatilises. The salt vapours settle on the wares in the kiln and react with the clay to form a sodium aluminosilicate glaze, which is acid and pollution resistant. Mainly used for sewer pipes and chimney pots but occasionally for tiles and architectural ceramics.

Sgraffito
The technique of incising through a layer of slip or glaze; fine lines were drawn with a stylus, bigger areas with a knife, colour added where needed. The term may be applied to the decorative finish of a wall, where it means a scratched pattern, often in plaster.

Silk-screen printing
Carter's of Poole carried out experiments with silk-screening before 1939, and were first to print on to the biscuit by this method, which became common from the 1950s. Silk-screening is essentially a method of pushing viscous colour through silk by means of a rubber leaf or squeegee.

Simulated mosaic
See *mosaic.*

Slip
Clay mixed with water to form a liquid of a smooth pouring consistency.

Specials
One-off designs, particularly in the production of terracotta and faience.

Stained body
Decoration achieved by staining the clay which made up the body of the tile. Pale blue, grey and green have been seen, with various forms of decoration printed or hand painted upon them.

Stencilling
Stencil decoration may be carried out using a fine grained sponge, spraying (when it is known as *aerography*) or a brush through a stencil; the finer lines were added by hand.

Stoneware
Ware made from very siliceous clay or a composition of clay and flint which can withstand extremely high firing temperatures. This results in a hard and glassy or vitrified body, which is impervious to water and thus suitable for external use. Polychrome stoneware, made by Doulton of Lambeth in the early twentieth century, used brightly coloured glazes on moulded stoneware.

Terracotta
Unglazed clay ware; from the Italian, meaning baked earth. Dried, shaped pieces are kiln-fired at 1150-1250°C, then allowed to cool gently before unloading. Terracotta normally ranges through buff to red in colour and is frequently used as a dressing on brick buildings.

Tesselated tiles
See *mosaic.*

Tesserae
See *mosaic.*

Tile press
See *dust-pressing.*

Tin glaze
A glaze made by adding tin oxide to lead glaze; when fired it becomes an opaque white colour.

Trade tile
An advertisement tile bearing the manufacturer's details on the upper side.

Transfer printing
The transfer of images to tiles from engraved copper plates, lithographic stone or wood block by means of gelatinous 'bats' or thin transfer paper. Transfer images can be applied on the glaze or under the glaze. John Sadler first used transfer printing on glazed tiles in Liverpool in 1756. During the 1830s Copeland produced under-glaze and on-glaze printed tiles. Printing flat colours (block-printing) from metal or stone using transfer paper was invented in 1848 by Collins and Reynolds, and developed for use on tiles by Minton. During the second half of the nineteenth century, transfer printing in its various forms became one of the main methods of decorating mass-produced tiles.

Tube-lining
Piping thin trails of slip onto a tile from the nozzle of a handheld rubber bulb to form raised lines separating areas of coloured glazes. This method was especially suitable for one-off designs and small runs such as pictorial panels. A similar but mass-produced effect (imitation tube-lining) was achieved by using metal dies on which the outlines were depressed, thus producing raised outlines on the tile.

Underglaze decoration

Printed or painted decoration applied to biscuit-fired tiles prior to a transparent glaze. Because the decoration is completely covered by the clear glaze, it is extremely durable.

Vitreous faience
See *glazed terracotta.*

Vitreous fresco
Unglazed, matt-surfaced faience with strong colours; introduced by Doulton's in 1885 and used for interior work, particularly murals.

Vitrified terracotta

See *glazed terracotta.*

Wedgwood's patent impressed tile
See *Marsden's patent.*

Wire-cut brick
Brick produced by cutting extruded clay into shape with taut wires.

Appendix 3

Bibliography

Mark Anders, *Burmantofts Architectural Faience,* in *Burmantofts Pottery,* (Bradford Art Galleries and Museums, Bradford, 1983), pp28-37.

Alastair Scott Anderson, 'Pierre Mallet (1836-1898) - Pioneer of French Aesthetic Ceramics in England', *Decorative Arts Society Journal,* 23 (1999), pp86-101.

Alastair Scott Anderson, 'Pierre Mallet - A Designer of Burmantofts Faience Tiles', *Glazed Expressions,* (1998) 36, pp7-9.

Katie Arber, *Patterns for Post-war Britain - the tile designs of Peggy Angus* (Middlesex University Press, London, 2002).

Katie Arber, 'Peggy Angus, designer of modern tiles for a modern Britain', *Decorative Arts Society Journal,* 26 (2002), pp120-134.

Liz Arthur, *Robert Stewart: Design 1946-95* (A. & C. Black, London, 2003).

Paul Atterbury and Louise Irvine, *The Doulton Story* (Royal Doulton Tableware, Stoke on Trent, 1979).

Paul Atterbury and Clive Wainwright, *Pugin: A Gothic Passion* (Yale University Press, New Haven and London, 1994).

J. Austwick and B. Austwick, *The Decorated Tile* (Pitman House Limited, London, 1980).

Julian Barnard, *Victorian Ceramic Tiles* (Studio Vista, London, 1972).

G. K. Beaulah, 'Samuel Wright of Shelton and his Tiles', *Journal of the Tiles and Architectural Ceramics Society,* 3 (1990), pp28-32.

G. K. Beaulah, 'Techniques used in tile decoration', *Glazed Expressions,* (1988) 17, pp5-12.

G. K. Beaulah, 'Church tile survey in Yorkshire', *Glazed Expressions,* (1981) 1, pp2-3.

Kenneth Beaulah and Hans van Lemmen, *Church Tiles of the Nineteenth Century* 2nd ed (Shire Publications, Princes Risborough, 2001).

Penny Beckett, 'George Swift and Liverpool's Swan Tile Works', *TACS Journal,* 10 (2004), pp24-31.

Penny Beckett, 'The Ceramic Murals of Philippa Threlfall', *Glazed Expressions,* (1999) 39, pp2-4.

Gilbert T. Bell, *The Monument That Moved: Springburn's Ornamental Column* (Springburn Museum Trust, Glasgow, 1999).

James Bettley, ''The Master of Little Braxted in his prime': Ernest Geldart and Essex, 1873-1900', *Essex Archaeology and History,* 31 (2000), pp169-194.

Ian M. Betts, *Medieval 'Westminster' floor tiles (MoLAS Monograph 11)* (Museum of London, London, 2002).

Ian M. Betts, Ernest T. M. Black and John L. Gower, 'A corpus of relief-patterned tiles in Roman Britain', *Journal of Roman Pottery Studies,* 7 (1997), pp1-167.

M. Biddle and B. Kjølbye-Biddle, 'Floor tiles' in G. Zarnecki, J. Holt and T. Holland, eds, *English Romanesque Art 1066-1200* (London, 1984), p392.

E. W. Black, 'The dating of relief-patterned flue-tiles', *Oxford Journal of Archaeology,* 4 (1985), pp353-376.

Chris Blanchett, *British Tiles of the Twentieth Century* (Schiffer, Atglen, Pennsylvania, 2005).

Chris Blanchett, 'The floor tiles at The Vyne, Hampshire, England', *Glazed Expressions*, (2000) 41, pp2-31.

Chris Blanchett, 'The Tiles of Dorchester Abbey', *TACS Journal*, 6 (1996), pp13-22.

Chris Blanchett, *William De Morgan Tiles at Knightscroft House, Rustington, West Sussex* (Buckland Books, Tring, 1992).

Michaela Braesel, 'The tile decoration by Morris & Co. for Queens' College, Cambridge', *Apollo*, 149 (1999) January, pp25-33.

Hugo Brown, 'A Minton floor rediscovered at Cliveden', *Apollo*, 157 (2003) April, pp22-3.

Philip and Dorothy Brown, 'Glass tiles', *Glazed Expressions*, (1994) 28, pp2-3.

Philip and Dorothy Brown, 'Cuenca tiles and Frederick Garrard', *Glazed Expressions*, (1993) 26, pp10-11.

Philip and Dorothy Brown, 'Spanish flavour in church tiles', *Glazed Expressions*, (1992) 25, pp9-10.

Philip and Dorothy Brown, 'Lancaster architects - church terracotta and tiles', *Glazed Expressions*, (1990) 21, pp8-10.

Philip and Dorothy Brown, 'Obliterating Butterfield', *Glazed Expressions*, (1989) 19, pp8-9.

Andrew Casey, *20th Century Ceramic Designers in Britain* (Antique Collectors' Club, Woodbridge, 2001).

Jon Catleugh, *William De Morgan Tiles* (Richard Dennis Publications, Shepton Beauchamp, 1983).

J. Cherry, 'Pottery and Tile' in J. Blair and N. Ramsay, *English Medieval Industries: Craftsmen, Techniques, Products* (London 1991), pp189-209.

Kenneth Clark, *The Tile: Making, Designing and Using* (Crowood Press, Marlborough, 2002).

Jane Cochrane, 'Medieval Tiled Floor Patterns', *TACS Journal*, 5 (1994), pp11-19.

Andrew Connolly, *Life in the Victorian brickyards of Flintshire and Denbighshire* (Gwasg Carreg Gwalch, Llanrwst, 2003).

Barry Corbett and Angela Corbett, *Tiles Tell the Tale* (Pilkington's Lancastrian Pottery Society, 2004).

Richard Cork, ed, *Eduardo Paolozzi Underground* (Royal Academy of Arts, London, 1986).

Chris Cox, 'The medieval tiles of Carew Cheriton Church, Pembrokeshire', *Glazed Expressions*, (1996) 32, pp6-7.

Chris Cox, 'Chamberlain floor tiles at Slebech Church, Wales', *Glazed Expressions*, (1994) 28, pp9-11.

A. J. Cross, *Pilkington's Royal Lancastrian Pottery and Tiles* (Richard Dennis, London, 1980).

Colin Cunningham, *The Terracotta Designs of Alfred Waterhouse* (Wiley-Academy, Chichester, 2001).

Colin Cunningham and Prudence Waterhouse, *Alfred Waterhouse, 1830-1905: Biography of a Practice* (Clarendon Press, Oxford, 1992).

Susan Degnan and Derek Seeley, 'Medieval and later floor tiles in Lambeth Palace Chapel', *London Archaeologist*, 6 (1988) Winter, pp11-18.

Michael J. Dillon, *Bricks, tiles and terracotta from Wrexham and Ruabon* (Wrexham Maelor Borough Council, Wrexham, 1985).

Max Donnelly, 'Daniel Cottier, Pioneer of Aestheticism', *Decorative Arts Society Journal*, 23 (1999), pp32-51.

Lesley Durbin, *Architectural Tiles: Conservation and Restoration* (Butterworth-Heinemann, 2004).

Elizabeth Eames, *English Tilers* (British Museum Press, London, 1992).

Elizabeth Eames, *English Medieval Tiles* (British Museum Publications, London, 1985).

Elizabeth S. Eames, *Catalogue of Medieval Lead-Glazed Earthenware Tiles in the Department of Medieval and Later Antiquities, British Museum* (British Museum Publications, London, 1980).

E. Eames and T. Fanning, *Irish medieval tiles* (Royal Irish Academy Monographs in Archaeology 2, Dublin 1998).

Ifor Edwards, 'Claymasters and Clayworkers in the old parish of Ruabon', *Transactions of the Denbighshire Historical Society*, 35 (1986), pp83-98.

John Elliott and John Pritchard, eds, *Henry Woodyer: Gentleman Architect* (Department of Continuing Education, University of Reading, Reading, 2002).

John Elliott and John Pritchard, eds, *George Edmund Street: a Victorian architect in Berkshire* (Centre for Continuing Education, University of Reading, Reading, 1998).

A. B. Emden, *Medieval decorated tiles in Dorset* (Phillimore, London & Chichester, 1977).

Desmond Eyles and Louise Irvine, *The Doulton Lambeth Wares* (Richard Dennis, Shepton Beauchamp, 2002).

Jean Farquhar and Joan Skinner, *The History and Architecture of the Turkey Cafe* (Sedgebrook Press, Leicester, 1987).

Jane Fawcett, ed, *Historic Floors: Their History and Conservation* (Butterworth-Heinemann, Oxford, 1998).

Margaret A. V. Gill, 'A Munificent Benefaction: Godwin tiles in St Peter's Church, Hereford', *TACS Journal*, 9 (2003), pp24-34.

Miranda F. Goodby, 'George Tinworth: an Artist in Terracotta', *TACS Journal*, 3 (1990), pp15-21.

Alun Graves, *Tiles and Tilework of Europe* (V & A Publications, London, 2002).

Betty Greene, 'The Godwins of Hereford', *TACS Journal*, 1 (1982), pp8-16.

John Greene, *Brightening the Long Days* (Tiles and Architectural Ceramics Society, 1987).

D. W. Hadley, 'From Rees mosaic to opus sectile: the development of opaque stained glass', *Glass Technology* 45 (2004), pp192-6.

Dennis W. Hadley, *James Powell & Sons: A listing of opus sectile, 1847-1973*, (2001, available from the TACS website at www.tilesoc.org.uk).

Malcolm Haslam, *The Martin Brothers: Potters* (Richard Dennis, London, 1978).

Leslie Hayward, *Poole Pottery: Carter & Company and their Successors, 1873-2002* 3rd edition, ed Paul Atterbury (Richard Dennis, Shepton Beauchamp, 2002).

Gwen Heeney, *Brickworks* (A & C Black, London, 2003).

Tony Herbert and Kathryn Huggins, *The Decorative Tile in Architecture and Interiors* (Phaidon Press, London, 1995).

Wendy Hitchmough, *The Michelin Building* (Conran Octopus, London, 1995).

B. Hurman and B. Nenk, 'The Gerald Dunning archive and the study of medieval ceramic roof furniture', *Medieval Ceramics* 24 (2000), pp63-72.

Louise Irvine, 'Ceramics for a Community', *Glazed Expressions*, (1986) 12, pp1-2.

Louise Irvine, 'Neatby's Work with Doulton', *Architectural Review*, 165 (1979) June, pp383-4.

Louise Irvine and Paul Atterbury, *Gilbert Bayes, Sculptor, 1872-1953* (Richard Dennis, Shepton Beauchamp, 1998).

Louise Irvine and Deborah Lambert, '"For present comfort and for future good" - Queen Alexandra's House, Kensington', *Decorative Arts Society Journal*, 21 (1997), pp27-34.

Lesley Jackson, '"Contempt and Contemporary" Attitudes in the Staffordshire Ceramics Industry during the 1950s', *Decorative Arts Society Journal*, 15 (1991), pp20-28.

Lesley Jackson and Kate Malone, *Kate Malone: A Book of Pots* (A. & C. Black, London, 2003).

Tony Johnson, *The Morris Ware, Tiles and Art of George Cartlidge* (Making Space, Whippingham, 2004).

David Jolley, *Architect Exuberant: George Skipper, 1856-1948* (Norwich School of Art, Norwich, 1975).

Robert Jolley, 'Edmund Sharpe and the 'Pot' Churches', *Architectural Review*, 146 (1969) December, pp426-31.

Joan Jones, *Minton: The first two hundred years of design and production* (Swan Hill Press, Shrewsbury, 1993).

Johan Kamermans and Hans van Lemmen, eds, *Industrial Tiles 1840-1940* (Nederlands Tegelmuseum, Otterlo, 2004).

Geoffrey Kay, 'The Peacock of Mysore: An account of the tiled floor of the Wedding Pavilion in the Mysore Palace, Karnataka State, India', *TACS Journal*, 7 (1998), pp3-9.

Geoffrey Kay, 'Charles Lynam - an Architect of Tile Factories', *TACS Journal*, 4 (1992), pp21-28.

L. Keen, 'Pre-Conquest Glazed Relief Tiles from All Saints Church, Pavement, York', *Journal British Archaeological Association*, 146 (1993), pp67-86.

J. Keily, 'The fabric of the medieval London house', in G. Egan, ed, *The Medieval Household: daily living c.1150-1450 (Medieval Finds from Excavations in London, 6)* (London, 1998).

Alison Kelly, *Mrs Coade's Stone* (Self Publishing Association, Upton-upon-Severn, 1990).

Tessa Kelly, 'The Morris Reredoses at St. John the Baptist Church, Findon, and The Church of The Blessed Virgin Mary, Clapham, West Sussex', *Journal of the William Morris Society*, 13 (2000) 4, pp30-34.

Michael Kerney, 'All Saints', Margaret Street: A Glazing History', *Journal of Stained Glass*, 25 (2001), pp27-52.

Rose Kerr, 'Hidden treasure at Sir John Soane's Museum', *Apollo*, 156 (2002) November, pp23-9.

Rose Kerr, 'Celestial Creatures: Chinese tiles in the Victoria and Albert Museum', *Apollo*, 149 (1999) March, pp15-21.

Elspeth King, *People's Pictures: The story of tiles in Glasgow* (Glasgow Museums, Glasgow, 1991).

Peter Larkworthy, *Clayton and Bell, Stained Glass Artists and Decorators* (Ecclesiological Society, London, 1984).

David Lawrence, *Underground Architecture* (Capital Transport, Harrow, 1994).

David Leboff, *The Underground Stations of Leslie Green* (Capital Transport Publishing, Harrow Weald, 2002).

J. M. Lewis, *The medieval tiles of Wales* (National Museum of Wales, Cardiff, 1999).

Barbara J. Lowe, *Decorated Medieval Floor Tiles of Somerset* (Somerset Archaeological and Natural History Society and Somerset County Museums Service, Taunton, 2003).

John Malam, 'A newly recognised Doulton interior, Manchester', *Glazed Expressions*, (1993) 27, pp1, 12.

A. McWhirr, ed, *Roman Brick and Tile; Studies in Marketing, Distribution and Volume in the Western Roman Empire,* (Oxford, 1979).

A. McWhirr and D. Viner, 'The products and distribution of tiles in Roman Britain with particular reference to the Cirencester region', *Britannia* 9 (1978), pp359-376.

A. Middleton, 'Tiles in Roman Britain', in I. Freestone & D. Gaimster, *Pottery in the Making*, (London, 1997), pp158-163.

Nicholas A. D. Molyneux and John E. McGregor, *The Medieval Tiles at Great Malvern Priory* (Friends of Great Malvern Priory, Great Malvern, 1997).

Richard Myers and Hilary Myers, *William Morris Tiles - The tile designs of Morris and his Fellow-Workers* (Richard Dennis, Shepton Beauchamp, 1996).

Christopher Norton, *The Decorative Pavements of Salisbury Cathedral and Old Sarum*, in *Medieval Art and Architecture at Salisbury Cathedral*, eds Laurence Keen and Thomas Cocke, (British Archaeological Association, 1996) pp90-105.

Christopher Norton, *Medieval Floor Tiles in Scotland*, in *Medieval Art and Architecture in the Diocese of St Andrews*, ed John Higgitt, (British Archaeological Association, 1994) pp137-173.

Christopher Norton, *The Medieval Tile Pavements of Winchester Cathedral*, in *Winchester Cathedral: Nine Hundred Years, 1093-1993*, ed John Crook, (Phillimore, Chichester, 1993), pp167-176.

C. Norton, 'The origins of two-colour tiles in France and England', in D. Derœux, ed, *Terres Cuites Architecturales au Moyen Âge* (Arras, 1986), pp256-293.

Annabel Pears, *Maw and Company 1900-1910* (1989, Diploma in Industrial Archaeology, Ironbridge Institute, University of Birmingham).

Lynn Pearson, 'To Brighten the Environment: Ceramic Tile Murals in Britain, 1950-70', *TACS Journal*, 10 (2004), pp12-17.

Lynn Pearson, 'Memorial and Commemorative Tiles in Nineteenth and Early Twentieth Century Churches', *TACS Journal*, 9 (2003), pp13-23.

Lynn Pearson, 'The 'Revelations' tiles of John Pollard Seddon at Sunningwell Church, Oxfordshire', *Glazed Expressions*, (2003) 48, pp18.

Lynn Pearson, 'Decorative ceramics in the buildings of the British brewing industry', *TACS Journal*, 8 (2000), pp26-36.

Lynn Pearson, *Minton Tiles in the Churches of Staffordshire* (Tiles and Architectural Ceramics Society, 2000; available from the TACS website at www.tilesoc.org.uk).

John Physick, *Albertopolis:The Estate of the 1851 Commissioners*, in *The Albert Memorial*, ed Chris Brooks, (Yale University Press, New Haven and London, 2000), pp308-38.

John Physick, *The Victoria and Albert Museum: The history of its building* (Phaidon-Christie's, Oxford, 1982).

Venetia Porter, *Islamic Tiles* (British Museum Press, London, 1995).

Venetia Porter, 'William De Morgan and the Islamic Tiles of Leighton House', *Decorative Arts Society Journal*, 16 (1992), pp76-9.

John Price, ''Everyday heroes': The Memorial Tablets of Postman's Park', *TACS Journal*, 10 (2004), pp18-23.

Susan Rasey, 'Sylvia Packard and the tile mural at the Royal School, Bath', *Glazed Expressions*, (1997) 35, pp2-3.

Anthony Ray, *English Delftware Tiles* (Faber and Faber, London, 1973).

John S. Reynolds, 'Alfred Reynolds and the Block Process', *TACS Journal*, 5 (1994), pp20-26.

Lezli Richer, 'Training for Industrial Design and the Decline of Maw & Co', *Glazed Expressions*, (1996) 33, pp3-5.

Pauline Sargent, 'Painted tiles by William Burges', *Antique Collector*, 58 (1987) March, pp101-108.

Graham Scott, 'The Dream of City Architecture Expressed in Colourful Ceramics - the theories and architecture of Halsey Ralph Ricardo', *TACS Journal*, 7 (1998), pp11-17.

David Sherlock, *Medieval floor tiles in Suffolk churches* (Suffolk Historic Churches Trust, Ipswich, 1980).

Andrew Skelton, 'The Carshalton Water Tower Tiled Bath - a study in Anglo-Dutch tiles', *TACS Journal*, 7 (1998), pp31-4.

D. S. Skinner and Hans van Lemmen, eds, *Minton Tiles 1835-1935* (City Museum and Art Gallery, Stoke-on-Trent, 1984).

Joan S. Skinner, *Form and Fancy: Factories and Factory Buildings by Wallis, Gilbert & Partners, 1916-1939* (Liverpool University Press, Liverpool, 1997).

Joan Skinner, 'The Fancy Factories of Wallis, Gilbert & Partners', *TACS Journal*, 5 (1994), pp34-40.

Annamarie Stapleton, *John Moyr Smith 1839-1912: A Victorian Designer* (Richard Dennis, Shepton Beauchamp, 2002).

Peter Stoodley, 'David Ballantyne - Renaissance Man of Clay', *Ceramic Review*, (1991) 128, pp20-23.

Jennie Stopford, *Medieval Floor Tiles of Northern England: Pattern and purpose - production between the 13th and 16th centuries* (Oxbow Books, Oxford, 2004).

Jennie Stopford, 'The Yorkshire Medieval Tile Project', *TACS Journal*, 4 (1992), pp11-14.

Shirley Strachan, 'Henry Powell Dunnill: a Victorian Tilemaster', *TACS Journal*, 3 (1990), pp3-10.

Michael Stratton, *Clad is bad? The relationship between structural and ceramic facing materials*, in *Structure and Style: Conserving Twentieth Century Buildings*, ed Michael Stratton, (E. & F. N. Spon, London, 1997) pp164-92.

Michael Stratton, *The Terracotta Revival* (Victor Gollancz, London, 1993).

Michael Stratton, *William Watkins and the Terracotta Revival*, in *The Victorian Facade: W. Watkins and Son, Architects, Lincoln, 1859-1918*, (Lincolnshire College of Art & Design, Lincoln, 1990), pp24-28.

Michael Stratton, 'Science and Art Closely Combined: the organisation of training in the terracotta industry, 1850-1939', *Construction History*, 4 (1988), pp35-51.

Michael Stratton, 'The Terracotta Industry: its Distribution, Manufacturing Processes and Products', *Industrial Archaeology Review*, 8 (1986) 2, pp194-214.

Alan Swale, 'Carter & Co. and the First Screen Printed Tiles', *Glazed Expressions*, (2002) 45, p9.

Alan Swale, *Architectural terracotta - a critical appraisal of its development and deployment* (1998, MA dissertation, History of Ceramics, University of Staffordshire).

Alan Swale, 'The Terracotta of the Wedgwood Institute, Burslem', *Journal of the Tiles and Architectural Ceramics Society*, 2 (1987), pp21-27.

Jeanne Marie Teutonico, ed, *Architectural ceramics: their history, manufacture and conservation* (James & James (Science Publishers) Ltd, London, 1996).

Laura Trelford, *A Discussion of the Figurative Tile Panels in the Nave of All Saints', Margaret Street, designed by William Butterfield, 1873-91* (2004, MA dissertation, Courtauld Institute of Art).

Hans van Lemmen, *Ceramic Roofware* (Shire Publications, Princes Risborough, 2003).

Hans van Lemmen, *Delftware Tiles* (Laurence King, London, 1997).

Hans van Lemmen, *Tiles in Architecture* (Laurence King Publishing, London, 1993).

Hans van Lemmen, *Minton Hollins Picture Tiles* 2nd ed (Gladstone Pottery Museum, Stoke-on-Trent, 1985).

Hans van Lemmen and Chris Blanchett, *Twentieth Century Tiles* (Shire Publications, Princes Risborough, 1999).

Hans van Lemmen and John Malam, eds, *Fired Earth - 1000 Years of Tiles in Europe* (Richard Dennis Publications and TACS, Shepton Beauchamp, 1991).

Hans van Lemmen and Jose Montgomery, *Dutch Tiles at 'Farrago' and 'Farrago' - A History of the House and its Tiles* 2nd ed (Leeds Polytechnic, Leeds, 1990).

Hans van Lemmen and Bart Verbrugge, *Art Nouveau Tiles* (Laurence King, London, 1999).

Alfred L. Wakeling and Peter Moon, *Tiles of Tragedy: Brightlingsea's Unique Maritime Memorial* 2nd ed (Ellar Publications, Stockton-on-Tees, 2003).

Robert Prescott Walker, 'Conrad Dressler and the Medmenham Pottery', *Decorative Arts Society Journal*, (1994) 18, pp50-60.

Philip Ward-Jackson, *Gilbert Bayes* Essays in the Study of Sculpture (Henry Moore Institute, Leeds, 1998).

William Waters, *Stained Glass from Shrigley & Hunt of Lancaster and London* (Centre for North-West Regional Studies, University of Lancaster, Lancaster, 2003).

Kevin Wheelan, *The History of the Hathern Station Brick & Terra Cotta Company* (Mercia Cinema Society, Birmingham, 1982).

Norma R. Whitcomb, *The medieval floor-tiles of Leicestershire* (Leicestershire Archaeological and Historical Society, Leicester, 1956).

Jane A. Wight, *Mediaeval Floor Tiles* (John Baker, London, 1975).

Jane A. Wight, *Brick Building in England from the Middle Ages to 1550* (John Baker, London, 1972).

Williamson Art Gallery and Museum, *Della Robbia Pottery, Birkenhead, 1894-1906: An interim report* (Metropolitan Borough of Wirral, Department of Leisure Services, Birkenhead, 1980).

Julie Gillam Wood, 'Behind the Facade: An Insight into Burmantofts' Trading Ethos', *TACS Journal*, 10 (2004), pp3-11.

Russell Wright, *Signs of the Times: a guide to the materials of modernism 1927-1933* (Building Centre, London, 1981).

In addition, the *Pevsner Architectural Guides* have been an invaluable source of general architectural information.

Index
Artists, Designers and Manufacturers

Index of Places